WITHDRAWN
UTSA Libraries

The Economics of Taxation
Volume I

The International Library of Critical Writings in Economics

Founding Editor: Mark Blaug

>Professor Emeritus, University of London, UK
>Professor Emeritus, University of Buckingham, UK

This series is an essential reference source for students, researchers and lecturers in economics. It presents by theme a selection of the most important articles across the entire spectrum of economics. Each volume has been prepared by a leading specialist who has written an authoritative introduction to the literature included.

Wherever possible, the articles in these volumes have been reproduced as originally published using facsimile reproduction, inclusive of footnotes and pagination to facilitate ease of reference.

For a list of all Edward Elgar published titles visit our website at
www.e-elgar.com

The Economics of Taxation Volume I

Edited by

James Alm

Department of Economics
Tulane University, USA

THE INTERNATIONAL LIBRARY OF CRITICAL WRITINGS IN ECONOMICS

An Elgar Research Collection
Cheltenham, UK • Northampton, MA, USA

© James Alm 2011. For copyright of individual articles, please refer to the Acknowledgements.

All rights reserved. No part of this publication may be reproduced, stored in a retrieval system, or transmitted in any form or by any means, electronic, mechanical, photocopying, recording, or otherwise without the prior permission of the publisher.

Published by
Edward Elgar Publishing Limited
The Lypiatts
15 Lansdown Road
Cheltenham
Glos GL50 2JA
UK

Edward Elgar Publishing, Inc.
William Pratt House
9 Dewey Court
Northampton
Massachusetts 01060
USA

A catalogue record for this book is available from the British Library

Library of Congress Control Number: 2011924192

ISBN 978 1 84844 829 2 (2 volume set)

Printed and bound by MPG Books Group, UK

Contents

Acknowledgements ix
Introduction James Alm xi

PART I   ANALYZING THE EFFECTS OF TAXATION

    A   **Notions of Equity**

        1. Richard A. Musgrave (1976), 'ET, OT and SBT', *Journal of Public Economics*, **6** (1/2), July–August, 3–16   5
        2. H. Peyton Young (1990), 'Progressive Taxation and Equal Sacrifice', *American Economic Review*, **80** (1), March, 253–66   19
        3. Louis Kaplow (1989), 'Horizontal Equity: Measures in Search of a Principle', *National Tax Journal*, **XLII** (2), 139–54   33

    B   **Taxes and Income Distribution**

        4. Charles E. McLure, Jr (1975), 'General Equilibrium Incidence Analysis: The Harberger Model After Ten Years', *Journal of Public Economics*, **4** (2), February, 125–61   51
        5. Michael L. Katz and Harvey S. Rosen (1985), 'Tax Analysis in an Oligopoly Model', *Public Finance Quarterly*, **13** (1), January, 3–19   88
        6. Lawrence H. Summers (1983), 'The Asset Price Approach to the Analysis of Capital Income Taxation', *National Tax Association/Tax Institute of America, Proceedings of the Seventy-Sixth Annual Conference on Taxation*, 112–20   105
        7. James Davies, France St-Hilaire and John Whalley (1984), 'Some Calculations of Lifetime Tax Incidence', *American Economic Review*, **74** (4), September, 633–49   114
        8. Timothy J. Besley and Harvey S. Rosen (1999), 'Sales Taxes and Prices: An Empirical Analysis', *National Tax Journal*, **LII** (3), 157–78   131
        9. John B. Shoven (1976), 'The Incidence and Efficiency Effects of Taxes on Income from Capital', *Journal of Political Economy*, **84** (6), December, 1261–83   153
     10. David M. Cutler (1988), 'Tax Reform and the Stock Market: An Asset Price Approach', *American Economic Review*, **78** (5), December, 1107–17   176

C Taxes and Efficiency

11. Arnold C. Harberger (1964), 'The Measurement of Waste', *American Economic Review*, **54** (3), May, 58–76 — 189
12. Jerry A. Hausman (1981), 'Exact Consumer's Surplus and Deadweight Loss', *American Economic Review*, **71** (4), September, 662–76 — 208
13. Edgar K. Browning (1987), 'On the Marginal Welfare Cost of Taxation', *American Economic Review*, **77** (1), March, 11–23 — 223
14. Charles L. Ballard, John B. Shoven and John Whalley (1985), 'The Total Welfare Cost of the United States Tax System: A General Equilibrium Approach', *National Tax Journal*, **XXXVIII** (2), 125–40 — 236

D Taxes and Revenues

15. Don Fullerton (1982), 'On the Possibility of an Inverse Relationship Between Tax Rates and Government Revenues', *Journal of Public Economics*, **19** (1), 3–22 — 255

E Taxes and Growth

16. Larry E. Jones, Rodolfo E. Manuelli and Peter E. Rossi (1993), 'Optimal Taxation in Models of Endogenous Growth', *Journal of Political Economy*, **101** (3), June, 485–517 — 277

F Taxes and Politics

17. Kevin W.S. Roberts (1977), 'Voting Over Income Tax Schedules', *Journal of Public Economics*, **8** (3), December, 329–40 — 313
18. Walter Hettich and Stanley L. Winer (1988), 'Economic and Political Foundations of Tax Structure', *American Economic Review*, **78** (4), September, 701–12 — 325

PART II OPTIMAL TAXATION

19. Peter A. Diamond and James A. Mirrlees (1971), 'Optimal Taxation and Public Production II: Tax Rules', *American Economic Review*, **61** (3, Part 1), June, 261–78 — 339
20. P.A. Diamond (1975), 'A Many-Person Ramsey Tax Rule', *Journal of Public Economics*, **4** (4), November, 335–42 — 357
21. J.A. Mirrlees (1971), 'An Exploration in the Theory of Optimum Income Taxation', *Review of Economic Studies*, **38** (2), April, 175–208 — 365

22. Peter A. Diamond (1998), 'Optimal Income Taxation: An Example with a U-Shaped Pattern of Optimal Marginal Tax Rates', *American Economic Review*, **88** (1), March, 83–95 — 399
23. A.B. Atkinson and J.E. Stiglitz (1976), 'The Design of Tax Structure: Direct Versus Indirect Taxation', *Journal of Public Economics*, **6** (1–2), 55–75 — 412
24. N.H. Stern (1976), 'On the Specification of Models of Optimum Income Taxation', *Journal of Public Economics*, **6** (1–2), 123–62 — 433
25. Emmanuel Saez (2001), 'Using Elasticities to Derive Optimal Income Tax Rates', *Review of Economic Studies*, **68** (1), January, 205–29 — 473
26. Joel Slemrod (1990), 'Optimal Taxation and Optimal Tax Systems', *Journal of Economic Perspectives*, **4** (1), Winter, 157–78 — 498

PART III TAX REFORM

27. Martin Feldstein (1976), 'On the Theory of Tax Reform', *Journal of Public Economics*, **6** (1–2), July–August, 77–104 — 523
28. Alan J. Auerbach, Laurence J. Kotlikoff and Jonathan Skinner (1983), 'The Efficiency Gains from Dynamic Tax Reform', *International Economic Review*, **24** (1), February, 81–100 — 551
29. David Altig, Alan J. Auerbach, Laurence J. Kotlikoff, Kent A. Smetters and Jan Walliser (2001), 'Simulating Fundamental Tax Reform in the United States', *American Economic Review*, **91** (3), June, 574–95 — 571

Acknowledgements

The editor and publishers wish to thank the authors and the following publishers who have kindly given permission for the use of copyright material.

American Economic Association for articles: Arnold C. Harberger (1964), 'The Measurement of Waste', *American Economic Review*, **54** (3), May, 58–76; Peter A. Diamond and James A. Mirrlees (1971), 'Optimal Taxation and Public Production II: Tax Rules', *American Economic Review*, **61** (3, Part 1), June, 261–78; Jerry A. Hausman (1981), 'Exact Consumer's Surplus and Deadweight Loss', *American Economic Review*, **71** (4), September, 662–76; James Davies, France St-Hilaire and John Whalley (1984), 'Some Calculations of Lifetime Tax Incidence', *American Economic Review*, **74** (4), September, 633–49; Edgar K. Browning (1987), 'On the Marginal Welfare Cost of Taxation', *American Economic Review*, **77** (1), March, 11–23; Peter A. Diamond (1998), 'Optimal Income Taxation: An Example with a U-Shaped Pattern of Optimal Marginal Tax Rates', *American Economic Review*, **88** (1), March, 83–95; Walter Hettich and Stanley L. Winer (1988), 'Economic and Political Foundations of Tax Structure', *American Economic Review*, **78** (4), September, 701–12; David M. Cutler (1988), 'Tax Reform and the Stock Market: An Asset Price Approach', *American Economic Review*, **78** (5), December, 1107–17; H. Peyton Young (1990), 'Progressive Taxation and Equal Sacrifice', *American Economic Review*, **80** (1), March, 253–66; Joel Slemrod (1990), 'Optimal Taxation and Optimal Tax Systems', *Journal of Economic Perspectives*, **4** (1), Winter, 157–78; David Altig, Alan J. Auerbach, Laurence J. Kotlikoff, Kent A. Smetters and Jan Walliser (2001), 'Simulating Fundamental Tax Reform in the United States', *American Economic Review*, **91** (3), June, 574–95.

Blackwell Publishing Ltd for articles: J.A. Mirrlees (1971), 'An Exploration in the Theory of Optimum Income Taxation', *Review of Economic Studies*, **38** (2), April, 175–208; Alan J. Auerbach, Laurence J. Kotlikoff and Jonathan Skinner (1983), 'The Efficiency Gains from Dynamic Tax Reform', *International Economic Review*, **24** (1), February, 81–100; Emmanuel Saez (2001), 'Using Elasticities to Derive Optimal Income Tax Rates', *Review of Economic Studies*, **68** (1), January, 205–29.

Elsevier for articles: Charles E. McLure, Jr (1975), 'General Equilibrium Incidence Analysis: The Harberger Model After Ten Years', *Journal of Public Economics*, **4** (2), February, 125–61; P.A. Diamond (1975), 'A Many-Person Ramsey Tax Rule', *Journal of Public Economics*, **4** (4), November, 335–42; Richard A. Musgrave (1976), 'ET, OT and SBT', *Journal of Public Economics*, **6** (1/2), July–August, 3–16; A.B. Atkinson and J.E. Stiglitz (1976), 'The Design of Tax Structure: Direct Versus Indirect Taxation', *Journal of Public Economics*, **6** (1–2), 55–75; Martin Feldstein (1976), 'On the Theory of Tax Reform', *Journal of Public Economics*, **6** (1–2), July–August, 77–104; N.H. Stern (1976), 'On the Specification of Models of Optimum

Income Taxation', *Journal of Public Economics*, **6** (1–2), 123–62; Kevin W.S. Roberts (1977), 'Voting Over Income Tax Schedules', *Journal of Public Economics*, **8** (3), December, 329–40; Don Fullerton (1982), 'On the Possibility of an Inverse Relationship Between Tax Rates and Government Revenues', *Journal of Public Economics*, **19** (1), 3–22.

National Tax Association for articles: Lawrence H. Summers (1983), 'The Asset Price Approach to the Analysis of Capital Income Taxation', *National Tax Association/Tax Institute of America, Proceedings of the Seventy-Sixth Annual Conference on Taxation*, 112–20; Charles L. Ballard, John B. Shoven and John Whalley (1985), 'The Total Welfare Cost of the United States Tax System: A General Equilibrium Approach', *National Tax Journal*, **XXXVIII** (2), 125–40; Louis Kaplow (1989), 'Horizontal Equity: Measures in Search of a Principle', *National Tax Journal*, **XLII** (2), 139–54; Timothy J. Besley and Harvey S. Rosen (1999), 'Sales Taxes and Prices: An Empirical Analysis', *National Tax Journal*, **LII** (3), 157–78.

Sage Publications via the Copyright Clearance Center for article: Michael Katz and Harvey S. Rosen (1985), 'Tax Analysis in an Oligopoly Model', *Public Finance Quarterly*, **13** (1), January, 3–19.

University of Chicago Press via Copyright Clearance Center's Rightslink Service for articles: John B. Shoven (1976), 'The Incidence and Efficiency Effects of Taxes on Income from Capital', *Journal of Political Economy*, **84** (6), December, 1261–83; Larry E. Jones, Rodolfo E. Manuelli and Peter E. Rossi (1993), 'Optimal Taxation in Models of Endogenous Growth', *Journal of Political Economy*, **101** (3), June, 485–517.

Every effort has been made to trace all the copyright holders but if any have been inadvertently overlooked the publishers will be pleased to make the necessary arrangement at the first opportunity.

In addition the publishers wish to thank the Library at the University of Warwick, UK, and the Library of Indiana University at Bloomington, USA, for their assistance in obtaining these articles.

Introduction

James Alm

Pothinus: Is it possible that Caesar, the conqueror of the world, has time to occupy himself with such a trifle as our taxes?
Caesar: My friend, taxes are the chief business of a conqueror of the world.
(George Bernard Shaw (*Caesar and Cleopatra*))

Taxation… is eternally lively; it concerns nine-tenths of us more directly than either smallpox or golf, and has just as much drama in it; moreover, it has been mellowed and made gay by as many gaudy, preposterous theories.
(H.L. Mencken)

At the most basic level, the economic functions of government are twofold: government collects taxes, and it spends these revenues. This selection of articles examines one of these functions, taxation in its many dimensions.

The choice of taxes involves the pursuit of multiple *goals*. Taxation must generate the revenues necessary to finance government expenditures, what might be termed 'adequacy'. It must raise these revenues in a way seen as fair, the goal of 'equity'. It must not unduly distort the decisions of individuals and firms ('efficiency'), although there may be circumstances in which changing these decisions is in fact the intention of taxation. Balancing these goals – and other goals like encouraging economic growth or achieving political acceptance, even making taxes easy to collect and to pay or promoting economic stabilization – in designing and reforming taxes in an 'optimal' way is an enduring challenge.

Taxation also has multiple *effects*, largely through its effects on incentives facing individuals and firms. Taxes affect incentives via their effects on relative prices, and agents seem likely to respond in an incredible range of behaviours. Individual choices include labour supply, saving, portfolio choice, capital gains realizations, bequests, evasion, and reporting; business choices include especially investment and financial structure decisions.

The papers in these two volumes represent much of the accumulated wisdom over the last several decades of economists working on these many issues. The papers are divided into five broad parts:

- Analyzing the Effects of Taxation
- Optimal Taxation
- Tax Reform
- Taxes and Individual Decisions
- Taxes and Business Decisions

The first three parts constitute Volume I of *The Economics of Taxation*; the last two make up Volume II. Within each part, there are additional divisions into sections, in which papers on specific research issues (e.g., notions of equity, taxes and labour supply) are collected. Papers in Volume I establish the positive and normative foundations for the analysis of taxation. Papers in Volume II represent the application of these broad positive and normative principles to specific behavioural issues.

It should be emphasized at the start that the papers in these two volumes, while comprehensive in their coverage in many respects, cannot of course cover all issues in taxation. The focus of these papers is clearly on the normative and positive evaluation of individual and corporate income taxes. Even so, within the individual income tax there are omissions, such as discussions of the appropriate definition of 'income', tax preferences, the income tax treatment of the family, and tax policy uncertainty. Similarly, there is no discussion of the impact of the corporate income tax on some dimensions of corporate behaviour, such as mergers and acquisitions. Many other taxes are omitted entirely or are given reduced emphasis, including property taxes, wealth taxes, and sales and excise taxes (including the personal consumption tax and the value-added tax). The use of taxation to achieve environmental objectives is not considered at all. There is also little discussion of taxation issues at the subnational level, including the appropriate assignment of taxes between levels of government or the potential for tax competition, and no discussion of the international dimension of taxes (including the effects of the corporate income tax on foreign direct investment). The macroeconomic effects of taxes are not examined here, including automatic stabilization issues, the size of tax and fiscal multipliers, and deficit finance. Even so, many of the most essential issues in taxation are discussed, and discussed in detail.

These papers share many common themes. An important one is that the appropriate analysis of taxes starts – and *must* start – with theory: it is theory that clarifies our thinking about the effects of taxation, and it is theory that lays the foundation for empirical analysis. The last several decades have seen theoretical analyses in public economics expanded from the traditional reliance upon a single period model of a single 'representative' agent to incorporate issues like asymmetric information, game theory, general equilibrium considerations, intertemporal and dynamic issues, and political economy, and these papers demonstrate these many expanded applications of theory. However, theory can only take one so far, and the actual effects of taxes remain an empirical issue. Accordingly, these papers also demonstrate the increased sophistication with which empirical methods have been used in public economics, expanding from simple cross-sectional (or time series) regressions at some aggregated level, to cross-sectional regressions with micro-level data, to estimations that better control for endogeneity, measurement error, selection bias, and identification, to data based on controlled laboratory or field experiments, even to purely computational approaches (as in computable general equilibrium modelling). Finally, the papers in these volumes demonstrate the somewhat fragile nature of many empirical results: identification is always difficult and always rests on some untestable assumptions; results vary by period, method, focus, sample, and the like; and the external validity of any empirical study is debatable. Indeed, there remains significant disagreement about the magnitude of behavioural responses to taxation, as shown by the papers in these volumes that examine such dimensions as labour supply, saving, portfolio choices, capital gains realizations, income reporting, firm investment decisions, and firm financial decisions.

Even so, theoretical and empirical analyses remain the essential core of research in public economics, and the papers in these two volumes exhibit, I believe, the very best of this work.

Volume I

Part I of Volume I ('Analyzing the Effects of Taxation') begins with the attempt to establish 'Notions of Equity'. The modern view of equity in taxation is most often based upon either the 'benefits principle' of taxation (e.g., people should pay taxes in accordance with the benefits that they receive from government) or the 'ability to pay principle' (e.g., people should pay taxes in accordance with their ability to pay, with people having equal ability to pay paying equal taxes and with people having greater ability paying greater taxes, or 'horizontal equity' versus 'vertical equity'). Richard A. Musgrave (1976; Chapter 1) discusses and illustrates in detail the foundations of these concepts and the often somewhat obscure difficulties in their applications, making reference to his own 1959 classic treatise *The Theory of Public Finance*.[1]

Peyton Young (1990; Chapter 2) focuses on a narrower and unresolved aspect of *vertical equity*: what does 'equal sacrifice', or the concept that individuals at different income levels should make the same 'sacrifice' when paying taxes, imply for the actual degree of progressivity of a tax system? In particular, does equal sacrifice imply a tax system that is progressive, proportional, or regressive? Young derives a general answer to this question that involves mainly the specification of a societal measure of inequality aversion, and he then illustrates his answer to this question with a specific application to the United States tax system. He concludes that equal sacrifice provides a reasonably accurate model of how the US federal tax burden has been distributed among most taxpayers, at least until the Tax Reform Act of 1986. He finds similar results for the United Kingdom, Italy, Japan, and West Germany.

Louis Kaplow (1989; Chapter 3) looks instead at *horizontal equity*, and examines the welfare foundations of this seemingly obvious notion of fairness in taxation. He concludes that there are 'serious doubts' about its normative basis and that the pursuit of equal treatment of equals can actually be welfare detracting. Indeed, he criticizes attempts to quantify horizontal equity in that those attempts are not based firmly on the welfare maximization process that underlies the Pareto principle, although he also recognizes that 'equal treatment of equals' is compelling as a practical principle of tax policy, even if this is (in his view) mainly because horizontal equity serves as a useful proxy that identifies factors that have not been appropriately considered in the more fundamental welfare maximization process. One implication of these papers is that the welfare foundations of 'Notions of Equity', together with their implications for tax structure, remain on a somewhat unstable basis.

However, regardless of one's actual notion of a fair tax, the effects of taxation on the distribution of income, or the 'incidence' of taxation, will no doubt be a central consideration. The next selection of papers examines the theoretical and empirical effects of taxes on the distribution of tax burdens ('Taxes and Income Distribution').

For many years prior to 1962, the standard analysis of tax incidence was based on partial equilibrium models, in which the effects of a single tax in a single market were analyzed. This analysis gave such standard – and correct – results as, for example, the split of an excise tax between buyers and sellers of the taxed good depended upon the relative elasticities of demand and of supply. However, partial equilibrium analysis was clearly limited in what it could analyze. In particular, it could not, by its very nature, consider the interdependence of markets. Many taxes have effects in multiple markets, and partial equilibrium analysis could not analyze the effects of one tax in other, related markets. For example, a tax on a product will affect the use of factors used to produce the product; similarly, a tax on a factor of production in a specific sector (e.g., the corporate income tax) will affect both the price of the product that the factor produces and the demand for the same factor in other untaxed uses; and a general tax (e.g., an income tax or a general sales tax) necessarily affects multiple markets simultaneously. More fundamentally, partial equilibrium analysis could not 'go behind the supply curve' of a single market, and so it could not consider the effects of a tax in other markets that might be related to the taxed market. This basic limitation was well recognized, but public finance economists simply did not possess the tools necessary to expand their analyses beyond a single market.

The paper that cut this Gordian knot came in 1962 by Arnold C. Harberger, with his development of a general equilibrium model of tax incidence.[2] Charles E. McLure (1975; Chapter 4) presents the details of the original Harberger model, and explains the ways in which the model addresses the limitations of the partial equilibrium approach to tax incidence. The Harberger model made a number of restrictive assumptions: two products, two factors, perfectly competitive markets, full employment via flexible prices, zero initial taxes, a single 'representative' consumer, fixed factor supplies in total with perfect intersectoral factor mobility, constant returns to scale technology, and a static (or single-period) setting. These assumptions allow the general model to be linearized and then solved analytically. As demonstrated by McLure, the basic insight of the model is that the effects of a tax in markets other than those in which it is introduced are often crucial in tax incidence. McLure also lays the groundwork for the many ways in which the simple version of the Harberger model might be expanded to deal with its own shortcomings. Indeed, the evolution of general equilibrium modelling has followed closely the directions outlined by McLure.

A somewhat different extension of standard tax incidence analysis is by Michael Katz and Harvey S. Rosen (1985; Chapter 5). Just as most analyses of tax incidence were based on partial equilibrium analysis, most analyses were also based on a single perfectly competitive market. Katz and Rosen expand the standard analysis to incorporate a conjectural variations model of oligopoly, thereby demonstrating the ways in which tax incidence depends narrowly upon the nature of firm interaction and broadly upon the degree of market competition. Their approach has been widely copied in other subsequent models of tax incidence in imperfectly competitive markets.

Lawrence H. Summers (1983; Chapter 6) also extends the theoretical analysis of tax incidence by using an 'asset price approach'. Most existing analyses of tax incidence – whether partial or general equilibrium – assumed that resource adjustments (e.g., capital reallocations in response to the corporate income tax) are both costless and instantaneous. However, neither assumption is realistic. In the presence of costly and slow factor adjustment, tax incidence analysis must consider tax-induced changes in asset prices, which measure the windfall gains and losses that arise when taxes are changed. Summers suggests that such asset price changes may often be a more important determinant of incidence than the long-run, steady-state changes in factor prices that emerge in partial or general equilibrium analyses.

The remaining papers in 'Taxation and Income Distribution' apply these theoretical insights to specific empirical settings. James Davies, France St-Hilaire, and John Whalley (1984; Chapter 7) calculate the 'lifetime' tax incidence of the Canadian tax system, and find a mild degree of tax progressivity that is quite robust to alternative incidence assumptions. Timothy J. Besley and Harvey S. Rosen (1999; Chapter 8) estimate the actual incidence of sales taxes using price data for 12 narrowly defined commodities in 155 different US cities, with quarterly price data for the period 1982 to 1990 issued by the American Chamber of Commerce Researchers Association. They find full shifting for a number of the commodities, but they also find over-shifting for more than half the products, a result they attribute to imperfect competition in the retail sector. John B. Shoven (1976; Chapter 9) uses a more fully specified, numerical variant of the original Harberger model of corporate income taxation to re-examine the incidence and efficiency effects of the tax, and generally finds the original Harberger results confirmed; that is, the burden of the corporate income tax is largely borne by the owners of capital, even in an expanded and more detailed general equilibrium model. David Cutler (1988; Chapter 10) examines the impact of the 1986 Tax Reform Act on the distribution of income, using the Summers asset price approach. The reform increased the overall corporate income tax burden by an estimated $120 billion over five years, reduced the corporate income tax rate from 46 per cent to 34 per cent, and changed the tax treatment of 'old' versus 'new' capital by repealing the investment tax credit and increasing effective tax lives of capital assets. The standard cash flow approach to incidence suggests that the increased corporate tax burden should be reflected in lower corporate returns; the asset price approach suggests considerable heterogeneity in the reform's impact, given firm variation in capital stocks (e.g., equipment, structures). Consistent with the asset price approach, Cutler found that firms with greater shares of equipment in their capital stocks benefited significantly via their stock price returns from the tax changes, while firms with larger pre-reform investment rates experienced share declines.

Taxes also affect the efficiency of resource use, and these effects are analyzed in the next section of Volume I ('Taxes and Efficiency'). Taxes cause inefficiency as people respond to the imposition of taxes in order to try to limit paying taxes, by working less, saving less, investing less, and the like. These responses result in an 'excess burden' from taxes, or a reduction in welfare in excess of the 'direct burden' in taxes that individuals pay. More precisely, the excess burden of taxation is the amount by which people are made worse off, over and above the direct burden in taxes that they pay. This concept is an old one, going at least as far back as Jules Dupuit in 1844,[3] and it had received considerable attention over the years. However, the concept and the measurement of excess burden had remained unsettled. The use of uncompensated Marshallian demand curves, with their associated 'consumer surplus' measures, had increasingly been criticized for such problems as 'path dependence' (e.g., the order in which one 'imposes' the taxes affects the calculated excess burden) and the lack of 'correspondence' between excess burden measures and underlying welfare changes (e.g., the calculated excess burden may indicate an efficiency loss even in the presence of an improvement in welfare). Various fixes to these problems had often been suggested, mainly focusing on the use of utility-compensated measures, such as the Hicksian 'equivalent variation' or 'compensating variation', or the Hicksian 'equivalent surplus' or 'compensating surplus', but without resolution. It – again – took Arnold C. Harberger (1964; Chapter 11) to lay the intellectual foundation for the 'measurement of waste'.

Harberger formulated a general equilibrium model for the exact measurement of excess burden in single or in multiple markets. He then established the conditions under which the general equilibrium model could be linearized, thereby allowing the exact measures of excess burden to be approximated both in general equilibrium and in partial equilibrium settings. These linear measures of excess burden have come to be known as 'Harberger triangles', and are familiar to every introductory student in economics.

Jerry A. Hausman (1981; Chapter 12) built on this work by demonstrating that one can derive exact measures of welfare changes, such as the Hicksian equivalent variation, the Hicksian compensating variation, or indeed any utility-compensated measure; that is, he showed that no approximation is needed. These exact measures of welfare changes can then be used in turn to calculate exact measures of the excess burden of taxation; again, no approximation is needed, and these exact measures are not subject to the possible errors associated with approximate measures based on consumer surplus measures. Hausman's basic insight was to apply duality to the observed market demand curve, in order to derive the unobserved compensated demand curve either via a 'quasi' indirect utility function or a 'quasi' expenditure function. With either of these functions, exact measures of welfare changes and of excess burdens can be calculated, at least for changes in a single price or tax. All that is needed are estimates of the uncompensated demand function in order to produce exact estimates that correspond to the correct theoretical magnitude.

These measures then can be extended to measure the 'marginal excess burden' of a tax, or the change in excess burden arising from a given tax change. More precisely, as originally developed in 1976 by Edgar K. Browning (under the name the 'marginal cost of public funds'),[4] the marginal excess burden is the ratio of the *change* in excess burden associated with a change in taxation and the *change* in tax revenue resulting from the tax change; that is, it is the change in excess burden for an additional dollar of tax revenue. The concept was extended by Browning in his later 1987 work (Chapter 13). He argued that the 'true' cost of any change in taxation is most accurately measured not by the total excess burden of the tax, but by the amount of revenue raised plus the added distortion. It is this cost that is measured by the marginal excess burden of the tax. Browning derived a simple formula for its measurement, using labour taxation as the framework, and showed that it depends upon four parameters: the marginal tax rate, the labour supply elasticity, the degree of progressivity of the change in taxation, and labour earnings. He then estimated the marginal excess burden for a range of parameter values, and finds that it could vary between 10 cents and 300 cents per each additional dollar of revenue (with his preferred estimates between 32 cents and 47 cents). He concluded that it is not possible to estimate the marginal excess burden very accurately, given uncertainty about the relevant parameters.

Charles L. Ballard, John B. Shoven, and John Whalley (1985; Chapter 14) focus instead on measuring the total excess burden of taxation. They construct a computable general equilibrium (CGE) model to examine the effects of taxes on efficiency, with 19 production sectors and 12 consumer groups. They then calibrate it to the US economy using 1973 data, and simulate the replacement of distorting taxes with neutral lump-sum taxes. They find that the total excess burden of all taxes is quite substantial; that is, the replacement of all distorting taxes with neutral taxes generates welfare gains of 13.2 per cent to 23.8 per cent of baseline revenues, depending upon the elasticities of labour supply and of savings. They also estimate that the most distorting of the various taxes are those on capital and on labour income, largely because these taxes inhibit capital accumulation.

Aside from incidence and efficiency effects, the structure and level of taxes also affect the revenues that they generate, and the next section ('Taxes and Revenues') examines this connection. An ongoing policy debate examines whether a reduction in tax *rates* can lead to an increase in tax *revenues*. In a simple case, tax revenues R from a single tax are equal to the tax rate t times the value of the tax base b, so that $R = tb$. In a world where the tax base is fixed, a change in the tax rate leads to a corresponding change in tax revenues; that is, if the tax base is fixed, then a reduction in the tax rate of, say, 10 per cent necessarily leads to a reduction in tax revenues of 10 per cent. However, the tax base is most likely a negative function of the tax rate, or $b(t)$, with $b' < 0$. Consequently, the impact of a tax rate change on tax revenues becomes $\Delta R = b\Delta t + t\Delta b + \Delta t \Delta b$, or (ignoring the last term) $\%\Delta R = \%\Delta t + \%\Delta b$. In this world, the more does b increase with a reduction in the tax rate the more are additional revenues generated from a tax decrease. Indeed, the revenue-maximizing tax rate in this simple case is inversely proportional to the tax base response. In the special case where the tax base b is a constant-elasticity function, or $b = A(1 - t)^\eta$, where A is an arbitrary constant and η is the elasticity of the tax base with respect to the tax price $(1 - t)$, then the revenue-maximizing tax rate t^* equals $[1/(1 + \eta)]$.

The issue then becomes the level of the tax rates (or t) and the responsiveness of the tax base (or the tax base elasticity η). One school of thought, the so-called 'Supply Side' school, is often characterized as arguing that the tax rates are so high and that the base response is so large that a reduction in tax rates will actually lead to greater revenues. It is this thinking that lies behind the 'Laffer Curve', named for Arthur Laffer who suggested that reducing tax rates in the US economy in the late 1970s would increase revenues. Looking at historical, time series information on tax rates and tax revenues is not particularly instructive here, given the myriad factors that are likely changing along with tax rates. Don Fullerton (1982; Chapter 15) takes a different approach to this issue. Like Ballard, Shoven, and Whalley, he develops a CGE model to examine the effects of taxes on revenues, calibrates it to the US economy using 1973 data, and then simulates various changes in labour and capital income tax rates, in an attempt to generate the Laffer Curve and the position of the US economy on the curve. He finds that the 1973 US economy was almost certainly operating in the 'normal' region of the Laffer Curve, in which increases in tax rates lead to increases in tax revenues. In particular, given estimated labour supply elasticities, he calculates the revenue-maximizing tax rate on labour income was 78.8 per cent, far in excess of the actual calculated tax rate of 31.8 per cent. Fullerton also finds no 'prohibitive' region of the Laffer Curve for capital income taxes; that is, given reasonable values for savings and other elasticities, revenues always increased with increases in capital taxes.

The effect of taxes on economic growth is also increasingly an important issue in policy discussions ('Taxes and Growth'). Larry E. Jones, Rodolfo E. Manuelli, and Peter E. Rossi (1993; Chapter 16) employ an infinite-horizon, representative-agent dynamic model of endogenous growth to examine the impact on economic growth rates of changing the system of taxation from a distorting set of taxes on human and physical capital to one suggested by optimal Ramsey taxation. They solve different variants of their basic model numerically, and they consistently find large impacts on growth rates from a move to optimal taxation, especially a move toward less reliance on capital taxes and more reliance on consumption taxes. Put differently, their simulations demonstrate that distorting taxes have a large and negative impact on economic growth. Of some note, in their preferred variant they find that the limiting tax rate on physical capital is positive, in contrast to some other dynamic models that conclude that capital should not be taxed at all if the policy goal is to encourage higher rates of growth.

A decidedly different approach to taxation is taken in the papers on 'Taxes and Politics'. Just like any government policy, taxes are determined in the political arena. Considerations like equity, efficiency, and adequacy may certainly play a role here, but the forces shaping political outcomes are often different than the forces shaping the distributional, efficiency, or revenue effects of taxation. The papers by Kevin W.S. Roberts (1977; Chapter 17) and by Walter Hettich and Stanley L. Winer (1988; Chapter 18) explore these political forces and their effects on how taxes are voted upon and determined.

A standard result in political economy is the 'Median Voter Theorem', which states that under some conditions the outcome of majority voting is determined by the preferences of the median voter. These conditions include the requirement that each individual has 'single-peaked preferences' (e.g., utility declines as the level of government provision moves away from the individual's most preferred outcome) and that the vote is on a 'single-dimensional issue' (e.g., the level of government provision). When these conditions do not hold, then the so-called 'voting paradox' can arise in which there is no unique outcome in majority voting. Indeed, it is well-known that a political equilibrium may well fail to exist without some restrictions on individual preferences, as established by Kenneth J. Arrow in his 'Impossibility Theorem'.[5]

Roberts examines what happens when individuals vote on a distortionary linear income tax. In voting on taxes, he argues that the assumption of single-peaked preferences seems especially likely to be violated. Even so, he shows that, under some reasonable additional conditions that are typically imposed, a stable and most preferred outcome will likely exist under a wide class of voting rules, including majority voting.

Hettich and Winer also examine voting over taxation, but their focus is more on the political forces that determine the structure of any tax: its tax base, its tax rates, and any special provisions. They invoke a probabilistic voting process in which political actors attempt to maximize expected support (subject to raising some level of revenues), and also in which a voter's support for a politician depends upon the benefits and costs of government decisions. They are able to demonstrate how the political choice of tax base, tax rates, and special provisions can be viewed as the outcome of self-interested and maximizing decisions by public (and private) actors, dependent on political calculations, on administrative costs, and on individual responses to taxes. In particular, the politically optimal tax structure is one that equalizes across all taxpayers the marginal political cost of an additional dollar of taxation. A particularly striking feature of this result is that complexity of a tax system, while often bemoaned and criticized, is the clear politically rational response of political agents to the benefits and costs of the political process.

Part II of Volume I takes many of these separate themes (e.g., equity, efficiency, adequacy) and combines them in an attempt to determine a system of 'Optimal Taxation'. The choice of optimal taxes in a first-best world is an easy exercise: finance government expenditures via neutral lump-sum taxes to achieve efficiency goals, and redistribute via (again) neutral lump-sum taxes to achieve equity goals. The use of lump-sum taxes allows the government to finance any required expenditures; it also allows the government to achieve both the standard efficiency conditions for Pareto efficient allocation of resources and the required interpersonal equity conditions. In short, first-best taxation allows the economy to achieve the social welfare maximizing position on the economy's utility possibility frontier.

However, taxation becomes considerably more complicated when neutral lump-sum taxes are not possible. In the presence of distorting taxes, government must face squarely the possible tradeoffs between equity and efficiency (as well as adequacy); that is, taxes that achieve distributional goals may well come at the expense of efficiency goals (as well as revenue goals). The papers in 'Optimal Taxation' confront these tradeoffs in different ways.

Despite their different approaches, these papers have several common elements, reflective of the common methodology of optimal taxation. First, each paper assumes that the goal of government is to maximize some objective function, typically a social welfare function that depends upon the utilities of individuals. Second, each paper assumes that government must choice its policies subject to a set of constraints, especially a government budget requirement, but also including the requirements that each individual maximizes utility, that each firm maximizes profits, that markets clear, and that resource and technological constraints are satisfied. Put differently, largely because of information constraints, the government cannot simply require individuals and firms to behave in a particular way but must instead make its own choices consistent with the optimizing behaviour of individuals and firms. Third, each paper assumes that the government has available the choice of different tax instruments. It is here where different 'branches' of the optimal taxation literature emerge. When only commodity taxes are available, the results characterize the structure of optimal commodity taxation; when only income taxes are available, optimal income taxation emerges; and when both commodity and income taxes are available, the analysis generates the optimal tax mix.

There were in fact some early papers that examined optimal taxation, including one by Frank A. Ramsey in 1927 and another one by Paul A. Samuelson in 1950, that was unpublished until 1986.[6] However, the paper that largely launched the more recent optimal taxation literature is by Peter A. Diamond and James A. Mirrlees (1971; Chapter 19), who set the government problem of choosing distorting commodity and income taxes in a general equilibrium setting. Diamond quickly followed in 1975 (Chapter 20) with a paper that focused on optimal *commodity* taxes in an economy with many different individuals, in order to examine explicitly the tradeoffs between equitable taxation and efficient taxation, tradeoffs that were not capable of being examined in simpler models with only one representative consumer. Mirrlees also expanded the analysis to focus on optimal *income* taxation in his 1971 paper (Chapter 21), a problem also revisited by Diamond in 1998 (Chapter 22). In contrast, Anthony B. Atkinson and Joseph E. Stiglitz (1976; Chapter 23) considered the more general problem of the optimal tax mix; that is, when both direct taxes (e.g., income taxes) and indirect taxes (e.g., consumption taxes) are available, under what conditions will both taxes actually be used? Given the extreme difficulties in characterizing precisely the nature of the optimal income tax rates, Nicholas Stern (1976; Chapter 24) used numerical methods to solve for the optimal income tax rates. Similarly, Emmanuel Saez (2001; Chapter 25) built on his own empirical work in which he estimated individual reporting responses and then used these estimated elasticities to calculate optimal income tax rates.

The general results from all of this work can be summarized in several 'propositions', which relate to the different branches of the optimal taxation tree. Regarding *optimal commodity taxation*, if *efficiency* is the only consideration, then commodity tax rates should be chosen to achieve equal proportional reductions in the (compensated) demands for all commodities, so that goods with more elastic demands should be taxed at lower rates (e.g., the 'Ramsey Rule'); in the special case of zero cross effects, commodity tax rates should be inversely proportional to the compensated elasticity of demand. More generally, uniform or proportional tax rates are not typically optimal, except when labour supply is fixed or when preferences are homothetic and separable between leisure and consumption. However, when both *equity* and *efficiency* considerations enter, then the simple Ramsey Rule results are modified. Goods consumed more heavily by those whose welfare is weighted more heavily by society (such as lower income groups) should now be taxed at lower rates.

Regarding *optimal income taxation*, considerations only of *equity* require that income taxes should be higher on those with greater income; indeed, under some special conditions (e.g., fixed income, identical utility functions, diminishing marginal utility of income), income taxes should be chosen to equalize after-tax incomes, thereby implying marginal tax rates of 100 per cent. However, when both *equity* and *efficiency* matter, marginal tax rates should be lower the more responsive are individuals in their labour decisions, the smaller is the spread in the skills of the individuals, the less concerned with equality is society, and the lower is the amount of revenue that government must collect. In fact, the marginal tax rate on the single richest individual should (under some circumstances) be zero.

The results regarding the *optimal tax mix* also depend upon the objectives of government. When only *efficiency* matters, the optimal tax mix requires simply a lump-sum income tax, and commodity taxes are not even used. However, when *efficiency and equity* both matter, then both income and commodity taxes should be used in general; under some restrictive conditions (e.g., separability between leisure and consumption), the optimal form of commodity tax rates that are imposed in the presence of an optimal income tax requires that the commodity tax rates be uniform, so that taxation of commodities at different rates is not optimal and only the optimal income tax is effectively used.

However, despite these various insights and conclusions, the impact of optimal taxation on practical tax policy remains quite limited. Joel Slemrod (1990; Chapter 26) explores some of these reasons, arguing that the analysis of optimal taxation typically ignores a range of relevant practical considerations reflecting actual fiscal systems, all of which are essential elements in the normative and positive analysis of taxation. In particular, he suggests that the standard optimal taxation methodology often ignores the effects that arise because taxes must be collected, at some cost to both the tax agency and the taxpayer, and that this collection must be enforced, again at some cost to the agency and the individual. Slemrod argues that it is only when these real-world considerations of administration, enforcement, and compliance are appropriately considered that optimal taxation will become more relevant to the design and the reform of real-world tax systems. Incorporating these considerations remains a significant challenge to optimal tax theorists.

Part III of Volume I builds on this last insight – the relevance of real-world fiscal institutions in the formulation of tax policy – to examine a somewhat different issue: how can an existing tax system be optimally reformed? The *design* of a new tax system is decidedly different than the *reform* of an existing system. The papers in Part III examine the different sets of issues that arise when policy makers are required to work within the confines of an already existing tax system.

Martin Feldstein (1976; Chapter 27) argues that tax reform is a piecemeal and dynamic process, unlike the once-and-for-all nature of tax design. Given this fundamental difference between reform and design, he goes on to argue that tax reform will necessarily generate efficiency gains that justify the reform, but that it will also introduce both more uncertainties and more horizontal inequities than the once-and-for-all nature of tax design: more uncertainties since reform will change the parameters of the tax system over time, and more horizontal inequities since reform will change the 'rules of the game' under which commitments have already been made. The basic tax reform tradeoff is therefore between the efficiency gains (inclusive of uncertainties) that justify the reform versus the horizontal inequities that reform necessarily introduces. His 'intuition' is that the optimal tax reform will be one in which the tax reform is fully enacted (rather than partially enacted) but also one in which its implementation is postponed (rather than immediate or phased-in): the postponement allows individuals to adjust their commitments to reduce the horizontal inequities, while the full enactment allows the efficiency gains to be eventually and fully realized.

Alan J. Auerbach, Laurence J. Kotlikoff and Jonathan Skinner (1983; Chapter 28) examine tax reform using numerical methods. They construct a dynamic general equilibrium rational expectations model, based upon life-cycle-maximizing individuals, profit-maximizing producers, and a budget-constrained government, and they simulate the model over 55 overlapping generations of individuals intended to represent the life span of an adult. Given that they assume a single representative agent for each generation, their simulations determine the pure efficiency gains from tax reform. Their results indicate the presence of significant efficiency gains by changing from the existing US tax system to a proportional consumption tax, a change that increases welfare by roughly two per cent of lifetime resources. They also find that virtually any degree of progressivity in an income tax leads to substantial efficiency losses.

David Altig, Alan J. Auerbach, Laurence J. Kotlikoff, Kent A. Smetters, and Jan Walliser (2001; Chapter 29) use a similar but much extended version of a dynamic general equilibrium rational expectations model, in which 12 different types are introduced within each age cohort to examine both intragenerational and intergenerational redistributions. Their model also allows for a detailed representation of the existing fiscal system (e.g., tax preferences, social security, Medicare). They use their model to simulate the effects of five fundamental tax reforms, each of which replaces the then-existing tax system (1996) in a revenue-neutral manner with: a proportional income tax, a proportional consumption tax, a flat tax, a flat tax with transition relief, or an 'X tax' (e.g., a high rate flat tax with a progressive subsidy to wages). They find significant long-run increases in output for some reforms, such as the proportional income tax and especially the proportional consumption tax reforms. However, in both cases the efficiency gains come at the expense of lower income and older groups. Attempts to protect these groups from the redistributional effects of reform substantially reduce the long-run gains in output.

Volume II

Volume II of *The Economics of Taxation* focuses on two broad themes: 'Taxes and Individual Decisions' and 'Taxes and Business Decisions'. The common theme of both is the increasing use of empirical methods to estimate the behavioural effects of taxes.

The starting point for most analyses of individual responses to taxation is based on the standard model of consumer choice, in which a single representative individual faces a single-period budget constraint whose position and slope are affected by taxation. In this framework, a tax has both income and substitution effects, and it is via the effect on the relative price of goods that most of the impacts of taxes are derived. In the first section of Part I of Volume II ('Incentives'), Joel Slemrod (2001; Chapter 1) builds on this framework but also considerably generalizes it by allowing individuals to change both their 'real response' (e.g., via labour supply) to taxation and their 'financial form response' or 'accounting response' (e.g., via tax avoidance activities). (An additional dimension is a 'timing response', as discussed later under 'Capital Gains'.) The introduction of tax avoidance activities as an additional dimension of behaviour allows Slemrod to demonstrate that the income and substitution effects of taxes depend on the standard consideration (e.g., preferences) but also on the technology of tax avoidance activities. An important conclusion is that the behavioural response to a change in the net-of-tax price (or $p[1 + t]$) of an activity depends on whether the underlying driver is a change in p or a change in $[1 + t]$.

The next sections examine a range of individual responses to taxes, starting with 'Labour Supply'. The pioneering work on estimating the impact of taxes on labour supply is by Jerry A. Hausman (1981; Chapter 2). Prior to his work, most empirical analyses concluded that tax impacts on labour supply were small, based largely on the estimated impact of wages on hours worked. These studies typically found income and substitution effects from wages that were both small and often offsetting. It was recognized that these estimated effects demonstrated only the impact of (net) wages on hours worked, and not the direct impact of taxes on hours worked. It was also recognized that these estimated effects were plagued by numerous and serious econometric issues (e.g., selection bias, endogeneity, measurement errors, unobserved variables, identification). Even so, the appropriate method for estimating the direct impact of taxes on labour supply was elusive. Additional complications for empirical work stemmed from the progressive individual income tax and its interaction with the transfer system, both of which created a non-linear and potentially a non-convex budget constraint that underlay the individual optimization.

Hausman addressed many of these problems in several steps. He incorporated the progressive individual income by introducing the concept of a piece-wise linear budget constraint that depends on a set of 'virtual incomes' (or the levels of income implied by each segment of the progressive income tax). He combined income taxes and transfer systems in his specification of the non-convex budget constraint facing individuals. He allowed for the possibility of multiple outcomes that satisfied the standard first-order conditions for utility maximization by conducting a search of those labour supply choices that were both feasible and optimal (e.g., multiple tangencies, joint tangencies). Finally, he estimated the underlying behavioural responses using non-linear least squares methods. Hausman found that labour supply responses were characterized by large and significant compensated wage elasticities, especially for secondary workers but also for prime-age males; that is, unlike much previous work, his estimates suggested – essentially for the first time in empirical work – that taxes had a significant, negative impact on hours worked. Since then, his use of non-linear least squares estimation of the piece-wise linear budget constraint has been questioned, because this method necessarily imposes statistical constraints that imply large substitution responses (and low income responses).[7] Even so, Hausman is largely responsible for changing the perception of how taxes affect labour supply.

Hausman's approach was based on a static model of individual choice. James P. Ziliak and Thomas J. Kniesner (1999; Chapter 3) extend the framework to a life-cycle model of labour supply, allowing for intertemporally progressive taxes (along with uncertainty). They estimate their model with panel data using a two-stage, fixed-effects, generalized method-of-moments approach that also allows for wage endogeneity and worker-specific effects. Ziliak and Kniesner are able to estimate both intratemporal and intertemporal preferences. They find that taxes have substantial impacts on the labour supply of prime-age men, indeed larger effects than those of Hausman and others based on a static approach.

The next three papers also deal with intertemporal effects, or the impact of taxes on 'Saving'. Many analyses of saving start – and finish – with a focus on a single representative individual in a simple two-period life-cycle model. Lawrence H. Summers (1981; Chapter 4) argues that this approach is fundamentally misleading. The focus on two periods does not allow for the 'human wealth effect' that arises from the impact of changes in interest rates on the present value of future labour income. The focus on a single individual does not allow for the heterogeneity that arises in aggregate behaviour (e.g., savers versus dissavers, young versus old); it also does not allow for general equilibrium effects of saving on factors prices. Summers constructs a more 'realistic' model that addresses each of these limitations. He then uses it to generate an aggregate saving function, and simulates the effects of changes in interest rates on aggregate saving. His numerical results indicate quite large saving-interest rate elasticities, ranging (in his preferred estimates) from 1.89 to 3.36, estimates far above most empirical estimates of saving elasticities. A clear implication is that the excess burden of taxes on capital is significantly larger than most previous work suggests.

William G. Gale and John Karl Scholz (1994; Chapter 5) examine the impact of taxes on saving using empirical methods and focusing on the impact of Individual Retirement Accounts (IRAs). The specific features of IRAs have changed over time, but even so they typically allow individuals to make tax-deductible contributions to savings plans up to an annual limit, with tax-free accrual of interest and substantial penalties for early withdrawal before the age of 59.5. The main empirical issue is whether contributions to IRAs constitute 'new' saving (or saving that would not have been undertaken in the absence of the special provisions) or simply a reshuffling of 'existing' saving from non-tax-preferred accounts to tax-preferred IRA accounts; that is, do households view IRAs as good or poor substitutes for other assets? Gale and Scholz construct a formal model of dynamic utility maximization that generates closed-form equations for IRA and other saving. They then test their model using US data surrounding changes in IRA contribution limits between 1983 and 1986. Their data suggest that most contributors were likely to find IRAs and other saving to be very good substitutes, suggesting that IRA changes led mainly to portfolio reshuffling and not to new saving. Their empirical estimates are consistent with this finding, and indicate that raising the annual IRA contribution limit between 1983 and 1986 led to little new saving.

James M. Poterba, Steven F. Venti, and David A. Wise (1995; Chapter 6) also use empirical methods to examine the impact of taxes on saving, but examine a different tax preference, 401(k) contributions. These plans allow individuals working in firms that offer the programs to make deposits in 401(k) accounts, where the deposits are tax deductible and the returns accrue tax-free, with taxes paid only upon withdrawal. As with other saving incentive programs (like IRAs), the main policy issue is whether the deposits are new saving or a reshuffling of existing saving. Poterba, Venti, and Wise use US data from the 1984, 1987, and 1991 Surveys of Income and Program Participation to examine patterns of participation in and contributions to the 401(k) plans. Their empirical methods compare the growth of non-401(k) assets for both contributors and non-contributors, and also compare the level of wealth for families that are eligible for 401(k) plans with the level for families that are not eligible. Overall, they find little evidence that 401(k) contributions substitute for other forms of savings, suggesting that the contributions represent new saving.

The following section examines theoretical and empirical work on the allocation of saving between different assets ('Portfolio Choice'). In his classic 1969 paper (Chapter 7), Joseph E.

Stiglitz analyzes the effects of various taxes (income, wealth, capital gains) on risk-taking, using an expected utility model in which an individual can invest a fixed amount of saving in different assets, a 'safe' asset with a guaranteed and certain return and a 'risky' asset with an uncertain return. He finds in almost all cases that taxes of whatever type have theoretically ambiguous effects on the demand for the safe versus the risky asset. Each tax typically has income and substitution effects, whose directions often conflict and whose magnitudes depend on individual attitudes toward risk. Stiglitz also finds that the impact depends critically on features of the tax code (e.g., full loss offset versus no loss offset).

Empirical tests of taxes on portfolio choice are challenging, given especially the difficulties in finding reliable information on individual portfolios. James M. Poterba and Andrew A. Samwick (2003; Chapter 8) are able to address these challenges, using data from the US 1983, 1989, 1992, 1995 and 1998 Surveys of Consumer Finances from the Federal Reserve Board. They classify the financial assets of households into eight categories based on their tax treatment (taxable equity held directly, taxable equity held in mutual funds, equity held in tax-deferred accounts, bonds held in tax-deferred accounts, tax-exempt bonds, taxable bonds, interest bearing accounts, and other financial assets). They use these different categories to estimate the impact of a household's marginal tax rate (and other socioeconomic and demographic characteristics) on two aspects of the household portfolio problem: whether to allocate any funds to a given asset category (using probit models), and how much to allocate to each category with positive holdings (using tobit models). Their estimation results indicate that households with higher marginal income tax rates are more likely to own tax-advantaged assets such as publicly traded stock and tax-exempt bonds than are comparable households with lower marginal tax rates. They also find that taxes affect the shares of portfolios in different assets. High marginal tax rate households are more likely to hold assets in tax-deferred accounts (e.g., IRAs, Keoghs, and defined contribution pension plans) and in other tax-favored forms (e.g., corporate stock), and are less likely to hold their portfolio in heavily taxed assets like interest-bearing accounts.

Related to portfolio choice is the impact of taxation on the realization and the timing of 'Capital Gains'. Income from the realization of capital gains is typically taxed differently – and often preferentially – relative to other types of income like wages and salaries, although the precise form of capital gains taxation has varied significantly over the years. Martin S. Feldstein, Joel Slemrod, and Shlomo Yitzhaki (1980; Chapter 9) use a detailed sample of individual tax returns to estimate the impact of marginal tax rates on capital gains realizations. Their data are based on a probability sample of all US taxpayers who own stock (and not just of those who sold stock) in 1973, using taxpayer receipt of dividend income to identify stockholders. They estimate the impact of marginal tax rates and other individual characteristics like age, income, and portfolio size on the net realization of capital gains by each stockholder (as well as on the value of their stock sold); given that Feldstein, Slemrod, and Yitzhaki have cross-section data, they must use differences in income and the resulting differences in marginal tax rates to identify the impact of taxes on realizations. Their estimation results indicate that realizations are quite sensitive to the marginal tax rate, with a 10 percentage point change in the marginal tax rate changing the gain-to-dividend ratio by a factor of 4.97. Indeed, their results imply that a reduction in the tax rate on capital gains would actually increase the total revenues.

Leonard E. Burman and William C. Randolph (1994; Chapter 10) also examine the response of capital gains realizations to taxation, with a somewhat different approach. They distinguish between a 'permanent tax rate' change (or a change in the tax rate on long-term capital gains) and a 'transitory tax rate' change, arguing that transitory changes are likely to influence mainly the timing of realizations and not their permanent level and using state tax rates to distinguish permanent from transitory tax changes. They then estimate the impact of permanent tax rates on capital gains using a panel of roughly 11 000 US taxpayers for the period 1979 to 1983; they also use instrumental variable methods to control for possible endogeneity of marginal tax rates and for selection issues. Their main estimation results indicate that the elasticity of capital gains realizations to permanent tax changes (–0.18) is significantly smaller than the transitory response (–6.42), and much smaller than estimates from most other previous studies; that is, the main effect of taxes on capital gains realizations is via changes in the timing of realizations, not on their levels. Their results are consistent with a large 'timing response' of behaviour to changes in tax rates.

With an aging population, the effects of estate and gift taxes on behaviour, especially giving behaviour, is of increasing importance. These effects are examined by James Poterba (2001; Chapter 11) in 'Estate Taxes'. The federal estate (and gift) tax in the US is imposed on the value of assets transferred at the taxpayer's death, plus the value of taxable gifts that were made during the decedent's lifetime, with some exemptions. The various features of the estate and gift tax have changed significantly over time. For the data that Poterba examined (from the 1995 Survey of Consumer Finances), the tax was imposed at progressive rates that reached 60 per cent, but only on estates valued at more than $600 000; also, inter-spousal gifts and bequests were not taxed, and each individual was allowed while living to make an unlimited number of tax-free gifts of $10 000 per year per recipient (or *inter vivos* giving). Poterba focuses on the incentives for *inter vivos* giving, and he finds that the 1995 level of intergenerational transfers was much lower than the level that would be implied by simple models of dynastic utility maximization. Even among elderly households with net worth in excess of $2.5 million, over four times the net worth at which US households became liable for estate tax in 1995, he finds that only 45 per cent took advantage of the opportunity for tax-free *inter vivos* giving. His cross-sectional regressions using the 1995 data suggest that households with greater net worth make more transfers, that households with more net worth in illiquid forms are less likely to make transfers than those with more liquid wealth, and that those with substantial unrealized capital gains, for whom the benefits of 'basis step-up at death' under the income tax are greatest, are less likely to make large *inter vivos* transfers than similarly wealthy households with higher basis assets.

Nearly all of these papers assume that taxpayers comply fully with the tax system. However, there is little doubt that individuals do not like paying taxes, and they take a variety of actions to reduce their tax liabilities. Some of these actions are legal practices that take full advantage of the tax code (or 'tax avoidance'), such as income splitting, postponement of taxes, and tax arbitrage across income that faces different tax treatment. Others are illegal and intentional (or 'tax evasion'): underreporting incomes, sales, or wealth; overstating deductions, exemptions, or credits; or failing to file appropriate tax returns. Tax evasion is notoriously difficult to measure. Still, there is widespread evidence that tax evasion is extensive and commonplace in nearly all countries.

Tax evasion is important for many reasons. The most obvious is that its presence reduces tax collections, thereby affecting taxes that compliant taxpayers face and public services that citizens receive. Evasion creates misallocations in resource use when individuals alter their behaviour to cheat on their taxes, such as in their choices of hours to work, occupations to enter, and investments to undertake. As emphasized earlier by Slemrod, its presence requires that government expend resources to deter non-compliance, to detect its magnitude, and to penalize its practitioners. Non-compliance alters the distribution of income in unpredictable, arbitrary, and unfair ways. Evasion may contribute to feelings of unjust treatment and disrespect for the law. It affects the accuracy of macroeconomic statistics. More broadly, as argued by Alm (2010), it is not possible to understand the true impact of taxation without recognizing the existence of tax evasion.[8]

'Tax Evasion' is the focus of the three papers by Michael G. Allingham and Agnar Sandmo (1972; Chapter 12), Charles T. Clotfelter (1983; Chapter 13), and James Alm, Gary H. McClelland and William D. Schulze (1992; Chapter 14). Allingham and Sandmo launched the analysis of tax evasion in their theoretical paper, based upon an economics-of-crime approach. In their model, a rational individual is viewed as maximizing the expected utility of the tax evasion gamble, weighing the benefits of successful cheating against the risky prospect of detection and punishment. They show that the individual pays taxes because he or she is afraid of getting caught and penalized if he or she does not report all income. This 'portfolio' approach gives the plausible result that compliance depends upon audit rates and fine rates. Indeed, its central point is that an individual pays taxes because – indeed, *only* because – of this fear of detection and punishment.

The basic Allingham and Sandmo approach has since been extended in many dimensions: by expanding individual choices (e.g., labour supply occupational choice, sectoral choice, avoidance strategies); by introducing alternative penalty, tax, and tax withholding functions; by incorporating complexity and uncertainty about the relevant fiscal parameters; by allowing the use of paid preparers; by recognizing the provision of government services; giving individuals positive rewards for honesty; and by allowing systematic audit selection rules in which the tax authority uses information from the tax returns to determine strategically whom to audit. There has also been work to expand the basic Allingham and Sandmo model of individual choice beyond its economics-of-crime foundation, by introducing some aspects of behaviour considered explicitly by other social sciences. Many of these can be discussed under the rubric of 'Behavioural Economics', broadly defined as an approach that uses methods and evidence from other social sciences (especially psychology) to inform the analysis of individual and group decision making. Even so, the basic theoretical premise and result remain largely unaltered, at least in work based on expected utility: individuals focus mainly on the financial incentives of the evasion gamble, and individuals pay taxes *only* because they fear detection and punishment.

The Allingham and Sandmo model provides a convenient framework for empirical analysis of tax evasion. However, empirical analysis obviously requires some measure of non-compliance, and such measures are obviously difficult to find and subject to much criticism. After all, tax evasion is illegal, and individuals have strong incentives to conceal their cheating, given financial and other penalties that are imposed on individuals who are found cheating on their taxes. These limitations have not prevented researchers from attempting to estimate the determinants of evasion, whatever the source of data, and researchers have become increasingly sophisticated in their search for evasion data.

The most accurate source of information on individual compliance is based on 'direct' measurement of evasion via actual audits of individual returns. For example, from 1965 to

1988, the US Internal Revenue Service (IRS) conducted detailed line-by-line audits of a stratified random sample of roughly 50000 individual tax returns on a 3-year cycle via its Taxpayer Compliance Measurement Program (TCMP). These audits yielded an IRS estimate of the taxpayer's 'true' income, which when compared to actual reported items allowed the IRS to calculate measures of income tax evasion. The TCMP has now been replaced by the National Research Program (NRP), which examined roughly 46000 randomly selected individual returns for the year 2001 (but only some of which were subject to line-by-line audits). NRP data are now being analyzed in detail. Few other countries have systematic audit-based programs.

Clotfelter was the first to analyze systematically the impact of fiscal incentives on tax evasion. He had access to the individual TCMP data for 1969, and he used these data to estimate with tobit maximum likelihood methods the determinants of underreported income, for several different types of taxpayers and for several different audit classes. He found that non-compliance increases significantly with marginal tax rates, with an estimated underreported income-tax rate elasticity that ranged from 0.5 to 3.0. Given the nature of the TCMP data, Clotfelter was unable to estimate the impact of enforcement parameters like the fine rate or the probability of detection on underreported income; he was also unable to examine the behaviour of individuals who did not file any tax return.

Researchers have also used other direct measures of evasion, based on survey evidence or tax amnesty data. More indirect methods look for traces of evasion behaviour that are left in various indicators that can be identified (e.g., currency demand, electricity use, labour supply), so that evasion is not measured directly but rather indirectly via these measureable traces. More recent approaches use a variety of novel methods, using reported income from individual tax returns as a proxy for evasion (as discussed below), or using consumption-based or tax deduction-based measures as an indicator of tax evasion. All of these measures have some well-known flaws.

Given these difficulties, Alm, McClelland, and Schulze use a very different approach to examine evasion behaviour, experimental methods. Experimental economics involves the creation of a real microeconomic system in the laboratory, one that parallels the naturally occurring world that is the subject of investigation and one in which subjects (usually students) make decisions that yield individual financial payoffs whose magnitude depends on their decisions. The essence of such a system is control over the environment, the institutions, the incentives, and the preferences that subjects face.

Laboratory methods allow many factors suggested by theory to be introduced in experimental settings. Also, experiments generate precise data on individual compliance decisions, which allow econometric estimation of individual responses in ways that are simply not possible with field data. Indeed, laboratory methods have examined a wide range of factors in the compliance decision, factors that have not proven amenable to either theoretical analyses or empirical analyses with field data.

In the experimental design of Alm, McClelland, and Schulze, human subjects are given income and must decide how much income to report. They pay taxes at some rate on all reported, but not on underreported, income. However, underreporting is discovered with some probability, and an audited subject must then pay a fine on unpaid taxes. This process is repeated for a given number of rounds. At the completion of the experiment, each subject is paid an amount that depends on his or her performance during the experiment. Their interest is the impact on evasion of changes in audit probabilities and in the group payoff from taxes (e.g., a public good). They find that a higher (random) audit rate leads to more compliance, with an estimated reported income-audit rate elasticity ranging from 0.1 to 0.2 and with an impact that is small and non-linear, so that the deterrent effect of a higher audit rate eventually diminishes. They also find that many subjects appear to substantially overweight the probability of an audit, so that there is far more compliance than is predicted by expected utility theory, a result that is nearly universal across all experimental designs. Finally, they find that the presence of a public good financed by voluntary tax payments increases subject tax compliance, again in a non-linear manner.

Related but more broadly defined work is on estimating the response of 'Income Reporting' to changes in marginal tax rates. This reporting response is not the same as, say, a simple labour supply response. Although reporting behaviour will certainly be influenced by any changes in hours worked or in labour force participation rates that may occur in response to taxes, the reporting decision is a far broader decision. It is affected also by behavioural changes in such dimensions as tax evasion, and also includes changes in hours worked, labour force participation, employee compensation, itemized deductions, income realizations, tax shelter and other tax avoidance mechanisms, taxable form decisions, and the like.

Martin Feldstein (1995; Chapter 15) was the first to examine the reporting response to taxes, using the Tax Reform Act of 1986 (TRA86) as a 'natural experiment'. TRA86 reduced marginal tax rates for all taxpayers, but especially for high income taxpayers from 50 per cent to 28 per cent; these changes in marginal tax rates meant that the marginal net-of-tax income per dollar of pre-tax income rose from 50 cents to 72 cents, or by 44 per cent. (TRA86 also changed a number of other features of the income tax, most of which had the effect of expanding the income tax base.) Feldstein used a US Treasury Department panel data set with 4000 taxpayers, and applied a 'difference-in-difference' method to estimate the elasticity of taxable income with respect to the net-of-tax rate. His estimates showed an elasticity of at least one and likely higher.

Many additional studies have followed. Jonathan Gruber and Emmanuel Saez (2002; Chapter 16) use an especially long panel of individual tax returns that covers the many changes in tax laws in the 1980s, in order to identify taxpayer reporting responses in total and by income group. They find that the overall net-of-tax rate elasticity of taxable income is significantly smaller than that found by Feldstein, or approximately 0.4. They also estimate that this aggregate elasticity is primarily due to a very elastic response of taxable income for taxpayers who have incomes above $100 000 per year; those with lower incomes have a significantly lower elasticity. An implication of their estimates is that optimal tax structures may feature tightly targeted transfers to lower income taxpayers and a flat or even declining marginal rate structure for middle and high income taxpayers. Other studies also suggest that individuals respond to tax rates in their reporting decisions. Even so, these estimates are very sensitive to a range of issues: sample selection, adjustments for non-tax-related changes to taxable income, methods for dealing with endogeneity of the tax rate, methods for dealing with mean reversion, estimation methods, the period under examination, and the specific type of taxpayer income (e.g., all taxpayers, high income taxpayers, executives), among other things.

Part II of Volume II of *The Economics of Taxation* examines 'Taxes and Business Decisions'. Income generated in business can be taxed at the individual owner's level via the individual income. However, income can also be taxed in the business itself, and a common form of taxation here is the corporate income tax. The corporate income tax is intended to tax the profits of a corporation; in practice, the tax is imposed at various rates on net accounting profits, equal to a firm's gross revenues less its operating costs plus its capital adjustments. While this may seem a straightforward exercise in principle, there are many difficulties that considerably complicate the administration of the tax.

One complication is where profits originate; that is, what is the location of the tax base? Here there are several possibilities:

- 'Source-based' (or 'territorial-based') taxation, where a country taxes income arising within its own borders; that is, the tax base is corporate income earned in the source country in which production takes place.
- 'Residence-based' taxation, where a country taxes the worldwide income of the enterprise; that is, the tax base is corporate income earned in the residence country of the corporation's owner.
- 'Destination-based' taxation, where a country taxes sales (net of costs) to the destination country where final consumption of the company's products takes place.

Traditional corporate income taxes are either source-based or residence-based. Broadly, capital-exporting countries use the residence method, while capital-importing countries use the source method. A capital-importing country that does not impose a corporate tax simply loses tax revenues to the home country of the enterprise.

A second complication is the precise definition of 'income'; that is, what is the type of income subject to the tax? Again, there are several possibilities:

- Full return to equity (e.g., economic profit, including pure rent).
- Full return to capital only.
- Rent (e.g., economic profit in excess of the level needed to justify the investment).

The standard practice in the classical corporate income tax is to tax the full return to equity (e.g., corporate profits), again defined typically as net accounting profits.

Now a 'corporation' is a legal form of business organization whose main feature is that of limited liability of its owners. Although a corporation is a 'legal person', it is clear that only actual people can bear the burden of any tax, and so the corporation itself as a legal entity does not actually pay a tax itself but acts mainly as a tax collector. A natural question at the start is therefore 'Why Tax Corporations?' A related but somewhat narrower question is 'Why Tax Capital Income?', and it is this question that begins the final section.

Alan J. Auerbach (1983; Chapter 17) presents a comprehensive and detailed discussion of what is known and what is hypothesized about the effects of corporate income taxation, especially its effects on capital and the incentive to invest. Auerbach demonstrates that the effects of the tax depend intimately on the specific features by which it is structured, including such elements as depreciation provisions, interest expenses, and inventory adjustments, all of which determine the ways in which capital is taxed. His discussion sets the stage for the papers that follow.

To a large extent, the effects of the corporate income tax depend upon what kind of tax it actually is. Is it a tax on corporate capital? Is it a tax on entrepreneurship in the corporate sector?

Is it a tax on pure economic profits? Is it a tax on risk-taking? Is it simply an added cost (like wages or even an excise tax)? Joseph E. Stiglitz (1976; Chapter 18) argues that, given the particular institutional setting of the US corporate income tax, especially the tax deductibility of interest expenses, the tax is most accurately seen as a tax on pure economic profits. The main implication of this result is that the tax becomes a neutral, non-distorting tax.

Christophe Chamley (1986; Chapter 19) takes a much different view of the tax, viewing it as a tax on capital income. He then examines the optimal tax on capital income, using a general equilibrium model in which agents have infinite lives, the population is heterogeneous, and consumption levels have no impact on preferences in future periods. He shows that the optimal tax rate is zero in the long run. The main reason for this result is that a positive tax rate discourages capital accumulation and so economic growth; more precisely, optimality requires equality between the social and the private discount rates in the long run, and the capital tax prevents this equality from being satisfied. The obvious conclusion from the work of Chamley is that capital income (and by extension corporate income) should not be taxed due to the inefficiencies that its taxation generates. This result is in sharp contrast to the Stiglitz result that the tax is neutral.

Even so, however, all three papers – by Auerbach, Stiglitz and Chamley – demonstrate that the effects of the tax very much depend upon its specific features. The remaining papers demonstrate this result with even more clarity, by examining the effects of the corporate income tax on the 'real' decisions of the firm (e.g., its investment choices) and on its 'financial' decisions (e.g., its dividend policies, its financing decisions, its organizational form decisions).

The impact of the corporate income tax on 'Investment' decisions is examined in the next three papers. Robert E. Hall and Dale W. Jorgenson (1967; Chapter 20) use an intertemporal neoclassical model of the firm to examine its optimal capital accumulation. Here the firm is assumed to maximize firm value (e.g., the present value of its profits), by its choice over time of capital goods as an input into production. This optimization generates the classic expression for the 'user cost of capital' c, equal without taxes (and with no changes in the price of capital goods) to sum of the real interest r plus the rate of economic depreciation δ times the price of capital goods q, or $c = q(r + \delta)$. In the presence of a corporate income tax imposed on profits at rate u, with depreciation provisions whose present value per dollar of investment is z and with an investment tax credit at rate k, then the user cost becomes $c = q(r + \delta)(1 - k)(1 - uz)/(1 - u)$. This expression demonstrates clearly the impact of tax policy (or u, k, z) on investment via its impact on user of cost of capital. Hall and Jorgenson estimate the impact of various changes in actual US tax policy that work through the user cost (e.g., changes in depreciation provisions, the introduction of the investment tax credit) on actual investment, using data on manufacturing and on non-farm, non-manufacturing investments in equipment and structures over the period 1929 to 1963. Their estimates of investment demand based on the standard accelerator model of investment indicate that tax policy had important and significant effects on the level, the timing, and the composition of investment. For example, the liberalization of depreciation rules in 1954 resulted in a shift of investment from equipment to structures, while the introduction of an investment tax credit in 1962 shifted investment toward equipment.

Robin W. Boadway (1987; Chapter 21) builds on this theoretical foundation, but considerably expands the theory to develop the notion of an 'Effective Tax Rate' t on capital income, defined as the difference between the gross or pre-tax rate of return on the marginal investment (r_g) and its net or after-tax rate of return (r_n), so that $t = r_g - r_n$. Like Hall and Jorgenson, Boadway starts with the dynamic neoclassical model of a firm, from which the familiar user cost of capital formulations can be derived but which can also be used to calculate the pre- and after-tax rates of return. He then introduces in these calculations a wide range of relevant corporate tax considerations beyond the standard corporate tax rate, depreciation provisions, and investment tax credits: the firm's financial policy (the cost of equity finance, the cost of debt finance, the relative shares of each), individual income tax rates, different types of depreciation provisions, different types of investments, variable holding periods for inventories, adjustment costs, monopoly versus competitive firms, depletable resources, the rate of inflation, and so on. Boadway illustrates these calculations with representative data on Canadian firms. Subsequent work has expanded the concept of an effective tax rate to many related but alternative measures, including the 'average effective corporate tax rate', the 'average effective total tax rate', the 'marginal effective corporate tax rate', the 'marginal effective total tax rate', the 'marginal effective corporate tax wedge', and the 'marginal effective total tax wedge'.

Alan J. Auerbach and Kevin Hassett (1992; Chapter 22) examine empirically the impact of tax policy on investment decisions, in a framework based on a structural model that allows direct estimates of the impact of tax policy variables on investment and that more fully incorporates firm (rational) expectations about future tax policy changes. Their model is based on the assumption of forward-looking investment behavior by a value-maximizing firm that is constrained by adjustment costs in smoothing its capital expenditures over time (e.g., the 'q' theory of investment, where 'q' is the ratio of the market valuation of the firm to the replacement cost of its capital stock). They estimate their model with annual data on US fixed non-residential investment in equipment and structures over the period 1956 to 1988. Auerbach and Hassett find clear evidence that tax factors, when properly specified, influence investment, although they also find that cash flow affects the level and the pattern of investment and that tax policy via its effects on investment has in fact not stabilized investment.

The final section looks at a different dimension by which taxes may affect business decisions, or the effects of taxes on a firm's 'Financial Structure'. For example, consider a firm's use of profits. In a simple case, the firm can keep the profits within the firm as retained earnings; the firm can also pay the profits to its owners via dividends. In the absence of any taxes, the firm (and its owners) should be indifferent between the two uses. However, in the presence of corporate – and individual – income taxes, retained earnings will be reflected in untaxed appreciation of the firm's value, while dividends will be taxed at the individual level via the individual income tax. This gives rise to the 'dividend paradox': why do corporations pay dividends? A similar paradox arises in a firm's choice of equity versus debt finance: given that interest is deductible as a capital adjustment while dividends are not deductible, why do corporations ever use equity as a source of finance? A final paradox relates to the very organizational structure of the firm: if income can be taxed at lower rates at the individual level rather than at the corporate level (via such legal entities as a publicly traded partnership or an S-corporation), why do some businesses choose the corporate form of organization when these other forms are available? The final papers examine the impact of the corporate income tax on such 'financial' decisions.

George R. Zodrow (1991; Chapter 23) provides a comprehensive discussion and analysis of dividend taxation and its effects. There is little question that income taxation of dividends at the individual level reduces the return to investment financed with *new share issues*; that is, the combination of dividend taxation at the individual level plus taxation at the corporate level leads to 'double taxation' of income financed via equity shares. However, there are quite different views about the impact of dividend taxation at the individual level and its impact on investment income financed via *retained earnings*. In the 'traditional' view of dividend taxation, dividend taxation at the individual level results in 'double taxation' of investment income attributable to investments financed with retained earnings. In contrast, under the 'new' view, dividend taxation at the individual level has no effect on marginal investments financed with retained earnings, largely because equity is 'trapped' within the corporation; that is, shareholders can recoup returns on equity-financed investment only if the corporation pays dividends, which are taxable at the individual level under the individual income tax. However, returns on retained earnings-financed investment are taxed only at the corporate level. Consequently, as long as capital gains are taxed at a lower rate than are dividends, new investment financed with retained earnings is subject to a lower tax burden than investment financed with new share issues. If the 'new' view is correct, then many of the distorting effects of the corporate income tax (especially on dividend payouts and on investment decisions) are effectively eliminated or at least substantially reduced. Indeed, if the 'new' view is correct, the case for individual/corporate income tax integration essentially disappears. Zodrow carefully reviews the theory behind both views, as well as the somewhat mixed empirical tests of the views. He concludes the debate is 'far from resolved', and suggests ways in which the debate may be clarified via future research. Indeed, he argues that a more appropriate theoretical model of the firm would incorporate some aspects of both views, especially extending the 'new' view to allow the possibility of share repurchases as a means of distributing profits to shareholders.

It is in fact this suggestion that underlies the paper by B. Douglas Bernheim (1991; Chapter 24). He constructs a 'signalling' model in which firms attempt to 'signal' their profitability by distributing cash (via dividends) to shareholders. Both dividends and share repurchases can be used to signal profitability of the firm, and dividends send the signal at a higher (tax) cost than share repurchases, given their tax treatment at the individual level. However, the dividend signal is especially desirable (despite its cost) to 'high quality' firms (or firms with greater cash flow, financial strength, or future profitability) because the payment of dividends allows the firm to more clearly differentiate itself from lower quality firms. Consequently, Bernheim is able to show that corporations will pay dividends under various plausible conditions. He is also able to explain the impact of various corporate tax provisions on firm financial decisions.

Raj Chetty and Emmanuel Saez (2005; Chapter 25) present empirical evidence on the impact of dividend taxes, using the 2003 US dividend tax cut as a natural experiment. The Jobs and Growth Tax Relief Reconciliation Act of 2003 reduced the tax rate on individual dividend income to 15 per cent instead of the regular progressive individual income tax schedule with a top rate of 35 per cent. Chetty and Saez use this dividend tax cut to estimate the effect of dividend taxes on dividend payments by publicly traded corporations (excluding financial and utility companies), using data on dividend payments from the Center for Research in Security Prices. Their empirical strategy is essentially a before- versus after-comparison, coupled with a test for confounding trends using firms owned primarily by non-taxable institutions as a control group. They find that dividend initiations surged in the quarters immediately following enactment of the reform, especially for non-financial and non-utility publicly traded corporations and for firms with strong principals whose tax incentives changed significantly (e.g., firms with large taxable institutional owners, firms with independent directors with large share holdings). They also find that dividend-paying firms were significantly more likely to increase their regular dividend payments after the reform, and that the number of special (i.e., one time, non-recurring) dividend payments increased following the 2003 tax reform. Aggregating the various changes, they calculate an implied elasticity of regular dividend payments with respect to the marginal tax rate on dividend income of –0.5. Overall, their evidence is largely consistent with the 'traditional' view of dividend taxation, although Chetty and Saez caution that the response seems too rapid to be entirely explained by the 'traditional' view.

Jeffrey K. Mackie-Mason (1990; Chapter 26) examines the impact of taxes on the corporation's choice of debt versus equity finance. His theoretical framework focuses on effects of a 'tax shield' (or the reduction in taxes from utilizing a specific tax provision) on the marginal or incremental investment decision of a firm. Tax shields should matter to a firm's marginal investment decisions only if they affect the marginal tax rate on interest deductions. Although tax deductions and tax credits always lower the *average* tax rate, they only lower the *marginal* rate if they cause the firm to have no taxable income and thus to face a zero marginal rate on interest deductions. Consequently, most tax shields have only a negligible effect on the marginal tax rate for most firms. His empirical methodology uses a large dataset of 1747 firm registrations (SEC Registered Offerings Statistics tape records) that includes the registration of every security for public offering from 1977 to 1987. These data have information on incremental decisions affected by two tax shields: tax loss carry forwards (TLCF) and investment tax credits (ITC). His results provide strong evidence that the relationship between tax shields and the marginal tax rate is important and that the marginal tax rate has a large impact on financing decisions. Firms with high TLCF are much less likely to use debt, while ITC does not reduce the probability of a debt issue; that is, tax shields affect financing but only when they change the marginal tax rate on interest deductions.

William M. Gentry (1994; Chapter 27) also examines the impact of taxes on financial decisions, by focusing on differences in financial behaviour between corporations and publicly traded partnerships (PTPs), also known as master limited partnerships. PTPs are similar to corporations and possess some of their advantages (e.g., liquidity, diversification of risk via public trading of equity), but they are not subject to corporate taxes, so that they escape double taxation of income. Given their mixture of corporate and partnership characteristics, PTPs provide a natural experiment for studying taxation and firm financial decisions, and Gentry uses this feature to compare the financial structure and dividend policies of PTPs and corporations, with data on the oil and gas exploration industry in 1987 and 1988. Simple comparisons of the mean financial behavior of PTPs and corporations indicate that PTPs pay more dividends and borrow less than similar corporations; these results also hold when controlling for other determinants of financial decisions (including possible endogenous choice of business form) via econometric analyses. These results are consistent with the hypotheses that the corporate income tax discourages dividend payouts and encourages debt.

Conclusions: Lessons and Future Directions

It is difficult, and probably foolhardy, to summarize the many lessons from all of these – and many other – papers on *The Economics of Taxation*. One approach here could simply offer some general recommendations on how 'best' to design taxes, such as 'To minimize excess burdens, impose taxes on activities where responses are smaller', or 'In reforming tax systems, impose taxes at low rates on broadly defined bases', or 'Keep taxes as simple as possible'. Rather than present such prescriptions, I instead offer my own perspective on the broader lessons from all of this work. These 'lessons' from taxation can, I believe, be distilled into several main conclusions.

First, incentives matter in individual and firm decisions, and taxes affect incentives. Second, behavioural responses to taxes can take several main forms: 'real' responses, 'financial form' (or 'accounting) responses, or 'timing' responses. The largest of these is likely to be timing responses and the smallest are real responses. Third, taxes have 'unintended consequences'. Fourth, the effects of a *single* tax depend both upon its specific structural features (e.g., its base, its rate structure, its administration) and upon the ways that the tax interacts with the entire *system* of taxes; that is, analyzing taxation requires analyzing tax systems. Finally, empirical evidence clearly shows that individuals and firms respond to the incentive effects of taxes, but these empirical estimates are often controversial and unsettled, dependent upon such things as the specific period, method, focus and sample that are used in the empirical work. Put differently, agents exhibit immense complexity in their behaviour, and the impact of taxes (and other policies) is often dominated by many other factors that cannot be easily modeled or analyzed. Indeed, there are limits to what tax policy can achieve.

In short, we have learned much about *The Economics of Taxation*. However, there is much that we do not, and probably cannot, ever really know.

I conclude with some thoughts about areas in which future research efforts on taxation could be – and should be – usefully directed.

First, theory is essential, and new theories will continue to be developed. However, I believe that there will be growing recognition and acceptance that one theory may not fit all individuals at all times, or even the same individual at different times. Individuals in their infinite variety exhibit a 'full house' of behaviours, behaviours that cannot be neatly captured by a single methodology. Indeed, I believe that the theoretical analysis of taxation will increasingly turn to other social sciences in the efforts to help understand the behavioural effects of taxation. The obvious area is 'Behavioural Economics', which has already made important contributions to tax analysis. The potential for other social sciences like sociology and anthropology to help researchers understand better which features of naturally occurring settings are likely to affect individual and group decisions is a likely direction of future research. For example, the notion of 'reciprocity' arises in large part from anthropology, and that of 'adherence to group norms' from sociology. Using alternative perspectives on human behaviour cannot help but expand our understanding of individual behaviour.

Second, empirical methods will continue to evolve. Laboratory experiments seem likely to play a decisive role in developing and testing theory, and controlled field experiments will also continue to increase in use. Such approaches offer a better avenue for achieving 'identification' of the separate and independent effects of taxes than the use of naturally occurring field data that has characterized the vast bulk of previous empirical research. Also, most existing research on the effects of taxes has been in developed countries, and indeed in the USA. The dramatic improvement in the availability of information about many other countries, especially developing countries, opens up the possibility of a significant expansion of research into the effects of taxation in many other parts of the world, and into the effects of many different types of taxes.

Third, and more specifically, research efforts will continue in such enduring yet still unresolved areas as those already covered in these two volumes, including such issues as the theoretical analysis of the dynamic and intertemporal effects of taxes, empirical estimates of the impact of taxes on individual and firm decisions (e.g., labour supply, investment), and the appropriate design of 'optimal' taxes. The well-documented rise in inequality across most countries in the last several decades suggests that additional research into the ways in which taxes and tax systems affect the distribution of income is sorely needed. Similarly, the nearly universal forecast of enormous and growing public sector deficits, in combination with current economic problems, suggests that additional research is also needed on ways that deficit reduction can be balanced with economic growth.

However, recent and emerging trends present some especially promising areas for future theoretical and empirical work in taxation. Here are five such areas that will and should, I believe, become the focus of new research efforts:

- *Institutions:* What is the role of 'institutions' – political institutions (e.g., political economy), administrative institutions (e.g., tax administration), social institutions (e.g., social capital, social norms) – in determining the effects of taxation, and how can these institutions best be incorporated and analyzed? The social context of decisions seems an especially fruitful area for research.
- *Demographics:* How will changes in population structure, such as an aging population, a growing diversity in 'family' structures, a changing workforce composition, or a shifting racial/ethnic/gender mix of the population, affect the design of taxes?
- *Technology:* What are the effects on taxes of a changing technology, especially changes in the way that information is collected and transmitted? How does the growing presence of the internet – and the growing use of the internet for many economic transactions – affect the design of tax systems?
- *Globalization:* How will globalization, and the resulting dramatic increase in product and factor mobility that is a defining characteristic of globalization, affect the design of taxes? Most tax systems were designed in a world in which production and consumption were primarily of *tangible goods*, in which the sale and consumption of these goods generally occurred in the *same location*, and in which the factors of production used to make the goods were for the most part *immobile*. Globalization changes all of these features: tax bases are significantly more mobile; trade increasingly involves intangible goods; and the measurement, identification, and assignment of tax bases are much more difficult. Will there emerge a 'vanishing taxpayer', or can ways be found to combine, say, the improvements in information and technology with improvements in taxation?
- *Environment:* How should taxes be designed in a world in which environmental issues (e.g., global warming, cross-border pollution) are becoming more prominent? What are the effects of 'green taxes' (e.g., carbon taxes, cap-and-trade programmes, Pigouvian

taxes), and how should taxes be designed, especially in a world in which externalities spill across subnational and national borders?

These issues are not simple ones.

Even so, to return to an earlier conclusion, there is much that we do not, and probably cannot, ever really know. This conclusion is a particularly apt one. It suggests that we should always be modest in our claims, even if not in our aspirations:

Teach the tongue to say 'I do not know', and thou shalt progress.

(Maimonides)

Acknowledgements

Overall 30 years ago, I was a graduate student at the University of Wisconsin-Madison, trying to make it through the core courses in the graduate sequence and then trying to choose a field of specialization. Wisconsin had superb professors in virtually all areas of economics, but I gravitated toward public economics (called "welfare economics" in the somewhat idiosyncratic nature of Wisconsin at the time). And I did so largely because of the inspiration provided by the extraordinary cadre of public economics professors whose classes I took, for whom I worked, or from whom I learned at the weekly seminars and workshops: Burt Weisbrod, Martin David, Gene Smolensky, Yves Balcer, Lee Hansen ... Most of all, I learned from Bob Haveman, who supervised my dissertation, who spent much time with me on a weekly basis despite his own frenetic schedule, and who showed me what it really took to teach and to do research in public economics.

Since then, I have been privileged to work with many other exceptional public economics scholars, including Mike McKee, Leslie Whittington, Dave Sjoquist, Jorge Martinez-Vazquez, Matt Murray, Roy Bahl, Richard Bird, Charlie McLure, Jerry Miner, Jesse Burkhead, Larry Schroeder, Bill Schulze, Jim Follain, Bob Buckley, and, more recently, Benno Torgler, Fritz Schneider, Sally Wallace, Mikhail Melnik, Mark Skidmore, and Edward Sennoga. I have learned much from all of these individuals, and I am still learning today.

It is to all of these individuals – professors, colleagues, mentors, and friends – that I am indebted.

Notes

1. Richard A. Musgrave (1959), *The Theory of Public Finance – A Study in Public Economy* (New York, NY: McGraw-Hill Book Company).
2. Arnold C. Harberger, 'The Incidence of the Corporation Income Tax', *Journal of Political Economy*, **70** (2), 215–240.
3. Arsène Jules Etienne Juvénal Dupuit (1844), 'De la mesure de l'utilité des travaux publics', *Annales des Ponts et Chaussées*, translated by R.H. Barback (1952) as 'On the Measurement of the Utility of Public Works', *International Economic Papers*, **2** (1), 83–110, and reprinted in Kenneth J. Arrow and Tibor Scitovsky (eds) (1969), *Readings in Welfare Economics* (Homewood, IL: Richard D. Irwin, 255–283).

4. Edgar K. Browning (1976), 'The Marginal Cost of Public Funds', *Journal of Political Economy*, **84** (2), 283–298.
5. Kenneth J. Arrow (1950), 'A Difficulty in the Concept of Social Welfare', *Journal of Political Economy*, **58** (4), 328–346.
6. Frank A. Ramsey (1927), 'A Contribution to the Theory of Taxation', *Economic Journal*, **37** (145), 47–61; Paul A. Samuelson (1950), 'Theory of Optimal Taxation', US Department of the Treasury Working Paper, published in 1986 in the *Journal of Public Economics*, **30** (2), 137–143.
7. Thomas MaCurdy, David Green and Harry Paarsch (1990), 'Assessing Empirical Approaches for Analyzing Taxes and Labor Supply', *Journal of Human Resources*, **25** (3), 415–490.
8. James Alm (2010), 'Measuring, Explaining, and Controlling Tax Evasion: Lessons from Theory, Experiments, and Field Studies', Keynote Address at the 66th Annual Congress at the International Institute of Public Finance, 'Tax Evasion, Tax Avoidance, and the Shadow Economy', held at Uppsala University in Uppsala, Sweden in August 2010.

Part I
Analyzing the Effects of Taxation

A
Notions of Equity

ET, OT and SBT

Richard A. MUSGRAVE*

Harvard University, Cambridge, MA 02138, U.S.A.

Revised version received October 1975

Until recently, the normative theory of taxation has focussed on the issue of horizontal equity, i.e. the equal treatment of equals. Based on the Schanz–Haig–Simons tradition, a definition of taxable income as accretion has been developed and applied to financial and legal institutions. This work has yielded important results, but certain basic problems which arise in defining an index of equality have been neglected. This paper addresses these problems as well as certain conflicts which arise in combining horizontal equity with efficiency considerations. This theory of equitable taxation is compared with the more recent writings on optimal taxation, where the issue of horizontal equity is bypassed but a more explicit reconciliation between vertical equity and efficiency considerations is achieved.

1. Introduction

The normative theory of taxation has a long history, with the concept of a 'good tax structure' developed along two lines. One is the ability-to-pay or sacrifice approach, the other that of benefit taxation. The ability-to-pay school takes a 'taxation only' view of the problem. While transfers can be included as negative taxes, the design for a good tax structure is drawn apart from the provision for social goods. Taxes should be equitable, i.e. in line with ability to pay, whatever the revenues are used for. In this respect, the traditional theory of equitable taxation (henceforth referred to as ET) resembles the new writings on optimal taxation (henceforth referred to as OT). Both incorporate transfers qua negative taxes, but do not provide an analytical link between the provision for social goods and the determination of the tax structure by which they are financed. OT and ET are both inferior in this respect to the benefit tradition. This tradition, especially in its Wicksellian version, has the great advantage of linking the tax to the expenditure side of the problem and of emphasizing the integral role of taxation in the provision for social goods.[1] Both ET and OT, to

---

*I am indebted to Roger Brinner, Michell Polinsky and James Medoff for helpful comments. I am also indebted to Karl Rosskamp for having directed my attention to the crucial role of the equal-preferences assumption in the context of optimal taxation theory.

[1]It is ironic that this inherent advantage should have been lost in the modern theory of social goods. In integrating social goods into the Paretian efficiency system, the problem has been viewed as one of deriving the efficient set of allocation between private and social goods in a de novo, predistribution state, where all preferences are known to an omniscient referee. As a

use my terminology, are essentially theories of the distribution branch, without inclusion of allocation branch taxes. Nevertheless, it remains convenient in some respects to consider the tax-transfer process in isolation and, for purposes of this paper, I shall follow the ET–OT pattern in this respect.

2. The ET concept of horizontal equity

The ET view of the good tax structure rests on the central proposition that the tax system should be equitable. More specifically, it should meet the double criteria of horizontal and vertical equity.[2]

2.1. The role of 'equal position'

Horizontal equity calls for equal tax treatment of people in equal positions. ET holds this to be a basic requirement for a good tax structure. It is called for by the principle of equal justice under the law and is accepted as a value judgment or ethical axiom, not as a proposition in economic efficiency. Vertical equity calls for a meaningful pattern of differentiation between people in unequal positions, related to society's evaluation of various states of well-being. Both concepts are interrelated and neither has priority over the other. In the absence of vertical equity norms, the case for horizontal equity is reduced to providing protection against malicious discrimination, an objective which might be met more simply by a tax lottery. Vertical equity in turn cannot be defined without horizontal equity norms, as it must deal with differential treatment of people who, to begin with, have been grouped on horizontal equity grounds.

Horzontal equity calls for equal treatment of people in equal positions. The general rule is plausible, but how should one define 'equal position' and 'equal treatment'? The basic meaning of 'equal position' must be that people enjoy equal levels of welfare, somehow defined; and that of 'equal treatment' that people in equal pre-tax positions should also be left in post-tax equality.[3] But this is only a statement of the problem, not its solution. As a first step, operational

---

result, taxation remains outside the model, except in its most barren form of lump-sum transfers. Yet, taxation is an essential part of the fiscal problem in the real world setting, where a resource transfer from the private to the public sector is called for, where consumer preferences for social goods are not known and where there exists a distribution of income to which effective preferences must be related. As Wicksell had stressed to begin with, it is through coordinated decisions on taxes and public services that consumers and voters must be induced to reveal their preferences, thus giving a central role to taxation. The suitability of various taxes in serving this revelation function then becomes an important normative criterion for what constitutes a good tax structure, just as allowance for the political process of preference determination becomes an integral part of a positive theory of the public sector. On this aspect see the paper by Buchanan in this issue.

[2] Without using the terms 'horizontal' and 'vertical' explicitly, this distinction is drawn clearly by Simons (1938, p. 30), who states that 'tax burdens should bear similarly upon persons whom we regard as in substantially similar circumstances, and differently where circumstances differ.'

[3] This distinction is similar to that drawn by Feldstein in his paper in this issue.

meaning must be given to the concept of equal position. One must devise an 'objective' index of welfare before addressing the problem of how to compare levels of welfare derived by people in unequal positions.

ET writers have tended to define economic position in terms of income, and to interpret equal treatment of people with equal income as calling for equal amounts of tax. The Edgeworth–Pigou-type sacrifice theory [Edgeworth (1897), Pigou (1951)] was developed in terms of sacrifice incurred when surrendering income, just as the Schanz–Haig–Simons tradition [Simons (1938)] of tax-base definition proceeded to interpret income in terms of accretion. ET writers, in following up this lead, adapted the accretion concept to the complexities of economic institutions [Simons (1940), Vickrey (1947), Bittker et al. (1968)] and arrived at some normative findings for the direction of income tax design. These include: (1) capital gains should be treated as ordinary income, whether realized or not, provided that appropriate allowance is made for averaging and loss offset; (2) gifts and bequests should be treated similarly; (3) corporate source income should be integrated into the individual income tax base, whether or not distribution occurs, without a separate or 'absolute' tax being imposed on corporate income; (4) appropriate treatment of homeowners calls for the taxation of imputed rent, combined with deduction of depreciation and mortgage interest; and (5) income should be defined in real terms, thus calling for inflation adjustment. While these and other rules may have to be modified in application, they nevertheless offer criteria for applying horizontal equity norms and provide guidance to tax policy. Leaving aside these matters of application, which have been discussed at length, we here turn to certain more basic difficulties inherent in the definition of equal position – difficulties which have not been scrutinized sufficiently. This is surprising, since the concept of equal position is at the heart of horizontal equity, and horizontal equity is central to the entire ET approach.

In order to derive an acceptable measure of equal position or equal welfare, we consider consumers who may choose between the consumption of two commodities X and Z and leisure L, with L defined as the use of time for non-income-earning activity, be it sleeping, playing or the enjoyment of literature. We also introduce a variable P which stands for psychic income or the pleasure or displeasure associated with particular jobs. To simplify matters, we begin with a one-period model so that the distinction between income and consumption may be disregarded for the time being. The definition of equal position is now examined under various assumptions regarding the equality or inequality of available options and preferences.

2.2. Equal preferences and options

No problem arises if all people have both equal options and preferences. Individuals A and B will be confronted with the same set of options (consumption packages of X, Z and L) as given by the surface DCE in fig. 1. Since they also have similar tastes, they will locate at the same point, say at F. It is a matter of indifference in this case how economic position is measured, whether in terms of X, Z, L or some composite expression. Indeed, there is no problem of defining equal position since all people choose the same mix of X, Z and L. Horizontal equity being met by any of the various indices of taxable capacity, the choice of tax base may be made on efficiency grounds. In this simplest case, taxes may be imposed in head-tax form, thus avoiding any problem of dead-weight loss. The same holds if differences in P are allowed for. Since the same job is chosen and the same P is experienced by all, the problem of its measurability does not arise.

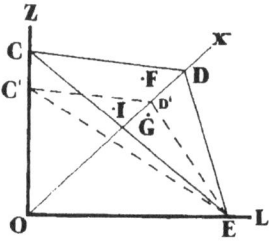

Fig. 1

Nevertheless, one difficulty must be noted. While rates of substitution between X, Z and L are similar across individuals in this simplest case, the 'level' of utility which A and B derive from the same bundles of X, Z and L may differ. If some absolute comparison could be drawn, they may prove to be in dissimilar positions. Since individuals vary in most other respects, such would not be a surprising finding. But no operational test is available (utility comparisons based on risk aversion are of no help since they address the slope, not the level of utility schedules) so that the best society can do is to adopt the hypothesis that the 'ability to enjoy' consumption (be it of X, Z or L) is the same for all. Justice is taken to call for treating individuals as if they were the same in this respect, i.e. derived equal welfare from similar baskets. Given this initial hypothesis, the conclusion for the equal-option – equal-preference case remains that people should pay the same amount of tax.[4]

[4]While most people will accept this way of short-circuiting the 'differences in capacity' problem, there remains the question of whether certain differences in need should not be accounted for. This includes the obvious issue of size of taxpaying unit, as reflected in the granting of differential exemptions under the income tax. Beyond this, one may argue that an allowance should be made for extra costs resulting from such handicaps as blindness. The latter may not only affect earnings abilities (this being allowed for automatically by reducing the level of taxable income) but also give rise to additional costs (the seeing-eye dog). A good case can be made in the ET context that such a cost should be allowed for. In other words, A and B should be considered in equal position if they consume equal bundles of X, Z and L, while B is allowed the additional cost of a seeing-eye dog. Of course, it is difficult to decide just what disabilities should be allowed for, and no clear line can be drawn. It does not follow, however, that the issue should be dismissed. A degree of arbitrariness is inevitable whenever normative concepts are applied to complex institutions.

2.3. Equal preference with unequal options

Next we allow for differences in available options while retaining the assumption of equal preferences or utility functions. Suppose first that P is the same for all jobs, so that only differences in earning capacities need be considered. In this case, individuals $(A_1, A_2, \ldots)$ may be confronted with the opportunity set given by CED in fig. 1, while individuals $(B_1, B_2, \ldots)$, who earn less, confront the lower set $C'ED'$. Since they have the same utility functions, all members of A group will choose the same mix, say F, located on CED while all members of the B group choose a mix, such as I, located on $C'ED'$. The A's may then be grouped as equals and so may the B's, following our earlier rule that people with identical baskets are considered to be in equal positions. As in the equal-options case, horizontal equity is met equally well whether we choose X, Z, L or a composite as base.

But now there arises the additional problem of vertical equity. On what basis are we to conclude that the B's are better off than the A's? If L, X and Z are all superior goods, the baskets of individuals with a superior option set will contain more of each X, Z and L, and they can be ranked accordingly. But such will hardly be the case. Even though the opportunity set of the A's is higher, they may consume less of some good. We must therefore be satisfied with saying that the B's are in a better position because their opportunity set lies above that of the A's, without insisting that they have more of each commodity. A higher opportunity set in turn means that a higher level of welfare can be achieved. This level may be measured in terms of income defined broadly to include the imputed earnings from leisure (or consumption broadly defined to include the consumption of leisure) and individuals may be ranked accordingly. Income thus defined is given by $Y_b = wK$, where w is the *observed* wage rate and K is a constant such as 16 or 24 hours. Or, we may write $Y_b = Y + wL$, where $Y = wH$ is earnings (or income as usually defined) and $H = K - L$ is hours worked. With leisure thus allowed for, wK becomes an operational measure of options and is clearly superior to Y or outlays on $X + Z$. Horizontal equity calls for people with equal values of wK to pay the same amount of tax. The tax base, accordingly, is to be defined as wK, which is also an optimal base on efficiency grounds.

Assuming the value of P to be the same for all jobs, a person will choose the job with the highest wage rate. The observed wage rate, therefore, equals the potential wage rate and $Y_b = wK$ is an operational concept. But matters are more difficult if a variable P is allowed for. Options now differ regarding P as well as w and a person's observed wage rate no longer reflects a unique potential wage rate. This is no trivial matter since P's do in fact vary widely. Moreover, differences in options with regard to P are a major form in which job discrimination occurs. Using only one commodity Z, the choice between Z, L and P is now given by a surface such as HIM in fig. 2. Assuming this to reflect the options available to the A's, they might choose a point such as Q on the plane HIM. The set of options available to the B's might be given by the lower plane $H'IM'$. They might then choose a point such as N. The difference in the position of the A's and B's is no longer reflected correctly by wK (with w the observed wage rate) because w differs with P. The definition of Y_b needs to be expanded to $(w+\alpha)K$, where w is the observed wage rate and α (which may be positive or negative) is the supplementary 'psychic' wage rate. Since α is not given by observable market behavior, the correct definition of Y_b ceases to be operational. This being the case, the quest for an index of horizontal equity has to be satisfied with a second-best solution. Treating people with equal wK's as equals now involves a discrimination against the person whose option set is limited to lower values of P.[5]

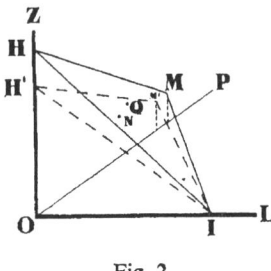

Fig. 2

2.4. Unequal preferences with equal options

Consider now a setting where available options are the same but preferences differ. The P variable is disregarded to begin with. People confronted with the same choice set on surface CED in fig. 1 now select different positions. A may choose point F while B chooses G. The criteria of equal baskets no longer yields a measure of equal position. While wK remains an operational measure of equal options, it is no longer obvious that the equal option criteria can be taken as index of equal position. To do so now involves more than our earlier hypothesis that individuals with similar baskets derive equal satisfaction. We must now accept a broader and intuitively less plausible hypothesis that people with equal options but different baskets derive the same satisfaction. Differences in welfare which result from difference in tastes (with similar options) are to be disregarded.

[5]If the opportunity sets, such as given by HIM in fig. 2, were revealed, the psychic wage rate might be measured by the difference between a person's hourly earnings at his chosen job and at the highest-paying job available to him. This position could then be measured in terms of potential earnings at that job. The difficulty arises because potentially available (as distinct from chosen) wage rates are not observable. Further difficulties may arise even in the absence of psychic income, since the leisure-income choice will frequently be constrained by institutional arrangements. Assuming that a person would like to consume less leisure than arrangements permit, valuation of leisure as wL is an overstatement.

While one feels uneasy with this construction, it seems the best that can be done in deriving an operational measure of economic position. Horizontal equity, once more, is satisfied by using wK as the tax base, with equity and efficiency considerations again in accord. No substitution effects result and individuals with equal options, in paying the same amount of tax, may also be taken to receive equal treatment, i.e. to bear the same burden.

Matters are more complex as P is allowed for. Even if options are similar, differences in preferences with respect to P will result in different job choices. The proper tax base $(w+\alpha)K$ is not an operational measure since the values of α, applicable to A and B respectively, are not observable. If the tax is imposed on wK only, A and B will experience the same change in their option set but it would be difficult to argue that they experience the same burden. Depending on their preferences, they pay more or less tax, with the person who values goods highly relative to job satisfaction bearing the heavier burden. An even greater bias results if the tax is limited to wH, where an equal change in options benefits the individual with high leisure preferences. Whereas equal pre-tax positions (given acceptance of the broader hypothesis) can be defined in terms of equal options, equal treatment evidently can no longer be defined in terms of equal changes in options. As a second-best solution, equal tax treatment (among pre-tax equals) might be measured in terms of equal changes in real income, with the consumption pattern (pre- or post-tax) for each taxpayer used as weights. But if this were done, different tax formulae would have to be applied to pre-tax equals; different amounts of tax would be paid by them, and the equal option criteria (though applicable to the pre-tax setting) could no longer be used to define equal post-tax positions.

As unequal options are combined with unequal preferences it becomes difficult to distinguish the impact of the two on actual behavior. Difficulties of defining equal pre-tax position are compounded with those of defining equal tax treatment. In all, it is evident that the concept of horizontal equity requires more scrutiny and careful thought than it has been given in the literature. Not only is α unobservable, but differences in preferences make it difficult to define pre-tax equality and equal treatment consistently. This, I hasten to add, does not mean that the search for horizontal equity should be abandoned: an orderly tax system has to be placed on a reasonable index of equality; and many of the departures therefrom can be identified as such even though certain aspects of the equality concept remain short of precise specification.

3. Time dimension of horizontal equity

Thus far the concept of horizontal equity has been viewed in the context of a single-period model, thus bypassing the distinction between income and consumption. We now allow for a time dimension, and with it the choice between income and consumption as the proper index of equality. Around seminar tables the debate has been over whether or not the income tax involves 'double taxation of savings.' In the political forum, the issue has been less ethereal. The debate has been basically one over progressive taxation, since the income base has developed historically as the instrument of progressive taxation while the consumption base has been associated with the use of regressive taxes. We are here concerned with the former issue only, keeping in mind that the consumption base (through a personalized expenditure tax) could be rendered progressive. Specifically, what does the equal option approach tell us about the appropriate choice between the income and consumption base?

In addressing this topic, a distinction needs to be drawn between asking (1) which base is preferable on efficiency grounds and (2) which offers the more meaningful index of equality in the ET context. Under highly simplified assumptions, a clear case can be made for the consumption base on efficiency grounds. A tax on income discriminates against future consumption, whereas the tax on consumption is neutral. Under more realistic assumptions, this conclusion need not follow, but in any case this line of reasoning, which pertains to efficiency only, does *not* tell us which of the two bases is preferable on equity grounds, i.e. as an index of equal position in the ET context.

To view the problem in its simplest setting, we assume leisure to be fixed and consider two individuals, A and B, who receive a given endowment or initial accretion M at the beginning of period 1. We may think of this as a gift, bequest, or as wage income which will not reoccur. They may use their M for consumption in period 1 or they may save, receive interest and enjoy increased consumption in period 2. All income is consumed in the course of lifetime (the two-year period), with bequests excluded for the time being. To simplify matters, we further assume that A consumes his entire M in period 1 while B saves and consumes in period 2 only.

3.1. Period-by-period view

One approach is to apply the standard of horizontal equity to each period separately, without continuity between periods. Thus, in period 1 both A and B receive an endowment (or wage income) of M which they may consume or save. They therefore have the same option and should pay the same tax. This they do if the tax is on M but not if it is on consumption since, in that case, only A would pay. Equal treatment, therefore, calls for a tax on M, i.e. an income tax. In the next period, A receives no income and has no consumption, while B receives interest income. The two are in unequal positions and the entire tax should be paid by B since only he receives income. Again this is accomplished by an income tax. While it is evident for period 1 that B prefers the consumption tax and A the income tax (with both indifferent in period 2), it does not follow that B suffers 'double taxation' under the income tax. With each period considered by itself, B's period-2 income presents a new option and he is properly taxed thereon.

	Period	(α) Accretion	Change in net worth	+	(β) Consumption	= Total
A	1	M	–		M	M
	2	–	–		–	–
B	1	M	M		–	M
	2	$i(1-t)M$	$-M$		$[1+i(1-t)]M$	$i(1-t)M$

This reasoning holds whether income is defined (α) as accretion, i.e. additions to a person's net worth before counting withdrawals for consumption or (β) as the change in net worth (additions minus withdrawals) plus consumption. Under the (α) concept, the period-1 tax base equals M for A and B, while the period-2 base equals zero for A and $i(1-t)M$ for B. Under the (β) concept, the period-1 base for A equals consumption of M (with change in net worth of zero), while that for B consists of increase in net worth by M (with consumption zero). The period-2 base equals zero for A, who has neither a change in net worth nor consumption. B's base in turn combines a reduction in net worth of M with consumption of $[1+i(1-t)]M$, which nets out to $i(1-t)M$. Thus, the bases under the (β) concept equal those recorded under the (α) concept. The two formulations of the income concept lead to identical results. What matters is not whether the income tax is interpreted under the (α) or (β) concept. What matters is whether a tax is to be imposed on income or on consumption.

3.2. Lifetime view

Though implicit in most of the literature on income tax, the above differs from the economists' view of income, based on Fisherian capital theory, as permitting a consumption stream, present and future. Having received equal initial endowments in period 1, A and B have the same consumption options over time, i.e. the two periods combined. This is what matters, not how each chooses to distribute his consumption over his lifetime. Since the present value of lifetime consumption is the same whatever the timing, both should pay the same present value tax for the period as a whole. This condition is met by a currently collected tax on consumption, where A pays $t_c M$ in period 1 and nothing in period 2, while B pays $t_c(1+i)M$ in period 2, the present value of which (as viewed in period 1) is again $t_c M$.

Relating the lifetime view to the concept of income tax as commonly understood, no difficulty arises with regard to taxpayer A, whose income base is M in period 1 and zero in period 2. The present value of his tax base equals M under both the income and consumption tax. Turning to B, the present value of his consumption tax base again equals M, but the present value of his income tax base,

$$\left[1+\frac{i(1-t)}{1+i}\right]M,$$

is larger. For the present value of the income tax base to equal M, accretion (or change in net worth) would have to be measured so as to exclude interest income, or the entire tax would have to be asessed at the end of the period.

3.3. Conclusion

Both the period-by-period and lifetime views can be made compatible with the equal option criteria, and it is not obvious which of the two offers the more meaningful base in the context of tax equity. However, if the lifetime view is chosen, it becomes essential to revise the assumption that all income is consumed during the entire period and to allow for bequests. The leaving of bequests offers an alternative option and therefore should be included in the tax base along with consumption. Since bequest rates differ among people with equal lifetime incomes, this is of obvious importance for horizontal equity; and since the ratio of bequests to lifetime income appears to rise with lifetime income (a matter on which little data are available) it is of importance for vertical equity as well. The definition of an equal options tax base must thus include bequests along with consumption. The rationale for this is not that bequeathing constitutes consumption, but that both uses of funds are alternative options. It is somewhat misleading, therefore, to refer to our 'equal options tax' as a consumption tax. Given such a restatement of the consumption tax base, the distinction between it and the income tax base is greatly reduced. While A will still prefer the income tax, whereas B prefers the consumption tax, the remaining difference merely relates to their chosen time-path of disposal.

The argument so far has been based on the assumption that the utility of income derives from consumption, including the leaving of bequests. But savings may be for the sake of security, social position or power rather than for future consumption. If so, should not a tax on holding of wealth be added to that on consumption? Evidently a person will save more, in response to a given rate of interest, if he values the holding of wealth as well as future consumption. Moreover, the benefits from holding of wealth accrue currently as wealth is held, and thus suffer less from discounting. Do these facts justify an additional tax being imposed on the holding of wealth? We believe not, since gains from both sources will be equated at the margin with the rate of interest and will thus be captured by discounting the value of future consumption or accumulation. Individuals whose savings motivation leans largely on the benefits from accumulation will derive a higher consumer surplus, due to the earlier accrual of accumulation benefits, then those whose savings motivation is directed mainly toward future consumption. This, however, does not seem to justify an extra tax on accumulation, as it reflects the more general problem of differences in consumer surplus which arises once differences and preferences are allowed for.

Finally, note should be taken of the fact that the lifetime model as here discussed is based on the assumption that consumers are free to arrange their time-paths of consumption within their lifetime budget constraint. Given the fact that the availility of borrowing and lending facilities may differ among individuals, the consumption base may impose hardships by imposing the heaviest taxes when taxpayers can least afford to pay, a consideration speaking in favor of the income option.

4. Equity and efficiency: ET and OT compared

The preceding discussion of ET has been in terms of horizontal equity, with little emphasis on efficiency aspects. We now consider how efficiency fits into ET analysis and how the equity norms of ET can be related to OT.

Efficiency and horizontal equity

ET literature, preoccupied with the quest for horizontal equity, has gone light in allowing for efficiency considerations. But this is not inherent in the horizontal equity concept. Proper interpretation of 'equal treatment of equals' calls for the imposition of equal burdens, measured not simply by tax dollars paid but by welfare losses incurred. This means inclusion of losses of consumer surplus or excess burden suffered. Moreover, it is only reasonable that the requirement of ET thus defined should be supplemented by the further requirement that excess burdens be minimized. Just as efficiency considerations do not suffice without allowance for equity (in which case the ideal tax would simply be a head tax), equity considerations cannot be dealt with without allowance for efficiency aspects. This is obvious enough, but the question is whether both goals can be met at the same time.

If utility functions were the same for all individuals, the same tax formula would impose equal excess burdens on A and B. People in equal positions (confronted with equal options) would incur the same burden when exposed to the same tax formula. But if preferences differ, a uniform formula, short of one which covers the entire vector of options, will not minimize burdens and also equalize them among individuals. Different formulae would have to be used, with each person's formula tailored to his particular preference set. This, however, is not an operational proposition. Tax theory, to be relevant to tax policy, must accept the constraint that the same tax base or formula is applied to all individuals; but closer consideration shows that there is no single formula that will be wholly satisfactory in both respects. A tax formula designed to avoid inefficiency will discriminate against products with low elasticities of substitution, whereas one designed to avoid inequities will discriminate against products whose share in consumer budgets (at given levels of income or consumption) shows a low degree of dispersion. The two sets of products will hardly be the same.

This being the case, a tradeoff between equity and efficiency becomes necessary, and to carry it out two tasks of measurement arise. First, it is no longer sufficient to rank taxes by efficiency cost. The absolute cost of various tax formulae must be determined. Secondly, the quality of various formulae in terms of horizontal equity must be measured [White (1975)] and evaluated so that it can be balanced against excess burden incurred or avoided. Solving for the good tax structure is to strike this balance but even then, only a second-best solution (SBT) can be found.

Seen in this perspective, the essential difference between ET and OT is not merely that the former has been more closely related to the institutional setting of taxation while the latter has been more abstract and technical in its reasoning. It lies in the fact that ET has been preoccupied with horizontal equity at the cost of neglecting efficiency, while OT (especially in its commodity tax branch) has been concerned primarily with efficiency while neglecting horizontal equity. As I see it, horizontal equity has been defined out of existence by assuming all individuals to be subject to identical utility functions. Essentially, the problem is viewed in terms of a one-consumer economy, with taxes tailored to *his* particular preference function, thereby eliminating the distinction between using a generally applicable tax formula and the tailoring of tax bases in line with the preferences of different individuals. The ET and OT approaches thus move in quite different conceptual worlds. They come together only if it is realized that efficiency must be accounted for more fully by ET, while the horizontal equity issue must be faced by OT. The heart of the matter is how to apply equal treatment to a world of unequals, and OT will be of little help to policymakers until this is recognised. My OT friends tell me that the allowance for differential tastes would render the problem too unwieldy for a neat solution, but I shall leave it to their ingenuity to find it.

5. Efficiency and vertical equity

We have noted that horizontal and vertical equity are closely linked concepts. Without criteria for differential treatment of unequals, there is little reason for worrying about the treatment of equals. ET writers have tended to interpret vertical equity in terms of equal sacrifice which (as applied to people in unequal positions) was taken to call for progressive taxation. Closer consideration, however, showed that this may or may not be the case, depending on the shape of the marginal income utility schedule and on how equal (absolute, proportional or marginal) sacrifice is defined. Moreover, the very assumption of objectively measurable, comparable and similar utility schedules became subject to increasing criticism. Eventually, the entire approach was replaced by a socially-postulated marginal income utility schedule with all individuals treated *as if* they were subject thereto.[6] Cognizant that progressive taxation aggrevates the problem of dead-weight loss, ET writers have hastened to add that vertical equity considerations in support of progression must be tempered by an allowance for adverse efficiency effects, a call for penance dating back to Edgeworth and Pigou. In all, the argument was left in a murky state and no clear conclusion emerged, with vertical equity analysis giving way to concern with horizontal equity.

OT, in its optimal income tax branch, has brought new life to the old issue of vertical equity. In postulating a utility function which specifies the taxpayer's choice between goods and leisure, his responses to tax or transfer rates are determined; and in postulating a social welfare function which permits alternative states of distribution to be ranked, an optimal structure of income tax is deduced (assuming a given distribution of earnings capacities) which will maximize social welfare under that function. Making the distribution of the tax-transfer burden progressive results in a social welfare gain since the high-income loss is valued less heavily than the low-income gain. But the higher marginal tax and transfer rates needed to accomplish this also impose an efficiency cost or welfare loss. The optimal degree of progression is reached where the former gain at the margin falls short of the latter loss. The model may then be applied not only to the optimal distribution of a given tax bill but also to the broader problem of redistribution through the inclusion of taxes and transfers in the context of a negative income tax. As distinct from the theoretical aloofness of the OT work on commodity taxes, this branch of OT has arrived at specific conclusions, results which place narrower limits on progressive taxation than might have been expected. The results, however, depend in large part on the underlying assumptions, including the stipulated utility function as well as the particular social welfare function which is assumed [Cooter and Helpman (1974)]. While the analysis is superior to the old sacrifice approach, one's view as to the optimal tax structure remains in substantial part a matter of value judgment.

Most important in our context, identical utility functions are again taken to apply to all individuals. This assumption not only eliminates the horizontal equity issue but thereby bypasses an essential aspect of the redistribution problem. Since in fact people have different income–leisure preferences, any solution which assigns roles in the redistribution process (whether as taxpayer or as transfer recipient) in terms of actual earnings discriminates against persons

---

[6]As the slope of the schedule remains unknown, so is the degree of progression called for to secure equal sacrifice. While efforts have been made to reverse the problem by deriving the shape of the utility function from the existing income tax, this would seem an excessively optimistic procedure [Mera (1969)].

with high goods preference and in favor of persons with high L and P preference. Thus vertical equity (defined in terms of X and Z but without regard for L and P) is implemented at the cost of violating horizontal equity. Iniquities, moreover, are to be found throughout the capacity scale, as persons with high income preference stand to suffer discriminatory treatment under the OT model. The OT standard, by postulating equal utility functions, offends horizontal equity and falls short of being optimal, as I would use the term. The scholar who likes to think of himself as pursuing the higher things of life (rather than money income) may be inclined to overlook this defect, but the public at large may not. It is not surprising that, in the end, the failure to choose a satisfactory index of equality proves to be troublesome in the derivation of vertical as well as horizontal equity norms.

References

Bittker, B.I., C.O. Galvin, R.A. Musgrave and J.A. Pechman, 1968, A comprehensive income tax base? A debate (Federal Tax Press, Branford, CT).

Cooter, R. and E. Helpman, 1974, Optimal income taxation for transfer payments under different social welfare criteria, Quarterly Journal of Economics.

Edgeworth, F.Y., 1897, The pure theory of taxation, Economic Journal 7. Reprinted in R.A. Musgrave and A. Peacock as Classics in the theory of public finance (International Economic Association, Macmillan, London, 1958).

Mera, K., 1969, Experimental determination of relative marginal utilities, Quarterly Journal of Economics.

Pigou, A.C., 1951, Studies in public finance, 3rd edition (Macmillan, London).

Simons, H., 1938, Personal income taxation (University of Chicago Press, Chicago).

Simons, H., 1940, Federal tax reform (University of Chicago Press, Chicago).

Vickrey, W., 1947, Agenda for progressive taxation.

White, M. and A. White, 1965, Horizontal inequity in the federal income tax treatment of home ownership and tenants, National Tax Journal, September.

[2]

Progressive Taxation and Equal Sacrifice

By H. Peyton Young*

Fairness is the dominant theme in almost every political debate about income tax policy.[1] Yet when it comes to actually assessing the treatment of different income groups, there is little or no agreement on how, or even whether, fairness can be meaningfully measured. The difficulty is that most criteria of vertical equity are based on the notion of equal sacrifice. While this idea was influential around the turn of the last century, it is now considered quite unfashionable, if not downright disreputable, since it relies heavily on interpersonal utility comparisons (Paul Samuelson, 1947; Richard Musgrave, 1959; Anthony Atkinson and Joseph Stiglitz, 1980). In spite of its dubious theoretical foundations, however, we propose to examine whether equal sacrifice may explain why observed tax rates have the particular structure that they do. In other words, is it a valid empirical principle?

Equal sacrifice is an elaboration of the notion that a rich person should pay more in taxes than a poor person because the former feels a given monetary loss to a lesser degree.[2] The case for it was put most succinctly by John Stuart Mill:

> As a government ought to make no distinction of persons or classes in the strength of their claims on it, whatever sacrifices it requires from them should be made to bear as nearly as possible with the same pressure upon all ...Equality of taxation, therefore, as a maxim of politics, means equality of sacrifice. [1848, p. 804]

This passage spawned a large and illustrious literature on sacrifice theory around the turn of the century (Henry Sidgwick, 1883; Arnold Jacob Cohen Stuart, 1889; Gustav Cassell, 1901; F. Y. Edgeworth, 1897, 1919; Arthur Pigou, 1928). Below we shall briefly review the various interpretations that have been given to the term "equal sacrifice." The point that bears emphasizing here is that Mill was suggesting the concept as a *political* principle. Equal sacrifice is a natural corollary of egalitarianism. If we consider Mill's statement in this light, then it is reasonable to ask whether equal sacrifice is discernible in the way that legislators actually do distribute the tax burden. Specifically, we shall ask whether different income groups give up approximately the same amount (alternatively, the same proportion) of their utility in paying taxes. The credibility of the answer will depend, of course, on whether the estimated form of the utility function accords well with estimates of utility derived from other sources, such as the finance literature. We shall find that it does.[3]

---

*H. Peyton Young is Professor of Public Policy, School of Public Affairs, University of Maryland, College Park, MD 20742. This work was completed while the author was a guest scholar in the Economic Studies Program at the Brookings Institution, Washington, DC 20036. The manuscript benefited from helpful comments by Marcus Berliant, Richard Musgrave, Joseph Pechman, Wolfram Richter, Michael Wallerstein, Stan Winer, and two anonymous referees. The author thanks Dean Foster and Eric Munz for assistance in analyzing the tax data. The research was supported by NSF grant no. SES-831-9530.

[1] For example, the title of the recent U.S. tax reform proposal was *Tax Reform for Fairness, Simplicity, and Economic Growth* (U.S. Department of the Treasury, 1984).

[2] Equal sacrifice does not necessarily imply (as some early authors erroneously assumed) that the rich should pay *proportionally* more of their incomes in tax (Samuelson, 1947, p. 247).

[3] An early attempt to estimate the marginal utility of income from tax data is due to Koichi Mera (1969). Irving Fisher (1927) suggested the reverse procedure: estimate the marginal utility of income from consumption data, and then substitute this into an equal sacrifice formula to determine the "just" rate of income tax progression. For related work, see Gabrielle Preinreich (1948), Otto Eckstein (1961), Robert H. Haveman (1965), and Burton Weisbrod (1968).

The data on which we test this hypothesis consist of federal income tax schedules in the United States over the period 1957–1987. During this period the income tax underwent a half-dozen substantial reforms.[4] The top bracket dropped from 91 percent in 1957 to 38.5 percent in 1987 to 33 percent today. In spite of these dramatic shifts, the distribution of the tax burden is explained quite well by the equal sacrifice model in most years. The post-1986 tax reform schedule is, however, a notable exception, as we shall presently see. In every case where a good fit is obtained, the estimated utility function exhibits constant proportional risk aversion with a coefficient between 1.5 and 1.7. These values are in good agreement with recent estimates based on cross-sectional studies of household demand for risky assets (Irwin Friend and Marshall E. Blume, 1975.) Similar results are obtained for recent nominal tax schedules in West Germany, Japan, and Italy.

The United Kingdom, like the United States, deviates significantly from the equal sacrifice model however. A possible explanation for this is that in both cases the schedules resulted from tax reforms in which great importance was attached to reducing the *number* of distinct tax brackets (so-called "tax simplification"). A small number of distinct brackets, with sizable jumps between the brackets, results in a choppy pattern for the average tax rate that does not fit the equal sacrifice model nearly as well as a gradually rising series of brackets.

Although we cannot draw definitive conclusions from such a limited set of data, the results suggest that equal sacrifice provides a reasonably accurate model of how the U.S. federal tax burden has been distributed among most taxpayers, at least until recently. It is also significant (or at least a remarkable coincidence) that the estimated elasticity of the utility of income is in agreement with estimates based on the demand for risky assets. At the lower and upper ends of the distribution, however, the equal sacrifice model does not fit the data well. One explanation is that at lower incomes the need to raise revenue forces an initial rate that is higher than equal sacrifice requires, whereas at higher incomes the need to preserve economic incentives holds the marginal rates below what equal sacrifice requires. These results appear to generalize to other industrialized countries, but more work on this aspect remains to be done.

I. Concepts of Equal Sacrifice

Any empirical test of the equal sacrifice hypothesis is complicated by the existence of several competing versions of the concept (Musgrave, 1959). The idea originally advanced by Mill was that everyone should suffer the same absolute loss of utility. That is, if $U(x)$ represents the utility corresponding to income level x, then the tax t as a function of x should satisfy

$$(1) \qquad U(x) - U(x-t) = s,$$

where s is the constant level of sacrifice for all income classes, x. This implies that the tax schedule takes the form

$$(2) \quad t = x - U^{-1}[U(x) - s] \quad \text{for all } x > 0.$$

Ideally, individuals should be differentiated according to their particular utility functions. But this is impossible in practice, and, even if it were possible, would be based on false premises because it requires making fine-tuned interpersonal utility comparisons. A more plausible point of view is to consider $U(x)$ as a social norm—the utility function of a "representative" member of society (Lionel Robbins, 1938; Musgrave, 1959). In this sense no interpersonal utility comparisons are being made; rather, individuals are being treated as if they were all alike. This is a typical assumption in many types of economic models, including most treatments of optimal taxation.

Mill proposed using the Bernoullian utility function, which was the standard of his day. In this case a fixed percentage decrease in

---

[4]In each of the periods 1954–1963, 1964, 1965–1976, 1977–1978, 1979–1981, U.S. individual income tax schedules remained fairly stable. From 1982–1987 major tax reforms were instituted through a series of transition schedules.

income represents the same loss of utility at every income level. Therefore, everyone sacrifices the same amount of utility if each person pays the same percent of income in tax.[5] It is noteworthy that this solution, which is considered by many to be the simplest and fairest, can be justified on equal sacrifice grounds.

Subsequent to Mill, the equal sacrifice doctrine was elaborated in several directions. Cohen Stuart (1889) proposed that everyone should suffer the same *relative* loss in utility. If r is the rate of loss in utility, then for all $x > 0$,

(3) $U(x-t)/U(x) = 1 - r.$

This criterion is known as "equal proportionate sacrifice."

For present purposes there is no need to distinguish the case of equal absolute from equal proportionate sacrifice, because equal proportionate sacrifice is nothing but equal absolute sacrifice relative to a different utility function. Namely, if we take the logarithm of both sides of (3), then we see that equal proportional sacrifice with respect to $U(x)$ amounts to equal absolute sacrifice with respect to $\ln U(x)$.[6]

II. A Test for Equal Sacrifice

To make any progress on testing equal sacrifice, it would appear that we must first specify the form of the utility function. Actually, this is not so. Instead, we shall postulate that equal sacrifice holds for some (unknown) utility function, and then show that important information about the utility

[5]Mill defined taxable income to be income net of subsistence requirements as well as savings.

[6]A third variation of the equal sacrifice theme is to minimize aggregate sacrifice. This means that taxes should be distributed so as to minimize the total loss of utility summed over all individuals. The solution (assuming that the utility of income is increasing and strictly concave) is to equalize everyone's after-tax income (Edgeworth, 1897). This welfare maximization approach can be made much more appealing by employing a more realistic utility function—one that incorporates, for example, the tradeoff between income and leisure (James A. Mirrlees, 1971; J. K. Seade, 1977).

function can be derived directly from the tax data. The equal sacrifice hypothesis will be plausible if: (i) the estimated utility function is reasonably consistent with utility theory; and (ii) the equal sacrifice schedule derived from this utility function fits the empirical tax data.

In the modern theory of risk bearing, two parameters play a key role in defining the utility function: the coefficient of absolute risk aversion $R(x) = -U''(x)/U'(x)$ and the coefficient of proportional risk aversion $C(x) = -xU''(x)/U'(x)$ (John Pratt, 1964, Kenneth J. Arrow, 1971.) It is now generally accepted that the coefficient of absolute risk aversion is decreasing, while the coefficient of proportional risk aversion is more or less constant. Constant proportional risk aversion implies that people hold a constant *proportion* of their wealth in any one class of risky assets as their wealth varies. Empirical studies of household wealth have tended to support this hypothesis, and the coefficient C has been estimated to be greater than 1, and probably in the general neighborhood of 2 (Friend and Blume, 1975). This implies that the utility function is of the form:

(4) $U(x) = -A(x)^{1-C} + B,$

$A > 0, \quad C > 1.$

Turning now to the test for equal sacrifice, the first step is to examine the behavior of C as a function of x. It turns out that C can be estimated directly from the tax data. To see this, consider an empirically given tax schedule $t = f(x)$, where t is the amount of tax paid by persons at income level x. Assume that there exists a utility function $U(x)$ such that the loss of utility at all levels of income x is approximately constant:

$$U(x) - U(x-t) = s.$$

Dividing both sides by t, we obtain

(5) $[U(x) - U(x-t)]/t = s/t.$

By the Mean Value Theorem, the left-hand side of (5) is equal to the derivative of U at some intermediate value, w, between x and

$x - t$. Of course, w cannot be known precisely unless we know $U(x)$, which is what we are trying to estimate. Nevertheless, it turns out that w can be estimated quite accurately without knowing U. To see this, assume that the coefficient C is more or less constant in some neighborhood that includes x and $x - t$. Then, in this neighborhood, $U(x) = -Ax^{1-C} + B$, and without loss of generality we may take $A = 1$ and $B = 0$. Thus $U'(x) = (C-1)x^{-C}$ and the defining equation for w is

$$U'(w) = (C-1)w^{-C}$$
$$= [U(x) - U(x-t)]/t,$$
$$= [(x-t)^{1-C} - x^{1-C}]/t.$$

After some algebraic manipulation, we find that

$$w/x = \left(\frac{(C-1)(t/x)}{(1-t/x)^{1-C} - 1}\right)^{1/C}.$$

Take a typical value of t/x, say $t/x = 0.2$, and substitute in various plausible values for C. As the following table shows, the resulting value of w/x (and hence of w, given a specific value of x) is quite insensitive to the choice of C.

C	w/x
3	0.893
2.5	0.894
2.0	0.894
1.5	0.895
1.1	0.896

The upshot is that we may safely choose any value of C in this range in order to estimate w. The value $C = 2$ seems like a good choice and leads to the particularly simple formula $w = \sqrt{x(x-t)}$. From this and equation (5) we therefore have

$$U'\left(\sqrt{x(x-t)}\right) = s/t.$$

Without loss of generality we may take $s = 1$.

Taking logarithms we obtain

(6) $\quad \ln U'\left(\sqrt{x(x-t)}\right) = -\ln t.$

Recall now that we are attempting to estimate the coefficient of proportional risk aversion $-zU''(z)/U'(z)$. This is the rate of change of $-\ln U'(z)$ with respect to $\ln z$, which is $d(-\ln U'(z)/d(\ln z) = -[U''(z)/U'(z)]/[1/z]$. Let $X = \ln z$ and let $Y = -\ln U'(z)$. If we regress Y against X, then the slope of the regression line will be an estimate of C.

Let $z = \sqrt{x(x-t)}$. Then

$$X = \ln z = \ln\sqrt{x(x-t)}$$

and, by (6), $Y = -\ln U'(\sqrt{x(x-t)}) = \ln t$. Thus, we wish to regress $Y = \ln t$ against $X = \ln \sqrt{x(x-t)} = (1/2)\ln x(x-t)$ for various levels of tax t and pre-tax income x. The higher the R^2 is, the more plausible is the hypothesis that C is independent of x, and that the tax equalizes sacrifice relative to an isoelastic utility function.

III. Empirical Results

We illustrate the approach for United States tax data in 1957. Table 1 shows tax paid as a function of Adjusted Gross Income, which is the closest approximation we have to the effective tax schedule.[7]

The first step is to estimate the coefficient of proportional risk aversion as described in the preceding section. Let $Y = \ln t$ and $X = (1/2)\ln x(x-t)$ for the various values of x and t in the table. If the equal sacrifice hypothesis is correct relative to an isoelastic utility function, then we would expect to see an approximately linear relationship between X and Y, and the slope of the regression line will be an estimate of the coefficient C. Figure 1a shows that this hypothesis is

---

[7] It would be far better, of course, to make this estimation relative to total personal income rather than Adjusted Gross Income. Unfortunately, these data are not available.

TABLE 1—FEDERAL TAX PAID AS A FUNCTION OF ADJUSTED GROSS INCOME (AGI)
UNITED STATES, 1957[a]

Income Class	Percent of Total Returns in the Class	Average Income	Tax Paid	Percent
Under $600	6.5	328	0	0
600– 1,000	5.0	798	13	1.6
1,000– 1,500	7.0	1,241	48	3.9
1,500– 2,000	6.2	1,752	90	5.1
2,000– 2,500	6.5	2,252	136	6.0
2,500– 3,000	6.4	2,748	188	6.8
3,000– 3,500	6.5	3,246	247	7.6
3,500– 4,000	6.6	3,751	309	8.2
4,000– 4,500	6.7	4,250	370	8.7
4,500– 5,000	6.5	4,748	431	9.1
5,000– 6,000	11.0	5,474	525	9.6
6,000– 7,000	7.9	6,472	690	10.7
7,000– 8,000	5.4	7,466	870	11.7
8,000– 9,000	3.5	8,467	1,065	12.6
9,000– 10,000	2.2	9,458	1,257	13.3
10,000– 15,000	3.7	11,744	1,740	14.8
15,000– 20,000	0.9	17,112	3,013	17.6
20,000– 25,000	0.4	22,256	4,468	20.1
25,000– 50,000	0.6	33,373	8,472	25.4
50,000–1000,000	0.2	65,652	23,262	35.4
Above 100,000	0.3	–	–	–

[a]*Source:* Statistics of Income, U.S. Internal Revenue Service, 1957.

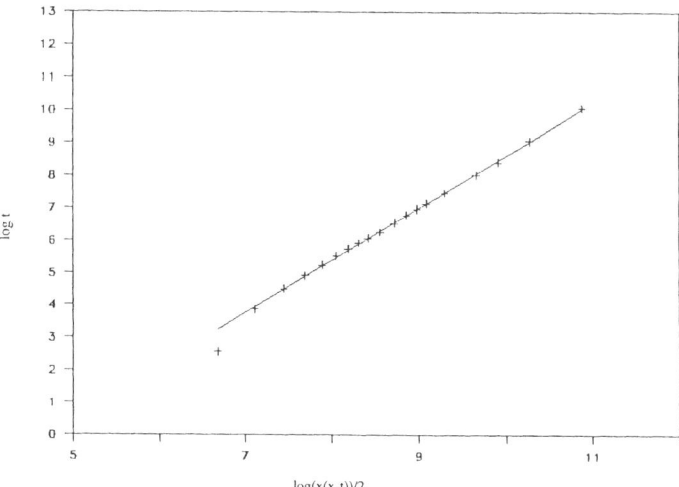

FIGURE 1a. SLOPE ESTIMATE OF C, U.S. EFFECTIVE TAX SCHEDULE, 1957, $C = 1.61$, S.E. $= 0.008$, $R^2 = 99.9$

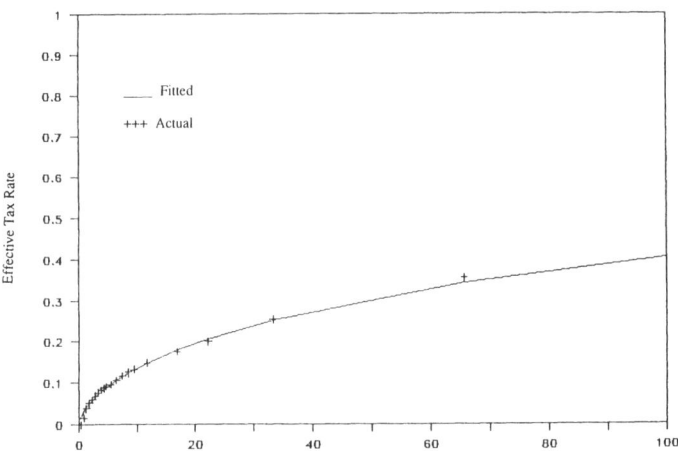

FIGURE 1b. EQUAL SACRIFICE TAX FITTED TO U.S. EFFECTIVE SCHEDULE, 1957. ES TAX = $x - (x^{-0.610} + 0.000337)^{-1/0.610}$. INCOME RANGE: $\$1,000 \leq x \leq \$100,000$. COEFFICIENT OF VARIATION OF ES TAX/ACTUAL TAX = 3.8 PERCENT

strongly confirmed for adjusted gross incomes above $1,000, which represents 88.2 percent of all returns in 1957.[8] The estimated value of C is 1.61, the standard error of the estimate is 0.008, and the R^2 is 99.9 percent. This finding does not confirm the hypothesis of equal sacrifice itself; it merely gives us confidence in the estimated value of C and the isoelasticity of the utility function *assuming* that equal sacrifice holds. To a good approximation, therefore, the utility function may be written as $U(x) = -x^{-0.61}$.

Next, we plot the differences $U(x) - U(x-t)$ to estimate the level of sacrifice, s. The value of s has no absolute significance,

of course, since it depends on the scaling of the utility function. Nevertheless, it is a necessary parameter for computing the equal sacrifice tax, given that the utility function has been specified. Again, treating incomes below $1,000 as outliers, the estimated mean level of sacrifice is $s = 3.37 \times 10^{-4}$ and the standard deviation is 0.1×10^{-4}, which is about 3 percent of the mean.

The final step is to use the estimated values of C and of s to compute a fitted tax schedule $t = x - (x^{1-C} + s)^{1/(1-C)}$. This is shown in Figure 1b. For incomes between $1,000 and $100,000, the ratio of the equal sacrifice tax to the actual tax has a coefficient of variation of ±3.8 percent. To a very good approximation, therefore, the effective tax rate in 1957 is consistent with equal absolute sacrifice relative to the isoelastic utility function $U(x) = -x^{-0.61}$.[9]

---

[8] The data point corresponding to the income class $600–$1,000 is treated as an outlier (see Figure 1a). If this point is included in the estimation, then the estimated value of C is 1.67 and the standard error is 0.033. As noted earlier, there are good reasons to expect a departure from the equal sacrifice model at the lower end of the income distribution. Hence we have estimated C after excluding the lower tail, where linearity does not appear to be confirmed.

[9] It should be noted that these results are also consistent with equal *proportionate* sacrifice relative to the utility function $U(x) = \exp[-Ax^{-0.61} + B]$. While this

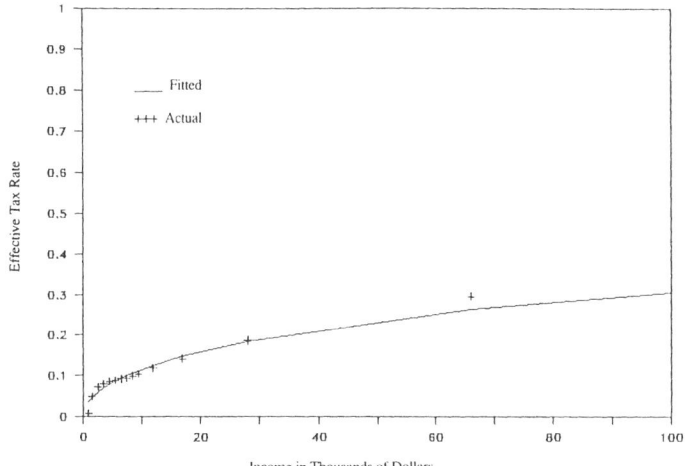

FIGURE 2. EQUAL SACRIFICE TAX FITTED TO U.S. EFFECTIVE SCHEDULE, 1967.
ES TAX = $(x^{-0.519} + 0.000566)^{-1/0.519}$. INCOME RANGE: $\$3,000 \leq x \leq \$100,000$.
COEFFICIENT OF VARIATION OF ES TAX/ACTUAL TAX = 7.2 PERCENT

Similar results are obtained for the tax years 1967 and 1977, though the fit is somewhat less good. (See Figures 2 and 3). The estimation for 1987 could not be done because the relevant data are not yet available from the Internal Revenue Service. The nominal tax schedules are available, however, and this is the estimation we turn to next.

It is quite conceivable that the schedule of published rates (the nominal schedule) is also consistent with equal sacrifice. The hypothesis here is that the public is at least as sensitive to the apparent distribution of tax rates as they are to the effective rates. In other words, the appearance of equity may be as important as equity in fact. Certainly, the question seems worthy of investigation. Furthermore, the nominal schedules have a distinct advantage over the effective schedules in that they are not subject to measurement error.

For purposes of this analysis we chose U.S. Schedule X, which applies to individuals. A good fit is obtained for the years 1957, 1967, and 1977, except at the very lower and upper ends of the income scale (Figure 4 is illustrative.)[10] The estimated elasticities are somewhat higher than for the corresponding effective schedules, as is to be expected, since the higher the elasticity of marginal utility, the greater the progressivity of the schedule (see Table 2).

---

is a less standard representation of utility than the isoelastic functions, it is not wholly unreasonable. In fact, the coefficient of proportional risk aversion for $U(x) = \exp[-Ax^{-p} + B]$ is $1 + p - Ap/x^p$, which is slightly increasing but very close to the coefficient for $-Ax^{-p} + B$ when x is large relative to A. In other words, the two functions are scarcely distinguishable with respect to risk aversion, and hence the model cannot really say whether equal absolute or equal proportionate sacrifice is more credible. Given the general preference for the isoelastic representation of utility in the literature, we shall interpret our results as implying equal absolute sacrifice relative to an isoelastic utility function.

[10] The coefficient of variation for the equal sacrifice tax divided by the actual tax is 8.8 percent for 1957, 5.6 percent for 1967, and 6.9 percent for 1977.

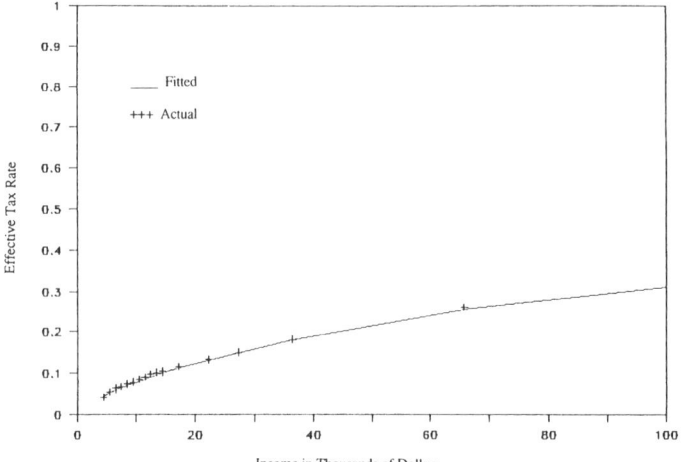

FIGURE 3. EQUAL SACRIFICE TAX FITTED TO U.S. EFFECTIVE SCHEDULE, 1977.
ES TAX = $x - (x^{-0.718} + 0.00008)^{-1/0.718}$. INCOME RANGE:
$\$4,000 \leq x \leq \$100,000$. COEFFICIENT OF VARIATION OF ES TAX/ACTUAL
TAX = 4.0 PERCENT

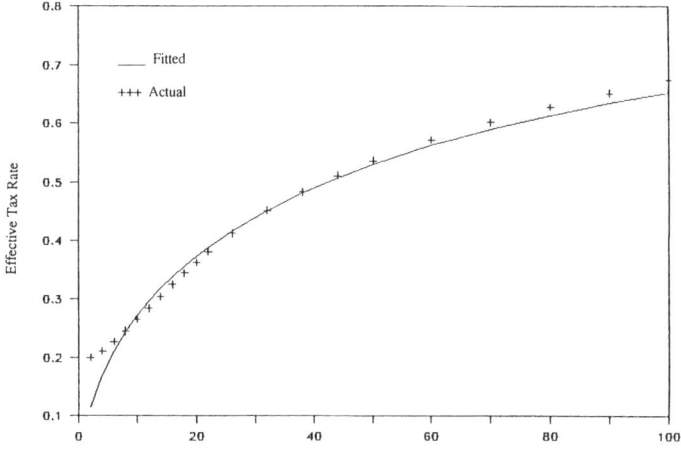

FIGURE 4. EQUAL SACRIFICE TAX FITTED TO U.S. NOMINAL SCHEDULE, 1957.
ES TAX = $x - (x^{-0.631} + 0.000664)^{-1/0.631}$. INCOME RANGE:
$\$3,000 \leq x \leq \$100,000$.
COEFFICIENT OF VARIATION OF ES TAX/ACTUAL TAX = 5.2 PERCENT

TABLE 2—ESTIMATED ELASTICITY OF MARGINAL UTILITY, U.S. NOMINAL AND EFFECTIVE TAX SCHEDULES, 1957–1987.

	Nominal	Effective
1957	1.63	1.61
1967	1.53	1.52
1977	1.79	1.72
1987	1.37	n/a

By contrast, the 1987 nominal schedule does not fit the equal sacrifice model very well (see Figure 5). The reason is that the tax is nearly flat-rate for incomes up to $16,800 and hence progressivity is almost nil in this range.[11] Above $16,800 progressivity is modest but fairly steady as marginal rates rise from 15 percent to 38.5 percent. This example clearly demonstrates that the equal sacrifice model does not explain all tax schedules. But it also shows that the model is not tautological: There exist perfectly reasonable tax schedules that do *not* support an equal sacrifice interpretation, at least not relative to an isoelastic utility function.

A possible explanation for the departure from equal sacrifice in 1987 (as compared with prior years) is the emphasis placed in the 1986 Tax Reform Act on "simplifying" the tax structure. One of the supposed simplifications was to reduce the number of brackets. But no schedule composed of just two or three marginal rates will fit the equal sacrifice model well, because equal sacrifice relative to any smooth utility function implies a continuously varying marginal rate.[12] The converse is not true: just because a tax schedule exhibits a continuously increasing marginal rate, does not imply that it is "almost" an equal sacrifice tax. Indeed, an equal sacrifice tax relative to an isoelastic utility function (with $1 < C < 2$) has a very special shape: the effective tax rate t/x is concave, increases continuously from zero and is asymptotic to 100 percent as income goes to infinity. Actually, more is true: once two points on the schedule are chosen—that is, once the tax is specified for two distinct incomes—then the equal sacrifice schedule and the corresponding utility function are fully determined. So, it would be highly coincidental if an arbitrarily chosen tax rate schedule (even one with many brackets) were to meet these requirements. For example, a tax rate schedule in which the effective rate t/x is first concave, then convex, then concave (as in the 1987 U.S. Schedule) does not fit the equal sacrifice model that we have described.

While earlier U.S. tax schedules are generally consistent with the equal sacrifice hypothesis over most of the income distribution, they do not fit the model at the lower end. The reason is that the tax brackets are not graduated finely enough for low incomes. Indeed, the equal sacrifice model (with $C > 1$) requires that the marginal tax rate decrease continuously to zero as income approaches zero. Any schedule based on a finite number of brackets obviously violates this condition. Given that the initial brackets in the U.S. schedules varied between 11 percent and 20 percent during the period 1957–1987, it can hardly be expected that the fit would be good at the lower end of the income scale. The reason for such large initial rates is a matter of fiscal arithmetic: In order to capture enough revenue, one must tax where the income is, and the lion's share of taxable income lies in the income brackets just above the minimum exemption level. So it is almost necessary for the initial marginal rate to be large, or at least to rise very steeply. This constraint may override considerations of fairness at the bottom of the income scale.

At the upper end of the income distribution we find departures from the equal sacrifice model for quite a different reason. Marginal tax rates must be truncated well below 100 percent in order to provide adequate incentives for people to work and invest. This is inconsistent with equal sacrifice

---

[11] Income up to $1,800 is taxed at 11 percent, then at 15 percent up to a total of $16,800. The fit is even worse for 1988, where the initial rate is 15 percent on the first $17,850, 28 percent up to $43,150, and 33 percent up to $89,560 (Internal Revenue Service, 1987, 1988.)

[12] From $U(x) - U(x - t) = s$ it follows by differentiation that $dt/dx = 1 - U'(x)/U'(x - t)$. Hence, if U' is continuous, then so is the marginal rate dt/dx.

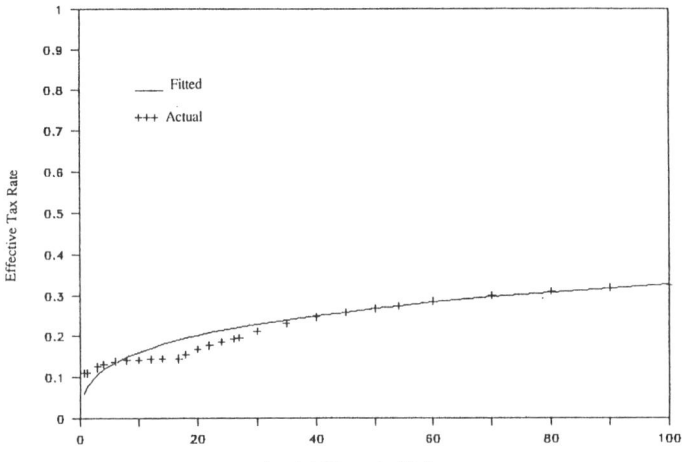

FIGURE 5. EQUAL SACRIFICE TAX FITTED TO U.S. NOMINAL SCHEDULE, 1987.
ES TAX $= x - (x^{-0.373} + 0.00218)^{-1/0.373}$. INCOME RANGE:
$\$3{,}000 \leq x \leq \$100{,}000$.
COEFFICIENT OF VARIATION OF ES TAX/ACTUAL TAX $= 10.3$ PERCENT

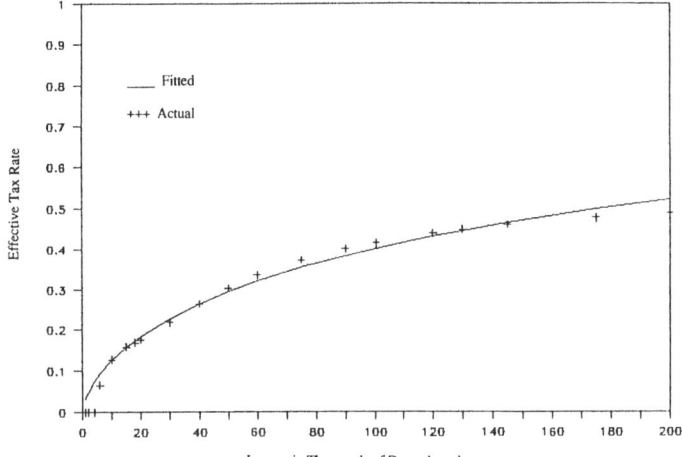

FIGURE 6. EQUAL SACRIFICE TAX FITTED TO WEST GERMAN NOMINAL
SCHEDULE, 1984. ES TAX $= x - (x^{-0.633} + 0.000260)^{-1/0.633}$. INCOME RANGE:
DM $10{,}000 \leq x \leq$ DM $200{,}000$. COEFFICIENT OF VARIATION OF ES
TAX/ACTUAL TAX $= 3.2$ PERCENT

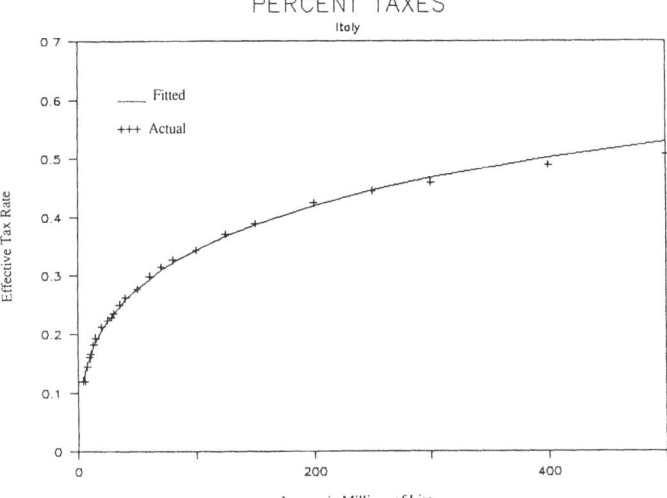

FIGURE 7. EQUAL SACRIFICE TAX FITTED TO ITALIAN NOMINAL SCHEDULE, 1987. ES TAX $= x - (x^{-0.403} + 0.00179)^{-1/0.403}$. INCOME RANGE: $4 \leq x \leq 500$ MILLION LIRE. COEFFICIENT OF VARIATION OF ES TAX/ACTUAL TAX = 3.9 PERCENT

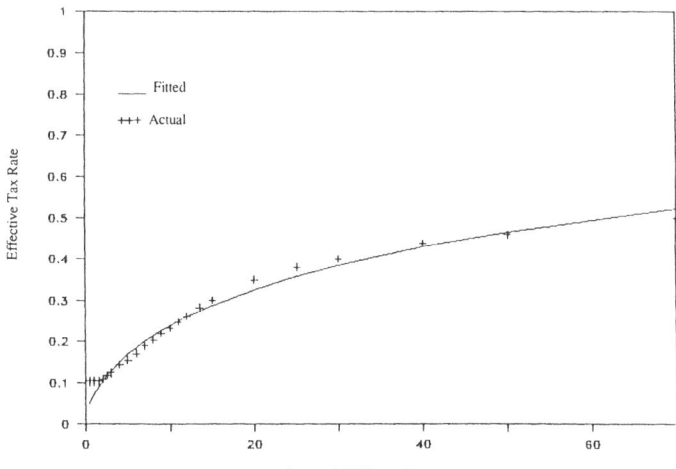

FIGURE 8. EQUAL SACRIFICE TAX FITTED TO JAPANESE NOMINAL SCHEDULE, 1987. ES TAX $= x - (x^{-0.587} + 0.0448)^{-1/0.587}$. INCOME RANGE: $1.5 \leq x \leq 70$ MILLION YEN. COEFFICIENT OF VARIATION OF ES TAX/ACTUAL TAX = 5.4 PERCENT

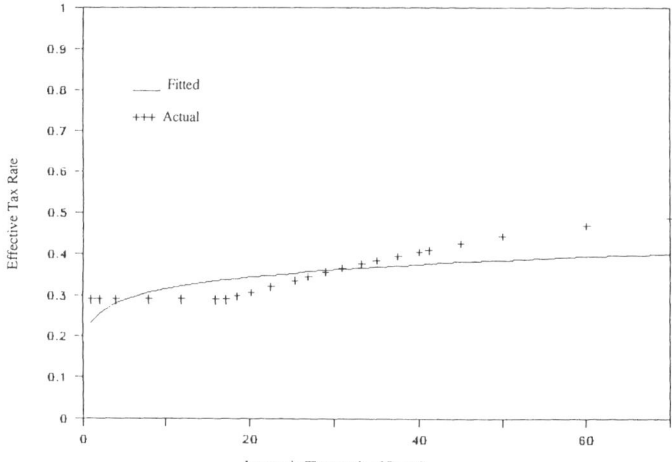

FIGURE 9. EQUAL SACRIFICE TAX FITTED TO U.K. NOMINAL SCHEDULE, 1987.
ES TAX $= x - (x^{-0.163} + 0.0143)^{-1/0.163}$. INCOME RANGE: $1 \leq x \leq 70$
THOUSAND POUNDS. COEFFICIENT OF VARIATION OF ES TAX $= 10.4$ PERCENT

relative to an isoelastic utility function, however, which requires that tax rates gradually approach 100 percent. For high incomes, therefore, the departure from equal sacrifice may be due to efficiency considerations, whereas for low incomes it is probably due to revenue requirements. The middle- to upper-middle income range is where considerations of vertical equity can be given somewhat freer rein.

IV. Data from Other Countries

It is natural to ask whether the preceding results are in some way peculiar to the United States. To investigate this possibility in a preliminary way, we chose four major industrialized countries—West Germany, Italy, Japan, and the United Kingdom—and analyzed the most recent nominal tax schedules available to us. The results are illustrated in Figures 6–9. The equal sacrifice model gives an excellent fit for West Germany, Italy, and Japan, and the estimated coefficients are 1.63, 1.40, and 1.59, respectively. It is rather remarkable that these values all lie within such a narrow range, and that they are so similar to the U.S. results. Italy is particularly noteworthy because the nominal schedule fits the equal sacrifice model very closely even at the low end of the income scale. All three countries exhibit a much more finely graduated rate structure than the current U.S. schedule does. The United Kingdom, however, is similar to the United States in that the 1987 schedule does not fit the equal sacrifice model at all well. The reason is that it employs a flat-rate tax on taxable income up to £17,200. and a mildly progressive series of rates thereafter. As in the case of the recent U.S. tax reform, this appears to be the result of a political compromise in which the drive toward a flat-rate tax had to be modified by demands for progressive treatment of the well-to-do.

V. Conclusion

In this paper we have described a general method for testing whether a tax schedule exhibits equal sacrifice relative to an isoelastic utility function. The technique can be applied to any schedule, whether nominal or effective, and even to particular portions of a given schedule. The method estimates the coefficient of risk aversion in the utility function, the level of sacrifice at each level of income, and the tax function that would be implied by equal sacrifice. The latter may then be compared with the actual schedule to see how far the actual tax deviates from equal sacrifice on different portions of the income distribution.

Over much of the postwar period, the observed tax rates in the United States conformed to the equal sacrifice model quite closely, and the estimated curvature of the utility function was fairly stable. Of course, obtaining a reasonably good fit does not prove causation. Nor do we have any direct evidence that legislators actually invoked equal sacrifice arguments in proposing the rate structures that we observe. It seems likely, however, that intuitive notions of "relative sacrifice" and "ability to pay" are one factor in the way that legislators evaluate the fairness of tax proposals. And it does not seem too far-fetched to suppose that the aggregate of these intuitions, as expressed in a majority vote, might come close to an equal sacrifice tax relative to an "average" utility function.

Several questions remain to be explored. First, it would be interesting to know whether these results hold up when we analyze the effective rather than the nominal schedules in other industrialized countries. Even for the United States, it would be far better to carry out the analysis relative to full income, rather than Adjusted Gross Income, as we were forced to do because of lack of data.

Second, it may well be that some other theory can explain why tax schedules merely look like equal sacrifice schedules. Such a theory would need to explain why effective rates t/x tend to be concave, and more specifically why they tend to fit functions of the form

$$(7) \quad t = x - [x^{-p} + s]^{-1/p},$$

$$s > 0, \quad 0 < p < 1.$$

Third, it may be that equal sacrifice has some other explanation or justification than the traditional utilitarian one. One idea along these lines is the following. If we hypothesize that taxes are distributed according to *some* measure of ability to pay (not necessarily a utilitarian one), and if we suppose further that the criterion applies not only to the distribution of the whole tax, but to every tax increase (or decrease), then the measure of ability to pay must be equal sacrifice relative to a social utility of income (Young, 1988).[13] This argument suggests that the equal sacrifice "look" might result from legislators trying to balance equity in incremental changes that they make to the tax distribution with equity in the overall result.

Resolving these issues is beyond the scope of the present paper. The evidence suggests, however, that equal sacrifice may play a significant role in the way that people think about taxation, and that it needs to be taken more seriously as the 'maxim of politics' that Mill claimed it to be.

---

[13] We assume here that taxes are positive, continuous, strictly increasing in income, strictly increasing as a function of the total tax burden, and that marginal rates are less than 100 percent.

REFERENCES

Arrow, Kenneth J., *Essays in the Theory of Risk Bearing*, Amsterdam: North-Holland, 1971.

Atkinson, Anthony and Stiglitz, Joseph, *Lectures on Public Economics*, New York: McGraw-Hill, 1980.

Cassell, Gustav, "The Theory of Progressive Taxation," *Economic Journal*, December 1901, *11*, 481–91.

Stuart, Cohen and Cohen, Arnold Jacob, 1889, "On Progressive Taxation," in R. A. Musgrave and A. T. Peacock, eds., "*Classics in the Theory of Public Finance*," New York: MacMillan, 1958.

Eckstein, Otto, "A Survey of the Theory of Public Expenditure Criteria," National Bureau of Economic Research, *Public Finances: Needs, Sources, and Utilization*, Princeton: Princeton University Press, 1961.

Edgeworth, F. Y., "The Pure Theory of Taxation," in R. A. Musgrave and A. T. Peacock, eds., *Classics in the Theory of Public Finance*, New York: MacMillan, 1958.

_____, "Methods of Graduating Taxes on Income and Capital," *Economic Journal*, 1919, *29*, 138–53.

Fisher, Irving, "A Statistical Method for Measuring Marginal Utility and Testing the Justice of a Progressive Income Tax," *Economic Essays in Honor of John Bates Clark*, New York: MacMillan, 1927.

Friend, Irving and Blume, Marshall E., "The Demand for Risky Assets," *American Economic Review*, December 1975, *65*, 900–22.

Haveman, Robert H., *Water Resource Investment and the Public Interest*, Nashville: Vanderbilt University Press, 1965.

Ishi, Hiromitsu, *The Japanese Tax System*, Oxford: Clarendon Press, 1989.

Mera, Koichi, "Expermental Determination of Relative Marginal Utilities," *Quarterly Journal of Economics*, August 1969, *83*, 464–77.

Mill, John Stuart, *Principles of Political Economy* (1848), London: Longmans Green, 1917.

Mirrlees, James A., "An Exploration in the Theory of Optimum Income Taxation," *Review of Economic Studies*, April 1971, *38*, 175–208.

Musgrave, Richard, *The Theory of Public Finance*, New York: McGraw-Hill, 1959.

Pfingsten, Andreas, *The Measurement of Tax Progression*, unpublished doctoral dissertation, Karlsruhe, West Germany: University of Karlsruhe, 1985.

Pigou, Arthur, *A Study in Public Finance*, London: MacMillan, 1928.

Pratt, John, "Risk Aversion in the Small and in the Large," *Econometrica*, January-April 1964, *32*, 122–36.

Preinreich, Gabrielle, "Progressive Taxation and Proportionate Sacrifice," *American Economic Review*, March 1948, *38*, 103–17.

Price Waterhouse, *Individual Taxes: A Worldwide Summary*, New York: Price Waterhouse, 1987.

Robbins, Lionel, "Interpersonal Comparisons of Utility," *Economic Journal*, December 1938, *48*, 635–41.

Samuelson, Paul, *Foundations of Economic Analysis*, Cambridge: Harvard University Press, 1947.

Seade, J. K., "On the Shape of Optimal Tax Schedules," *Journal of Public Economics*, April 1977, *7*, 203–35.

Sidgwick, Henry, *The Principles of Political Economy*, London: MacMillan, 1983.

Weisbrod, Burton, "Income Redistribution Effects and Benefit-Cost Analysis," in: S. B. Chase ed., *Problems in Public Expenditure Analysis*, Washington: The Brookings Institution, 1968.

Young, H. Peyton, "Distributive Justice in Taxation," *Journal of Economic Theory*, April 1988, *44*, 321–35.

U.S. Treasury Department, *Statistics of Income: Individual Tax Returns*, 1957–1977.

_____, *Tax Reform for Fairness, Simplicity, and Economic Growth*. Washington, DC: USGPO, 1984.

_____, Internal Revenue Service, Form 1040, Schedule X, Washington, DC: USGPO, 1987, 1988.

[3]

HORIZONTAL EQUITY: MEASURES IN SEARCH OF A PRINCIPLE**

LOUIS KAPLOW*

ABSTRACT

Horizontal equity—the command that equals be treated equally—has received increasing attention, particularly in attempts to assess the desirability of tax reform proposals. It is demonstrated that recent attempts to implement horizontal equity are inconsistent with its stated foundations. More thorough examination raises serious doubts as to whether there is any alternative justification of horizontal equity that would support many common applications of the concept. Examples typically offered to motivate support for horizontal equity are shown to resonate with our intuition only because of the concept's congruence (in such cases) with conventional understandings of risk and vertical equity. Many remaining practical uses of horizontal equity are noted.

1. Introduction

HORIZONTAL equity (HE) is the command that equals be treated equally. The concept arises most frequently in discussions of tax policy alongside the more frequently addressed concerns for equality—denominated as vertical equity (VE)—and efficiency. The structure of analysis is that each of the three criteria has independent significance and must in some way be balanced against the others. (See Atkinson 1980; Feldstein 1976a, 1976b; King 1983).

Despite HE being mentioned in the same breath as VE in Musgrave's (1959) and (although not by name) in Shoup's (1969) pioneering treatises on public finance, HE had long received less serious attention among public finance economists than VE or efficiency, both in theoretical development and empirical elaboration. More recently, there has been a rapidly growing interest in the concept. An often-cited article by Feldstein (1976a) exploring HE in the context of tax reform, joined by an article by Musgrave (1976) that explores all three evaluative criteria, has led the way. Additional work such as that by Brennan (1971), King (1983), Plotnick (1981, 1982, 1984), and Rosen (1978) has focused primarily on refining the measurement of HE.

This rise in prominence may seem surprising since HE, as it has more recently been developed, is in conflict with the social welfare tradition, whereas VE and efficiency are included within it. Moreover, recent applications of HE do not involve the direct use of clearly irrelevant or invidious factors—as in varying tax rates by one's height or race—the sorts of discrimination that motivate the concern for equal protection of the law. Nor do they present arbitrary distinctions in sources or uses of income when defining a tax base, which was the central concern of Simons (1938) when invoking the notion of equal treatment. Rather, the question is whether one should object to *prima facie* reasonable tax reforms, motivated by concerns of efficiency or distribution, because of the incidental, inevitable, and often unavoidable effects of such reforms on the pre-reform distribution of income. Violations of HE are understood as being measured without regard to the origin or justification of the initial distribution of income—including, for example, the possibility that it merely reflects the incidental or even capricious effects of previous reforms.

The thesis of this paper is that recent work on HE has in an important sense jumped the gun. HE is now frequently measured and applied even though there has been virtually no exploration of why one should care about the principle in the contexts and in the manner in which it is now being used. Although the notion of equal treatment of equals is hardly new, it generally has been analzyed and ad-

---

*Harvard Law School and National Bureau of Economic Research, Cambridge, MA 02138.

vanced in contexts that bear little resemblance to those in which HE is now being avidly discussed. Mosts papers considering HE refer briefly to familiar remarks by Musgrave (1959) or Shoup (1969) without directly considering the connection between the original motivations and current applications.

Two problems arise from the failure to identify the normative justification for current uses of HE. First, if there is no normative basis for a measure of HE, efforts directed toward applying it are misspent and will lead policymakers astray when they are encouraged to sacrifice other values in the pursuit of HE. Second, if there is some normative basis, one cannot properly develop and choose among measures for a concept and methods for weighing it along with other objectives until that basis is specified. It is not always possible to be precise in matters of equity, but neither should ambiguity be accepted without complete investigation, as in some instances ambiguity can be reduced and in others it may indicate that deeper problems remain unresolved.

Section 2 compares traditional definitions and recently offered indexes of HE, suggesting that there exist serious difficulties even before one considers directly the foundations of HE. Section 3 assesses the extent to which the persuasive force often thought to support more recent invocations of HE in the context of tax reform can be understood better in the traditional social welfare framework. This section seeks to illuminate the connection between HE and VE first emphasized by Musgrave and to link the application of HE to the study of risk. Section 4 considers whether recent uses of HE can be defended by attributing normative significance to preserving the status quo or by invoking other theories of justice. Concluding remarks emphasize the practical uses of HE in light of this criticism.

2. Definitions and Indexes of Horizontal Equity

It seems backwards to criticize definitions and indexes of HE before exploring the motivation for the concept. Stiglitz (1982) has aptly characterized some past studies as "ad hoc approaches defining an index of horizontal inequity and an index of vertical equity, and positing a social welfare function giving trade-offs between the two[, which] seems close to assuming what is to be analyzed." Yet, even before considering foundations directly, it can be demonstrated that traditional definitions of HE are insufficient for current uses, recently developed HE indexes do not follow from these definitions, and such indexes are almost certainly inconsistent with any reasonable normative basis for HE. These defects are not, however, inherent in the concept of HE or in the motivations for extending it; thus, the section closes by offering an index of HE that seeks to capture the relevant features.

2.1. Problems with Simple Definitions of Horizontal Equity

Most generally, and most commonly, HE is said to require the equal treatment of equals. (Musgrave 1959, 1976; Atkinson and Stiglitz 1980.) Feldstein (1976a) defines HE for evaluating tax reform: "if two individuals would have the same utility level if the tax remained unchanged, they should also have the same utility level if the tax is changed." In contrast, VE calls for an appropriate pattern of differentiation (inequality in treatment) among people who are not equals. (See Musgrave 1959, 1976.)

The notion of equal treatment by itself is insufficient. (Similar analysis applies to the expanded version of HE that would require almost equal treatment of those who are almost equal.[1]) First, unless HE is taken to be an absolute constraint,[2] one needs to add some measure of the degree to which HE is violated by any action. Second, HE applies only to equals; it provides no judgment with regard to individuals whose positions are not initially alike, even though the motivations usually suggested for the concept extend more broadly. Related to both of these problems, even an infinitesimal difference in treatment beyond whatever range is deemed "equal treatment" counts as a violation, while further deviations, no matter how significant, are ignored. Thus, once it is recognized that virtually all effects of any action are on individuals who are unequal—either initially or after even modest change—the core definition of HE is inapplicable.[3] All further analysis is *by definition* in the realm of VE, which addresses the appropriate treatment of unequals.

2.2. Failures of Modified Definitions and Indexes of Horizontal Equity

Recognizing some of these limitations has led investigators to develop measures of HE that go beyond its traditional definition. Most commonly, indexes measure the number or magnitude of order reversals or the rank correlation between the pre- and post-reform distribution of income. (See Atkinson 1980; King 1983; Plotnick 1982, 1984; and Rosen 1978; also discussed by Feldstein 1976a.) Of course, according to the classic definition, these are really VE judgments since they address the proper treatment of unequals — which suggests that the implicit value judgment must be specified and defended (see Shoup 1969), something that has not been done.

These elaborations are subject to many of the criticisms applicable to the initial definition: Minute movements leading to order reversals count as full violations of HE while substantial disturbances in the initial distribution that result in no order reversal are ignored.[4] The basic problem is that these measures, because they are based on reranking, do not vary continuously with the magnitude of the effect on each individual (or groups of individuals).

To illustrate these shortcomings, consider King's (1983) index, which measures affronts to HE by using a scaled order statistic (s_i) for each individual, defined as follows:

$$s_i = \frac{|y_{pi} - y_{ai}|}{y},$$

where y_{ai} and y_{pi} denote, respectively, "the *ex post* income levels corresponding to the rank of individual i in the ex ante and ex post distributions," and y denotes the mean income. This measure has some remarkable properties that are not noted by King (or by others taking this approach). First, consider two individuals, A and B, such that A has one cent more income in the ex ante income distribution than B, but two times the income of B in the ex post income distribution. Since there is no rank reversal, $s_A = s_B = 0$. Contrast this with the same situation, except that in the ex ante distribution, A has one cent less than B rather than one cent more. Now, $s_A = s_B = .67$. This large jump (in a two-person example, the maximum value of the indicator is 2) demonstrates how the proposed indicator is discontinuous in ex ante income levels. Moreover, it should be clear that, except at the point of the discontinuity, the indicator is totally unaffected by ex ante income levels. The indicator also has surprising properties in terms of changes in ex post income levels. Until there is a cross-over, $s_A = s_B = 0$. After the cross-over, the s_i's increase smoothly as the gap in income increases, with a discontinuity in the derivative at the cross-over point (the derivative jumps from zero to a strictly positive number).[5] The analysis and indexes of many others have reflected a very similar approach.[6] It is hard to conceive of the normative principle that could justify measures with such properties.

2.3. On the Inconsistency Between Concerns for Horizontal Equity and Economic Mobility

Before continuing with an analysis of the justification for HE, this section comments briefly on recent indexes of economic mobility (MOB); the striking contrast between analysis of this concept and of HE reinforces the sense of weakness in the conceptual foundations of HE indexes. Despite the substantial sophistication devoted to measuring MOB, little attention has been given to why one cares about the concept in the first place—a problem emphasized in Shorrocks' (1978b) investigation. MOB has been said to be valued for a variety of reasons; these must be distinguished because each implies different definitions and measures. The most relevant interpretation for present purposes,[7] offered by Atkinson (1981), simply would consider MOB to be a good thing in its own right. Basically, this view of MOB is the mirror image to recent implementations of HE. Change from the status quo is preferred (rather than disliked) for its own sake. It turns out that many past attempts to examine MOB more precisely have implicitly adopted this characterization: Measures simply capture changes from the status quo distribution, which are assumed to be desirable.

The most obvious, yet most startling point is simply that, under a variety of interpretations, HE and MOB are direct opposites. The simple example of a reform that gives everyone an equal probability of taking the position of any individual in the income distribution is a massive affront to HE and, at the same time, the maximum possible degree of MOB (according to some measures). This opposition can be seen most clearly by examining King's (1983) article entitled "An Index of Inequality: With Applications to Horizontal Equity and Social Mobility." In one section, he offers and explores a particular index for HE. In the next, he claims to overcome prior difficulties in developing a satisfactory index for MOB by constructing "a normative index along the lines pursued above [i.e., in developing an index for HE]. The only difference is that it is usual *in the context of social mobility* to *favor* changes in the ordering of the distribution." Thus, he simply adopts his HE index as his MOB index, just changing the direction of the effect.[8] If he had attempted to combine VE, HE, and MOB into his total equity index all at the same time, the HE and MOB terms would essentially collapse.

This connection is not as apparent as it might be because King discusses VE and HE in one section, and pairs VE and MOB in the next. Immediately thereafter, he uses his approach to consider optimal taxation and offers an empirical application of his indexes; in both instances he measures overall inequity by using his combined index of VE and HE, making no comment indicating why the just-derived MOB index has been left out of the computation. King's conclusion suggests that his proposed index allows "horizontal equity *or* social mobility to be taken into account," without noting the importance and exclusive nature of the "or" in avoiding normative contradiction.

The idea that there is some connection between HE and MOB has not gone unnoticed by others (Atkinson 1980, Plotnick 1982). But the notion that those writing about HE and those writing about MOB were writing the same things, just switching signs and reversing normative positions whenever switching terminology, seems to have remained quite far from sight. Yet this connection between MOB and HE *measures* should hardly be surprising if some of the simplest motivations for the two *concepts* arise, respectively, from the ad hoc assumption of social preferences for and against changes from the status quo distribution. This suggests that all who use one measure or the other when evaluating proposed reforms are implicitly advocating one of these preferences at the expense of the other, although this underlying value choice typically remains hidden.

2.4. Toward a Working Definition of Horizontal Equity

Having raised doubts about recent applications of HE, the remainder of this investigation examines possible justifications. Initially, however, it is necessary to offer an index with *prima facie* plausibility. To avoid the difficulties specified in subsections 2.1 and 2.2, a measure of violations of HE must in some way reflect the number of individuals affected, weighted by the degree of the effect (i.e., distance of movement). Consider

$$I_{HE} = \frac{1}{2} \sum_i \sum_j [(y_{ai} - y_{aj}) - (y_{pi} - y_{pj})]^2,$$

where y_{ai}, y_{aj}, y_{pi}, and y_{pj} refer to the incomes of individuals i and j before (ante) and after (post) a reform. This measure sums the (squared) change in distance separating all pairs of individuals.[9]

The following discussion can be simplified by analyzing the five ways a pair of individuals can be affected by a reform. They can:
1. Move further apart (if initially unequal).
2. Move closer together (still remaining unequal).
3. Move apart from an initially equal position.
4. Move together, ending at an equal position.
5. Begin apart, cross over, and end up apart.

Possibility 5 is simply the combination of others (4 and 3).[10] In addition, there seems to be no compelling reason to attach much significance to 3 or 4, as distinguished from 1 or 2, since the latter pair encompass the former except for an infinitesimal movement at either the beginning or the end.

This index thus can be seen to have two central properties. First, in order to avoid the problems of other indexes it was necessary that no particular significance be attached to starting or ending at precise equality or to the cross-over point itself. Second, attaching negative weight to movements in both directions is central to HE. Since unequal treatment of equals most clearly violates HE, moving apart (1 or 3) must be registered by any HE index. But if HE were limited to being an objection to moving individuals further apart in the income distribution, it would solely be an objection to increased income inequality, subsumed in conventional notions of VE. *Hence, the central defining characteristic of HE—and its central force in policy applications—is that it also condemns moving individuals closer together in the income distribution (2 or 4), directly contrary to VE.* Note how distant this core feature is from the original definition of equal treatment of equals that most investigators abandon after introductory remarks—a definition that concerns the preservation of equality rather than opposition to enhanced equality. The next section demonstrates how this aspect of HE, although incorporated in various indexes, has been ignored in past attempts to motivate the concept when assessing the effects of reform on the distribution of income.

3. Horizontal Equity and the Welfarist Approach

Feldstein (1976a) has stated that "equal taxation of equals is implied directly by utilitarianism and does not require a separate principle of horizontal equity" when all individuals are assumed to have the same preferences. (See also Atkinson and Stiglitz 1980, Stiglitz 1982.) In simple examples this is often true because whatever reasons motivate a particular treatment of one individual will require the same treatment of another individual who is equal in all relevant respects.[11] (See Westen 1982.) Requiring HE would be redundant. Yet, in many instances, some incidental unequal treatment will be inevitable. For example, although purely random taxes can be avoided, some randomness in enforcement or mistakes in administration are unavoidable, and often significant. In addition, arbitrary distinctions may be necessary for reasons of convenience (for example, not all fringe benefits that conceptually are income can feasibly be taxed), and individuals with equal incomes may have acted differently, so that they may be differentially affected by a given reform.[12] In such instances, giving weight to HE—understood here to refer to any disruption in the pre-reform distribution of income—is in conflict with the social welfare tradition.[13] The previous section indicated how such an implementation of HE departs from its original motivations. This section suggests that much of the intuitive force behind recent considerations of HE is already accounted for in the economist's traditional use of a social welfare function, which involves evaluating policies based on their effects on individuals' utility.

3.1. Horizontal Equity as an Implicit Appeal to Vertical Equity

Feldstein's (1976a) major example illustrates how the intuitive appeal of HE can be traced to traditional considerations of VE and risk. He considers a tax reform that imposes costs in terms of HE as follows: 1000 taxpayers gain $10 each, at a cost of $1000 to each of 9 taxpayers (a net gain of $1000, but the losses are concentrated). All taxpayers begin with equal incomes and have identical utility functions. He demonstrates that the unequal treatment offsets part of the benefit of the reform; the greater the rate at which the marginal utility of income declines and the lower the initial level of income, the less desirable is the reform. But this result is all too familiar. The reform increases aggregate income but causes inequality in the distribution. The utilitarian framework he employs, like many others, is sensitive to income inequality: The greater is the loss in social welfare due to the resulting inequality, the less desirable is the reform. The only difference is that we generally refer to this effect under the rubric of VE, not HE.[14]

Note that in this example the choice of the status quo—which is the centerpiece of most definitions of HE, including Feldstein's—is clearly irrelevant to the comparative evaluation of the two states. In particular, if one considered the unequal state as the status quo and imagined moving back to what was originally considered to be the initial state, Feldstein's approach would lead to the same evaluation of each state; in this case, the distributive effects of the reform would be seen as desirable. Yet movement back to the initial state equally offends HE using the index I_{HE} offered above, and similar indications would follow from virtually all other definitions and indexes if his example were modified even slightly.[15] This suggests that the persuasive force behind Feldstein's example is captured in the standard social welfare framework whereas his earlier definitions of HE are inconsistent both with that framework and with his example. HE would register a loss from implementing both changes consecutively, while his example (and the social welfare approach more generally) indicate no net effect.[16]

This illustration can be generalized as follows. First, consider two individuals who are moved further apart in the income distribution as a result of a reform. I_{HE} will register some loss, and the loss will vary directly with the significance of the movement. Thus, the greater the increase in inequality caused by the reform, the greater the loss in HE. But, just as was the case with Feldstein's example, we find that HE seems to be measuring just what we are accustomed to considering under the guise of VE. HE and VE have the same sort of measure (distance-related)[17] for the same sort of change (moving apart) and both deem it undesirable.

Next, consider two individuals who are moved closer together in the income distribution as a result of a reform. Just as in the preceding instance, our measure of HE will register some loss, and the loss will vary directly with the significance of the movement. Thus, the more equality is enhanced by the reform, the greater the loss in HE. We again find that HE seems to be measuring just what we are accustomed to considering under the guise of VE. HE and VE again have the same sort of measure (distance-related) for the same sort of change (moving together). But here, HE indicates that the equity impact of the change is negative whereas VE indicates a positive evaluation. But what is the justification for this implication of HE? Examples offered to illustrate violations of HE typically begin with the assumption that all individuals initially have equal incomes, as was the case in Feldstein's illustration as well as those offered by others (e.g., Brennan 1971, Zodrow 1981).[18] This starting point is hardly surprising since the basic definition of HE requires equal treatment *of equals*. The separation of changes into movements together and movements apart, however, suggests that this set of examples has largely missed the issue. By starting with all being equal, all movements are apart; hence, HE yields the same verdict that VE would in any event.[19] It is revealing that those exploring HE, in attempting to motivate their analysis, have not chosen examples involving increased equality, which section 2 has shown to be the relevant application if HE is to have independent significance.

3.2. Horizontal Equity as an Implicit Appeal to Risk Analysis

HE arguably could be reinterpreted as an expression of concern for avoiding the imposition of risk. For example, a random tax's arbitrary unequal treatment of equals is welfare reducing, even setting aside for the moment the earlier argument that VE provides a basis for this conclusion. The random tax and a certain tax on each group that raises the same revenues[20] produce the same expected income in the post-reform state, yet the random tax is associated with a lower expected utility precisely because of the risk that is imposed.

Unlike the purely random tax, Feldstein's (1976a) example of the reform producing benefits of $10 to most individuals but a loss of $1000 to a few is similar in its effects to many realistic reforms. Feldstein discovers, however, that he must specify the degree of risk aversion (and the level of ex ante income) in order to evaluate the proposed reform and various modifications thereof. Now one might question whether risk is really implicated here, because it was clear from the beginning who the gainers and losers would be. Yet if an earlier announcement had been made describing the general distributive impact of the reform, but not indicating who the gainers and losers would be, followed the next day by a revelation of the complete proposal and its incidence, our judgment as to the equities or impact on social welfare surely would be unchanged. Thus, most government reforms, which have the characteristic that they impose both benefits and losses, can be analogized, for example, to a change in climate that results in substantial benefits but imposes significant losses through changes in asset values. Whether imposed by the government, nature, or a casino, there is risk all the same. This connection between risk from uncertainty concerning future government policy and other sources of risk is explored in Kaplow (1986, 1987).

Consider further this connection between the imposition of risk and evaluation of the effect of reforms on the distribution of income. It is well known that the statistical measure of variance can be used to describe the probability distribution that characterizes an uncertain prospect or as a summary statistic to describe the distribution of some attribute of a population—e.g., income—after the results of some event (even one not embodying any uncertainty). The frequency interpretation of probability presents a familiar connection between ex ante uncertainty and resulting distributions. One can describe the relevant situations from either an ex ante or an ex post perspective without changing the underlying phenomenon—the former perspective is more in accord with risk analysis, the latter with VE.[21]

Previous discussions of HE contain a number of clues suggesting some connection between HE and risk, although the claim that there is a direct linkage has never, to my knowledge, been asserted. In addition to Feldstein's use of the Arrow-Pratt measure of relative risk aversion, he also sometimes talks of gambles and future risks. Rosen (1978) and Stiglitz (1982) use a random tax as their primary example. King (1983) notes that his HE index bears some resemblance to a risk premium. Hettich (1979) uses a variance measure to capture the loss in HE. Brennan's (1971) discussion of HE frequently refers to variance and related characteristics of probability distributions, and the arguments he uses to motivate his HE measure resemble those often used in motivating statistical measures of dispersion. Moreover, he derives the result that a government choosing among a variety of tax sources—each of which affronts HE to some degree—will always do best by using a combination of all of them, including those causing the greatest affront to HE. Brennan fails to note, however, that this is *precisely* the well known result of standard portfolio theory with regard to how diversification reduces risk. Despite such indications, none of these authors suggests that HE amounts to another way of talking about risk in a particular context.

Risk is a concept that economists (and others) have studied much more carefully than they have studied HE. Using the terminology associated with risk and uncertainty invokes certain intuitions, as well as particular measures, that aid in one's analysis. In contrast, HE is coming to be associated with conflicting indexes that fail to provide even a remotely accurate measure or judgment concerning risk, if that is really the basis for concern.

4. Horizontal Equity Outside the Social Welfare Framework

4.1. Normative Significance of the Status Quo

In order to support more recent applications of HE in the context of tax reform, it is necessary to accord direct normative significance to the status quo distribution of income, independent of the welfare consequences in the post-reform state. After all, HE indexes are measures of the degree to which reform modifies the pre-reform distribution of income. A major justificatory problem posed by any such formulation concerns why the status quo is to be intrinsically valued, thus supporting a preference against all changes in position, when the status quo was itself the product of countless changes throughout history. This cannot be viewed as a mere "definitional" problem, because the very thing to be defined is to be given direct normative significance if HE indexes are to be justified.[22]

The issue is well illustrated by the previous example that involved a reform (moving, say, from state A to state B), followed by a later reform that had the effect of restoring the initial situation. For the latter reform, the status quo is B, producing a double loss in HE from changing and then moving back again. A more extended example reinforces the point. Consider a parent raising two children. One child starts our story with 10, the other with 8. The parent periodically has some discretionary income that can be used to benefit the children—by purchasing books, sending them to summer camp, taking them to the dentist, and the like. As it turns out, the discretionary income usually becomes available 4 at a time, and most relevant purchases are lumpy, also costing 4 each. On the first occasion, the parent decides to spend the 4 on the child who started with 8, thinking that such treatment is more fair since that child is then less well off and the resulting distribution is more equal than if the opposite choice is made. Sometime later when 4 more is available, it is spent on the other child, for the same reasons. This pattern continues. I doubt anyone would describe the parent's decision rule as remotely inequitable. Yet the effect at each stage is a loss in HE by any reasonable measure.

The most obvious response if one hopes to defend HE measures is to describe this not as a number of separate actions but rather as a single action: the adoption of a decision rule for the period during which the children are cared for by the parent. This recharacterization essentially treats the situation (10,8) as the status quo throughout. But how is this definition to be justified? Which "reforms" should be combined? Why not all reforms, past and future? Note that any such combinations would require a wholly different application of HE indexes than has been conventional. Does it matter how much time passes between the periods? Not that much time passes between many reforms—the recent sequence of major tax reforms being but one example. Would we feel the same way if the status quo, instead of being (10,8), were (100,1)? Or if the status quo, regardless of the income levels, has arisen as a result of theft? Or if one of the children was extremely sick and needed medical care for five periods in a row? Should the notion of HE count as a reason against rectifying theft or caring for a sick child first? Moreover, even if all these problems were overcome, one still would have to determine which point in the past decade, century, or era corresponds to the place of (10,8) in the above example. Thus, one must determine why it is that some pre-existing (or never-existing) "status quo" is important and then analyze what relationship such a hypothetical state bears to the actually existing status quo.

Even if some of these questions seem to demand excessive precision, it must be emphasized that some sort of answer to each is required before HE, understood as a desire to maintain the status quo distribution of income, could be assessed in the context of a particular tax reform. In the literature, such assessments are never attempted. Moreover, there remains the question of the independent weight to be given to the status quo. Returning to the illustration, once the parent has evaluated the relative needs of the two children, their merits, relevant considerations of equality, and the like, one must then ask why and when (if ever) the parent should make a different decision than indicated by these factors on the ground that the otherwise desirable result incidentally changes the existing distribution of welfare between the two children. (Furthermore, recall that, as developed in section 2.4, if one is to decide differently on this account, one's decision should change regardless of whether this incidental effect is in the direction of further inequality or further equality. VE objects to inequality and favors equality whereas HE constitutes an objection to change itself.)

Another alternative to attaching direct significance to the status quo would involve attempting, in the manner of Nozick (1974), to portray the status quo as the result of an intrinsically justified *process*. Thus, the status quo can be defined as the distribution that results from this process. This gambit, however, is subject to essentially the same problems just described. There must be some prior "status quo" from which that process began, again raising the foundational problem. In dealing with the neverending sequence of changes that occur in any society, one would have to isolate all those that violated the just process and recompute what the world would have been like had those changes never occurred, modified by any desire to accord some respect to actions that arguably were justified given the imperfect circumstances in which they were made.[23]

Thus, the status quo as conventionally defined and as traditionally used in measuring HE—which consists of the income distribution moments before the pending reform, and shortly after countless previous reforms—would only by the most extreme of repeated historical coincidence be very relevant under this process approach. The appropriate comparison would much more closely resemble the comparison of the post-reform state with some externally specified distribution, or at least results that could be speculatively derived therefrom. Finally, even if the external distribution from this process perspective were specified, it is not clear how violations of HE would be measured. Arguably, all reforms would have to be prohibited (which apparently is Nozick's (1974) position)—an extreme approach criticized in note 2, and one in contradiction with prior attempts to develop indexes of HE. Moreover, in an imperfect world where such an absolute constraint had often been violated, it might be thought appropriate to adopt reforms that made the resulting distribution conform more closely to the ideal. But such an approach also has little to do with recent implementations of HE. The status quo is now devalued; reforms can increase HE. These problems are pursued further in the next subsection's examination of broader attempts to justify HE outside of the traditional social welfare framework.

4.2. Horizontal Equity and Distributions External to the Status Quo

The difficulties just described arose from our attempt to give intrinsic significance to the status quo itself. It may not be the status quo that we care about after all, but rather some other distribution that is capable of independent justification. (A pre-existing normatively significant status quo could be viewed simply as an instance of this more general class.) Some authors discussing HE in the context of tax reform in fact use as their reference point not the status quo, but some other distribution such as that existing if the ideal tax system were in place or if there were no taxes.[24] Departures from the status quo would no longer be deemed relevant, and some reforms could be seen as increasing HE.[25]

Yet any approach relying upon an external distribution is hard to reconcile with the traditional concept and measures of HE. The status quo generally would be irrelevant; social welfare—including all equity concerns—would be measured solely by reference to the final distribution. In addition, there would be no particular reason to expect the idea of equal treatment to have special significance. If the post-reform state is not ideal, there would be no *a priori* implication following from the fact that the shortcoming arose from unequal treatment of equals rather than, for example, equal treatment of unequals. Of course, it might well be an improvement if two "ideal world equals" that were formerly treated in a less than ideal manner, and unequally, were instead treated equally, by taking the average treatment that both received. But gains from moving individuals closer together are already encompassed in VE and, in many instances, by considerations of efficiency.[26]

There also is only a modest connection between more complex measures of HE that have been developed and an externally specified ideal. To be sure, an index of HE such as that suggested in subsection 2.4 (where the external distribution is substituted for the status quo distribution) would tend to be positively correlated with the degree to which a state fell short of the external ideal. But it would be more natural (and more accurate) to measure the degree to which one failed in achieving the ideal by reference to the objectives used in generating the external distribution. More fundamentally, even if an index of HE were useful as a proxy, such an index would hardly be indicating a value to be traded off *against* optimal achievement of the objectives that generated the external distribution. Rather, it indicates the degree to which these other stated goals *are being achieved*. Finally, to the extent one's reference distribution was derived in a second-best framework that balances a number of factors—as is often the case—it would be inappropriate to base a measure of inequity on deviations from that second-best distribution rather than from the unattainable first best.

All these considerations indicate that HE as embodied in recent indexes would be a totally derivative concept, not an independent normative consideration. To the extent HE departs from such a role, it is not only outside of the traditional social welfare framework, but inconsistent with more general notions of optimally achieving any set of stated objectives. In sum, the closer one gets to a plausible justification, the further one moves from recent implementations of HE. It thus seems appropriate to consider more carefully various concepts of equity that appear to merit attention and develop pragmatic measures tailored directly to those concepts.

5. Concluding Remarks

The familiar definition of HE is inconsistent with attempted applications, and more elaborate indexes often produce paradoxical results. In addition, the illustrations that have been offered to motivate recent implementations of HE involve precisely those instances where traditional concerns for risk and VE are sufficient to explain the intuition against the distributive effects that arise. Finally, it is doubtful that current approaches could be based upon attempts to attribute normative significance to the status quo or derived from other intrinsically valued distributions. In either case, the command for equal treatment was seen to be a *by-product* of the optimization process, not an independent factor to *trade off against* whatever normative principle is represented by the posited distribution. It thus appears that the desire to capture our intuitive sense of justice cannot be met by continued attempts to derive ever more complex measures of HE that are not grounded in the original motivation of the concept or some other principles that are identified and defended.

In the tax reform contexts in which HE

indexes are applied, pre-reform equals in the income distribution are often equal by happenstance or as a result of undesirable aspects of the status quo that the reform is designed to change. Post-reform inequality thus may be an appropriate result, there being relevant differences between individuals that justify unequal treatment. Much unequal treatment is, however, more incidental. Yet, so long as such inequality is not capricious and is justified—often by the excessive administrative cost or other adverse effects of attempting to remedy it—there is no obvious affront to the principles of justice originally offered to motivate the HE concept. After all, HE demands equal treatment only when there is no legitimate basis for inequality. To be sure, unequal treatment does raise concerns for overall economic inequality and may involve the imposition of risk (as when there is the prospect of reform that will produce "windfall" gains and losses). When that is the case, such effects should be identified and subject to the sort of analysis that has been developed to address these concerns, rather than being measured by an index not designed for this purpose.

From a practical perspective, it will often be useful to pay particular attention to the unequal treatment of equals, even though the measures offered by HE indexes are not of independent normative significance. First, to the extent that equal treatment of equals is often implied by the maximizaton of any quasi-concave objective function, unequal treatment may indicate the potential to improve upon the existing situation. For example, in much of the tax reform debate, discovering violations of HE entails identifying wedges that create inefficiency or making appropriate relative income determinations among individuals that are necessary to determine the degree of inequality for application of VE norms.

Second, violation of HE on a repeated basis might have adverse effects on incentives. And, independent of the effects on behavior, the simple imposition of risk (or increase in dispersion of the income distribution) is generally undesirable, so we should be attentive to unequal treatment to the extent it is connected to these effects. These and related issues are studied in the context of assessing transition policy in Kaplow (1986, 1987).

Third, Atkinson (1980) and Jenkins (1986) have noted that in attempting to measure the degree of equality (VE) resulting from a reform, one can be misled by examining the post-reform averages for groups of pre-reform equals to the extent equals are not treated equally.

Fourth, the status quo orientation of HE could be motivated by intuitions relating to endogenous preferences—for example, that utility is determined not only by the absolute level of income or wealth, but changes in that level.[27] The rationale might be that, over time, individuals and households make investments in tangible assets, human capital, and information that are most valuable at a certain level of well-being, making unanticipated adjustment costly. Alternatively, support may be found in various psychological interpretations of the sources of utility, particularly those—such as Veblen's (1899) original formulation or more recent interpretations such as Yitzhaki (1982)—that emphasize relative incomes within reference groups.[28] Empirical evidence concerning disparities in offer and asking prices that exceed what can be explained by wealth effects, such as that offered by Knetsch and Sinden (1984), as well as asymmetric treatment of gains and losses in situations involving uncertainty, as documented and modeled by Kahneman and Tversky (1979), similarly suggest modifications in the typical formulation of the utility function. Of course, even if different utility functions were deemed appropriate to employ in welfare analysis, the resulting formulation is still within the welfarist tradition. Moreover, the most direct implication of such modifications is that welfare analysis should not treat all individuals—particularly those at different income levels—as if they have the same utility functions, since the function itself would depend upon current income or wealth.[29] These implications, although arising from justifications for giving independent weight to the status quo distribution, are not aspects of HE as generally understood and implemented.

Fifth, as suggested by Atkinson (1980) and Plotnick (1984), political advisors would certainly care about HE. This is true, of course, since how people are treated is highly relevant to how they will react.[30] It is a bit surprising, however, that this justification for the concept would be offered without further explanation amidst what appear to have been intended as normative discussions.

Finally, quite apart from the effects of violating HE on individuals, imposing requirements of equal treatment as a constraint might limit actions by imperfect government institutions that do not in fact advance social welfare. For example, Stiglitz (1982) suggests on these grounds that permitting unequal treatment may make arbitrary discrimination favoring certain interest groups more likely. He is correct that this view implies that analysis of HE such as that "contained in Feldstein, Rosen and King may not be focusing on the critical issues" since his argument, like the others noted in this section, relates to determining the likely effects of government action, not to evaluating them. (This application is considered further in note 2.)

That violations of HE can have so many implications helps to explain the attention the concept has received. It must be emphasized, however, that these reasons have one thing in common: They are not reasons why HE in itself is valued in any normative sense. Rather, each are reasons why unequal treatment may provide information as to the actual motivations for or effects of a given reform, whether such effects are to be evaluated by a maximizer of social welfare (who cares about risk, incentives, and VE), a politician on the move, or anyone else using whatever criteria are justified in a particular context. Each rationale may warrant further analysis in some instances, but none supports implementations of HE of the sort now in use.

ENDNOTES

**A prior version appeared as NBER Working Paper No. 1697. Comments from Lucian Bebhuk, Martin Feldstein, John Parsons, Steven Shavell, Lawrence Summers, and the anonymous referees are gratefully acknowledged. Support was received from the John M. Olin Foundation through the Harvard Program in Law and Economics.

[1] The problems raised in the text would arise at whatever boundaries were to be drawn to separate the almost equal from the not sufficiently equal. As will be clear in section 2.2, these problems inhere in any measure that is not continuous in the degree of change caused by reform.

[2] Atkinson and Stiglitz (1980) suggest that imposing HE as a constraint that cannot be violated in reaching other objectives may in fact be the most appealing interpretation of HE. This lexicographic preference, in addition to being subject to the criticism developed in the text, has little appeal as applied to the context considered here. It seems implausible that the slightest inequality in treatment of status quo equals would be thought more important than even substantial gains in overall welfare levels (including to the individuals treated unequally) and significant improvements in equality or other objectives. Similarly, this lexicographic approach would accord no weight to inequitable treatment of whatever magnitude to individuals that were not precise equals in the status quo. Finally, typical reform proposals inevitably involve at least *some* violation of HE—and, admitting various differences among individuals (see Feldstein 1976a) or unavoidable administrative error, this would be true of all reforms. Similarly, it is necessary to rely on enforcement strategies that have random aspects in virtually all policy contexts. HE used as a constraint thus virtually forbids reform—and the enforcement of most existing laws and policies.

Interpreting HE as a side constraint may have some force in terms of prohibiting arbitrary discrimination, for example among individuals of different race. See Musgrave (1976). Justification for such an approach would probably rest on assumptions concerning the fallibility of human institutions, since nondiscrimination would typically be implied by social welfare maximization in any event. The criticism that the side constraint imposes an unjustifiable lexicographic ordering and that the constraint is generally violated by making virtually any reform would be less powerful since the constraint would typically be satisfied in such cases at no—or little—cost in social welfare. It is the application of the side constraint approach to any change in income or wealth that results directly or indirectly from any change in government policy that leads to crippling implications.

Shleifer and Waldmann (1985) have defended HE as a constraint on the ground that it might assist in addressing the time consistency problems of the sort developed by Kydland and Prescott (1977). They examine the well-known problem that, ex post, it is optimal to adopt a complete capital levy, which, ex ante, will destroy investment incentives. Since in their basic model HE prohibits any reform, assuming adherence to HE does imply that a capital levy will not be employed ex post. (For an alternative approach to this problem, see Kotlikoff, Persson, and Svensson (1986).) Despite their contrary claim, however, this approach is little different than simply positing specific abilities to commit. HE is broader, as they argue, but precisely because it rules out all desirable ex post actions

³For example, Schmalensee (1984) admits that his measure of horizontal inequity is zero if no two individuals are exactly alike, yet attributes significance to the magnitude of inequality in treatment among those who are identical, and insists that this magnitude is of a different normative order than similar differences arising between individuals who initially are different, regardless of how small that initial difference might be.

⁴Part of this problem has been noted by Plotnick (1982) and Rosen (1978). Yet Rosen's distance-sensitive measure has some bizarre properties—for example, a complete reversal in the income distribution registers no loss in HE. Only the absolute value of the distances, measured before and after the reform, not the total change in distance, is used; his approach sharply differs from a direct distance measure when there are crossovers.

⁵Essentially, negative weight is attached only to any "overshooting," i.e., movements apart after the reform has reached the point of equality in ex post income. This might be viewed as a sort of VE measure since, as will be discussed in subsection 3.1, HE and VE give the same indications when individuals are moved further apart in the distribution. This does not fully hold, however, since movement apart absent a cross-over is ignored by King's index, and the index also places no beneficial weight on movements together up to the cross-over point.

⁶For example, Feldstein (1976a) simply asserts that "the introduction of a tax should not alter the *ordering* of individuals by utility level" (emphasis added) and later criticizes one possible measure of order reversals because it "would be distorted . . . if the utilities were altered by a nonlinear function" that preserved ranking perfectly, not noticing the somewhat bizarre judgments implicit in such criticism. Feldstein's implicit defense of a discontinuous index is most surprising in light of his criticism of Rawls' (1971) difference principle on the basis of its discontinuity.

Plotnick explicitly advocates the need for distance measures (1982, page 383 and note 17, page 388; 1984, page 5). But elsewhere, Plotnick (1984, note 7) states that: "Useful measures will *not* be concerned between initial and actual final levels of well-being, nor between initial and final rank-preserving levels. These comparisons may also be of interest, but they are not appropriate for assessing horizontal inequity." (See also 1984, page 11.) He never resolves this tension. Four of the five indexes Plotnick (1984) examines exhibit precisely the character of King's index. The fifth, based on the Spearman rank correlation coefficient, takes no account of distance, which he agrees makes it less satisfactory.

⁷There exist others as well. MOB may be desired because, as stated by Atkinson (1981), "it is instrumental in leading to greater efficiency." From this perspective, MOB is seen primarily as a symptom of a freely functioning economy or as a policy instrument that can be directly manipulated (increased) in order to improve the efficiency of the economy, either interpretation being wholly consistent with the traditional social welfare framework and thus of no further interest here. This should be contrasted with a decision to place intrinsic value on greater equality of opportunity. Of course, observed MOB would only be a symptom of such equality, as MOB can also be generated, for example, by arbitrary fiat or random events, neither of which would indicate that opportunities are more equal in the relevant sense. This interpretation of MOB, therefore, calls more for a direct evaluation of the processes by which individuals' positions are endogenously determined before and after a reform, rather than measurement of the actual change in welfare positions directly resulting from a reform. In particular, equal opportunity in this sense can be understood as a preference for equality in ex ante positions, where ex ante refers not to before a particular reform, but to before the processes permitted as a result of any reforms have produced particular outcomes for different individuals. MOB also can be interpreted as a dynamic analog of VE, the idea being that the greater the movement within the income distribution over an individual's lifetime, the more likely highs and lows average out in some manner. See Shorrocks (1978a).

⁸Compare conditions 1–3 (1983, pages 105–06) with conditions 1'–3' (page 109); equation 23 with equation 30; and Theorem 2 with Theorem 3.

⁹It may be noted that the expression for I_{HE} includes the terms for where $i = j$, but since those terms equal zero, they can be ignored. Simple manipulation shows that

$$I_{HE} = \sum_i (\Delta y_i)^2 - (\Delta y)^2,$$

where Δy_i is the change in income of individual i caused by the reform and Δy is the change in total income caused by the reform. One could weight the index by the inverse of the population to compare relative inequality among societies of differing sizes. With this final modification, this function is in the class axiomatized by Cowell (1985, expression 59). See also Russell (1985).

¹⁰This is not to say that any particular measure will be separable in that each of the two movements can be weighed without regard to the magnitude of the other. Rather, my claim is that the *character* of the measure—i.e., whether a movement is good or bad and why—in instance 5 can be understood from how one evaluates instances 3 and 4.

¹¹Exceptions to this general proposition due to diversities in tastes (see Feldstein 1976a, Musgrave 1976), offsetting the incentive to substitute labor for leisure (see Weiss 1976), or nonconvexities in the feasible set (see Stiglitz 1982) are not relevant for present purposes.

¹²See also note 11. With respect to the latter instances, which account for a large portion of the unequal treatment that is the focus of attention when measuring the HE brought about by tax reform, one might simply say that the individuals are not equal in all relevant respects and thus the concept of HE, as traditionally understood, is inapplicable. So long as the inequality in treatment is rationally based on the differences in circumstances, there is no inequity. Thus, it becomes clear that many of the problems discussed in the text are not in the original motivation for HE, but rather in recent attempts to equate changes in the pre-reform income distribution with inequity,

regardless of the cause of the distributive effects.

In some instances, resulting unequal treatment could be rectified by a complex compensation or grandfathering scheme. For present purposes, this is assumed to be prohibitively costly. More generally, the issue arises so long as perfect compensation involves some cost, for then it would be necessary to consider the magnitude of the HE violation and the weight to be attributed to HE in order to determine whether the compensation was justified.

[13]Technically, HE can be seen as violating the social welfare tradition in two ways. First, it introduces nonwelfare information (see Sen 1977)—in this case positions in the distribution of income in a state (the status quo) other than the one being evaluated. In social choice theory discussions, this would be termed a violation of the anonymity condition. Second, as discussed in note 26, increases in an individual's welfare, ceteris paribus, can reduce social welfare. Analysis in section 4 suggests, moreover, that existing conceptions of HE also seem inconsistent with the notion of optimization more generally.

[14]This example is interpreted further in section 3.2 as illustrating the imposition of risk. It will then be argued that both of these interpretations are interchangeable since both arise from the assumed concavity of the utility function. Feldstein (1976a) claims that "[t]he concavity of the utility functions *together with the assumption* that everyone should be treated as if they had the same utility function and the same initial income imply that the optimal tax change may be smaller than if horizontal equity is ignored." The important point here is that concavity alone is what drives his conclusion—i.e., the concept of HE is superfluous. To prove that it is a necessary condition, simply consider (1) where utility functions are linear, in which case his social welfare measure simply reflects the net gain of $1000, independent of the distribution, and (2) where utility functions are convex, in which case the unequal treatment actually would improve welfare under his measure. Concavity will often be sufficient as well, for even if individuals had different initial incomes or different utility functions, the unequal incidence would tend to lower social welfare. The exception would be where the losers happened to be those with the lowest marginal utility of income and the gainers those with the highest—which typically would be a redistribution from the rich to the poor. But that is precisely what is captured by VE. The assumption that all should be treated as if they have the same utility function is usually justified either as an approximation for an unmeasurable reality or as dictated by egalitarian principles, which are directly linked to economists' references to VE. (The "as if same initial income" assumption is discussed further in the text that follows.)

Yet, in addition to the fact that this equal income assumption does not really drive the analysis, the assumption is inappropriate, particularly in the context of tax policy. Feldstein's argument that, for example, courts often ignore unequal income seems beside the point for tax policy, which is explicitly concerned with the allocation of tax burden according to income level, is not wholly true; e.g., damage awards do reflect the income level of the victim; and, where true, is typically capable of independent justification (ignoring the income level of the injurer is often supported by administrative concerns) or simply may be wrong.

[15]Consider, for example, moving back to Feldstein's initial situation, but overshooting by 1 cent for each person. There would be a complete order reversal between the two groups.

[16]Consider the well known example in which there exist two groups of individuals with different abilities. The utilitarian solution may well entail a reversal in ranking from the pre-tax status quo. (See Atkinson and Stiglitz 1980, Mirlees 1971, King 1983.) Achieving VE in this example clearly affronts HE. Plotnick (1984) advances the general argument that "[u]nless the socially optimal distribution is one of full equality, those earning more initial well-being should surely have greater final well-being than those earning less." Yet one might ask why the status quo distribution should be given normative weight. Since it is assumed in the example that individuals did not determine their own abilities, it seems no more unfair for the less able to be better off due to accident of birth than for the more able to be better off due to the same accident. The problem of justifying normative weight being attributed to the status quo is pursued further in subsection 4.1.

[17]Both HE and VE could be interpreted as being concerned not with absolute changes, but relative changes, measured for example by proportions relative to the mean. Similar analysis would apply.

[18]A modification with very similar effects is when the population is divided into large groups, all perfectly equal within each, as is the case in White and White (1965).

[19]At most, HE can be said to give added weight to this preference, but when there are no movements together being considered and no explicit formula is offered to combine the HE judgments with other factors, the difference in weighting has no operational significance.

[20]A strictly random tax might not, but one can similarly imagine a tax that is random as to each individual but designed to raise a specified amount of revenue overall. Incentive effects are ignored here.

[21]That the same phenomena can be interpreted equally well in terms of risk or VE should hardly be surprising. At least in the utilitarian framework, concerns for VE traditionally have been justified by reference to the decreasing marginal utility of income, which is precisely the source of risk aversion. In fact, Harsanyi (1953, 1977) has modeled the VE issue by using the methods of decisionmaking under uncertainty, taking as the starting point a hypothetical situation in which individuals do not know which person they will be in any possible social state. This framework suggests that each would choose states by maximizing expected utility, implying unanimous agreement upon the utilitarian criterion. States with greater inequality (lower in VE) are opposed because of the risk to each that they would be one of the individuals at the low end of the income distribution. In addition, Harsanyi (1955, 1977) has shown that acceptance of the axioms for rational choice under uncertainty for both social and individual preferences also leads to the utilitarian criterion.

[22]Plotnick (1981) advocates using the status quo—despite philosophical objections—"on pragmatic grounds [since] it may not be too bad. If, despite the contrary arguments that can be offered, most persons

tacitly accept the fairness of the preredistributive rankings when making judgments on redistributive equity, a useful measure of [horizontal] inequity must also accept this ranking." But redistributive judgments usually reject the preredistributive situation— almost by definition. In addition, by this analysis, violations of HE from past reforms are ignored. Thus, if a reform were enacted over Plotnick's objections on HE grounds, even that post-reform distribution would be given normative significance in evaluating the next reform—including the repeal of the reform just (inappropriately) enacted. Finally, whatever norms provide the *basis* for any such tacit acceptance of the fairness of the status quo should provide the foundation for equity measures, as discussed later in this section.

Plotnick (1984) discusses how different initial positions should be selected for analyzing various policies. He concedes "that whatever the initial measure selected by the analyst, he or she is implicitly assuming the initial ranking to be fair." The problem, however, is that in each of his examples a different initial position is selected, and thus the set of implicit fairness assumptions are directly contradictory. He does not explain how inconsistent normative assumptions can simultaneously be maintained in analyzing a single normative concept.

[23] Nozick (1974) is often referenced for a process defense of the status quo. Yet his process theory is applicable only if original entitlements and all subsequent transfers have been in accord with his justifications. If not, he supports rectification to account for past injustice, and willingly notes that such reparations could justify substantial government action that disturbs the status quo distribution (1974, pages 152–53, 230–31). The argument in the text suggests that most process approaches one can envision would be subject to precisely these limitations in attempting to justify giving weight directly to the status quo distribution.

[24] For examples of the latter, see Brown (1983), King (1983), Plotnick (1982). The latter approach raises the distinction sometimes made in the HE literature, traced to Feldstein (1976a), between tax *design* and tax *reform*. Reform, which has been referred to throughout, defines the status quo as that which exists prior to the change. Subject to the numerous problems noted in the text, this admits of some definition, even if lacking in normative significance. By contrast, design takes as the reference point not the status quo itself, but a hypothetical world in which no tax exists. Choosing the perspective of design versus reform is not a matter that should be taken lightly since the two definitions can lead to contradictory results—i.e., design A can have better HE than design B, yet reforming from B to A can only diminish HE by the reform-oriented definition. Similarly, one would not simultaneously advocate that, in the case of a "reform," the status quo (in particular, characterized by the existing tax system) has great normative significance whereas in the case of greater change—tax (re)design—the normative significance of the status quo would disappear altogether (to be replaced by some other reference point). Any of the choices suggested by the tax *design* way of thinking are purely arbitrary in normative terms, except to the extent they refer to some independently justified ideal and the corresponding distribution thereby implied, in which case the discussion in the text would apply.

[25] As he operates in this context, it is not clear why Hettich (1979) claims that his index is a measure of HE and not VE. His external reference distribution is chosen based on preferences concerning progressivity and his index measures departures from that distribution. (See also Hettich 1983.) His argument that partial expansions of a less-than-comprehensive tax base may rationally be rejected based on pursuit of the goals of HE and VE can surely be supported based on VE considerations alone. (His argument is a simple application of the theory of second best.) In fact, his index registers a substantial loss in HE when equals are treated perfectly equally, but unequals are taxed in proportions that deviate from the optimal distribution of the tax burden, which clearly is a VE concern. If his measure were truly to capture VE, however, it would measure VE directly rather than measuring departures from a distribution derived in part based on VE considerations. Hettich's (1979, 1983) conclusion that VE and HE cannot be separated in making policy judgments is not a "result," but rather an interpretation of his arbitrarily selected aggregate equity index that was not derived from any clear statement of the basis for or meaning of VE and HE concerns.

[26] It is not clear why upward deviations are deemed undesirable in the HE context. With VE, this is the case only to the extent that others at lower points in the income distribution are made worse off. In contrast, the HE concept would attach independent *negative* weight to gains regardless of their adverse effects on others. Hettich (1983) is typical: "With regard to [horizontal] equity, no cancellation occurs, *of course*. According to the principle of equal treatment of equals, paying too little [tax] is as undesirable as paying too much." No further motivation or justification for this normative approach is offered.

[27] As a simple, though extreme illustration, it can be demonstrated that, for a reform that does not change total income, but only the distribution, the index I_{HE} presented in subsection 2.4 corresponds to the traditional utilitarian social welfare function in the case where individual utility is a quadratic function of the *change* in income—i.e., $U = \alpha + \beta\Delta y - \gamma\Delta y^2$.

[28] Within each reference group, the relevant concept is VE—i.e., unequal treatment of equals involves increasing the degree of inequality in the group, and increasing equality within the reference group is considered to be desirable, contrary to the dictates of HE.

[29] Implementing such an approach in practice would be even more complex than suggested by the discussion in the text. For such concerns, it would surely matter whether the effects of a reform were permanent, what the trend of income was over time, and if additional prospects affecting the same individuals were on the horizon.

[30] Since the concept of equal treatment of equals has so much surface appeal, the unequal treatment in itself may have intrinsic political significance even if it lacks intrinsic normative significance. People are often quite attached to the status quo, regardless of the degree of justice entailed in producing it. Independently, the cry of unequal treatment derives much rhetorical power from its force in unrelated contexts, such as those involving racial discrimination.

REFERENCES

Atkinson, A. B., 1980, "Horizontal Equity and the Distribution of the Tax Burden," in: H. Aaron and M. J. Boskin, eds., *The Economics of Taxation* (Brookings Institution, Washington, D.C.), 3–18.

Atkinson, A. B., 1981, "The Measurement of Economic Mobility," in: A. B. Atkinson, *Social Justice and Public Policy* (MIT Press, Cambridge), 61–75.

Atkinson, A. B. and J. E. Stiglitz, 1980, *Lectures on Public Economics* (McGraw-Hill, New York).

Brennan, G., 1971, "Horizontal Equity: An Extension of an Extension," *Public Finance* 26, 437–456.

Brown, E., 1983, "Comment: Bequests and Horizontal Equity Under a Consumption Tax," *National Tax Journal* 36, 511–513.

Cowell, F. A., 1985, "Measures of Distributional Change: An Axiomatic Approach," *Review of Economic Studies* 52, 135–151.

Feldstein, M., 1976a, "On the Theory of Tax Reform," *Journal of Public Economics* 6, 77–104.

Feldstein, M., 1976b, "Compensation in Tax Reform," *National Tax Journal* 29, 123–130.

Harsanyi, J. C., 1953, "Cardinal Utility in Welfare Economics and in the Theory of Risk-Taking," *Journal of Political Economy* 61, 434–435.

Harsanyi, J. C., 1955, "Cardinal Welfare, Individualistic Ethics, and Interpersonal Comparisons of Utility," *Journal of Political Economy* 63, 309–321.

Harsanyi, J. C., 1977, *Rational Behavior and Bargaining Equilibrium in Games and Social Situations* (Cambridge University Press, Cambridge).

Hettich, W., 1979, "A Theory of Partial Tax Reform," *Canadian Journal of Economics* 12, 692–712.

Hettich, W., 1983, "Reforms of the Tax Base and Horizontal Equity," *National Tax Journal* 36, 417–427.

Jenkins, S., 1986, "Reranking and the Analysis of Income Redistribution," University of Bath Papers in Political Economy 86/01.

Kahneman, D. and A. Tversky, 1979, "Prospect Theory: An Analysis of Decision Under Risk," *Econometrica* 47, 263–291.

Kaplow, L., 1986, "An Economic Analysis of Legal Transitions," *Harvard Law Review* 99, 509–617.

Kaplow, L., 1987, Optimal Transition Policy: Replacing Horizontal Equity with an Ex Ante Incentives Perspective (dissertation, Harvard University).

King, M. A., 1983, "An Index of Inequality: With Applications to Horizontal Equity and Social Mobility," *Econometrica* 51, 99–115.

Knetsch, J. L. and J. A. Sinden, 1984, "Willingness to Pay and Compensation Demanded: Experimental Evidence of an Unexpected Disparity in Measures of Value," *Quarterly Journal of Economics* 99, 507–521.

Kotlikoff, L. J., T. Persson, and L. E. O. Svensson, 1986, "Social Contracts as Assets: A Possible Solution to the Time Consistency Problem," *American Economic Review* 78, 662–677.

Kydland, F. E. and E. C. Prescott, 1977, "Rules Rather than Discretion: The Inconsistency of Optimal Plans," *Journal of Political Economy* 85, 473–491.

Mirlees, J., 1971, "An Exploration in the Theory of Optimal Income Taxation," *Review of Economic Studies* 38, 179–208.

Mueller, D. C., 1979, *Public Choice* (Cambridge University Press, Cambridge).

Musgrave, R. A., 1959, *The Theory of Public Finance* (McGraw-Hill, New York).

Musgrave, R. A., 1976, "Optimal Taxation, Equitable Taxation and Second-Best Taxation," *Journal of Public Economics* 6, 3–16.

Nozick, R., 1974, *Anarchy, State and Utopia* (Basic Books, New York).

Plotnick, R., 1981, "A Measure of Horizontal Inequity," *Review of Economics and Statistics* 63, 283–288.

Plotnick, R., 1982, "The Concept and Measurement of Horizontal Equity," *Journal of Public Economics* 17, 373–391.

Plotnick, R., 1984, "A Comparison of Measures of Horizontal Inequity Using Alternative Measures of Well-Being," Institute for Research on Poverty Working Paper 752–84.

Rawls, J., 1971, *A Theory of Justice* (Harvard University Press, Cambridge).

Rosen, H. S., 1978, "An Approach to the Study of Income, Utility, and Horizontal Equity," *Quarterly Journal of Economics* 92, 307–322.

Russell, R. R., 1985, "A Note on Decomposable Inequality Measures," *Review of Economic Studies* 52, 347–352.

Schmalensee, R., 1984, "Imperfect Information and the Equitability of Competitive Prices," *Quarterly Journal of Economics* 99, 441–460.

Sen, A., 1977, "On Weights and Measures: Informational Constraints in Social Welfare Analysis," *Econometrica* 45, 1539–1572.

Shleifer, A. and R. Waldmann, 1985, "Horizontal Equity as a Socially Valuable Taboo," mimeo.

Shorrocks, A. F., 1978a, "Income Inequality and Income Mobility," *Journal of Economic Theory* 19, 376–393.

Shorrocks, A. F., 1978b, "The Measurement of Mobility," *Econometrica* 46, 1013–1024.

Shoup, C. S., 1969, *Public Finance* (Aldine Publishing Company, Chicago).

Simons, H. C., 1938, *Personal Income Taxation: The Definition of Income as a Problem of Fiscal Policy* (University of Chicago Press, Chicago).

Stiglitz, J., 1982, "Utilitarianism and Horizontal Equity: The Case for Random Taxation," *Journal of Public Economics* 18, 1–33.

Veblen, T., 1899, *The Theory of the Leisure Class* (Macmillan, New York).

Weiss, L., 1976, "The Desirability of Cheating Incentives and Randomness in the Optimal Income Tax," *Journal of Political Economy* 84, 1343–1352.

Westen, P., 1982, "The Empty Idea of Equality," *Harvard Law Review* 95, 537–596.

White, M. and A. White, 1965, "Horizontal Inequality in the Federal Income Tax Treatment of Homeowners and Tenants," *National Tax Journal* 18, 225–239.

Yitzhaki, S., 1982, "Relative Deprivation and Economic Welfare," *European Economic Review* 17, 99–113.

Zodrow, G., 1981, "Implementing Tax Reform," *National Tax Journal* 34, 401–418.

B
Taxes and Income Distribution

Journal of Public Economics 4 (1975) 125-161. © North-Holland Publishing Company

GENERAL EQUILIBRIUM INCIDENCE ANALYSIS
The Harberger model after ten years

Charles E. McLURE, Jr.*

Rice University, Houston, Texas 77001, U.S.A.

Received January 1974, revised version received September 1974

This survey paper summarizes and appraises the Harberger model of tax incidence and its extensions, modifications, and applications. It considers the shortcomings of Marshallian partial equilibrium incidence analysis and early efforts to overcome them, exposits a late vintage version of the Harberger model, explains how this relatively simple general equilibrium model overcomes many of the shortcomings of earlier analysis, and describes several existing and potential modifications and applications and several inherent shortcomings of the model. It concludes that Harberger performed an invaluable service in providing public finance economists with an easily manageable general equilibrium incidence model.

1. Introduction

Just over ten years ago, Arnold C. Harberger (1962) introduced to the field of public finance the two-sector general equilibrium model of tax incidence that, with various modifications and extensions, has since become the standard tool of incidence analysis in situations requiring a general equilibrium framework. In so doing, he provided the theoretical breakthrough from partial to general equilibrium analysis of tax incidence that numerous public finance economists had long recognized as being essential and for which many had been searching. It is the purpose of the present paper to take a retrospective view of the

---

*The author is professor of economics at Rice University. A preliminary version of this paper was written while the author was visiting the University of Wyoming during the summer of 1972 for presentation at the annual meetings of the Western Economic Association in Santa Clara, California, August 24-25, 1972. Though the passage of time has rendered the original title somewhat inaccurate, there seems to be no compelling reason to replace 'ten' with 'eleven' or 'twelve'. An effort has, however, been made to include references to the literature of one more year in the final revision of the paper. The present version has benefitted significantly from comments on earlier drafts by Greg Ballentine, Richard Bird, Michael Boskin, John Due, Robert Floyd, Arnold Harberger, Robert Klein, Mel Krauss, Joseph Pechman, David Roberts, Maria Schmundt, Carl Shoup, Wayne Thirsk, Wayne Vroman, and two referees for this journal. A final important debt is to George Break, who originally urged the writing of the paper. Of course, none of the persons named above is responsible for the opinions stated here.

Harberger model after ten years in order to summarize it and its extensions, modifications, and applications and assess its importance.[1]

Several distinct topics are discussed. Section 2 describes briefly early attempts to improve both the methodology and the tools of incidence analysis and then some of the very real problems encountered in the application of traditional Marshallian partial equilibrium incidence analysis in certain situations. Section 3 describes a late vintage version of the Harberger model, and section 4 the ways in which the model handles the problems described in section 2. In this section many of the various modifications and extensions of the original Harberger model are discussed explicitly. Sections 5–7, respectively, describe briefly several applications and other extensions of the Harberger model, several directions in which the Harberger model needs yet to be extended, and several inherent shortcomings of the model. The final section offers as concluding remarks a brief assessment of the importance of the Harberger model.

Throughout this paper, the emphasis is primarily upon methodology, though some results are reported. Thus the primary focus is upon the ways in which the basic theoretical model presented by Harberger in 1962 has been modified, extended, and applied to particular problems, rather than upon the analytical results and policy implications of those modifications, extensions, and applications. Both for this reason and because this review does not extend beyond the literature based on the Harberger model (and its precursors), the present paper is not intended to be a complete review of the literature on either tax incidence or two-sector general equilibrium models.[2]

---

[1]Some readers will undoubtedly question reference to 'the Harberger model' since (as Harberger has readily acknowledged) the general equilibrium model given an explicit formulation by Harberger in his 1962 article had been used in a somewhat different form for years before 1962, especially in the theory of international trade [see especially the classic Stolper–Samuelson article (1941) and the literature on factor–price equalization], and since 1962 has been extended by other economists, again particularly those working on the theory of international trade. The answer sheds some light upon the development of economic thought and the cross-fertilization of disciplines. First, as is discussed further below, it was Harberger who provided public finance with the easily understood general equilibrium incidence model it had long needed. That Harberger did not invent general equilibrium analysis or that parallel developments were proceeding apace in the field of international trade made this development no less important for the field of public finance. The relevance of this comment can perhaps best be appreciated by noting that the author has been asked why this model is attributed to Harberger primarily by relatively young economists whose training has included substantial doses of international trade theory, and never by an established economist with a standard public finance background dating from before 1962. Second, it seems reasonable to call this 'the Harberger model' if only because Harberger first wrote a system of equations describing changes in the standard economy of neoclassical economics in a particular way.

[2]Another assessment of the Harberger approach to incidence analysis is contained in Break (forthcoming). For a recent review of the literature on the theory of tax incidence, see Mieszkowski (1969). Writings on two sector general equilibrium models are, of course, too voluminous to be summarized in a survey of this kind. Two useful references are, however, Johnson (1971), and Jones (1965).

2. Partial equilibrium analysis

Tax incidence analysis before 1962 was partial equilibrium analysis, though economists such as Brown, Rolph, Musgrave, and Wells had attempted to place incidence analysis in a general equilibrium context. Brown (1939) and Rolph (1954), for example, emphasized (and perhaps overemphasized) the effects taxes have upon factor incomes, as well as upon product prices. Musgrave (1953a,b and 1959) extended this reasoning, distinguishing what he called changes in income on the side of sources of income, which result from tax-induced movements in relative factor rewards, from changes on the side of uses of income, which result from shifts in relative product prices. Wells (1955) presented a provocative diagrammatic analysis of tax incidence in a general equilibrium context. His clear understanding of the advantages of general equilibrium analysis and the determinants of incidence in a general equilibrium setting are indicated by the following quotation (1955, p. 345):

'The main conclusions of this paper are: (a) that an excise tax exerts both a burden – an aspect of excise taxes long recognized and much discussed in the literature – and a benefit, an aspect of excise taxes that has been little discussed in the literature; and (b) that these burdens and benefits fall on individuals as buyers and sellers of goods and services, and that the degree to which the burdens and benefits of an excise tax spread out from one individual or group of individuals to another individual or group of individuals will depend upon the preference functions of all individuals, the asset structure of all individuals, the tax and expenditure policy of the taxing agency, and the nature of the transformation functions of the commodities produced.'

Despite the important insights and some qualitatively correct answers provided by these and other pioneers in general equilibrium incidence analysis, there was no theoretical model of sufficient detail that could be used by most economists to obtain precise answers – even qualitatively – to questions of tax incidence in a general equilibrium setting.[3] In his treatise, Musgrave (1959, p. 347) described the situation as follows:

'These partial adjustments are strategic elements in the overall change, but nothing more. They have repercussions upon the market setting within which any adjusting unit operates, thus giving rise to a chain of adjustments until a new equilibrium is reached. The final result of the adjustment process is the product of the interaction of these individual moves.... It is necessary, therefore, that we push beyond the partial equilibrium view and consider the

---

[3]The analyses of Brown and Wells, while highly suggestive, lacked the precision of a fully specified mathematical model. On the other hand, the sophisticated mathematical models of Meade (1955) and Shepard (1944) lacked the simplicity necessary to make them readily available to all public finance specialists. One of the chief advantages of the Harberger model is its combination of precision with relative simplicity. Among the most advanced thinking on the subject of tax incidence was that by the Italians; see de Viti de Marco (1936) and the summary by Buchanan (1960).

general equilibrium adjustment process as a whole. This is a difficult task. One may readily understand the general interdependence of the pricing system as a concept or as a formal statement within the framework of the Walrasian equilibrium system. But it is quite another matter to formulate the problem so as to obtain specific results. ... A workable system of this sort remains to be devised before it can be applied to the determination of incidence.'

Thus by 1962, except for the methodological insights and qualitative conclusions mentioned above and the extensions of partial equilibrium analysis to cases of imperfect competition following the theoretical breakthroughs of the 1930s by Chamberlin and Robinson, the theory of tax incidence had not advanced greatly beyond what is found in Marshalls' *Principles of economics*.[4] This standard analysis, while extremely useful and illuminating under the proper circumstances, is simply not adequate for some purposes and is adequate for others only if handled with extreme care. The rest of this section is devoted to a discussion of these inadequacies.[5] Primary attention is, of course, devoted to those deficiencies that can be remedied by the Harberger analysis. Throughout this and the next section, all references are to the case of perfect competition in all markets, except where explicitly noted, since that is the context in which the Harberger model has most commonly been used. Similarly, almost all references are to a world of fixed total supplies of every factor, since that is the world of the Harberger model in its usual form.

2.1. Behind the supply curve

Perhaps the most pervasive fault of traditional partial equilibrium analysis is the difficulty of taking into account the interdependence among markets and of what occurs in product and factor markets simultaneously when a tax is imposed. This is most easily seen by examining a traditional diagram of supply and demand analysis of an excise tax. The shape of the demand curve – which is a description of consumer behavior – is determined directly from the preferences of the consumers in the market and poses no great problem. (But the demand curve may be affected by redistributions of income; see the discussion of expenditure effects below.) The problem, rather, is that in partial equilibrium analysis we cannot ordinarily 'go behind' the supply curve for the taxed product to the underlying causes of its shape.[6] Unlike the demand curve, the supply curve is not merely

---

[4]For a summary of the literature on tax incidence at the end of the 1960s, including Musgrave's own important contributions, see Musgrave (1959, chs. 10, 13, 15, 16).

[5]See Shoup (1969, pp. 7–19) for a discussion of these and other problems of general equilibrium incidence analysis.

[6]Stated differently, the question involves the shape of the production-possibility frontier or transformation curve. Seen from the factor market end, the problem is that we must know the determinants of the derived demand for factors. Going behind the product supply curve involves the same considerations as going behind the factor demand curve. But since incidence

behavioral. Rather, it describes the supply response of one industry to changes in relative product prices, taking into account interactions in markets for other products and for factors. The supply curve might slope upwards to the right for any number of reasons, including (a) decreasing returns to scale in the production of the taxed good, (b) fixity of supply of one factor to the taxed industry and imperfect factor substitution in production, and (c) unequal factor proportions in the two industries, even if both factors are mobile. Which of these (or others) causes the positive slope is not important in the determination of the effects of the tax on relative product prices.[7] But the standard partial equilibrium analysis does not ordinarily spell out how the tax affects the real incomes of the suppliers of factor services, because it does not go behind the supply curve.[8] In fact, ordinarily the formal analysis does not go much beyond determining the split of the tax burden between consumers and 'producers', the further split of the latter portion between wages, rents, interest, and profits being considered only through the *ad hoc* examination of a series of special cases.[9] Moreover, there is usually no explicit consideration of the tendency of tax effects to be felt by owners of factors employed in untaxed industries or by purchasers of untaxed products. (See the quote from Wells above for a clear qualitative description of these effects.)

2.2. Factor taxes

The inability to go behind the supply curve to the production function and conditions in factor markets is even more troublesome when a partial tax on one use of a factor is being examined. The mobility of both taxed and untaxed factors, the scale economies and ease of factor substitution inherent in the production functions, and the initial factor endowments or shares, as well as conditions of demand for the product, determine the incidence of a tax on one use of a factor. But traditional partial equilibrium analysis has virtually nothing to say on these matters.[10] In his treatise, Musgrave (1959, p. 311) has only two

---

analysis has traditionally been framed in terms of product supply curves, the discussion in this part of the text refers only to going behind the supply curve. For the analysis of factor taxes, discussed in the next part of this section, it may be more useful to think of going behind the derived demand curves for the various factors.

[7]Strictly speaking, even this is of interest. Some kinds of factor immobility may be overcome by the passage of time, but other types of immobility and (for a given state of technology) decreasing returns to scale or unequal factor proportions will not be.

[8]Thus in Musgrave's terminology (1959, ch. 10), partial equilibrium analysis may be adequate in determining effects of excises on relative product prices and thus incidence on the side of uses of income, but it is gravely deficient on the side of sources of income, since it cannot determine changes in relative factor returns.

[9]Naturally enough, these special cases often involve factors specific to the taxed industry – a case of fixity of factor supply in the taxed industry. Moreover, some of the difference between the long-run and short-run effects of a tax are matters of factor mobility, as noted in footnote 7.

[10]Wells' diagrammatic analysis (1955), which was corrected by Johnson (1956), contains the germ of the Harberger analysis for excise taxes, even though specific results could not easily be drawn from it. But factor taxes were not incorporated in the analysis as originally presented.

paragraphs in his section on 'partial taxes on selected factors'. The second of those, quoted in full, while accurate, is indicative of the dearth of analysis of these taxes:

'If the production function is such that it requires fixed proportions of factor inputs, there is no difference between a tax on total cost payments and a tax on cost payments to certain factors only. If factor proportions are variable, imposition of a tax on the purchase of certain factors will lead to substitution of tax-free factors for taxed factors, until an equality between gross factor prices (including tax) and marginal-value products is restored. Depending upon the supply elasticities of the various factors and the production function, the resulting upward shift in the cost schedule may be more or less severe.'

2.3. Analysis of general taxes

A further problem with the traditional partial equilibrium analysis is that it cannot properly be applied to general taxes levied on the entire output of an economy. This inadequacy is particularly troublesome as a practical matter, for one often reads prospective assessments of the price effects of a newly imposed federal value-added tax that are expressed in terms of the elasticities of supply and demand for various goods. The Harberger analysis – and even conventional general equilibrium analysis done without the benefit of a formal mathematical model – shows that this line of reasoning is inappropriate. A tax levied at uniform rates on all consumption (or income) has no effect upon relative prices (except the interest rate, under an income-type value added tax), and therefore is borne in proportion to consumption (income), regardless of the elasticities of supply and demand for various products.[11]

A similar problem involves the incidence of a tax on all uses of one factor, such as a payroll tax. Using reasoning similar to what might be applied to the incidence of a partial tax on labor (that is, a tax on labor in only some of its uses) – which in itself is likely to be defective for the reasons noted above – it is sometimes concluded that a general tax on payrolls deters the employment of labor, is shifted in part, and affects prices differently, depending upon the elasticity of labor demand and the labor intensities of various industries. The Harberger analysis shows the fallacy of this argument. In the standard neoclassical model, a general tax on all uses of one factor is borne entirely by that factor, so long as the factor is inelastic in supply to the economy as a whole, regardless of the values of other parameters.[12]

[11]Musgrave (1959, ch. 15) is still among the best references on this subject, which is considered in greater detail below. In a world of imperfect markets, the reaction to a value added tax may not be what neoclassical theory, as characterized by the Harberger model, tells us it is. But most authors who have made the kind of statement described in the text seem not to have had this point in mind.

[12]Proper application of partial equilibrium analysis, using labor as an inelastically supplied good, also produces the correct result – that labor bears the entire burden of the tax. Of course, if the labor–leisure choice is not fixed, the result stated here is likely to be altered.

2.4. Expenditure effects

Another problem related to the use of general taxes involves the use of the proceeds from the tax. In the analysis of selective excises that are imposed upon a 'small' portion of the total output of an economy and that yield a relatively 'small' amount of revenue, the use of the revenues can reasonably be ignored.[13] Under most circumstances the effect the tax has upon prices will be far more important than the effect of the expenditure of the funds. But when more general taxes are involved and the amount of revenue is substantial, the use of the tax receipts cannot be ignored. Assuming that the receipts are simply withdrawn from the economy and are therefore the cause of a continuous deflation or disinflation (*specific* incidence analysis) is clearly unsatisfactory, unless the tax policy under examination is obviously an alternative to open inflation. And even if that were the relevant alternative, we would need to compare the distributional effects of the tax with those of inflation (or combine them with those of deflation).

A more reasonable alternative is to assume that a given pattern of public expenditures is to be financed (or that the government has a particular demand schedule for public goods), independently of the method of financing chosen, so that a *differential* analysis (i.e., comparison) of the incidence of various taxes can be conducted. This approach is, of course, perfectly compatible with the standard partial equilibrium analysis, though as a matter of fact this seems rarely to be what practitioners of the latter have in mind. Finally, there are cases in which it is useful to engage in *balanced-budget* incidence analysis, that is, to ask the distributional implications of a given tax–expenditure package. This can never be revealed by the standard partial equilibrium analysis, unless the expenditure is so small as to be unimportant or is distributionally neutral (which can be known only through the use of some fairly sophisticated analysis).[14] The Harberger model is particularly well suited to both differential incidence analysis and balanced-budget incidence analysis, as is shown in the next section.[15]

---

[13]But by the same token, we could probably also ignore the incidence of the tax. Certainly we cannot use traditional partial equilibrium analysis to examine the incidence of large balanced budget increases in taxes and expenditures.

[14]If the government and the private sector have the same income-compensated elasticity of demand for the taxed good, government expenditures are distributionally neutral if at the margin the government spends tax proceeds in the same way as that tax money would have been spent in the private sector, that is, if public and private marginal propensities to consume the various goods are the same. See McLure (1972).

[15]As a matter of fact, the Harberger model is quite capable of handling the specific incidence analysis of the case of continual deflation, since only relative prices can be determined, and it is assumed that no assets are fixed in money terms. The three italicized terms in the text are from Musgrave (1959, ch. 10). Among early efforts to account for the effects of government expenditures in incidence analysis are de Viti de Marco (1936), Jaskari (1960), and Rolph (1954). Note that the discussion here is not concerned with who benefits from public provision of services or how these services affect production possibilities or the demand for private goods. On this point, see section 6.2.

Related to the question of how the government disposes of the revenues from the tax in question is that of how changes in the distribution of private incomes resulting from the tax have 'second-round' impacts upon demand, the composition of output, relative prices, and income distribution. These too, are easily analyzed with the Harberger model.

2.5. Deflationary excises

A final problem that has bothered some incautious users of partial equilibrium analysis involves the question of how an excise or sales tax can at the same time raise the price of the taxed good, as shown by microeconomic analysis, and be deflationary, as suggested by macroeconomic analysis. The answer is, as Musgrave has masterfully argued (1959, ch. 15), that tax incidence is primarily a matter of changes in *relative* prices, whereas inflation and deflation involve changes in price *levels*.[16] This proposition is easily demonstrated using the Harberger model.

3. The Harberger model

The Harberger model, in its general form, is based upon standard neoclassical assumptions, with several important exceptions. The equations of the model are discussed at some length by Harberger (1962) and Mieszkowski (1967), and derived explicitly by Shoven and Whalley (1972, appendix B). Thus there is no need to describe them at great length. But a brief description may be worthwhile, especially for variants of the original Harberger equations.[17]

Two competitive industries, x and y, are assumed to employ two factors, capital (K) and labor (L) under conditions of constant returns to scale and to pay them gross (i.e., tax-inclusive) returns equal to the value of their marginal products. Factors are generally assumed to be fixed in total supply and fully employed. [See McLure (1971b) and Mieszkowski (1972) for exceptions.] This implies that prices of factor services, and especially the wage rate, are completely flexible. Under alternative assumptions about factor mobility between industries, both factors are mobile, as in the original Harberger formulation, or one or both factors may be immobile.

In the original Harberger formulation all prices of goods and factors were assumed to be unity for the sake of expositional convenience. That convention is followed here. But two important and easily overlooked implications of that

---

[16]Of course, if all prices are inflexible downward and the tax raises some prices, it cannot reduce the price level. But disinflation can mean a slower rate of growth of prices.

[17]This description draws heavily upon McLure (1971a). Readers for whom the algebraic presentation causes difficulty may find McLure and Thirsk (1973) a useful reference. However, the Cobb–Douglas assumptions employed there are inevitably restrictive and an understanding of the mathematics of the more general version is necessary for a full appreciation of the model.

convention should be noted explicitly. First, any change in a price (dP) is also a fractional or (multiplying by 100) percentage change in that price. Second, what appear to be taxes levied on a per unit basis (dT) are really also ad valorem taxes, since all initial prices are assumed to be unity. While this convention of choosing units of factors and products in such a way that all initial prices are unity should create no problems if these two points are kept in mind, some readers might wish to substitute dP/P for dP and dT/T for dT in the equations below (with the relevant subscripts in both cases).

Changes in various variables are indicated by differential notation. Thus strictly speaking, we are considering infinitesimally small changes in taxes and their comparative statics impacts upon other variables. Though this has not always been made clear, the analysis as usually presented is thus applicable only for 'small' changes in taxes, and for discrete changes is only a local approximation. Moreover, strictly speaking, it is correct only if there are no pre-existing taxes or other distortions in the system and the economy is in equilibrium before the imposition of the tax being analyzed. These points are discussed more fully in section 6.6 below.

The basic demand equation in simple versions of the Harberger model is

$$\frac{dx}{x} = -E \frac{d(P_x/P_y)}{P_x/P_y},$$

where E is the income-compensated elasticity of demand for good x with respect to relative product prices.[18] Differentiation and use of the convention that all prices are initially unity produces the standard Harberger equation,

$$dx/x = -E(dP_x - dP_y). \qquad (1)$$

That demand depends only on changes in relative product prices results from the simplifying assumption that 'small' taxes are imposed in a distortion-free world and that at the margin all economic groups (including the government) spend their incomes in exactly the same way. Thus any redistribution of purchasing power from the private sector to the government or within the private sector has no effect upon demand. Ignoring the income loss resulting from the excess burden of taxes, we can identify E in eq. (1) with the Hicksian substitution term in the Slutsky equation.[19]

---

[18]Note that the sign convention adopted here for elasticities is opposite from that used by Harberger and Mieszkowski. It seems easier to define the elasticity of demand (or later, the elasticity of factor substitution) to be a positive number.

[19]Though it seems to be implicit in Harberger (1962), Mieszkowski (1967) was the first to make this identification explicit. More recently in conversation with the author, Harberger has argued that he did not intend for E to be the 'fully compensated' elasticity of demand. Rather, E would be compensated for changes in income resulting from redistributions of income, but would be a 'reduced form' elasticity in that it would include effects on demand resulting from such excess burdens as may result from changes in relative prices.

(continued on next page)

The next five equations result directly from the assumptions that firms are competitive and that the production functions are linear homogeneous. The first describes changes in the output of industry x resulting from changes in factor inputs to the industry:

$$\frac{dx}{x} = f_L \frac{dL_x}{L_x} + f_K \frac{dK_x}{K_x}, \qquad (2)$$

where f_L and f_K are the initial shares of capital and labor in industry x. Simply stated, the percentage change in the output of good x is the weighted average of the percentage changes in the two inputs, where the weights are initial factor shares. Stated in still another way, f_L and f_K are the partial elasticities of output with respect to the two inputs. The analogous equation for industry y is not necessary, as any factors not employed in x are automatically employed in y.[20] Finally, by Walras' law, we know that a demand equation for good y is redundant.

The possibilities of factor substitution in production are indicated by the elasticities of substitution in the two industries, S_x and S_y,[21]

$$\frac{d(K_x/L_x)}{K_x/L_x} = -S_x \frac{d(P^*_{Kx}/P^*_{Lx})}{P^*_{Kx}/P^*_{Lx}},$$

and

$$\frac{d(K_y/L_y)}{K_y/L_y} = -S_y \frac{d(P^*_{Ky}/P^*_{Ly})}{P^*_{Ky}/P^*_{Ly}},$$

where asterisks on price variables indicate factor prices as entrepreneurs see them, that is, factor prices inclusive of factor taxes.[22] The gross factor prices in industry x can be related to the corresponding net factor prices in the following way:

It might be wondered why E, rather than the more familiar elasticity of substitution in consumption is used. As Harberger has shown (1957), so long as there are no first order income effects, this elasticity, C, and E are related in the following simple way: $E = Cy/(x+y)$. But it is difficult to reconcile this demonstration (which requires that E exclude first order income effects) with Harberger's more recent interpretation of E as reported in the previous paragraph.

It is common to assume that all economic units also have the same elasticity of demand. But as shown by McLure (1969), E can just as well be a weighted average of individual elasticities (and the government's elasticity). Finally, implicit in this approach is the assumption that the government pays tax on its purchases, just as private buyers do.

[20] However, if the elasticity of substitution in consumption, C, is employed, rather than E, the equation analogous to (2) must be added to the system.

[21] It is a characteristic of linear homogeneous production functions that under perfect competition the wage–rental ratio is uniquely related to the labor–capital ratio.

[22] This definition of starred price variables implies nothing about the incidence of factor taxes. It is simply to distinguish the starred versions from the unstarred versions, introduced immediately, which are the prices factor owners receive, that is, factor prices net of all factor taxes.

$$P^*_{Kx} = P_{Kx} + T_{Kx} + T_K,$$

and

$$P^*_{Lx} = P_{Lx} + T_{Lx} + T_L.$$

Analogous relations hold for the prices of factors used in industry y.

Differentiating the above equations defining the elasticities of substitution and the relationships between gross and net factor prices, substituting for the starred price variables, setting all factor taxes initially equal to zero, and making use of the convention that all initial prices are unity, we derive the following standard equations:

$$\frac{dK_x}{K_x} - \frac{dL_x}{L_x} = -S_x(dP_{Kx} + dT_{Kx} + dT_K - dP_{Lx} - dT_{Lx} - dT_L), \quad (3)$$

and

$$\frac{dK_y}{K_y} - \frac{dL_y}{L_y} = -S_y(dP_{Ky} + dT_{Ky} + dT_K - dP_{Ly} - dT_{Ly} - dT_L). \quad (4)$$

The relation of changes in product prices to changes in tax-inclusive factor prices and sales taxes is given by the following version of Euler's theorem:[23]

$$dP_x = f_L dP^*_{Lx} + f_K dP^*_{Kx} + dT_x + dT_c,$$

and

$$dP_y = g_L dP^*_{Ly} + g_K dP^*_{Ky} + dT_y + dT_c.$$

In common-sense terms these equations state that the percentage change in the price of a product is the weighted average of the percentage changes in the tax-inclusive prices of factors (where the weights are factor shares), plus any ad valorem excise tax on the product itself and any general ad valorem retail sales tax (T_c). Substituting into these equations we have the standard Harberger expressions for the relationship between product prices, net factor returns and various kinds of taxes,

$$dP_x = f_L(dP_{Lx} + dT_{Lx} + dT_L) + f_K(dP_{Kx} + dT_{Kx} + dT_K) + dT_x + dT_c, \quad (5)$$

and

$$dP_y = g_L(dP_{Ly} + dT_{Ly} + dT_L) + g_K(dP_{Ky} + dT_{Ky} + dT_K) + dT_y + dT_c. \quad (6)$$

---

[23]Again, we make use of the assumptions that all taxes are initially zero and all prices are initially unity. See Harberger (1962) or Shoven and Whalley (1972) for the derivation of this type of equation.

The next four equations describe the fixity of total factor supplies and alternative mobility assumptions. Eqs. (7) and (8) simply state that in total both factors are fixed in supply,

$$dK_x + dK_y = 0, \tag{7}$$

and

$$dL_x + dL_y = 0. \tag{8}$$

It is important to note that these two equations imply that there is no net saving (or if a longer-range view is taken, that the rate of saving is not economically determined) and that there is no labor–leisure choice (and that growth of the labor force is exogenous, in a long-run context).

Alternative assumptions about the inter-industry mobility of the two factors are described by eqs. (9a) and (9b) for capital and by eqs. (10a) and (10b) for labor,

$$dP_{Kx} = dP_{Ky} = dP_K, \tag{9a}$$

or

$$dK_x = 0; \tag{9b}$$

and

$$dP_{Lx} = dP_{Ly} = dP_L, \tag{10a}$$

or

$$dL_x = 0. \tag{10b}$$

Eq. (9a) implies that capital is completely mobile between sectors, and therefore receives a common rate of return, net of tax. The alternative formulation (9b) states that capital is completely immobile between sectors. Therefore, sectoral subscripts on the net return to capital must be maintained.[24] Analogous statements apply to eqs. (10a) and (10b), which describe the mobility of labor.

Thus far we have ten equations to solve for eleven unknowns. In order to close the system we must either choose one good or one factor to serve as numéraire or add to the model a simple description of macroeconomic policy. If the former route is chosen we can solve for changes in relative product and factor prices. If the latter, we can solve for changes in absolute prices, given an assumed

---

[24]It may be useful to comment at this point on the assumption that all initial prices are unity since there is no reason to believe that an immobile factor will receive the same reward in both industries. The point is that if the factor is immobile between industries different units can be used to measure input of the factor in the two industries, both choices being made to produce a factor price of one. For analytical purposes, an immobile factor used in two industries is simply two different factors.

macroeconomic policy. In either event, we can solve the system for changes in relative prices, which is the essence of incidence analysis. [See Musgrave (1959) and McLure (1970b).] Eqs. (11a) to (11d) show several of the myriad ways in which the system can be closed that have actually been employed in the literature,

$$dP_L = 0, \tag{11a}$$

$$dP_y = 0, \tag{11b}$$

$$L_x dP_{Lx} + L_y dP_{Ly} + K_x dP_{Kx} + K_y dP_{Ky} = VdM, \tag{11c}$$

$$xdP_x + ydP_y = VdM. \tag{11d}$$

In the first of these, the original Harberger formulation, labor is taken to be the numéraire. In the second, product y, usually the untaxed product, is chosen as the numéraire. In the third and fourth alternative descriptions, in which V is the velocity of money and M the money supply, it is assumed that the monetary authorities act to stabilize (or otherwise affect) the value of either disposable income [eq. (11c)] or net national product [eq. (11d)]. The relative advantages of these various formulations (and others) are discussed further below. In any event, if only one of the alternatives given for each of eqs. (9) – (11) is chosen, there are eleven equations to solve for eleven unknowns. Since methodology, and not solutions, is the subject of the present paper, we shall turn in the next section to the reconsideration of the problems partial equilibrium analysis handles inadequately. But first it will be convenient to make one final methodological point before leaving the description of the basic Harberger model. This has to do with the equivalence of taxes.

Musgrave (1959, ch. 15) noted that under certain circumstances (perfect competition, constant returns to scale, and no saving) – which are also descriptive of the world of the Harberger model – the following equivalences hold between taxes levied at a given ad valorem rate:

T_{Kx} and T_{Lx} are equivalent to T_x

and and and

T_{Ky} and T_{Ly} are equivalent to T_y

are are are

equivalent equivalent equivalent

to to to

T_K and T_L are equivalent to $T_c = T_I$.

Mieszkowski (1967) demonstrated these equivalences for the case in which both factors are mobile. Eqs. (3) – (6), which are the only ones that contain tax terms, can be employed to prove that these equivalences hold regardless of mobility assumptions. For example, equal ad valorem taxes on capital and labor in x would cancel in eq. (3) and together would enter eq. (5) in exactly the same way as an excise on product x. The other equivalences are readily demonstrated in a similar way.

Because of the equivalences, it is necessary to examine in detail the incidence of only three taxes, T_{Kx}, T_K and T_x, for example. (The three cannot come from the same row or column.) As noted above, a tax levied at the same ad valorem rate on capital and labor in producing good x is equivalent to a tax levied at that rate on good x itself. Thus, if we know the incidence of T_x and T_{Kx}, we automatically know that of T_{Lx} by subtraction. Similarly, if we know the incidence of T_K and T_{Kx}, the incidence of T_{Ky} follows immediately, since capital has only two uses. Finally, if we know the incidence of T_x and T_K, we can learn the incidence of T_y and T_L if we know the incidence of a general tax on all income (T_I) or consumption (T_c). (In a world of fixed factor supplies there is no saving, so income and consumption are identical.) But there is no need for explicit analysis of the general income or consumption tax. We know that it affects no relative product prices or relative factor rewards. Rather, it simply drives a uniform wedge between factor payments and product prices, and hence is borne in proportion to initial shares in income or consumption.

4. Improvements over partial analysis

Having described the equations of the Harberger model at some length, we can now return to the problems that partial equilibrium analysis can handle only imperfectly, if at all, in order to see the usefulness of the Harberger model. In each case we see that problems for which partial equilibrium analysis is in some way unsuited can be handled with the Harberger analysis.

4.1. Behind the supply curve

First, it is readily apparent that in this model the interdependence of markets is taken into account and that there is no problem in determining how an excise tax affects individuals in their roles as recipients of factor incomes by changing the relative net returns to factors, as well as how it affects them in their roles as consumers through variations in relative product prices. The Harberger model allows us to 'go behind' the supply curve through its explicit inclusion of the returns to the various factors as variables and constant returns to scale, initial factor endowments and factor shares, elasticities of factor substitution, and the mobility of factors as assumptions or parameters of the model. A supply curve that takes into account the interactions between markets can be derived for the taxed good, if desirable. In any case, detailed analysis indicates how the values of the various parameters influence the incidence of particular excise taxes.[25]

It may be instructive at this point simply to write out the expressions for the elasticity of supply of good x with respect to relative product prices in the cases of complete factor mobility and of one factor (capital) mobile and one (labor) immobile, so that we can see how the various parameters influence the supply response to price changes:

Complete mobility case

$$\frac{dx/x}{dP_x - dP_y} = \frac{S_y + S_x(f_K(L_x/L_y) + f_L(K_x/K_y))}{(f_K - g_K)((K_x/K_y) - (L_x/L_y))}. \tag{12}$$

Imperfect mobility case (labor immobile)

$$\frac{dx/x}{dP_x - dP_y} = \frac{f_K S_x S_y}{f_L S_y + g_L S_x K_x/K_y}. \tag{13}$$

We see immediately that in the imperfect mobility case supply is completely fixed if factor substitution is impossible in either industry. On the other hand, the elasticity of supply is zero in the complete mobility case only if both elasticities of factor substitution are zero. So long as factor substitution is possible in one industry, output can respond to changes in relative prices, even if the other industry employs factors in fixed proportions. In either case, the elasticity of supply is greater, the greater is either elasticity of factor substitution.

The second important feature of these supply curves is the different roles played by factor intensities, on the one hand, and by factor shares and the initial division of the mobile factor between the two industries, K_x/K_y, on the other. In the complete mobility case the elasticity of supply is inversely proportionate to the square of the difference between the factor intensities in the two industries. In the extreme case of equal factor intensities, supply is perfectly elastic, as this is the case of constant opportunity costs of x in terms of y.

In the imperfect mobility case relative factor intensities have no immediate bearing on the value of the elasticity of supply. Rather, the important things in this case are labor's share of output in both industries and the fraction of all capital employed in industry x. Supply is more elastic the smaller is labor's share

---

[25] For detailed analyses of the incidence of various kinds of taxes and the role of the various parameters, see McLure (1971a) and Mieszkowski (1967). The original Harberger model considered only the case of perfect factor mobility. Imperfect factor mobility was introduced in the following publications by McLure: (1969, 1970a, 1971a, b, 1972 and 1974). McLure (1974), upon which the remainder of this subsection is based, represents the first attempt in the literature on the Harberger model to derive the elasticity of the product supply curve explicitly from the underlying production functions and mobility assumptions and then 'go behind' the supply curve to interpret the results of the earlier mathematical treatments. But see Jones (1965).

in either industry (i.e., the less important the immobile factor is in production) and the smaller is the fraction of the total capital stock initially invested in industry x (that is, the smaller the fraction of the mobile factor initially utilized in the taxed industry).

Finally, it should be noted that for any reasonable values of the parameters of the model the elasticity of supply is much greater in the complete mobility case than in the imperfect mobility case, as one would expect. The immobility of one factor simply imposes a considerable degree of inelasticity upon supply, unless factors are good substitutes.

4.2. Partial factor taxes

It is equally apparent that the analysis can be extended to partial factor taxes, rather than being confined to excise taxes. Because of the inclusion of the equations describing the conditions underlying the supply of products, examining the incidence of a tax on one use of a factor poses no problem. In fact, Harberger's initial use of the model (1962) was to examine the effects of the corporation income tax, which he found to be borne by capital in both the corporate and non-corporate sectors. In his 1967 article Mieszkowski (1967, pp. 252–253) showed how, in the complete mobility case, the effects of a partial factor tax can be split into two components, the 'output effect' and the 'factor substitution effect'. The former is simply the effect of an equal yield tax on the output of the industry in which the factor is taxed. It occurs because taxation is related only to that industry. The factor substitution effect, on the other hand, occurs because only one factor is taxed in that industry, and can be isolated as the differential incidence of equal yield taxes on (a) the output of the industry and (b) one factor employed in that industry.[26]

4.3. Analysis of general taxes

Third, the Harberger model gives straightforward answers to questions of the incidence of general taxes, assuming fixed total factor supplies. In particular, it indicates that a general tax on income or consumption is borne in proportion to initial shares in income or consumption, regardless of the elasticities of demand and supply of the various goods. Moreover, it indicates that a general tax on all uses of one factor (such as a payroll or property tax) is borne by that factor, rather than being shifted in part to consumers or owners of other factors. This result holds independently of demand conditions for the factor, the factor-intensity of production in the various sectors, and the mobility of both factors.

---

[26]Of course, if the excess burdens created by the two taxes are not similar, this comparison may be difficult or misleading. See also Mieszkowski (1969, pp. 1108–1109) and McLure (1971a, pp. 41–44). Krauss and Johnson (1972) question the usefulness of this distinction. As suggested by McLure's discussion, this distinction may be particularly unsatisfactory if both factors are not mobile.

Of course the results for both the general income or consumption tax or a general tax on all uses of one factor may be modified by relaxation of the assumption that all factor supplies are completely inelastic.

4.4. Expenditure effects

The Harberger model also lends itself directly to explicit consideration of the effects of government disposal of tax revenues. In his original article Harberger (1962, p. 224) simply assumed 'for the sake of simplicity that the way in which the government would spend the tax proceeds, if the initial prices continued to prevail, would just counterbalance the reductions in private expenditures on the two goods'. Thus, Harberger explicitly stated his problem in terms of balanced-budget incidence, but for convenience in isolating the redistributional implications of taxes, he also explicitly assumed away any redistributional effects arising from differences in marginal public and private expenditure patterns. Moreover, he assumed that 'redistributions of income among consumers do not change the pattern of demand', which implies that all consumers have the same marginal spending patterns. But he also assumed that all 'individual consumers have the same expenditure pattern as the average of all consumers'. Thus there can be no effect on income distribution from the side of uses of income in the original Harberger formulation.[27]

In his extension of Harberger's work, Mieszkowski (1967, pp. 257–259 and 262) relaxed the assumption of identical public and private expenditure patterns and obtained what he called 'demand effects'. These arise if the spending propensities of the government and all segments of the private sector are not identical. If the *average* propensities of individuals to purchase the two goods are not identical, income redistributional effects are caused on the side of uses of income by a change in relative product prices. And if all *marginal* propensities to spend on the two goods are not identical, effects on product demand and relative prices result from the transfer of purchasing power (real income) from the private to the public sector and within the private sector. In his work McLure [see especially (1970b) and (1971a, pp. 31–34)] has found it convenient for analytical purposes to assume that consumers have equal marginal propensities to spend on the two goods, but not necessarily equal average propensities. This allows us to ignore the second round effects on demand and relative prices resulting from unequal marginal expenditure patterns without also forcing us to ignore changes in income on the uses side.

McLure (1972) has also extended Mieszkowski's reasoning in a recent paper. It examines (a) the distributional implications of balanced-budget increases in

[27]Harberger (1962, p. 219) recognized that 'insofar as individual consumers differ from the average, they gain if they spend a larger fraction of their budget on y than the average, and lose if they spend a larger fraction of their budget on x than the average'. But in the formal analysis of the model no further mention is made of the necessary qualifications resulting from redistributions occurring on the side of uses of income.

various types of neutrally financed expenditures and (b) the differential effects of changes in the composition of a given amount of public expenditures, both under various assumptions of factor mobility.[28] Thus the former analysis is the analog on the expenditure side of Harberger's analysis of the incidence of taxes used to finance distributionally neutral expenditures. The second, differential expenditure incidence analysis, is analogous to the differential analysis of the incidence of various taxes used to finance a given pattern of expenditures. Of course, the tax and expenditure analysis can be combined to determine the incidence of non-neutral financing of non-neutral expenditures.

4.5. Deflationary excises

The final inadequacy of the traditional partial-equilibrium analysis noted in the previous section is its apparent inability to reconcile the tendency of excise taxes to raise the price of the taxed good with the use of excise taxes as tools of deflationary fiscal policy. If either eq. (11c) or (11d), which are quantity theory specifications of macroeconomic conditions in the economy, is chosen from among the four listed alternative numéraire and monetary eqs. (11a) – (11d), the reconciliation is easily effected. Tax incidence, which is a matter of changes in *relative prices* (except to the extent of the existence of assets and liabilities fixed in money terms), depends upon the *structure* of taxation (and its effects on relative prices), whereas changes in the *price level* depend upon the *level* of taxes and other *macroeconomic* variables. Though one should be a bit chary about carrying these strong theoretical conclusions over to policy making in the real world, using excise taxes to restrain inflationary forces clearly involves no logical inconsistency.[29]

Of course, Harberger realized clearly that the primary interest of incidence analysis was in changes in relative prices. In his initial article (1962, p. 226) he wrote the following about his choice of our equation (11a) to complete his system: 'The equations of the model contain absolute price changes as variables, while in the underlying economic theory it is only relative prices that matter.

---

[28]In both this and Mieszkowski's extension, the demand function in eq. (1) must be modified to allow for the effects of the redistribution of purchasing power among individuals and to the public sector; see Mieszkowski (1967, p. 262) and McLure (1972, pp. 438–439). Moreover, McLure's analysis admits the possibility that the government hires factors as well as purchasing finished goods. For a diagrammatic exposition of the incidence of expenditures on final products, see McLure (1974). Ballentine and Eris (1973) also consider the case in which private and government spending patterns differ at the margin.

Distributionally neutral financing involves taxation that does not affect the initial distribution of income. One example of such a tax that is borne in proportion to initial shares in national income would be a general income or sales tax, as noted above.

[29]See McLure (1970b). McLure also shows that eqs. (1)–(10), like most other general equilibrium models, can be solved directly for changes in relative prices without specifying any numéraire or monetary equation. Partial equilibrium analysis, properly applied, gives this result. If demand functions are assumed to be homogeneous of degree zero in prices and income, only relative prices can be determined.

We have need of some sort of *numéraire*, a price in terms of which the other prices are expressed, and equation (9) chooses the price of labor as the *numéraire*. This choice places no restrictions on the generality of our results.' Harberger's eq. (9) and eq. (11a) above are identical.

In much of his work McLure has chosen the untaxed good as the numéraire by using eq. (11b). This choice has the attraction of both convenience and intuitive appeal. First, Harberger's numéraire equation cannot be carried over unchanged to the examination of cases of imperfect mobility of labor. Since imperfectly mobile labor may earn different wage rates in the two sectors, at the very least labor in only one sector would need to be chosen as the numéraire. But this choice renders very difficult the comparison of price effects in cases of complete and incomplete factor mobility.[30] No similar difficulty is involved in interpreting the results if eq. (11b) is used; it is equally applicable under any assumption of factor mobility. In addition, this numeraire equation has the further intuitive advantage that results of the general equilibrium analysis take the same form as those of partial equilibrium analysis. That is, we solve for changes in the price of the taxed good x and in the returns to all the factors in their various uses, where each price is expressed in terms of the untaxed numéraire good. Thus changes on the side of uses of income appear directly as involving changes in the price of the taxed good and those on the sources side as involving changes in the returns to the various factors.[31]

5. Further extensions and applications of the Harberger analysis

In the last ten years the Harberger analysis has taken its place alongside the traditional Marshallian partial equilibrium analysis in the toolkit of the public finance specialist. It has been applied to a number of practical problems of tax policy, and in the process has been extended in several directions not mentioned in the previous section. This section reviews briefly those applications and extensions that have come to the attention of the author.[32]

5.1. Federal tax policy

Perhaps the clearest sign of the acceptance of the Harberger model by public

---

[30]In McLure (1970a), the numéraire equation $dP_{Lx} = 0$ was employed. But that article was concerned with factor movements between sectors (regions), which do not depend even nominally upon the choice of numéraire equation. The interpretation and comparison of price effects, which do depend nominally upon the choice of numéraire equation, would have been much more difficult, even though in real terms the choice of numéraire equation is irrelevant. In McLure (1974), mobile capital was used as the numéraire, primarily because of convenience in carrying out the diagrammatic analysis.

[31]As noted in McLure (1971a, pp. 31–32), because there is no uniquely correct numéraire equation, there seems to be no singularly appropriate division of effects on the distribution of income available for private use between the sources and uses sides. Eq. (11b) is simply one choice that is convenient and has intuitive appeal.

[32]Of course, general equilibrium analysis of taxation has existed quite independently of Harberger's model, as noted earlier. In this section only that literature that can be traced directly to the Harberger model is reviewed.

finance specialists is the explicit use of the model as the underlying theoretical framework for two recent monographs on federal tax policy published by the Brookings Institution.[33] The authors of these works recognized that for questions of such pervasive economic importance as federal subsidies to housing and the payroll taxes used to finance social security, partial equilibrium analysis simply would not suffice, and they turned to the Harberger model of general equilibrium analysis.

Brittain (1972) concluded that social security taxes are almost certainly borne largely by all workers, the primary qualification having to do with the elasticity of supply of labor. This result for a tax on labor in covered industries is analogous to Harberger's result for a tax on capital in the corporate sector. One benefit of applying the Harberger approach to this problem is the recognition that the burden of the tax extends to all labor, if labor is mobile, rather than falling only on the labor statutorily subject to taxation. Of course, a partial payroll tax may also raise the price of goods produced in covered industries, relative to the price of goods from industries that are not covered. But as Brittain notes, these effects on relative product prices (the side of uses of income) are likely to be quite unimportant from a distributional point of view, since it is not clear that consumption of goods from covered industries is closely linked with any other relevant partitioning of the population.

Aaron (1972) employs the Harberger approach (though he suppresses the equations) to examine the incidence of federal subsidies to housing, which for analytical purposes can simply be treated as a negative excise tax on one sector, housing. Since both capital and labor are assumed to be mobile, the impact of housing subsidies depends crucially upon whether housing is more or less capital intensive than the remainder of the economy.[34] And, to repeat a constant theme of a Harberger literature, any effects on the returns to labor and capital will be felt by all owners of the two factors, due to the complete mobility assumption.

5.2. Regional tax analysis

Perhaps the most widespread use of the Harberger model has been in the investigation of the effects of taxes levied in an open-economy setting. In one sense this is not surprising, since the model had its immediate intellectual origins in the Heckscher–Ohlin theory of international trade. But some of the adaptations of the model to interregional problems have changed it considerably from the original international trade model.

Among the early applications of the Harberger model to open-economy problems were McLure's theoretical investigations (1969, 1970a and 1971b) of the interregional incidence and effects upon industrial location of general taxes

[33]A similar application of the Harberger model in the appraisal of tax reform proposals for Canada is reported in Krauss (1971).

[34]The analysis of housing is complicated by the fact that the production of the housing stock is labor intensive, but the rendering of housing services is quite capital intensive.

levied in one region. The model was adapted to this problem by treating sectors x and y as two regions completely specialized in the production of one good and investigating the effects of various general taxes levied on the output and use of one or both factors in the region under various conditions of interregional mobility of capital and labor. Among the useful insights provided by this analysis is an appreciation of the determinants of the extent to which taxes on the output of a region or upon capital invested in a region will be borne by labor if labor is immobile and capital is mobile. This analysis is also suggestive of the extent to which various local taxes might be borne by land if both capital and labor are mobile or by both land and labor if only capital is mobile.

This analysis suffered from the necessity to lump the entire output of each region together into one aggregate commodity and the concomitant inability to consider partial taxes on only some products or some uses of a given factor in the region. In this sense these applications represented a significant step backward from the standard international trade model.[35]

At roughly the same time Mieszkowski was approaching a similar problem from the other end. In a paper on the relative efficiency of tariffs and other tax–subsidy schemes (1966) he assumed that a small economy characterized by incomplete specialization and the assumptions and equations of the Harberger model (including immobility of factors between nations) was trading with the outside world. Thus Mieszkowski got away from the complete specialization assumption, but he did so only at the expense of assuming that the nation (region) in question faced fixed terms of trade. Again, the application of the Harberger model to open-economy problems fell somewhat short of the generality of the standard international trade model.

The next step clearly was a two-country model of international trade in which each of the two countries was characterized by the Harberger assumptions, plus the additional assumptions needed to close the system. Then the Harberger model would have come full circle. In a doctoral dissertation on the welfare effects of the treatment allowed under the General Agreement on Tariffs and Trade of internal taxes levied on goods (and on factors used to produce goods) entering international trade, Floyd (1971) has examined such a model. In it, the traditional assumption of international trade theory that factors are geographically immobile is maintained.

Other open-economy applications of the Harberger model have followed

---

[35]In defense of early work in the area of interregional incidence analysis, one can quote the following statement about the analysis of the effects of internal tax policy from Bhagwati's review of the literature of international trade theory (1964, p. 43):

'Such questions have rarely been posed *directly* in trade theory.... Practically the only direct analysis of such problems, however, is due to Mundell, who has extended his survey of pure theory to include an original contribution on the effect of consumption and production taxes on the terms of trade (at market prices and factor costs).' (Emphasis in original.)

More recently, trade theorists have come to pay considerable attention to these problems; see, for example, Magee (1971).

various lines of development. In a theoretical paper on regional tax incentives written for the Musgrave Commission for fiscal reform in Colombia, McLure (1971b) applied the model to the determination of the effects of various kinds of regional incentives on the level of income in low income regions, on the assumption that labor is immobile out of the depressed region. If full employment is guaranteed automatically by a flexible wage rate, the analysis simply repeats that of his earlier work (1969) on interregional incidence. But if there is a floor on (real or money) wages in the backward region, say because of a traditional idea as to a 'reasonable' wage rate or an extended family system, unemployment may occur, and the analysis is different. In this case various kinds of subsidy can be used in the effort to increase employment. It is shown that if there is a floor on money wages, for a given cost a subsidy to the use of labor in the depressed area has a greater positive effect on employment than a subsidy to either production or the use of capital in the region.[36] The analogous applications of this theoretical analysis to the problem of regional development in developed countries are obvious.

Finally, in a recent article on the incidence of the local property tax, Mieszkowski (1972) has employed the reasoning of the Harberger model to examine a situation in which three factors of production are employed in a local community using the property tax as a source of revenue. This analysis takes into account explicitly the mobility of the three factors and interlocality differentials in property tax rates. Though the results of this study are far too numerous and too complicated to summarize briefly, we might note some of the key results.

The most important result is that, seen as a national tax levied at some uniform average rate, the local property tax reduces the net return to capital by roughly the amount of the tax, rather than being 'shifted' to consumers or reducing the rents paid on land. On the other hand, due to the mobility of capital, local differentials in property tax rates not matched by service differentials are likely to have what Mieszkowski calls 'excise effects' by raising (or lowering) the cost of capital to the local area imposing differentially higher (lower) taxes on property. Such excise effects are likely to be particularly important for so-called 'home' products, as opposed to 'export' goods. Finally, differential property taxes are also likely to be reflected in lower (or higher) returns to immobile factors such as land, and perhaps labor, than would otherwise be the case. The extent to which (or whether) this occurs depends crucially upon the cross-partial elasticities of demand for the three factors, the elasticity of supply of

---

[36]Though one would not ordinarily expect such a result, it is even possible that a subsidy linked to the use of capital in the depressed area would reduce regional employment. Like all the results derived from this model, the accuracy of any policy prescription depends upon the extent to which the assumptions of the model reflect the real world. McLure (1971b) has mentioned briefly some of the qualifications to the model that seem especially important for the discussion of incentives to regional development.

labor, and the elasticity of demand for the output of the local area. Given reasonable values of these parameters, it seems likely that land will be burdened relatively more than labor. Mieszkowski's best estimate is that labor is not likely to bear (or benefit from) an important part of differentials in local property taxes, that land is not likely to bear more than 40 per cent of such differentials, and that consumers are likely to bear 75 per cent or more of the differentials. But all this should not be allowed to obscure the basic presumption that on the average property taxes are borne by owners of capital.

5.3. Excess burden of taxes

One of the early applications of the Harberger model, by the original author of that model (1966), was to the measurement of the welfare loss resulting from the differential taxation of capital employed in the corporate sector. Harberger estimated that in 1953–1959 the welfare loss resulting from the differential taxation of capital in the corporate sector (excluding the favorably treated petroleum industry) averaged about $2 billion annually. In a related analysis, Hoffman (1972) has examined the downward bias introduced into this kind of estimate of tax-induced welfare loss by aggregation over industry classes.

Because the Harberger model, as usually written, is only a linear local approximation, it cannot with complete legitimacy be employed to examine the effects of taxes of finite size. An attempt to get around this problem and test the sensitivity of Harberger's results to relaxation of the linearity assumption has been made by Shoven and Whalley (1972) in an important recent article in this journal. These authors have utilized an algorithm for computing general equilibrium prices that does not require any linearity assumptions and that allows substantially more disaggregation than the Harberger model. Moreover, it allows the relaxation of the assumptions that factor endowments are fixed and that no other distortions exist. Unfortunately, however, Shoven and Whalley can only bracket estimates of the welfare loss, by evaluating it in terms of distorted and non-distorted prices. The discrepancy between the two sets of estimates corresponds to the range of uncertainty involved in using the Paasche index, rather than the Laspeyres index, and is fairly large.

5.4. Unions and income distribution

Extending the Harberger model to yet another set of problems, Johnson and Mieszkowski (1970) have examined the impact of unionization upon the distribution of income. (The wage differential between union and non-union labor is treated as analytically similar to a tax on labor in the unionized sector.) Inserting reasonable values for the parameters of the model into the equations, they conclude (p. 560) that '... most, if not all, of the gains of union labor are made at the expense of non-unionized workers, and not at the expense of earnings on capital'. Ballentine and Thirsk (1974) have reexamined the Johnson–Mieszkowski analysis, taking account of preexisting distortions (differential taxation of the unionized and non-unionized sectors). They find that the earlier numerical estimates may be in error by 2 to 12 per cent and that the Johnson–Mieszkowski findings on income distribution and welfare effects of unionization are questionable once allowance is made for initial distortions.

5.5. Mechanization of agriculture

In one of the most ambitious applications of the Harberger model to date Thirsk (1972) has examined the distributional effects and efficiency implications of a Colombian program to encourage the mechanization of agriculture through low interest loans. In the more complicated of his two models, which requires computer simulation for its solution, he considers four factors (labor, capital, and two types of land) and four products (non-agricultural products, cattle, and the outputs of small and large farms). In a somewhat simpler model that allows an analytical solution, the cattle sector is suppressed. In both cases Thirsk found that the credit policy under examination worsened both the allocation of resources and the distribution of income.

5.6. Preferential taxation of household activity

Boskin (1973) has used the Harberger model in an imaginative way to examine the distributional and allocational effects of the preferential treatment of economic activity occurring within the household, rather than in the market sector. Analytically, his approach is simply to use the two-sector division of the standard Harberger model to distinguish between the market (M) and household (H) sectors, rather than between corporate and non-corporate sectors, unionized and non-unionized industries, different regions, etc., as in previous studies. But he does assign to one factor (capital or labor) in each of the two sectors part of each of the following taxes: individual and corporate income taxes, payroll taxes, property taxes, and indirect taxes. According to his calculations, factors bear the following tax rates (calculated as a percentage of gross factor rewards) in the two sectors: $T_{KM} = 43\%$; $T_{LM} = 24\%$; $T_{KH} = 24\%$; $T_{LH} = 0$. Compared to the average rate of tax of about 23%, capital in the market sector can be seen to be seriously overtaxed and labor in the household sector seriously undertaxed.

Using the results of his theoretical analysis, the average tax rates listed above, and suggestive values of various other parameters, he estimates both the distributional effects ('quite modestly progressive') and the excess burden or welfare loss (about $20 billion) involved in the existing differential taxation of market and household activity in the United States. The estimate of excess burden is of special interest because it utilizes the formula derived by Harberger (1964) for the calculation of the excess burden resulting from the imposition of taxes at different rates on several sectors or factors. He then examines the question of the optimal taxation of capital in the two sectors, assuming that labor in the household sector is inherently untaxable and that the existing taxation of labor in the market sector is not to be altered. He finds that the traditional partial equilibrium prescription of equal taxation of capital in the two sectors produces 90 per cent of the welfare gain involved in going to the optimal taxation of capital – which would involve a reversal of the present pattern of unequal taxation of capital in the two sectors.

6. Potential additional modifications

The usefulness of the Harberger model has been demonstrated in the last two sections. This brief section outlines several further modifications of the model that are likely to prove useful in the analysis of tax incidence.[37] The various modifications discussed here and in the previous section are, in most cases, not mutually exclusive; more than one can be made at one time. Finally, one potential modification which seems unlikely to be of great value and one of the inherent shortcomings of the model are discussed in section 7.

6.1. Three goods

Thirsk's work (1972) provides a natural starting point for one of the most obvious extensions of the Harberger analysis, that to the case of three goods. This extension would permit the examination of the effects of taxation upon the prices of complements, as well as substitutes, and the effects through them on real incomes.[38] Extension to more than three products would be extremely laborious, and probably not very rewarding.

6.2. Public goods and private demand

An especially intriguing candidate for inclusion in the model as the third good would be one provided publicly. It was noted above that when balanced-budget incidence is examined it is necessary to consider explicitly how tax revenues are utilized, and that it is often analytically convenient to assume that marginal public and private expenditure patterns are identical. This allows us to abstract

---

[37]Time and space limit discussion of potential modifications to the field of tax analysis. The scope of more general application is, of course, as wide as the realm of general equilibrium comparative statics and policy analysis.

[38]Presumably complementarity would be defined in net terms – that is, excluding the income effect – since the elasticity of demand in the standard Harberger model is for income-compensated demand. Of course, if two products are so complementary in consumption as to be required in fixed proportions, they can be collapsed into one product for analytical purposes. Musgrave (1959, pp. 301–302) discusses several 'peculiar' cases of value based on complementarity and attributable to Edgeworth.

from effects on prices resulting from differences in expenditure patterns, unless we want to consider them explicitly.

But while we may want to assume for convenience that transfer of purchasing power from the private sector to the public sector does not have second-round effects on income distribution, ideally we need not assume as well that the government simply provides the same goods and services that individuals would have bought for themselves in the absence of the tax–expenditure operation. Presumably some publicly provided services are close substitutes for private goods (police protection as opposed to locks and watchdogs), some are complementary to private goods (marinas and roads used by owners of boats and automobiles), and some might be effectively unrelated to the demands for private goods. Yet it has been the practice in all papers on balanced-budget incidence up to now to neglect the effects the provision of public services has upon private demand for the two products in the Harberger model. For example, McLure (1971a) has assumed for analytical convenience 'that government services are neither substitutes for nor complements to either product of the private sector...'.[39] A far more satisfactory approach would be to assume explicit relationships between demands for the public and private goods. We know, for example, that a tax on good x used to finance a given public service would raise the relative price of good x more if that private good were a complement to the public service than if it were a substitute. But it would be useful to investigate in a formal model just how the relationships between demands for public and private goods interact with the various other parameters in the model.[40] In a similar vein, we could examine the effects of public expenditures that tend to substitute for or be complementary to, one or the other of the factors of production. But we could not consider government capital formation without using a growth model.

6.3. Factor supply and mobility

As noted above, Mieszkowski (1972) has extended the Harberger analysis to a world with three factors, and Thirsk (1972) to a world with four factors. But there are surely additional useful results to be obtained. For example, assuming land to be immobile, the incidence of various taxes can be examined under the alternative assumptions that both labor and capital are mobile and that only one is mobile. A particularly straightforward application would be to assume that

---

[39]Krzyzaniak (1967, p. 474) goes even further by assuming (again for analytical convenience) that government spending is 'complete waste'. The author is indebted to Carl Shoup for pointing out to him that balanced-budget analysis cannot be truly general equilibrium analysis unless one considers explicitly the nature of the goods and services the government supplies and how their provision affects demands for private goods. See also Shoup (1969, p. 9).

[40]We know, after all, the relevant parameters of general equilibrium incidence analysis without using the Harberger model. Nevertheless, the Harberger model is a tremendous improvement over Wells' diagrammatic analysis (1955) because it allows us to understand the determinants of incidence in a particular situation better than the diagrammatic approach.

the mobile factors are used in fixed – but different – proportions in the two sectors. This allows use of well-known propositions about price relations in the two-by-two model without restricting analysis to only two factors. Beyond that, the three-factor analysis can be applied on the expenditure side. As always, the exigencies of policy situations should dictate the modifications and applications of the model.

Relaxing the assumption that labor is inelastic in supply poses no major problem. [See Mieszkowski (1972).] The supply of labor need only be made to depend upon the real wage rate net of tax. Income effects would result from any tax policy changing the real incomes of workers, including taxes on labor income, taxes on capital income (if workers receive capital income), and partial and general excise taxes. Substitution effects on work effort would result from any tax altering the real wage rate received by workers. The results of this analysis should be fairly straightforward modifications of the results for the fixed factor supply case and should affirm standard results for the effects of taxation on work effort.[41] Relaxing the assumption that saving is zero or insensitive to economic rewards is more involved and is considered in the next section.

6.4. Monopoly

In his seminal paper, Harberger (1962, pp. 238–240) considered the possibility that the corporate sector is characterized by constant mark-up pricing, and found the results little different from those for perfect competition, so far as the portion of the tax that applies to the normal return to capital is concerned. That portion that falls directly on monopoly profits is simply reflected in lower profits after tax. More generally, Mieszkowski (1969, pp. 1115–1116) has noted that, except insofar as the level of monopoly rents are concerned, the results for the competitive case are little affected by the existence of profit maximizing monopoly or by constant mark-up pricing.

Johnson and Mieszkowski (1970) in their analysis of union behavior, have laid the groundwork for the analysis of tax incidence in the case of monopoly in the labor market. But it should be recognized, that, strictly speaking, it is inadmissible to employ the Harberger specification of demand if a partial tax is levied in the context of a pre-existing distortion, such as mark-up pricing or unionization in one sector, even if differential (small change) analysis is employed. The problem is that in such a case excess burdens involve income losses that are not second-order effects, and it does not suffice to assume that all economic units have identical tastes at the margin. These first-order losses of welfare must be considered explicitly in the formulation of the demand equation. (But see

---

[41]See Musgrave (1959, ch. 11) for a provocative discussion of the effects taxes have on work effort. Of particular interest would be the effects on work effect of imposing excise taxes on goods complementary to leisure; see, for example, Corlett and Hague (1953–54), Harberger (1964), and the recent synthesis by Andersen (1972).

D

footnote 19 above on an alternative interpretation of demand conditions in the model.) Ballentine and Eris (1973) examine the monopoly mark-up case, taking account of income effects due to excess burdens.

Despite this problem, it seems as though fruitful theoretical analysis of taxation in a world of imperfect competition is possible. Several potentially valuable pieces of analysis can be indicated. First, it may be possible to examine the incidence of taxes in a world with profit maximizing monopolists and constrained sales maximizing monopolists in the context of the Harberger model. Second, the case of monopoly in the labor market probably has not been exhausted, and the case of monopsony in the labor market has not even been mentioned. Of course, as a practical matter there may be relatively little payoff to any of the extensions just mentioned, in that sufficiently small portions of the economy are effected that partial equilibrium analysis may be quite adequate. Finally, the possibilities for conscious use of tax policy by a political jurisdiction to maximize the welfare of its citizens – which is related to the tax exporting question and is essentially analogous to the optimum tariff problem – has also not been treated in the context of the Harberger model.

6.5. Non-constant elasticities and returns

Another kind of extension of the model involves modification of the production function. Though in its traditional form the model deals only with production functions characterized by constant elasticities of factor substitution, there is no real obstacle to using production functions not characterized by a constant elasticity of substitution.[42] However, this particular modification would be unimportant, so long as only differential analysis is used. On the other hand, if analysts move increasingly to adapt the model for the examination of finite changes, it might be worthwhile to consider cases in which both the elasticity of demand and the elasticities of factor substitution are variable.

The possibility of extending the model to include production functions not exhibiting constant returns to scale also deserves examination. Decreasing returns to scale should involve relatively minor problems, except that changes in profits would need to be accounted for, since the sum of factor payments falls short of the value of output in such a case, and profit would be a residual. On the other hand, increasing returns to scale would be more troublesome. For one thing, if factors are paid the value of their marginal products, the sum of factor payments exceeds the value of output in this case. Second, any industry operating under increasing returns to scale tends naturally to monopolization (or oligopoly), unless regulated or operated publicly (with a subsidy, if at an efficient level). Whether the model can be fruitfully adapted to apply to taxes on monopolists

---

[42]Similarly, there is no inherent reason to assume that the elasticity of demand with respect to relative product prices is constant.

6.6. Discrete changes and existing distortions

At several points it has been noted that the Harberger model is written formally in terms of differentials (infinitely small changes) and assumes (often implicitly) that there are no pre-existing taxes or other distortions. Thus, strictly speaking, it can legitimately be applied only to the analysis of infinitesimally small taxes (and expenditures) imposed in a zero-tax world. To use it to examine the effects of real world taxes, which in most interesting cases are imposed in the presence of other taxes and distortions and are far from 'small', is therefore risky.

The crucial problem involved in using the Harberger model to examine taxes imposed in a context of pre-existing distortions (which includes the analysis of taxes of discrete size) is that it is not valid to assume that in total there are no income effects, even if all economic units have identical marginal propensities to consume the two goods. One way of seeing this if there are taxes on x, y, K_x and K_y is to differentiate totally the following expression for national income:

$$xP_x + yP_y = LP_L + KP_K + K_x T_{Kx} + K_y T_{Ky} + xT_x + yT_y.$$

Thus,

$$xdP_x + ydP_y + P_x dx + P_y dy = LdP_L + KdP_K + P_K dK + P_L dL$$
$$+ K_x dT_{Kx} + T_{Kx} dK_x + K_y dT_{Ky} + T_{Ky} dK_y$$
$$+ xdT_x + T_x dx + ydT_y + T_y dy.$$

Making use of eqs. (5) – (10), we can rewrite the resulting expression as follows if there are no initial taxes or if $T_x = T_y$ and $T_{Kx} = T_{Ky}$:

$$P_x dx + P_y dy = 0.$$

This equation says that the Laspeyres index of real national income (i.e., using initial prices) is unchanged. But if we use the analogue of eqs. (5) and (6) for the case of initial taxes, we discover that this Laspeyres index is now

$$P_x dx + P_y dy = (T_{Kx} - T_{Ky}) dK_x + (T_x - T_y) dx,$$

where the term on the right-hand side of the equation is simply the excess burden of the differential tax on capital in x (relative to capital in y) or the differential excise tax on x. Thus, when taxes on x or K_x are raised, real income falls by the amount of the tax-induced excess burden, if $T_{Kx} > T_{Ky}$ or $T_x > T_y$, respectively.[43]

---
[43]I am grateful to Wayne Thirsk for this particular formulation of the problem.

Yet another more intuitive explanation of the problem utilizes fig. 1 in the partial equilibrium analysis of an excise tax imposed on a constant-cost industry. Consider the imposition of a specific excise of T_1 on each unit of output and the subsequent raising of the excise to T_2. Imposition of excise T_1 changes price, and quantity from P_0 and Q_0 to P_1 and Q_1. Excess burden equals $(P_1-P_0)(Q_0-Q_1)/2$ and is a second-order phenomenon for a 'small' tax. Raising of the excise further from T_1 to T_2 produces the price–quantity relations P_2, Q_2 and increases excess burden to $(Q_0-Q_2)(P_2-P_0)/2$, or by $[(P_2-P_0)+(P_1-P_0)]\,(Q_1-Q_2)/2$. This increase can be rewritten as $T_1\cdot(Q_1-Q_2)+(T_2-T_1)(Q_1-Q_2)/2$, which is *not* a second-order expression if T_1 is finite, even

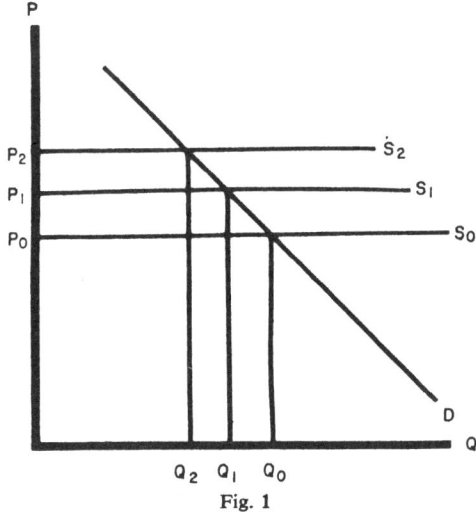

Fig. 1

if the change from T_1 to T_2 is 'small'. Thus if there are pre-existing distortions (such as the T_1 in this example or monopoly elements) and for finite taxes (in which case the 'last' 'small' tax change occurs in the presence of existing distortions, so that in total T_2 is 'large'), it is not admissible to ignore the income effects arising from excess burdens. See Harberger (1964) for a more detailed elaboration of the analysis presented here. Shoven and Whalley (1972) and Ballentine and Eris (1973) have also noted that the net income effect is zero only if there are initially no non-neutral taxes or other distortions and only for 'small' tax changes.

One upshot of this analysis is that excise taxes of discrete size have consumer excess burdens that must be taken into account. Even worse, in the complete mobility case, partial factor taxes (such as T_{Kx}) of finite size distort decisions as to optimal factor intensities and cause the transformation curve to be less concave to the origin, and they could even cause it to become convex. This kind of dead weight loss, which results from tax-induced production inside the production-possibility frontier, clearly cannot simply be ignored if a tax of discrete size is under consideration.[44] Moreover, a partial factor tax shares with an excise tax the distortion of consumption choices, but this distortion occurs along the already inefficient transformation curve.[45]

This distortion can be seen in fig. 2, in which the final consumption point chosen, A, is characterized by two kinds of distortion. First, the production possibility curve FF' has been moved toward the origin by the partial factor tax. In addition, relative product prices are distorted, even given the inferior production possibility curve, as shown by the intersection of the indifference curve and the cum-tax production-possibility curve at A. The marginal rate of substitution (MRS) does not equal the marginal rate of transformation (MRT) at A, as it does at B.

Further problems arise in using initial factor shares, factor intensities, factor endowments, consumption patterns, and prices for the numerical evaluation of effects of discrete taxes.[46] Nor can cum-tax values of those variables be employed, since we then have an index number problem as to which set of values is most suitable. What is needed, of course, is integration of the relevant differential equations over the range of the variables under consideration.[47]

---

[44]Thus one could reasonably question the kind of reasoning that allows Harberger (1966) and Boskin (1973) to calculate the excess burden of a given tax structure after having assumed that excess burden is small enough to be ignored. At the least, whether the calculated excess burden is in fact small enough to be ignored should be reexamined.

What seems to be one clear-cut error in analysis (aside from the common practice of using the equations for a local approximation to estimate effects of taxes of finite size) is to be found in Harberger's (1962) analysis of monopoly. Reasoning from analogy with the zero-distortion case, Harberger does not modify his demand equation to allow for the income effects caused by imposing a tax in the face of the pre-existing distortion caused by mark-up pricing. It would appear that this error resulted from Harberger's attempt to modify his analysis of the competitive case in a simple way so that he could deal with the monopoly case. But, as noted in footnote 19, Harberger has argued that his E is a reduced-form elasticity which subsumes such income effects due to excess burdens.

Mieszkowski and Johnson (1973) seem to make a similar error in their paper on unionization, since they refer repeatedly to *changes* in the degree of unionization. But a previous unpublished version of that paper (1967) and the calculations of the effects of unionization on relative prices make clear that in their mathematical model they are dealing with unionization occurring in a world without prior unionization. Of course, they are subject to the usual criticism of using the equations for a local approximation to calculate the effects of a distortion of discrete size. See Ballantine and Thirsk (1974) for a more complete discussion of these matters.

[45]In the case in which only one factor is mobile, a tax on the mobile factor in one use has exactly the same effects as an equal ad valorem tax on the product, except with regard to the immobile factor; see McLure (1969 and 1971a).

[46]Elasticities of demand and factor substitution may also vary over an interval in response to taxation.

[47]Krauss (1972) recognizes that factor shares may not be constant, as did Harberger (1962 and 1966). But the attempt by Krauss to deal with the problem is not wholly successful. He considers only how factor shares change over a discrete interval, since that affects the equal yield requirement for the comparison of an excise and a partial factor tax. He fails to note that the two equations to be integrated will vary over the interval of integration, as well.

Economists have only recently begun to examine the importance of the zero-tax starting point and the extent to which results for a differentially small tax (expenditure) fail, either qualitatively or quantitatively, to reflect accurately the results of a discrete tax (expenditure) change. Ballentine and Eris (1973) constitutes the only complete analysis of these problems to date in the public finance literature, though similar problems have been examined for several years by international trade theorists. [See, for example, Jones (1971), Magee (1971 and 1973)] Ballentine and Eris examine the validity of several general theoretical propositions and estimate the price effects and incidence of the corporation income tax, taking account of the usually neglected income effects.[48] Shoven and Whalley (1972) have, as noted before, employed an iterative approximation to overcome the limitations imposed by the linearity assumptions and ignoring

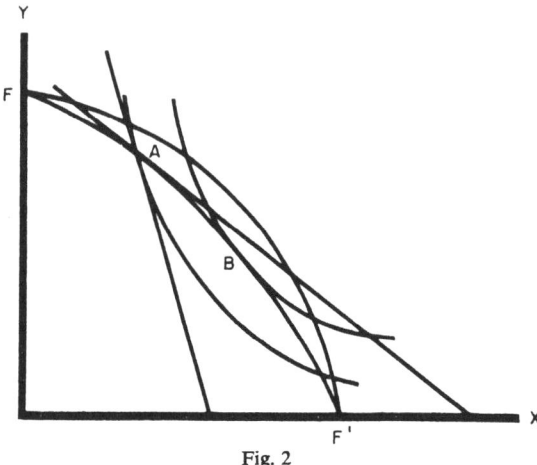

Fig. 2

[48]Ballentine and Eris' demand equation contains terms which are readily identified as the change in the Laspeyres index of real national income described earlier in this section.

In a paper that reached the author only after the present paper was essentially completed, Vandendorpe and Friedlaender (1973) examine the implications of allowing for the income effects, deadweight loss, and effects on the budget constraint that result when differential incidence analysis is undertaken for taxes levied in the context of preexisting distortions. Thus, although it utilizes the Jones model, rather than the Harberger model, and focusses upon the adjustments to tax rates that are necessary if real government spending is to be constant, rather than upon the deadweight loss of taxes, it duplicates some of the analysis of Ballentine and Eris (1973). One can question their assertion that the general equilibrium analysis of the Harberger model only re-affirms what we already knew from partial equilibrium analysis, and that the addition of income effects to the model is crucial. It is the message of sections 2.1 and 4.1 of this paper that one of the real contributions of general equilibrium analysis is the allowance for market interactions that partial equilibrium analysis places in the stockade of *ceteris paribus*. How important including excess burdens, income effects, etc. will be as a practical matter remains to be seen, it seems.

of income effects, as well as others. They find that Harberger's estimate of tax incidence does not differ drastically from their own, and that his estimate of the excess burden of the corporation income tax falls within their two estimates based on initial and cum-tax prices. But it is still too early to judge the extent to which the Harberger model will, as a practical matter, need to be altered for the estimation of the economic effects of taxes of discrete size in policy discussions. The answer to this important question is likely to be a fertile field for researchers over the next several years. Depending upon the outcome of the examination, the Harberger model as a policy tool may need to be modified in significant ways. If so, much of its simplicity is likely to be lost. Of course, there is no doubt that in theoretical discussions the qualifications necessary when analyzing finite taxes will increasingly be recognized.

7. Inadequacies of the model

Applied with care under the proper circumstances, the Harberger model can be an extremely useful tool of analysis. But there are several problems upon which this particular model is unlikely to shed much light. This section mentions two of these.

7.1. Compensatory setting

One set of problems that probably cannot be treated satisfactorily in the context of the Harberger model is that of incidence in a compensatory setting. [See Musgrave (1959, pp. 215–217).] At one level of sophistication, the Harberger model can be modified in a fairly straightforward way to include the possibilities of unemployment (by making wages downward rigid) and losses from inflation (by including initial endowments of assets and liabilities fixed in money terms). But unless the modifications are done quite carefully (e.g., to allow for behavioral response to expected inflation), they are likely to remain merely mechanical and rather artificial adaptations of the model and to offer no substantial insights. What is needed is a full-blown general equilibrium macro-model of tax incidence in a world in which both unemployment and inflation can occur, and can even occur together. For this the tax specialist will probably be forced to wait upon developments in the field of macroeconomics and upon the more complete integration of microeconomic and macroeconomic theory.

7.2. Saving and growth

The second kind of question the Harberger model probably cannot answer satisfactorily involves tax incidence in the context of capital accumulation and growth. Because the Harberger model is a comparative statics model based on the assumption that the capital stock is fixed, it is not well suited to questions of tax effects on capital formation and the long-run incidence of taxation, which require a dynamic analysis. For these problems a growth model, including a description of saving and investment, is needed.[49] Thus, it seems as though the tax specialist must have a triad of incidence models in his toolbox: (a) Marshallian partial equilibrium analysis for cases in which its use is warranted, (b) the Harberger general equilibrium analysis for cases in which partial equilibrium analysis will not suffice, but in which it is reasonable to ignore the effects of taxation upon capital accumulation, and (c) growth models of incidence for cases in which effects on capital accumulation cannot be ignored. It should be noted that whereas approaches (a) and (b) are intended to provide answers to the same question and can utilize basically the same general concepts, approach (c) involves a quite different question and different concepts of tax burdens, incidence, etc. For a discussion of some of these conceptual issues, see Krzyzaniak (1967).

A related problem involves the long-run effects of the creation of human capital and infrastructure through expenditures of the public sector. In this case government spending can be seen as changing the available amount of factor supplies or the production function of the economy over time. The Harberger model may give a rough idea of how this public investment expenditure affects income distribution in a comparative-statics framework. But for a truly satisfactory answer it is likely that the analysis should be conducted in the dynamic context of a model of economic growth.

8. Concluding remarks

Since this paper is itself a survey of the advantages and disadvantages and the past and prospective applications and extensions of the Harberger model, there is little to be gained from trying to summarize its contents. Nor is it necessary to dwell upon the author's belief that the Harberger model has been an extremely valuable contribution to the literature of economics in general and of public finance in particular. Suffice it to say that Arnold Harberger performed an invaluable service in cutting the Gordian knot that had effectively stymied economists attempting general equilibrium analysis of tax incidence. Once that

---

[49]See Mieszkowski (1969, pp. 1113–1114) for references to literature on the incidence of taxation in a growth context. Harberger (1962) has suggested that savings may be sufficiently insensitive to taxation to make the model useful even in the analysis of the long-run incidence of taxes. But this proposition is questionable at best. Finally, a referee has questioned the asymmetrical judgments made here about the ease of including the labor–leisure and saving–consumption choices in the model. He suggests that a third commodity, a durable capital good, could be introduced, with demand for it related to its price and the return to capital. This approach deserves attention. Though this cannot be known with certainty, in the absence of a detailed study of the issue, it seems likely that a satisfactory description of saving and investment would be more complicated than the analogous description of the labor–leisure choice mentioned above.

knot was cut, it was possible for others to begin to extend the analysis in various directions – many of which they have not yet followed very far. Thus the ten years following the 1962 appearance of Harberger's model have been most fruitful ones in the field of tax incidence analysis. And given the large number of potential extensions and applications of the model that remain, a few of which have been described briefly in this paper, it seems likely that the next ten years of work on the Harberger model will be equally productive.

Having said this, however, it is necessary to condition this high praise for the Harberger model with a healthy and respectful skepticism. The Harberger model is a simple, yet elegant description of the economy of neoclassical economics. And to the extent that the real world resembles the world of the neoclassical economist, the model is a useful guide to policy. But the world clearly contains a great many non-neoclassical elements, over and above those that have been mentioned above. The list of such elements is too long and too familiar to be recited here. But the user of the Harberger model must never forget those deviations from the neoclassical description of the economic world. He must constantly be ready to leaven the results flowing from his formal model to take account of what he knows about the world about him. This is not to say that the model is not an extremely useful analytical tool. It is to say that the model almost certainly does not describe the world exactly and that we can only err by assuming blindly that it does.

References

Aaron, H.J., 1972, Shelter and subsidies: Who benefits from Federal housing policies (Brookings Institution, Washington, D.C.).
Andersen, P.S., 1972, The optimum tax structure in a three good one consumer economy, Swedish Journal of Economics 74, 185–200.
Ballentine, J.G. and I. Eris, 1973, On the general equilibrium analysis of tax incidence, Discussion Paper no. 38 of the Program of Development Studies (Rice University, Houston, Texas).
Ballentine, J.G. and W.R. Thirsk, 1974, Labor unions and income distribution reconsidered, xeroxed (Rice University, Houston, Texas).
Bhagwati, J., 1964, The pure theory of international trade: A survey, Economic Journal 74, 1–84.
Boskin, M.J., 1973, Efficiency and equity aspects of the differential tax treatment of market and household economic activity, Memorandum no. 149 of the Center for Research in Economic Growth (Stanford University, Stanford, Calif.).
Break, G.F., forthcoming, Taxation (Brookings Institution, Washington, D.C.).
Brittain, J. A., 1972, The payroll tax for social security (Brookings Institution, Washington, D.C.).
Brown, H.G., 1939, The incidence of a general output or a general sales tax, Journal of Political Economy 47, 254–262.
Buchanan, J.M., 1960, La scienza delle finanze: The Italian tradition in fiscal theory, in: J.M. Buchanan, ed., Fiscal theory and political economy (University of North Carolina Press, Chapel Hill, N.C.) 24–74.
Corlett, W.J. and D.C. Hague, 1953–54, Complementarity and the excess burden of taxation, Review of Economic Studies 21, 21–30.
de Viti de Marco, A., 1936, First principles in public finance (Jonathan Cape, London).

Floyd, R.H., 1971, Domestic tax systems and the provisions of the general agreement on tariffs and trade: A theoretical analysis of their implications for economic efficiency, unpublished doctoral dissertation (Rice University, Houston, Texas).

Harberger, A.C., 1957, Some evidence on the international price mechanism, Journal of Political Economy 65, 506–521.

Harberger, A.C., 1962, The incidence of the corporation income tax, Journal of Political Economy 70, 215–240.

Harberger, A.C., 1964, Taxation, resource allocation, and welfare, in: J. Due, ed., The role of direct and indirect taxes in the federal revenue system (Princeton University Press, Princeton, N.J.) 25–131.

Harberger, A.C., 1966, Efficiency effects of taxes on income from capital, in: M. Krzyzaniak, ed., Effects of corporation income tax (Wayne State University Press, Detroit) 107–117.

Harberger, A.C., 1968, Taxation: Corporation income taxes, in: D.L. Sills, ed., International encyclopedia of the social sciences (New York) 538–545.

Hoffman, R., 1972, Disaggregation and calculations of the welfare cost of a tax, Journal of Political Economy 80, 409–417.

Jaskari, O.V., 1960, A study in the theory of incidence of taxation (Finnish Academy of Science, Helsinki).

Johnson, H.G., 1956, General equilibrium analysis of excise taxes, comment, American Economic Review 46, 151–156.

Johnson, H.G., 1971, The two sector model of general equilibrium (Aldine-Atherton Press, Chicago, Ill.).

Johnson, H.G. and P. Mieszkowski, 1967, The effects of unionization on the distribution of income, Cowles Foundation Prenumbered Paper 83102.

Johnson, H.G. and P. Mieszkowski, 1970, The effects of unionization on the distribution of income: A general equilibrium approach, Quarterly Journal of Economics 84, 539–561.

Jones, R.W., 1965, The structure of general equilibrium models, Journal of Political Economy 73, 557–572.

Jones, R.W., 1971, Distortions in factor markets and the general equilibrium model of production, Journal of Political Economy 79, 437–459.

Krauss, M., 1971, General equilibrium aspects of Canada's White Paper on tax reform, Canadian Journal of Economics 4, 256–263.

Krauss, M., 1972, Differential tax incidence: Large vs. small tax changes, Journal of Political Economy 80, 193–197.

Krauss, M.B. and H.G. Johnson, 1972, The theory of tax incidence: A diagrammatic analysis, Economica 39, 357–382.

Krzyzaniak, M., 1967, The long-run burden of a general tax on profits in a neoclassical world, Public Finance 22, 472–491.

Magee, S.P., 1971, Factor market distortions, production, distribution and the pure theory of international trade, Quarterly Journal of Economics 85, 623–643.

Magee, S.P., 1973, Factor market distortions, production and trade: A survey, Oxford Economic Papers 25, 1–43.

McLure, C.E., Jr., 1969, Interregional incidence of general regional taxes, Public Finance 24, 457–483.

McLure, C.E., Jr., 1970a, Taxation, substitution, and industrial location, Journal of Political Economy 78, 112–132.

McLure, C.E., Jr., 1970b, Tax incidence, macroeconomic policy, and absolute prices, Quarterly Journal of Economics 84, 254–267.

McLure, C.E., Jr., 1971a, The theory of tax incidence with imperfect factor mobility, Finanzarchiv 30, 27–48.

McLure, C.E., Jr., 1971b, The design of regional tax incentives for Colombia, in: M. Gillis, ed., Fiscal reform for Colombia (Harvard Law School, Cambridge, Mass.) 545–556.

McLure, C.E., Jr., 1972, The theory of expenditure incidence, Finanzarchiv 30, 432–453.

McLure, C.E. and W.R. Thirsk, 1973, A numerical exposition of the Harberger model of tax and expenditure incidence, Discussion Paper no. 48 of the Program of Development Studies (Rice University, Houston, Texas).

McLure, C.E., Jr., 1974, A diagrammatic exposition of the Harberger model, Journal of Political Economy 82, 56–82.

Meade, J.E., 1955, Mathematical supplement to trade and welfare (Oxford University Press, Oxford).

Mieszkowski, P.M., 1966, The comparative efficiency of tariffs and other tax–subsidy schemes as a means of obtaining revenue or protecting domestic production, Journal of Political Economy 74, 587–599.

Mieszkowski, P.M., 1967, On the theory of tax incidence, Journal of Political Economy 75, 250–262.

Mieszkowski, P.M., 1969, Tax incidence theory: The effects of taxes on the distribution of income, Journal of Economic Literature 7, 1103–1124.

Mieszkowski, P.M., 1972, The property tax: An excise or a profits tax?, Journal of Public Economics 1, 73–96.

Musgrave, R.A., 1953a, General equilibrium aspects of incidence theory, American Economic Review 43, 504–517.

Musgrave, R.A., 1953b, On incidence, Journal of Political Economy 61, 306–323.

Musgrave, R.A., 1959, The theory of public finance (McGraw-Hill, New York).

Rolph, E.R., 1954, The theory of fiscal economics (University of California Press, Berkeley, Calif.).

Shepard, R.W., 1944, A mathematical theory of the incidence of taxation, Econometrica 12, 1–18.

Shoup, C.S., 1969, Public finance (Aldine, Chicago, Ill.).

Shoven, J.B. and J. Whalley, 1972, A general equilibrium calculation of the effects of differential taxation of income from capital in the U.S., Journal of Public Economics 1, 281–321.

Stolper, W.F. and P.A. Samuelson, 1941, Protection and real wages, Review of Economic Studies 9, 58–73.

Thirsk, W., 1972, The economics of farm mechanization in Colombia, unpublished doctoral dissertation (Yale University, New Haven, Conn.).

Vandendorpe, A.L. and A.F. Friedlaender, 1973, Differential incidence and distorting taxes in a static general equilibrium framework, Working Paper no. 46 (Boston College, Chestnut Hill, Mass.).

Wells, P., 1955, General equilibrium analysis of excise taxes, American Economic Review 45, 345–359.

[5]

In this article we analyze taxation using the conjectural variations model of oligopoly. We demonstrate the way in which the incidence of a tax depends on the pattern of firm interaction. The results obtained have important implications for the controversy surrounding the question of whether a tax on corporate income can be overshifted. We also study normative aspects of taxation. The focus here is on the errors that can arise in excess burden calculations when incorrect assumptions on market structure are made.

TAX ANALYSIS IN AN OLIGOPOLY MODEL

MICHAEL L. KATZ
HARVEY S. ROSEN
Princeton University

Taxation usually is studied in models that postulate a perfectly competitive market structure.[1] Analyses that deviate from this rule tend to focus on the opposite polar case of monopoly. Given that the "in-between" situation—oligopoly—is of major importance in Western industrial countries, it might appear surprising that oligopoly has received such scant attention. Of course, at least as far back as Musgrave (1959) it has been recognized that the impact of a tax may depend on market structure. There is no definite model of oligopolistic behavior, however, and different stories can have quite different implications for tax shifting. The tendency has been to ignore oligopoly on the grounds that either "anything can happen," so that formal analysis yields no insights, or oligopoly falls somewhere in between the polar cases of monopoly and perfect competition and, thus, no new analysis is needed. In this article we attempt to counter both of these claims.

Any model of industry behavior must specify both the nature of entry into the industry and the form of interaction among existing firms. We examine a market into which entry by new firms is blocked and in which the incumbent producers interact

AUTHORS' NOTE: *We are grateful to two referees for useful comments.*

with one another according to the well-known conjectural variations model. Although the conjectural variations model is not the unique solution to the oligopoly problem, it allows us to study a wide variety of firm interactions, ranging from price-taking to joint-profit maximization.[2] Thus, this model provides a simple and useful analytical framework with which to examine the ways that the nature of oligopolistic interaction influences the incidence and efficiency consequence of a tax.

Using this framework we examine the effects of taxation on after-tax industry profits. We demonstrate that oligopoly does not fall between perfect competition and monopoly. For nonpathological cases, taxation may raise industry after-tax profits, a result that never arises under either perfect competition or monopoly in the long run. The intuition behind this result is the following: The firms in the industry would like to achieve the joint-profit maximizing, or cartel, outcome. This outcome may not be sustainable, however, due to each firm's incentives to increase its output and thus earn greater profits for itself at the expense of other firms. The firm's incentives to cheat by expanding its level of output depend on its marginal revenue and marginal cost schedules. A tax that in effect raises marginal costs induces firms to reduce their level of output, moving the oligopolistic equilibrium closer to the cartel level of output and raising before-tax profits. This increase in before-tax profits may exceed the level of tax revenues collected, with the result that after-tax profits are increased by the tax.

This result cannot arise in the long run for a perfectly competitive market because free entry will drive profits to zero. When the market is monopolized the single producer is able to attain the profit-maximizing level of industry output; the imposition of a tax can only lower before-tax and, hence, after-tax profits.

Note that there is nothing within this story that is peculiar to any particular model of oligopolistic behavior. Specifically, although our formal analysis is conducted within the simple framework provided by the conjectural variations model, there is every reason to believe that the basic results carry over to other models of oligopoly.

In the next section we review the essential aspects of the conjectural variations model. The following section shows how an industry's output, price, and profits are affected by the presence of a factor or output tax. It is demonstrated that, under quite reasonable conditions, the imposition of a tax can lead to an increase in industry profits. We explore the way that this result depends on the industry's tax and cost structures. Using a similar model, Seade [1983] provides an elegant and extensive analysis of the demand conditions required for overshifting under the assumption of linear costs. We also discuss the normative analysis of taxation in a conjectural variations model. Our focus here is on the errors that can arise in excess burden calculations when incorrect assumptions on market structure are made. We show that these errors can be quite substantial. In the final section we summarize our results and discuss some implications for future research.

A CONJECTURAL VARIATIONS MODEL OF OLIGOPOLY

Consider an industry comprising n firms producing a homogeneous product with a market inverse demand function $P[\cdot]$. Firm i produces x_i units of output and incurs costs $C[x_i, t]$, where t is a tax parameter. The firm's profits are as follows:

$$\Pi^i[x_i] = P\left[x_i + \sum_{j \neq i} x_j\right] x_i - C[x_i, t] \qquad [2.1]$$

A given firm's output decision will depend upon its expectations concerning the response of its rivals to any change in the firm's level of production. We assume that all firms have identical "conjectural variations" equal to δ. That is, each firm believes that when it raises its outputs by Δx_i, the other firms will raise their output by a total of $\delta \Delta x_i$:

$$\left[\frac{d \sum_{j \neq i} x_j}{dx_i}\right]^{con} \equiv \delta \qquad [2.2]$$

where the superscript "con" denotes that it is the conjectured rather than actual response.

Suppose that firm i's current level of output is x_i^o, and the rest of the industry produces

$$\sum_{j \neq i} x_j^o.$$

Firm i's conjectured inverse demand function, $P^{con}[\cdot]$, gives the price that the firm perceives will be associated with each level of its output, conditional on the current levels of its output and the total output of the other firms:

$$P^{con}\left[x_i; x_i^o, \sum_{j \neq i} x_j^o\right] \equiv P\left[x_i + \sum_{j \neq i} x_j^o + \delta(x_i - x_i^o)\right] \quad [2.3]$$

Each firm sets its level of output to maximize its profits, taking $P^{con}[\cdot]$ as the inverse demand function. The first order conditions state that each firm's conjectured change in profits due to a change in its output is equal to zero:

$$0 = \left[\frac{d\Pi^i}{dx_i}\right]^{con} = P\left[x_i + \sum_{j \neq i} x_j\right]$$

$$+ (1 + \delta)P'\left[x_i + \sum_{j \neq i} x_j\right]x_i - C_x[x_i, t] \quad [2.4]$$

The second order necessary condition for a firm's optimization problem is

$$0 \geq \left[\frac{d^2\Pi^i}{dx_i^2}\right]^{con} = 2(1 + \delta)P'\left[x_i + \sum_{j \neq i} x_j\right]$$

$$+ (1 + \delta)^2 P''\left[x_i + \sum_{j \neq i} x_j\right]x_i - C_{xx}[x_i, t] \quad [2.5]$$

Because all firms have identical cost functions, we will restrict our attention to symmetric equilibria (i.e., those equilibria in which $x_i = x$ for all firms).[3] Thus, the firms' necessary conditions, equations 2.3 and 2.4 yield the following equilibrium conditions:

$$P[nx] + (1 + \delta)P'[nx]x - C_x[x,t] = 0 \qquad [2.6]$$

and

$$2(1 + \delta)P'[nx] + (1 + \delta)^2 P''[nx]x - C_{xx}[x,t] \leq 0 \qquad [2.7]$$

The equilibrium level of output depends on the number of firms, the conjectural variation, and the level of taxes.

This framework affords great flexibility in modelling firm behavior and the degree of competition within the industry. If $\delta = -1$, for example, each firm believes that if it contracts its output by one unit in an effort to raise price, other firms will expand by an equal amount, leaving the market price unchanged. Firms will behave as price takers. Equation 2.6, the equilibrium condition, becomes

$$P[nx] - C_x[x,t] = 0$$

and each firm will set its output at a level at which price is equal to marginal cost.

At the other extreme, if $\delta = n - 1$, each firm has a conjectured inverse demand curve that is $1/n$ of the industry curve, and each firm believes that it will receive $1/n$ of total industry profits. Hence, the firms will behave like a joint profit maximizing cartel.[4] The equilibrium is characterized by

$$P[nx] + nxP'[nx] - C_x[x,t] = 0 \qquad [2.8]$$

the monopoly condition that market marginal revenue equals marginal cost.

THE OUTPUT AND PROFIT EFFECTS OF TAX CHANGES

A shift in the tax parameter that affects marginal costs generally will induce changes in the equilibrium levels of price, output, and profits. In this section we derive comparative statics results for an infinitesimal tax change.

To derive these comparative statics, we totally differentiate the equilibrium condition,[5] equation 2.6, which yields

$$\{(n+1+\delta)P'[nx] + (1+\delta)P''[nx]nx - C_{xx}[x,t]\}dx$$

$$- C_{xt}[x,t]dt = 0$$

Rearranging terms,[6]

$$\frac{dx}{dt} = \frac{C_{xt}}{(n+1+\delta)P' + (1+\delta)nxP'' - C_{xx}} \qquad [3.1]$$

Marginal costs are assumed to be a nondecreasing function of the level of taxes; $C_{xt} \geq 0$. Local stability of the equilibrium implies that the denominator of equation 3.1 is negative. Thus, dx/dt is negative. An increase in t leads to a fall in output and an increase in the market price.

The tax change has two effects on profits: It induces shifts in price and output that change the level of before-tax profits; and it alters the level of per-firm tax payments.

Algebraically, the change in profits is given by the following:

$$(P-C_x)\frac{dx_i}{dt} + x_i\frac{dP}{dt} - C_t = \{P - C_x + nxP'\}\frac{dx}{dt} - C_t \qquad [3.2]$$

where we have used the equilibrium condition equation 2.6 and the fact that the equilibrium is symmetric.

The first term on the right-hand side of equation 3.2 represents the change in before-tax profits, and the second term is the increase in tax payments. Comparing equations 2.6 and 3.2, we see that the change in before-tax profits due to a tax increase is zero for $\delta = n - 1$ and positive for all $\delta < n - 1$.

The intuition behind this result is the following: When $\delta = n - 1$, the oligopolists behave like a cartel and x is set at the joint profit maximizing level; $d\Pi^i/dx = 0$. Hence, to the first order, the tax-induced change in output has no effect on before-tax profits. When $\delta < n-1$, the oligopolistic equilibrium entails a firm output level that is greater than the one at which joint profits are maximized: $d\Pi_i/dx < 0$. Thus, a tax increase that raises marginal costs and reduces the equilibrium level of output moves the industry toward the joint profit maximizing outcome. The tax-induced contraction of output leads to greater before-tax profits. Depending on the patterns of taxes, tastes, and technology, a tax increase may lead either to a fall or a rise in after-tax profits. The net effect cannot be known a priori.

The result that a tax increase may raise after-tax profits in an oligopoly model is neither a pathology nor an artifact of the particular model that we have used to illustrate it. When the firms behave noncooperatively and are not able to restrict output to the joint-profit maximizing level, there will be scope for a tax increase to induce a profitable output contraction. For particular forms of taxes, the change in after-tax profits may be positive or negative in any model of oligopoly in which the firms are not able to sustain the cartel output level. To see this point, consider two extreme types of taxes.

First, suppose that a per-firm lump sum tax is imposed. Such a tax will have no effect on firms' output incentives as long as the lump sum is smaller than before-tax profits. This tax has no output effect, but it does have a tax-revenue effect. Thus, before-tax profits will be unaffected by the tax, and after-tax profits will decline by the full amount of the tax.

Now consider a tax change at the opposite extreme, one that has an output effect, but has no tax revenue effect. Let $C(x;0)$ denote the no-tax cost function, and impose a tax, $\hat{t}$, with the following form on each firm

$$C[x;\hat{t}] = \begin{cases} C[x;0] & x \leqslant \text{cartel output} \\ \infty & x > \text{cartel output} \end{cases}$$

Under this tax each firm will produce its share of the cartel output and will pay no taxes. The only effect is to enforce a collusive output restriction and, thus, raise after-tax profits.

Actual taxes fall somewhere between the two extremes above; tax revenues will be collected and output will be affected. Which effect dominates depends, in part, on the tax and cost structures. From equations 3.1 and 3.2 we see that $d\Pi^i/dt$ is greater than zero if and only if

$$\left\{\frac{P - C_x + nxP'}{(n+1+\delta)P' + (1+\delta)P'' - C_{xx}}\right\} C_{xt} - C_t > 0$$

As shown above, the term in curly brackets is positive. The larger is C_{xt} relative to C_t, therefore, the more likely is $d\Pi^i/dt > 0$. Intuitively, the output reduction effect (and, thus, the change in before-tax profits) depends on the change in marginal cost, C_{xt}. On the other hand, because the tax affects the costs of producing inframarginal units, the change in after-tax profits depends on the change in total costs, C_t. Thus, the tax is more likely to raise profits when it has a smaller effect on costs on average than at the margin.

We have seen that after-tax profits may rise or fall. A natural question is whether an increase in after-tax profits is plausible or is merely a theoretical curiosity. Economists often take linear demand curves and quadratic cost functions as approximations of actual demands and costs. When demands and costs have these forms, $d\Pi_i/dt$ may be positive for reasonable values of the parameters.

Suppose, for example, that the market inverse demand function is

$$P[nx] = 200 - 8(nx)$$

and each firm has a cost function

$$C[x,t] = w(1+t)x^2$$

where w is an index of factor prices. Such a cost function arises when the tax is levied proportionately on all factor prices and production is homogeneous of degree 1/2.[7] For the calculations, w was taken to be equal to 1 and t equal to zero.

	δ			
	-1	-.61	0	1
$X = 2x$	22.2	18.9	14.4	11.8
$P[2x]$	22.2	48.5	76.9	105.9
$C[x,t]$	123.5	89.6	59.2	34.6
π^i	123.5	369.7	532.6	588.2
$\frac{dX}{dt} = 2\frac{dx}{dt}$	-2.5	-1.8	-1.2	-0.7
$\frac{dP}{dt}$	19.7	14.3	9.5	5.5
$\frac{dC}{dt}$	123.5	89.6	59.2	34.6
$\frac{d\pi^i}{dt}$	96.0	19.7	-22.8	-34.6

Figure 1

Using equations 2.6, 3.1, and 3.2, the tax-induced changes in per-firm output and after-tax profits were calculated for a duopoly under several different conjectural variations. The results are presented in Figure 1. When $\delta = -1$, each firm sets its price equal to marginal cost; output is pushed beyond the joint profit maximizing level. Here, the increase in before-tax profits due to the output restriction dominates the increase in taxes; $d\Pi_i/dt > 0$. In this example, when firms have Cournot conjectures ($\delta = 0$), the direct effect of increased tax payments dominates; $d\Pi_i/dt < 0$. At $\delta = 1$, the duopolists act to maximize joint profits and the only effect of a tax rise on profits is the decrease due to the increase in tax payments.

Recently, several authors have analyzed the notion of "consistent" or "rational" conjectures. Firms are said to have consistent conjectures when, in equilibrium, the conjectured local responses are equal to the true responses. For the case of duopolists with quadratic costs and a linear demand curve, Bresnahan (1981) has developed a closed-form expression for the consistent value of δ. Applying his formula to our example, the consistent conjecture is approximately -0.61. For this conjecture $d\Pi^i/dt = 19.7 > 0$. Thus, the result that a tax increase can increase profits does not rely on irrationality on the part of firms, at least in this narrowly defined sense.[8]

Our example illustrates the shortcomings of attempting to analyze oligopoly by looking at the polar cases of monopoly and competition. As noted above, for monopoly before-tax profits are not increased by the tax-induced reduction in output, and $d\Pi^i/dt = -C_t < 0$. At the other pole, under perfect competition free entry leads to $d\Pi^i/dt = 0$. In some oligopolistic markets the change in profits due to a change in taxes is positive and does not fall between the values of $d\Pi^i/dt$ for the cases of monopoly and perfect competition.

This discussion of competition raises the question of entry in the present model. In our analysis we have taken the number of firms to be fixed exogenously. One may think of the model in two ways. First, it can be viewed as a short-run analysis of a market in which capital stocks are fixed. Second, it can be viewed as a long-run analysis of a market in which existing firms can adjust the levels of all productive inputs but sufficiently high barriers exist to preclude the entry of new firms. Krzyzaniak and Musgrave (1963: 2) suggested that a positive value of $d\Pi^i/dt$ was likely to be a short-run phenomenon, in the sense that it depended on the inability of firms to adjust their capital stocks. When there are barriers to entry, "overshifting" can occur in the long run as well.

WELFARE ANALYSIS

It is well-known that the presence of a preexisting distortion complicates the welfare analysis of a tax. Typically, monopoly is

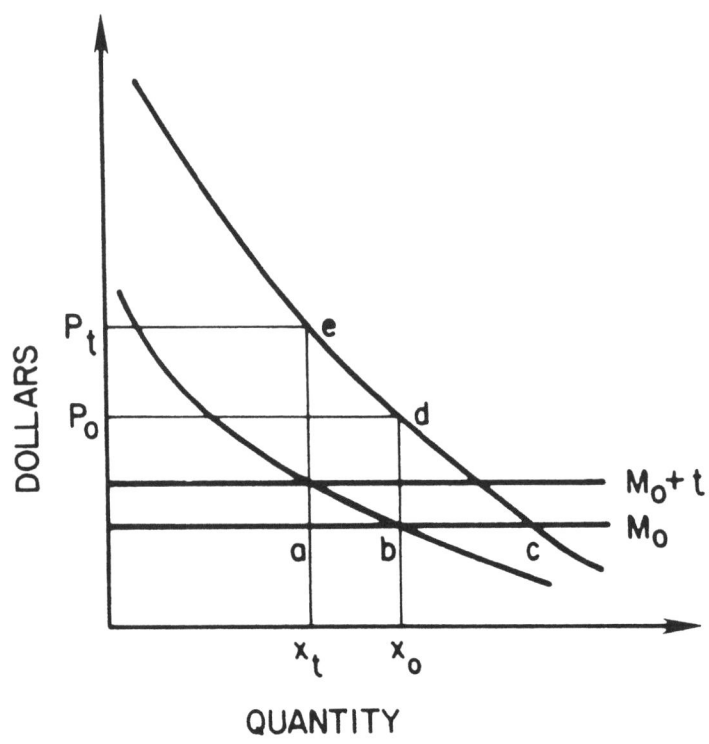

Figure 2

the only distortion induced by market structure that public finance economists study.[9] In this section we discuss the errors that might be made in estimating the incremental excess burden of a tax if one erroneously assumes that the firms behave as a perfect cartel, or monopolist, ($\delta = n - 1$) when in fact the oligopolists do not maximize joint profits ($\delta < n - 1$).

Consider an investigator who has the following information about an industry: It has constant marginal costs $C_x \equiv M_0$, price P_0, and market output X_0. The investigator notes that the industry is composed of several large firms, so that the competitive assumption is untenable. Instead, he assumes that the firms behave like a monopolist. A unit tax of t is imposed on the output of the industry. What is the incremental excess burden of the tax?

There are a number of ways to proceed. Our investigator might begin by using a diagram such as Figure 2, on which the horizontal axis measures industry output $X \equiv nx$. Conventional market demand and market marginal revenue curves are illustrated. The curves are sketched so that the marginal revenue curve intersects the marginal cost curve at X_0 and the associated price is P_0. Prior to imposition of the tax there is a monopoly excess burden of cbd that is a consequence of the fact that price exceeds marginal cost.[10] After the tax is imposed, price and output are P_t and X_t, respectively, and the incremental excess burden is abde.

Algebraically, the area abde can be approximated by the following:

$$abde \cong (P_0 - M_0) \left|\frac{dX}{dt}\right| \Delta t + \frac{1}{2} \left|\frac{dX}{dt}\frac{dP}{dt}\right|(\Delta t)^2$$

$$= (P_0 - M_0) \left|\frac{dX}{dt}\right| \Delta t + \frac{1}{2} \left|\frac{dP}{dX}\left(\frac{dX}{dt}\right)^2\right|(\Delta t)^2 \qquad [4.1]$$

where Δt is the change in the tax rate. Let us call the estimates of dP/dX and dX/dt made under the (incorrect) assumption of monopoly $d\hat{P}/dX$ and $d\hat{X}/dt$, respectively. A natural way to compute $d\hat{P}/dX$ is to manipulate equation 2.8, the first-order condition for the monopolist's equilibrium:

$$\frac{d\hat{P}}{dX} \equiv \hat{P}' = \frac{C_x - P}{X} \qquad [4.2]$$

Hence,

$$\hat{P}' = \frac{M_0 - P_0}{X_0}$$

The next step is to compute dX/dt. Under the monopoly assumption this is found by substituting $\delta = n - 1$ in equation 3.1:

$$\frac{d\hat{X}}{dt} = \frac{n}{2n\hat{P}' + nX\hat{P}''} = \frac{1}{2\hat{P}' + X\hat{P}''} \qquad [4.3]$$

where $\hat{P}''$ is the value of d^2P/dX^2 assumed by the investigator. Recall that $C_{xt} = 1$ and $C_{xx} = 0$.

In contrast, the correct value of dX/dt (from equation 3.1) is as follows:

$$\frac{dX}{dt} = \frac{n}{(n+1+\delta)P' + (1+\delta)XP''} \quad [4.4]$$

A comparison of equations 4.3 and 4.4 suggests that the investigator's belief that the industry behaves as a monopoly when actually it is a conjectural variation oligopoly leads to two errors.

First, there is an "econometric" error that results from using $\hat{P}'$ and $\hat{P}''$ instead of their true values. Specifically, from equation 2.6, the erroneous $\hat{P}'$ and the correct P' are related by the following:

$$\hat{P}' = \frac{1+\delta}{n} P' \quad [4.5]$$

Because $\delta < (n-1)$, $|\hat{P}'| < |P'|$. By incorrectly assuming monopoly, the investigator is lead to believe that the demand curve is (locally) flatter than it really is. Intuitively, the price-cost margin is driven below the cartel level by competition among firms, but the investigator attributes this low margin to demand being more elastic than it actually is.

As noted above, use of the incorrect value of the second derivative of the inverse demand function also contributes to the "econometric" error. However, unlike the case of the first derivative of the inverse demand curve, there is no necessary relationship between P'' and $\hat{P}''$.

The second problem is a "behavioral" error that is a consequence of using equation 4.3 to estimate how market output will respond to a tax increase. Note that even if the econometric error were eliminated so that correct values of P' and P'' were available, problems would still arise due to the use of equation 4.3 instead of equation 4.4.

In general, the direction of the bias introduced by the two errors cannot be determined a priori. However, in the important case in which both the actual and estimated demand curves are linear, the incorrect assumption of cartel behavior unambiguously leads to an overestimate (in absolute value) of the incremental excess burden. To see why, note that under linearity,

$$\frac{dX}{dt} = \frac{n}{(n+1+\delta)P'} \qquad [4.6]$$

and

$$\frac{d\hat{X}}{dt} = \frac{1}{2\hat{P}'} = \frac{1}{2\left(\frac{1+\delta}{n}\right)P'} = \frac{n}{2(1+\delta)P'} \qquad [4.7]$$

Because $\delta < n-1$, $|dX/dt| < |d\hat{X}/dt|$—the monopoly estimate of the tax-induced output reduction exceeds the true value. Therefore, the true value of the first term of the excess burden calculation, $(P_0 - M_0) dX/dt$, is less in absolute value than the erroneous monopoly value. Similarly, it can be shown that

$$\left| P' \left(\frac{dX}{dt}\right)^2 \right| < \left| \hat{P}' \left(\frac{d\hat{X}}{dt}\right)^2 \right|$$

so that the second term of the excess burden formula also is greater in the monopoly case.[11] Therefore, in the case of linear demand and constant marginal costs, the incorrect assumption of monopoly leads to overestimates of the incremental excess burden of a tax.

More generally, however, when P'' and $\hat{P}''$ are nonzero, $|dX/dt|$ may exceed $|d\hat{X}/dt|$.[12] Coupling this observation with the fact that $|P'| > |\hat{P}'|$, the estimated incremental excess burden (found by substituting $\hat{P}'$ and $d\hat{X}/dt$ into equation 4.1) can be less in absolute value than the actual. Ignoring market structure can lead to overestimates or underestimates of the incremental excess burden of a tax.

CONCLUSION

We have discussed some positive and normative aspects of taxation using a conjectural variations model of oligopoly. The assumption that an oligopolistic industry acts as if it is competitive or monopolistic can produce misleading results. For example, it is quite possible that a tax on a factor used by oligopolists will raise their economic profits, although this result never could arise in the polar cases. More generally, we have shown that impacts of a tax upon an oligopolistic industry need not lie between those of monopoly and competition.

In their famous econometric study published 20 years ago, Krzyzaniak and Musgrave (1963) asserted that there was a positive relationship between the corporate income tax rate and corporate profits. The finding was roundly attacked. Although our concern here is not the merits of their particular statistical procedure, other economists' comments on the theoretical plausibility of the result are of some interest. Cragg et al. (1969: 811-812) observed the following:

> Not only does this result run counter to most economists' judgments of plausibility, it also opens questions concerning the pricing behavior of corporations which have wide ramifications beyond the specific issue of corporation tax incidence. Indeed, it is certainly not far from the truth to say that if we accept the Krzyzaniak-Musgrave results at face value, we must also accept the task of rebuilding the foundations of the theory of the behavior of the firm.

We have shown that far from being outside the pale of economic theory, the Krzyzaniak-Musgrave result can be rationalized using fairly conventional neoclassical tools.

Since the time of the debate over the Krzyzaniak-Musgrave study, virtually all of the work on taxation has assumed perfect competition. Within this framework authors have studied the effects of alternative assumptions concerning production technologies and demand structures. General equilibrium responses have been carefully taken into account, as have been dynamic considerations.[13] Our results suggest that there might be a high payoff to analyzing models that are perhaps simpler along these dimensions but include a more realistic description of market behavior. For example, it could be instructive to fit a basic conjectural variations model to industry data.[14] The estimated coefficients could then be used to conduct positive and normative analyses of taxation along the lines suggested here. "Anything can happen" is not an excuse for ignoring the empirically important case of oligopoly in the study of tax policy.

NOTES

1. See, for example, the discussion of tax theory in Tresch (1981). Important exception are Stern (1982), who considers the problem of dual pricing in an oligopoly model, and Seade (1983).

2. The conjectural variations model is discussed by Bresnahan (1981) and Seade (1980).

3. Asymmetric equilibria may arise in cases in which a firm's profit function achieves its maximum at two distinct output levels. Hence, under the conventional assumption that each firm's profit function is strictly concave, only symmetric equilibria will exist.

4. Assuming that costs are convex.

5. Observe from equation 2.3 that each firm's conjectural demand curve depends upon the x_j^o's of the other firms, which will in equilibrium vary with the tax parameter. Hence, although δ is constant, the firm's conjectural demand curve generally will shift with changes in the tax parameter—it is not maintained that each firm believes that only it will respond to the tax.

6. Hereafter for the sake of clarity, we will suppress the arguments of the inverse demand and cost functions where there is no ambiguity.

7. A similar cost function can arise when only a subset of factors is taxed.

8. In general, the constant δ is a function of the tax rate. If we allow δ to adjust to a change in t, this adjustment only reinforces our result. Intuitively, the consistent conjectural variation increases with t, and a larger δ increases profits, ceteris paribus.

9. See, for example, Harberger (1974: 160-162).

10. It is assumed throughout that the structure of demand is such that consumer surplus measures provide good approximations to welfare changes.

11. Proof: Using equations 4.5, 4.6, and 4.7,

$$P'\left(\frac{d\hat{X}}{dt}\right)^2 - P'\left(\frac{dX}{dt}\right)^2 =$$

$$\frac{1}{P'}\left\{\frac{n}{4(1+\delta)} - \frac{n^2}{(n+1+\delta)^2}\right\} = \frac{1}{P'}\frac{n(n-1-\delta)^2}{4(1+\delta)(n+1+\delta)^2} < 0.$$

12. A necessary and sufficient condition for $\left|\frac{dX}{dt}\right| > \left|\frac{d\hat{X}}{dt}\right|$ is

$$\frac{1}{n}\left\{(n-1-\delta)P' + (1+\delta)XP'' - nX\hat{P}''\right\} > 0.$$

13. For some examples of the former, see Fullerton et al. (1978). For the latter, see Feldstein (1974).

14. See, for example, Gollop and Roberts (1979).

REFERENCES

BRESNAHAN, T. F. (1981) "Duopoly models with consistent conjectures." Amer. Econ. Rev. 71, 5: 934-945.

CRAGG, J. G., A. C. HARBERGER, and P. MIESZKOWSKI (1967) "Empirical evidence on the incidence of the corporation income tax." J. of Pol. Economy 75, 6: 811-821.

FELDSTEIN, M. S. (1974) "Tax incidence in a growing economy with variable factor supply." Q. J. of Economics 88: 551-573.

FULLERTON, D., J. B. SHOVEN, and J. WHALLEY (1978) "General equilibrium analysis of U.S. taxation policy," pp. 23-58 in 1978 Compendium of Tax Research. Washington, DC: Office of Tax Analysis, Department of the Treasury.

GOLLOP, F. M. and M. J. ROBERTS (1979) "Firm interdependence in oligopolistic models." J. of Econometrics 10: 313-331.

HARBERGER, A. C. (1974) "The incidence of the corporation income tax," pp. 135-162 in A. C. Harberger (ed.) Taxation and Welfare. Boston: Little, Brown.

KRZYZANIAK, M. and R. A. MUSGRAVE (1963) The Shifting of the Corporation Income Tax. Baltimore: Johns Hopkins Univ. Press.

MUSGRAVE, R. A. (1959) The Theory of Public Finance. New York: McGraw-Hill.

SEADE, J. (1983) "Prices, profits, and oligopoly." University of Warwick. (mimeo)

——— (1980) "On the effects of entry." Econometrica (March): 479-489.

STERN, N. (1982) Market Structure, Dual Pricing, and Taxes. Discussion Paper 13. University of Warwick.

TRESCH, R. W. (1981) Public Finance: A Normative Theory. Plano, TX: Business Publications.

Michael L. Katz is Assistant Professor of Economics at Princeton University. His research interests are in applied microeconomic theory, particularly the field of Industrial Organization.

Harvey S. Rosen is Professor of Economics at Princeton University and Research Associate at the National Bureau of Economic Research. His research focuses on theoretical and empirical issues in Public Finance.

[6]

THE ASSET PRICE APPROACH TO THE ANALYSIS OF CAPITAL INCOME TAXATION

LAWRENCE H. SUMMERS
Harvard University
(Co-winner of the 1982 NTA-TIA Outstanding Doctoral Dissertation Award)

[*EDITOR'S NOTE: Because of prior commitments to the President's Council of Economic Advisors, this summary was not available for publication in the PROCEEDINGS OF THE SEVENTY-FIFTH ANNUAL CONFERENCE (1982).*]

This paper summarizes and attempts to place in a broader context my recent research directed at developing an asset price approach to the analysis of the effects of capital income taxation.[1] The link between asset markets and real investment decisions has been an important theme of much recent research in macroeconomics dating at least from Tobin's seminal q theory of investment. However, asset markets have been subordinate in most previous theoretical and empirical efforts to model the effects of capital income taxation on economic behavior. Although changes in asset prices are the proximate determinants of who gains and loses following tax reforms, asset markets are suppressed in standard models used to study tax incidence.

A recurring theme in much of the empirical work described here is the effect of inflation on the tax system. Empirical work on the macroeconomic effects of tax reforms has always been difficult because of the paucity of statutory changes. In this limited respect, inflation has been salutary, because its frequent increases during the 1970's and recent sharp decreases have significantly altered the effective taxation of real income because of nominal accounting practices. Indeed, it is fair to say that most of the variation in tax rates on corporate capital over the last two decades can be traced to the effects of inflation.

Beyond its scientific interest, an analysis of capital income taxation and particularly its interactions with inflation is highly pertinent in light of recent economic events. The inflationary decade of the 1970's witnessed important changes in traditional patterns of capital accumulation and valuation in the American economy. The real price of corporate capital relative to consumption goods declined by almost 50 percent. Almost as dramatic was the real appreciation in the relative price of owner-occupied housing and land. As a consequence of these changes, the relative value of the two principal forms of wealth in the economy changed by a factor of more than two. During late 1982, the rate of expected inflation fell very sharply, and the stock market rose very dramatically, while real housing prices remained relatively stable. These large changes in relative prices were reflected in movements in rates of investment. The growth rate of nonresidential business capital employed per man hour declined from 3.4 percent during the 1949–74 period to .2 percent during the 1976–80 interval, while the share of net investment devoted to residential capital rose significantly.

The first section of this paper describes in more detail what is meant by the asset price approach to capital income taxation and discusses its advantages for studying certain public finance questions.

The second section illustrates how the effects of tax reforms on both asset prices and investment can be estimated in a simple partial equilibrium setting. The third and final section of the paper summarizes research on the relationship between taxes and the pricing of capital assets and suggests directions for future research.

I. The Asset Price Approach

The asset price approach to capital income taxation provides a united framework in which three traditional issues in the analysis of capital income taxation can be addressed. These issues include the short-run effects of tax reforms on investment, their long-run effects on capital accumulation and growth and their effects on horizontal and vertical equity. The relationship between the asset price and traditional approaches to each of these issues is discussed below.

Taxation and Investment

Before discussing the advantages of focusing on asset prices in analyzing the effects of capital income taxes on investment, it is useful to review briefly more standard approaches to the problem. There exists a large literature attempting econometric evaluation of the effects of investment incentives.[2] This literature which is extensively summarized in Eisner and Chirinko (1980) is all based on extensions of the flexible accelerator approach to investment developed in the seminal work of Hall and Jorgenson (1967). These studies all model investment as an adjustment process to a desired capital stock. The desired capital stock is postulated to be a function of the past levels of real output and the cost of capital. Often, as in Jorgenson's work, theory is used to tightly constrain this function. As Eisner and Chirinko illustrate, there is room for substantial disagreement about these constraints and the specification of the cost of capital. Here I leave these issues aside, and consider two more fundamental problems with the use of flexible accelerator-type econometric investment equations to model the effects of investment incentives.

The major conceptual difficulty with flexible accelerator approaches is that they treat output as predetermined from the point of view of the firm's investment decision. The desired capital stock is chosen conditional on output rather than being simultaneously determined. This is an important problem. Presumably, government's reason for offering investment tax incentives is the belief that reductions in the cost of capital will raise the level of output firms desire to supply. This in turn leads to increased investment. It is difficult to imagine how investment incentives could be beneficial, if they have no impact on the level of output firms expect to produce. Yet this constraint is imposed *a priori* in studies using flexible accelerator approaches to model investment.

This objection is sometimes met by embedding equations of this type in large scale Keynesian models, and simulating the path of the economy, under alternative assumptions about tax policy. This approach brings with it all the well-known problems with such models. More importantly, it does not really meet the objection that meaningful evaluation of the effects of investment incentives requires analysis of their effects on the desired supply of output. In standard Keynesian models, output is demand determined with essentially no role left for the effects of policies on aggregate supply.

A second problem with flexible accelerator models is the treatment of expectations. Presumably the desired capital stock should be a "forward looking variable" depending on expectations about the future marginal product and cost of capital. Standard approaches assume that these variables can be adequately proxied by lagged values of output and the cost of capital. This seems implausible. Announced but not yet implemented tax policies will clearly have effects on the level of investment, but this possibility is precluded in standard investment equations. A second example is provided by changes in the production function through time. Flexible accelerator approaches typically assume that the marginal product of capital is a stable function of the capital output ratio. The substantial variation in observed rates of profit suggests that this assumption is unwarranted. These examples are merely illustrations of Robert Lucas's (1976) famous critique of standard large scale econometric models. In general, the estimated parameter will be complex combinations of underlying structural parameters, and the stochastic processes followed by policy and other exogenous variables. It is unlikely that the estimates will be stable from period to period, especially when policy rules are altered.

The asset price approach to analyzing the effects of capital taxation relied on here takes as its point of departure a different strand of the literature on investment. A number of authors including Eisner and Strotz (1963), Lucas (1967), Treadway (1968), and Abel (1980) have recognized the *ad-hoc* character of the delivery lags introduced in many models of investment, and developed models of investment in which costs of adjustment enter explicitly. In these models, the level of investment depends on the shadow price associated with the capital accumulation constraint. When the value of capital rises, firms are willing to incur more adjustment costs in order to rapidly increase their capital stock. As Hayashi's (1982) important paper demonstrates, these models of competitive firms facing adjustment costs, are under constant returns to scale assumptions, closely related to q investment models of the type pioneered by Tobin (1969). In models the rate of investment is a function of q, the ratio of the market value of the capital stock to its replacement cost. In fact, the observed q ratio can be used to infer the shadow price of capital goods in the model of a firm facing costs of adjustment.

These linkages are important because they imply that an asset price approach can avoid the difficulties with standard econometric evaluations of investment incentives which were considered above. When adjustment costs are introduced, it is possible to develop a meaningful theory of supply even for firms with constant returns to scale. In any given period, the firm will choose its desired level of output depending on its previous capital stock. The growth rate of the capital stock will depend on the return on capital investment. Thus the asset price approach is supply based and so can be used to evaluate the effects of investment incentives.

The link between the observable q ratio and the shadow price of capital in the firm's dynamic optimization problem also solves the problem of modelling expectations. The q ratio will summarize the expectations of future profitability and costs of capital on which investment depends. Thus it obviates the need to adopt complex procedure for estimating expectations about these future variables. The relationship between investment and q, is structural in the sense that it should be invariant with respect to changes in policy rules, depend only on technology. Therefore the asset price approach can be used to estimate the effects of policy announcements, and temporary measures, which are not susceptible to analysis using alternative econometric approaches.

Taxation and Capital Accumulation

The asset price approach also bears on the literature in public finance examining the long-run effects of capital income taxation on both the accumulation and allocation of capital, and the long-run efficiency and incidence implications of capital income taxation. This literature originating in Harberger's (1962) seminal paper on the corporate income tax has largely ignored the process of investment. The models employed are not well suited to analyzing the short and intermediate-run response of the economy to changes in tax policy since they assume that there are no costs of adjustment impeding the accumulation or reallocation of capital. As a consequence, sectoral marginal products of capital are always equated. This means that there is essentially no scope for variation in the asset price of existing capital goods.

The evident volatility of observed asset prices demonstrates the unrealism of the maintained assumption of instantaneous adjustment. In order for large relative price changes to occur, it is necessary that adjustment be slow so that divergences of the marginal product of capital and its cost endure. The asset price approach developed here provides a basis for explicitly estimating the extent of these adjustment costs and modeling more realistically the transition of the economy following tax changes.

Tax Incidence

The presence of large adjustment costs also has important implication for the analysis of the incidence of capital income taxation. The implausibility of standard models without adjustment costs may be seen by noting that they imply that corporate shareowners would not gain relative to homeowners from an equalization of the tax rates on residential and corporate capital. This is because the standard approach to tax incidence ignores an important aspect of the actual economy's response to such a tax change. In the short run, the price of existing corporate capital would rise, and of existing homes would fall, as investors adjusted their portfolios. The price changes would capitalize the expected present value of the effects of the tax reform on future returns, conferring windfall gains on the owners of corporate capital, and losses on homeowners. These price changes would act as signals to the suppliers of new capital, calling forth more plant and equipment and fewer homes, until their relative prices were again equated to their relative long-run marginal costs of production.

Because an essential step in the asset price approach is the estimation of the effects of tax reforms on the market valuation of existing assets, it is ideally suited for evaluating the short-run incidence of tax policy changes. Such an analysis is important to evaluating the effects of tax reforms on both vertical and horizontal equity. Given information on the effects of tax reforms on asset prices, and the distribution of wealth holding, it is possible to evaluate the vertical equity effects of tax reforms. As Feldstein (1976) pointed out, horizontal equity is best achieved by avoiding reforms that give rise to windfall gains and losses.

The asset price approach also highlights the very different incidence of reforms that reduce taxes on all capital income and those which benefit only new investments. While appropriately chosen reforms of these two types may have an equal impact on investment, they are likely to have very different effects on existing wealthholders. Measures that reduce the tax burden on all capital are likely to substantially raise the market value of existing assets, conferring a windfall gain on the holders of existing assets. On the other hand, measures that subsidize only new capital may well actually reduce the wealth of owners of the existing capital which must compete with newly subsidized capital. These distinctions are not recognized within standard analyses which focus on the effects of tax policy changes on after tax rates of return but not on the value of existing assets.

II. The Dynamics of Investment and Market Valuation

The asset price approach to public finance and its implications for investment and market valuation can be illustrated in the context of simple stylized model. A more complex version of this framework is used in much of the research described in the next section.

The dynamics of investment and market valuation are considered in a model in which there is no inflation, capital does not depreciate, investment is financed through retained earnings, and the only tax is a proportional levy on corporate income. In this setting it is reasonable to assume that investment depends on the ratio of the market value of existing capital to its replacement cost. Unless an investment of one dollar increases the market value of the firm by more than one dollar, there is no reason to invest. Given the costs of adjustments and lags in recognition and implementation, there is no reason to expect that all investments that increase market value by more than their cost will be made immediately. As Tobin argued, these considerations lead to an investment equation of the form:

$$I = I\left(\frac{V}{K}\right)K \qquad (1)$$

$$I(1) = 0 \qquad I' > 0$$

where I represents gross investment and V/K is the q ratio of market value to replacement cost. Since inflation is assumed to be zero, the price of capital can be taken to be 1. The assumption that the ratio of I/K depends on q ensures that the growth rate of the capital stock is independent of the scale of the economy. It is important to recognize that the investment schedule given by equation (1) is a technological relation that depends on the adjustment cost function.

It is assumed that equity owners require a fixed real rate of return to induce them to hold the existing stock of equity. This return comes in the form of dividends—equal to after-tax profits minus retained earnings for new investment—and capital gains. Hence the condition,

$$\rho = \frac{\text{Div}}{V} + \frac{\dot{V}}{V} \qquad (2)$$

which implies:

$$\dot{V} = \rho V - (1 - \tau)F'(K)K + I\left(\frac{V}{K}\right)K, \qquad (3)$$

where τ is the corporate tax rate, and the production function, with labor input fixed, is given by F(K). Because it is assumed that the economy's fixed labor force is fully employed, the rate of profit, F'(K), declines as the capital stock increases. It will be convenient to examine the dynamics in terms of K and q. Equations 2 and 3 imply that the system's equations of motion are:

$$\dot{K} = I(q)K \qquad (4)$$

$$\dot{q} = [\rho - I(q)]q + I(q) - (1 - \tau)F'(K) \qquad (5)$$

The steady state properties of the model are easily found by imposing the conditions $\dot{K} = 0$ and $\dot{q} = 0$. These imply:

$$q = I^{-1}(0) = 1 \tag{6}$$

$$\rho = (1 - \tau)F'(K) \tag{7}$$

Equation 6 indicates that in the steady state, the value of q must equal 1 so that the market value of capital goods equals their replacement cost. Equation 7 indicates that, in equilibrium, firms equate their net marginal product of capital to the cost of capital. Inspection of 6 and 7 makes clear that a change in the corporate tax rate affects the steady-state capital stock but has no effect on steady-state q because the change does not influence the cost to the firm of acquiring new capital goods.

The dynamics of adjustment following a tax change are illustrated in Figure 1, a phase diagram representing equations 4 and 5. In the figure, the arrows depict the equations of motion of the system when it is not in equilibrium. The dark line represents the saddle-point path along which the system will converge to a steady state. A reduction in the corporate tax rate does not immediately affect the capital stock. The value of q jumps from E_1 to B, as shown in Figure 2. As capital is accumulated, the marginal product of capital falls and the system converges to E_2, where q is again equal to its equilibrium value. This path assumes that investors have perfect foresight and take account of the capital losses that occur as capital is accumulated. An alternative assumption is that the investors have myopic expectations and fail to foresee the effects of capital accumulation. In this case, the system jumps from E_1 to A and then converges to E_2 along the q = 0 schedule; along this transition path investors consistently earn less than their required rate of return.

An alternative type of tax reform benefits only new investment. Consider the introduction of a subsidy at rate s, a new investment. This reduces the effective purchase price of capital goods to firms. It also reduces corporate tax payments for any firm that invests. The effects of such a subsidy are displayed in Figure 3. Unambiguously, the steady state level of capital intensity increases. However, the short-run effect of the tax change on the market valuation of existing capital is unclear as illustrated in Figure 3.[3] There are two offsetting effects. The investment subsidy reduces tax payments tending to increase market valuation, but it also increases the competition for old capital tending to reduce the value

Dynamics of Investment and Market Valuation

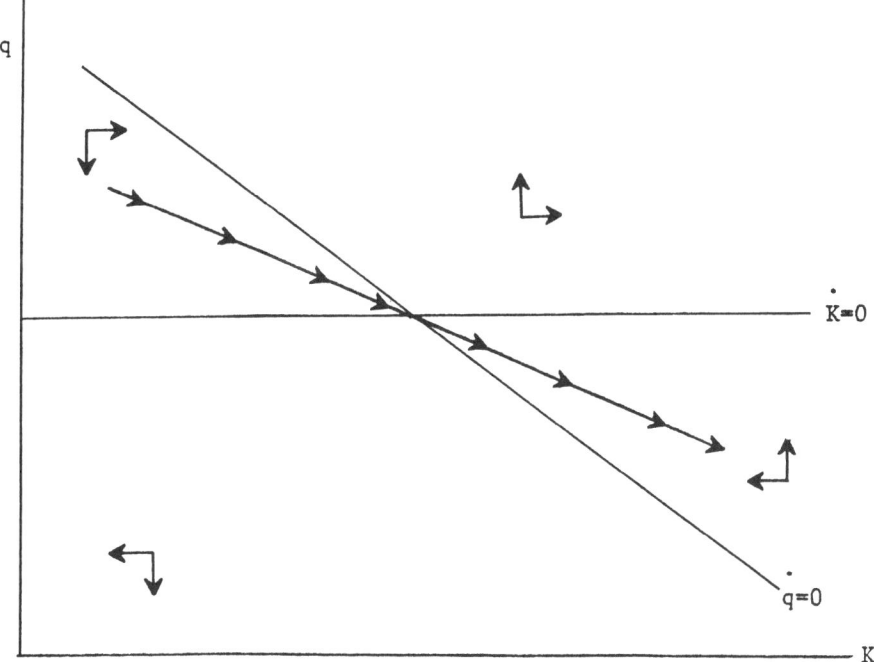

Figure 1

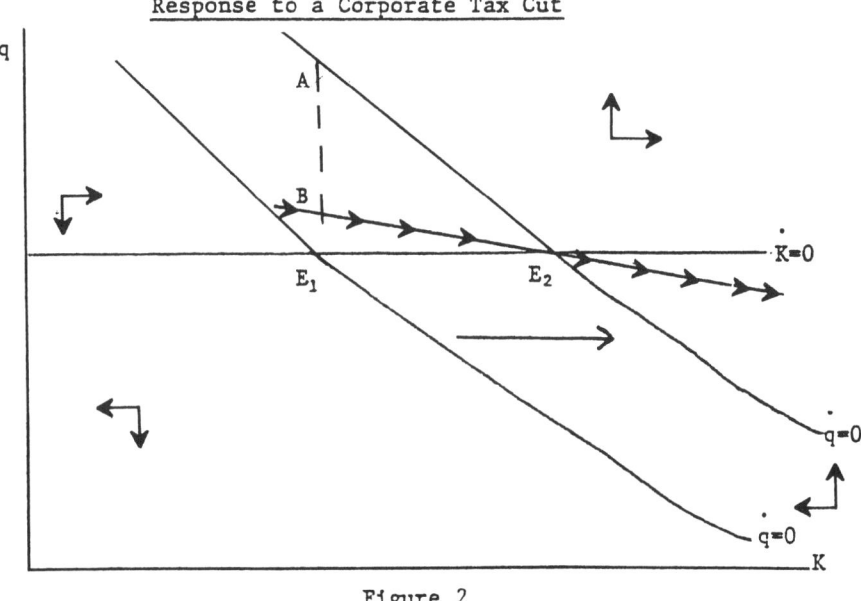

Figure 2

of existing capital. The crucial distinction between tax reforms which benefit all capital, and those which benefit only new capital, discussed in the previous section can be readily observed by comparing Figures 2 and 3.

This discussion illustrates the asset price approach to the analysis of tax policy in a particular simple context. Note that all that is necessary to evaluate the effects of implementing any given tax policy path, is knowledge of the profit function F(k) and the investment schedule I(q). Both are estimable from observable data and do not depend on commeasurable expectations. Given knowledge of these functions, equations (3) and (4), together with an initial condition on the capital stock and the terminal condition (6) can be used to calculate the evolution of V, K, and I. Formally, solution of a two-point boundary value problem is involved. While this can be difficult in models with multiple assets, Lipton, Poterba, Sachs, and Summers (1982) have developed an algorithm that can be used to solve problems of moderate size.

III. SUMMARY OF RESEARCH ON TAXATION AND ASSET PRICES

In Summers (1981),[4] I developed a q theory of investment. The linkage between the "average q" as measured on financial markets, and marginal q, the shadow price of investment in a dynamic model of firm investment decisions when adjustment is costly is established. The model considered is stochastic and includes a fairly detailed tax structure. The performance of standard q investment equations, and equations using a q variable which is adjusted for the effect of taxation, in explaining fluctuations in investment at both the firm and the aggregate level are then contrasted. The econometric results support the theory. The tax adjusted q variable outperforms the standard variable in explaining both aggregate and firm investment. These results are confirmed using data on individual firms in Salinger and Summers (1983).

The next stage in this research also described in Summers (1981) involves using these econometric results to calibrate a partial equilibrium simulation model capable of examining the effects of alternative tax reforms on investment and stock market valuation. The model used is partial equilibrium in the sense that it takes as exogenously fixed the real after tax rate of return required by equity investors. Results of simulations suggest that the interaction of inflation and the tax system can significantly reduce investment and the level of the stock market. The estimates suggest that indexation of the tax system would raise the stock market by about 20 percent and investment by about 15 percent. Various statutory tax reforms are then considered. The results suggest that measures directed at reducing capital gains

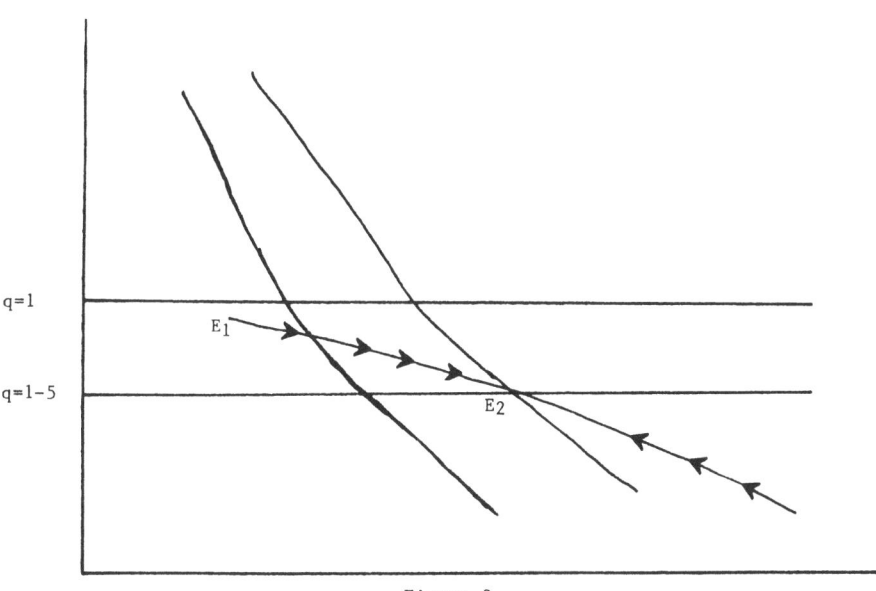

Figure 3

taxes and accelerating depreciation have the largest impact on investment per dollar of revenue foregone.

Summers (1982) takes a first step towards the construction of a general equilibrium model in which the effect of taxation on asset prices and investment can be studied.[5] The model incorporates owner-occupied housing and land as well as corporate capital. In the model, consumption is determined by intertemporal optimization. The model is designed to capture the wealth effects of fiscal policies which are ignored in standard models used in public finance. Three substantive conclusions emerge from the analysis. First, the supply of funds to the nonfinancial corporate sector is likely to be highly elastic so that tax policies will have relatively little impact on required rate of return. Second, indexation of the tax system would generate significant windfall gains for equity owners and stimulate corporate investment. Large losses would be suffered by bond owners. Home owners and landowners would also lose as portfolio reallocations towards corporate capital reduced the value of their investment. Third, the form of tax incentives has a major impact. The elimination of the corporate income tax, and the implementation of an accelerated depreciation program like that recently enacted, have similar effects on long-run corporate capital intensity. However, they have very different effects on the stock market in the short-run. The former measure raises the value of the market by about 80 percent relative to the latter. The consumption caused by the greater increase in wealth leads to higher interest rates, so the crowding out effects of eliminating corporate taxes are much greater than those of instituting accelerated depreciation.

The research described so far is directed at developing estimates of the effects of tax reforms; assuming the validity of the assumptions underlying the asset price approach. A major virtue of working with asset price information is that it can be used to provide tests of alternative models of the effects of tax changes.

Microeconomic tests of the asset price model are presented in Summers (1981).[6] The tests rely on differences between the firms in the tax effects on inflation. The "tax effects" hypothesis predicts that high leverage firms, using LIFO inventory accounting, for which depreciaton is a small part of cash flow, should benefit from increases in inflation relative to firms with opposing characteristics. The "inflation illusion" view of Modigliani and Cohn, has the opposite implications. These hypotheses are tested using a sample of 1,200 firms drawn from the compustat tapes. The econometric results are generally favorable to the tax effects hypothesis. The data suggest that FIFO firms lose substantially from inflation, relative to others. Highly levered firms appear to benefit from inflation. The evidence on depreciation is more mixed, with the results suggesting that inflation illusion was present in the 1960's but had almost vanished by the late 1970's. The cross-sectional results are then used to try to explain the disastrous performance of the market during the 1970's. I conclude that tax effects can explain about a 15 percent decline, with another 25 percent potentially attributable to increasing awareness of the need to adjust reported historic cost depreciation.

The adjustment of nominal interest rates to changes in expected inflation plays a critical role in any analysis of inflation-tax interactions. This issue is taken up in Summers (1982b).[7] A simple general equilibrium model in which the effects of taxation on the Fisher relationship can be studied is developed. Theoretical analysis with almost any plausible parameter values suggests that in the presence of taxes, steady inflation should raise nominal interest rates by more than point for point. Theoretical analysis does not identify the short-run relationship between interest rates and inflation, which depends on the sources of stochastic shocks. Standard econometric procedures are therefore not well suited to testing the predictions of the model. Tests of the Fisher relationship are presented which use band-spectrum regression to filter out high frequency movements in the variables. The results are disappointing in suggesting the failure of nominal interest rates to adjust for inflation as fully as theory would predict. This conclusion is robust, holding over 120 years of American data. The possibility that the failure of interest rates to rise with inflation, is the result of correlation between inflation and measures of either the marginal product of capital or the measures of risk is considered and rejected. The possibility that financial markets exhibit inflation illusion is entertained tentatively.

Recognition of the importance of changes in asset prices has crucial implications for the analysis of the effects of taxation of risky assets. Bulow and Summers (1982) demonstrate that previous analyses which have typically assumed that depreciation rates are constant and that the future price of capital goods is known with certainty are very misleading as guides to the effects of corporate taxes. In an environment where asset prices are variable, the concept of economic depreciation requires careful definition. We show that an appropriate *ex ante* depreciation schedule depends on future asset price risk. Some empirical calculations suggest that the appropriate adjustments for risk are large and greatly affect the estimated burden of the corporate income tax.

Data on asset prices can also be used to test alternative hypotheses regarding corporate financial policy. Poterba and Summers (1983) exploit the substantial variations in British dividend taxation that have occurred over the last 30 years, to contract the "tax capitalization" and "traditional" models of the effects of dividend taxation. The tests rely on the specification of investment equations based on alternative specifications of "tax adjusted q" variable.

Asset prices can also be used to study questions in other areas of public finance. Rosen (1982) uses information on housing prices to assess the effects of California's Proposition 13 on individual localities. Potentially this approach could be extended to consider other types of governmental spending programs. These might include agricultural measures whose incidence is reflected in changes in the price of farm land, and direct or indirect subsidies to industries which affect stock prices. The research described here illustrates two propositions. First, the effect of tax policies on asset prices can be estimated and used to measure their incidence. Second, asset price data can be used to answer otherwise very difficult empirical questions in public finance. Future research on the issues mentioned here and others will contribute to our understanding of the effects of the functioning of taxation on our economy.

Footnotes

[1] Much of this research was contained in my doctoral dissertation. It has also appeared in the various papers cited in the references and will ultimately appear in my forthcoming book.

[2] While the discussion here focuses on corporate investment incentives, it is more widely applicable. The flexible accelerator approach criticised here is a standard tool in analyses of housing investment.

[3] The figure is drawn for the case where the price of existing capital declines.

[4] The research described in the next two paragraphs is presented as Chapters 1 and 2 of my thesis.

[5] A version of this paper appears as Chapter 3 of my thesis.

[6] This work appears as Chapter 4 of my doctoral thesis.

[7] This work appears in Chapter 5 of my dissertation.

References

Abel, Andrews B., 1980, Empirical investment equations: An integrative framework, in: Karl Brunner and Alan H. Metzler, eds., *On the State of Macro-Economics*, Carnegie-Rochester Conference Series on Public Policy, 12 (Amsterdam: North Holland) 39–91.

Bulow, Jeremy I. and L. Summers, 1982, Risk and taxes reconsidered, mimeo.

Eisner, Robert and Robert Chirinko, 1980, Tax policy and business investment, unpublished.

Eisner, Robert and R. H. Strotz, 1963, Determinants of business investment, in Commission on Money and Credit, *Impacts of Monetary Policy* (Prentice-Hall, Englewood Cliffs, NJ) 59–337.

Feldstein, Martin, 1976, Toward a theory of tax reform, *Journal of Public Economics*. (need vol., mo., & pp.)

Hall, Robert E. and Dale W. Jorgenson, 1967, Tax policy and investment behavior, *American Economic Review* 57, June, 391–414.

Harberger, Arnold, 1962, The incidence of the corporation income tax, *Journal of Political Economy* (need vol., mo, pp.)

Hayashi, Fumio, 1982, Tobin's marginal q and average q: A neoclassical interpretation, *Econometrica* 50, Jan., 213–224.

Lipton, David and James Poterba, Jeffrey Sachs, Lawrence Summers, 1982, Multiple shooting in rational expectations models, *Econometrica*, Sept.

Lucas, Robert E., Jr., 1967a, Adjustment costs and the theory of supply, *Journal of Political Economy* 75, Aug., 321–334.

Lucas, Robert E., Jr., 1976, Econometric policy evaluation: A critique, ed., *The Phillips Curve and Labor Markets*, Carnegie-Rochester Conference Series on Public Policy, 1 (Amsterdam: North Holland) 19–46.

Poterba, James and Lawrence Summers, 1983, Dividend taxes, corporate investment and q, forthcoming, *Journal of Public Economics*.

Rosen, Kenneth T., 1982, The impact of proposition 13 on house prices in Northern California, *Journal of Political Economy*, Feb., 191.

Salinger, Michael and Lawrence Summers, 1983, Corporate tax reform and securities prices; A simulation approach, forthcoming in National Bureau of Economic Research Conference Volume on *Tax Simulation Analysis*.

Summers, Lawrence, 1981, Taxation and corporate investment: A q theory approach, *Brookings Papers on Economic Activity*, January, 67–127.

Summers, Lawrence, 1983, Taxation and asset prices in a general equilibrium model, unpublished.

Summers, Lawrence, 1983, The non-adjustment of nominal interest rates: A study of the Fisher effect, in: J. Tobin, ed., *Macroeconomics: Prices and quantities*, Brookings Institution, 201–247.

Summers, Lawrence, 1982, Inflation and the valuation of corporate equities, National Bureau of Economic Research Working Paper.

Tobin, James, 1969, A general equilibrium approach to monetary theory, *Journal of Money, Credit and Banking* 1, Feb., 15–29.

Treadway, Arthur B., 1969, On rational entrepreneurial behavior and the demand for investment, *Review of Economic Studies* 36, 227–239.

[7]

Some Calculations of Lifetime Tax Incidence

By James Davies, France St-Hilaire, and John Whalley*

This paper reports a set of lifetime tax incidence calculations using a life cycle simulation model for Canada due to Davies (1979a, 1982). A repeatedly stated qualification to annual calculations in the empirical tax incidence literature is that it would be more satisfactory to make calculations on a lifetime basis. Even though it is acknowledged that lifetime tax incidence could well differ from annual, it is widely believed that data and other difficulties make such calculations next to impossible. Indeed, the widespread acceptance of the data problems of lifetime calculations seems also to have inhibited speculation about how lifetime tax incidence might differ from annual. As a result, redistributive tax policy judgments continue to be based on annual incidence calculations in spite of the reservations many have about their usefulness. Our paper is intended to reorient discussion towards lifetime tax incidence by providing some initial null hypotheses about the shape of lifetime tax profiles.

Our main finding is that under the standard competitive assumptions common in the incidence literature, lifetime and annual incidence calculations both produce mild progression in tax rates across household deciles (ignoring the bottom decile in the annual calculation). While the income tax is less progressive in lifetime than in annual calculations, other taxes are for the most part less regressive. Also, lifetime incidence calculations are much more robust to alternative shifting assumptions than annual calculations. In the lifetime context, key distributions such as earnings, transfer payments, and consumption are less heavily concentrated in particular percentiles of the population than is true in annual data. As a result, changing the allocative series for any particular tax does not have the large effect on incidence results found in annual calculations.[1]

Each component of the tax system is allocated to households grouped by lifetime income using particular distributive series following a procedure similar to that employed in annual incidence calculations (for example, Richard Musgrave et al., 1974; Joseph Pechman and Benjamin Okner, 1974; Edgar Browning and William Johnson, 1979; W. Irwin Gillespie, 1980). In the process we are able to compare lifetime and annual incidence calculations using the same data set.

In both lifetime and annual calculations, we allocate five groups of taxes among households using distributive series which come partly from the 1971 Statistics Canada Survey of Consumer Finances (*SCF*) and partly from our life cycle simulation model. The *SCF* data are used to construct synthetic longitudinal lifetime profiles of earnings and transfer payments for a sample of 500 households. The latter are assigned inheritances by simulating patterns of mortality and bequest. These data are then used in the life cycle model to generate lifetime consumption profiles and bequests. The earnings, transfer, and inheritance data, plus the model output provide the distributive series on which alternative incidence calculations are based.

While the incidence calculations presented in this paper use Canadian data, results would likely be similar for the United States

---

*Department of Economics, University of Western Ontario, London, Canada N6A 5C2. We thank participants in workshops at McMaster University and the University of Western Ontario, as well as an anonymous referee, for useful comments. St-Hilaire and Whalley gratefully acknowledge financial support from the Social Sciences and Humanities Research Council of Canada.

[1] See St-Hilaire and Whalley (1982) for an investigation of the impact of changing incidence assumptions in annual tax incidence calculations. We note that several of the issues raised by St-Hilaire and Whalley, including the implications of the open economy and the treatment of human capital for tax incidence calculations, are not taken up in this paper. Lifetime calculations may well be sensitive to the way these are treated, and this should be explored in future work.

as is true of annual calculations (see St-Hilaire and Whalley, 1982). Relative to overall tax revenue, personal and corporate income taxes are of roughly the same importance in the two countries. The personal income tax in Canada has a flatter rate profile, less significant exemptions and deductions, and more extensive tax shelters than its U.S. counterpart (for example, mortgage interest is not deductible, but there are larger shelters for savings for retirement). Taxes levied by the provinces are relatively more important than those at state level in the United States. Finally, sales and excise taxes are higher than in the United States, but social security taxes are considerably lower. This latter feature produces an offsetting effect in standard incidence calculations where both taxes are largely regressive.

I. Annual Incidence Calculations and Lifetime Issues

A. *Annual Incidence Studies*

Tax incidence calculations which use annual data typically focus on five key taxes or tax groups: income, corporate, sales and excise, property, and social security. Each tax is treated as having sources (income) side and/or uses (expenditure) side effects for each group of households who, in turn, are usually stratified by income. Incidence calculations for whole tax systems use a separate tax burden calculation for each tax by income range. The overall redistributive effect of the tax system is usually evaluated by examining the pattern of combined average tax rates across income ranges.

Three main income sources—capital, labor, and transfer income—can bear the burden of taxes either singly or jointly. In annual data, transfers are heavily concentrated in the lower tail of the income distribution. Capital income is a relatively high proportion of total income in the upper tail, but also in the lower tail due to the presence of retirees. Labor income increases sharply as a fraction of total income for the bottom few deciles, but is approximately proportional to income for about 70 percent of the population. Thus, on the sources side, widely varying patterns of progressivity or regressivity can result depending upon whether a tax is allocated to capital, labor, or transfer income, or to income in general.

On the uses side, the strongest effects occur through differences in household saving rates. This is because a tax assumed to be forward shifted in higher prices is treated as borne by households out of consumption. In annual data, saving rates differ sharply by income range, with around 70 to 80 percent of household saving commonly concentrated in the top 10 percent of the income distribution.[2] Forward shifted taxes allocated to consumption are therefore regressive.

One of the most widely cited annual incidence studies is Pechman and Okner, which uses detailed merged data involving approximately 87,000 1966 U.S. income tax returns and 30,000 households appearing in a Survey of Economic Opportunity data file. Alternative incidence calculations are made using different shifting assumptions as to the burden of certain taxes. Their main conclusion is that "regardless of the incidence assumptions, the tax system is virtually proportional for the vast majority of families in the United States" (p. 64).[3] This, however, omits the bottom 10 and top 3 percent of the population (see Pechman and Okner, pp.

---

[2] St-Hilaire and Whalley (1983, Table 9, p. 195) indicates saving of the top decile of Canadian households in 1972 made up 73 percent of aggregate saving. Browning and Johnson (Table 18, p. 73) have a saving rate of 34.4 percent of disposable income for their top decile of 1974 U.S. households. From their Table 9 on page 56 it appears that the top decile would have had about 30 percent of aggregate disposable income. This implies a share of about 76 percent of aggregate saving.

[3] Musgrave et al. also report rough proportionality using assumptions close to Pechman and Okner's least progressive variant and a different data set. Gillespie (1980) obtains comparable results for Canada, and performs sensitivity analysis similar to that of Pechman-Okner. The similarity of results to the U.S. studies is obscured by the use of an income concept which excludes transfer payments. Excluding transfers significantly increases tax rates for bottom income groups, and tends to make the overall tax system appear regressive. When Gillespie's results are presented using an income base comparable to that of Pechman-Okner or Musgrave et al., the similarity in results is more evident. See either St-Hilaire and Whalley (1982, Table 1), or Gillespie (1976, Table A-7, p. 445).

5-6), which has an effect on the conclusions. In their most progressive variant, for example, where corporate and property taxes are borne by capital, the total effective tax rate for the bottom 10 percent is much lower than for other deciles and that for the top 3 percent far above average (see Tables 4.4 and 4.9 on pp. 51 and 61, respectively).

This "proportionality" view of overall tax incidence has been questioned in recent work by Browning (1978) and Browning and Johnson (1979). The main difference concerns the treatment of sales and excise taxes which are regressive in Pechman-Okner and progressive in Browning-Johnson. Browning and Johnson argue that uses side effects of sales and excise taxes due to different saving rates by income range are insignificant when consumption out of normal or permanent income is considered. They therefore only consider the sources side effects of sales and excise taxes, pointing out that since transfers are largely indexed for price level changes, only factor incomes can bear the burden of taxes. The concentration of transfers in the lower tail of the income distribution, and saving in the upper tail means that sales and excise taxes which appear as strongly regressive in Pechman-Okner are strongly progressive in Browning-Johnson.[4]

The incidence assumptions used in this literature are crucial to the extent of progressivity in results. The income tax is universally treated as paid by income recipients and is progressive. However, widely varying assumptions for other taxes are examined in the literature. Social security is treated either exclusively or predominantly as a payroll tax on labor and (outside of the lower tail of the income distribution) is regressive due to ceilings on contributions. Corporate and property taxes are regressive if treated as shifted forward onto consumption, but mainly progressive if assumed shifted backwards onto capital income.[5] Finally, sales and excise taxes are regressive if borne by consumers, and progressive if treated as borne by recipients of factor incomes. Depending on the combination of shifting assumptions the tax system can be made to appear regressive or progressive in annual calculations. (See St-Hilaire and Whalley, 1982.)

B. *Lifetime Incidence — Expected Contrasts with Annual Calculations*

Despite the extensive literature reporting annual incidence calculations, it is widely acknowledged that lifetime calculations would be preferable.[6] Data limitations are usually cited as precluding such an approach. (See, for example, Browning and Johnson, p. 81.) The lack of incidence calculations on a lifetime basis is especially unfortunate, since on a priori grounds there are several reasons to believe there may be significant differences between annual and lifetime incidence results. First, much of the observed inequality in earnings and transfer payments disappears when we examine lifetime rather than annual distributions. According to the estimates of Jacob Mincer (1974), Lee Lillard (1977), and Nils Blomqvist (1981), about one-half of annual earnings inequality (according to conventional measures) disappears when one looks at lifetime earnings.[7] Social security and other in-

---

[4]An intermediate case would ignore the indexation of transfers on the sources side but include consumption out of permanent income on the uses side. Sales and excise taxes may then have uses side effects arising from differing taxes on different consumer goods. See David Davies (1959) for an early study of sales and excise tax incidence that proceeds along these lines.

[5]Corporate taxes are more progressive if treated as borne by capital specific to taxed industries rather than capital in general, because of light tax treatment of widely held housing capital. In some of the literature, this observation motivates the use of dividends rather than capital income in general as a more progressive distributive series for allocating corporate taxes.

[6]See, for example, Browning and Johnson (pp. 24-26 and 80-84) and Anthony Atkinson and Joseph Stiglitz (1980, p. 286). Acknowledgement that lifetime calculations would be preferable is also implicit in the repeated argument that the uses side effects of sales and excise taxes should be evaluated on the basis of patterns of consumption out of permanent income. See, for example, D. Davies, and Pechman-Okner (pp. 52-55).

[7]Mincer (p. 119) argues that about half the log variance of earnings is attributable to transitory components and age-related differences. Lillard's panel evidence indicates a Gini coefficient for lifetime earnings about 25-40 percent below that in age-specific annual earnings (see p. 50). The short-fall below the annual Gini for all

come support payments, in particular, are much more equally distributed when examined on a lifetime rather than an annual basis. Lifetime transfers are therefore not concentrated chiefly in the hands of the poor as is true in annual data. These differences imply less progressivity of personal income taxes in the lifetime context. Also, with transfers less important and earnings more important in the bottom tail the significance of the indexation issue stressed by Browning and Johnson is weakened.

A second issue relevant to lifetime calculations is the treatment of capital income. This important element in annual incidence calculations is not part of a household's discounted lifetime income. It therefore cannot bear the burden of taxes on the sources side in the same way as in annual calculations since it is not part of the income base. As a result, a fundamentally different treatment of taxes thought to be borne by capital (for example, corporate, property) is required.

A third important difference between annual and lifetime calculations arises from the differing time profiles of taxes over the life cycle. Taxes on labor income, for example, are paid until retirement, but those on consumption are paid until death. Hence the relative lifetime importance of various taxes may differ significantly from their relative annual importance, due to the effect of discounting.

Finally, the profile of consumption as a proportion of income will differ considerably between annual and lifetime data. While there is reason to expect higher income groups to save a larger proportion of their lifetime resources for bequests, the lifetime profile of savings rates by income range ought to be much flatter than the annual. Therefore sales and excise taxes treated as borne by consumers should appear less regressive in the lifetime calculations. Also, switching the incidence assumption for corporate or property taxes from full burden on capital income to partial forward shifting should produce a less dramatic shift towards regressivity.

II. A Life Cycle Approach to Incidence Analysis

Later in the paper we report tax incidence calculations based on lifetime rather than annual data. Our approach is similar to that used in annual calculations in that we adopt alternative distributive series for the allocation of various taxes between household groups. The main differences are that distributive series are generated using lifetime rather than annual data, households are grouped by lifetime income, and taxes paid over the lifetime rather than in a single year are allocated.

Our distributive series rely on the data used in, and the output from, a micro-simulation model of life cycle saving and bequest behavior of Canadian households reported in Davies (1982). In Davies' model, each household includes a husband and wife who start economic life together at age 20 and die together at age 75.[8] Households are assigned realistic (exogenous) streams of earnings, transfer payments, and inheritances over the lifetime, as described below. The simulation generates lifetime paths of consumption and investment income which along with the lifetime income data provide the distributive series for our incidence calculations.

A. The Behavioral Model

Each household receives an exogenously determined stream of earnings, E_t, and government transfers, G_t (depending on age, t) over its lifetime. We refer to the sum of earnings and transfers as noninvestment income, N_t. Real interest before tax on wealth, W_t, is received at a constant rate, r, giving rise to investment income, $M_t = rW_t$. Annual

---

ages taken together would be higher. Finally, Blomqvist estimates that the Gini for lifetime earnings is about 45–55 percent below that in age-specific annual earnings (see p. 255).

[8]Each married couple has a number of children. Children are taken into account in the determination of bequests and in the simulation of saving behavior. The earnings hump in middle age produces less life cycle saving than would occur in a model without children since up to age 45 most families' consumption requirements are increased by children. The number and spacing of children is designed to be quasi realistic. See Davies (1982) for details.

income gross of (direct) tax, Y_t, is thus given by

(1) $\quad Y_t = E_t + G_t + M_t = N_t + M_t.$

This income is divided between consumption, C_t (gross of indirect taxes); direct taxes, T_t, and saving, S_t.[9] The annual budget constraint is thus:

(2) $\quad Y_t = C_t + S_t + T_t.$

Over the lifetime, resources are augmented by an exogenous stream of capital transfers, I_t, which we refer to as inheritances. Denoting discounted present values over the lifetime by dropping the t subscript, lifetime income or lifetime resources, L, is given by

(3) $\quad L = E + G + I = N + I,$

where discounting occurs at a family's after-tax discount rate, r^*.[10]

Like annual income Y_t, lifetime resources L are gross of direct tax. However, because lifetime investment income M is not included in L, direct taxes on investment income are not included in the lifetime measure of direct taxes on $L(\tilde{T})$ as they are in the annual measure of direct taxes on $Y_t(T_t)$. The $\tilde{T}$ represents direct taxes on E and G (I is net of estate taxes). With this definition, and denoting the discounted value of bequests as B, we have the lifetime budget constraint:

(4) $\quad L = C + B + \tilde{T}.$

Households generate a time path of C_t and a value of B by maximizing an intertemporal utility function defined over consumption and bequests, subject to (4). The utility function is of the familiar additive iso-elastic form (see, for example, Alan Blinder, 1974) but with parents' consumption and children's expected lifetime income (which depends partly on parents' bequests) as arguments. Bequests have a compensatory element since they are directly related to parents' income, but inversely related to children's anticipated earnings. Because the latter regress to the mean, on average, bequests rise as a proportion of parents' income. Lifetime consumption C therefore declines as a proportion of L, although to a much smaller extent than does annual consumption as a fraction of annual income.

B. *The Simulation*

The simulation model assumes that Canada is in balanced growth with labor force growth in efficiency units of 2 percent. Per capita earnings, transfer payments, taxes, and other flows all grow at the same rate, and successive cohorts are identical except for a proportional increase in their resources and expenditures. The balanced growth assumption makes it possible to infer time paths of the distributions of all the annual flows (E_t, G_t, Y_t, etc.) for each cohort from the observed values of a representative cross section at a point in time. The before-tax interest rate r is set at 6 percent.[11]

Lifetime paths of E_t, G_t, T_t, and $\tilde{T}_t$ are generated for each cohort by taking random samples of 500 households for each of 11 different age groups (20-24, 25-29,...,70-74) from the 1971 Statistics Cana-

---

[9]Direct taxes, T_t, include employees' share of social security premiums (imputed on the basis of reported E_t and the statutory rate schedule), and personal income taxes.

[10]As explained in Section I, Part B, r^*s differ slightly between households as we assume a common before-tax rate of interest, r, and use different marginal tax rates across households. In the tax incidence calculations, where comparisons between households must be made, it is necessary to discount lifetime streams for all families using the same interest rate. This is done using the common rate, r (see Section III, Part B).

[11]An overall before-tax average rate of return of 6 percent for households was used by Blinder in his pioneering study of life cycle behavior and income distribution. Although lower rates are sometimes thought more realistic, we find support for such a rate in some of our earlier work. St-Hilaire and Whalley (1983, Table 10) estimate that aggregate comprehensive household investment income in 1972 was $16.5 billion. When adjusted to a 1970 basis for growth and inflation, at $13.0 billion, this is approximately 6 percent of the estimate of aggregate household net worth for 1970 in Davies (1979, Table 2)—$216.9 billion.

da Survey of Consumer Finances (*SCF*).[12] The data are adjusted to a 1970 basis, correcting for inflation and growth, to make them consistent with the rest of the model data base. Households are ranked according to total reported income in each age group. They are then linked across age groups in order to construct 500 life histories for E_t and G_t. The linking procedure contains a random element, whose strength may be varied to produce more or less earnings mobility. We parameterize this process to reproduce the degree of earnings mobility implicit in Lillard's study of the relationship between annual and lifetime earnings in the United States.[13] Sensitivity of the incidence results to the assumed degree of earnings mobility is checked by repeating our calculations assuming zero and free (random) mobility.

The 1971 *SCF* does not contain any information on inheritances. In order to model this, Davies (1982) produces a cohort distribution of inheritances by simulating the mortality of the Canadian population.[14] Estimates of the size distribution of wealth by age groups for 1970 are available for Canada in the data described by Davies (1979a, b). Assuming that the 1970 data provide a snapshot of a point on a balanced growth path, the age-specific distribution of wealth at any date can be inferred. Simulation of mortality, along with estate division practices and taxes based on observed patterns, produces a size distribution of net inheritances which can be fed into the life cycle saving simulation. This is done in such a way that the correlation between parents' lifetime noninvestment incomes and (assumed) inheritances is close to that between children's income and (simulated) inheritances.

The simulation assigns each household a constant marginal tax rate, u, on investment income over its lifetime.[15] Hence the after-tax rate of interest, $r^* = (1-u)r$. The rate u is calculated by examining each household's reported income tax payment when aged 45-49 in the 1971 *SCF* data. The 1971 tax tables indicate the corresponding marginal tax rate. Since taxable investment income is affected by various exclusions (for example, nontaxation of imputed rent and capital gains on owner-occupied houses, and one-half of all other capital gains), and the lack of accounting for inflation, this legal rate does not correspond to the effective tax rate on true investment income. Legal rates are transformed into effective marginal tax rates as follows. Comparison of aggregate taxable, and simulated total, investment income for 1970 shows that the former was approximately 15 percent of the latter. We make the strong assumption that this ratio is the same for all households. The effective tax rate on broadly defined investment income is therefore set at 15 percent of the legal rate for each household.

III. Implementing Incidence Calculations in the Life Cycle Framework

Our life cycle incidence calculations use the data and the output from the model described above in a procedure commonly used in annual incidence calculations. As a central case we use a set of standard competitive incidence assumptions adapted to the lifetime context and employ alternative

---

[12] Ideally, $\tilde{T}_t$ would be found by computing the personal income tax (and social security taxes) payable on $N_t = E_t + G_t$ if M_t were zero. (This is appropriate since N_t is exogenous.) Since this computation cannot be made with the *SCF* data (numerous deductions and exclusions are not reported) we have instead prorated the total income tax paid between N_t and M_t. Given the progressivity of the income tax this means that $\tilde{T}_t$ is slightly overstated for each household. This is not a major effect since reported M_t is typically small compared with N_t.

[13] In our central case, the ratio of the Gini coefficient for lifetime earnings to that for age-specific annual earnings is almost precisely the same as found in Lillard. For the age groups 25-34, 35-44, and 45-54, we have ratios of .73, .68, and .60. Lillard obtains ratios of .75, .68, .67, and .61 for groups aged 30-34, 35-39, 40-44, and 45-49, respectively.

[14] The procedure is similar to that employed by Laurence Kotlikoff and Lawrence Summers (1981, Section V).

[15] A varying tax rate would preclude a closed-form solution to the household's consumption plan, and require a more complex simulation model. Given the relatively light overall taxation of capital income, use of constant tax rates on capital income is probably not an important defect in the present exercise.

lifetime distributive series for the five major tax groups listed earlier.

In contrast to the annual calculations where investment income N_t is an important distributive series, and inheritances I_t do not appear, the key distributive series on the sources side in the lifetime calculations are discounted lifetime earnings, E; inheritances, I; and transfers, G. These series sum to the gross of tax lifetime income base, L. On the uses side, two rather than the one key series in the annual calculations (C_t) are used: lifetime investment income M, and lifetime consumption C.

A. Obtaining Comparable Annual Results

We not only generate lifetime incidence calculations but also annual estimates. A natural method of generating comparable annual incidence calculations is to use annual cross sections from the life cycle simulation to produce distributive series. However, in the simulation model, households are free from liquidity constraints and dissave rapidly when transitory income is negative. The consumption pattern across annual income deciles is therefore more extreme than in actual annual data. Thus while the simulation provides useful information on patterns of saving over the lifetime, it is not as reliable a guide to patterns of saving on an annual basis.

In order to obtain annual tax incidence results we have used the same primary data source (the 1971 SCF) as far as possible to produce the distributive series for allocating taxes.[16] The only series that cannot be obtained in this way is consumption, which we generate by simulation. We have found that when zero earnings mobility is assumed—greatly reducing the importance of transitory income—the simulated annual consumption profile becomes reasonably similar to that reported in other data sources.[17] The annual consumption profile obtained in the zero mobility simulation run was therefore used in the annual incidence calculations reported below.

B. Lifetime vs. Annual Distributive Series

Table 1 shows the main features of both the lifetime and annual data used in the incidence calculations reported in the next section.[18] The following contrasts between the annual and lifetime data should be highlighted:

1) There is less inequality in the distribution of lifetime income L, than in that of annual income Y. (Both distributions are gross of direct taxes.) It is therefore not surprising that the lifetime data show a lower variance of personal income tax rates over households ranked by income than the annual data.

---

[16] However, the investment income concept in these data is different from the broad concept in the life cycle simulation. It excludes imputed rental income on housing and durables, and retained earnings. We have made a rough adjustment to compensate for these exclusions by multiplying up the reported SCF investment incomes by the ratio of household broad investment income as reported in St-Hilaire and Whalley (1983) to the aggregate investment income indicated by the 1971 SCF. (The St-Hilaire and Whalley data are for 1972, and were adjusted for growth and inflation to put them on a 1971 basis.) A further, downward adjustment was made to this total so that it would underestimate the National Accounts figure by the same fraction as other forms of SCF income. This prevents capital income from taking on an unrealistic significance in these computations.

[17] Using this procedure, consumption declines from 157 percent of income for the bottom decile to 49 percent for the top decile (see Table 1). St-Hilaire and Whalley (1983), in comparison, find that consumption varied from 117 to 64 percent of income from the bottom to top income groups (17 and 9 percent of households, respectively) in the 1972 Canadian data. See their Tables 9 and 10. Others have found considerably higher consumption to income ratios at the bottom end. Browning and Johnson (p. 73), for example, have a consumption to *disposable* income ratio of 149 percent for the bottom decile.

[18] All lifetime magnitudes in this and subsequent tables are discounted using the before-tax rate of return r. We cannot make comparisons across households using the after-tax rate r^* since the latter differs between households. There is little difference between r and r^* on average since the tax rates u on investment income are low—in the range 0–10 percent. Our results are therefore unlikely to be affected by the use of r instead of some average of the r^*s. (Note that to use an average of the r^*s some arbitrary weighting scheme for averaging across households would have to be selected.)

TABLE 1—BASIC DATA IN LIFETIME AND ANNUAL INCIDENCE CALCULATIONS[a]

Decile	Share of Total L	Composition of L			Uses of L			
		E/L	G/L	I/L	C/L	B/L	$\tilde{T}/L$	M/L
A. Lifetime								
1	4.2	81.2	15.3	3.5	86.7	4.4	8.9	9.4
2	6.2	86.8	10.4	2.8	82.3	5.2	12.5	12.2
3	7.3	89.2	7.9	2.8	81.5	4.7	13.8	10.9
4	8.3	91.2	6.6	2.2	80.4	5.0	14.6	12.8
5	9.1	90.3	6.2	3.5	79.4	5.2	15.4	12.4
6	9.7	92.7	4.5	2.8	77.9	6.0	16.1	14.1
7	10.7	91.6	4.7	3.7	78.4	5.1	16.5	14.0
8	12.0	92.5	3.3	4.3	76.7	6.1	17.1	17.5
9	14.0	91.3	3.0	5.7	76.2	5.6	18.2	14.2
10	18.4	88.3	2.3	9.4	71.7	8.6	19.7	21.8
All	100.0	90.1	5.2	4.7	77.7	6.0	16.4	15.1

Decile[b]	Share of Total Y_t	Composition of Y_t			Uses of Y_t		
		E_t/Y_t	G_t/Y_t	M_t/Y_t	C_t/Y_t	S_t/Y_t	T_t/Y_t
B. Annual							
1	1.0	44.2	51.5	4.3	157.2	−62.4	5.2
2	3.1	50.1	44.2	5.7	117.0	−21.1	4.1
3	4.8	77.2	15.8	7.0	91.4	−0.3	8.9
4	6.4	85.6	7.7	6.7	84.2	−4.0	11.9
5	7.7	90.0	5.1	5.0	80.9	5.1	14.0
6	9.0	89.8	4.3	5.9	77.6	7.1	15.4
7	10.4	91.3	3.4	5.3	77.9	6.4	15.7
8	12.1	90.2	2.6	7.2	76.3	7.2	16.5
9	14.9	86.6	2.1	11.3	73.8	9.3	16.9
10	30.6	57.5	1.2	41.4	49.2	34.4	16.4
All	100.0	77.1	5.3	17.7	71.6	13.5	15.0

Sources: E_t, G_t, T_t, E, G, and $\tilde{T}$ are based on data from the 1971 Statistics Canada Survey of Consumer Finances (*SCF*), as described in the text. All other variables are from the authors' simulations.

Notes: Part A: Gini coefficient of $L = .218$; Part B: Gini coefficient of $Y_t = .410$. Part A: L, E, G, I, C, B, $\tilde{T}$, and M are all present discounted lifetime values; L = lifetime resources, E = earnings, G = transfers, I = inheritances, C = consumption, B = bequest, $\tilde{T}$ = direct taxes on L, and M = investment income.

Part B: Y_t, E_t, G_t, M_t, C_t, S_t, and T_t are all annual flows; Y_t = income, E_t = earnings, G_t = transfers, M_t = investment income, C_t = consumption, S_t = saving, and T_t = direct taxes on Y_t.

[a] Shown in percent.
[b] Deciles are sorted by annual income as reported in the 1971 Statistics Canada *SCF*.

2) Over the lifetime transfers are less heavily concentrated in the bottom two deciles of the population than in the annual data. The decline in the relative importance of transfers as income rises is also less marked. This tends to reduce the quantitative importance of Browning and Johnson's argument regarding the impact of indexed transfers in a lifetime calculation.

3) Variation in consumption to income ratios is smaller in lifetime than in annual data. This reduces the regressivity of taxes assumed to be borne out of consumption, such as sales and excise.

4) There is less variation in the relative importance of earnings as we move up the income scale in lifetime data as against annual data. This is partly associated with the more even distribution of government transfers in the lifetime data. A consequence is that the progressivity of social security taxes over the low deciles in annual data is replaced by rough proportionality in the lifetime calculations. (In addition, regressivity over the upper deciles is reduced.) Also, the flatter earnings series again means that the Browning and Johnson procedure of allocating sales and excise taxes to factor incomes

has less tendency to produce progressivity for these taxes.

5) Overall, lifetime earnings are larger in relation to lifetime consumption than are annual earnings compared with annual consumption. This reflects the fact that, on average, earnings occur earlier in the lifetime and are less heavily discounted. We see in the next section that this factor tends to make overall lifetime incidence slightly more progressive than annual, since the relative importance of taxes falling on consumption is smaller and that of taxes on earnings is increased.

C. Central Case Lifetime Incidence Assumptions

The lifetime distributive series can be used in alternative ways to allocate the various taxes across deciles. Our central case uses standard competitive assumptions: the income tax is assumed to be borne by income recipients; corporate and property taxes by recipients of investment income; social security taxes by earnings recipients; and sales and excise taxes in proportion to consumption.

While for the most part it is clear from the central case incidence assumptions which distributive series should be used for which taxes, this is not true for taxes borne by capital in the lifetime context. In lifetime incidence, taxes on capital income have both sources and uses side effects rather than just a sources side impact as assumed in annual calculations.[19] By reducing the rate of interest they increase the relative lifetime incomes of those whose receipts occur later in life (via the discounting effect)—a sources side effect. In addition, they reduce the relative real incomes of persons who consume more later in the lifetime by increasing the price of future consumption—a uses side effect. While the sources and uses side effects of taxes

[19] The nature of the uses side effect over the lifetime was pointed out by Browning and Johnson: "...corporation income taxes and property taxes reduce the net interest rate that savers receive. Consequently, these taxes harm savers and benefit consumers on the uses side..." (p. 27).

borne by capital could be accounted for separately in the lifetime incidence calculations, it is simpler to net them out. This can be seen in the case of a family which consumes its total income in each year and is unaffected by taxes borne by capital, since it never saves and therefore feels no effect of a reduced interest rate. In contrast, a family which saves suffers from the reduced reward for abstinence.

Thus, taxes borne by capital reduce the welfare of families which defer consumption. In any year, in the absence of taxes borne by capital, a family which accumulated savings could consume more than with those same taxes present. The amount of additional consumption would equal the reduction in current investment income due to the taxes borne by capital. The appropriate distributive series for taxes borne by capital in lifetime incidence calculations is therefore the discounted value of all investment income received over the lifetime, M.

D. Computing Tax Burdens

As mentioned earlier, personal income tax payments are taken directly from the primary data source—the 1971 *SCF*. Social security tax payments are imputed using the applicable rates and ceilings under both the Canada Pension Plan (*CPP*) and Unemployment Insurance (*UI*) programs to determine employer and employee contributions on the basis of earnings reported in the 1971 *SCF* by simulation households. Other taxes must be imputed by establishing an overall tax rate and applying this to the appropriate distributive series.

For corporate and property taxes, rates are determined using 1970 tax collections and an estimate of total 1970 household investment income. We estimate the sales and excise tax rate by comparing actual 1970 tax collections with observed aggregate consumption. Lifetime capital and sales and excise tax burdens are calculated by applying these tax rates to discounted lifetime investment income M, and consumption C, respectively, for each simulation household.

E. *Sensitivity Analyses*

In addition to lifetime incidence calculations under standard competitive assumptions, we present further results using a number of alternative assumptions to explore the robustness of our central case. We not only alter incidence assumptions, but also vary earnings mobility and other parameters in a sensitivity testing procedure. The calculations are kept on a comparable equal yield basis by using the aggregate tax collections from the central case,[20] and reallocating these by household according to the alternative assumptions used.

Our first variant on incidence assumptions is a "noncompetitive" version of the central case, comparable to that used in many annual studies. It is assumed that 50 percent of corporate and property taxes is shifted to consumers rather than to recipients of investment income. A second variant we refer to as the "Browning and Johnson Case." As discussed earlier, the argument of Browning and Johnson is that uses side effects of sales and excise taxes can be ignored and that transfers, being indexed, remain unaffected. The tax must therefore be borne by other sources of income. In this case, under competitive assumptions, sales and excise taxes are allocated using the distributions of lifetime earnings and inheritances instead of lifetime consumption.

Finally, we examine the sensitivity of our results to variations in key features of the life cycle model. We pay particular attention to the dependence of our results on the parameter which determines household mobility across the age specific distributions of earnings. Incidence results based on zero mobility (households occupy the same rank order in each age specific distribution) and free mobility (households' positions in each age distribution are random) are contrasted with the central case. We also rerun the life cycle simulation which generates our distributive series and recompute tax incidence using alternative long-run balanced growth rate assumptions of 1 and 4 percent, and interest rates of 4 and 8 percent. Results of these runs appear in the Appendix.

IV. Lifetime Tax Incidence Results

Our central case lifetime tax incidence results are displayed in Table 2, Part A, with comparable annual tax incidence calculations reported in Part B. Several interesting points emerge from a comparison of these results.

First, the overall tax system appears mildly progressive in both the annual and lifetime calculations. While in the annual results there is regressivity from the bottom to the second decile, from the second to the ninth deciles rates increase slowly, and in the top decile a significant increase occurs. In the lifetime data there is progressivity throughout—with moderate increases in overall rates from the first to the fourth deciles, a slow rise from the fourth to the ninth deciles, and once more a larger increase for the top decile. While the regressivity at the bottom end in the annual run is an important feature, we conclude that both profiles show mild progression overall across the income ranges.

An alternative method of summarizing differences in tax profiles is to examine the proportional impact on a summary measure of income inequality. Following the suggestion of Musgrave and Tun Thin (1948), this is often done using the Gini coefficient.[21] The pre-tax Gini of .218 in the lifetime run is reduced to .184 by the tax system; in contrast, the annual Gini falls only 10 percent —from .410 to .370. On this basis it might be claimed that the lifetime tax structure is significantly more progressive than the annual.

The reason that our lifetime taxes give a larger proportional reduction in the Gini than in annual data, while the range of tax rates across the deciles is similar in both cases, lies in the smaller inequality in the pre-tax lifetime income distribution. Figure 1 provides

---

[20] The tax yield needs to be adjusted only in the cases where the interest rate or the rate of growth is altered.

[21] Alternative approaches employing inequality indexes, intended to provide purely descriptive measures of overall progressivity were presented by Nanak Kakwani (1976) and Daniel Suits (1977). For a rigorous defense of the original Musgrave-Thin measure as a normative index and comments on Kakwani and Suits, see Pak-Wai Liu (forthcoming).

TABLE 2—AVERAGE TAX RATES OF CANADIAN HOUSEHOLDS BY DECILE, CENTRAL CASE ASSUMPTIONS

	1	2	3	4	5	6	7	8	9	10	All Deciles
A. Lifetime Incidence (Deciles Ranked by Lifetime Resources (L))											
Corporate Income Tax	2.2	2.9	2.6	3.0	2.9	3.3	3.3	4.1	3.4	5.1	3.6
Property Tax	2.4	3.1	2.8	3.3	3.2	3.6	3.6	4.5	3.7	5.6	3.9
Sales and Excises	15.0	14.3	14.1	13.9	13.8	13.5	13.6	13.3	13.2	12.4	13.5
Social Security	3.9	4.0	3.9	4.0	3.8	3.8	3.6	3.6	3.4	2.8	3.6
Personal Income Tax	7.3	11.3	12.5	13.5	14.5	15.1	15.7	16.7	17.7	20.5	15.8
All Taxes	30.9	35.5	35.9	37.7	38.1	39.3	39.8	42.2	41.3	46.5	40.2
B. Annual Incidence (Deciles Ranked by Annual Income (Y_t))											
Corporate Income Tax	1.0	1.3	1.6	1.6	1.2	1.4	1.2	1.7	2.7	9.8	4.2
Property Tax	1.1	1.5	1.8	1.7	1.3	1.5	1.3	1.9	2.9	10.6	4.5
Sales and Excises	27.2	20.3	15.8	14.6	14.0	13.4	13.5	13.2	12.8	8.5	12.4
Social Security	1.7	2.5	4.1	4.3	4.2	3.9	3.8	3.4	3.0	1.4	2.9
Personal Income Tax	4.3	2.8	6.8	9.7	11.9	13.4	13.8	14.8	15.4	15.7	13.5
All Taxes	35.4	28.4	30.1	31.9	32.6	33.6	33.7	35.0	36.8	46.0	37.5

Source: Computations performed by the authors. See text.

an illustration of how this works. Suppose that both annual and lifetime income are uniformly distributed, and that lifetime and annual tax profiles are both linear and have the same range. It is clear that the relative range of tax rates in the lifetime case is higher. Hence, for an index like the Gini which is concerned with relative differences in income, taxes appear more equalizing over the lifetime.[22]

A second interesting point evident from Table 2 is that there is considerably less variation in incidence patterns across taxes in the lifetime calculation. Lifetime income taxes while progressive are less so than in the annual case; sales and excise are less regressive; social security is initially less progressive and subsequently less regressive by income range, and corporate and property taxes are less progressive (especially at the top end). This reflects a greater flatness of the underlying lifetime distributive series and means that changes in incidence assumptions have less impact on lifetime, than on annual incidence results.

[22] We are indebted to an anonymous referee for suggesting the use of the Musgrave-Thin measure, and for providing the diagram in Figure 1. Since inequality in underlying income distributions frequently varies in incidence studies due to experiments with income definition, more general use of the Musgrave-Thin measure seems to us desirable.

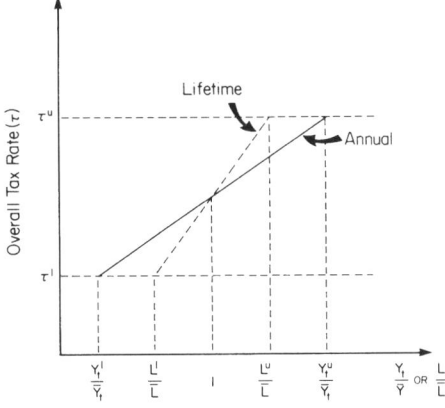

FIGURE 1. HYPOTHETICAL LIFETIME AND ANNUAL TAX PROFILES

Note: Y_t and L are annual and lifetime income, respectively. The bars indicate mean value; u and l superscripts denote upper and lower bounds, respectively.

Table 3 confirms this by showing how use of noncompetitive assumptions makes surprisingly little difference to overall tax rates. In this case, corporate and property taxes are treated as partially forward shifted and are allocated one-half to consumption and one-half to capital income in general. In this noncompetitive variant, overall progressivity

TABLE 3—SENSITIVITY OF LIFETIME INCIDENCE RESULTS TO ALTERNATIVE INCIDENCE ASSUMPTIONS

	Deciles[a]										All Deciles
	1	2	3	4	5	6	7	8	9	10	
A. Central Case Results[a]											
Corporate Income Tax	2.2	2.9	2.6	3.0	2.9	3.3	3.3	4.1	3.4	5.1	3.6
Property Tax	2.4	3.1	2.8	3.3	3.2	3.6	3.6	4.5	3.7	5.6	3.9
Sales and Excises	15.0	14.3	14.1	13.9	13.8	13.5	13.6	13.3	13.2	12.4	13.5
Social Security	3.9	4.0	3.9	4.0	3.8	3.8	3.6	3.6	3.4	2.8	3.6
Personal Income Tax	7.3	11.3	12.5	13.5	14.5	15.1	15.7	16.7	17.7	20.5	15.8
All Taxes	30.9	35.5	35.9	37.7	38.1	39.3	39.8	42.2	41.3	46.5	40.2
B. Noncompetitive Assumptions											
Corporate Income Tax	3.1	3.3	3.2	3.4	3.3	3.4	3.4	3.8	3.4	4.2	3.6
Property Tax	3.4	3.6	3.4	3.6	3.9	3.7	3.7	4.2	3.7	4.6	3.9
Sales and Excises	15.0	14.3	14.1	13.9	13.8	13.5	13.6	13.3	13.2	12.4	13.5
Social Security	3.9	4.0	3.9	4.0	3.8	3.8	3.6	3.6	3.4	2.8	3.6
Personal Income Tax	7.3	11.3	12.5	13.5	14.5	15.1	15.7	16.7	17.7	20.5	15.8
All Taxes	32.8	36.4	37.1	38.4	39.2	39.5	40.1	41.6	41.4	44.6	40.2
C. Browning and Johnson Case											
Corporate Income Tax	2.2	2.9	2.6	3.0	2.9	3.3	3.3	4.1	3.4	5.1	3.6
Property Tax	2.4	3.1	2.8	3.3	3.2	3.6	3.6	4.5	3.7	5.6	3.9
Sales and Excises	12.0	12.7	13.1	13.3	13.3	13.6	13.5	13.7	13.8	13.9	13.5
Social Security	3.9	4.0	3.9	4.0	3.8	3.8	3.6	3.6	3.4	2.8	3.6
Personal Income Tax	7.3	11.3	12.5	13.5	14.5	15.1	15.7	16.7	17.7	20.5	15.8
All Taxes	27.9	34.0	34.9	37.0	37.6	39.4	39.8	42.6	41.8	48.0	40.2

Source: Computations performed by the authors. See text.

[a] Deciles ranked by lifetime resources.

of the tax system hardly changes at all. This is in sharp contrast to the results from annual studies where similar forward shifting assumptions produce marked reductions in progressivity.[23]

Finally Table 3 indicates that while Browning-Johnson assumptions make the tax profile more progressive, the change is small —markedly less than occurs in annual calculations. Denying the uses side effect of sales and excise taxes removed less regressivity in the lifetime than in annual calculations, because, over the lifetime, consumption is much flatter as a proportion of income across the income ranges. Recognizing the indexation of transfers increases progressivity less since transfers are less concentrated in the lower deciles in the lifetime data. The change in tax rates reported here is thus small when compared to the changes reported by Browning and Johnson. These results qualify the claim that changing the treatment of sales and excise taxes, as Browning and Johnson suggest transforms the overall incidence pattern from proportionality to sharp progressivity.

In Table 4 we report the impacts of changes in mobility assumptions on our incidence results. Not surprisingly, altering the degree of household mobility through the age-specific distributions of earnings changes measured lifetime inequality considerably. While in our central case, with mobility parameterized according to the best available empirical evidence (as explained earlier) we have a Gini coefficient for lifetime resources of .218, with fixed earnings ranks (zero mobility) the Gini rises to .326, and with completely random ("free") mobility it falls to .135. The altered inequality is reflected directly in the progressivity of personal income taxes. While in the central case the personal tax rate on a lifetime basis varies from 7 to 21 percent across deciles, with zero mobility

---

[23] See, for example, Pechman and Okner (Table 4.4, p. 51). Their variants 1a and 3b differ principally in that 3b shifts one-half of corporate and payroll taxes forward onto consumers (see p. 38).

TABLE 4—SENSITIVITY OF LIFETIME RESULTS TO ALTERNATIVE MOBILITY ASSUMPTIONS

	Percent of Total Lifetime Resources Accruing to Decile					
Deciles[a]	Zero Mobility Assumption		Central Case		Free Mobility Assumption	
A. Size Distribution of Lifetime Resources						
1	1.7		4.2		6.4	
2	4.1		6.2		7.7	
3	5.9		7.3		8.4	
4	7.3		8.3		8.9	
5	8.6		9.1		9.4	
6	9.9		9.7		9.9	
7	11.3		10.7		10.4	
8	12.8		12.0		11.1	
9	15.2		14.0		12.2	
10	23.2		18.4		15.5	
Gini Coefficient	.326		.218		.135	
	Income Tax	Total Taxes	Income Tax	Total Taxes	Income Tax	Total Taxes
B. Tax Rate Profiles						
1	2.1	28.9	7.3	30.9	12.7	36.7
2	5.2	30.8	11.3	35.5	13.1	37.7
3	8.4	33.7	12.5	35.9	14.1	38.0
4	11.1	35.8	13.5	37.7	14.1	37.2
5	13.2	38.7	14.5	38.1	15.7	40.5
6	14.0	38.3	15.1	39.3	15.6	40.5
7	14.9	39.7	15.7	39.8	15.2	39.1
8	16.6	42.7	16.7	42.2	15.8	40.4
9	17.4	41.4	17.7	41.3	17.4	43.1
10	22.7	47.4	20.5	46.5	18.8	46.1
All Deciles	15.8	40.7	15.8	40.2	15.8	40.6

Source: Computations performed by the authors. See text.

[a] Deciles ranked by lifetime resources.

the range widens from 2 to 23 percent, and with free mobility it narrows from 13 to 19 percent. Although the change in personal income tax progressivity has a limited effect on the overall incidence pattern,[24] it is clear that the assessment of lifetime tax incidence depends to a significant extent on the degree of mobility assumed.

Calculated overall progressivity of the tax system is relatively insensitive to the rate of interest and long-run balanced growth rate which are assumed, as shown in Table A1 in the Appendix. Choosing a higher growth rate slightly reduces progressivity, while the higher the interest rate the more progressivity we have. These effects operate via changes in the time paths of earnings relative to consumption. A higher growth rate skews earnings toward the future, reducing saving in early periods and therefore raising consumption and reducing investment income as a fraction of lifetime income. Sales and excise taxes (regressive) become more important and capital taxes (progressive) less. A higher interest rate works in the opposite direction, skewing consumption toward the future and increasing saving when households are young.

V. Conclusion

In this paper we report a set of lifetime tax incidence calculations which combine the data and output from a life cycle, microsimulation model for Canada due to Davies

---

[24] Offsetting changes occur in the incidence of the corporate and property, and sales and excise taxes. These are largely due to changes in saving patterns resulting from the altered age profiles of noninvestment income across the deciles.

(1979, 1982) with incidence assumptions comparable to those used in previous annual incidence studies. While incidence calculations have several limitations, previous annual calculations have received so much attention in policy debate that it is important to analyze to what extent they correspond to the more interesting case of lifetime tax incidence.

We offer two main findings. The first is that using standard "competitive" shifting assumptions, lifetime and annual incidence patterns both display mild progression of overall tax rates across income ranges (ignoring the bottom decile in the annual calculation). While the personal income tax becomes less progressive in a lifetime context, offsetting changes occur in the incidence of other taxes. Sales and excise taxes, for example, become less regressive since the fraction of income saved rises less sharply with income. The regressivity often found at the bottom end of the income scale in annual calculations is not present in the lifetime calculations. This is largely the result of the reduced regressivity of sales and excise taxes.

Our second finding is that lifetime incidence results are far more robust to alternative incidence assumptions than is true of annual results. The principal distributive series in the lifetime context—transfers, earnings, and consumption, as a fraction of lifetime income—are all closer to uniform across income ranges than corresponding annual series. As a result, changes in incidence assumptions such as the indexing of transfers (suggested by Browning and Johnson), or the forward shifting of capital taxes have much less impact on the overall progressivity of the tax system than in annual calculations. Our results thus indicate that we can perhaps be more confident than on the basis of annual incidence calculations alone that the incidence of the overall tax system is mildly progressive.

Several qualifications are in order, however. First, lifetime saving behavior by household is simulated rather than observed. While Davies (1982) found that the patterns of intergenerational saving generated are consistent with available evidence, our empirical knowledge of intergenerational transfers is not as well developed as that in other areas of consumer behavior. It would be valuable to compare our results with those obtained using alternative models of saving, or longitudinal data sets. Secondly, results are sensitive to the degree of earnings mobility assumed in our simulations. While mobility has been carefully parameterized with reference to studies using longitudinal data on earnings, more direct use of such data would be preferable.

Finally, the incidence assumptions behind our central (competitive) case are only correct under strong assumptions about factor supplies and technology. General equilibrium computations allowing differential incidence calculations under more interesting assumptions would clearly be more revealing. Adoption of the lifetime framework in detailed general equilibrium computations of tax incidence would seem to be a promising direction for future research to explore.

Appendix

Here we investigate the sensitivity of our central (competitive) case to changes in the rates of interest and growth rates which are assumed. Table A1 shows the overall lifetime incidence patterns obtained with alternative values of these parameters.

The table shows that overall progressivity falls slightly as higher growth rates are used, and rises somewhat with a higher rate of discount. Also, the average total tax rate falls with the rate of growth and rises with the rate of interest. The changes in progressivity are all fairly small, providing an indication that results of the paper would not be greatly altered with significantly different rates of interest and growth.

Raising the growth rate skews households' earnings more towards the future without altering the shape of their optimal consumption profiles significantly.[25] The result is lower saving at earlier ages, and a general

[25] There would be no change in shape (only in level) if households were not constrained to have nonnegative wealth. Skewing earnings more toward the future will result in this constraint being effective for more households.

TABLE A1—SENSITIVITY OF LIFETIME RESULTS TO THE CHOICE OF PARAMETERS

Deciles[a]	Total Tax Rate Profiles[b]		
A. Rate of Growth	1 Percent	2 Percent	4 Percent
1	31.6	30.9	29.8
2	36.5	35.5	33.6
3	36.9	35.9	34.8
4	39.8	37.7	35.7
5	38.6	38.1	36.8
6	42.0	39.3	36.8
7	42.1	39.8	37.8
8	44.8	42.2	38.6
9	43.7	41.3	38.9
10	49.5	46.5	43.4
All Deciles	42.3	40.2	37.9
B. Discount Rate	4 percent	6 Percent	8 Percent
1	29.0	30.9	33.5
2	33.2	35.5	38.4
3	33.5	35.9	39.0
4	34.7	37.7	41.1
5	35.6	38.1	41.0
6	36.2	39.3	44.7
7	36.0	39.8	44.2
8	37.4	42.2	47.2
9	38.3	41.3	45.4
10	42.1	46.5	52.1
All Deciles	36.9	40.2	44.5

Source: Computations performed by the authors. See text.

[a] Deciles ranked by lifetime resources.

[b] Part A: Assuming a rate of growth as shown; Part B: Assuming a discount rate as shown.

increase in discounted lifetime consumption as a fraction of lifetime income. There is also a general reduction in discounted lifetime investment incomes (due to lower saving when households are young).

The general rise in consumption as a fraction of lifetime income caused by increasing the growth rate, means that any given rate of sales and excise tax will translate into a higher tax as a proportion of lifetime income. Thus sales and excise taxes, which are fairly regressive (see Table 2) increase in importance. The general decline in lifetime investment income as a fraction of lifetime income similarly lowers corporate and property taxes as a proportion of lifetime income. In addition to the increased importance of the regressive sales and excise taxes, we thus have a somewhat reduced importance of progressive capital taxes (again see Table 2). It is therefore not surprising that overall progressivity declines somewhat. The slight decline in the average total tax rate is the result of capital taxes declining fairly sharply as a fraction of lifetime income.[26]

When we reduce the growth rate, the two mechanisms described work in reverse. We skew earnings more toward the present, and saving goes up considerably when households are young. Consumption falls and investment income rises as a fraction of lifetime income. Sales and excise taxes become less important, and capital taxes more. Overall progressivity therefore is somewhat increased.

Finally, as noted, Table A1 also shows that a higher rate of discount raises progres-

[26] In the central case (growth rate = 2 percent) capital taxes average 7.5 percent of lifetime income, and other taxes 32.5 percent. In the variant we are considering with a growth rate of 4 percent, capital taxes average 4.5 percent, and other taxes 33.4 percent of lifetime income.

sivity, and the average total tax rate slightly. The explanation runs along lines similar to that for changes in the growth rate. A higher rate of interest skews planned consumption more toward the future, without altering the time path of earnings. Saving in early periods therefore goes up, leading to a decline in consumption, and a rise in investment income as a proportion of lifetime income. Sales and excise taxes become less important, and capital taxes more. Overall progressivity therefore rises. The increase in average total tax rates is somewhat larger than when the growth rate is reduced, however. The reason is that the rise in investment income as a fraction of lifetime income is greater than when the growth rate is reduced, leading to a larger rise in capital taxes as a proportion of lifetime income.[27]

[27]When we raise the interest rate to 8 percent, on average discounted lifetime investment income rises to 23.6 percent of lifetime income, whereas reducing the growth rate to 1 percent only produces a rise to 20.1 percent. (Investment income averages 15.1 percent of lifetime income in the central case—see Table 1.) The result is that capital taxes rise to 11.7 percent on average, from 7.5 percent, when the interest rate is raised, as compared with a rise to 9.8 percent when the growth rate is reduced to 1 percent.

REFERENCES

Atkinson, Anthony B. and Stiglitz, Joseph E., *Lectures in Public Economics*, London: McGraw-Hill, 1980.

Blinder, Alan S., *Toward an Economic Theory of Income Distribution*, Cambridge: MIT Press, 1974.

Blomqvist, Nils S., "A Comparison of Distributions of Annual and Lifetime Income: Sweden Around 1970," *Review of Income and Wealth*, September 1981, 27, 243–64.

Browning, Edgar K., "The Burden of Taxation," *Journal of Political Economy*, August 1978, 86, 649–71.

_____ and Johnson, William R., *The Distribution of the Tax Burden*, Washington: American Enterprise Institute, 1979.

Davies, David G., "An Empirical Test of Sales-Tax Regressivity," *Journal of Political Economy*, February 1959, 67, 72–78.

Davies, James B., (1979a) "Life-Cycle Savings, Inheritance, and the Distribution of Personal Income and Wealth in Canada," unpublished doctoral dissertation, London School of Economics, 1979.

_____, (1979b) "On the Size Distribution of Wealth in Canada," *Review of Income and Wealth*, September 1979, 25, 237–59.

_____, "The Relative Impact of Inheritance and Other Factors on Economic Inequality," *Quarterly Journal of Economics*, August 1982, 97, 471–98.

Gillespie, W. Irwin, "On the Redistribution of Income in Canada," *Canadian Tax Journal*, July-August 1976, 24, 419–50.

_____, *The Redistribution of Income in Canada*, Ottawa: Gage Publishing, Ltd., 1980.

Kakwani, Nanak C., "Measurement of Tax Progressivity: An International Comparison," *Economic Journal*, March 1976, 87, 71–80.

Kotlikoff, Laurence J. and Summers, Lawrence H., "The Role of Intergenerational Transfers in Aggregate Capital Accumulation," *Journal of Political Economy*, August 1981, 89, 706–32.

Lillard, Lee A., "Inequality: Earnings vs. Human Wealth," *American Economic Review*, March 1977, 67, 42–53.

Liu, Pak-Wai, "Lorenz Domination and Global Tax Progressivity," *Canadian Journal of Economics*, forthcoming.

Mincer, Jacob, *Schooling, Experience and Earnings*, New York: Columbia University Press, 1974.

Musgrave, Richard A. and Musgrave, Peggy B., *Public Finance in Theory and Practice*, New York: McGraw-Hill, 1980.

_____, Case, Karl E. and Leonard, Herman B., "The Distribution of Fiscal Burdens and Benefits," *Public Finance Quarterly*, July 1974, 2, 259–311.

_____ and Thin, Tun, "Income Tax Progression, 1929–48," *Journal of Political Economy*, December 1948, 56, 498–514.

Pechman, Joseph A. and Okner, Benjamin A., *Who Bears the Tax Burden?*, Washington: The Brookings Institution, 1974.

St-Hilaire, France and Whalley, John, "What Have We Learned from Tax Incidence Calculations?," mimeo., University of

Western Ontario, 1982.

_____ and _____, "A Microconsistent Equilibrium Data Set for Canada for Use in Tax Policy Analysis," *Review of Income and Wealth*, June 1983, *29*, 175–204.

Suits, Daniel B., "Measurement of Tax Progressivity," *American Economic Review*, September 1977, *67*, 747–52.

Statistics Canada Survey of Consumer Finances (SCF), *1971 Income Distribution by Size in Canada*, Publication No. 13-207, Ottawa: Ministry of Supply and Services, 1973.

[8]

Sales Taxes and Prices: An Empirical Analysis

Abstract - We employ a unique data source to examine the incidence of sales taxes. The main idea is to take information on the prices of specific commodities in different U.S. cities and to examine the extent to which differences in tax rates and bases are reflected in prices, controlling for other factors (such as costs). We find a surprising variety of shifting patterns. For some commodities, the after-tax price increases by exactly the amount of the tax, a result consistent with the standard competitive model. However, taxes on other commodities are overshifted—an increase in tax revenue of one dollar per unit increases the price by more than one dollar.

INTRODUCTION

One of the most fundamental questions in public finance is who bears the burden of taxes—the "incidence of taxation." This question has received a great deal of attention, especially at the theoretical level. However, it seems fair to say that the empirical evidence on incidence is still quite meager. Indeed, there seems to be little evidence, even in the case that is theoretically the easiest—partial equilibrium commodity taxes. Are taxes levied on commodities completely shifted into their prices, or does the incidence also fall on firms? This question is just as important to policymakers as it is to academics. Current debates in Europe about the effects of tax harmonization hinge crucially on the way in which prices relate to taxes. In the United States, recent debates on whether to increase reliance on consumption-based taxes have revealed an intense concern over the distributional effects of such taxes. Technical staffs in both the Administration and the Congress have prepared detailed analyses of how the various taxes would be distributed among income classes. The differences in these technical analyses—which grow into important political disputes—are due in part to differences in assumptions about who would ultimately bear the various taxes. We stress the word "assumptions," because in the absence of empirical evidence, all the technicians can do is assume how the various taxes would be distributed.

In this paper, we employ a unique data source to examine the incidence of sales taxes. The main idea is to take information on the prices of specific commodities in different U.S.

Timothy J. Besley
Department of Economics, London School of Economics, London, England WC2A 2AE

Harvey S. Rosen
Department of Economics, Princeton University, Princeton, NJ 08544-1021.

NBER, Cambridge, MA 02138

cities and to examine the extent to which they are affected by taxes, controlling for other factors (such as costs) that also affect prices. The next section discusses some previous work in this area. The third section provides a framework for thinking about how changes in commodity taxes may affect prices, particularly when markets are not competitive. We discuss the data in the fourth section and present the results in the fifth section. A major finding is that there is a surprising variety of shifting patterns. For some comodities, the after-tax price increases by just the amount of the tax, a result consistent with the standard competitive model. However, some taxes are overshifted, which is difficult to reconcile with the assumption of perfect competition. The final section concludes with a summary and discussion of the policy implications of this study.

BACKGROUND

A compendium of the theory of tax incidence can be found in Kotlikoff and Summers (1987). As they note, many factors determine how taxes are shifted in a particular industry, including the responsiveness of supply and demand to changes in price. In addition, recent work has paid much attention to the consequences of market structure. (See, e.g., Besley (1989), Delipalla and Keen (1992), Katz and Rosen (1985), Seade (1985), and Stern (1987).) An important implication of this literature is that in an imperfectly competitive market, varying degrees of shifting are possible in the long run. Indeed, even *overshifting* is a distinct possibility; i.e., the price of the taxed commodity can increase by more than the amount of the tax. These results contrast markedly with those that emerge from a competitive model. With competition, after-tax prices increase by just the amount of the tax if the long-run supply curve is horizontal, and by less than the amount of the tax if the supply curve is upward sloping.

While economists are now in command of a better understanding of the theory of tax incidence, knowledge at the empirical level has not progressed so easily. The government's technical staffs typically assume (1) that shifting is the same for all goods and (2) that shifting is full, i.e., consumers bear the full burden. This has also been the assumption in most academic studies of sales tax incidence, where it is assumed that prices fully reflect taxes, so that the only important empirical question is how these price increases affect members of different income groups. (See, e.g., Pechman and Okner (1974) and Metcalf (1994).) While the full-shifting hypothesis is reasonable in the absence of further evidence, the conclusions reached on the basis of it have the potential to be seriously misleading if it turns out to be incorrect. For example, imagine trying to determine who bears the burden of a set of commodity taxes as in a value-added tax. If there is differential shifting across commodities, then the answer will be quite different than the answer found under the standard assumption.

There have, in fact, been a few empirical studies designed to examine the full-shifting hypothesis.[1] Harris (1987) carefully examines cigarette prices before and after an increase in the federal excise tax on cigarettes in 1983. He finds that the 8-cent per pack tax led to a price increase of 16 cents per pack. In contrast to Harris's case-study approach, several studies apply structural econometric methods to the problem. Examples are Sumner's (1981) and Sullivan's (1985) studies of the effects

---

[1] These studies all employ microlevel data. Poterba, Rotemberg, and Summers (1986) use macrodata to investigate a question related to but distinct from ours—do direct and indirect taxes have different effects on the price level? They interpret the results as a test of rigidities in nominal prices and do not focus on tax incidence issues. Dornbusch (1987) uses aggregate data to examine the relationship between the prices of imported goods and exchange rates.

Sales Taxes and Prices

of cigarette taxation and Karp and Perloff's (1989) examination of the effect of taxes on television set prices in Japan. They make assumptions about the functional form of costs and demand in the industry to estimate the underlying parameters that go into the industry's "mark-up" equation. Having done so, they can explicitly calculate the implied relationship between taxes and prices.

We cannot implement this kind of approach here since we have only price data. Instead, we estimate reduced form models. Evidently, this precludes us from drawing precise inferences about market conduct. In this, we follow the important contribution of Poterba (1996), who surveys earlier empirical work going back to the 1930s. He examines quarterly data on tax rates and prices in eight SMSAs over the period 1947–77 for three commodity groups: women and girls' clothing, men and boys' clothing, and personal care items.[2] Poterba estimates reduced form equations and never rejects the view that prices react one-for-one to tax changes.

Our approach is similar in spirit to that of Poterba (1996), although we employ more disaggregated data. He uses Bureau of Labor Statistics (BLS) city-specific consumer price indices. Such data, however, exist for only 28 cities. Moreover, for most commodity groups, one cannot obtain city-specific price indices over periods of more than a decade; hence the need to analyze only three commodity groups, as noted above. Finally, although the BLS characterizes these prices as being "disaggregated," they are really quite broad. "Women and girls' clothing," for example, encompasses a plethora of products. Lumping together all of these commodities makes it difficult to interpret the results, if for no other reason than the weights on the components of such a composite are likely to vary from area to area and across time.[3] In contrast, we study very specific items—a dozen large Grade A eggs or a three-pack of boy's underwear, for example. In addition, our data set has information on 155 cities; with more data, we expect to obtain more precise results.

FRAMEWORK

The U.S. federal system of government provides a natural setting for examining tax shifting, since different states and cities levy different tax rates and use very different tax bases. On the null hypothesis that all industries are competitive and in long-run equilibrium with horizontal supply curves, we should expect to observe that all post-tax prices adjust to reflect only differences in taxes, other things being the same. According to this view, pretax prices in different jurisdictions should reflect only differences in costs of delivering the commodity and taxes. Conversely, to the extent that the after-tax prices in various jurisdictions differ by amounts that are greater or less than the associated taxes, it suggests that this paradigm is inappropriate, and our views on the incidence of taxes must be modified accordingly.

There is a large number of potential models available for thinking about the link between taxes and prices with different market structure, some of which were referred to above. Our analysis is not structural, in that we do not appeal to any particular model in interpreting the results. However, it is useful to lay out a simple model in order to motivate the econometric specification that we adopt.

Consider a firm operating in market i in city j at time t. We assume that the firm

---
[2] A number of other papers have focused on price variation within cities in order to determine how a neighborhood's prices depend on the incomes of its members. (See MacDonald and Nelson (1991) and Alcaly and Klevorick (1971).)
[3] Further, as noted by Carlton (1986), the use of BLS data has been criticized because these data are not accurate measures of transaction prices.

in which we are interested chooses a variable x_{ijt}[4] to maximize profits, which is the difference between costs $c^{ij}(x_{ijt}; z_{ijt}, \tau_{ijt})$, and revenues $R^{ij}(x_{ijt}; z_{ijt})$, where z_{ijt} is a vector representing the behavior of other firms in the market and τ_{ijt} is the *ad valorem* tax rate. We assume that the firms choose variables to form a Nash equilibrium and denote the equilibrium values as ($\dot{z}_{ijt}(\tau_{ijt})$, $\dot{x}_{ijt}$ (τ_{ijt})). A natural way to write the solution to the maximization problem is:

[1] $q_{ijt} = \phi_{ijt}[m_{ijt}(1 + \tau_{ijt})]$

where

q_{ijt} = tax-inclusive price of good i in city j at time t,

ϕ_{ijt} = mark-up on good i in city j at time t, and

m_{ijt} = marginal production cost of good i in city j at time t.

This is the standard formula, which says that price is equal to a mark-up over marginal cost. Equation 1 is not particularly useful for empirical purposes. First, the left-hand side is a tax-inclusive price, which often times we do not observe (in our data, we do not). It will be useful to have an explicit expression for the tax-exclusive price, p_{ijt}:

[2] $p_{ijt} = \phi_{ijt} m_{ijt}$.

Second, the mark-up parameter ϕ_{ijt} (and possibly m_{ijt}) is typically a function of the tax, so that equation 2 can be written as:

[3] $p_{ijt} = f^{ijt}(\tau_{ijt}, \theta_{ijt})$

where θ_{ijt} are factors that affect the underlying cost of producing the commodity and will typically vary across location and across time.

Our method is to study reduced form relationships of the kind illustrated in equation 3. Let C_{ijt} be those observable variables that may reflect intertemporal and spatial differentials in costs. In addition, we assume that there are unchanging characteristics of the communities themselves that affect costs (e.g., location and climate), as well as changes in the macroeconomic environment that affect the costs of all cities the same way each period. Under these assumptions, we augment the equation with fixed effects for city and for time. Assuming a semilogarithmic specification for equation 3, we obtain:

[4] $\ln p_{ijt} = \beta_{1i} \tau_{ijt} + \beta_{2i} C_{ijt} + CITY_{ij}$

$+ TIME_{it} + \varepsilon_{ijt}$

where $CITY_{ij}$ represents the city effects, $TIME_{it}$ represents the time effects (i.e., quarterly dummy variables), and ε_{ijt} is a white noise error.

From the viewpoint of tax incidence, the key parameter is β_{1i}. In interpreting its value, it is useful to relate β_{1i} back to the question of whether taxes are under- or overshifted into prices, which is a statement about tax-inclusive prices q_{ijt}. Imagine an increase of dx in the tax revenue raised from a particular commodity (i.e., the specific tax equivalent of a given *ad valorem* tax increase). By how much does the tax-inclusive price rise? One can show that:

[5] $\dfrac{\partial q_{ijt}}{\partial x} = 1 + \dfrac{\beta_{1i}}{1 + \beta_{1i}\tau_{ijt}}$.

The conventional assumption is that $\beta_{1i} = 0$ so that the tax-inclusive price perfectly reflects any taxes levied on it in dollar terms. Assuming that the tax rate, τ_{ijt}, is small relative to one, then we can think of β_{1i} as a coefficient of under- or overshifting. With competitive markets

---

[4] This could be a vector. In the scalar case, it can be interpreted as price or quantity.

Sales Taxes and Prices

and constant costs, $\beta_{li} = 0$ for all i. In this context, it is important to note our implicit assumption that β_{li} is independent of i—it is the same in every city. This is clearly a restrictive assumption, and below we discuss some possible ways of relaxing it.

A further conceptual issue concerns market dynamics. Our discussion so far has, in effect, focused only on the ultimate or long-run impact of a tax. There are, however, a host of reasons why tax incidence may differ in the long and short runs in competitive and other market structures. These include entry and exit of firms and changes in capacity choices by existing firms. It seems reasonable to allow for the possibility that such effects take place only slowly. More generally, numerous theories suggest that firms' prices will not respond instantaneously to changes in their economic environments. (See, e.g., Ball and Mankiw (1994).) Mindful of these concerns, we also estimate several models that include some dynamic component.

DATA

Price Data

Our price data are from publications issued by the American Chamber of Commerce Researchers Association (ACCRA). ACCRA's objective is to construct quarterly price indices for each of a large group of U.S. cities. The ACCRA data gathering teams are instructed to select establishments and neighborhoods used by a "mid-management executive household." Schoeni (1996) compared an ACCRA-based price index to an index based on BLS data for 23 cities. The two indices agree fairly closely, with a correlation of 0.715.[5] (As Schoeni notes, one would not expect the two indices to correspond exactly because they cover somewhat different commodities and the geographic boundaries of the communities are not quite the same.)

We use the raw data upon which the price indices are based, reported in volumes that are published each quarter. The series is available from 1975 second quarter to the present. However, the set of cities surveyed and the array of commodities whose prices are sampled grow through time. In the end, we chose 12 commodities and 155 cities. The commodities were chosen because the data for them existed over a reasonably long period of time.[6] We converted the prices into real terms by deflating with the consumer price index. They are listed in Table 1 along with the years for which the data exist and summary statistics. The proxies for cross-city variation in costs, detailed below, are available only after the second quarter of 1982, so that our econometric work is based on observations from 1982 second quarter through 1990 third quarter (about 4,200 observations per commodity).

Three aspects of the table are noteworthy. (1) The commodities are narrowly defined. In some cases, we even have specific brand names. (2) The characteristics of some of the commodities change during our time period. The time effects in equation 4 adequately capture such changes.[7] (3) There is substantial spatial

---

[5] Consistent with this finding, when Card and Krueger (1995) used the ACCRA data in some of their work on the minimum wage, they found that using ACCRA data and the (limited) BLS data on city price indices produces very similar results.

[6] In addition to the commodities in the table, we also collected data on cigarettes, alcohol, gasoline, and tobacco products. However, due to the complex tax regulations governing these items, we do not have results for them at the present time.

[7] Consider, for example, the change in the spin balance from two wheels to one. In effect, this is a one time change in the price of the "commodity" spin balance, which increases the intercept of the regression line in every subsequent quarter. Since each quarter has its own dichotomous variable, this effect is automatically captured.

TABLE 1
SUMMARY OF PRICE DATA (1982 DOLLARS)

Item	Mean (in 1982 Dollars)	Standard Deviation	Number of Observations	Quarters (Year/Quarter)
Bananas: 1 pound	0.36	0.07	4,626	1982/26–1990/3
Bread: 24 ounce loaf	0.57	0.12	4,626	1982/26–1990/3
Big Mac: Quarter Pounder with cheese (McDonalds)	1.26	0.09	4,444	1982/26–1990/3
Crisco: 3 pound can	2.24	0.28	4,626	1982/26–1990/3
Eggs: 1 dozen large Grade A	0.78	0.16	4,626	1982/26–1990/3
Kleenex (facial tissues)				
200 count	0.86	0.07	849	1982/26–1983/3
175 count	0.85	0.07	3,777	1983/46–1990/3
Milk: 1/2 gallon carton	1.07	0.13	4,626	1982/26–1990/3
Monopoly (board game) Parker Brothers, No. 9 edition	8.25	1.11	4,582	1982/26–1990/3
Shampoo: 11 ounce bottle	2.50	0.32	4,581	1982/26–1990/3
Soda: 1 liter Coke	1.20	0.25	4,626	1982/26–1990/3
Spin balance				
2 wheels	10.41	1.54	849	1982/26–1983/3
1 wheel	4.83	0.71	3,638	1983/46–1990/3
Underwear (boys): 3 briefs, cotton (lowest price)	3.78	0.68	4,312	1982/26–1990/3

and temporal variation in prices, as indicated by relatively large standard deviations.

Similarly, we selected the cities mainly on the criterion that they be in the data set for a sufficiently long period.[8] The set of cities that reports to ACCRA varies over time because some local Chambers of Commerce choose not to collect the data in some quarters. We have no reason to believe that this biases the sample. However, the fact that the panel is unbalanced suggests that heteroskedasticity may be an issue in the estimation of equation 4. In all of our estimates, therefore, we report t-statistics calculated from robust (Huber) standard errors.

The ACCRA publications report the average, net-of-tax price for each commodity in each city. The samples used to construct a "representative" price for each commodity in each city are relatively small—the price for each city is generally based on the average of a sample of between 3 and 12 stores. This reduces the signal-to-noise ratio in this variable as a representation of the true mean price in each city. Since the price variable appears on the left-hand side, measurement error of this kind should not bias the results. In particular, even if the samples of stores were "unrepresentative," we can think of no plausible reason that this should induce a correlation between the regression error and any of the right-hand-side variables in equation 4.

Tax Data

Our tax rate variable, τ_{ijt}, includes all sales taxes levied on the commodity (state,

---
[8] We chose cities that appeared in the data for at least one quarter every year between 1982 and 1990.

Sales Taxes and Prices

county, and local). We also need information about the tax status of each of the goods in our data set. For example, many jurisdictions subject food to a lower rate of tax or exempt it altogether. Some of the tax information was available in the series *Significant Features of Fiscal Federalism*, published by the Advisory Council on Intergovernmental Relations. However, many of the required county and city tax rates were not included in this series. We obtained the remainder of the tax data from Vertex, Inc., a firm near Philadelphia that provides advice to companies relating to compliance with state and local taxes. In this context, it is important to note that the total tax rate on a commodity is not necessarily the simple sum of the state, county, and local rates. Rather, in a few states, such as New Mexico, the state in effect reduces its component of the total tax rate on a commodity if a given locality decides to levy its own tax on that commodity.

The mean tax rates and standard deviations for different commodity groupings are given in Table 2. The figures suggest that taxes are lowest on repairs and food. The coefficient of variation of taxes is lowest for clothing and greatest for the general tax rate. The ranges of the tax rates are fairly similar for all the cases.

With respect to temporal variation, it will not surprise most readers to know that mean tax rates have been increasing through time. The average general tax rate is close to 4.5 percent at the beginning of the sample period and trends upward to almost 6 percent by the end. However, food and repairs have been largely exempt from this tendency (and average tax rates on food even fell in the early 1980s). Tax rates appear to vary more in the cross section than they do through time. The intertemporal coefficient of variation in mean general tax rates is just 0.11, while the cross-sectional variation in 1988 quarter 1 (a typical quarter) is 0.21. This will be important in our discussion below on some of the issues associated with dynamics. To get a feel for the cross-sectional dispersion in tax rates and its intertemporal variation, consider the histograms in Figure 1, which record the variation in tax rates on two commodities (food and clothing) at two points in time, five years apart. This pictorially reinforces the point that there is variation both in the cross section and in the time series. We will be getting our identification of tax rate effects from intertemporal variation/deviations from city-specific means.

Cost Data

Our model also requires that we account for measurable differences in costs across jurisdiction and time, C_{ijt}. There are no really satisfactory quarterly data on input costs at the community level. However, the ACCRA data contain several variables that may serve at least as rough proxies in this context. Specifically, we attempt to proxy for differences in rental, wage, and energy costs as follows: For rental costs, we use the rental value of a typical two-bedroom apartment. In principle, it would have been desirable to have

TABLE 2
SUMMARY OF TAX RATES

Item	Mean	Standard Deviation	Minimum	Maximum
Food tax rate	0.019	0.028	0	0.0825
Soda tax rate	0.051	0.019	0	0.085
Clothes tax rate	0.052	0.017	0	0.085
Repairs tax rate	0.022	0.028	0	0.0825
General tax rate	0.055	0.012	0	0.085

Notes: The rates in this table and the commodities in our sample correspond as follows: food tax rate applies to milk, eggs, bananas, bread, and Crisco; soda tax rate to soda; clothes tax rate to underwear; repairs tax rate to spin balance; and general tax rate to Big Mac, Monopoly, Kleenex, and shampoo.

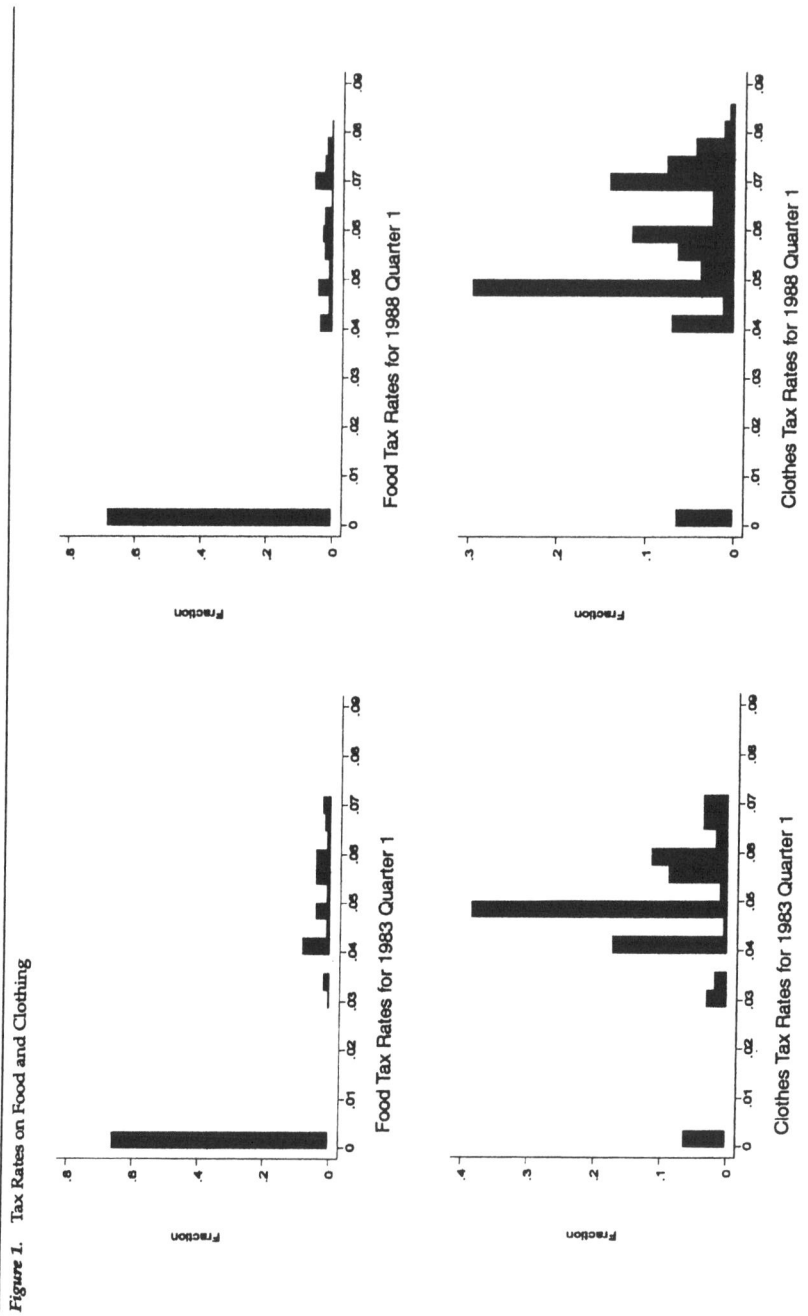

Figure 1. Tax Rates on Food and Clothing

Sales Taxes and Prices

a measure of commercial rather than residential rents. However, we were unable to obtain a series on this for our cities. For wage costs, we use the minimum labor charge for a home-service call to repair a clothes washing machine. Clearly, this need not be representative of the general wage level, but it may be correlated with it. For energy costs, we used the price of one gallon of unleaded gasoline. Again, there are many other dimensions to energy costs, but we expect this to be a significant component of total costs.[9]

We believe that the inclusion of these three variables together with time effects and city fixed effects should pick up a very substantial fraction of intercity cost variation. While the cost variables are far from ideal, our confidence in them is somewhat bolstered by the fact that, for every commodity we study, whenever the coefficient on one of these cost variables is statistically significant, it is also positive. This is just what one would expect if they are indeed proxying for costs. In any case, if we omit these variables from the analysis, our results are basically unchanged. (For specifics, see the Appendix.) As a further check, we re-estimated the model with some possibly better cost data that are available for a subsample of our cities on an annual basis. This exercise, which is described in greater detail below, also does not affect our substantive findings.

RESULTS

We begin by discussing the estimates of equation 4 and then analyze some alternative specifications to assess the robustness of the results.

Results from the Canonical Specification

To begin, we estimated equation 4 for each of our commodities.[10] This specification includes city effects, time effects, and the three cost variable described above.

The first column in Table 3 shows the number of observations used to estimate the regressions for the associated commodity. (The sample sizes vary somewhat across commodities because some data are missing during certain time periods.) The second column shows the estimate β_{li} for the corresponding commodity and the associated t-statistic. Recall from the third section that in the commonly assumed case of full shifting, β_{li} is zero. We cannot reject the standard model of full shifting for several of our commodities—Big Macs, eggs, Kleenex, Monopoly games, and spin balances. However, more than half of our commodities exhibit overshifting. The coefficients in the bananas, bread, Crisco, milk, shampoo, soda, and boys' underwear equations are all positive and exceed their standard errors by more than a factor of two.

From a quantitative standpoint, how important is overshifting for the commodities that exhibit it? One can obtain an answer by recalling from equation 5 that if the tax rate is relatively small, then β_{li} measures the extent of overshifting. For example, the estimate of β_{li} for bananas is 0.83, suggesting that an increase in the tax rate that is sufficient to raise 10 cents of revenue per pound increases the tax-inclusive price by about 18 cents. Some of the overshifting parameters are less than one, but those for bread, Crisco, shampoo, soda, and boys' underwear exceed one—raising a dime of revenue per unit sold increases the price per unit by more than 20 cents.

---

[9] The means and standard deviations of the three cost variables are rent: mean = 322, standard deviation = 64; wage: mean = 22.07, standard deviation = 3.58; gas: mean = 0.97, and standard deviation = 0.20.

[10] We also augmented equation 4 with a quadratic term in the tax rate. In a few cases, the quadratic term was statistically significant, but did not affect the substantive conclusions.

TABLE 3
ESTIMATED SHIFTING PARAMETERS FROM THE CANONICAL MODEL*

	(1) Observations	(2) Shifting Parameter
Bananas	4,057	0.828 (2.37)
Bread	4,057	2.42 (4.90)
Big Mac	4,020	−0.0963 (−0.514)
Crisco	4,057	1.03 (6.26)
Eggs	4,057	0.0443 (0.233)
Kleenex	4,158	0.0818 (0.319)
Milk	4,057	0.525 (3.61)
Monopoly	4,158	0.698 (1.66)
Shampoo	4,157	1.042 (3.17)
Soda	4,158	1.29 (4.38)
Spin balance	4,158	−0.0416 (−0.077)
Underwear	3,888	1.51 (3.07)

*Column (1) shows the number of observations; column (2) shows β_t, the coefficient on the tax rate from equation 4. (All figures in parentheses are t-statistics calculated from heteroskedasticity consistent standard errors.) All regressions include city effects; time effects; and measures of real rental, wage, and energy costs.

Making Sense of the Results

For some commodities, our results are consistent with the competitive paradigm. For the others, they are not, and it is natural to wonder if the results are plausible. There are two main ways in which one can make sense of overshifting.

Imperfect Competition

As we stressed in the third section, recent developments in incidence theory in imperfectly competitive markets indicate that overshifting is by no means a pathological phenomenon.[11] There are, of course, many models of imperfect competition. Not all of them are plausible representations of the retail sector. A model with free entry and decreasing average cost seems a sensible starting point for this section. Can overshifting occur in such a model? As shown by Delipalla and Keen (1992), the answer is yes. Indeed, in a conjectural variations model with fixed costs, constant marginal costs of production, entry, and locally constant price elasticity of demand, overshifting *must* occur, at sufficiently low tax rates. While we do not know if these assumptions on parameters are correct in the markets of the commodities we study, they are certainly the kinds of assumptions that economists are comfortable building into their models.

A closely related question is whether it is plausible for the after-tax prices of different commodities in the same store to react very differently to the same change in their tax rates. To form an intuitive basis for understanding this result, think about the standard competitive model. In that model, provided that the supply curve is upward sloping, the effect of a tax upon price depends on the elasticities of the supply and demand curves, and there is no reason to believe that these are the same across commodities. Indeed, in the familiar monopoly model, even if marginal costs are constant, the price response depends on the elasticity of the demand curve—there is no presumption that this elasticity is constant across commodities, and hence there is no presumption that the price responsiveness to tax rates is the same. In the same spirit,

---

[11] Even in the absence of oligopoly, overshifting is possible in a decreasing cost industry because of scale economies external to the firm. However, most plausible models of scale economies would introduce some kind of imperfect competition.

Sales Taxes and Prices

Delipalla and Keen (1992) show that the extent of overshifting depends on the elasticity of the slope of the demand curve and the change in marginal cost as output increases. Even for three commodities as "similar" as milk, eggs, and bread (they are often near each other in the grocery store), there is no reason to believe that demand and cost conditions (including elasticities of slopes) are the same.[12] In short, from a theoretical standpoint, neither overshifting nor differential responses to taxes are unexpected phenomena. Rather, they can occur in a variety of models, including ones in which long-run profits are bid to zero.

In the Delipalla–Keen and related models, the producer of the commodity in effect sells it directly to the consumer. Given that many of our commodities are retailed in common outlets, it might be worthwhile to distinguish between market structures at the retail and upstream levels. For commodities whose prices are set in national or global markets, the relevant effect is that coming from the retail market. For commodities that are priced and produced locally, the results we observe could be due to noncompetitive behavior at both levels. This is another reason why differences among commodities might occur. It is tempting to try to rationalize the findings for the various commodities in Table 3 on the basis of guesses about the nature of the various market structures. But without details on the individual markets, this would be a perilous exercise.[13]

Given the potential importance of noncompetitive retail markets in the interpretation of some of our results, it behooves us to ask whether it is reasonable to characterize retail trade as being a noncompetitive industry. It turns out that a number of papers in the industrial organization literature have made just this claim. These papers, which are reviewed in Anderson (1990), examine the relationship between grocery store prices or grocery store profits and market concentration. They find a positive and statistically significant effect and conclude that many local markets are indeed imperfectly competitive. This finding has been questioned by other work, also surveyed in Anderson (1990). The critics argue that the positive correlation between grocery prices and market concentration may be due to higher costs in more concentrated markets, not market power. Our goal is not to assert that one side or the other is correct in this debate. Rather, we want to point out that the claim that local retail markets are imperfectly competitive is taken seriously by industrial organization economists.

Finally, we note that Hall (1988), using an entirely different data set and methodology, also finds that retail trade is not competitive. Using aggregate data on output and labor input changes, he estimates for a variety of industries a parameter that is equal to the ratio of price to marginal cost. Under competition, of course, this ratio is unity; for retail trade, Hall reports a value of 2.355. This is not only consistent with our qualitative finding of noncompetitive behavior, but the quantitative results are remarkably consistent with several of our estimated shifting parameters.

Common Effects on Taxes and Prices

The interpretation of our results has implicitly assumed that the year effects and fixed effects adequately capture changes

---

[12] Indeed, the literature suggests that the elasticities of demand of these commodities are rather different from each other, let alone the elasticities of the slopes of the demand curves. An estimate of the elasticity of demand for milk is –1.63 (Boehm, 1975); for eggs –0.15 (Tomek and Robinson, 1981); and for bread –0.372 (Mariak and Logan, 1971). Hence, even in the basic textbook model of taxation in short-run competitive markets, we would expect these commodities to be associated with different amounts of tax shifting.

[13] That said, it may be useful to point out that our results are *not* the kind that would be obtained in a competitive model with an upward sloping supply curve.

in demand across space and time. Suppose, however, that as cities grow, two phenomena occur simultaneously. First, the demand for public spending rises and tax rates increase, and second, the demand for certain commodities increases. To the extent that the commodities are characterized by increasing marginal costs, tax rates and prices rise together. We observe prices rising with tax rates, but this is due to the demand shift, and not the change in the tax rate per se. Hence, it tells us little or nothing about whether overshifting has occurred. Related to this, it is possible that governments increase taxes only during periods of high demand since political resistance will tend to be lower at those times. Again, this could suggest a positive link between taxes and prices, which has nothing to do with incidence.

While it is certainly plausible that sales tax *revenues* will increase with population, it is much less plausible that sales tax *rates* will do so. This notion was confirmed when we analyzed the relationship between tax rates and population density in another data set and found that a doubling of density does not show up even in the fourth decimal place of the tax rate.[14]

Nevertheless, the possibility remains that *some* variable is simultaneously driving prices and tax rates.[15] To investigate this notion, we begin by observing that, if it is correct, then the *ratio* of the price of commodity i to the price of some untaxed good should not depend on the tax rate for commodity i, ceteris paribus. Now it happens that about 65 percent of our observations had no tax on spin balances.[16] We re-estimated each of our basic equations using this subsample with the log of the ratio of the price of the particular good to the price of a spin balance on the left-hand side. In effect, spin balances served as an untaxed numeraire. We found that the commodities that exhibited statistically significant coefficients on the tax rate variable in Table 3 continued to do so.[17] We believe that this constitutes fairly compelling evidence that our results are not being driven by city-specific or time-varying shocks.[18]

---

[14] We were unable to examine this question using our data because quarterly population data on cities are not available. The data for this exercise contained annual observations on all 48 continental states from 1950 to 1990 and are described in Besley and Case (1995). We measured the state tax rate as sales tax revenues divided by state income. We estimated a regression of this on state fixed effects, year effects, and the population density by state (1,440 observations in total).

[15] Perhaps, for example, prices tend to be high in cities with inelastic demand and sales taxes tend to be higher in cities with inelastic demand because rates are being set according to the Ramsey rule. Or, in the case of a regulated commodity like milk, a state may allow higher milk prices through regulation and in exchange impose higher taxes on it.

[16] A spin balance is a device that spins wheels with tires mounted on them and senses whether they are in dynamic (spinning) balance. It produces readouts that allow the placement of lead weights on the rims that even things out.

[17] See column (1) of Table A.1 in the Appendix for details.

[18] Another possible problem along the same lines stems from the fact that some proportion of the sales tax falls on intermediate purchases of firms. Indeed, Ring (1999) estimates that, on average, about 41 percent of sales tax revenues are from intermediate goods. If such taxes raise the cost of final goods and services, then the tax-induced increases in prices that we observe may have nothing to do with overshifting. More formally, suppose that we can write the cost of production of commodity i in city j in year t as $C_{ijt} = \alpha_{ijt} + \gamma_i \tau_{ijt}$, where γ_i is a parameter that measures the dependence of costs upon (intermediate goods) taxation. If so, the estimate of β_{1i} generated by the regression in equation 4 will be biased upward providing that γ_i is positive. Note that by itself the fact that a substantial proportion of state sales taxes are comprised of taxes on intermediate goods tells us little about the magnitude of γ_i. For example, if input prices are set in competitive national markets, then these taxes are borne by input suppliers, and $\gamma_i = 0$. Of course, we do not know the extent to which the inputs are purchased in national as opposed to local markets; further, the national markets might not be competitive. Hence, the possibility that our overshifting results are due to intermediate goods taxation remains a real one.

Sales Taxes and Prices

As a further test of robustness against the possibility of common shocks, we re-ran the canonical specification including time-varying demographic, economic, and political variables. Since quarterly, city-specific time-varying regressors are not available, we had to rely on the yearly state level data from Besley and Case (1995). This will, at least partially, control for common influences on prices and taxes at the state level, especially given that a substantial portion of tax variation is at the state level. This led to almost no changes in the basic results.[19]

Alternative Specifications

Dynamics

One possible problem with our canonical specification is that it assumes that the full effect of a change in the tax rate occurs instantaneously. As noted in the third section, however, it might take time for changes in tax rates to become fully incorporated into prices. The most straightforward way to allow for this possibility is to include lagged values of the tax rates in addition to their contemporaneous values. We augmented equation 4 with 20 lagged values of the tax rate, placing no restrictions on the pattern of the lags.

Our initial hope was that this exercise would yield useful information about the time pattern of the response of prices to tax rates. However, this hope was frustrated by the relatively small amount of intertemporal variation in tax rates (see the fourth section, above). This made it impossible to estimate with any precision the coefficients on the lagged tax rates. However, the long-run incidence, which is given by the sum of the coefficients on the lags, can be estimated with some precision. The sums of the lag coefficients are reported in column (1) of Table 4. Qualitatively, the results tend to be in line with those from Table 3—generally, commodities that were characterized by overshifting in the canonical model are also characterized by overshifting in the model with lags. These commodities include bananas, Crisco, milk, and underwear. Similarly, most of the commodities that had insignificant coefficients in Table 3 also have insignificant coefficients in column (1) of Table 4: eggs, Monopoly games, and spin balance. The main differences are in Big Macs and Kleenex (where the coefficients go from insignificant to positive significant) and shampoo and soda (from positive significant to positive insignificant). In no case is there a statistically significant change in signs. We conclude that incorporating some simple dynamics does not seriously affect the substantive finding—a substantial number of commodities exhibit overshifting.

To sharpen these results and be able to say something useful about timing issues requires that one impose some restrictions on the lag structure.[20] The simplest restriction is that the weights on the lagged variables decline geometrically. As is well known (see Maddala (1977)), one can transform an equation with a geometric lag pattern to obtain a specification that

---

[19] This exercise and the others in this section address the possibility that a common shock is affecting all tax rates and prices in a given jurisdiction. Another possibility is that some shock is affecting the price and the tax rate on a *given commodity* in a jurisdiction. To deal with such a possibility, one would need an instrument that, on a city-by-city basis, is correlated with tax rates and not with prices. It is hard to think of such an instrument. In this context, it is natural to think of a model in which communities use Ramsey pricing principles to set tax rates. Since Ramsey pricing is best thought of as trying to achieve a target post-tax price, this will induce a negative correlation between tax rates and tax-exclusive prices, so that our estimates of the coefficients on the various tax rates would be biased downward.

[20] Of course, to the extent that the wrong structure is imposed, the resulting coefficients will be inconsistent. Nevertheless, dozens of previous studies in a variety of contexts have found this to be a useful way to proceed.

TABLE 4
ALTERNATIVE SPECIFICATIONS

	(1) Unrestricted Lag Structure	(2) Short-Run Coefficient	(3) Lag Coefficient	(4) Long-Run Coefficient	(5) Autocorrelated Errors	(6) F-Statistic p-value (on Interactions)	(7) Coefficient with Interactions
Bananas	2.10 (2.80)	0.620 (1.70)	0.224 (12.0)	0.799	1.02 (3.41)	0.054	1.28 (3.28)
Bread	1.78 (1.65)	1.52 (3.10)	0.312 (14.9)	2.21	1.38 (2.95)	0.81	—
Big Mac	0.868 (3.04)	−0.0342 (−0.178)	0.366 (11.3)	−0.0539	−0.149 (−.928)	0.49	—
Crisco	1.21 (2.70)	0.612 (4.47)	0.519 (25.8)	1.27	0.870 (5.04)	0.059	0.813 (3.83)
Eggs	−0.684 (−1.35)	−0.0136 (−0.070)	0.342 (16.5)	−0.0207	0.244 (1.20)	0.024	0.00199 (0.003)
Kleenex	0.866 (2.09)	−0.190 (−0.078)	0.338 (17.0)	−0.287	−0.281 (−1.14)	0.41	—
Milk	0.771 (1.98)	0.284 (2.42)	0.550 (26.5)	0.631	0.189 (1.65)	0.045	0.483 (2.50)
Monopoly	−0.663 (0.838)	0.461 (1.10)	0.397 (12.7)	0.765	0.643 (1.57)	0.23	—
Shampoo	0.339 (0.578)	0.760 (2.34)	0.332 (15.7)	1.14	1.02 (3.38)	0.38	—
Soda	1.05 (1.58)	0.831 (3.00)	0.307 (16.7)	1.20	0.631 (2.15)	0.65	—
Spin balance	−0.306 (−0.463)	0.107 (0.211)	0.455 (18.3)	0.196	−1.11 (−2.20)	0.001	0.346 (0.548)
Underwear	2.23 (2.68)	0.883 (1.91)	0.455 (20.8)	1.62	1.28 (2.68)	0.41	—

Note: All figures in parentheses are t-statistics calculated from heteroskedasticity consistent standard errors. Column (1) shows the sum of the coefficients on τ_{it} and its lags in a specification without any lag structure imposed. Columns (2), (3), and (4) are from a specification with a geometric lag structure: (2) shows the coefficient on the contemporaneous tax rate, (3) shows the coefficient on the lagged price, and (4) shows the long-run coefficient on the tax rate. Column (5) shows the value of β_1 when the model is estimated with a first-order autocorrelated error structure; the correlation coefficient varies across cities. Column (6) is the p-value on the F-statistic testing the joint significance of closeness to the border and land area variables interacted with the tax rate. Column (7) gives the derivative of the log-price with respect to the tax rate evaluated at the means. All specifications include city effects; time effects; and measures of real rental, wage, and energy costs.

Sales Taxes and Prices

includes on the right-hand side all of the original variables plus the lagged dependent variable.

The coefficient on the lagged dependent variable, which we denote λ_i, measures the rate of decay in the lag distribution—the lower the value of λ_i the faster the decay, i.e., the greater the proportion of the impact that is felt immediately. In this specification, the coefficient on the contemporaneous value of the variable (here, the coefficient on τ_{ijt}) gives the short-run impact on the dependent variable. The long-run impact is the short-run impact divided by $(1 - \lambda_i)$.[21]

The results are summarized in columns (2), (3), and (4) of Table 4. Column (2) shows the coefficient on the contemporaneous tax rate. Note that for most commodities, the sign of the coefficient is the same as that on the corresponding coefficient in the canonical specification in Table 3. (The only exceptions—eggs, Kleenex, and spin balances—have imprecisely estimated coefficients in both specifications.) All the coefficients that were insignificant stay that way, and only one of the coefficients that was significant becomes insignificant (bananas). Moreover, for each commodity with a precisely estimated coefficient, the coefficient in column (2) is smaller in absolute value than its counterpart in Table 3. This is consistent with an interpretation of the coefficients in the canonical specification as being an amalgam of the long- and short-run effects, while those in column (2) are short run.

The lag coefficients (λ_i) are shown in column (3). They all fall between 0.22 and 0.55. We discuss the implications for the speed of adjustment below. Column (4) shows the long-run effects of taxes on prices, the column (2) parameter divided by one minus the column (3) parameter. There is a quite striking similarity to the results in Table 3. We conclude that allowing for dynamics in a conventional fashion does not affect our basic result, that taxes on a number of commodities are overshifted.

Let us now turn to the estimates of λ_i in column (3), which are of independent interest. As noted above, these coefficients determine speeds of adjustment. Specifically, the average lag length is given by $\lambda_i/(1 - \lambda_i)$. Hence, according to our estimates, the mean lags vary from 0.29 to 1.27 quarters. Prices react very quickly to changes in tax rates.

This finding is relevant to the debate over price stickiness in the macroeconomics literature. The New Keynesian view assumes adjustment costs to explain price rigidity, while the New Classical macroeconomists favor models with no rigidities in wages or prices. Ultimately, the question of who is right must be answered empirically. Carlton (1986) investigates this issue using data on transactions prices. He finds evidence of relatively long periods of price stickiness. However, he does not look at how shocks to costs get transmitted into prices. Cecchetti (1986) looks at evidence from magazine prices and finds that, during periods of inflation, price adjustments are more frequent, although there are considerable reductions in real prices before some adjustment. However, again, he is not looking at the effect of a price shock. Blinder (1991) uses interview data on price setting behavior of firms. He asks about hypothetical responses to cost shocks and estimates that these are passed through to prices in about three months. Remarkably, this is about the mean lag that we

---

[21] In a panel data context, biases may arise in estimating specifications with a lagged dependent variable. However, provided that the error term is not autocorrelated and there is a relatively large number of time-series observations (as is the case here), such biases are likely to be inconsequential. For further discussion, see Hsiao (1986). The assumption of temporally uncorrelated errors seems reasonable given that we have taken out city and time effects. Nevertheless, we also estimated the equations using lagged values as instrumental variables. This led to somewhat less precise estimates, but the substantive story was the same.

estimate. In short, while the speed of adjustment is not central for the issue of tax shifting, our results provide some support for the view that prices are quite flexible at the microlevel.

A final issue relating to dynamics concerns the regression error in equation 4. We have been assuming that the error is uncorrelated across time periods, but, to the contrary, there might be persistence of shocks. We therefore re-estimated the canonical equation with an AR(1) error and allow the correlation coefficient to vary across cities. The results are shown in column (5) of Table 4. The general patterns exhibited in the canonical model are maintained, although the shifting parameters tend to be somewhat smaller in absolute value.[22]

Including Other Tax Rates

Our specification assumes that only a commodity's own tax rate affects its price. In principle, however, the tax rates on all commodities might affect any given commodity's price through either demand or cost interactions. This observation is particularly relevant because the tax rates on various commodities tend to change at the same time. This might call into question our interpretation of β_{ii} as the independent tax effect.

To investigate this possibility, we re-estimated the canonical model including all the tax rates on the right-hand side. Unfortunately, multicollinearity among the tax rates led to absurd findings. We thereupon re-estimated the equation, without allowing the clothing rate and the general rate to appear together. We found that in only about half the cases were the tax rates that applied to the "other" commodities jointly significant. Even in these cases, the coefficients on the own tax rates were about the same size as those reported above. Patterns of significance were also preserved. In short, our interpretation of the coefficient on the own tax rate as an overshifting parameter seems legitimate.

Interactions with the Tax Variable

Another possible problem with the canonical specification is the implicit assumption that the shifting parameter is the same for each city. There are many ways in which one might relax this assumption. One natural possibility is suggested by the fact that consumers in one jurisdiction may choose to shop in another jurisdiction if the tax rates there are lower (see Trandel (1992)). The extent to which taxes could be shifted to consumers might be less in communities that are closer to jurisdictions with other tax rates, *ceteris paribus*. Another possibility is that the area of a jurisdiction might be related to the size of the retail market and hence affect the extent of shifting.

We were able to obtain the areas of 130 of our cities.[23] Using atlases, we also computed for each city the distance from the nearest state border, which we converted into a dichotomous variable taking a value of one if the distance is less than five miles and zero otherwise. We then augmented the specification in Table 3 with each of these variables interacted with the tax rate. Our first step after re-estimating the regressions was to test the joint significance of the interaction variables. The results are shown in column (6) of Table 4. These results indicate that, for most of the commodities, the interaction terms are jointly insignificant. For the cases in which they are significant (bananas, Crisco, eggs, milk, and spin balances), we report the shifting coefficient evaluated at the means

---

[22] The spin balance parameter is –1.11, which suggests the implausible result that the after-tax price falls after imposition of a tax. One cannot, however, reject the hypothesis that the coefficient is one.

[23] The data on area as well as the other variables discussed below were obtained from the *City and County Fact Book* for 1988.

Sales Taxes and Prices

in column (7).[24] The commodities that exhibited overshifting in the canonical specification continue to do so when interactions are included.

We used distance from the border and area of the city largely because these variables are available and can plausibly be regarded as fixed through time. Of course, time-changing variables might also be candidates for interacting with the tax rate. However, we do not have quarterly or even annual data on any relevant city characteristics. We experimented with several variables whose values, though not fixed through time, were available at least for 1985. These are income per capita, population, population density, and retail stores per square mile. These variables might proxy for the state of retail competition and, hence, are candidates for interacting with the tax rate. Since these variables are not likely to be constant through time, including them in the analysis introduces possible measurement errors into the regression. Thus, we must be careful in placing too much weight on these results.

We find that, in almost all cases, the interaction terms are jointly significant. However, most of the results from the canonical model continue to hold. In the few cases in which they do not, this might be due to measurement error in jurisdiction characteristics. Clearly, this issue merits investigation in future work, but given the quality of the data on city characteristics, we find the results to be encouraging to the view that our initial findings are robust.[25]

Cost Variables

As noted above, our cost variables—the rental value of a typical two-bedroom apartment, the minimum labor charge for a home-service call to repair a clothes washing machine, and the price of one gallon of unleaded gasoline—are far from ideal proxies for differences in production costs across jurisdictions. It is possible to obtain somewhat better data on labor and energy prices for a subset of the communities in our sample. Specifically, from the Bureau of Labor Statistics volume *Employment and Earnings* and the Department of Energy's publication *Typical Electricity Bills*, we can obtain wage and commercial electricity rate data, respectively, on a city-by-city basis. The problem is that both the wage and electricity data are available for only 57 out of the 155 cities in our sample. Further, the electricity data are available only annually. This leaves us with many fewer observations to estimate the regression parameters. (The number of observations in a typical equation falls from about 4,200 to 390.) Nevertheless, it seemed worthwhile to re-estimate the model with this subsample.

We found that four of the commodities that were characterized by overshifting in Table 3 now have insignificant coefficients on their tax-rate variables—Crisco, milk, shampoo, and underwear. On the other hand, bananas, bread, and soda continue to have the positive and statistically significant coefficients associated with overshifting. (Detailed results are reported in column (2) of the Appendix table.) What is one to make of these findings? With a dramatically smaller sample size, one expects larger standard errors—*ceteris paribus*, when the sample size decreases by a factor of n, standard errors increase by a factor of the square root of n. Hence, it is no surprise that some of our coefficients are rendered insignificant by this exercise. The fact that several commodities nevertheless continue to exhibit positive and statistically significant values of β_{li} suggests that our finding of tax overshifting in some commodities is not due to inadequate con-

---

[24] The shifting coefficient is $\beta_h + \beta_{n}\bar{x}$, where β_{li} is the vector of means of the interaction terms and β_n is the associated parameter vector.

[25] It should also be observed that the joint significance of the interaction variables is per se evidence against the long-run competitive model with constant costs, which would predict identical shifting across jurisdictions.

trols for cost differences across cities. In this context, it is important to recall that our equations all contain city effects, and these probably pick up the important across-city differences in production costs.

Comparison with Poterba's Specification

As noted earlier, Poterba (1996) employed a similar approach to ours, but was unable to reject the hypothesis of one-for-one shifting predicted by the competitive model. In an attempt to reconcile our results with Poterba's, we focused on the major differences between his specification and our own.

First, Poterba estimates his equation in first differences rather than with city dichotomous variables. We examined whether a first-difference specification is consistent with our data. Specifically, for each commodity, we re-estimated the canonical equation deleting the city dichotomous variables and including on the right-hand side the lagged value of the left-hand side variable, as well as the lagged values of each of the right-hand side variables. If the first-difference specification is correct, then the lagged dependent variable should have a coefficient of one, and the lagged value of each right-hand side variable should be the negative of the coefficient of the associated contemporaneous variable. This joint hypothesis was strongly rejected for each commodity. We conclude that a first-difference specification is not consistent with our data.

Second, Poterba does not include time effects, although he does use the economy-wide inflation rate to control for changes in the macroeconomic environment. However, we continue to find overshifting for several commodities when we replace the time effects with the inflation rate.

Finally, Poterba's commodities are more aggregated than ours. To investigate the possible effects of aggregation, we formed a composite "grocery" commodity by taking a weighted average of the relevant individual items' prices.[26] If we estimate our canonical model using the composite, we find overshifting. The coefficient on the tax rate is 1.21 with a t-statistic of 5.21. Further, if we estimate the model with the composite *and* impose differencing (despite the results of the statistical test discussed above), we continue to find a positive and statistically significant coefficient—1.70 with a t-statistic of 9.03. This is the closest approximation to Poterba's setup allowed by our data.

Where does this leave us? For some commodities, we obtain results consistent with Poterba's—full shifting of taxes. However, unlike Poterba, we find that taxes on some commodities are overshifted, and this result holds even when we use his specification. Given that the commodities that we analyze are simply not the same as those in Poterba's sample, ultimately, it is difficult to reconcile the two sets of results.

CONCLUSIONS

A time-honored question in public finance is how prices react to the imposition of taxes. Although there is a vast theoretical literature on this question, there has been surprisingly little empirical work. In this paper, we follow a simple and obvious strategy for addressing this issue: we examine the relationship between the prices of particular commodities and the taxes levied upon them. Specifically, we assemble a panel of quarterly data for 12 commodities and 155 cities over the period 1982–90. Importantly, such data allow us to control for fixed effects across jurisdictions that might affect prices, and for shocks in the macroeconomic environment that might affect all cities similarly.

---

[26] The items included are milk, eggs, bananas, bread, Kleenex, and soda. The weights are taken from the ACCRA data and are the same as they use to construct their price indices.

Sales Taxes and Prices

At the same time, this strategy allows us to avoid problems associated with aggregation and small samples that have bedeviled the few previous efforts in this area.

We find a variety of shifting patterns. For some commodities, we cannot reject that taxes are shifted on a one-for-one basis. For others, commodity taxes are overshifted—a ten-cent increase in the revenue extracted from the sale of these commodities leads to an increase in their prices of more than a dime. The finding that some commodities exhibit overshifting is robust to a number of reasonable alternative specifications of the estimating equation. It is consistent with the predictions of certain theoretical models of imperfect competition that seem like reasonable characterizations of the retail sector. What do our results say about the markets for the commodities that exhibit overshifting? They do *not* imply that any particular model of market structure is correct, but they are inconsistent with perfect competition. Hall (1988) also found that many markets, and the retail market in particular, are not competitive. We also find that prices respond quite rapidly to the imposition of taxes—the mean lag length is only about one-quarter. This finding may have implications for the price-flexibility debate in the macroeconomics literature.

The policy implications of our results are striking. Distributional tables for proposed policy changes typically assume that commodity taxes increase consumer prices on a one-for-one basis. If, in fact, prices on some commodities go up more than on a one-for-one basis, then taxes on these items are more burdensome than the usual analyses would suggest. To the extent that our findings for food items hold more generally, taxes that fall on them are likely to be more regressive than is conventionally thought. Such considerations might be important in thinking about recent proposals to introduce a value-added tax in the United States. In the same way, these findings are relevant for evaluating European proposals to harmonize value-added tax rates across countries.

Acknowledgments

The authors are grateful to the team of research assistants, lead by Don Dale and Matthew Liao, who helped to prepare the price data. Vertex Incorporated of Philadelphia provided much useful information about state and local tax systems. Andrew Clarkson, Theresa Osborne, and Abigail Payne ably assisted in analyzing the data. The authors thank the Center for Economic Policy Studies at Princeton, the NBER, and the National Science Foundation for financial support. We are also grateful to two anonymous referees, Laurence Ball, Ben Bernanke, David Bradford, David Card, Stephen Cecchetti, Dennis Epple, William Gentry, Douglas Holtz-Eakin, Bo Honoré, Alan Krueger, Gilbert Metcalf, Joel Slemrod, James Poterba, Greg Trandel, and participants in seminars at Princeton and the Institute for Fiscal Studies for helpful comments and discussions.

REFERENCES

Alcaly, Roger E., and Alvin K. Klevorick.
"Food Prices in Relation to Income Levels in New York City." *Journal of Business* 44 (October, 1971): 380–97.

Anderson, Keith B.
A Review of Structure-Performance Studies in Grocery Retailing. Washington, D.C.: Bureau of Economics, Federal Trade Commission, 1990.

Ball, Laurence, and N. Gregory Mankiw.
"A Sticky Price Manifesto." *Carnegie-Rochester Series on Public Policy* 41 (1994): 127–51.

Besley, Timothy.
"Commodity Taxation and Imperfect Competition: A Note on the Effects of Entry." *Journal of Public Economics* 40 (1989): 359–67.

Besley, Timothy, and Anne C. Case.
"Does Electoral Accountability Affect Economic Policy Choices? Evidence from Gubernatorial Term Limits." *Quarterly Journal of Economics* 105 (August, 1995): 769–98.

Blinder, Alan.
"Why Are Prices Sticky? Preliminary Results from an Interview Study." *American Economic Review* 81 (May, 1991): 89–96.

Boehm, William T.
"The Household Demand for Major Dairy Products in the Southern Region," *Southern Journal of Agricultural Economics* 7 No. 2 (1975): 187–96.

Card, David, and Alan Krueger.
Myth and Measurement: The New Economics of the Minimum Wage. Princeton: Princeton University Press, 1995.

Carlton, Dennis.
"The Rigidity of Prices." *American Economic Review* 76 (September, 1986): 637–58.

Cecchetti, Stephen.
"The Frequency of Price Adjustment: A Study of the Newsstand Prices of Magazines." *Journal of Econometrics* 31 (August, 1986): 255–74.

Delipalla, Sofia, and Michael Keen.
"The Comparison Between Ad Valorem and Specific Taxation Under Imperfect Competition." *Journal of Public Economics* 49 (December, 1992): 351–68.

Dornbusch, Rudiger.
"Exchange Rates and Prices." *American Economic Review* 77 No. 1 (March, 1987): 93–106.

Hall, Robert E.
"The Relationship Between Price and Marginal Cost in U.S. Industry," *Journal of Political Economy* 96 No. 5 (October, 1988): 921–47.

Harris, Jeffrey E.
"The 1983 Increase in the Federal Cigarette Excise Tax." in *Tax Policy and the Economy*, edited by Lawrence H. Summers, 87–111. Cambridge: MIT Press, 1987.

Hsiao, Cheng.
Panel Data. Cambridge: Cambridge University Press, 1986.

Karp, Larry S., and Jeffrey M. Perloff.
"Estimating Market Structure and Tax Incidence: The Japanese Television Market." *Journal of Industrial Economics* 37 No. 3 (March, 1989): 225–39.

Katz, Michael, and Harvey S. Rosen.
"Tax Analysis in an Oligopoly Model." *Public Finance Quarterly* 13 No. 1 (January, 1985): 3–19.

Kotlikoff, Laurence, and Lawrence Summers.
"The Theory of Tax Incidence." In *Handbook of Public Economics*, edited by Alan Auerbach and Martin Feldstein. Amsterdam: North-Holland, 1987.

Maddala, G.S.
Econometrics. New York: McGraw-Hill, 1977.

MacDonald, James M., and Paul E. Nelson.
"Do the Poor Still Pay More? Food Price Variations in Large Metropolitan Areas." *Journal of Urban Economics* 30 No. 3 (November, 1991): 344–59.

Mariak, Theo F., and Samuel H. Logan.
"Monthly Retail Demand for Bread." *Agricultural Economics Research* 23 No. 3 (July, 1971): 58–62.

Metcalf, Gilbert E.
"The Lifetime Incidence of State and Local Taxes: Measuring Changes During the 1980s." In *Tax Progressivity and Income Inequality*, edited by Joel Slemrod, 59–88. New York: Cambridge University Press, 1994.

Pechman, Joseph A., and Benjamin A. Okner.
Who Bears the Tax Burden? Washington, D.C.: The Brookings Institution, 1974.

Poterba, James M.
"Retail Price Reactions to Changes in State and Local Sales Taxes." *National Tax Journal* 49 No. 2 (June, 1996): 165–76.

Poterba, James M., Julio Rotemberg, and Lawrence H. Summers.
"A Tax-Based Test for Nominal Rigidities." *American Economic Review* 76 (September, 1986): 659–75.

Ring, Raymond J.
"Consumers' Share and Producers' Share of the General Sales Tax." *National Tax Journal* 52 No. 1 (March, 1999): 71–90.

Schoeni, Robert F.
"The Effect of Immigrants on the Employment and Wages of Native Workers: Evidence from the 1970s and 1980s." RAND Discussion Paper, 1996.

Seade, Jesus.
"Profitable Cost Increases and the Shifting of Taxation: Equilibrium Responses of Markets to Oligopoly." University of Warwick Discussion Paper, 1985.

Stern, Nicholas H.
"The Effects of Taxation, Price Control and Government Contracts in Oligopoly."

Sales Taxes and Prices

Journal of Public Economics 32 (1987): 133–58.

Sullivan, Daniel.
"Testing Hypotheses About Firm Behavior in the Cigarette Industry." *Journal of Political Economy* 93 No. 3 (June, 1985): 586–98.

Sumner, Daniel A.
"Measurement of Monopoly Behavior: An Application to the Cigarette Industry." *Journal of Political Economy* 89 (October, 1981): 1010–19.

Tomek, William G., and Kenneth L. Robinson. *Agricultural Product Prices*. Ithaca: Cornell University Press, 1981.

Trandel, Gregory A.
"Evading the Use Tax on Cross-Border Shopping: Pricing and Welfare Effects." *Journal of Public Economics* 49 No. 3 (December, 1992): 313–32.

Appendix

In Table A.1, we report the shifting parameters for several variations on our canonical model, equation 4. In column (1), the price of a spin balance is used as a numeraire. That is, the left-hand-side variable is the logarithm of the price of the relevant commodity minus the logarithm of the price of a spin balance. Column (2) uses alternative measures for the wage rate and energy costs. (These equations are estimated on an annual rather than a quarterly basis.) In column (3), the model is estimated without any cost variables.

TABLE A.1
SHIFTING PARAMETERS UNDER ALTERNATIVE SPECIFICATIONS

	(1) Spin Balance as Numeraire	(2) Alternative Cost Measures	(3) No-Cost Variables
Bananas	0.665 (2.27)	1.72 (3.29)	0.823 (2.31)
Bread	1.42 (3.207)	3.90 (4.03)	2.46 (4.93)
Big Mac	−0.282 (−1.86)	0.530 (1.26)	−0.137 (−0.748)
Crisco	0.816 (3.76)	0.625 (1.06)	1.01 (6.06)
Eggs	0.172 (0.827)	0.107 (0.224)	0.0002 (0.001)
Kleenex	0.121 (0.599)	−1.08 (−1.57)	−0.0895 (−0.368)
Milk	0.489 (3.63)	0.338 (1.08)	0.510 (3.44)
Monopoly	0.357 (0.831)	0.403 (0.344)	0.961 (2.36)
Shampoo	1.03 (3.51)	0.111 (0.118)	0.944 (2.94)
Soda	0.930 (2.45)	2.27 (3.29)	1.32 (4.42)
Spin balance	— —	0.961 (0.567)	−0.259 (−0.479)
Underwear	0.779 (1.93)	−1.14 (−0.767)	1.47 (3.02)

Notes: Column (1) shows β_{t}, the coefficient on the tax rate, when equation 4 is estimated with the left-hand-side variable as the log of the price of the respective commodity minus the log of the price of a spin balance. (All figures in parentheses are *t*-statistics calculated from heteroskedasticity consistent standard errors.) Column (2) shows the coefficients when alternative measures of wage and energy costs are used for a subsample of the communities. Column (3) shows the coefficients when no-cost variables are included, using the same samples as in Table 3.

LIST OF CITIES

AL	Birmingham, Dothan, Gadsden, Huntsville, Mobile, Montgomery
AR	Fayetteville, Fort Smith, Jonesboro
AZ	Phoenix
CA	Blythe, Fresno, Indio, Palm Springs, Riverside, Sacramento, San Diego, San Jose, Visalia
CO	Colorado Springs, Denver, Grand Junction, Pueblo
CT	Hartford
FL	Gainesville, Lakeland, Miami, Pensacola, West Palm Beach
GA	Albany, Americus, Atlanta, Augusta, Columbus, Macon
IA	Cedar Rapids, Fort Dodge
ID	Boise
IL	Champaign, Charleston, Decatur, Peoria, Rockford, Springfield
IN	Anderson, Bloomington, Fort Wayne, Indianapolis, Marion, South Bend, Warsaw
KS	Great Bend, Wichita
KY	Bowling Green, Lexington, Louisville, Murray, Owensboro, Somerset
LA	Baton Rouge, Lake Charles, New Orleans
MD	Baltimore
MI	Benton Harbor, Jackson, Marquette, Traverse City
MN	Minneapolis
MO	Clinton, Columbia, Jefferson City, Joplin, Kansas City, Springfield, St. Joseph, St. Louis
NC	Charlotte, Durham, Greensboro, Greenville, Hickory, Marion, Rocky Mount, Wilmington, Winston-Salem
NE	Hastings, Lincoln, Omaha
NM	Alamagordo, Albuquerque
NV	Las Vegas, Reno
NY	Binghamton, Buffalo, Elmira, Syracuse
OH	Akron, Canton, Cincinnati, Columbus, Newark, Youngstown
OK	Oklahoma City, Tulsa
OR	Portland
PA	Harrisburg, Lancaster, Waynesboro, Wilkes-Barre, York
SC	Greenville
SD	Rapid City, Vermillion
TN	Chattanooga, Dyersburg, Jackson, Knoxville, Memphis, Morristown, Nashville
TX	Abilene, Amarillo, El Paso, Harlingen, Houston, Kerrville, Killeen, Lubbock, McAllen, Odessa, San Antonio, Sherman, Temple, Texarkana, Tyler, Waco, Wichita Falls
UT	Provo, Salt Lake City
VA	Norfolk, Roanoke
WA	Richland, Tacoma, Yakima
WI	Appleton, Fond Du Lac, Green Bay, Janesville, La Crosse, Marinette, New London, Oshkosh, Wausau
WY	Casper, Charleston

[9]
The Incidence and Efficiency Effects of Taxes on Income from Capital

John B. Shoven
Stanford University

This article reexamines the incidence and efficiency cost of the discriminatory taxation of capital income in the United States. It is argued that Harberger's 1966 estimates of the static welfare loss were subject to two important mistakes. Their correction lowers the efficiency cost estimates approximately 38 percent. The paper also compares the corrected results of the Harberger model with those achieved with an algorithmic solution procedure for a general equilibrium model. When the latter approach is used with the same two-sector division of production, the results are very similar to those of Harberger's model. With disaggregation to 12 production sectors, however, the loss estimates increase by an average of 40 percent.

I. Introduction

There has developed over the past 15 years or so a very extensive literature regarding the taxation of income from capital, particularly the corporation income tax. On issues regarding the distributional incidence and inefficiency of these capital income levies, the works of Arnold Harberger (1959, 1962, 1966) have been particularly influential and important. His models and results often serve as a reference with which other approaches to these questions are compared. The 1959 and 1966 articles by Harberger deal with estimating the efficiency cost or dead-weight loss of these taxes resulting from the misallocation of resources. The latter of these pieces is somewhat more complete, in that it attempts to include all taxes on capital income rather than just the corporation income tax. Harberger's 1962 article describes his theoretical framework and addresses the question

This work was supported by National Science Foundation grant GI-39319 at the Institute for Mathematical Studies in the Social Sciences, Stanford University. The author wishes to thank J. G. Ballentine, John Whalley, and Mark Gertler for helpful comments.

of the incidence of the corporation income tax on the functional distribution of income. On this issue, Harberger concludes that capital bears close to the full burden of the tax for realistic estimates of the elasticity parameters of his model.

Despite the attention economists have given the corporation income tax and other capital income taxes, nothing near a consensus has emerged regarding their economic impact. The importance of the subject is often rejuvenated by suggestions that the corporation income tax be integrated into the personal income tax structure.

This article has two primary purposes with respect to capital income taxation. The first of these is to correct two serious flaws in Harberger's 1966 article. One error is purely arithmetic, while the other is conceptual; but they both significantly affect his widely referred to inefficiency estimates. In the second section of this paper, I briefly describe the Harberger model,[1] comment on its shortcomings, illustrate the sources of the two mistakes, and present the corrected results for the Harberger approach. The importance of this section derives from the fact that the corrected inefficiency estimates of Harberger's model amount to only 32–63 percent of the published figures for the same elasticity parameterizations. On the other hand, it will be argued that the usual reporting of these dead-weight loss results as a trivial fraction of GNP is misleading. The section is also of value in displaying how important consistent units definitions are in applying data to the Harberger model.

The second purpose of this paper is to compare the corrected results of the Harberger model with those derived from an algorithmic solution of a general equilibrium model. One advantage of such an approach is that, in not using calculus, the changes which one is trying to gauge need not be assumed small in the model itself. The task of comparing the results of such a procedure with those of the Harberger model was undertaken in an earlier work (Shoven and Whalley 1972), but a recalculation is now in order, for several reasons. First, the earlier article used the data and the results of the Harberger 1966 article in evaluating the two techniques. However, the data and therefore the results were incorrect (as shown here in Sec. II). Second, the algorithmic approach has been greatly improved in the interim, as is detailed in Shoven and Whalley (1973) and Shoven (1976). And finally, third, another advantage of the algorithmic approach is that it is capable of evaluating an n sector rather than a two-sector model. Therefore, in order to provide a feel for the effects of aggregated analysis, the impact of the uneven capital income tax levies is estimated for a 12- as well as a two-sector breakdown of the production side of the U.S. economy. With the algorithmic approach, the flat tax rate necessary to generate the same real yield as the current system is calculated.

[1] The model has been elaborately specified several times in the literature. See, e.g., Harberger (1962); appendix B of Shoven and Whalley (1972); McLure (1974); or McLure (1975).

II. Harberger Model, Data, and Results

The Harberger model, as detailed in his 1962 article and in several subsequent studies, is sufficiently well known and documented that it need not be completely specified here. However, since a primary purpose of this section is to correct the results of his 1966 paper concerning the efficiency losses of the taxes, it is appropriate that we review the approach of that study.

In his model, Harberger makes an empirical distinction between a heavily and lightly taxed sector. These sectors are sometimes referred to as the "corporate" and "non-corporate" sectors, due to the major role played by the corporation income tax in causing the differential rates, although the sectoral division does not exactly correspond to the legal distinction between incorporated and unincorporated enterprises. Harberger assumes that each sector employs two factors, capital services and labor, in the production of homogeneous outputs.

In order to estimate the efficiency loss due to the differential taxation of the return to capital, Harberger applies a form of welfare analysis in the tradition of Marshallian producer surplus. It is assumed that the marginal product of capital schedules for each sector are linear, as drawn in figure 1. Output units are chosen so that both commodity prices are unity, and therefore the schedules in figure 1 can be thought of as marginal revenue product schedules. The total quantity of both capital and labor in the economy is assumed fixed and always fully employed. With these assumptions, the changes in the capital allocation can be used to generate a measure of the social waste imposed by the distortion. In the absence of any taxes, capital will allocate itself in a market economy such that the rate of return $\bar{r}$ is equal for the two sectors and the capital endowment is fully employed. Upon the imposition of a tax on capital income in sector X, the gross rate of return r_g in that sector must be such that the net rate of return r_n is equalized across the sectors and capital is again fully employed. The difference between r_g and r_n is by definition the tax T per unit of capital utilized in sector X.

Referring to figure 1, the area $ABEF$ can be interpreted as the value of the lost output in sector X when K_X decreases from K_{X0} to K_{X1} upon the imposition of the tax. Analogously, $GHIJ$ is the value of increase in output in sector Y. Since we know that capital is fully employed both in the presence and absence of the tax, it must be true that $K_{X0} - K_{X1} = K_{Y1} - K_{Y0}$. The area $FECD$ represents the social loss of the tax in the producer surplus sense (it is simply $ABEF - GHIJ$) and is given by

$$\tfrac{1}{2}(r_g - \bar{r})(K_{X0} - K_{X1}) + \tfrac{1}{2}(\bar{r} - r_n)(K_{Y1} - K_{Y0}) = -\tfrac{1}{2}T\Delta K_X, \quad (1)$$

where $\Delta K_X = K_{X1} - K_{X0} = K_{Y0} - K_{Y1}$ and $T = r_g - r_n$.

Now, in order to estimate the magnitude of the social efficiency loss, an expression for ΔK_X is required. In order to obtain such a solution,

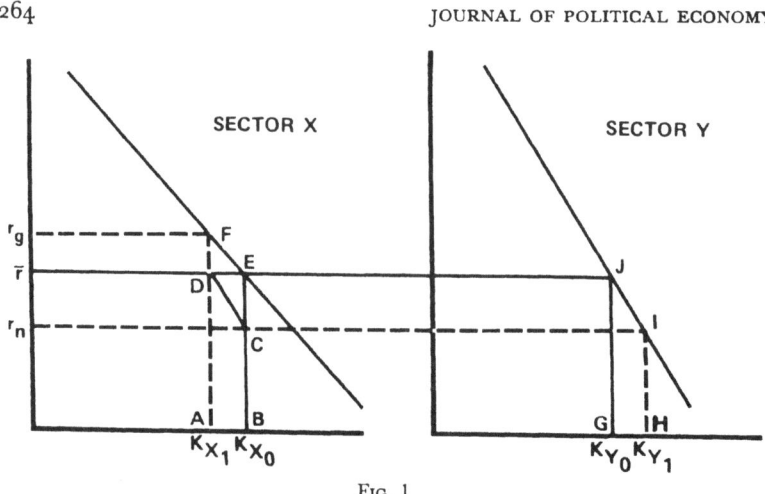

Fig. 1

Harberger calls upon the static two-sector, two-factor, general equilibrium model of his 1962 paper. The use of this model in conjunction with the Marshallian approach above has several shortcomings, particularly if the purpose involves measurement of economic changes. The primary problem is that local or "small change" assumptions are made repeatedly in the analysis. For example, in solving for the efficiency loss formula (eq. [1]), it has been assumed that the marginal product of capital varies linearly with the amount of capital for each of the sectors. In addition, either the labor allocation must be assumed to be unaltered, or the marginal product of capital must be taken as independent of the amount of labor employed in each sector. Without either of these conditions, the marginal product curves themselves will not be stationary. At the same time, in the model used to solve for the capital shift, ΔK_X, constant returns to scale in production is assumed. The joint assumptions of linear marginal product schedules, constant returns to scale, and separable marginal products (or an unchanged labor allocation) are inconsistent for large changes. Given that the purpose of the analysis is to determine the magnitude of the effects of distortionary taxation, assumptions such as these which are consistent only locally are undesirable.

Solving through the equations of the Harberger (1962) model, the following solution for ΔK_X is obtained:

$$\Delta K_X = \frac{K_X T \{-E[g_K S_X(L_X/L_Y) + f_K S_Y] - S_X S_Y f_L\}}{E(g_K - f_K)[(K_X/K_Y) - (L_X/L_Y)] - S_Y - S_X[f_L(K_X/K_Y) + f_K(L_X/L_Y)]}, \quad (2)$$

where E = compensated price elasticity of demand for X; $S_X(S_Y)$ = elasticity of factor substitution in sector $X(Y)$; $f_K(g_K)$ = share of capital in sector $X(Y)$; and $f_L(g_L)$ = share of labor in sector $X(Y)$. So, as one would expect, the capital shift depends on the various elasticities and factor intensities and is also proportional to T. This last point is emphasized, as it later becomes important in that it, along with equation (1), implies that the social cost varies with the square of the tax rate.

Harberger similarly solves this system of equations for the change in the net price of capital (i.e., $\Delta P_K = r_n - \bar{r}$) and obtains

$$\Delta P_K = \frac{T\{Ef_K[(K_X/K_Y) - (L_X/L_Y)] + S_X[f_L(K_X/K_Y) + f_K(L_X/L_Y)]\}}{E(g_K - f_K)[(K_X/K_Y) - (L_X/L_Y)] - S_Y - S_X[f_L(K_X/K_Y) + f_K(L_X/L_Y)]}. \quad (3)$$

He uses this figure to evaluate the incidence of the burden, reasoning that, if $\Delta P_K = -(TK_X)/(K_X + K_Y)$, capital could be said to bear the full burden of the tax in that its gross return would be unchanged, while if $\Delta P_K = 0$ both net input prices would be unaffected, and thus the share of national income going to capital and labor would remain constant.

In order to evaluate expressions (2) and (3) for the 1953–59 U.S. economy, Harberger uses and supplements the data of Rosenberg (1969). However, in carrying this out, two mistakes are made. Estimates of K_X, K_Y, and T are drawn from table 1, reproduced from Harberger (1966). Columns 1 and 2 are derived from Rosenberg's disaggregated study, while column 3 is meant to reflect the personal income taxes on capital income. Appealing to columns 4 and 5, Harberger notes that total taxes on net income in the "non-corporate" and "corporate" sectors average, respectively, 45 percent and 168 percent.[2] Thus he asserts that the taxation of income from capital in the United States during this period may be approximated by a general tax of 45 percent on all net income from capital and an 85 percent surtax on the net income from capital originating in the heavily taxed sector ($1.45 \times 1.85 = 2.68$).

The first flaw in Harberger's 1966 application of this data to his model is an inconsistency between the calculation of tax rates above and the units of measurement of capital chosen in the study. Harberger takes as one unit of capital that amount which earned an average annual flow of $1.00 net of all taxes. Thus, appealing to column 5 of table 1, he sets K_Y as 18,510 million and K_X as 19,547 million. In models such as this, with a fixed quantity of aggregate capital, a general tax on all capital income is nondistortionary. Therefore Harberger proceeds to evaluate only the 85 percent surtax applying to the capital income of the "cor-

---

[2] The use of average tax data to evaluate distortions has been questioned by Stiglitz (1975). The implied assumption that the marginal gross cost of capital equals the average gross cost can be defended on the grounds that investment decisions are often made using average capital costs (see, e.g., Van Horne 1971).

TABLE 1

TAXES ON INCOME FROM CAPITAL, BY MAJOR SECTORS
(Annual Averages, 1953-59, in $ Millions)
(Reproduced from Harberger 1966, p. 110)

	Total Income* from Capital (1)	Property & Corp. Income Taxes (2)	Other Tax Adjustments (3)	Total Tax on Income from Capital (4)	Net Income from Capital (5)
"Non-corporate" sector	26,873	6,639	1,724	8,363	18,510
Agriculture	7,481	1,302	927[a]	2,229	5,252
Housing	18,429	5,140	797[b]	5,937	12,492
Crude Oil and Gas	963	197	...[c]	197	766
"Corporate" sector..	52,399	22,907	9,945[d]	32,852	19,547
Total..........	79,272	29,546	11,669	41,215	38,057

* "Income" (Rosenberg 1969, p. 125) is defined as income from capital for nonfinancial industry and includes
 (1) Corporate sector net income before corporate profits tax liability and property tax payments.
 (2) For the unincorporated enterprise that is a return on equity capital, plus property tax payments.
 (3) Net monetary interest paid by businesses on borrowed capital in the form of debt obligations.
 (4) Net rent paid by an industry to persons for the use of physical capital.
 (5) Net realized capital gains by the corporate sector that are considered as income to an industry.
[a] Assumes a 15% effective tax on income from capital in agriculture after payment of property and corporate income taxes (i.e., [3][a] = 15% of [1] − [2]).
[b] Assumes that 70% of income from capital in the housing sector is generated by owner-occupied housing, on which no personal income tax liability is incurred. It is assumed that the remaining 30% of capital income from housing is subjected to a 20% income tax rate after the deduction of property and corporate income taxes incurred (i.e., [3][b] = 6% of [1] − [2]).
[c] Assumes personal tax offsets on account of oil depletion allowances and similar privileges offset any taxes on dividends and capital gains in this sector.
[d] Assumes a 50% dividend distribution rate and a "typical" effective tax rate of 40% on dividend income (i.e., [3][d] = 20% of [1] − [2]).

porate" sector (i.e., he set $T = 0.85$ in equations (1), (2), and (3)). The problem is that the surtax is in fact applied not to the net capital income of the heavily taxed sector (indicated in table 1 to be 19,547 million) but to the capital income in that sector gross of the neutral 45 percent tax ($28,379 million). Harberger is thus evaluating a smaller tax than his data reveals! The social marginal product of each of Harberger's units of capital is $1.45, not the $1.00 he recognizes. In order to rectify this problem, one either has to evaluate *both* the 45 percent and 168 percent taxes simultaneously or to evaluate only the surtax and take as a unit of capital that amount which earns $1.00 net of the surtax but gross of the neutral tax. The dead-weight loss estimates are identical with either convention, and I have chosen the latter simply because the previous figure and equations have been for the surtax case. Under this approach, table 1 shows $K_Y = 26,873$ million and $K_X = 28,379$ million. As the estimate of the capital shift and the dead-weight loss are proportional to K_X, this correction alone would increase Harberger's inefficiency results 45 percent.

Unfortunately, the problem with units above is not the most serious error related to the data of Harberger (1966). They contain a simple arithmetic mistake, which also greatly affects his results. The entry superscripted d in column 3 should be 5,898 rather than 9,945, and, with this correction, the net income from capital in the "corporate" sector becomes $23,589 rather than $19,547 million. The total tax on capital income in the "corporate" sector should be $28,805 million. The source of the error is obvious. In determining the column 3 entry for the "corporate" sector, the arithmetic was mistakenly done on the first two entries in the total row. Note that 9,945 is 20 percent of 79,272 less 29,546.[3]

Table 2 contains the corrected factor input and capital tax data for both a two- and a 12-sector level of aggregation for averaged data for the same 1953–59 period. The capital income and tax data are again drawn from Rosenberg (1969), and the "Other Capital Tax Adjustments" column was constructed upon the assumptions listed in the footnotes to table 1. The labor data are derived from National Income and Product Accounts. At the two-sector level of aggregation, the main difference between the two tables is caused, of course, by the arithmetic mistake just noted. The surtax rate, which Harberger figures as 85 percent, is, according to table 2, only 53 percent ($1.45 \times 1.53 = 2.22$). The effect of this error is magnified, since, as was pointed out earlier, the loss estimate varies as the square of the rate of distortionary taxation. The capital data, using the consistent definition of units mentioned above, now indicates that $K_Y = 26,878$ million and $K_X = 34,244$ million.

Subject to these two mistakes, Harberger uses the data of table 1 augmented with labor data[4] to estimate ΔK_X and $-(1/2)T\Delta K_X$ for several different elasticities of factor substitution (S_X and S_Y) and for two different compensated elasticities of demand for the "corporate" product X. The two demand elasticities E are based on the elasticity of substitution between X and Y, which is labeled V, being assigned values of 1 and $\frac{1}{4}$. The relationship between V and the compensated demand for X is

$$E = Vr_Y, \qquad (4)$$

where r_Y is the share of national income spent on Y. Thus the $V = 1$ case is consistent with demands derived from a Cobb-Douglas–type utility function. Harberger takes r_Y as 0.17, although my revised data (col. 3, table 2) suggests that r_Y is just slightly under 0.15.

Many different estimates have been made of the elasticities of substitution between labor and capital for various sectors, often concluding with contradictory results. Most of the work based on cross-section data

---

[3] There are two other errors in table 1. The total income figure from capital in the noncorporate sector should be 26,878 rather than 26,873, and in the corporate sector the figure should be 52,394 rather than 52,399. The total of the two is correct in table 1.

[4] Harberger takes L_X to be $200 billion and L_Y to be $20 billion. Col. 1 of table 2 agrees very closely with his L_X figure but shows L_Y to be only $17,471 billion (or units).

TABLE 2

FACTOR PAYMENTS AND CAPITAL INCOME TAXES, BY MAJOR SECTORS
(Annual Averages, 1953–59, in $ Million)

Sector	Total Return to Labor (1)	Total Return to Capital (2)	Total Factor Return (1) + (2) (3)	Property and Corporate Income Tax (4)	Other Capital Tax Adjustments (5)	Total Capital Tax (4) + (5) (6)	Net Return to Capital (2) − (6) (7)	Capital Tax as a Fraction of Total Return to Capital (6)/(2) (8)	Capital Tax as a Fraction of Net Return to Capital (6)/(7) (9)
"Non-corporate"	17,471	26,878	44,349	6,639	1,724	8,363	18,515	0.3111466	0.4516878
Agriculture	8,800	7,481	16,281	1,302	927	2,229	5,252	0.2979548	0.4244097
Real estate	6,869	18,429	25,298	5,140	797	5,937	12,492	0.3221552	0.4752641
Crude oil and gas	1,802	968	2,770	197	...	197	771	0.2035123	0.2555123
"Corporate"	199,871	52,394	252,265	22,907	5,898	28,805	23,589	0.5497766	1.2211220
Mining*	2,528	688	3,216	305	77	382	306	0.5552325	1.2483660
Contract construction	16,670	1,195	17,865	435	152	587	608	0.4912133	0.9654605
Manufacturing†	79,626	24,665	104,291	12,488	2,435	14,923	9,742	0.6050273	1.5318209
Lumber and wood products	2,426	718	3,144	206	102	308	410	0.4289693	0.7512195
Petroleum and coal products	1,846	3,028	4,874	770	452	1,222	1,806	0.4035667	0.6766334
Trade	43,590	10,897	54,487	3,493	1,481	4,974	5,923	0.4564559	0.8397771
Transportation	14,078	2,683	16,761	1,230	291	1,521	1,162	0.5669027	1.3089500
Communication and public utilities	7,394	6,489	13,883	3,290	640	3,930	2,559	0.6056403	1.5357561
Services	31,713	2,031	33,744	690	268	958	1,073	0.4716888	0.8928238
Total	217,342	79,272	296,614	29,546	7,622	37,168	42,104	0.4688666	0.8827664

* Other than crude oil and gas.
† Other than lumber and wood products and petroleum and coal products.

INCIDENCE AND EFFICIENCY EFFECTS OF TAXES 1269

suggests that, for most two-digit manufacturing industries, S is not significantly different from 1 (see, e.g., Solow 1964 and Minasian 1961). On the other hand, time-series studies yield estimates significantly less than 1 (see Lucas 1969). Given this situation, Harberger looks at several combinations of S_X and S_Y.

Table 3 contains Harberger's published results, appropriately qualified as only rough estimates, and the impact on them of the two errors just discussed. Their importance is readily apparent, although the net effect is somewhat reduced, as they cut in opposing directions. The 45 percent increase in the inefficiency estimates due to the units-definition problem is apparent in comparing column 7 with column 5. The independent effect of the arithmetic mistake and Harberger's use of other data which are only roughly correct is seen by contrasting columns 9 and 7. The range of the estimates is lowered from the published $1.0 billion–$2.9 billion to the $0.625 billion–$1.79 billion shown in column 9 of table 3 and based on the data of table 2. Surprisingly, Harberger's numerical estimates of the outflow of capital from the "corporate" sector due to the discriminatory taxation shown in column 4 are almost identical with the corrected figures given in column 8 except in case 11, where he has made a serious computational error. The equivalency is less comforting and more coincidental, however, when it is recalled that each of Harberger's units of capital is equivalent to 1.45 units under the revised system of accounts.

It may be claimed that all that has been done is to lower further Harberger's already small loss estimates, widely reported as between 0.5 and 1 percent of GNP (or NNP). This presentation of the results as a percentage of national product seems misleading, however. Perhaps a more natural benchmark is the net revenue yield of the surtax. This alternative, also not without some interpretational difficulties, suggests a "coefficient of inefficiency" which can be defined as the ratio of the deadweight loss of the surtax (in this case the 53% additional tax paid by sector X) to the net surtax revenue. This additional revenue due to the presence of the surtax amounts to between $9.3 billion and $13.9 billion, depending on the factor-elasticity assumptions. The yield of a flat 45 percent tax on net income depends upon the net price of capital in the nondistortionary situation. For the revised results of column 9, table 3, the coefficient of inefficiency ranges from 0.06 to 0.15. Column 10 of table 3 records the values for ΔP_K, the change in the price of capital in moving from the nondistortionary to the distortionary situation. This variable sheds some light on the functional incidence of the taxation, particularly when it is noted that $-TK_X/(K_X + K_Y) = -0.297$. This is the value of ΔP_K at which capital can be said to bear the entire tax, as its net return is reduced by the amount of the tax proceeds. For those cases in which the price falls by more than this figure, capital can be said to be bearing more than 100 percent of the tax burden.

TABLE 3

ESTIMATES OF EFFICIENCY COST OF EXISTING TAXES ON INCOME FROM CAPITAL (1953–59), USING HARBERGER'S MODEL

CASE	S_X (1)	S_Y (2)	V (3)	HARBERGER'S ESTIMATES*		ESTIMATES WITH REVISED UNITS†		ESTIMATES WITH REVISED UNITS AND REVISED DATA‡		
				ΔK_X (4)§	$-(1/2)T\Delta K_X$ (5)‖	$\Delta K_X'$ (6)§	$-(1/2)T\Delta K_X'$ (7)‖	$\Delta K_X''$ (8)§	$-(1/2)T\Delta K_X''$ (9)‖	ΔP_K (10)
1	−1.0	−1.0	−1.0	−6.9	2.9	−9.7	4.1	−6.76	1.79	−0.326
2	−1.0	−0.5	−1.0	−5.9	2.5	−8.4	3.6	−5.85	1.55	−0.362
3	−0.5	−1.0	−1.0	−5.2	2.2	−7.4	3.1	−5.20	1.38	−0.221
4	−0.5	−0.5	−1.0	−4.8	2.0	−6.7	2.9	−4.75	1.26	−0.261
5	−1.0	0.0	−1.0	−4.7	2.0	−6.6	2.8	−4.71	1.25	−0.408
6	−0.5	0.0	−1.0	−3.9	1.7	−5.7	2.4	−4.09	1.08	−0.318
7	−1.0	−1.0	−0.5	−5.3	2.3	−7.5	3.2	−5.13	1.36	−0.365
8	−1.0	−0.5	−0.5	−4.2	1.8	−5.8	2.5	−4.00	1.06	−0.408
9	−0.5	−1.0	−0.5	−4.1	1.7	−5.8	2.5	−4.06	1.08	−0.272
10	−0.5	−0.5	−0.5	−3.5	1.5	−4.9	2.1	−3.38	0.896	−0.326
11	−1.0	0.0	−0.5	−5.0	2.1	−3.6	1.5	−2.55	0.676	−0.464
12	−0.5	0.0	−0.5	−2.4	1.0	−3.3	1.4	−2.36	0.625	−0.408

NOTE.—S_X (S_Y) = elasticity of factor substitution in "corporate" ("non-corporate") sector; V = elasticity of substitution between products X and Y.
* Based on K_X = 20, K_Y = 20, L_X = 200, L_Y = 200, f_K = 0.2, f_L = 0.8, g_K = 0.8, g_L = 1.1.
† Based on K_X = −2.5 and −(1/2)$T\Delta K_X$ = 0.54, r_Y = 0.17, r_Y = 0.85.
have gotten ΔK_X = −2.5 and −(1/2)$T\Delta K_X$ = 1.1.
‡ Based on K_X = 28.5, K_Y = 27.0, L_X = 200, L_Y = 20, f_K = 0.2, f_L = 0.8, g_K = 0.54, r_Y = 0.17, T = 0.85. Harberger made a computational error in case 11, where he should
§ Based on K_X = 34.244, K_Y = 26.878, L_X = 199.871, L_Y = 17.471, f_K = 0.20769, f_L = 0.79231, g_K = 0.60606, r_Y = 0.14952, T = 0.53003.
§ In billions.
‖ In $ billion.

III. Results of the Algorithmic Approach

Using the revised data of table 2, the efficiency cost of the distortionary taxation of capital income has been recomputed using a solution algorithm for a general equilibrium model. It is, of course, the corrected results of columns 9 and 10 of table 3 which will serve as a basis for comparison. Such additional questions as the impact of the taxes on the supply of labor, on the functional and personal distribution of income, and the flat capital income tax rate which would be required to generate the same real revenue as the existing taxes can be addressed using the algorithmic approach. In most cases the assumptions of Harberger have been followed, although the models of course are not strictly comparable. Production functions are assumed to be of the CES form, while both CES and Cobb-Douglas utility functions were analyzed for consumers. Two classes of consumers were incorporated, one representing the top 10 percent of the income recipients in the United States, the other the bottom 90 percent. The model was solved both with and without the inclusion of a labor-leisure choice, although detailed results will be presented only for the fixed-labor-supply case.

Just as there is no need to respecify the Harberger model completely each time it is employed, it is likewise unnecessary to review fully the Scarf (1973) general equilibrium algorithm utilized here to derive the results of this section. For that reason, only a brief sketch of the mechanics of the approach is presented.

The basic idea of the algorithmic approach of this section is to specify an Arrow-Debreu general equilibrium model with and without taxes. The existence of an equilibrium for a model with such ad valorem taxes is assured in Shoven (1974). In order to parameterize the model, some extraneous estimates are required. These are the same factor substitution and demand elasticities which must be specified in the Harberger approach described in the last section. Given these estimates, which comprise perhaps one-third of the total number of parameters, the model is solved "backward" to determine the values that the remaining variables must take in order to replicate exactly the prechange economy. The technique of carrying out this parameterization approach is more fully described in Shoven (1973) and Whalley (1973). Once all the parameters are set, the model is solved "forward" for a new equilibrium in the presence of the new tax environment. In the case of this study, the new system involves the removal of the surtax on capital income in the heavily taxed sector (or sectors with the 12-sector level of aggregation). The solution technique is a version of Scarf's algorithm modified to include taxes and continuous production functions. This method is detailed in Shoven (1973) and Shoven and Whalley (1973). The degree of approximation is greatly improved with a Newton-type termination routine similar to that described in appendix A of Shoven and Whalley (1972). The advantages of this general approach over that of Section II are that (1) no localization assumptions are required; (2) it is simple to incorporate many commodities and several classes of consumers; and (3) it is unnecessary to assume fixed factor supplies. A more abstract advantage is that the model need not be kept sufficiently simple so as to be analytically tractable.

On the production side of the economy, each sector's technological production possibilities are characterized by a CES production function such as

$$Q_i = \gamma_i [\alpha_i L_i^{-\rho_i} + (1 - \alpha_i) K_i^{-\rho_i}]^{-1/\rho_i}. \tag{5}$$

Noting the discussion in the previous section of plausible estimates of the elasticity of substitution (in this case $S_i = -1/[1 + \rho_i]$), seven cases were considered: three in line with Harberger, and four others. They may be listed as

Case	S_X	S_Y
1	-1.00	-1.00
2	-1.00	-0.50
3	-1.00	-0.25
4	-0.75	-0.25
5	-0.50	-0.50
6	-0.50	-0.25
7	-0.25	-0.25

As previously mentioned, two consumers were considered; the first heuristically represents the upper 10 percent of the income recipients, while the second represents the lower 90 percent. The first is endowed with approximately 23 percent of the economy's labor (corresponding to the observed share of labor income going to the top decile of income receivers) and 40 percent of total stock of capital (both figures from Projector and Weiss 1966). This latter figure roughly corresponds to the share of capital income going to the top 10 percent of the income receivers, although it is much lower than the share of capital income going to the top 10 percent of wealth holders. Endowing the high-income receivers with more than 10 percent of the labor appeals to an equal endowment of labor in natural units but a disproportionate endowment in efficiency units.

Each consumer's demand functions are of the form

$$x_{ij} = \frac{I_j}{\sum_{i=1}^{n} a_{ij} P_i^{(1-V_j)}} \frac{a_{ij}}{P_i^{V_j}}, \quad i = 1, \ldots, n; j = 1, 2, \tag{6}$$

where x_{ij} is consumer j's demand for commodity i, a_{ij} measures the intensity of his desire for commodity i, P_i is the price of the ith good, V_j

INCIDENCE AND EFFICIENCY EFFECTS OF TAXES 1273

is individual j's elasticity of substitution between commodities, and I_j is his income given by

$$I_j = \sum_{i=1}^{n} P_i w_{ij}, \qquad (7)$$

where the w_{ij} are his initial asset holdings, including labor.

In the recomputations, two values for the consumer's elasticities of substitution (i.e., the V_j's) are examined: 1.0 and 0.5. With V_j equal to 1.0, the demand functions (6) are of the familiar Cobb-Douglas type.

Using the demand functions (6) permits one to impose the observed aggregate 5.69–1.0 expenditure ratio for the outputs of the heavily and lightly taxed sectors. Approximately $252 billion a year was spent on "corporate" products, while only $44 billion was spent on the output of the "non-corporate" sector. If each individual's tastes were such that $a_{ij} = 5.69 a_{2j}$, $j = 1, 2$, where the "corporate" product is labeled commodity 1 and the "non-corporate" product commodity 2, the expenditure ratios of the model would exactly correspond to the 5.69–1.00 figure with unitary prices. However, in the examples investigated here, lower-income individuals are taken to place a relatively higher weight on the output of the lightly taxed sector than higher-income individuals. This is consistent with observed higher budget shares allocated to food expenditures (agricultural output) by lower-income people. The ratios a_{1j}/a_{2j} used are 7.00 for the higher-income consumer and 5.30 for the lower-income consumer.

The total endowments of the economy are taken from table 2 of the last section. Again, we need to clarify units conventions. The approach taken in this section is to analyze all capital income taxes, and not simply the surtax. This implies taking as a unit of capital that amount which earns $1.00 net of all taxes, Harberger's original units. The advantage of this convention here is that it readily permits disaggregation, and it explicitly recognizes that the government's tax collections rise (even from neutral taxes) when the net price of capital services increase. It is a perfectly acceptable units convention, provided all taxes are incorporated into the model. Relative price changes and real output effects are independent of which of the two consistent units definitions is chosen. Only in comparing absolute quantities of capital must the appropriate conversion (1.45) be applied. With this settled and in the absence of a labor-leisure choice, the total labor endowment is taken to be 217.342 billion units, while the capital-services endowment is 42.104 billion units. In the presence of the surtax, 23.589 billion units of capital and 199.871 billion units of labor are allocated to the "corporate" sector (from table 2, columns 1 and 7). To focus solely on the impact of the tax, the fraction of government tax proceeds returned to each consumption class is assumed equal to that class's fraction of the total capital endowment.

Thus the potential redistributionary effects of the expenditure of the tax proceeds are not considered here.

Table 4 contains a summary of the efficiency loss and incidence results for the two production-sector cases. What is compared in this table is the observed equilibrium (the equilibrium in the presence of distortionary capital income taxes) with the equilibrium which would prevail in the absence of the distortionary taxes (i.e., in the absence of what Harberger refers to as the surtax). Also reported are the equilibrium prices and the tax rate (on net income) which would prevail if the replacement were a flat tax designed to have the same real yield as is realized in the distortionary situation. A Paasche price index is used in determining real rather than nominal revenue equivalency. The technique of determining this equal-yield tax rate is described in Shoven and Whalley (1975). The entry termed the "shift factor" is presented to give some insight into the incidence of the distortionary capital taxation with respect to the functional distribution of income.[5] The definition of the term is shift factor $= 1 + (\Delta P_K K)/(\Delta R)$, where K is the total endowment of capital, ΔP_K is the change in the net price of capital in moving from the nondistortionary to the distortionary tax regime (thus this term is negative in all cases), and ΔR is the change in nominal government revenue (which is of course positive). If this shift factor is zero, the decrease in the net return to capital is equal to the increase in government revenue due to the distortionary surtax, and in this sense capital may be said to bear the full burden. A negative value for this shift factor would indicate that capital bears more than 100 percent of the burden of the surtax, while a positive value would reflect the fact that labor is sharing in its costs.

Table 4, part A, presents the results for the cases in which both consumer classes have demand elasticities of substitution (V_j's) equal to 1. As one would expect, the removal of the surtax involves a decrease in the price of X, the "corporate" output, and an increase in the price of Y (due to the increase in the net price of capital). It might be noted that these price changes tend to benefit the higher-income consumer class more than the lower-income class, as the former spends a larger fraction of its income on products which decrease in price (i.e., X). As is done in Harberger's work, labor is taken as the numéraire commodity and thus always has a price of unity. The "X" and "Y" rows show that the output of sector X increases by 2–3 percent, while the output of sector Y decreases by as much as 15 percent. Factor substitution occurs, and the "corporate" sector switches to a more capital-intensive technology with the removal of the surtax, while the lightly taxed sector becomes more labor intensive. One interesting aspect of this particular problem is that the sector whose capital income is currently heavily taxed is relatively

---

[5] Of course the reader also can compute ΔP_K from the tables.

INCIDENCE AND EFFICIENCY EFFECTS OF TAXES 1275

labor intensive. This fact opens the possibility that labor may bear a large fraction of the burden of the surtax, particularly in cases with low elasticities of factor substitution. Indeed, the "shift factor" row of this section shows that, in cases 5, 6, and 7, labor's share of the burden is significant. In fact, in case 7 the relative share of the rich consumer class (whose assets are capital intensive) is 0.4 percent higher in the presence of the distortionary tax than in its absence. The efficiency loss estimates are shown to be sensitive to the specification of the production parameters and range between $0.435 billion and $2.344 billion. These figures amount to 2.8–18.7 percent of the revenue generated by the surtax. For each parameterization, two loss estimates (or changes in NNP)[6] are given: one evaluated at the observed prices and one at the new, nondistortionary prices. As is known from index number theory, under "reasonable" assumptions it can be shown that the estimate based on the new prices gives by a lower bound for welfare losses, while that based on the old, observed prices provides an upper bound.

As capital services are fixed in aggregate supply by assumption, any flat-rate tax on capital income is nondistortionary. Further, since the tax proceeds are distributed according to one's ownership of capital, the distribution of income is unaffected by flat-rate capital income taxes. It is for these reasons that the only price which changes in moving from a flat 45.16878 percent tax (the surtax-removal cases) to a flat tax at an equal-yield rate is the net price of capital. For each of the seven production parameterizations, the new net price of capital and the equal-yield tax rate applying to net capital income are shown in the "P_K" and "tax rate" rows, respectively.

Part B of table 4 presents the same seven factor-elasticity cases where the consumers' elasticities of substitution are now specified as 0.5. As is shown, the efficiency loss estimates are reduced by 10–40 percent, and the shift factors are substantially lower, indicating that labor bears a smaller share of the burden of the surtax. The sensitivity of this incidence of the distortion on the functional distribution of income to different parameterizations seems to be far greater than expected or indicated by Harberger.

In comparing the estimates of the two parts of table 4 with Harberger's corrected results, one arrives at the general conclusion that the magnitudes are similar. The capital reallocation caused by the discriminatory capital income taxation is estimated to be smaller with the algorithmic approach of this section. Recalling the inequality of the units of measurement, the figures can best be interpreted by comparing the percentage increase in the amount of capital allocated to sector X which would occur in moving from the distortionary to a neutral tax situation. The six comparable

---

[6] What is referred to here as NNP is the value of the product of the two (or 12) sectors. The efficiency loss is the value of the change in production.

TABLE 4
SUMMARY OF TWO-SECTOR RESULTS

A. Consumer Demand Elasticities = 1; Fixed Factor Supplies

Case	Observed Equilibrium	1	2	3	4	5	6	7
S_X	...	−1.0	−1.0	−1.0	−0.75	−0.5	−0.5	−0.25
S_Y	...	−1.0	−0.5	−0.25	−0.25	−0.5	−0.25	−0.25
Surtax removal:								
P_X	1.00000	0.96626	0.97136	0.97419	0.96834	0.95607	0.95921	0.94337
P_Y	1.00000	1.17068	1.19455	1.20842	1.18378	1.13088	1.14478	1.07529
P_L	1.00000	1.00000	1.00000	1.00000	1.00000	1.00000	1.00000	1.00000
P_K	1.00000	1.29695	1.33027	1.34900	1.30727	1.22027	1.24145	1.12495
R	37.168	24.665	25.299	25.655	24.861	23.207	23.610	21.394
X^*	252.265	261.074	261.495	261.741	261.070	259.666	259.971	257.884
Y^*	44.349	37.883	37.374	37.082	37.541	38.614	38.310	39.624
K_X^*	23.589	27.828	27.318	27.043	26.815	26.585	26.431	25.665
K_Y^*	18.515	14.276	14.786	15.061	15.289	15.519	15.673	16.439
L_X^*	199.871	199.871	201.250	202.026	201.916	201.165	201.731	201.366
L_Y^*	17.471	17.471	16.092	15.316	15.426	16.177	15.611	15.976
Shift factor	...	0.00000	−0.17158	−0.27634	−0.05125	0.33570	0.25018	0.66648
Relative share of rich	0.273	0.273	0.274	0.275	0.274	0.271	0.272	0.269
ΔNNP†	...	0.943	0.633	0.450	0.467	0.591	0.477	0.435
ΔNNP‡	...	2.344	2.255	2.209	1.997	1.666	1.666	1.094
Equal yield replacement:								
P_X	1.00000	0.96626	0.97136	0.97419	0.96834	0.95607	0.95921	0.94337
P_Y	1.00000	1.17068	1.19455	1.20842	1.18378	1.13088	1.14478	1.07529
P_L	1.00000	1.00000	1.00000	1.00000	1.00000	1.00000	1.00000	1.00000
P_K	1.00000	1.00692	1.04901	1.07269	1.01902	0.90749	0.93441	0.78472
R	37.168	36.877	37.141	37.289	36.998	36.376	36.538	35.719
Tax rate	1.22112/0.45169	0.86983	0.84091	0.82795	0.86232	0.95204	0.92871	1.08108

TABLE 4 (Continued)

B. Consumer Demand Elasticities = 0.5; Fixed Factor Supplies

S_x	...	−1.0	−1.0	−1.0	−0.75	−0.5	−0.5	−0.25
S_y	...	−1.0	−0.5	−0.25	−0.25	−0.5	−0.25	−0.25
Surtax removal:								
P_x	1.00000	0.97166	0.97842	0.98230	0.97781	0.96531	0.97032	0.95551
P_y	1.00000	1.18989	1.22155	1.24078	1.22182	1.16734	1.18994	1.12585
P_L	1.00000	1.00000	1.00000	1.00000	1.00000	1.00000	1.00000	1.00000
P_K	1.00000	1.33226	1.37745	1.40398	1.37175	1.28306	1.31769	1.20961
R	37.168	25.337	26.196	26.701	26.088	24.401	25.060	23.004
X^*	252.265	257.426	257.618	257.740	257.460	256.760	256.979	255.969
Y^*	44.349	40.879	40.502	40.279	40.462	41.044	40.783	41.470
K_x^*	23.589	26.862	26.180	25.800	25.693	25.760	25.506	25.096
K_y^*	18.515	15.242	15.924	16.304	16.411	16.344	16.598	17.007
L_x^*	199.871	198.180	199.707	200.595	200.583	199.872	200.562	200.511
L_y^*	17.471	19.162	17.635	16.747	16.759	17.470	16.780	16.830
Shift factor	...	−0.18240	−0.44843	−0.62499	−0.41262	0.06652	−0.10472	0.37689
Relative share of rich	0.273	0.274	0.276	0.275	0.273	0.274	0.271
ΔNNP†	...	0.885	0.539	0.328	0.331	0.481	0.330	0.305
ΔNNP‡	...	1.690	1.507	1.405	1.308	1.190	1.148	0.831
Equal yield replacement:								
P_x	1.00000	0.97166	0.97842	0.98230	0.97781	0.96531	0.97032	0.95551
P_y	1.00000	1.18989	1.22155	1.24078	1.22182	1.16734	1.18994	1.12585
P_L	1.00000	1.00000	1.00000	1.00000	1.00000	1.00000	1.00000	1.00000
P_K	1.00000	1.04987	1.10675	1.14016	1.09892	0.98588	1.02976	0.89152
R	37.168	37.039	37.594	37.809	37.575	36.913	37.183	36.397
Tax rate	1.221122/0.45169	0.84215	0.80675	0.78759	0.81211	0.88928	0.85760	0.96964

* Billions of units.
† $ billion. Calculated at new (i.e., nondistortionary) prices.
‡ $ billion. Calculated at old (i.e., observed) prices.

TABLE 5

% Increase in Capital Allocated to "Corporate" Sector with Neutral Capital Income Taxation

S_X	S_Y	V	Estimate of Harberger Model (%)	Scarf Algorithm Estimate (%)
−1.0	−1.0	−1.0	19.74	17.97
−1.0	−0.5	−1.0	17.08	15.81
−0.5	−0.5	−1.0	13.87	12.70
−1.0	−1.0	−0.5	14.98	13.88
−1.0	−0.5	−0.5	11.68	10.98
−0.5	−0.5	−0.5	9.87	9.20

cases are shown in table 5.[7] The algorithmic estimates indicate that the discriminatory taxes cause slightly less resource misallocation and therefore a slightly smaller dead-weight loss. These facts are confirmed by noting that table 4 also indicates a smaller change in the price of capital services than do the comparable cases in column 10 of table 3. In all cases the percentage of deviation between the two approaches correctly implemented is small, indicating that, despite its several shortcomings, Harberger's model does not give a poor approximation, even for analyzing tax distortions as large as these.

Somewhat more ambiguity occurs in comparing the dead-weight loss estimates, although again the answers do not conflict. I would argue, however, that, in giving a point estimate, the Harberger approach may give the user of that technique a false sense of precision. While Harberger qualifies his results as rough estimates, the approach of this section gives an explicit upper and lower bound for the welfare loss.[8] In the six comparable cases, the Harberger corrected point estimate is always well within the upper and lower bounds prescribed in table 4 and is somewhat larger than their arithmetic or geometric mean. The geometric mean, of course, forms the Fisher "ideal" index (Fisher 1927). Again, however, the point estimate provided by the Harberger method does not deviate far from what one would arrive at with the technique of this section.

---

[7] The two models are not strictly comparable. One difference is the fact that two consumer classes are dealt with in this section, while the Harberger approach encompasses only a single-consumer or market demand relationship. The Scarf algorithm method was also run with a single consumer, and the results in terms of resource allocation across the two production sectors, prices, and dead-weight loss were nearly identical with the examples with two consumer classes reported here. So this does not account for the small differences in the results between Harberger's method and those of this section. The differences are due to the local assumptions of the Harberger model and the lack of an income effect in its demand specification.

[8] Of course, for a multitude of reasons, the numerical accuracy of these bounds themselves needs qualification.

INCIDENCE AND EFFICIENCY EFFECTS OF TAXES

The Scarf algorithm approach of this section allows the incorporation of a labor-leisure choice in the model. A fairly simple and possibly unrealistic demand function for leisure was analyzed in Shoven (1973) and Shoven and Whalley (1972). The more recent study covered the same elasticity cases reported on here. The general results were that the welfare loss estimates were approximately the same as in the fixed-labor-supply case, as long as leisure was valued at the wage rate. It is possible that the value of production can actually be higher in the presence of the distortion than in its absence. That is, the inefficiency of the distortion can be manifested totally in a decreased consumption of leisure. The lesson from that earlier analysis, then, is that the change in NNP is likely to be a poor estimate of the efficiency loss if there is a substantial elasticity in the supply of labor.

Given that the two approaches, when applied correctly to two production-sector data, are in broad agreement as to the incidence and efficiency effects of capital income taxes, the major advantage of the Scarf algorithmic method is its capability to analyze a more disaggregated description of production. The Harberger producer-surplus approach can likewise be disaggregated, but the general equilibrium model he uses to solve for the capital reallocation cannot easily incorporate more than a two-way division of production, except for the case in which all elasticities of substitution are the same (Hoffman 1972).

In order to evaluate the impact of disaggregation, the 12-sector data of table 2 were analyzed using the Scarf algorithm. The results for a selective subset of the 12 production-sector cases are contained in table 6. As intermediate products are not explicitly considered, it is necessary to interpret consumers as demanding value added from each of the 12 sectors. What is compared is the current tax situation (with each of the 12 sectors facing the different effective tax rates, as shown in column 9, table 2) with a flat-tax regime, with the tax rate set at 45.16878 percent (for comparability with the two-sector results just presented). As above, the equal-yield tax rate and the corresponding net price of capital were computed and are reported. Compared with the two-sector results shown in the previous set of tables, the loss estimates for these 12-sector cases are 10–70 percent higher. The efficiency cost as a percentage of the surtax yield now goes as high as 24.4 percent. The restrictiveness of the two-sector bifurcation of production is seen by noting that large relative price differentials develop between sectors which had previously been aggregated together in the "corporate" sector. In particular, the price of petroleum and coal products is shown to rise as much as 24 percent relative to the price of communication and public utilities with the switch to neutral capital income taxation. While the two-sector results had indicated that the price of the "corporate" sector's output would fall, it is seen in table 6 that the price of some components of that sector would rise relative to the

TABLE 6
Selective Summary of 12 Sector Results

Case*	Observed Equilibrium	1	2	3
A. Consumer Demand Elasticities = 1; Fixed Factor Supplies				
$S_{1,2,3}$	...	−1.0	−0.75	−0.25
S_{4-12}	...	−1.0	−0.25	−0.25
Surtax removal:				
P_1/Y_1	1.00000/ 16.281	1.13667/ 14.322	1.14850/ 14.197	1.07483/ 14.680
P_2/Y_2	1.00000/ 25.298	1.19444/ 21.180	1.20492/ 21.027	1.09027/ 22.487
P_3/Y_3	1.00000/ 2.770	1.15212/ 2.404	1.17168/ 2.368	1.10970/ 2.419
P_4/X_4	1.00000/ 3.216	0.96275/ 3.340	0.96454/ 3.339	0.94226/ 3.304
P_5/X_5	1.00000/ 17.865	0.99713/ 17.916	0.99753/ 17.937	0.98936/ 17.480
P_6/X_6	1.00000/104.291	0.93235/111.859	0.93539/111.670	0.91523/110.309
P_7/X_7	1.00000/ 3.144	1.01668/ 3.092	1.01817/ 3.093	0.98789/ 3.081
P_8/X_8	1.00000/ 4.874	1.07470/ 4.535	1.07906/ 4.524	0.99339/ 4.750
P_9/X_9	1.00000/ 54.487	1.00463/ 54.236	1.00582/ 54.257	0.98013/ 53.816
P_{10}/X_{10}	1.00000/ 16.761	0.96786/ 17.318	0.96940/ 17.317	0.95340/ 17.019
P_{11}/X_{11}	1.00000/ 13.883	0.87008/ 15.956	0.87479/ 15.895	0.83382/ 16.118
P_{12}/X_{12}	1.00000/ 33.744	0.99968/ 33.755	1.00003/ 33.796	0.99244/ 32.915
P_L	1.00000	1.00000	1.00000	1.00000
P_K	1.00000	1.29695	1.30453	1.14267
R	37.168	24.665	24.809	21.731
Shift factor	...	0.00000	−0.03749	0.610853
ΔNNP†	...	1.344	0.774	0.477
ΔNNP‡	...	3.300	2.808	1.762
Equal yield:				
P_K	1.00000	1.00971	1.01792	0.80915
R	37.168	36.759	36.877	35.774
Tax Rate	...	0.86466	0.86044	1.05006
B. Consumer Demand Elasticities = 0.5; Fixed Factor Supplies				
$S_{1,2,3}$	...	−1.0	−0.75	−0.25
S_{4-12}	...	−1.0	−0.25	−0.25
Surtax removal:				
P_1/Y_1	1.00000/ 16.281	1.14982/ 15.276	1.17555/ 15.144	1.10548/ 15.371
P_2/Y_2	1.00000/ 25.298	1.21625/ 23.079	1.24727/ 22.845	1.13786/ 23.542
P_3/Y_3	1.00000/ 2.770	1.16216/ 2.585	1.19441/ 2.556	1.13551/ 2.580
P_4/X_4	1.00000/ 3.216	0.96788/ 3.290	0.97361/ 3.289	0.95204/ 3.270
P_5/X_5	1.00000/ 17.865	0.99879/ 17.993	1.00053/ 18.025	0.99278/ 17.790
P_6/X_6	1.00000/104.291	0.93784/108.395	0.94490/108.277	0.92506/107.588
P_7/X_7	1.00000/ 3.144	1.02246/ 3.130	1.02890/ 3.128	1.00064/ 3.119
P_8/X_8	1.00000/ 4.874	1.09141/ 4.696	1.11011/ 4.669	1.02938/ 4.767
P_9/X_9	1.00000/ 54.487	1.00963/ 54.580	1.01501/ 54.581	0.99086/ 54.311
P_{10}/X_{10}	1.00000/ 16.761	0.97172/ 17.114	0.97616/ 17.121	0.96059/ 16.968
P_{11}/X_{11}	1.00000/ 13.883	0.88024/ 14.894	0.89270/ 14.829	0.85279/ 14.916
P_{12}/X_{12}	1.00000/ 33.744	1.00118/ 33.944	1.00276/ 34.008	0.99561/ 33.555
P_L	1.00000	1.00000	1.00000	1.00000
P_K	1.00000	1.32957	1.36463	1.20969
R	37.168	25.286	25.952	23.006
Shift factor	...	−0.16777	−0.36883	0.37659
ΔNNP†	...	1.298	0.657	0.390
ΔNNP‡	...	2.363	1.857	1.164
Equal yield:				
P_K	1.00000	1.04844	1.09151	0.89259
R	37.168	37.122	37.452	36.357
Tax rate	...	0.84094	0.81494	0.96741

* Sector 1, agriculture; 2, real estate; 3, crude oil and gas; 4, mining; 5, contract construction; 6, manufacturing; 7, lumber and wood products; 8, petroleum and coal products; 9, trade; 10, transportation; 11, communication and public utilities; 12, services.
† $ billion. Calculated at new (i.e., nondistortionary) prices.
‡ $ billion. Calculated at old (i.e., observed) prices.

TABLE 7

FISHER INDEX OF SOCIAL WASTE
CONSUMER DEMAND ELASTICITIES = 1.0; FIXED FACTOR SUPPLIES

2 SECTORS			12 SECTORS		
S_X	S_Y	$ Billion	$S_{1,2,3}$	S_{4-12}	$ Billion
−1.00	−1.00	1.49	−1.00	−1.00	2.11
−1.00	−0.50	1.19	...	...	...
−1.00	−0.25	1.00	...	...	...
−0.75	−0.25	0.97	−0.75	−0.25	1.47
−0.50	−0.50	0.99	...	...	...
−0.50	−0.25	0.89	...	...	...
−0.25	−0.25	0.69	−0.25	−0.25	0.92

price of labor. The added detail of this disaggregated analysis thus gives a somewhat different picture and information which may be valuable in the making of policy decisions.

As has been shown in tables 4 and 6, a change in tax rates causes a vector of changes in outputs which must be aggregated to arrive at a single-number dead-weight loss estimate. This condensation of information is subject to the usual index number problems, and I have presented the Paasche and Laspeyres measures of the inefficiency resulting from the distortionary taxation of capital income in the 1953–59 U.S. economy. Nonetheless, policy makers often want a single number, and not a range of numbers (they want the impossible solution to the index number problem). One technique of combining the Paasche and Laspeyres indices into a single loss estimate is to form the Fisher "ideal" index (Fisher 1927), which is the square root of their product. The results of such a procedure for the cases shown in part A of tables 4 and 6 are shown in table 7. If personally asked to give a point estimate of the efficiency loss due to the U.S. capital income taxes, I would refer to the $S_X = -0.75$, $S_Y = -0.25$ 12-sector model. The Fisher index shows a loss of $1.47 billion in this case, or 11.9 percent of the surtax revenue. The point estimate is somewhat smaller than what one would arrive at from Harberger's published estimates, although, given the magnitude of his two mistakes and the fact that this is for a 12-sector rather than a two-sector analysis, the number is remarkably close to the $2.0–$2.5 billion figure one might get from his work. Needless to say, one would still want to qualify heavily any such point estimate.

IV. Conclusion

This paper has reexamined the results of the Harberger model concerning the static efficiency cost of the U.S. taxation of capital income during the 1953–59 period. I have asserted that Harberger made two significant mistakes in his earlier evaluation of this question, each of which substantially altered his results. The net effect of correcting these errors is to lower the dead-weight loss estimates previously published as ranging from $1.0 billion to $2.9 billion approximately 38 percent to a range of $0.625 billion–$1.79 billion. The correct results are thus an even smaller fraction of GNP or NNP than previously thought, but the efficiency loss does amount to between 6 and 15 percent of the revenue generated by the distortionary surtax on capital income originating from the "corporate" sector.

Using the corrected data, I have computed the incidence and deadweight loss using an algorithmic-solution technique for a general equilibrium model. In the two-sector analyses, the results do not differ substantially from the corrected Harberger figures, showing, if anything, that the unequal tax treatment causes less resource reallocation. The conclusion is that, at least in this case, the second-order approximations made in the Harberger analysis are reasonably accurate, even for tax distortions as large as those of this study. The algorithmic approach does explicitly remind one of the fundamental index number problems in describing the static inefficiency effects of a tax distortion with a single number.

One of the advantages of the algorithmic method is its capability of solving a disaggregated general equilibrium model. In order to evaluate the effect of moving to a less aggregated description of production, a 12-sector analysis was presented. The dead-weight loss estimates increased an average of approximately 40 percent from what they were in the two-sector cases. The model also implied that differential capital income taxes caused significant relative output price distortions among sectors which were previously lumped together. It was stated that the added richness of the results of the disaggregated analysis should be valuable to those involved in tax policy evaluation and formation.

The final point which should be made is that, in comparing the Harberger model and approach with the algorithmic-solution procedure in this study, I have not pressed the latter method anywhere near its capabilities. Because of its ability to handle models with many commodities and consumers, detailed incidence studies are feasible. Further, the additional disaggregation may allow studying several distortions simultaneously or, by time-dating commodities, permit a dynamic evaluation of policy alterations. The purpose here was to correct Harberger's errors in his study of the efficiency cost of uneven capital income taxation and to examine how different the results of a similar simple analysis would be with this algorithmic approach. The implementation of the further capabilities of the algorithmic technique in conjunction with more recent economic data is an area of active research for this author and others but is beyond the scope of this study.

References

Fisher, I. *The Making of Index Numbers: A Study of their Varieties, Tests, and Reliability.* 3d ed. New York: Houghton Mifflin, 1927.

Harberger, A. C. "The Corporation Income Tax: An Empirical Appraisal." In *Tax Revision Compendium*. Vol. 1. Washington: House Committee on Ways and Means, Government Printing Office, 1959.

———. "The Incidence of the Corporation Income Tax." *J.P.E.* 70, no. 3 (June 1962): 215–40.

———. "Efficiency Effects of Taxes on Income from Capital." In *Effects of Corporation Income Tax*, edited by M. Krzyzaniak. Detroit: Wayne State Univ. Press, 1966.

Hoffman, R. F. "Disaggregation and Calculations of the Welfare Cost of a Tax." *J.P.E.* 80, no. 2 (March/April 1972): 409–17.

Lucas, R. E. "Labor-Capital Substitution in U.S. Manufacturing." In *The Taxation of Income from Capital*, edited by A. C. Harberger and M. J. Bailey. Washington: Brookings Inst., 1969.

McLure, C. E., Jr. "A Diagrammatic Exposition of the Harberger Model with One Immobile Factor." *J.P.E.* 82, no. 1 (January/February 1974): 56–82.

———. "General Equilibrium Incidence Analysis: The Harberger Model after Ten Years." *J. Public Econ.* 4 (February 1975): 125–61.

Minasian, J. R. "Elasticities of Substitution and Constant-Output Demand Curves for Labor." *J.P.E.* 69, no. 3 (June 1961): 261–70.

Projector, D. S., and Weiss, S. *Survey of Financial Characteristics of Consumers*. Federal Reserve Technical Papers. Washington: Government Printing Office, 1966.

Rosenberg, L. C. "Taxation of Income from Capital, by Industry Group." In *The Taxation of Income from Capital*, edited by A. C. Harberger and M. J. Bailey. Washington: Brookings Inst., 1969.

Scarf, H. E., with the collaboration of Hansen, T. *The Computation of Economic Equilibria*. New Haven, Conn.: Yale Univ. Press, 1973.

Shoven, J. B. "General Equilibrium with Taxes: Existence, Computation, and a Capital Income Taxation Application." Ph.D. dissertation, Yale Univ., 1973.

———. "A Proof of the Existence of a General Equilibrium with Ad Valorem Commodity Taxes." *J. Econ. Theory* 8 (May 1974): 1–25.

———. "Applying Fixed Point Algorithms to the Analysis of Tax Policies." In *Fixed Points: Algorithms and Applications*, edited by C. B. Garcia and S. Karamardian. New York: Academic Press, 1976.

Shoven, J. B., and Whalley, J. "A General Equilibrium Calculation of the Effects of Differential Taxation of Income from Capital in the U.S." *J. Public Econ.* 1 (November 1972): 281–321.

———. "General Equilibrium with Taxes: A Computational Procedure and an Existence Proof." *Rev. Econ. Studies* 60 (October 1973): 475–90.

———. "Equal Yield Tax Alternatives: A General Equilibrium Computational Technique." Technical Report no. 150(R), Stanford Univ., Inst. Math. Studies Soc. Sci., 1975.

Solow, R. M. "Capital, Labor, and Income in Manufacturing." In *The Behavior of Income Shares*. Princeton, N.J.: Princeton Univ. Press (for Nat. Bur. Econ. Res.), 1964.

Stiglitz, J. E. "The Corporation Tax." Technical Report no. 162, Stanford Univ., Inst. Math. Studies Soc. Sci., 1975.

Van Horne, J. C. *Financial Management and Policy*. Englewood Cliffs, N.J.: Prentice-Hall, 1971.

Whalley, J. "A Numerical Assessment of the April 1973 Tax Changes in the United Kingdom." Ph.D. dissertation, Yale Univ., 1973.

[10]

Tax Reform and the Stock Market: An Asset Price Approach

By DAVID M. CUTLER*

The incidence of the corporate income tax has been a subject of much dispute. Traditionally, the debate has focused on the importance of general equilibrium effects in evaluating tax burdens. In applied work, incidence analysis has often consisted of estimating the changes in future tax payments from tax reforms. These "cash flow" models of incidence implicitly assume that the relative price effects of tax reforms are unimportant. In general equilibrium analyses, however, these relative price effects, particularly changes in the price of existing capital, are important determinants of the tax burden. "Asset price" models of incidence can consequently yield predictions quite different from those of cash flow models. In theory, the general equilibrium effects associated with the asset price approach are well understood, but little is known about their empirical magnitude.[1]

This paper assesses these asset price effects by examining the stock market's reaction to the Tax Reform Act of 1986. The 1986 Tax Act presents a unique natural experiment for studying asset pricing theories. The Act changed the overall corporate tax burden (a $120 billion increase over five years), the tax rate on corporate income (a decrease from 46 percent to 34 percent), and the relative treatment of old and new capital (the repeal of the investment tax credit and lengthening of depreciation lifetimes). These changes could produce substantial cross-firm heterogeneity in the reaction to tax news.

The paper uses a "differential effects" event study to evaluate the market response.[2] The analysis focuses on two key events in the tax bill's progress: the vote by the House of Representatives for the bill in December 1985, and the vote for a similar bill by the Senate Finance Committee in May 1986. Both events came as surprises to the financial community and are therefore well suited to an event study.

The analysis leads to two conclusions. First, there is some evidence confirming the predictions of the asset price model. After accounting for changes in future cash flows, firms with greater shares of equipment in their capital stocks benefit from the tax change, while firms with greater pre-reform investment rates suffer share declines. These results suggest that the differential taxation of new and old capital could have substantial effects on market values. Second, however, the paper finds little evidence of a large market response to tax news. Excess returns on days containing similar tax news are essentially uncorrelated, and overall market

---

*Department of Economics, Massachusetts Institute of Technology, Cambridge, MA 02139. I am grateful to Alan Auerbach, Larry Katz, Greg Mankiw, Peter Reiss, two anonymous referees, and especially Martin Feldstein, Jim Poterba, and Lawrence Summers for useful discussions and comments on an earlier draft. Financial support from a National Science Foundation graduate fellowship is gratefully acknowledged.

[1] Formal discussions of the asset price model and its relation to other incidence methods are in Andrew Abel, 1982; Alan Auerbach, 1986; and Lawrence Summers, 1981, 1985; though the distinction between taxes on new and old assets was noted at least by Richard Musgrave: "In the long run, this [tax on new investment] may lead to a decline or increase in the supply of capital, with resulting changes in yield of new assets. These, in turn, give rise to a revaluation of existing assets, and may involve changes in the relative yields and capital values of various assets." [1959, p. 384]. One cash flow model which does allow for many of the general equilibrium effects is Thomas Downs and Patric Hendershott, 1987. Empirical studies of the asset price approach include Andrew Lyons, 1986; and Downs and Hassan Tehranian, 1988.

[2] See Nancy Rose, 1985, for a comparison of this approach with alternative methods of estimating the effects of changes in policy on corporate returns.

reactions to the tax news are small. These results leave unanswered questions about what the tax news meant to the market, and whether the news was efficiently incorporated in stock prices.

The structure of the paper is as follows. Section I discusses the asset price approach to incidence, as well as a competing cash flow approach. Sections II and III detail the methodology employed and identify dates of changing tax expectations. Section IV examines cross-sectional incidence tests. Section V considers more general tests of market movements. Section VI concludes.

I. Tax Reform and Market Value

Two approaches have traditionally been advanced for studying the effects of tax reform on market value. The first is a cash flow approach. Cash flow analyses evaluate tax incidence by estimating changes in after-tax income. While reform-induced demand shifts are sometimes incorporated in these analyses, other general equilibrium effects typically are not. More commonly, the focus is on computing changes in corporate tax payments.

The cash flow approach predicts a substantial market fall in response to the 1986 Act. The House of Representatives' (1986) forecast of corporate tax payments indicates that the Act should raise $84 billion in real terms over its first five years.[3] The effect of this increase on share values should be tempered by the reduced taxation of corporate dividend payments. Estimates by Jerry Hausman and James Poterba (1987) suggest that the marginal tax rate on dividends will fall by 8.1 percent under the new law, which, assuming historical average real dividend growth of 3.4 percent per year, yields a five-year tax savings of $35 billion. The net effect of the reform is thus an increase of $49 billion in the shareholder tax burden, or about 2.5 percent of the end of 1985 value of the stock market.

While the cash flow approach correctly focuses on after-tax returns, it ignores many general equilibrium effects. These are highlighted in the asset price model of incidence. The asset price approach stresses changes in the value of existing assets from tax reform, in addition to the change in future tax payments. Policies that alter future marginal products also affect the value of existing assets through their impact on the supply of capital-intensive goods and thus on product market prices. If these general equilibrium effects are large, they can reverse the partial equilibrium analysis. Consider, for example, the repeal of the investment tax credit. This change reduces the after-tax return to new equipment,[4] but increases the value of existing equipment, which now competes with more expensive (after-tax) new equipment. Higher returns on old capital therefore partly offset the higher taxes that firms must pay on new capital. The net effect on share values is ambiguous, depending on specific technological and adjustment cost assumptions. The asset price approach does, however, offer cross-sectional predictions about the response to tax news. These are detailed in the next section.[5]

II. Methodology and Data

To measure the impact of tax reform on market value, I examine the excess returns caused by tax news. I use the market model

---

[3] See Alan Auerbach and James Poterba, 1987, for details of the calculation.

[4] Since the investment tax credit applied only to equipment, the tax change hurt equipment investment more than structures investment. Auerbach, 1987, estimates that the tax reform increased the effective tax rate on equipment from −3.3 percent to 38.0 percent, and lowered the rate on structures from 45.6 percent to 37.0 percent.

[5] The 1986 Act also changed the taxation of personal income, which could affect the value of corporate distributions. I consider some of these changes in the empirical work, but concentrate on the corporate tax changes. I also ignore the implications of the asset price model for the transition after the tax news. Since the two events I consider contained similar news, the change in prices after each should be similar; the transitions after the votes, in contrast, need not be. Further, the phasing in of many of the tax changes and the retroactive repeal of the investment tax credit make the determination of the transition path difficult.

to measure these returns:

(1) $R_{it} = \alpha_i + \beta_i R_{mt} + \varepsilon_{it}$,

where R_{it} and R_{mt} are the return to stock i and the market (m) at time t. The coefficient $\beta_i = \text{cov}(R_i, R_m)/\text{var}(R_m)$ is the share of the return that cannot be fully diversified. The excess return is then the residual, ε_{it}.[6] The firm sample is the 1985 Fortune 500 largest industrial corporations.[7]

To examine the incidence hypotheses, I model the excess returns as a function of firm asset and financial characteristics:

(2) $ERET_i = \tau_0 + \tau_1 M\&ESHARE_i$

$+ \tau_2 INV_i + \tau_3 NETK_i + \tau_4 ATR_i$

$+ \tau_5 \Delta CASHFLOW_i + \xi_i$,

where $ERET_i = \varepsilon_{i,H} + \varepsilon_{i,S}$, the combined excess return from the days or weeks around the House and Senate Finance Committee votes.[8] The first three variables are measures of the firm's assets. M&ESHARE is the percentage of the 1985 gross book value of the capital stock accounted for by machinery and equipment (found in the annual report of each company).[9] INV and NETK are the average growth rate of the net capital stock from 1982 to 1985 and the net book value (in millions of dollars) of the capital stock in 1985. Both variables are from COMPUSTAT.

The last two variables highlight the tax payments of the firm. ATR is the firm's 1985 average tax rate, while $\Delta CASHFLOW$ is the projected change in annual tax payments from the tax reform. $\Delta CASHFLOW$ is found by recomputing the corporation's 1985 average tax rate under 1988 tax rules and multiplying this change by the ratio of the tax base of the firm to the value of equity.[10] The data on average tax rates and changes in average tax rates are from Tax Analysts (1985, 1986).[11] The other variables are from COMPUSTAT.

The two incidence hypotheses offer different predictions about the importance of these explanatory variables. The cash flow approach predicts that the projected change in tax payments should be positively related to the firm's excess stock return, but that the other variables should not. After controlling for future taxes, no pre-reform aspects of the corporation should influence share prices.[12]

The asset price approach similarly suggests that the change in cash flow should be positively related to excess returns, since this measures the direct effects of the reform on tax liabilities. The other variables capture the relative price effects. Holding constant future taxes and the stock of existing capital, an increase in the equipment share of the capital stock increases the amount of the

---

[6] I use daily return data from January 1985 to November 1986. The data were adjusted for dividend payments and stock splits. The return on the Standard & Poor's Composite Stock Index was employed as a proxy for the market return.

[7] An industrial corporation is one in which over 50 percent of the sales are from mining or manufacturing. The Fortune list was selected because annual reports are more readily available for these firms, and because the companies in the Fortune survey are ranked on sales, not profits. The sample thus should not be self-selected for profitability. In fact, a record number of firms (70) lost money in 1985. Due to missing data, the sample was reduced to 336 of the 500 firms.

[8] I report OLS estimates of equation (2), though differential variances of the error terms in equation (1) would result in heteroskedastic errors in equation (2). Using weighted least squares has no significant effects on the estimates.

[9] A more appropriate specification would use the percentage of equipment in the net capital stock. Firms only report asset types by gross value, however.

[10] The tax base is imputed as the sum of federal and foreign tax payments and investment tax credits utilized, divided by the statutory tax rate in 1985 (46 percent).

[11] Tax Analysts did not compute the average tax rate or projected change in the average tax rate for a small number of firms. For these firms, the variables utilized were the weighted average estimates for the relevant industry. The results do not change across samples.

[12] If the tax bases of firms grow at different rates, or if the 1986 and 1987 transition rules differ greatly from the fully implemented provisions, the recalculations of the average tax rates may not be a complete estimate of the total changes in cash flow. While part of these differences may be captured by the industry dummies, the noise in the estimates suggests that the coefficients on the change in cash flow could be downward biased.

firm's existing capital that is in competition with the less subsidized new equipment, and thus should positively affect excess returns. Similarly, the investment rate should be negatively related to excess returns, because faster-growing firms have younger capital stocks and thus generate larger depreciation deductions. The reduced corporate rate decreases the value of these deductions, so that, for equal final capital stocks, higher growth firms should experience larger windfall losses. Finally, the pre-reform average tax rate should have a negative effect on excess returns. Low average tax rates are associated with tax loss firms, or firms nearing tax losses. Since the tax act increases overall corporate tax payments, the value of existing tax losses should rise.[13]

III. Expectations of Tax Changes

Two events dominated the history of the 1986 Tax Act. In December 1985, the House of Representatives voted for major tax reform, and in May 1986, the Senate Finance Committee voted for a substantially similar bill. Both of these votes came as surprises to the financial community.[14]

For most of 1985, the tax reform bill was stuck in the House of Representatives. As late as mid-December, the full House had not yet received the bill for consideration. On December 11, two tax bills were introduced on the House floor. The first (Republican) bill was defeated as projected, but in a surprise move, the second (Democratic) bill failed to pass. The headlines on December 12 proclaimed "Reagan Loses Key Tax Vote," and the House adjourned for the weekend "with the prospects growing dimmer that a tax bill can clear the House this year." [*New York Times*, December 13, 1985, IV, 1:3]

---

[13] This effect is partly mitigated by the repeal of the General Utilities doctrine and the strengthening of ownership requirements to utilize acquired operating losses, both of which make the transfer of tax losses more difficult. It is difficult to find proxies to control for these effects, however.

[14] The discussion of the tax bill here is necessarily brief. For a narrative of the bill's history, see Jeffrey Birnbaum and Alan Murray, 1987.

Lobbying over tax reform continued that weekend and early the next week. On December 17 (Tuesday), the bill was reintroduced in the House. It was passed later that day, although the vote was not held until 11:00 P.M. The timing of the change in expectations is unclear. It is conceivable that investors anticipated the outcome on Tuesday, though it was not until the discussion of Wednesday's market movement (on Thursday) that the *New York Times* mentioned the bill influencing traders. "Another negative for the stock market was the House passage Tuesday night of its version of the tax-revision bill," it reported. [December 19, 1985, IV, 14:4] Accordingly, I use the return on December 18 (Wednesday) as the immediate response to tax news.

After passing the House, the tax bill was sent to the Senate Finance Committee, where it remained for almost half a year. For most of this period, little progress was made toward approval. As late as May 4, 1986, the *New York Times* noted that the prospects for passage looked dim. Powerful lobbyists were strongly against the bill. After working all day on May 6 (Tuesday), however, the Senate Finance Committee voted on and passed a tax bill. As with the House passage, the vote was not taken until late at night, this time at 12:30 A.M. on May 7. The *New York Times* noted that the outcome was uncertain until a late-night agreement was reached leaving in oil and gas tax shelters. Thursday's paper carried the headline "Tax Revision in 1986 is Almost Assured, Lawmakers Insist," and reported that, "Leading Senators and Representatives from both parties said today (May 7) that the Senate Finance Committee's unanimous approval of a tax bill meant that comprehensive tax revision legislation would almost certainly be enacted by the end of this year." [May 8, 1986, I, 1:6] As with the House vote, I use the day after the vote (May 7) as the immediate response to tax news.

IV. The Effect on Market Values

The most natural test of the reaction to tax news is the change in aggregate share values. The cash flow hypothesis predicts a large decline from the capitalization of the increased taxes, while the predictions of the asset price model are ambiguous. The actual response to the votes was negative but small in magnitude. On the day after the House vote, the S&P 500 fell by 0.40 percent; after the Senate Finance Committee vote, the index fell by 0.49 percent. These responses do not appear to stem from mis-specified dates of expectations changes. On the previous days, the index fell by 0.65 and 0.21 percent. In fact, for the 10-day period spanning the two votes, the index fell by 0.65 percent for the House vote, but actually rose by 1.19 percent for the Senate Finance Committee vote.[15] The aggregate market statistics thus seem inconsistent with large share declines, though the overall movements do little to estimate the relative price effects. The remainder of this section examines excess returns using industry- and firm-specific returns.

A. *Industry-Based Tests*

Most incidence analyses are conducted on industry aggregates. This is both because demand shifts from the tax reform would plausibly be concentrated along industry lines,[16] and because firms in an industry may be similar enough to merit common treatment. To test these hypotheses, Table 1 presents the average excess returns for the firms in each industry. The industries are grouped into "winners" and "losers" based on newspaper and magazine discussions of the bill's likely effects. The first column reports the predicted changes in one year's net income from one of the quantitative assessments of the tax bill, the Shearson-Lehman Brothers projections (Walter Dolde, 1986, and Allen Sinai, 1986). The Shearson projections are similar to other discussions in the financial press.

The remaining three columns present the industry average return for different time periods: the day after both votes, the 10-day (6-market day) period encompassing the weekend before and after each vote, and the one-month period beginning the Friday before the vote and extending after the vote. The industry returns provide little evidence that reactions to tax reform fell along industry lines. For most industries, one cannot reject the hypothesis of zero excess return. Further, the predicted and actual effects seem only weakly correlated. The industries with above-average predicted changes in income do not appear to have above-average excess returns. In fact, most of the industries in the "losers'" category were consistent winners in the stock market,[17] although the predicted winners fared well on average. The results are generally unsupportive of industry-based measures of tax incidence.

B. *Firm-Specific Tests*

Since industry-level predictions are only partly consistent with the observed reaction, I examine returns on a firm-specific basis. Table 2 presents the results for estimating equation (2). I include industry dummies to control for industry effects and estimate the equations over different time periods to examine the timing of the market reaction.

The estimates in Table 2 lead to three conclusions. The most significant result is the distinction between high growth firms and firms with large existing equipment shares. Exclusive of the one-day return, firms with high investment rates suffer from the tax reform; the effects are significant and increase in magnitude with longer time periods. In contrast, firms with large shares of

---

[15]Other measures of market activity also show little movement. Market volume on the day after both votes (138 million and 130 million shares for the House and Senate Finance Committee votes) was near average for that week (154 and 125 million shares) and only average for that month (137 and 127 million shares). The same is true of the 10-day volume moving average, the number of new highs and lows, and the number of advances and declines.

[16]A common prediction was that the shift in the tax burden from households to corporations would increase demand for consumer goods and decrease demand for corporate equipment.

[17]The oil and gas industry did well after the Senate Finance Committee vote because of the already noted depletion provisions included in the bill. For the other industries, however, special provisions do not appear to be important.

TABLE 1—ESTIMATED AND ACTUAL TAX REFORM WINNERS AND LOSERS[a]

Industry	Predicted Change in Net Income (percent)	Excess Returns Over		
		One Day	Ten Days	One Month
Predicted Winners				
Appliances	8.40	1.35	2.55	6.02
		(1.45)	(3.02)	(5.00)
Apparel	5.10	0.36	2.54	7.13
		(1.02)	(2.14)	(3.54)
Wholesale and Retail Trade	4.50	0.37	0.98	−0.27
		(1.12)	(2.34)	(3.87)
Service	1.80	1.76	1.27	−3.20
		(1.77)	(3.70)	(6.12)
Media	1.10	0.76	1.00	1.70
		(0.72)	(1.51)	(2.50)
Predicted Losers				
Electrical Machinery	−5.65	−0.03	−2.20	−2.03
		(0.54)	(1.12)	(1.85)
Aerospace	−5.82	0.30	−0.30	−2.65
		(0.65)	(1.35)	(2.24)
Machinery and Equipment	−6.39	1.46	3.48	4.29
		(0.50)	(1.05)	(1.77)
Communication	−15.00	−0.38	−0.08	−4.11
		(0.95)	(1.98)	(3.27)
Metals and Mining	−18.50	0.24	−0.96	0.36
		(0.58)	(1.23)	(2.04)
Oil and Gas	−20.30	1.33	3.97	2.98
		(0.46)	(0.26)	(1.61)
Heavy Industry	−76.43	−0.53	0.09	1.09
		(0.76)	(1.58)	(2.61)
Indeterminate				
Dairy Products	14.78	−0.08	−5.60	−6.06
		(1.45)	(3.02)	(5.00)
Stone, Clay, and Plastics	13.12	−0.32	−0.34	−2.38
		(0.67)	(1.40)	(2.31)
Drugs	9.60	−0.86	−1.99	−2.30
		(0.70)	(1.45)	(2.40)
Furniture	8.40	−0.49	−0.23	0.03
		(2.51)	(5.23)	(8.66)
Measuring Instruments	7.83	−1.32	−3.76	2.59
		(0.79)	(1.65)	(2.74)
Food and Tobacco	6.00	−0.18	−0.48	−2.79
		(0.51)	(1.07)	(1.77)
Textiles	5.10	0.44	0.74	7.55
		(0.89)	(1.85)	(3.06)
Beverages	3.40	−0.53	−3.54	−1.37
		(0.95)	(1.98)	(3.54)
Engines and Turbines	1.10	−0.11	2.70	8.89
		(1.12)	(2.34)	(3.87)
Office Machinery	−0.02	0.25	0.27	−0.31
		(0.65)	(1.40)	(2.31)
Automobiles	−13.30	−1.15	−4.39	−3.14
		(0.63)	(1.35)	(2.16)
Miscellaneous Manufacturing	−15.60	−0.97	−0.97	6.16
		(1.12)	(2.34)	(3.87)
Chemicals	−23.20	0.02	0.10	0.10
		(0.45)	(0.94)	(1.56)
Paper and Lumber	−25.80	−0.29	−0.09	1.48
		(0.58)	(1.20)	(2.04)

TABLE 1—CONTINUED

Industry	Predicted Change in Net Income (percent)	Excess Returns Over		
		One Day	Ten Days	One Month
Rubber	−34.20	−0.16	−3.13	−2.03
		(0.89)	(1.85)	(3.06)
R^2		0.09	0.17	0.12
N		336	333	330

Sources: Stock return data are from Data Resources, Inc. Changes in net income are from Dolde (1986) and Sinai (1986). Periodicals used in grouping industries were the *New York Times*, *Wall Street Journal*, *Fortune*, and *Business Week*.

[a] This table shows predicted change in net income and mean excess return for each industry. Excess returns are the sum of the returns for the House and Senate Finance Committee votes. Industries were grouped by newspaper and magazine discussions of tax reform. Industries in the "Indeterminate" category either had no predictions made about them, or were predicted as a winner by some analysts and a loser by others. Standard errors are in parentheses.

---

formerly ITC-qualifying equipment increase in value in response to tax news, though the estimates are less significant when industry effects are included. Both of these results support the predictions of the asset price model of incidence.

The equipment share and investment rate coefficients are broadly consistent with the predictions of the asset price theory.[18] The coefficient on the investment rate measures the difference in the losses on existing depreciation allowances for firms with different rates of investment. Using aggregate data, it is possible to provide an estimate of these effects. For a given nominal discount rate (8 percent), it is possible to calculate the present value of depreciation allowances (under the 1985 tax law) for a unit of equipment and structures of every vintage. Given constant depreciation rates, the stock of depreciation deductions on existing assets can then be computed for different rates of investment. Evaluated at the 1982–85 average net investment rates, a 1 percent increase in investment, split between equipment and structures in the ratio of the outstanding stocks (70 percent equipment in the sample) results in a 3.1 percent increase in the stock of depreciation allowances. The rate cut, then, reduces the value of these allowances by 0.37 percent. Empirically, the largest estimate of this effect is about one-third this magnitude. The predicted changes are larger than the observed changes, though allowing for the less favorable tax law before 1981, slower growth in the 1970s, and an effective tax rate change of less than 12 percent would reduce the differences in the stocks of allowances.

The coefficient on the equipment share is more difficult to evaluate because it depends on how quickly the capital stock adjusts to the tax change. A quick adjustment would imply large windfalls from the repeal of the investment tax credit but smaller windfalls from the rate cut. It is possible to provide some estimates of these magnitudes. Auerbach (1986) solves the asset price model analytically and simulates the impact of the 1986 tax reform. He finds that the tax change should result in equal revaluations of equipment and structures when adjustment costs are large, but that each dollar of equipment should increase in value by 0.07 percent more than a dollar of structures when adjustment

---

[18] It is possible that firms with large amounts of net investment suffer because their returns to shareholders are conveyed in the form of capital gains, which are taxed more heavily under the new law. Including the dividend-earnings ratio to measure these payout effects, however, does not change the estimated coefficients. Further, the coefficient on the dividend-earnings ratio is small in magnitude and insignificant statistically.

TABLE 2—TAX CHANGES AND MARKET VALUE[a]

Period	Machinery and Equipment Share	Rate of Investment	Net Capital Stock	Average Tax Rate	Predicted Change In Cash Flow	Industry Dummies	R^2	N
One Day	.018 (.012)	−.004 (.006)	.037 (.033)	−.002 (.004)	−.045 (.064)	No	.022	336
One Day	.000 (.015)	−.003 (.006)	.032 (.036)	−.003 (.005)	−.044 (.066)	Yes	.097	336
Ten Days	.083 (.025)	−.029 (.013)	.068 (.070)	−.009 (.010)	−.126 (.141)	No	.061	333
Ten Days	.035 (.031)	−.028 (.013)	.044 (.075)	−.011 (.010)	−.166 (.139)	Yes	.205	333
One Month	.064 (.043)	−.131 (.042)	−.025 (.117)	−.028 (.016)	−.173 (.318)	No	.052	330
One Month	.024 (.051)	−.158 (.044)	−.027 (.124)	−.028 (.016)	.115 (.323)	Yes	.174	330

Sources: See Table 1 for source of stock returns. Machinery and equipment share is from the footnote of the annual report for each company. Rate of investment and net capital stock are from COMPUSTAT. Average tax rates and predicted changes in cash flow are from Tax Analysts (1985, 1986) and COMPUSTAT.

[a] This table shows results of OLS estimation of equation (2) in the text. The dependent variable is the sum of the excess returns from the House of Representatives and Senate Finance Committee votes. The independent variables are the share of machinery and equipment in the gross capital stock, the average rate of investment, the net capital stock (in millions of dollars), the pre-reform average tax rate, and the predicted change in cash flow as a percent of total value of equity. The industry dummy variables are the same as in Table 1. Industry estimates are not reported. The final column reports the sample size for the estimate. Firms were omitted from longer period regressions when newspapers reported significant nontax news (generally merger activity) in the period. Standard errors are in parentheses.

costs are small. The estimates of this differential using 10-day and one-month returns (0.03 to 0.08 percent) are thus in line with the Auerbach results.[19]

In contrast to the equipment share and investment rate effects, however, there is no evidence that either average tax rates or predicted changes in future tax payments affect excess returns. The latter result is particularly surprising. Under both approaches, measures of changes in cash flow should be positively related to excess returns; this coefficient is generally negative and insignificant, however. Similarly, the coefficient on the average tax rate provides little evidence for windfall gains from more effective shielding of future liabilities.

These results are quite robust. Replacing the cash flow change with the change in the average tax rate, to eliminate potential tax base problems, does not affect the estimated coefficients. Further, the estimates change little when measures of explicit tax provisions such as minimum tax payments are included in the regression separately or in tandem with the cash flow variable.[20]

---

[19] These estimates suggest two additional points about the asset price model. First the size of the equipment share coefficient implies a much shorter adjustment period than previous studies have found. In the investment function associated with these adjustment costs, Auerbach's 0.07 estimate suggests that the rate of investment increases by 2 percent for a 1-point increase in Tobin's q; the estimates of Summers, 1981, in contrast, are of an increase of 0.031 in the investment rate (see Huntley Schaller, 1987, for larger estimates of the responsiveness to q). Second, the results imply that increases in the value of old capital are consistent with relatively small changes in equilibrium product market prices. With Cobb-Douglas production functions and a capital share of 25 percent, the output of equipment-only firms would have to increase in price by just 1.5 percent more than the output of structures-only firms to produce the 6 percent windfall.

[20] An alternative hypothesis about the tax variables is that, due to incomplete foreign tax credit utilization, firms with large foreign tax payments (essentially min-

TABLE 3—THE CORRELATION OF EXCESS RETURNS[a]

	Dec 16	Dec 17	Dec 18*	Dec 19	Dec 20	Dec 23
May 5	0.115	0.027	0.104	−0.071	−0.002	−0.014
	(0.056)	(0.057)	(0.056)	(0.057)	(0.057)	(0.057)
May 6	−0.045	0.002	0.036	0.176	−0.019	0.036
	(0.057)	(0.057)	(0.057)	(0.055)	(0.057)	(0.057)
May 7*	−0.208	−0.044	0.036	0.124	0.055	−0.071
	(0.054)	(0.057)	(0.057)	(0.056)	(0.057)	(0.056)
May 8	−0.005	−0.022	0.168	−0.003	0.022	0.026
	(0.057)	(0.057)	(0.055)	(0.057)	(0.057)	(0.057)
May 9	0.050	−0.005	0.097	0.087	−0.018	0.021
	(0.057)	(0.057)	(0.056)	(0.056)	(0.057)	(0.057)
May 12	−0.076	0.057	0.121	−0.022	0.036	0.004
	(0.057)	(0.057)	(0.056)	(0.057)	(0.057)	(0.057)

Source: See Table 1.
[a] This table shows correlation of excess returns for the days around the two tax votes. Sample size is 310 firms for all correlations. The excluded firms had missing return data for one or more days. The first day after the vote is indicated with an asterisk. Standard errors are in parentheses.

One final point about Table 2 is troubling as well. The immediate reaction to tax news, shown in the first two rows of the table, cannot be explained by any of the firm characteristics included. All of the estimated coefficients are small in magnitude and statistically insignificant. The same is true when returns on the day before the evening vote are utilized as the dependent variable. At short horizons, returns seem unrelated to the tax news. I take up some implications of this puzzle next.

V. General Tests of the Market Response

The cross-sectional results are consistent with two hypotheses: either tax reform had large effects that are not captured by the included variables; or the news of major tax reform did not significantly affect market valuations. This section explores these possibilities.

As a first test of the importance of tax news, Table 3 presents correlations of excess returns for the two votes. If tax news had a large impact on the market, returns on days of similar news release should be positively correlated. Table 3 provides little evidence of large tax effects. The correlation on the days immediately after the votes is only 0.036, with a standard error of 0.057. This result is striking; on the two most important days in the process of tax reform, stock returns show no indication of common movement. Other days show a larger correlation than this, but there is little evidence of a pervasive reaction to tax news.[21]

Over a 10-day horizon, the results are more promising but still rather weak. The correlation of 10-day excess returns is 0.197, with a standard error of 0.055. While this estimate is statistically significant, it does not indicate when in the period the adjust-

---

ing and oil companies) have much greater tax bases than firms with only U.S. tax liabilities, so that their cash flow projections are understated relative to the other firms. Further, given the large changes in world commodity prices, the effective capital stocks for these firms might be farthest from market value. Re-estimating the equations without these firms, or including the ratio of foreign taxes to total taxes paid as a proxy for these understatements however, does not change the results.

[21] One potential explanation for these results is that the β_i coefficients in equation (1) were changed by the tax reform, and thus the residuals reflect both tax reform news and errors from the change in the covariance. When correlations are estimated using either nominal returns or industry stock returns, where the β_i seem less likely to change greatly, however, the same pattern of correlations results.

ment occurred. Indeed, the within-week correlation of excess returns, like the cross-event correlations in Table 3, are generally very small.

A second test of the response to tax reform is the dispersion of excess returns around the tax votes. If tax reform news was a large part of the market movement, measures of the dispersion of returns on these days should be greater than similar measures on non-news days. This does not appear to be the case, however. The average standard deviation of returns in the weeks of the two votes are 1.81 percent for the House vote and 1.74 percent for the Senate Finance Committee vote. For the 30 days prior to May 1986, a period of no consistently large tax or other news, the average standard deviation is 1.93 percent. Even on the days immediately after the votes, both standard deviations are only 1.96 percent, slightly above the longer period average.

The same finding is true with one-week returns. The Monday-to-Monday return standard deviations are 3.54 percent and 4.01 percent for the two votes, while for the 14 weeks prior to May 1986, the average is 4.41 percent.

There findings are consistent with two possibilities about market expectations of tax changes. Unfortunately, however, neither possibility seems very plausible. First, the events considered might not have changed the expectations of market participants. The long discussions of the tax bill in Congress, or the support for tax reform by President Reagan might have convinced investors that tax reform was soon to occur. Both the immediate attention paid to the votes and the chronicles of journalists who covered the bill's progress (Jeffrey Birnbaum and Alan Murray, 1987), however, make it difficult to believe that tax reform was anticipated long in advance.

Second, the importance of the tax bill might have been reduced because further tax changes were expected after this bill passed. If, for example, investors felt that the bill would be quickly repealed or that tax rates would return to their previous levels soon, the reaction to the tax news would not be large. Evidence for this explanation is found in the statements of congressmen who had hoped to raise revenue from the tax bill, and in the newspaper articles that cautioned against accepting this as the last major tax change. Again, however, the length of the process seems to belie the hypothesis of quick tax revisions.

VI. Conclusions

The stock market response to the 1986 Tax Act suggests a mixed conclusion about the impact of tax reform. First, there is some microeconomic evidence for the predictions of the asset price model of incidence. The revaluation of share prices from the differential taxation of new and old capital and the reduced value of existing depreciation allowances do appear to be empirically important. Second, however, there is little evidence of positive responses to changes in cash flows, or of significant reactions to the tax news more generally. Tests of the variances and covariances of excess returns consistently reject the hypothesis of large, immediate changes in share values. Further, plausible explanations for the small response do not appear to be consistent with the tax reform process.

These latter results especially suggest that an explanation for the observed reaction may be inefficient pricing of the tax news by the market. Recent evidence indicates that changes in macroeconomic fundamentals cannot explain much of the variation in stock returns, and that even large legislative and diplomatic events that are not captured in macroeconomic time-series cannot account for a significant part of the residual variation (David Cutler, Poterba, and Summers, 1988). The limited reaction to the tax news could thus be indicative of this more general inexplicability of stock returns with economic fundamentals.

REFERENCES

Abel, Andrew, "Temporary and Permanent Tax Changes in a q Model of Investment," *Journal of Monetary Economics*, March 1982, 9, 353–73.

Auerbach, Alan J., "Tax Reform and Adjustment Costs: The Impact on Investment and Market Value," NBER Working Paper No. 2103, 1986.

_____, (1987a) "The Tax Reform Act of 1986 and the Cost of Capital," *Journal of Economic Perspectives*, Summer 1987, *1*, 73-86.

_____ and Poterba, James M., (1987b) "Why Have Corporate Tax Revenues Declined?," in Lawrence H. Summers, ed., *Tax Policy and the Economy*, Cambridge: MIT Press, 1987, 1-28.

Birnbaum, Jeffrey H. and Murray, Alan S., *Showdown at Gucci Gulch: Lawmakers, Lobbyists, and the Unlikely Triumph of Tax Reform*, New York: Random House, 1987.

Cutler, David M., Poterba, James M. and Summers, Lawrence H., "What Moves Stock Prices?," NBER Working Paper No. 2538, March 1988.

Dolde, Walter, "The Impact of Corporate Tax Reform by S&P Industry," *Shearson-Lehman Brothers Prospects*, May 23, 1986.

Downs, Thomas and Hendershott, Patric H., "Tax Policy and Stock Prices," *National Tax Journal*, June 1987, *40*, 183-90.

_____ and Tehranian, Hassan, "Predicting Stock Price Responses to Tax Policy Changes," *American Economic Review*, December 1988, *78*, 1118-30.

Gordon, Roger H., Hines, James R., Jr. and Summers, Lawrence H., "Notes on the Tax Treatment of Structures," in Martin Feldstein, ed., *The Effects of Taxation on Capital Accumulation*, Chicago: University of Chicago Press, 1986, 223-54.

Hausman, Jerry A. and Poterba, James M., "Household Behavior and the Tax Reform Act of 1986," *Journal of Economic Perspectives*, Summer 1987, *1*, 101-19.

Lyons, Andrew, "How Do Stock Prices Change When Corporate Tax Laws Change? An Empirical Analysis of the Effect of Tax Laws on the Value of the Firm," Princeton University, unpublished doctoral dissertation, 1986.

Musgrave, Richard A., *The Theory of Public Finance*, New York: McGraw-Hill, 1959.

Poterba, James M., "Explaining the Yield Spread Between Taxable and Tax-Exempt Bonds: The Role of Expected Tax Policy," in Harvey S. Rosen, ed., *Studies in State and Local Public Finance*, Chicago: University of Chicago Press, 1986, 5-49.

Rose, Nancy L., "The Incidence of Regulatory Rents in the Motor Carrier Industry," *Rand Journal of Economics*, Autumn 1985, *16*, 299-318.

Schaller, Huntley, "Investment and Acquisitions: The Evidence from U.S. Firm Data," MIT mimeo., November 1987.

Sinai, Allen, "The Tax Reform Act of 1986: Winners and Losers," *Shearson Lehman Brothers Economic Studies Series*, Report No. 22, 1986.

Summers, Lawrence H., "Taxation and Corporate Investment: A q-Theory Approach," *Brookings Papers on Economic Activity*, 1:1981, 67-140.

_____, "The Asset Price Approach to the Analysis of Capital Income Taxation," in George R. Felwil, ed., *Issues in Contemporary Macroeconomics and Distribution*, London: Macmillan, 1985, 429-43.

Tax Analysts, *Effective Corporate Tax Rates*, Arlington, VA, 1985.

_____, *Quantifying the Impact of the Tax Reform Act of 1986 on Effective Corporate Tax Rates*, Arlington, VA, 1986.

U.S. Congress, House of Representatives, *Tax Reform Act of 1986: Conference Report to Accompany H.R. 3838*, Report 99-841, Washington: USGPO, 1986.

C
Taxes and Efficiency

[11]

THE MEASUREMENT OF WASTE

By ARNOLD C. HARBERGER[*]
University of Chicago

I

The subject of this paper might be called "The Economics of the nth Best." This would distinguish the approach taken here from that taken by Lipsey and Lancaster in their fine article, "The General Theory of Second Best" [6], as well as from the conventional concern of economic analysis with the characteristics of fully optimal situations. To state the differences briefly, the conventional approach is concerned with how to get to a Pareto-optimal position, the Lipsey-Lancaster approach is concerned with how to make the best of a bad situation (i.e., how to get to a position which is optimal subject to one or more constraints which themselves violate the conditions of a full optimum), while this paper is concerned with measuring the deadweight loss associated with the economy's being in any given nonoptimal position.

The measurement of deadweight losses is not new to economics by any means. It goes back at least as far as Dupuit; and more recently Hotelling [4], Hicks [3], Debreu [2], Meade [10], and H. Johnson [5] [6] have made important contributions. Nonetheless I feel that the profession as a whole has not given to the area the attention that I think it deserves. We do not live on the Pareto frontier, and we are not going to do so in the future. Yet policy decisions are constantly being made which can move us either toward or away from that frontier. What could be more relevant to a choice between policy A and policy B than a statement that policy A will move us toward the Pareto frontier in such a way as to gain for the economy as a whole, say, approximately $200 million per year, while policy B will produce a gain of, say, about $30 million per year? What could be more useful to us as a guide to priorities in tax reform than the knowledge that the deadweight losses stemming from the tax loopholes (percentage depletion and capital gains) open to

---

[*] I wish to express my indebtedness to Martin J. Bailey, Donald V. T. Bear, Milton Friedman, John Hause, and Harry G. Johnson for helpful discussions during the preparation of this paper. In addition, I am grateful to the members of the Workshop in Mathematical Economics and Econometrics at the University of Chicago for comments made at a seminar on this subject. Needless to say, all errors that remain are my own responsibility.

explorers for oil and gas are probably greater in total magnitude than the deadweight losses associated with all the other inefficiencies induced by the corporation income tax? What could be more tantalizing than the possibility (which I believe to be a real one) that the U.S. tariff, whose indirect effect is to restrict the equilibrium value of U.S. exports, produces by this route a gain for the U.S. from a partial exploitation of U.S. monopoly power in world markets which nearly offsets (or perhaps fully or more than fully offsets) the efficiency-losses produced by tariff-induced substitution of more expensive domestic products for cheaper imports? These and similar questions seem to me so interesting, so relevant, so central to our understanding of the economy we live in, that I find it hard to explain why the measurement of deadweight losses should be the province of only a handful of economists rather than at least the occasional hobby of a much larger group. Let me simply suggest four possible reasons for the apparent unpopularity of the loss-measurement game:

1. Even the simplest attempts to measure the deadweight loss (or, as I prefer to call it, the welfare cost) associated with particular distortions involve the use of numerical values for certain key parameters (elasticities of demand, of substitution, etc.), which may be impossible to obtain at all, or which may be estimated but with substantial error. Workers in this field must be ready to content themselves with results that may be wrong by a factor of 2 or 3 in many cases. But, on the other hand, it is a field in which our professional judgment is so poorly developed that the pinning down of an answer to within a factor of 2 can be very helpful. Be that as it may, one cannot expect the field to attract colleagues who prefer their results to be meticulously exact.

2. While it is relatively easy to measure the welfare costs of a particular distortion when one assumes other distortions to be absent, it is much more difficult to carry through the measurement in a way which takes account of the presence of other distortions. One of the profound lessons taught us by earlier workers in this field (Hotelling [4], Viner [11], Lipsey-Lancaster [7], Corlett and Hague [1], Little [8], and others) is that an action (i.e., imposing a tax of T_1 per unit on good X_1) which would take us away from a Pareto optimum if we were starting from that position can actually bring us toward such an optimum if we start from an initially distorted situation. Crude measures can thus mislead us, while correct measures are hard to come by.

3. Many people find it difficult to isolate the measurement of efficiency-losses due to particular distortions from the changes in the distribution of income that they conceive would ensue if the distortions were actually removed. Of these, some are undoubtedly not willing to make the kind of assumptions they have to make in order to compare the changes in welfare of different individuals or groups.

4. Consumer surplus, in spite of its successive rehabilitations, is still looked upon with suspicion by many economists. In spite of the fact that it is possible to formulate measures of welfare cost which do not directly involve the use of the consumer surplus concept, the most convenient and most frequently cited measures of welfare cost do involve this concept. Thus, I venture to guess, another group of potential workers (or at least tasters) in the vineyard do not venture to enter.

II

The main purpose of this paper is to explore a variety of possible ways of formulating measures of deadweight losses. All the ways considered are members of a single family. This section begins by expounding a widely accepted approach to the problem and then proceeds to extend this approach to what I believe are new areas.

Let us begin by assuming that the only distortions present in the economy are taxes. Monopoly elements, externalities, and other market imperfections will be introduced at a later stage. We shall assume that the economy will seek and find a unique full employment equilibrium once its basic resource endowments, the distribution of income, the quantities of goods purchased by the government, and the set of distortions (taxes) are known. Letting X represent the vector of equilibrium quantities, D be a vector representing the proportion of total income received by each spending unit, G be a vector representing the quantities of the different goods and services purchased by government, and T be a vector representing the tax levied per unit of the different goods and services produced in the economy, we have $X=f(D, G, T)$.

Now to isolate the efficiency effects of distortions, we must hold D and G constant. Thus, with respect to D, we conceive of the possibility of keeping the percentage share of each spending unit in the total national income constant by means of neutral taxes and transfers. With respect to G, we assume that, in any pair of situations being compared, the government buys the same bundle of goods and services. Even though the comparison of two actual situations might be between $X=f(D, G, T)$ and $X'=f(D', G', T')$, we split up the move from X to X' into a minimum of two steps. The first step is from $X=f(D, G, T)$ to $X^*=f(D, G, T')$. This step isolates the efficiency aspects of the change. The move from X^* to X' entails no change in the distortions affecting the economy, and involves only shifts in the distribution of income and in the level of government expenditures. To the extent that the tax yield produced by the vector T is insufficient or more than sufficient to finance the expenditure vector G, we assume that neutral taxes or transfers will be called upon to make up the difference. (Should fiscal policy measures be necessary to provide full employment, neutral taxes and transfers would be the instruments used to bring the total tax take to the required level. Government expenditures, on our assumptions, would be held fixed.)

The above assumptions have the effect of setting first-order income effects (whether caused by redistributions or changes in the size of government purchases) to one side so as to isolate the efficiency effects of alternative tax patterns. They put us in a world of substitution effects and of relative prices. When dealing with relative price phenomena, it is customary to treat a single product as the numeraire. This procedure is, however, not essential. One could normalize by holding any desired index of prices constant, or in a variety of different ways. For our purposes, it is convenient to normalize by holding the money national income constant as among all possible situations being compared. We could alternatively hold constant money net national product, gross national product, gross national product less excise taxes, or any of a variety of other possible aggregates. But, as will be seen, holding money national income constant is exceedingly convenient for the problems with which we shall deal.

Let us consider first a case that has been frequently dealt with in the literature. Assume that the production function of the economy is linear and that only one factor of production, in fixed supply, is involved in production.

The fact that the only distortions present in our system are per unit excise taxes assures us that when the vector $T=0$, we are at a Pareto optimum. (In this case the government is raising all its revenue by taxes that are by definition neutral; e.g., head taxes.) Thus if we set up an index of welfare W as a function of the tax vector T, we have that $W_{max} = W(0)$. We can take money national income, $\overline{Y}$, as the measure of $W(0)$. We can, therefore, indicate the level of welfare associated with any tax vector T by $\overline{Y}$ plus a deviation ΔW, depending on T and expressed in the same units as Y. The relevant expression for ΔW, in a wide class of cases, is

$$(1) \qquad \Delta W = \sum_{i=1}^{n} \int_{0}^{T_i} \sum_{j \leq i} T_j \frac{\partial X_j}{\partial T_i} dT_i,$$

Two basic rules underlie this expression.

First, if as a result of an increment dT_i in the unit tax on X_i, there is an increment or decrement dX_j in the equilibrium quantity of a good X_j in the market for which no distortion exists, the change dX_j carries with it no direct contribution to the measure of ΔW. For each successive minute increment of X_j, demand price is equal to marginal cost, and the gain to demanders of having more of X_j is just offset by the costs of producing the extra amount.

Second, if as a result of an increment dT_i in the unit tax on X_i there is an increment dX_j in the equilibrium quantity of good X_j, in the market for which a distortion T_j already exists, there is a social gain associated with the change dX_j equal to $T_j dX_j$. Here demand price exceeds marginal cost, on each unit increment of X_j, by the amount T_j. Likewise if dX_j is negative, there is a social loss involved equal in magnitude to $T_j dX_j$.[1]

Obviously, the second rule given above contains the first, but I have set them out as two rules to emphasize the neutrality of changes taking place in undistorted sectors. Once this fact is appreciated, the rest of the road is easy.

Let me emphasize at this point that up to now there is nothing new in what has been said. Expression (1), and the rules behind it, say only that

$$(2) \quad \frac{\partial W}{\partial T_i} = \sum_j T_j \frac{\partial X_j}{\partial T_i}$$

This expression pops up in one form or another all through the literature on the measurement of welfare costs, the economics of second best, the theory of customs unions, etc. It appears, or can be derived from what appears, in Corlett and Hague [1], Hotelling [4], H. Johnson [5] [6], Meade [10], and Lipsey and Lancaster [7], among others.

Let us now linearize expression (1) by setting

$$\frac{\partial X_j}{\partial T_i} = R_{ji}.$$

With this substitution, (1) evaluates at

$$(3) \quad \Delta W = \frac{1}{2} \sum_{i=1}^{n} R_{ii} T_i^2 + \sum_{i}^{n} \sum_{j<i} R_{ji} T_j T_i$$

Expression (3) can be simplified, however, using the integrability condition

$$\frac{\partial X_i}{\partial T_j} = \frac{\partial X_j}{\partial T_i},$$

[1] Another way of looking at this problem is to consider that consumers, in transferring their demand to X_j are indifferent between what they get and what they give up for each marginal unit of purchasing power transferred; and that suppliers of factor services are likewise, for each marginal unit of services transferred, on the borderline of indifference. But if X_j goes up by dX_j, the government will obtain an increase in tax receipts of $T_j dX_j$, which (under our assumptions) will permit either a corresponding reduction in associated lump-sum taxes or a corresponding increase in lump-sum transfers. In short, "the people" gain to the tune of $T_j dX_j$.

which translates in the linearized form into $R_{ij}=R_{ji}$. In economic terms, this same condition derives from the fact that the welfare cost of a set of taxes should not, in a comparative static framework such as this, depend on the order in which those taxes are conceived to be imposed. Thus if we impose T_1 first and follow it by T_2, we have $\Delta W = \frac{1}{2}R_{11}T_1^2+\frac{1}{2}R_{22}T_2^2+R_{12}T_1T_2$. If on the other hand we impose T_2 first and follow it by T_1, we have $\Delta W = \frac{1}{2}R_{22}T_2^2+\frac{1}{2}R_{11}T_1^2+R_{21}T_2T_1$. Hence if the linearized expression (3) is to be invariant with respect to order of imposition of taxes, R_{12} must equal R_{21}, and in general R_{ij} must equal R_{ji}. This enables (3) to be simplified to

(4) $$\Delta W = \frac{1}{2} \sum_i \sum_j R_{ij}T_iT_j.$$

For each $R_{ji}(j<i)$ appearing in (3), we simply substitute $\frac{1}{2}R_{ji}+\frac{1}{2}R_{ij}$, to obtain (4).

A further condition on the R_{ij} can be established by noting that a set of taxes with some $T_i \neq 0$ can at best produce an equal level of welfare as an undistorted situation. This yields

(5) $$\Delta W = \frac{1}{2} \sum_i \sum_j R_{ij}T_iT_j \leq 0 \quad \text{for all possible values of } T_i, T_j.$$

As a special case of (5) we have

(6) $$R_{ii} \leq 0 \quad \text{for all } i.$$

This is obtained when $T_i \neq 0$, while $T_j = 0$ for all $j \neq i$.

We are by now quite close to establishing the Hicksian substitution conditions by the back door, so to speak. What we need to finish the job is the adding-up property. Suppose it to be true that a proportional tax at the rate t on all the X_i would indeed be a neutral tax. We can define $T_i = t_i c_i$, where c_i = marginal cost, and t_i = percentage rate of tax on X_i, to obtain:

(7) $$\Delta W = \frac{1}{2} \sum_i \sum_j c_ic_jR_{ij}t_it_j.$$

If an equal percentage tax on all commodities is neutral, we have

(8) $$\sum_i \sum_j c_ic_jR_{ij} = 0.$$

But we actually have much more than this. If a proportional tax at the rate t is truly neutral, then, given our assumptions about the constancy of income distribution and of government purchases, it simply substitutes for the head tax that would have to exist if all the T_i were zero. It must produce the same equilibrium quantity for each and every commodity. Thus we have that

(10) $$\frac{\partial X_i}{\partial t} = \sum_j c_j R_{ij} = 0 \quad \text{for all } i.$$

This is the counterpart of the Hicksian adding-up property.

However, a tax at the rate t on all X_i will be neutral only in certain cases.

Case A) Suppose that, as was assumed above, the production frontier of the economy is linear—

$$\sum_i c_i X_i = \text{a constant}.$$

This means that total production is in inelastic supply, and therefore that a tax which strikes the value of all production at a constant rate will be neutral. In this case all the X_i must be final products; the R_{ij} here turn out to be precisely the Hicksian substitution terms.

Case B) Suppose that all the X_i are final products, and that the production frontier of the economy is convex from above. Suppose, moreover, that all basic factors of production are fixed in total supply. So long as a tax at the rate t on final products is in effect a tax at a fixed rate on the net earnings of all factors of production, it will be neutral, and condition (9) will hold. In this case, the R_{ij}, while obeying the properties of the Hicksian substitution terms, are actually quite different from them. Here the R_{ij} are really the "reduced form" coefficients showing how the equilibrium value of X_i (with supply and demand equal for all commodities) depends on T_j.

Case B presents no problem when capital is not among the basic factors of production, or when the relation between gross and net earnings of capital is the same in all uses. However, when capital is among the basic factors and when the relationship between gross and net earnings does (because of different depreciation patterns) differ among uses, then an equal tax on all final products will not be neutral, even though capital and other factors of production are fixed in total supply. This is because increases in the rate of proportional tax, t, will create incentives which would relatively favor the longer-lived applications of capital. An equal tax on value added in all industries, however, would be neutral in these circumstances, because we assume the net rate of return on capital to be equalized among all uses of capital. (This, of course, assumes that the stock of capital and the supplies of other basic factors of production are fixed.)

Problems quite similar to those presented by different depreciation

PRINCIPLES OF EFFICIENCY 65

patterns in different applications of capital arise when the possibility of taxing intermediate products is introduced. As McKenzie [9] has forcefully pointed out, an equal percentage tax on all products will generally be nonneutral if any of the products in question are intermediate or primary products not in fixed supply. A tax at an equal percentage rate on value added in every activity will, on the other hand, be neutral so long as the basic factors of production are in fixed supply.

Case C) When considering taxes on value added we let X_i represent the volume of final product of industry (or activity) i, v_i represent value added per unit of the product of activity i, and T_i represent the tax per unit of final product in industry. (Although the tax is levied on value added, T_i is here expressed per unit of product.) Once again letting $R_{ij} = \partial X_i/\partial T_j$, we have (5) as the expression for ΔW. To reflect the neutrality of an equal percentage tax on value added everywhere, we require that the response of any X_i to such a tax be zero; i.e., that

$$\sum_j v_j R_{ij} t_j = 0 \quad \text{when} \quad t_j = t \quad \text{for all } j.$$

Here v_j = value added per unit of the product X_j, t_j = percentage rate of tax on value added in industry j, $v_j t_j = T_j$. Hence we have

$$\sum_j v_j R_{ij} = 0; \ R_{ij} = R_{ji}; \ \sum_i \sum_j R_{ij} T_i T_j \leq 0 \text{ for all } T_i, T_j; \ R_{ii} \leq 0 \text{ for all } i$$

as before.

Case C deals rather neatly with problems of differential depreciation and taxes on nonfinal products. However, case C assumes that indirect taxes are levied on value added, whereas most frequently in the real world they are levied on the final product.

Fortunately, it is possible to translate product taxes into value-added taxes, and still stay within the framework of case C so long as inputs other than labor and capital enter their respective products in fixed proportions. The reason for this is obvious. All the effects of a tax at the rate t_i on product i can be replicated by a tax at the same rate on all factor shares (including materials input) entering into the production of product i. These are simply two ways of imposing the same tax. Suppose that with a tax of 10 percent on all factor shares in the ith industry an equilibrium is reached in which materials inputs account for half the value of product and labor and capital the other half. So long as materials inputs must be used in fixed proportions per unit of product, a shift from a 10 percent tax on all factor shares in the ith industry to a 20 percent tax on value added in the ith industry would introduce no incentive to change the equilibrium reached with a 10 percent tax on all factor shares. Purchasers could pay the same price for the product;

labor, capital, and materials sellers could get the same net reward; and the government could get the same tax take. Moreover, since the taxes on labor and capital shares would still be at equal percentage rates, there would be no inducement for substitution between them. In short, so long as materials are used in fixed proportions to output, we can translate any given tax on output into a tax on value added that is equivalent in all respects relevant for this analysis.

We now turn to a broader set of problems—all of which take into account the possibility of different rates of tax on the return to capital and to labor in any given activity. Consider first the set of possible taxes B_i per unit of capital in activity i. The change in welfare associated with such taxes can be written, assuming no other nonneutral taxes in the system, as

(11) $$\Delta W = \frac{1}{2} \sum_i \sum_j G_{ij} B_i B_j,[2]$$

where

$$G_{ij} = \frac{\partial K_i}{\partial B_j},$$

and K_i represents the number of units of capital employed in activity i. Correspondingly, if we consider the set of possible taxes E_i per unit of labor in activity i, and assume no other nonneutral taxes, we can write:

(12) $$\Delta W = \frac{1}{2} \sum_i \sum_j M_{ij} E_i E_j,$$

where

$$M_{ij} = \frac{\partial L_i}{\partial E_j},$$

and L_i represents the number of units of labor employed in activity i. The G_{ij} and the M_{ij} will obey the following properties:

$G_{ij} = G_{ji}$; $\quad \sum_i \sum_j G_{ij} B_i B_j \leq 0$ for all B_i, B_j; $\quad G_{ii} \leq 0$ for all i

$M_{ij} = M_{ji}$; $\quad \sum_i \sum_j M_{ij} E_i E_j \leq 0$ for all E_i, E_j; $\quad M_{ii} \leq 0$ for all i.

---

[2] We could here have explicitly set out an equation corresponding to (1); i.e.,

$$\Delta W = \sum_{i=1}^{n} \int_0^{Bi} \sum_{i \leq i} B_i \frac{\partial X_i}{\partial B_i} dB_i,$$

linearized this expression as in (3), and then used the symmetry property to obtain (11) or its counterpart. These steps are not presented explicitly in this and the other cases treated in this section.

Moreover, with fixed supplies of capital and labor we have

$$\sum_i G_{ij} = 0, \qquad \sum_i M_{ij} = 0.$$

When nonneutral taxes are levied only on capital in different activities, (11) measures the cost of the distortions involved; when only labor is affected by nonneutral taxes, (12) is the relevant measure. But when nonneutral taxes are levied on both labor and capital in different activities, the interaction between them must be taken into account. Let us define

$$H_{ij} = \frac{\partial K_i}{\partial E_j} \quad \text{and} \quad N_{ij} = \frac{\partial N_i}{\partial B_j}.$$

Here symmetry exists between H_{ij} and N_{ji}. Suppose for example, we impose first a tax of B_1 and then one of E_2. We obtain $\tfrac{1}{2}G_{11}B_1^2 + M_{22}E_2^2 + H_{12}B_1E_2$ as our measure of ΔW. If we conceive of E_2 being imposed first, and then B_1, we obtain $\tfrac{1}{2}M_{22}E_2^2 + \tfrac{1}{2}G_{11}B_1^2 + N_{21}E_2B_1$. If we think of imposing a set of taxes B_i first and then a set of taxes E_i, we have

$$(13) \quad \Delta W = \frac{1}{2}\sum_i\sum_j G_{ij}B_iB_j + \frac{1}{2}\sum_i\sum_j M_{ij}E_iE_j + \sum_i\sum_j H_{ij}B_iE_j.$$

If we think of it the other way around, we have

$$(14) \quad \Delta W = \frac{1}{2}\sum_i\sum_j M_{ij}E_iE_j + \frac{1}{2}\sum_i\sum_j G_{ij}B_iB_j + \sum_j\sum_i N_{ji}E_jB_i.$$

For a reason that will be apparent later, it is most convenient to write:

$$(15) \quad \Delta W = \frac{1}{2}\sum_j\sum_i M_{ji}E_jE_i + \frac{1}{2}\sum_j\sum_i N_{ji}E_jB_i + \frac{1}{2}\sum_i\sum_j G_{ij}B_iB_j + \frac{1}{2}\sum_i\sum_j H_{ij}B_iE_j.$$

Now, when labor is in fixed supply, a tax on capital in industry i can only redistribute the existing amount of labor. Hence

$$\sum_j N_{ji} = 0.$$

Likewise, when capital is in fixed supply, a tax on labor in industry j can only redistribute the available capital, so that

$$\sum_i H_{ij} = 0.$$

The interaction terms disappear for neutral taxes because in this case $E_i = \bar{E}$ for all i, $B_i = \bar{B}$ for all i. (Since the wage is assumed to be equalized in all uses of labor and since the net rate of return is assumed to be equalized in all uses of capital, an equal tax per unit of labor is also an equal percentage tax on value added by labor in different activities, and likewise for capital.)

Thus we have:

Case D) When labor and capital are in fixed supply, expression (15) measures the change in welfare due to any pattern of taxes on labor and capital in different activities. The M_{ji} and the G_{ij} obey the Hicksian conditions, with the adding-up property in this case

$$\sum_j M_{ij} = 0 = \sum_i G_{ij}.$$

All terms vanish for taxes on labor that are equal all uses together with taxes on capital that are equal in all uses. The interaction terms can in general be positive or negative, but the whole expression (15) must always be ≤ 0. In this case the coefficients reflect not only conditions of final demand and supply but also conditions of factor substitution.

We now attempt to allow for the fact that the supply of labor in the market may itself be a function of the pattern of taxation. This question has been dealt with in the literature of second-best by Little, Corlett, and Hague, Lipsey and Lancaster, and Meade, among others. The key to at least the last three of these treatments is the substitution of the assumption (!) that the number of hours in the year is fixed for the assumption that the number of man-hours offered in the market is fixed. We can do this simply by adding another activity for labor—labeled "leisure" or "nonmarket activity." If there are n market activities, we add an $n+1$st, and have

$$\sum_{j=1}^{n+1} L_j = \bar{L}.$$

This does not change the form of equation (12) but it does alter the definition of a neutral tax. Now an equal tax on all labor in market activities is not neutral, because it neglects the $n+1$st activity. However, a tax that struck all hours equally (including leisure hours) would be neutral. Hence we have

$$\sum_{j=1}^{n+1} M_{ji} = 0 = \sum_{j=1}^{n+1} M_{ij}$$

To measure the welfare cost of an equal tax of $\bar{E}$ on all activities except leisure we take

(16) $$\Delta W = \frac{1}{2} \sum_{j=1}^{n} \sum_{i=1}^{n} M_{ji} \overline{E}^2$$

but

$$\sum_{i=1}^{n+1} M_{ji} = 0, \quad \text{so} \quad \sum_{i=1}^{n} M_{ji} = -M_{j,n+1}.$$

Hence (16) reduces to

(17) $$\Delta W = -\frac{1}{2} \sum_{j=1}^{n} M_{j,n+1} \overline{E}^2$$

But

$$\sum_{j=1}^{n+1} M_{j,n+1} = 0, \quad \text{so that} \quad \sum_{j=1}^{n} M_{j,n+1} = -M_{n+1,n+1},$$

Thus (17) reduces to

(18) $$\Delta W = \tfrac{1}{2} M_{n+1,n+1} \overline{E}^2,$$

where $M_{n+1,n+1}$ represents the responsiveness of leisure to a change in the tax rate on leisure (or to the negative of a change in the tax rate on work). This exercise illustrates, I think, the usefulness of properties of the kind that we have been establishing in the various cases examined. (16) taken by itself looks hard to interpret; with the aid of the adding-up properties, however, it can be reduced to (18), which is easy to interpret and perhaps even to measure.

The general expression for ΔW, for a fixed capital stock and for a fixed amount of labor-plus-leisure, is

(19) $$\Delta W = \frac{1}{2} \sum_{j=1}^{n+1} \sum_{i=1}^{n+1} M_{ji} E_j E_i + \frac{1}{2} \sum_{j=1}^{n+1} \sum_{i=1}^{n} N_{ji} E_j B_i + \frac{1}{2} \sum_{i=1}^{n} \sum_{j=1}^{n} G_{ij} B_i B_j$$
$$+ \frac{1}{2} \sum_{i=1}^{n} \sum_{j=1}^{n+1} H_{ij} B_i E_j$$

Its properties are basically the same as those of (15), modified only to take account of the fact that labor has $n+1$ activities available to it while capital has only n. Thus, in the interaction terms we have

$$\sum_{j=1}^{n+1} N_{ji} = 0; \quad \sum_{i=1}^{n} H_{ij} = 0.$$

Hence we have:

Case E) Where capital is in fixed supply to market activities, but labor is in fixed supply only to market-plus-nonmarket activities, and where taxes are considered which strike labor and capital differentially in different activities, (19) measures the change in welfare stemming from any set of such taxes. Neutral taxes in this case are taxes striking each unit of capital (or each dollar of net return from capital) equally, and taxes striking each hour of a worker's day equally. This last set of taxes could equivalently be called head taxes, but, as was shown above, convenient results can be obtained using properties derived from the neutrality of an equal tax per hour.

The formulation of case E is quite versatile. It can deal with proportional income taxation (equal percentage taxes on the income from labor and capital), and can recognize the nonneutrality of ordinary income taxation as regards the choice between labor and leisure. It can also cope with progressive income taxation, simply by using the effective marginal rate of tax to apply to income from labor and capital (here one has to assume that each individual's supply of capital is constant). It can cope with indirect taxes on intermediate as well as final products, provided that one is prepared to make the assumption that materials inputs bear fixed relationships to final products. And, most important of all, it can cope with property and corporation income taxes, which have widely differing burdens on the income from capital in different industries. Finally, it is possible to deal with situations in which all the above-mentioned taxes are simultaneously present, amalgamating those taxes (including allocations of excise tax receipts) falling on income from capital in each activity, and those falling on income from labor.

III

This section consists of three "appended notes" to the earlier analysis. The first (A) reduces the expressions derived in Section II to a common simplified form. The second (B) discusses how distortions other than taxes can be incorporated in the analysis. The third (C) discusses the problems that arise when one eliminates the assumption of a constant capital stock.

A. The cases dealt with in the preceding section all have in common a simple property. Since, in (4)

$$\sum_j R_{ij} T_j \text{ can be expressed as } \Delta X_i,$$

(4) itself can be rewritten:

(4') $$\Delta W = \frac{1}{2} \sum_i T_i \Delta X_i.$$

For cases A and B, T_i refers to taxes on final products only, and the X_i's are final products. For case C, (4') might better be written

$$(4'') \qquad \Delta W = \frac{1}{2} \sum_i v_i t_i \Delta X_i,$$

where the X's are now final or intermediate products, the v_i represent value added per unit of product in activity i, and the t_i are percentage taxes on value added in activity i. Since

$$\sum_j G_{ij} B_j \text{ can be expressed as } \Delta K_i,$$

(11) can be written:

$$(11') \qquad \Delta W = \frac{1}{2} \sum_i B_i \Delta K_i$$

Similarly, (12) can be written:

$$(12') \qquad \Delta W = \frac{1}{2} \sum_i E_i \Delta L_i.$$

In (15),

$$\sum_i M_{ji} E_i + \sum_i N_{ji} B_i$$

can be expressed as ΔL_j, while

$$\sum_j G_{ij} B_j + \sum_j H_{ij} E_j$$

can be expressed as ΔK_i, so that (15) can be written:

$$(15') \qquad \Delta W = \frac{1}{2} \sum_j E_j \Delta L_j + \frac{1}{2} \sum_i B_i \Delta K_i.$$

(15') also serves as an alternative form for (19), with the index j going from 1 to $n+1$ and the index i going from 1 to n. Thus all of the cases discussed here are extensions of the "triangle-under-the-demand-curve" that emerges in textbook discussions of the excess burden of taxation. But I believe that for actual work the simplified forms presented above are not as useful as those presented in Section II of this paper, in which explicit account is taken of how the reaction coefficients R_{ij}, G_{ij}, H_{ij}, M_{ij} and N_{ij} enter into the determination of the result. One can conceive, at least hypothetically, of measuring these reaction coefficients by experimental movements in individual tax rates. Once measured, they will enable us to estimate the changes in welfare associated with any arbitrary combination of taxes.

In practice one cannot expect to measure all the relevant reaction coefficients, but one can place reasonable bounds on their orders of magnitude and thus get estimates of the order of magnitude of the welfare costs of a given set of taxes, or of particular changes in the existing tax structure. In dealing with practical problems, the presumptive dominance of the diagonal elements in the matrices of reaction coefficients can be put to good use. Consider, for example, the case of a tax of T_1 on X_1, in case A or B of Section II. If there are no other taxes present in the system, the change in welfare associated with this tax will be $\Delta W = \frac{1}{2} R_{11} T_1^2$. If there are other taxes already present in the system, the effect on welfare of adding a tax of T_1 on X_1 will be

$$(20) \qquad \frac{\partial W}{\partial T_1} T_1 = \frac{1}{2} R_{11} T_1^2 + \sum_{i=2}^{n} R_{i1} T_i T_1, \text{ or}$$

$$(20') \qquad \frac{\partial W}{\partial T_1} T_1 = \frac{1}{2} c_1^2 R_{11} t_1^2 + \sum_{i=2}^{n} c_1 c_i R_{i1} t_i t_1.$$

Since

$$\sum_{i=2}^{n} c_i R_{i1} = -c_1 R_{11},$$

(20') can be rewritten as

$$(21) \qquad \frac{\partial W}{\partial T_i} T_1 = \frac{1}{2} c_1^2 R_{11} t_1 \left[t_1 - 2 \sum_{i=2}^{n} (c_i R_{i1} / - c_1 R_{11}) t_i \right].$$

Thus, t_1 has to be compared with a weighted average of the tax rates on other commodities. Even though we cannot measure the R_{i1}, so as to know the precise weights to apply, in many cases it is possible to set reasonable limits within which the true weighting pattern is likely to lie. We are likely to have a good idea of which, if any, of goods X_2 to X_n are very close substitutes or complements to good X_1. After making allowance for the plausible degree of substitution or complementarity here, we are not likely to go far wrong if we assume that the remaining commodities are remote, "general" substitutes for X_1. Thus the procedure would be first to estimate $-c_1 R_{11}$; then to estimate $c_2 R_{21}$ and $c_3 R_{31}$, say, if goods 2 and 3 were particularly close substitutes or complements to good one; and finally to distribute the remaining total weights $(-c_1 R_{11} - c_2 R_{21} - c_3 R_{31})$ to commodities X_4 to X_n, say, in proportion to their relative importance in the national income. Obviously this procedure is not exact, but it is unlikely to lead to a result that is of an erroneous order of magnitude.

B. We now attempt to take account of distortions other than taxes. These can be treated as "autonomous" taxes or subsidies. If a monopoly is present in industry i, which prices its products at 20 percent above marginal cost, it is as if a 20 percent tax existed on the product of industry i, or, perhaps, a 40 percent tax on the value added by labor and by capital in industry i. If activity j has positive external effects, leading to an excess of 10 percent of social benefit over marginal cost (at the margin) it is once again as if a tax of 10 percent existed on the value produced in industry j, or of an appropriately greater percentage on the value added in industry j. Correspondingly, if an industry's product has negative external effects, it is as if a subsidy existed on the value produced or the value added in that industry (i.e., the economy, by itself, tends to produce too much of that industry's product).

To see how these other distortions would be taken into account, assume that a monopoly exists in industry 1, such that price is $(1+m_1)$ times marginal cost. Suppose, moreover, that a tax of t'_1 percent exists (or is contemplated) on this product. To take account of the combined effect of the monopoly and the tax, we would simply set $t_1 = [(1+m_1)/(1-t'_1)] - 1$, and then use this value for t_1 in (7).

It seems to me that most distortions other than taxes can be taken into account in the way just indicated. There is no intrinsic difficulty, however, in dealing with more complicated cases in which the percentage excess of social value over marginal cost is a function of output rather than a constant. Cases in which the external effects of an industry or activity are independent of its output or level, and depend only on the existence of the industry, need not be dealt with within the framework of this analysis. If the industry or activity is to exist in all situations being compared, external effects of this sort will be equal in all such situations. If, on the other hand, one contemplates eliminating an industry with a given negative external effect, one can calculate by an analysis of the type used in this paper what would be the efficiency-cost of a tax which was just barely prohibitive of the activities of the industry, and see whether this cost outweighed the negative external effect or not.

C. We now turn to a problem which was consciously avoided in Section II. There we maintained the assumption that the capital stock was given. Now we must investigate the possibilities of eliminating this restrictive assumption.

In the first place, we can recognize that, for the analysis of Section II, we do not need to assume that the capital stock remains fixed through time. Both population and capital stock can change through time, and the analysis of Section II can be modified to take account of these changes, so long as the changes (in population and in capital stock) are not dependent on tax rates and other distortions. The difficulties appear when we try to allow for the effects of changes in tax rates, etc., on the level of capital stock (and/or population).

Particularly since I have no really satisfactory solution to the problem posed, I am inclined to defend the assumption that the level of capital stock is reasonably independent of tax rate changes (at least of the sorts of tax rate changes that we have observed in the past). Here I rely on the secular constancy of the rate of net saving in the United States, in the face of substantial savings in the rate of return and in the face of significant alterations in the tax structure. I would not expect, given this historical experience, that the neglect of an effect of taxation upon savings would introduce large errors into the measures derived in Section II.

Obviously, however, this answer, though perhaps adequate for many practical applications, really begs the fundamental question. As I see it, there are three main roads to a solution.

1. One could attempt to extend the "models" of Section II to many time periods, building in all of the relevant dynamics. This, I think, would be scientifically the most satisfying approach to take. However, I am afraid that this approach is likely to complicate the analysis to the point where it will be hard to apply it to real-world problems. Nonetheless, I feel that this is a line worth pursuing.

2. One could attempt to separate the "comparative static" from the "dynamic" costs of alternative tax set-ups. Suppose that changing from tax vector T to tax vector T' leads to a change in the rate of saving from s to s'. We could measure the change in welfare due to the change in taxes first on the assumption that the rate of saving was unaffected, and then attempt to measure the additional cost or benefit associated with the change in the rate of saving. This approach has a particular appeal because, given the assumption that the net rate of return to capital is equalized in all uses, it is reasonable to assume the rate of saving depends only on the level of real income and the net rate of return.

One can go quite some distance with this approach without greatly complicating the analysis. The present value to the saver of a dollar of saving at the margin is $\$1.00 = \rho(1-t)/r$, where ρ is the social rate of marginal net productivity of capital and r (which at least in uncomplicated situations should equal $\rho(1-t)$) is the after-tax rate of discount which the individual uses to obtain present values, and t is the expected future rate of tax on income from saving. The present value of the social yield of capital is simply ρ/r, so that a dollar's worth of savings should have a social value of $\$1.00/(1-t)$. The change in welfare due to the difference in this year's savings stemming from a tax rate of t rather than a tax rate of zero would then be $\frac{1}{2}t\Delta s/(1-t)$, where Δs is the tax-induced change in the amount of this year's savings. If we call this expression $\Delta_2 W$, and expression (19), say, $\Delta_1 W$, we can express ΔW as $\Delta_1 W + \Delta_2 W$. $\Delta_1 W$ expresses the cost this year of misallocating the resources that would be present this year if the rate of savings were unaffected by tax changes. $\Delta_2 W$ measures the present value of the future benefit foregone because the economy—for tax reasons—did not save "enough" this year. One could correspondingly estimate the ΔW stemming from a particular tax structure for a series of future years, and estimate the present value of the future stream of welfare costs associated with that tax structure.

The principal difficulty with approach number 2 is, I believe, that it requires the assumption that ρ will remain constant in the future. The approach could of course be modified so as to impose a particular non-constant time-path for ρ in the future, but the basic difficulty remains that the model does not itself tell us what that time-path should be. As a practical matter, however, I believe that changes in the marginal net productivity of capital are likely to be sufficiently slow so that the assumption of constancy will not introduce serious errors in the estimation of ΔW.

3. One could attempt to incorporate tax-induced changes in capital stock directly into the analysis. This approach requires two changes in the analysis of cases D and E of Section II. First the assumptions that

$$\sum_i G_{ij} = 0 \quad \text{and} \quad \sum_i H_{ij} = 0$$

must be abandoned; and second, we must eliminate the assumption of the neutrality of any tax striking equally the income from capital in all uses. In effect this means that the only neutral tax treatment of the income from capital would be not to tax it at all.[3] These two adjustments could easily be incorporated into the framework developed in Section II. One additional step would also be necessary. Since the savings-effects of a tax change are likely to go on indefinitely, one would have to decide on the specific time period over which one was measuring the effect of tax changes on the capital stock. This would enable one in principle to deal with specific values for

$$\sum_i G_{ij} \quad \text{and} \quad \sum_i H_{ij},$$

whereas otherwise these values could be almost anything, depending on the time period over which the reactions were being measured. This last requirement—of measurement over a specific time period—is to my mind the most serious disadvantage of approach number 3.

I shall not go into more detail here on the possible merits and disadvantages of the three approaches to the savings problem that I have

---

[3] Though I find the nontaxation of income from capital repugnant as a policy prescription, there is no doubt that even proportional income taxation is nonneutral in respect of the decision to save. The social yield of saving is the gross of tax return to capital, while the private yield is net of tax.

suggested. This problem is, as I have indicated, the most serious "open end" in the analysis of Section II, and I hope that further work in the field, following one or more of the approaches outlined above, will help close this important gap.

REFERENCES

1. W. J. Corlett and D. C. Hague, "Complementarity and the Excess Burden of Taxation," *Rev. of Econ. Studies,* 1953, pp. 21-30.
2. Gerard Debreu, "The Coefficient of Resource Utilization," *Econometrica,* July, 1951, pp. 273-92.
3. J. R. Hicks, *Value and Capital* (2d ed.; Oxford: Clarendon Press, 1946), esp. pp. 330-33.
4. Harold Hotelling, "The General Welfare in Relation to Problems of Taxation and of Railway and Utility Rates," *Econometrica,* July, 1938.
5. Harry G. Johnson, "The Cost of Protection and the Scientific Tariff," *J.P.E.,* Aug., 1960, pp. 327 ff.
6. Harry G. Johnson, "The Economic Theory of Customs Unions," in *Money, Trade and Economic Growth* (London: George Allen and Unwin, 1962), pp. 48 ff.
7. R. G. Lipsey and K. Lancaster, "The General Theory of Second Best," *Rev. of Econ. Studies,* XXIV, No. 63. (1956-57), pp. 11-32.
8. I. M. D. Little, "Direct versus Indirect Taxes," *Econ. J.,* Sept., 1951.
9. L. W. McKenzie, "Ideal Output and the Interdependence of Firms," *Econ. J.,* Dec,. 1951, pp. 785-803.
10. J. E. Meade, *Trade and Welfare,* Vol. II (Mathematical Supplement [London: Oxford Univ. Press, 1955]).
11. Jacob Viner, *The Customs Union Issue* (Carnegie Endowment for Int. Peace, 1950).

[12]

Exact Consumer's Surplus and Deadweight Loss

By Jerry A. Hausman*

Consumer's surplus is a widely used tool in applied welfare economics. Both economic theorists and cost benefit analysis often use consumer's surplus despite its somewhat dubious reputation. The basic idea is to evaluate the value to a consumer or his "willingness to pay" for a change in price of a good from say price p^0 to price p^1. Because price changes affect consumer welfare, an evaluation of this effect is often a key input to public policy decisions. Yet consumer's surplus is probably the most controversial of widely used economic concepts. Both Paul Samuelson and Ian Little conclude that the economics profession would be better off without it.

It is my feeling of the situation that substantial agreement exists on the correct quantities to be measured: the amount the consumer would pay or would need to be paid to be just as well off after the price change as he was before the price change. The quantities correspond to John Hicks' compensating variation measures. An alternative measure which takes *ex post* price change utility as the basis of comparison is Hicks' equivalent variation.[1] The controversy arises in the measurement of these quantities. The usual measurement procedure is to use the area to the left of the Marshallian (market) demand curve between two price levels. Jules Dupuit originated this measure of welfare change, and Alfred Marshall and Hicks derived appropriate conditions for its use. The primary condition for the area to the left of the demand curve to correspond to the compensating variation is to have constant marginal utility of income. Marshall gave this condition, and if it holds, the same quantity will be derived as the area to the left of the compensated (Hicksian) demand curve. This area to the left of the compensated demand curve is exactly what the compensating variation and equivalent variation measure. Thus the constant marginal utility of income is a sufficient condition for Marshallian consumer's surplus to be equal to Hicks' consumer's surplus. In this case Arnold Harberger's plea to use the welfare triangle as one-half times the product of the price change times the quantity change to measure deadweight loss corresponds to the correct theoretical amount of welfare change.

In a recent paper, Robert Willig derives bounds for the percentage difference between the correct measure of either the compensating or equivalent variation and the Marshallian measure derived form the market demand curve. His bounds, which depend on the income elasticity of demand for the single good in the region of price change being considered as well as the proportion of the consumer's income spent on the good, demonstrate that the Marshallian consumer's surplus is often a good approximation to Hicks' consumer's surplus. The fact that the proportion of the consumer's income spent matters as well as the income elasticity was first pointed out by Harold Hotelling. Willig contends that the approximation error will be less than the errors involved in estimating the demand curve. Thus he hopes to remove the need for apology that applied economists often need to give to theorists who remark on the inappropriateness of using Marshallian consumer's surplus to measure welfare change.

However, in this paper I show that for the case primarily considered by Willig of a single price change, which is also the situation in which consumer's surplus is often used in applied work, no approximation is necessary.

---

*Professor of economics, Massachusetts Institute of Technology, and research associate, National Bureau of Economic Research. I would like to thank Peter Diamond, Erwin Diewert, Daniel McFadden, Robert Merton, Robert Solow, Hal Varian, Joel Yellin, and the referees for help and comments. Research support from the National Science Foundation is acknowledged.

[1] The reason that we still have two, rather than one, of Samuelson's six measures of consumer's surplus arises from an index number problem of the correct basis for the welfare comparison. I will give both measures but plan to concentrate on the compensating variation.

From an estimate of the demand curve, we can derive a measure of the *exact* consumer's surplus, whether it is the compensating variation, equivalent variation, or some measure of utility change. No approximation is involved. While this result has been known for a long time by economic theorists, applied economists have only a limited awareness of its application. Furthermore, for the majority of cases the calculations are simple enough for a hand calculator. It seems preferable to remove completely any approximation argument from so important a matter as consumer's surplus. Also, my exact formulae allow calculation of the precision of our estimated consumer's surplus in terms of a standard error of estimation. Since unknown parameters for the demand curve will usually be estimated by econometric procedures, standard error formulae allow construction of confidence regions for the estimated compensated variation. These confidence regions might well be an important input to policy decisions. In most empirical applications we would like to account for the error in estimating the demand curve rather than including it in the approximation error as Willig implicitly does. Lastly, for some important uses of consumer's surplus, Willig's approximation argument is not useful. For instance, in assessing the welfare loss from taxation of labor income or capital income the proportion of total income can become so large that the Marshallian measure could differ markedly form the Hicks' measure of compensating variation or equivalent variation.[2]

However, a more important shortcoming of the use of the Marshallian measure (and Willig's approximation argument) arises in measuring deadweight loss. Here we are not interested in the complete compensating variation, which is a trapezoid to the left of the appropriate demand curve, but rather the triangle which corresponds to the excess of the compensating variation over the tax revenue collected from an individual. This triangle corresponds to the welfare measure that Harberger has used in his many studies of the effect of taxation on the U.S. economy. Even in cases where Willig's approximations hold for the complete compensating variation, the Marshallian deadweight loss can be a very poor approximation for the theoretically correct Hicksian measure of deadweight loss based on the compensated demand curve. Thus the Marshallian measure of deadweight loss is not accurate for the important measurements often undertaken in applied welfare economics and public finance studies. But, again, given an estimate of the uncompensated demand curve we can derive the exact measure of deadweight loss. As the example in the concluding section of the paper shows, the traditional measurement of the welfare triangle can lead to badly biased estimates of the true deadweight loss even when the conditions for Willig's approximation argument hold true for measurement of consumer's surplus.

The basic idea used in deriving the exact measure of consumer's surplus is to use the *observed* market demand curve to derive the *unobserved* compensated demand curve. It is this latter demand curve which leads to the compensating variation and equivalent variation.[3] In the two-good case using modern duality theory, I begin with the market demand curve and derive the corresponding indirect utility function. These two functions permit exact calculation of the compensating variation, equivalent variation and deadweight loss. In the many-good case when a single price changes, I derive the "quasi" indirect utility function and the "quasi" expenditure function. I denote the appropriate functions as quasi since they do not corre-

---

[2] For recent uses of consumer's surplus in these situations, see Michael Boskin and Martin Feldstein. Many important applications in public finance have the feature that a large proportion of an individual's income is involved.

[3] Hal Varian derives the compensating variation as the area under the Hicksian compensated demand curve. He then remarks that "unfortunately, since the Hicksian demand curves are unobservable these expressions do not appear to be useful" (p. 210). Herbert Mohring considers the properties of different welfare measures and uses a technique similar to mine to derive the compensating variation for the Cobb-Douglas case. G. W. McKenzie and I. F. Pearce and Y. O. Vartia use somewhat similar approaches but use different methods of analysis.

spond exactly to the individual's indirect utility function and expenditure function. To derive these functions, one would require estimates of the complete system of demand equations. The complete demand system usually cannot be estimated due to lack of data. Instead, I use Hicks' aggregation theorem to demonstrate that the quasi functions which correspond to the assumption of a two-good world would give exactly the same measure of consumer's surplus as the actual functions for a single price change. Thus, the estimates of the uncompensated demand curve are all that is required to produce estimates which correspond to the correct theoretical magnitude.

My approach differs from much recent work in that I begin with the observed market demand curve and then derive the unobserved indirect utility function and expenditure function. The more common approach is to start from a specification of the utility function, for example, Stone-Geary or translog, and then estimate the unknown parameters from the derived market demand functions. The method used here seems preferable on two grounds. First, the only observable data are the market demand data so good econometric practice would indicate finding a function that fits the data well. Thus, different specifications of the demand curve, not the utility function, would be fit with the best-fitting demand equation chosen to base the applied welfare analysis on. Second, specifications such as the translog functions force all the demand curves to have the same functional form which are often difficult to fit econometrically. Since here I consider only partial-equilibrium welfare analysis, I need only estimate a single demand function. Again, alternative specifications of the demand curve allow consideration of the robustness of the results to the chosen specification. The demand curve approach offers considerably more flexibility than does the utility function approach in obtaining good econometric results given the available market data.

In the next section, I derive the indirect utility function and expenditure function for the two-good case. It is shown how the use of these functions leads to correct measure of the compensating variation and equivalent variation. Section II then extends the analysis to the many-good case when only one price changes. There I show that the two-good analysis can be applied with only slight modifications. The functions for the case of a general quadratic demand curve are also derived. Lastly, in Section III, I provide an example of labor supply where the Marshallian approximation is inaccurate for the true compensating variation. I also provide an example of the calculation of deadweight loss to demonstrate that even when the Marshallian measure of the compensating variation is reasonably accurate, the Marshallian measure of deadweight loss can be incorrect by a relatively large amount. Section IV provides a brief conclusion to the paper.

I. The Compensating Variation and Equivalent Variation in the Two-Good Case

The basic tools which I will use in the analysis emerge from the dual approach to consumer behavior. The conventional treatment of consumer behavior considers the maximization of a strictly quasi-concave utility function defined over n goods, $x = (x_1, \ldots, x_n)$, subject to a budget constraint.

$$(1) \quad \max_x u(x) \text{ subject to } \sum_{i=1}^n p_i x_i = p \cdot x \leq y$$

where p_i are prices and y is (nonlabor) income.[4] The dual approach to the problem is to consider the associated minimization problem which defines the expenditure function

$$(2) \quad e(p, \bar{u}) \equiv \min_x p \cdot x \text{ subject to } u(x) \geq \bar{u}$$

The expenditure function was introduced into the literature by Lionel McKenzie; for recent

---

[4]Local nonsatiation will be assumed throughout the analysis so that the budget constraint will hold as an equality.

analysis and applications see Leo Hurwicz and Hirofumi Uzawa and Peter Diamond and Daniel McFadden. Charles Blackorby and W. Erwin Diewert have recently studied local properties of the expenditure function. The important property of the expenditure function which we will find extremely useful is that the partial derivative with respect to the jth price gives the Hicksian compensated demand curves.[5]

$$(3) \quad \frac{\partial e(p, \bar{u})}{\partial p_j} = h_j(p, \bar{u})$$

These unobservable Hicksian demand curves should be distinguished from the observable market uncompensated demand curves $x(p, y)$. At an optimum solution to equations (1) and (2) the demands coincide at maximum utility u^*, $h(p, u^*) = x(p, y)$.

The other function we will use which connects the utility function of equation (1) and the expenditure function of equation (2) is the indirect utility function which is the solution to the maximization problem

$$(4) \quad v(p, y) \equiv \max \left[u(x): p \cdot x \leq y \right]$$

Properties of the indirect utility function are derived in Diewert. An important property of the indirect utility function which we will use is René Roy's identity which yields the observed market demand curves as partial derivatives of $v(p, y)$.

$$(5) \quad x_j(p, y) = -\partial v(p, y)/\partial p_j / \partial v(p, y)/\partial y$$

It is the difference between equation (3) for the compensated demand curve and equation (5) for the uncompensated demand curve that induces the difference between Marshallian consumer's surplus and exact Hicks'

consumer's surplus when a price change occurs. Since the indirect utility function of equation (4) is monotonically increasing in income while the expenditure function of equation (2) is monotonically increasing in utility, either function can be inverted to derive the other corresponding function.

Let us now consider a change in the price vector from p^0 to p^1 and formally define the exact measures of consumer's surplus, the compensating variation, and equivalent variation, using the expenditure function.[6] Holding nonlabor income constant at y^0, the compensating variation $CV(p^0, p^1, y^0)$ is the minimum quantity required to keep the consumer as well off as he was in the initial state characterized by (p^0, y^0) as he is in the new state $(p^1, y^0 + CV)$. In terms of the expenditure function

$$(6) \quad CV(p^0, p^1, y^0) = e(p^1, u^0) - e(p^0, u^0)$$
$$= e(p^1, u^0) - y^0$$

where $u^0 = v(p^0, y^0)$ from the indirect utility function. Equivalently the compensating variation can be defined through the indirect utility function as $v(p^1, y^0 + CV) = v(p^0, y^0)$. An alternative measure of welfare change is the equivalent variation, $EV(p^0, p^1, y^0)$, which uses utility after the price change as the basis of comparison:[7]

$$(7) \quad EV(p^0, p^1, y^0) = e(p^1, u^1) - e(p^0, u^1)$$

Using either the compensating variation or equivalent variation, it can be shown that the area under the compensated Hicksian demand curve corresponds to consumer's surplus.

---

[5]The other useful property of the expenditure function which will be utilized in subsequent analysis is that the second derivatives of the expenditure function yield the elements of the Slutsky matrix $S_{ij} = \partial^2 e(p, \bar{u})/\partial p_i \partial p_j = \partial h_j(p, \bar{u})/\partial p_i$.

[6]Willig and Avinash Dixit and P. A. Weller do a similar derivation.

[7]The compensating variation and equivalent variation always have the same sign because of the monotonicity of $e(p, u)$ in prices so long as the net demands do not change sign. Except for the single price change case, no inequality relationship holds in general.

Let us consider the case when only the first price changes from p_1^0 to p_1^1 with all other prices held constant. Equation (3) gives the compensated demand curve, and integrating it between the two price levels gives

(8) $CV(p^0, p^1, y^0) = e(p^1, u^0) - e(p^0, u^0)$

$= \int_{p_1^0}^{p_1^1} h_1(p, u^0) dp_1 = \int_{p_1^0}^{p_1^1} \frac{\partial e(p, u^0)}{\partial p_1} dp_1$

The equivalent variation is derived in an identical manner where u^0 is replaced by u^1.[8]

Let us now compare this measure of welfare change with the traditional measure of Marshallian consumer's surplus as the area under the uncompensated demand curve of equation (5).[9] The integral has the form

(9) $A(p^0, p^1, y^0) = \int_{p_1^0}^{p_1^1} x_1(p, y^0) dp_1$

$= -\int_{p_1^0}^{p_1^1} \frac{\partial v(p, y^0)/\partial p_1}{\partial v(p, y^0)/\partial y} dp_1$

This integral in general differs from the integral for the compensating variation in equation (8). To keep the individual on the same indifference curve, y^0 which enters both the numerator and denominator of equation (9) must be constantly adjusted along the path of the price change. Since y^0 is kept constant, this produces the difference between the uncompensated market demand curve with its Marshallian measure of consumer's surplus and the compensated demand curve with its measure of the compensating variation.

It is the supposed constancy or near constancy of the marginal utility of income which has often served as a basis for using Marshal-

---

[8] An alternative but equivalent method of interpreting our procedure is to use equation (3) to write $\partial e/\partial p_j = h_j(p, \bar{u}) = x_j(p, e(p, \bar{u}))$. In principle this implicit equation can always be numerically integrated from p^0 to p^1 to find the exact compensating variation. Vartia gives a computer algorithm for the numerical integration method. My technique to find closed-form solutions uses Roy's identity to derive a differential equation which can be explicitly solved in many cases.

[9] Varian (pp. 209 ff.) does a similar analysis.

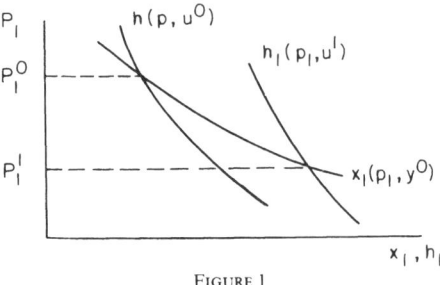

FIGURE 1

lian consumer's surplus as a measure of welfare change. However, equations (6) and (9) in general do not give the same measure. The difference between the compensated Hicksian demand curve which forms the basis for equation (6) and the uncompensated Marshallian demand curve which forms the basis for equation (9) follows from Slutsky's equation

(10)

$\frac{\partial h_1(p, u^0)}{\partial p_1} - \frac{\partial x_1(p, y^0)}{\partial p_1} = x_1 \cdot \frac{\partial x_1(p, y^0)}{\partial y}$

A sufficient condition for equation (10) to equal zero is that both $\partial^2 v(p, y^0)/\partial y \partial p$ and $\partial^2 v(p, y^0)/\partial y^2$ equal zero. These conditions correspond to the case of constant marginal utility of income. For the case of a normal good, the compensated demand curve has steeper slope than the market demand curve so Figure 1 demonstrates the inequalities for a single price change $EV(p^0, p^1, y^0) \leq A(p^0, p^1, y^0) \leq CV(p^0, p^1, y^0)$, an inequality found in Willig. His paper shows that even when the marginal utility of income is not constant that the percentage difference, $(CV-A)/A$, is not large under certain conditions.

Let us now turn to the empirical application of consumer's surplus. It turns out that for many applications no approximation is needed since equation (6) or (7) can be computed exactly. I begin with the simplest case, two goods only with prices $p^0 = (p_1^0, 1)$. Thus I use the second good as numeraire and consider a price change to p_1^1. Both the price of the first good and income are normalized with respect to the price of the second good, which does not change. While this case is very simple, it is not totally unrealistic. It is often used in empirical analysis, especially when a separability assumption between the good whose price changes and the other goods is appropriate. A very general treatment of separability is contained in Blackorby, Primont, and Russell, but for use herein, a simple interpretation of separability which allows us to write the utility function of equation (1) as $u(x_1,\ldots,x_n) = u(x_1, g(x_2,\ldots,x_n))$ is adequate. The appropriate price index which corresponds to the structure of $u(\cdot)$ provides the numeraire good. Separability of the indirect utility function is defined in an analogous manner, $v(p_1, k(p_2,\ldots,p_n))$ where $k(\cdot)$ provides the price index. In general separability of $u(\cdot)$ does not imply separability of $v(\cdot)$ or vice versa.

Separability utility functions justify specification and estimation of demand curves that have only a single price in them. An important example often used in empirical studies is the linear labor supply relationship

(11) $\quad x_j = \alpha w_j + \delta y_j + z_j \gamma + \varepsilon_j; \quad j = 1,\ldots, J$

estimated over a sample of J individuals where w_j is the commodity price deflated (net after tax) wage, y_j is the commodity price deflated nonlabor income, Z_j is a vector of socioeconomic characteristics, and ε_j is a stochastic disturbance. Numerous other commodity demand equations are specified in this form where the wage is replaced by the price of the commodity.

To derive the exact compensating variation is straightforward and provides an exact welfare measure. The basic idea is to take the *observed* market demand curve and to use Roy's identity from equation (5) to integrate and derive the indirect utility function.[10] Inversion of the indirect utility gives the expenditure function which allows calculation of the compensating variation. Equivalently, using equation (3) we can derive the *unobservable* compensated demand curve.

And equation (8) shows that the area under the compensated demand curve yields the exact consumer's surplus.

In principle we can always perform this integration for a well-specified demand function. This statement is the essence of the famous integrability problem in consumer demand.[11] So long as the derivatives of the *compensated* demand functions satisfy the properties of symmetry and negative semi-definiteness of the Slutsky matrix and the adding-up condition, the indirect utility function can be recovered by integration.[12] In practice, many commonly used demand functions in empirical work yield explicit solutions so that exact welfare analysis is easily done.

Returning to the two-good example, consider the nonstochastic demand function (where both p_1 and y are deflated by the price of the other good, p_2):[13]

(12) $\quad x_1 = \alpha p_1 + \delta y + z\gamma$

$\quad\quad = -\partial v(p_1, y)/\partial p_1/\partial v(p_1, y)/\partial y$

I solve this linear partial differential equation by applying the method of characteristic curves which assures a unique solution, given an initial condition.[14] To make welfare comparisons we will want to be on a given indifference curve. As the price changes I will use the equation $v(p_1(t), y(t)) = u_0$ for some u_0; for example, initial utility in the compensat-

---

[10] This technique has been used in estimating demand with nonlinear budget constraints by Gary Burtless and myself, and in my earlier article.

[11] See Samuelson and Hurwicz and Uzawa.

[12] In addition a regularity condition is needed. A Lipschitz-type condition is given by Hurwicz and Uzawa. A stronger sufficient condition that often holds is for the demand function to be continuously differentiable.

[13] It has been pointed out to me by Diewert that this demand specification corresponds to a flexible functional form for the underlying preferences as discussed in Blackorby and Diewert. Basically, three independent parameters are needed for the demand function in the two-good case, which equation (12) has, so that the value of demand, the uncompensated price derivative, and the income derivative can attain arbitrary values.

[14] See Fritz John or Richard Courant and David Hilbert. Given that along an initial curve (here an indifference curve), the initial values are continuously differentiable then a unique solution to the partial differential equation exists.

ing variation case. Along a path of price change to stay on the indifference curve, we have

$$(13) \quad \frac{\partial v(p_1(t), y(t))}{\partial p_1(t)} \frac{dp_1(t)}{dt}$$
$$+ \frac{\partial v(p_1(t), y(t))}{\partial y(t)} \frac{dy(t)}{dt} = 0$$

Then, using the implicit function theorem and Roy's identity from equation (12),

$$(14) \quad \frac{dy(p_1)}{dp_1} = \alpha p_1 + \delta y + z\gamma$$

I have now expressed y as a function of p_1 and can solve the ordinary differential equation (14) to find

$$(15) \quad y(p_1) = c e^{\delta p_1} - \frac{1}{\delta}\left(\alpha p_1 + \frac{\alpha}{\delta} + z\gamma\right)$$

where c, the constant of integration, depends on the initial utility level u_0. In fact, I simply choose $c = u_0$ as our cardinal utility index. Therefore, solving equation (15), we find the indirect utility function[15]

$$(16)$$
$$v(p_1, y) = c = e^{-\delta p_1}\left[y + \frac{1}{\delta}\left(\alpha p_1 + \frac{\alpha}{\delta} + z\gamma\right)\right]$$

Then the corresponding expenditure function (again normalized by the price of the second good) follows simply from equation (16) by interchanging the utility level with the income variable

$$(17) \quad e(p_1, \bar{u}) = e^{\delta p_1}\bar{u} - \frac{1}{\delta}\left(\alpha p_1 + \frac{\alpha}{\delta} + z\gamma\right)$$

It is important to note that this procedure yields a *local solution* to the differential equation over some domain in price space. It is not always the case that there exists a global solution to equation (12) which satisfies the integrability conditions. However, we need only a local solution to make the welfare calculations that we are interested in. That is, we only want to compute a welfare measure at two price points, sat p_1^0 and p_1^1, which equations (16) and (17) permit us to do.

We now have a solution to Roy's identity, but we need to check whether we have a valid indirect utility function which arises from consumer maximization.[16] The indirect utility function of equation (16) is continuous and homogeneous of degree zero in prices and income by my normalization condition using p_2 as numeraire. It is also decreasing in prices if $\alpha \leq 0$ and increasing in income if $\delta \geq 0$. The other condition $v(p_1, y)$ must satisfy is quasi concavity which is equivalent to the Slutsky condition

$$(18) \quad s_{11} = \frac{\partial h_1(p_1, \bar{u})}{\partial p_1}$$
$$= \alpha + \delta(\alpha p_1 + \delta y + z\gamma) \leq 0$$

where the compensated demand curve $h_1(p_1, \bar{u})$ follows from the expenditure function of equation (17) by differentiation with respect to p_1. So long as the sign conditions are satisfied by the demand function we can calculate exact consumer's surplus and deadweight loss using the expenditure function of equation (17) and indirect utility function of equation (16).

To compute the compensating variation we use equation (17) and equation (6) to find

$$(19) \quad CV(p_1^0, p_1^1, y_0)$$
$$= e^{\delta(p_1^1 - p_1^0)}\left[y_0 + \frac{1}{\delta}\left(z\gamma + \frac{\alpha}{\delta} + \alpha p_1^0\right)\right]$$
$$- \frac{1}{\delta}\left(z\gamma + \frac{\alpha}{\delta} + \alpha p_1^1\right) - y^0$$
$$= \frac{1}{\delta}e^{\delta(p_1^1 - p_1^0)}\left[x_1^0(p_1^0, y_0) + \frac{\alpha}{\delta}\right]$$
$$- \frac{1}{\delta}\left[x_1^1(p_1^1, y^0) + \frac{\alpha}{\delta}\right]$$

---

[15]Any monotonic transformation of this equation will of course satisfy the differential equation since ordinal utility is determined only up to a monotonic transformation. The only change would be in c, the constant of integration.

[16]Diewert discusses the appropriate conditions.

This expression for the compensating variation, while certainly more complicated than the Marshallian triangle formula, is still straightforward to calculate. The corresponding equivalent variation would be calculated from equation (7). Furthermore, since the parameters for equation (17) are presumably estimated by econometric methods, well-known methods allow calculation of the large sample standard error for the compensating variation in equation (19) (for example, see Rao, p. 323). Note, also that the compensating variation now varies across individuals by their socioeconomic characteristics and their income levels while the corresponding Marshallian expressions neglects these factors in its approximation. Use of the compensating variation or equivalent variation ends all arguments about the appropriateness of the Marshallian approximation since they give the exact measure of welfare change.

Another commonly used demand curve specification in the two-good case is the constant elasticity specification[17]

$$(20) \quad x_1 = e^{z\gamma} p_1^\alpha y^\delta$$

$$= -\partial v(p_1, y)/\partial p_1 / \partial v(p_1, y)/\partial y$$

$$\delta \neq 1$$

which is often estimated in *log*-linear form as $\log x_{1j} = z_j \gamma + \alpha \log p_{1j} + \delta \log y_j + \varepsilon_j$ for $j = 1, \ldots, J$.[18] To find the indirect utility function we use the technique of separation of variables and integrate to find

$$(21) \quad v(p_1, y) = c = -e^{z\gamma} \cdot \frac{p_1^{1+\alpha}}{1+\alpha} + \frac{y^{1-\delta}}{1-\delta}$$

where c, the constant of integration, has again been set at the initial utility level. The Slutsky condition is $s_{11} = x_1(\alpha/p_1 + \delta x_1/y)$. The expenditure function (again normalized by p_2) is

$$(22)$$

$$e(p_1, \bar{u}) = \left[(1-\delta)\left(\bar{u} + e^{z\gamma} \frac{p_1^{1+\alpha}}{1+\alpha}\right)\right]^{1/1-\delta}$$

so that the compensating variation for a change in price from p_1^0 to p_1^1 is the quantity

$$(23) \quad CV(p_1^0, p_1^1, y^0) = \left\{(1-\delta)\left[\frac{e^{z\gamma}}{1+\alpha}\right.\right.$$

$$\left.\left.\left(p_1^{1\ 1+\alpha} - p_1^{0\ 1+\alpha}\right)\right] + y^{0(1-\delta)}\right\}^{1/1-\delta} - y^0$$

$$= \left\{\frac{(1-\delta)}{(1+\alpha)y^{0\delta}}\left[p_1^1 x_1^1(p_1^1, y^0)\right.\right.$$

$$\left.\left. -p_1^0 x_1^0(p_1^0, y^0)\right] + y^{0(1-\delta)}\right\}^{1/1-\delta} - y^0$$

Again an exact formula for the compensating variation is derived for which a standard error could be straightforwardly calculated given a covariance matrix for the estimated parameters. No approximation argument is required in using the compensating variation as a measure of welfare change. It is interesting to note that while the denominator of equation (9) is constant for the demand specification of equation (20) so that in this case the Marshallian area also gives an exact measure of welfare change, it is not equal to either the compensating variation or the equivalent variation. The income effect from equation (10) is not zero so that the compensated demand derivative and uncompensated demand derivative differ by a positive amount. Thus, use of the Marshallian measure still involves an error of approximation if either the compensating variation or the equivalent variation are the desired measure.

II. The Many-Good Case and More General Demand Specifications

The welfare measures developed at the beginning of Section I were all fully general in the sense that they considered n different

---

[17]Again this demand curve provides a flexible functional form for the underlying preferences.

[18]Willig considers a constant income elasticity demand specification in deriving his approximations. For $\delta = 1$ the indirect utility function has the same form as equation (19) except that the last term is replaced by $\log y$.

goods and allowed all n prices to change. In particular, the compensating variation of equation (6) and the equivalent variation of equation (7) used the expenditure function whose arguments are the complete price vector and the appropriate utility level. In this section I generalize the methods of calculating the compensating variation to the many-good case but continue to consider only one price change.[19] While we cannot recover the complete expenditure function as before, we can still recover the quasi-expenditure function whose derivative yields the appropriate compensated demand curve. Thus again the compensating variation and equivalent variation can be estimated exactly given information on the market demand curve for the good whose price has changed.

A complete specification of a system of demand equations would have the general form

(24) $\quad x_i = x(p, y, z, \varepsilon_i); \qquad i = 1, \ldots, N$

where p is the price vector, z is a vector of socioeconomic characteristics, and ε_i is a stochastic disturbance. So long as the estimated coefficients of the demand system have the property that the Slutsky matrix is symmetric and negative semidefinite and that the function $x(\cdot)$ is regular in p and y, then in principle the system can be integrated and the expenditure functions derived. However, the usual case is that we do not have information on all quantity demands at the individual level. But suppose we do have information on demand for, say, the first good whose price is expected to change as a result of the public policy measure being considered. A first-order Taylor expansion of equation (24) would lead to the econometric specification[20]

(25) $\quad x_1(p, y) = z\gamma + \sum_{i=2}^{N} \frac{\delta_i y}{p_i} + \sum_{i=2}^{N} \frac{\alpha_i p_1}{p_i} + \varepsilon_1$

The important point to note about equation (25) is that by assumption only p_1 will change due to the contemplated policy measure, while z, y, and $p_2, \ldots, p_n$ will remain constant. Thus, all prices except the first can be written as a scalar multiple of a price index, $p_2 = \lambda_2 q, \ldots, p_N = \lambda_N q$ where $\lambda_2, \ldots, \lambda_N$ are known fixed positive constants. We can now apply Hicks' composite commodity theorem.[21] Rewrite equation (25) as

(26) $\quad x_1(p_1, q, y)$

$= z\gamma + \left(\sum_{i=2}^{N} \frac{\delta_i}{\lambda_i} \right) \frac{y}{q} + \left(\sum_{i=2}^{N} \frac{\alpha_i}{\lambda_i} \right) \frac{p_1}{q}$

$= z\gamma + \delta \frac{y}{q} + \alpha \frac{p_1}{q}$

where $\quad \delta = \sum_{i=2}^{N} \delta_i / \lambda_i \quad \text{and} \quad \alpha = \sum_{i=2}^{N} \alpha_i / \lambda_i$

Since equation (26) is the same as equation (12) except that the composite price q has replaced p_2, I can repeat the analysis of the last section with the welfare analysis based on equations (16) and (17). Note that the resulting functions might best be referred to as a quasi-indirect utility function and a quasi-expenditure function. We have not recovered the complete indirect utility function or expenditure function, but the "quasi" functions lead to exact welfare measures when all other prices are constant. But they cannot be used to analyze the welfare change when more than one price changes (except proportionately) without further analysis.

Let us now briefly consider some extensions of our techniques to more general cases. First, we can generalize the log-linear demand specification of equation (20) to the many good consumer

(27) $\quad x_1(p, y) = e^{z\gamma} \prod_{i=2}^{N} \left(\frac{p_1}{p_i} \right)^{\alpha_i} \prod_{i=2}^{N} \left(\frac{y}{p_i} \right)^{\delta_i}$

---

[19] The one-price-change situation is the case considered by Willig.

[20] I am indebted to Diewert for help in improving this section of the paper from an earlier version.

[21] For other references and developments of this theorem, see Terrance Gorman and Blackorby et al. and Diewert.

Again, if only the first price changes, we can obtain the quasi-expenditure function corresponding to equation (22) by the application of Hicks' composite commodity theorem to obtain

$$(28) \quad x_1(p_1, q, y) = e^{z\gamma} \left(\frac{p_1}{q}\right)^{\sum_{i=2}^{N} \alpha_i} \left(\frac{y}{q}\right)^{\sum_{i=2}^{N} \delta_i}$$

Use of the quasi-expenditure function allows exact welfare measures to be calculated.

I now return to the two-good case to present some generalizations of the demand specification with the observation that they can be expanded to the N good case by the techniques which lead to equations (26) and (28). Thus, I again normalize by the second price so that p_1 and y are divided by p_2. I return to the linear demand specification of equation (12) but allow the price and income coefficients of the demand specification, as well as the intercept, to depend on individual socioeconomic characteristics. Let $\delta = zd$ and $\alpha = za$ which leads to the demand specification[22]

$$(29) \quad x_1(p_1, y) = z\gamma + zdy + zap_1 + \varepsilon_1$$

Calculation of the welfare measures proceeds in the same way except that δ and α vary across individuals. Perhaps a more important generalization is to allow interactions among the price terms to move away from the linear demand curve specification. A demand function quadratic in prices is

$$(30) \quad x_1(p_1, y) = z\gamma + \delta y + \beta_1 p_1 + \beta_2 p_1^2 + \varepsilon_1$$

so long as the Slutsky term is negative we can integrate the corresponding differential equation by parts to find the indirect utility function

$$(31) \quad v(p_1, y) = e^{-\delta p_1} \left[y + a_1 p_1 + a_2 p_1^2 + a_3\right]$$

where $a_1 = \beta_1/\delta + 2\beta_2/\delta^2$, $a_2 = \beta_2/\delta$, and a_3

[22] Stochastic terms can be added of the type $\delta = Zd + v$, which lead to a random coefficients specification. The resulting heteroscedasticity can be accounted for in the estimation procedure. This type of demand function is estimated in my article with Burtless.

$= z\gamma/\delta + 2\beta_2/\delta^3$. With equation (31) exact welfare analysis is again straightforward since the expenditure function, compensating variation, and equivalent variation all follow from equation (31).

The last and most general demand curve that is considered is fully quadratic in both prices and income. The demand function is

$$(32) \quad x_1 = \beta_0 + \beta_1 y + \beta_2 p_1 + \beta_3 y^2 + \beta_4 p_1^2 + \beta_5 p_1 y + \varepsilon_1$$

where $\beta_0 = z\gamma$. Using Roy's identity we have the nonlinear differential equation

$$(33) \quad \frac{dy}{dp_1} + Qy + Ry^2 + S = 0$$

where $R = -\beta_3$, $Q = -(\beta_1 + \beta_5 p_1)$ and $S = -(\beta_0 + \beta_2 p_1 + \beta_4 p_1^2)$. It turns out that this equation can be transformed by changes of variables to the famous Schrodinger wave equation of physics. I give the derivation in the Appendix where the indirect utility function is found to have the form

$$(34) \quad v(p, y) = \left(h\tilde{W}_1 - \tilde{W}_1^1\right)/\left(\tilde{W}_2^1 - h\tilde{W}_2\right)$$

where $h = -\beta_3 y + (\beta_5/2)(\beta_1 + \beta_5 p)^2$ and $\tilde{W}_1$ and $\tilde{W}_2$, functions of the β parameters of equation (32) and prices, which are straightforward to calculate. Their exact form is given in the Appendix. Again, the expenditure function and exact welfare measures follow directly from equation (34). Thus, we have a very general demand specification with associated exact welfare measures. In fact, the demand function may well provide a third-order flexible function form in the sense of Blackorby and Diewert.

III. Calculation of the Compensating Variation and of the Deadweight Loss

In the previous section, I have given formulae for calculating the exact welfare change by deriving the unobservable compensated demand curve given market information. Here I consider two examples to demonstrate use of the formulae. I can also assess how accurate the Marshallian approximations are for the exact welfare measures. The first example of labor supply shows that the approximation may be quite poor for goods which form a large proportion of total expenditure. Since Willig showed that the approximation might not do well in this case, the finding is not surprising. However, the second example raises severe doubt about the use of uncompensated market demand for a commodity which is only a small proportion of the budget when we calculate the deadweight loss from the imposition of a tax. Even though the conditions for an accurate approximation to the compensating variation hold, the approximation to the deadweight loss is very inaccurate. In fact, this finding seems to hold in general. While the Marshallian approximation is adequate in certain situations for the compensating variation, it is often *not* accurate under these conditions for measurement of the deadweight loss. Since measurement of the deadweight loss is often the goal in applied welfare economics, this finding strongly recommends use of the exact measure deadweight rather than the Marshallian approximation.

The first example used, is a linear labor supply function of the form of equation (11). The estimates used are taken from a study of wives' labor supply functions in my forthcoming paper. The estimated values used for the jth individual are

(35) $\quad h_j = 495.1 w_j - .1250 y_j + 765.1$

The left-hand side variable is hours per year of work, w_j is market wage which has a mean of \$4.15 per hour, y_j is after tax income of the husband which has a mean of \$8,236, and the constant takes account of demographic factors such as age and children.

Here I calculate the required compensating variation after the imposition of a 20 percent proportional tax on labor earnings. Compared to a no-tax situation, the expenditure takes the form

(36) $\quad e(w, \bar{u}) = e^{-\delta w} \bar{u} - \frac{\alpha}{\delta} w + \frac{\alpha}{\delta^2} - \frac{z\gamma}{\delta}$

Calculating u^0 from the corresponding indirect utility function and using it in equation (36) leads to a required expenditure of \$9485 per year. I find that the compensating variation is \$2,056. Using the formula for distribution of a nonlinear function, I find one standard error for the compensating variation to be plus or minus \$481. Then to find the aggregate compensating variation for the complete population, a sample enumeration would be done allowing the wages, husband's income, and socioeconomic variables to differ across individuals.

Calculations of the Marshallian approximation is straightforward since we use the estimates of equation (35) and measure the area to the left of the labor supply curve between the initial and final net wages of \$4.15 per hour and \$3.32 per hour. The Marshallian approximation is \$1,315 per year so that the two measures differ by 44.6 percent. Thus, the Marshallian measure provides a very poor approximation to the exact measure of welfare change. That the Marshallian measure provides a poor approximation in this case is in line with Willig's results since the Marshallian area is large with respect to base income. Hence, the Taylor approximation which provides Willig's bounds demonstrates that the derivation between the two measures can be substantial. It is worth emphasizing again that the exact welfare change is easily calculated from the indirect utility function and the expenditure function. Then no worry about the accuracy of the approximation is needed.

The last example I consider is the more important one, since it involves a quite common use of consumer's surplus in applied welfare economics. I consider the deadweight loss from imposition of a commodity tax.

Consider the compensated demand curve $h(p, u_0)$ shown in Figure 2. The compensating variation is the area to the left of the demand curve between the initial price p^0 and the final, post tax, price p^1. But we are often *more* interested in the welfare triangle which measures the efficiency loss from the use of distorting taxes. This triangle corresponds to the Harberger measure. Therefore, I define the deadweight loss to be the difference of the compensating variation minus

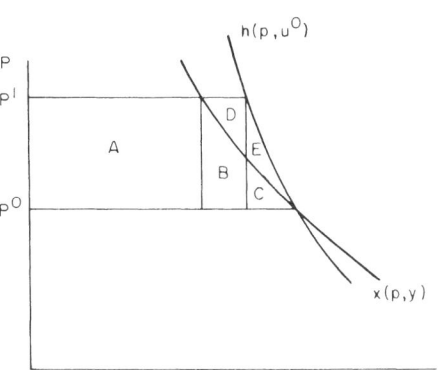

FIGURE 2

the tax revenue collected. The rectangle in Figure 2 thus has only distributional consequences while the triangle is the deadweight burden which cannot be undone. Optimal tax policy typically tries to minimize the sum of the deadweight losses to achieve a second best optimum, for example, see Diamond and Mirrlees.

The particular example I consider is meant to approximate the long-run demand for gasoline, although the numbers used are hypothetical. The demand function is

(37) $\quad q_j = -14.22 p + .082 y_j + 4.95$

Choosing income for the mean person to be $720 per month and initial price to be $.75 per gallon, the price elasticity is .2 with an income elasticity of 1.1. Both elasticities are similar to elasticities which have been found in empirical studies. Let us now consider imposition of a tax which raises the price of gasoline to $1.50 per gallon. Using equation (17) we find that the compensating variation equals $37.17 per month. The Marshallian approximation equals $35.99 per month, so that the two measures differ by only 3.2 percent. Thus, the Willig results are confirmed since demand for gasoline is only a small part of the total budget for the individual.

However, when we compare the two measures of deadweight loss we find a substantial difference. The compensated measure of the deadweight loss is $2.88 while the Marshallian measure is $3.96. The two measures differ by 31.7 percent, even though the approximation is good for the compensating variation. Why can the approximation be so poor for the deadweight loss? Using order arguments somewhat loosely, the compensating variation is composed of two pieces, the rectangle which is a first-order quantity of demand times change in price while the deadweight loss is a second-order quantity of one-half the changes in demand times the change in price. While the Marshallian approximation does reasonably well for the first-order part of the compensating variation under certain conditions given by Willig, its performance on the second order part may still be quite bad.

In Figure 2 we see that both measures of the compensating variation have rectangle A in common, which is a large part of the whole. In measuring the first-order effect they differ only by triangle D, which is small compared to the whole. However, in measuring the deadweight loss, the percentage difference will depend on the difference of area B and triangle E compared to the area of triangle C. Figure 2 shows that this difference can often be substantial. Thus, the Marshallian approximation is not accurate for measurement of the deadweight loss. Instead, the exact Hicksian measure should be used. While the Willig results will hold for the compensating variation, if the goal of the calculation is deadweight loss, the Marshallian approximation should not be used. In many cases it is a very inaccurate measure of the true deadweight loss.

IV. Conclusion

In empirical situations where a measure of either the compensating variation, equivalent variation, or deadweight loss is needed, economists often work with relatively simple demand specifications. For these types of specifications we have developed the exact measures of welfare change. While it has been known that use of the compensated demand curves lead to the appropriate welfare measures, it has not been generally recognized how straightforward it is to derive the compensated demand curves from observed market demand curves. I derived methods which are easily applied to the two-good case. These methods are then extended to the many-good case with one price change. The quasi-indirect utility function and expenditure function provide the appropriate compensated demand curve and thus the appropriate welfare measure. While our measures tell us the appropriate compensation, they, of course, do not necessarily give the correct measurement of the loss in social welfare if no compensation is paid.

Through two examples I attempt to assess the accuracy of the Marshallian approximation. For a good which forms a small part of the total budget, the Marshallian area is reasonably accurate as proven by Willig. But if the good forms a large part of the budget, the approximation may be quite inaccurate as our labor supply example shows. A more important finding is the high level of inaccuracy when the deadweight loss, or welfare triangle, is measured. For deadweight loss, the Marshallian area can often be quite far off even though it is reasonably accurate for the compensating variation in the same situation. The gasoline example shows that the deadweight loss measures differ by 32 percent even though the compensating variation measures differ by 3.2 percent. Thus, it seems *inappropriate* to measure deadweight loss by using the market demand curve. But since the exact deadweight loss measure can be often calculated by use of the compensated demand curve, no special problem arises. The formulae given in this paper permit exact calculation of both the compensating variation and of the deadweight loss.

APPENDIX

Let us consider derivation of the indirect utility function and expenditure function which corresponds to the fully quadratic demand curve of Section II.[23]

The demand function that I consider is

$$x_1 = \beta_0 + \beta_1 y + \beta_2 p_1 + \beta_3 y^2 + \beta_4 p_1^2 + \beta_5 p_1 y + \varepsilon_1$$

where $\beta_0 = Z\gamma$. Using Roy's identity this demand equation may be written as the nonlinear differential equation

$$y' + Qy + Ry^2 + S = 0$$

where $R = -\beta_3$, $Q = -(\beta_1 + \beta_5 p_1)$ and $S = -(\beta_0 + \beta_2 p_1 + \beta_4 p_1^2)$. I do one change of dependent variable $y = (1/R)(u'/u)$ and one change of independent variable $t = \beta_1 + \beta_5 p_1$ calling the resulting function $\phi(t)$ to find

$$\phi'' + \beta_5 t \phi' + q\phi = 0$$

where $q = \beta_5^2 SR$. Thus, I have transformed the nonlinear equation, a Ricatti equation, to a second-order differential equation of the form studied by physicists. I then transform by $W = \phi e^{\beta_5 t^2/4}$ to put the equation in parabolic cylinder form $W'' + WM = 0$ where $M = \delta_0 + \delta_1 t + \delta_2 t^2$ and the δ_i's are easily calculated functions of the β_i's. I have thus transformed the original equation into the famous Schrodinger wave equation. One last change of independent variable $x^2 = 4(\delta_1 t + \delta_2 t^2)$ and we have the final form

$$W'' + W\big(\delta_0 + (x^2/4)\big) = 0.$$

Define the functions $W_1 = 1 + \delta_0(x^2/2) + (\delta_0^2 - (1/2)(x^4/4!) + \ldots$ and $W_2 = x + \delta_0(x^3/3!) + (\delta_0^2 - 3/2)(x^5/5!) + \ldots$, which converge quickly for values likely to be encountered in economics.[24] Now define $\gamma_0 = \delta_1 \beta_1 + \delta_2 \beta_1^2$, $\gamma_2 = \delta_1 \beta_5 + 2\delta_2 \beta_1 \beta_5$, and $\gamma_3 = \delta_2 \beta_5^2$ and we have the W_i function in terms of prices $\tilde{W}_1 = 1 + 2\delta_0(\gamma_1 + \gamma_2 p_1 + \gamma_3 p_1^2) + (2/3)(\delta_0^2 - 1/2)(\gamma_1 + \gamma_2 p_1 + \gamma_3 p_1^2)^2 + \ldots$ and $W_2 = 2\delta_0(\gamma_2 + 2\gamma_3 p_1) + (1/3)(\delta_0^2 - 1/2)(\gamma_1 + \gamma_2 p_1 + \gamma_3 p_1^2)(\gamma_2 + 2\gamma_3 p_1) + \ldots$ which again converge

---

[23] Generalization to the many-good case is straightforward. Only a sketch of the derivation is provided here. Further details may be obtained by writing the author.

[24] Description and analysis of the parabolic cylinder functions is found in Milton Abramowitz and Irene Stegum (ch. 19). The successive coefficients of the expansion have a simple recursive formula which eases calculation.

quickly. The indirect utility function thus takes the form

$$(A1) \quad v(p, y) = \frac{h\tilde{W}_1 - \tilde{W}_1'}{\tilde{W}_2' - h\tilde{W}_2}$$

where $h = -\beta_3 y + \beta_5 t^2/2$. The expenditure function also takes a simple form in terms of the W functions

$$(A2) \quad e(p_1, \bar{u}) = \frac{t\beta_5^2}{2\beta_3} - \frac{1}{\beta_3} \left(\frac{\tilde{W}_1' + \bar{u}\tilde{W}_2'}{\tilde{W}_1 + \bar{u}\tilde{W}_2} \right)$$

Then equation (A1) is used to compute utility at original prices p_1^0 and equation (A2) is used to compute $e(p_1^1, \bar{u})$ so that after subtracting off y_0 we find the compensating variation. The W functions are straightforward to calculate and both tables and computer routines exist to do the calculation.

I might note that it is straightforward to generate demand functions and corresponding indirect utility functions and expenditure functions that are closed form and contain quadratic terms in both prices and incomes. But I have not yet found demand functions of this type which can be estimated using linear regression techniques. The specification leading to (A1) and (A2) has this advantage although specialized computer routines then become necessary to evaluate the consumer's surplus and deadweight loss measures.

REFERENCES

Milton Abramowitz and Irene Stegum, *Handbook of Mathematical Functions*, Washington 1964.

Charles Blackorby and W. E. Diewert, "Expenditure Functions, Local Duality, and Second Order Approximations," *Econometrica*, May 1979, 47, 579–601.

_____, Daniel Primont, and Robert Russell, *Duality Separability and Functional Structure*, New York 1978.

M. J. Boskin, "Taxation, Saving and the Rate of Interest," *J. Polit. Econ.*, Apr. 1978, 86, S3–S28.

G. Burtless and J. Hausman, "The Effect of Taxation on Labor Supply," *J. Polit. Econ.*, Feb. 1978, 86, 1103–30.

Richard Courant and David Hilbert, *Methods of Mathematical Physics, II.*, New York 1962.

P. Diamond and D. McFadden, "Some Uses of the Expenditure Function in Public Finance," *J. Public Econ.*, Feb. 1974, 3, 3–21.

_____ and J. Mirrlees, "Optimal Taxation and Public Production," *Amer. Econ. Rev.*, Mar. 1971, 61, 8–27.

W. E. Diewert, "Applications of Duality Theory" in Michael. D. Intriligator and David A. Kendrick, eds., *Frontiers of Quantitative Economics, II*, Amsterdam 1974.

_____, "Hicks Aggregation Theorem and the Existence of a Real Value Added Function," mimeo, 1976.

A. Dixit and P. A. Weller, "The Three Consumer's Surpluses," *Economica*, May 1979, 46, 125–35.

J. Dupuit, "On the Measurement of the Utility of Public Works," in Kenneth Arrow and Tibor Scitovsky, eds., *Readings in Welfare Economics*, Homewood 1969.

M. Feldstein, "The Welfare Cost of Capital Income Taxation," *J. Polit. Econ.*, Apr. 1978, 86, S29–S52.

W. M. Gorman, "Community Preference Fields," *Econometrica*, Jan. 1953, 21, 63–80.

A. Harberger, "Three Basic Postulates for Applied Welfare Economics: An Interpretive Essay," *J. Econ. Lit.*, Sept. 1971, 9, 785–97.

J. A. Hausman, "The Effect of Wages, Taxes, and Fixed Costs on Women's Labor Force Participation," *J. Public Econ.*, Oct. 1980, 14, 161–94.

_____, "The Effects of Taxes on Labor Supply," in Henry Aaron and Joseph Pechman, *How do Taxes Affect Economic Behavior*, forthcoming 1981.

J. R. Hicks, *Value and Capital*, Oxford 1939.

_____, *A Revision of Demand Theory*, London 1956.

H. Hotelling, "The General Welfare in Relation to Problems of Taxation and of Railway and Utility Rates," *Econometrica*, July 1938, 6, 242–69.

J. Hurwicz and H. Uzawa, "On the Integrability of Demand Functions," in John S. Chipman, ed., *Preferences, Utility and Demand*, New York 1971.

Fritz John, *Partial Differential Equations*, New

York 1978.
I. M. D. Little, *A Critique of Welfare Economics*, London 1957.
G. McKenzie and I. Pearce, "Exact Measures of Welfare and the Cost of Living," *Rev. Econ. Stud.*, Oct. 1976, *43*, 465–68.
L. W. McKenzie, "Demand Theory Without a Utility Index," *Rev. Econ. Stud.*, June 1957, *24*, 185–89.
Alfred Marshall, *Principles of Economics*, New York 1961.
H. Mohring, "Alternative Welfare Gain and Loss Measures," *Western Econ. J.*, Dec. 1971, *9*, 349–68.
C. R. Rao, *Linear Statistical Inference*, New York 1973.

R. Roy, "La Distribution du revenue entre les divers biens," *Econometrica*, July 1947, *15*, 205–25.
Paul A. Samuelson, *Foundations of Economic Analysis*, Cambridge, Mass. 1947.
_____, "The Problem of Integrability in Utility Theory," *Economica*, Nov. 1950, *17*, 355–85.
Hal Varian, *Microeconomic Analysis*, New York 1978.
Y. O. Vartia, "Efficient Methods of Measuring Welfare Change and Compensated Income," mimeo., 1978.
R. Willig, "Consumer's Surplus without Apology," *Amer. Econ. Rev.*, Sept. 1976, *66*, 589–97.

[13]

On the Marginal Welfare Cost of Taxation

By EDGAR K. BROWNING*

This paper develops a rigorous partial-equilibrium analysis of the determinants of the marginal welfare cost (MWC) of taxes on labor earnings. It shows that four key parameters interact to determine the magnitude of MWC. Using aggregate data and plausible ranges of values for the parameters, MWC can vary from under 10 percent to more than 300 percent of marginal tax revenue, suggesting that, given available evidence, we cannot estimate MWC with much precision.

The marginal welfare cost of raising tax revenue is now understood to be an important factor in the analysis of government expenditure policies, and several recent studies have developed estimates suggesting its size is substantial.[1] In general, these studies have concluded that the marginal welfare cost is significantly larger than I found in my early study (1976). For example, I concluded that marginal welfare cost was likely to be between 9 and 16 percent of additional revenue raised, but Charles Ballard, John Shoven, and John Whalley (1985) suggest that it is in the 15 to 50 percent range, with Charles Stuart (1984) reporting similar results. Developing an analysis that clarifies why the estimates differ so markedly is a major purpose of the present paper.

Both Stuart and Ballard et al. employ general-equilibrium methodologies, while I used a simple partial-equilibrium formulation based on Arnold Harberger's (1964) approach. It is apparently widely believed that this difference in methodologies is responsible for the difference in results, with the general-equilibrium approaches capturing some essential elements that are missing in the partial-equilibrium approach. I do not believe that this is the case; almost all of the differences in results can be traced to different assumptions about key parameter values.

To support this assertion, this paper develops the partial-equilibrium approach in a more careful and usable form, and shows that modest variations in four key parameters can account for much of the apparent differences in results. One of the virtues of the partial-equilibrium approach is that it clarifies the contribution these key parameters make to the final estimate, something that is often obscured in large-scale general-equilibrium models.[2]

Section I develops the theory necessary to estimate the total welfare cost due to labor supply distortions of the tax system. It also corrects an error in the original Harberger formulation that I used, which led to an underestimate of total and marginal welfare costs in my 1976 paper. Section II applies the theory to the calculation of the marginal welfare cost of raising tax revenue and shows that by varying four parameter values over a relatively narrow range, the estimated marginal welfare cost varies from under 10 percent to well over 100 percent.

I. The Total Welfare Cost

Here I will consider only the welfare cost that results from taxes on labor incomes, both because the theory is less controversial and because there is a greater consensus

---

*Department of Economics, Texas A&M University, College Station, TX 77843. I thank Charles Ballard, Donald Deere, Charles Stuart, and anonymous referees for comments on previous drafts.

[1] See Charles Ballard et al. (1985), Ingemar Hansson and Charles Stuart (1983), Stuart (1984), and David Wildasin (1984).

[2] This is especially true in the case of Ballard et al. (1985), where the model is a multisector, dynamic computational general-equilibrium model. On the other hand, the far simpler two-sector general-equilibrium model of Stuart does a better job of focusing on the importance of key parameter values. The model in the present paper is more in the spirit of Stuart's approach.

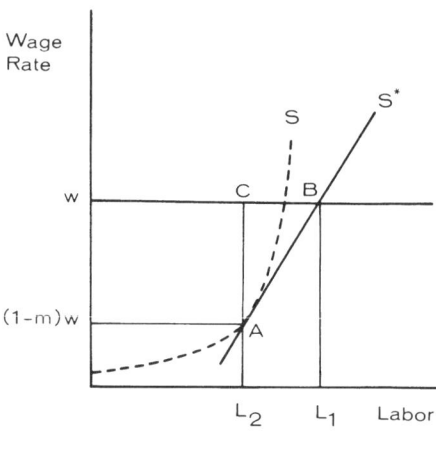

FIGURE 1

concerning empirical magnitudes than for taxes that fall on capital income. Figure 1 illustrates the usual representation of the welfare cost that results from a tax on labor income. The worker's wage rate is w (assumed to equal the marginal value product of his labor services), and labor earnings are subject to a tax at a marginal rate of m, so that the net marginal wage rate confronting the worker is $(1-m)w$. The equilibrium in the presence of the tax is at point A, where the quantity of labor supplied is L_2.[3] The compensated labor supply curve drawn for the utility level realized by the worker with the tax in place is S^*.[4] (Ignore supply curve S for the moment.) Thus, the total welfare cost is shown by area ACB, equal to the increase in earnings if the marginal tax rate is reduced to zero (but with the worker kept on the same indifference curve), CBL_1L_2, less the value of leisure given up in generating that increment in earnings, ABL_1L_2.[5]

It is important to recognize that area ACB is an exact measure of the welfare cost of the tax within the context of this model; there is no approximation involved. The key point is that I am using the compensated labor supply curve, which is necessary when evaluating welfare effects of changes in labor supply. However, note that this analysis is based on the assumption that the market wage rate remains unchanged when labor supply changes from L_2 to L_1. This assumption, common but not essential in partial-equilibrium models, differs from the general-equilibrium treatment in which the market wage rate is endogenously determined. The appropriateness of the fixed wage rate assumption will be discussed later.

To derive a formula that can be used to calculate the total welfare cost, it is assumed that the compensated labor supply curve is linear between L_2 and L_1. Then the welfare cost, W, equals one-half $CB \times AC$, or,

$$(1) \qquad W = \tfrac{1}{2}(dL)wm.$$

The compensated change in the quantity of

---

[3] It is important to understand that the line between $(1-m)w$ and A in Figure 1 should not be interpreted to mean that the marginal tax rate is necessarily constant regardless of the level of earnings. The welfare cost depends on the marginal tax rate at the actual earnings level, which is identified here as m; the marginal tax rate(s) that applies to inframarginal earnings may differ from this. Thus, Figure 1 should not be taken to imply a proportional tax, but only to emphasize that it is the tax rate at the margin (evaluated at the worker's actual equilibrium position) that produces the distortion in the allocation of resources. In particular, note that if the tax is progressive, tax revenue will not be equal to the rectangle $wCA(1-m)w$; it will be smaller than this because the marginal tax rate that applies to earnings below wL_2 is less than m.

[4] This compensated supply curve is drawn for the utility level realized by the worker after adjustment to the tax and whatever benefits are received from government expenditures. Government expenditures are held constant along the compensated supply curve.

[5] Although Peter Diamond and Daniel McFadden (1974) have proposed a different measure of welfare cost, I believe this continues to be the standard measure. Put differently, area ACB is equal to the difference between the tax revenue actually collected and the revenue that could be collected with a lump sum tax that leaves the taxpayer on the same indifference curve that he attains under the actual tax. This is equivalent to the measure defended by J. A. Kay (1980) in his criticism of Diamond and McFadden; Kay describes the measure as the difference between tax revenue and the equivalent variation measure of the loss in consumers' surplus from the tax. By contrast, the Diamond-McFadden measure uses the compensating variation measure of the change in consumers' surplus and the tax revenue that would hypothetically be collected at the compensated equilibrium.

labor supplied can be expressed as the inverse of the slope of the compensated supply curve, dL/dw, times the change in the marginal wage rate, wm, so

$$(2) \qquad W = \tfrac{1}{2}\left[\frac{dL}{dw}wm\right]wm.$$

Multiplying by $L_2(1-m)/L_2(1-m)$ yields

$$(3) \qquad W = \tfrac{1}{2}\left[\frac{dL}{dw}\frac{w(1-m)}{L_2}\right]\frac{m^2}{1-m}wL_2.$$

Note that the term in brackets equals the elasticity of the compensated supply curve evaluated at the net of tax wage rate (point A in Figure 1). Expressing this compensated labor supply elasticity as η, equation (3) can be conveniently written as[6]

$$(4) \qquad W = \tfrac{1}{2}\eta\frac{m^2}{1-m}wL_2.$$

In contrast to equation (4), the widely used Harberger formula for calculating the welfare cost is

$$(5) \qquad W = \tfrac{1}{2}\eta m^2 wL.$$

It is easily shown that the Harberger formula correctly evaluates the welfare cost if we measure the compensated elasticity and the level of labor earnings at their undistorted levels, that is, at point B in the diagram. However, these values are not observable, and available estimates pertain to elasticities and earnings evaluated in the presence of distorting taxes, that is, at point A in the diagram. Consequently, equation (4) will generally be the appropriate way to estimate the total welfare cost of a tax on labor earnings.

In my earlier paper (1976), I started with (Harberger's) equation (5) and from it developed expressions to estimate the marginal welfare cost. This procedure led to an underestimate of total and marginal welfare costs; my earlier estimates should be multiplied by (approximately) $1/(1-m)$ to correct for this error. This is one reason why recent general-equilibrium studies have generally found larger welfare costs—an error in my use of, rather than a true shortcoming of, the partial-equilibrium approach.[7] I avoid this error here by not relying on the Harberger formula.

Before turning to the issue of marginal welfare cost, it will be helpful to consider the application of this approach to the estimation of the total welfare cost, in part because this clarifies several points that are also relevant for the estimation of marginal welfare costs. For this purpose, I propose to use equation (4) with aggregate rather than individual data. If all households confronted the same marginal tax rate and had the same labor elasticity, this approach would yield the correct result. However, as can easily be shown, when marginal rates and/or elasticities differ, this common approach understates the welfare cost, and the understatement is larger the greater the dispersion in marginal tax rates and elasticities. Although I do not believe the actual dispersion is large enough to greatly affect the estimates (at least relative to the other factors I wish to emphasize here), the downward bias of this approach should be kept in mind.[8]

---

[6] Note that the average tax rate does not enter into the determination of the welfare cost according to equation (4). However, this does not mean that the average tax rate plays no role; it can influence the welfare cost through its indirect effect on the labor supply elasticity and earnings. For example, for an unchanged marginal tax rate, a higher average tax rate will increase the wL term if leisure is normal, and since the worker ends up on a different indifference curve, the compensated supply elasticity may also be affected. To apply equation (4) correctly, we do not need to know the average tax rate, but we do need to know the compensated supply elasticity and earnings at the worker's actual equilibrium position, thereby incorporating whatever effect the average tax may have through these terms.

[7] This error in the use of the Harberger formula has been pointed out in Christopher Findlay and Robert Jones (1981).

[8] Jerry Hausman (1981) uses disaggregated data in his work estimating welfare costs. Potentially, this approach will yield more accurate estimates, but there are some serious problems with his implementation of this approach (see my 1985b paper), and he does not provide estimates that permit a comparison of the dif-

To apply equation (4), we require estimates of aggregate labor earnings, a weighted-average compensated labor supply elasticity for workers as a group, and a weighted-average marginal tax rate for workers as a group. Although the greatest uncertainty surrounds the appropriate value for the labor supply elasticity, there is no point in reviewing once again the econometric literature, and I will simply use values of 0.2, 0.3, and 0.4 here. While values substantially larger than 0.4 have been used in the literature, it seems unlikely to me that a value much in excess of this figure is plausible.[9]

The only subtle point to recognize in choosing a value for aggregate labor earnings is that labor supply should be valued at the marginal value product of labor since the theory is based on the tax wedge between the marginal value product and the net wage received by workers. (See Figure 1 where w is the marginal value product.) In the absence of indirect taxes collected from firms (and some other factors mentioned below), wage earnings received by workers would represent the appropriate magnitude. However, because of the employer portion of the Social Security payroll tax, fringe benefits, and indirect output taxes (sales and excise taxes), reported wage and salary incomes must be grossed up to a broader measure of before-tax labor compensation. A rough estimate of the required figure for 1984 is $2400 billion.[10] This compares with wage and salary income of only $1800 billion.

The weighted-average marginal tax rate should reflect the combined effect of all taxes and transfers in reducing the net marginal wage rate received by workers below the marginal value product of labor. Thus, the marginal tax rate should be measured relative to the broad before-tax measure of labor income. This means that statutory tax rates are not the appropriate values to use. To see this, consider the Social Security payroll tax which was levied at a 14.1 percent combined employer-employee rate in 1984. If a worker increases his labor supply sufficiently to receive an additional $100 from his employer, he actually had to generate $107.05 in additional product since the employer portion of the tax ($7.05) is remitted to the government before the worker is paid. Thus, the marginal tax rate that applies to the worker's marginal value product is $14.10/$107.05, or 13.2 percent rather than 14.1 percent (assuming no other indirect taxes, fringe benefits, and so on).

Similarly, the effective marginal tax rate of personal income taxes is below the statutory

---

ference when aggregate data are used. An example of how sensitive the results are to dispersion in marginal tax rates is provided by the following. Consider three workers with respective earnings of $10,000, $20,000, and $30,000, who confront marginal tax rates of 30, 37, and 44 percent, respectively. With a compensated labor supply elasticity of 0.3, using equation (4) with the individual data and summing yields an estimate of $2400 for the total welfare cost. Using aggregate data—$60,000 for earnings, 0.3 for the elasticity, and the weighted-average (weights equal to share of total labor income) marginal tax rate of 39.4 percent—the estimate is $2305, only 4 percent less than the correct figure. Of course, the difference will be larger if the differences in marginal tax rates are greater. However, my paper with William Johnson (1984, Table 3) found that the average effective marginal tax rates for the top four quintiles of households range only from 39 to 47 percent when all taxes and implicit marginal tax rates of transfers are taken into account. Of course, there is also variation in marginal tax rates within quintiles, so the degree of understatement may be larger than these figures suggest.

[9] Numerous references to the relevant literature are contained in my paper with Johnson, Ballard et al. (1985), and Stuart. It should be noted that both Stuart and Ballard et al. use upper bound values for the compensated labor supply elasticity that exceed the 0.4 figure used in this paper. Stuart uses a value of 0.836; while Ballard et al. do not explicitly give the value they use, based on Table 1 of Ballard et al. (1982), the figure is apparently about 0.6. These figures seem too high to me, although there is some empirical evidence to support such values. Note that with a marginal tax rate of 43 percent, a compensated labor supply elasticity of 0.6 implies that reducing the marginal tax rate to zero in a compensated fashion would increase labor supply by 45 percent.

[10] The *Economic Report of the President* (1985, Table B-21) gives total compensation of employees (which includes the employer contribution to Social Security and some fringe benefits) for 1984 as $2173 billion. To this can be added the approximate $147 billion in sales and excise taxes which, according to M. Kevin McGee (1985), can be taken to fall on labor income. In addition, I assume that $80 billion of the $155 billion in proprietors' income represents labor compensation.

marginal tax rate that applies only to taxable income as defined by the tax laws. The significance of this point is evident from a comparison of the results of recent studies by Robert Barro and Chaipat Sahasakul (1983) and John Seater (1984). Barro and Sahasakul estimate a weighted-average marginal tax rate in 1980 for the federal individual income tax of 30.4 percent; this is simply an average of statutory marginal tax rates weighted by adjusted gross income. For the same year, Seater estimated a weighted-average marginal tax rate of 22.2 percent, but he arrived at his estimate by relating actual tax payments to variations in adjusted gross income (rather than to taxable income). For purposes of evaluating the labor supply distortions of taxes, the Seater approach comes closer to measuring the effective marginal tax rate that applies to the marginal value product of labor.[11]

In addition to measuring each tax's effective marginal tax rate consistently with respect to the same broad base, it is the combined marginal tax rate due to all factors that depress the marginal net wages received by workers that is relevant. Thus, the implicit marginal tax rates of means-tested transfer programs must also be included. One study that does measure marginal tax rates due to all taxes and transfers relative to a broad measure of income is my paper with William Johnson, which provides estimates for each quintile of households for 1976. A weighted average (weights equal to each quintile's share of labor income, broadly measured) of these marginal tax rates is 43 percent, and I will use this as my benchmark estimate for the effective marginal tax rate in 1984.[12]

There are, however, greater difficulties involved in accurately estimating the effective marginal tax rate than are commonly recognized, and the 43 percent figure should be viewed as subject to a significant margin for error.[13] For example, the Browning-Johnson estimate, as well as most others, treats the Social Security payroll tax as fully a distortion at the margin (except for those earning above the ceiling on taxable earnings). But if workers view, correctly or not, an additional dollar in Social Security taxes as purchasing deferred labor compensation in the form of a pension with a present value of a dollar, then the effective marginal tax rate of this tax would be zero.[14]

In view of this consideration, as well as others, it is appropriate to consider a range of values for the weighted-average effective marginal tax rate. Consequently, I use values of 38, 43, and 48 percent in the calculations. These estimates, together with the compensated labor supply figures (0.2, 0.3, and 0.4) and gross labor compensation ($2400 billion), can be inserted into equation (4) to estimate the total welfare cost of distorted labor supply decisions in 1984.

Table 1 displays the results, with the total welfare cost as a percentage of tax revenues from taxes that fall on labor income shown in parentheses.[15] What is perhaps most strik-

---

[11] To the extent that some exclusions and deductions are worth less at the margin than after-tax cash income, the approach used by Seater would understate the effective marginal tax rate to some degree.

[12] The Browning-Johnson estimate for 1976 is really a weighted-average marginal tax rate for labor and capital taxes together as they apply to an increment of labor and capital income. Insofar as the marginal tax rate on labor income is lower than the marginal tax rate on capital income, this figure would overstate the rate on labor income. However, since 1976, labor income has come to be taxed more heavily.

[13] See myself and Johnson, Barro-Sahasakul, and Seater for discussions of some of the technical problems.

[14] Three recent studies have investigated the linkage between social security taxes and future benefits (Roger Gordon, 1983; myself, 1985a; and Richard Burkhauser and John Turner, 1985), but with conflicting results. It seems quite possible, however, that the effective marginal tax rate of Social Security is somewhat less than the approximate 9 percentage point contribution it makes to the overall 43 percent rate cited above.

[15] Total tax revenues from taxes on labor income in 1984 are approximately $745 billion. This is the sum of Social Security payroll taxes ($242 billion), sales and excise taxes ($147 billion), state income taxes ($60 billion), and the federal individual income tax ($296 billion). Treating personal income taxes as falling fully on labor income rather than labor and capital income is something of an exaggeration, but because of the many special provisions favoring capital income contained in the income tax laws, the overstatement is probably not very large.

TABLE 1—TOTAL AND AVERAGE WELFARE COSTS, 1984
(Billions $)

m	η		
	0.2	0.3	0.4
0.38	$55.9	$83.8	$111.8
	(7.5)	(11.2)	(15.0)
0.43	77.9	116.8	155.7
	(10.5)	(15.7)	(20.9)
0.48	106.3	159.5	212.6
	(14.3)	(21.4)	(28.5)

Note: Percentages of tax revenues that fall on labor income are shown in parentheses.

ing is the wide range of the estimates: the welfare cost when $\eta = 0.4$ and $m = 48$ percent is nearly four times as large as when $\eta = 0.2$ and $m = 38$ percent. Varying the marginal tax rate alone from 38 to 48 percent approximately doubles the total welfare cost. The wide range of estimated welfare costs that results from use of a relatively narrow range of values for the two key parameters, η and m, shows how far we are from having reliable and precise estimates of the total welfare cost. Although my preferred parameter values are 43 percent and 0.3, the available empirical evidence certainly does not rule out the other possibilities; indeed, evidence can be cited to support a higher labor supply elasticity than 0.4.

Before turning to the extension of the analysis to marginal welfare costs, two reasons why this framework may overstate the total welfare cost should be discussed. (Recall, in addition, that use of aggregate data tends to work in the opposite direction.) First, this partial-equilibrium approach assumes the marginal value product of additional hours of work is constant. With a fixed capital stock, however, an increase in labor will reduce the marginal product of labor. How large a bias is introduced by assuming a fixed wage rate depends on the elasticity of the marginal product curve relative to the labor supply elasticity. With the demand elasticity high relative to the labor supply elasticity, the degree of overstatement is small. For example, with $\eta = 0.3$ and $m = 43$ percent, assuming the marginal value product curve has an elasticity of two implies that the true welfare cost would be about 15 percent less than estimated using equation (4) and assuming the wage is constant. Moreover, the actual elasticity of the marginal value product curve is likely to be higher than two. For example, with a Cobb-Douglas technology and a labor share, α, equal to 0.75, the elasticity of the marginal product of labor curve is $1/(1-\alpha)$, or 4.0. Thus, the partial-equilibrium assumption of a fixed wage is not likely to have a quantitatively important effect on the estimation of welfare cost.[16]

The second problem is potentially more troublesome, and relates to the assumption that the compensated labor supply curve is linear which underlies the derivation of equation (4). When the supply curve is not linear, equation (4) does not provide an exact estimate of welfare cost. If, as seems likely, the actual compensated supply curve is concave, as illustrated by S in Figure 1, the estimate provided by equation (4), area ACB, will overstate the true welfare cost. The available evidence provides little basis for determining how much of a bias the assumption of linearity introduces. However, for my purposes, it is most important to note that when the approach developed here is extended to the measurement of marginal welfare cost, it is not necessary to assume linearity. Thus, estimates of marginal welfare cost may be more reliable than those of total welfare cost.

---

[16] Taking into account possible changes in the market wage rate when labor supply varies raises one other potentially important issue that is ignored here. When labor supply rises, the wage rate falls and the rate of return to the fixed capital stock rises. Thus, capital income rises and tax revenue from capital taxes will also rise. This general-equilibrium effect is potentially important for the estimation of marginal welfare costs that relate welfare costs to changes in revenue. Note that Stuart does not take this relationship into account in his model since he assumes that there are no taxes on capital income. It is not clear whether this effect is incorporated in the Ballard et al. (1985) model or not. Assuming a fixed wage rate, as here, sidesteps this issue since capital income is then unaffected by changes in labor supply, but the importance of this point deserves further investigation.

II. Marginal Welfare Cost

The marginal welfare cost is the ratio of the change in total welfare cost to the change in tax revenue produced when tax rates are varied in some specified way. With W representing the total welfare cost and R total tax revenue, it is simply dW/dR. Figure 2 illustrates the numerator, dW, of the marginal welfare cost ratio. When the marginal tax rate rises from m to m', there is a reduction in the quantity of labor supplied along the compensated supply curve to L_3. The increment in the total welfare cost produced by this increase in the marginal tax rate is shown by area $CDEA$.[17] Area $CDEA$ is dW; dividing this by the increase in tax revenues —which is not shown in the diagram since it does not identify what happens to either the average tax rate or the actual (as distinct from the compensated) quantity of labor—measures the marginal welfare cost of raising additional revenue from taxes falling on labor income.

An expression to estimate the marginal welfare cost can be derived easily. Note that[18]

(6) $\qquad dW = \tfrac{1}{2}(wm + wm')dL_2.$

Since m' equals $m + dm$ and dL_2 equals $[\eta L_2/(1-m)]dm$, (6) can be rewritten as

(7) $\qquad dW = \left[\dfrac{m + 0.5\,dm}{1-m}\right]\eta w L_2\,dm.$

---

[17]This assumes that the incremental government expenditure restores the individual to the same indifference curve, and that the benefits from marginal government spending are a perfect substitute for disposable income, assumptions to be explained more fully later. Under these conditions, the compensated supply curve doesn't shift. Different assumptions regarding the incremental expenditures require a different interpretation of marginal welfare cost, as explained later in this section.

[18]Equation (6) depends on the assumption that the compensated supply curve is linear for the change in labor produced by the change in the marginal tax rate (dm), that is, between points E and A in Figure 2. In developing the results that follow, I assume $dm = 0.01$. However, dm can be assumed to be as small as desired, and in the limit as dm approaches zero, it is, of course, not necessary to assume linearity at all.

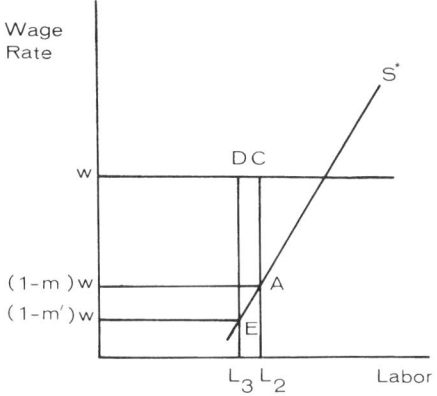

FIGURE 2

The change in tax revenue depends on how the average tax rate changes and on the change in actual labor income. It can conveniently be expressed as the sum of the additional tax revenue produced if earnings do not change and the revenue lost due to any reduction in earnings. Thus,

(8) $\qquad dR = wL_2\,dt + w\,dL(m + dm),$

where dt is the change in the average tax rate evaluated at the initial level of earnings, wL_2. The first term in (8) thus gives the additional revenue produced if the average rate rises by dt and labor income remains unchanged. The second term in (8) gives the revenue lost when earnings fall by wdL. Note that dL in (8) need not be equal to $L_3 - L_2$ in Figure 2; $L_3 - L_2$ is the compensated change in labor supply while dL is the actual change in labor supply.

Combining (7) and (8) gives us a simple expression for marginal welfare cost:

(9) $\qquad \dfrac{dW}{dR} = \dfrac{\left[\dfrac{m + 0.5\,dm}{1-m}\right]\eta w L_2\,dm}{wL_2\,dt + w\,dL(m+dm)}.$

In principle, equation (9) can be used to evaluate marginal welfare cost for any discrete change in tax rates, but to do so requires knowledge of how actual labor earnings, the wdL term, will be affected. In considering the effect on actual earnings, I should begin by noting that the conceptual experiment underlying the notion of marginal welfare cost is a balanced-budget operation in which the government spends the increment in tax revenue. This implies that the marginal welfare cost of raising additional tax revenue does not depend solely on the change in the tax system, but also on how the government spends the funds.[19]

The simple theory underlying equation (9) does not take into account the full range of possible ways expenditure side effects could reinforce or offset the added tax distortions of labor supply. It can, however, take into account government expenditures in an important special case. If the marginal government spending provides benefits that are a perfect substitute for the disposable incomes of taxpayers, then the spending has only an income effect that is equivalent to a lump sum transfer. (In other words, the marginal spending can be analyzed as a parallel shift in the after-tax budget constraint.) In this case, the income effect of the spending can be taken into account through its effect on the wdL term in equation (9). For example, if the marginal spending, in combination with the tax change, leaves taxpayers' utilities unchanged, the actual reduction in labor earnings, wdL, will equal the compensated change in labor earnings and can therefore be calculated using the assumed parameter values.

Although the assumption that government spending is a perfect substitute for disposable income is restrictive, it may be more widely applicable than it first appears. Note that the marginal change in government spending does not have to take the form of cash transfers for the assumption to be valid. In particular, if the government provides a service that taxpayers would otherwise have purchased on their own, then the spending would be a perfect substitute for disposable income. This may be largely correct in cases involving government provision of schooling, medical care, pensions, and other things taxpayers would purchase with their disposable incomes if the government did not provide them. Thus, treating government expenditures as a perfect substitute for disposable income appears reasonable and permits the simple framework employed here to incorporate expenditure side effects.

Granted this assumption, there are two polar cases that seem likely to span the range of plausible outcomes. First, marginal government spending is taken to provide no benefits to taxpayers, so there is an income effect from the balanced-budget operation that acts to counter the substitution effect. I assume that the net effect on actual labor earnings is zero, so the second term in the denominator of equation (9) is zero. In this case, the formula for marginal welfare cost simplifies to

$$(10) \quad \frac{dW}{dR} = \left[\frac{m + 0.5\,dm}{1 - m}\right] \eta \frac{dm}{dt}.$$

The second polar case to be considered is when marginal government spending provides benefits that return taxpayers to their initial (i.e., before the tax and expenditure change) utility levels. When this is so, the wdL term in equation (9) is equal to the change in compensated labor earnings, or $-[dm/(1-m)]\eta wL_2$. Substituting this for wdL in (9) and simplifying yields the following expression for marginal welfare cost in this case:

$$(11) \quad \frac{dW}{dR} = \frac{\left[\dfrac{m + 0.5\,dm}{1 - m}\right] \eta \dfrac{dm}{dt}}{1 - \left[\dfrac{m + dm}{1 - m}\right] \eta \dfrac{dm}{dt}}.$$

Equations (10) and (11) can be used to estimate marginal welfare cost for a discrete change in marginal tax rates under the assumed conditions. This analysis indicates

---

[19]Several recent papers have investigated the issue of balanced-budget changes and labor supply, both from the point of view of a positive analysis of labor supply (Assar Lindbeck, 1982; James Gwartney and Richard Stroup, 1983; Arthur Snow and Ronald Warren, 1985) and in connection with the determinants of marginal welfare cost (Wildasin).

that there are four key factors that interact to determine marginal welfare cost. Two of these, η and m, were also relevant in the estimation of total welfare cost. In addition, there are two other factors that were irrelevant for total welfare costs. The first is how the balanced-budget operation affects actual labor earnings, as reflected in the wdL term in equation (9) or in the choice between equations (10) and (11) for the two special cases I will examine. Second, equations (10) and (11) show that marginal welfare cost depends also on the parameter dm/dt. This term measures the progressivity of the *change* in the tax structure that produces the incremental tax revenue. As the equations show, the more progressive the tax change (the larger dm/dt is), the greater marginal welfare cost will be.

Since there are many different ways the tax structure could be modified to produce a change in revenue, dm/dt will depend on exactly how the tax structure is changed. Thus, we must consider the range of values that dm/dt could plausibly take on. The type of change in the tax system that would probably yield the smallest value for dm/dt would be to change the rates of sales or excise taxes, or to change the Social Security payroll tax rate. Raising additional revenue by increasing the rates of these taxes implies that the marginal tax rate would rise by less than the average tax rate;[20] a reasonable assumption might be that dm/dt equals 0.8.

At the other extreme, use of the federal individual income tax will typically imply that dm/dt is greater than one since this tax is progressive. With the marginal tax rate of the federal income tax nearly twice its average rate at most income levels, it seems reasonable to assume marginal tax revenue from this source implies $dm/dt = 2.0$.[21]

Between these two extremes, two other possibilities merit consideration. One is to consider a proportionate increase in the rates of all taxes simultaneously so that m/t remains unchanged. Since m equals 43 percent in my benchmark case and t equals 31 percent, this sort of change implies $dm/dt = 1.39$. The other possibility is to consider some change where dm/dt equals one; this would be appropriate if a proportional tax were added to the present tax structure. While these four values for dm/dt do not exhaust the possibilities, they probably encompass most changes we are likely to see in the tax system.

At this point, a graphical treatment of marginal welfare cost for the case in which the benefit from the expenditure returns the taxpayer to his (her) initial indifference curve may prove helpful. In Figure 3, the before-tax budget constraint relating income and leisure is YN, and the initial tax—drawn as a proportional tax for simplicity—produces the constraint Y_1N. The worker is initially at point E, with tax revenue equal to HY since HH is drawn parallel to YN. Now let us consider a small increase in the tax rate which, ignoring expenditure side effects, produces the constraint Y_2N, drawn exaggerated for clarity. Assume that the expenditure is a perfect substitute for disposable income and the benefit from the expenditure returns the

---

[20] An increase in the rates of sales and excise tax will reduce the real tax base of personal income taxes, and so the increment in the effective combined marginal tax rate will decline with income. To see this, suppose a general sales tax is introduced at a rate of 10 percent, and this reduces factor prices by 10 percent while the price level is unchanged. For a person in a 50 percent income tax bracket, the 50 percent rate now applies only to 90 percent of his marginal value product, so the effective marginal rate of the income tax is reduced to 45 percent, and the combined rate is 55 percent. Thus, the sales tax increased this person's effective marginal tax rate from 50 to 55 percent. By contrast, for a person initially in a 20 percent income tax bracket, the increase would be from 20 to 28 percent. For the Social Security payroll tax, the ceiling on taxable earnings implies that an increase in its rate would increase the overall average tax rate more than its weighted-average marginal tax rate.

[21] In 1984, the average tax rates at one-half median income, the median income, twice median income, and five times median income were, respectively, 5.9, 11.9, 16.0, and 26.1 percent. The corresponding marginal tax rates were 14.0, 22.0, 33.0, and 45.0 percent (Congressional Budget Office, 1984, Table VI-3). These are, however, statutory rates; the effective rates would be lower. It is also worth noting that Seater's estimate of a weighted-average marginal tax rate for the income tax in 1980 is 22.9 percent, nearly double its average rate of about 12 percent.

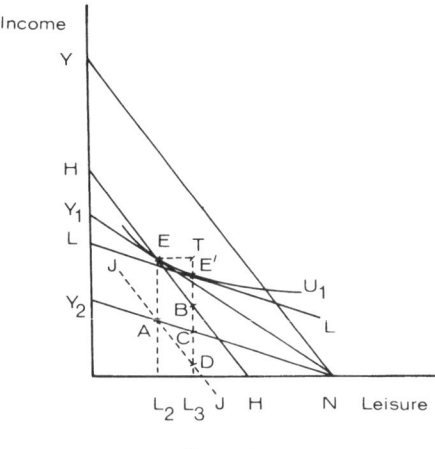

FIGURE 3

(BE'/CB) per dollar spent if taxpayers are to be benefited on balance.[22] Other definitions of marginal welfare cost are possible. Stuart, for example, defines marginal welfare cost as the loss that results when the incremental tax revenue is returned to the worker as a lump sum payment. This produces a measure of the loss when outlays are valued at their budgetary cost, but it is not the appropriate definition to use in conducting a cost-benefit analysis of an expenditure policy.[23]

Note that equation (9) will estimate BE'/CB exactly. The numerator measures dW as the difference between the compensated reduction in earnings using the market wage rate, TB, less the increment in the value of leisure, TE'. The denominator

worker to his initial indifference curve. Then the effect of the expenditure can be shown as a parallel shift in $Y_2 N$ to LL, with LL tangent to U_1 at point E'.

Since the additional tax revenue is CB given the new equilibrium with labor of NL_3, the benefit from the expenditure of CB must be valued at CE' to return the worker to his initial indifference curve. Note that the required benefit, CB, is BE' greater than the additional tax revenue; BE' is the additional welfare cost. Thus, the marginal welfare cost, dW/dR, is BE'/CB. It is a compensating variation measure of the change in surplus, and shows how much greater the benefits from government spending must be than the tax revenues collected if the balanced-budget operation is to keep the worker on his initial indifference curve.

This particular way of defining marginal welfare cost produces a measure that is relevant for determining whether government expenditures combined with the taxes that finance them will leave taxpayers on balance better or worse off. In Figure 3, note that if the benefit from the expenditure of CB is anything less than CE', the worker will be worse off than he was at E, while if it is anything greater than CE', he will be better off. Put more generally, the marginal benefits from government spending must be more than one plus the marginal welfare cost

---

[22] Note that this measure of marginal welfare cost, based on the compensating variation, is similar to that proposed by Diamond and McFadden. The only difference is that my definition uses the utility level actually achieved with existing taxes and expenditures, whereas theirs uses the before-tax utility level. Note also that it is not inconsistent to use an equivalent variation measure of total welfare cost (as in Section I) and a compensating variation measure of marginal welfare cost. When the analysis is intended to provide a measure of marginal welfare cost useful for cost-benefit analysis, as explained in the text, the compensating variation measure is appropriate.

[23] Stuart's measure and mine yield the same result in the special case of zero income effects. In this case, if the incremental tax revenue is returned as a lump sum, the final equilibrium in Figure 3 will be at point B since an indifference curve will be tangent to the budget constraint (incorporating the lump sum transfer) that is parallel to $Y_2 N$ and passes through B. Stuart's measure is then the loss, BE', divided by the incremental tax revenue, CB. However, if leisure is a normal good, work effort will be greater than NL_3 when the tax revenue is returned as a lump sum due to the worker's loss in real income. The final equilibrium will then lie to the left of point B on the EB portion of HH, and Stuart's measure of marginal welfare cost will be smaller than BE'/CB since incremental tax revenue will be greater and the additional welfare cost will be smaller. For this case, Stuart's measure has the defect that even when the marginal expenditure is valued at one plus marginal welfare cost, the final equilibrium involves the worker being worse off than at point E because the income effect of the expenditure will lead to less work effort than the lump sum transfer. Thus, Stuart's measure does not identify how much the benefits of the expenditure must exceed additional tax revenue to exactly compensate the worker.

TABLE 2—MARGINAL WELFARE COST PER DOLLAR OF REVENUE
(Percentages)

		$m =$	0.38			0.43			0.48		
	$\dfrac{dm}{dt}$	$\eta =$	0.2	0.3	0.4	0.2	0.3	0.4	0.2	0.3	0.4
Earnings	0.8		9.9	14.9	19.9	12.2	18.3	24.4	14.9	22.4	29.8
Constant	1.0		12.4	18.6	24.8	15.3	22.9	30.5	18.7	28.0	37.3
	1.39		17.3	25.9	34.5	21.2	31.8	42.4	25.9	38.9	51.9
	2.0		24.8	37.3	49.6	30.5	45.8	61.1	37.3	56.0	74.6
Earnings	0.8		11.0	17.6	24.9	13.9	22.5	32.4	17.6	28.9	42.7
Decline	1.0		14.2	23.0	33.2	18.0	29.8	44.2	23.0	39.0	59.9
	1.39		20.9	35.1	53.1	27.0	46.9	74.3	35.1	64.1	108.9
	2.0		33.2	59.8	100.0	44.1	85.2	159.7	59.9	128.8	303.1
Average Welfare											
Cost			7.5	11.2	15.0	10.5	15.7	20.9	14.3	21.4	28.5

measures dR as the sum of the increment in tax revenue if earnings remain unchanged, EA ($=DB$, since JJ is parallel to HH), less the reduction in taxes due to the actual (and compensated, in this case) reduction in labor supply, CD.[24]

III. Results

To sum up, the range of values for the four key parameters that will be used here are:

m: .38, .43, and .48;
η: 0.2, 0.3, and 0.4;
dm/dt: 0.8, 1.0, 1.39, and 2.0;
wL: Unchanged, and reduced by the compensated change.

Table 2 displays the results of using equations (10) (Earnings Constant) and (11) (Earnings Decline) to calculate the marginal welfare cost for the 72 possible combinations of parameter values for an increase in the marginal tax rate on one percentage point ($dm = 0.01$). The estimates range from a low of 9.9 percent to a high exceeding 300 percent! (Note, however, that only one combination of parameter values yields an estimate exceeding 159.7 percent.) If, as I believe to be the case, our empirical evidence and theory do not allow us to narrow substantially the range of possible parameter values from those used here, then we cannot provide a very precise estimate of the marginal welfare cost. My preferred estimates are based on $\eta = 0.3$, $m = 43$ percent, and $dm/dt = 1.39$, implying that marginal welfare cost would lie between 31.8 and 46.9 percent, depending on what assumption is made about the extent to which tax payers benefit from the marginal government spending. It would be difficult, however, to defend these parameter values as necessarily more accurate than others used in the table.

The results here suggest that marginal welfare cost is significantly larger than implied by my 1976 paper. In part, the difference is due to correction of the error discussed above in Section I. The 9 to 16 percent range of my earlier paper was based on parameter values of (approximately) $\eta = 0.2$, $m = .43$, $dm/dt = 1.0$ and 1.39, with earnings constant. Table 2 shows the corrected estimates for these values would be 15.3 and 21.2 percent. The remaining difference in results, however, is due to the use here of a wider range of parameter values. What was not clear in my earlier paper, but Table 2 brings out forcefully, is how sensitive the results are to the combination of parameters used.

Even though this model is far simpler than the general-equilibrium models of Stuart and

---

[24] For a graphical treatment that can be used to show marginal welfare cost when the taxpayer is not returned to his original indifference curve, in which case an equivalent variation measure is used; see Figure 3 in my paper with Johnson. In this diagram, marginal welfare cost is DE/AH.

Ballard et al. (1985), the results seem quite similar for comparable parameter values. The approach used here yields estimates that are moderately larger than the Stuart model, but corrected for two differences in assumptions the results differ only negligibly.[25] Comparison with Ballard et al. is more difficult, since they are not explicit concerning all the parameter values emphasized here and their model also evaluates distortions other than the labor supply distortion. However, their general conclusion that marginal welfare cost is likely to be in the range of 15 to 50 percent accords well with the results in Table 2.

IV. Concluding Remarks

Other things the same, general-equilibrium results are to be preferred to partial-equilibrium results. Until it is shown that the general-equilibrium models provide significantly different and more accurate estimates (for the same parameter values), however, the partial-equilibrium approach has some advantages. First, it is easily understood, so it is less likely that critical assumptions will be obscured. The sensitivity of the results to the four key parameter values is quite apparent in this treatment, for example. Second, it is simple for other investigators to perform sensitivity analysis by modifying the assumptions regarding parameter values if such changes seem appropriate. Finally, on a more substantive matter, the results here seem to imply that arriving at a more precise estimate of marginal welfare cost may well depend more on empirical investigation that narrows the range of possible parameter values than on developing more rigorous models that yield slightly better estimates for given parameter values.

An important point concerning the proper use of estimates of marginal welfare cost is in order. These estimates are intended to provide the basis for comparing the costs with the benefits of government expenditure policies that do not have as a major consequence or goal a redistribution of income. Marginal welfare costs are relevant in analyzing redistributive programs, but the estimates here do not indicate how large the relevant effects are. For this purpose, it is necessary to estimate the costs borne by the group that loses separately from the benefits received by the group that gains, along the lines suggested by myself and Johnson.[26] In general, the relevant marginal welfare costs of redistribution are several times larger than the marginal welfare costs reported here. Basically, the reasons are that both the taxpayer's and recipient's decisions are distorted by a redistributive policy, and marginal tax rates necessarily rise quite sharply in comparison to the amounts redistributed.[27]

Finally, it should be recalled that the estimates relate only to the labor supply distortions of taxes. Actual taxes distort behavior on a number of other margins of choice, and ignoring these probably means that the estimates here understate the marginal welfare cost of raising tax revenue, subject to the usual second-best qualifications. Further research to incorporate these effects into the analysis would be worthwhile.

REFERENCES

Ballard, Charles L., Shoven, John B. and Whalley, John, "General Equilibrium Computations of the Marginal Welfare Costs of Taxes in the United States," *American Economic Review*, March 1985, 75, 128–38.

---

[25] The first difference is that Stuart defines marginal welfare cost as the loss resulting when the expenditure is a lump sum transfer back to taxpayers. The second difference is that Stuart's general-equilibrium model effectively incorporates a downward-sloping marginal value product curve. These are not the only differences in the models, but they appear to account for most of the differences in results.

[26] In this connection, it is unfortunate that Stuart refers to one of his marginal welfare cost measures as relevant for analyzing redistributional social programs. In Stuart's model, this refers to the case where the revenues are returned to the taxpayer as a lump sum payment. Since Stuart's model is based on a single aggregate household, there is no real redistribution involved in this case, and this measure of marginal welfare cost gives no clue to the relevant distortions produced by redistributive programs.

[27] I have explained in greater detail the relationship between the marginal welfare cost of raising tax revenue as discussed here and the marginal welfare cost of redistributing income in my 1986 paper (Section IV).

———, ———, and ———, "The Welfare Cost of Distortions in the United States Tax System: A General Equilibrium Approach," NBER Working Paper No. 1043, 1982.

Barro, Robert J. and Sahasakul, Chaipat, "Average Marginal Tax Rates from Social Security and the Individual Income Tax," NBER Working Paper No. 1214, 1983.

Browning, Edgar K., "The Marginal Cost of Public Funds," *Journal of Political Economy*, April 1976, *84*, 283–98.

———, (1985a) "The Marginal Social Security Tax on Labor," *Public Finance Quarterly*, July 1985, *13*, 227–51.

———, (1985b) "A Critical Appraisal of Hausman's Welfare Cost Estimates," *Journal of Political Economy*, October 1985, *93*, 1025–34.

———, "The Marginal Cost of Raising Tax Revenue," in Phillip Cagan, ed., *Essays in Contemporary Economic Problems*, Washington: American Enterprise Institute, 1986.

——— and Johnson, William R., "The Trade-Off between Equality and Efficiency," *Journal of Political Economy*, April 1984, *92*, 175–203.

Burkhauser, Richard V. and Turner, John A., "Is the Social Security Payroll Tax a Tax?," *Public Finance Quarterly*, July 1985, *13*, 253–67.

Diamond, P. A. and McFadden, D. L., "Some Uses of the Expenditure Function in Public Finance," *Journal of Public Economics*, February 1974, *3*, 3–21.

Findlay, Christopher C. and Jones, Robert L., "The Marginal Costs of Australian Income Taxation," manuscript, Australian National University, 1981.

Gordon, Roger H., "Social Security and Labor Supply Incentives," *Contemporary Policy Issues*, April 1983, *3*, 16–22.

Gwartney, James and Stroup, Richard, "Labor Supply and Tax Rates: A Correction of the Record," *American Economic Review*, June 1983, *73*, 446–51.

Hansson, Ingemar and Stuart, Charles, "Tax Revenue and the Marginal Cost of Public Funds in Sweden," manuscript, University of California-Santa Barbara, 1983.

Harberger, Arnold C., "Taxation, Resource Allocation, and Welfare," in *The Role of Direct and Indirect Taxes in the Federal Revenue System*, NBER Other Conference Series No. 3, University Microfilms, 1964.

Hausman, Jerry A., "Labor Supply," in Henry J. Aaron and Joseph A. Pechman, eds., *How Taxes Affect Economic Behavior*, Washington: Brookings Institution, 1981.

Kay, J. A., "The Deadweight Loss from a Tax System," *Journal of Public Economics*, February 1980, *13*, 111–19.

Lindbeck, Assar, "Tax Effects Versus Budget Effects on Labor Supply," *Economic Inquiry*, October 1982, *20*, 473–89.

McGee, M. Kevin, "The Burden of Taxation Revisited," manuscript, University of Wisconsin-Oshkosh, 1985.

Seater, John J., "On the Construction of Marginal Federal Personal and Social Security Tax Rates in the U.S.," manuscript, North Carolina State University, 1984.

Snow, Arthur and Warren, Ronald S., Jr., "Labor Supply and Tax Rates in General Equilibrium," manuscript, Georgetown University, 1985.

Stuart, Charles, "Welfare Costs per Dollar of Additional Tax Revenue in the United States," *American Economic Review*, June 1984, *74*, 352–62.

Wildasin, David E., "On Public Good Provision with Distortionary Taxation," *Economic Inquiry*, April 1984, *22*, 227–43.

U.S. Congress, Congressional Budget Office, *Reducing the Deficit: Spending and Revenue Options*, Washington, USGPO, February 1984.

U.S. Council of Economic Advisers, *Economic Report of the President*, Washington: USGPO, 1985.

[14]

THE TOTAL WELFARE COST OF THE UNITED STATES TAX SYSTEM: A GENERAL EQUILIBRIUM APPROACH****

CHARLES L. BALLARD,* JOHN B. SHOVEN,** AND JOHN WHALLEY***

ABSTRACT

We use a computational general equilibrium model of the United States economy to examine the combined welfare cost of all taxes in the U.S. revenue system. We estimate that the present value of the gain from replacing the distortionary tax system with certain lump-sum taxes would be between 13 cents and 24 cents per dollar of revenue, depending on elasticity assumptions. Corporate taxes and income taxes generate the greatest welfare losses. Equalization of tax rates across sectors would lead to large gains, as would replacing the existing tax system with a consumption-type value-added tax.

1. Introduction

THE purpose of this paper is to provide estimates of the welfare cost of various parts of the tax system in the United States, as well as estimates of the welfare cost of the entire system. Most earlier studies[1] have focused on only one portion of the tax system at a time. However, because of the interdependencies among different taxes within the economic system, it is not possible to analyze a single tax in isolation in a satisfactory way. The estimates here are produced by a medium-scale computational general equilibrium model of the economy and tax system. By using such a model, we are able to assess the different taxes in a consistent fashion. We account simultaneously for all interactions in the economy, and we do not have to ignore income effects or use approximations.

A problem in the interpretation of welfare loss estimates is that they frequently are reported as a fraction of GNP. Against this yardstick, the cost of any distortion is likely to appear quite small. We feel that the appropriate procedure is to compare the welfare loss with the revenue that is gained from the tax. When we divide the welfare loss by the revenue, we get the "coefficient of inefficiency." (See Shoven [1976]). In this paper, we present the welfare losses in dollar terms, but we also present the coefficient of inefficiency for each portion of the tax system. If all distortionary taxes were replaced with a set of lump-sum levies, the present value of the welfare gain is in the range of $1.86 trillion to $3.36 trillion, in 1973 dollars,[2,3] for values of factor supply elasticities that we consider most reasonable. The annual value of these efficiency costs is from 13 to 24 percent of revenues raised. We also consider replacement of different parts of the tax system with lump-sum taxes. The most distortionary taxes are those which fall on capital and personal income, while the labor or payroll taxes such as those on Social Security are the least distortionary. This suggests that the tax system could be made more efficient by increasing some taxes and decreasing others.[4]

Obviously, replacing the existing tax system with lump-sum taxes is not a realistic policy option. However, we have also experimented with replacing the existing tax system with broadly-based but still distortionary taxes. If the only tax were a value-added tax of the consumption type, more than half of the welfare cost of the tax system could be eliminated. We also simulate the effects of equalizing tax rates across sectors. These policies also produce sizable welfare gains.

Our calculations suggest that the economic efficiency of the tax system is very important. If the welfare costs of distortionary taxes are this large, then it is difficult to accept the view that microeconomic issues are of secondary importance compared to macroeconomic ones. Our results indicate that Harberger triangles may not be nearly as small as Harberger (1964) himself believed them to be.

---
*Michigan State University.
**Stanford University and National Bureau of Economic Research.
***University of Western Ontario.

2. A General Equilibrium Model of the U.S. Economy and Tax System

A. Basic Model Structure

To keep the focus of this paper on results and policy implications, only a brief overview of model structure is given here. We provide a very detailed description of our model in Chapters 3-7 of Ballard, Fullerton, Shoven, and Whalley (1985).

First, we summarize the production side of the model. In any single period, there are 19 producer good industries that use capital and labor in constant elasticity of substitution (CES) value-added functions. They also use the outputs of other industries through a matrix of fixed input-output coefficients. Tax rates on labor for each industry are derived by taking payroll taxes and other contributions as a proportion of labor income, while tax rates on capital for each industry are derived by taking corporate income, corporate franchise, and property taxes as a proportion of capital income. Each of these 19 producer goods is used directly for investment, for net exports, and by the government. The transformation of producer goods into consumer goods is represented by a matrix of fixed coefficients. This procedure is necessary because the goods classification of consumer expenditure data is different from the classification of the outputs of the 19 production sectors.

On the consumer side of the model, we have 12 consumer groups, which are distinguished by their money income[5] in 1973 (the basic data year for the model). Each consumer group has an initial endowment of capital and labor. Consumer decisions regarding factor supplies are made jointly with their consumption decisions. Each household at any point in time has a nested CES utility function of the form:

$$U = U\left[H\left(\prod_{i=1}^{15} X_i^{\lambda i}, \ell\right), C_f\right] \quad (1)$$

where H is the instantaneous utility function defined over current consumption commodities X_i and leisure ℓ, and the function U determines the allocation between current welfare and expected future consumption, C_f. Current consumption commodities X_i are aggregated using a Cobb-Douglas function, whereas both U and H are CES functions. When U is maximized subject to a budget constraint, we get a desired level of C_f for each consumer. The demand for C_f is then translated into demand for saving in the current period. The latter is, in turn, translated into a vector of investment demands for the 19 industry outputs.[6]

With the utility structure of equation (1), the consumer divides current income between current consumption and saving. This process is repeated for infinite time, since we assume that the consumers are infinitely-lived. This approach stands in contrast to the approach of Summers (1981), Auerbach and Kotlikoff (1983), and others, who use a lifetime utility function that is maximized subject to a lifetime wealth constraint. Their formulation is elegant, but it has its disadvantages. As Starrett (1982), Evans (1983), and Ballard (1985) have pointed out, the approach of Summers and others can generate implied saving elasticities that are extremely high. The implied saving elasticity in these models is not very robust to changes in assumptions and parameters. On the other hand, with the approach used here, any saving elasticity can be specified exactly and imposed on the model. The same is true with the labor supply elasticity. Thus, with our type of model, the researcher has more control over the elasticities. This is a distinct advantage.

B. Sources of and Adjustments to the Data

Government collects taxes from both the production and demand sides of the economy and uses the revenue to purchase producer goods (with constant expenditure shares), make direct transfer payments to consumers, and subsidize government enterprises. The government always balances its budget in the model. A simple trade sector closes the model.

We specify our model with data from 1973 because this is the most recent year during which the Department of Labor conducted a Consumer Expenditure Survey. In addition to this survey, we use four other major data sources. These are the July, 1976, *Survey of Current Business*, the Bureau of Economic Analysis Input-Output Matrix, unpublished worksheets of the U.S. Department of Commerce National Income Division, and the U.S. Treasury Department's Merged Tax File. Adjustments are made so that the data are mutually consistent. All data on industry and government uses of factors are accepted as given, while the data on consumer factor incomes and expenditures are correspondingly adjusted. Tax receipts, transfers, and government endowments are accepted as given, and government expenditures are adjusted in order to yield a balanced budget. Similar adjustments guarantee that supply equals demand for all goods and factors, and that trade is balanced.

The fully consistent data set defines a single-period benchmark equilibrium in terms of transactions. These observations on values are separated into prices and quantities by assuming that a physical unit of a good or factor is the amount that sells for one dollar. All benchmark equilibrium prices are $1, and observed values are the benchmark quantities.

The equilibrium conditions of the model are then used to determine the behavioral equation parameters, consistent with the benchmark data set. This procedure calibrates the model to the benchmark data, in the sense that the benchmark data can be reproduced as an equilibrium solution to the model before any policy changes are considered. In order to implement this procedure, we specify the elasticities of substitution between capital and labor in each industry, on the basis of the econometric literature. We also specify labor supply and saving elasticities, to which substitution elasticities in preferences are calibrated. Factor employments by industry are used to derive production function weights, and expenditure data are used to derive utility function weights. This calibration procedure allows for a test of the solution and ensures that the various agents' behaviors are mutually consistent in our benchmark data before we evaluate policy changes.

C. Parameter Selection

The elasticities of labor supply and saving are important for our results, so it is appropriate to discuss our choices. There are a large number of estimates for the uncompensated elasticity of labor supply with respect to the real, net-of-tax wage. Reviews of the literature can be found in Borjas and Heckman (1978), Ballard, Fullerton, Shoven, and Whalley (1985), Killingsworth (1982), and Stuart (1984). Many of the studies of male labor supply behavior find negative uncompensated elasticities. Female labor supply elasticities are positive and often very large. Some of the larger estimates have come in recent studies that deal carefully with a variety of econometric issues.

We choose a central case value of 0.15 for each of our consumer groups, which we take as a weighted average of plausible estimates for males and females. We use this value to select the elasticity of substitution between present consumption and present leisure for the "H" function in equation (1) for each consumer. To test the sensitivity of the model, we also use a zero uncompensated labor supply elasticity. Even though we specify the labor supply decision in our model on the basis of an uncompensated elasticity, we still can compute the implied compensated elasticities. The compensated elasticities differ among our different consumer groups but they tend to exceed the uncompensated elasticities by about 0.3 for the functional forms and parameter values employed here.

The other key parameter is the elasticity of saving with respect to the real, after-tax rate of return. We use the value of this elasticity to choose values for the elasticity of substitution between present consumption, H, and future consumption, C_f, for each consumer.

There is considerable controversy in the econometric literature regarding the value of the uncompensated saving elasticity.

For a long time, the consensus appeared to favor a zero value for this elasticity. This proposition was termed Denison's Law, after Denison (1958). In more recent work, Boskin (1978) has estimated this elasticity to be approximately 0.3 to 0.4. On the other hand, Summers (1981) derives savings elasticities between 1.5 and 3.0, by parameterizing an overlapping generations life cycle model. Each of these studies has problems of technique and interpretation. In particular, for reasons outlined in the paper by Starrett (1982), Summers's elasticity figures may be high. We report simulations using the values of 0.0 and 0.4 for the saving elasticity. As is to be expected, the excess burdens increase as the saving elasticity increases. If the elasticity were in the range suggested by Summers, the welfare gains from removing all distortions would be more than twice as great as those reported here.

Another important parameter is the steady-state growth rate of the benchmark equilibrium sequence. To derive this rate, we compare the amount of observed 1973 saving to the capital stock. This gives us a rate of growth of capital, which is 2.8 percent per year. We then assume that the number of effective units of labor grows at the same rate. The 2.8 percent labor growth rate is assumed to be equally divided between Harrod-neutral technical change and population growth. Our welfare measures of tax changes are adjusted to account only for the initial size of population.

A final important parameter is the real net-of-tax return to capital in the benchmark data. Since this value is used to calibrate preference parameters under the assumption of intertemporal utility maximization, it also determines the rate of time preference in the benchmark sequence of equilibria. We use four percent for the average value of the parameter, but each income class receives a net-of-tax return that depends on its own marginal tax rate.

D. Model Treatment of Taxes

In order to help the reader assess the validity of our results, it is important to explain our treatment of the various taxes in the model.

In Table 1, we present a summary of the way in which we model the effects of the various taxes and a brief description of problems with each case. Even with a model of this complexity it is impossible to completely capture the operation of each tax. Further, for some (like the corporate tax) the profession has not reached consensus on the appropriate way to model it. On the basis of this modeling, we calculate tax rates. Table 2 includes some summary information about these tax rates. The figures in Table 2 suggest that capital taxes should be candidates for being major sources of welfare cost. Defining capital tax rates as a proportion of gross income, we find that the *average* tax rate on capital at the industry level is about 45 percent. (Note that we do not incorporate the reduction in capital tax rates which was part of the 1981 Economic Recovery Tax Act. For a study of the effects of these changes, see Fullerton and Henderson [1983].)[7]

In contrast to capital taxes, labor taxes (Social Security and other contributions) raise a large amount of revenue, without rates which are high or widely dispersed. Marginal income tax rates are high, on average. In addition, the income tax rates differ substantially among consumers. In our model, each of the 12 consumer groups faces a linear income tax schedule. The rates rise from 0.01 for the poorest group to 0.41 for the richest.

Consumer sales and excise tax rates average about 6.7 percent, and the rates for most goods are reasonably low. However, there are three notable exceptions. The tax rate on alcoholic beverages is 0.875, on tobacco, 0.958, and on gasoline and other fuels, 0.295.

Now that we have discussed the levels of the various types of taxes, we shall consider their economic effects. The key distortions created by the income tax deal with factor supplies. It is widely recognized that the income tax distorts labor supply decisions. In addition, the supply of new capital through saving is affected by the "double taxation" of saving. Double taxation is mitigated partially by tax

TABLE 1

United States Taxes and Their Treatment in the Model

Tax	Treatment	Difficulties of Model Treatment
1. Corporate taxes (including state and local) and corporate franchise taxes	Ad valorem tax on use of capital services by industry	Some argue for treatment as a lump sum tax; model treatment ignores role of financial instruments
2. Property taxes	Ad valorem tax on use of capital services by industry	Differential rates across jurisdictions ignored
3. Social Security taxes, Unemployment Insurance, and Workmen's Compensation	Ad valorem tax on use of labor services by industry	Benefit related nature of contributions; arbitrary distinction between public and private insurance programs
4. Motor vehicles tax	Ad valorem tax on use of motor vehicles by producers	In practice, a yearly registration fee and not a purchase tax; averaging over jurisdictions
5. Retail sales taxes	Ad valorem tax on purchases of producer goods	Averaging of rates over states
6. Excise taxes	Ad valorem tax on output of producer goods	Taxes often expressed as charge per unit physical measure such as volume
7. Other indirect business taxes and non-tax payments to government	Ad valorem tax on output of producer goods	Payments depend on output levels by industry to only limited extent; averaging of rates over states
8. Personal income taxes (including state and local)	Linear function for each consumer; thirty percent of savings currently tax sheltered	Detailed deductions and exemptions not specifically considered in model

TABLE 2

LEVEL AND DISPERSION OF TAX RATES IN 1973

Type of Tax	Sectors on Which Tax is Levied	Weights	Weighted Statistics		
			Mean of Marginal Tax Rates	Standard Deviation	Coefficient of Variation[b]
Capital Taxes at Industry Level	19 Industries	Capital Use	0.452	0.136	0.300
Labor Taxes at Industry Level	19 Industries	Labor Use	0.092	0.008	0.086
Consumer Purchase Taxes	15 Goods	Total Consumption	0.053	0.080	1.531
Output Taxes	18 Industries[a]	Output	0.010	0.017	1.641
Motor Vehicle Taxes[c]	Intermediate Use of Motor Vehicles in 19 Industries	Use of Motor Vehicles	0.050	0.000	0.000
Personal Income Taxes	12 Consumer Groups	Income	0.239	0.101	0.424

[a]The statistics shown here are for all of the industries except the government enterprises industry. This industry receives a subsidy, which we model as a negative tax rate. If we were to calculate these statistics for all 19 industries, the mean would be 0.008, the standard deviation 0.018, and the coefficient of variation 4.612.

[b]Coefficients of variation will not equal the quotients of the corresponding standard deviations and means because of rounding in the standard deviations and means.

[c]The motor vehicle tax is uniform across industries.

shelters (such as Individual Retirement Accounts). We model the U.S. tax system of 1973 by assuming that 30 percent of saving is sheltered through pension funds, insurance companies, and other forms of retirement-saving.

Another aspect of the effect of the income tax on factor supplies is the fact that consumers with higher incomes face higher marginal tax rates. Since saving is heavily concentrated in the top tail of the income distribution, much of the saving in the economy occurs where the tax rates are highest.[8] On the other hand, labor supply is much more widely diffused. Consequently, the effective rates on labor income are lower, on average, than those facing capital income.

In addition to factor supply decisions, the income tax also has important features which distort choices among industries and commodities. The most prominent of these is the preferential treatment of housing which results from the absence of tax on the imputed income of owner-occupied housing. This is compounded by preferential treatment for capital gains on houses. These features of the tax law combine to create substantial static resource allocation and intertemporal distortions.

In modeling the corporate tax, we follow in the tradition of Harberger (1962, 1966) who treats it as a partial factor tax. More recently, this treatment has been the subject of active debate. It has been argued that the corporate tax acts as a tax on the return to equity, rather than on the total return to capital invested in the corporation. Stiglitz (1973) has argued further that if all marginal investments by firms are debt financed, the corporate tax operates as a lump-sum tax. However, so many features of corporate financial behavior remain unexplained that we follow Harberger's procedure of treating the corporate tax as an *ad valorem* tax on capital, with average and marginal rates the same. Thus the corporate tax misallocates capital services among industries in the economy, since tax rates differ by industry. In addition, the tax affects saving decisions, since savers who acquire corporate equity have to pay a higher tax rate on the return to their saving than they would pay in the absence of the tax.

Similarly to the corporate tax, we treat the property tax as a differential tax on capital by sector. This falls most heavily on residential housing, but structures in other capital-using industries in the economy are also liable for the tax. As with the corporate income tax, both static and dynamic distortions occur.

Consumer sales taxes have a variety of effects. Even if the sales tax system covers all commodities evenly, it still distorts labor supply decisions. Additional distortions come from the nontaxation of food and other exempted items. The specific excises on alcohol, tobacco, and gasoline are sharply discriminatory in our model, since we treat them (along with sales taxes) as *ad valorem* taxes. However, we recognize that this treatment could be challenged. The taxes on alcohol and tobacco could be defended as externality-correcting, and the gasoline tax defended as a benefit-related fee for the use of the highway system.

The last major component of the tax system consists of payroll taxes for Social Security, unemployment insurance taxes, and workmen's compensation taxes. We treat these as *ad valorem* taxes on labor at the industry level, rather than as benefit-related charges, because the correspondence between taxes and benefits for any individual is very rough.

E. Calculations

Through their interaction, utility-maximizing consumers and profit-maximizing producers are assumed to reach a single-period competitive equilibrium where all profits are zero and supply equals demand for each good and factor. Starting with data on endowments, tax rates, preferences, and production parameters, we use either Merrill's (1972) algorithm (a revised version of Scarf's (1973) algorithm) or the Factor Price Revision Rule of Kimbell and Harrison (1984) to calculate prices that satisfy these conditions at each point in time. These algorithms can accommodate any number of sectors and agents. The model can handle a number of large distortions and evaluate the effects of simultaneous changes in any of them without linearity assumptions and without ignoring income effects. This allows us to appraise tax policy changes which are of sufficient magnitude to cause interactive effects throughout the economy.

Many of the general equilibrium models which exist today can calculate only a single equilibrium. Consequently, they are poorly equipped to analyze the relative importance of intertemporal and intersectoral distortions. Our model calculates a sequence of equilibria, covering an arbitrarily long period of time. The equilibria are tied together by endogenous saving decisions and exogenous growth of labor endowments. This allows us to assess intertemporal distortions as well as intersectoral ones.

For the benchmark sequence of equilibria, we assume that the economy was on a balanced growth path in 1973. The first equilibrium in the sequence replicates the 1973 data. Subsequent equilibria are merely scaled-up versions of the initial equilibrium. Prices remain constant, and all quantities grow at the same rate (the rate of growth of the effective labor force). We then alter tax parameters and calculate a revised sequence of equilibria. Since we compute a complete set of prices and quantities under alternative tax policies, we can estimate the changes in utility or income for each consumer group, changes in national income, and all new factor allocations among industries.

Clearly, we cannot calculate an infinite sequence of equilibria. Instead, we calculate equilibria a certain number of years into the future and then calculate a termination term. The welfare evaluation in the termination term will be precisely correct if the economy is on a steady-state growth path, as is the case in our base case sequence of equilibria. In a revised case sequence, the tax change causes a transition toward a new steady-state growth path. In this case, the termination term calculations will only be approximate, with the accuracy of the approximation becoming better as the economy settles more closely toward the new steady-state growth path. Our calculations of average excess burden involve huge changes in relative prices, so that the approach to the new steady-state takes a very long time. In order to improve the accuracy of the approximation in the termination term, we carry our equilibrium calculations 100 years into the future, by calculating 21 equilibria spaced five years apart. The results would not change greatly if we were to choose a different number of years between equilibrium calculations. See Ballard and Goulder (1982) for a discussion of the sensitivity of the results from this model to changes in the spacing of equilibria.

We calculate each consumer's utility in each period from current consumption and leisure. Then we take the present value of these utilities, for the before-change sequence and the after-change sequence. For each consumer, we compute the financial transfer necessary to equate the present values in the absence and presence of the tax change. The sum of these figures across the 12 households is our measure of the dynamic welfare change. This calculation is in the spirit of the static Hicksian equivalent variation.

3. Calculations of Total and Average Welfare Costs of Distortionary Taxes

For most of the simulations reported in this section, we remove all taxes, and replace them by lump-sum levies in proportion to personal income taxes and sales taxes paid. These are the only two parts of the tax system for which the legal incidence (although not the economic incidence) can be attributed to consumers directly. By assigning the lump sums in this manner, we make a crude attempt to abstract from income effects and concentrate on the efficiency aspects of the tax system.

In Table 3, we report the welfare gain from this tax change for four different combinations of factor supply elasticities. It seems to us that these welfare gains are very substantial, even for the case in which both the uncompensated labor supply elasticity and the uncompensated saving elasticity are zero. Even under these fairly

TABLE 3

WELFARE GAINS FROM REPLACING EXISTING DISTORTIONARY TAXES
WITH LUMP SUM TAXES IN PROPORTION TO INCOME AND
SALES TAXES PAID, FOR DIFFERENT ELASTICITIES

Saving Elasticity	Labor Supply Elasticity	Welfare Gain (in billions of 1973 dollars)	Gain as Percentage of Base Case Revenues	Gains as Percentage of Base Case GNP
0.4	0.15	$3,357.1	23.8%	6.9%
0.4	0.0	2,692.4	19.1	5.6
0.0	0.15	2,333.3	16.6	4.8
0.0	0.0	1,862.0	13.2	3.8

inelastic assumptions, the welfare gain from replacing the distortionary taxes exceeds one-eighth of revenues. For comparison purposes, we also report the gains as a proportion of GNP, even though we have argued that GNP is not the most appropriate yardstick against which to measure the welfare changes. We see that the welfare cost of distortionary taxes is in the range of four to seven percent of GNP. This result is consistent with results from Piggott and Whalley (1985), for a model of the UK tax system.

Of all the changes in behavior which contribute to this welfare improvement, the most notable are those dealing with the accumulation of capital. In the case of the first simulation in Table 3, saving is 80 percent higher in the initial equilibrium than it was in the initial period of the base sequence. In addition, saving continues at high levels: saving after 100 years of the revised sequence outstrips the corresponding figure for the base sequence by 70 percent. The continued high level of saving is the result of two offsetting forces. First, as capital becomes more abundant, its relative price decreases. Since we have a positive saving elasticity, this causes less saving, *ceteris paribus*. However, the increased capital stock makes the economy wealthier. Given our functional form assumption for the saving decision, this leads to an increase in saving, *ceteris paribus*. In the 100 years covered by this sequence of equilibria, the capital/labor ratio increases by 31 percent.

As we have said, this simulation involves large movements in relative prices. In the first period, the price of capital relative to the price of labor rises from 1.0 in the base case to 2.133 in the revised case. (Recall that prices are defined as *net* of taxes.) Capital deepening then causes the price to fall, steeply at first and less steeply later on as the economy approaches its new steady-state growth path. The price of capital ultimately settles down at about 1.16. This time path of capital prices implies that, in the short run, capital taxes are borne by capital, as suggested by Harberger's (1962) incidence analysis of the corporate tax. In the longer run, however, as Feldstein's (1974) work on variable factor supply indicates, the burden of these taxes is increasingly shifted to labor.

In short, the system of distortionary taxes causes the economy to have much less capital than it would otherwise have, even if the revenues were recovered by lump-sum taxes. The return to capital is lower than it would be in the absence of distortionary taxes, and there is a substantial welfare loss.

Labor supply increases in response to the removal of tax distortions, but the increase is not nearly so large (relatively) as the increase in saving. Of course, this flows directly from our assumptions about factor supply elasticities. Labor supply in the revised sequence is higher than in the base sequence by more than 18 percent in the first period and more than 15 percent in the final period. Consumption of goods rises instantaneously by eleven percent. This is possible, despite the large increase in saving, because of the increase in labor supply. In the final period of the revised sequence (i.e., after 100 years), consumption is 33 percent higher than in the base sequence.

The simulations indicate that the lightly-taxed agriculture and real estate industries are larger under the present tax system than they would otherwise be, while the heavily-taxed metals and machinery industry is smaller.

In Table 4, we break down the results of Table 3 by calculating the welfare gains associated with removing the major groups of distortionary taxes, using the same combinations of labor supply and saving elasticities. A complication is caused by the fact that one of the output tax rates is negative. We model the subsidies to government enterprises as a negative tax on the output of that industry. To avoid difficulties in the interpretation of the coefficients of inefficiency, our simulations of the removal of output taxes only involve industries other than government enterprises.

Table 4 indicates that capital taxes at the industry level and income taxes are the most important causes of distortion on average. This is not surprising in view of the fact that growth of the capital stock is so important for long-term welfare improvements. Also, as seen in Table 2, these taxes are the ones with the highest rates.

From Table 4, we see that the coefficient of inefficiency of each part of the tax system rises as the assumed factor supply elasticities rise. The rank order of the coefficients of inefficiency barely changes when we consider different elasticities. Generally speaking, the capital taxes and income taxes are very costly in efficiency terms, while the output taxes and labor taxes (such as the Social Security payroll tax) are more efficient producers of revenue.

Because lump-sum levies are so unlikely ever to be adopted in practice, it is interesting to ask whether a broadly-based tax system, with relatively undifferentiated rates, can give similarly large gains. We simulate replacing the existing distortionary system with a value-added tax (VAT) of the consumption type.[9] The VAT leads to substantial capital deepening. The welfare gain from the adoption of a VAT is very substantial. In the case of a labor supply elasticity of 0.15 and a saving elasticity of 0.4, the gain is nearly 55 percent of the gain from replacing the tax system with a lump-sum tax. In the case of zero factor supply elasticities, the VAT gain is nearly 85 percent of the lump-sum gain. This may seem surprisingly high. The reason for this is that the income effects from the lump-sum simulation and the simulation of the VAT are substantially different. In our model, the upper income groups have the highest propensities to save. Consequently, highly progressive lump-sum schemes like the one we have used here will lead to less saving than less progressive schemes. We therefore ran another simulation, in which the existing tax system is replaced by a set of lump-sum taxes allocated according to income in the base case.[10] The welfare gain associated with this type of lump-sum replacement is substantially higher, ranging from 28 percent to 52 percent greater than the gain from the other type of lump-sum replacement, depending on the elasticities. This illustrates an important point. In a model with many consumers who have different endowments and preferences, the effect of a lump-sum tax will depend upon the distribution of the lump-sum tax among the consumers. Each consumer is a unique "distortion filter," and the ability of a policy change to offset existing distortions will depend upon the amount of tax owed by each of the consumers in the new situation. When consumers face different marginal tax rates, the social

TABLE 4

WELFARE GAIN FROM REPLACING DIFFERENT PORTIONS
OF THE TAX SYSTEM WITH LUMP-SUM TAXES

	Welfare Gain in Billions of 1973 Dollars				Coefficient of Inefficiency: Welfare Gain per Dollar of Revenue			
Labor Elasticity	0.0	0.0	0.15	0.15	0.0	0.0	0.15	0.15
Saving Elasticity	0.0	0.4	0.0	0.4	0.0	0.4	0.0	0.4
Taxes Removed								
1. All Distortionary Taxes	$1862.0	$2692.4	$2333.3	$3357.1	13.2¢	19.1¢	16.6¢	23.8¢
2. Capital Taxes at the Industry Level	558.5	1194.3	582.8	1314.5	15.0	32.1	15.7	35.5
3. Labor Taxes at the Industry Level	249.9	291.9	391.4	444.8	8.1	9.5	12.7	14.5
4. Personal Income Taxes	948.3	1293.9	1354.3	1723.3	21.3	28.0	29.4	37.4
5. Output Taxes	87.5	116.2	123.1	156.8	10.9	13.9	15.2	19.4
6. Consumer Sales and Excise Taxes	273.6	314.9	372.4	423.6	13.3	15.3	18.2	20.6
a. Taxes on Alcohol, Gasoline, and Tobacco Only	229.8	252.8	282.6	311.0	23.6	26.2	29.3	32.3
b. Taxes on Other Goods	21.6	39.8	71.5	94.2	1.8	3.7	6.4	8.7

marginal utility of a dollar of income will depend on which consumer receives the income.

Because we do not use an explicit lifecycle model, we do not emphasize the distributional results of these simulations. Nevertheless, it is important to recognize that the changes that lead to the greatest welfare gains often are highly regressive. In many cases, the richest group is the only one to reap significant gains. In these cases, there is a strong tradeoff between equity and efficiency. We plan to explore the equity/efficiency issue in greater detail in the near future.

The gains from these policies are summarized in Table 5. We also consider another type of broad-based replacement tax. This is a proportional wage tax. Table 5 shows that, under all but one of our elasticity combinations, this policy is actually a welfare-losing proposition. There are two main reasons for this, each of which is similar to the reasons for the results in Auerbach, Kotlikoff, and Skinner (1983).

The VAT taxes the return to old capital. Thus, the VAT has a lump-sum component that is missing from the wage tax. Moreover, since the wage tax involves a narrowing of the tax base, the tax rates necessary to maintain equal revenue yield are very high (in the vicinity of 55 percent). When the entire tax burden is placed on a single margin (the labor-leisure choice in this case), it can cause severe distortions.

Not only the level but also the dispersion of tax rates is important to the welfare cost of taxation. For each major portion of the tax system, we would like to know how much welfare loss is due to *high* taxes, and how much is due to taxes which discriminate among industries, goods, or consumer goods. In the case of taxes on capital at the industry level, this amounts to an analysis of intertemporal distortions versus interindustry distortions.

We have already reported that the taxes on capital at the industry level have a welfare cost of $559 billion to $1,315 billion in present value terms, depending on the elasticities. The coefficients of inefficiency range from 15 cents per dollar of revenue to 35 cents per dollar. How much of an improvement would we have if we were to equalize these rates at the average level? (In other words, what is the welfare cost of maintaining a tax system with differentiated rates?) As shown in Table 6, these welfare costs range from $415 billion to $461 billion, or from 11.2 cents to 12.4 cents per dollar of revenue, depending on the elasticity assumptions. In the case of zero uncompensated elasticities, the gain from rate equalization is nearly 75 percent as great as the gain from replacing the capital taxes with lump-sum taxes. If the assumed factor supply elasticities are higher, the gain from rate equalization is only about 35 percent of the gain from removal of the capital taxes. This difference is explained as follows. By far the most important effect of equalizing the capital tax rates is intersectoral; there is relatively little dynamic effect. If the saving elasticity is assumed to be small, then dynamic effects are relatively less important, so that the effects of rate equalization comprise a large portion of the total effects.

Intersectoral distortions are relatively important for the consumer sales taxes. Just the opposite is true of the taxes on labor at the industry level. Equalization of these rates produces a negligible effect. These results are not surprising in light of the data in Table 2. That table showed that the coefficient of variation of labor taxes is minuscule, while capital tax rates are moderately variable and consumer purchase tax rates are highly variable. It might seem surprising that equalization of the output tax rates has so small an effect. However, it should be noted that, since we do not change the tax rate on the government enterprises industry, we do not reduce the variation in these tax rates as much as we might have. More importantly, the output taxes feed through the imput-output matrix to create an ultimate pattern of tax incidence that is very widely dispersed by industry.

Finally, we can ask what would happen if the rates were equalized within every portion of the tax system (i.e., capital tax rates, income tax rates, etc., are all set to their average values). We see that the gains are greater than $1 trillion in pres-

TABLE 5

WELFARE GAINS FROM REPLACING THE ENTIRE EXISTING
TAX SYSTEM WITH VARIOUS TYPES OF TAXES

	Welfare Gain in Billions of 1973 Dollars				Coefficient of Inefficiency: Welfare Gain per Dollar of Revenue			
Labor Elasticity	0.0	0.0	0.15	0.15	0.0	0.0	0.15	0.15
Saving Elasticity	0.0	0.4	0.0	0.4	0.0	0.4	0.0	0.4
Type of Tax Replacement								
1. Lump-Sum Tax in Proportion to Income and Sales Taxes Paid	$1862.0	$2692.4	$2333.3	$3357.1	13.2¢	19.1¢	16.6¢	23.8¢
2. Lump-Sum Tax in Proportion to Income	2836.5	3526.3	3392.8	4288.9	20.1	25.0	24.0	30.4
3. Consumption-Type Value-Added Tax	1581.4	1847.7	1458.3	1834.7	11.2	13.1	10.4	13.0
4. Proportional Wage Tax	-74.8	675.4	-1320.5	-253.6	-0.5	4.8	-9.4	-1.8

TABLE 6
WELFARE GAINS FROM EQUALIZING TAX RATES FOR VARIOUS GROUPS OF TAXES

Type of Tax Equalized		Welfare Gain In Billions Of 1973 Dollars		Gains As Percentage Of Gain From Replacing This Group Of Taxes With Lump-Sum Taxes	
	Labor Elasticity	0.0	0.15	0.0	0.15
	Savings Elasticity	0.0	0.4	0.0	0.4
Capital Taxes at the Industry Level		$415.4	$460.6	74.4%	35.0%
Consumer Sales Taxes		254.3	266.5	92.9	62.9
Personal Income Taxes		486.6	577.1	51.3	33.5
Output Taxes[a]		16.7	16.6	19.1	10.6
All Groups of Taxes[b]		1139.2	1280.9	61.2	38.2

[a] Tax rates are set to the mean value for the 18 industries other than government enterprises. The subsidy to government enterprises is not changed.

[b] This includes equalization of labor tax rates by industry which are not reported separately because the gains from equalization are negligible.

ent value terms. This is more than 60 percent of the gain from replacing the tax system with lump-sum taxes, if the assumed factor supply elasticities are zero, and nearly 40 percent in the case of the larger elasticities. The implication for tax policy is clear: large welfare gains could accrue if we were to equalize tax rates.

4. Conclusion

Most of the earlier studies using this model have focused on specific policy proposals, such as corporate tax integration or the consumption tax. The present paper is designed to give more general guidance to policy. The central message of this paper is that the welfare losses caused by distortionary taxation can be very large. We estimate that the gain from replacing the distortionary tax system with certain lump-sum taxes would be in the range of 13 cents to 24 cents per dollar of revenue. Replacing the existing system with a consumption-type value-added tax would also yield very large gains.

The greatest causes of inefficiency are the heavy taxation of capital at the industry level, and of personal incomes. Each of these leads to substantial intertemporal distortion. Both intertemporal distortions and intersectoral distortions are quite large. We should note, however, that these results were achieved with data from 1973, when capital taxes were higher than they are now. The tax changes passed in 1981 amounted to a substantial reduction in marginal taxes on corporate capital. These changes will move us in the right direction (see Fullerton and Henderson [1983]). Nevertheless, we believe that there is still a good deal of room for improvement in the efficiency of the tax code. For one thing, under one set of elasticity assumptions we find that equalizing the tax rates across sectors, goods, or consumers for the various parts of the tax system would lead to gains with a present value of almost $1.3 trillion, or about nine percent of revenue.

It is hoped that the numbers presented here will give the reader some perspective on the relative magnitudes of the welfare costs of distortionary taxes. This will help to judge the results from other studies. We also hope that our results on the different efficiency costs of high and variable tax rates in different parts of the tax system will help the reader to assess different types of distortions. However, we suggest using some caution in interpreting the results. The welfare costs of the tax system are certainly very large, but equity considerations should also be taken into account when judging any tax change. We have not emphasized the equity effects of our simulations, in part because the present model does not capture lifecycle effects. Still, there is reason to believe that some of the tax changes reported here would be substantially disequalizing. For example, when we replace the entire tax system with a value-added tax, we remove the progressive personal income tax and replace it with an indirect tax that is likely to be regressive. Nevertheless, the main result of this paper is that total efficiency costs of distortionary taxes are very large. Sensible economic policymaking ought to take these efficiency costs into account.

FOOTNOTES

****We are grateful to Don Fullerton, Karl Scholz, and Joel Slemrod for helpful comments. We are responsible for any remaining errors. We thank Karen Platz and Debby Baer for preparing the manuscript. Thanks for financial support are expressed to the National Bureau of Economic Research and its Project on the Government Budget and the Private Economy and to Stanford University's Center for Economic Policy Research.

[1] See, for example, Harberger (1964).

[2] We will report our results in 1973 dollars, because our model is specified with 1973 data.

[3] The lump-sum taxes in question were assigned in proportion to income and sales taxes paid by the 12 consumer groups in our model. Different methods of assigning the lump-sums lead to different welfare gains. This point is discussed further in our results section.

[4] A similar conclusion is reached in another paper (Ballard, Shoven, and Whalley [1985]) in which we calculate *marginal* excess burdens. Our results here accord generally with our marginal excess burden results. The marginal excess burdens are larger than the average excess burdens, as the theory would predict. Also, those parts of the tax system that have the largest average excess burdens also tend to have the largest marginal excess burdens. However, the uses to which the two types of calculations can be put are somewhat different. The marginal excess burden figures tell us the incremental welfare cost of increasing overall government spending, and financing the spending with distortionary taxes. The figures in the present paper tell us the welfare gains that would result from replacing existing distortionary taxes with lump-sum taxes. Thus, they give us an upper bound for the gains that could be realized by rearranging the system of distortionary taxes. In future work, we plan to continue this line of research by calculating the set of taxes that would be optimal in the model.

[5] These are incomes as defined for the 1973 Consumer Expenditure Survey.

[6] The simulations reported here employ the assumption of myopic expectations. Because of this assumption, the current rate of return and other current prices are all that we require to formulate a budget in terms of prices for present and future consumption. In an earlier paper (Ballard, Shoven, and Whalley [1982]), we used the algorithm developed by Ballard and Goulder (1982) to study the sensitivity of our results with respect to the expectational structure. We found that our results are fairly robust with respect to the assumptions on consumer beliefs about future prices. Therefore, our calculations are of myopic sequences of equilibria, since these are less expensive to compute.

[7] Our 45 percent rate of taxation of capital at the industrial level contrasts with the 37 percent figure of King and Fullerton (1984) for the U.S. corporate sector and their 29 percent average figure for total capital stock. Their numbers were derived by examining the tax law for 81 combinations of investors, financial instruments, assets, and industries and taking a weighted average of the 81 tax rates. Our number is simply a ratio of taxes paid to gross income. Our figures are for 1973 and theirs 1980. It may be that the average tax rate on capital income declined over that period, and, if so, the dead weight loss of those taxes would have also declined. However, it should be pointed out that the variance in the rates across sectors and asset types has, if anything, increased, thereby offsetting to some extent the efficiency gain from the lower average rates.

[8] Our model exaggerates this effect, since we do not capture life-cycle differences among households.

[9] We get the same results, regardless of whether we model an origin-based or destination-based VAT. For an explanation of this equivalence, see Goulder, Shoven, and Whalley (1983). Note that the model of the VAT here does not include deductions for certain favored classes of commodities. Therefore, this version of a VAT is likely to be more efficient than some of the versions suggested in popular proposals.

[10] Allocation according to income has been used in some of the earlier papers using this model, e.g., Fullerton, King, Shoven, and Whalley (1981).

REFERENCES

Auerbach, Alan J., and Laurence J. Kotlikoff. "National Savings, Economic Welfare, and the Structure of Taxation." In Martin S. Feldstein (ed.), *Behavioral Simulation Methods in Tax Policy Analysis*. Chicago: University of Chicago Press, 1983.

Auerbach, Alan J., Laurence J. Kotlikoff, and Jonathan Skinner. "The Efficiency Gains from Dynamic

Tax Reform." *International Economic Review* 24 (February 1983): 83–100.

Ballard, Charles L. "Comment on Auerbach and Kotlikoff, 'Simulating Alternative Social Security Responses to the Demographic Transition.'" *Mathematical Programming Study*, (1985), forthcoming.

Ballard, Charles L., Don Fullerton, John B. Shoven, and John Whalley. *A General Equilibrium Model for Tax Policy Evaluation*. Chicago: University of Chicago Press, 1985, forthcoming.

Ballard, Charles L., and Lawrence H. Goulder. "Expectations in Numerical General Equilibrium Models." Factor Markets Workshop Research Paper No. 31, Stanford University, (1982).

Ballard, Charles L., John B. Shoven, and John Whalley. "The Welfare Cost of Distortions in the United States Tax System: A General Equilibrium Approach." National Bureau of Economic Research Working Paper No. 1043, December, 1982.

Ballard, Charles L., John B. Shoven, and John Whalley. "General Equilibrium Computations of the Marginal Welfare Costs of Taxes in the United States." *American Economic Review*, 1985, forthcoming.

Borjas, George J., and James J. Heckman. "Labor Supply Estimates for Public Policy Evaluation." *Proceedings* of the Industrial Relations Research Association (1978): 320–31.

Boskin, Michael J. "Taxation, Saving, and the Rate of Interest." *Journal of Political Economy* 86 (April 1978): S3–S27.

Denison, Edward F. "A Note on Private Saving." *Review of Economic Statistics* 40 (August 1958): 261–67.

Evans, Owen J. "Tax Policy, the Interest Elasticity of Saving, and Capital Accumulation." *American Economic Review* 73 (June 1983): 398–410.

Feldstein, Martin. "Incidence of a Capital Tax in a Growing Economy with Variable Savings Rates." *Review of Economic Studies* 41 (October 1974): 505–13.

Fullerton, Don, and Yolanda K. Henderson. "Long Run Effects of the Accelerated Cost Recovery System." Discussion Paper No. 20R, Woodrow Wilson School, Princeton University, February, 1983.

Fullerton, Don, A. Thomas King, John B. Shoven, and John Whalley. "Corporate Tax Integration in the United States: A General Equilibrium Approach." *American Economic Review* 71 (September 1981): 677–91.

Goulder, Lawrence H., John B. Shoven, and John Whalley. "Domestic Tax Policy and the Foreign Sector: The Importance of Alternative Foreign Policy Formulations to Results from a General Equilibrium Tax Analysis Model." In Martin S. Feldstein (ed.), *Behavioral Simulation Methods in Tax Policy Analysis*. Chicago: University of Chicago Press, 1983.

Harberger, Arnold C. "The Incidence of the Corporation Income Tax." *Journal of Political Economy* 70 (June 1962): 215–40.

———. "Taxation, Resource Allocation, and Welfare." In John F. Due, ed., *The Role of Direct and Indirect Taxes in the Federal Revenue System*. Princeton, N.J.: Princeton University Press, 1964.

———. "Efficiency Effects of Taxes on Income from Capital." In Marian Krzyzaniak (ed.), *Effects of Corporation Income Tax*. Detroit: Wayne State University Press, 1966.

Killingsworth, Mark R. *Labor Supply*. New York: Cambridge University Press, 1982.

Kimbell, Larry J., and Glenn W. Harrison. "General Equilibrium Analysis of Regional Fiscal Incidence." In Herbert E. Scarf and John B. Shoven (eds.), *Applied General Equilibrium Analysis*. New York: Cambridge University Press, 1984.

King, Mervyn A., and Don Fullerton (eds.), *The Taxation of Income from Capital: A Comparative Study of the U.S., U.K., Sweden, and West Germany*. Chicago: University of Chicago Press, 1984.

Merrill, O. H. "Applications and Extensions of an Algorithm that Computes Fixed Points to Certain Upper Semi-Continuous Point-to-Set Mappings." Unpublished Ph.D. dissertation, University of Michigan, 1972.

Piggott, John, and John Whalley. *Efficiency and Distributional Aspects of U.K. Taxes: An Applied General Equilibrium Approach*. New York: Cambridge University Press, 1985, forthcoming.

Scarf, Herbert E. (with collaboration of Terje Hansen). *The Computation of Economic Equilibria*. New Haven, Conn.: Yale University Press, 1973.

Shoven, John B. "The Incidence and Efficiency Effects of Taxes on Income from Capital." *Journal of Political Economy* 84 (December 1976): 1261–84.

Starrett, David A. "Long Run Savings Elasticities in the Life Cycle Model." Factor Markets Workshop Research Paper No. 24, Stanford University (1982).

Stiglitz, Joseph E. "Taxation, Corporate Financial Policy, and the Cost of Capital." *Journal of Public Economics* 2, No. 1 (1973): 1–34.

Stuart, Charles E. "Welfare Costs Per Dollar of Additional Tax Revenue in the United States." *American Economic Review* 74 (June 1984): 352–62.

Summers, Lawrence H. "Capital Taxation and Accumulation in a Life Cycle Growth Model." *American Economic Review* 71 (September 1981): 533–44.

D
Taxes and Revenues

ON THE POSSIBILITY OF AN INVERSE RELATIONSHIP BETWEEN TAX RATES AND GOVERNMENT REVENUES

Don FULLERTON*

Princeton University, Princeton, NJ 08544, USA
The National Bureau of Economic Research

Received December 1980, revised version received December 1981

When Arthur Laffer and other 'supply side advocates' plot total tax revenue as a function of a particular tax rate, they draw an upward-sloping segment called the normal range, followed by a downward-sloping segment called the prohibitive range. A brief literature review indicates that tax rates on the prohibitive range in theoretical and empirical models have been the result of particularly high tax rates, high elasticity parameters, or both. The labor tax rate which maximizes total revenue, for example, will depend on the assumed labor supply elasticity. This paper introduces a new curve which summarizes the tax rate and elasticity combinations that result in maximum revenues, separating the 'normal area' from the 'prohibitive area'. A general-purpose empirical U.S. general equilibrium model is used to plot the Laffer curve for several elasticities, and to plot the newly introduced curve using the labor tax example. Results indicate that the U.S. could conceivably be operating in the prohibitive area, but that the tax wedge or labor supply elasticity would have to be much higher than most estimates would suggest.

1. Introduction

Ever since Arthur B. Laffer first drew his famous curve on a napkin in a Washington restaurant seven years ago, there has been considerable public debate about the possibility of an inverse relationship between tax rates and government revenue. Pictured in fig. 1, the curve plots total revenue against the tax rate and claims to show that there are two rates at which a given revenue can be collected. The tax rate of fig. 1 generally refers to any particular tax instrument, while revenues generally refer to total tax receipts. An increase in the payroll tax rate, for example, could affect not only its own revenue, but work effort and thus personal income tax revenues.

---

*I am indebted to my colleagues John B. Shoven and John Whalley with whom I developed the general equilibrium taxation model used in this paper. I am grateful to the Treasury Department's Office of Tax Analysis for financial assistance. This version of the paper incorporates changes suggested by David F. Bradford, Shantayanan Devarajan, Ronald E. Grieson, Michael Kaufman, Mark Killingsworth, Arthur B. Laffer, R. David Ranson, James E. Rauch, Harvey S. Rosen, Joel Slemrod, Nicholas H. Stern, and Norman B. Ture. I retain full responsibility for errors and for the views expressed.

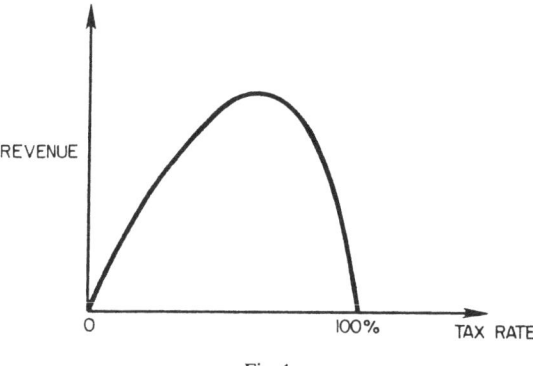

Fig. 1

The upward-sloping portion of the curve is called the 'normal' range and the downward-sloping segment is the 'prohibitive' range. No rational government would knowingly operate on the latter range in the long run, because the same revenue could be obtained with a lower tax rate. However, with adjustment lags in the private sector and a high social discount rate, such tax rates might be used in the short run. The prohibitive range is said to exist because the high tax rates stifle economic activity, force agents to barter, and encourage leisure pursuits. It is also made plausible by remembering that excess burden varies with the square of the tax rate.

The debate has been conducted mostly in the spheres of politics and journalism, and it includes a wide variety of unsupported claims and opinions. These range all the way from the assertion that the prohibitive range does not exist to the claim that 'we are well within this range at present'.[1] Simple theoretical models can show that the prohibitive range does indeed exist, but the U.S. position on the curve is clearly an empirical matter. Despite the obvious importance of this issue for fiscal policy, there has been no serious estimation of the curve using an economic model.[2] This paper attempts to correct this deficiency by using a general equilibrium taxation

---

[1]Michael Kinsley (1978) correctly claims that there is no logical necessity for revenues to be zero at 100 percent tax rates, due to nonmonetary incentives for work effort, but he incorrectly infers that 'there's no logical reason to assume without proof that the Laffer curve ever reverses direction at all' (p. 38). Laffer (1980) points out that even if a motivated person still works with a 100 percent tax rate, there must be some higher rate that will make him stop. The curve will still have the shape of fig. 1. The quote in the text is from Laffer (1977, p. 79).

[2]Several papers have described models in which there exists the possibility of a prohibitive range. See Canto, Joines and Laffer (1978) and Beck (1979) for examples. Other empirical papers have found governments operating in this range, as seen in the next section. Also, Kiefer (1978) provides estimates of revenue effects from the DRI, Wharton, and Chase Econometric models. None of these papers plots out the Laffer curve, however, nor do they estimate its relationship to various elasticity parameters.

model to address two questions. First, what is the position of the U.S. on the curve today? Second, what is the relationship between the location of the curve itself and critical parameters like the appropriate factor supply elasticity?[3]

The next section offers a brief review of some salient points from the debate. A common aspect of previous studies is that a prohibitive range for some local or national economy is always associated with particularly high tax rates, high factor supply elasticities, or both. Section 3 sets out the conditions under which a lower tax rate could result in higher revenues. These conditions are summarized in a new curve, plotting the appropriate factor supply elasticity against the tax rate. Section 4 describes the general equilibrium model used to simulate the effects of various tax rates. These estimations are performed in section 5, and the two curves are plotted for an example with a labor tax and labor supply elasticity. Section 6 provides some evidence on the value of the critical labor supply elasticity, and the final section concludes that to operate in the prohibitive range, the tax wedge must be very high, or the factor supply elasticity must be very high, or there must be some combination of the two.

2. A brief literature review

The idea of an inverse relationship between tax rates and revenue is not entirely new. In *The Wealth of Nations* (1776), Adam Smith could hardly be more explicit:

> High taxes, sometimes by diminishing the consumption of the taxed commodities, and sometimes by encouraging smuggling, frequently afford a smaller revenue to government than what might be drawn from more moderate taxes (Book V, Chapter II).

The trade literature, as exemplified by Caves and Jones (1973), has always understood the existence of a revenue maximizing tariff. This pre-Laffer edition contains a hump-shaped tariff revenue curve which looks just like fig. 1. With respect to internal taxes, Jules Dupuit in 1844 states:

> By thus gradually increasing the tax it will reach a level at which the yield is at a maximum ... Beyond, the yield of tax diminishes ... Lastly a tax [which is prohibitive] will yield nothing [Dupuit (1844)].

After the introduction of the Laffer curve (or perhaps the reintroduction of the Smith–Dupuit curve) in 1974, the quality of debate deteriorates

---

[3]In general, the location of the curve depends on both supply and demand elasticities, consumption and production parameters, and other circumstances in the economy. In wartime, for example, individuals might be willing to work harder at high tax rates to generate larger tax revenues. Later sections estimate the curve using a model of the 1973 U.S. economy.

significantly. Wanniski (1978) chronicles every fiscal catastrophe from the fall of the Roman Empire to the Great Depression and attributes each of them to some tax hike occurring within a few years in either direction. He states that the peak of the curve 'is the point at which the electorate desires to be taxed' (p. 98). On the same page, Wanniski suggests that 'if the tax rate is zero ... production is maximized' and that 'revenues plus production are maximized at [the peak of the curve]'.[4] The welfare maximizing government would instead operate somewhere on the normal range with the size of its budget determined by marginal cost–benefit analysis.

For the opposition, Kiefer (1978) comments that there is no tax rate for the overall economy which can be measured on the horizontal axis, and that 'the Laffer Curve represents a gross simplification of a major portion of macro-economics into a single curved line' (p. 15). These arguments are not compelling, either, in view of the large number of economic models which oversimplify in order to comprehend and convey economic phenomena. Kiefer also begrudges the supply side concentration, reminding us that income and substitution effects tend to be offsetting. 'By concentrating primarily on incentive and supply side effects, the Laffer Curve largely ignores the actual mechanism by which fiscal policy exerts its biggest and most immediate impact — demand side effects' (p. 16). One gets the feeling that these antagonists are talking past one another, using different models that are not comparable. Take for example the claim that the existence of a prohibitive range implies a marginal propensity to consume of greater than one. This Keynesian wisdom assumes no distorting taxes, no accelerator mechanism, and no incentive effects, all of which are central to the supply side argument.[5]

Canto, Joines and Laffer (1978) build a simple equilibrium model with one output, two factors, and a labor/leisure choice on the part of a single consumer group. Their utility function includes discounted consumption and leisure of each future period, a formulation which is very similar to the larger empirical general equilibrium model used later in this paper. Another similarity is that capital is inelastically supplied in any one period, but can grow over time. Labor taxes in these models place a wedge between the wage paid by producers and net wage received by workers. Individuals react to this wedge with an income effect and a substitution effect. In their model, however, government revenues are returned through transfers or are used to

---

[4]Walter Heller (1978) has his own complaints about Wanniski's evidence: 'At a time when only a few million Americans paid income taxes and federal spending was less than 5% of GNP, we are asked to believe that federal income tax cuts alone powered the growth of GNP from £70 billion in 1921 to $103 billion in 1929' (p. 47).

[5]Also, supply side advocates typically assume an equivalence between bond and tax financed spending, so that spending itself creates a wedge. Debates over the rationality of consumers and the net wealth of government bonds are best conducted elsewhere. For the purposes of this paper, I grant this equivalence.

buy goods that are perfect substitutes for private goods. This modelling cancels out the income effect and leaves the economy with an unambiguously positive substitution effect and an upward-sloping labor supply curve.

There are three points raised by this modelling. First, as recognized by these authors, if transfers are given to individuals other than those who pay taxes, and if individuals have different preferences, then income effects do not necessarily cancel. Second, if a government does nothing other than place a distorting wedge into the labor/leisure choice of homogeneous consumers and then return revenues in lump-sum fashion, of course output and welfare would both fall. These authors have not allowed for any positive contribution of a government budget. Their model does not account for the income effect of an efficiency gain that can be associated with correcting market failure by providing a public good. Third, they fail to allow for any complementarity between private and public outputs. Clearly there are public goods such as police protection and transportation systems which act to encourage private production, more than offsetting the adverse effects of the necessary tax wedge. Thus, the 'balanced budget' labor supply curve does not have to be upward sloping as these authors insist. Positive and negative estimates for the aggregate uncompensated labor supply elasticity will be surveyed in a later section.[6]

In empirical work, Grieson et al. (1977) find the possibility of an inverse relationship between tax rates and revenue for local government in New York: 'The inclusion of state taxes lost when economic activity leaves both the city and state would ... raise the possibility of a net revenue loss as a result of an increase in business income taxes' (p. 179). They find that the nonmanufacturing sector has fewer alternatives to the New York City location and should be taxed more heavily relative to the manufacturing sector whose response to tax is more elastic. Grieson (1980) finds the two sectors reversed for Philadelphia, where nonmanufacturing is under greater competitive pressure. Still, 'Philadelphia may have been at or very close to the revenue maximizing point ... before the recent income tax increase, which raises the possibility of it having been in excess of the socially optimal one' (p. 135).

For Sweden, Stuart (1981) uses a fairly simple two-sector model to find that the current 80 percent marginal tax wedge exceeds the revenue maximizing rate. For the U.S., Canto, Joines and Webb (1979) evaluate the 1964 Kennedy tax cuts which included the reduction of the top personal rate from 91 to 70 percent. They find that the Kennedy tax cuts may have increased or decreased revenues, equally likely possibilities.

Perverse revenue effects are more likely from selected tax cuts than from

---

[6]These three shortcomings of the Canto, Joines and Laffer (1978) theoretical model are not explicitly corrected in the empirical model used below, but they are implicitly corrected through the possibility of positive or negative labor supply elasticities.

general tax cuts, if they can be directed at individuals or activities that are unusually sensitive to tax rates. Hausman (1982) simulates tax cuts separately for husbands and for wives, finding less revenue loss from the latter group because of their higher labor supply elasticity. Feldstein, Slemrod and Yitzhaki (1980) find that capital gain realizations are very sensitive to the effective tax rate: 'An important implication of this high coefficient is that a reduction in the tax rate on capital gains would actually increase the total revenue collected' (p. 786).[7] On the other hand, Minarik (1981) finds that capital gain realizations respond to ordinary fluctuations in individual effective tax rates. As a result of this self-averaging over time, statutory rate reductions cannot be expected to generate enough additional realizations to increase revenues.

3. Another simple curve

Two prominent themes from this debate are high marginal tax rates and implicit or explicit reference to high factor supply elasticities.[8] Offsetting income and substitution effects merely imply that the relevant uncompensated supply elasticity might be low or negative. The emphasis on large incentive effects in the supply side argument implies a large elasticity. The open nature of a local economy implies mobile factors and a more elastic response to a local tax. Indeed, the entire debate reduces to the empirical matter of determining the relevant parameter values. If supply elasticities are high enough, the economy could be on the prohibitive range.

The very location of Laffer's curve in the rate-revenue space of fig. 1 depends on the supply elasticity of the factor being taxed. If that elasticity were fairly low, the total revenue maximizing point would be at a high tax rate for that factor, and conversely. One can imagine a third dimension on that diagram giving different elasticity values. The hill would then be converted into a ridge, running from a low tax rate and high elasticity combination to a high rate and low elasticity pair. The crest of that ridge is plotted in fig. 2. Everything to the southwest of that curve signifies the 'normal area', where raising rates increases revenue, and northeast of the curve is the 'prohibitive area', where no rational government would

---

[7]Three points serve to mitigate the strength of this result. First, a capital gains tax cut might unlock a flood of realizations in the short run, without necessarily increasing revenues in the long run. Second, increased selling of corporate stock does not necessarily imply increased saving and capital formation (i.e. buying of corporate stock). Third, the capital gains tax cut is likely to increase corporate retained earnings, decrease the dividends paid out, and thus reduce personal tax revenue from dividends.

[8]Other themes from this literature include minimum wage laws, regulation of business, nonmarket activity, and the complexity of tax rules. The Laffer curve itself focuses on tax rates, however, so this paper will consider different tax rates and assume unchanged complexity. The relevant elasticity for this exercise would provide not just the response of labor supply, but the response of taxable labor supply.

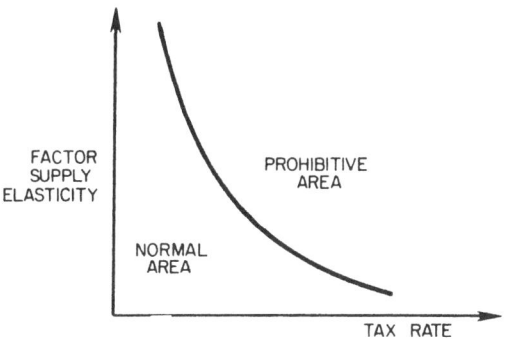

Fig. 2

knowingly operate. Each point on the curve shows the tax rate which maximizes total revenue for a given elasticity.

Suppose, for a simple example, that homogeneous labor L is taxed at the proportional rate t. Labor demand and supply are based, respectively, on the gross-of-tax wage w and the net-of-tax wage $w(1-t)$, in constant elasticity forms:

$$L_d = Aw^\eta, \qquad \eta < 0, \tag{1}$$

$$L_s = B[w(1-t)]^\varepsilon, \qquad \varepsilon > 0. \tag{2}$$

Tax revenue R is equal to twL, so differentiation and algebra provide:

$$\frac{\partial R}{\partial t} = wL\left[1 + \frac{\partial L}{\partial t}\cdot\frac{t}{L} + \frac{\partial w}{\partial t}\cdot\frac{t}{w}\right]. \tag{3}$$

Setting (3) equal to zero, we have three equations that can be solved for w, L, and the revenue-maximizing tax rate t. Since $L_s = L_d$ in this partial equilibrium system, we can use (1) and (2) to express w as a function of t. Substituting that w back into (1), we can also express L as a function of t. Differentiating these expressions, substituting into (3), and solving for t, we have:[9]

$$t = \frac{\eta - \varepsilon}{\eta(1+\varepsilon)}. \tag{4}$$

If $\eta > -1$ (demand is inelastic), then higher tax rates can always achieve

[9]Eq. (4) is derived somewhat differently in Blinder (1981).

more revenue. If $\eta < -1$, however, then the relationship between t and ε will look like fig. 2:

$$\frac{\partial t}{\partial \varepsilon} = \frac{-1}{(1+\varepsilon)^2}\left(\frac{1+\eta}{\eta}\right) < 0 \qquad (5)$$

and

$$\frac{\partial^2 t}{\partial \varepsilon^2} = \frac{2}{(1+\varepsilon)^3}\left(\frac{1+\eta}{\eta}\right) > 0, \qquad (6)$$

so the curve slopes down and is convex to the origin. The easiest case to see is where $\eta = -\infty$, so that $t = 1/(1+\varepsilon)$. Then the revenue maximizing rate approaches one as ε goes to zero, and it approaches zero as ε becomes infinite.[10]

We can now reconcile conflicting claims of the previous section. Those who find an inverse relationship between tax rates and revenues must believe that the relevant elasticity is high, that the relevant tax rate is high, or both. Those who find a normal range must believe that one or both of these parameters is low. Finally, those who deny the existence of an inverse relationship at any tax rate might really just believe that the uncompensated supply elasticity is zero or negative (or that demand is inelastic).[11]

4. The general equilibrium model

To simulate the effects of different tax rates for a variety of factor supply elasticities, a previously developed general equilibrium taxation model is employed. This model has been used to evaluate various tax reform proposals, but it was built as a general purpose model. Its features are surprisingly well suited for this application, as no adjustments were required to obtain the following estimates. Since more thorough descriptions of the model are available elsewhere, only an essential outline of it is provided here.[12]

---

[10]Several points are manifest. First, this analysis oversimplifies by using a given elasticity for all tax rates to find the revenue maximizing point. As the tax rate varies, so would equilibrium prices, incomes, and preference parameters like the factor supply elasticity. Second, a given time frame is implied since elasticities might increase as more time is allowed for adjustment. Third, neither elasticities nor tax rates have to be positive. The southwest quadrant contains a symmetrical curve showing the maximum revenue loss from a subsidy. Finally, note that similar analyses can be performed with respect to η, the labor demand elasticity.

[11]A zero uncompensated elasticity can mask a high compensated elasticity, however. Hausman (1981) points out that while the former is relevant to determine actual factor supply (and thus the tax base and revenues), the latter is relevant for the efficiency cost of distortions.

[12]See Fullerton, Shoven and Whalley (1978) and Fullerton, King, Shoven and Whalley (1981). This model provides more detailed features than would be necessary to demonstrate the relationships of figs. 1 and 2. Some form of general equilibrium model is required, however, to capture indirect effects. Although certain aspects of this model have been updated since the calculations for this paper were performed, the changes do not significantly affect these results.

The economy is divided into 19 profit-maximizing producers, 15 consumption commodities, and 12 consumer groups differentiated by income class. Each industry has a Cobb–Douglas or Constant Elasticity of Substitution (CES) production function, where the elasticity of substitution between capital and labor is chosen as a 'best-guess' value from evidence in the literature. Each output can be used as an intermediate input through a fixed coefficient input–output matrix. Outputs can be purchased by government, used for investment, or converted into consumer goods. There is also a simple foreign trade sector, though this model of the U.S. economy should be considered closed for purposes of this paper.

Each consumer has initial endowments of labor and capital services which can be sold for use in production. Because of perfect mobility and competition, the net-of-tax return to each factor is equal among industries. A consumer can also choose to buy some of his own labor endowment for leisure. The capital stock is fixed in any one period, but the dynamic version of the model allows the savings response to augment the stock in later periods. Demand functions are based on CES utility functions with double nesting. The choice between present and future consumption is represented by the outside nest, and the elasticity of substitution between them is based on an estimate of the uncompensated savings elasticity with respect to the net-of-tax rate of return. For this value we use 0.4 as found by Boskin (1978). The breakdown of present consumption into commodities and leisure is represented by the inside nest, and the elasticity of substitution in this choice is based on an estimate of the uncompensated labor supply elasticity with respect to the net-of-tax wage. For this value we typically use 0.15, but relationships for different labor elasticity values will be derived below.[13]

The various federal, state, and local taxes are typically modelled as ad valorem tax rates on purchases of appropriate products or factors. Corporate income taxes and property taxes are modelled as different effective rates of tax on use of capital by industry.[14] Social security, workmen's compensation and unemployment insurance appear as taxes on use of labor. These rates differ slightly by industry because different proportions of workers hit the social security maximum, but they average 10 percent of payments to labor. Personal income taxes operate as different linear schedules for each consumer group, with marginal tax rates increasing from an average of 1 percent for

---

[13]Leisure in the baseline is taken as three-fourths of observed labor, reflecting the assumption that 40 hours are worked out of a possible 70 hours each week. Because of the CES form, the income elasticity of demand for leisure is one. From the Slutsky equation, it can then be shown that the compensated labor supply elasticity is equal to the uncompensated elasticity plus 3/7. A tax increase alone will cause a reaction based on the uncompensated elasticity, but if revenues are returned to consumers then their net behavior will approximate the larger compensated response.

[14]The effective tax rate in each industry is equal to capital taxes paid divided by capital income. For a comparison of this 'average' tax rate with an alternative 'marginal' treatment in this model, see Fullerton and Gordon (1982).

the lowest income group to an average marginal tax rate of 40 percent for the highest income group.

The model is parameterized for 1973 using data from the National Income and Product Accounts, the Bureau of Labor Statistics' Consumer Expenditure Survey, and the Treasury Department's Merged Tax File. These data are adjusted for known inaccuracies of government collection procedures and for general equilibrium consistency requirements. This 'benchmark' data set is used to solve backwards for relevant preference parameters and tax rates, so that the model solution can replicate the benchmark equilibrium. The user can specify different tax rates to calculate a simulated equilibrium with different resource allocations for comparison with the benchmark. The model is solved using a variant of Scarf's algorithm for an equilibrium price vector where excess demands and profits are zero.

The model does not include involuntary unemployment, endogenous inflation, or other aspects of disequilibria. It is essentially a microeconomic model, expressing all prices in relative terms. Voluntary unemployment is captured through the labor/leisure choice, however, and the interaction of inflation with effective marginal tax rates is modelled by adjusting those rates appropriately. The modelling of capital gains, for example, accounts for the nominal gains that are subject to tax.

Of potential controversy, however, is the modelling of government transfers as essentially lump-sum payments to consumer groups in proportion to their observed 1973 receipts from social security, unemployment compensation, food stamps, and other welfare programs. Supply side advocates may like to model these payments as additional work disincentives, increasing the wedge betweeen labor's marginal product and leisure's implicit price. Though lawmakers probably do not intend to subsidize leisure, some programs have that effect. The incentive depends on the program's ability to isolate important characteristics such as age, disability, and number of dependents which make the recipient unable to work. If this intention is successful, the payments will not have a substitution effect. The income effect of transfer programs could also reduce labor supply, but this effect is captured in the model.[15]

---

[15]The difference between paying people who do not work, and paying people not to work, is the difference between a marginal payment with incentive effects, and a lump-sum payment. Legally, an employee must be laid off to be eligible for unemployment compensation. A worker can ask to be laid off, but employers may be reluctant to circumvent the intent of the law. These transfers are not automatically and fully available to nonworkers. Similarly, AFDC payments are designed to select recipients by particular characteristics, maximizing the lump-sum effect and minimizing disincentive effects. Social security payments are higher for the blind or disabled. Finally, note that these transfers, to the extent that they are disincentives, do not always apply to marginal hours. Most individuals who take an extra hour of leisure do not become eligible for transfers at all. Laffer (1980) is correct, however, that if transfer payments include a means test, work disincentives can be large for some individuals. Another more thorough study could undertake to measure incentive effects of transfers.

5. Estimation

Supply side advocates refer to several different types of taxes when they claim an inverse relationship betwen a particular tax rate and government revenue. The curve in fig. 2 could be plotted by varying a product tax rate against the price elasticity of demand for that product, or by plotting capital tax rates against the elasticity of savings with respect to the net-of-tax return to capital. The latter example was attempted with the empirical model, but no prohibitive area was discovered.[16] For this reason, the example used here is the labor tax against the labor supply elasticity.

In our basic model, the tax on labor used by industry averages 10 percent of net factor payments. The personal income tax takes another 24.9 percent of marginal labor income, weighting the twelve marginal tax rates by labor income of each group. The total wedge thus takes 31.8 percent of marginal labor income gross of all tax.[17] This overall marginal rate is the relevant single parameter for summarizing incentive effects in the model, and this is the parameter varied in simulations for the horizontal axes of figs. 1 and 2. The overall average rate is 19.2 percent, dividing total labor taxes by gross labor income.

Marginal tax rates determine incentives, but average tax rates by definition determine revenues. A more progressive tax structure will therefore attain an earlier revenue maximum. For this reason, progressivity should not be altered in simulating alternative tax rates. Unfortunately, however, there is no unambiguous measure of progressivity. Simulations in this paper will hold constant the first of three possible progressivity measures defined in Musgrave and Musgrave (1980). The effect of this selection is that the same number of percentage points are added to or subtracted from all average *and* marginal labor tax rates of all consumers when a rate change is simulated. Such changes are summarized by referring to changes in the 31.8 percent

---

[16]Over forty simulations were performed in seeking a prohibitive area for capital taxes. Using the dynamic version of the model, tax rates were raised to 83 percent of gross capital income, savings elasticities were increased to 4.0, and equilibria were calculated out 50 years in the future. Normally, discount rate problems arise in determining whether the present value of revenues has increased or decreased. In this case, however, there was not a single period of the raised-tax sequence of equilibria which had lower revenues than the corresponding period of the benchmark sequence. Inverse relationships may exist for high effective rates of tax on certain types of real capital income for certain individuals. No overall inverse relationship was discovered in this model, however, because the tax distortion applies to the savings decision, while savings are only an increment to the capital tax base. More than 50 years would be required for the tax base reduction to offset a tax rate increase and result in lower revenues.

[17]The model defines labor income as net of the 10 percent factor tax on industries, but gross of the personal income tax on individuals. For a marginal dollar of this labor income, $1.10 is the gross-of-tax payment, $0.10 is the payroll tax, and $0.249 is the marginal personal tax paid, averaged over the 12 groups. The total marginal tax rate is thus $(0.1+0.249)/1.10$, which equals 31.8 percent, except for rounding. By the same formula for different groups, personal marginal rates between 1 and 40 percent imply total marginal rates between $(0.1+0.01)/1.10$, which equals 10 percent, and $(0.1+0.4)/1.10$, which equals 45.5 percent.

overall marginal rate on gross labor income.[18]

The consistent 1973 data set also shows a total tax revenue of $360 billion and a national income of $1,252 billion. Our expanded notion of welfare, including leisure valued at the net-of-tax wage, is $1,690 billion. These values are replicated for any possible labor supply elasticity as long as tax rates are unchanged. Simulations with labor tax rates other than 31.8 percent will have revenues which depend on the elasticity, and it becomes necessary to specify the disposition of extra revenues. One possibility is simply to allow a budget surplus or deficit. If a surplus implies lower future taxes, however, individuals may react to an effective tax rate that is different from the specified rate for the simulation. Higher revenues must eventually be spent or returned (see footnote 5). A second possibility is to increase public expenditure on the 19 industry outputs of the model. Though government spending has no macroeconomic effects on inflation or unemployment in this model, it does have a microeconomic effect on the pattern of demands for commodities. It indirectly affects the demand for capital and labor through the different factor ratios of production. Instead, additonal revenues are returned to consumers in lump-sum fashion, in proportion to their original after-tax incomes.[19]

The results from over sixty simulations are summarized in table 1.[20] The first column shows the total revenue resulting from different labor tax rates using the basic model's value of 0.15 for the labor supply elasticity with respect to the net-of-tax wage. The 'observed' total revenue of $360 billion corresponds to the basic tax rate of 31.8 percent, and total revenues are positively related to tax rates up to a tax which is 78.8 percent of gross labor income. Beyond that rate, revenues start to fall.[21]

---

[18]Thus, labor tax rate changes can be thought of as changes in the proportional payroll tax rate or as changes in all average and marginal personal tax rates, on labor income only.

[19]This lump-sum rebate has no direct effect on prices since no tax rates are altered. It could have an indirect effect on prices of the simulated equilibrium, however, since consumers include the income in their expanded budgets for purchase of commodities and leisure according to their own preference patterns. This disposition of revenues corresponds exactly to that of Canto, Joines and Laffer (1978), reviewed in section 2. By symmetry, a decrease in revenue is accompanied by a lump-sum charge on consumers in the same proportions. Total government tax revenues are defined to be inclusive of income returned to consumers, and exclusive of any lump-sum charges necessary to keep government spending on commodities constant.

[20]These simulations are static in the sense that total endowments of labor and capital are fixed. Labor can be sold to industry or retained for leisure in the simulation, while both factors can be reallocated among industries.

[21]Like Canto, Joines and Laffer (1978), this model ignores production-encouraging aspects of any public goods made possible through increased revenue. As a result, national income (GNP) falls by $292 billion when the elasticity is 0.15 and the tax rate is raised to 78.8 percent. Though the return to the fixed capital stock rises, labor supply falls off by almost half. The gross-of-tax wage rises, but the net-of-tax wage falls by 40 percent in the new equilibrium. If the increased leisure is valued at the net-of-tax wage, then the $292 billion income fall is offset by a $177 billion leisure gain, with a $115 billion net loss in real terms. These calculations use a Laspeyres index, valuing old and new quantities at base prices.

Table 1
Total revenue associated with each labor tax rate (in billions of 1973 dollars).

Rate on gross labor income[a]	Labor supply elasticity with respect to net-of-tax wage								
	0.15	0.50	1.00	1.50	1.75	2.00	2.50	3.00	4.00
0.166									341.79
0.249								355.82	365.57
0.285						354.00	357.46	360.56	365.93
0.318	360.00	360.00	360.00	360.00	360.00	360.00	360.00	360.00	360.00
0.347					364.00	361.98	358.23		349.18
0.374				369.80	365.17	360.85			
0.399				370.82	363.62	356.91			
0.422	439.48		391.82	369.60		350.57			295.40
0.464			396.49	361.52					
0.482			396.60						
0.499	503.71		395.43						
0.531			389.75						
0.558	555.56	474.13	380.36						
0.605	597.41	481.65							
0.615		481.98							
0.625	615.16	481.78	336.60						
0.674	657.84	476.01							
0.700	678.84								
0.722	694.90								
0.750	711.16								
0.772	719.58								
0.779	720.89								
0.785	721.53								
0.788	721.60								
0.791	721.52								
0.797	720.92								
0.812	715.79								
0.833	697.79								
0.850	670.19								
0.875	593.30								

[a]Simulations were made selectively to save computational expense. Not all possible rates are reported. These rates on gross income include social security taxes and personal income taxes at the overall marginal rate, all as a fraction of gross labor income.

Any column of data from table 1 can be used to plot an example of fig. 1, as is done in fig. 3 for the 0.15 elasticity. In any of these Laffer curve diagrams, the modelled U.S. economy is represented by 0.318 on the labor tax rate axis. If the various tax rates, transfers, and elasticities are reasonable, as modelled, then the U.S. economy is well down the normal range of the curve. For those who prefer a high elasticity, fig. 4 plots another Laffer curve.

The 4.0 labor supply elasticity and current tax rates place the U.S. well onto the prohibitive range.[22]

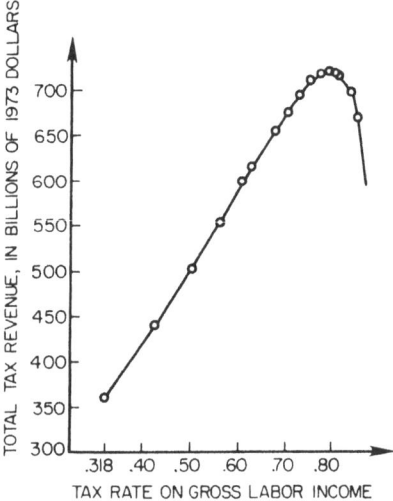

Fig. 3. Laffer curve with a 0.15 labor elasticity.

Underlined in each column of table 1 is the maximum revenue point for that elasticity. These tax rate and elasticity combinations correspond to points on a curve like fig. 2. When plotted for this example, the curve is shown in fig. 5. On this curve, with tax rates as modelled, the labor supply elasticity would have to be at least 2.5 to put the U.S. over the peak and onto the prohibitive range. Alternatively, if the supply elasticity were at least 1.0 and the true overall tax rate were at least 48.2 percent, then again U.S. taxes could be operating irrationally. The continuum of fig. 5 allows the reader to select a plausible tax rate and elasticity combination to determine whether the U.S. is now in the prohibitive area.

6. What is the labor supply elasticity?

The empirical model was fairly careful in establishing all of the basic tax

[22]In the 4.0 elasticity case, even the small jump from a 31.8 percent labor tax rate to a 34.7 percent rate causes a 9 percent fall in labor supply, a $70 billion reduction in national income, a $44 billion increase in the value of leisure, and a net welfare loss of $26 billion in real terms. A small tax cut with this high elasticity results in symmetrical increases in labor supply, output, and welfare. All tax cuts increase welfare in this model because revenue is replaced with lump-sum charges as in Canto, Joines and Laffer (1978). Such opportunities may not in fact be available.

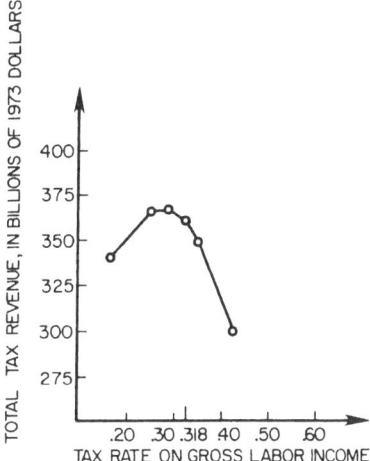

Fig. 4. Laffer curve with a 4.0 labor elasticity.

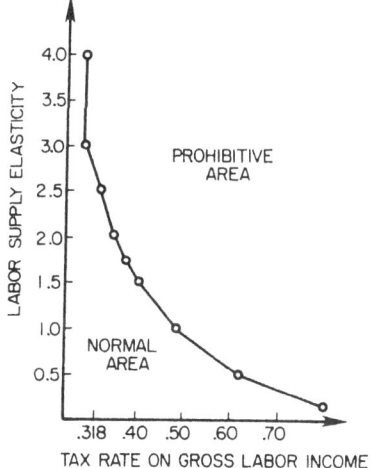

Fig. 5. Elasticity and tax rate combinations.

Table 2
Estimates of the uncompensated labor supply elasticity.

Authors	Data subset	Type of data	Range of estimates
A. For males			
Finegan (1962)	Male family heads	Inter-occupational	−0.35 to −0.25
Rosen (1969)	Male family heads	Inter-industrial	−0.30 to −0.07
Kalachek–Raines (1970)	Male family heads	U.S. cross-section	+0.05 to +0.30
Owen (1971)	Male family heads	U.S. time-series	−0.24 to −0.11
Greenburg–Kosters (1973)	Poor male family heads	U.S. cross-section	−0.16 to −0.05
Boskin (1973)	Different male subgroups	U.S. cross-section	−0.07 to +0.18
Hill (1973)	Poor male family heads	U.S. cross-section	−0.32 to −0.07
Ashenfelter–Heckman (1973)	Male family heads	U.S. cross-section	−0.15
Fleisher–Parsons–Porter (1973)	Male ages 45–59	U.S. cross-section	−0.25 to −0.10
Ashenfelter–Heckman (1974)	Married males	U.S. cross-section	Zero
Burtless–Hausman (1978)	Low-income males	Gary NIT cross-section	Zero
Hausman (1981)	Married males	U.S. cross-section	Zero
B. For females			
Finegan (1962)	Females	Inter-occupational	−0.095
Leuthold (1968)	Females	U.S. cross-section	−0.067
Kalachel–Raines (1970)	Females	U.S. cross-section	+0.20 to +0.90
Boskin (1973)	Different female subgroups	U.S. cross-section	−0.04 to +1.60
Ashenfelter–Heckman (1974)	Married females	U.S. cross-section	0.87
Hausman (1981)	Married females	U.S. cross-section	0.9
Hausman (1981)	Female household heads	U.S. cross-section	0.5
C. Aggregate			
Winston (1966)	Aggregate	International cross-section	−0.11 to −0.05
Lucas–Rapping (1970)	Short run aggregate	Time-series	1.35 to 1.58
Lucas–Rapping (1970)	Long run aggregate	Time-series	Zero to 1.12

rates, including the 31.8 percent labor rax rate, but it is much less explicit about the aggregate labor supply elasticity. The econometric literature gives many estimates for population subgroups, since different individuals will typically have different rates of response to a new net-of-tax wage. Finegan's (1962) occupational study found managers, craftsmen, and clerical workers varying from a -0.29 to a $+0.42$ labor supply elasticity, while Boskin's (1973) division by sex, race, and age found estimates from -0.07 (for prime-age white males) to $+1.60$ (for elderly black women). Since taxes do not distinguish among these characteristics, the relevant elasticity parameter is an aggregate one. Table 2 summarizes a number of econometric studies and is based mostly on discussion in Killingsworth (1982).

A certain injustice is perpetrated against these authors by reporting their results in such summary fashion. Each study has its own measure of the wage, its own data-year or time-period, its own mean values, and its own functional forms. The studies differ as to whether they account for labor participation rates and as to whether they account for the balanced budget effects of government spending, discussed above.[23] The numbers in table 2 are provided only to give the reader a framework for choosing a plausible aggregate labor supply elasticity. Since few aggregate studies are available, male and female estimates can be roughly combined.

Elasticity estimates for males are mostly small and negative, ranging from -0.40 to zero. Borjas and Heckman (1978) review the econometrics of these studies and reduce the bounds to -0.19 and -0.07. The estimates for females are more often positive, and can be large in absolute value. Killingsworth finds that females' elasticity estimates are mostly between 0.20 and 0.90 in cross-section studies. To obtain the model's 0.15 aggregate labor supply elasticity, perform a rough numerical calculation. The *Statistical Abstract* shows that the median money income of male employed civilians has consistently been twice that of females. It also shows about a 1.7 ratio of males to females in the labor force, a ratio which is decreasing with time. By multiplication, the ratio of total male to female labor income would be about 3.4 (though decreasing). Taking a relatively high male elasticity of -0.10 and a relatively high female elasticity of $+0.90$, the three-to-one weighted average is a 0.15 aggregate elasticity.

7. Conclusion

This paper investigates a number of analytical and empirical arguments

[23]The most recent and perhaps the most thorough estimates are provided in Hausman (1981). His methodology includes consideration of progressivity, transfer programs, labor force participation, fixed costs of working, and a market wage which depends on the hours worked. These features can result in budget sets that are nonconvex and labor supply that is discontinuous. However, the study still excludes choices with respect to the type of job, the intensity of work on the job, nonpecuniary rewards, on the job training, and intertemporal considerations.

about the relationship between tax rates and government revenues. A general equilibrium tax model is used to plot this relationship as well as another relationship between tax rates and factor supply elasticities. This new curve shows that the U.S. economy could conceivably be operating in the 'prohibitive range' for taxes on labor, but that reasonable estimates of an aggregate labor supply elasticity and of an overall marginal labor tax rate are both low enough to suggest that broad-based cuts in labor tax rates would not increase revenues.

The tax rate and elasticity relationship can be applied to other federal, state, or local taxes to find circumstances where a particularly high tax rate on real income or a particularly high elasticity could place a tax in the prohibitive area. A tax on purely nominal capital gains, for example, or an underallowance for depreciation can result in high effective tax rates on some types of real capital income. Future research could investigate the responsiveness of these particular investments to high effective rates. The 'marriage penalty' which places a secondary worker in the higher marginal tax bracket of his or her spouse may represent another high rate of tax on an elastically supplied factor.[24] Welfare programs that make recipients ineligible at a given income level imply effective marginal tax rates of 100 percent or higher. Also, the high elasticity argument is particularly applicable for state and local governments since factors are generally more mobile within national boundaries. McGuire and Rapping (1968, 1970) find labor supply elasticities of 20–100 for particular states or industries. This mobility implies that one jurisdiction cannot charge higher tax rates than its neighbors and may apply increasingly to international factor flows.

Finally, although the results of this paper tend to reject the notion of an inverse relationship between major U.S. tax rates and government revenues, they do not necessarily invalidate the claim that these tax rates and revenues should be lowered. Even on the normal range, taxes may be higher than desired by voters. Preferences can change over time, fewer public goods may now be demanded, and the electorate can legitimately request a tax decrease. Although incentive effects can still be important without perverse revenue effects, the point is that the 'economics of the tax revolt' are less the economics of incentive effects and more the economics of public choice.

[24]Feenberg and Rosen (1982) simulate the effects of four proposals to reduce or eliminate the marriage penalty. Each has its own welfare effects and redistributions, but none implies higher revenue.

References

Ashenfelter, Orley and James J. Heckman, 1973, Estimating labor supply functions, in: Glen G. Cain and Harold W. Watts, eds., Income maintenance and labor supply (Rand McNally, Chicago).

Ashenfelter, Orley and James J. Heckman, 1974, The estimation of income and substitution effects in a model of family labor supply, Econometrica 42, January, 73–85.

Beck, John H., 1979, An analysis of the supply-side effects of tax cuts in an IS–LM model, National Tax Journal 32, December, 493–499.

Blinder, Alan S., 1981, Thoughts on the Laffer curve, in: Laurence H. Meyer, ed., The supply-side effects of economic policy (Center for the Study of American Business, Federal Reserve Bank of St. Louis, and Washington University, St. Louis).

Borjas, George J. and James J. Heckman, 1978, Labor supply estimates for public policy evaluation, Proceedings of the industrial relations research association, 320–331.

Boskin, Michael J., 1973, The economics of the labor supply, in: Glen G. Cain and Harold W. Watts, eds., Income maintenance and labor supply (Rand McNally, Chicago).

Boskin, Michael J., 1978, Taxation, saving and the rate of interest, Journal of Political Economy 86, April, S3–S27.

Burtless, Gary and Jerry A. Hausman, 1978, The effect of taxation on labor supply: Evaluating the Gary negative income tax experiment, Journal of Political Economy 86, December, 1103–1130.

Canto, Victor A., Douglas H. Joines and Arthur B. Laffer, 1978, An income expenditure version of the wedge model, mimeo (University of Southern California, Los Angeles).

Canto, Victor A., Douglas H. Joines and Robert I. Webb, 1979, Empirical evidence on the effects of tax rates on economic activity, Proceedings of the Business and Economic Statistics Section (American Statistical Association, Washington, D.C.).

Caves, Richard E. and Ronald W. Jones, 1973, World trade and payments (Little-Brown and Co., Boston).

Dupuit, Jules, 1844, On the measurement of the utility of public works, translation in: K.J. Arrow and T. Scitovsky, eds., Readings in welfare economics (published for the American Economic Association by Richard D. Irwin, Inc., Homewood, Illinois, 1969).

Feenberg, Daniel and Harvey S. Rosen, 1982, Alternative tax treatment of the family: Simulation methodology and results, in: Martin Feldstein, ed., Simulation methods in tax policy analysis (The University of Chicago Press, Chicago, forthcoming).

Feldstein, Martin, Joel Slemrod and Shlomo Yitzhaki, 1980, The effects of taxation on the selling of corporate stock and the realization of capital gains, Quarterly Journal of Economics 94, June, 777–791.

Finegan, T. Aldrich, 1962, Hours of work in the United States — A cross-sectional analysis, Journal of Political Economy 70, October, 452–470.

Fleisher, Belton M., Donald O. Parsons and Richard D. Porter, 1973, Asset adjustment and labor supply of older workers, in: Glen G. Cain and Harold W. Watts, eds., Income maintenance and labor supply (Rand McNally, Chicago).

Fullerton, Don and Roger H. Gordon, 1982, A reexamination of tax distortions in general equilibrium models, in: Martin Feldstein, ed., Simulation methods in tax policy analysis (The University of Chicago Press, Chicago, forthcoming).

Fullerton, Don, John B. Shoven and John Whalley, 1978, General equilibrium analysis of U.S. taxation policy, in: 1978 compendium of tax research, U.S. Treasury Department, Office of Tax Analysis (U.S. Government Printing Office, Washington, D.C.) 23–58.

Fullerton, Don, A. Thomas King, John B. Shoven and John Whalley, 1981, Corporate tax integration in the United States: A general equilibrium approach, American Economic Review 71, September, 677–691.

Greenberg, David H. and Marvin Kosters, 1973, Income guarantees and the working poor: The effect of income maintenance programs on the hours of work of male family heads, in: Glen G. Cain and Harold W. Watts, eds., Income maintenance and labor supply (Rand McNally, Chicago).

Grieson, Ronald E., 1980, Theoretical analysis and empirical measurements of the effects of the Philadelphia income tax, Journal of Urban Economics 8, July, 123–137.

Grieson, Ronald E., William Hamovitch, Albert M. Levenson and Richard D. Morgenstern, 1977, The effect of business taxation on the location of industry, Journal of Urban Economics 4, April, 170–185.

Hausman, Jerry A., 1981, Labor supply, in: Henry J. Aaron and Joseph A. Pechman, eds., How taxes affect economic behavior (The Brookings Institution, Washington, D.C.).

Hausman, Jerry A., 1982, Stochastic problems in the simulation of labor supply, in: Martin Feldstein, ed., Simulation methods in tax policy analysis (The University of Chicago Press, Chicago, forthcoming).

Heller, Walter, 1978, The Kemp–Roth–Laffer free lunch, in: The Wall Street Journal, July 12, p. 20. Reprinted in Arthur B. Laffer and Jan P. Seymour, eds., The economics of the tax revolt: A reader (Harcourt, Brace, Jovanovich, New York, 1979) 46–49.

Hill, C. Russell, 1973, The determinants of labor supply for the working urban poor, in Glen G. Cain and Harold W. Watts, eds., Income maintenance and labor supply (Rand McNally, Chicago).

Kalachek, Edward D. and Fredric Q. Raines, 1970, Labor supply of lower income workers, in: President's Commission on Income Maintenance Programs, Technical Studies (U.S. Government Printing Office, Washington, D.C.) 159–186.

Kiefer, Donald W., 1978, An economic analysis of the Kemp/Roth tax cut bill H.R. 8333: A description, an examination of its rationale, and estimates of its economic effects, Congressional Record, August 2, pp. H7777–H7787. Reprinted in Arthur B. Laffer and Jan P. Seymour, eds., The economics of the tax revolt: A reader (Harcourt, Brace, Jovanovich, New York, 1979) 13–27.

Killingsworth, Mark R., 1982, Labor supply (Cambridge University Press, New York, forthcoming).

Kinsley, Michael, 1978, Alms for the rich, in: The New Republic 179, August 19, pp. 19–26. Reprinted in Arthur B. Laffer and Jan P. Seymour, eds., The economics of the tax revolt: A reader (Harcourt, Brace, Jovanovich, New York, 1979) 35–43.

Laffer, Arthur B., 1977, Statement prepared for the Joint Economic Committee, May 20. Reprinted in Arthur B. Laffer and Jan P. Seymour, eds., The economics of the tax revolt: A reader (Harcourt, Brace, Jovanovich, New York, 1979) 75–79.

Laffer, Arthur B., 1980, An equilibrium rational macroeconomic framework, in: Nake M. Kamrani and Richard Day, eds., Economic issues of the eighties (Johns Hopkins University Press, Baltimore, Maryland).

Leuthold, Jane H., 1968, An empirical study of formula income transfers and the work decision of the poor, Journal of Human Resources 3, Summer, 312–323.

Lucas, Robert E. and Leonard A. Rapping, 1970, Real wages, employment and inflation, in: Edmund S. Phelps et al., Microeconomic foundations of employment and inflation theory (W.W. Norton Co., New York) 257–305.

McGuire, Timothy W. and Leonard A. Rapping, 1968, The role of market variables and key bargains in the manufacturing wage determination process, Journal of Political Economy 76, September–October, 1015–1036.

McGuire, Timothy W. and Leonard A. Rapping, 1970, The supply of labor and manufacturing wage determination in the United States: An empirical examination, International Economic Review 11, June, 258–268.

Minarik, Joseph J., 1981, Capital gains, in: Henry J. Aaron and Joseph A. Pechman, eds., How taxes affect economic behavior (The Brookings Institution, Washington, D.C.).

Musgrave, Richard A. and Peggy B. Musgrave, 1980, Public finance in theory and practice (McGraw-Hill, New York).

Owen, John D., 1971, The demand for leisure, Journal of Political Economy 79, January–February, 56–76.

Rosen, Sherwin, 1969, On the interindustry wage and hours structure, Journal of Political Economy 77, March–April, 249–273.

Smith, Adam, 1776, The wealth of nations (J.M. Dent & Sons, Ltd., London, reprinted 1975).

Stuart, Charles, 1981, Swedish tax rates, labor supply, and tax revenues, Journal of Political Economy 89, October, 1020–1038.

Wanniski, Jude, 1978, The way the world works: How economies fail and succeed (Basic Books, New York).

Winston, Gordon C., 1966, An international comparison of income and hours of work, Review of Economics and Statistics 48, February, 28–39.

E
Taxes and Growth

[16]

Optimal Taxation in Models of Endogenous Growth

Larry E. Jones
Northwestern University

Rodolfo E. Manuelli
Stanford University

Peter E. Rossi
University of Chicago

> We study the problem of optimal taxation in three infinite-horizon, representative-agent endogenous growth models. The first model is a convex model in which physical and human capital are perfectly symmetric. Our second model incorporates elastic labor supply through a Lucas-style technology. Analysis of these two models points out the danger of assuming that government expenditures are exogenous. In our third model, we include government expenditures as a productive input in capital formation, showing that the limiting tax rate on capital is no longer zero. In numerical simulations, we find similar effects on growth and welfare in all three models.

I. Introduction

In recent years, considerable interest has developed in the determinants of the divergent paths of development both across countries at

---

We would like to thank Tony Braun, Christophe Chamley, V. V. Chari, Ken Judd, Robert King, Robert Lucas, Richard Rogerson, Paul Romer, Tom Sargent, Nancy Stokey, and an anonymous referee for their comments and the National Science Foundation for financial support. Remaining errors are our own.

the same time and within the same country at different times. A body of research has developed that traces differences in development paths to differences in government policies. This literature has emphasized simple convex models of the growth process. Examples of this line of work are Eaton (1981), Barro (1990), Jones and Manuelli (1990, 1992), King and Rebelo (1990), and Rebelo (1991).

In this paper, we continue the study of the connection between government policies and growth. Specifically, we present a quantitative assessment of the effects of making drastic changes in the structure of fiscal policies relative to the current situation. We explore the effects of the switch to this optimal tax scheme on both the growth rate and level of welfare in a representative-agent calibrated economy.

Recent examples of work on the quantitative effects of dynamic tax policies in a general equilibrium framework include Chamley (1981), Judd (1987, 1990), Auerbach and Kotlikoff (1987), Chari, Christiano, and Kehoe (1990), King and Rebelo (1990), Lucas (1990), and Yuen (1990). These studies differ greatly in both the models that they analyze and the types of fiscal experiments undertaken. Chamley (1981) explores the effects of both marginal and global effects on tax changes in a model with exogenous growth and a representative agent. Judd (1987) treats the case of the effects of marginal changes for a wide variety of different time paths for tax changes with exogenous growth. Auerbach and Kotlikoff (1987) consider global changes in taxes in an overlapping generations setting with exogenous growth. Judd (1990) and Chari et al. (1990) consider Ramsey optimal taxation problems in stochastic environments with exogenous growth. Both of these studies compare the business cycle frequency properties of optimal state-contingent tax policies with U.S. tax policies. King and Rebelo (1990) consider the effects of tax policy changes in a simple model of endogenous growth and compare them to tax effects in an exogenous growth model. Lucas (1990) examines the growth effects of Ramsey optimal taxation in a model of endogenous growth driven by a human capital externality. He uses an approximation to characterize the steady-state behavior of the optimal tax policy conditional on an exogenously specified level of steady-state debt service. Yuen (1990) analyzes a similar problem, using a linear approximation around the steady state to study optimal taxation.

We examine three separate models of the process of growth. The first is a fully convex model with no externalities in which physical and human capital are perfectly symmetric both in their usage and in their accumulation laws. The second model deviates from the first in that there is a nonconvexity at the household level in the production of "effective labor" (following Heckman [1976], Rosen [1976],

OPTIMAL TAXATION 487

and Lucas [1988]), and the human capital accumulation process depends on both market goods and nonmarket goods. In both of these models we follow the standard public finance practice of assuming that the flow of government expenditure is viewed as exogenous by the planner.

In both of these models, the growth effects of the switch to optimal tax policies cause government expenditures to shrink to a negligible fraction of output. A more realistic approach includes government expenditures as a productive input. Our third experiment makes the sequence of government expenditures endogenous to the planner's problem. This has drastic effects on the nature of optimal taxes. It is shown that, in a setting in which government spending has direct positive effects on investment, the asymptotic tax rate on capital income is strictly positive. These results contrast with those of the existing literature, which shows that the limiting tax rate on capital income is zero in the Ramsey optimal tax scheme in cases in which government spending is unproductive.

The models that we study do not admit closed-form solutions. Hence, our strategy is to compute exact solutions to finite-horizon versions of an optimal taxation problem in a deterministic setting with endogenous growth. We study the full solution to the optimal policy choice problem, which includes the determination of debt service as part of the optimal policy.

For all three models, we find large growth and welfare effects from a switch to optimal tax policies. This occurs regardless of whether the supply of labor is inelastic or elastic and whether government expenditures are taken as exogenous or endogenous. Moreover, the sizes of both the growth and welfare effects that we find are similar for the three models examined. Finally, we find a shift from a reliance on labor to consumption taxes in the second model examined (the only place in which this can be considered).

An important omission is consideration of issues of time consistency. Would new governments in power in the future choose to adopt the continuation of the policies we find as Ramsey optimal? Or in "resolving" the Ramsey problem from their point of view, would they choose to adopt different policies? (See Chari and Kehoe [1989, 1990] and Stokey [1991] for a discussion of these issues.) Throughout, we ignore the constraints these considerations impose on governments. Again, a more complete treatment of the problem including these considerations would be of considerable interest.

In all these exercises, we assume that both solutions to the planner's problems exist (in particular, the feasible set of policy plans is nonempty) and that the time paths of these solutions converge to steady-state growth paths. Neither of these assumptions is innocuous. In the case in which government spending is taken as exogenous (as in the models in Secs. II and III below), it is a simple exercise to choose time paths for spending that give rise to either nonexistence or nonstationary behavior. In addition, a recent example (Chamley 1990) shows that optimal policy can be nonstationary even if government policies are both exogenous and stationary.

The remainder of the paper is organized as follows. In Section II, we analyze a simple convex model of endogenous growth. In Section III, we modify the model to allow for a nonconvexity at the individual level in the production of effective labor from human capital and raw labor. In addition, we allow for a more general formulation of the human capital accumulation process. Section IV contains the results of the experiments when government expenditure is allowed to be endogenous. Finally, Section V offers some concluding remarks.

II. A Simple Version of the Problem: Model 1

Throughout the paper, we study variants of the following Ramsey problem: Choose tax rates to maximize the welfare of the representative agent subject to the constraints that the government's budget be balanced (in the present value sense) and that the resulting allocation is a competitive equilibrium.

In this section, we examine a simple case of this problem in which labor is inelastically supplied and physical and human capital are treated symmetrically. The representative household solves

$$\max \sum_t \beta^t u(c_t) \quad \text{subject to}$$

(i) $k_{t+1} \leq (1 - \delta_k)k_t + x_{kt}$,

(ii) $h_{t+1} \leq (1 - \delta_h)h_t + x_{ht}$,

(iii) $\sum_t p_t(c_t + x_{kt} + x_{ht}) \leq \sum_t p_t[(1 - \tau_{Kt})r_t k_t + (1 - \tau_{Ht})w_t h_t + T_t]$,

where k_t is physical capital and h_t is the stock of human capital. We interpret the household as supplying effective labor (as in Heckman [1976] and Lucas [1988]) given by $u_t h_t$, where u_t is the number of hours worked in the market sector and the household inelastically supplies the total raw labor endowment of one unit. The term T_t captures transfers from the government that are treated as lump sum by the household. The terms r_t and w_t are the rental prices of capital and labor in terms of time t consumption, and p_t is the price of time t consumption in terms of the numeraire. Finally, τ_{jt}, $j = H, K$, are the tax rates on the two factors.

OPTIMAL TAXATION

The firm solves

$$\max p_t[F(k_t, z_{2t}) - w_t z_{2t} - r_t k_t],$$

where $z_{2t} = u_t h_t$ is the number of effective labor hours purchased by the firm from the market.

Simple manipulations coupled with standard no-arbitrage conditions allow us to rewrite the consumer's budget constraint as

$$\sum_t p_t(c_t - T_t) \leq W_0 \equiv k_0[(1 - \tau_{K0})r_0 + 1 - \delta_k]$$

$$+ h_0[(1 - \tau_{H0})w_0 + 1 - \delta_h],$$

where we have normalized $p_0 = 1$ and have assumed throughout that the solution is interior: $x_{ht} > 0$ and $x_{kt} > 0$ for all t. Since we shall want to impose this later on, we restrict the planner to choices of taxes that guarantee that this will hold in equilibrium.

The planner's problem can be phrased as choosing time paths of the variables c_t, k_t, h_t, x_{ht}, x_{kt}, τ_{Kt}, τ_{Ht}, p_t, w_t, and r_t to maximize the representative agent's welfare subject to the constraints embodied in the conditions describing competitive equilibrium. Following the approach of Lucas and Stokey (1983) and Lucas (1990), we can simplify the problem to eliminate p_t, w_t, r_t, τ_{Kt}, and τ_{Ht}.

After this is done, the planner's problem becomes

$$\max \sum_t \beta^t u(c_t) \quad \text{subject to}$$

(a) $\sum_t \beta^t (c_t - T_t) u'(t) = W_0,$

(b) $c_t + x_{ht} + x_{kt} + g_t = F(k_t, h_t),$ \hfill (P1)

(c) $k_{t+1} = (1 - \delta_k)k_t + x_{kt},$

(d) $h_{t+1} = (1 - \delta_h)h_t + x_{ht},$

(e) all variables nonnegative, h_0 and k_0 given.

Here

$$W_0 = [(1 - \tau_{K0})F_k(0) + 1 - \delta_k]k_0 + [(1 - \tau_{H0})F_h(0) + 1 - \delta_h]h_0,$$

and the sequences g_t and T_t are viewed as fixed.

Given the time paths for the variables c_t, x_{ht}, x_{kt}, k_t, h_t, τ_{H0}, and τ_{K0}, which solve this problem, the remainder of the variables (i.e., prices and tax rates) can be reconstructed using the conditions describing competitive equilibrium.

As is, this problem has a very simple solution: to set τ_{K0} or τ_{H0} high enough to finance the entire sequence of government expenditures and to set taxes to zero thereafter (this may involve $\tau_{K0} > 1$ for some choices of g_t and T_t). Of course, this is simply a form of lump-sum taxation since h_0 and k_0 are in fixed supply. Since there is more interest in the solution to (P1) in environments in which lump-sum taxation is not available, we shall have to put some restrictions on how the planner can set taxes. To this end, we set τ_{K0} and τ_{H0} at their historical levels and restrict the size of τ_{Kt} and τ_{Ht}. Further, the bounds on tax rates must be chosen with care. If the tax rate bounds are too high, then investment at time 0 will be zero, with the period 1 capital stocks fixed at their depreciated time 0 levels. Given this, capital taxation in period 1 takes on a lump-sum character. To avoid this problem, we choose our bounds on tax rates low enough so as to guarantee that investment will remain strictly positive in all periods.

To implement tax bounds, we use the fact that bounding tax rates above is equivalent to bounding consumption growth rates below. The bound we use in our simulations is a zero consumption growth rate.

It is worth noting that versions of the results of Judd (1985) and Chamley (1986) (which can be easily extended to the setting of endogenous growth) apply to this case. These imply that $\lim_{t\to\infty} \tau_{Kt} = 0$. Moreover, if $T_t = 0$ for all t, the tax rate bounds will be attained at the optimum for some finite number of periods after which (plus one period) $\tau_{Kt} = 0$. Because of the symmetry of the model, it follows that $\lim_{t\to\infty} \tau_{Ht} = 0$ as well. This is true in spite of the fact that labor is inelastically supplied. Roughly, although the planner would like to tax the inelastically supplied labor endowment, his only avenue to accomplish this is to jointly tax the (in the limit perfectly elastically supplied) stock of human capital as well. Because of this, the planner taxes neither labor nor capital income in the limit.

A. Computational Methods

In choosing a method for numerical solution of variations on the Ramsey planner's problem, we confront two major difficulties. First, we know very little about the qualitative nature of the solution path. What we do know is limited largely to the steady-state behavior of the system. For some variants of the problem, this is dependent on steady-state revenue requirements of the solution, which is, in turn, determined by the revenue raised in the initial periods. Second, the Ramsey planner's problem cannot be posed as a time-invariant dynamic program; if we follow the strategy of Chari et al. (1990) of conditioning on the budget constraint multiplier, we can write the

OPTIMAL TAXATION

problem as a dynamic program only from the first period forward. Even if this is done, the addition of constraints on the maximum tax rate complicates the behavior of the policy functions. Finally, this strategy requires iteration over the budget constraint multiplier and the time 0 investment choices.

To numerically solve these infinite-horizon Ramsey problems, we form truncated versions of the problems with T periods. We experimented with different values of T to obtain accurate solutions of the problem. As is standard, dropping returns after period T gives rise to "end effects" on the capital stock and consumption path due to the implicit understatement of the value (in the truncated version of the problem) of the terminal capital stocks. Even in an undistorted problem (i.e., with no taxes) with $T = 50$, this effect is felt throughout the entire time path. To compensate for this problem, we added a term to the objective function reflecting the continuation value of the terminal capital stocks. We assumed that after period T, the economy would follow the theoretically calculated steady-state growth path from then on (as in Auerbach and Kotlikoff [1987]). A similar correction was made to the last period of the constraints that are infinite horizon in nature (i.e., the Ramsey budget constraints). In some of the problems that we shall solve below, the steady-state growth behavior of the system is dependent on the solution in the first few periods. In these cases, adjustments to this procedure are used. See the discussion in Sections III and IV for details.

Once the truncated versions of the Ramsey problems are formed, they are simply nonlinear programming problems in which the value function is maximized subject to linear, nonlinear, and bounds constraints. We chose nonlinear programming methods to solve these problems. We made this choice for three reasons: (1) the modern methods that are available have known error properties, (2) experience with these techniques on a very wide variety of problems has shown them to be very robust to even extremely ill-behaved objective functions, and (3) the code for these techniques has been extensively tested and is available on a wide variety of computers from personal computers to supercomputers. The exact nonlinear programs solved for the models considered are presented in the Appendix.

We employed a sequential quadratic programming method each iteration of which uses a quadratic approximation to each problem to obtain a search direction for minimization of an augmented Lagrangian merit function (see Gill, Murray, and Wright [1981] for a discussion of this method). We used the implementation of the NPSOL algorithm in the NAG subroutine library routine E04UCF. Analytical objective function gradients and constraint Jacobians were used for all solutions. We used SUN SparcStation 330 and IBM

RS6000/520 work stations to perform all computations. Computer programs are available on request from the authors.

B. Simulations of the Simple Model

For the simulations, we use a calibrated version of the model outlined above. In particular, we assume that

$$u(c) = \frac{c^{1-\sigma}}{1-\sigma}, \quad F(k, h) = Ak^\alpha h^{1-\alpha}.$$

It can be shown (see Jones and Manuelli 1990) that for certain values of the parameters the tax-distorted equilibrium of this economy converges to a steady-state growth path. When δ_h and δ_k are equal, the characteristics of this path are

$$\frac{h_t}{k_t} = \frac{(1-\alpha)(1-\tau_H)}{\alpha(1-\tau_K)} \tag{1}$$

and

$$\gamma \equiv \frac{c_{t+1}}{c_t} = \frac{k_{t+1}}{k_t} = \frac{h_{t+1}}{h_t}$$
$$= (\beta\{A[(1-\alpha)(1-\tau_H)]^{1-\alpha}[\alpha(1-\tau_K)]^\alpha + 1 - \delta_k\})^{1/\sigma}, \tag{2}$$

where τ_K and τ_H are the limiting tax rates on human capital and physical capital income, respectively, and γ is the growth rate.

Given this, we chose parameters for the model consistent with U.S. time-series observations. Thus we set $\alpha = .36$, $\beta = .98$, $\delta_k = \delta_h = .1$, $\tau_K = .21$, $\tau_H = .31$, and $\gamma = 1.02$. This estimate of α comes from a computation of capital's share in national income, which includes durables as part of the capital stock (see Prescott 1986). Kydland and Prescott (1982) use $\delta_k = .1$ as their estimate. Data from Jorgenson and Yun (1991) suggest a smaller value, near .06. On the other hand, in a calculation using capital consumption allowances, Judd (1987) estimates $\delta_k = .12$. Heckman's (1976) estimates of δ_h range from 4 percent to 9 percent but seem very sensitive to the specification of the model. Rosen's (1976) estimates vary from 5 percent (high school graduates in 1960) to 19 percent (college graduates in 1970). Because of the wide variance in these estimates, we decided initially to treat human and physical capital symmetrically, setting $\delta_k = \delta_h = .1$. Kydland and Prescott (1982) estimate $\beta = .96$. However, empirical studies in both macroeconomics and finance find higher values (exceeding one in some cases). We chose $\beta = .98$ as an intermediate value. Given that we have fixed β in this way, different values for other parameters of preferences imply different rates of return. These are presented in table 1 below for the purpose of reference. The value of τ_H that we have selected is consistent with the estimates given in Barro and Sahasakul (1986). Given this, τ_K is given by the requirement that the government budget constraint be satisfied. Below we investigate the sensitivity of model solutions to changes in depreciation and tax rates.

Given these choices for parameter values, equation (2) then gives a joint restriction on σ and A. We experimented with various values along this frontier for comparative purposes. We chose $\sigma = 1$ (the log case), 1.5, 2.0, and 2.5. These give rise to A's of .37, .40, .43, and .46, respectively. It follows that the asymptotic growth rates of consumption in these cases are 1.072, 1.057, 1.049, and 1.044, respectively (these can be calculated using [2] with $\tau_K = \tau_H = 0$).

All calculations were done with the initial share of government spending on consumption in gross national product equal to .20 and transfers' share of output equal to .0726 with (the U.S. historical) 2 percent growth, $T = 50$, and the same initial capital stocks. Note that this figure for transfer payments is less than that reported in most sources. The difference amounts to approximately 50 percent of social security taxes. The idea behind this difference is that individuals treat at least some portion of social security as forced savings (for retirement) rather than transfer payments in the strict sense.[1]

An example of the time paths of a Ramsey solution is given in figure 1. The top half of the figure shows the paths of the real variables in the solution to the problem. The bottom half shows the corresponding paths of the tax rate, government revenues, and expenditures. As can be seen, consumption stays constant during the first few periods as the planner builds a surplus of revenue over expenditure because of our particular implementation of the tax bounds constraints. Following this initial phase, c, h, and k asymptotically ap-

---

[1] The figures we used for government spending are based on spending and revenue data for government at all levels. Government expenditure as a fraction of GNP has varied over the period from .266 to .349. We chose as our base case .33. Of this quantity, government consumption has been about 20 percent of GNP. Thus the figure we used in our calculations for g_t is .2 of output. The remainder of government expenditures is made up of transfer payments and interest payments. Of this quantity, approximately 1.8 percent of GNP over the period has been devoted to interest payments. Transfer payments have been growing over the period and are currently approximately 11.1 percent of GNP. These payments are made up of two parts, social security and other payments. Social security payments are complicated because they correspond in part to what is called transfer payments in the model and part savings since payments are linked (indirectly) to contributions. To handle this problem, as a first step, we attributed half of social security payments to forced savings, with the remainder being treated as true transfer payments. Since social security tax payments are approximately 12 percent of labor income, this gives forced savings through social security of approximately $.06 \times .64 = 3.84$ percent of GNP (.64 is labor's share in output). This gives transfers of 7.26 percent of GNP ($= 11.1 - 3.84$). This is the number we used for T_t in our calculations.

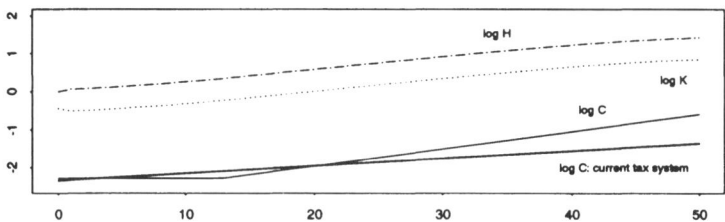
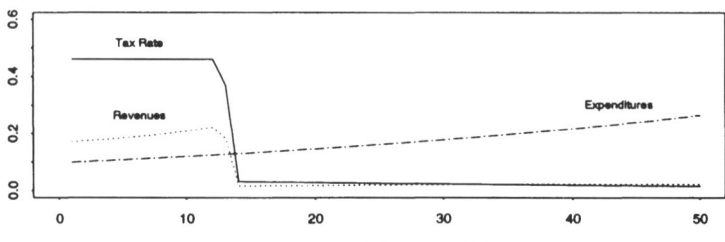

Fig. 1.—Model 1, $\sigma = 2.0$

proach the steady-state growth levels. Because of the symmetry of human and physical capital in the model, $\tau_{Kt} = \tau_{Ht}$ along the optimal path for all t. After an initial stage of high taxation, there is a one-period transition in which the tax rate declines dramatically, followed by a gradual reduction to zero.

A summary of the results obtained from different parameter settings is presented in table 1. In the table, N denotes the number of periods during which the taxes are at their theoretical upper bound, $\bar{\tau}$ denotes the tax rate upper bound that is implied by the consumption growth constraints, γ_1 is the calibrated growth rate (always 2 percent), and γ_2 is the asymptotic growth rate under optimal taxation. The term r_1 denotes the before-tax rate of return on capital along the

TABLE 1

CALCULATIONS FOR THE SIMPLE MODEL

σ	γ_1	A	r_1	γ_2	r_2	N	$\bar{\tau}$	Welfare*
1.01	1.02	.37	.05	1.072	.09	16	.38	3.92
1.50	1.02	.40	.06	1.057	.11	15	.42	1.37
2.00	1.02	.43	.08	1.049	.12	12	.46	1.15
2.50	1.02	.46	.09	1.044	.14	10	.49	1.09

* This is the factor by which the $\{c_t\}$ path of consumption must be raised in order to bring utility under the current system up to the level attained in the Ramsey resolution of tax paths.

OPTIMAL TAXATION

steady-state growth path under the current fiscal system, and r_2 denotes the rate of return to capital in the steady state of the Ramsey solution. It should be emphasized that r_1 represents the rate of return paid to households for rental of capital in a world in which there is no firm-level taxation of capital income. For this reason, comparison of these rates of return with interest rates measured on existing assets in the economy should be done with caution.

There are several important qualitative features of the solutions. First, there is a substantial realignment in the ratios of physical to human capital arising from the differences between effective marginal tax rates on income derived from human and physical capital. The resulting "static" realignment gives rise to an increase in growth rates. In addition to this, the fact that the limiting tax rates are zero diminishes the intertemporal distortion present in the current system and causes faster accumulation of both types of capital.

Second, as σ is increased, the limiting growth rate (γ_2 in table 1) decreases monotonically. The nature of our model calibration induces two competing effects. As σ increases, for a given technology the growth rate falls. In contrast, as A increases for a given σ, the growth rate increases. In our simulation studies, the growth effects of changes in σ dominate those of A, resulting in a reduction in limiting growth as σ increases. As can be seen, the welfare impact of the tax reform envisaged in this exercise is substantial. Further, in our experiments, the welfare gains from tax reform are highly sensitive to and decreasing in σ.

To test the sensitivity of these results to our choice of parameters, we performed several additional computations with different choices for the depreciation rates on human and physical capital and for the tax rates on the two types of income. We performed three sets of additional computations. In the first two, we adjusted tax rates to increase capital's share of revenue; the cases considered were $\tau_K = \tau_H = .274$ and $\tau_K = .31$ with $\tau_H = .254$. For the final experiment, we reduced depreciation rates on both types of capital to $\delta_k = .07$ and $\delta_h = .05$. In all cases, σ was held fixed at two and α at .36. The results of these computations suggest that the findings reported in table 1 are fairly robust. In particular, these changes in tax rates result in almost no change in either the welfare gain or the limiting growth rate. The estimated growth rates are all close to 4.9 percent with welfare increases between 13 and 14 percent. These estimates should be compared with 4.9 percent for the growth rate and 15 percent as the welfare change in table 1. Changes in the depreciation rates also have little effect on the growth results presented in table 1. We find a limiting growth rate of 4.2 percent and a welfare gain of 20 percent for the case corresponding to a reduction in depreciation rates.

For comparative purposes, additional simulations excluding transfers were performed. We left the initial share of government spending on consumption at 20 percent of initial GNP, which was again increased by the historical average of 2 percent per year. In order that the government would be running a roughly balanced budget in the pre-Ramsey state, taxes were reduced to $\tau_K = .13$ and $\tau_H = .24$. To maintain the steady-state growth rate of 2 percent, the values of A were adjusted down accordingly. In this case, the tax rates in the optimal solution take on a "bang-bang" character in which the tax rates achieve the bound for an initial phase and after a one-period transition are set to zero. These computations give rise to similar growth and welfare effects.

In the case that excludes transfers, there is no time consistency problem because of the special form of the optimal taxes. That is, at any date t, if the problem were resolved, the resulting solution would agree with the time path from the first solution. This result holds only for the special case in which the two capital goods are perfectly symmetric and labor is inelastically supplied.

The estimates of the welfare changes that we obtain from this exercise are both large and highly sensitive to assumptions about the intertemporal elasticity of substitution in consumption. For the log case, we find a 390 percent gain with a marked decline down to 15 percent for the case in which $\sigma = 2$. To our knowledge, no directly comparable results exist in the literature. There is, however, a large related literature. King and Rebelo (1990) consider both exogenous and endogenous growth models in which the government finances a transfer policy using capital income taxation. They study the effect of using lump-sum taxes to reduce the tax rate from 30 percent to 20 percent and find very different results depending on whether the model is one with exogenous or endogenous growth. In the exogenous growth case, the gain is less than 2 percent, whereas in the endogenous growth case it exceeds 60 percent using logarithmic utility and inelastic labor supply. They find that changes in the elasticity of substitution do not have significant effects on their estimates. Chamley (1981) uses an exogenous growth model to evaluate the welfare gain in an exercise similar to that of King and Rebelo. He computes estimates of both the effects of a global tax reform from the elimination of capital income taxes and the marginal effect of small reductions in tax rates. His estimates of the welfare gain due to global changes range from 3.19 percent (when the capital tax rate is 50 percent) to less than 1 percent (when the capital tax rate is 30 percent) with logarithmic preferences. Judd (1987) estimates the marginal effect of lowering both capital and labor income tax rates. For this calculation,

OPTIMAL TAXATION 497

he obtains estimates roughly four times as large as those of Chamley for a similar exercise. Even if we use this factor to inflate Chamley's results for the global case, we obtain estimates of welfare change that are less than 13 percent for the log case.

Our own results indicate a much larger effect than the estimates given by the exogenous growth literature cited above. They are more in line with the findings of King and Rebelo (1990) for the endogenous growth case. A key difference is the greater sensitivity to σ that we find.

III. Complications of the Simple Model: Model 2

In this section, we add two features to model 1: a labor-leisure choice and a modification of the human capital accumulation process. In doing this we introduce some asymmetries between physical and human capital.

These changes have three qualitatively important effects on the model. First, they change the model from a one-sector one to a two-sector one. That this can have important impacts on the growth process is well known (see Rebelo 1991; Jones and Manuelli 1992). Second, some parts of the human capital accumulation process go untaxed. Specifically, direct labor services used in the production of human capital (i.e., a student's time spent in school) are untaxed. This is the sense in which "nonmarket" goods are introduced. Third, because of the form of the production function assumed for effective labor (see below), there is now an intrinsic source of inelasticity in the supply of human capital. Although there are two inputs into the production of effective labor, we allow the planner to use only one tax on labor income. The effect of this is to add a set of constraints not found in the existing optimal taxation literature to the Ramsey problem. These added constraints complicate the computation of the solution to the Ramsey problem.

As discussed in Section II, we assume that effective labor is supplied to both market activities and investment in human capital. Specifically, let $v_t h_t$ and $u_t h_t$ be the amount of effective labor supplied to the formation of human capital and market work, respectively. Then the problem faced by the consumer is to choose time paths for c_t, u_t, v_t, h_t, k_t, x_{kt}, and x_{ht} to maximize

$$\sum_t \beta^t u(c_t, 1 - u_t - v_t) \quad \text{subject to the constraints}$$

(a) $k_{t+1} \leq (1 - \delta_k)k_t + x_{kt}$,

(b) $h_{t+1} \leq (1 - \delta_h)h_t + G(x_{ht}, v_t h_t)$,

(c) $\sum_t p_t[(1 + \tau_{ct})c_t + x_{kt} + x_{ht}]$

$\leq \sum_t p_t[(1 - \tau_{Kt})r_t k_t + (1 - \tau_{Ht})w_t u_t h_t + T_t]$,

(d) all variables nonnegative, h_0 and k_0 fixed.

As before, if $x_{kt} > 0$ for all t, considerable simplification occurs in constraint c. After simplification using the conditions defining competitive equilibrium, the planner's problem can be reformulated as

$$\max \sum_t \beta^t u(c_t, 1 - u_t v_t) \text{ subject to}$$

(a) $\sum_t \beta^t \left[u_1(t)c_t - u_2(t)\frac{T_t}{h_t}\frac{G_1(t)}{G_2(t)} + u_2(t)\frac{x_{ht}}{h_t}\frac{G_1(t)}{G_2(t)} - u_2(t)u_t \right]$

$= W_0 \frac{u_2(0)}{h_0}\frac{G_1(0)}{G_2(0)}$,

(b) $k_{t+1} = (1 - \delta_k)k_t + x_{kt}$, \hfill (P2)

(c) $h_{t+1} = (1 - \delta_h)h_t + G(x_{ht}, v_t h_t)$,

(d) $c_t + x_{kt} + x_{ht} + g_t = F(k_t, u_t h_t)$,

(e) $\frac{u_2(t)}{u_2(t+1)} = \beta \frac{G_2(t)}{G_2(t+1)}\frac{h_t}{h_{t+1}}[1 - \delta_h + G_2(t+1)(u_{t+1} + v_{t+1})]$,

where $W_0 = [1 - \delta_k + (1 - \tau_{K0})F_k(0)]k_0$ and part e captures the constraint that the same tax rate, τ_{Ht}, must be used for both raw labor, u_t, and human capital, h_t.

Again, there is a problem with lump-sum taxation if the planner is allowed to set taxes without any restrictions. To solve this problem, we impose constraints on the maximum tax rate.

As before, one can show that under the optimal plan, $\tau_{Kt} \to 0$. However, since human and physical capital are no longer perfectly symmetric, it is no longer necessarily true that $\tau_{Ht} \to 0$. However, if transfers disappear asymptotically, then for the functional forms that we use, the labor tax rate and the consumption tax rate converge to zero. See Bull (1992) and Jones, Manuelli, and Rossi (1992) for a derivation.

For the purposes of calibration, we used the following specific func-

OPTIMAL TAXATION

tional forms:

$$u(c, 1 - u - v) = \frac{[c(1 - u - v)^\eta]^{1-\sigma}}{1 - \sigma},$$

$$F(k, uh) = A_1 k^\alpha (uh)^{1-\alpha},$$

$$G(x_h, vh) = A_2 (x_h)^\psi (vh)^{1-\psi}.$$

Under these assumptions, the steady-state equations of the competitive system are given by

$$\gamma^\sigma = \beta \left[1 - \delta_k + (1 - \tau_K)\alpha A_1 u^{1-\alpha} \left(\frac{h}{k}\right)^{1-\alpha} \right], \quad (3)$$

$$\gamma^\sigma = \beta \left[1 - \delta_h + A_2(1 - \psi) \left(\frac{x_h}{h}\right)^\psi v^{1-\psi} \right.$$
$$\left. + (1 - \tau_H) A_2 \psi \left(\frac{x_h}{h}\right)^{\psi-1} v^{1-\psi} A_1 (1 - \alpha) \left(\frac{k}{h}\right)^\alpha u^{1-\alpha} \right], \quad (4)$$

$$\frac{c}{h} \frac{\eta}{1 - u - v} = \frac{1 - \tau_H}{1 + \tau_c} (1 - \alpha) \frac{A_1}{u^\alpha} \left(\frac{k}{h}\right)^\alpha, \quad (5)$$

$$\frac{c}{h} \frac{\eta}{1 - u - v} = \frac{1 - \psi}{\psi} \frac{x_h}{h} \frac{1}{v} \frac{1}{1 + \tau_c}, \quad (6)$$

$$\gamma = 1 - \delta_k + \frac{x_k}{k}, \quad (7)$$

$$\gamma = 1 - \delta_h + A_2 \left(\frac{x_h}{h}\right)^\psi v^{1-\psi}, \quad (8)$$

$$\frac{c}{h} + \frac{x_h}{h} + \frac{x_k}{k}\frac{k}{h} + \frac{g}{h} = A_1 \left(\frac{k}{h}\right)^\alpha u^{1-\alpha}. \quad (9)$$

To calibrate the model, we fix $\beta = .98$, $\delta_h = \delta_k = .1$, $A_2 = 1$, $u = .17$, $v = .12$, $\gamma = 1.02$, and $\alpha = .36$.[2] The tax and government spending variables are the same as those in model 1 with the excep-

---

[2] To obtain estimates of the quantities of work in the market sector and in human capital formation, we first estimated the number of hours available in total:

hours avail = (pop over 16) × 14.5 (hrs/day) × 7 (days/wk) × 52 (wks/yr)
+ (pop 5–15) × 8 (hrs/day) × 7 (days/wk) × 52 (wks/yr).

This gives an estimate of the (aggregate) time available. Note that we allotted less usable time to younger individuals. Second, we constructed series of actual hours

tion that we added $\tau_c = .083$.[3] The steady-state equations are used to solve for η, ψ, and A_1 for a grid of σ values. For the parameters chosen in our calibrations, the implied intertemporal elasticity of labor supply ranges from 1.3 (for $\sigma = 1.1$ and $\eta = 7.09$) to .67 (for $\sigma = 2.5$ and $\eta = 4.38$). These values are within the upper range of the estimates reported in MaCurdy (1985) and are slightly lower than Lucas and Rapping's (1969) preferred estimate of 1.4.

Numerical solution of this problem is considerably more difficult than the inelastic labor supply case discussed in Section II. The labor supply decisions increase the number of variables twofold. In addition, the form for effective labor supply introduces nonconvexities into the problem. For this reason, we started with an initial problem with zero fiscal activity and gradually increased government expenditures to the desired level, resolving the problem at each intermediate step. Having obtained a solution for one set of parameter values, we deformed the problem by gradual shifts in the parameters. This allowed us to trace the solution over an interesting region of the parameter space.

Figures 2 and 3 show the time path of the solution to the optimal tax problem for the case of $\sigma = 2.0$ (with $\eta = 4.99$, $\psi = .44$, and $A_1 = 1.60$). The solutions are qualitatively similar for the other values of the parameters we studied. The top half of figure 2 shows the time path of the two capital variables h and k as well as the path of consumption. These paths converge very quickly to the limiting growth rate of 5.5 percent.

---

worked from the *Economic Report of the President*. Our estimate of u is then (hours worked)/(hours avail). This has fluctuated from .169 to .176 over the period 1960–85. This was the basis of the calibrated value we chose of $u = .17$. To obtain an estimate of v, we used the hours avail estimate above in conjunction with estimates of the hours used in human capital formation. This last quantity was formed by

$$\text{hcap1} = (\text{pop 5--19}) \times 30 \text{ (hrs/wk)} \times 40 \text{ (wks/yr)},$$

$$\text{hcap 2} = (\text{number employed}) \times 9 \text{ (hrs/wk)} \times 52 \text{ (wks/yr)}.$$

These are estimates of time spent in schooling and on-the-job training, respectively (see Juster and Stafford 1990). Our estimate of v is then given by $v = (\text{hcap1} + \text{hcap2})/(\text{hours avail})$. This has varied from .104 to .123 over the period 1960–85 and forms the basis of our estimate of $v = .12$.

[3] In keeping with our discussion concerning our tax rates given in conjunction with model 1, we chose tax rates of .37 for labor income and .21 for capital income. This tax on labor income includes social security payments; thus, in keeping with our treatment of social security payments outlined above, .31 is the effective rate affecting marginal decisions and .06 is the component we are treating as forced savings through the social security system. This gives revenue of 31.24 percent of GNP. The remainder of revenue is made up of a variety of tariffs and excise, sales, and other indirect business taxes. To handle this last part, we attributed the entire quantity to general taxes on consumption. Since consumption taxes are lump sum in the model of Sec. II, we ignored this source in that section. Here, we used a tax rate of 8.3 percent on consumption to account for this extra source of revenue.

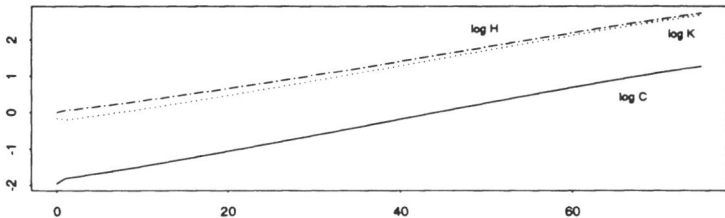

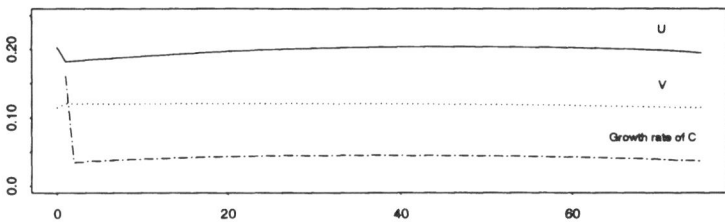

Fig. 2.—Model 2, $\sigma = 2.0$

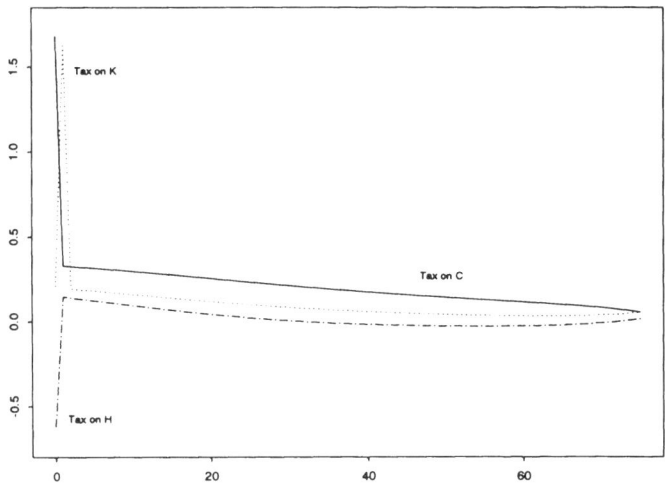

Fig. 3.—Model 2, $\sigma = 2.0$

The bottom half of figure 2 shows the time paths of some of the variables that are converging to constants along the optimal path, u, v, and γ. These are very well behaved and smoothly approach their limiting values. Also, the steady-state growth path values of u and v are considerably above those from the current calibration. It can be seen from the steady-state equations that both u and v have an effect on the limiting growth rate. This is one source of the very large change in the growth rate from 2 to 5.5 percent. Lower taxes result in a significant increase in the number of hours devoted to market work with a higher utilization of human capital.

Figure 3 shows the time paths of the tax rate variables in the calculated Ramsey solution. All tax rates converge to zero in the limit after an initial phase of high taxation. As in model 1, there is a very high time period 1 capital tax rate followed by a smooth decline to zero. The tax on consumption follows a similar path with an even higher initial tax rate. In contrast, the initial labor tax rate is negative immediately followed by positive and smoothly declining tax rates. The time 0 labor subsidy accounts for the initial high values of u and v, which are immediately adjusted downward. The high time 0 consumption tax delays consumption, resulting in an abnormally high time 0 consumption growth rate.

The results of experiments involving changes in σ are contained in tables 2–4. As in the experiments conducted with model 1, we have adjusted the values of η, ψ, and A_1 so as to maintain a growth rate of 2 percent under the current tax system. Alternatively, given the nature of the experiment, this exercise can be viewed as adjusting η and altering σ, ψ, and A_1 accordingly.

Table 2 contains limiting growth rates calculated from the 75-period approximate solution. For all values of σ, there are large growth and welfare effects of a change to the optimal tax system. As in model 1, there is a general reduction in the level of limiting taxation. This by itself results in a substantial increase in the growth rate through its effect on investment decisions. There are both dynamic

TABLE 2

Growth and Welfare: Elastic Labor Supply

σ	η	A_1	ψ	γ_1	γ_2	Welfare*
1.1	7.09	1.29	.51	1.02	1.103	3.52
1.5	5.91	1.42	.48	1.02	1.055	1.46
2.0	4.99	1.60	.44	1.02	1.040	1.20
2.5	4.38	1.80	.41	1.02	1.034	1.13

* This is the factor by which the $\{c_t\}$ path of consumption must be raised in order to bring utility under the current system up to the level attained in the Ramsey resolution of tax paths.

OPTIMAL TAXATION

TABLE 3
STEADY-STATE VARIABLES: ELASTIC LABOR SUPPLY

σ	γ_2	u_1	u_2	v_1	v_2	$(k/h)_1$	$(k/h)_2$	$(c/y)_1$	$(c/y)_2$
1.1	1.103	.17	.25	.12	.18	.74	.71	.24	.21
1.5	1.055	.17	.20	.12	.13	.79	.84	.29	.35
2.0	1.040	.17	.19	.12	.12	.85	.94	.34	.44
2.5	1.034	.17	.19	.12	.12	.93	1.04	.39	.51

TABLE 4
REVENUE SHARES: ELASTIC LABOR SUPPLY

σ	γ_2	rev_1^c	rev_2^c	rev_1^k	rev_2^k	rev_1^h	rev_2^h
1.1	1.103	.07	.31	.26	.47	.68	.22
1.5	1.055	.08	.49	.25	.41	.67	.11
2.0	1.040	.09	.56	.25	.39	.66	.05
2.5	1.034	.11	.62	.25	.39	.65	−.01

and static components to these investment decision effects. In addition to these investment effects, there is an additional effect of the switch to optimal taxes. This is the labor supply response to the reduction in distortion on the labor-leisure margin. In fact, for a given σ, the welfare effects seen here are larger than those calculated in model 1 (see table 1).

In tables 3 and 4, a subscript 1 denotes values corresponding to the current tax system, and a subscript 2 refers to limiting values in the optimal tax system.

The reduction in labor and consumption taxes results in an increase in $u + v$, as can be seen in table 3. For all σ, u is larger in the optimal tax system by at least 11 percent over the current value. This increase in u enhances the effectiveness of h in production, resulting in higher growth as can be seen from (3). This labor intensity effect on growth is a direct by-product of our choice of the technology for effective labor. (Any production function of the form $z = \phi(u)h$ will have this type of effect.) A similar argument could be made for v.

Reductions in any of the tax rates have complicated effects on all the steady-state variables of the system. For example, the tax reductions induce an increase in u but not always in v, which have opposite growth effects. This can be seen by comparing the results for $\sigma = 1.1$ and $\sigma = 2.5$. In the first case, the change in tax systems increases u and v and decreases c/y (a reflection of the increase in the fraction of output devoted to investment), all of which are growth enhancing.

When σ = 2.5, we still see an increase in u. However, v is slightly reduced (in the third digit) and c/y increases. These last two changes serve to temper the growth effect of the increase in u.

Table 4 shows one of the most dramatic effects of the switch to the optimal tax system. This is the change in reliance on differing sources of revenue relative to the current system. The terms rev^c, rev^k, and rev^h are, respectively, the fraction of government revenue raised through taxation of consumption, capital income, and labor income. These are calculated as present values of revenue streams in time 0 consumption units. Most striking is the switch from a labor tax–based system to one that relies heavily on consumption taxes.[4]

As is the case with model 1, we obtain large growth and welfare effects from a switch to the Ramsey optimal solution. It is interesting to note that we obtain similar magnitudes in both the inelastic and elastic labor supply cases. Our results for the elastic labor supply case differ from the findings of Lucas (1990), in which a related model is studied. He estimates the maximal gain in welfare from this experiment to be 2.7 percent using the value σ = 2. However, his policy experiment is slightly different in that he reduces the tax on capital income to zero while increasing both the labor tax rate (to keep the level of debt roughly constant) and the level of government spending (to account for the growth effect of tax changes). The requirement in Lucas's exercise that the budget be balanced in the steady state is probably the main source of the differences in growth and welfare effects.

IV. Endogenous Government Expenditure

The reader will note that in the experiments we have performed to this point, we have taken the Ramsey program very literally. Specifically, we have held a sequence of government expenditures on consumption and transfers as fixed exogenously (in real terms) and asked the question, Is there an alternative tax system that would finance this expenditure sequence more efficiently?

In particular, because of the way in which the Ramsey scheme differs from the current one, it follows that following the Ramsey scheme would give rise to long-run growth rates of output different from those we are currently experiencing. Because of this fact, it follows that the sequence of fixed g's tends to a negligible fraction of output. There is no obvious reason to think that g is an inferior good.

---

[4] From a policy perspective, switching to a consumption-based tax has been advocated in Bradford (1984). The results concerning welfare comparisons among alternative tax bases in Auerbach and Kotlikoff (1987) are also relevant.

OPTIMAL TAXATION

This suggests that g should be adjusted at the same time that taxes are realigned. In this respect, there are both qualitative and quantitative issues that deserve attention. On the qualitative side, it is of interest to explore how different technological specifications involving productive public goods affect both the path and the asymptotic properties of optimal tax policies. From a quantitative perspective, it is important to identify those aspects of technology that are crucial in determining the effects of tax reform. This is the focus of this section.

Alternative methods for endogenizing g include explicitly introducing g into either the utility function or the production function (or both). For these versions of the Ramsey problem, the planner chooses both the tax rates and the g_t sequence. Any of the several different alternatives for introducing productive government spending would be controversial. As a start, we treat government spending as though it had a direct impact on the effectiveness of investment. Examples of this would include the provisions of roads or dams and expenditures on education and health.[5]

In order to isolate the effects of this change on the form of optimal taxes in infinite-horizon growth models, we simplify the models considered above. To do this, we consider the case of a simple one-sector model of capital accumulation and delete labor from the model entirely. The notion of equilibrium used given a time path of government expenditures is identical to that introduced in Section II. Consumers treat the sequence g_t as given when making their investment decisions.

This gives rise to the following problem for the consumer to solve:

$$\max \sum_t \beta^t u(c_t) \quad \text{subject to}$$

$$(a) \sum_t p_t(c_t + x_t) \leq \sum_t p_t(1 - \tau_{Kt}) r_t k_t,$$

$$(b) \ k_{t+1} \leq (1 - \delta_k) k_t + G(x_t, g_t),$$

where we assume that G is homogeneous of degree one in x and g jointly, concave, and smooth.

As formulated, the problem assumes that government spending is a publicly provided private good. This is not a necessary assumption. Alternatively, one could view g as a common input that is shared by each of n productive units. The qualitative character of the solution

---

[5] For empirical evidence concerning the effect of government spending on productivity, see Aschauer (1989) and Munnell (1990).

of the Ramsey problem presented below would not be affected by this change.

Following the same strategy as in previous sections and using the arbitrage condition that $p_t/G_1(t) = p_{t+1}\{(1 - \tau_{Kt+1})r_{t+1} + [(1 - \delta_k)/G_1(t+1)]\}$, we can write the Ramsey problem for this economy as

$$\max \sum_t \beta^t u(c_t) \text{ subject to}$$

(a) $\sum_t \beta^t \left[u_1(t)c_t - u_1(t)g_t \frac{G_2(t)}{G_1(t)} \right] = \frac{u_1(0)}{G_1(0)}$ (P3)

$$\times \left\{ [1 - \delta + G_1(0)(1 - \tau_{K0})F_k(0)]k_0 + \sum_t \beta^t u_1(t) \frac{G_1(0)}{u_1(0)} F_L(t) \right\},$$

(b) $c_t + x_t + g_t = F(k_t, 1)$,

(c) $k_{t+1} \leq (1 - \delta_k)k_t + G(x_t, g_t)$,

where the planner is choosing time paths for c, k, x, and g.

It is straightforward to show that the first-best allocation in this environment involves only lump-sum taxes. It follows from this fact that the Ramsey equilibrium will not be first-best in most cases of interest. Exceptions include situations in which τ_{K0} is viewed as variable and unlimited (so that lump-sum taxation is available to the planner) or situations in which g is sufficiently unproductive (i.e., $G_2() = 0$). (In this regard, the recent work of Barro and Sala-i-Martin [1990] on the relative benefits of lump-sum and income taxation in an unconstrained environment should be noted.)

As it turns out, this change has significant impacts on the limiting nature of taxes. In contrast to the results with models 1 and 2 above, it can be shown that in certain cases, the limiting tax on capital income is strictly positive. To study this issue and ensure that stationary growth paths can be equilibria, we restrict attention to cases in which $u(c) = c^{1-\sigma}/(1 - \sigma)$, $F(k, 1) = bk$. Any other production function consistent with long-run growth will give rise to the same limiting behavior. In Jones et al. (1991), the following proposition is proved.

PROPOSITION. The form of the solution to (P3) is determined by the following inequality:

$$\sum_t \beta^t u_1^*(t) g_t^* > k_0 [\tau_{K0} u_1^*(0) F_k^*], \quad (10)$$

where asterisks indicate that variables are evaluated at their first-best quantities.

OPTIMAL TAXATION

i) If (10) is satisfied, then the limiting tax on capital income is strictly positive.
ii) If (10) is not satisfied, then the Ramsey allocation is first-best and involves only lump-sum taxation.

Expression (10) has a very simple interpretation: that the planned government spending in the first-best solution exceeds the government's ability to raise taxes in the first period by taxing time 0 capital income.

It is possible to show (see Jones et al. 1992) that the reason why asymptotic tax rates on capital income are positive is that pure profits result in our formulation. Both the limiting g (as a fraction of output) and the limiting x affect the size of these profits. The planner has full control over g but can influence the choice of x only indirectly through the choice of capital tax rates. This is the reason why limiting tax rates are positive.

Alternative formulations of productive public goods (see Judd 1991; Zhu 1991) have been suggested. Under these specifications, profits do not result from the inclusion of public goods, and because of this, the limiting tax rate on capital income is zero. These are only a few of many possible specifications for the incorporation of productive public goods. A comprehensive investigation of optimal tax and spending policies across these formulations would be an interesting direction for future research.

A. Simulations

In this subsection, we describe the results of some simple simulation experiments based on the model outlined above. To do this, we shall simplify the model by choosing the following functional forms:

$$u(c) = \frac{c^{1-\sigma}}{1-\sigma},$$

$$f(k) = bk,$$

$$G(x, g_x) = A[\alpha x^{-\rho} + (1-\alpha)g_x^{-\rho}]^{-1/\rho}.$$

The constant elasticity of substitution functional form was chosen to enable us to study the relationship between the elasticity of substitution between public and private investment ($\epsilon = 1/[1+\rho]$) and both the limiting tax rate on capital income and the limiting share in output of government investment expenditure.

Given these choices, the steady-state growth equations for the model are

$$\gamma^\sigma = \beta[(1-\delta) + (1-\tau_k)bG_1], \tag{11}$$

$$\gamma = 1 - \delta + G_1 \frac{x}{k} + G_2 \frac{g_x}{k}, \qquad (12)$$

$$\frac{c}{k} + \frac{x}{k} + \frac{g_c}{k} + \frac{g_x}{k} = b. \qquad (13)$$

To calibrate the model, we chose $\beta = .98$, $\delta = .1$, $\gamma = 1.02$, $\tau_k = .2$, $g_c/k = .08b$, $g_x/k = .12b$, $A = 1$, $\sigma = 2$, and $\alpha = .6$. Given these choices, the steady-state equations given above determine b, c/k, and x/k as a function of ρ.

To avoid lump-sum taxation, it is necessary to bound taxes. This bound is referred to as $\tau_{\max}$ below.

In contrast to models 1 and 2, the limiting behavior of the system is dependent on the path of the solution in the first few periods. The reason is that the long-run rate of growth depends on steady-state revenue requirements. This (and hence the limiting tax rate) depends on the ability of the planner to raise revenue in the beginning of the problem. To handle this problem, we followed a procedure in which the limiting government choice variables (τ_k and g_x/k) are chosen, and then the problem is solved to give calculated values for τ_k and g_x/k from the end of the solution. We iterate on these values until a fixed point is found.

Figure 4 shows the time path of capital taxes and the share in output of government investment spending for the base case: $\sigma = 2$, $\delta = .1$, $A = 1$, $\beta = .98$, $\rho = -.5$ ($\epsilon = 2$), $\tau_{\max} = .65$, $b = .416$, and

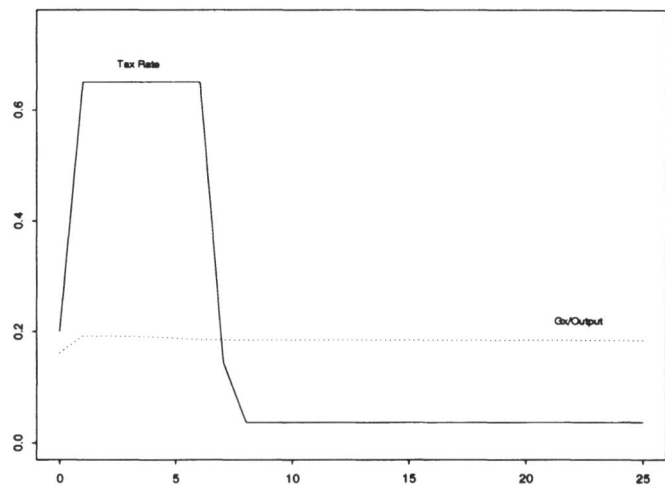

FIG. 4.—Model 3, $\sigma = 2.0$, elasticity of substitution $= 2$

OPTIMAL TAXATION

$\alpha = .6$. There is a substantial increase in the limiting growth rate of output due to two separate effects. First, because of our choice of $\alpha = .6$, there is a substantial realignment of the ratio of public to private spending on investment. In addition to this, there is a change in the limiting tax rate on capital income that also increases the growth rate.

The dynamic behavior of taxes mimics that of the model considered in Section II. An initial period of high taxation is followed by a reduction of taxes to their steady-state levels. In contrast to the results in Section II, however, this limiting tax rate is strictly positive. This is in keeping with the proposition above.

In order to test the sensitivity of our numerical results to our choice of parameter values, experiments were done adjusting σ and ϵ independently. These experiments involved one-dimensional parametric adjustments around a base case in which $\sigma = 2$, $\delta = .1$, $A = 1$, $\beta = .98$, $\rho = -.5$ ($\epsilon = 2$), $\tau_{max} = .65$, $b = .416$, and $\alpha = .6$. The results of two of these experiments are included in tables 5 and 6 below.

In the first experiment, we changed σ while adjusting b to maintain a 2 percent growth rate in the steady state under the current tax system. The results of this experiment are summarized in table 5. As in the experiments in the previous sections, we see that the change to the Ramsey optimal tax system gives rise to substantial increases in both welfare and the growth rate. In contrast to the results in the previous section, however, there are now two independent reasons for these changes. First is the standard increase due to realignment across time of the tax burden. This effect is present in the models of Sections II and III as well. In this case, there is an additional effect due to the misalignment of the relative sizes of government and private investment spending in the current system as discussed above. As σ increases, the limiting rate of growth decreases for the standard intertemporal elasticity of substitution reasons. (The subtlety here is that as σ is increased, b is increased as well. These changes have opposing effects on growth, with the net effect of a decrease in

TABLE 5

CHANGING σ

σ	b	γ_1	γ_2	c/y	x/y	g_x/y	N	τ_x	Welfare*
1.01	.37	1.02	1.042	.26	.58	.17	9	.098	2.24
1.50	.39	1.02	1.042	.31	.51	.18	7	.065	1.57
2.00†	.42	1.02	1.041	.35	.47	.19	6	.037	1.37
2.50	.44	1.02	1.038	.39	.43	.18	4	.022	1.27

NOTE.—For all cases, $\delta = .1$, $A = 1$, $\beta = .98$, $\rho = -.5$ ($\epsilon = 2$), $\tau_{max} = .65$, and $\alpha = .60$.
* This is the factor by which the $\{c_t\}$ path of consumption must be raised in order to bring utility under the current system up to the level attained in the Ramsey resolution of tax paths.
† Signifies results for the base case.

TABLE 6

Changing ϵ

ϵ	b	γ_1	γ_2	c/y	x/y	g_x/y	N	τ_∞	Welfare*
.66	.62	1.02	1.082	.42	.31	.27	4	.134	1.84
.99	.53	1.02	1.060	.39	.34	.26	5	.115	1.54
2.00†	.42	1.02	1.041	.35	.47	.19	6	.037	1.37
4.00	.37	1.02	1.038	.31	.59	.10	3	.002	1.34

Note.—For all cases, $\sigma = .1$, $\delta = .1$, $A = 1$, $\beta = .98$, $\alpha = .6$, and $\tau_{max} = .65$.
* This is the factor by which the $\{c_t\}$ path of consumption must be raised in order to bring utility under the current system up to the level attained in the Ramsey resolution of tax paths.
† Signifies results for the base case.

growth.) In addition to this, both the limiting tax rate and the limiting share of government in output are decreasing in σ. As both the limiting rate of growth of output falls and the share of government spending in output falls, a higher percentage of the necessary government budget can be raised through the initial phase of high taxation, giving rise to lower steady-state revenue requirements and hence lower steady-state tax levels.

The second experiment involves adjusting the elasticity of substitution between private and public expenditures on investment. These results are contained in table 6. As ϵ is increased, public and private investment become better substitutes. Thus the higher ϵ is, the less important is any misalignment between these two sources of investment expenditure. In line with this intuition, the sizes of the welfare and growth effects are lower when ϵ is higher. For the same reason, the higher ϵ is, the lower is the limiting tax rate on income and the fraction of output devoted to public investment.

In addition, we conducted experiments in which α and τ_{max} were varied while σ and ϵ were held constant. Varying α changes the size of the realignment between x and g_x in the optimal regime. Because of this, an increase in α results in lower levels of the limiting growth rate and welfare change. The tax bound was varied between .5 and .8. As the constraint is relaxed, a higher level of the required revenue is raised at the beginning of the problem, giving rise to lower limiting tax rates and higher limiting growth rates. In addition, as is to be expected, increasing this bound increases the size of the welfare effect. While the range of tax bounds considered is fairly substantial, the differences in the welfare and growth effects across the cases are quite small, changing the limiting growth rate by less than 0.2 percent over the entire range.

In summary, the key parameters for determining the size of the growth and welfare effects of a switch to the Ramsey optimal policy are those of the production function for investment and the intertemporal elasticity of substitution. The fact that the production function parameters are so crucial in determining the size of the effects is unfortunate since our knowledge about these is particularly sparse. This suggests a high payoff to further research on the identification and estimation of these parameters.

V. Conclusions

Our goal in this paper has been to provide a quantitative assessment of the size of the effects on welfare and growth rates of radical tax reform in the Ramsey spirit in a calibrated model of the U.S. economy. In all experiments, we found large growth and welfare effects. This holds for all the cases we have studied with inelastic or elastic labor supply and with exogenous or endogenous government spending.

However, these improvements in welfare have been attained by qualitatively different tax policies. Thus the structure of optimal tax policy is highly dependent on the formulation of the model. What the models considered in Section IV suggest is that the program of strict separation between the spending and revenue sides of the government's problem envisaged in the Ramsey approach should be viewed with some skepticism. If the solution to the Ramsey problem causes a large enough realignment of private resources to necessitate a reconsideration of the planned expenditure pattern, the resulting tax policy may be seriously misleading. In more concrete terms, in the calibrated models of Sections II and III, there is a substantial increase in investment in both human and physical capital. If accomplishing this requires an increase in publicly financed activities (e.g., schooling or roads), models of the sort explored in Section IV are of considerable interest. However, in models with endogenous government spending, the limiting capital tax rate depends critically on the specification of the production technology (cf. Judd 1991; Zhu 1991; Jones et al. 1992).

Our findings contrast markedly with many of the results in the dynamic taxation literature. Chamley (1981), Judd (1987), and King and Rebelo (1990) find much smaller welfare effects from various tax reform experiments in exogenous growth settings. Our results are most similar in magnitude to those of the endogenous growth case studied in King and Rebelo. This suggests that endogenous growth is an important contributing factor to the quantitative character of the effects of optimal tax experiments.

The nature of the solutions to the Ramsey problems that we study raises several concerns about the practicality of their implementation. One consideration that arises because of the dynamic path of the taxes is time consistency. This is clearly a problem with the solutions presented in connection with the models we have analyzed (the solutions in Sec. II without transfers are time consistent). In addition to this, in a tax system with significant differences in marginal tax rates across either time or factors, tax arbitrage schemes might arise, limiting government revenue.

Finally, the solutions to all the Ramsey problems that we study in this paper are characterized by an initial phase of relatively high taxation followed by much lower (often zero) asymptotic taxes. If this feature is endemic to all dynamic Ramsey problems, the relevance of the Ramsey experiment might be called into doubt. However, further work is required on alternative technological specifications and more complicated sets of constraints suggested by implementation concerns before definitive methodological conclusions can be drawn.

Appendix

In this Appendix, we outline the nonlinear programming problems actually solved in performing the simulations.

Simple Symmetric Model with Inelastic Labor Supply (Sec. II)

Maximize over $\{k_1, \ldots, k_{T+1}; h_1, \ldots, h_{T+1}\}$

$$\sum_{t=0}^{T} \beta^t u(f(k_t, h_t) - k_{t+1} + (1 - \delta_k)k_t - h_{t+1} + (1 - \delta_h)h_t - g_t) + f^*(k_{T+1})$$

subject to

$$k_t - (1 - \delta_k)k_{t-1} \geq 0, \quad t = 2, \ldots, T,$$

$$h_t - (1 - \delta_h)h_{t-1} \geq 0, \quad t = 2, \ldots, T,$$

$$k_1 \geq (1 - \delta_k)k_0,$$

$$h_1 \geq (1 - \delta_h)h_0,$$

$$\frac{h_{T+1}}{k_{T+1}} = hk^*,$$

$$f(k_t, h_t) - k_{t+1} + (1 - \delta_k)k_t - h_{t+1} + (1 - \delta_h)h_t - g_t$$
$$\geq f(k_{t-1}, h_{t-1}) - k_t + (1 - \delta_k)k_{t-1} - h_t + (1 - \delta_h)h_{t-1} - g_{t-1}, \quad t = 1, \ldots, T$$

(this constraint ensures positive consumption growth),

$$\sum_{t=0}^{T} \beta^t [f(k_t, h_t) - k_{t+1} + (1 - \delta_k)k_t - h_{t+1}$$
$$+ (1 - \delta_h)h_t - g_t - T_t]u'(t) + g^*(k_{T+1}) = W_0,$$

where

$$W_0 = [(1 - \delta_k) + (1 - \tau^k)f_1(k_0, h_0)]k_0 + [(1 - \delta_h) + (1 - \tau^h)f_2(k_0, h_0)]h_0$$

(budget constraint).

OPTIMAL TAXATION

End corrections are made to the objective function and the budget constraint by assuming that after period T consumption and the capital stocks grow at the steady-state rate. In the steady state, both capital taxes are zero, h and k are in a fixed ratio, g has dropped to a negligible fraction of output, and consumption is linear in k:

$$f^*(k_{T+1}) = \sum_{t=T+1}^{\infty} \beta^t u(\gamma^{t-T-1} ck^* k_{T+1}),$$

$$g^*(k_{T+1}) = \sum_{t=T+1}^{\infty} \beta^t (\gamma^{t-T-1} ck^* k_{T+1}) u'(\gamma^{t-T-1} ck^* k_{T+1}),$$

where hk^* is the steady-state ratio of h to k and ck^* is the steady-state ratio of c to k when all taxes are zero (see eqq. [1] and [2] above).

Elastic Labor Supply Model (Sec. III)

In this model, we think of the planner as solving a constrained infinite-horizon problem under the restriction that after period T consumption and the capital stocks must grow at a constant rate and labor supply is constant. To implement this, we pose a planner problem in which the steady-state growth rate, γ, labor supplies (u_{T+1} and v_{T+1}), and terminal values of consumption (c_{T+1}) and investment (x_{hT+1}) are explicit choice variables. Additional constraints are introduced to ensure that the terminal variable choices are feasible and satisfy the dynamic constraints. The problem can be stated as

maximize over $\{k_1, \ldots, k_{T+1}; h_1, \ldots, h_{T+1}; u_0, \ldots, u_{T+1}; v_0, \ldots, v_{T+1};$
$x_{h0}, \ldots, x_{hT+1}; c_0, \ldots, c_{T+1}; \gamma\}$

$$\sum_{t=0}^{T} \beta^t u(c_t, 1 - u_t - v_t) + f^*(c_{T+1}, u_{T+1}, v_{T+1}, \gamma)$$

subject to

$$k_t \geq (1 - \delta_k) k_{t-1}, \quad t = 1, \ldots, T,$$

$$c_t \geq c_{t-1}, \quad t = 1, \ldots, T,$$

$$(1 - \delta_h) h_t + G(x_{ht}, v_t h_t) - h_{t+1} = 0, \quad t = 0, \ldots, T,$$

$$F(k_t, u_t h_t) - k_{t+1} + (1 - \delta_k) k_t - x_{ht} - g_t - c_t \geq 0, \quad t = 0, \ldots, T,$$

$$\frac{u_2(c_t, 1 - u_t - v_t)}{u_2(c_{t+1}, 1 - u_{t+1} - v_{t+1})} - \beta \frac{G_2(x_{ht}, v_t h_t)}{G_2(x_{ht+1}, v_{t+1} h_{t+1})} \frac{h_t}{h_{t+1}}$$

$$\times [1 - \delta_h + G_2(x_{ht+1}, v_{t+1} h_{t+1})(u_{t+1} + v_{t+1})] = 0,$$

$$t = 0, \ldots, T \ (h_t \ \text{Euler constraint}),$$

$$\sum_{t=0}^{T} \beta^t \left[u_1(t) c_t - u_2(t) \frac{T_t}{h_t} \frac{G_1(t)}{G_2(t)} + u_2(t) \frac{x_{ht}}{h_t} \frac{G_1(t)}{G_2(t)} - u_2(t) u_t \right]$$

$$+ g^*(c_{T+1}, u_{T+1}, v_{T+1}, \gamma) = W_0 \frac{u_2(0)}{h_0} \frac{G_1(0)}{G_2(0)},$$

where $W_0 = [(1 - \delta_k) + (1 - \tau^k) F_1] k_0$ (budget constraint).

To ensure that the choices of terminal variables (γ, c_{T+1}, u_{T+1}, v_{T+1}, and x_{hT+1}) satisfy feasibility and the h_t Euler constraints from period $T + 1$ on, we impose three additional constraints:

$$\gamma^\sigma v_{T+1} - \beta\{(1 - \delta_h) + (1 - \psi)[\gamma - (1 - \delta_h)](u_{T+1} + v_{T+1})\} = 0$$

(h_t Euler from period $T + 1$ on),

$$F(k_{T+1}, u_{T+1} h_{T+1}) - [\gamma - (1 - \delta_k)]k_{T+1} - x_{hT+1} - c_{T+1} \geq 0$$

(consumption feasibility), and

$$(1 - \delta_h)h_{T+1} + G(x_{hT+1}, v_{T+1} h_{T+1}) - \gamma h_{T+1} \geq 0$$

(feasibility of x_{hT+1}).

Given the choice of steady-state growth and labor supply, we can compute the continuation value of the objective and budget constraints:

$$f^*(c_{T+1}, u_{T+1}, v_{T+1}, \gamma) = \sum_{t=T+1}^{\infty} \beta^t u(c_{T+1} \gamma^{t-T-1}, 1 - u_{T+1} - v_{T+1}),$$

$$g^*(c_{T+1}, u_{T+1}, v_{T+1}, \gamma) = \frac{\beta^{T+1}(c_{T+1})^{1-\sigma}}{1 - \beta\gamma^{1-\sigma}}$$

$$\times \left[1 + \frac{\eta\psi v_{T+1}}{(1 - \psi)(1 - u_{T+1} - v_{T+1})} - \frac{\eta u_{T+1}}{1 - u_{T+1} - v_{T+1}} \right].$$

Endogenous Government Spending Model (Sec. IV)

Maximize over $\{c_0, \ldots, c_T; k_1, \ldots, k_{T+1}; x_0, \ldots, x_T; g_0, \ldots, g_T\}$ given k_0

$$\sum_{t=0}^{T} \beta^t u(c_t) + f^*(k_{T+1})$$

subject to

$$f(k_t) - c_t - x_t - g_t - g_{ct} \geq 0, \quad t = 0, \ldots, T,$$

$$k_t = (1 - \delta_k)k_{t-1} + G(x_{t-1}, g_{t-1}), \quad t = 1, \ldots, T + 1,$$

$$\sum_{t=0}^{T} \beta^t \left[u_1(t) c_t - u_1(t) g_t \frac{G_2(t)}{G_1(t)} \right] + g^*(k_{T+1})$$

$$= \frac{u_1(0)}{G_1(0)}[(1 - \delta_k) + G_1(0)(1 - \tau^k)F_k(0)]k_0$$

(budget constraint), and

$$1 - \frac{1}{F_k(t)} \left[\frac{u_1(t)}{G_1(t)\beta u_1(t+1)} - \frac{1 - \delta_k}{G_1(t+1)} \right] \leq \tau_{\max}, \quad t = 1, \ldots, T$$

(tax bounds).

For this model, we face an additional problem. We know that the steady-state taxes are nonzero; however, the steady-state revenue requirements are determined by the initial portion of the solution path. We adopt a different strategy here: (1) we fix values of the steady-state tax rate and the size of government investment relative to output; (2) we calculate the steady-state values of growth, consumption relative to output, and private investment relative to output conditional on these estimates of steady-state taxes and government investment; (3) we make end corrections assuming these values of steady-state variables; and (4) we iterate this procedure until the growth rate and tax rate from the end of the solution agree with the assumed steady-state values. The continuation corrections to the objective and the budget constraint are

$$f^*(k_{T+1}) = \sum_{t=T+1}^{\infty} \beta^t u(ck^* k_{T+1} \gamma^{t-T-1}),$$

$$g^*(k_{T+1}) = \beta^{T+1} \frac{(ck^* k_{T+1})^{1-\sigma}}{1 - \beta\gamma^{1-\sigma}} \left[1 - \frac{gk^*}{ck^*} \frac{1-\alpha}{\alpha} \left(\frac{xk^*}{ck^*}\right)^{\rho+1} \right],$$

where gk^* is the asymptotic ratio of government investment spending to capital and ck^* is the asymptotic ratio of consumption to the capital stock given by solving steady-state equations (11)–(13) conditional on an assumed tax rate and g/k ratio.

References

Aschauer, David A. "Is Public Expenditure Productive?" *J. Monetary Econ.* 23 (March 1989): 177–200.

Auerbach, Alan J., and Kotlikoff, Laurence J. *Dynamic Fiscal Policy.* New York: Cambridge Univ. Press, 1987.

Barro, Robert J. "Government Spending in a Simple Model of Endogenous Growth." *J.P.E.* 98, no. 5, pt. 2 (October 1990): S103–S125.

Barro, Robert J., and Sahasakul, Chaipat. "Average Marginal Tax Rates from Social Security and the Individual Income Tax." *J. Bus.* 59, no. 4, pt. 1 (October 1986): 555–66.

Barro, Robert J., and Sala-i-Martin, Xavier. "Public Finance in Models of Economic Growth." Working Paper no. 3362. Cambridge, Mass.: NBER, May 1990.

Bradford, David F. *Blueprints for Basic Tax Reform.* 2d ed. Arlington, Va.: Tax Analysts, 1984.

Bull, N. "When the Optimal Dynamic Tax Rate Is None." Manuscript. Minneapolis: Fed. Reserve Bank, 1992.

Chamley, Christophe. "The Welfare Cost of Capital Income Taxation in a Growing Economy." *J.P.E.* 89 (June 1981): 468–96.

———. "Optimal Taxation of Capital Income in General Equilibrium with Infinite Lives." *Econometrica* 54 (May 1986): 607–22.

———. "The Last Shall Be First: Foreign Borrowing and Growth with Human Capital in an Open Economy." Manuscript. Boston: Boston Univ., 1990.

Chari, V. V.; Christiano, Lawrence; and Kehoe, Patrick J. "Dynamic Ramsey Taxation in a Stochastic Growth Model." Manuscript. Minneapolis: Fed. Reserve Bank, 1990.

Chari, V. V., and Kehoe, Patrick J. "Sustainable Plans with Debt." Manuscript. Minneapolis: Fed. Reserve Bank, 1989.

———. "Sustainable Plans." *J.P.E.* 98 (August 1990): 783–802.
Eaton, Jonathan. "Fiscal Policy, Inflation and the Accumulation of Risky Capital." *Rev. Econ. Studies* 48 (July 1981): 435–45.
Gill, Philip E.; Murray, Walter; and Wright, Margaret H. *Practical Optimization.* New York: Academic Press, 1981.
Heckman, James J. "A Life-Cycle Model of Earnings, Learning, and Consumption." *J.P.E.* 84, no. 2, pt. 2 (August 1976): S11–S44.
Jones, Larry E., and Manuelli, Rodolfo. "A Convex Model of Equilibrium Growth: Theory and Policy Implications." *J.P.E.* 98, no. 5, pt. 1 (October 1990): 1008–38.
———. "Finite Lifetimes and Growth." *J. Econ. Theory* 58 (December 1992).
Jones, Larry E.; Manuelli, Rodolfo; and Rossi, Peter E. "Optimal Taxation in Models of Endogenous Growth." Working paper no. 91-108. Chicago: Univ. Chicago, 1991.
———. "On the Optimal Taxation of Capital Income." Manuscript. Chicago: Univ. Chicago, 1992.
Jorgenson, Dale W., and Yun, Kun-Young. *Tax Reform and the Cost of Capital.* Oxford: Clarendon, 1991.
Judd, Kenneth L. "Redistributive Taxation in a Simple Perfect Foresight Model." *J. Public Econ.* 28 (October 1985): 59–83.
———. "The Welfare Cost of Factor Taxation in a Perfect-Foresight Model." *J.P.E.* 95 (August 1987): 695–709.
———. "Optimal Taxation in Dynamic Stochastic Economies: Theory and Evidence." Manuscript. Stanford, Calif.: Hoover Inst., 1990.
———. "Optimal Taxation with Government Investment." Manuscript. Stanford, Calif.: Hoover Inst., 1991.
Juster, F. Thomas, and Stafford, Frank P. "The Allocation of Time: Empirical Findings, Behavioral Models and Problems of Measurement." Manuscript. Ann Arbor: Univ. Michigan, Survey Res. Center, Inst. Soc. Res., 1990.
King, Robert G., and Rebelo, Sergio. "Public Policy and Economic Growth: Developing Neoclassical Implications." *J.P.E.* 98, no. 5, pt. 2 (October 1990): S126–S150.
Kydland, Finn E., and Prescott, Edward C. "Time to Build and Aggregate Fluctuations." *Econometrica* 50 (November 1982): 1345–70.
Lucas, Robert E., Jr. "On the Mechanics of Economic Development." *J. Monetary Econ.* 22 (July 1988): 3–42.
———. "Supply-Side Economics: An Analytical Review." *Oxford Econ. Papers* 42 (April 1990): 293–316.
Lucas, Robert E., Jr., and Rapping, Leonard A. "Real Wages, Employment, and Inflation." *J.P.E.* 77 (September/October 1969): 721–54.
Lucas, Robert E., Jr., and Stokey, Nancy L. "Optimal Fiscal and Monetary Policy in an Economy without Capital." *J. Monetary Econ.* 12 (July 1983): 55–93.
MaCurdy, Thomas E. "Interpreting Empirical Models of Labor Supply in an Intertemporal Framework with Uncertainty." In *Longitudinal Analysis of Labor Market Data,* edited by James J. Heckman and Burton Singer. Cambridge: Cambridge Univ. Press, 1985.
Munnell, Alicia H., ed. *Is There a Shortfall in Public Capital Spending?* Conference Series no. 34. Boston: Fed. Reserve Bank, 1990.
Prescott, Edward C. "Theory Ahead of Business Cycle Measurement." *Fed. Reserve Bank Minneapolis Q. Rev.* 10 (Fall 1986): 9–22.

Rebelo, Sergio. "Long-Run Policy Analysis and Long-Run Growth." *J.P.E.* 99 (June 1991): 500–521.

Rosen, Sherwin. "A Theory of Life Earnings." *J.P.E.* 84, no. 4, pt. 2 (August 1976): S45–S67.

Stokey, Nancy L. "Credible Public Policy." *J. Econ. Dynamics and Control* 15 (October 1991): 627–56.

Yuen, C. W. "Taxation, Human Capital Accumulation and Economic Growth." Manuscript. Chicago: Univ. Chicago, 1990.

Zhu, X. "Optimal Taxation with Endogenous Government Expenditures." Manuscript. Chicago: Univ. Chicago, 1991.

F
Taxes and Politics

Journal of Public Economics 8 (1977) 329–340. © North-Holland Publishing Company

VOTING OVER INCOME TAX SCHEDULES

Kevin W.S. ROBERTS*

St. John's College, Oxford OX1 3JP, England

Received February 1977, revised version received June 1977

In many voting situations, preferences over options may fail to be single-peaked. This is especially true when options consist of different amounts of a good which is provided through distortionary taxation. In this paper, voting over linear income tax schedules is considered. Although preferences may fail to be single-peaked, a choice set is shown to exist when only mild restrictions are imposed. For many choices in the public domain, the conditions required for this result are likely to be satisfied.

1. Introduction and summary

It may appear unrealistic to consider that choices made in the public domain are the outcome of some voting process. However, if political parties make choices so as to maximise the likelihood of being elected then it is possible to view the chosen options as being determined, albeit indirectly, by a voting process. The point is not whether choices in the public domain are made through a voting mechanism but whether choice procedures mirror some voting mechanism.

The problem then arises as to whether there will exist a 'best' policy. If individual preferences are unrestricted then it is well known [see Arrow (1963)] that choice sets may fail to exist under many mechanisms, e.g. majority rule. But it is also well known [see Black (1958)] that if individual preferences are single-peaked then majority rule will operate in a satisfactory manner. The following question arises: How likely is it that preferences over issues in the public domain will be single-peaked?

Consider a decision being made about the level of provision of some public good. If each individual must pay a constant percentage of the cost of provision then single-peakedness will follow from the assumption of convex production sets and quasi-concave preferences. In many instances, both of these assumptions are questionable. For instance, consider the case where a municipal body is deciding upon the level of public transport facilities. If an individual owns an automobile then his preferences over the level of provision may be expected

---

*This paper is based upon chapter 4 of Roberts (1975). I am grateful to two anonymous referees for their comments.

to be single-peaked. Similarly if he does not own an automobile. But at some level of provision, the individual may switch from owning to not owning an automobile. It is then quite possible for individual preferences to be double-peaked. Various other examples of a similar nature could be cited, e.g. public replacing private schooling – on which see Stiglitz (1974).

The results of this paper could be applied to the situation just mentioned, but our main interest will centre upon cases where individual preferences over goods are well-behaved although preferences over options can fail to be single-peaked. To be more specific, we shall consider the problems that arise when provision is made through distortionary taxation and, in particular, preferences over linear income tax schedules will be considered; these may be viewed as a (distortionary) tax on income which is used to finance a lump-sum subsidy.

It is not immediately clear why single-peakedness over tax schedules should fail to hold, given that preferences are well-behaved. At the risk of oversimplification, the following example illustrates the nature of the problem: an individual may dislike a small increase in the marginal tax rate because the increase in the tax rate causes a large reduction in the work effort of others and so the lump-sum subsidy must decrease. However, further increases in the tax rate may cause little shifting and so the individual may agree with these further increases in the tax rate. Finally, with a marginal tax rate of 100%, nobody will choose to work and the lump-sum subsidy will be at its minimum level so that, eventually, the individual will dislike further increases in the tax rate. Thus, because there is distortionary taxation of a heterogeneous population, preferences for tax rates may fail to be single-peaked, even though each individual's preferences map, considered in isolation, is well-behaved. In fact, restrictive assumptions may be necessary to ensure single-peakedness in these circumstances. Even when individuals have identical preferences over consumption and leisure and differ with respect to the wage rate that they receive, Itsumi (1974) and Romer (1975) have shown that single-peakedness is not guaranteed.

It is not the purpose of this paper to investigate the likelihood of single-peakedness. Instead, the problem to be investigated is whether, in the circumstances that have been described, it is likely that voting mechanisms will give rise to a most preferred outcome, irrespective of whether single-peakedness is satisfied or not. It will be shown that if preferences are such that the ordering of individuals by income is independent of the tax schedule in operation, an assumption which is termed Hierarchical Adherence in the text, then a most preferred outcome will exist under a wide class of voting mechanisms. For the class of income tax models first developed by Mirrlees (1971), hierarchical adherence is a consequence of the assumptions which are generally imposed. Thus relative to other work in this area, hierarchical adherence may be viewed as a mild assumption.

The results obtained in this paper are applicable to many situations. Essentially, if, say, the provision of some public good is being considered then an assumption similar in effect to hierarchical adherence is that the ordering of individuals in terms of their marginal preference for the public good is independent of the level of provision of the public good. This would seem to be a reasonable assumption for the example of public transport provision mentioned earlier. It may be noted that the assumption requires that there be a 'natural' ordering of individuals, whereas single-peakedness requires that there be a 'natural' ordering of options.

In section 2, individual preferences for tax schedules are considered. The class of voting mechanisms being admitted is considered in section 3. The main results of the paper are obtained in section 4 and most preferred tax schedules under the majority decision rule are briefly considered in section 5.

2. Individual preferences for tax schedules

It will be assumed throughout that all prices are unaffected by changes in tax rates and that the only tax in operation is one on income. Consider an individual who is deciding how much labour to supply. As prices are fixed, it may be assumed that he has preferences over post-tax income (consumption) c and pre-tax income (labour supply) y. Preferences are assumed to be representable by a differentiable utility function $u(c, y)$ with $u_c > 0$ and $u_y < 0$.

The government, or municipal body, implements a linear income tax. The tax paid by an individual with income y is given by

$$T(y) = ty - \alpha, \tag{1}$$

where t is the marginal tax rate and α is a lump-sum subsidy. Usually, the tax implemented will have to satisfy the property that total receipts can finance some fixed revenue requirement G, i.e.

$$\sum_i T(y_i) \geq G, \tag{2}$$

where y_i is the income of individual i (if there is a continuum of individuals then summation could be replaced by integration). If y_i is continuous in α then we may expect that for any t, α is made as large as possible so that (2) is satisfied with equality. In this case, combining (1) and (2):

$$\alpha = t\bar{y} - G/n, \tag{3}$$

where $\bar{y}$ is the mean pre-tax income and n is the number of individuals in the community. If leisure is a normal good so that $\bar{y}$ decreases with α, for any value of t there will be a unique value of α which satisfies (3).

It will be assumed that for all tax schedules to be considered, all individuals can attain a position inside their consumption sets. An individual chooses y so as to maximise $u(\alpha+(1-t)y, y)$. First-order conditions of maximisation give

$$(1-t)u_c + u_y \leqq 0, \qquad (4)$$

with equality if $y > 0$. Consider how a small change in the tax schedule affects an individual. Totally differentiating the utility function with respect to t and α:

$$du = dy[u_c(1-t) + u_y] + u_c[d\alpha - y\,dt]. \qquad (5)$$

Making use of (4):

$$du = u_c[d\alpha - y\,dt], \qquad (6)$$

which is basically Roy's identity. If (3) defines α as a differentiable function of t, then

$$\frac{d\alpha}{dt} = \bar{y} + t\frac{d\bar{y}}{dt}. \qquad (7)$$

This equation may be used in conjunction with (6) (notice that it is an implicit relationship because $\bar{y}$ and $d\bar{y}/dt$ are influenced by changes in α).

When incomes are unaffected by a change in the tax schedule, (6) and (7) combine to give:

$$\frac{du}{dt} = u_c[\bar{y} - y]. \qquad (8)$$

Thus an individual with an income y less than the mean income $\bar{y}$ will always prefer a higher to a lower tax rate and preferences will be reversed if y is greater than $\bar{y}$. In this situation, the consequences of majority voting, say, are easily analysed. If the median income is less than the mean income, so that the income distribution is positively skewed (using Pearson's second coefficient of skewness), then majority voting will lead to the tax schedule with the highest marginal tax rate being adopted. This result has been obtained by Foley (1967).

3. Voting mechanisms

The underlying structure of the problem being analysed is best brought out if a more general class of voting mechanisms than majority rule is considered. The existence of a most preferred outcome (choice set) for mechanisms satisfying decisiveness, neutrality, and nonnegative responsiveness will be investigated. A complete description of the economy is provided when the two parameters α and t are specified. In fact, if (3) is imposed, say, then it will generally only be necessary to specify t but such an assumption is not required for the results that will be obtained. Individual preferences over tax schedules may be obtained by integration of (6). R_i will denote individual i's ordering of tax schedules, i.e. $(\alpha_1, t_1)R_i(\alpha_2, t_2)$ iff individual i weakly prefers schedule (α_1, t_1) to (α_2, t_2). For notational convenience the α term will be suppressed and so $t_1 R_i t_2$ will be written. Corresponding to R_i, P_i and I_i will denote strict preference and indifference respectively.

The voting mechanism is assumed to provide a binary relation R over a set of tax schedules τ, and R will be some function f of the list $\langle R_i \rangle_{i=1,n}$ over τ. We have:

A.1. Decisiveness: R is decisive iff for every logically possible list $\langle R_i \rangle_{i=1,n}$ it is complete ($t_1 R t_2 \veebar t_2 R t_1$) and reflexive ($t_1 R t_1$).

A.2. Neutrality: Consider any quadruple t_1, t_2, t_3, t_4. If for all i:

$$t_1 R_i t_2 \leftrightarrow t_3 R'_i t_4 \quad \text{and} \quad t_2 R_i t_1 \leftrightarrow t_4 R'_i t_3,$$

for two lists $\langle R_i \rangle$ and $\langle R'_i \rangle$, then:

$$t_1 R t_2 \leftrightarrow t_3 R' t_4 \quad \text{and} \quad t_2 R t_1 \leftrightarrow t_4 R' t_3,$$

where $R = f(\langle R_i \rangle)$ and $R' = f(\langle R'_i \rangle)$.

A.3. Nonnegative responsiveness: Consider any pair t_1, t_2. If for all i:

$$t_1 R_i t_2 \to t_1 R'_i t_2 \quad \text{and} \quad t_1 P_i t_2 \to t_1 P'_i t_2,$$

then $t_1 R t_2 \to t_1 R' t_2$.

These three assumptions are much used in the theory of social choice [see Sen (1970) and Pattanaik (1971)]. Mechanisms that satisfy A.1–A.3 include the method of majority decision, the method of nonminority decision, and variants of these methods which do not treat individuals in an anonymous manner.

4. Analysis

So far, we have only considered a single individual's preference over tax schedules. No assumption has yet been imposed upon the class of utility functions which is permissible. Instead of pinning down any one individual's utility function, we impose a condition which restricts the set of preferences that individuals in society may have, relative to each other:

A.4. Hierarchical adherence: For all i, j: either $y_i(\alpha, t) \leq y_j(\alpha, t)$ for all α, t, or $y_i(\alpha, t) \geq y_j(\alpha, t)$ for all α, t, where $y_i(\alpha, t)$ is the pre-tax income that i *chooses* to obtain under the tax schedule (α, t).

Thus hierarchical adherence states that there exists an ordering of individuals such that pre-tax income is monotonically increasing irrespective of the tax schedule which is in operation. If all individuals have identical preferences over consumption and leisure but differ with respect to the wage rate that they receive then A.4 will be satisfied if the elasticity of labour supply (in terms of hours worked) is not less than minus unity (pre-tax income will increase with the wage rate). Further, in this case, A.4 holds even when, under some tax schedules, there are individuals who choose not to work, a situation which creates problems when single-peakedness is being analysed [see Romer (1975, section 5)].

It is a remarkable feature of the problem under consideration that A.4 is a sufficient condition on preferences for the existence of a choice set to be proved. The analysis proceeds in stages, the implications of A.4 for individual preference orderings being considered first.

With A.4 satisfied, it will be useful to adopt the labelling convention that if i is greater than j then $y_j(\alpha, t)$ is no greater than $y_i(\alpha, t)$ for all (α, t).

Lemma 1. Under A.4, if $t_2 > t_1$ then for all i:

(1) $t_1 I_i t_2 \rightarrow \begin{cases} t_1 R_j t_2 & \text{for all } j > i, \\ t_2 R_j t_1 & \text{for all } j < i, \end{cases}$
(2) $t_1 P_i t_2 \rightarrow t_1 P_j t_2$ for all $j > i$,
(3) $t_2 P_i t_1 \rightarrow t_2 P_j t_1$ for all $j < i$.

Proof
(1) Consider i's indifference map in (α, t) space which is derived from his indirect utility function $v^i(\alpha, t) \equiv u^i(\alpha + (1-t)y_i(\alpha, t), y_i(\alpha, t))$. An indifference curve connects (α_1, t_1) to (α_2, t_2) and, from (6), its slope is given by

$$\frac{d\alpha}{dt} = y_i(\alpha, t).$$

Consider $j > i$. Moving along the indifference curve, (6) gives

$$\frac{du^j}{dt} = u_c^j [y_i(\alpha, t) - y_j(\alpha, t)] \leq 0$$

by A.4. Hence,

$$u^j(\alpha_2, t_2) - u^j(\alpha_1, t_1) = \int_{t_1}^{t_2} u_c^j[y_i(\alpha, t) - y_j(\alpha, t)]dt \leq 0,$$

i.e. $t_1 R_j t_2$. When $j < i$, the inequalities are reversed and $t_2 R_j t_1$.

(2) As $t_1 P_i t_2$, there exists an $\varepsilon > 0$ such that $(\alpha_1 - \varepsilon, t_1) I_i(\alpha_2, t_2)$. Now, for $j > i$:

$$u^j(\alpha_1 - \varepsilon, t_1) < u^j(\alpha_1, t_1).$$

Applying the first part of the lemma:

$$u^j(\alpha_1 - \varepsilon, t_1) \geq u^j(\alpha_2, t_2).$$

Combining these inequalities we obtain $t_1 P_j t_2$.

(3) In a symmetrical manner to (2).   Q.E.D.

Thus A.4, by itself, imposes an interesting set of restrictions on individual preferences. For instance, if everybody has a unique most preferred tax schedule then lemma 1 implies that individuals with higher incomes have most preferred schedules with lower marginal tax rates.

A result similar to lemma 1 has interesting implications in welfare theoretic analyses. For such analyses, interest centres not upon individuals as such but upon their utilities. Consider replacing A.4 by the following adherence condition:

A.5: For all i, j, for all (α, t):

$$y_i(\alpha, t) \geq y_j(\alpha, t) \leftrightarrow v_i(\alpha, t) \geq v_j(\alpha, t),$$

where v is the indirect utility function.

Under A.5, lemma 1 holds with R_I replaced by R^i, where R^i is the ordering by positions in the income (or utility) hierarchy, i.e. $(\alpha_1, t_1) R^i (\alpha_2, t_2)$ iff the individual who is the ith worst-off when the schedule (α_1, t_1) is in operation is at least as well off under (α_1, t_1) as the individual who is the ith worst-off under (α_2, t_2) when (α_2, t_2) is in operation. For although as we integrate around a positional indifference curve the relevant individuals may be changing, A.5 ensures that there is no change in utility just because of this.

Thus the amended lemma 1 now states that if a schedule with a higher marginal tax rate is adopted, the utility distribution will alter so that the lowest utilities will increase, utilities in the middle of the distribution will remain constant, and the highest utilities will decrease. It is therefore to be expected that more inequality averse SWFs will prefer schedules with higher marginal tax rates. Following on from the work of Rothschild and Stiglitz (1970) and Diamond and Stiglitz (1974), define a SWF $W = \sum_{i=1}^{n} G(u^i)$ to be more inequality averse than $W' = \sum_{i=1}^{n} u^i$ if G is increasing and strictly concave (u^i could obviously be viewed as a function of individual utilities). Let ρ be an index of inequality aversion and let R_ρ be the ordering of schedules by a SWF W_ρ with inequality aversion ρ. Assume that

$$(\alpha_1, t_1) I_{\rho_1}(\alpha_2, t_2), \qquad t_2 > t_1.$$

Define $\alpha(t)$ so that $(\alpha(t), t) I_{\rho_1}(\alpha_1, t_1)$. From the discussion above we know that if $W_{\rho_1} = \sum u^i$, then an increase in t, with a change in α given by $\alpha(t)$, will lead to a mean preserving reduction in the inequality of the u^i, to adopt the terminology of Rothschild and Stiglitz (1970). By their well-known equivalence theorem (theorem 2), a more inequality averse SWF will prefer the increase in the marginal tax rate. Thus we shall have

$$(\alpha_2, t_2) R_{\rho 2}(\alpha_1, t_1),$$

where $\rho_2 > \rho_1$. We may thus obtain a dual result to lemma 1:

Theorem 1. Under A.5, if $t_2 > t_1$ then for all ρ_1:

(1) $t_1 I_{\rho_1} t_2 \to \begin{cases} t_1 R_{\rho_2} t_2 & \text{for all } \rho_2 < \rho_1, \\ t_2 R_{\rho_2} t_1 & \text{for all } \rho_2 > \rho_1, \end{cases}$
(2) $t_1 P_{\rho_1} t_2 \to t_1 P_{\rho_2} t_2 \quad \text{for all } \rho_2 < \rho_1,$
(3) $t_2 P_{\rho_1} t_2 \to t_2 P_{\rho_2} t_1 \quad \text{for all } \rho_2 > \rho_1.$

Theorem 1 also has interesting implications. For instance, the theorem implies that SWFs with a greater degree of embodied inequality aversion will choose schedules with higher marginal tax rates [see Roberts (1975) and Helpman and Sadka (1976)]. It is important to notice that the driving force of this result is condition A.5. Further, if individuals' voting behaviour is based upon some form of ethical preference, as captured by a SWF, then the structure of individuals preference will be basically identical to the structure implied by A.4 as long as it is possible to order individuals in terms of the inequality aversion that is embodied in their preferences.

Returning explicitly to voting procedures, the outcome of voting mechanisms may be considered by utilizing lemma 1:

Lemma 2. If the voting mechanism satisfies A.1–A.3 and preferences satisfy A.4, then for all $t_1, t_2, t_3, t_1 < t_2 < t_3$:

(1) $t_1 R t_2$ and $t_2 R t_3 \to t_1 R t_3$,
(2) $t_3 R t_2$ and $t_2 R t_1 \to t_3 R t_1$,

(3) t_1Pt_2 and $t_2Pt_3 \rightarrow t_1Pt_3$,
(4) t_3Pt_2 and $t_2Pt_1 \rightarrow t_3Pt_1$,

where $R = f(\langle R_i \rangle)$.

Proof.
(2) is proved in a symmetrical manner to (1); (3) and (4) may be proved as in (1) and (2), strict replacing weak preference. Thus we concentrate upon (1). Consider individual preferences over the pair t_1, t_2. By lemma 1, preferences must be of the form: $t_2P_it_1 \forall i \leq \beta$; $t_2I_it_1 \forall \beta < i < \gamma$; $t_1P_it_2 \forall i \geq \gamma$, for some $\beta, \gamma, \beta < \gamma$. Similarly, over the pair t_2, t_3: $t_3P_it_2 \forall i \leq \delta$; $t_3I_it_2 \forall \delta < i < \varepsilon$; $t_2P_it_3 \forall i \geq \varepsilon$, for some $\delta, \varepsilon, \delta < \varepsilon$. There are six cases to be considered:
(i) $\beta < \gamma \leq \delta < \varepsilon$; (ii) $\beta \leq \delta \leq \gamma \leq \varepsilon$; (iii) $\beta \leq \delta < \varepsilon \leq \gamma$; (iv) $\delta < \varepsilon \leq \beta < \gamma$;
(v) $\delta \leq \beta \leq \varepsilon \leq \gamma$; (vi) $\delta \leq \beta < \gamma \leq \varepsilon$.

(i) Let $\beta < \gamma \leq \delta < \varepsilon$. Therefore, $t_3P_it_1$ for all $i < \gamma$. Assume that $\sim t_1Rt_3$ so, by A.1, t_3Pt_1. Consider the following preference profile: $t_3P'_it_1 \forall i \leq \beta$; $t_3I'_it_1 \forall \beta < i < \gamma$; $t_1P'_it_3 \forall i \geq \gamma$. Applying A.3, $t_3P't_1$. By A.2, $t_3P't_1 \rightarrow t_2Pt_1$ which gives a contradiction. Thus t_1Rt_3.

(ii) Let $\beta \leq \delta \leq \gamma \leq \varepsilon$. Therefore: $t_3P_it_1 \forall i \leq \delta$; $t_1R_it_3 \forall \delta < i < \varepsilon$; $t_1P_it_3 \forall i \geq \varepsilon$. Assume that $\sim t_1Rt_3$ so, by A.1, t_3Pt_1. Consider the following preference profile: $t_3P'_it_1 \forall i \leq \delta$; $t_1I'_it_3 \forall \delta < i < \varepsilon$; $t_1P'_it_3 \forall i \geq \varepsilon$. Applying A.3, $t_3P't_1$. By A.2, $t_3P't_1 \rightarrow t_3Pt_2$ which gives a contradiction. Thus t_1Rt_3.

(iii) Let $\beta \leq \delta < \varepsilon \leq \gamma$. Therefore: $t_3P_it_1 \forall i \leq \delta$; $t_3I_it_1 \forall \delta < i < \varepsilon$; $t_1P_it_3 \forall i \geq \varepsilon$. Assume that $\sim t_1Rt_3$ so, by A.1, t_3Pt_1. By A.2, t_3Pt_2 which gives a contradiction. Thus t_1Rt_3.

Cases (iv), (v) and (vi) replicate, mutatis mutandis, cases (i), (ii) and (iii) respectively.   Q.E.D.

Lemma 2 may now be applied and the main result of the paper obtained:

Theorem 2. If the voting mechanism satisfies A.1–A.3 and preferences satisfy A.4 then the social preference relation is quasi-transitive, i.e. for all t_1, t_2, t_3:

$$t_1Pt_2 \text{ and } t_2Pt_3 \rightarrow t_1Pt_3.$$

Proof. Let the antecedent hold but assume that t_3Rt_1. There are six cases where the marginal tax rates differ to be considered:

$$t_1 < t_2 < t_3; \quad t_1 < t_3 < t_2; \quad t_2 < t_1 < t_3;$$
$$t_3 < t_2 < t_1; \quad t_3 < t_1 < t_2; \quad t_2 < t_3 < t_1.$$

The last three cases are essentially the same as the first three so that we concentrate upon the first three cases. For each case we obtain a contradiction:

Case (i)   by lemma 2, $t_1 P t_3$;
Case (ii) applying lemma 2, $t_2 P t_3$ and $t_3 R t_1 \to t_2 R t_1$;
Case (iii) applying lemma 2, $t_3 R t_1$ and $t_1 P t_2 \to t_3 R t_2$.

When $t_1 = t_2$, say, as $t_1 P t_2$ it must be the case, by A.2 and A.3, that $\alpha_1 > \alpha_2$ and $t_1 P_i t_2$ for all i. The desired result then follows from a simple application of A.2 and A.3. The other cases where two or three of the marginal tax rates are equal may be treated in a similar way.   Q.E.D.

A sufficient condition for a choice set to exist is that the underlying binary relation is complete, reflexive and quasi-transitive, and the set of social states is finite [see Sen (1970, ch. 1*)]. Completeness and reflexivity follow from A.1 so that as a corollary to the above theorem we have:

Corollary. If the voting mechanism satisfies A.1–A.3, preferences satisfy A.4, and τ is finite then $C(\tau)$, the choice set of τ under the voting mechanism, is non-empty.

Given this result, the question arises as to whether there is any connection between the structure of preferences implied by A.4 and the structure implied by other preference restrictions used in the social choice literature. Consider the condition of *value restriction* (VR) which ensures the existence of a choice set. VR states that over any triple, all concerned individuals agree that some option is either not best (NB), not medium (NM), or not worst (NW) (an individual is concerned if he is not indifferent between the three options). Single-peakedness corresponds to NW [see Sen (1970, ch. 10)]. Although the restrictions imposed by A.4 do not imply VR, consider the following strengthening of A.4:

A.6. For all i, j, $i \neq j$: either $y_i(\alpha, t) > y_j(\alpha, t)$ for all α, t, or $y_i(\alpha, t) < y_j(\alpha, t)$ for all α, t.

A.6 is clearly an unattractive condition in the present context; for instance, it is compatible with only at most one individual not working. Applying A.6 instead of A.4 in lemma 1, the effect of the change is that if (α_1, t_1), (α_2, t_2), $t_1 < t_2$, are such that $t_1 I_i t_2$ then $t_1 P_j t_2$ for all $j > i$, and $t_2 P_j t_1$ for all $j < i$. The following result provides the reason for looking at A.6:

Theorem 3. If preferences satisfy A.6 then they satisfy VR.

Proof. Consider any triple (α_1, t_1), (α_2, t_2), (α_3, t_3). If $t_1 = t_2$, say, then with $\alpha_1 \neq \alpha_2$ there will be strict domination and NB and NW will be satisfied. Thus assume that $t_1 < t_2 < t_3$. It will be shown that (α_2, t_2) is either NB or NW. Assume not so that there exist i, j, who are concerned, such that: i finds

(α_2, t_2) best, i.e. $t_2 R_i t_3$ and $t_2 R_i t_1$; j finds (α_2, t_2) worst, i.e. $t_1 R_j t_2$ and $t_3 R_j t_2$.
With A.4 replaced by A.6 in lemma 1, we have: as $t_2 < t_3$, $t_2 R_i t_3$ and $t_3 R_j t_2 \rightarrow i \geq j$; as $t_1 < t_2$, $t_2 R_i t_1$ and $t_1 R_j t_2 \rightarrow i \leq j$. Therefore, $i = j$ and $t_1 I_i t_2 I_i t_3$ which contradicts the assumption that i and j are concerned. Q.E.D.

Thus hierarchical adherence is weaker than one particular form of value restrictiveness.

5. Majority voting

As an example of a voting mechanism which satisfies A.1–A.3, the method of majority decision may be briefly considered. Assume that the number of individuals is odd or individuals form a continuum so that, under A.4, there will exist an individual m with a median income level. Utilizing lemma 1, it is easy to see that if m shows a strict preference between two schedules then a majority will have the same preference. Thus the choice set under majority voting will be a non-empty subset of m's choice set.

To consider m's most preferred schedule, assume that α and t are related as in eq. (7). Combining (6) and (7):

$$\frac{du^m}{dt} = u_c^m \left[\bar{y} + t \frac{d\bar{y}}{dt} - y_m \right]. \tag{9}$$

If $y_m < \bar{y}$, i.e. the distribution of income is positively skewed, and $d\bar{y}/dt < 0$ so that the adoption of a more progressive tax schedule leads, because of disincentive effects, to a reduction in national income, then the median voter will most prefer a schedule with a positive marginal tax rate. Of course if G, the government revenue requirement, is positive, then it is still possible that the lump-sum subsidy α will be negative.

From lemma 1, the median individual has a most preferred tax schedule with a marginal tax rate below that which is desired by an individual with zero income; from (6), this will be the schedule where α is maximised. As nobody will work when the marginal tax rate is 100%, α will be maximised at a tax rate below 100%. Hence, the median individual will most prefer a schedule with a marginal tax rate below 100%.

To be able to say anything further about the tax schedule which will be chosen under a majority voting rule, further assumptions must be imposed. Assume that aggregate labour supply is given by the constant elasticity function

$$Y = n\bar{y} = nk(1-t)^\beta \alpha^{-\gamma}, \tag{10}$$

where k is a constant and β and γ are the relevant elasticities. This equation is clearly unacceptable when α is small. However, it may be assumed to hold locally around m's most preferred tax schedule. Assuming that $G = 0$, m's most preferred tax schedule will be given by

$$t = \frac{1-(1+\gamma)\delta}{1-(1+\gamma)\delta+\beta}, \qquad (11)$$

where $\delta = y_m/\bar{y}$ (assuming second-order conditions are satisfied). As an example, let $\beta = 0.5$, $\gamma = 0.2$ and $\delta = \frac{2}{3}$. Then the tax schedule which will be chosen will have a marginal tax rate of 29%. Assuming that the worst-off individual does not work, this may be compared to the maximin tax rate which will be given by (11) with δ set at zero. Thus the maximin tax rate will be 67%. By lemma 1, no individual will prefer a schedule with a higher marginal tax rate to this schedule.

References

Arrow, K.J., 1963, Social choice and individual values, 2nd ed. (Yale University Press, New Haven, CT).
Black, D., 1958, The theory of committees and elections (Cambridge University Press).
Diamond, P.A. and J.E. Stiglitz, 1974, Increases in risk and in risk aversion, Journal of Economic Theory 8, 337–360.
Foley, D., 1967, Resource allocation and the public sector, Yale Economic Essays 7, 45–98.
Helpman, E. and E. Sadka, 1976, The optimal income tax: Some comparative statics results, Foerder Institute for Economic Research Working Paper No. 15–76.
Itsumi, Y., 1974, Distributional effects of linear income tax schedules, Review of Economic Studies 41, 371–381.
Mirrlees, J.A., 1971, An exploration in the theory of optimum income taxation, Review of Economic Studies 38, 175–208.
Pattanaik, P.K., 1971, Voting and collective choice (Cambridge University Press).
Roberts, K.W.S., 1975, Aspects of the theory of optimal income taxation, B.Phil. thesis, Oxford University.
Romer, T., 1975, Individual welfare, majority voting, and the properties of a linear income tax, Journal of Public Economics 4, 163–186.
Rothschild, M. and J.E. Stiglitz, 1970, Increasing risk: 1, A definition, Journal of Economic Theory 2, 225–243.
Sen, A.K., 1970, Collective choice and social welfare (Holden Day, San Francisco).
Stiglitz, J.E., 1974, Demand for education in public and private school systems, Journal of Public Economics 3, 349–386.

[18]

Economic and Political Foundations of Tax Structure

By WALTER HETTICH AND STANLEY L. WINER*

The paper derives the essential elements of tax systems as the outcome of rational behavior in a model where government maximizes expected support and where opposition to taxation depends on the loss in full income. The analysis treats the level of expenditures as endogenous and integrates the influence of administration costs with that of political and economic factors. Tax structure is shown to be a system of related components in equilibrium.

While the theoretical literature on taxation has flourished in the past fifteen years, tax theory continues to suffer from important limitations. Perhaps the most serious shortcoming is a dichotomy in assumptions on what motivates public and private decisions. While private behavior is modeled as self-interested in the way common in other areas of economics, public decision makers are assumed in much of the tax literature to choose and implement policies according to general social criteria such as efficiency and equity. The conflicting treatment of private and public choices restricts the ability of economists to understand the operation of actual tax systems and to explain why they have the characteristics and structure that we commonly observe.

We show in this paper that the essential facts of tax systems can be explained as the natural outcome of self-interested decision making if such behavior is assumed in both the private and public sectors. Actual tax systems are complicated and often elaborate. Underneath their rather baroque appearance lies a simple skeleton, however, consisting of a limited number of parts or components. The main elements in all tax systems are tax bases, rate structures, and special provisions, such as exemptions and deductions. A theoretical analysis of tax structure must show how these elements arise as a result of private and public choices and what determines their design and their importance within the system as a whole.

The emphasis in the paper is on the reasons for the emergence of the tax skeleton with a given set of political institutions. An alternative approach to positive tax theory is to assume the existence of one particular aspect of tax structure and to allow voters to choose relevant parameters through majority rule (Thomas Romer, 1975; K. W. S. Roberts, 1977; A. H. Meltzer and S. F. Richard, 1981, 1983). While focusing on one feature permits more detailed analysis of that component, it avoids the broader question of why tax structure as a whole exists and how different parts of the tax skeleton are related. A similar limitation also affects work which emphasizes particular determinants, such as administration costs and opportunities to tax (Richard Musgrave, 1969).[1]

The paper starts with the presentation of a basic model in which a government maximizing expected support sets tax rates for N

---

*Department of Economics, California State University, Fullerton, CA 92634, and School of Public Administration, Carleton University, Ottawa, Canada K1S 5B6. The authors are indebted to participants in seminars at Carleton University, the Universities of Toronto, Western Ontario, Montreal and Rochester, and the Claremont Graduate School. In addition, they would like to acknowledge stimulating discussions with George Warskett and helpful comments by Peter Coughlin and referees of this *Review*. The research was supported by a grant from the Social Sciences and Humanities Research Council of Canada.

[1] Musgrave refers to tax handles, a term which appears to include the changing opportunities to levy taxes as well as tax administration costs. Some authors, such as Harley Hinrichs (1966) also rely on exogenous cultural and political factors. For an attempt to base the explanation of tax structure primarily on political factors, see Susan Hansen (1983).

individuals who have different economic and political responses but who engage in the same type of economic activity. The resulting equilibrium serves as a reference solution for later parts of the paper where the analysis is generalized to include many activities by taxpayers and to account for the creation of bases, rate structures, and special provisions. The paper also contains a discussion of the relationship of tax rates and tax revenues and a comparison with two well-known alternative approaches, optimal taxation and the Leviathan model.

I. A Basic Model

The approach to political economy adopted here relies on the modeling of political equilibrium rather than of the political process. There is a successful literature that uses models of this type, including work by George Stigler (1971), Sam Peltzman (1976), and Gary Becker (1983), and having its roots in the writings of Joseph Schumpeter (1950) and Anthony Downs (1957). This literature has focused on the implications of different equilibrium outcomes for government policy while bypassing questions concerning the existence and stability of political equilibrium and the explicit derivation of government objective functions in a game-theoretic context. Political equilibria are interpreted as the outcome of a competitive process and no independent role is assigned to bureaucracy.[2] Our paper can be viewed as a further formalization and extension of this literature.

A second important tradition of analysis has taken a quite different direction, emphasizing theoretical questions of existence and stability (see for example, Peter Ordeshook, 1986, ch. 4). This tradition has not been concerned with developing institutional implications, perhaps because problems of existence and stability are sufficiently difficult

in their own right. While we see no general solution emerging as yet from this literature which could serve as a basis for modeling tax structure, we will suggest briefly how our objective function could be derived from the solution to a particular electoral game described in a recent paper by Peter Coughlin (1986).

We assume that the government's objective in designing a tax structure is to maximize expected support, a term which can be interpreted in both a narrow and broad manner. In the "narrow" version, individual support for the government depends (i) on the benefits from public goods and the loss in full income resulting from taxation and (ii) on characteristics which determine how a particular individual's net economic benefit from the fiscal system is translated into a probability of voting for the government. Examples of relevant such characteristics include the cost of voting, age, and the taste for civic duty. The government's objective in this model can be interpreted as the maximization of expected votes, an objective often used in the literature since Downs. Maximization of expected votes can be regarded as a simple way of capturing the motivation of a government which is unsure of the identity or characteristics of its opponents in future elections (Arthur Denzau and Michael Munger, 1986; David Mayhew, 1974).

A broader interpretation of the term support which we have found useful in empirical research (Walter Hettich and Stanley Winer, 1984; Winer and Hettich, 1987) is also possible. In this view, support has a third component in addition to those already mentioned. As seen by the government, effective support depends not only on the likelihood that an individual will cast a favorable vote in the next election but also on the individual's relative political influence in a world where equality of franchise differs from equality of influence. As a result, the government maximizes the weighted sum of expected votes where weights depend on voter characteristics such as interest group membership and strength and on individual attributes such as personal wealth.

In the model presented below, the probability of any individual's voting for the

---

[2] The underlying assumptions for this approach are that political competition is sufficiently strong to force convergence to an optimal strategy and that the ensuing equilibrium is stable.

government is influenced positively by the services received from a pure public good G and negatively by his loss in full income v (including deadweight loss) from taxation. Voters base their decision on whether to support the government on how they are affected by benefits and taxes and are not influenced by how others are treated. Moreover, individual taxpayers see no connection between the level of services provided and their own tax burden. This implies that there is no direct link between expenditure structure and tax structure, even though the level of expenditures is endogenous and affects tax structure indirectly through the government's budget constraint. The separation of taxes and expenditures is an important characteristic of modern fiscal systems, and for this reason, a good starting point in constructing a positive theory of tax structure. One may also note that assuming such separation helps to simplify a rather complex theoretical problem and has proven useful in empirical research.

Given the above assumptions, we can represent the ith voter's support for the government as:

(1) $\quad \{b_i(G) - c_i(v_i)\} \quad i = 1, 2, \ldots, N$

where N is the number of taxpayers and where $\partial b_i/\partial G > 0$ and $\partial c_i/\partial v_i > 0$. In the narrow view, (1) normalized appropriately represents the probability of voting for the government, while in the broader interpretation it is that probability weighted by additional factors determining effective political influence.[3] The term b_i in (1) represents benefits for individual i while c_i can be interpreted as effective opposition to taxation by the rational voter. The greater is c_i, the smaller is the expected support from the ith voter. Opposition depends positively on the loss in full income v_i which may be written as

(1a) $\qquad v_i = T_i + d_i,$

where T_i is the tax payment and d_i is the deadweight loss or welfare cost of taxation for the ith voter.

We shall also assume that taxation of the ith voter is proportional at rate t_i, that B_i, the level of the taxable activity of the ith voter, is related negatively to t_i, while the welfare loss d_i depends positively on t_i and on exogenous factors x_i that determine the nature of the supply function for the taxable activity. (If the taxable activity is work, for example, an important component of x_i will be the taste for leisure.) Hence for $i = 1, 2, \ldots, N$,

(1b) $\qquad T_i = t_i \cdot B_i,$

(1c) $\qquad B_i = B_i(t_i, x_i) \quad \partial B_i/\partial t_i < 0$

and

(1d) $\qquad d_i = (t_i, x_i) \quad \partial d_i/\partial t_i > 0$

with $d_i = 0$ and $v_i = T_i$ if taxes did not disturb behavior.[4] Equations (1c) and (1d) reflect the voter's utility-maximizing response to taxation. For simplicity it is assumed that all taxpayers engage in the same type of activity (but that they are otherwise unique) and that their economic and political responses to taxation are known to the government without cost.

The government chooses the level of public expenditure G and tax rates $t_1, t_2, \ldots, t_n$, so as to maximize expected support

(2) $\qquad \sum_{i=1}^{N} \{b_i(G) - c_i(v_i)\},$

---

[3] One approach to the narrow interpretation of (1) is to define an index of support $I_i = b_i(G) - c_i(v_i)$. Then let p_i be an increasing function of I_i which translates the support index into a voting probability, $0 \le p_i(I_i) \le 1$. The standard logit or probit model could be used to define p_i.

[4] Putting deadweight costs (1d) explicitly into the model is a convenient method of incorporating the full consequences of taxation for individual welfare. See Becker (1983) for a similar construction.

subject to the government budget restraint

(2a) $$G - \sum_{i=1}^{N} t_i \cdot B_i = 0,$$

and subject to taxpayers' responses to taxation reflected by equations (1c) and (1d).

While we shall not further develop this aspect of the analysis, it is of interest to note that maximization of (2) can be viewed as describing the outcome of a particular two-candidate game. Coughlin (1986) has constructed such a game where every voter has a finite probability of voting for any one of the two candidates. Equilibrium can be represented by the maximization of any candidate's expected vote over the policy space available to him.[5] Candidates use a binomial logit model to determine the probabilities that they will receive the support of particular voters. These probabilities and hence the candidate's expected vote are related positively to the net effect of government policy on the welfare of voters. Since we can write (2) more generally as

(2') $$\sum_{i=1}^{N} p_i \{ f_i(G, \underline{t}) \},$$

where p_i is the ith voter's probability of voting for the government and f_i represents the effect of fiscal policy on his welfare (f depends positively on public services G and negatively on tax rates $\underline{t}$), maximization of (2) or (2') and the equilibrium of the voting game characterize the same policy choices.[6]

In the basic model, the first-order conditions for a solution to the government's problem consist of equations (2a), (3a), and (3b):

(3a) $$\sum_i \partial b_i / \partial G - \lambda = 0,$$

(3b) $$-(\partial c_i / \partial v_i \cdot \partial v_i / \partial t_i)$$
$$+ \lambda (B_i + t_i \cdot \partial B_i / \partial t_i) = 0$$
$$i = 1, 2, \ldots, N.$$

The first term in brackets in (3b) is the growth in opposition that results from increasing t_i. The second term in brackets represents $\partial T_i / \partial t_i$, the additional revenue raised by this rate increase. The meaning of these results can be understood more easily if we restate the first-order conditions (3) for each i as

(4) $$\frac{\partial c_i / \partial v_i \cdot \partial v_i / \partial t_i}{B_i \cdot (1 + \varepsilon_i)} = \lambda,$$

where $\varepsilon_i = \partial B_i / \partial t_i \cdot t_i / B_i$ is the elasticity of the ith taxpayer's activity with respect to his tax rate.[7] Thus the politically optimal tax structure in the basic model requires a choice of tax rates that equalizes marginal political costs per dollar of additional revenue across all taxpayers. This tax structure will finance a total expenditure such that the marginal political benefit of another dollar of expenditure λ is equal to the common marginal political cost per dollar of additional revenue.[8]

---

[5] Coughlin states his results in terms of the maximization of expected plurality. However, his assumptions about candidates' beliefs concerning voter behavior imply that the maximization of expected plurality and of expected votes are equivalent objectives. One should note that in Coughlin's game, candidates propose after-tax incomes subject to a constraint on the sum of their incomes. This can also be viewed as the proposing of tax payments subject to a government budget constraint.

[6] We can think of f as the voter's post-fisc utility relative to his pre-fisc utility, the level of which is assumed given. (2') could also be written as $\sum p_i \{ U_i(G, \underline{t}) - \hat{U}_i \}$, where $\hat{U}_i$ is pre-fisc welfare.

[7] We only consider interior solutions where everybody's support is solicited to some extent. This is consistent with the type of equilibrium considered in the probabilistic voting literature referred to above, where in equilibrium every voter has a positive probability of voting for each candidate.

[8] Second-order conditions for a unique solution to the government's problem include, in addition to assumptions about derivatives made above, (i) $b_i^{GG} < 0$, (ii) $v_i^{t_i t_i} > 0$, (iii) $c_i^{v_i v_i} > 0$, and (iv) $B_i^{t_i t_i} < 0$. Superscripts denote partial derivatives. Note that the separation of expenditures and taxes and the independence of taxpayers assumed in the text implies that cross-partial derivatives of the objective function with respect to

While the first-order conditions above integrate economic and political behavior, they yield only a very simple tax structure which still misses several essential elements of observed tax systems. Tax structure in (4) consists of N rates on one activity, with each taxpayer being taxed at a unique rate. As yet, voters are not grouped into rate brackets, activities are not grouped into bases, and there are no special provisions. In subsequent sections we extend the basic model to account for these additional elements.

We are interested primarily in establishing a set of sufficient conditions for the existence of a stylized tax structure. Since we can accomplish this without endogenizing interest group formation and without relaxing the assumption of independence among net political benefit functions of voters, or the assumption that their economic and political responses to taxation are known to the government without cost, we shall maintain all three assumptions throughout the paper.

II. Taxation of Many Activities

In this section we demonstrate that the taxation of many activities is a natural outcome of expected support maximization. The loss in full income given by (1a) can be generalized to $v_i = v_i(T_{i1}, T_{i2}, \ldots, T_{iJ}, d_i)$ in the case in which each taxpayer conducts J activities and faces tax rates $t_{i1}, t_{i2}, \ldots, t_{iJ}$. Equations (1c) and (1d) may also be similarly generalized. In this case, the government budget restraint (2a) becomes

$$(2a') \quad G - \sum_{i=1}^{N} \sum_{j=1}^{J} t_{ij} \cdot B_{ij} = 0,$$

and the first-order conditions for the government's problem (4s) change to

$$(4') \quad \frac{\partial c_i / \partial v_i \cdot \partial v_i / \partial t_{ij}}{B_{ij} \cdot (1 + \varepsilon_{ij}) \sum_{h \neq j} t_{ih} \cdot \partial B_{ih} / \partial t_{ij}} = \lambda$$

$$i = 1, 2, \ldots, N; \; j, h = 1, 2, \ldots, J$$

where $\varepsilon_{ij} = \partial B_{ij} / \partial t_{ij} \cdot t_{ij} / B_{ij}$. The second term in the denominator on the left side of (4') represents the effect of taxing activity j on other activities conducted by a given taxpayer.[9] Activities of different taxpayers are, however, assumed to be independent in this formulation.[10]

Equation (4') generalizes the conditions stated in (4). It implies that the politically optimal tax structure requires marginal political opposition per dollar of tax revenue to be equalized across taxable activities for each taxpayer, as well as to be equalized across taxpayers for each activity.

The above argument indicates that the evolution of tax structure is closely related to economic change and development. Minimization of opposition to taxation requires the adjustment of tax structure whenever the broad nature of activities conducted by taxpayers changes. The same argument also explains why tax structure is complex—disregarding differences in the welfare consequences of taxation across activities conducted by any taxpayer or across all taxpayers increases opposition to taxation because such disregard makes voters worse off. This may be the reason why tax simplification remains elusive although it appears to be universally endorsed as a good idea.

Equation (4') indicates that complexity in tax structure is politically rational. In fact, it implies even greater complexity than is usually observed. The task is thus not only to justify the existence of complexity, but also to delineate its limits.

---

policy instruments are zero. It is also assumed that taxable activities are independent across taxpayers. Conditions (ii) and (iii) imply that marginal opposition to taxation increases with tax rates. Conditions (i) to (iii) ensure the objective function (2) is strictly concave, while (iv) ensures that the constraint (2a) is strictly convex.

[9] If taxpayer i engages in J activities, equation (1c) must be reformulated as $B_{ij} = B_{ij}(t_{i1}, t_{i2}, \ldots, t_{iJ}, x_i)$.

[10] This last assumption is consistent with the simplification introduced earlier that net political benefit functions (1) are independent across taxpayers.

III. Grouping and the Choice of Rate Structures and Bases

In the solution to the government's problem in Section II we have N taxpayers, J activities, and $N \times J$ tax rates. This is unrealistic in two respects. First, activities are generally grouped into bases which consist of similar or related activities. In addition, taxpayers are sorted or grouped into rate brackets where despite interpersonal differences they pay the same tax rates.

Deviations from unique treatment of activities or of taxpayers will cause a loss in political support. What must be explained is why the government decides to accept such losses, that is, what offsetting advantage can be gained in exchange for the grouping. The answer lies in reduced administration costs. Resources released in this way can then be used to provide more public goods and therefore to obtain increased support. The government's problem is to balance the marginal loss in support from grouping with the marginal gain in support from spending resources not used in administration.

Since we developed the basic model using a framework with N taxpayers and one activity, it is convenient to begin the analysis by considering the sorting of taxpayers into rate brackets on one activity. We shall indicate later how the solution can also be interpreted as the rationale for combining different activities into bases.

Creation of rate brackets will mean that groups of individuals with differing levels of economic activity will be subject to the same tax rate. The government's problem is (i) to establish the politically optimal number of brackets and (ii) to assign individuals to these brackets in a manner that is consistent with its political objective.

The second part of the problem, that is, the assignment problem, is considered at length in the Appendix. We let the number of rate brackets or groups be fixed at some number $K < N$, the number of individuals. Levying the same rate on all members of a given group rather than taxing them at their unique politically optimal rates defined by first-order conditions analogous to (4) must result in a loss in expected support. If we linearize the N first-order conditions in the absence of grouping, we can show that the loss from grouping N unique individuals into K-rate brackets is minimized when taxpayers are assigned to brackets so as to minimize the within group variation in politically optimal rates.

By considering solutions of the sorting problem for different values of K, we can construct the "marginal tax discrimination" curve AA in Figure 1. For each K, this curve shows the maximum reduction in opposition possible from increasing the number of groups by one while simultaneously resorting individuals among the $K+1$ groups in the manner described above. AA lies above the horizontal axis when $K < N$ and intersects the horizontal axis at $K = N$, where all taxpayers are treated uniquely. It is assumed to decline continuously as K approaches N.

The optimal number of rate brackets K^* is shown in Figure 1 where AA intersects BB, the "marginal tax administration curve," reflecting the opportunity cost to the government of treating individuals differently when this creates administration costs.[11] For each K, BB shows the fall in political support resulting from an increase in the number of rate brackets from K to $K+1$ and a reduction in public services by an amount equal to the corresponding growth in administration costs. When λ in (4) is constant, BB will slope upward as long as the increase in administration costs rises with K when another tax instrument is added.[12]

The general solution when each taxpayer is taxed on all of his J activities involves four elements: the reduction in votes lost

---

[11]Administration costs include: (i) the cost of processing tax payments, (ii) the cost of monitoring compliance and enforcing tax codes, (iii) the cost of coordinating administrative personnel, and (iv) the costs of acquiring knowledge about taxpayers' characteristics. The last type of cost is not generally incorporated into the analysis in this paper except that lump-sum taxation is considered infeasible.

[12]It is possible that administration costs depend on the nature of the tax instruments employed, as well as on their number, as in W. P. Heller and Karl Shell (1974). We do not explore that possibility in this paper. We also rule out possible discontinuities and nonconvexities introduced by administration costs.

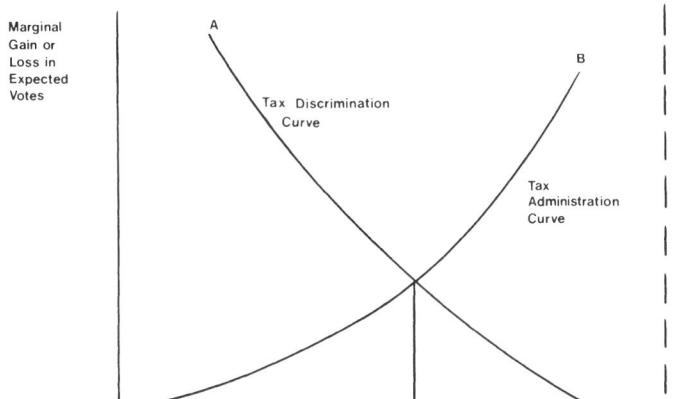

FIGURE 1. THE POLITICALLY OPTIMAL NUMBER OF RATE BRACKETS

(i.e., the marginal gain in support) when the number of rate brackets k_j on any activity is increased $\partial S/\partial k_j$, the resulting increase in administration costs $\partial A/\partial k_j$ and in total revenue $\partial R/\partial k_j$, and the additional support from spending one more dollar on public goods λ. In equilibrium,

$$(5) \quad \frac{\partial S/\partial k_j}{(\partial A/\partial k_j - \partial R/\partial k_j)} = -\lambda$$

$$j = 1, 2, \ldots, J$$

that is, the marginal reduction in opposition per "net" dollar of administration costs must be equal across activities.[13]

---

[13] First-order conditions (5) can be derived by choosing G and $(k_1, k_2, \ldots, k_J)$ to minimize the loss in support from grouping N taxpayers into k_j rate brackets for each of J activities, that is, min $\Sigma_i \{b_i(G^*) - b_i(G)\}$ + $S(k_1, k_2, \ldots, k_J; t^*)$, subject to $R(k_1, \ldots, k_J) = G + A(k_1, \ldots, k_J)$, where S is decreasing in each k_j and (G^*, t^*) represent the optimal G and the vector of $N \times J$ tax rates defined in the absence of administration costs. The first term in the objective function is the loss in support from the revenue implications of grouping relative to the (G^*, t^*) solution. $S(\cdot)$ represents the

As pointed out, the analysis has a second important application to the grouping of activities into tax bases. Consider a model with one representative taxpayer who engages in J different activities. The government can save on administration costs by combining related activities into a limited number of bases, such as occurs when incomes from different labor activities are included in the same tax base. Grouping leads to an increase in political opposition in this case since it will raise a taxpayer's deadweight loss associated with any given tax payment. On the other hand, the government receives additional support by spending resources saved in administration on the provision of public goods. The solution illustrated in Figure 1 again describes the nature of the equilibrium where K^* now refers to the number of bases for each individual rather than to rate brackets.

The preceding analysis for the first time formally integrates administration costs into

---

minimum increase in opposition to taxation from (optimally) grouping taxpayers into rate brackets, as discussed in the Appendix.

political optimization.[14] In doing so, it provides a new basis for understanding the evolution of tax systems. In his pioneering work on fiscal systems, Musgrave (1969) argues that tax handles are crucial for explaining the formation and growth of tax structure. If we conceive of the term "tax handles" in a broad sense that includes opportunities to tax and to escape taxation as well as administration costs, the theory presented here formalizes what so far has mainly been implicit. In an analysis over time, changes in economic activities and in the conditions under which they are carried out will be of crucial importance together with administration costs since the nature of such activities and conditions determines the characteristics according to which the government sorts taxpayers to create bases, rate structures, and (as argued below) special provisions. The development of tax structure results therefore from an interaction between the changing ways in which people work, transact, and consume on the one hand, and the cost of administering the collection of revenues on the other. To this is added a third element, namely the influence of those factors that determine how benefits from public goods and losses in full income from taxation are translated into political action.

IV. Special Provisions

The final feature of the skeleton that remains to be explained is the existence of special provisions such as exemptions, deductions, and tax credits. Consider the grouping of activities into tax bases in the case with N taxpayers, each of whom engages in J activities. According to the preceding analysis, the government will create separate bases for each of the N taxpayers. The composition of bases will differ among taxpayers unless there is an additional cost, not considered so far, in administering different bases for each individual. Such costs

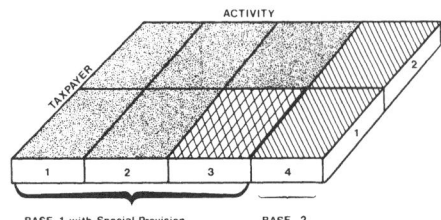

FIGURE 2. SPECIAL PROVISIONS IN TAX STRUCTURE

introduce a further constraint on the grouping process leading to bases that coincide for large numbers of individuals and in rate structures that are defined on bases rather than on separate activities.

The argument is illustrated in Figure 2 which is drawn for two taxpayers, each of whom engages in four activities. When there are no additional costs in having separate bases for each taxpayer, the grouping process results in person 1's being taxed on two bases consisting of activities 1 and 2 and activities 3 and 4, respectively. For person 2, the two bases will consist of a combination of the first three activities and of activity 4. When there are costs to having separate bases for each individual, it may be preferable to define the first base for both individuals to include 1, 2, and 3 while making activity 4 into a second base.[15] However, it will be politically undesirable to tax activity 3 in the same way for both taxpayers. A special provision such as an exemption or a deduction in the first base will allow the government to differentiate tax treatment of activity 3 depending on the taxpayer involved.

The argument can also be approached from a second angle. The general solution in (5) specifies a different rate structure for each activity. This, no doubt, would be administratively costly. It may be preferable to define rate structures across bases compris-

---

[14]See Shlomo Yitzhaki (1979) for a consideration of administration costs in an optimal tax setting. Yitzhaki does not explore the implications of heterogeneity.

[15]An additional base generally requires a new set of collection points and separate administrative arrangements.

ing several activities, but to introduce some differentiation in the tax treatment of each activity in any base by having special provisions that are specific to particular activities.[16]

We have now shown that the government's optimizing behavior generates all essential elements of tax structure. The skeleton is complete. The analysis also demonstrates that all the parts are interdependent. This is an important point since tax policy or tax reform often focuses only on one aspect of the system without taking account of the repercussions that must follow intervention in other parts. Rate structures, bases, and special provisions are all determined jointly. The government will furthermore try to establish a new political equilibrium each time there are shocks to the system such as changes in the factors (x_i) determining the supply of taxable activities, or in the nature of heterogeneity among taxpayers. The analysis strongly suggests that tax systems should be studied as integrated systems of essential elements and not merely as collections of unrelated or ill-designed components.

V. The Relationship Between Tax Rates and Tax Revenues

The model developed in this paper throws new light on the much discussed relationship between tax rates and tax revenues. In the basic model of Section II, this relationship will differ for each individual. While each long-run "Laffer" curve may have a backward-bending portion, political optimization in the basic model precludes tax rates which push taxpayers onto that portion, provided that political opposition increases continuously with tax rates and that the vote productivity of additional public expenditure is positive.

Opposition to taxation will always increase with tax rates if both terms in the numerator of (4) are positive. It seems reasonable to assume this to be the case, even though increases in tax rates may lower tax revenues after some point (Geoffrey Brennan et al., 1984). Then, as long as $B_i > 0$ and $\partial b_i / \partial G > 0$, the first-order conditions (4) require that ε_i exceed -1. In other words, choice of a tax rate placing a voter on the backward-bending portion of his Laffer curve would imply that the government is foregoing revenues which could be used to generate further support and that the affected voter is at the same time opposing the government more strongly than he would at lower rates.[17]

In a world of heterogeneous taxpayers and positive administration costs, this conclusion may no longer hold for some individual taxpayers. When grouping occurs, the original optimal conditions no longer apply, with the result that some individuals may become subject to a group rate placing them on the backward-bending portion of their individual rate-revenue curve. This will occur if assignment to any other group would lower the government's overall expected support. (Two factors are relevant in assigning individuals to groups: revenue collected, which can be turned into political support through production of public goods, and the expected support from the individual himself. Assuming the number of groups to be fixed, the government will assign individuals so as to maximize net support from these two sources.)

---

[16] There may be further reasons for special provisions if there is a more direct link between the expenditure and tax sides. Expression (1) assumes that expected support by a particular individual is separable in G and v_i. In actual tax systems, we do observe some provisions which may represent a more direct link between the two sides of the budget. One can imagine a government creating a tax structure based initially on (1) and then amending it subsequently for certain broad classes of individuals having similar evaluations of public output. For example, people over 65 years of age may be given a special exemption to acknowledge a lower evaluation of public services. We would expect the cost of adjusting the definition of tax bases to exceed the cost of creating special provisions. As a result, the link between expenditures and taxes—as far as it exists—will be expressed primarily through the introduction of additional special provisions.

[17] It should be pointed out that there is no difference in the time horizon of voters and the government in the model. For a discussion of the Laffer curve that focuses on such differences, see Buchanan and Dwight Lee (1983).

The argument shows that we may expect to observe some individuals whose tax payments would increase if *they alone* faced lower tax rates. One should note, however, that the same conclusion does not apply to groups. No group will be on the backward-bending part of its aggregate rate-revenue relationship. Otherwise, the government could collect more revenues from the group as a whole by lowering the group's rate, while at the same time reducing opposition from all of its members.

VI. Comparison with Other Approaches

It is useful to compare the implications of our analysis to results derived from models that are based on different premises. We shall comment on the two approaches that have been most influential in recent years, the Leviathan model and the theory of optimal taxation.

In their work on taxation, Brennan and James Buchanan (1980) put major emphasis on underlying political forces while also making the level of expenditures endogenous. Nevertheless, their approach differs in an essential aspect from ours; they are concerned with a government attempting to maximize revenues and facing no significant political constraint. The government in our model has a different objective function and is effectively constrained by political forces even to the extent that opposition by unorganized voters will be reflected in tax structure.[18]

Brennan and Buchanan do not address the problem of how tax structure is created when bases as well as other major structural elements are endogenous. Presumably, Leviathan would also combine activities and individuals into groups, but the sorting would differ in two essential respects. Grouping in our framework reflects political factors determining how losses in full income are translated into political action in addition to the abilities of taxpayers to escape taxation which are Leviathan's major concern. Furthermore, the government has an incentive to economize on administration costs, while no such motivation exists in a world where government is not constrained politically in setting tax policy.

Both these differences have implications for empirical work. Statistical research based on our model requires a more explicit treatment of the $c(v)$ function and thus the development of proxy variables for the determinants of political influence. In addition, it is necessary to formulate variables reflecting administration costs (Winer and Hettich, 1987). Presumably, no such variables would be included in a model based on the existence of Leviathan-type behavior. Wallace Oates (1985) investigates such behavior by looking at whether or not decentralization constrains the size of government. Our theory suggests a more direct test, namely whether the evolution of tax structure and revenue composition is influenced by political and administrative factors in addition to economic ones.

While there are formal similarities between the theory of optimal taxation (OT) and the analysis developed here, there are also important substantive differences. In OT, the government maximizes a welfare function, usually written as a weighted sum of individual utilities, with the weights reflecting exogenously given distributional preferences. To our knowledge, writers on OT have not dealt with the creation of tax structure when tax bases are endogenous. While their work could be extended to include an analysis of sorting, the resulting equilibrium would differ since factors determining how losses in full income are translated into political support have no role in OT.

Optimal taxation is generally conceived of as a normative theory not concerned with explaining actual government behavior, but intended to provide a standard of reference which abstracts from the political setting in which tax policy is made. In this context, the interesting comparison concerns the efficiency of equilibrium.

---

[18] For this reason, our model also differs from that of Becker (1983) in which only the interests of organized groups are reflected in policy choices by the government.

If the optimal tax problem is stated as the maximization of social welfare subject to the raising of a fixed budget, efficiency in taxation requires that the change in social welfare per dollar of additional revenue be equalized across revenue sources. Efficiency of this kind is not a general characteristic of the model presented here, where as in equation (4), a support-maximizing government equalizes the change in expected political support per dollar of additional revenue across revenue sources. As a result, support-maximizing governments will create tax structures that differ significantly from solutions envisioned in the OT literature.

We may still ask whether a tax system of the kind described in the paper can be considered globally efficient. If we interpret tax structure as the long-run equilibrium of a competitive political system in which political opposition depends on the loss in full income, no political party can offer an alternative tax system generating the same political support with a lower welfare loss for any individual. In this sense tax structure is efficient for the existing set of political institutions. This does not mean that an alternative set of institutions could not yield a better tax system. The argument does, however, direct debate on tax reform toward the redesign of political institutions.

VII. Concluding Remarks

Existing tax systems are composed of a limited number of basic elements which have been combined to form complicated structures. To understand why tax systems have the appearance and characteristics that we observe, we must explain why the basic elements are used as building blocks and why they are combined in particular ways.

The paper demonstrates that the essential stylized facts of observed tax systems can be viewed as the outcome of optimizing political and economic behavior. It further shows that the way in which these elements are combined into different structures depends on administration costs and on the nature of political and economic responses to taxation among individuals.

Tax structure is a system of related parts in equilibrium, not merely a collection of separate and ill-designed components. This has important implications for the understanding of tax policy. Changes must pass a political as well as an economic test and reforms in one part of the system may lead to unexpected repercussions elsewhere as the government attempts to establish a new equilibrium. The analysis also suggests that the evolution of tax systems can be viewed as a sequence of responses to changing economic, administrative, and political factors. Future empirical work should adopt a framework that can account for the systematic influence of these determinants on tax history.

APPENDIX: GROUPING OF TAXPAYERS INTO RATE BRACKETS (OR ACTIVITIES INTO BASES)

Let the number of rate brackets be some number $K < N$, the number of taxpayers, and assume that first-order conditions in the absence of grouping can be written as

(A1) $$a_{ik} + m \cdot t_{ik} = g_{ik} - h \cdot t_{ik}.$$

The left side of (A1) represents the marginal political cost of taxing person i ($i = 1, 2, \ldots, n_k$) in group k ($k = 1, 2, \ldots, K$), analogous to the numerator in (4), while the right side stands for the marginal benefit of raising t_{ik} and spending the extra revenue. Heterogeneity of behavior is captured by differences in the constant terms. Imposing a rate t_{ik}, differing from the politically optimal rate t_{ik}^* found by solving (A1), results in a loss in support from each taxpayer equal to the integral of the difference between marginal political costs and benefits over the interval from t_{ik}^* to t_{ik}. Given (A1), this integral is equal to $v \cdot (t_{ik} - t_{ik}^*)^2$ where $v = (m+h)/2$. Similarly, the loss in support from taxing all members of any group k alike at rate t is equal to $v \cdot \Sigma_i (t - t_{ik}^*)^2$. The rate t that minimizes this loss is the least squares solution $t_{\cdot k} = \Sigma_i t_{ik} / n_k$. Thus with K brackets or groups the total loss in support from grouping can be reduced to $v \cdot \Sigma_k \Sigma_i (t_{\cdot k} - t_{ik}^*)^2$. This loss can be made as small as possible if taxpayers are assigned among groups so as to minimize the variation of the t_{ik}^*'s within each group.

REFERENCES

Atkinson, A.B. and Stiglitz, J.E., *Lectures on Public Economics*, New York: McGraw-Hill, 1980.

Becker, Gary S., "A Theory of Competition Among Pressure Groups for Political Influence," *Quarterly Journal of Economics*, August 1983, *98*, 371–400.

Brennan, Geoffrey and Buchanan, James M., *The Power to Tax*, Cambridge MA: Cambridge University Press, 1980.

_____, **Bohanon, Cecil and Carter, Richard,** "Public Finance and Public Prices; Towards a Reconstruction of Tax Theory,"*Public Finance*, 1984, *39*, 157–79.

Buchanan, James and Lee, Dwight, "Politics, Time and Laffer Curve," *Journal of Political Economy*, August 1982, *90*, 816–19.

Coughlin, Peter J., "Elections and Income Redistribution," *Public Choice*, 1986, *50*, 27–91.

Denzau, Arthur T. and Munger, Michael C., "Legislators and Interest Groups: How Unorganized Interests Get Represented," *American Political Science Review*, March 1986, *80*, 89–106.

Downs, Anthony, *An Economic Theory of Democracy*, New York: Harper & Row, 1957.

Hansen, Susan B., *The Politics of Taxation: Revenue Without Representation*, New York: Praeger, 1983.

Heller, W.P. and Shell, Karl, "On Optimal Taxation with Costly Administration," *American Economic Review Proceedings*, May 1974, *64*, 338–45.

Hettich, Walter and Winer, Stanley L., "A Positive Model of Tax Structure," *Journal of Public Economics*, June 1984, *24*, 67–87.

_____ and _____, "Blueprints and Pathways: The Shifting Foundations of Tax Reform," *National Tax Journal*, December 1985, *38*, 423–45.

_____ and _____, "Federalism, Special Interests and the Exchange of Policies for Political Resources," *European Journal of Political Economy*, 1987, *3*, Special Issue, 33–54.

Hinrichs, Harley H., *A General Theory of Tax Structure Change During Economic Development*, Cambridge, MA: Harvard Law School, 1966.

Mayhew, David R., *Congress: The Electoral Connection*, New Haven: Yale University Press, 1974.

Meltzer, A.H. and Richard S.F., "A Rational Theory of the Size of Government," *Journal of Political Economy*, October 1981, *89*, 914–27.

_____ and _____, "Tests of a Rational Theory of the size of Government," *Public Choice*, 1983, *41*, 403–18.

Musgrave, Richard A., *Fiscal Systems*, New Haven: Yale University Press, 1969.

Oates, Wallace E., "Searching for Leviathan: An Empirical Study," *American Economic Review*, September 1985, *75*, 748–57.

Ordeshook, Peter C., *Game Theory and Political Theory: An Introduction*, Cambridge, MA: Cambridge University Press, 1986.

Peltzman, Sam, "Toward a More General Theory of Regulation," *Journal of Law and Economics*, August 1976, *19*, 219–40.

Roberts, K.W.S., "Voting over Income Tax Schedules," *Journal of Public Economics*, December 1977, *8*, 329–40.

Romer, Thomas, "Individual Welfare, Majority Voting, and the Properties of a Linear Income Tax," *Journal of Public Economics*, February 1975, *4*, 163–85.

Schumpeter, Joseph A., *Capitalism, Socialism, and Democracy*, 3rd ed., New York: Harper & Row, 1950.

Stigler, George J., "The Economic Theory of Regulation," *Bell Journal of Economics*, Spring 1971, *3*, 3–21.

Winer, Stanley L. and Hettich, Walter,"The Evolution of Revenue Systems: A Theoretical and Empirical Investigation," Carleton Economics Papers, No. 87-04, May 1987.

Yitzhaki, Shlomo, "A Note on Optimal Taxation and Administration Costs," *American Economic Review*, June 1979, *69*, 475–80.

Part II
Optimal Taxation

[19]

Optimal Taxation and Public Production II: Tax Rules

By Peter A. Diamond and James A. Mirrlees*

In Part I of this paper which appeared in the March 1971 issue of this *Review*, we set out the problem of using taxation and government production to maximize a social welfare function. We derived the first-order conditions, and considered the argument for efficiency in aggregate production. Here in Part II we consider the structure of optimal taxes in more detail. Part I contained five sections, and Part II begins at Section VI. In the sixth and seventh sections we consider commodity taxation in one- and many-consumer economies. In the eighth section we consider other kinds of taxes; and in the ninth, public consumption. In the tenth section we consider a rigorous treatment of the problem, giving a sufficient condition for the validity of the first-order conditions. To begin, we shall restate the notation and basic problem.

Notation

- p producer prices
- q consumer prices
- t taxes ($t = q - p$)
- $x^h(q)$ net demand by consumer h (incomes are assumed to equal zero) $h = 1, 2, \ldots, H$
- $u^h(x^h)$ utility function of consumer h
- $v^h(q)$ indirect utility function of consumer h $v^h(q) = u^h(x^h(q))$
- $X(q)$ aggregate net demand $X(q) = \sum_h x^h(q)$

* Massachusetts Institute of Technology and Nuffield College, respectively. The remainder of the matching footnote in Part I is appropriate here too.

- $U(x^1, \ldots, x^H)$ social welfare function
- $V(q)$ indirect social welfare function $V(q) = U(x^1(q), \ldots, x^H(q))$
- $W(u^1, \ldots, u^H)$ special case of an individualistic social welfare function, assumed for some of the analysis below.

With this notation before us again, we can restate the welfare maximization problem as that of selecting q to

$$\text{Maximize } V(q)$$
(33)
$$\text{subject to } G(X(q)) \leq 0$$

where G represents the aggregate production constraint. This problem gave rise to the first-order conditions ((19) and (22)) which were equivalently stated as

(34)
$$\frac{\partial V}{\partial q_k} = \lambda \sum_i p_i \frac{\partial X_i}{\partial q_k}$$
$$= -\lambda \frac{\partial}{\partial t_k}\left(\sum_i t_i X_i\right)$$
$$(k = 1, 2, \ldots, n)$$

Equations (34) were derived only for $k=2, \ldots, n$. But we can see that they hold also for $k=1$; for, on multiplying by q_k and adding, we have

$$\sum_{k=1}^{n}\left[\frac{\partial V}{\partial q_k} - \lambda \sum_i p_i \frac{\partial X_i}{\partial q_k}\right] q_k = 0$$

by the homogeneity of degree 0 of V and the X_i. Equation (34) states that the impact of a price rise on social welfare is proportional to the cost of meeting the change in demand induced by the price rise. Alternatively the impact of a tax increase on social welfare is proportional to the induced change in tax revenue (all calculated at fixed producer prices).

VI. Optimal Tax Structure— One-Consumer Economy

For one consumer and an individualistic welfare function (so that V coincides with v, the indirect utility function of the only consumer in the economy), we can express directly the derivative of social welfare with respect to q_k ($v_k = -\alpha x_k$ where α is the marginal utility of income—see equation (5) of Part I). For this case we can then explore the structure of taxation in more detail. The formulation of the first-order conditions using compensated demand derivatives is due to Paul Samuelson (1951). We begin by stating the familiar Slutsky equation:

$$(35) \quad \frac{\partial x_i}{\partial q_k} = s_{ik} - x_k \frac{\partial x_i}{\partial I}$$

where s_{ik} is the derivative of the compensated demand curve for i with respect to q_k, and $\partial x_i/\partial I$ is the derivative of the uncompensated demand with respect to income (evaluated at $I=0$ in our case). We shall make use of the well-known result that $s_{ik} = s_{ki}$.

Substituting into the first-order conditions (34) we have:

$$(36) \quad \begin{aligned} -\alpha x_k &= -\lambda \frac{\partial}{\partial t_k} \left(\sum t_i x_i \right) \\ &= -\lambda \left(x_k + \sum t_i \frac{\partial x_i}{\partial t_k} \right) \\ &= -\lambda x_k - \lambda \sum t_i s_{ik} \\ &\quad + \lambda x_k \sum t_i \frac{\partial x_i}{\partial I} \end{aligned}$$

$$k = 1, 2, \ldots, n$$

Rearranging terms, we can write this in the form:

$$(37) \quad \frac{\sum_i t_i s_{ik}}{x_k} = \frac{\alpha + \lambda - \lambda \sum_i t_i \frac{\partial x_i}{\partial I}}{\lambda}$$

The point to be noticed is that the right-hand side of this equation is independent of k. Call it $-\theta$. Finally, using the symmetry of the Slutsky matrix, we write the first-order conditions as:

$$(38) \quad \frac{\sum_i s_{ki} t_i}{x_k} = -\theta$$

Multiplying by $t_k x_k$ and summing, we obtain

$$(39) \quad \theta \sum_k t_k x_k = -\sum_{k,i} t_k s_{ki} t_i \geq 0,$$

by the negative semi-definiteness of the Slutsky matrix. Thus θ has the same sign as net government revenue.

The left-hand side of (38) is the percentage change in the demand for good k that would result from the tax change if producer prices were constant, the consumer were compensated so as to stay on the same indifference curve, and the derivatives of the compensated demand curves were constant at the same level as at the optimum point:

$$(40) \quad \begin{aligned} \Delta x_k &= \sum_i \int_0^{t_i} \frac{\partial x_k}{\partial t_i} dt_i = \sum_i \int_0^{t_i} s_{ki} dt_i \\ &= \sum_i s_{ki} \int_0^{t_i} dt_i = \sum_i s_{ki} t_i \end{aligned}$$

In fact, it is not possible for all these derivatives to be constant. But if the optimal taxes are small, it is approximately true that the optimal tax structure implies an equal percentage change in compensated demand at constant producer prices.

We can also calculate the actual changes in demand arising from the tax structure (assuming price derivatives of demand and production prices are constant) by resubstituting from the Slutsky equation (35). Then, upon substitution, we have:

DIAMOND AND MIRRLEES: OPTIMAL TAXATION

$$\sum_i \frac{\partial x_k}{\partial q_i} t_i + \frac{\partial x_k}{\partial I} \sum t_i x_i = -\theta x_k;$$

or

(41) $$\frac{\sum_i \frac{\partial x_k}{\partial q_i} t_i}{x_k} = -\theta - x_k^{-1} \frac{\partial x_k}{\partial I} \sum t_i x_i$$

The actual changes in demand (again assuming constant derivatives) induced by the tax structure differ from proportionality with a larger than average percentage fall in demand for goods with a large income derivative.

Three-Good Economy

In the case of a three-good economy, we can obtain an expression for the relative ad valorem tax rates of the two taxed goods. This argument is similar to that of W. J. Corlett and D. C. Hague, who discussed the direction of movement away from proportional taxation that would increase utility. In the three-good case, with good one untaxed, the first-order conditions (38) become

(42) $$\begin{aligned} s_{22} t_2 + s_{23} t_3 &= -\theta x_2 \\ s_{32} t_2 + s_{33} t_3 &= -\theta x_3 \end{aligned}$$

Solving these equations we have

(43) $$t_2 = \theta \frac{s_{23} x_3 - s_{33} x_2}{s_{22} s_{33} - s_{23}^2}, \quad t_3 = \theta \frac{s_{32} x_2 - s_{22} x_3}{s_{22} s_{33} - s_{23}^2}$$

Notice that the denominator here is positive, by the properties of the Slutsky matrix. We convert these into elasticity expressions, defining the elasticity of compensated demand by

(44) $$\sigma_{ij} = \frac{q_j s_{ij}}{x_i}$$

Equation (43) can then be written

(45) $$\frac{t_2}{q_2} = \theta'(\sigma_{23} - \sigma_{33}), \quad \frac{t_3}{q_3} = \theta'(\sigma_{32} - \sigma_{22}),$$

where

$$\theta' = \frac{\theta x_2 x_3}{q_2 q_3 (s_{22} s_{33} - s_{23}^2)}$$

We now substitute for σ_{23} and σ_{33}, using the adding-up properties of compensated elasticities,

(46) $$\begin{aligned} \sigma_{23} &= -\sigma_{22} - \sigma_{21}, \\ \sigma_{32} &= -\sigma_{33} - \sigma_{31} \end{aligned}$$

This gives us

(47) $$\begin{aligned} \frac{t_2}{q_2} &= \theta'(\sigma_{21} + \sigma_{22} + \sigma_{33}), \\ \frac{t_3}{q_3} &= \theta'(\sigma_{31} + \sigma_{22} + \sigma_{33}) \end{aligned}$$

The interesting case to consider is where labor ($x_1 < 0$) is the untaxed good, while goods 2 and 3 are consumer goods ($x_2 > 0$, $x_3 > 0$). Then θ' has the same sign as net government revenue. For definiteness, suppose that government revenue is positive so that $\theta' > 0$. Equation (47) shows that

(48) $$\frac{t_2}{q_2} \gtreqless \frac{t_3}{q_3} \quad \text{according as} \quad \sigma_{21} \lesseqgtr \sigma_{31}$$

The tax rate is proportionally greater for the good with the smaller cross-elasticity of compensated demand with the price of labor. (It is possible that one commodity is subsidized, but it has to be the one with the greater cross-elasticity.)

Examples

The implications of the above model are very diverse, depending upon the nature of the demand functions. A simple example will show how the theory can be used. If we define ordinary demand elasticities by the usual formula

(49) $$\epsilon_{ik} = q_k x_i^{-1} \frac{\partial x_i}{\partial q_k},$$

we can rewrite the optimal taxation formula in the form

(50) $$v_k = q_k^{-1} \lambda \sum p_i x_i \epsilon_{ik}$$

When the welfare function is individualistic, equation (5) applies, so that equation (50) may be written as

$$-\alpha q_k x_k = \lambda \sum p_i x_i \epsilon_{ik} \tag{51}$$

or

$$q_k p_k^{-1} = -\frac{\lambda}{\alpha} \sum_i \frac{p_i x_i}{p_k x_k} \epsilon_{ik}$$

If we have a good whose price does not affect other demands (implying a unitary own price elasticity), equation (51) simplifies to yield the optimal tax of that good:

(52) If $\epsilon_{ik} = 0$ $(i \neq k)$ and $\epsilon_{kk} = -1$, then $q_k p_k^{-1} = \lambda \alpha^{-1}$

where $q_k p_k^{-1}$ equals one plus the percentage tax rate. Recalling that α is the marginal utility of income while λ reflects the change in welfare from allowing a government deficit financed from some outside source, their ratio gives a marginal cost (in terms of the numeraire good) of raising revenue. Thus the optimal tax rate on such a good gives the cost to society of raising the marginal dollar of tax.

An example of a utility function exhibiting such demand curves is the Cobb-Douglas, where only labor is supplied. As an example consider:

$$u(x) = b_1 \log(x_1 + \omega_1) + \sum_{i=2}^n b_i \log x_i \tag{53}$$

If we choose labor as the untaxed numeraire, all other goods satisfy (52) and we see that the optimal tax structure is a proportional tax structure.

It is easy to exhibit examples where the optimal tax structure is not proportional. Consider the example:

$$u(x) = \sum b_i \log(x_i + \omega_i), \tag{54}$$
$$\sum b_i = 1, \quad \omega_i \neq 0$$

The demands arising from these preferences are:

$$x_i = q_i^{-1} b_i \sum q_j \omega_j - \omega_i \tag{55}$$

Therefore the demand elasticities are:

$$\epsilon_{ik} = b_i \omega_k x_i^{-1} \frac{q_k}{q_i} \quad (k \neq i)$$

(56)

$$\epsilon_{kk} = -b_k x_k^{-1} \sum_{j \neq k} \omega_j \frac{q_j}{q_k}$$

Substituting in the formula for the optimal taxes,

$$(57) \quad -\alpha q_k x_k =$$

$$\lambda \left[\sum_{j \neq k} b_j \frac{p_j}{q_j} \omega_k q_k - b_k \frac{p_k}{q_k} \sum_{j \neq k} \omega_j q_j \right]$$

$$= \lambda \sum_j \left[b_j \omega_k \frac{p_j q_k}{q_j} - b_k \omega_j \frac{p_k q_j}{q_k} \right]$$

Since the assumption $\sum b_j = 1$ allows us to write the demand functions (55) in the form:

$$q_k x_k = \sum_j [b_k \omega_j q_j - b_j \omega_k q_k], \tag{58}$$

we can deduce from (57) and (58) that

$$(59) \quad \sum_j \left[b_j \omega_k q_k \left(\frac{p_j}{q_j} - \frac{\alpha}{\lambda} \right) \right.$$
$$\left. - b_k \omega_j q_j \left(\frac{p_k}{q_k} - \frac{\alpha}{\lambda} \right) \right] = 0$$

These equations allow us to calculate p for any given q, and in that way give the optimal taxation rules. In general, taxes will not be proportional. As one example of this, consider the following three-good case.

Sample Calculation

Let us combine the above two examples by considering a three-good economy (one-consumer good and two types of labor) with preferences as in (54). This example will be used to show that limited tax possibilities (represented by the same proportional tax on goods 2 and 3) introduces the desirability of aggregate production inefficiency.

Example e. Assume that preferences satisfy

(60a) $\quad u = $

$$\log x_1 + \log (x_2 + 1) + \log (x_3 + 2)$$

$$x_1 > 0, \quad x_2 > 1, \quad x_3 > -2;$$

while private production possibilities are

(60b) $\quad y_1 + y_2 + y_3 \leq 0,$

$$y_1 \geq 0, \quad y_2 \leq 0, \quad y_3 \leq 0;$$

and the government constraint is

(60c) $\quad 1.02 z_1 + z_2 \leq 0$

$$z_1 \geq 0, \quad z_2 \leq 0, \quad z_3 \leq -0.1$$

Thus the government needs good 3 for public use and can produce good 1 from good 2, but only less efficiently than the private sector can.

Since we know that production efficiency is desired, we have

$$q_1 = p_1 = p_2 = 1, \quad z_1 = z_2 = 0$$

From the first-order conditions (59) and market clearance given the demands (58), we obtain two equations to determine q_2 and q_3:

$$q_2(q_3^{-1} - 1) = 2q_3(q_2^{-1} - 1)$$

$$(q_2 + 2q_3)(q_2^{-1} + q_3^{-1} + 1) = 8.7$$

These have a unique positive solution

$$q_2 = 0.94494, \quad q_3 = 0.90008$$

which give

$$x_1 = 0.9150, \quad x_2 = -0.0316, \quad x_3 = -0.9834$$

$$u = -0.1045$$

If we now require the same tax rate on goods 2 and 3 and at the same time impose production efficiency, then $q_2 = q_3 = q$, and the tax rate is determined by the market clearance equation. We obtain

$$3q + 6 = 8.7; \quad \text{i.e., } q = 0.9$$

Then demands are

$$x_1 = 0.9, \quad x_2 = 0, \quad x_3 = -1$$

and

$$u = -0.1054$$

Notice that the economy is still on the production frontier even though both input prices are lower in this case. If we introduce inefficiency with $p_2 > 1$, so that $y_2 = 0$ and $x_2 = z_2$, we can increase utility. Market clearance now requires

$$(q_2 + 2q_3)((1.02)^{-1} q_2^{-1} + q_3^{-1} + 1) = 8.7$$

At prices $q_2 = .92$, $q_3 = .90008$ for example, we have, $x_1 = 0.9067$, $x_2 = -0.0144$, $x_3 = -0.9926$, and $u = -0.1051$.

VII. Optimal Tax Structure— Many-Consumer Economy

As we noted in Section III of Part I, the equations for optimal taxation with a single consumer which do not reflect the particular form of V are also valid for many consumers. To pursue the analysis further, we must find an expression for V_k, the derivative of social welfare with respect to the kth consumer price.

With an individualistic welfare function, we have

(61) $\quad V(q) = W(v^1(q), v^2(q), \ldots, v^H(q))$

Differentiating with respect to q_k, we obtain

(62) $\quad V_k = \sum_h \dfrac{\partial W}{\partial u^h} v_k^h = -\sum_h \dfrac{\partial W}{\partial u^h} \alpha^h x_k^h$

The term α^h is the marginal utility of income of consumer h. Therefore

(63) $\quad \beta^h = \dfrac{\partial W}{\partial u^h} \alpha^h$

is the increase in social welfare from a unit increase in the income of consumer h. We have

(64) $\quad -V_k = \sum_h \beta^h x_k^h,$

or the derivative of welfare with respect to a price equals the "welfare-weighted" net consumer demand for commodity k. The necessary condition for optimal taxation makes V_k proportional to the marginal contribution to tax revenue from raising the tax on good k.

(65) $$\sum_h \beta^h x_k^h = \lambda \frac{\partial T}{\partial t_k},$$

where $T = \sum t_i X_i$ is total tax revenue, and the derivative is evaluated at constant producer prices (i.e., on the basis of consumer excess demand functions alone). We also have the alternative formula

(66) $$\sum_h \beta^h x_k^h = -\lambda \sum_i p_i \frac{\partial X_i}{\partial q_k}$$

Example f. Before turning to interpretations of the optimal tax formulae like those above, let us consider an example.

We will assume that each consumer has a Cobb-Douglas utility function,

(67) $$u^h = b_1^h \log(x_1^h + \omega^h)$$
$$+ \sum_2^n b_i^h \log x_i^h, \qquad \sum_1^n b_i^h = 1$$

Choosing good 1 as numeraire, we saw in Section VI that with a one-consumer economy, taxation would be proportional. This will not, in general, be true in a many-consumer economy where each consumer has this utility function. The individual demand curves arising from this utility function are:

(68) $$x_i^h = q_i^{-1} b_i^h q_1 \omega^h, \qquad i = 2, 3, \ldots, n$$
$$x_1^h = -(1 - b_1^h)\omega^h$$

Notice that $\partial x_i^h/\partial q_k = 0$ $(k \neq i \neq 1)$ and $\partial x_i^h/\partial q_1 = -x_i^h/q_i$ $(i \neq 1)$.

Assuming an individualistic welfare function, the first-order conditions (66) are in this case

(69) $$\sum_h \beta^h x_k^h = \lambda p_k q_k^{-1} \sum_h x_k^h$$
$$(k = 2, \ldots, n)$$

This implies the following formula:

(70) $$\frac{q_k}{p_k} = \lambda \frac{\sum_h x_k^h}{\sum_h \beta^h x_k^h} = \lambda \frac{\sum_h b_k^h \omega^h}{\sum_h \beta^h b_k^h \omega^h}$$
$$(k = 2, \ldots, n)$$

To complete the determination of the optimal taxes, we must find the relationship between λ, p_1, and q_1. This is obtained from the Walras identity. The value of net consumer demand in producer prices is equal to minus the profit in production. (Alternatively, we could determine λ so that the government budget is balanced.) That is

(71) $$-p_1 \sum_h (1 - b_1^h)\omega^h$$
$$+ \sum_{i=2}^n \sum_h p_i q_i^{-1} b_i^h q_1 \omega^h = \gamma,$$

where γ is the maximized profit of production net of government needs $(= \sum_{i=1}^n p_i z_i)$. Substituting from (70) and rearranging, we obtain

(72) $$\frac{q_1}{p_1} = \lambda \frac{\sum_h (1 - b_1^h)\omega^h + \gamma p_1^{-1}}{\sum_{i=2}^n \sum_h \beta^h b_i^h \omega^h}$$
$$= \lambda \frac{\sum_h (1 - b_1^h)\omega^h + \gamma p_1^{-1}}{\sum \beta^h (1 - b_1^h)\omega^h}$$

The number γp^{-1} is determined by the technology and the government expenditure decision, and therefore depends on p (unless $\gamma = 0$).

Equations (70) and (72) determine the optimal tax rates. If the social marginal utilities, β^h, are independent of taxation, the optimal tax rates can be read off at once. This is true if W has the special form $\sum_h v^h$; for in that case $\beta^h = 1/\omega^h$. It should be noticed that, although each household's social marginal utility of income is unaffected by taxation, it is desirable to have taxation in general. If households with relatively low social marginal utility of income predominate among the purchasers of a commodity, that commodity should be relatively highly taxed. Although such taxation does nothing to bring social marginal utilities of income closer together, it does increase total welfare.

In general, taxation does affect social marginal utilities of income. The β^h depend on the tax rates, and equations (70) do not, therefore, give explicit formulae for the optimum taxes. In the case $W = -\mu^{-1}\sum_h e^{-\mu v^h}$, $\mu > 0$, so that there is a stronger bias toward equality than in the additive case, it can be verified quite easily that the optimum taxes have to satisfy

$$(73) \quad \frac{q_k}{p_k} \sum_h b_k^h(\omega^h)^{-\mu} \prod_{i=2}^n (b_i^h)^{-\mu b_i^h} q_i^{\mu b_i^h}$$

$$= \lambda \sum_h b_k^h \omega^h \quad (k = 2, 3, \ldots, n)$$

In this case, marginal utilities of income are brought closer together.[1] It is not immediately obvious from the equations (10) that the q are determined given the p. However, it can be shown that, in the present example, the first-order conditions must have a unique solution.[2] In fact, the

---

[1] If $\mu < 0$, utilities and marginal utilities are moved further apart.
[2] It is easily verified that $v^h = \delta_h + \sum_i b_i \log(q_1/q_i)$, where the δ_h are constants. Consequently

$$V(q) = -\mu^{-1} \sum_h e^{-\mu \delta_h} \prod_i (q_1/q_i)^{-\mu b_i^h}$$

which is a concave function of $(q_1/q_2, q_1/q_2, \ldots, q_1/q_n)$. Also, aggregate demand is

$$X_i(q) = \sum_h b_i^h \omega^h \cdot (q_1/q_i), \quad X_1(q) = -\sum_h (1 - \alpha^h)\omega^h$$

If the production set is convex, the set of $(q_1/q_2, \ldots, q_1/q_n)$ for which $(X_1, X_2, \ldots, X_n)$ is feasible is also convex. Thus the optimum q is obtained by maximizing a

relations (70) (along with (72)) would, if followed by government, certainly lead to maximum welfare if production were perfectly competitive, since any state of the economy satisfying these conditions maximizes welfare, and the maximum is unique for the welfare function considered. Unfortunately this convenient property is not general.

From equation (70) we can identify two cases where optimal taxation is proportional. If the social marginal utility of income is the same for everyone ($\beta^h = \beta$, for all h), then equation (70) reduces to $q_k p_k^{-1} = \lambda/\beta$. In this case there is no welfare gain to be achieved by redistributing income, and so no need to tax differently (on average) the expenditures of different individuals. Thus the optimal tax formula has the same form as in the one-consumer case. When the β^h do differ, taxes are greater on commodities purchased more heavily by individuals with a low social marginal utility of income. If, for example, the welfare function treats all individuals symmetrically and if there is diminishing social marginal utility with income, then there is greater taxation on goods purchased more heavily by the rich.

The second case leading to proportional taxation occurs when demand vectors are proportional for all individuals, $x^h = \rho^h x$, and thus $b_k^h = b_k$ for all h. With all individuals demanding goods in the same proportions, it is impossible to redistribute income by commodity taxation implying that the tax structure again assumes the form it has in a one-consumer economy.

Optimal Tax Formulae

The description in Section VI of some possible interpretations of the optimal tax formula carries over to the many-consumer case. Thus, as was true there con-

---

concave function of $(q_1/q_2, \ldots, q_1/q_n)$ over a convex set, and is therefore uniquely defined by the first-order conditions.

sumer price elasticities but not producer price elasticities enter the equations, and at the optimum the social marginal utility of a price change is proportional to the marginal change in tax revenue from raising that tax, calculated at constant producer prices. Analysis of the change in demand can also be carried out, but is naturally more complicated. Assuming an individualistic welfare function, the first-order conditions can be written[3]

$$(74) \quad \sum_h \beta^h x_k^h = \lambda \sum_h \sum_i t_i \frac{\partial x_i^h}{\partial q_k} + \lambda \sum_h x_k^h$$

From the Slutsky equation, we know that

$$(75) \quad \begin{aligned} \frac{\partial x_i}{\partial q_k} &= s_{ik} - x_k \frac{\partial x_i}{\partial I} = s_{ki} - x_k \frac{\partial x_i}{\partial I} \\ &= \frac{\partial x_k}{\partial q_i} - x_k \frac{\partial x_i}{\partial I} + x_i \frac{\partial x_k}{\partial I} \end{aligned}$$

Substituting from (75) in (74) we can write the optimal tax formula as equation (76). Rearranging terms we can write equation (76) as (77). With constant producer prices, equation (77) gives the change in demand as a result of taxation for a good with constant price-derivatives of the demand function (or for small taxes). Considering two such goods, we see that the percentage decrease in demand is greater for the good the demand for which is concentrated among:

---
[3] We neglect the possibility of a free good when the first-order condition would be an inequality.

(1) individuals with low social marginal utility of income,
(2) individuals with small decreases in taxes paid with a decrease in income,
(3) individuals for whom the product of the income derivative of demand for good k and taxes paid are large.

VIII. Other Taxes

Thus far we have examined the combined use of public production and commodity taxation as control variables. It is natural to reexamine the analysis when additional tax variables are included in those controlled by the government. In particular, in the next subsection we will briefly consider income taxation; but first, let us examine a general class of taxes such that the consumer budget constraint depends on consumer prices and on tax variables. We shall replace the budget constraint $\sum q_i x_i = 0$ by the more general constraint $\phi(x, q, \zeta) = 0$, where ζ represents a shift parameter to reflect the choice among different systems of additional taxation (for example, the degree of progression in the income tax). Let us note that this formulation continues to assume that all taxes are levied on consumers and that there are no profits in the economy.

The key assumption to permit an extension of the analysis above is an independence of the two constraints on the planner. We need to assume that the choice of tax variables does not affect the production

$$(76) \quad \sum_h \beta^h x_k^h = \lambda \sum_h \sum_i t_i \frac{\partial x_k^h}{\partial q_i} + \lambda \sum_h \sum_i t_i \left(x_i^h \frac{\partial x_k^h}{\partial I} - x_k^h \frac{\partial x_i^h}{\partial I} \right) + \lambda \sum_h x_k^h$$

$$(77) \quad \frac{\sum_h \sum_i t_i \frac{\partial x_i^h}{\partial q_i}}{\sum_h x_k^h} = \frac{1}{\lambda} \frac{\sum_h \beta^h x_k^h}{\sum_h x_k^h} - 1 + \frac{\sum_h \left(\sum_i t_i \frac{\partial x_i^h}{\partial I} \right) x_k^h}{\sum_h x_k^h} - \frac{\sum_h \left(\sum_i t_i x_i^h \right) \frac{\partial x_k^h}{\partial I}}{\sum_h x_k^h}$$

possibilities, and further that the choice of a production point does not affect the set of possible demand configurations. In particular, this formulation implies that producer prices do not affect consumer budget constraints. Thus the income tax, to fit this formulation, needs to be levied on the wages that consumers receive, not on the cost of wages to the firm. Similarly it is assumed that there are no sales tax deductions from the income tax base.

We know already that in such a case, optimal production is efficient. We may therefore concentrate upon the case in which all production is controlled by the government, and the production constraint is that $x_1 = g(x_2, x_3, \ldots, x_n)$. We have to choose $q_2, q_3, \ldots, q_n, \zeta$ to

(78)   maximize $V(q, \zeta)$ subject to $X_1(q, \zeta)$
$$= g(X_2(q, \zeta), \ldots, X_n(q, \zeta))$$

As before we introduce a Lagrange multiplier λ. Differentiation with respect to q_k yields the familiar

(79) $V_k = \lambda \sum_i p_i \dfrac{\partial X_i}{\partial q_k}$,

where the producer price p_i is $\partial g / \partial x_i$ ($i = 2, 3, \ldots, n$), and $p_1 = 1$. Differentiation with respect to the new tax variable provides the similar equation

(80) $\dfrac{\partial V}{\partial \zeta} = \lambda \sum_i p_i \dfrac{\partial X_i}{\partial \zeta}$

We have an alternative form for (79), namely,

(81) $V_k = -\lambda \dfrac{\partial T}{\partial t_k}$

In exactly the same way, we obtain from (80) a formula involving the effect of the new tax on total tax revenue,

(82) $V_\zeta = -\lambda \dfrac{\partial T}{\partial \zeta}$

Income Taxation

Nothing that we have said suggests that commodity taxation is superior to income taxation. The analysis has only considered the best use of commodity taxation. It is natural to go on to ask how one employs both commodity taxation and income taxation. The formulation of income taxation raises a problem. If the planners are free to select any income tax structure and if there are a finite number of tax payers, the tax structure can be selected so that the marginal tax rate is zero for each taxpayer at his equilibrium income (although this does not necessarily bring the economy to the full welfare maximum). This eliminates much of our problem, but like lump sum taxation, seems to be beyond the policy tools available in a large economy. The natural formulation of this problem is for a continuum of tax payers, since then no man can have a tax schedule tailor-made for him. (This approach is taken by Mirrlees.) However, we shall here take the alternative route by assuming a limited set of alternatives for the income tax structure.

If only commodity taxation is possible, the tax paid by a household that purchases a vector x^h is

(83) $T^h = \sum_i t_i x_i^h$

To add income taxation to the tax structure, we can select a subset of commodities, L, e.g., labor services, and tax the value of transactions on this subset, so that

$$I^h = \sum_{i \text{ in } L} q_i x_i^h$$

where I is "taxable income." Then

(84) $T^h = \sum_i t_i x_i^h + \tau(I^h, \zeta)$,

where τ is a fixed continuously differentiable function depending on a parameter ζ, and is the same for all consumers. With a tax on services (x_1 negative) we would expect τ to be decreasing in its tax base, with a derivative between zero and minus one. In terms of the notation employed above, we can define the budget constraint $\phi(x^h, q, \zeta)$ by

(85) $$\phi(x^h, q, \zeta) = \sum p_i x_i^h + T^h$$
$$= \sum q_i x_i^h + \tau\left(\sum_{i \text{ in } L} q_i x_i^h, \zeta\right)$$

Here we can regard q and ζ as the policy variables. Thus the consumer's budget constraint can be expressed in a form depending on consumer prices and independent of producer prices.

The first-order conditions for optimal income taxation are just the conditions (79) and (80), interpreted for this special case. The social marginal utility of a tax variable change is proportional to the marginal change in tax revenue calculated at constant producer prices. In the case of an individualistic welfare function, we can give more explicit formulae for the welfare derivatives, V_k and V_ζ:

(86) $$V_k = \sum_h \beta^h x_k^h \left(1 + \delta_k \frac{\partial \tau^h}{\partial I}\right)$$

(87) $$V_\zeta = \sum_h \beta^h \frac{\partial \tau^h}{\partial \zeta},$$

where $\delta_k = 1$ if k is in L, 0 if k is not in L; and $\tau^h = \tau(I^h, \zeta)$.

These equations are derived from the first-order conditions for maximizing u^h subject to $\phi = 0$, noticing that, for example, the budget constraint implies that

$$\sum_k \frac{\partial \phi}{\partial x_k} \frac{\partial x_k}{\partial \zeta} + \frac{\partial \phi}{\partial \zeta} = 0$$

Combining (82) and (87), we obtain

(88) $$\sum \beta^h \frac{\partial \tau^h}{\partial \zeta} = \lambda \frac{\partial T}{\partial \zeta}$$

Thus, at the optimum, for any two different kinds of change in the income tax structure, the social-marginal-utility weighted changes in taxation (consumer behavior held constant) are proportional to the changes in total tax revenue (both income and commodity tax revenue, calculated at fixed producer prices, with consumer behavior responding to the price change).

IX. Public Consumption

From the start, we have considered the government production decision as constrained by $G(z) \leq 0$. The presence of a fixed bundle of public consumption was therefore included in the model (and would show itself by $G(0)$ being positive). This is unsatisfactory and was assumed to keep as uncluttered as possible a naturally complicated problem. We can now consider a choice among vectors of public consumption which affect social welfare directly. (We shall assume that the government controls all production, thus ignoring public expenditures which affect private production rather than consumer utility.) Let us denote by e the vector of public consumption expenditures. (Items of public consumption which are difficult to measure can be described by the inputs into their production.) The presence of public consumption alters our problem in three ways. First, public consumption represents public production (or purchases) which are not supplied to the market. Thus market clearance becomes $X = z - e$.

Second, the presence of public consumption affects private net demand, which must now be written $X(q, e)$. Third, the level of public consumption directly affects the social welfare function (by affecting individual utility in the case of an individualistic welfare function).

We can restate the basic maximization problem as

(89) $\underset{q,e}{\text{Maximize}}\ V(q, e)$

subject to $G(X(q, e) + e) \leq 0$

The presence of e in the problem will not affect the equations obtained by differentiating a Lagrangian expression with respect to q. Thus the presence of alternative bundles of public consumption does not alter the rules for the optimal tax structure. Nor would we expect it to affect the conditions which imply production efficiency at the optimum. We can therefore replace the inequality in (89) with an equality and differentiate the Lagrangian expression with respect to e_k:

(90) $\dfrac{\partial V}{\partial e_k} - \lambda \left[\sum G_i \dfrac{\partial X_i}{\partial e_k} + G_k \right] = 0$

Since

(91) $\sum G_i \dfrac{\partial X_i}{\partial e_k}$

$= \sum p_i \dfrac{\partial X_i}{\partial e_k} = \sum (q_i - t_i) \dfrac{\partial X_i}{\partial e_k}$

$= \dfrac{\partial}{\partial e_k} (\sum q_i X_i - \sum t_i X_i)$

$= - \dfrac{\partial}{\partial e_k} (\sum t_i X_i),$

we can write (90) as

(92) $\dfrac{\partial V}{\partial e_k} = -\lambda \dfrac{\partial}{\partial e_k} (\sum t_i X_i) + \lambda G_k$

Equations (92) show how the optimal level of public consumption depends on:
 (i) the direct contribution of public consumption to welfare (measured by $\partial V/\partial e_k$);
 (ii) the effect of public consumption on tax revenue (measured by $\partial \sum t_i X_i / \partial e_k$); and
 (iii) the direct cost of public consumption (G_k).
There are three differences between this theory and that of public goods in the presence of lump sum taxation (as developed, for example, by Samuelson (1954)). Because social marginal utilities of income are not equated, the expression $\partial V/\partial e_k$ cannot be reduced to a sum of marginal rates of substitution, but depends on the weights given to the different beneficiaries of public consumption:

(93) $\dfrac{\partial V}{\partial e_k} = \sum_h \dfrac{\partial W}{\partial u^h} \dfrac{\partial u^h}{\partial e_k}$

Second, the cost associated with the raising of government revenue implies that the impact of public consumption on revenue is a relevant part of the first-order conditions. Third, for the same reason, the cost of public consumption is measured in terms of the cost to the government of raising revenue to finance the expenditures (in terms of the one-consumer equation, λ may not be equal to α, the marginal utility of income).

The first-order conditions for the provision of public goods can be expressed in another way, showing the relationships between the marginal cost and "willingness to pay." Write r_k^h for the marginal rate of substitution between public good k and income for the hth household. Then $\partial u^h/\partial e_k = \alpha^h r_k^h$, where α^h is the hth household's marginal utility of income. The social marginal utility of the hth household's income, β^h, is $(\partial W/\partial u^h)\alpha^h$. Consequently, from (93)

(94) $\dfrac{\partial V}{\partial e_k} = \sum_h \beta^h r_k^h$

Then, from (92)

(95) $G_k = \sum_h \left[\dfrac{\beta^h}{\lambda} r_k^h + \dfrac{\partial}{\partial e_k} \sum_i t_i x_i^h \right]$

Thus the marginal cost of producing the public good should be equated to a sum, over all households, of the price which the household is just willing to pay for a marginal increment in the level of provision, weighted by the marginal "social worth" of the household's income, and adjusted for the effect of the level of provision on net tax payments by the household.[4]

In the discussion of public consumption thus far it has been assumed that there were no possible fees associated with the provision of public goods. This would be appropriate for national defense or preventive medicine, but not for goods where licenses can be required from users. The optimal level of license fees will not, in general, be zero. Indeed we may be able to associate with any good more complicated pricing mechanisms than the single fixed price considered above. In particular, there are the familiar examples of two-part tariffs (a license fee for use of a facility plus a per unit charge on the amount of use), and prices depending on quantity of sales. Formally these can be treated in a fashion similar to the income taxes considered above; the set of goods over which the tax is defined is now a consumption good rather than labor. With a two-part tariff, this would imply a tax function which was not continuous at the origin.

Presumably the introduction of more general pricing and taxing schemes gives an opportunity for increasing social welfare, just as the progressive income tax gives such an opportunity. In practice, the ignored costs of tax administration may severely limit the number of complicated pricing schemes which can increase welfare. We would expect the analysis done above to be basically unchanged by the addition of these possibilities, although a two-part tariff will cause aggregate demand to have discontinuities. In practice we would expect these discontinuities to be small relative to aggregate demand, and formally, they could be eliminated by the device of a continuum of consumers.

X. The Optimal Taxation Theorem

In the earlier discussion, we employed calculus techniques to obtain the first-order conditions for the optimal tax structure. However, the valid use of Lagrange multipliers is subject to certain restrictions, which in the present case have no very obvious economic significance. This section provides a rigorous analysis of conditions under which the tax formulae (34) are indeed necessary conditions for optimality, and in particular provides economically meaningful assumptions that ensure their validity. The reader should be warned that the discussion is highly technical.

One might hope to provide a rigorous analysis by using the well-known Kuhn-Tucker theorem for differentiable (not necessarily concave) functions. This theorem requires a certain "constraint qualification" to be satisfied. Let us apply it and see how far we get. We wish to

$$\text{Maximize } V(q)$$
$$\text{subject to } g(X(q)) \leq 0 \text{ and } q \geq 0,$$

where g is a (vector) production constraint such that $g(X) \leq 0$ if, and only if, X is in G. Given that V, X, and g are differentiable, and that the Kuhn-Tucker constraint qualification is satisfied, we have the first-order conditions

$$(96) \quad V'(q^*) = \frac{\partial V}{\partial q} \leq p \cdot \frac{\partial X}{\partial q} = p \cdot X'(q^*),$$

where $p = \lambda \cdot g'(X(q^*))$ for a vector of Lagrange multipliers λ, and is therefore a support or tangent hyperplane to G at $X(q^*)$. Since V and X are homogeneous

---

[4] Another case can be treated in a similar manner: that of limited government production of a good, which is also being produced privately, when government production is given away rather than being sold. Since the government production rule given above does not reduce to the first-order condition in producer prices, we would not find aggregate production efficiency for the sum of these two sources of production.

of degree zero, $[V'(q^*) - p \cdot X'(q^*)] \cdot q^* = 0$: consequently $\partial V/\partial q_i = p \cdot (\partial X/\partial q_i)$ for i such that $q_i^* > 0$.

To express the first-order conditions in this form, we naturally expect to assume that V and X are continuously differentiable: to that extent, the differentiability assumptions are innocuous. The assumption that the production set can be described by a finite number of continuously differentiable inequality constraints that satisfy the constraint qualification is less satisfactory. The constraint qualification is an assumption about the functions g: one can violate it by changing the functions g without changing the actual constraint set, G. Some such assumption is required to avoid not unreasonable counter-examples, as we shall see below. But it is not at all obvious how one would check whether a particular example that failed to satisfy the constraint qualification could be put right by describing G by a better behaved set of inequalities. We should like to use a constraint qualification that depends on the properties of the set G (and X) rather than the particular functions g; and we should like the assumption to be more amenable to economic interpretation. The theorem we prove below contains such an assumption, for the case where G is convex and has an interior.

Before stating the theorem let us consider an example in which the first-order conditions are not satisfied at the optimum.

Example g. Consider the one-consumer economy. In the case shown in Figure 10, the offer curve is tangent to the production frontier at the optimum production point. As q varies, the vector $X(q)$ traces out the offer curve. Thus, holding q_2 constant, the vector $\partial X(q)/\partial q_1$ is tangent to the offer curve at $X(q^*)$. Therefore if p is the vector of producer prices, which is tangent to the production frontier at $X(q^*)$, $p \cdot \partial X(q^*)/\partial q_1 = 0$. The same is true for the derivatives with respect to q_2. But there is no reason why $V'(q^*)$ should be zero: therefore the above first-order conditions may not be satisfied at the optimum.

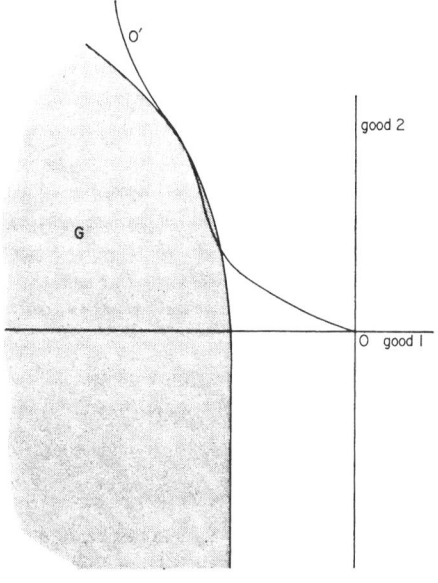

FIGURE 10

We shall make an assumption ruling out tangency between the frontier of the production set and the offer curve:

For any p, q ($q \geq 0$, $p \neq 0$) such that $X(q)$ is in G and $p \cdot X(q) \geq p \cdot x$ for all x in G, $p \cdot X'(q) \geq 0$.

The qualification takes this particular form because we also have the constraint $q \geq 0$. Let us note that for $q > 0$ the condition $p \cdot X(q) \geq 0$ is equivalent to $p \cdot X'(q) \neq 0$, because X is homogeneous of degree zero. The qualification asserts that *for any possible competitive equilibrium (under commodity taxation) there is a consumer price change which will decrease the value of equilibrium demand, measured in producer* prices. By the aggregate consumer budget constraint, $q \cdot X = (p+t) \cdot X = 0$. Therefore the assumption says that at any possible equilibrium point on the production frontier, it is possible to increase tax revenue. Thus the first-order conditions may not be applicable if the optimal point represents a local tax revenue maximum. Returning to example g, we see that $p \cdot X' = 0$ at the optimum, or equivalently $\partial(t \cdot X)/\partial t = 0$, although the derivatives of V are not necessarily zero there.

We now state and prove the theorem.[5]

THEOREM 5: *Assume an optimum, (X^*, q^*) exists; that $V(q)$ and $X(q)$ are continuously differentiable; and that G is convex and has a nonempty interior. Assume furthermore that there is no pair of price vectors (p, q) for which*

$X(q)$ maximizes $p \cdot x$ for x in G,

(97) $\qquad p \neq 0$, and

$$p \cdot X'(q) \geq 0$$

Then there exists p^* such that

X^* maximizes $p^* \cdot x$ for x in G, and

$$V'(q^*) \leq p^* \cdot X'(q^*)$$

PROOF:

Let $P = \{p \mid p \cdot X^* \geq p \cdot x, \text{ all } x \text{ in } G\}$. P is the cone of normals to G at X^*, including the zero vector. It is a nonempty, closed, convex cone.

---

[5] It should be noticed that when the constrained optimum is (locally) an unconstrained maximum, the producer prices satisfying the theorem are zero. This happens if optimal production is in the interior of the production set and may happen if it is on the frontier. The theorem can be weakened in a complicated manner by replacing the nontangency qualification by two conditions. One is an analog of the Kuhn-Tucker Constraint Qualification providing for the existence of an arc in the attainable set. The other use of nontangency occurs when V' is in $\bar{B}$ but not in B. If it is assumed that when there is tangency, the cone of normals is polyhedral, B will be closed. The Kuhn-Tucker theorem is then a special case of the weakened version of theorem 5 when G is the nonnegative orthant. The Kuhn-Tucker theorem is very much easier to prove, however.

We write V' for $V'(q^*)$ and X' for $X'(q^*)$. Consider the set

$$B = \{v \mid v \leq p \cdot X', \text{ some } p \text{ in } P\}$$

We have to show that V' is in B. We do this by showing first, that if V' is in $\bar{B}$, the closure of B, in fact V' is in B; and then that V' must be in $\bar{B}$.

If V' is in $\bar{B}$, there exist sequences $\{v_n\}$ and $\{p_n\}$, p_n in P, such that

(98) $\qquad v_n \leq p_n \cdot X',$
$\qquad v_n \to V' \quad (n \to \infty)$

Either $\{p_n\}$ is bounded or it is not. If not, we can find a subsequence on which

$$\|p_n\| \to \infty, \qquad \frac{p_n}{\|p_n\|} \to \bar{p} \neq 0$$

Then, dividing (98) by $\|p_n\|$ and letting $n \to \infty$ on the subsequence, we obtain $\bar{p} \cdot X' \geq 0$ while $\bar{p}, \neq 0$, is in P. This possibility is excluded by assumption (97). Therefore $\{p_n\}$ is bounded, and has a limit point p, in P. Equation (98) implies that $V' \leq p \cdot X'$. The conclusion of the theorem is thus established on the assumption that V' is in $\bar{B}$.

Suppose, on the contrary, that V' is not in $\bar{B}$. We shall derive a contradiction by a sequence of lemmas.

LEMMA 5.1:

$\bar{B}$ *is pointed. That is, v and $-v$ both belong to $\bar{B}$ only if $v = 0$.*

PROOF:

If $v, -v$ is in $\bar{B}$, we have sequences such that

(99) $\qquad v_n^1 \leq p_n^1 \cdot X', \qquad v_n^2 \leq p_n^2 \cdot X',$

(100) $\qquad v_n^1 \to v, \qquad v_n^2 \to -v$

If $v \neq 0$, it cannot be the case that p_n^1 and p_n^2 both tend to zero. Suppose, for example, p_n^1 does not, and take a subsequence on which

$$\|p_n^1\| \to \pi_1 \leq \infty,$$

$$p_n^1/\|p_n^1\| \to p^1, \neq 0$$

If $p_n^1 + p_n^2 \to 0$, $p_n^2/\|p_n^1\| \to -p^1$, and therefore $-p^1$ is in P. This is impossible, since, G having a nonempty interior, P is pointed. (If $p, -p$ are in P, $p \cdot x$ is constant for x in G, but a hyperplane has no interior.) We can therefore take a subsequence on which

$$\|p_n^1 + p_n^2\| \to \pi, \quad 0 < \pi \leq \infty,$$

$$\frac{p_n^1 + p_n^2}{\|p_n^1 + p_n^2\|} \to p, \neq 0, \in P$$

From (99) (adding and dividing by $\|p_n^1 + p_n^2\|$) and (100), we now have

$$(101) \quad p \cdot X' \geq \operatorname{Lim} \frac{v_n^1 + v_n^2}{\|p_n^1 + p_n^2\|} = 0$$

This contradicts (97), since p is in P and $p \neq 0$, and thereby establishes the lemma.

LEMMA 5.2: *If C is a pointed, closed, convex cone, there exists a vector p such that for all non-zero z in C, $p \cdot z < 0$.*

PROOF:

By the duality theorem for convex cones $C^{++} = C$, where C^+ is the dual cone, $\{p \mid p \cdot z \leq 0, z \text{ is in } C\}$. Clearly, if C^+ is pointed, C has a nonempty interior: for if interior C is empty, $p \cdot z = 0$ for some non-zero p and all z in C, and then p and $-p$ both belong to C^+. Under the assumptions of the theorem, C is closed and pointed. Therefore C^{++} is pointed, and C^+ has an interior point p.

$$p \cdot z < 0 \quad \text{(all nonzero } z \text{ in } C)$$

Otherwise, if $p \cdot z = 0$, we can easily find a sequence $\{p_n\}$ on which $p_n \to p$ and $p_n \cdot z > 0$, so that p_n is not in C^+.

LEMMA 5.3: *If V' is not in $\overline{B}$, there exists r such that*

(102) $\quad V' \cdot r > 0$

(103) $\quad v \cdot r < 0 \quad (v \in B)$

PROOF:

The closed convex cone $\overline{B} + \{\lambda V' \mid \lambda \leq 0\}$ is pointed. Thus there exists an r such that

$$v \cdot r + \lambda V' \cdot r < 0$$

$$(v \in \overline{B}, \lambda \leq 0, v, \lambda \text{ not both zero})$$

Putting $v = 0$ and $\lambda = -1$ we obtain (102); putting $\lambda = 0$ we obtain (103).

LEMMA 5.4: *Let r be a vector satisfying (102) and (103). For some $\delta > 0$,*

(104) $\quad X(q^* + \theta r) \in G \quad (0 \leq \theta \leq \delta)$

PROOF:

Assume not. Then for some sequence $\{\theta_n\}$, $\theta_n > 0$, $\theta_n \to 0$,

$$X(q^* + \theta_n r) \notin G$$

Since G is convex, this implies that

$$X(q^*) + \frac{\lambda}{\theta_n} [X(q^* + \theta_n r) - X(q^*)] \notin G$$

for $\lambda \geq \theta_n$. Letting $n \to \infty$, we deduce, for any $\lambda > 0$, that

$$X(q^*) + \lambda X' \cdot r$$
$$= \operatorname*{Lim}_{n \to \infty} \left[X(q^*) + \lambda \frac{X(q^* + \theta_n r) - X(q^*)}{\theta_n} \right]$$

is not in the interior of G. It follows that the half-line $\{X(q^*) + \lambda X' \cdot r \mid \lambda > 0\}$ can be separated from the interior of G by a hyperplane with normal $p \neq 0$:

$$p \cdot X(q^*) + \lambda p \cdot X' \cdot r \geq p \cdot x$$

$$(\lambda > 0, x \in \text{Int } G)$$

Letting $\lambda \to 0$ we have $p \in P$. Letting $x \to X^*$ we have

$$p \cdot X' \cdot r \geq 0,$$

which contradicts (103) since $p \cdot X'$ is in B. The lemma is proved.

Since q^* is optimal, (104) implies that

$$V(q^* + \theta r) \leq V(q^*) \qquad (0 \leq \theta \leq \delta)$$

Therefore,

$$V' \cdot r = \lim_{\theta \to 0} \frac{1}{\theta} [V(q^* + \theta r) - V(q^*)]$$

$$\leq 0$$

This, however, contradicts (102). The hypothesis of Lemma 5.3, that $V' \in \overline{B}$, is therefore false. The proof of the theorem is thus complete.

In reaching our results that the first-order conditions for optimum taxes (96) hold in general, we have assumed that the production set, G, is convex. But one common argument for government control of production is nonconvexity of the production set. This is not a question we are primarily concerned with in this paper. However, some extensions of the theorem do hold. As an example, assume the frontier of G is differentiable at X^*, so that p can be uniquely defined as the normal at X^* and that G is not thin in the neighborhood of X^*—i.e., there exists a ball with center on the normal through X^*, contained in G and containing X^*. Applying the theorem to this ball we get the validity of the first-order conditions (96) using the producer prices defined by the normal.

As in general welfare economics, two uniqueness problems may arise when considering the application of the first-order conditions to achieve an optimum. In the first place, there may be more than one pair of price vectors, (p, q), that satisfy the first-order conditions and allow markets to be cleared. This is similar to the problem that arises when we attempt to define optimum production and distribution by first-order conditions in the presence of a non-convex production set. It is noteworthy that, if lump sum transfers are excluded as a feasible policy, this problem may arise even when the production set is convex. There is no reason why the demand functions should have any of the nice convexity properties which ensure that first-order conditions imply global maximization. Only in particular cases, such as that discussed in footnote 2 above (where rigorous argument is possible without appeal to theorem 5), will the first-order conditions lead to a unique solution.

The second problem is that the tax policies one might like to employ may not uniquely determine the behavior of the system. The lump sum redistribution of wealth required in standard welfare economics does not carry with it any guarantee that the desired competitive equilibrium is the unique one consistent with the optimal wealth distribution (although if the wrong equilibrium is achieved, this should be easily noticed). Similarly, in the present case, if we employ taxes rather than consumer prices as the government control variables, the equilibrium of the economy may not be unique.[6] But if consumer prices are used as the control variables—and why not?—the demand functions give us a unique equilibrium position, so long as preferences are strictly convex.

XI. Concluding Remarks

Welfare economics has usually been concerned with characterizing the best of attainable worlds, accepting only the basic technological constraints. As economists have been aware, the omitted constraints on communication, calculation, and administration of an economy (not to mention political constraints) limit the direct applicability of the implications of this theory to policy problems, although great insight into these problems has certainly been acquired. We have not at-

---

[6] For a discussion of multiple equilibria in a related problem, see E. Foster and H. Sonnenschein.

tempted to come directly to grips with the problem of incorporating these complications into economic theory. Instead, we have explored the implications of viewing these constraints as limits on the set of policy tools that can be applied. There are many sets of policy tools which might be examined in this way. Specifically, we have assumed that the policy tools available to the government include commodity taxation (and subsidization) to any extent. For these tools we have derived the rules for optimal tax policy and have shown the desirability of aggregate production efficiency, in the presence of optimal taxation. We have also considered expansion of the set of policy tools in such a way that we continue to have the condition that production decisions do not change the class of possible budget constraints. For example, this condition is still preserved when one includes poll taxes, progressive income taxation, regional differences in taxation, taxation on transactions between consumers, and most kinds of rationing. This type of expansion of the set of policy tools does not alter the desirability of production efficiency, nor does it alter the conditions for the optimal commodity tax structure, although in general the tax rates themselves will change. We have, unfortunately, ignored the cost of administering taxes. Presumably optimization by means of sets of policy tools that do not, because the cost of administration, include the full scope of commodity taxation, will not lead to the same conclusions.

Let us briefly consider the type of policy implications that are raised by our analysis. In the context of a planned economy our analysis implies the desirability of using a single price vector in all production decisions, although these prices will, in general, differ from the prices at which commodities are sold to consumers.

As an application of this analysis to a mixed economy, let us briefly examine the discussion of a proper criterion for public investment decisions. As has been widely noted, there are considerable differences in western economies between the intertemporal marginal rates of transformation and substitution. This has been the basis of analyses leading to investment criteria which would imply aggregate production inefficiency because they employ an interest rate for determining the margins of public production which differs from the private marginal rate of transformation. One argument used against these criteria is that the government, recognizing the divergence between rates of transformation and substitution, should use its power to achieve the full Pareto optimum, bringing these rates into equality. When this is done, the single interest rate then existing will be the appropriate rate to use in public investment decisions. We begin by presuming that the government does not have the power to achieve any Pareto optimum that it chooses. Then from the maximization of a social welfare function, we argued that the government will, in general, prefer one of the non-Pareto optima to the Pareto optima, if any, that can be achieved. At the constrained optimum, which is the social welfare function maximizing position of the economy for the available policy tools, we saw that the economy will still be characterized by a divergence between marginal rates of substitution and transformation, not just intertemporally, but also elsewhere, e.g., in the choice between leisure and goods. However, we concluded that in this situation we desired aggregate production efficiency. This implies the use of interest rates for public investment decisions which equate public and private marginal rates of transformation.

We have obtained the first-order conditions for public production, but we have not considered the correct method of evaluating indivisible investments. This is one problem that deserves examination. In examining the optimal tax structure, we have briefly considered the tax rates implied by particular utility functions. This analysis should be extended to more general and more interesting sets of consumers. Further, we have not examined in any detail the uniqueness and stability of equilibrium, that is, the question whether there are means of achieving in practice an equilibrium which is close to the optimum.

Finally, we would like to emphasize the assumptions which seem to us most seriously to limit the applications of this theory.[7] We have assumed no costs of tax administration and no tax evasion. And we have assumed constant-returns-to-scale and price-taking, profit-maximizing behavior in private production. Pure profits (or losses) associated with the violation of these assumptions imply that private production decisions directly influence social welfare by affecting household incomes. In such a case, it would presumably be desirable to add a profits tax to the set of policy instruments. Nevertheless, aggregate production efficiency would no longer be desirable in general; although it may be possible to get close to the optimum with efficient production if pure profits are small. We hope, nevertheless, that the methods and results of this paper have shown that economic analysis need not depend on the simplifying, but unrealistic, assumption that the perfect capital levy has taken place.[8]

REFERENCES

W. J. Corlett and D. C. Hague, "Complementarity and the Excess Burden of Taxation," *Rev. Econ. Stud.*, 1953, *21*, No. 1, 21–30.

E. Foster and H. Sonnenschein, "Price Distortion and Economic Welfare," *Econometrica*, Mar. 1970, *38*, 281–97.

H. Kuhn and A. Tucker, "Nonlinear Programming," in J. Neyman, ed., *Proceedings of the Second Berkeley Symposium on Mathematical Statistics and Probability*, Berkeley 1951.

J. A. Mirrlees, "An Exploration in the Theory of Optimum Income Taxation," *Rev. Econ. Stud.*, Apr. 1971, *38*, forthcoming.

C. C. Morrison, "Marginal Cost Pricing and the Theory of Second Best," *Western Econ. J.*, June 1969, *7*, 145–52.

P. A. Samuelson, "Memorandum for U.S. Treasury, 1951," unpublished.

———, "The Pure Theory of Public Expenditure," *Rev. Econ. Statist.*, Nov. 1954, *36*, 387–89.

---

[7] These assumptions are viewed in the context of equilibrium theory. There is no need here to go into the limitations inherent in current equilibrium theory.

[8] A recent paper by Clarence Morrison also deals with marginal cost pricing as a special case of optimal pricing.

Journal of Public Economics 4 (1975) 335-342. © North-Holland Publishing Company

A MANY-PERSON RAMSEY TAX RULE

P.A. DIAMOND*

Massachusetts Institute of Technology, Cambridge, Mass. 02139, U.S.A.

Received January 1975, revised version received February 1975

Define the social marginal utility of an individual's income as the gain to society of a unit of consumption by the individual plus the value of his marginal propensity to pay taxes out of income. This concept rather than the social marginal utility of consumption (equal to the first term above) seems helpful in understanding optimal tax first order conditions. For example, with many consumers (and a poll tax as well as excise taxes) the change in aggregate compensated quantity demanded is proportional to the covariance between individual quantities demanded and social marginal utilities of income.

1. Introduction

In setting out the first-order conditions for optimal excise taxes in a one person (or many identical individuals) economy, it has become standard to use the Ramsey (1927) formulation[1] that the optimal taxes induce (approximately) equal percentage reductions in (compensated) demands for all commodities (with the approximation being valid for small amounts of tax revenue). Mirrlees (1975) has given an alternative interpretation of these same conditions – that at the optimum, a small proportional increase in all tax rates results in a proportional decrease in all (compensated) demands. Consideration of the first-order conditions for optimal excise taxes in a general many-person economy has not yet yielded similarly simple interpretations when cast into a similar quantity change form. In considering the two-class economy, (i.e., two types of consumers), Mirrlees (1975) has modified the standard problem by considering simultaneously excise taxes and a poll tax. For this problem he gets a generalized Ramsey formulation that the induced changes in aggregate demand be proportional to demand differences between typical members of the two classes. This paper will examine the Ramsey rule for a many-person economy with excise taxes and a poll tax. Instead of using the social marginal utilities of consumption (i.e., increase in social welfare from increased consumption of the numeraire good by different individuals), the interpretation will use the

---

*Financial support by the National Science Foundation is gratefully acknowledged.

[1] The directly derived first-order conditions have the form that at the optimum the impact of any tax increase on social welfare is proportional to the marginal tax revenue collected, or alternatively to the cost of producing the induced changes in demand.

social marginal utilities of income (i.e., gain in social welfare from provision of additional income in numeraire units, which is the sum of gains from individual consumption and from the marginal propensity to pay taxes out of income). The many-person Ramsey rule is that the (approximate) percentage change in (compensated) demands depends on the social marginal utilities of income, being positive (negative) for goods demanded on average by individuals with above (below) average social marginal utilities of income.[2] Denoting the social marginal utility of man h by γ^h, and his consumption of good k by x_k^h, the many-person Ramsey rule is

$$\frac{\Delta X_k}{X_k} = \frac{\sum (\gamma^h - \lambda) x_k^h}{\lambda X_k}, \qquad (1)$$

where λ is the average of γ^h (and also equals the Lagrangian on the government budget constraint) and X_k is aggregate demand for good k.

This modification of familiar first-order conditions might appear to be simply replacing a complicated expression by an arbitrary definition, γ^h, which thereby automatically simplified the expression. However, by briefly considering three problems already analyzed in the literature, we shall see that the use of the social marginal utility of income seems to give more natural interpretations than use of the social marginal utility of consumption. We shall see that in the two-class model of Mirrlees the individuals in the class with lower social marginal utility of income pay more in excise taxes. In the many-consumer economy this generalizes to a negative covariance between social marginal utilities of income and excise taxes paid. The same statement does not appear to hold generally with consumption replacing income. Without using this terminology, Atkinson and Stern (1974) have noted that in the one-consumer economy the relative size of social marginal utility of consumption and of the Lagrangian on the government budget constraint appears to depend on the choice of numeraire. As they noted, the sign of the social marginal utility of income less the government Lagrangian, however, is the opposite of that of tax revenue, independent of choice of numeraire. In addition we will consider the rules for optimal public good expenditures, expressed in terms analogous to the social marginal utility of income.

2. Many-person Ramsey rule

Since optimal tax derivations are now so familiar we will proceed directly. For convenience in later use we shall set up the model with public goods.

q vector of consumer prices,
p vector of producer prices,

[2]This result has also been developed by Atkinson and Stiglitz (1974).

$t = q - p$ vector of taxes,
I lump-sum income (the same for all consumers),
e level of public good expenditures,
$v^h(q, I, e)$ indirect utility function for consumer h,
$\alpha^h = \dfrac{\partial v^h}{\partial I}$ marginal utility of income (consumption),
$W(v^1, \ldots, v^H)$ social welfare function depending on utilities of the H consumers,
$\beta^h = \dfrac{\partial W}{\partial v^h} \alpha^h$ social marginal utility of consumption,
$x^h(q, I, e)$ vector of consumer h demands,
$X = \sum_h x^h$ aggregate demand,
$F(X, e)$ production constraint.

We can now set up the welfare function maximization as

$$\text{Max } W(v^1(q, I, e), \ldots, v^H(q, I, e)), \qquad (2)$$

subject to

$$F(X(q, I, e), e) = 0.$$

Forming a Lagrangian expression with multiplier λ we are in a position to generate first-order conditions. Assuming I and e are given and zero, we can calculate the first-order conditions for q,

$$\sum_h \frac{\partial W}{\partial v^h} \frac{\partial v^h}{\partial q_k} = \lambda \sum_i F_i \frac{\partial X_i}{\partial q_k}. \qquad (3)$$

Choosing good one as numeraire and selecting units appropriately we shall write $p_1 = F_1 = 1 = q_1$. Using the properties of the indirect utility function we can write this in the familiar form (e.g., see, Diamond and Mirrlees (1971))

$$-\sum_h \beta^h x_k^h = \lambda \sum_h \sum_i p_i \frac{\partial x_i^h}{\partial q_k}. \qquad (4)$$

Replacing p_i by $q_i - t_i$, noting that $\sum_i q_i (\partial x_i^h / \partial q_k) = -x_k^h$ (from the individual's budget constraint), and using the Slutsky equation, we have

$$\sum_h \beta^h x_k^h = \lambda \sum_h \left(x_k^h + \sum_i t_i \left(s_{ik}^h - x_k^h \frac{\partial x_i^h}{\partial I} \right) \right), \qquad (5)$$

where s_{ik}^h is the derivative of the compensated demand curve.

Defining the social marginal utility of income, γ^h, as the gain to society from additional income given to consumer h, we see that γ^h is made up of two parts. One part is the social evaluation of the increased utility of h made possible by higher income. This equals β^h. The second part is the social evaluation of the additional tax revenue collected, $\sum t_i (\partial x_i^h/\partial I)$, as a consequence of his having more income. We shall elaborate on this definition in section 4. Thus

$$\gamma^h = \beta^h + \lambda \sum_i t_i (\partial x_i^h/\partial I). \tag{6}$$

Using this definition we can write the first-order conditions (5) as

$$\sum_h (\gamma^h - \lambda) x_k^h = \lambda \sum_i \sum_h t_i s_{ik}^h. \tag{7}$$

From the symmetry of the Slutsky matrix, so that $s_{ik}^h = s_{ki}^h$, this has the form of eq. (1), where

$$\Delta X_k = \sum_h \sum_i s_{ki}^h t_i \tag{8}$$

is the change in compensated aggregate demand for good k as a result of a marginal proportional increase in all tax rates. Eq. (7) holds as a consequence of the optimal excise taxes. The interpretation of (7) becomes more interesting if we also have an optimal poll tax. From (2) the first-order condition coming from differentiation with respect to I is

$$\sum_h \beta^h = \lambda \sum_i F_i (\partial X_i/\partial I). \tag{9}$$

Following the same sequence of steps as before we can write this as

$$\sum_h \beta^h = \lambda \sum_i \sum_h p_i \frac{\partial x_i^h}{\partial I} = \lambda \sum_h \sum_i (q_i - t_i) \frac{\partial x_i^h}{\partial I} = \lambda \sum_h \left(1 - \sum_i t_i \frac{\partial x_i^h}{\partial I}\right). \tag{10}$$

Thus we have the result that λ is equal to the average of γ^h in the economy

$$\sum_h \gamma^h = \lambda H. \tag{11}$$

With λ equal to the average of the γ^h, we can interpret (1) as a covariance formula, since we can subtract $\sum (\gamma^h - \lambda) \bar{x}_k$ from the left hand side, where $\bar{x}_k$ is the average of x_k^h. Thus, for each good, the change in aggregate compensated quantity demanded is proportional to the covariance between individual quantities demanded and social marginal utilities of income. The percentage change in demand equals the covariance divided by the product of the two means.

3. Two-class economy

We can move directly from (7) and (11) to the results of Mirrlees. Assume there are m consumers of type 1 and n consumers of type 2. Then, from (11),

$$(m+n)\lambda = m\gamma^1 + n\gamma^2. \tag{12}$$

Thus using (12), eq. (7) becomes

$$\lambda \sum_i \sum_h t_i s_{ik}^h = m(\gamma^1 - \lambda)x_k^1 + n(\gamma^2 - \lambda)x_k^2$$

$$= n(\lambda - \gamma^2)x_k^1 + n(\gamma^2 - \lambda)x_k^2$$

$$= n(\gamma^2 - \lambda)(x_k^2 - x_k^1). \tag{13}$$

Thus the induced changes in compensated aggregate demand are proportional to the differences in demand between the two types. Multiplying (13) by t_k and summing over k we have

$$n(\gamma^2 - \lambda)\left(\sum_k t_k x_k^2 - \sum_k t_k x_k^1\right) = \lambda \sum_h \sum_i \sum_k t_i s_{ik}^h t_k \leq 0. \tag{14}$$

The sign follows from the negative semidefiniteness of the Slutsky matrix. Since the signs of $\gamma^2 - \lambda$ and $\gamma^2 - \gamma^1$ are the same, we see that an individual with greater social marginal utility of income pays less in excise taxes under the optimal excise and poll tax regime.

Applying the same procedure to the general economy, from (7) we have the result that with optimal excise taxes

$$\sum_h \left((\gamma^h - \lambda) \sum_k t_k x_k^h\right) \leq 0. \tag{15}$$

If we add an optimal poll tax we can again go to a covariance formulation. With $\sum (\gamma^h - \lambda)$ equal to zero we can multiply it by the average over h of $\sum_k t_k x_k^h$ and subtract it from (15).

Denoting average values by a bar we thus have the result that with optimal excise and poll taxes,

$$\sum_h \left\{(\gamma^h - \bar{\gamma})\left(\sum_k t_k x_k^h - \overline{\sum_k t_k x_k}\right)\right\} \leq 0. \tag{16}$$

That is, with optimal excise and poll taxes there is a negative covariance between social marginal utility of income and excise taxes paid.

4. One-consumer economy

Consider an outside agency planning to give aid to a one-consumer economy with optimal excise taxes. The agency might give the aid to the consumer directly or to the government, and the aid might be given in any commodity. One would expect that it is better to give the aid to the government if revenue is being raised by distorting taxes, whatever the good being considered. (And to give it to the consumer if the government is disposing of a surplus by distorting subsidies.) This is precisely the answer given by (15), evaluating the social worth of aid to the consumer and government respectively by γ and λ. From the definition of γ, it is clear we are evaluating aid assuming it is provided while markets are still open. Thus the consumer engages in trade with the income provided him, generating a change in tax revenue, as well as a direct utility rise for the consumer.

Suppose, alternatively, that aid is provided 'after markets are shut'. That is, no changes in trades are allowed after aid is provided. For arbitrarily small amounts of aid, the fact that the consumer was at a utility maximizing consumption plan implies that his direct gain in utility from the aid is unaffected by the prohibition of further trading. Thus the value to society of aid provided to the consumer in this way is β. The question of the comparative advantage of giving this aid to the consumer rather than the government is a comparison of β with λ.[3] However, the government's rate of substitution between different commodities is equal to the ratio of producer prices, p, while the consumer's rate of substitution is equal to the ratio of consumer prices q. Thus a change in units in which aid is given (corresponding to a change in choice of numeraire) has the potential of altering the answer to the question of the choice of recipient which most increases social welfare.

5. Public good expenditures

The first-order condition for public expenditures, like any equation, can be arranged with different terms on either side of the equation. We shall consider a rearrangement which parallels the structure considered above. For some of the interpretations, it will not be necessary to assume that all taxes are optimally set since the equations derived will also hold when those taxes not being optimally set are held constant at given levels. Let us define δ^h to be the value to society of providing the public good to consumer h. It is made up of two parts, the social evaluation of his utility increase, $(\partial W/\partial v^h)(\partial v^h/\partial e)$, and the value of any change in taxes paid, $\lambda \sum_i t_i (\partial x_i^h/\partial e)$,

---

[3]Atkinson and Stern (1974) discuss this issue in terms of α and λ. These are obviously the same where, in the one-consumer economy, the social welfare function and the utility function are the same.

$$\delta^h = \frac{\partial W}{\partial v^h}\frac{\partial v^h}{\partial e} + \lambda \sum_i t_i \frac{\partial x_i^h}{\partial e} \tag{17}$$

$$= \beta^h \frac{\partial v^h/\partial e}{\partial v^h/\partial I} + \lambda \sum_i t_i \frac{\partial x_i^h}{\partial e}.$$

Returning to the problem of social welfare maximization, (2), differentiation with respect to the public good expenditure gives

$$\sum_h \frac{\partial W}{\partial v^h}\frac{\partial v^h}{\partial e} = \lambda \sum_i F_i \frac{\partial X_i}{\partial e} + \lambda F_e \tag{18}$$

$$= \lambda \sum_h \sum_i (q_i - t_i)\frac{\partial x_i^h}{\partial e} + \lambda F_e.$$

Since $\sum_i q_i (\partial x_i^h/\partial e)$ is zero by the consumers budget constraint, we can write the first-order condition for public expenditures as

$$\sum_h \delta^h = \lambda F_e. \tag{19}$$

Thus, for the optimum, the sum over individuals of the value to society of providing each of them with the public good is equated to the resource cost of public provision of the public good, measured in units of social welfare. Put this way, this is an obvious first-order condition. The complication is to measure correctly the value to society of provision of the public good to the individual. Dividing (19) by λ we can, alternatively, express the first-order condition in units of numeraire. The right-hand side is the resource cost of public good provision. Since the public good expenditure comes out of the government budget it makes sense that the left-hand side is the sum over individuals of the marginal rate of substitution between the social cost of expenditure from the public budget and the social gain from the individual's enjoyment of the public good. This first-order condition is valid whatever mix of excise and poll taxes and other public expenditures is varied optimally, the remaining government choice variables being held constant.

To get an expression more closely resembling that in the lump-sum tax world, we can assume that the poll tax is among the variables being optimally set. Then λ is the average of social marginal utilities of income in the economy, and the first-order condition for public goods equates the marginal rate of transformation in production to the sum over consumers of social marginal rates of substitution between public good consumption by the consumer and income averaged over the population.

We are still a long way from having an intuition for resource allocation questions in economies with distorting taxes which parallels the level of intuition in first-best economies. Perhaps by using the social marginal utility of income rather than the seemingly more natural social marginal utility of consumption we can develop such a level more rapidly.

References

Atkinson, A.B. and N.H. Stern, 1974, Pigou, taxation and public goods, Review of Economic Studies 41, 119–128.
Atkinson, A.B. and J.E. Stiglitz, 1974, Alternative approaches to the redistribution of income, unpublished.
Diamond, P.A. and J.A. Mirrlees, 1971, Optimal taxation and public production, American Economic Review 61, 8–27 and 261–278.
Mirrlees, J.A., 1975, Optimal commodity taxation in a two-class economy, Journal of Public Economics 4, 27–33.
Ramsey, F.P., 1927, A contribution to the theory of taxation, Economic Journal 37, 47–61.

[21]
An Exploration in the Theory of Optimum Income Taxation[1,2]

J. A. MIRRLEES
Nuffield College, Oxford

1. INTRODUCTION

One would suppose that in any economic system where equality is valued, progressive income taxation would be an important instrument of policy. Even in a highly socialist economy, where all who work are employed by the State, the shadow price of highly skilled labour should surely be considerably greater than the disposable income actually available to the labourer. In Western Europe and America, tax rates on both high and low incomes are widely and lengthily discussed[3]: but there is virtually no relevant economic theory to appeal to, despite the importance of the tax.

Redistributive progressive taxation is usually related to a man's income (or, rather, his estimated income). One might obtain information about a man's income-earning potential from his apparent I.Q., the number of his degrees, his address, age or colour: but the natural, and one would suppose the most reliable, indicator of his income-earning potential is his income. As a result of using men's economic performance as evidence of their economic potentialities, complete equality of social marginal utilities of income ceases to be desirable, for the tax system that would bring about that result would completely discourage unpleasant work. The questions therefore arise what principles should govern an optimum income tax; what such a tax schedule would look like; and what degree of inequality would remain once it was established.

The problem seems to be a rather difficult one even in the simplest cases. In this paper, I make the following simplifying assumptions:

(1) Intertemporal problems are ignored. It is usual to levy income tax upon each year's income, with only limited possibilities of transferring one year's income to another for tax purposes. In an optimum system, one would no doubt wish to relate tax payments to the whole life pattern of income,[4] and to initial wealth; and in scheduling payments one would wish to pay attention to imperfect personal capital markets and imperfect foresight. The economy discussed below is timeless. Thus the effects of taxation on saving are ignored. One might perhaps regard the theory presented as a theory of " earned income " taxation (i.e. non-property income).

(2) Differences in tastes, in family size and composition, and in voluntary transfers, are ignored. These raise rather different kinds of problems, and it is natural to assume them away.

---
[1] *First version received Aug.* 1970; *final version received October* 1970 (*Eds.*).
[2] Work on this paper and its continuation was begun during a stimulating and pleasurable visit to the Department of Economics, M.I.T. The influence of Peter Diamond is particularly great, and his comments have been very useful. Earlier versions were presented at the Cowles Foundation, to the Economic Study Society, at the London School of Economics, and to CORE. I am grateful to the members of these seminars and to A. B. Atkinson for valuable comments. I am also greatly indebted to P. G. Hare and J. R. Broome for the computations.
[3] Discussions on (usually) orthodox lines, including many important points neglected in the present paper, can be found in [7], [1], [5, Chapters 5, 7, 8], and [6, Chapters 11 and 12]. [2] is close in spirit to what is attempted here.
[4] Cf. [7, Chapter 6].

(3) Individuals are supposed to determine the quantity and kind of labour they provide by rational calculation, corresponding to the maximization of a utility function, and social welfare is supposed to be a function of individual utility levels. It is also supposed that the quantity of labour a man offers may be varied within wide limits without affecting the price paid for it. The first assumption may well be seriously unrealistic, especially at higher income levels, where it does sometimes appear that there is consumption satiation and that work is done for reasons barely connected with the income it provides to the " labourer ".

(4) Migration is supposed to be impossible. Since the threat of migration is a major influence on the degree of progression in actual tax systems, at any rate outside the United States, this is another assumption one would rather not make.[1]

(5) The State is supposed to have perfect information about the individuals in the economy, their utilities and, consequently, their actions. In practice, this is certainly not the case for certain kinds of income from self-employment, in particular work done for the worker himself and his family; and in some countries, the extent of uncertainty about incomes is very great. Yet it seems doubtful whether the neglect of this uncertainty is a simplification of much significance.

(6) Various formal simplifications are made to render the mathematics more manageable: there is supposed to be one kind of labour (in a special sense to be explained below); there is one consumer good; welfare is separable in terms of the different individuals of the economy, and symmetric—i.e. it can be expressed as the sum of the utilities of individuals when the individual utility function (the same for all) is suitably chosen).

(7) The costs of administering the optimum tax schedule are assumed to be negligible.

In sections 2-5, the more general properties of the optimum income-tax schedule, and the rules governing it, are discussed. The treatment is not rigorous. Nevertheless a reader who wants to avoid mathematical details can omit the last page or two of section 3, and will probably want to glance through section 4 rather rapidly. In section 6, I begin the discussion of special cases. The mathematical arguments in sections 6-8 are frequently complicated. If the reader goes straight to section 9, where numerical results are presented and discussed, he should not find the omission of the previous sections any handicap. He may, nevertheless, find it interesting to look at the results and conjectures presented at the beginning of section 7, and at the diagrams for the two cases discussed in section 8.

Rigorous proofs of the main theorems will be given in a subsequent paper, [4].

2. MODEL AND PROBLEM

Individuals have identical preferences. We shall suppose that consumption and working time enter the individual's utility function. When consumption is x and the time worked y, utility is

$$u(x, y).$$

x and y both have to be non-negative, and there is an upper limit to y, which is taken to be 1. In fact, it is assumed that: u is a strictly concave, continuously differentiable, function (strictly) increasing in x, (strictly) decreasing in y, defined for $x>0$ and $0 \leq y<1$. u tends to $-\infty$ as x tends to 0 from above or y tends to 1 from below.

The usefulness of a man's time, from the point of view of production, is assumed to vary from person to person. To each individual corresponds a number n such that the quantity of labour provided, per unit of his time, is n. If he works for time y, he provides a quantity of labour ny. There is a known distribution of skills, measured by the parameter n, in the population. The number of persons with labour parameter n or less is $F(n)$. It

---

[1] The relation of optimum tax schedules to propensities to migrate is discussed in another paper under preparation.

will be assumed that F is differentiable, so that there is a density function for ability, $f(n) = F'(n)$. Call an individual whose ability-parameter is n an n-man.

The consumption choice of an n-man is denoted by (x_n, y_n). Write $z_n = ny_n$ for the labour he provides. Then the total labour available for use in production in the economy is

$$Z = \int_0^\infty z_n f(n) dn, \qquad \ldots(1)$$

and the aggregate demand for consumer goods is

$$X = \int_0^\infty x_n f(n) dn. \qquad \ldots(2)$$

In order to avoid the possibility of infinite labour supply, I assume that

$$\int_0^\infty n f(n) dn < \infty. \qquad \ldots(3)$$

Each individual makes his choice of (x_n, y_n) in the light of his budget constraint. Using an income tax, the government can arrange that a man who supplies a quantity of labour z can consume no more than $c(z)$ after tax: the government can choose the function c arbitrarily. It makes sense to impose the restriction on the government's choice of c, that c be upper semi-continuous, for then all individuals have available to them consumption choices that maximize their utility, subject to the budget constraint[1]:

$$(x_n, y_n) \text{ maximizes } u(x, y) \text{ subject to } x \leq c(ny). \qquad \ldots(4)$$

Notice that (x_n, y_n) may not be uniquely determined for every n.[2] I write:

$$u_n = u(x_n, y_n). \qquad \ldots(5)$$

Proposition 1. *There exists a number $n_0 \geq 0$ such that*

$$y_n = 0 \quad (n \leq n_0),$$
$$y_n > 0 \quad (n > n_0). \qquad \ldots(6)$$

Proof. If $m < n$, and $y_m > 0$, $u[c(my_m), y_m] < u\left[c\left(n \cdot \frac{m}{n} y_m\right), \frac{m}{n} y_m\right] \leq u_n$. Consequently, $y_m = 0$ if $y_n = 0$, since then $y_m = 0$ gives the utility u_n to n-man. Thus

$$n_0 = \inf[n \mid y_n > 0]$$

has the desired properties. ∥

Proposition 2. *Any function[3] of n, (x_n, y_n), that satisfies (4) for some upper semi-continuous function c also satisfies (4) for some non-decreasing, right-continuous function c'.*

---

[1] To say that c is upper semi-continuous means that
$$\limsup c(z_i) = c(z) \text{ when } \lim_{i \to \infty} z_i = z.$$
If
$$u_n = \sup \{u(x, y) \mid x \leq c(ny)\}, \text{ and } u(x_i, y_i) \to u_n, x_i \leq c(ny_i)$$
we can suppose that $x_i \to x$ and $y_i \to y$ (since $\{y_i\}$ and therefore $\{x_i\}$ is bounded). By the upper semi-continuity of c,
$$x \leq \limsup c(ny_i) = c(ny);$$
and by the continuity of u, $u(x, y) = \lim u(x_i, y_i) = u_n$. Therefore the supremum is attained.

[2] In other words, we have a *correspondence*, providing a set of utility maximizing choices for n-men. It arises when the consumption function c coincides with the indifference curve for part of its length. It is convenient nevertheless to use the notation of the text, despite its suggestion that we are dealing with a function.

[3] It is easy to see that the result is true for a correspondence also.

Proof. Define $c'(z) = \sup_{z' \leq z} c(z')$. If $x'_n \leq c'(ny'_n)$, then, for any $\varepsilon > 0$, there exists $y''_n \leq y'_n$ such that $x'_n - \varepsilon \leq c(ny''_n)$. Thus $u(x'_n - \varepsilon, y''_n) \leq u_n$, which implies, since u is a decreasing function in y, that $u(x'_n - \varepsilon, y'_n) \leq u_n$. Letting $\varepsilon \to 0$, $u(x'_n, y'_n) \leq u_n$. It follows that (x_n, y_n) maximizes u subject to $x \leq c'(ny)$.

c' is clearly a non-decreasing function of z. To prove that it is right-continuous, take a decreasing sequence $z^i \to z$. $c'(z^i)$ is a non-increasing sequence, and therefore tends to a limit, which is not less than $c'(z)$. If it is equal to $c'(z)$, there is no more to prove. Suppose it is greater. Then for some $\varepsilon > 0$ each $c'(z^i) > c'(z) + \varepsilon$. Therefore, there exists a sequence $(\bar{z}^i)$ such that $\bar{z}^i \leq z^i$ and $c'(z^i) \geq c(\bar{z}^i) > c'(z) + \varepsilon$. The second inequality implies that $\bar{z}^i > z$. Thus $\bar{z}^i \to z$. Yet $\limsup c(\bar{z}^i) > c(z)$, which contradicts upper semi-continuity. Thus in fact, c is right-continuous. ∥

This proposition says that the marginal tax rate may as well be not greater than 100 per cent. We shall consider later whether it should be positive.

The government chooses the function c so as to maximize a welfare function

$$W = \int_0^\infty G(u_n) f(n) dn. \qquad \ldots(7)$$

I use the function G here, rather than writing u_n alone, because I shall later want to devote special attention to the case $u_{xy} = 0$ (when u can be written as the sum of a function depending only on x and a function depending only on y). In maximizing welfare, the government is constrained by production possibilities: it must be possible to produce the consumption demands, X, arising from its choice of c, with labour input no greater than Z. The production constraint is written

$$X \leq H(Z). \qquad \ldots(8)$$

We have not yet fully specified the possibilities available to the government, since, if (x_n, y_n) is not uniquely defined, it is not clear whether the government or the consumer is allowed to choose the particular utility-maximizing point. Perhaps it is reasonable to suppose that the government can choose, and that the necessity for market-clearing will make its choices actual. But it will turn out that the issue is of no significance when we make the following assumption, as we shall:

(A) y_n is uniquely defined for all n except for a set of measure 0.

Thus the class of functions c from which the government chooses is further restricted by the requirement that the function lead to choices satisfying (A). It will appear in due course that (A) is satisfied for *all* functions c in the particular cases we shall be most concerned with.

3. NECESSARY CONDITIONS FOR THE OPTIMUM

On the assumption that an optimum for our problem exists, we shall now obtain conditions that it must satisfy. The mathematical argument will not be rigorous. To do the analysis properly, one must attend to a number of rather tricky points. Since these technical details tend to obscure the main lines of the argument, rigorous proofs will be presented separately, in the continuation of this paper. The nature of these neglected difficulties will be discussed briefly in the next section.

The key to a reasonably neat solution of the problem is to find a convenient expression of the condition that each man maximizes his utility subject to the imposed " consumption function " c. If we suppose that c is differentiable, the derivative of $u[c(ny), y]$ with respect to y must be zero. Denoting the derivative of u with respect to its first and second arguments by u_1 and u_2, respectively, we have

$$u_1 n c'(ny) + u_2 = 0. \qquad \ldots(9)$$

Recollect that u_n is the utility of n-man. Then a straightforward calculation, using the first-order condition (9), yields

$$\frac{du_n}{dn} = u_1 y c' = -\frac{y u_2}{n}. \qquad \ldots(10)$$

(The expressions on the right are, of course, alternative expressions for the *partial* derivative of u with respect to n, evaluated at the maximum. The case where n enters u in a more general manner can be analyzed by using this more general equation. We shall return to this point later.)

Our problem is to maximize w subject to the constraint of the production function, $X \leq H(Z)$, the differential equation (10), and the definition $u_n = u(x_n, y_n)$. Those who are familiar with the Pontriyagin Maximum Principle will see that this is a form of problem fairly suitable for treatment by it. Shadow prices p and w have to be introduced for X and Z. Then we would like to maximize

$$W - pX + wZ = \int [G(u_n) - px_n + wy_n n] f(n) dn \qquad \ldots(11)$$

subject to (10). u_n is to be regarded as the state variable, y_n (say) as the control variable, while x_n is determined as a function of u_n and y_n from the equation $u_n = u(x_n, y_n)$. The Hamiltonian is

$$M = G[(u_n) - px_n + wy_n n] f(n) - \phi_n \frac{y_n u_2}{n},$$

where ϕ_n is a function of n satisfying the differential equation

$$\frac{d\phi}{dn} = -\frac{\partial M}{\partial u}$$

$$= -\left[G'(u_n) - \frac{p}{u_1} \right] f(n) + \phi \frac{y_n u_{12}}{n u_1}. \qquad \ldots(12)$$

y_n should then be chosen so as to maximize M:

$$\left[wn + \frac{pu_2}{u_1} \right] f(n) + \phi_n \frac{\psi_y}{n} = 0, \qquad \ldots(13)$$

where the function $\psi(u, y)$ is defined by

$$\psi(u, y) = -yu_2(x, y), \quad u = u(x, y), \qquad \ldots(14)$$

and ψ_y is its partial derivative with respect to y. (Notice, at the same time, that

$$\psi_u = -yu_{12}/u_1.)$$

Equation (12) can now be integrated to obtain an expression for ϕ_n; which, when substituted in (13), provides us with an equation to be satisfied by the optimum we seek. Before going on to use this equation, however, we shall derive it in a different way, by a more explicit use of the methods of the calculus of variations. The use of the Maximum Principle has a number of serious disadvantages. It does not show us how to obtain certain important supplementary conditions on the optimum. The analysis provides no hint as to how it could be made rigorous. It does not provide any insight into the kind of maximization that is going on. When we have done a more explicit variational analysis, we shall be better able to see where the logical holes are, and to understand why things come out the way they do.

For this purpose, I prefer to write (10) in integrated form:

$$u_n = -\int_0^n y_m u_2(x_m, y_m) \frac{dm}{m} + u(c(0), 0),$$

$$= \int_0^n \psi(u_m, y_m) \frac{dm}{m} + u_0, \qquad \ldots(15)$$

using the notation ψ introduced above, and denoting the utility allowed to a man who does no work by u_0. Suppose first that ψ is independent of u (corresponding to the sepcial case $u_{12} = 0$). If we consider a variation from the optimum which changes the functions u_n and y_n by " small " variations δu_n and δy_n, we deduce from (15) that these variations must be related by

$$\delta u_n = \int_0^n \psi_y \delta y_m \frac{dm}{m} + \delta u_0. \qquad \ldots(16)$$

This variation will bring about changes in W, X, and Z. As before, introduce shadow prices (in terms of welfare) for X and Z. Then the variation must leave (11) stationary:

$$0 = \delta \int [G(u_n) - px_n + wy_n n] f(n) dn$$

$$= \int \left[G'(u_n) \delta u_n - p \left(\frac{1}{u_1} \delta u_n - \frac{u_2}{u_1} \delta y_n \right) + w \delta y_n n \right] f(n) dn, \qquad \ldots(17)$$

where the variation in x is calculated as follows:

$$\delta u_n = \delta u(x_n, y_n) = u_1 \delta x_n + u_2 \delta y_n. \qquad \ldots(18)$$

It remains to substitute (16) in (17), yielding,

$$0 = \int_0^\infty \left\{ \left[G'(u_n) - \frac{p}{u_1} \right] \left[\int_0^n \psi_y \delta y_m \frac{dm}{m} + \delta u_0 \right] + \left[wn + p \frac{u_2}{u_1} \right] \delta y_n \right\} f(n) dn$$

$$= \int_0^\infty \left\{ \int_n^\infty \left[G'(u_m) - \frac{p}{u_1} \right] f(m) dm \cdot \frac{\psi_y}{n} + \left(wn + p \frac{u_2}{u_1} \right) f(n) \right\} \delta y_n dn$$

$$+ \int_0^\infty \left[G'(u_n) - \frac{p}{u_1} \right] f(n) dn \cdot \delta u_0. \qquad \ldots(19)$$

The second equation is obtained by inverting the order of integration in the double integral.[1] (19) is to be satisfied for all possible variations of the function y_n, and the number u_0. Since u_0 can be either increased or decreased at the optimum (if, as is to be expected in general, some people will do no work at the optimum),

$$\int_0^\infty \left[G'(u_n) - \frac{p}{u_1} \right] f(n) dn = 0 \qquad \ldots(20)$$

at the optimum.

[1] The double integral is

$$\int_0^\infty \left[G'(u_n) - \frac{p}{u_1} \right] f(n) \int_0^n \psi_y \delta y_m \frac{dm}{m} . dn.$$

The region over which the integration takes place is defined by $0 \leq m \leq n$. Thus, when the order of integration is inverted, n ranges between m and ∞ for given m. The integral can therefore be written

$$\int_0^\infty \int_m^\infty \left[G' - \frac{p}{u_1} \right] f(n) dn . \psi_y \delta y_m . \frac{dm}{m},$$

which is seen to justify (19) on permuting the symbols m and n.

If all variations in y_n were possible—and this is a question we shall take up shortly—we could also claim that the expression within curly brackets ought to be zero:

$$\left(wn + p\frac{u_2}{u_1}\right)f(n) = \frac{\psi_y}{n}\int_n^\infty \left[\frac{p}{u_1} - G'(u_m)\right]f(m)dm. \qquad \ldots(21)$$

It should be noticed that this equation will only be valid for $n \geq n_0$: it does not apply to n for which $y_n = 0$ (except n_0) because, there, not all variations of the function y_n are possible, since y_n cannot be negative.

Finally we know that the marginal product of labour should be equal to the shadow wage:

$$pH'(Z) = w. \qquad \ldots(22)$$

These equations, (20) and (21), have been worked out under the special assumption that ψ is independent of u. In the more general case, we have to replace (16) by

$$\delta u_n = \int_0^n T_{mn}\psi_y \delta y_m \frac{dm}{m} + \delta u_0, \qquad \ldots(23)$$

where

$$T_{mn} = \exp \int_m^n \psi_u \frac{dm'}{m'}. \qquad \ldots(24)$$

To show this, we can go back to the differential equation (10). Applying the variation, we obtain from it,

$$\frac{d}{dn}\delta u_n = \frac{1}{n}\psi_u \delta u_n + \frac{1}{n}\psi_y \delta y_n. \qquad \ldots(25)$$

This is a first order linear equation, and can therefore be solved by the standard method to give the solution (23).

Having replaced (16) by (23), we can now go through the rest of the calculation as before. We find that (20) is generalized into

$$\int_0^\infty [G'(u_n) - p/u_1]T_{0n}f(n)dn = 0; \qquad \ldots(26)$$

while (21) becomes

$$(wn + pu_2/u_1)f(n) = \frac{\psi_y}{n}\int_n^\infty [p/u_1 - G'(u_m)]T_{nm}f(m)dm. \qquad \ldots(27)$$

Notice that we have T_{nm} here, although it was T_{mn} that appeared in (23).

If these equations are correct, the two integral equations, (15) and (27) may be thought of as determining the two functions u_n and y_n, given the three parameters $u_0, w,$ and p. The values of these parameters are fixed by the three equations (26), (22), and (8). We have enough relations to determine the optimum tax schedule, since the function c can be determined once we know u_n and y_n.

4. NECESSARY CONDITIONS: A COMPLETE STATEMENT

The argument used to derive these conditions for the optimum tax schedule had a number of weak points. It is indeed unlikely that the relationships derived above hold in general. Among the weak points of the argument, notice that

(i) the existence of the shadow prices p and w was assumed without proof;
(ii) the optimum tax schedule, and the resulting functions $x_n, y_n,$ and u_n were assumed to be differentiable;
(iii) the application of the variation was quite heuristic; and
(iv) no justification was provided for assuming that the function y_n could be varied arbitrarily (for $n > n_0$).

I shall not comment on (i) and (iii), which, though important, are technical matters: they can be justified. (ii) is not satisfied in general: there was no reason to suppose that it would be. When (ii) is not satisfied, the first-order condition, (9), for maximization of utility ceases to be meaningful. Finally, (iv) is never justified. The function y_n is derived from the imposition of the consumption function c, and we have no *a priori* information about it. We must expect that some conceivable functions y_n can never arise from the imposition of a consumption function. The class of possible y-functions is no doubt quite complicated in certain cases. Fortunately it is possible to specify that class quite simply in the realistic cases, and it is then possible to use the variational argument rigorously.

Problem (ii) is dealt with in the rigorous analysis by depending on equation (15) instead of the differential first-order condition (9). It is a remarkable fact that this condition holds if and only if the various functions arise from utility-maximization under an imposed consumption function, even when that function is not differentiable. For proof, the reader is referred to [4].

To deal with problem (iv), we have to restrict the class of utility functions considered. We assume that

(B) $V(x, y) = -yu_2/u_1$ is an increasing function of y for each $x > 0$ (and bounded in $0 \leq x \leq \bar{x}, 0 \leq y \leq \bar{y}$ for any $\bar{x} < \infty$ and $\bar{y} < 1$).

It will be noticed that this is an assumption about preferences, not just about the form of the utility function used to represent preferences. The second part of the assumption is readily acceptable. The first, and main part of the assumption holds if and only if, for a given level of consumption x, a one per cent increase in the amount of work done requires a larger increase in consumption to maintain the same utility level, the greater is the amount of work being done. It is equivalent to assuming that (in the absence of taxation) the consumer's demand for goods is an increasing function of the real wage rate (at any given non-wage income.[1] Few individuals appear to have preferences violating (B), and intuitively it is rather plausible. We shall later use the fact that (B) holds if preferences can be represented by an additive utility function. (It will be noticed that, as $y \to 1$, $V \to +\infty$, so that the assumption must hold for some ranges of y.) If the assumption does not hold, the theory of optimum taxation is more complicated.

The point of the assumption is indicated in

Theorem 1. *Under Assumption* (B), $z_n = ny_n$ *maximizes utility for every* n *under some consumption function* c *if and only if*

(i) z_n *is a non-decreasing function defined for* $n > 0$;

(ii) $0 \leq z_n < n$ *for all* $n > 0$.

---

[1] This equivalence is fairly obvious from an indifference curve diagram. For a formal proof that (B) implies that consumption is an increasing function of the wage rate, let w be the wage rate, and m non-labour income (both measured in terms of goods). (B) states that wy, regarded as a function of x and y, is an increasing function of y. Write x and y as functions of w and m, putting $x = x(w, m)$, $y = y(w, m)$ and $x' = x(w', m)$, $y' = y(w', m)$ where $w' > w$. I shall show that $x' > x$. To do this, choose w'' and m'' such that $x'' = x(w'', m'') = x$, and

$$y'' = y(w'', m'') = \frac{w}{w''} y.$$

Since $x'' - w'y'' = m$, (x', y') is preferred to (x'', y''); and therefore

$$x' - x > w''(y' - y'')$$
$$= \frac{w''}{w'}(w'y' - w'y'') = \frac{w''}{w'}(w'y' - wy)$$
$$= \frac{w''}{w'}(x' - x),$$

since $x' - w'y' = m = x - wy$. This implies, with our assumption $w'' < w'$, that $x' > x$.
The converse proposition can be proved by reversing the steps.

For a rigorous proof of this theorem, the reader is referred to [4]. For a heuristic justification, suppose that z_n is differentiable, and that c is twice differentiable. The first order condition, (9), can be written

$$\frac{\partial}{\partial z} u(c(z), z/n) = \frac{u_1}{z} [zc'(z) - V(c(z), z/n)] = 0. \qquad \ldots(28)$$

Furthermore, we have the second-order condition, that the derivative is non-increasing at z_n. Since it is zero there, this is also true when we drop the positive factor u_1/z. In other words,

$$\frac{\partial}{\partial z} [zc'(z) - V(c(z), z/n)] \leq 0, \text{ at } z = z_n. \qquad \ldots(29)$$

Now differentiate the equation $z_n c'(z_n) - V(c(z_n) z_n/n) = 0$ with respect to n:

$$\frac{\partial}{\partial z} [zc' - V]\big|_{z=z_n} \cdot \frac{dz_n}{dn} = -V_y(c(z_n), z_n/n) z/n^2. \qquad \ldots(30)$$

It follows from (29) and assumption (B) that

$$\frac{dz_n}{dn} > 0 \qquad \ldots(31)$$

unless $z_n = 0$. In fact z_n is strictly increasing when $n > n_0$ and c is differentiable; a corner in c causes z_n to be constant for a range of values of n. (An indifference curve diagram makes this clear.) Condition (ii) of the theorem clearly has to be satisfied by the utility maximizing choice.

To prove that a suitable consumption function exists for a given z-function satisfying the two conditions, one defines c by the first-order condition (28). (30) then shows (nearly) that the second-order condition for a maximum is satisfied. This does not yet prove global maximization of utility, but that also is true.

It should be noticed that, as a corollary of Theorem 1, condition (A) holds when condition (B) holds, for z_n is shown to be non-decreasing even if it is a correspondence. It therefore takes a single value for all but a countable set of values of n. A fortiori, condition (A) is satisfied in this case.

Theorem 1 at once implies that z_n and therefore also x_n are non-decreasing functions when the optimum tax schedule is imposed. Furthermore, it shows us quite straightforwardly what changes in the function y_n we are allowed to contemplate when applying the variational argument that allowable small changes should make only a second-order difference to the maximand. The rigorous argument is still complicated, in part because one has to allow for the possibility that z_n is constant over some intervals, and discontinuous at some values of n. The full statement of the result, which is proved in [4], is as follows:

Theorem 2. *If preferences satisfy assumption (B) and (u_n, x_n, y_n) arise from optimum income taxation, then*

(i) $z_n = n y_n$ *is a non-decreasing function of n;*

(ii) $u_n = u_0 - \int_0^n [y_m u_2(x_m, y_m)/m] dm \quad (n \geq 0);$ ...(32)

(iii) *at all points of increase of z_n (i.e., where $z_n > z_{n'}$ for all $n' < n$, or $z_n < z_{n'}$ for all $n' > n$)*

$$A_n \equiv [w + u_2^{(n)}/n u_1^{(n)}] f(n) - \frac{\psi_y}{n^2} \int_n^\infty \left[\frac{1}{u_1^{(m)}} - \lambda G'(u_m)\right] T_{nm} f(m) dm = 0, \qquad \ldots(33)$$

where superscripts "(n)", etc. indicate that the function is evaluated at n-man (etc.)'s utility-maximizing choice, and

$$\psi_y = -u_2^{(n)} - y_n u_{22}^{(n)} + y_n u_2^{(n)} u_{12}^{(n)}/u_1^{(n)}, \qquad \ldots(34)$$

$$T_{nm} = \exp\left[-\int_n^m y_{m'} u_{12}(x_{m'}, y_{m'})/u_1(x_{m'}, y_{m'}) \cdot dm'\right]; \qquad \ldots(35)$$

(iv) If $n \in [n_1, n_2]$, where z is constant on $[n_1, n_2]$, and $[n_1, n_2]$ is a maximal interval of constancy for z,

$$\int_{n_1}^n A_m dm \geq 0, \quad \int_n^{n_2} A_m dm \leq 0; \qquad \ldots(36)$$

(v) If z is discontinuous at n, $\bar{y}_n$ is defined to be $\lim_{m \to n-} y_m$, $\bar{x}_n$ is defined by

$$u(\bar{x}_n, \bar{y}_n) = u_n = u(x_n, y_n),$$

and $\bar{u}_1$, etc., denote u_1 evaluated at $\bar{x}_n, \bar{y}_n$, while u_1, etc., denote evaluation at x_n, y_n,

$$\frac{(wy_n - x_n/n) - (w\bar{y}_n - \bar{x}_n/n)}{\bar{y}_n \bar{u}_2 - y_n u_2} = \frac{w + u_2/nu_1}{\psi_y} = \frac{w + \bar{u}_2/n\bar{u}_1}{\bar{\psi}_y}. \qquad \ldots(37)$$

If ψ_y is a non-decreasing function of y for constant u, z_n is continuous for all n.

(vi) $\displaystyle\int_0^\infty \left[\frac{1}{u_1} - \lambda G'(u_m)\right] T_{0m} f(m) dm = 0, \qquad \ldots(38)$

(vii) $X = H(Z), \qquad \ldots(39)$

$w = H'(Z). \qquad \ldots(40)$

It will be noticed that in this statement w is the commodity shadow wage rate (w/p in the earlier notation), while λ ($1/p$ in the previous notation) is the inverse of the marginal social utility of commodities (national income). The second part of (v) should be particularly noted, since we are quite likely to be willing to assume that ψ_y is a non-decreasing function of y, and it is a great advantage not to have to worry about possible discontinuities in z_n. It does not seem possible, unfortunately, to delimit a class of cases in which one can be sure that $[0, n_0]$ will be the only interval of constancy for z. It should be mentioned that, when ψ_y is not non-decreasing, and the equations (37) may possibly apply, the conditions of Theorem 1 may define more than one candidate for optimality, and then only direct comparison of the welfare generated by the alternative paths so defined will solve the problem.

5. INTERPRETATION

If n is not in an interval of constancy for z, and $c(.)$ is therefore a differentiable function at z_n, the first-order condition (9) applies. It can be written

$$-u_2/nu_1 = c'(z). \qquad \ldots(41)$$

If we denote the marginal tax rate, $\dfrac{d}{d(wz)}[wz - c(z)]$, by θ, we have

$$w\theta = \frac{d}{dz}[wz - c(z)] = w + u_2/nu_1$$

$$= \frac{\psi_y}{n^2 f(n)} \int_n^\infty \frac{1 - \lambda G' u_1}{u_1} T_{nm} f(m) dm, \qquad \ldots(42)$$

by (33). (42) suggests the considerations that should influence the magnitude of the marginal tax rate. First, it can tell us something about the sign of θ: we already know that θ will not be greater than 1, but we were not previously able to say anything about its sign. Of course, we expect that it will not usually be negative. Using (42) and the conditions in Theorem 1, we can establish this rigorously.

Note first that $1 - \lambda G'u_1$ is a non-decreasing function of n, since x_n is a non-decreasing function of n, and $\frac{\partial}{\partial x} G = G'u_1$ a decreasing function of x. If $1 - \lambda G'u_1$ were always positive or always negative, Equation (38) could not be satisfied. Therefore

$$\int_n^\infty \frac{1}{u_1}(1 - \lambda G'u_1) T_{nm} f(m) dm$$

is increasing in n for n less than some $\bar{n}$, and decreasing for $n > \bar{n}$; but in any case positive for $n > \bar{n}$. (Here we use the properties $u_1 > 0$, $T_{mn} > 0$.) Since the integral is zero when $n = 0$, it is non-negative for all n. Consequently the marginal tax rate is non-negative at all points of increase of z. If n is not a point of increase of z, c is not differentiable at z_n. It is easily seen that, if $[n_1, n_2]$ is a maximal interval of constancy of z, $-u_2/nu_1$ is equal to the left derivative of c at n_1, and the right derivative at n_2. Thus both the "right" and "left" marginal tax rates are non-negative in this case. Summarizing:

Proposition 3.[1] *If assumption (B) is satisfied, $wz - c(z)$ (the "tax function") is a non-decreasing function for all z that actually occur (and may therefore be taken to be a non-decreasing function for all z).*

Having established that the integral in Equation (42) is non-negative for all n, we can see that the marginal tax rate will be greater if there are relatively few n-men than otherwise; or if the utility-value of work, $-yu_y$, is more sensitive to work done (utility being held constant); or if n is closer to $\bar{n}$, the value of n at which $1 = \lambda G'u_1$ (and the integral is therefore a maximum). If f is a single-peaked distribution, the first consideration suggests that marginal tax rates should be greatest for the richest and the poorest; but the last consideration tells the other way.

In any case, it is important to note than n_0, the largest n for which $y_n = 0$, may be quite large: if the number who do not work in the optimum regime is large, the marginal tax rate may not be high at zero income. Explicitly, we can rewrite Equation (38) in the form

$$\left[\frac{1}{u_1(x_0, 0)} - \lambda G'(u_0) \right] F(n_0) + \int_{n_0}^\infty \left[\frac{1}{u_1} - \lambda G' \right] T_{n_0 m} f(m) dm = 0 \quad \ldots(43)$$

which, when combined with Equation (33) (for $n = n_0$) gives

$$w + \frac{u_2(x_0, 0)}{n_0 u_1(x_0, 0)} = \psi_y(u_0, 0) \frac{F(n_0)}{n_0^2 f(n_0)} \left[\lambda G'(u_0) - \frac{1}{u_1(x_0, 0)} \right]. \quad \ldots(44)$$

Unfortunately, one cannot get much information from these "local" conditions, at least for small n. For any detail, and in particular for numerical results, one must examine the whole system of equations. It is easier to do that for particular examples of the general problem, and that is what we shall do in succeeding sections. It may be noted, however, that Equation (44) does provide us with *some* information about n_0 and x_0. For example, it is clear that n_0 can be zero only if F/nf tends to 0 as n tends to 0; indeed, since the left hand side of Equation (44) is bounded, $n_0 = 0$ only if $x_0 = 0$, and therefore $1/u_1 = 0$. It follows that $n_0 = 0$ only if $F/(n^2 f)$ is bounded as $n \to 0$, which means that F tends to zero faster than $\exp(-1/n)$. This excludes the cases usually considered by economists. We

---

[1] The analysis and result can be generalized to the utility function $u(x, z, n)$ where the parameter n can indicate variations in tastes as well as skill. The extension is fairly routine and will not be discussed here.

may conclude at this stage that it will be optimal, in the most interesting cases, to encourage some of the population to be idle.

A number of conclusions have been obtained, but they are fairly weak: the marginal tax rate lies between zero and one; in a large class of cases, consumption and labour supply vary continuously with the skill of the individual; there will usually be a group of people who ought to work only if they enjoy it. The main feature of the results is that the optimum tax schedule depends upon the distribution of skills within the population, and the labour-consumption preferences of the population, in such a complicated way that it is not possible to say in general whether marginal tax rates should be higher for high-income, low-income, or intermediate-income groups. The two integral equations that characterise the optimum tax schedule are, however, of a reasonably manageable form. One expects to be able to calculate the schedule in particular cases without great difficulty. In the next sections of the paper, we shall show how this can be done in certain special cases, and obtain further properties of the optimum tax in these cases.

6. ADDITIVE UTILITY

An interesting case arises when, for all x and y,

$$u_{12} = 0. \qquad \ldots(45)$$

Thus u_1 depends only on x, and u_2 only on y.

Proposition 4. *If assumption (45) is satisfied, $V(x, y)$ is an increasing function of y, bounded for small x and y.*

Proof. $V = -yu_2(y)/u_1(x)$, and $V_2 = (-u_2 - yu_{22})/u_1 > 0$. Boundedness is obvious. ‖

Corollary. *Under assumption (45), Theorem 1 applies.*

In particular we know, from statement (v) of that Theorem that y_n is continuous provided that ψ_y is non-decreasing. In the present case, this condition is equivalent to the requirement that

$$-yu_2(y) \text{ is convex.} \qquad \ldots(46)$$

There is no reason why this assumption should hold in general, but it is easily checked for any particular case. We shall now restrict attention to cases for which (46) holds.[1]

If we restrict attention also to cases where z is strictly increasing when $n > n_0$, the optimum situation will be a solution of the equations

$$\left\{ \left(w + \frac{u_2}{nu_1} \right) n^2 f(n) = \psi_y \int_n^\infty \left(\frac{1}{u_1} - \lambda G' \right) f(m) dm, \qquad \ldots(47)$$

$$\left\{ u_n = u_0 - \int_0^n y_m u_2 \frac{dm}{m}. \qquad \ldots(48)$$

We shall further assume that f is continuously differentiable. Since x_n, y_n are continuous in this case, it follows that u_n and $\left(w + \frac{u_2}{nu_1} \right) / \psi_y$ are differentiable functions of n. Write

$$v = \frac{w + \frac{u_2}{nu_1}}{\psi_y}. \qquad \ldots(49)$$

---
[1] In [4] a theorem is proved which states that the conditions of Theorem 2 are in fact *sufficient* (as well as necessary) for an optimum in the special case now being considered.

u and v are continuously differentiable functions of x and y. Since $\frac{\partial u}{\partial x}>0$, $\frac{\partial u}{\partial y}<0$, and, as can easily be seen, $\frac{\partial v}{\partial x}<0$, $\frac{\partial v}{\partial y}<0$, the Jacobian $\frac{\partial(u,v)}{\partial(x,y)}$ is always negative. Consequently x and y can be expressed as continuously differentiable functions of u and v, and are therefore themselves differentiable functions of n.

We can now write Equations (47) and (48) as differential equations:

$$\frac{dv}{dn} = -\frac{v}{n}\left(2+\frac{nf'}{f}\right) - \frac{1}{n^2 u_1} + \frac{\lambda G'}{n^2}, \qquad \ldots(50)$$

$$\frac{du}{dn} = -\frac{yu_2}{n}; \qquad \ldots(51)$$

which, as we have just shown, can be thought of as equations in u and v. The particular solution we seek, and the particular value of λ, are defined by the boundary conditions, Equations (39), (40),

$$v_{n_0} = \frac{F(n_0)}{n_0^2 f(n_0)}\left[\lambda G'(u_{n_0}) - \frac{1}{u_1(x_{n_0})}\right], \qquad \ldots(52)$$

which is the form (38) takes here, and

$$v_n n^2 f(n) \to 0 \quad (n \to \infty), \qquad \ldots(53)$$

which is apparent from Equation (47). Provided that z_n is strictly increasing for $n \geq n_0$, a solution that satisfies all those conditions will, by Theorem 2 of [4], provide the optimum.

Equations (39) and (40), the production function and the marginal productivity equation, may be ignored in the calculations. Corresponding to the particular values of w and λ used in the calculation, one obtains values for X and Z. Thus we know the optimum tax schedule when the marginal product is w and the average product is X/Z. In this way one could obtain a range of tax schedules corresponding to different average products and marginal products—which is what one wants. Of course, it is desirable to choose λ so that the average product will be related to the marginal product, w, in a reasonable way. This should not present any great difficulty.

To determine the sign of $\frac{dz_n}{dn} = y_n + n\frac{dy_n}{dn}$, we calculate, from Equation (49),

$$\psi_y \frac{dv}{dn} = \left(\frac{u_{22}}{nu_1} - v\psi_{yy}\right)\frac{dy}{dn} - \frac{u_2}{n^2 u_1} - \frac{u_2 u_{11}}{nu_1^2}\frac{dx}{dn}$$

$$= \left(\frac{u_{22}}{nu_1} - v\psi_{yy}\right)\frac{dy}{dn} - \frac{u_2}{n^2 u_1} + \frac{u_2^2 u_{11}}{nu_1^3}\frac{dy}{dn} - \frac{u_2 u_{11}}{nu_1^3}\frac{du}{dn}$$

$$= \frac{1}{n}\left(\frac{u_{22}}{nu_1} - v\psi_{yy} + \frac{u_2^2 u_{11}}{nu_1^3}\right)\frac{dz}{dn} - \frac{y_n}{n}\left(\frac{u_{22}}{nu_1} - v\psi_{yy}\right) - \frac{u_2}{n^2 u_1}, \qquad \ldots(54)$$

substituting from (51). Therefore, using (50)

$$\left[\frac{u_{22}}{nu_1} - v\psi_{yy} + \frac{u_2^2 u_{11}}{nu_1^3}\right]\frac{dz}{dn} = \frac{yu_{22}}{nu_1} - yv\psi_{yy} + \frac{u_2}{nu_1} - \left(2+\frac{nf'}{f}\right)v\psi_y - \frac{\psi_y}{nu_1} + \frac{\lambda\psi_y G'}{n}$$

$$= -\psi_y\left\{\left(2+\frac{nf'}{f} + \frac{y\psi_{yy}}{\psi_y}\right)v + \frac{2}{nu_1} - \frac{\lambda G'}{n}\right\}. \qquad \ldots(55)$$

We may therefore check the assumption $\frac{dz}{dn} \geq 0$ by examining the solution to see whether

$$\left(2 + \frac{nf'}{f} + \frac{y\psi_{yy}}{\psi_y}\right)v + \frac{2}{nu_1} - \frac{\lambda G'}{n} \geq 0. \qquad \ldots(56)$$

Equation (56) is equivalent to $\frac{dz}{dn} \geq 0$ because the expression in square brackets in Equation (55) is negative, term by term.

In computation, one can proceed as follows:—

[1] A value of λ is chosen. To get the right order of magnitude, one can calculate $\int_0^\infty u_1^{-1} f \, dn / \int_0^\infty G' f \, dn$ (cf. (38)) for some particular feasible, and *a priori* plausible, allocation of consumption and labour.

[2] A trial value of $n_0 > 0$ is chosen. (It should be borne in mind that the inequality $v_{n_0} \geq 0$ may, with (52), restrict the range of possible n_0.)

[3] Bearing in mind that $y_{n_0} = 0$, the values of v_{n_0} and u_{n_0} are obtained from (49) and (52).

[4] The solution of equations (50) and (51) is calculated for increasing n until either (56) fails to be satisfied, or it becomes apparent that (53) will not be satisfied (see [6] below).

[5] If (56) fails to be satisfied, z_n is kept constant, u_n (and v_n) being calculated from (49) until (56) is satisfied again, when z_n is allowed to increase and the solution pursued as in [4].

[6] The attempted solution should be stopped if u_n or x_n begins to decrease, or v_n or y_n fall to zero, or x_n, y_n cannot be calculated (e.g. because u_n exceeds the upper bound of u, if there is one). Other stopping rules can be given for particular examples, depending on the structure of the solutions of the equations.

[7] A range of trial values of n_0 must be used to find the one that most nearly provides a solution satisfying (53). Efficient rules for iteration might be obtained in particular cases.

7. FEATURES OF SOLUTIONS

Solutions may, for all I know, be very diverse in their characteristics; but examination of the equations suggests a number of comments. First we note that v_n will always lie between 0 and $\frac{1}{\psi_y(0)}$, since

$$0 \leq \frac{1 + \frac{u_2}{nu_1}}{\psi_y} \leq \frac{1 + \frac{u_2}{nu_1}}{\psi_y(0)} < \frac{1}{\psi_y(0)}. \qquad \ldots(57)$$

We are therefore led to expect that v tends to a limit as $n \to \infty$. (It might cycle for certain forms of f, of a kind one would perhaps be unlikely to use.) y is also bounded, by 0 and 1, and is therefore likely to tend to a limit. One is then led to certain conjectures about the limits, which ought to hold for sufficiently regular f and u.

Let
$$\frac{nf'}{f} \to \gamma + 2 \leqq \infty. \qquad \ldots(58)$$

(Since $\int_0^\infty nf\,dn < \infty$, $\gamma \geqq 0$: otherwise $n^2 f$ is increasing for large n, therefore bounded below.) Further, suppose
$$u_1 \sim \alpha x^{-\mu} \quad (\mu > 0) \qquad \ldots(59)$$

as $x \to \infty$. Then there appear to be three cases; in each of which one expects the following results to hold.

(i) $\mu < 1$. As $n \to \infty$,
$$y_n \to 1 \qquad \ldots(60)$$
and
$$v_n \to 0. \qquad \ldots(61)$$
The marginal tax rate,
$$\theta \to 1. \qquad \ldots(62)$$

(ii) $\mu = 1$. As $n \to \infty$,
$$y_n \to \bar{y}, \qquad \ldots(63)$$
where $\bar{y}$ is defined (uniquely) by
$$\bar{y} u_2(\bar{y}) = -\alpha, \qquad \ldots(64)$$
and
$$v_n \to [-(1+\gamma)u_2(\bar{y}) - \bar{y} u_{22}(\bar{y})]^{-1}. \qquad \ldots(65)$$
Furthermore,
$$\theta \to \frac{1+v}{1+v+\gamma}, \qquad \ldots(66)$$
where
$$v = \frac{\bar{y} u_{22}(\bar{y})}{u_2(y)}. \qquad \ldots(67)$$

(iii) $\mu > 1$. As $n \to \infty$,
$$y_n \to 0, \qquad \ldots(68)$$
and
$$v_n \to [-(1+\gamma)u_2(0)]^{-1}. \qquad \ldots(69)$$
$$\theta \to \frac{1}{1+\gamma}. \qquad \ldots(70)$$

(It may be noted that, in a natural sense, (66) holds for all cases.)

Before indicating the reasons for these conjectures, a few words of interpretation may be in place. On the whole, the distribution of income from employment appears to be of Paretian form at the upper tail[1]: Equation (58) holds with γ between 1 and 2, roughly speaking. It is not improbable, however, that marginal productivity per working year is distributed differently from actual incomes: the lognormal distribution is the most plausible simple distribution. For this, $\gamma = \infty$, and
$$-\frac{nf'}{f} \sim \frac{\log n}{\sigma^2} \qquad \ldots(71)$$
for large n; (σ^2 is the variance of the distribution of logarithm of incomes).

---
[1] See the general assessment by Lydall [3].

The realism of alternative assumptions about utility may be assessed by calculating the response of the consumer to a linear budget constraint, $x = wy + a$. It is easy to see that utility-maximization requires (since $u_{12} \equiv 0$)

$$-\frac{u_1(x)}{u_2(y)} = \frac{1}{w}, \quad x = wy + a. \qquad \ldots(72)$$

If $u_1 = \alpha x^{-\mu}$, we have to solve

$$\alpha w = -(a + wy)^\mu u_2(y). \qquad \ldots(73)$$

(If $\alpha w \leq -a^\mu u_2(0)$, $y = 0$.) Clearly the solution has the following properties:

$$\left.\begin{array}{l} y \to 1 \text{ as } w \to \infty \text{ if } \mu < 1, \\ y \to 0 \text{ as } w \to \infty \text{ if } \mu > 1. \end{array}\right\} \qquad \ldots(74)$$

(Cf. (61) and (68).) Also

$$\left.\begin{array}{l} x \sim a + w \quad (\mu < 1), \\ x \sim \left(\dfrac{aw}{u_2(0)}\right)^{\frac{1}{\mu}} \quad (\mu > 1) \end{array}\right\}. \qquad \ldots(75)$$

These asymptotic properties suggest that the case $\mu = 1$ is particularly interesting. When $\mu = 1$, since, by (73)

$$\frac{a}{w} = -\frac{\alpha}{u_2} - y,$$

$$-yu_2 \to \alpha \text{ as } w \to \infty;$$

i.e.

$$y \to \bar{y}, \qquad \ldots(76)$$

where $\bar{y}$ is defined by (64). (Cf. (63).) If in addition,

$$u_2(y) = -(1-y)^{-\delta} \quad (\delta > 0), \qquad \ldots(77)$$

we have

$$\bar{y}(1-\bar{y})^{-\delta} = \alpha,$$
$$\bar{y}(1-\bar{y})^{-1} = v.$$

The choice of α may be influenced by considering that $y = 0$ when $w/a \leq 1/\alpha$. It is interesting to note that, if

$$\alpha = 2, \quad \delta = 1, \quad \gamma = 2,$$
$$\bar{y} = 2/3, \quad v = 2,$$

and, if our conjectures are correct,

$$\theta \to 60 \text{ per cent.}$$

This case is perhaps not completely unrealistic; but it should be remembered that the homogeneous form for u means that the decision not to work depends only on the *ratio* of earned to unearned income, which is not a very realistic assumption.

It will be noticed that, in this case, the asymptotic marginal tax rate is very sensitive to the value of μ (in the neighbourhood of 1).

The reasons for the conjectures Equations (60)-(70) (in fact, I can provide a proof of (iii) and will do so below) are as follows. One expects that, as $n \to \infty$, the relevant solution of the differential equations will tend towards a singularity of the equations: not only will y and v tend to limits, but $n\dfrac{dy}{dn}$ and $n\dfrac{dv}{dn}$ will tend to zero. Denote the postulated limit of y_n by $\bar{y}$. Consider first the case $u_1 = \alpha x^{-\mu} (\mu < 1)$.

In this case utility is unbounded. I shall show that $\bar{y} = 1$. If not, u_2 and ψ_y tend to finite limits, and, from (51), we have

$$nu_1 \frac{dx}{dn} = -u_2\left(y + n\frac{dy}{dn}\right) \to -\bar{y}u_2(\bar{y}). \qquad \ldots(78)$$

Therefore, since $u_1 \dfrac{dx}{dn} = \alpha \dfrac{d}{dn}\left[\dfrac{1}{1-\mu} x^{1-\mu}\right]$,

$$\frac{\alpha}{1-\mu} x^{1-\mu} = -\bar{y}u_2(\bar{y}) \log n [1 + o(1)]. \qquad \ldots(79)$$

This implies that

$$nu_1 = 0[n(\log n)^{-\frac{\mu}{1-\mu}}] \qquad \ldots(80)$$

$$\to \infty. \qquad \ldots(81)$$

Therefore

$$\frac{1}{n^2 f(n)} \int_n^\infty \left[\frac{1}{u_1} - \lambda\right] f(m) dm = \frac{1}{\psi_y}\left[1 + \frac{u_2}{nu_1}\right] \to \frac{1}{\psi_y(\bar{y})} > 0, \qquad \ldots(82)$$

which is readily seen to be inconsistent with (80) if the distribution is either Paretian or lognormal.

We must therefore expect that $\bar{y} = 1$. Suppose now that $1 + \dfrac{u_2}{nu_1}$, the marginal tax rate, tends to a limit $\bar{\imath} < 1$. Then

$$\frac{dx}{dn} = -\frac{u_2}{nu_1}\left(y + n\frac{dy}{dn}\right) \to 1 + \bar{\imath}, \qquad \ldots(83)$$

and consequently

$$\frac{x}{n} \to 1 - \bar{\imath}. \qquad \ldots(84)$$

This implies that

$$\frac{1}{u_1} = \frac{1}{\alpha}(1-\bar{\imath})^\mu n^\mu [1 + o(1)], \qquad \ldots(85)$$

from which we can deduce the behaviour of

$$I = \frac{u_1}{nf}\int_n^\infty \left(\frac{1}{u_1} - \lambda\right) f(m) dm \qquad \ldots(86)$$

as $n \to \infty$. In the Paretian case, $f \sim n^{-2-\gamma}$, it is easily seen that

$$I \to (2 + \gamma - \mu)^{-1} > 0. \qquad \ldots(87)$$

Since $1 - \bar{\imath} = \lim \dfrac{\psi_y}{u_2} \cdot \dfrac{u_2}{nu_1} \cdot I$, and $\dfrac{\psi_y}{u_2} = -1 - \dfrac{d}{dy}\log|u_2|$ tends to $-\infty$ as $y \to 1$ (if it tends to a limit at all), we must have $\dfrac{u_2}{nu_1} \to 0$, which is inconsistent with the assumption $\bar{\imath} < 1$. In the lognormal case, one obtains

$$1 - \bar{\imath} = \lim \frac{\psi_y}{u_2} \cdot \frac{u_2}{nu_1} \cdot \frac{\text{constant}}{\log n}. \qquad \ldots(88)$$

If $\dfrac{\psi_y}{u_2} \dfrac{1}{\log n}$ tended to a finite limit, since

$$\log|u_2| \sim \log(1-\bar{\imath}) + \log(nu_1) \sim (1-\mu)\log n,$$

$\dfrac{1}{\log|u_2|}\dfrac{d}{dy}\log|u_2|$ would tend to a finite limit as $y\to 1$; which is clearly impossible. Thus in the lognormal case too, we expect that $\bar{\imath}=1$. This explains the conjectures in the case $\mu<1$.

If $\mu=1$,
$$\alpha\frac{d(\log x)}{d(\log n)}=nu_1\frac{dx}{dn}=-u_2\left(y+n\frac{dy}{dn}\right), \qquad \ldots(89)$$

which therefore cannot tend to ∞, since in that case $u_1^{-1}=\dfrac{x}{\alpha}>n^M$ eventually for any finite M, so that $\dfrac{1}{n^2f(n)}\displaystyle\int_n^\infty \dfrac{1}{u_1}f(m)dm$ becomes unbounded as $n\to\infty$.

We can expect, therefore, that $y\to\bar{y}<1$ and
$$\alpha\frac{\log x}{\log n}\to -\bar{y}u_2(\bar{y}). \qquad \ldots(90)$$

It is easily seen that the only plausible value of $\bar{y}$ is that for which $\log x/\log n\to 1$, i.e.
$$\bar{y}u_2(\bar{y})=-\alpha. \qquad \ldots(91)$$

Then if $1+\dfrac{u_2}{nu_1}\to \bar{\imath}$, we shall have
$$n\alpha x^{-1}\to\frac{-u_2(\bar{y})}{1-\bar{\imath}},$$

and
$$\frac{\psi_y}{n^2f(n)}\int\left(\frac{1}{u_1}-\lambda\right)f(m)dm\to\frac{(1-\bar{\imath})\psi_y(\bar{y})}{-u_2(\bar{y})}\frac{1}{\gamma};$$

which suggests that
$$\bar{\imath}=(1-\bar{\imath})\frac{\psi_y(\bar{y})}{-u_2(\bar{y})}\frac{1}{\gamma}$$
$$=(1-\bar{\imath})(1+v)/\gamma, \qquad \ldots(92)$$

in the notation (57). This is equivalent to (56). In particular, we expect that $\bar{\imath}=0$ in the lognormal case.

When $\mu>1$, the utility function is bounded above, and a more general and rigorous treatment is easy. u_n is an increasing function, and being now bounded tends to a finite $\bar{u}$. We shall write
$$u(x,y)=\chi(x)+\rho(y). \qquad \ldots(93)$$

Since x is an increasing function, $\chi(x)$ also tends to a finite limit $\bar{\chi}$. Thus $\rho(y)$ tends to a limit, and so does y. The limit of y must be zero, since otherwise (32) implies $u\to\infty$, which is now impossible.

Now
$$v+\frac{1}{nu_1}=\frac{1}{\psi_y}+\left(1+\frac{u_2}{\psi_y}\right)\frac{1}{nu_1}$$
$$\to\frac{1}{-u_2(0)} \qquad \ldots(94)$$

in this case $\left(\text{since } \dfrac{1}{nu_1}, \text{ being} \leq \dfrac{1}{-u_2}, \text{ is bounded}\right)$. Therefore Equation (50) becomes

$$n\frac{dv}{dn} = (\gamma+1+o(1))v + \frac{1}{u_2(0)} + o(1) \qquad \ldots(95)$$

in the Paretian case. From (95) one deduces, by the usual method of solving a first-order linear differential equation, that

$$v \to \frac{1}{-u_2(0)(\gamma+1)}, \qquad \ldots(96)$$

from which it follows at once that the marginal tax rate tends to $(\gamma+1)^{-1}$. It is easily checked that in the lognormal case the marginal tax rate tends to zero.

In the next section, a particular case is examined in detail, and provides confirmation for some of our conjectures.

8. AN EXAMPLE

Case I. Let us, by way of illustration, analyze the following case:

$$\left.\begin{array}{l} u = \alpha \log x + \log(1-y) \\[2pt] G(u) = -\dfrac{1}{\beta} e^{-\beta u} \quad (\beta \geq 0)\ ^1 \\[2pt] f(n) = \dfrac{1}{n} \exp\left[-\dfrac{(\log n+1)^2}{2}\right]. \end{array}\right\} \qquad \ldots(97)$$

(The last assumes a lognormal distribution of skills: the average of n is $\dfrac{1}{\sqrt{e}} = 0{\cdot}607\ldots$).
We put $w = 1$. With these assumptions, Equations (50) and (51) become

$$\frac{dv}{dn} = v \frac{\log n}{n} - \frac{x}{\alpha n^2} + \frac{\lambda}{n^2} e^{-\beta u},$$

$$\frac{du}{dn} = \frac{y}{n(1-y)},$$

where

$$v = \left[1 + \frac{u_2}{nu_1}\right] / \psi_y = \frac{1 - \dfrac{x}{\alpha n(1-y)}}{1/(1-y)^2} = (1-y)\left(1 - y - \frac{x}{\alpha n}\right),$$

and

$$e^u = x^\alpha(1-y).$$

For simplicity, we consider the case $\beta = 0$ first, and put

$$s = 1-y,$$
$$t = \log n.$$

The equations become, since $u = \alpha \log(\alpha n) + \alpha \log\left(s - \dfrac{v}{s}\right) + \log s$,

$$\frac{dv}{dt} = v\left(t + \frac{1}{s}\right) - s + \lambda e^{-t}, \qquad \ldots(98)$$

$$\frac{ds}{dt} = \frac{[1-\alpha-(1+\alpha)s](s^2-v) + \alpha s(vt + \lambda e^{-t})}{(1+\alpha)s^2 - (1-\alpha)v}. \qquad \ldots(99)$$

[1] In the case of $\beta = 0$, we define $G = u$.

Solutions of these equations are depicted in Fig. 1. We now establish their properties. We remember that, in the optimum solution, $0 < v < s^2$ (for the marginal tax rate, v/s^2, is between 0 and 1). Using this fact, we can deduce from the first equation that

$$v \to 0 \quad (t \to \infty).$$

Suppose that, for some t, $vt \geq 1$. Then

$$\frac{d}{dt} v \geq vt + \frac{v-s^2}{s} > vt - 1 \geq 0,$$

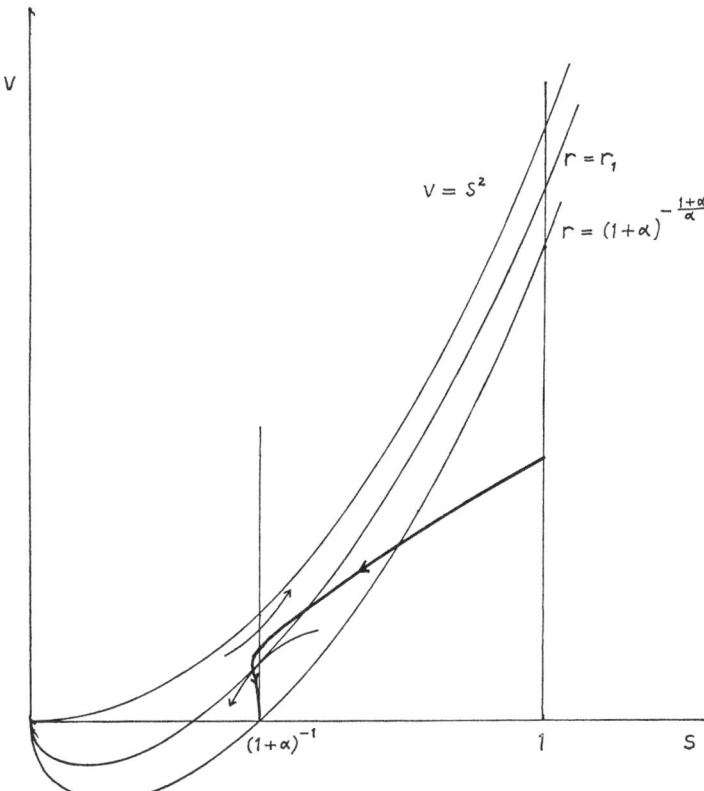

FIGURE 1

since $v > 0$, and $s \leq 1$. Therefore v is increasing at an increasing rate, contradicting $v < s^2 \leq 1$. This shows that, in fact,

$$0 < v < 1/t. \qquad \ldots(100)$$

The two equations together imply that

$$\frac{d}{dt}[s^{\frac{1-\alpha}{\alpha}}(s^2-v)] = \frac{1-(1+\alpha)s}{s} s^{\frac{1-\alpha}{\alpha}}(s^2-v), \qquad \ldots(101)$$

as one may see if one multiplies the first by αs, and the second by $[(1+\alpha)s^2 - (1-\alpha)v]$, and subtracts. Write

$$r = s^{\frac{1-\alpha}{\alpha}}(s^2-v). \qquad \ldots(102)$$

so that
$$\alpha \frac{dr}{dt} = \frac{1-(1+\alpha)s}{s} r. \qquad \ldots(103)$$

When $s < \frac{1}{1+\alpha}$, r increases; when $s > \frac{1}{1+\alpha}$, r decreases. For this reason s cannot tend to a limit other than $1/(1+\alpha)$: we shall show more, that $s \to 1/(1+\alpha)$. (Cf. Fig. 1.) Since $v \to 0$, given $\varepsilon > 0$, there exists t_0 such that $0 < v_t < \varepsilon$ for all $t \geq t_0$. Then
$$s^{\frac{1+\alpha}{\alpha}} - \varepsilon s^{\frac{1-\alpha}{\alpha}} < r < s^{\frac{1+\alpha}{\alpha}} \quad (t \geq t_0). \qquad \ldots(104)$$

If $r_t > (1+\alpha)^{-\frac{1+\alpha}{\alpha}}$, the right hand inequality implies that
$$s_t > \frac{1}{1+\alpha}. \qquad \ldots(105)$$

Therefore r is decreasing. If
$$r_t < (1+\alpha)^{-\frac{1+\alpha}{\alpha}} - \varepsilon \max\left[1, (1+\alpha)^{-\frac{1-\alpha}{\alpha}}\right], \qquad \ldots(106)$$
we obtain from the left hand inequality (104),
$$s_t^{\frac{1+\alpha}{\alpha}} < (1+\alpha)^{-\frac{1+\alpha}{\alpha}} - \varepsilon\{\max\left[1, (1+\alpha)^{-\frac{1-\alpha}{\alpha}}\right] - s_t^{\frac{1-\alpha}{\alpha}}\} \leq (1+\alpha)^{-\frac{1+\alpha}{\alpha}} \qquad \ldots(107)$$

if, either $\alpha \leq 1$ (in which case $\{\ldots\} \geq 0$ since $s \leq 1$), or $\alpha > 1$ and $s_t \geq \frac{1}{1+\alpha}$. Thus, in fact
$$s_t < \frac{1}{1+\alpha}, \qquad \ldots(108)$$
and, by (98), r_t is increasing. Combining these two results, we deduce that
$$r_t \to (1+\alpha)^{-\frac{1+\alpha}{\alpha}},$$
which in turn implies, since $v > 0$, that
$$s_t \to \frac{1}{1+\alpha}. \qquad \ldots(109)$$

Our demonstration that v and s tend to limits 0 and $\frac{1}{1+\alpha}$, respectively, confirms the conjectures for the special case. It is readily checked that exactly the same arguments apply to the case $\beta > 0$. As we have noted previously, the marginal tax rate is v/s^2. Thus, as $t \to \infty$
$$\theta \to 0. \qquad \ldots(110)$$

It is a striking result; but we should note at once that 0 is a poor approximation to v/s^2 even for large t. This becomes apparent when we demonstrate that $vt \to \frac{1}{1+\alpha}$.

Suppose the contrary, that $\left|vt - \frac{1}{1+\alpha}\right| > \varepsilon > 0$ for an unbounded set of values of t.

If $vt > \frac{1}{1+\alpha} + \varepsilon$, and t is large enough to imply that $s_t < \frac{1}{1+\alpha} + \tfrac{1}{2}\varepsilon$,
$$\frac{dv}{dt} > \tfrac{1}{2}\varepsilon. \qquad \ldots(111)$$

Thus vt continues greater than $\frac{1}{1+\alpha}+\varepsilon$, and $\frac{dv}{dt} > \frac{1}{2}\varepsilon$ for all larger t: but this implies that $v \to \infty$, which we have already shown to be false. If on the other hand $vt < \frac{1}{1+\alpha} - \varepsilon$, and t is greater than $\frac{2}{\varepsilon}$, and is large enough to imply

$$v_t < \frac{1+\alpha}{4}, \quad \lambda t e^{-t} < \frac{1+\alpha}{4}, \quad s_t > \frac{1}{1+\alpha} - \frac{1}{2}\varepsilon,$$

then

$$\frac{d}{dt}(vt) = v + t(vt-s) + \frac{vt}{s} + \lambda t e^{-t}$$

$$< \frac{1+\alpha}{2} + \frac{\frac{1}{1+\alpha}-\varepsilon}{\frac{1}{1+\alpha}-\frac{1}{2}\varepsilon} - \frac{1}{2}\varepsilon t$$

$$< 1 - \frac{3}{2} = -\frac{1}{2}. \qquad \ldots(112)$$

This implies that vt becomes negative, which is impossible. Therefore $\left| vt - \frac{1}{1+\alpha} \right| < \varepsilon$ for all large enough t:

$$vt \to \frac{1}{1+\alpha}. \qquad \ldots(113)$$

Thus

$$\theta = v/s^2 \sim \frac{1+\alpha}{t}. \qquad \ldots(114)$$

Only 1 per cent of our population have $t \geq 1\cdot 7$ (one in a thousand have $t \geq 2\cdot 4$). Since one might want to have α as low as 1, the above approximation is clearly rather bad even at $t = 2$.[1,2] How bad will become apparent in the next section.

Case II. It is also of interest to examine the case of a skill-distribution with Paretian tail:

$$\frac{nf'}{f} \to \gamma + 2, \quad \gamma > 0. \qquad \ldots(115)$$

The equations for the optimum become (with $\beta = 0$),

$$\frac{dv}{dt} = v\gamma(t) + \frac{v}{s} - s + \lambda e^{-t}, \qquad \ldots(116)$$

$$\frac{ds}{dt} = \frac{[1-\alpha-(1+\alpha)s](s^2-v) + \alpha s(v\gamma(t) + \lambda e^{-t})}{(1+\alpha)s^2 - (1-\alpha)v}; \qquad \ldots(117)$$

[1] In this example, $\sigma^2 = 1$: that is, the standard deviation of $\log n$ is 1. This is done merely for convenience in manipulations. A precisely similar theory holds for a general lognormal distribution.
  It can be shown, by continuing the methods of the text, that $vt \sim \frac{1}{1+\alpha} - \frac{1}{t}$ while $s = \frac{1}{1+\alpha} + o\left(\frac{1}{t^2}\right)$.
The fact that the optimum path is tangential to the vertical at $(s, v) = \left(\frac{1}{1+\alpha}, 0\right)$ implies that $s < \frac{1}{1+\alpha}$, for large t, since otherwise r would be decreasing, and that, as can be seen from the diagram, is inconsistent with $\frac{dv}{ds} \to \infty$. Thus we have the situation portrayed in Fig. 1.
[2] The case $\beta > 0$ can be treated in a precisely similar way, to obtain the same qualitative results.

MIRRLEES   OPTIMUM INCOME TAXATION

and, exactly as before, one has the equation

$$\frac{dr}{dt} = \frac{1-(1+\alpha)s}{s}r \qquad \ldots(118)$$

where $r = s^{\frac{1+\alpha}{\alpha}}(s^2 - v)$. The situation is portrayed in Fig. 2. The broken curves have equations

$$s^{\frac{1-\alpha}{\alpha}}(s^2 - v) = r_i \quad (i = 1, 2, 3) \qquad \ldots(119)$$

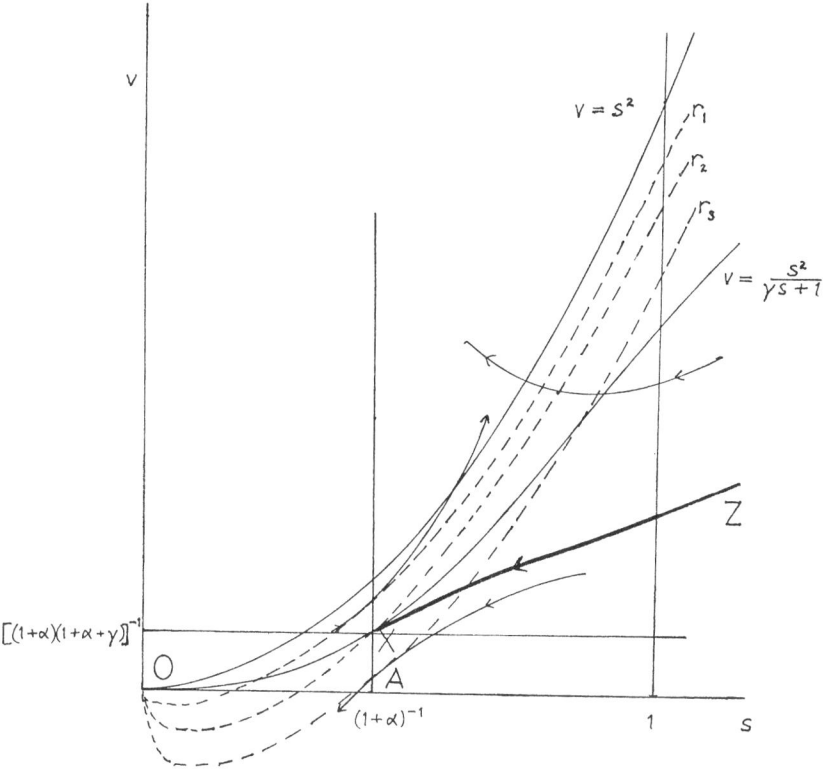

FIGURE 2

with $0 < r_1 < r_2 < r_3$. It will be noted that such a curve, with equation

$$v_1 = s^2 - rs^{\frac{1-\alpha}{\alpha}} \quad (r \text{ constant}), \qquad \ldots(120)$$

always cuts from below the curve

$$v_2 = \frac{s^2}{\gamma s + 1} + p \quad (p \text{ constant}) \qquad \ldots(121)$$

that passes through the same point. This follows from the calculation,

$$\frac{dv_1}{ds} - \frac{dv_2}{ds} = \frac{d}{ds}\left(\frac{\gamma s^3}{\gamma s + 1} - rs^{\frac{1-\alpha}{\alpha}}\right) > 0. \qquad \ldots(122)$$

This remark will prove very useful; but first we want to establish that, for large t, the sign of $\dfrac{dv}{dt}$ is nearly the same as the sign of $v - \dfrac{s^2}{\gamma s + 1}$.

Let ε' be a positive number, and let t_1 be so large that $|v\gamma(t) + \lambda e^{-t} - v\gamma| > \varepsilon'$ when $t \geq t_1$. Since $s = 1$ at $t_0 = \log n_0$, $s < \dfrac{1}{1+\alpha}$ at t only if $s = \dfrac{1}{1+\alpha}$ for some previous t_1; if (for the given t) t_1 is the greatest such, we have from Equation (118)

$$r_t > r_{t_1} = (1+\alpha)^{-\frac{1-\alpha}{\alpha}}\left(\frac{1}{(1+\alpha)^2} - v_{t_1}\right)$$

$$\geq (1-\alpha)^{-\frac{1-\alpha}{\alpha}} \inf\left\{\frac{1}{(1+\alpha)^2} - v_t \,\bigg|\, s_t = \frac{1}{1+\alpha},\, \frac{dv_t^!}{dt} < 0\right\}$$

$$= \Delta > 0, \qquad \qquad \ldots(123)$$

since as $t \to \infty$, $0 > \dfrac{dv}{dt}$ implies

$$v_t < \frac{s_t^2}{\gamma s_t + 1} + o(1)$$

$$< s_t^2 - \gamma s_t^3 + o(1). \qquad \qquad \ldots(124)$$

Therefore s_t is positively bounded below, say

$$s_t \geq \Delta' > 0. \qquad \qquad \ldots(125)$$

Hence, when $t \geq t_1$,

$$\frac{dv}{dt} = v\gamma(t) + \frac{v}{s} - s + \lambda e^{-t}$$

$$> \left(v - \frac{s^2}{\gamma s + 1}\right)\left(\gamma + \frac{1}{s}\right) - \varepsilon'$$

$$> \varepsilon', \qquad \qquad \ldots(126)$$

if

$$v > \frac{s^2}{\gamma s + 1} + \frac{2\varepsilon'}{\gamma + \dfrac{1}{\Delta'}}. \qquad \qquad \ldots(127)$$

Similarly, we can show that

$$\frac{dv}{dt} < -\varepsilon' \qquad \qquad \ldots(128)$$

if

$$v < \frac{s^2}{\gamma s + 1} - \frac{2\varepsilon'}{\gamma + \dfrac{1}{\Delta'}}. \qquad \qquad \ldots(129)$$

Now write $\varepsilon = \varepsilon'/\left(\gamma + \dfrac{1}{\Delta'}\right)$. It is clear that, if, for some $t \geq t_1$,

$$v > \frac{s^2}{\gamma s + 1} + \varepsilon \quad \text{and} \quad s \geq \frac{1}{1+\alpha},$$

then $\frac{dv}{dt} > 0$ and also $\frac{dr}{dt} < 0$. Therefore, by the properties of the two sets of curves (cf. Fig. 3), $v - \frac{s^2}{\gamma s + 1}$ is increasing. Thus for all subsequent t, $\frac{dv}{dt} > \varepsilon'$, and $v \to \infty$. Such a path cannot be optimum. Consequently on the optimum path, if $t \geq t_1$,

$$\text{either } s < \frac{1}{1+\alpha} \text{ or } v \leq \frac{s^2}{\gamma s + 1} + \varepsilon. \qquad \ldots(130)$$

Similarly, for $t \geq t_1$,

$$\text{either } s > \frac{1}{1+\alpha} \text{ or } v \geq \frac{s^2}{\gamma s + 1} - \varepsilon. \qquad \ldots(131)$$

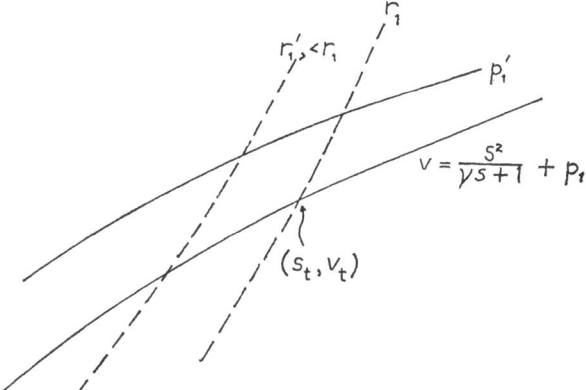

FIGURE 3

Suppose that at t_1, $s > \frac{1}{1+\alpha}$. (An exactly similar argument applies if $s < \frac{1}{1+\alpha}$.) Then r is decreasing, and continues to do so until

$$r = r' = (1+\alpha)^{-\frac{1-\alpha}{\alpha}} \left(\frac{1}{(1+\alpha)^2} \frac{\gamma}{(1+\alpha+\gamma)} + \varepsilon \right).$$

Only then can s become less than $\frac{1}{1+\alpha}$. (Cf. Fig. 4.) Once $s < \frac{1}{1+\alpha}$, r increases again. Therefore at no time is

$$r < r'' = (1+\alpha)^{-\frac{1-\alpha}{\alpha}} \left(\frac{\gamma}{(1+\alpha)^2(1+\alpha+\gamma)} - \varepsilon \right).$$

Nor can we have $r > r'$ at any later time. Thus we have found t_2 such that, when $t \geq t_2$, (s_t, v_t) lies in the curvilinear parallelogram $LMPQ$ in Fig. 4, which contains X, and can be made as small as we please by suitable choice of ε'. Therefore as $t \to \infty$,

$$s_t \to \frac{1}{1+\alpha}, \quad v_t \to \frac{1}{(1+\alpha)(1+\alpha+\gamma)}. \qquad \ldots(132)$$

The optimum path is indicated by XZ in Fig. 2. On it, the marginal tax rate,

$$\theta = \frac{v_t}{s_t^2} \to \frac{1+\alpha}{1+\alpha+\gamma}; \qquad \ldots(133)$$

which confirms our conjecture in this special case.[1,2]

It should be noted that we have not shown, in either of these cases, that s diminishes (nor even that $z = ny = e^t(1-s)$ increases) all along the path: the possibility that z is constant for some range of n, in the optimum regime, remains in both the examples we have discussed. Calculation of specific cases is required to settle this issue. Such calculation is not difficult with the information about the solution that we now have.

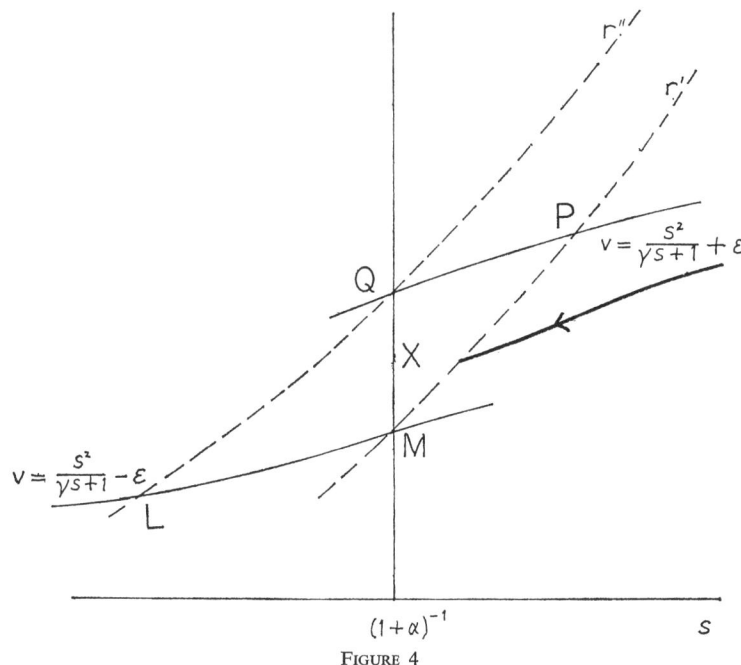

FIGURE 4

9. A NUMERICAL ILLUSTRATION

The computations whose results are presented in the tables below were carried out for the first case examined above, with $\alpha = 1$, but with a more realistic value for σ^2. Computations have also been carried out for the case $\sigma^2 = 1$, and these provide an interesting contrast to the main set of calculations. In all cases, we take $w = 1$; and for computational convenience, the average of $\log n$ is -1. This means that the average marginal product of a full day's work is $e^{\frac{1}{2}\sigma^2 - 1}$, but it amounts only to a choice of units for the consumption good. The results show, for particular values of the average product of labour, X/Z, what is the optimum tax schedule, and what is the distribution of consumption and labour in the population.

[1] The case $\beta > 0$ can be treated in a precisely similar way, to obtain the same qualitative results.
[2] It is possible to calculate optimum tax schedules explicitly for a uniform (rectangular) distribution of skills; but since that distribution is of no great interest in the present context, the analysis is omitted.

For purposes of comparison, one naturally wants to know what would have been the optimum position if it had been possible to use lump-sum taxation (or, equivalently, direction of labour). Let us consider this first for the case $\beta = 0$. We shall assume a linear production function

$$X = Z + a \qquad \ldots(134)$$

(which one thinks of as applying only over a certain range of values of Z, including all those that are to be considered). In the full optimum, we maximize

$$\int [\log x + \log (1-y)] f(n) dn$$

subject to

$$\ldots(135)$$

$$\int xf(n) dn = \int nyf(n) dn + a.$$

It is clear that x will be the same for everyone:

$$x = x^0, \qquad \ldots(136)$$

and that y_n must maximize

$$\log (1-y) + ny/x^0, \qquad \ldots(137)$$

for otherwise we could improve matters by changing y_n (for a set of n of positive measure, of course) and changing the constant x correspondingly. Maximization of (137) yields

$$y_n^0 = [1 - x^0/n]_+, \qquad \ldots(138)$$

where the notation $[\ldots]_+$ means max $(0, \ldots)$.

It is worth noticing that in the full optimum, only men for whom $n > x^0$ actually work, and an interesting curiosity that, with the particular welfare function specified in (135), utility will be less for more highly skilled individuals. This is, as we have seen, impossible under the income-tax. The value of x^0 is determined by the production constraint:

$$x^0 = \int_{x^0}^{\infty} (n - x^0) f(n) dn + a, \qquad \ldots(139)$$

where, for convenience, we have taken $\int_0^{\infty} f(n) dn = 1$. In the case of the special lognormal distribution used here, it can be shown that this equation reduces to

$$2x^0 - x^0 F(x^0) - e^{\frac{1}{2}\sigma^2 - 1}[1 - F(e^{-\sigma^2} x^0)] = a. \qquad \ldots(140)$$

Solution of this equation gives the consumption level in the full optimum, and also the skill-level below which no work is required of a man, namely that at which a full day's labour would provide a wage equal to the consumption level.

When $\beta > 0$, a similar theory holds. In that case, $x > x^0$ for men with $n > x^0$, but it is still the case that such men are made to have a lower utility level than their less skilled neighbours. The equation corresponding to (140) is a little more complicated and will not be reproduced. For $n > x^0$, consumption and labour are

$$x_n = (x^0)^{(1+\beta)/(1+2\beta)} n^{\beta/(1+2\beta)},$$

$$y_n = 1 - (x^0/n)^{(1+\beta)/(1+2\beta)}. \qquad \ldots(141)$$

In the tables, certain features of the optimal regime under income taxation are given, along with x^0 for the full optimum for the same linear production function. In Tables I-X, the lognormal distribution has parameters $\sigma = 0.39$. This figure is derived from Lydall's figures for the distribution of income from employment for various countries ([3], p. 153). It is intended to represent a realistic distribution of skills within the population. In each

TABLE I
(Case 1)

$\alpha = 1, \beta = 0, \sigma = 0\cdot 39$, mean $n = 0\cdot 40$, $X/Z = 0\cdot 93$.
Full optimum for $X = Z - 0\cdot 013$: $x^0 = 0\cdot 19$, $F(x^0) = 0\cdot 045$.
Partial optimum (income-tax): $x_0 = 0\cdot 03$, $n_0 = 0\cdot 04$, $F(n_0) = 0\cdot 000$.

$F(n)$	x	y	$x(1-y)$	z	full optimum x
0	0·03	0	0·03	0	0·19
0·10	0·10	0·42	0·05	0·09	0·19
0·50	0·16	0·45	0·08	0·17	0·19
0·90	0·25	0·48	0·13	0·29	0·19
0·99	0·38	0·49	0·19	0·45	0·19
Population average	0·17			0·18	0·19

TABLE II
Same case as Table I.

z	x	Average tax rate per cent	Marginal tax rate per cent
0	0·03		23
0·05	0·07	−34	26
0·10	0·10	−5	24
0·20	0·18	9	21
0·30	0·26	13	19
0·40	0·34	14	18
0·50	0·43	15	16

TABLE III
(Case 2)

$\alpha = 1, \beta = 0, \sigma = 0\cdot 39$, mean $n = 0\cdot 40$, $X/Z = 1\cdot 10$.
Full optimum for $X = Z + 0\cdot 017$: $x^0 = 0\cdot 21$, $F(x^0) = 0\cdot 075$.
Partial optimum (income-tax): $x_0 = 0\cdot 05$, $n_0 = 0\cdot 06$, $F(n_0) = 0\cdot 000$.

$F(n)$	x	y	$x(1-y)$	z	Full optimum x
0	0·05	0	0·05	0	0·21
0·10	0·11	0·36	0·07	0·08	0·21
0·50	0·17	0·42	0·10	0·15	0·21
0·90	0·27	0·45	0·15	0·28	0·21
0·99	0·40	0·47	0·21	0·43	0·21
Population average	0·18			0·17	0·21

TABLE IV
Same case as Table III.

z	x	Average tax rate per cent	Marginal tax rate per cent
0	0·05		
0·05	0·09	−80	21
0·10	0·13	−30	20
0·20	0·21	−5	19
0·30	0·29	3	17
0·40	0·37	6	16
0·50	0·46	8	15

TABLE V
(Case 3)

$\alpha = 1, \beta = 1, \sigma = 0{\cdot}39$, mean $n = 0{\cdot}40, X/Z = 1{\cdot}20$.
Full optimum for $X = Z + 0{\cdot}030$: $x^0 = 0{\cdot}16, F(x^0) = 0{\cdot}016$.
Partial optimum (income-tax): $x_0 = 0{\cdot}07, n_0 = 0{\cdot}09, F(n_0) = 0{\cdot}000$.

$F(n)$	x	y	$x(1-y)$	z	Full optimum x
0	0·07	0	0·07	0	0·16
0·10	0·12	0·28	0·08	0·07	0·18
0·50	0·17	0·37	0·11	0·14	0·21
0·90	0·26	0·43	0·15	0·26	0·25
0·99	0·39	0·46	0·21	0·42	0·29
Population average	0·18			0·15	0·21

TABLE VI
Same case as Table V.

z	x	Average tax rate per cent	Marginal tax rate per cent
0	0·07		23
0·05	0·11	−113	28
0·10	0·14	−42	27
0·20	0·22	−8	25
0·30	0·29	2	23
0·40	0·37	7	21
0·50	0·45	10	19

TABLE VII
(Case 4)

$\alpha = 1, \beta = 1, \sigma = 0{\cdot}39$, mean $n = 0{\cdot}40, X/Z = 0{\cdot}98$.
Full optimum for $X = Z - 0{\cdot}003$: $x^0 = 0{\cdot}14, F(x^0) = 0{\cdot}007$.
Partial optimum (income-tax): $x_0 = 0{\cdot}05, n_0 = 0{\cdot}07, F(n_0) = 0{\cdot}000$.

$F(n)$	x	y	$x(1-y)$	z	Full optimum x
0	0·05	0	0·05	0	0·14
0·10	0·10	0·33	0·07	0·08	0·17
0·50	0·15	0·41	0·09	0·15	0·20
0·90	0·24	0·46	0·13	0·28	0·23
0·99	0·37	0·48	0·19	0·44	0·26
Population average	0·16			0·17	0·19

TABLE VIII
Same case as Table VII.

z	x	Average tax rate per cent	Marginal tax rate per cent
0	0·05		30
0·05	0·08	−66	34
0·10	0·12	−34	32
0·20	0·19	7	28
0·30	0·26	13	25
0·40	0·34	16	22
0·50	0·41	17	20

TABLE IX
(Case 5)

$\alpha = 1, \beta = 1, \sigma = 0.39$, mean $n = 0.40$, $X/Z = 0.88$.
Full optimum for $X = Z - 0.021$; $x^0 = 0.13$, $F(x^0) = 0.004$.
Partial optimum (income-tax): $x_0 = 0.04$, $n_0 = 0.06$, $F(n_0) = 0.000$.

$F(n)$	x	y	$x(1-y)$	z	Full optimum x
0	0.04	0	0.04	0	0.13
0.10	0.09	0.36	0.06	0.08	0.15
0.50	0.14	0.43	0.08	0.16	0.18
0.90	0.23	0.48	0.12	0.29	0.22
0.99	0.36	0.50	0.18	0.45	0.25
Population average	0.15			0.17	0.19

TABLE X
Same case as Table IX.

z	x	Average tax rate per cent	Marginal tax rate per cent
0	0.04		35
0.05	0.07	−43	39
0.10	0.10	−3	36
0.20	0.17	15	31
0.30	0.24	20	27
0.40	0.31	22	24
0.50	0.39	21	21

TABLE XI
(Case 6)

$\alpha = 1, \beta = 1, \sigma = 1$, mean $n = 0.61$, $X/Z = 0.93$.
Full optimum for $X = Z - 0.013$: $x^0 = 0.25$, $F(x^0) = 0.35$.
Partial optimum (income-tax): $x_0 = 0.10$, $n_0 = 0.20$, $F(n_0) = 0.27$.

$F(n)$	x	y	$x(1-y)$	z	Full optimum x
0	0.10	0	0.10	0	0.25
0.10	0.10	0	0.10	0	0.25
0.50	0.14	0.15	0.11	0.06	0.28
0.90	0.32	0.41	0.19	0.54	0.44
0.99	0.90	0.49	0.46	1.84	0.62
Population average	0.18			0.20	0.32

TABLE XII
Same case as Table XI.

z	x	Average tax rate per cent	Marginal tax rate per cent
0	0.10		50
0.10	0.15	−50	58
0.25	0.20	20	60
0.50	0.30	40	59
1.00	0.52	48	57
1.50	0.73	51	54
2.00	0.97	51	52
3.00	1.47	51	49

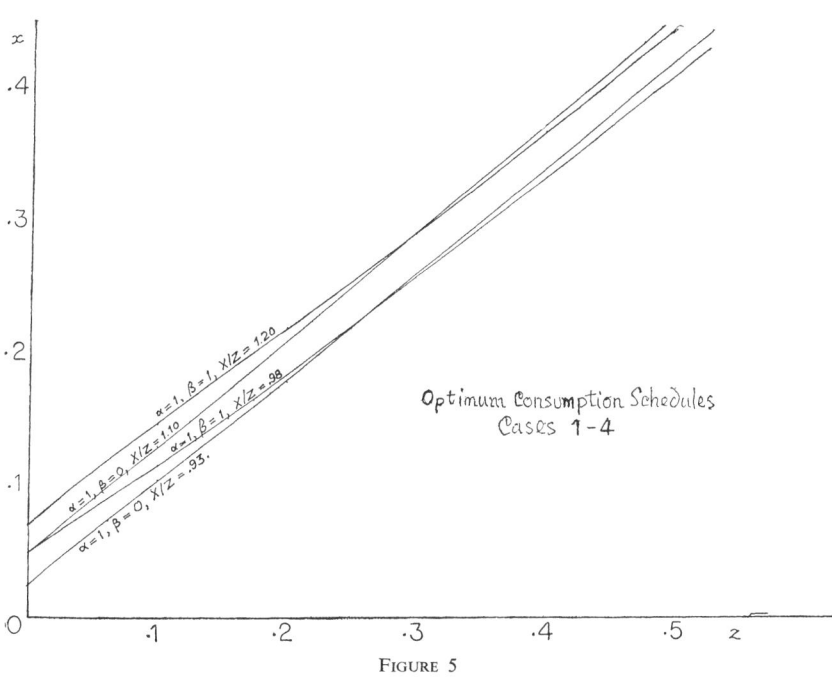

FIGURE 5

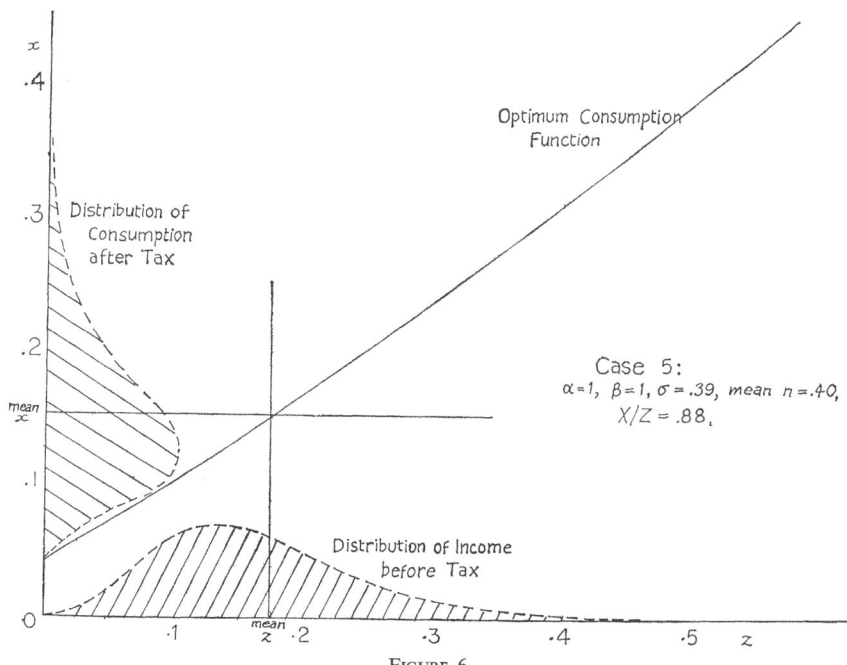

FIGURE 6

case, x_0, n_0, and the values of x, y and $x(1-y)$ (which measures utility) at the 10 per cent, 50 per cent, 90 per cent and 99 per cent points of the skill-distribution are given. In separate tables, the average and marginal tax rates are given for a representative range of values of z. Graphs of the optimal consumption schedule ($x = c(z)$) are given in Figs. 1 and 2. In Fig. 2, the distributions of x_n and z_n are displayed in case 5.

It will be noticed at once that, under the optimum regime, practically the whole population chooses to work in each of these cases: this contrasts, in some cases, with the full optimum, where sometimes a substantial proportion of the population is allowed to be idle. In most cases, a significant number work for less than a third of the time. It is also somewhat surprising that tax rates are so low. This means, in effect, that the income tax

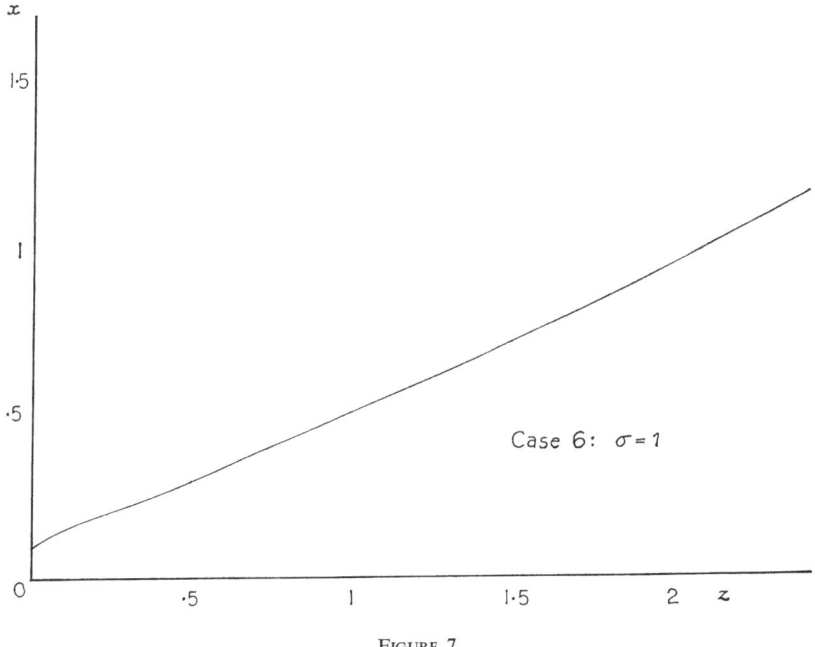

FIGURE 7

is not as effective a weapon for redistributing income, under the assumptions we have made, as one might have expected. It is not surprising that tax rates are higher when $\beta = 1$. When objectives are more egalitarian, more output is sacrificed for the sake of the poorer groups. Nevertheless, the difference between the optimum when only an income tax is available, and the full optimum, is rather large.

The examples have been chosen for X/Z fairly large: this corresponds to economies in which the requirements of government expenditure are largely met from the profits of public production, or taxation of private profits and commodity transactions. Tax rates are, as one might expect, fairly sensitive to changes in X/Z (i.e. to the production possibilities in the economy, and the extent to which income taxation is used to finance government expenditure as well as for " redistribution "). Tax rates are mildly sensitive to the choice of β. (When $\alpha = \frac{1}{2}$, the main features are unchanged).

Perhaps the most striking feature of the results is the closeness to linearity of the tax schedules. Since a linear tax schedule, which may be regarded as a proportional income tax in association with a poll subsidy, is particularly easy to administer, it cannot be said that the neglect of administrative costs in the analysis is of any importance, except that considerations of administration might well lead an optimizing government to choose a perfectly linear tax schedule. The optimum tax schedule is certainly not exactly linear, however, and we have not explored the welfare loss that would arise from restriction to linear schedules: nevertheless, one may conjecture that the loss would be quite small. It is interesting, though, that in the cases for which we have calculated optimum schedules, the maximum marginal tax rate occurs at a rather low income level, and falls steadily thereafter.

This conclusion would not necessarily hold if the distribution of skills in the population had a substantially greater variance. The sixth case presented has $\sigma = 1$. So great a dispersion of known labouring ability does not seem to be at all realistic at present, but it is just conceivable if a great deal more were known to employers about the abilities of individual members of the population. The optimum is in almost all respects very different. Tax rates are high: a large proportion of the population is allowed to abstain from productive labour. The results seem to say that, in an economy where there is more intrinsic inequality in economic skill, the income tax is a more important weapon of public control than it is in an economy where the dispersion of innate skills is less. The reason is, presumably, that the labour-discouraging effects of the tax are more important, relative to the redistributive benefits, in the latter case.

10. CONCLUSIONS

The examples discussed confirm, as one would expect, that the shape of the optimum earned-income tax schedule is rather sensitive to the distribution of skills within the population, and to the income-leisure preferences postulated. Neither is easy to estimate for real economies. The simple consumption-leisure utility function is a heroic abstraction from a much more complicated situation, so that it is quite hard to guess what a satisfactory method of estimating it would be. Many objections to using observed income distributions as a means of estimating the distribution of skills will spring to mind. Yet the assumptions used in the numerical illustrations seem to fit observation fairly well, and are not in themselves implausible. It is not probable that work decisions are entirely, or even, in the long run, mainly, determined by social convention, psychological need, or the imperatives of cooperative behaviour: an analysis of the kind presented is therefore likely to be relevant to the construction and reform of actual income taxes.

Being aware that many of the arguments used to argue in favour of low marginal tax rates for the rich are, at best, premissed on the odd assumption that any means of raising the national income is good, even if it diverts part of that income from poor to rich, I must confess that I had expected the rigorous analysis of income-taxation in the utilitarian manner to provide an argument for high tax rates. It has not done so. I had also expected to be able to show that there was no great need to strive for low marginal tax rates on low incomes when constructing negative-income-tax proposals. This feeling has been to some extent confirmed. But my expectation that the minimum consumption level would be rather high has not been confirmed. Instead, virtually everyone is brought into the workforce. Since this conclusion is based on the analysis of an economy in which a man who chooses to work can work, I should not wish to see it applied in real economies. So long as there are periods when employment offered is less than the labour force available, one would perhaps wish to see the minimum income-level, assured to those who are not working, set at such a level that the number who choose not to work is as great as the excess of the labour force over the employment available. A rigorous analysis of this situation has still to be attempted. The results above do at least suggest that we should allow the least skilled to work for a substantially shorter period than the highly skilled.

I would also hesitate to apply the conclusions regarding individuals of high skill: for many of them, their work is, up to a point, quite attractive, and the supply of their labour may be rather inelastic (apart from the possibilities of migration). There is scope for further theoretical work on this problem too. I conclude, for the present, that:—

(1) An approximately linear income-tax schedule, with all the administrative advantages it would bring, is desirable (unless the supply of highly skilled labour is much more inelastic than our utility function assumed); and in particular (optimal!) negative income-tax proposals are strongly supported.[1]

(2) The income-tax is a much less effective tool for reducing inequalities than has often been thought; and therefore

(3) It would be good to devise taxes complementary to the income-tax, designed to avoid the difficulties that tax is faced with. In the model we have been studying, this could be achieved by introducing a tax schedule that depends upon time worked (y) as well as upon labour-income (z): with such a schedule, one can obtain the full optimum, since one can, in effect, construct a different z-schedule for each n.[2] Such a tax would not be fully practicable, but we have other means of estimating a man's skill-level—such as the notorious I.Q. test: high values of skill-indexes may be sought after so much for prestige that they would not often be misrepresented. With any such method of taxation, the risks of evasion are, of course, quite great: but if it is true, as our results suggest, that the income tax is not a very satisfactory alternative, this objection must be weighed against the great desirability of finding some effective method of offsetting the unmerited favours that some of us receive from our genes and family advantages.

REFERENCES

[1] Blum, W. J. and Kalven, H. Jr. *The Uneasy Case for Progressive Taxation* (University of Chicago Press, 1953).

[2] Diamond, P. A. " Negative Income Taxes and the Poverty Problem—a Review Article ", *National Tax Journal* (September 1968).

[3] Lydall, H. F. *The Structure of Earnings* (Oxford, 1968).

[4] Mirrlees, J. A. " Characterization of the Optimum Income Tax " (unpublished).

[5] Musgrave, R. A. *The Theory of Public Finance* (McGraw-Hill, 1959).

[6] Shoup, C. S. *Public Finance* (Weidenfeld and Nicolson, 1969).

[7] Vickrey, W. *Agenda for Progressive Taxation* (Ronald Press, N.Y., 1947).

[1] The essential point of these proposals is that the marginal tax rate (as represented by rules for deductions from social security benefits) should be significantly less than 100 per cent. Proposals of this kind have sometimes been put forward in terms that suggest—quite wrongly of course—that any plausible-sounding negative income-tax proposal is better than a system in which all earnings are deducted from social security benefits. It was a major intention of the present study to provide methods for estimating desirable tax rates at the lowest income levels, and a surprise that these tax rates are the most difficult to determine, in a sense. They cannot be determined without at the same time determining the whole optimum income-tax schedule. To put things another way, no such proposal can be valid out of the context of the rest of the income-tax schedule.

[2] I am indebted to Frank Hahn for pointing this out. It would seem to be true that lump-sum taxation is possible in any formal model where uncertainty is not introduced explicitly.

Optimal Income Taxation: An Example with a U-Shaped Pattern of Optimal Marginal Tax Rates

By Peter A. Diamond*

Using the Mirrlees optimal income tax model with quasi-linear preferences, the paper examines conditions for marginal tax rates to be rising at high income levels and declining in an interval containing the modal skill. It examines conditions for the marginal tax rate to be higher at a low skill level than at the high skill level with the same density—an argument only holding for skill levels above a cutoff where resources of a worker are marginally of the same value as resources of the government. Data on earnings rates are presented. (JEL H21)

The trade-off between efficiency and income distribution plays a central role in analyzing tax policy.[1] The modern framework for analyzing this trade-off using nonlinear income taxes was created in James A. Mirrlees (1971). While this formulation crystallized a presentation of the income tax problem and derived some of the properties of optimal income taxation, the implications for policy have been somewhat limited. For example, the *Financial Times* (September 11, 1995 p. 24) has summarized the policy impact of the optimal income tax literature as: "A few general principles none the less gained the status of received wisdom, for example that marginal tax rates should be constant and modest over most of the income range, but zero at the top and bottom." The public finance community has recognized that the results deriving zero marginal tax rates at the top and the bottom of the income distribution are of little or no relevance for policy. This paper argues that the case for nonconstant and high marginal tax rates in the Mirrlees model is considerably stronger than has been realized. The technical contribution of this paper is very modest, being primarily a rearrangement of terms in the standard first-order condition for optimal income taxation. This rearrangement leads to a different way of approaching the combinations of assumptions that will sign the change in marginal tax rates with income level. In addition, by concentrating on the case where there is a zero income derivative of labor supply, the intuition behind the first-order condition becomes clearer.

Section I reviews some of the previous literature. Section II presents the optimal income tax problem. Section III examines conditions for marginal tax rates to be rising at income levels above the modal skill level. Section IV examines the level of marginal tax rates on very high incomes. Section V examines conditions for the marginal tax rate to be declining and to be higher at a skill level below the modal skill than at the skill level above the mode with the same density of skills. These arguments apply for skill levels above a cutoff level, where resources are of the same value in the hands of the government and in the hands of a worker with the cutoff skill level. Section VI considers another example. Section VII looks at data on earnings rates to suggest the relevance of alternative empirical assumptions on the distribution of skills. Some closing remarks are in Section VIII.

---

* Department of Economics, Massachusetts Institute of Technology, Cambridge, MA 02139. I am grateful to Jon Gruber for suggesting the inclusion of data in this paper and providing me with the figures presented below, and to Marcus Berliant, Svetlana Danilkina, Jim Mirrlees, Eytan Sheshinski, Jay Wilson, and anonymous reviewers for helpful suggestions. I am also grateful to the National Science Foundation for research support under Grant SBR-9307876.

[1] If part of the population has potential income below per capita government expenditures, then it is impossible to finance government spending without some distorting taxes. This paper assumes that concern for the income of the poor is large enough that there is a positive transfer to those with zero income.

I. Review of the Literature

Formal results about the optimal income tax are fairly limited. (For recent expositions, see Matti Tuomala, 1990 Ch. 6 or Gareth D. Myles, 1995 Ch. 5.) Assuming that labor supply can be continuously adjusted, there is no gain from having marginal tax rates above 100 percent since no one will have such a tax at the margin. That is, the same outcome can be achieved with taxes no greater than 100 percent. It is usually assumed that preferences are such that consumption is an increasing function of the wage. Then, earnings will be nondecreasing in skill. It then follows that the optimal tax structure has nonnegative marginal rates (Mirrlees, 1971) and positive rates in the interior of the income distribution (Jesus K. Seade, 1982).

Assuming that there is a finite maximum to the skill distribution, the marginal tax rate should be zero at the income level of the top skill (Efraim Sadka, 1976; Seade, 1977). The argument for this result is quite intuitive. Assume this were not the case, then, extending the tax function to higher incomes with a zero tax rate would lead the top earner to work more, raising social welfare without losing any tax revenue. However, this condition need not convey information about optimal taxes over any significant region of incomes — the optimal rates need not approach zero until very close to the top. This point has been made by the numerical calculations in Tuomala (1984).

At the bottom of the skill distribution, in the presence of optimal taxes, there may or may not be an atom of individuals doing no work. If everyone works, then the argument for a zero marginal tax rate carries over (Seade, 1977). However, if there is an atom of nonworkers, the optimal tax has a positive marginal tax rate at the level where earnings begin (Udo Ebert, 1992). This latter case seems empirically more relevant.

In addition to these analytical results, presentation of the first-order condition for optimal taxes has generally been accompanied by observations on the factors leading to high or low rates, ceteris paribus. Considerable effort has gone into simulations, starting with that by Mirrlees. In his simulation Mirrlees assumed a utility function $u = \log[x] + \log[1 - y]$, where x is consumption and y is labor supply (in percentage terms), a social evaluation $G(u) = -\exp(-bu)/b$ ($b > 0$), and a lognormal distribution of skills. He concluded (p. 206) that "Perhaps the most striking feature of the results is the closeness to linearity of the tax schedules." As seen in the survey in Tuomala (1990), similar results followed with some other simulations, but some simulations have shown other patterns, including a significantly inverse-U shaped pattern (e.g., Ravi Kanbur and Tuomala, 1994). As will be clarified below, simulation results are sensitive to both the utility function and the family of distributions of skills assumed, opening up the possibility of different conclusions.

II. Optimal Income Tax Problem

The Mirrlees optimal income tax problem is the maximization of the integral over the population of a concave function of individual utilities, subject to an aggregate budget constraint and subject to the constraint that individuals optimize in their choice of labor supply given the relationship between work and after-tax income. The only difference across individuals in the model is a difference in skills, with an individual of skill n having a marginal product equal to n. The model is a one-period model with only labor income. It is assumed that the government can observe income received but not hours worked or skill. Denoting consumption of someone with skill n by $x(n)$, labor (in percentage terms) by $y(n)$, and the concave utility function by $u(x, y)$, the social objective function can be stated as

$$(1) \quad \int_{n_0}^{n_1} G\{u[x(n), y(n)]\} f(n) \, dn,$$

where $G(u)$ is an increasing and strictly concave function of utility, with G independent of n, and the distribution of skills is written as $F(n)$, with density $f(n)$. It is assumed that the distribution of skills is single-peaked, with a mode at n_m. The density is assumed to be positive and continuous between the bottom and the top skill levels, n_0 and n_1.

The resource constraint on this maximization can be stated in terms of output—that aggregate consumption be less than aggregate production minus government expenditures, E:

$$(2) \quad \int_{n_0}^{n_1} x(n)f(n)\,dn$$

$$\leq \int_{n_0}^{n_1} ny(n)f(n)\,dn - E.$$

This constraint can be stated alternatively in terms of taxes. Denoting taxes as a function of earnings as $T[ny(n)]$, consumption equals the difference between earnings and taxes, $x(n) = ny(n) - T[ny(n)]$. In this case, the government budget constraint is that taxes cover government expenditures:

$$(3) \quad \int_{n_0}^{n_1} T[ny(n)]f(n)\,dn \geq E.$$

That the resource constraint can be stated equivalently in terms of government budget balance or in terms of aggregate supply and demand is a consequence of Walras Law.

In addition to the resource constraint, there is an incentive compatibility constraint. The government observes earnings, not hours worked or skill. Thus the government is restricted to setting taxes as a function only of earnings. The incentive compatibility constraint is that the selected labor supply, $y(n)$, maximizes utility, given the tax function, $u\{ny(n) - T[ny(n)], y(n)\}$. The relevant part of the tax function is just the part that is selected by someone—taxes can be set arbitrarily high at earnings levels that no one chooses with the optimal tax structure. Thus the incentive compatibility constraint can be stated in the familiar form that a worker with skill n does not prefer to imitate the earnings of a worker with a different skill level:

$$(4) \quad u\{ny(n) - T[ny(n)], y(n)\} \geq$$

$$u\{n'y(n') - T[n'y(n')], n'y(n')/n\}$$

for all n and n'.

That is, someone of skill n would have to work n'/n times as much as someone with skill n' in order to have the same earnings level.

This paper will concentrate on the special case where there are no income effects on labor supply.[2] That is, it is assumed that utility is linear in consumption (referred to as quasi-linear):

$$(5) \quad u(x, y) = x + v(1 - y)$$

$$= ny - T(ny) + v(1 - y),$$

where v is assumed to be strictly concave.[3] This assumption seems appropriate at very high income levels, since people at the top of the income distribution are likely to leave large estates—with a linear utility of bequests, neither consumption nor earnings vary with the exact level of estate. (The receipt of such bequests is not part of the model.) In addition, this assumption removes a source of considerable complication in tax analysis. In the presence of distorting taxes, income effects imply that lump-sum taxes have efficiency effects since they change distorted labor supply decisions.

This problem has some complexity in the derivation of the first-order condition for an optimal tax function, but is familiar from a number of mechanism design problems.[4] The simplest way to proceed is to replace the incentive compatibility conditions, (4), with the first-order condition for individual choice, which, from (5), can be written:

$$(6) \quad v'[1 - y(n)] = n\{1 - T'[ny(n)]\},$$

where T' is the marginal tax rate. For later use, it is convenient to note that for the quasi-linear utility function the elasticity of labor supply

---

[2] For a discussion of this case with a constant elasticity of labor supply, see Anthony B. Atkinson (1990). The complementary case where utility is linear in leisure has been studied; see Stefan Lollivier and Jean-Charles Rochet (1983) and John A. Weymark (1987).
[3] I assume that $G'[v(1)]$ is infinite, so that someone doing no work is given positive consumption and the non-negativity constraint on consumption can be ignored.
[4] For an exposition of the mechanism design problem, see Drew Fudenberg and Jean Tirole, 1991 Ch. 7.

evaluated at the chosen labor supply of a worker of skill n, $e(n)$, satisfies

(7) $e(n) = -v'[1 - y(n)]$

$\div \{y(n)v''[1 - y(n)]\}$.

Since the wage equals the skill level, this is the elasticity with respect to the wage, evaluated at the labor supply level that is chosen by someone with skill n.

More complicated than deriving the first-order condition is the problem of checking when the first-order condition does indeed characterize an optimum. The complication comes from the need to check that individual labor supplies satisfying the first-order conditions are globally optimal choices, and not just the solution to a first-order condition. This problem arises since the budget set is not convex when marginal tax rates are declining over some income levels. For any particular economy, one can check whether individual labor supplies are optimal. This issue raises the possibility that with the optimal tax, the distribution of skills results in a distribution of incomes that either has bunching at some income level (an atom of workers choosing the same income level) or a gap in the distribution of incomes. (Bunching at zero income or a gap between zero and the lowest positive income are not issues for the interpretation of the optimal tax structure below.) I do not explore this issue for this particular class of preferences, but proceed with analysis of the first-order condition; the analysis holds where the equilibrium distribution of incomes has no bunching and no gap, since generically the equation is a necessary condition for the optimal tax where this is true.

The first-order condition for the optimal tax can be calculated by specializing the condition in Mirrlees (1971) for quasi-linear preferences or deriving it directly, as is done in the Appendix. As usually written, the condition is:

(8) $p(n - v')f$

$= [(v' - yv'')/n]$

$\times \left[\int_n^{n_1} (p - G') dF\right],$

where p is the Lagrange multiplier on the government's budget constraint and the functions v and G are evaluated at the appropriate labor supplies and consumption levels.

It is convenient to use the elasticity of labor supply and the marginal condition for individual choice, (6), to rewrite (8) as

(9) $T'/(1 - T')$

$= [(e^{-1} + 1)/n]$

$\times \left[\int_n^{n_1} (p - G') dF\right] \Big/ [pf].$

Multiplying and dividing (9) by $(1 - F)$ to turn the integral into an average term, (9) can be rewritten as:

(10) $T'/(1 - T') = A(n)B(n)C(n)$

where $A(n) = e^{-1}(n) + 1$;

$B(n) = \int_n^{n_1} (p - G') dF / \{p[1 - F(n)]\}$;

$C(n) = [1 - F(n)]/[nf(n)]$.

The analysis below examines these three functions, $A(n)$, $B(n)$, and $C(n)$, under alternative assumptions on the functions $e(n), f(n)$ and $G(u)$.

The absence of income effects allows an intuitive grasp of the factors that determine the optimal tax structure. Increasing the marginal tax rate affecting some skill level involves an increase in the deadweight burden for people at this skill level. Thus, the optimal marginal tax rate at some income level depends on the elasticity of labor supply at that income level, since this is important for marginal distortions. Increasing the marginal tax rate also transfers income from all individuals with higher skills to the government, without changing the distortions of their labor supplies. The weights on these two elements depend on the ratio of individuals with skills above this level to individuals with skills at this level and on the level of skill which links the tax on hours to the tax on income. This intuition is displayed in equation (10), where the first-order condition for the optimal income tax is written as a product of these three terms.

The same approach to signing the change in marginal tax rates can be used with the assumption of additive preferences, $u_{xy} = 0$, without the further assumption of quasi-linear preferences. The mathematical conditions for signing the change in the marginal tax rate are similar, although the economic interpretation of the conditions is more complex. $A(n)$ no longer depends only on the compensated elasticity of labor supply, but also has a term involving the second derivative of the utility-of-consumption, which is no longer assumed to be zero. Thus different economic assumptions are needed to sign the mathematical expressions.

III. Increasing Marginal Tax Rates

I turn now to analysis of (10), the first-order condition for the optimal income tax in the presence of quasi-linear preferences. In general, the variation in the elasticity of labor supply with skill will depend on the tax function, since taxes will affect the level of labor supplied and the elasticity varies with the quantity of labor supplied. One obvious exception, making for simpler analysis, is that of a constant elasticity of labor supply. In this case the utility of leisure satisfies $v(1 - y) = c\{1 - [1 - (1 - y)]^k\} = c(1 - y^k)$ for some constants c and k.

LEMMA A: *If $v(1 - y) = c\{1 - [1 - (1 - y)]^k\} = c(1 - y^k)$, then $A(n)$ is a constant.*

With quasi-linear preferences, a uniform transfer from the government to all workers has no effect on labor supply, and so no extra impact on the government budget. The welfare impact of such a transfer is the average of G' over the entire population. Thus one can conclude that the Lagrangian on the government budget constraint, p, is equal to the average of G':

(11) $$p = \int_{n_0}^{n_1} G'(n) f(n) \, dn.$$

Thus, $B(n_0)$ is equal to zero.

Given the incentive compatibility constraint, utility must be nondecreasing in skill and increasing where earnings are positive, since a worker can always have the same consumption as a worker with lower skill while doing less work, provided the level of work is positive. That is, above the skills at which there is no work, utility is increasing in n. With G a concave function, G' is then decreasing in n. Since $B(n)$ is the average of $[p - G']$ from the level n to the top of the skill distribution, $B(n)$ is increasing in n.[5]

Since p is equal to the average of G' and G' is nonincreasing, there is a critical value of n, denoted n_C, at which G' is equal to p:

(12) $$G'[u(n_C)] = p.$$

If n_C occurs at a level of skill where there is positive work, then n_C is unique; otherwise n_C is set equal to the highest skill at which there is no work. The level of n_C is endogenous, varying with both the structure of the economy and the nature of the social welfare function. To simplify the statement of results, analysis is restricted to economies where this critical level is below the modal level of skill:

(13) $$n_C < n_m.$$

This seems like the more interesting case, assuming that the mode of skills is near the median and the government would like to redistribute toward a fraction of the labor force well below one-half.

I note that $[1 - F(n)]B(n)$ is increasing in n up to n_C and then decreasing in n. These results are summarized as:

LEMMA B: *$B(n)$ is increasing in n. $[1 - F(n)]B(n)$ decreases in n for $n > n_C$.*

I turn now to the shape of the distribution of skills. Given the assumption of a single-

---

[5] Formally, differentiating $B(n)$, the derivative has the same sign as the average of $(p - G')$ from n to n_1 minus the value $[p - G'(n)]$. Since G' is decreasing in n, this difference is positive.

peaked density of skills, $nC(n)$ is decreasing in n for n below the modal level, n_m. For values of n above the modal level, the shape of $C(n)$ depends on the family of distributions assumed for skills. With a Pareto distribution above the modal skill level, (i.e., the density is proportional to $1/n^{1+a}$ for $a > 0$), then $C(n)$ is a constant above the modal skill level.

LEMMA C: *For $n < n_m$, $nC(n)$ is decreasing in n. For $n > n_m$, $C(n)$ is constant if $F(n)$ is the Pareto distribution above n_m.*

One can now put these lemmas together to identify sufficient conditions for marginal tax rates to be increasing with income for incomes above the modal level. Where all three of $A(n)$, $B(n)$, and $C(n)$ are nondecreasing and at least one is increasing, then marginal tax rates are increasing.

PROPOSITION 1: *Marginal tax rates are increasing above the modal skill if, above this skill, the elasticity of labor supply is constant and the distribution of skills is Pareto.*

With the conditions in Proposition 1, $A(n)$ and $C(n)$ are constants, so that $T'/(1 - T')$ varies with n as $B(n)$ varies with n. With $B(n)$ increasing, so too is T'. The result carries over if the elasticity of labor supply falls with skill at the equilibrium labor supplies. Similarly, it is sufficient to have a distribution of skills such that $[1 - F(n)]/[nf(n)]$ is increasing. Moreover, the result of rising tax rates will hold for part of the skill distribution (above the mode) if the conditions are met for that part; one does not need conditions on the entire distribution.

IV. Asymptotic Marginal Tax Rates

With a known finite top to the distribution of skills, the optimal marginal tax rate is zero at the top of the income distribution. As noted in the review of the literature and is clear from the argument behind Proposition 1, this need not imply that rates approach zero until very close to the top. Thus it is natural to consider the case of an unbounded distribution of skills and to consider the behavior of the optimal marginal tax rate as skills rise without limit.

In addition to assumptions on the distribution of skills and the elasticity of labor supply, the shape of the social welfare of individual utility, $G(u)$, needs to be examined. One possibility is that the marginal welfare weight of consumption of those at the top tends to zero as skill rises without limit[6]. For example, this is the case in the example in Mirrlees (1971) where $G = -\exp(-bu)/b$ ($b > 0$) and $u = a\log(x) + \log(1 - y)$. Similarly, it is the case in Martin Feldstein's (1985) study of social security, where $G = u$ and $u = \log(x)$. If G' goes to zero as n rises without limit, then $B(n)$ goes to 1. Alternatively, one might assume that G' has a positive lower bound which is approached as n rises without limit. For example, Atkinson (1990) considers the case of a "charitable Conservative" position, where the marginal welfare weight of consumption takes on two values—a high one for "poor" people and a low one for "nonpoor" people. I denote by g the ratio of the lower bound on G' to the Lagrangian on the government budget constraint, which is equal to the average of G' in the entire population. Thus, $B(n)$ converges to $1 - g$ as skill rises without limit.

Assuming a constant elasticity of labor supply, e, and a Pareto distribution for skills above the mode with coefficient a, so that $C(n)$ equals $1/a$, (10) becomes

(14) $\quad T'/(1 - T') = (e^{-1} + 1)B(n)/a.$

Solving for T' and taking the limit as n rises, one has:

PROPOSITION 2: *Assuming a Pareto distribution of skills above the modal skill and a constant elasticity of labor supply, as skill rises without limit the optimal tax rate converges to*

(15) $\quad T' = (e^{-1} + 1)(1 - g)$

$\qquad \div [a + (e^{-1} + 1)(1 - g)].$

---

[6] In this case, the tax rate tends to the revenue-maximizing rate, since, in the limit, the only effect of taxes on welfare is through the budget constraint.

TABLE 1—ASYMPTOTIC MARGINAL TAX RATES

	$g = 0$			$g = 0.25$			$g = 0.5$		
$a =$	0.5	1.5	5.0	0.5	1.5	5.0	0.5	1.5	5.0
e									
0.2	92	80	55	90	75	47	86	67	38
0.5	86	67	38	82	60	31	75	50	23

Notes: Asymptotic marginal tax rates, in percent, with a constant elasticity of labor supply, e, a Pareto distribution of skills with parameter a, and a ratio of social marginal utility with infinite income to average social marginal utility of g.

To examine the implications for the taxation of very high earners, values need to be selected for a, e, and g. Identifying skill with the wage yields an elasticity based on adjusting hours of labor supply; identifying skill with an underlying ability suggests a larger elasticity since education is also variable. With a zero income effect, compensated and ordinary labor supply elasticities are the same. Presumably it is the compensated elasticity that one would want to use for illustrative purposes. Recognizing that I am seeking an elasticity for high earners, looking at the elasticity for prime-age males provides an approximation. Based on the survey by John Pencavel (1986), calculations are done for a range of elasticities from 0.2 to 0.5. A range of g from 0 to 0.5 seems very wide. For the coefficient of the Pareto distribution, using tax data Daniel R. Feenberg and James M. Poterba (1993) find a varying between 0.5 and 1.5 over the years 1951–1990 for the incomes of the top 0.5 percent of the population. The calculations reported below suggest the possibility of a considerably higher value for the distribution of skills, perhaps as large as 5. Values of the asymptotic marginal tax rate [from (15)] are shown in Table 1. Thus I conclude that there is a case for high marginal tax rates in the quasi-linear Mirrlees model with plausible empirical parameters.

V. Decreasing Marginal Tax Rates

In considering decreasing marginal tax rates, I consider only the levels of skills above n_C, the level at which G' equals p. At skill levels above n_C, it would be desirable to transfer resources away from this skill level (if it could be done costlessly). It is now convenient to work with equation (9), which I rewrite

(9) $\quad T'/(1 - T')$

$$= [e^{-1} + 1]\left[\int_n^{n_1} (p - G')\, dF\right]$$

$$\div [pnf(n)].$$

As noted in Lemma B, at skill levels above n_C, the integral in (9) is decreasing with skill. Below the mode, the density is rising and so $1/[nf(n)]$ is falling with skill. Thus with a constant or rising elasticity of labor supply, the marginal tax rate is declining with skill. This argument also goes through above the mode where $nf(n)$ is rising with skill. This is summarized in:

PROPOSITION 3: *Above the critical skill level, n_C, marginal tax rates are decreasing where the elasticity of labor supply is constant and the distribution of skills has $nf(n)$ rising with skill.*

While one would expect $nf(n)$ to be increasing in n just above the modal skill, empirically, this seems unlikely at high skills, as is indicated in the data discussed below.

One can also use (9) to compare tax rates at two income levels above n_C, on either side of the modal skill and such that the density is equal at the two points. With G' less than p at the lower of the two skill levels being compared, the marginal tax rate would be higher at the lower income level with a constant or rising elasticity of labor supply. This is summarized in:

PROPOSITION 4: *Above the critical skill level, n_C, marginal tax rates are higher at the lower of two skill levels that have the same density and the same the elasticity of labor supply at the chosen labor supplies.*

Combining results, one can see the pattern of tax rates when the density of skills is single-peaked (and such that the workers with the modal skill work and have G' less than p in equilibrium). With a constant elasticity of labor supply and the Pareto distribution of skills where the density is falling, the pattern of marginal tax rates is U-shaped above n_C, with the minimum of marginal rates occurring at the modal skill. Moreover, marginal rates are higher at the lower income levels. Plausibly, the density of skills does not have a kink at the mode, but changes smoothly from rising to declining as a Pareto density. Then, with the conditions in Proposition 3 the minimum of the tax rate (over the range above n_C) occurs above the modal skill. It is worth reiterating that the range with declining marginal rates need not begin at zero earned income.

VI. Another Example

The assumption of a constant elasticity of labor supply relates the optimal tax to a familiar concept in the analysis of deadweight burdens. By moving the term "n" from $C(n)$ to $A(n)$, one finds another example with similar conclusions. Consider the logarithmic case, $v(1 - y) = \log(1 - y)$. In this case, the elasticity of labor supply is equal to $(1 - y)/y$. Thus one has:

LEMMA A': *If $v(1 - y) = \log(1 - y)$, then $A(n) = n(1 - T')$.*

If, above the modal skill level, the distribution is the exponential distribution, then $nC(n)$ is a constant.

LEMMA C': *For $n < n_m$, $nC(n)$ is decreasing in n. For $n > n_m$, $nC(n)$ is constant if $F(n)$ is the exponential distribution above n_m.*

I can now put together Lemmas A', B, and C'.

PROPOSITION 1': *Marginal tax rates are increasing above the modal skill if, above this skill, the utility-of-leisure is logarithmic and the distribution of skills is exponential.*

For Proposition 1', it is noted that $T'/(1 - T')^2$ varies with n as $B(n)$ does. With $B(n)$ increasing, so too is T'. As above, from the arguments that led to Proposition 1', one can see that the result carries over if, at the equilibrium labor supplies, the elasticity of labor supply falls with skill more than in the stated condition. Similarly, it is sufficient to have a distribution of skills such that $[1 - F(n)]/f(n)$ rises. Moreover, the result of rising tax rates will hold for part of the skill distribution (above the mode) if the conditions are met for that part; one does not need conditions on the entire distribution.

For the case just analyzed, the asymptotic marginal rate is calculated. With a logarithmic utility-of-leisure function and an exponential distribution of skills (above the mode) with coefficient b, (10) becomes:

$$(16) \quad T'/(1 - T')^2 = B(n)(1 - F)/f$$
$$= B(n)/b.$$

Solving for T' and taking the limit, one has:

PROPOSITION 2': *Assuming an exponential distribution of skills above the modal skill with parameter b and logarithmic utility-of-leisure, as skill rises without limit the optimal tax rate converges to*

$$(17) \quad T' = 1 - [(b'^2 + 4b')^{1/2} - b']/2,$$

where $b' = b/(1 - g)$.

For g equal to 0 and $(1 - F)/f$, that is, $1/b$, of 5, 10, and 15 (see Figures 1 and 2), the optimal marginal tax rate tends to 64, 73, and 77 percent. For g equal to 0.5 and the same values of $1/b$, the optimal marginal tax rate tends to 54, 64, and 70 percent.

Similarly, one can examine conditions for declining marginal tax rates with the log-

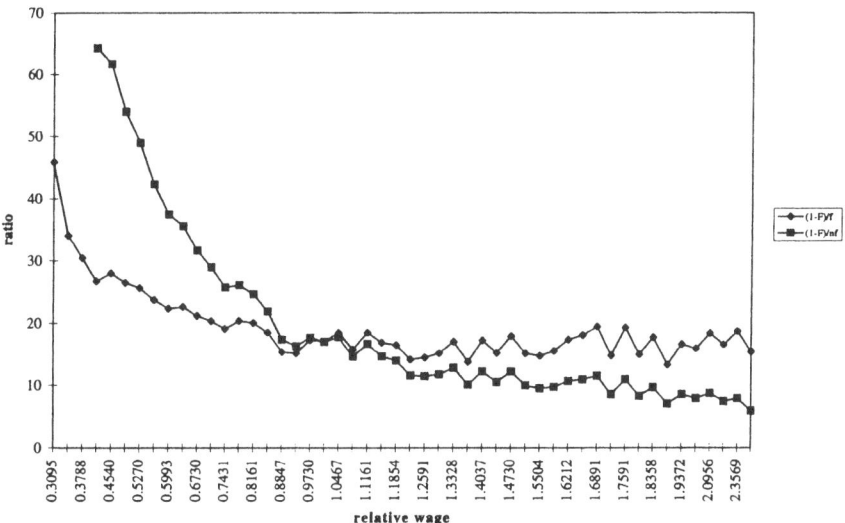

FIGURE 1. RATIOS $[1 - F(n)]/f(n)$ AND $[1 - F(n)]/[nf(n)]$ CALCULATED FROM RELATIVE WAGES

arithmic utility-of-leisure. In this case, (9) becomes:

(18) $\quad T'/(1 - T')^2$

$$= \left[\int_n^{n_1} (p - G') \, dF \right] \bigg/ [pf].$$

From Lemma B, it can be concluded that the tax rate is declining above n_C and below the mode.

PROPOSITION 3': *Between the critical skill level, n_C, and the mode, n_m, marginal tax rates are decreasing if the utility-of-leisure is logarithmic.*

Similarly, from (18) one can conclude:

PROPOSITION 4': *Above the critical skill level, n_c, marginal tax rates are higher at the lower of two skill levels that have the same density if the utility-of-leisure is logarithmic.*

VII. Data on the Distribution of Skills

While a careful attempt to fit this model to available data is beyond the scope of this paper, it does seem interesting to examine the distribution of wages. For this purpose, calculations have been done using the March 1992 CPS. This survey asked individuals for annual earnings in 1991, as well as weeks worked and typical hours per week. From these numbers one can calculate an implied average wage.[7] Using these wages, calculations were made of the mean wage per cell; the number of observations per cell, adjusted by interval width in order to be proportional to the density; and the number of observations with higher wages. Approximately 17 percent of the sample report wages below $1 or no work and are omitted. In order to have reasonable cell sizes, the wage intervals are first $0.50, but are expanded above a wage of $26. As expected, a smoothing of the data would show a single-peaked distribution, as assumed in the analysis above. In Figure 1 is shown the ratios $(1 - F)/f$ and $(1 - F)/(nf)$, where n is measured as the wage relative to the mean wage. Because the series are very noisy, the graph is a centered three-cell moving average.

---

[7] No attempt was made to consider both earners in a two-earner family or wages of single females.

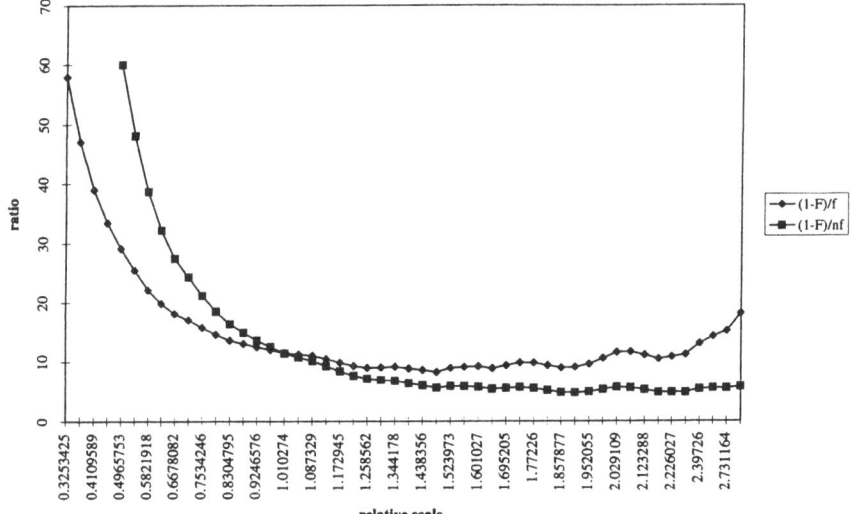

FIGURE 2. RATIOS $[1 - F(n)]/f(n)$ AND $[1 - F(n)]/[nf(n)]$ CALCULATED FROM RELATIVE SKILLS

For readability, the lowest wages are dropped from the graph since the ratios are very large. The figure shows sharply falling values of $(1 - F)/f$ through the range where the density is first rising and then roughly flat, that is, up to a wage of roughly $13, a little below the mean of $13.70. Beyond this point $(1 - F)/f$ is roughly constant at a value around 15. This implies a downward trend in $(1 - F)/(nf)$. A constant value of $(1 - F)/f$ is consistent with an exponential distribution over this range of values.

With a longer time horizon than one year, one would consider education to be an endogenous variable somewhat responsive to tax incentives. One might also be interested in the distribution of skills within a cohort. Thus a further calculation was done by regressing the log of the wage on education, age, and age squared, and plotting the exponentiated residuals. In Figure 2 are the same curves for this distribution as shown in Figure 1 for the distribution of wages (except that a moving average was not used). This distribution shows a fatter tail than the distribution of wages, with $(1 - F)/f$ rising and $(1 - F)/(nf)$ roughly constant for the top 15 percent of the skill distribution. A constant value of $(1 - F)/(nf)$ is consistent with a Pareto distribution over this range of values.

VIII. Concluding Remarks

The absence of income effects allows an intuitive grasp of the factors that determine the optimal tax structure. Increasing the marginal tax rate affecting some skill level involves an increase in the deadweight burden for people at this skill level. Thus, the optimal marginal tax rate at some income level depends on the elasticity of labor supply at that income level, since this is important for marginal distortions. Increasing the marginal tax rate also transfers income from all individuals with higher skills to the government, without changing the distortions of their labor supplies. The weights on these two elements depend on the ratio of individuals with skills above this level to individuals with skills at this level and on the level of skill which links the tax on hours to the tax on income. This intuition is displayed in the equations above, where the first-order condition for the optimal income tax is written with a product of these three terms.

The rewriting of the first-order condition also highlights the critical role of the assumed family of distributions for the upper tail of skills, as opposed to just the value of the parameters. With the Pareto distribution, $(1 - F)/(nf)$ is a constant and the change in the marginal tax rate reflects the rate of decline in social marginal utility of income as well as the change in labor supply elasticity with skill. With the exponential distribution, $(1 - F)/(nf)$ declines at the rate $1/n$. Thus either the elasticity of labor supply or the social marginal utility of income needs to be falling sufficiently rapidly to have constant or rising marginal tax rates. In the simulations in Mirrlees (1971), it was assumed that the distribution of skills was lognormal, so that $(1 - F)/(nf)$ declines at the rate $1/\log(n)$. Presumably the relatively constant marginal tax rate in the those simulations would have had a different shape with a different assumed family of distributions. Exploration of the shape of this distribution is clearly important for the normative case for different degrees of income tax progressivity.

There is not a simple route between the Mirrlees model and policy implications for annual income taxes levied repeatedly on families and covering both capital and labor incomes. The assumption of a zero income elasticity of labor supply and the limited information on both the shape of the skill distribution and the pattern of elasticities of labor supply by skill level would limit inferences even if there were a simple route. Nevertheless there are some lessons from the analysis. The sharp fall in $(1 - F)/f$ as skills approach the mode of the skill distribution from below seems highly relevant, especially if one wants to redistribute from people near the mode, rather than to them. This finding on the shape of an optimal (negative) income tax seems relevant in thinking about the phaseout of the earned income tax credit, and, possibly, welfare reform. That is, labor supply depends on the net return to earnings, which, in turn, depends on both the income tax and the phaseout of income-tested benefits. The presence of high marginal tax rates in the region of phaseout of benefits is not necessarily a basis for criticism of the programs—the optimal program may well have such a shape because of the advantage of higher marginal rates over a shorter range of skills where the skill density is large and rising. In other words, a sizable implicit marginal tax rate where benefits are being phased out is consistent with the U-shaped pattern of marginal rates and may well be optimal.

Second, this model confirms the implication of Mirrlees' calculations that the optimality of a zero tax rate at the highest income level is not a finding that sheds much light on optimal taxes, especially in the absence of knowledge of exactly where the top is. That is, if one replaced an unbounded distribution of skills by a bounded one with the same distribution up to some level and a concentration of skills at the highest levels, the result of rising marginal tax rates continues to hold until the concentration at the top is reached. There is no need for tax rates to decline slowly toward zero as one approaches the absolute top of the skill distribution.

Third, the sensitivity of the pattern of marginal rates to the measure of skill seems relevant, although different formulations of "skill" will be associated with different estimates of the elasticities of labor supply as well as different estimates of the shape of the distribution of skills. This analysis emphasizes the importance of the shape of the distribution of skills for optimal tax rates.

APPENDIX: HEURISTIC DERIVATION OF THE OPTIMAL TAX FIRST-ORDER CONDITION

Using just the first-order condition for labor supply for the quasi-linear utility function as a constraint, the optimal tax problem is

$$(A1) \quad \text{Max} \int_{n_0}^{n_1} G\{u[x(n), y(n)]\} f(n) \, dn,$$

$$\text{subject to:} \int_{n_0}^{n_1} x(n) f(n) \, dn$$

$$\leq \int_{n_0}^{n_1} ny(n) f(n) \, dn - E;$$

$$v'[1 - y(n)] = n(1 - T'[ny(n)]).$$

With $x(n) = ny(n) - T[ny(n)]$, and using the first-order condition for labor supply, the change in consumption with skill satisfies:

(A2) $\quad x'(n) = y(n)(1 - T')$

$\qquad\qquad + n(1 - T')y'(n)$

$\qquad = [y(n) + ny'(n)]v'/n.$

With the quasi-linear utility function, one can calculate the derivative of u with respect to n:

(A3) $\quad u'(n) = x'(n) - v'y'(n)$

$\qquad = y(n)v'/n.$

Treating $u(n)$ as a state variable and $y(n)$ as a control variable, the optimal tax problem can be rewritten as

(A4) $\quad \text{Max} \int_{n_0}^{n_1} G[u(n)]f(n)\,dn,$

subject to:

$\int_{n_0}^{n_1} \{u(n) - v[1 - y(n)]\}f(n)\,dn$

$\leq \int_{n_0}^{n_1} ny(n)f(n)\,dn - E;$

$u'(n) = y(n)v'[1 - y(n)]/n.$

Forming a Hamiltonian for this expression,

(A5) $\quad H = \{G[u(n)] - p[u(n)$

$\qquad\qquad - v[1 - y(n)] - ny(n)]\}$

$\qquad\qquad \times f(n) + h(n)y(n)$

$\qquad\qquad \times v'[1 - y(n)]/n,$

where p and $h(n)$ are multipliers. The derivative of h is equal to minus the partial derivative of the Hamiltonian with respect to u:

(A6) $\quad h'(n) = -\{G'[u(n)] - p\}f(n).$

Maximizing the Hamiltonian with respect to $y(n)$,

(A7) $\quad -p\{n - v'[1 - y(n)]\}f(n)$

$\qquad = h(n)\{v'[1 - y(n)]$

$\qquad\qquad - y(n)v''[1 - y(n)]\}/n.$

Recognizing that $h(n_1)$ is equal to zero, (A6) can be integrated from n to n_1 to have an expression for $h(n)$. Substituting in (A7), one then has the first-order condition in the text, (8).

REFERENCES

Atkinson, Anthony B. "Public Economics and the Economic Public." *European Economic Review*, May 1990, *34*(2–3), pp. 225–48.

Ebert, Udo. "A Reexamination of the Optimal Nonlinear Income Tax." *Journal of Public Economics*, October 1992, *49*(1), pp. 47–73.

Feenberg, Daniel R. and Poterba, James M. "Income Inequality and the Incomes of Very High-Income Taxpayers: Evidence from Tax Returns," in James Poterba, ed., *Tax policy and the economy*. Cambridge, MA: MIT Press, 1993, pp. 145–77.

Feldstein, Martin. "The Optimal Level of Social Security Benefits." *Quarterly Journal of Economics*, May 1985, *100*(2), pp. 303–20.

Financial Times. "The Markets: Still Waiting for Answers on Tax—Economics Notebook." September 11, 1995, p. 24.

Fudenberg, Drew and Tirole, Jean. *Game theory.* Cambridge, MA: MIT Press, 1991.

Kanbur, Ravi and Tuomala, Matti. "Inherent Inequality and the Optimal Graduation of Marginal Tax Rates." *Scandinavian Journal of Economics*, June 1994, *96*(2), pp. 275–82.

Lollivier, Stefan and Rochet, Jean-Charles. "Bunching and Second-Order Conditions: A Note on Optimal Tax Theory." *Journal of Economic Theory*, December 1983, *31*(2), pp. 392–400.

Mirrlees, James A. "An Exploration in the Theory of Optimum Income Taxation." *Review of Economic Studies*, April 1971, *38*(114), pp. 175–208.

Myles, Gareth D. *Public economics.* Cambridge: Cambridge University Press, 1995.

Pencavel, John. "Labor Supply of Men: A Survey," in Orley Ashenfelter and Richard Layard, eds., *Handbook of labor economics.* Amsterdam: North-Holland, 1986, pp. 3–102.

Sadka, Efraim. "On Income Distribution, Incentive Effects and Optimal Income Taxation." *Review of Economic Studies*, June 1976, *43*(2), pp. 261–67.

Seade, Jesus K. "On the Shape of Optimal Tax Schedules." *Journal of Public Economics*, April 1977, *7*(2), pp. 203–35.

———. "On the Sign of the Optimum Marginal Income Tax." *Review of Economic Studies*, October 1982, *49*(4), pp. 637–43.

Tuomala, Matti. "On the Optimal Income Taxation: Some Further Numerical Results." *Journal of Public Economics*, April 1984, *23*(3), pp. 351–66.

———. *Optimal income tax and redistribution.* Oxford: Clarendon Press, 1990.

Weymark, John A. "Comparative Static Properties of Optimal Nonlinear Income Taxes." *Econometrica*, September 1987, *55*(5), 1165–85.

THE DESIGN OF TAX STRUCTURE: DIRECT VERSUS INDIRECT TAXATION*

A.B. ATKINSON

University of Essex, Wivenhoe Park, Colchester, England

J.E. STIGLITZ

Stanford University, Stanford, CA 94305, U.S.A.

Revised version received February 1976

1. Introduction

The recent literature on optimal taxation may be seen as attempting to clarify the structure of the arguments advanced to support changes in the tax system, tracing the implications of taxes and quantifying (analytically) the trade-offs between the various objectives of tax policy. This literature has examined the optimal structure for particular types of taxation taken in isolation, such as the optimal rates of excise tax and the optimal income tax schedule. Our purpose, on the other hand, is to provide a broader framework and to consider the interaction between different kinds of taxation. To illustrate this, we reexamine the age-old question of direct versus indirect taxation and the relationship of these taxes to the goals of efficiency, vertical equity and horizontal equity.

After describing in section 2 the general framework of the analysis, and arguing that any treatment of the choice of tax structures must be centrally concerned with distributional considerations, we begin in section 3 with the extension of the classic Ramsey formula for optimal excise taxation to include vertical equity objectives. This was considered by Diamond and Mirrlees (1971), but the results

---

*This is a revised and condensed version of the paper given at the ISPE meeting under the title 'Alternative approaches to the distribution of income.' This in turn was based on part II of 'The structure of indirect taxation,' Cowles Foundation, 1970 [part I appeared as Atkinson and Stiglitz (1972)] and on the draft of chapter 15 of *Lectures on Public Economics*, University of Essex, 1971. Parts of the paper have been presented by the first author at seminars at the universities of Essex, Harvard and Namur, and by the second author at Chicago, National Bureau of Economic Research–West and Stanford, and they are grateful to participants in these seminars for their helpful comments. This work was supported in part by National Science Foundation Grant SOC74-22182 at the Institute for Mathematical Studies in the Social Sciences at Stanford University, and in part by the Guggenheim and Ford Foundations.

given here are in a rather different form.[1] The rest of the paper is concerned with the case where the government can employ both income and excise taxes. In section 4 it is shown that the existence of an optimal linear income tax may lead to quite different results. Section 5 introduces the possibility of a general non-linear income tax, and argues that under a relatively wide class of conditions – separability between leisure and consumption – the optimal tax system can rely solely on income taxation. This brings out clearly the importance of considering simultaneously the whole range of tax instruments open to the government. Finally, section 6 examines the relationship between vertical and horizontal equity, and the implications of differences in tastes.

2. The basic framework for taxation

The general problem of taxation of individuals may be posed as follows. There are a large number of people in any economy who differ with respect to a number of characteristics, in particular their endowments and tastes. On the basis of certain ethical premises, it is decided that individuals with different characteristics should pay varying amounts of tax. If we could observe these characteristics costlessly and perfectly, that would be the end of the analysis: we would simply impose a lump sum tax on individuals, with the amount differing according to their characteristics. The theory of optimal taxation would then be concerned simply with deriving, on the basis of the specified ethical premises, what the functional relationship between characteristics and taxes 'ought to be.'[2]

It is the difficulties associated with observing characteristics which make the theory of taxation an interesting and difficult problem. The theory may be seen as being concerned with the choice of certain easily observable characteristics which are related systematically to the unobservable characteristics in which we are really interested. It is thus part of what has come to be called the 'theory of screening.' The use of these surrogate characteristics gives rise to a number of problems similar to those discussed in the screening literature [see, for example, Spence (1973) and Stiglitz (1975)].

(1) Many of the characteristics which may be used for screening are, at least to some extent, under the control of the individual, and basing a tax on these is inevitably distortionary.

(2) Almost all characteristics which may be used for screening are imperfect; that is, the surrogate characteristics employed to determine tax liability are not perfectly correlated with the characteristics with which we are really concerned.

---

[1]This section includes the distributional results referred to in our earlier paper [Atkinson and Stiglitz (1972)].
[2]Another potentially important function of the tax system – to provide signals concerning the demand for public goods – is not discussed here.

(3) There are costs (e.g. of administration) associated with even nondistortionary screening systems.

This general view of taxation shows that the analysis of tax systems must be inherently concerned with individual differences. As a consequence, the treatment of, say, optimal excise taxation in a world where individuals are assumed to be identical is at best of limited relevance. In what follows we assume that people differ with respect to their abilities (earning power) and their tastes, although for the main part of the paper (sections 3–5) we concentrate on differences in ability. For simplicity, we assume that this can be measured by a single parameter, n, so that an individual of ability n_1 can do in $1/n_1$ hours what an individual of ability n_2 can perform in $1/n_2$ hours. We assume, however, that ability is not observable directly. What one can identify depends on the nature of the employment relationship. The following are three of the most important possibilities, where L is the number of labor hours worked, e is the level of effort, and income is given by $Y = neL$.

(i) Income is observable, but effort and labor time are not. This makes sense for unincorporated businesses, although not necessarily for employees.

(ii) Wages per hour ($w \equiv ne$) are observable, but not labor hours and hence not income. This applies where individuals may have several jobs and it may be difficult to keep track of them. It should be noted that where effort is unobservable, one cannot infer ability, even when one can observe the wage rate.

(iii) Both wages and hours are observable, but since effort is not, ability cannot be inferred.

Case (i) corresponds to that where income taxation is employed (Y is the surrogate characteristic), case (ii) to that where there is a wage tax (w is the surrogate characteristic), and in case (iii) there is a choice of screening devices.

In addition to income and wages, other economic variables on which taxation might be based are purchases by different individuals of different commodities. In a world where income and wages are unobservable, but purchases of certain luxuries are observable, the latter may provide the best screening device. Whether such purchases remain good screening devices when income and wages *are* observable is one of the questions to which we address ourselves in this paper. Still other economic variables that may be useful as screening devices are the sources of income: e.g. the government could distinguish between salaried and wage workers, between earned and unearned income, or, within unearned income, between dividends and capital gains. For the purposes of this paper, however, we consider only labor income and do not distinguish among types of jobs, except in terms of the wages they pay. There are certain other distinctions, such as the sex, age, and marital status of the worker, which are relatively costless to observe. An argument can be made for differentiation on this basis [see Boskin (1973)], but again, for present purposes, we ignore these distinctions.

Thus, if x_i are the individual's purchases of commodity i, we can describe a general tax system as a relationship between potentially observable characteristics, x_i, Y and w, and his tax payments:

$$T = T(x, Y, w).$$

In practice, almost all tax systems possess a high degree of separability, and indeed are often linear in some or all of the arguments. There are good reasons why this is so. Not only are there greater costs of calculating tax liabilities when nonseparable and nonlinear tax systems are employed, but also there are significantly higher costs of record-keeping and enforcement (with linear commodity taxes, for example, no record of the number of units purchased by a given person need be kept). Thus although separability and linearity have great analytical advantages, and will be assumed in much of what follows, there are also strong economic grounds for making these assumptions.

Within this framework, we can consider the following taxes.

Excise tax: $T = \sum_i t_i x_i = t \cdot x,$

where $t \cdot x$ denotes the inner product of the two vectors. In the simplest case the tax rates t_i are constant, but in certain situations (e.g. housing subsidies) the tax may be nonproportional. Taxes may also be income-related, $t_i(x_i, Y)$, or wage-related $t_i(x_i, w)$, the latter applying, for example, to job-related subsidies.

Income tax: $T = T(Y).$

In certain cases the tax base may depend on the consumption of commodities (e.g. medical care), so that $T = T(Y, x_i)$; it may be constrained to be linear (constant marginal tax rate) or allowed to vary freely.

Wage tax: $T = \tau(w)L.$

Again the tax schedule may be constrained to be linear. (The problem of the optimal wage structure in a socialist country may be viewed as determining the function τ.)

Thus the theory of optimal taxation must be concerned with the choice of tax base as well as the structure of taxes imposed. A full analysis would, of course, begin with the general function $T(x, Y, w)$ and examine its properties. The difficulty with such a completely general approach is that it does not appear – at least at this juncture – to lead to any simple or clear prescriptions. In this paper we attempt a less ambitious task and focus primarily on the relationship between excise and income taxation. This piecemeal approach has obvious limitations, but we hope that it is sufficient to demonstrate the importance of a unified treatment of the choice of tax base and the optimal design of tax rates. As a preliminary to this, we review in the next section the main results regarding excise taxes viewed in isolation; then, in sections 4–6, we examine the interaction with income tax.

3. Excise taxes and distribution

The optimal structure of indirect taxation, and particularly whether there should be differential rates of tax, is an old issue which has recently be re-examined in a series of papers. Much of this literature has ignored differences in endowments and has concentrated on efficiency aspects. At the same time, it has been recognized that the policy prescriptions would need to be modified when distributional considerations were introduced. This aspect of the problem was first discussed by Diamond and Mirrlees (1971); their treatment was, however, somewhat different from that given below.

We assume that there are N individuals, denoted by a superscript h. Each individual has a well-behaved utility function defined over the n commodities and labor,[3]

$$U^h = U^h(x, L). \tag{1}$$

The individual maximizes utility subject to the budget constraint

$$q \cdot x = w^h L^h, \tag{2}$$

where q is the price of the commodity to the consumer, and w^h is his after-tax wage. The solution leads to individual demand and labor supply functions. Substituting these back into the utility function gives the indirect utility function $V^h(q, w^h)$. There is no loss of generality (with the assumptions made below) in letting labor be the numeraire and in assuming it to be untaxed (a proportional tax on labor income is simply equivalent to a uniform commodity tax). This will be done throughout the analysis. Finally, we denote by X_i the total demand for good i summed over all individuals ($\Sigma_h x_i^h$).

At this stage it is assumed that the only taxes open to the government are proportional excise taxes at the rate t_i on commodity i, and that no lump-sum taxes or subsidies are allowed.[4] For simplicity, we take producer prices as fixed and normalize them at unity, so that $q_i = 1 + t_i$. We assume that the govern-

---
[3]The labor variable may be treated more generally as a vector, including elements such as hours, effort, etc.

[4]Such a restriction makes sense in the context of the general approach taken in this paper only if 'individuals' are not directly observable as individuals: e.g., with a lump-sum subsidy, they could collect twice under different 'names' or with a lump-sum tax they disappear into the bush.

ment wishes to raise a given amount of revenue,

$$R \equiv \sum_h t \cdot x^h \geq \bar{R}, \tag{3}$$

and that subject to this constraint it aims to maximize a social welfare function of the Bergson form $G(U^1, \ldots, U^N)$, where G is increasing in all its arguments. Forming the Lagrangian

$$\mathscr{L} = G(V^h) + \lambda \left[\sum_h t \cdot x^h - \bar{R} \right], \tag{4}$$

straightforward manipulation yields the result that the first-order conditions imply[5]

$$\frac{\sum_h \left[\sum_k t_k (S^h_{ik}) \right]}{X_i} = -\left[1 - \sum_h b^h \left(\frac{x^h_i}{X_i} \right) \right], \quad i = 1, \ldots, n, \tag{5}$$

where

$$S^h_{ik} = \left(\frac{\partial x^h_i}{\partial p_k} \right)_U,$$

the compensated price derivative;

$$b^h = \frac{\beta^h}{\lambda} + \frac{\partial R}{\partial I^h},$$

the *net* social marginal utility of income for household h, using government income as numeraire;

$$\beta^h = \frac{\partial G}{\partial V^h} \frac{\partial V^h}{\partial I^h},$$

the gross social marginal utility of income (consumption) accruing to household h; and

$$\frac{\partial R}{\partial I^h} = \sum_k t_k \frac{\partial x^h_k}{\partial I^h},$$

the marginal tax paid by household h on receiving an extra dollar of income.

[5]This by making use of the fact that $\partial V/\partial q_i = -x_i^h \alpha^h$, where α^h is the private marginal utility of income of individual h, and of the Slutsky equation

$$\frac{\partial x_k}{\partial q_i} = S_{ki} - x_i \frac{\partial x_k}{\partial I},$$

where $\partial x_k/\partial I$ is the derivative with respect to income (evaluated at $I = 0$ in this case) and S_{ki} is the compensated price term.

In interpreting b^h, note that there are two effects of transferring a dollar to the hth household: the direct effect, which is just β^h/λ measured in government revenue, plus an indirect effect – the effect of the transfer on government income. It may also be noted that the mean ($\bar{b}$) is the net value of giving an equal lump-sum payment to everyone. Thus, if uniform lump-sum payments or taxes were allowed, the government would set them at a level such that $\bar{b} = 1$. The implications of this are explored in the next section.

The left-hand side of (5) has the usual interpretation of the proportional reduction of the consumption of the ith commodity along the compensated demand schedules. We can immediately see that this is no longer necessarily the same for all commodities. Sufficient conditions for it to be independent of i are *either* that b^h be the same for all h *or* that x_i^h/X_i be the same for all commodities (there are no goods which are consumed disproportionately by rich or poor). In general, where these are not satisfied, the compensated reduction in demand with the optimal tax structure is smaller:[6] (1) the more the good is consumed by individuals with a high net social marginal utility of income, (2) the more the good is consumed by households with a high marginal propensity to consume taxed goods.

Eq. (5) can be rewritten in two ways which will prove useful in the subsequent discussion:

$$\sum_h \sum_k t_k S_{ik}^h = -X_i(1-\bar{b}r_i), \qquad i = 1,\ldots,n, \tag{5'}$$

where

$$r_i = \sum_h \left(\frac{x_i^h}{X_i}\right)\left(\frac{b^h}{\bar{b}}\right); \tag{6}$$

and

$$\sum_h \sum_k t_k S_{ik}^h = -X_i[(1-\bar{b})-\bar{b}\phi_i], \qquad i = 1,\ldots,n, \tag{5''}$$

where $\phi_i \equiv r_i - 1$ is the normalized covariance between the consumption of the ith commodity and the net social marginal utility of income [a result derived independently by Diamond (1975)]. In the first of these formulae, r_i is a generalization of the 'distributional characteristic' of Feldstein (1972a) and (1972b). It shows that if $\bar{b}$ is large, i.e. if there would be large gains from a uniform lump-sum payment, then distributional considerations are to be weighted more heavily.

---

[6]Diamond and Mirrlees (1971) derived the analogous expression for the uncompensated changes. Since the uncompensated reductions in demand with the optimal tax structure are not the same even without distributional considerations, to make comparisons with the Ramsey results more direct, we have employed compensated derivatives. In the uncompensated form, Diamond and Mirrlees have identified a third factor determining the percentage reduction in demand: it will be greater the more the demand for the commodity is concentrated among individuals for whom the product of the income derivative of demand for that good and total taxes paid is large.

A.B. Atkinson and J.E. Stiglitz, The design of tax structure

The extension of the Ramsey formula given above is relatively general. In particular, it allows individuals to differ with respect to both tastes and endowments; other taxes (e.g. a lump-sum tax) may be imposed; and not all commodities need be taxed. (As in the earlier Ramsey analysis, the result does, however, depend on there being either constant returns to scale in production or 100 per cent profits taxes – see Stiglitz and Dasgupta (1971).) However, to obtain detailed results on the optimal tax structure, we need to make more specific assumptions about the nature of differences between individuals and the form of the utility function. Here, and until section 6, we assume that everyone has the same tastes, that effort is not a variable, and that individuals differ solely with respect to their ability (wage rate). For ease of analysis, we assume a continuum of individuals, and replace the summation signs in the previously derived formulae by integrals. We let F represent the distribution function of abilities, where we normalize such that $F(\infty) = 1$. The special case of the utility function we consider for purposes of illustration is that where all individuals have independent compensated demand schedules. Eqs. (5') and (5") then give

$$\frac{t_i}{1+t_i} = \frac{1-\bar{b}r_i}{\bar{\varepsilon}_i} = \frac{(1-\bar{b})-\bar{b}\phi_i}{\bar{\varepsilon}_i}, \tag{7}$$

where $\bar{\varepsilon}_i$ is the weighted average compensated price elasticity, the weights being the consumption of the different individuals.[7]

In the case where everyone is identical, (7) reduces to the familiar formula that taxes should be inversely proportional to demand elasticities. Eq. (7) provides a simple adjustment to this formula for distributional considerations. The value of r_i depends now solely on the social marginal valuation of income received by different households and on the proportion of total consumption which goes to them. In particular, it depends on the degree of aversion to inequality. If β is constant, i.e. society is indifferent with regard to the distribution, then the optimal tax formula is the familiar one. But if the social marginal valuation of income falls with w, this tends to increase the tax rate on goods which are primarily consumed by those at the top of the scale.[8]

---

[7]The first-order conditions need careful interpretation since they may not lead to a unique solution. Where the price elasticity varies with q_i there may be multiple solutions, and the optimal tax structure may involve taxing at different rates two goods with identical demand curves.

[8]That is, letting r_i be a function of ρ, some measure of inequality aversion with $\rho = 0$ corresponding to no inequality aversion, then $r_i(0) = 1$, for all i, and

$$r_i(\rho) - r_i(0) = \frac{\Sigma (x_i^h - \bar{x}_i)(b^h - \bar{b})}{\bar{b}X_i} \gtreqless 0 \quad \text{as} \quad \frac{\partial x^h}{\partial b^h} \gtreqless 0,$$

i.e. households which consume more of x_i (relative to mean consumption $\bar{x}_i$) have a higher or lower valued net marginal social utility of income. (For the meaning of inequality aversion, see Atkinson (1970) and Diamond–Stiglitz (1974).) Because of our normalization, $\bar{x}_i = X_i$.

A formula similar to (7) was given by Feldstein (1972a,b), but he did not bring out the inherent conflict between equity and efficiency considerations. With an additively separable utility function and constant marginal utility of leisure, demands depend on the ratio of commodity price to wage. This means that a commodity with a low elasticity of demand appears from an efficiency standpoint to be a good candidate for taxation but that since the consumption of such a commodity rises only slowly with w, this points to low tax rates for equity reasons. Which of these factors will predominate depends on the form of the social welfare function and on the shape of the distribution of abilities.

One especially simple case to examine is that where the government maximizes the sum of utilities – the classical utilitarian case – and where the compensated demand curves have constant elasticity. In table 1, we present the value of ϕ_i and the associated form of eq. (7) for the Pareto and lognormal distributions. For the Pareto distribution, it follows that where the government would like to make a uniform lump-sum transfer to everyone ($\bar{b} > 1$), the tax

Table 1
Values of distributional characteristics: Pareto and lognormal distributions.

(a) Pareto distribution: $f = \delta \bar{w}^\delta w^{-(1+\delta)}$ (where it is required that $\delta > \varepsilon_i$):

$$\phi_i = \frac{-\varepsilon_i}{\delta(1+\delta-\varepsilon_i)}, \quad \frac{t_i}{1+t_i} = -\frac{(\bar{b}-1)}{\varepsilon_i} + \frac{\bar{b}}{\delta(1+\delta-\varepsilon_i)}.$$

(b) Lognormal distribution (where $(e^{\sigma^2}-1)^{1/2}$ is the coefficient of variation):

$$\phi_i = e^{-\varepsilon_i\sigma^2} - 1, \quad \frac{t_i}{1+t_i} = -\frac{(\bar{b}-1)}{\varepsilon_i} + \frac{\bar{b}(1-e^{-\varepsilon_i\sigma^2})}{\varepsilon_i}.$$

rate rises with the elasticity of demand; this is therefore a sufficient condition for equity to outweigh efficiency considerations and for goods with a high price elasticity to be taxed more heavily. It may also be noted that the magnitude of the distributional term falls with δ, or as the distribution of abilities becomes less unequal [for the same mean, see Chipman (1974)]. For the lognormal distribution, if $\bar{b} > 1$ and σ is small, then again the distributional considerations dominate; but if σ is not small, then as the elasticity of demand increases, the tax rate may at first increase (for low elasticities, distributional considerations are more important) and then decrease (for high elasticities, efficiency dominates).[9]

4. Excise taxes with an optimal linear income tax

Thus far we have considered indirect taxation in isolation from the rest of the tax system, and in particular we have not examined how the possibility of

---

[9] This may be seen by expanding the term $\exp(-\varepsilon_i\sigma^2)$ and first considering terms of order σ^2, and then of order σ^4 (it is assumed that $\sigma^2\varepsilon_i < 1$).

employing *direct* taxes affects the optimal structure of *indirect* taxation. How does the existence of a progressive income tax affect the balance between equity and efficiency considerations in determining the optimal rates of excise taxation?

A first step towards considering the interaction between direct and indirect taxation may be taken by a relatively straightforward modification of the analysis of the previous section. The simplest progressive income tax is that where there is an exemption level and a proportional rate of tax both above and below this level (the tax below the exemption level being a negative income tax, so that the taxpayer receives a supplement from the revenue). Such a linear income tax schedule can readily be incorporated into the model we have been discussing, since wages are the only source of income and a uniform tax on all commodities is equivalent to a proportional tax on wages. The only difference therefore is in the exemption level, which can be introduced by supposing that the government provides a lump-sum payment identical in amount (E) to all individuals (if E is negative, it is a lump-sum tax). We assume an additive, symmetric, social welfare function and write the Lagrangian

$$\mathscr{L} = \int_0^\infty [G\{V(t, E)\} + \lambda\{t \cdot x - E - \bar{R}\}] \mathrm{d}F. \tag{8}$$

The indirect utility function now depends on E, where $\partial V/\partial E = \alpha$, the marginal utility of income. The first-order conditions give:

$$\frac{\partial \mathscr{L}}{\partial t_i} = \int_0^\infty \left[(\lambda - G'\alpha)x_i + \lambda \sum_k t_k \frac{\partial x_k}{\partial t_i}\right] \mathrm{d}F = 0, \quad i = 1, \ldots, n, \tag{9}$$

$$-\frac{\partial \mathscr{L}}{\partial E} = \int_0^\infty \left[(\lambda - G'\alpha) - \lambda \sum_k t_k \frac{\partial x_k}{\partial I}\right] \mathrm{d}F = 0. \tag{10}$$

Since $\beta = G'\alpha$, (10) is equivalent to $\bar{b} = 1$, as the previous section indicated. Thus, with an optimal linear income tax, the percentage reduction of consumption along the compensated demand schedule is simply *equal* to the normalized covariance between consumption of the commodity and the net marginal social utility of income (eq. (5″) with $\bar{b} = 1$).

If β were constant, that is, if society were indifferent regarding the distribution, then $\{t_i = 0, \text{all } i\}$ would provide a solution to the first-order conditions, and if there were a positive revenue requirement, it would all be raised by a poll tax ($E < 0$). This is a quite intuitive result, since we should expect that efficiency considerations taken on their own would dictate using solely a lump-sum tax. Where the government is concerned with the distribution of income, i.e. β is a decreasing function of w, then indirect taxes would in general be employed. The question, however, is whether they would be employed with differential rates, since, as we have seen, a uniform indirect tax is equivalent – in this model – to a proportional income tax.

The point at issue may be illustrated by one very special example. Suppose that the utility function is quadratic (an example used by Ramsey), that the cross-terms are zero, and that the marginal utility of leisure is constant:

$$U = \sum_i \left(a_i x_i - \frac{c_i}{2} x_i^2 \right) - vL. \tag{11}$$

In the absence of the income tax, it may be shown that the optimal tax rates vary according to $a_i(1-\bar{b})$, and would in general differ across commodities. However, the introduction of an income tax with the exemption level E means that $\bar{b} = 1$, and that the optimal tax structure is uniform. It follows that no indirect taxation need be employed, and that the optimum may be achieved simply through a linear income tax. (Another example is the linear expenditure system.)

Where the utility function is more general, but the compensated demands are still independent, we can see from eq. (7) that $t_i/(1+t_i) = -\phi_i/\bar{\varepsilon}_i$. We may note two features of this result. Firstly, it implies that there is no case for subsidizing normal goods; an increase in the lump-sum subsidy is always superior. Secondly, the tax rates depend on the level of revenue to be raised only through the dependence on the covariance of x_i with net marginal social utility of income. With a constant marginal utility of leisure and $G' = 1$, ϕ_i is independent of the level of revenue to be raised – any increase in $\bar{R}$ is met by a reduction in E. Hence for sufficiently large $\bar{R}$, the tax system is regressive.

From table 1 we can derive the optimal tax rates in the constant elasticity case. For the Pareto distribution, the tax is higher on goods with a higher price elasticity (which is also the elasticity with respect to w). With $\delta = 3.0$, the tax rates vary from 9.5 percent with $\varepsilon = 0.5$ to 16.7 percent with $\varepsilon = 2.0$. In the case of the lognormal, it is quite possible for the tax rate to fall with ε: for example, if $(\sigma^2 \varepsilon)$ is sufficiently less than 1 for third and higher powers to be neglected, then the tax rate may be approximated by $\sigma^2 - \varepsilon\sigma^4/2$, which gives the following results (where all individuals work).

σ^2	ε		
	0.5	1.0	2.0
0.16	15%	15%	13%
0.24	23%	21%	18%

The fact that the tax structure may be regressive (i.e. the rates fall with ε) may appear to conflict with the intuitive notion discussed above that efficiency considerations would point to the use of a poll tax and that it is concern for the distribution which leads to the use of commodity taxes. However, when distributional objectives are relevant, indirect taxes play two roles. Firstly, by taxing luxuries at a higher rate they may increase the progressitivity of the tax system; secondly, they provide an alternative source of revenue, allowing the regressive poll tax to be reduced or converted into a lump-sum payment. In the latter case, the revenue would be raised in the distortion-minimizing way, and the final tax structure would balance the two sets of considerations.

Going back to the general formulation (5″), we can see that

$$\int_0^\infty \left(\sum_k S_{ik} t_k\right) dF = \int_0^\infty (x_i - X_i)(b - \bar{b}) dF, \tag{12}$$

so that the reduction of consumption along the compensated demand curve is simply equal to the covariance between the consumption of that good and the net marginal social utility of income. For small variance, the tax structure may be approximated by taking a Taylor series expansion of the RHS of (12),

$$x_i \phi_i \approx \frac{dx_i}{dw} \frac{\partial b}{\partial w} \sigma_w^2,$$

where σ_w^2 is the variance of wages (abilities). Thus, the percentage reduction (along the compensated demand curve) in consumption is exactly proportional to the uncompensated derivative of the commodity with respect to the wage. If there is constant marginal utility of leisure and separable demand functions, we obtain

$$x_i \phi_i \approx q_i \left(\frac{\partial x_i}{\partial q_i}\right)_U \frac{\partial b}{\partial w} \sigma_w^2,$$

so

$$\frac{t_i}{1 + t_i} \approx \frac{\partial b}{\partial w} \sigma_w^2,$$

independent of i: i.e. to the first order of approximation, there should be uniform taxation.

Expanding ϕ_i further shows that to the second order of approximation, differences in tax rates depend on the concavity or convexity of the demand functions ($\partial^2 x_i / \partial q_i^2$) and the third moment of the ability distribution, parameters for which we are unlikely to obtain robust estimates.

The examples given above show that the results described in the previous section may need significant modification where the government is able to employ income taxation, even where this is restricted to a simple linear schedule. In the next section we examine the relationship between direct and indirect taxation where the income tax schedule may be freely varied.

5. Excise taxes and optimal income taxation

We assume that the income tax schedule is differentiable,[10] but apart from that may be of any form. We also allow for the possibility that the tax rate on commodities may be a function of the level of consumption.[11] The individual with wage w faces a budget constraint

$$\sum_i (x_i + t_i(x_i)) = wL - T(wL), \qquad (13)$$

and the first-order conditions for utility maximization are[12]

$$U_i = \frac{(1+t_i')(-U_L)}{w(1-T')}, \qquad i = 1, \ldots, n. \qquad (14)$$

The government maximizes the social welfare function subject to

$$\int_0^\infty \left[\sum_i t_i(x_i) + T(wL) \right] dF = \bar{R},$$

or

$$\int_0^\infty \left[wL - \sum_i x_i - \bar{R} \right] dF = 0. \qquad (15)$$

This problem may be treated in a number of different ways. In the heuristic argument which follows, we take $x_2, \ldots, x_n$ and L as the control variables, treating U as a state variable, and making use of the fact that x_1 depends on $U, x_2, \ldots, x_n$ and L. Moreover,

$$\frac{dU}{dw} = \frac{-U_L L}{w} \equiv -U_L \theta(w, L). \qquad (16)$$

The Hamiltonian may then be written

$$H = \left[G(U) + \lambda(wL - \sum_i x_i - \bar{R}) \right] f - \mu \theta U_L, \qquad (17)$$

---

[10]See Mirrlees (1971). In general this need not be the case. For an analysis of such non-differentiabilities within the context of this class of 'screening' problems, see Stiglitz (1974a).

[11]Actually we could have considered a general tax function of the form $T(x, L, w)$. In fact, for this particular problem, the results for the more restrictive, but practically more important, tax structure involving separability assumed here are identical to those in which the separability is dropped. This may be seen most easily by observing that nowhere in the analysis is the separability restriction on the tax function actually used.

[12]For an interior solution; we do not consider the case where labor supply is zero, although the analysis could easily be modified.

where f is the density function. Maximizing H with respect to x_i, we obtain as necessary conditions

$$-\lambda\left[\left(\frac{\partial x_1}{\partial x_i}\right)_U + 1\right] - \frac{\mu}{f}\left[U_{L1}\left(\frac{\partial x_1}{\partial x_i}\right)_U + U_{Li}\right]\theta = 0.\tag{18}$$

From (14) it is immediate that

$$\left[\frac{\partial x_1}{\partial x_i}\right]_U = -\frac{U_i}{U_1} = -\frac{(1+t_i')}{(1+t_1')}.\tag{19}$$

Thus we can rewrite (18) as

$$\lambda\left[\frac{1+t_i'}{1+t_1'} - 1\right] = \frac{\mu\theta U_i}{f}\frac{\mathrm{d}\log\left(\frac{U_i}{U_1}\right)}{\mathrm{d}L}.\tag{20}$$

Without loss of generality, we set $t_1' = 0$. Hence

$$\frac{t_i'}{1+t_i'} = \frac{\mu\theta\alpha}{\lambda f}\frac{\mathrm{d}\log\left(\frac{U_i}{U_1}\right)}{\mathrm{d}L}.\tag{21}$$

Tax rates are simply proportional to the rate at which the marginal rate of substitution between commodity i and commodity 1 changes with a change in the consumption of leisure.

From this analysis we obtain at once an interesting result. If the utility function is weakly separable between labor and all consumption goods (taken together), then no commodity taxation need be employed ($t_i = 0$). It is immediate that we could have allowed U to depend on n as well, as long as we maintain our separability hypothesis: $U = U(V(x_1, \ldots, x_n), L, n)$. With the greater flexibility provided by the nonlinear income tax schedule, the result found for special cases in the previous section now holds for much more general utility functions. The assumption of separability between consumption and labor may well be regarded as a reasonable first approximation for our purpose; and even if it is in fact empirically rejected, it is a useful benchmark case.[13] From the results given above, it follows that goods which are complementary (in the Edgeworth, not the more usual Hicksian, sense) with leisure ($U_{iL} < 0$) will face lower tax rates, whereas substitutes face higher tax rates. Finally, it is interesting to note that relative tax rates are independent of the social welfare function, so that they may be viewed as conditions for constrained Pareto optimality.[14]

---

[13] Where a subset of commodities is separable from labor, then the commodities in this group should all be taxed at the same rate.

[14] We are indebted to J.A. Mirrlees for pointing this out in his discussion of the paper at the Paris conference.

There are three interesting applications of the results given above which should be mentioned briefly [see also Atkinson (1974)]. First, if the goods are interpreted as consumption at different dates, then the analysis shows that the conventional presumption in favor of consumption rather than income taxation may be interpreted as assuming separability between leisure and consumption. Perhaps a more reasonable structure of preferences in this context is

$$U = U_1(c_1, L) + U_2(c_2),$$

in which case whether there should be an interest income tax or subsidy depends on the complementarity or substitutability (in the Edgeworth sense) between the first-period consumption and labor. The second application is to the question of the differential treatment of safe and risky assets: x_i is then treated as purchases of the ith security. Our theorem then says that where the individual maximizes $V(L) + EU(Y)$, there should be no differential treatment of risky assets [Stiglitz (1970) and Atkinson and Stiglitz (1972)].

The third application is to the use of quotas of specific allocations for distributing certain goods. Some economists [e.g. Tobin (1970)] have argued that there exist certain inelastically supplied commodities (medical care, at least in the short run) where quotas might be desirable. Such quota systems can be viewed as an extreme nonlinear commodity tax-subsidy scheme: below the quota the price is zero, above the quota, infinite. Viewed this way, the question of the desirability of quotas is equivalent simply to the question of whether it is optimal to have such an extreme form of progression for some particular commodity. The import of our theorem is that, provided the separability assumption is satisfied, not only should no quota be employed for such commodities, but not even a tax should be imposed. The result does not depend on the supply elasticities for the commodities in question.[15]

The basic intuition behind the argument that quotas might be desirable for inelastic commodities was that, if commodities are elastically supplied, then individuals should be allowed to trade off consumption of one good against the other: an individual's increased consumption of vanilla ice cream cones does not deprive someone else of his consumption of vanilla ice cream cones. When commodities are inelastically supplied, then there is no production inefficiency introduced by quotas. But prices serve as signals not only for the production of goods but also for the allocation of goods among individuals (the conventional exchange model). So long as tastes differ, the use of quotas will result in exchange inefficiency.

But, it might be argued, if we had a separable utility function, a first-best

---

[15]In our proof, we assume an elastic supply of all commodities, but it is easy to establish that, provided profits (rents) are fully taxed, the results are true for any production technology (including the limiting case of a perfect inelastically supplied commodity).

solution would entail allocating the same amount of the given good to everyone (if they had the same utility function) and hence we could achieve a first-best allocation of this particular good, with no loss of production efficiency. Such an argument, though plausible at first sight, fails to recognize the second-best nature of the problem we are considering: satisfying one of the first-best conditions (equating marginal utilities of consuming this particular good) does not necessarily represent an improvement when the other conditions are not satisfied.

A more plausible argument is that if we are able to discriminate among those with higher incomes by charging them a higher price (e.g. by having price an increasing function of quantity consumed) we would improve welfare, since such a differential price imposes a higher cost on those with lower marginal utilities of income. But there is a cost in deadweight loss from such differential pricing, and the import of our theorem is that in the central case examined, the cost outweighs the gains.[16]

6. Differences in tastes and horizontal equity

The existence of differences in tastes among individuals of the same ability raises issues in the design of the tax structure which we have not yet taken into account. In the conventional treatment, the principle of horizontal equity – that people who are in all relevant senses identical ought to be treated identically – plays an important role. In this section, we discuss, necessarily briefly, the nature of this principle as well as its implications for the design of tax policy. We first point out that the principle of horizontal equity may be in direct conflict with the utilitarian maximum even when tastes are identical; next we examine the case where tastes differ and show that the principle does not imply, as some have suggested, uniform taxation; finally, we consider more generally the status of horizontal equity as an objective of government policy.

The literature on optimal taxation has typically assumed that the redistributive goals of the government may be represented by maximizing a Bergsonian social welfare function, such as $G(U)$ defined above, and has not discussed the relationship between this and the concept of horizontal equity. Some earlier authors have taken the view that there is no conflict: 'the requirements of horizontal and vertical equity are but different sides of the same coin' [Musgrave (1959, p. 160)]. However, this need not be so. It is quite possible that the maximization of a Bergsonian social welfare function may indicate that individuals with identical tastes and endowments should be taxed at different rates (if this

[16]Spence (1975) and Weitzman (1974) have discussed this issue in a partial equilibrium context. The fact that their results differ from those given here is attributable to the fact that the presence of the optimal income tax has important implications for the role to be played by other distributive mechanisms, as we have emphasized throughout this paper.

is feasible), thus violating conventional notions of horizontal equity [see Atkinson and Stiglitz (1976)].[17]

The point is that if the feasible set of allocations is not convex (as it may be when only indirect taxes are employed), optimality may entail treating otherwise identical individuals differently.[18] An even stronger conflict has been noted by Stiglitz (1974b), where horizontal equity may conflict with the principle of Pareto optimality. Even before we introduce taste differences, therefore, there is a possible conflict between horizontal equity and the maximization of a social welfare function of the type usually assumed.

If we now introduce differences in tastes, the immediate consequence is that we must confront the interpersonal comparability question, which we have ignored thus far. When individuals have the same indifference curves, it is natural simply to use the same cardinal number of the indifference curves for different individuals. But when tastes differ, this is no longer so. Even if everyone had the same homothetic indifference maps, we must still decide which indifference curve for individual 1 corresponds to a given curve for individual 2.

The point is that the utilitarian system evaluates taxes in terms of the individual's ability to derive utility from goods and leisure, and in this respect may be contrasted with the alternative criterion of 'ability to pay,' that is, of basing taxation on opportunity sets. When the only differences are those in the ability to produce, then a utilitarian ethic leads to redistribution from those with 'better' opportunity sets to those with 'poorer'. There is no conflict between it and the ability-to-pay approach. But this may arise as soon as tastes differ. Suppose individual 1 has a higher productivity, so that his budget constraint lies outside

---

[17]Consider the simplest possible case of labor and a single consumption good (C), with two identical individuals. We assume that lump-sum taxes (poll taxes) are not admissible. The utilitarian problem may be formulated as

$$\max V(q_1) + V(q_2),$$

subject to

$$\tau_1 C_1 + \tau_2 C_2 = R,$$

with first-order conditions

$$V_{q_i}(q_i) = -\lambda \left(C_i + \tau_i \frac{\partial C_i}{\partial q_i} \right),$$

where λ is the Lagrange multiplier associated with the constraint. It is obvious that

$$q_1 = q_2 = q^* = 1 + \tau^*,$$

where

$$2\tau^* C(q^*) = R,$$

satisfies the first-order conditions. But

$$V_{qq} + \lambda \left(\tau_i \frac{\partial^2 C_i}{\partial q_i^2} + \frac{2 \partial C_i}{\partial q_i} \right)$$

may well be positive at $q_i = q^*$, which would mean that this represents a local minimum.

[18]Analogous results in different contexts have been noted by Stiglitz (1974b) and Mirrlees (1972).

that of individual 2. The ability-to-pay criterion would indicate that individual 1 paid more tax, but there are obviously numberings of their indifference curves which lead to the opposite result with the utilitarian objective.

In order to contrast these two approaches, let us suppose that tastes may be represented by a single parameter, γ, so that the indirect utility function may be written as $V(q, w, \gamma)$. The utilitarian principle recognizes such taste differences as a legitimate basis for discrimination, and the government maximizes $G[V(q, w, \gamma)]$. On the other hand, if we introduce the concept of horizontal equity and interpret this as meaning that differences in tastes are not 'relevant' characteristics on which discrimination ought to be based, then this has two implications. Firstly, it introduces a cardinalisation $V(1, w, \gamma) = \tilde{V}(1, w)$, so that only endowments, w, and consumer prices (normalized at unity before tax) are relevant. Secondly, it constrains the government in levying taxes ($q \neq 1$) to maintain

$$V(q, w, \gamma) = \tilde{V}(q, w). \qquad (22)$$

Suppose that the government were to adopt this version of horizontal equity; what would be the implications for the optimal tax structure? It is popularly believed that it would require uniform taxation. If two individuals are identical in all respects except that one likes chocolate ice cream and the other likes vanilla, a system which taxes chocolate ice cream at a higher rate is felt to be horizontally inequitable.[19] This is not however necessarily correct, as may be seen from the following example:

$$U = \sum_i (A_i(\gamma))^{(1/\varepsilon_i)} \frac{x_i^{1-(1/\varepsilon_i)}}{1-(1/\varepsilon_i)} - vL.$$

(It should be noted that we are assuming that there are no differences between people in the marginal utility of leisure, and that ε_i is independent of γ.) Let us further assume that A_i is independent of γ, for $i = 3, \ldots, n$, and that $A_1 = \gamma$. The requirement of normalization is then that $A_2(\gamma)$ is such that $V(1, w, \gamma) = V(1, w)$: i.e. that all those with the same w have the same pre-tax utility. Using this, it can be shown that the horizontal equity condition (22) requires that[20]

$$q_1^{1-\varepsilon_1} = q_2^{1-\varepsilon_2}. \qquad (23)$$

---

[19] Pigou (1947) gives a nice example: 'When England and Ireland were united under the same taxing authority, it was strongly argued that, owing to the divergent tastes of Englishmen and Irishmen, it was improper to subject them to the same tax formulae in respect of beer and whiskey.' The tax on spirits, more generally consumed in Ireland, was more than two-thirds of the price, whereas the tax rate on beer was only about one-sixth of the price.

[20] It may be noted that (for $\varepsilon_i \neq 1$).

$$V(q, w, \gamma) = \sum_i \frac{A_i(\gamma)}{(\varepsilon_i - 1)} \left[\frac{(vq_i)}{w}\right]^{1-\varepsilon_i}.$$

The condition for horizontal equity is not, therefore, uniform taxation; only if the price elasticity is the same – as it may well be in the chocolate/vanilla ice cream case – would uniform tax rates be horizontally equitable. This may be related to the argument made by Pigou (1947, p. 77):

> Suppose that there are two persons of equal income and general economic status, that in the aggregate of their tastes they are similar, in the sense that they would get equal satisfactions from equal incomes if they were permitted to spend them as they chose, but that one likes and purchases commodity A and not commodity B, the other commodity B and not commodity A. Suppose, further, that taxes are imposed upon commodities A and B in such ways that both these persons pay the same amount of tax. It will not necessarily follow that they suffer equal real burdens. If the demand of one for his commodity is more elastic than the demand of the other for his, the former will suffer the larger hurt.

The model just described is a very simple one, but it brings out clearly the conflict between horizontal equity and the maximization of a social welfare function of the Bergson type. For example, where $G' = 1$ (the classical utilitarian case), the latter leads to the first-order condition,

$$1 - \frac{1}{q_i} = \frac{1 - \bar{b} r_i}{\varepsilon_i},$$

as before. This is not in general consistent with the requirement of horizontal equity, eq. (23).

This raises the important issue of the status of the horizontal equity principle. It is often suggested that horizontal equity is in some sense prior to vertical equity: 'it is sometimes said that the horizontal aspect is more basic and less controversial' [Musgrave and Musgrave (1973, p. 199)]. Most authors, including Musgrave and Musgrave, go on to argue that neither is more basic than the other; however, this ignores the conflict which we have seen to arise between the two principles, at least in the form presented here. Faced with this potential conflict, it might seem more reasonable to view the social welfare function as lexicographic. For certain classes of goods, probably those marked by considerable diversity of tastes, the horizontal equity requirement is imposed, and the government then maximizes a Bergsonian social welfare function subject to this constraint. As Pigou (1947, p. 51) put it, 'the ideal of least sacrifice has to be pursued subject to a handicap.' The optimal structure of taxation, and the choice between direct and indirect taxes, will depend on how wide is the range of goods covered by constraints such as (23).

7. Concluding comments

In this paper, we have attempted to present a framework within which we can evaluate the appropriateness of different tax bases and to apply this framework to the classical question of the use of direct versus indirect taxation.

The general framework employed may be summarized as follows. The necessity for any form of taxation other than a uniform lump-sum tax arises from the fact that individuals have differing characteristics (endowments or tastes). If we could observe all relevant characteristics costlessly and perfectly, we should be able to achieve a first-best solution. However, in practice we have to make use of surrogate characteristics, which are related systematically to the characteristics on which we would like to differentiate individuals, but which are not perfectly correlated and which are, to some extent, under the control of the individual. Certain ethical principles, notably those which fall under the rubric of horizontal equity, limit further the set of surrogates which may be used. Having established an admissible class of characteristics, the problem then becomes one of determining which are to be employed (the choice of tax base) and the structure of the tax schedule.

The application of this framework to the direct/indirect tax problem led to the following results. Firstly, if the government had no distributional objectives and was concerned solely with efficiency, it may employ only direct taxation and this would take the form of a poll tax. This is a very straightforward prescription, but it has the implication, which runs counter to much popular belief, that the use of indirect taxation stems from a pursuit of distributional objectives. The extent to which indirect taxes are employed to this purpose – that is, purchases of different commodities are used as a screening device – depends on the form of consumer preferences and on the restrictions (if any) on the type of income taxation employed. If a general income tax function may be chosen by the government, we have shown that, where the utility function is separable between labor and all commodities, no indirect taxes need be employed. In this case, the use of consumption of particular commodities as a screening device offers no benefit. Finally, we have seen that horizontal equity considerations may impose constraints on the structure of taxes which may be levied.

Throughout the paper, we have stressed the importance of the interactions between different taxes, and the fact that a piecemeal approach may be misleading. In section 4, for example, it was shown that in the quadratic case considered by Ramsey (plus constant marginal utility of leisure and independence) the introduction of an optimal linear income tax meant that indirect taxation was no longer necessary. The Ramsey-style results would, therefore, only be relevant where there were constraints on the use of income taxation. Such interactions are equally a warning that the results given in this paper should be treated with considerable caution. For this and other reasons, such as the failure to incorporate the costs of administration,[21] the theory may be more useful in illuminating the structure of the argument than in providing definite answers to policy issues.

[21]See Heller and Shell (1974) for an attempt to introduce administration costs into the analysis of optimal taxation.

References

Atkinson, A.B., 1970, On the measurement of inequality, Journal of Economic Theory 2, 244–263.
Atkinson, A.B., 1974, Housing allowances, income maintenance and income taxation, International Economic Association conference, Turin.
Atkinson, A.B., and J.E. Stiglitz, 1972, The structure of indirect taxation and economic efficiency, Journal of Public Economics 1, 97–119.
Atkinson, A.B. and J.E. Stiglitz, 1976, Lectures on Public Economics, forthcoming.
Boskin, M.J., 1973, Optimal tax treatment of the family, Memorandum 143 (Center for Research in Economic Growth, Stanford University, Stanford, CA).
Chipman, J.S., 1974, The welfare ranking of Pareto distributions, Journal of Economic Theory 9, 275–282.
Diamond, P.A., 1975, A many-person Ramsey tax rule, Journal of Public Economics 4, 335–342.
Diamond, P.A. and J.A. Mirrlees, 1971, Optimal taxation and public production, American Economic Review 61, 8–27 and 261–278.
Diamond, P.A. and J.E. Stiglitz, 1974, Increases in risk and in risk aversion, Journal of Economic Theory 9, 337–360.
Feldstein, M.S., 1972a, Distributional equity and the optimal structure of public prices, American Economic Review 62, 32–36.
Feldstein, M.S., 1972b, Equity and efficiency in public pricing, Quarterly Journal of Economics 86, 175–187.
Heller, W.P. and K. Shell, 1974, On optimal taxation with costly administration, American Economic Review 74, papers and proceedings, 338–345.
Mirrlees, J.A., 1971, An exploration in the theory of optimum income taxation, Review of Economic Studies 38, 175–208.
Mirrlees, J.A., 1972, Population policy and the taxation of family size, Journal of Public Economics 1, 169–198.
Musgrave, R.A., 1959, The theory of public finance (McGraw-Hill, New York).
Musgrave, R.A. and P.B. Musgrave, 1973, Public finance in theory and practice (McGraw-Hill, New York).
Pigou, A.C., 1947, A study in public finance (Macmillan, London).
Spence, M., 1973, Job market signalling, Quarterly Journal of Economics 87, 355–379.
Spence, M., 1975, Nonlinear prices and welfare, Technical Report 158, (IMSSS, Stanford University, Stanford, CA).
Stiglitz, J.E., 1970, Taxation, risk-taking and the allocation of investment in a competitive economy, in: M. Jensen, ed., Studies in the theory of capital markets (forthcoming).
Stiglitz, J.E., 1974a, Monopoly and imperfect information (Oxford and Stanford University) mimeo.
Stiglitz, J.E., 1974b, The efficiency wage hypothesis, surplus labor and the distribution of income in LDCs, Technical Report 152 (IMSSS, Stanford University, Stanford, CA).
Stiglitz, J.E., 1975, The theory of 'screening', education and the distribution of income, American Economic Review 65, 283–300.
Stiglitz, J.E. and P.S. Dasgupta, 1971, Differential taxation, public goods, and economic efficiency, Review of Economic Studies 38, 151–174.
Tobin, J., 1970, On limiting the domain of inequality, Journal of Law and Economics 13, 263–278.
Weitzman, M.L., 1974, Is one price system or rationing more effective in meeting true needs for a deficit economy? (MIT, Cambridge, MA) mimeo.

ON THE SPECIFICATION OF MODELS OF OPTIMUM INCOME TAXATION

N.H. STERN*

St. Catherine's College, Oxford, England

with programming by D. Deans

Revised version received September 1975

The main concerns of the paper are the problems of estimating labour supply functions for use in models of optimum income taxation, and the calculation of the effect on the optimum linear tax rate of varying the elasticity of substitution, ε, between leisure and goods from 0 to 1. Backward sloping supply curves are commonly observed and they imply $\varepsilon < 1$. Our calculation of ε from estimates of supply curves by Ashenfelter and Heckman gives $\varepsilon = 0.4$. Optimum marginal rates decrease with ε when taxation is purely redistributive but may be nonmonotonic if positive revenue is to be raised. It is proved that optimum (linear or nonlinear) taxation involves a marginal rate of 100 percent when $\varepsilon = 0$.

1. Introduction

There are four main ingredients for a model of optimum income taxation: an objective function, a preference relation or supply function for individuals, a skill structure and distribution, and a production relation. They are closely intertwined. An individualistic social welfare function would take into account the preference structure of individuals. The supply of various kinds of skills will depend on individuals' wishes or ability to produce these skills. The production relation must state how skills of different kinds are combined to produce outputs.

The optimum income taxation problem as usually posed is to maximise a social welfare function, which depends on individual utilities, subject to two constraints. The first is that each individual should consume goods and supply factors in amounts which maximise his utility subject to the constraint of the tax function, which describes how much post-tax consumption can be acquired from pre-tax earnings. We are searching for the optimum function. The second is that the total labour supplied can produce the total quantity of goods

---

*This paper has benefited greatly from discussions with A.B. Atkinson, D.L. Bevan, P.A. Diamond, J.S. Flemming, J.A. Mirrlees and K.W.S. Roberts. The comments of participants at a seminar in Cambridge were also helpful. Responsibility for all errors is mine.
The paper was presented to the ISPE Conference on taxation in Paris, January 18–20, 1975. The comments of the discussants at that conference, E. Malinvaud and M. Bruno, were helpful. The support of the SSRC under grant HR 3733 is gratefully acknowledged.

demanded. It is the former constraint which characterises the optimum income taxation problem and which makes it a problem of the second best. Without this constraint, that individuals are on their supply curves, we have a first-best problem.

When taxation is discussed it is often in terms of a trade-off between equality and efficiency, or the distribution of the cake and its size. The optimum income taxation problem is one way of formalising this trade-off and it is, perhaps, surprising that it was not until Mirrlees (1971) that a suitable model was developed. We are still at the stage of understanding the structure of these models and the importance of the various components. It should be clear at the outset that the purpose of this paper is not to make recommendations to the Treasury as to appropriate tax rates, but to contribute to the understanding of the discussion of equality versus efficiency through examination of a particular model.

The particular concern of this paper is the supply function, and attention is focussed on the special case of labour supply. We shall examine the problem of estimation, which preference structures obtain support from the empirical literature on labour supply, and then the influence such estimates should have on our view of the appropriate level of income taxation. It will be suggested that most previous calculations of optimum tax rates may have been biased low.

The next section presents the models of Mirrlees (1971) and Atkinson (1972) and contains a brief discussion of their numerical results.[1] The problems of specifying and estimating skill distributions are discussed in section 3, together with calculations of the elasticity of substitution (ε) between leisure and goods, based on empirical estimates of labour supply functions.

The calculations of section 3 suggest that elasticities of substitution around $\frac{1}{2}$ are of interest, and in section 4 the optimum linear income tax, for values of ε between 0 and 1, is calculated in a model similar to that of Mirrlees (1971). The extreme case of $\varepsilon = 0$ is examined, in the Mirrlees model, in section 5 and we find the optimum income taxation (linear or nonlinear) involves marginal taxation at 100 percent. It is not surprising, therefore, that the calculations of section 4 show that, for small ε, the optimum linear tax rate increases to 100 percent as ε decreases to zero. However, where taxation is imposed to raise revenue, as well as to redistribute, the optimum marginal rate may increase as ε increases over a certain range. In section 6 the numerical discussion is evaluated.

The remainder of this section is devoted to a brief examination of those elements of the model, the objective function and the production relation, which receive no further attention in the later discussion.

Most previous writers have worked with a concave transformation of individual cardinal utilities. The transformation ranges from the linear utilitarian sum to the case where the 'degree of concavity' goes to infinity – the maximin,

---

[1] I originally intended to do a survey of theoretical and empirical work in progress but became more involved with my own investigations.

or Rawlsian, solution. Some might wish to claim that one is merely specifying the value judgements of the decision-maker by using an arbitrary numbering of individual indifference curves together with a method by which individual utilities are aggregated. The specification of a particular cardinal numbering for individuals and the form of the social preference relation over utilities may well be difficult, if not impossible, to disentangle, but I find it hard to understand a quantitative comparison between different forms of social welfare function for the same indifference structure (for individuals) if some benchmark of cardinality is not involved.

The cardinality problem is much less severe when a one argument utility function is used – see, for example, Atkinson (1973a). One can then suppose that the government defines its values over the vectors whose components are household incomes. However, when supply functions are central to the model a one-argument utility function seems out of place. It then becomes more difficult to wriggle out of the problem of numbering individual indifference curves. It is possible that part of the attraction of maximin objective functions is that the cardinality problem is less troublesome – maximising the lowest utility level will give the same policy whichever cardinalisation is used when the same monotonic increasing transformation of utilities is applied to all individuals.

The above discussion and most of the literature has supposed that the Bergson–Samuelson social welfare function (nondecreasing in each argument) is the appropriate tool for capturing social values in such analyses. Leaving aside the question of whether it *should* be used, it is possible that many people have some different underlying notion of welfare or distributional justice when they discuss income taxation. We illustrate the possible phenomenon with a few quotations and arguments which might be thought plausible and yet imply *non-Paretian* objectives. We begin with three quotations on inequality each of which clearly involves a non-Paretian position.

Tawney:[2]

When the press assails them with the sparkling epigram that they desire not merely to make the poor richer but to make the rich poorer, instead of replying, as they should, that, being sensible men, they desire both, since the extremes of both of riches and poverty are degrading and anti-social, they are apt to take refuge in gestures of depreciation.

Simons:[3]

The case for drastic progression in taxation must be rested on the case against inequality – on the ethical or aesthetic judgement that the prevailing distribu-

---

[2] See Atkinson (1973b, p. 19). I am grateful to Kevin Roberts for drawing my attention to this quote.
[3] See Simons (1938, p. 15). Kevin Roberts drew my attention to this quote too.

tion of wealth and income reveals a degree (and/or kind) of inequality which is distinctly evil or unlovely.

Fair (1971) quotes Plato as follows:

Plato felt that no one in a society should be more than four times richer than the poorest member of society for 'in a society which is to be immune from the most fatal disorders which might more properly be called distraction than faction, there must be no place for penury in any section of the population, nor yet for opulence, as both breed either consequence.'

Certain arguments on tax proposals and structures might seem plausible to many and also involve non-Paretian judgements. For example, Sadka (1973) has shown that with a finite number of individuals or skill levels the optimum marginal tax rate at the very top is zero. One can express his argument verbally as follows. Suppose that a given tax structure is a candidate for the optimum and it results in the most skilled person earning $£Y$. Consider the announced marginal tax on the $(Y+1)$ pound and suppose it is positive. Reduce it to zero. The most skilled person may work more and if he does he is better off. Similarly, others of lower skill may also work more. If they do, then they are better off (exploiting opportunities that were not available to them before) and they pay more tax since they move through tax brackets with nonnegative marginal rates. Thus, our change has produced more tax revenue and has made everyone at least as well off as before.[4] A Paretian should approve. Many, however, might regard a zero marginal rate at the top as offensive. It is conceivable that they may wish to retain this view even after they have understood the above argument. We should note that one cannot deduce that, where the skill distribution has positive density, for all positive skill levels the optimum marginal tax rate tends to zero. Indeed, Mirrlees (1971) gives examples where it does not. The structure of the model is similar to an optimum growth model where we cannot infer from the result that a finite horizon model should have zero capital stock at the end, the conclusion that the capital stock tends to zero on the infinite horizon path.

Some might propose a 100 percent tax on inheritance on the grounds of equality of opportunity for children. It is non-Paretian (if one rules out envy as the basis of the argument), since the ability to confer the inheritance makes the parent better off (the desire is to give rather than consume) and, presumably, the offspring as well.[5]

Many have found[6] the 'equal absolute sacrifice' proposal an attractive basis for optimum income taxation. This abstracts from incentive problems and states that to raise a given revenue everyone should give up that amount of his income

---

[4]One can throw away the extra tax revenue if it is so desired. The argument is clearly rather general. 'Better off' has been used here in the weak sense of 'at least as well off.'
[5]Mirrlees drew my attention to this argument.
[6]This principle is discussed and fitted to U.K. tax schedules in Stern (1973).

which makes the sacrifice of utility equal. It turns out that one can choose a utility function which fits the U.K. income tax structure rather well.[7] Although it does not violate the Paretian condition, the proposal cannot be based on any symmetric strictly concave Bergson–Samuelson welfare function since, abstracting from incentive effects, such welfare functions lead to equal post-tax incomes.

The above examples indicate that the standard welfare economics procedure based on the usual welfare functions would not be regarded as the obvious starting point by many who might be prepared to comment on income tax structures.

Most of this paper will use a production structure with one basic input – labour in efficiency units – with a fixed wage. This does not mean that we are assuming constant returns to scale. We can regard the wage as the marginal product at the level of optimum total production and any profits that accrue as lump sum income for the government. Nevertheless, the assumption of one basic input is worrying. It is often asserted that a particular skill is lacking (say, management in the U.K.) and this carries with it a strong notion of complementarity with other factors rather than the complete substitutability assumed in the case of labour in efficiency units. Feldstein[8] has made a start in this direction and incorporates two different kinds of labour into his model.

The frequent assumption of public ownership seems less serious. If, for example, there are profits in the system, one can carry out an analysis of the optimum levels (presumably subject to some constraints). The constraints on income taxation would then take account of the presence of these other taxes. Further work is necessary, however, and Atkinson and Stiglitz (1976) have begun an examination of appropriate combinations of various taxes.

The absence of further discussion of the production assumptions should not be taken as a belief that they do not matter. The specification of the way different skills interact in the production process embodies an aspect of income taxation that many would regard as crucial. It is an important area for further research.

The models discussed here will all be static and will not, therefore, involve capital and the elasticity of its supply in any essential way. These models allow the discussion of the important questions of labour supply and raise sufficient significant and difficult questions to warrant study. Some progress has been made with dynamics but the components of the models have to be kept rather simple.[9]

2. The model and numerical results of the studies of Mirrlees and Atkinson

This discussion is not intended as a comprehensive survey since Atkinson (1973a) has recently provided a thorough discussion of previous numerical

---
[7]See Stern (1973).
[8]Feldstein (1973). The different types of labour combine through a Cobb–Douglas production function to produce output.
[9]See, e.g., Feldstein (1973).

work. The main purpose of this section is to draw attention to the levels of calculated optimum marginal tax rates, in models similar to those of section 4 which are, on the whole, lower than one might have predicted. Indeed Mirrlees (1971, p. 207) remarked '..., I must confess that I had expected the rigorous analysis of income-taxation in the utilitarian manner to provide arguments for high tax rates. It has not done so.'[10] A partial response to these results has been the use of strongly egalitarian ('highly concave') social welfare functions and the limiting case the 'maxi-min welfare function.'[11] We shall suggest later that there is no need to use these more extreme social welfare functions to obtain tax rates that seem closer to observed rates, and that one has merely to use labour supply functions which seem closer to those which are usually estimated. For the moment, however, we give a brief sketch of these earlier results and, in the process, set out the model of income taxation to be used later.

The original work on the current models of income taxation was that of Mirrlees (1971). In his model individuals supply labour of different qualities and hence face different pre-tax wage rates. They choose how much to supply by maximising $u(c, l)$ subject to $c = g(nlw)$, where c is consumption, l the hours worked, nw the hourly wage of an n-man – he produces n efficiency hours per hour worked – w is the wage per efficiency hour and $g(\cdot)$ the tax function giving post-tax income as a function of pre-tax income.

The aggregate production constraint is $X = \int cf(n) \, dn = H(\int nlf(n) \, dn) = H(Z)$, where X (total consumption) is a function $H(Z)$ of effective labour Z, and $f(n)$ is the density of the distribution of individuals. The problem is to vary $g(\cdot)$ to maximise $\int G(u)f \, dn$, where $G(\cdot)$ is a concave function and the constraints are that the amounts individuals choose to supply of labour and consume of goods be compatible with the production relation. Note that the formulation involves taxation of nlw and does not require (nw) and l to be separately observable. If one can identify an n-man without affecting his behaviour, then the first-best optimum can be achieved by levying an appropriate lump sum tax for each n with a zero marginal rate of taxation.

Mirrlees provided detailed calculations for the cases where $u(c, l) = \log c + \log(1-l)$, n distributed lognormally (parameters of the associated normal distribution being $\bar{\mu}$ and σ), H linear and $G(u) = u$ or $-e^{-u}$. Using a value of $\sigma = 0.39$, derived from the work of Lydall,[12] *on the distribution of earnings*, he obtained median marginal tax rates for the case of $G(u) = u$ of 22% and 20%.[13] The higher rate was for the case where 7% of product was required by the government and the lower where 17% could be added – the additions or subtractions corresponding respectively to cases where profits or revenues

---

[10]The utilitarian optimum ignoring incentives involves 100 percent taxation. One is initially surprised therefore when the introduction of incentives drops the rate down to 20 percent.
[11]See Atkinson (1972).
[12]See Lydall (1968) and Mirrlees (1971).
[13]Interpolated from Mirrlees (1971, tables I–IV, p. 202).

elsewhere outweighed or were outweighed by fixed costs, or necessary expenditure. With a net government expenditure of 12% of product and $G(u) = -e^{-u}$, the median marginal rate rises to 33%.

The highest marginal rates for the three cases respectively are 26%, 21% and 39%. The marginal rates rise at first but begin falling before the median is reached. Mirrlees proves that, for the log-normal distribution and where the elasticity of substitution between consumption and leisure is less than one, the marginal rate tends to zero as n tends to ∞. There is a higher limit in the case of the Pareto distribution where, with the same condition on the substitution elasticity, the marginal rate tends to $1/(1+\gamma)$ as $n \to \infty$ when $(nf'/f) \to -(\gamma+2)$. Examination of distributions of earnings (see section 3.2) suggests values of γ from 0.5 to 2.5 giving limiting marginal rates from 67% to 29%.

Higher rates can also be produced by widening the distribution of skills – if σ in the log normal case is increased to 1.0 (from 0.39), the median rate is 56% for the case $G(u) = -e^{-u}$ and a government requirement of 7% of product. Presumably with a wider distribution of skills, inequality considerations increase relative to those concerned with incentives. However, Mirrlees (1971, p. 207) suggests that such a σ 'does not seem to be at all realistic...' since it gives a dispersion of skills too wide to be compatible with observed distributions of earnings.[14]

There are two main features of the calculated tax schedules which look different from actual income tax structures.[15] Marginal rates are not monotonically increasing – most of the population is in the region where they are falling – and the highest marginal rates are low. For the 'realistic' case of $\sigma = 0.39$, applying to 5 out of 6 of Mirrlees' examples, the highest marginal rate is 39%.

Atkinson (1972) and (1973a) discusses the effect of increasing the concavity of $G(\cdot)$ and the limiting case of maximin. It seems clear that he was in part influenced by the low rates in the Mirrlees calculations – see Atkinson (1972, p. 2) and (1973a, pp. 390–391). The maximin criterion in the Mirrlees model yields tax rates around 50% for the median person [see Atkinson (1972, p. 28)].

We have already given the Sadka argument which explains why, for a finite population, we should expect zero marginal tax rates at the top of the distribution. This argument may also have some intuitive force for distributions with an infinite domain, provided the weight in the tail is not too big. We have noted, for example, that the log-normal gives a limiting marginal rate of zero but the Pareto does not. The zero limit of the marginal rate for certain distributions suggests that a declining rate at the upper end may be a feature of many models of optimum income taxation. We shall say no more (except for the special case of section 5) about the shape of the tax funtion, and concentrate on the labour supply function and its relation to optimum linear taxation.

[14]We discuss in section 3.2 whether the distribution of earnings gives a misleading impression of the distribution of skills.
[15]These are announced rates rather than effective rates.

3. The estimation of supply functions and skill distributions

3.1. Supply functions[16]

The work on optimum income taxation has dealt exclusively with situations where individuals have the same preference relation but differ in their earnings capacity. One can also imagine cases where individuals differ in their preference relations but face the same earnings function which is determined, as far as they are concerned, exogenously. In this subsection we shall be discussing such alternative specifications, and the different problems they pose for estimation.

We shall suppose, for the moment (but see section 3.2) that the number of hours of work is the appropriate argument of an individual's utility function and that the pre-tax wage measures the skill or efficiency of a worker per hour of work. For estimation (but not taxation) purposes we suppose that the wage and hours are separately observable.

To make some of our formulae explicit we shall consider utility functions of the constant elasticity of substitution (CES) form, although it is clear that many of the problems we shall discuss do not depend on the particular form of the utility function.

We suppose an individual maximises

$$u(c, l) = [(1-\alpha) \, c^{-\mu} + \alpha(h(L-l))^{-\mu}]^{-1/\mu}, \tag{1}$$

subject to the budget constraint

$$c = A + (nw)l. \tag{2}$$

We thus have a linear tax schedule. The individual is characterised by the triple (h, n, L) and one could consider a distribution of this triple over the population. We shall be discussing some special cases. We should think of L as the number of hours available to the individual for allocation between work and leisure, given his family commitments, sleeping requirements, physical attributes and so on. The parameter h measures the ability to enjoy leisure and n the ability to produce efficiency hours of work from clock hours. Different specifications of the relations between h, n and L may lead to very different interpretations of data on wages and hours.

The first-order condition for maximisation of utility subject to the budget constraint is

$$\frac{(A+(nw)l)}{h^{1-\varepsilon}(L-l)} = \left[nw \cdot \frac{(1-\alpha)}{\alpha}\right]^{\varepsilon}, \tag{3}$$

where $\varepsilon = 1/(1+\mu)$.

---
[16]The comments of A.B. Atkinson on this subsection were particularly useful.

In the Mirrlees case individuals have identical preferences so that h and L are constant over the population. Putting $h = 1$ and taking logarithms, we have

$$\log\left(\frac{A+(nw)l}{L-l}\right) = \varepsilon \log (nw) + \varepsilon \log\left(\frac{1-\alpha}{\alpha}\right). \quad (4)$$

We see immediately that where the total quantity of hours available (L) is known or specified, we can estimate ε and α by regressing consumption per hour of leisure on the wage rate (nw).

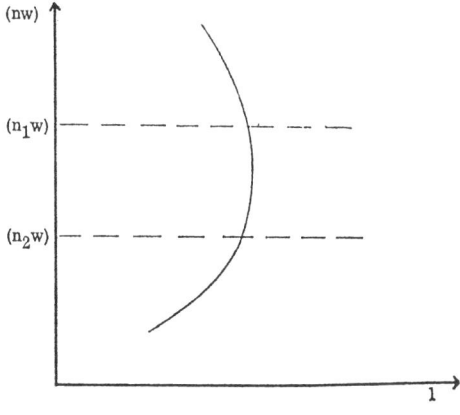

Fig. 1

Note that our assumption of identical preferences enables us to identify the supply function by merely plotting the relation between l and the post-tax wage rate per clock hour (nw) (see fig. 1). This formulation is, therefore, especially convenient for estimation purposes (see section 3.3). The skill distribution is then given by the distribution of wage rates.

The above procedure is very sensitive to the assumption of identical preferences. We give two examples to illustrate this point. First, suppose L is constant in the population but $h = n$. In other words, individuals have identical available hours but those who produce more efficiency hours of work obtain a similarly increased satisfaction per hour of leisure. And suppose, for the sake of illustration, that $A = 0$. We see from (3) that l is independent of n. In other words, everyone works the same number of hours. Thus we might infer, on seeing a distribution of wages and no variation of hours, that the supply curve was inelastic when an increase in w (the wage per efficiency hour) would change hours worked.

A second example has been used by Hall (1974). He supposes $h = n = 1$ but L varies in the population. He deals in particular with the case where $\varepsilon = 1$ (equivalent to $\mu = 0$ or $u(c, l) = c^{1-\alpha}(L-l)^{\alpha}$) so that we have $(L-l) = \alpha(A+wL)/w$. He assumes $L = (1-\theta)\bar{L}$, where θ has the beta density on $[0, 1]$: $f(\theta) = 6\theta(1-\theta)$. He applies the model to the Penn–New Jersey negative income tax (NIT) experiment. Families were offered a choice between (A_0, w_0) (participation) and (A, w) (nonparticipation) with $A_0 > A$, $w_0 < w$. His model predicts both participation rates and changes in hours given participation fairly well. Hall argues that the representative individual is not a sensible concept when we see a dispersion of hours worked for a given (A, w), and that a theory of labour supply should account for this dispersion.

3.2. Some problems of estimating the skill distribution

In the previous subsection we suppose for our discussion of estimation that nw and l were separately observable. We had been interpreting l as clock-hours and regarding l as the relevant argument for the disutility of labour and as the basis of the productivity measure. The problem is more complicated than this, however. Both disutility and productivity of labour may be a function primarily of the effort required rather than the number of hours, although the latter is obviously of importance. In the absence of a direct measurement of effort we should discuss estimation problems when we can observe nwl, total pre-tax labour income, and not nw and l separately. Here we interpret l as effort.

There is one special formulation[17] which makes the problem disappear. If individuals maximise $(1-\alpha) \log c + \alpha \log (1-l)$ subject to $c = a(nwl)^{\delta}$, where a and δ define the tax function, then l is constant and (pre-tax) incomes are distributed as a constant times n. We can, therefore, read off the distribution of skills from the distribution of labour income. Since l is not directly observable, the assumption that it is constant is not violated, although we cannot estimate α. It is clear, however, that the trick is rather special and will not work for more general utility and tax functions.

In general then, if l is not directly observable, we cannot pass from a distribution of labour income to a distribution of n unless we have full knowledge of the utility function and the tax function, when l can be deduced. We can, however, gain information on the utility function and skill distribution separately if the tax schedule *changes*. We can illustrate this as follows. Put $\varepsilon = 1$ in (3), and we have

$$(nwl) = (1-\alpha)nwL - \alpha A. \qquad (5)$$

We can now use (5) to estimate α. Let us suppose that the current post-tax wage

---

[17] The formation was used by Vickrey (1947) and Bevan (1974).

per effective hour is one (where the model presumes a linear tax schedule). This is merely choosing a linear scale for n. A tax change occurs which increases A to A_0 and decreases w from 1 to w_0 – as in the Penn–New Jersey NIT experiment. We observe only nwl and A in both cases but we know that nw has decreased from n to nw_0, where w_0 is known – since $1-w_0$ is the increase in the marginal tax rate. For a given individual we then have two equations in two unknowns (α, n) which we can solve for α and n. Given a population subject to the experiment we could find the distribution of n (and of α) in the population.

The kind of experimental information we have just been discussing is rather rare.[18] Usually we have a given tax structure, a distribution of labour income and we may be uneasy about measuring effort by hours worked. We should like to know if the income distribution is a good proxy for the skill distribution. We saw at the beginning of this subsection a special case where the distributions were identical. This case is unusual, however, and the income distribution may be very misleading as an estimate of the distribution of skills. For example, one can imagine a utility function where an individual has a target level of consumption or income (c_0) upon which he insists, but he is not prepared to work to raise his consumption beyond this level,

$$u(c, l) = \begin{cases} 1-l & \text{if } c \geq c_0, \\ -\infty & \text{otherwise.} \end{cases}$$

If we have a community of individuals of different skills, all of whom have this utility function, we should observe a completely equal distribution of incomes. However, some individuals would have to exert a great deal of (unobservable) effort to achieve c_0 and consequently would have low utility. Others would achieve c_0 with comparative ease.

This is an extreme example but it illustrates the point that where the unobserved supply curve of effort l with respect to nw is backward sloping, the distribution of skills is more unequal than the distribution of incomes. We shall see in section 3.3 that supply curves of hours are usually found to be backward sloping for much of their range.

On the other hand there may be many factors in actual situations which affect wage rates but should not be described as innate ability: for example, age, education, luck or power. In ideal circumstances one would examine a population which had constant values of these complicating factors. While this may be possible for age or education it is difficult in the case of luck or power. Note that if the acquisition of education is sensitive to earnings, education should be included in supply functions and not 'skill' distributions. We return to this briefly below.

---

[18]Hall (1974) makes use of the experimental Penn–New Jersey NIT data for his actual estimation (see section 3.1).

Suppose the wage rate m is equal to an (additive) combination of innate ability n and some other factor x. Then

$$\text{var}(m) = \text{var}(n) + \text{var}(x) + 2\,\text{cov}(n, x).$$

If the covariance is zero or positive the distribution of wage rates is more unequal than the distribution of abilities. It seems more likely that the factors mentioned are positively correlated with ability.

We have seen that the relevant evidence for skill distribution must, therefore, be based on labour earnings and, where possible, rates, and be corrected for age and education. It is clear that a casual examination of the distribution of (earned plus unearned) income is insufficient. This is an important area for further research.

One of the main problems for this research will be the specification of the functional form of the distribution to be fitted. Pareto (1897) found that $N_x = JX^{-\alpha}$, where N_x is the number of incomes above X, gave a remarkably good fit for several countries. He estimated α and found that it was around 1.5. On the other hand, Lydall examines the upper tail of the distribution of employment incomes for different countries and finds α ranging from 2.27 for France in 1964 to 3.4 for Germany in 1964 (1968, p. 133). Lydall does examine employment incomes and, in some cases (1968, p. 33) tries to work with populations with given numbers of hours per week. He suggests further that, for precisely defined occupational characteristics (1968, p. 33), the log-normal distribution fits rather well.

An interesting approach to the problem is the recent study by Schwartz (1975). He finds, disaggregating populations by race and years of education, that the power transformation of income which gives the closest approximation to normality is the cube root of income.

We can come to no firm conclusions as to whether the current distribution of income gives an accurate picture of the distribution of skills. We saw that there were two powerful influences, backward bending supply curves and non-skill factors, pulling in opposite directions. It must be emphasised that the non-skill factors include a multitude of variables which depend on the institutions and organisation of society, and that the relative productivity of different skills depends on the capital stock. Further it is clear that the one-dimensional model of the skill distribution is a very crude representation of reality. But the problem is deeper than this. If skills are acquired, the motivation may be the potential reward, as for example in human capital models. We should then include acquired skills in the supply function rather than the skill distribution. This forces us to think of n as innate ability, a notion which is both slippery and controversial. And, what if skills (and effort) are not acquired (or supplied) for monetary reward? We have to reexamine our concepts of supply. Theoretical and empirical research on these problems is still in its infancy.

3.3. Supply curves as estimated

Empirical estimates of the response of labour supply to changes in wages and income are usually expressed in terms of a supply function. For models of optimum income taxation we usually wish to work with explicit utility functions. The purpose of this section is to describe the calculation of the parameters of a CES utility function from the estimates of income and wage responses which have been found by others.

We showed in section 3.1 that for the Mirrlees case we can estimate the labour supply function directly by assuming that everyone has the same supply function and differences in skills result in differences in wage rates (see fig. 1). We suppose that such an estimation has been performed and we have estimates of the (uncompensated) wage and income elasticities at some level of wages and for some lump-sum incomes. We want to infer a CES utility function.

We suppose the individual problem is to maximise $[(1-\alpha)c^{-\mu}+\alpha(L-l)^{-\mu}]^{-1/\mu}$, where c is consumption of goods, l is labour supply and L the maximum possible level of work. We assume that consumption is $c = A+wl$. We are, therefore, assuming a linear tax schedule where w is the post-tax wage. We are not concerned here with the reason for the level of w so we suppress the 'n' factor.

The first-order condition for the above problem is obtained by putting $h = n = 1$ in eq. (3); we then have

$$\left[\frac{L-l}{A+wl}\right]^{\mu+1} = \frac{\alpha}{(1-\alpha)w}. \tag{6}$$

It is obvious from (6) that

$$\frac{-\partial \log\left[\frac{L-l}{A+wl}\right]}{\partial \log w} = \frac{1}{1+\mu} = \varepsilon,$$

the elasticity of substitution. We differentiate eq. (6) logarithmically with respect to w and A in turn, and after a little manipulation obtain

$$\frac{\partial l}{\partial w} = \frac{(A-\mu wl)(L-l)}{w(\mu+1)(A+wL)}, \tag{7}$$

$$\frac{\partial l}{\partial A} = -\frac{(L-l)}{A+wL}. \tag{8}$$

Given w, l, $(w/l)(\partial l/\partial w)$, $(A/l)(\partial l/\partial A)$, we can solve (6), (7) and (8) for L, α, μ.

Ashenfelter and Heckman (1973) estimate income and substitution effects from a cross-section of 3,203 male heads of families from the national probability sample component of the 1967 U.S. Survey of Economic Opportunity. They restricted their sample to men not receiving welfare payments and whose wives were present but not working. They write (my notation),

$$\Delta l = S\Delta w + B[l^*\Delta w + \Delta A]. \qquad (9)$$

Δ represents differences from sample means, S is the substitution term, and l^* is the average of the mean labour supply of the sample and l, so that $l^*\Delta w$ represents an approximation to the income compensation and thus B an approximation to $\partial l/\partial A$. Eq. (9) is then estimated.[19] Hours were calculated using annual earnings divided by hourly wage rates. Dummy variables for race, region and size of town were included as well as age and age squared. The age terms give an increase in hours to age 44 and a decline thereafter.

They find, for the mean of their sample, that $w = 3.86$ dollars per hour, $l = 2272$ hours per year, $A = 800$ dollars per year,[20] $(w/l)(\partial l/\partial w) = -0.15$ and $\partial l/\partial A = -0.07$. These numbers give values of L, α and μ of 3190, 0.994 and 1.45 (to 3 significant figures), respectively. Note that the value of α depends on the units of measurement of labour and income. The value of the elasticity of substitution, $\varepsilon = 1/(1+\mu)$, is 0.408.

This is a rather striking result since the income tax models discussed in section 2 concentrated attention on the addilog case where $\mu = 0$ and $\varepsilon = 1$. We discuss the qualifications which must be attached to this estimate at the end of this subsection. For the moment, we examine its sensitivity to the values of A, $(w/l)(\partial l/\partial w)$ and $\partial l/\partial A$ - presumably the wage and hours of work at the mean of the sample can be taken as given.

It is rather hard to measure the lump sum income A available to an individual. One has to make many judgements as to how to treat social security benefits,[21] returns on durable assets and so on. We therefore allowed A to vary across a large range, $0-2000. The results are shown in table 1. The estimates are rather insensitive to changes in A. For $A = 0$, we obtain $\varepsilon = 0.444$; and for $A = 2000$, $\varepsilon = 0.362$.

Ashenfelter and Heckman compare the figure of -0.15 for $(w/l)(\partial l/\partial w)$ with 'Sherwin Rosen's (1969) estimates of -0.07 to -0.30 from inter-industrial data, T. Aldrich Finegan's (1962) estimates of -0.25 to -0.35 from inter-occupational data, Gordon Winston's (1966) estimates of -0.07 to -0.10 from inter-country data, and John Owen's (1971) estimates of -0.11 to -0.24 from U.S.

---

[19]Instrumental variable techniques were used since l^* is correlated with the disturbance term [see Ashenfelter and Heckman (1973)]. The income compensation term should really allow for any differences between marginal and average tax rates.

[20]I am grateful to Professor Ashenfelter for supplying me with this estimate of A.

[21]In fact, workers receiving social security benefits were excluded from the sample.

time-series data.' The Ashenfelter–Heckman figure of -0.15 is calculated from the sum of a substitution effect and an income effect. The former is estimated at 0.12 and the latter $[3.86 \times (-0.07)]$ at -0.27. The standard error of the substitution coefficient is 26.0% of its estimated value and of the income coefficient 13.4% of its estimated value.[22]

Given this breakdown of the -0.15 estimate, the range of the other estimates and the standard errors, we examine the sensitivity of the ε estimate by using 4 ways of changing $(w/l)(\partial l/\partial w)$ so that it ranges over -0.05 to -0.30. In table 2, col. (a), we vary $(w/l)(\partial l/\partial w)$ holding the income term constant at -0.27. All the adjustment occurs in the substitution term and ε decreases to 0.0685

Table 1

Central estimates of ε.[a]

A	L	$1-\alpha$	ε
(Dollars per year)	(Hours per year)		
0	3113	0.9903	0.4449
400	3152	0.9926	0.4255
800	3190	0.9944	0.4077
1200	3228	0.9957	0.3913
1600	3267	0.9967	0.3762
2000	3305	0.9975	0.3622

[a]$(w/l)(\partial l/\partial w) = -0.15$, $\partial l/\partial A = -0.07$, $w = \$3.86$, $l = 2272$ hours, as in Ashenfelter–Heckman (1973).

for $(w/l)(\partial l/\partial w) = -0.25$ (and $A = 800$). A value of $(w/l)(\partial l/\partial w)$ below -0.27 would, of course, give negative ε and is not, therefore, entered in the table.

In table 2, col. (b), we vary $(w/l)(\partial l/\partial w)$ holding the substitution term constant. In col. (c) we vary $(w/l)(\partial l/\partial w)$ by changing the income and substitution terms in the same proportion. For $(w/l)(\partial l/\partial w) = -0.30$, for example, the income term contributes -0.54 and the substitution term $+0.20$. Finally, in col. (d), we vary $(w/l)(\partial l/\partial w)$ so that the modulus of the substitution and income terms moves in the same direction by equal proportions. The sensitivity was analysed in terms of the income and substitution terms since these are the coefficients estimated by Ashenfelter and Heckman and are the natural parameters for an analysis based on utility. Different methods of variation are used since we have two parameters and thus must consider errors scattered on a plane. Movements along the axes of this plane are represented in table 2, cols. (a) and (b).

The row of table 2 corresponding to -0.15 replicates the central estimates since there is no change in income or substitution effects. Column (c) gives a

[22]See Ashenfelter and Heckman (1973, table 7.1, line 4).

constant value of ε – it is clear from dividing eqs. (7) and (8) that given A, w and l, μ (and hence ε) depends only on

$$\left(\frac{w}{l}\frac{\partial l}{\partial w}\right)\bigg/\left(\frac{\partial l}{\partial A}\right).$$

It appears that our ε estimate of 0.408 is, if anything, a little above the 'average' value one would obtain using the estimates of the authors cited by Ashenfelter and Heckman.

Table 2

Sensitivity of ε estimate to assumptions on income and substitution effects.[a]

$\frac{w}{l}\frac{\partial l}{\partial w}$	(a)[b]		(b)[c]		(c)[d]		(d)[e]	
	ε	L	ε	L	ε	L	ε	L
−0.05	0.7468	3190	0.6471	2780	0.4077	2517	0.6884	2895
−0.10	0.5772	3190	0.5002	2972	0.4077	2816	0.5274	3036
−0.15	0.4077	3190	0.4077	3190	0.4077	3190	0.4077	3190
−0.20	0.2381	3190	0.3441	3439	0.4077	3668	0.3152	3359
−0.25	0.0685	3190	0.2977	3730	0.4077	4303	0.2415	3546
−0.30	not applicable		0.2623	4070	0.4077	5187	0.1816	3754

[a]$A = \$800$, $w = \$3.86$, $l = 2272$ hours; Ashenfelter-Heckman estimate $(w/l)(\partial l/\partial w) = +0.12 - 0.27 = $ substitution term + income term.
[b]Col. (a): vary $(w/l)(\partial l/\partial w)$ holding income term constant.
[c]Col. (b): vary $(w/l)(\partial l/\partial w)$ holding substitution term constant.
[d]Col. (c): vary $(w/l)(\partial l/\partial w)$ by changing income and substitution terms in same proportion.
[e]Col. (d): vary $(w/l)(\partial l/\partial w)$ by changing income and substitution terms so that they contribute to the changes in the same direction and in proportion to their absolute magnitudes.

Twice the standard error of the substitution term is $2 \times 0.12 \times 0.26$, i.e. 0.062; and twice the standard error of the income term is, in absolute value, $2 \times 0.27 \times 0.13$, i.e. 0.069. The sensitivity of the ε estimate to errors in the Ashenfelter – Heckman substitution term alone can be examined by looking down column (a), and to the income term alone by looking down column (b).

The estimates for ε of this subsection are, of course, qualified by the discussion of the preceding two subsections. Our use of the Mirrlees specification is important.

We should also be aware that the nature of the sample, men with nonworking wives, is likely to produce a supply function of hours that is rather inelastic [see Hall (1973)]. It is a subgroup of considerable numerical importance, however. Rosen (1976) estimates for a sample whose supply would be rather more elastic than average, women with working husbands, elasticities around 0.8.

We have used estimates from a particular source, but they do seem to be representative of findings on labour supply both in terms of parameter estimates and that the supply curve is backward sloping over much of its range. It is clear from eq. (7) that this phenomenon requires $\mu > 0$, and so $\varepsilon < 1$, in which case we have a backward sloping curve for $L > l > A/\mu w$. If one believes that supply curves are backward sloping over some range and that the CES is a good specification, then one must conclude that ε is less than one.

Finally, we should reiterate that it may not be labour supply in hours that is changed when the wage is changed but, for example, enthusiasm or effort. If the discouragement of these factors is seen as important by governments they may regard the estimates of ε appearing here as too low for a model of the decision problem they face.

4. The optimum linear tax in the Mirrlees model for constant elasticity of substitution

4.1. The model and computation of optima

The problem is to choose t and G to maximise

$$\frac{1}{v}\int_0^\infty u^v(c_n, l_n)f(n)\,dn,$$

subject to

$$\int_{n_t}^\infty nl_n f(n)\,dn = G + R. \tag{10}$$

The wage rate for an efficiency unit is one, there is a lump sum grant G, no other lump sum income, and a constant marginal tax rate t, so that the individual budget constraint is

$$c = (1-t)nl + G. \tag{11}$$

Skills are distributed with density function $f(n)$ and we normalise so that $\int_0^\infty f(n)\,dn = 1$. The skill level n_t is that below which individuals do no work, where c_n, l_n are chosen by the individual to maximise $u(c, l)$ subject to (11).

$$u(c, l) = [\alpha(1-l)^{-\mu} + (1-\alpha)c^{-\mu}]^{-1/\mu}, \tag{12}$$

where $\varepsilon = 1/(\mu+1)$ and hence, manipulating the first-order conditions,

$$l_n = \frac{1 - Gk(1-t)^{-\varepsilon}n^{-\varepsilon}}{1 + k(1-t)^{1-\varepsilon}n^{1-\varepsilon}},$$

where $k = [\alpha/(1-\alpha)]^\varepsilon$. Then

$$n_t = \frac{G^{1/\varepsilon} k^{1/\varepsilon}}{1-t}.$$

We have written the government constraint as a revenue constraint. This procedure is equivalent (see below) to using a production relation. We can interpret R as a fixed cost of production. Units are such that the marginal product of an efficiency hour is one. For a comparison of optima for different parameter values we should think of the marginal product as constant. For a single problem we can suppose that the unit is given by the marginal product at the optimum. An alternative view of R is as a public good. Note, however, that the public good does not influence labour supply or the distribution of utilities. For the case $v = 1$, for example, we could have $u_0(c_n, l_n, R) = u(c_n, l_n) + p_n(R)$, and the optimum for the u_0 problem for given R would be the same as the one we have posed. For the calculation for a particular ε and v, one can think of the given R as being optimum and the tax rate must then be chosen given that R. One can obviously extend the model to include optimisation with respect to R, although this will be more complicated in the case where R influences labour supply.

The equivalence between the production constraint specification and that of a tax revenue constraint is seen as follows:

tax revenue = wages − consumption

= output − profit − consumption.

The production constraint is that

output = consumption + government expenditure.

Combining the above two equations, we have

tax revenue + profit = government expenditure.

If we count any fixed cost of production as government expenditure, measure profit before any fixed cost, and write R = government expenditure − profit, we have eq. (10).

Optimum taxation was calculated for the two Mirrlees log-normal cases where $\bar{\mu}, \sigma$ (the mean and standard deviation of the associated normal distribution) are taken as $(-1, 0.39)$ and $(-1, 1)$ with the former regarded as the more realistic case,

$$f(n) = \frac{1}{n\sigma \sqrt{(2\pi)}} \exp\left\{\frac{-(\log_e n - \bar{\mu})^2}{2\sigma^2}\right\}.$$

The parameter α was set so that in the absence of taxation or grants the individual with mean skill would work for $\frac{2}{3}$ of the day in the case $\varepsilon = \frac{1}{2}$. Values of ε ranged from 0.1 to 0.9 and 0.99. The tax rate (t) was varied between 0 and 1 to search for the maximum. The maximand was calibrated using ^0C and $^{\frac{1}{2}}C$ defined as follows:

$$\frac{1}{v} u^v(^0C, 0) = \frac{1}{v} u^v(^{\frac{1}{2}}C, \tfrac{1}{2}) = \frac{1}{v}\int_0^\infty u^v(c_n, l_n) f(n) \, dn. \tag{13}$$

In other words, ^0C is that consumption which, if equally distributed with zero work hours, would give the same social welfare integral as the allocation $\{(c_n, l_n)\}$ arising from a given tax rate t. A similar interpretation covers $^{\frac{1}{2}}C$, where we instead set work hours to half the day. Note that $^0C \geq G$, since the utility of each individual is at least $u(G, 0)$, and $^0C \leq Y$, where Y (total output) is $(G+R)/t$ (from (10)), because consumption is unequally distributed and positive work is required.

The values of v were $1, -1, -2$. The case $v = 1$ shows no preference for equality. The utility function (12) is homogeneous of degree 1 in $(c, 1-l)$, and hence the indirect utility function can be written $(w+G)v(w)$, where w is the post-tax wage, and it is easily checked that $v(w) = [(1-\alpha)^\varepsilon + \alpha^\varepsilon w^{1-\varepsilon}]^{-1/(1-\varepsilon)}$. Thus where $v = 1$, the social marginal valuation of a unit increase of lump-sum grant G to an individual facing wage w is $v(w)$, which is independent of G. One can determine which value of v captures one's values as follows. Consider two individuals, A and B, with the same wage, w, but A has a lump sum income of $3w$ and B of w. Thus, A's 'full' (lump sum plus w times endowment of hours (one)) income is twice that of B. If we considered one marginal unit of lump sum income to B twice as valuable as that to A, we should be opting for $v = 0$; and if we considered the marginal unit 4 times as valuable, we should be choosing $v = -1$ (since the social indirect valuation function is $(1/v)(w+G)^v v^v(w)$ and hence the marginal valuation is $(w+G)^{v-1} v^v(w)$). Note that at the optimum these marginal valuations are unequal. See Stern (1973), where the distribution is calculated explicitly.

The calculations of Mirrlees (1971) (see section 2) correspond to $\mu = v = 0$ and $\alpha = \tfrac{1}{2}$ since he worked with the utility function $\log c + \log(1-l)$.

The maximin, or Rawlsian welfare function, corresponds to $v = -\infty$. The objective becomes the maximisation of G since the worst-off individual, whose welfare is to be maximised, has a zero wage rate.

Where $R > 0$, there is a minimum feasible t, which we call t_b, which satisfies (10) with $G = 0$. Lower values of t would require negative G and this would prevent the worst-off individuals having positive consumption. Note that, for $0 \leq t < 1$ and $\varepsilon < 1$, $t \int_0^\infty n l_n f(n) \, dn$ is monotonic increasing in t for $G = 0$ since in this case the supply curve is backward sloping. Hence values of t larger than t_b allow a lump sum grant G, and thus there exists a $G \geq 0$ corresponding to each t: $t_b \leq t < 1$.

The computation procedure for a given ε was as follows. For a given t, the G satisfying (10) was calculated using Newton's method. Finite integrals were

K

Table 3

Optimum linear income taxation.[a]

ε	t_b	$v = 1$			$v = -1$			$v = -2$			$v = -\infty$		
		t_{opt}	$^oC_{opt}$	n_t	^oC_b	t_{opt}	$^oC_{opt}$	n_t	^oC_b	t_{opt}	$^oC_{opt}$	n_t	^oC_b	t_{opt}	$^oC_{opt}$	n_t	^oC_b

(a) $R = 0$

ε	t_b	t_{opt}	$^oC_{opt}$	n_t	^oC_b	t_{opt}	$^oC_{opt}$	n_t	^oC_b	t_{opt}	$^oC_{opt}$	n_t	^oC_b	t_{opt}	$^oC_{opt}$	n_t	^oC_b
0.1	0	0.546	0.264	0.000	0.262	0.753	0.242	0.000	0.237	0.784	0.260	0.000	0.232	≥0.950	0.242	0.000	0
0.2	0	0.362	0.247	0.000	0.246	0.627	0.228	0.000	0.223	0.670	0.240	0.000	0.219	0.926	0.212	0.000	0
0.3	0	0.274	0.229	0.000	0.228	0.541	0.211	0.000	0.207	0.590	0.221	0.000	0.203	0.882	0.188	0.000	0
0.4	0	0.223	0.211	0.000	0.210	0.477	0.195	0.000	0.191	0.527	0.202	0.000	0.187	0.839	0.167	0.000	0
0.5	0	0.191	0.194	0.000	0.193	0.428	0.179	0.000	0.175	0.478	0.185	0.000	0.172	0.797	0.150	0.000	0
0.6	0	0.170	0.178	0.000	0.178	0.389	0.164	0.000	0.160	0.438	0.169	0.000	0.157	0.756	0.135	0.000	0
0.7	0	0.154	0.164	0.000	0.164	0.357	0.151	0.000	0.147	0.404	0.155	0.000	0.144	0.717	0.122	0.001	0
0.8	0	0.141	0.152	0.000	0.151	0.331	0.139	0.000	0.135	0.376	0.142	0.000	0.133	0.682	0.111	0.003	0
0.9	0	0.133	0.141	0.000	0.140	0.309	0.128	0.000	0.125	0.352	0.131	0.000	0.122	0.648	0.101	0.007	0
0.99	0	0.127	0.131	0.000	0.131	0.291	0.119	0.000	0.116	0.334	0.122	0.000	0.114	0.621	0.094	0.012	0

(b) $R = 0.05$

0.1	0.175	0.595	0.230	0.000	0.228	0.791	0.227	0.000	0.210	0.818	0.226	0.000	0.200	≥0.950	0.209	0.000	0
0.2	0.177	0.406	0.215	0.000	0.214	0.681	0.209	0.000	0.197	0.720	0.208	0.000	0.189	0.938	0.182	0.000	0
0.3	0.180	0.309	0.198	0.000	0.198	0.600	0.192	0.000	0.183	0.646	0.190	0.000	0.175	0.903	0.159	0.000	0
0.4	0.183	0.254	0.182	0.000	0.181	0.540	0.174	0.000	0.167	0.588	0.172	0.000	0.160	0.867	0.139	0.000	0
0.5	0.186	0.217	0.165	0.000	0.165	0.490	0.158	0.000	0.153	0.541	0.155	0.000	0.146	0.832	0.122	0.000	0
0.6	0.189	0.189	0.151	0.000	0.151	0.450	0.143	0.000	0.139	0.501	0.140	0.000	0.133	0.798	0.107	0.000	0
0.7	0.193	0.193	0.137	0.000	0.137	0.417	0.129	0.000	0.126	0.467	0.126	0.000	0.120	0.766	0.094	0.000	0
0.8	0.197	0.197	0.125	0.000	0.125	0.389	0.117	0.000	0.114	0.438	0.114	0.000	0.109	0.736	0.082	0.001	0
0.9	0.201	0.201	0.114	0.000	0.113	0.366	0.106	0.000	0.104	0.414	0.103	0.000	0.099	0.709	0.072	0.002	0
0.99	0.206	0.206	0.104	0.000	0.104	0.347	0.096	0.000	0.095	0.395	0.094	0.000	0.091	0.685	0.064	0.003	0

N.H. Stern, Optimum income taxation

(c) R = 0.10

0.1	0.333	0.646	0.196	0.000	0.195	0.828	0.193	0.000	0.177	0.850	0.193	0.000	0.169	≧0.950	0.175	0.000	0
0.2	0.338	0.456	0.183	0.000	0.182	0.733	0.177	0.000	0.167	0.767	0.176	0.000	0.159	≧0.950	0.153	0.000	0
0.3	0.344	0.344	0.168	0.000	0.168	0.661	0.161	0.000	0.154	0.703	0.159	0.000	0.147	0.922	0.131	0.000	0
0.4	0.351	0.351	0.153	0.000	0.153	0.605	0.145	0.000	0.140	0.651	0.143	0.000	0.134	0.893	0.112	0.000	0
0.5	0.358	0.358	0.138	0.000	0.138	0.559	0.130	0.000	0.127	0.608	0.127	0.000	0.121	0.865	0.095	0.000	0
0.6	0.366	0.366	0.124	0.000	0.124	0.520	0.115	0.000	0.114	0.571	0.113	0.000	0.109	0.839	0.081	0.000	0
0.7	0.375	0.375	0.111	0.000	0.111	0.488	0.102	0.000	0.101	0.540	0.100	0.000	0.097	0.814	0.068	0.000	0
0.8	0.386	0.386	0.098	0.000	0.098	0.460	0.090	0.000	0.090	0.513	0.088	0.000	0.086	0.792	0.057	0.000	0
0.9	0.398	0.398	0.087	0.000	0.087	0.436	0.080	0.000	0.079	0.488	0.077	0.000	0.076	0.772	0.047	0.000	0
0.99	0.409	0.409	0.078	0.000	0.078	0.417	0.071	0.000	0.071	0.470	0.068	0.000	0.068	0.756	0.039	0.000	0

(d) R = 0.15

0.1	0.476	0.701	0.162	0.000	0.161	0.863	0.160	0.000	0.146	0.881	0.159	0.000	0.138	≧0.950	0.142	0.000	0
0.2	0.484	0.513	0.151	0.000	0.151	0.784	0.145	0.000	0.137	0.812	0.144	0.000	0.130	≧0.950	0.123	0.000	0
0.3	0.494	0.494	0.138	0.000	0.138	0.723	0.131	0.000	0.126	0.759	0.129	0.000	0.120	0.938	0.104	0.000	0
0.4	0.504	0.504	0.125	0.000	0.125	0.675	0.117	0.000	0.114	0.716	0.114	0.000	0.108	0.917	0.086	0.000	0
0.5	0.516	0.516	0.111	0.000	0.111	0.634	0.103	0.000	0.101	0.680	0.100	0.000	0.096	0.896	0.071	0.000	0
0.6	0.530	0.530	0.097	0.000	0.097	0.600	0.089	0.000	0.089	0.648	0.087	0.000	0.085	0.877	0.058	0.000	0
0.7	0.546	0.546	0.084	0.000	0.084	0.571	0.077	0.000	0.077	0.621	0.074	0.000	0.074	0.861	0.046	0.000	0
0.8	0.565	0.565	0.072	0.000	0.072	0.565	0.066	0.000	0.066	0.598	0.063	0.000	0.063	0.848	0.035	0.000	0
0.9	0.588	0.588	0.061	0.000	0.061	0.588	0.056	0.000	0.055	0.588	0.053	0.000	0.053	0.838	0.026	0.000	0
0.99	0.613	0.613	0.051	0.000	0.051	0.613	0.046	0.000	0.046	0.613	0.044	0.000	0.044	0.831	0.019	0.000	0

*Results are given to 3 decimal places. Where 0 is entered the figure is identically zero. An upper bound of 95 percent was placed on the optimum tax rate. Where the optimum is higher than this ≧0.950 is printed in the table. For $\nu = -\infty$, $^{\circ}C \equiv G$ and $^{\circ}C_b \equiv 0$. Symbols are defined in section 4 of the text.

Table 4a

$\mu = -1.0000 \quad \sigma = 0.3900, \quad R = 0.0500, \quad \bar{n} = 0.3969, \quad \alpha = 0.3864.$

ε		0.0000	0.1000	0.2000	0.3000	0.4000	t 0.5000	0.6000	0.7000	0.8000	0.9000
0.1000	G		INFEASIBLE	0.0073	0.0359	0.0643	0.0926	0.1207	0.1482	0.1749	0.1992
	n_t		INFEASIBLE	0.0000	0.0000	0.0000	0.0000	0.0000	0.0000	0.0000	0.0000
0.2000	G		INFEASIBLE	0.0065	0.0343	0.0617	0.0886	0.1147	0.1396	0.1622	0.1794
	n_t		INFEASIBLE	0.0000	0.0000	0.0000	0.0000	0.0000	0.0000	0.0000	0.0000
0.3000	G		INFEASIBLE	0.0056	0.0327	0.0590	0.0844	0.1085	0.1305	0.1488	0.1585
	n_t		INFEASIBLE	0.0000	0.0000	0.0000	0.0000	0.0000	0.0000	0.0000	0.0000
0.4000	G		INFEASIBLE	0.0047	0.0310	0.0562	0.0800	0.1020	0.1210	0.1349	0.1372
	n_t		INFEASIBLE	0.0000	0.0000	0.0000	0.0000	0.0000	0.0000	0.0000	0.0000
0.5000	G		INFEASIBLE	0.0038	0.0292	0.0533	0.0755	0.0953	0.1112	0.1207	0.1163
	n_t		INFEASIBLE	0.0000	0.0000	0.0000	0.0000	0.0000	0.0000	0.0000	0.0001
0.6000	G		INFEASIBLE	0.0029	0.0274	0.0503	0.0709	0.0884	0.1013	0.1067	0.0965
	n_t		INFEASIBLE	0.0000	0.0000	0.0000	0.0000	0.0000	0.0000	0.0000	0.0034
0.7000	G		INFEASIBLE	0.0019	0.0255	0.0472	0.0661	0.0814	0.0914	0.0930	0.0786
	n_t		INFEASIBLE	0.0000	0.0000	0.0000	0.0000	0.0000	0.0000	0.0007	0.0210

N.H. Stern, *Optimum income taxation*

ε								
0.8000	G	INFEASIBLE	0.0009	0.0441	0.0614	0.0745	0.0800	0.0629
	n_t	INFEASIBLE	0.0000	0.0000	0.0000	0.0000	0.0048	0.0567
0.9000	G		INFEASIBLE	0.0409	0.0565	0.0676	0.0680	0.0496
	n_t		INFEASIBLE	0.0000	0.0000	0.0000	0.0156	0.1010
			0.0217					
			0.0000					
0.9900	G		INFEASIBLE	0.0380	0.0522	0.0615	0.0581	0.0395
	n_t		INFEASIBLE	0.0000	0.0000	0.0002	0.0311	0.1389
			0.0200					
			0.0000					

ε	$t_{op}, v = -\infty$	G	Y	n_t	t_b
0.1000	$\geqq$ 0.9500	0.2085	0.27	0.0000E 00	0.1750
0.2000	0.9383	0.1820	0.25	0.1491E-40	0.1773
0.3000	0.9031	0.1585	0.23	0.1352E-16	0.1797
0.4000	0.8672	0.1386	0.22	0.3634E-09	0.1828
0.5000	0.8320	0.1215	0.21	0.5216E-06	0.1859
0.6000	0.7984	0.1067	0.20	0.2265E-04	0.1891
0.7000	0.7664	0.0937	0.19	0.1825E-03	0.1930
0.8000	0.7359	0.0824	0.18	0.6673E-03	0.1969
0.9000	0.7086	0.0724	0.17	0.1634E-02	0.2008
0.9900	0.6852	0.0643	0.17	0.2854E-02	0.2055

[a] See note from table 3. All columns to the left of an 'INFEASIBLE' statement are also infeasible. E-03, for example, means 'multiplied by 10^{-3}'.

Table 4b

$$\mu = -1.0000, \sigma = 0.3900, R = 0.0500, \bar{n} = 0.3969, \alpha = 0.3864, \nu = -1.0000.^a$$

ε		0.0000	0.1000]	0.2000	0.3000	0.4000	0.5000	0.6000	0.7000	0.8000	0.9000
0.1000	°C		INFEASIBLE	0.2108	0.2150	0.2186	0.2218	0.2245	0.2264	0.2271	0.2252
	$^{1/2}C$		INFEASIBLE	0.2108	0.2150	0.2186	0.2218	0.2245	0.2264	0.2271	0.2252
0.2000	°C		INFEASIBLE	0.1980	0.2017	0.2048	0.2073	0.2089	0.2094	0.2078	0.2012
	$^{1/2}C$		INFEASIBLE	0.1988	0.2025	0.2057	0.2082	0.2099	0.2104	0.2087	0.2020
0.3000	°C		INFEASIBLE	0.1834	0.1866	0.1892	0.1909	0.1916	0.1907	0.1868	0.1755
	$^{1/2}C$		INFEASIBLE	0.1873	0.1908	0.1936	0.1955	0.1962	0.1952	0.1910	0.1789
0.4000	°C		INFEASIBLE	0.1680	0.1708	0.1729	0.1740	0.1738	0.1716	0.1654	0.1499
	$^{1/2}C$		INFEASIBLE	0.1775	0.1808	0.1832	0.1845	0.1842	0.1816	0.1746	0.1569
0.5000	°C		INFEASIBLE	0.1530	0.1555	0.1572	0.1577	0.1567	0.1531	0.1448	0.1255
	$^{1/2}C$		INFEASIBLE	0.1693	0.1724	0.1744	0.1751	0.1738	0.1694	0.1594	0.1362
0.6000	°C		INFEASIBLE	0.1389	0.1412	0.1425	0.1424	0.1406	0.1357	0.1256	0.1032
	$^{1/2}C$		INFEASIBLE	0.1625	0.1654	0.1671	0.1671	0.1646	0.1584	0.1453	0.1172
0.7000	°C		INFEASIBLE	0.1260	0.1280	0.1289	0.1284	0.1257	0.1197	0.1079	0.0836
	$^{1/2}C$		INFEASIBLE	0.1569	0.1597	0.1609	0.1601	0.1565	0.1483	0.1323	0.1003

0.8000 $°C$	INFEASIBLE	0.1143	INFEASIBLE	0.1161	0.1166	0.1155	0.1121	0.1050	0.0918	0.0667
$1/2C$	INFEASIBLE	0.1523		0.1549	0.1557	0.1541	0.1492	0.1391	0.1205	0.0856
0.9000 $°C$			INFEASIBLE	0.1052	0.1054	0.1038	0.0997	0.0917	0.0775	0.0526
$1/2C$			INFEASIBLE	0.1508	0.1512	0.1488	0.1426	0.1307	0.1098	0.0734
0.9900 $°C$			INFEASIBLE	0.0963	0.0962	0.0942	0.0894	0.0807	0.0660	0.0420
$1/2C$			INFEASIBLE	0.1478	0.1477	0.1446	0.1373	0.1239	0.1012	0.0643

ε	t_{opt}	G	Y	n_t	$°C_{opt}$	$1/2C_{opt}$	t_b	$°C_b$	$1/2C_b$
0.1000	0.7914	0.1727	0.28	0.0000E 00	0.2271	0.2271	0.1750	0.2096	0.2096
0.2000	0.6805	0.1349	0.27	0.0000E 00	0.2094	0.2104	0.1773	0.1970	0.1977
0.3000	0.6000	0.1085	0.26	0.8098E-53	0.1916	0.1962	0.1797	0.1826	0.1865
0.4000	0.5391	0.0889	0.26	0.6348E-34	0.1741	0.1846	0.1828	0.1673	0.1767
0.5000	0.4898	0.0734	0.25	0.1287E-24	0.1577	0.1751	0.1859	0.1525	0.1687
0.6000	0.4500	0.0609	0.25	0.3161E-19	0.1426	0.1673	0.1891	0.1386	0.1621
0.7000	0.4172	0.0507	0.24	0.8481E-16	0.1290	0.1609	0.1930	0.1258	0.1565
0.8000	0.3891	0.0420	0.24	0.1578E-13	0.1166	0.1557	0.1969	0.1141	0.1521
0.9000	0.3656	0.0347	0.23	0.6383E-12	0.1055	0.1513	0.2008	0.1036	0.1485
0.9900	0.3469	0.0289	0.23	0.6460E-11	0.0964	0.1481	0.2055	0.0949	0.1457

[a]See notes from tables 3 and 4a.

calculated using Gauss–Legendre quadrature and infinite integrals using Gauss–Laguerre quadrature. With t and G known we can calculate the level of the maximand. In this manner tables (such as table 4) are constructed giving values of G and ${}^0C$ over a (one-dimensional) grid of tax rates t, for each ε.

We search, for each ε, over the grid of t to find the optimum. The procedure depends on the existence of at most one local maximum. It is clear from an inspection of tables 4a and 4b that this is satisfied for our problem. The existing grid is examined to find a triple of values of t such that the maximand is higher at the middle value t_2 than the two outer values t_1 and t_3. The optimum must then lie in the range (t_1, t_3). (There is an obvious modification if the largest value of the maximand lies at one of the boundaries of the grid.) A fourth point, t_4, is defined as the midpoint of the larger of the intervals between t_3 and t_1, t_2. One of the outer values (t_1 or t_3) is then replaced by t_4 so that we again have a triple with the maximand highest at the interior point. It is clear that in two moves we must have an interval at most half the length of that of the original. The process is continued until the length of the interval is less than a specified value (here 0.001) and then the interior point of the triple is taken as the opitmum. Thus our optimum tax rates are accurate to $\pm 0.1\%$.

The calculations presented in tables 3, 4a and 4b are for the case $\bar{\mu} = -1$, $\sigma = 0.39$. We have $v = 1, -1, -2, -\infty$; and $R = 0, 0.05, 0.10, 0.15$. A method for understanding how v measures our value judgements has already been given. The magnitude of R can be judged by comparison with the mean of the $f(n)$ distribution, $\bar{n} (= 0.3969$ in the case $\bar{\mu} = -1, \sigma = 0.39)$. Output $\bar{n}$ is the maximum conceivable output – it would be produced if everyone worked all day ($l_n = 1$, all n). Alternatively, one can compare R with output $Y (= (G+R)/t)$ which is given in table 4. ${}^0C_{opt}$ is the value of ${}^0C$ associated with t_{opt}, the optimum t, and ${}^0C_b$ is the value associated with t_b.

A pictorial expression of the results is given in the graphs of figs. 2 and 3.

4.2. Discussion of the results

The purpose of the calculations is to examine the sensitivity of the optimum tax rate to the parameters ε, v and R. We also report, but do not give details on, the results of changing σ, a measure of the dispersion of the distribution of skills.

Table 3(a) gives the optimum tax rates for different values of ε and v for the case $R = 0$ where taxation is *purely* redistributed. The results are illustrated in fig. 2a. As ε increases from 0 to 1, the optimum tax rate decreases (from 100 percent at $\varepsilon = 0$ for all v – see section 5) along a curve which is convex to the origin. Higher values of v (less egalitarian) give lower tax rates as one would expect. The calculations of Mirrlees correspond to the case ($v = 0, \varepsilon = 1$) and of Atkinson to the case ($v = -\infty, \varepsilon = 1$). The Mirrlees median rates of around 20 percent compare reasonably with the middle of the interval between $v = 1$ and $v = -1$. Atkinson found an optimum t of 64 percent for the linear case with

$R = 0$, and a value of α close to the one we are using [see Atkinson (1972, table 2, $a = 0.5$)]. Hence our results correspond with previous studies.

Results with higher values of R are given in tables 3(b), 3(c) and 3(d), and portrayed graphically in figs. 2b, 2c and 2d. It remains true that for a given R and ε, optimum tax rates increase with v and, understandably, for a given ε and v they increase with the expenditure requirement R. However, for a given R and v it is not necessarily true that the optimum tax rate decreases with ε.

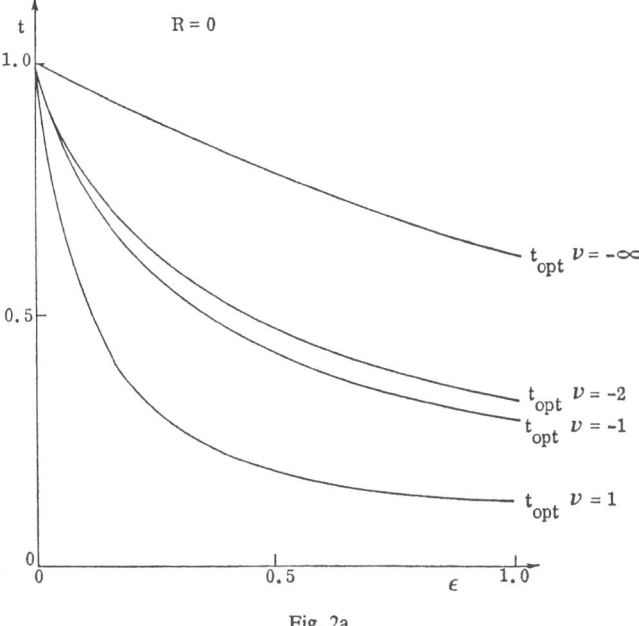

Fig. 2a

For example, for $v = 1$ and $R = 0.10$, the optimum tax rate, as a function of ε, has a minimum of approximately 35 percent around $\varepsilon = 0.35$. This failure of monotonicity is more likely the higher is v and the higher is R.

The reason for the nonmonotonicity is fairly straightforward and can best be understood by examining the behaviour of t_b, the minimum feasible tax rate, as a function of ε. From the calculations it can be seen that t_b increases with ε. The region below the t_b curve (see figs. 2b, 2c and 2d) is infeasible. For higher (less egalitarian) values of v the optimum has lower tax rates and lower G. When the optimum involves G very close to zero, the optimum tax rate is close to t_b, which *increases* with ε, and thus the optimum lying near to the frontier of the infeasible region also increases with ε.

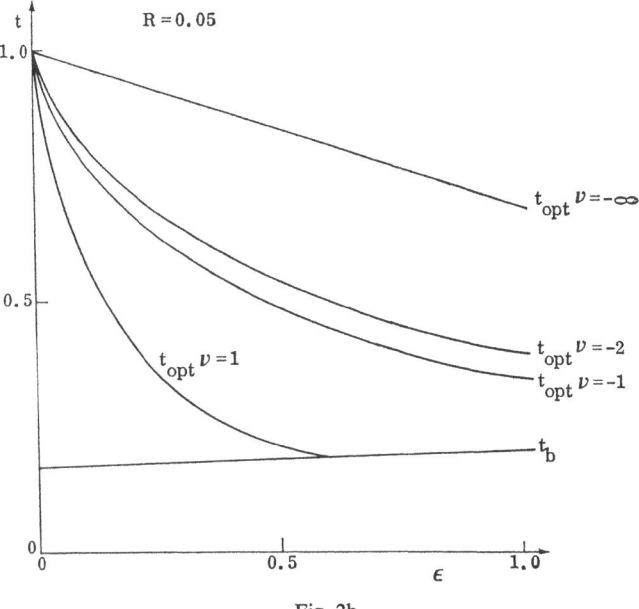

Fig. 2b

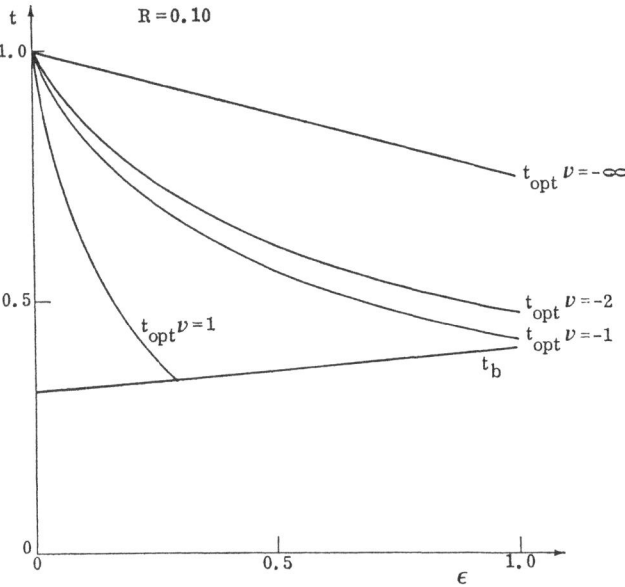

Fig. 2c

Mirrlees (1971, pp. 206–7) found that the use of a much wider dispersion of skills ($\sigma = 1$) gave tax rates which were very much higher. The same conclusion emerges here. For $v = 1$, $R = 0$, $\sigma = 1$, the optimum tax for $\varepsilon = 0.4$ was 62.3%, and for $\varepsilon = 0.99$ was 42.9%, compared with $\sigma = 0.39$, which gives a rate of 22.5% for $\varepsilon = 0.4$ and 12.5% for $\varepsilon = 0.99$. Further, the higher values of ε together with $\sigma = 1$ provided the only cases where the proportion of the population not working was high. For $R = 0$, $v = 1$, $\varepsilon = 0.99$, the optimum

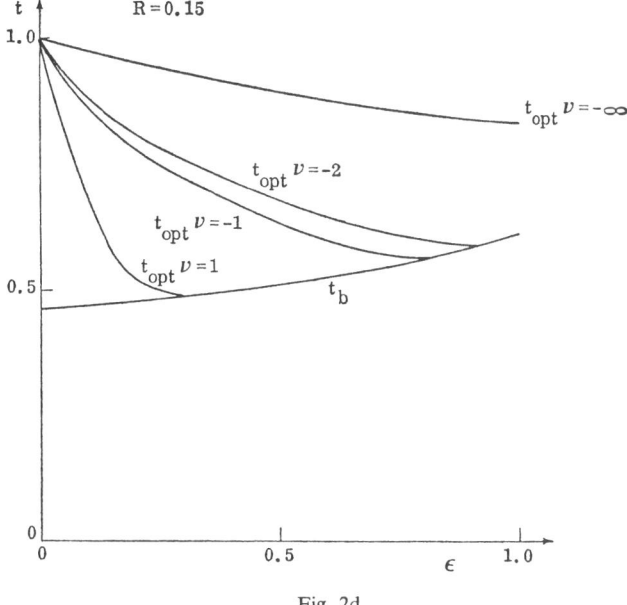

Fig. 2d

proportion of the population not working was 11% (and compare with the n_t figures in table 3).

The total product in our examples usually lies in the range 0.25 to 0.30 and thus a government revenue requirement of 0.15 is very large. Government expenditure on goods and services in the U.K. is approximately 20% of GNP.[23] Thus 0.05 might be viewed as an appropriate figure for R. We have argued that $v = 1$ represents no egalitarian preference and have given a method for judging which values of v capture one's values. I prefer $v = -1$, corresponding to an assertion that the social marginal valuation of income should decrease as the

---

[23]The major components of this 20 percent are health services, education and defence. It is arguable whether these should be classified as public goods – fixed costs since at least the first two in the list may also be productive and none are equally available to all.

square of income.[24] Our estimate of ε is 0.4 – see section 3. Our *central case*, therefore, is $\varepsilon = 0.4$, $R = 0.05$ and $v = -1$, which gives an optimum tax rate of 54%, a grant G of 0.089 and income Y of 0.257. Thus the minimum (0.089) below which no income is allowed to fall is 34% of the average income (total population is one, so Y is also the average income). The utilitarian approach therefore gives taxation rates which are rather high without any appeal to extreme social welfare functions, and need only invoke labour supply functions of the type which are commonly observed. Total net direct and indirect tax rates were around 50% for a broad range of British incomes in 1974 (see *Economic Trends*, Feb. 1976).

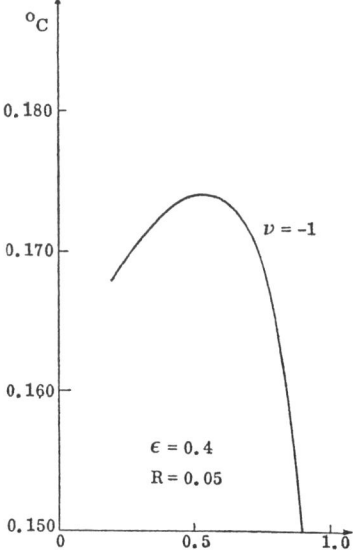

Fig. 3a. (Horizontal axis is tax rate (t).)

The redistributive benefits of taxation can be judged by the comparison of ^0C_b and $^0C_{opt}$ in table 3. The former gives the welfare level when taxes cover only R (and $G = 0$) and the latter gives the welfare level with the optimum linear income tax. In the central case we have $^0C_b = 0.167$ and $^0C_{opt} = 0.174$. Thus the redistributive benefits of taxation are worth approximately 5% of income.

It might be argued that such a figure is small when compared with the possible incentive and administrative costs of taxation. This argument would be mistaken. If R is positive, a tax system is necessary, with its administrative costs. The difference in administrative costs between a tax rate t_b and the optimum is that associated with a positive grant G. The incentive aspects of taxation are already

[24]See Stern (1973).

incorporated in the model. It would be reasonable to argue that our estimate of ε is too small because, for example, in a fully articulated model risk-taking, savings and effort should all be responsive to rewards, but that is a different position. Whichever value of ε one selects there will still be benefits to be obtained from redistribution and, if a tax system is necessary in any case, the benefits, if they are agreed to be such, should be taken. That being said it seems that the benefits are not large for our central case. It is clear that this conclusion is very sensitive to our specification of v. Where $v = -\infty$, the maximin welfare function, the

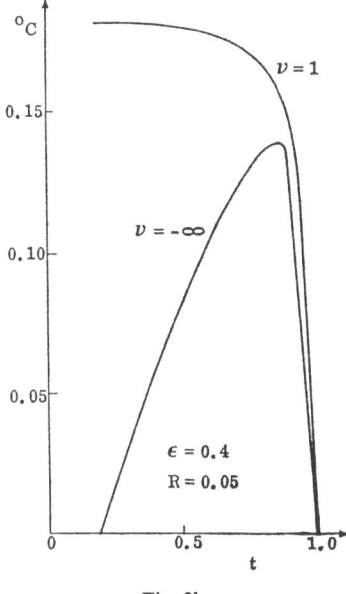

Fig. 3b

measure ^0C is equal to G. Hence, for this case, $^0C_b = 0$. The redistributive benefits of taxation, here raising the income of the least-skilled from zero, are very large. Where $v = 1$ and we have no special preference for equality the redistributive benefits are very small (see table 3 and fig. 3).

A further suggestion that emerges from the examination of the welfare measure ^0C is that uncertainty about the level of ε might lead us to choose a tax rate lower than the optimum (under certainty) associated with our mean estimate of ε, if our central estimates of ε are in a region where the optimum t falls with ε. The reason (see figs. 3a and 3b) is that, for a given ε, increases in taxation above the optimum seem to give larger welfare losses than deviations below the optimum. Further underestimates of ε lead to bigger changes in the choice of t than overestimates.

An example of the full set of results available from the author for each of the cases discussed here is given in tables 4a and 4b, for the case $v = -1$, $R = 0.05$. Table 4a shows the G available from given t, for each ε, together with the t giving maximum G (t_{opt} for $v = -\infty$). Table 4a is independent of v. The values of the maximand for ε, t (calibrated using ^0C and $^{\ddagger}C$) are shown in table 4b, followed by the optimum t and t_b with corresponding values of other figures associated with t and t_b.

The objective of this section has been to display the sensitivity of optimum tax schedules to the elasticity of supply (given by ε), social values (given by v) and the expenditure requirement (R). It would, perhaps, be misleading to say that rates are more sensitive to ε than to v and R since we have no precise measure of sensitivity. But we can claim that values of ε based on observation do give values of the optimum tax rate substantially higher than those which Mirrlees (1971) was surprised to find so low (see section 2) and that an argument for very high rates (say above 70%) must be based (if it is rooted in our model) on a claim that ε is very low (say less than 0.1 or 0.2) rather than an extreme view of values (v) or the government revenue requirement (R).

5. The optimum tax schedule in the Mirrlees model for the case $\varepsilon = 0$

We saw in section 2 that hitherto attention has been focussed on the addi-log case where the elasticity of substitution ε is one. We saw also in section 3.3 that current estimates of labour supply elasticities give ε around or less than one-half. We should, therefore, see $\varepsilon = 1$ as a polar case with $\varepsilon = 0$ as another polar case. It transpires, not surprisingly, that the case $\varepsilon = 0$ is much easier to work out than the case $\varepsilon = 1$, and the answer is independent of the production function and distribution of skills.

The result is that the optimum tax rate, amongst both linear and general schedules, is 100%. This is a fairly obvious result since consumption and leisure are consumed in fixed proportions and there are no dead-weight losses from income taxation. This does not mean that the first-best optimum can be achieved, however. We should emphasise however that a zero elasticity of substitution does *not* imply inelastic labour supply. The substitution effect of a wage change is zero, but we still have the income effect which gives a backward bending supply curve. An inelastic labour supply is the prerogative of the case $\varepsilon = 1$ where (in the absence of a lump sum income) substitution and income effects exactly cancel.

The CES utility function for the case $\varepsilon = 0$ is

$$u(c, l) = \text{Min}(c, 1-l). \qquad (14)$$

We consider first the optimum income taxation problem for the utilitarian maximand where individual utilities are given by (14). We pose this formally as:

Problem P. Find c_n, l_n and a function $g(\cdot)$ such that $\int_0^\infty u_n f(n)\, dn$ is maximised where $u_n = u(c_n, l_n)$ (u as (14)) and $g(\cdot)$ is such that (i) the individual problem maximise $u(c, l)$, subject to $c \leq g(nl)$ $c \geq 0, 1 \geq l \geq 0$, has a solution (c_n, l_n), (ii) $\int_0^\infty c_n f(n)\, dn \leq \int_0^\infty nl_n f(n)\, dn$. The density function $f(n)$ satisfies $f(n) \geq 0$, $\int_0^\infty f(n)\, dn = 1$ and $\infty > \bar{n} = \int_0^\infty nf(n)\, dn$.

We call an allocation $\{(c_n, l_n)\}$ which satisfies (i) and (ii) feasible. Note that as the problem is posed we are assuming that where there is more than one pair (c_n, l_n) which maximises u the government can select whichever such pair it wishes. Mirrlees (1971, proposition 2) shows that we can restrict attention to $g(\cdot)$ that are nondecreasing and right-continuous. Note that, as the problem is posed, units are such that the n-man produces n if he has zero leisure and the kinks in his indifference curves in (c, l) space lie on the line joining $(0, 1)$ and $(1, 0)$.

Theorem 1. An optimum for problem P is $c_n = \bar{n}/(\bar{n}+1)$, $l_n = 1/(\bar{n}+1)$, all n, and $g(x) = \bar{n}/(\bar{n}+1)$ all x.

Proof. Consider a feasible allocation $\{(c_n^0, l_n^0)\}$. If $1 - l_n^0 > c_n^0$, then we can replace l_n^0 by $l_n' = 1 - c_n^0$ and both (i) and (ii) remain satisfied. If $c_n^0 > 1 - l_n^0$, then we can replace c_n^0 by $c_n' = 1 - l_n^0$ and again (i) and (ii) remain satisfied. We can, therefore, confine attention to feasible allocations $\{(c_n, l_n)\}$ where $c_n = 1 - l_n$. The utility maximising (c_n, l_n) (where we now take $c_n = 1 - l_n$) satisfies

$$g(nl_n) \geq 1 - l_n \geq \lim_{a \to nl_n} g(a).$$

It is clear (see fig 4) that c_n is nondecreasing with n [see also Mirrlees (1971, theorem 1)].
Now

$$\int_0^\infty u_n f(n)\, dn = \int_0^\infty c_n f(n)\, dn \equiv A. \tag{15}$$

From (ii), we have, putting $l_n = 1 - c_n$,

$$A \leq \bar{n} - \int_0^\infty c_n n f(n)\, dn. \tag{16}$$

But c_n is a nondecreasing function of n, hence [25]

$$\int_0^\infty c_n n f(n)\, dn \geq \left(\int_0^\infty c_n f(n)\, dn\right)\left(\int_0^\infty n f(n)\, dn\right). \tag{17}$$

---

[25]Where c_n is continuous, write $c(n^*) = \bar{c}$, the average of c. Then since c is nondecreasing, $n(c - \bar{c}) \geq n^*(c - \bar{c})$ and

$$\int ncf - \bar{n}\bar{c} = \int n(c - \bar{c})f \geq n^* \int (c - \bar{c})f = 0.$$

c_n is continuous as defined here, but if not, a similar argument using lim inf in defining n^* will work.

(16) and (17) imply

$$A + A\bar{n} \leq \bar{n},$$

or

$$A \leq \frac{\bar{n}}{\bar{n}+1}.$$

But $\bar{n}/(\bar{n}+1)$ is exactly the utility integral obtained from putting c_n, l_n and $g(\cdot)$ as in the statement of the theorem. We, therefore, have the desired result.

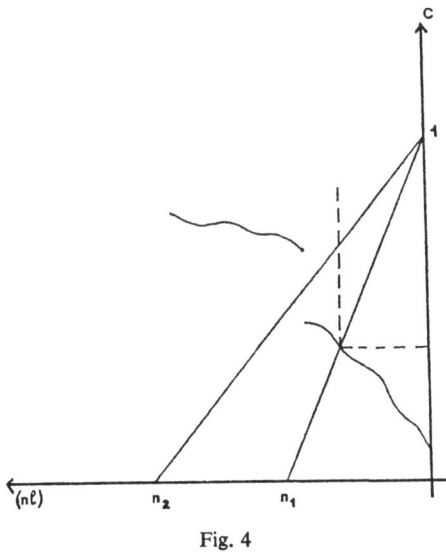

Fig. 4

Suppose the constraint (ii) in problem P is replaced by $\int_0^\infty c_n f(n) \, dn \leq H(\int_0^\infty n l n f(n) \, dn)$, where $H(\cdot)$ is a monotonic increasing function satisfying $H(\bar{n}) > 0$ (where everyone works full-time positive output is possible) and $H(0) < 1$ (satiation is not possible with zero work input). Call the modified problem P'.

Theorem 2. An optimum for the problem P' is $c_n = c^*$, $l_n = 1-c^*$, $g(x) = c^*$, all x, where c^* satisfies $c^* = H(\bar{n}-c^*\bar{n})$. Note that under the conditions imposed on $H(\cdot)$ the equation for c^* defines a unique c^* and $0 < c^* < 1$.

Proof. We follow the proof of theorem 1 but (16) becomes

$$A \leq H(\bar{n} - \int_0^\infty c_n n f(n) \, dn). \tag{16'}$$

(16') and (17) imply

$$A \leq H(\bar{n} - A\bar{n}).$$

Hence $A \leq c^*$ (check from the definition of c^* and the conditions on H – see fig. 5). But c^* can be achieved by putting c_n, l_n and $g(\cdot)$ as in the theorem, and we have the desired result.

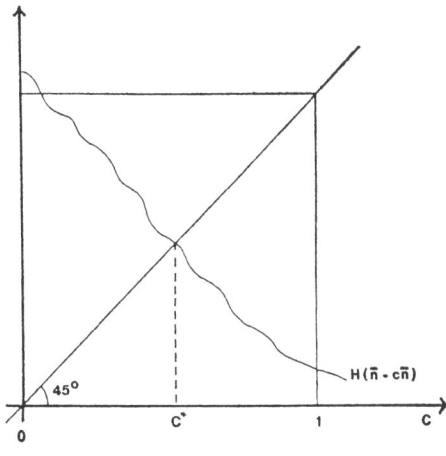

Fig. 5

One can easily see that c^* lies between 0 and 1 by plotting c and $H(\bar{n} - c\bar{n})$ against c and looking at the point of intersection (this also provides a demonstration that $A \leq c^*$) (see fig. 5).

Replace the maximand in problem P by $\int_0^\infty G(u) f(n) \, dn$, where $u(c, l)$ is as in eq. (14) and G is concave and increasing. Call this problem Q.

Theorem 3. An optimum for problem Q is given by the solution described in theorem 1.

Proof. We can again restrict attention to allocations where $c_n = 1 - l_n$ and where the maximand becomes

$$\int_0^\infty G(c_n) f(n) \, dn. \tag{18}$$

The problem Q^0: maximise (18) subject to $\int_0^\infty c_n f(n) \, dn \leq \bar{n}/(\bar{n}+1)$, has a solution with a higher utility integral than problem Q since $\bar{n}/(\bar{n}+1)$ is the maximum output obtainable under an income taxation scheme and Q^0 is, therefore, a less constrained problem than Q. But a solution to problem Q^0,

$$c_n = \frac{\bar{n}}{\bar{n}+1}, \quad (\text{and } l_n = 1/(\bar{n}+1)),$$

can be achieved with the tools of problem Q and we, therefore, have an optimum for problem Q.

Remark. A similar statement to theorem 3 applies if we modify problem P' to Q' by introducing $G(\cdot)$.

We should note two points about these theorems. First, if G is convex we should not expect a solution with 100% marginal tax rates. Presumably, one might be prepared to reduce total output for the 'benefits' of unequal consumption. Secondly, we are forced to rely rather heavily on the notion that the government can choose from the set of bundles that maximise utility for the individual.

The full optimum involves maximising $\int_0^\infty u_n f(n) \, dn$, subject to $\int_0^\infty c_n f(n) \, dn \leq \int_0^\infty n l_n f(n) \, dn$. As before, we can restrict attention to configurations where $c_n = 1 - l_n$ and hence $\int_0^\infty u_n f(n) \, dn = \int_0^\infty c_n f(n) \, dn$. Taking a Lagrange multiplier v for the constraint, we have

$$\left. \begin{array}{c} -1+(n+1)\,v \leq 0 \\ l \geq 0 \end{array} \right\}, \text{comp,}$$

$$\left. \begin{array}{c} -1+(n+1)\,v \geq 0 \\ l \leq 1 \end{array} \right\} \text{comp,}$$

$$\left. \begin{array}{c} \int_0^\infty c_n f(n) \, dn \leq \int_0^\infty n l_n f(n) \, dn \\ v \geq 0 \end{array} \right\} \text{comp,}$$

as necessary and sufficient conditions for optimality. Thus, the optimum requires[26] that for

$$n \leq \frac{1}{v^*} - 1, \quad c_n = 1, \quad l_n = 0,$$

$$n > \frac{1}{v^*} - 1, \quad c_n = 0, \quad l_n = 1,$$

[26] We need not be specific about c_n at $n = (1/v^*) - 1$ if there is no probability atom concentrated on this level of n.

with v^* determined by

$$\text{total consumption} = \int_0^{(1-v^*)/v^*} f(n) \, dn = \int_{(1-v^*)/v^*}^\infty nf(n) \, dn$$
$$= \text{total output}.$$

The l.h.s. decreases from 1 to 0 as v goes from 0 to 1, and the r.h.s. increases from 0 to $\bar{n}$ as v goes from 0 to 1, and we therefore have a unique solution for some $v^* > 0$.

The solution was calculated for n distributed log-normally with the parameters used by Mirrlees (1971). The cases are specified by $\bar{\mu} = -1$, $\sigma = 0.39$ and $\bar{\mu} = -1$, $\sigma = 1$, where $\bar{\mu}$ and σ are the mean and standard deviation of the underlying normal distribution. Mirrlees suggested $\sigma = 0.39$ was the more realistic. In the former case $v^* = 0.766$ and the proportion of the population not working is 32.0%. The ratio β of output in the optimum income taxation solution to output in this, the full optimum, is 0.889. Output is the obvious measure of welfare here since the utility function is linear in consumption and the Atkinson (1970) equally-distributed-equivalent (EDE) measure is equal to output itself.

The corresponding figures for $\bar{\mu} = -1$, $\sigma = 1$ are $v^* = 0.727$, 50.8% of the population not working, and a ratio β of output in the optimum income tax case to output in the full optimum of 0.744. With the wider spread of skills, more of the population is idle, yet the increased availability and use of skills at the upper end gives a greater proportional output increase in the movement from optimum income taxation to the full optimum.

The full optimum here provides an illustration of the Mirrlees result that the full optimum has utility decreasing with skill level, provided leisure is a normal good. The form of decrease is rather bizarre, however, with consumption dropping from its maximum, one, to its minimum, zero, at $n = (1/v^*)-1$.

The full optimum was also calculated for maximand $\int_0^\infty G(u)f(n) \, dn$, where $G(x) = \log_e x$ and $-1/x$. The analysis is similar and the solution, where $h(\cdot) \equiv G'^{-1}(\cdot)$, is

$$c_n = h((n+1)v^*) \quad \text{if} \quad h((n+1)v^*) \leq 1,$$
$$c_n = 1 \quad \text{if} \quad h((n+1)v^*) \geq 1,$$

with $l_n = 1 - c_n$ and v^* determined from

$$\int_0^\infty c_n f(n) \, dn = \int_{((x_0/v^*)-1)}^\infty nl_n f(n) \, dn,$$

if $(x_0/v^*) - 1 > 0$, where x_0 is defined by $h(x_0) = 1$, and

$$\int_0^\infty c_n f(n) \, dn = \int_0^\infty nl_n f(n) \, dn$$

if $(x_0/v^*) - 1 \leq 0$.

The solutions for the two log-normal cases and $G(x) = \log_e x$, and $G(x) = -1/x$, involved the whole population working. In all four cases $x_0 = 1$. The value of the maximand at the full optimum was calibrated by c^* where $G(c^*) = \int_0^\infty G(c_n) f(n) \, dn$ (again analogous to Atkinson's EDE). We then calculated the ratio β of output (equals consumption per head) in the optimum income tax case to c^*. For $\bar{\mu} = -1$, $\sigma = 0.39$, we have

$$\beta = 0.994, \quad G(x) = \log_e x,$$

$$\beta = 0.997, \quad G(x) = -1/x.$$

For $\bar{\mu} = -1$, $\sigma = 1$, we have

$$\beta = 0.935, \quad G(x) = \log_e x,$$

$$\beta = 0.963, \quad G(x) = -1/x.$$

In the case where $\varepsilon = 0$, therefore, a small amount of inequality aversion (concavity of $G(\cdot)$), brings the full optimum rather close to the (completely equal) optimum income tax solution. Presumably the increased availability and use of skills at the upper end is again giving bigger output increases, for the case $\sigma = 1$, when we move from optimum income taxation to the full optimum.

The small welfare difference between the full optimum and the optimum income taxation solutions contrasts with the impression one has from Mirrlees' (1971, p. 206) calculations that the full optimum gives substantial welfare differences from the optimum income taxation solution.

6. Concluding remarks

We have discussed most of the ingredients of a model of optimum income taxation both in terms of how the different components should be specified and the effects of varying the specifications of optimum tax schedules. It was suggested that the Bergson–Samuleson social welfare function, nondecreasing in each argument and which is almost universally adopted in the literature on welfare economics, may not be a good representation of the values of many who would wish to comment on appropriate income taxation. This did not involve the rejection of the criterion, and the usual form of welfare function was used in most of the paper. Our particular concern, however, was the elasticity of labour supply and the related problem of the skill distribution.

It was argued in section 3 that the assumption that individuals differ only in skills, and not in preferences between work and leisure, is very convenient for estimation purposes. Since backward bending supply curves of hours of work are generally observed in practice, such a specification must lead to estimates of the elasticity (ε) of substitution between work and leisure which are considerably less than one. We used the figure $\varepsilon = 0.4$. On the other hand, a specification where individuals differ in their preferences as well as their skills can produce very different results, and we saw how a completely inelastic labour supply might be inferred when supply was in fact sensitive to the wage rate (positively or negatively).

We suggested that it is hard to guess whether the distribution of earnings overestimates or underestimates the dispersion of the distribution of skills since backward bending supply curves make the earnings dispersion narrower, and nonskill factors wider, than the dispersion of skills.

There are deeper questions, however, concerning the supply of effort and skills. If a skill is acquired, then the motive for acquisition should be in the model. Thus any distribution of fixed skills in the model should be of unacquired skills. We do not know how to measure skill or the difference between acquired and unacquired skills, if indeed the distinction is sound. Similarly, the measurement of effort is extremely complex and very difficult to disentangle from skill. The motive for supply of effort may not always be monetary reward – for example, many work who would receive more on public welfare. It is precisely because of the incentives for the individual to conceal his levels of skill and effort, that we build models of income taxation rather than ability taxation.

Our central estimate (see section 4), using $\varepsilon = 0.4$, of the optimum linear income taxation rate was 54%, compared with levels of 20 or 30% which emerge from models where $\varepsilon = 1$. We found that the optimum tax rate was rather sensitive to ε and proved in general, (see section 5) that for $\varepsilon = 0$, the optimum tax rate (linear or nonlinear) is 100%.

Very high tax rates can only be justified by appeal to low ε and not to high revenue requirements or extreme preference for equality. The optimum tax rates are, however, rather sensitive to: ε, social values (v) and revenue requirements (R).

An interesting feature to emerge was, where there is a large revenue to be raised and values are not particularly egalitarian, that the optimum tax rate may not be monotonic in the elasticity of substitution. The reason is that the minimum tax required to raise the revenue increases with ε when the desired grant G is small.

We found that, in our central case, the gains from optimum linear taxation, as compared with minimum taxation to meet revenue requirements, were not large but that this conclusion was, not surprisingly, very sensitive to distributional values. On the other hand, in the case where $\varepsilon = 0$, there is no loss from a restriction to optimum linear income tax as opposed to nonlinear, and the optimum income tax solution gives welfare close to the full optimum.

Finally we should emphasise that the study of optimum income taxation is in its infancy, there is much work, empirical and conceptual as well as theoretical, to do, and therefore all our estimates and calculations must be viewed with circumspection and as attempts to understand the best model currently available rather than prescriptions for policy.

References

Ashenfelter, O. and J. Heckman, 1973, Estimating labour-supply functions, in: Cain and Watts (1973).
Atkinson, A.B., 1970, On the measurement of inequality, Journal of Economic Theory, and in Atkinson (1973b).
Atkinson, A.B., 1972, 'Maxi-min' and optimal income taxation, (mimeo) presented to the 1972 Budapest meeting of the Econometric Society.
Atkinson, A.B., 1973a, How progressive should income tax be?, in: Phelps (1973).
Atkinson, A.B., ed., 1973b, Wealth, income and inequality (Penguin, Harmondsworth).
Atkinson, A.B. and J.E. Stiglitz, 1975, The design of tax structure: Direct versus indirect taxation, Journal of Public Economics 6, 000–000 (this issue).
Bevan, D., 1974, Savings, inheritance and economic growth in the presence of earnings inequality, mimeo, Oxford.
Cain, G.C. and N.W. Watts, 1973, Income maintenance and labour supply (Rand McNally, Chicago).
Fair, R.C., 1971, The optimal distribution of income, Quarterly Journal of Economics.
Feldstein, M.S., 1973, On the optimal progressivity of the income tax, Journal of Public Economics 2, 357–376.
Finegan, T.A., 1962, Hours of work in the United States: A cross-sectional analysis, Journal of Political Economy.
Hall, R.E., 1973, Wages, income and hours of work in the U.S. labor force, in: Cain and Watts (1973, ch. 3).
Hall, R.E., 1974, Labour supply and the negative income tax experiment, mimeo, M.I.T.
Lydall, H.F., 1968, The structure of earnings (Oxford).
Mirrlees, J.A., 1971, An exploration in the theory of optimum income taxation, Review of Economic Studies.
Owen, J.D., 1971, The demand for leisure, Journal of Political Economy.
Phelps, E.S., 1973, Wage taxation for economic justice, Quarterly Journal of Economics.
Plato, 1960, The laws, translated by A.E. Taylor (E.P. Dutton, New York).
Roberts, K.W.S., 1974, On optimal linear income tax schedules, mimeo, Oxford.
Roberts, K.W.S., 1974, Calculations on the optimal linear income tax, mimeo, Oxford.
Rosen, H., 1975, A methodology for evaluating tax reform proposals, Journal of Public Economics 6, 000–000 (this issue).
Rosen, S., 1969, On the interindustry wage and hours structure, Journal of Political Economy.
Sadka, E., 1973, Income distribution, incentive effects and optimal income taxation, unpublished Ph.D. dissertation (M.I.T., Cambridge, MA).
Schwartz, J., 1975, An examination of some theoretical and methodological issues relating to the study of income, income distributions and inequality, mimeo.
Simons, H.C., 1938, Personal income taxation (University of Chicago, Chicago).
Stern, N.H., 1973, Welfare weights and the elasticity of the marginal valuation of income, (mimeo) presented to I.I.M. Berlin Symposium on Planning, 1973. Revised version to appear in the proceedings of the 1976 AUTE conference in Edinburgh.
Tawney, R.M., 1964, Equality (Allen and Unwin, London).
Vickrey, W., 1974, Agenda for progressive taxation (Ronald Press, New York).
Winston, G.C., 1966, An international comparison of income and hours of work, Review of Economics and Statistics.

Review of Economic Studies (2001) **68**, 205–229

Using Elasticities to Derive Optimal Income Tax Rates

EMMANUEL SAEZ
Harvard University and NBER

First version received June 1999; *final version accepted May* 2000 (*Eds.*)

This paper derives optimal income tax formulas using compensated and uncompensated elasticities of earnings with respect to tax rates. A simple formula for the high income optimal tax rate is obtained as a function of these elasticities and the thickness of the top tail of the income distribution. In the general non-linear income tax problem, this method using elasticities shows precisely how the different economic effects come into play and which are the key relevant parameters in the optimal income tax formulas of Mirrlees. The optimal non-linear tax rate formulas are expressed in terms of elasticities and the shape of the income distribution. These formulas are implemented numerically using empirical earning distributions and a range of realistic elasticity parameters.

1. INTRODUCTION

There is a controversial debate about the degree of progressivity that the income tax should have. This debate is not limited to the economic research area but also attracts much attention in the political sphere and among the public in general. At the centre of the debate lies the equity-efficiency trade-off. Progressivity allows the government to redistribute from rich to poor, but progressive taxation and high marginal tax rates have efficiency costs. High rates may affect the incentives to work and may therefore reduce the tax base, producing large deadweight losses. The modern setup for analysing the equity-efficiency tradeoff using a general nonlinear income tax was built by Mirrlees (1971). Since then, the theory of optimal income taxation based on the original Mirrlees framework has been considerably developed. The implications for policy, however, are limited for two main reasons.

First, optimal income tax schedules have few general properties: we know that optimal rates must lie between 0 and 1 and that they equal zero at the top and the bottom. These properties are of little practical relevance for tax policy. In particular the zero marginal rate at the top is a very local result. In addition, numerical, simulations show that tax schedules are very sensitive to the utility functions chosen. Second, optimal income taxation has interested mostly theorists and has not changed the way applied public finance economists think about the equity-efficiency tradeoff. Though behavioural elasticities are the key concept in applied studies, there has been no systematic attempt to derive results in optimal taxation which could be easily used in applied studies. As a result, optimal income tax theory is often ignored and tax reform discussions are centred on the concept of deadweight burden. Thus, most discussions on tax reforms focus only on the efficiency aspect of taxation and do not incorporate the equity aspect in the analysis.

This paper argues that there is a simple link between optimal tax formulas and elasticities of earnings familiar to empirical studies. It shows that using elasticities directly to derive optimal income tax rates is a useful method to obtain new results in optimal income taxation. First, a simple formula for the optimal tax rate for high incomes is derived as a function of both substitution and income effects and the thickness of the top tail of the income distribution. Second, deriving the general Mirrlees formula for optimal non-linear tax rates in terms of elasticities provides a clear understanding of the key economic effects underlying the formula. It shows that the shape of the income distribution plays a critical role in the pattern of optimal tax rates. Third, the optimal tax formulas derived using elasticities do not explicitly require the strong homogeneity assumptions about preferences usually made in the optimal income tax literature. Therefore the elasticity method might be robust to the introduction of heterogeneity in preferences. Last, because the formulas derived are closely related to empirical magnitudes, they can be easily implemented numerically using the empirical income distribution and making realistic assumptions about the elasticity parameters.

The paper is organized as follows. Section 2 reviews the main results of the optimal income tax literature. Section 3 derives a simple formula for optimal high income tax rates and relates it to empirical magnitudes. Section 4 considers the general optimal non-linear income tax problem. The formula of Mirrlees (1971) is derived directly in terms of elasticities. Section 5 presents numerical simulations of optimal tax schedules and Section 6 concludes.

2. LITERATURE REVIEW

The Mirrlees (1971) model of optimal income taxation captures the key efficiency-equity tradeoff issue of redistribution: the government has to rely on a distortionary nonlinear income tax to meet both its revenue requirements and redistribute income. General results about optimal tax schedules are fairly limited. Tuomala (1990) presents most of the formal results.

Mirrlees (1971) showed that there is no gain from having marginal tax rates above 100% because nobody will choose to have such a rate at the margin. Mirrlees (1971) also showed that optimal marginal rates cannot be negative. Seade (1982) clarified the conditions under which this result holds. The most striking and well known result is that the marginal tax rate should be zero at the income level of the top income level when the income distribution is bounded (Sadka (1976) and Seade (1977)). Numerical simulations have shown, however, that this result is very local (see Tuomala (1990)). This result is therefore of little practical interest. Mirrlees (1971) did not derive this simple result because he considered unbounded distributions of skills. He nonetheless presented precise conjectures about asymptotic optimal rates in the case of utility functions separable in consumption and labour. Nonetheless, these conjectures have remained practically unnoticed in the subsequent optimal income tax literature. This can be explained by two reasons. First, Mirrlees conjectures depend on the unobservable distribution of skills and on abstract properties of the utility function with no obvious intuitive meaning. Second, the zero top rate result was probably considered for a long time as the definitive result because the empirical income distribution is indeed bounded. The present paper argues that in fact unbounded distributions are of much more interest than bounded distributions to address the high income optimal tax rate problem.

A symmetrical zero rate result has been obtained at the bottom. Seade (1977) showed that if everybody works (and labour supply is bounded away from zero) then the bottom rate is zero. However, if there is an atom of non workers then the bottom tax rate is positive and numerical simulations show that, in this case, the bottom rate can be substantial (Tuomala (1990)).

A number of studies have tried to relate optimal income tax formulas to the elasticity concepts used in applied work. Using the tools of optimal commodity tax theory, Dixit and Sandmo (1977) expressed the optimal *linear* income tax rate in terms of elasticities. However, in the case of the non-linear income tax problem, the attempts have been much less systematic. Roberts (2000) uses a perturbation method, similar in spirit to what is done in the present paper, and obtains optimal non-linear income tax formulas expressed in terms of elasticities.[1] He also derives asymptotic formulas that are similar to the ones I obtain.[2] Recently, Diamond (1998) analysed the case of utility functions with no income effects and noticed that the Mirrlees formula for optimal rates is considerably simpler in that case and could be expressed in terms of the labour supply elasticity. He also obtained simple results about the asymptotic pattern of the marginal rates.[3] Piketty (1997) considered the same quasi-linear utility case and derived Diamond's optimal tax formulas for the Rawlsian criterion without setting a formal programme of maximization. He considered instead small local changes in marginal rates and used directly the elasticity of labour supply to derive the behavioural effects of this small reform. My paper clarifies and generalizes this alternative method of derivation of optimal taxes. Finally, the non-linear pricing literature, which considers models that are formally very close to optimal income tax models, has developed a methodology to obtain optimal price formulas based on demand profile elasticities that is also close to the method adopted here (see Wilson (1993)).

Another strand of the public economics literature has developed similar elasticity methods to calculate the marginal costs of public funds. The main purpose of this literature was to develop tools more sophisticated than simple deadweight burden computations to evaluate the efficiency costs of different kinds of tax reforms and the optimal provision of public goods (see *e.g.* Ballard and Fullerton (1992) and Dahlby (1998)). I will show that the methods of this literature can be useful to derive results in optimal taxation and that, in particular, Dahlby (1998) has come close to my results for high income rates.

Starting with Mirrlees (1971), considerable effort has gone into simulations of optimal tax schedules. Following Stern (1976), attention has been paid on a careful calibration of the elasticity of labour supply. Most simulation results are surveyed in Tuomala (1990). It has been noticed that the level of inequality of the distribution of skills and the elasticities of labour supply significantly affect optimal schedules. Most simulations use a log-normal distribution of skills which matches roughly the single moded empirical distribution but has also an unrealistically thin top tail which leads to marginal rates converging to zero. Nobody has tried to use empirical distributions of income to perform simulations because the link between skills and realized incomes was never investigated in depth.[4] The present study pays careful attention to this issue and presents simulations based on the empirical earnings distribution.

3. HIGH INCOME OPTIMAL TAX RATES

I show in this section that the classic method of the optimal *linear* income tax literature can be used to derive in a simple way an optimal tax rate formula for high income earners.

---

1. Revesz (1989) also attempted to express the Mirrlees formulas in terms of elasticities.
2. The link between Roberts (2000) and the present analysis is discussed in detail in Section 4.
3. Some of these results had been obtained by Atkinson (1990) in a more specialized situation.
4. However, Kanbur and Tuomala (1994) realized that it is important to distinguish between the skill distribution and the income distribution when calibrating the distribution of skills. Their work improved significantly upon previous simulations. I come back to their contribution in Section 5.

I will consider that the govenment sets a flat marginal rate τ above a given (high) income level $\bar{z}$ and then derive the welfare and tax revenue effects of a small increase in τ using elasticities. The optimal tax rate τ is obtained when a small change in the tax rate has no first-order effects on total social welfare.[5]

3.1. *Elasticity concepts*

I consider a standard two good model. Each taxpayer maximizes a well-behaved individual utility function $u = u(c, z)$ which depends positively on consumption c and negatively on earnings z. Individual skills or ability are embodied in the individual utility function. Assuming that the individual faces a linear budget constraint $c = z(1 - \tau) + R$, where τ is the marginal tax rate and R is virtual (non-labour) income. The first-order condition of the individual maximization programme, $(1 - \tau)u_c + u_z = 0$, defines implicitly a Marshallian (uncompensated) earnings supply function $z = z(1 - \tau, R)$. The *uncompensated* elasticity is defined such that

$$\zeta^u = \frac{1-\tau}{z}\frac{\partial z}{\partial(1-\tau)}. \tag{1}$$

Income effects are captured by the parameter

$$\eta = (1-\tau)\frac{\partial z}{\partial R}. \tag{2}$$

The Hicksian (compensated) earnings function is the earnings level which minimizes cost $c - z$ needed to reach a given utility level u for a given tax rate τ and is denoted by $z^c = z^c(1 - \tau, u)$. The *compensated* elasticity of earnings is defined by

$$\zeta^c = \frac{1-\tau}{z}\frac{\partial z}{\partial(1-\tau)}\bigg|_u. \tag{3}$$

The two elasticity concepts and the income effects parameter are related by the Slutsky equation

$$\zeta^c = \zeta^u - \eta. \tag{4}$$

The compensated elasticity is always non-negative and η is non positive if leisure is not an inferior good, an assumption I make from now on.

3.2. *Deriving the high income optimal tax rate*

The government sets a constant linear rate τ of taxation above a given (high) level of income $\bar{z}$. I normalize without loss of generality the population with income above $\bar{z}$ to one and I note $h(z)$ the density of the earnings distribution at the optimum tax regime.[6] To obtain the optimal τ, I consider a small increase $d\tau$ in the top tax rate τ for incomes

---

5. Dahlby (1998) considered piecewise linear tax schedules and used the same kind of methodology to compute the effects of a general tax rate reform on taxes paid by a "representative" individual in each tax bracket. By specializing his results to a reform affecting only the tax rate of the top bracket, he derived a formula for the tax rate maximizing taxes paid by the "representative" individual of the top bracket that is a special case of the one obtained here.
6. Note that the density $h(z)$ is endogenous to the tax schedule. I come back to this in detail later on.

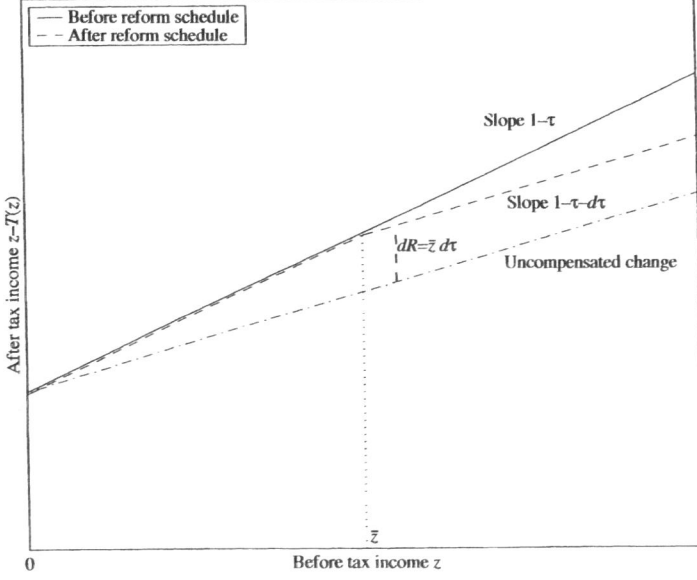

FIGURE 1
High income tax rate perturbation

above $\bar{z}$ as depicted on Figure 1. This tax change has two effects on tax revenue. First, there is a mechanical effect, which is the change in tax revenue if there were no behavioural responses, and second, there is a reduction in tax revenue due to reduced earnings through behavioural responses. Let us examine these two effects successively.

- *Mechanical effect.*

The mechanical effect (denoted by M) represents the increase in tax receipts if there were no behavioural responses. A taxpayer with income z (above $\bar{z}$) would pay $(z - \bar{z})d\tau$ additional taxes. Therefore, summing over the population above $\bar{z}$ and denoting the mean of incomes above $\bar{z}$ by z_m, the total mechanical effect M is equal to

$$M = [z_m - \bar{z}]d\tau. \tag{5}$$

- *Behavioural responses.*

As shown in Figure 1, the tax change can be decomposed into two parts; first, an overall *uncompensated* increase $d\tau$ in marginal rates (starting from 0 and not just from $\bar{z}$), second, an overall increase in virtual income $dR = \bar{z}d\tau$. Therefore, an individual with income z changes its earnings by

$$dz = -\frac{\partial z}{\partial (1-\tau)}d\tau + \frac{\partial z}{\partial R}dR = -(\zeta^u z - \eta \bar{z})\frac{d\tau}{1-\tau}, \tag{6}$$

where we have used definitions (1) and (2). The reduction in income dz displayed in equation (6) implies a reduction in tax receipts equal to τdz. The total reduction in tax receipts due to the behavioural responses is simply the sum of the terms τdz over all individuals earning more than $\bar{z}$

$$B = -(\bar{\zeta}^u z_m - \bar{\eta}\bar{z})\frac{\tau d\tau}{1-\tau}, \qquad (7)$$

where $\bar{\zeta}^u = \int_{\bar{z}}^{\infty} \zeta^u_{(z)} zh(z)dz/z_m$ is a weighted average of the uncompensated elasticity. The elasticity term $\zeta^u_{(z)}$ inside the integral is the average elasticity over individuals earning income z. Similarly, $\bar{\eta} = \int_{\bar{z}}^{\infty} \eta_{(z)} h(z)dz$ is the average income effect. Note that $\bar{\eta}$ and $\bar{\zeta}^u$ are not averaged with the same weights. It is not necessary to assume that people earning the same income have the same elasticity; the relevant parameters are simply the average elasticities at given income levels.[7]

In order to obtain the optimal tax rate, we must equalize the revenue effect obtained by summing (5) and (7) to the welfare effect due to the small tax reform. To obtain the welfare effect, let us consider $\bar{g}$ which is the ratio of social marginal utility for the top bracket taxpayers to the marginal value of public funds for the government. In other words, $\bar{g}$ is defined such that the government is indifferent between $\bar{g}$ more dollars of public funds and one more dollar consumed by the taxpayers with income above $\bar{z}$. The smaller $\bar{g}$, the less the government values marginal consumption of high incomes. Thus $\bar{g}$ is a parameter reflecting the redistributive goals of the government.

To compute the welfare effects, let us note $u((1-\tau)z(1-\tau, R) + R, z(1-\tau, R))$, the individual utility at the optimum labour supply choice for a top bracket taxpayer. Using the envelope theorem, the effect of the small tax change on u is $du = u_c(-zd\tau + dR) = -u_c(z-\bar{z})d\tau$ where $(z-\bar{z})d\tau$ is the mechanical increase in individual tax. As a result and by definition of $\bar{g}$, each additional dollar raised by the government because of the tax reform reduces on average social welfare of people in the top bracket by $\bar{g}$. Thus the total welfare loss due to the tax reform is equal to $\bar{g}M$. Consequently, the government sets the rate τ such that, $(1-\bar{g})M + B = 0$. Thus, using (5) and (7), the optimal rate is such that

$$\frac{\tau}{1-\tau} = \frac{(1-\bar{g})(z_m/\bar{z}-1)}{\bar{\zeta}^u z_m/\bar{z} - \bar{\eta}}. \qquad (8)$$

Equation (8) gives a strikingly simple answer to the problem of the optimal marginal rate for high income earners. Note that this formula does not require identical elasticities among taxpayers and thus applies to populations with heterogeneous preferences or elasticities. The only relevant behavioural parameters are the average elasticity $\bar{\zeta}^u$ and average income effects $\bar{\eta}$ for taxpayers with income above $\bar{z}$. Unsurprisingly, the optimal rate τ is a decreasing function of the social weight $\bar{g}$ put on high income taxpayers, the average elasticity $\bar{\zeta}^u$, and the absolute size of income effects $-\bar{\eta}$. Interestingly, the optimal rate is an increasing function of $z_m/\bar{z}$. The ratio $z_m/\bar{z}$ is a key parameter for the high income optimal tax problem. This parameter depends on the shape of the income distribution and has not been studied in the optimal tax literature.

If the distribution of income is bounded, then, when $\bar{z}$ is close to the top, the ratio $z_m/\bar{z}$ tends to one and thus, from (8), we deduce that the top rate must be equal to zero. This is the classical zero top rate result derived by Sadka (1976) and Seade (1977). The intuition for the result is straightforward. As can be seen comparing (5) and (7), close to the top, the mechanical increase in tax revenue M is negligible relative to the loss in tax

---

7. Note that, in deriving (7), I have implicitly assumed that the set of taxpayers who might jump discontinuously because of the small tax reform is negligible. This is expected to be true almost surely but constructing particular counter-examples might nonetheless be possible.

revenue B due to the behavioural response implying that the optimal rate must be close to zero.

3.3. Empirical earnings distributions and optimal top rate

To assess whether the zero top result is actually relevant, it is useful to examine the ratio $z_m/\bar{z}$ using empirical earnings distributions. Figure 2 plots the values of the ratios $z_m/\bar{z}$ computed using annual wage income reported on tax return data for years 1992 and 1993 in the U.S.[8] On Figure 2, the ratios $z_m/\bar{z}$ are reported as a function of $\bar{z}$ for incomes between \$0 to \$500,000 in the left panel and for incomes between \$10,000 to \$30 million in the right panel (using a semi-log scale). Figure 2 shows that the ratio is strikingly stable (and around 2) over the tail of the income distribution.[9] As discussed above, the ratio must be equal to one at the level of the highest income. However, Figure 2 shows that even at income level \$30 million, the ratio is still around 2. For example, if the second top income taxpayer earns half as much as the top taxpayer then the ratio is equal to 2 at the level of the second top earner. Thus the ratio might well come to one only in the vicinity of the top income earner. Consequently, the zero top result only applies to the very highest taxpayer and is therefore of no practical interest.

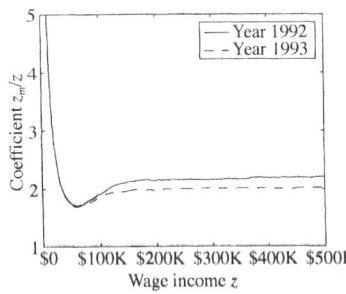 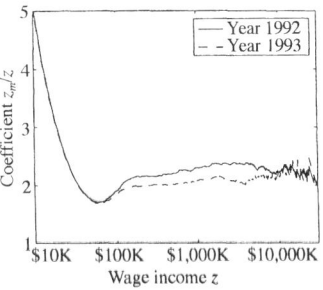

FIGURE 2

Ratio mean income above z divided by z, z_m/z, years 1992 and 1993

From \$150,000 to close to the very top, the ratio $z_m/\bar{z}$ is roughly constant around 2. This means that formula (8) can be applied by replacing $z_m/\bar{z}$ by 2 for any $\bar{z}$ above \$150,000. Distributions with constant ratio $z_m/\bar{z}$ are exactly Pareto distributions. Therefore, the tails of empirical earnings distributions can be remarkably well approximated by Pareto distributions.[10] More precisely, a Pareto distribution with parameter $a > 1$ is such that Prob(Income $> z$) = C/z^a for some constant C. For a Pareto distribution, $z_m/\bar{z}$ is constant and equal to $a/(a-1)$. The higher a, the thinner is the tail of the income distribution. For the U.S. wage income distribution, the ratio $z_m/\bar{z}$ is around 2 and thus the parameter a is approximately equal to 2.

---

8. The public use tax files prepared yearly by the Internal Revenue Service have been used for this exercise. This data is particularly fitted for this type of computations because it oversamples high income taxpayers. As many as one third of the highest income earners in the U.S. are included in the sample. The ratios have been computed using the amounts reported on the line Wages, Salaries and tips of Form 1040. The sample has been restricted to married taxpayers only.

9. The ratio becomes noisy above \$10 million because the number of taxpayers above that level is very small and crossing only one taxpayer has a non trivial discrete effect on the curves.

10. Pareto discovered this empirical regularity more than a century ago (see Pareto (1965)).

Assuming that the elasticity $\bar{\zeta}^u$ and income effects $\bar{\eta}$ converge as $\bar{z}$ increases, and assuming that the ratio $z_m/\bar{z}$ converges (to a limit denoted by $a/(a-1)$), the optimal tax rate (8) converges. Using the Slutsky equation (4), the limiting tax rate can be written in terms of the limiting values of the elasticities $\bar{\zeta}^u$ and $\bar{\zeta}^c$ and the Pareto parameter a

$$\bar{\tau} = \frac{1-\bar{g}}{1-\bar{g}+\bar{\zeta}^u+\bar{\zeta}^c(a-1)}. \qquad (9)$$

In that case, the government wants to set approximately the same linear rate $\bar{\tau}$ above any large income level and thus $\bar{\tau}$ is indeed the optimal non-linear asymptotic rate of the Mirrlees problem.[11]

The top rate $\bar{\tau}$ depends negatively of the thinness of the top tail distribution measured by the Pareto parameter a. This is an intuitive result, if the distribution is thin then raising the top rate for high income earners will raise little additional revenue. Interestingly, for a given compensated elasticity $\bar{\zeta}^c$, the precise division into income effects and uncompensated rate effects matters. The higher are absolute income effects $(-\bar{\eta})$ relative to uncompensated effects $(\bar{\zeta}^u)$, the higher is the asymptotic tax rate $\bar{\tau}$. Put in other words, what matters most for optimal taxation is whether taxpayers continue to work when tax rates increase (without utility compensation). In particular, though $\bar{\zeta}^c$ is a sufficient statistic to approximate the deadweight loss of taxation, same values of $\bar{\zeta}^c$ can lead to very different optimal tax rates.

The case $\bar{g}=0$ corresponds to the situation where the government does not value the marginal consumption of high income earners and sets the top rate so as to extract as much tax revenue as possible from high incomes (soak the rich). Formula (9) specialized to the case $\bar{g}=0$ is the high income tax rate maximizing tax revenue. In the case with no income effects ($\bar{\zeta}^c = \bar{\zeta}^u$), this "Laffer" rate is equal to $\bar{\tau} = 1/(1+a\bar{\zeta})$ with a around 2 for the U.S. This formula is a simple generalization of the well known formula for the flat tax rate maximizing tax revenue, $1/(1+\bar{\zeta})$, where $\bar{\zeta}$ is the average elasticity over all taxpayers.

As the income distribution is affected by taxation, a may depend on $\bar{\tau}$. I show in Section 4 that, in the Mirrlees model, the parameter a is independent of $\bar{\tau}$ as long as $\bar{\tau} < 1$ which implies that formula (9) can be applied using directly the empirical value of a. The intuition is the following. When elasticities are constant, changing the tax rate has the same multiplicative effect on the incomes of each high income taxpayer and therefore the ratio $z_m/\bar{z}$ is unchanged. Empirically, in the U.S. a does not seem to vary systematically with the level of the top rate.[12]

There is little consensus in the empirical literature on behavioural responses to taxation about the size of high income elasticities. Some studies have found estimates in excess of 1 while others have found elasticities very close to zero. Gruber and Saez (2000) summarize the empirical literature based on U.S. tax reforms and discuss the reasons for discrepancies.[13] They find elasticity estimates around 0·25 for gross income. It is unlikely, though not impossible, that the long-term compensated elasticity are bigger than 0·5. The uncompensated elasticity is probably even smaller.

Table 1 presents optimal asymptotic rates using formula (9) for a range of realistic values for the Pareto parameter of the income distribution, $\bar{\zeta}^u$ and $\bar{\zeta}^c$, (the asymptotic elasticities) and $\bar{g}$. Except in the cases of high elasticities, the optimal rates are fairly high. It is important to remember, though, that these optimal rates are the optimal tax rates on

---

11. This point is confirmed in Section 4.
12. See Saez (1999a) for an empirical examination.
13. The recent volume of Slemrod (2000) also provides a number of elasticity estimates for high incomes.

TABLE 1
Optimal tax rates for high income earners

	Uncompensated elasticity = 0			Uncompensated elasticity = 0·2			Uncompensated elasticity = 0·5	
	Compensated elasticity			Compensated elasticity			Compensated elasticity	
	0·2	0·5	0·8	0·2	0·5	0·8	0·5	0·8
	(1)	(2)	(3)	(4)	(5)	(6)	(7)	(8)
Panel A: Social marginal utility with infinite income $g = 0$								
Pareto parameter								
1·5	91	80	71	77	69	63	57	53
2	83	67	56	71	59	50	50	43
2·5	77	57	45	67	51	42	44	37
Panel B: Social marginal utility with infinite income $g = 0·25$								
Pareto parameter								
1·5	88	75	65	71	63	56	50	45
2	80	60	48	65	52	43	43	37
2·5	71	50	38	60	44	32	38	31

g is the ratio of social marginal utility with infinite income over marginal value of public funds. The Pareto parameter of the income distribution takes values 1·5, 2, 2·5. Optimal rates are computed according to formula (9).

income assuming that there are no other taxes distorting the leisure-consumption choice. Therefore, an optimal income tax rate τ derived from (9) should be reduced to $(1-t)\cdot\tau$ in the presence of a consumption tax at rate t. Comparing the rows in Table 1 shows that the Pareto parameter has a big impact on the optimal rate. Pareto parameters for income distributions vary across countries, the parameter is low in the U.S. compared to most European countries or Canada. A thorough investigation of Pareto parameters across countries would be relatively simple to carry out and would provide an important piece of information for tax policy discussions. Comparing columns (2), (5) and (7) (or columns (3), (6), (8)), we see also that, at fixed compensated elasticity, the optimal rate is very sensitive to the size of income effects.

4. OPTIMAL NON-LINEAR INCOME TAX RATES

The last section considered only the problem of optimal tax rates at the high income end. In this section, I investigate the issue of optimal rates at any income level using the same elasticity method. In order to contrast my approach to the original Mirrlees approach, I first present briefly the Mirrlees (1971) model.

4.1. *The Mirrlees model*

In the model, all individuals have the same utility function which depends positively on consumption c and negatively on labour supply l and is noted $u(c, l)$. Individuals differ only in their skill level (denoted by n) which measures their marginal productivity. Earnings are equal to $z = nl$. The population is normalized to one and the distribution of skills is written $F(n)$, with density $f(n)$ and support in $[0, \infty)$. c_n, $z_n = nl_n$, and u_n denote the consumption, earnings and utility level of an individual with skill n. The government cannot observe skills and thus is restricted to setting taxes as a function only of earnings,

$c = z - T(z)$. The government maximizes a social welfare function

$$W = \int_0^\infty G(u_n) f(n) dn, \qquad (10)$$

where $G(\cdot)$ is an increasing and concave function of utility. The government maximizes W subject to a resource constraint and incentive compatibility constraints. The resource constraint states that total consumption is less than total earnings minus government expenditures, E,

$$\int_0^\infty c_n f(n) dn \leqq \int_0^\infty z_n f(n) dn - E. \qquad (11)$$

I note p the multiplier of the budget constraint (11) which represents the marginal value of public funds. The incentive compatibility constraints state that, for each n, the selected labour supply l_n maximizes utility $u(nl - T(nl), l)$, given the tax function. The derivation of the first-order condition for optimal rates is sketched in the Appendix. Note that in the model, redistribution takes place through a guaranteed income level (equal to $-T(0)$) that is taxed away as earnings increase.

4.2. Optimal marginal rates

The general first-order condition Mirrlees obtained depends in a complicated way on the derivatives of the utility function $u(c, l)$ which are not related in any obvious way to empirical magnitudes (see equation (22) in Appendix). Moreover, it is derived using powerful but blind Hamiltonian optimization. Thus, the optimal taxation literature has not elucidated the key economic effects leading to the optimal formula. In this subsection, I derive a formula for optimal tax rates using elasticities of earnings and show precisely the key economics effects behind the optimal tax rate formula.

4.2.1. Results and derivation.
I denote by $H(z)$ the cumulated income distribution function (the total population is normalized to one) and by $h(z)$ the density of the income distribution at the optimum. I note $g(z)$ the social marginal value of consumption for taxpayers with income z, at the optimum, expressed in terms of the value of public funds.[14] It is again important to keep in mind that both $h(z)$ and $g(z)$ are endogenous to the tax schedule. I first present a simple preliminary result that is also useful to understand the relation between the income distribution and the distribution of skills in the Mirrlees economy.

Lemma 1. *For any regular tax schedule T not necessarily optimal, the earnings function z_n is non-decreasing and satisfies the following differential equation,*

$$\frac{\dot{z}_n}{z_n} = \frac{1 + \zeta^u_{(n)}}{n} - \dot{z}_n \frac{T''_{(n)}}{1 - T'_{(n)}} \zeta^c_{(n)}. \qquad (12)$$

If equation (12) leads to $\dot{z}_n < 0$ then z_n is discontinuous and (12) does not hold.

The proof, which is routine algebra, is presented in the Appendix. In the case of a linear tax ($T'' = 0$) the earnings equation (12) simplifies to $dz/z = (1 + \zeta^u) dn/n$. In the

---

14. This is $G'(u) u_c / p$ using the notation of the Mirrlees model.

general case, a correction term in T'' which represents the effect of the change in marginal rates is present. By definition, the income density and the skill density are related through the equation $h(z)\dot{z} = f(n)$. Consequently, for a given skill distribution and using Lemma 1, we see that a non-linear tax schedule produces a local deformation of the income distribution density $h(z)$.

In order to simplify the presentation of optimal tax rates formulas, I introduce $h^*(z)$ which is the density of incomes that would take place at z if the tax schedule $T(\cdot)$ were replaced by the linear tax schedule tangent to $T(\cdot)$ at level z.[15] I call the density $h^*(z)$ the *virtual* density. Applying Lemma 1 to the linearized schedule, we have $\dot{z}^*/z = (1 + \zeta^u)/n$ where $\dot{z}^*$ is the derivative of earnings with respect to n when the linearized schedule is in place. By definition, we also have $h^*(z)\dot{z}^* = f(n)$. Thus h and h^* are related through the following equation

$$\frac{h^*(z)}{1 - T'(z)} = \frac{h(z)}{1 - T'(z) + \zeta^c z T''(z)}. \tag{13}$$

Of course, the virtual density h^* is not identical to the actual density h. However, because the density h at the optimum tax schedule is endogenous (changes in the tax schedule affect the income distribution through behavioural responses), there is very little inconvenience in using h^* rather than h. Using h^* is a way to get rid of the deformation component induced by the non-linearity in the tax schedule. In that sense and as evidenced by Lemma 1, h^* is more closely related than h to the underlying skill distribution which represents intrinsic inequality.

The following proposition presents the optimal tax formula expressed in terms of the behavioural elasticities (same notations as in the previous section) and the shape of the income distribution using the concept of virtual density h^*.[16]

Proposition 1. *The first-order condition for the optimal tax rate at income level z^* can be written as follows,*

$$\frac{T'(z^*)}{1 - T'(z^*)} = \frac{1}{\zeta^c_{(z^*)}} \left(\frac{1 - H(z^*)}{z^* h^*(z^*)} \right) \int_{z^*}^{\infty} (1 - g(z)) \exp\left[\int_{z^*}^{z} \left(1 - \frac{\zeta^u_{(z')}}{\zeta^c_{(z')}} \right) \frac{dz'}{z'} \right] \frac{h(z)}{1 - H(z^*)} dz. \tag{14}$$

Alternatively, using the notations of the Mirrlees model, this equation can be rewritten as,

$$\frac{T'(z_n)}{1 - T'(z_n)} = A(n)B(n), \tag{15}$$

where

$$A(n) = \left(\frac{1 + \zeta^u_{(n)}}{\zeta^c_{(n)}} \right) \left(\frac{1 - F(n)}{nf(n)} \right), \tag{16}$$

$$B(n) = \int_n^{\infty} \left(1 - \frac{G'(u_m)u_c^{(m)}}{p} \right) \exp\left[\int_n^m \left(1 - \frac{\zeta^u_{(s)}}{\zeta^c_{(s)}} \right) \frac{dz_s}{z_s} \right] \frac{f(m)}{1 - F(n)} dm. \tag{17}$$

In equations (16) and (17), sub or superscripts (n) mean that the parameter is computed at the skill level n.

---

15. This linearized tax schedule is characterized by rate $\tau = T'(z)$ and virtual income $R = z - T(z) - z(1 - \tau)$.
16. The proof of the proposition makes clear why introducing h^* is a useful simplification.

Obtaining (15) in the context of the Mirrlees model is possible using the Mirrlees first-order condition. This derivation is presented in the Appendix.[17] This rearrangement of terms of the Mirrlees formula is a generalization of the one developed by Diamond (1998) in the case of quasi-linear utility functions. This method, however, does not show the economic effects which lead to formula (14). Formula (14) can, however, be fruitfully derived directly in terms of elasticities using the same method as in Section 3. The formula is commented in the light of this direct derivation just after the proof.

Direct proof of Proposition 1. I consider the effect of the following small tax reform perturbation around the optimal tax schedule. As depicted on Figure 3, marginal rates

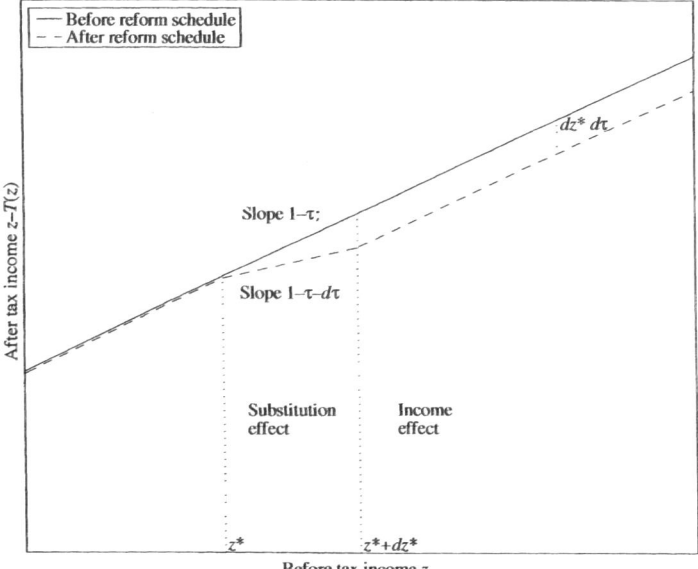

FIGURE 3
Local marginal tax rate perturbation

are increased by an amount $d\tau$ for incomes between z^* and $z^* + dz^*$. I also assume that $d\tau$ is second order compared to dz^* so that bunching (and inversely gaps in the income distribution) around z^* or $z^* + dz^*$ induced by the discontinuous change in marginal rates are negligible. This tax reform has three effects on tax receipts: a mechanical effect, an elasticity effect for taxpayers with income between z^* and $z^* + dz^*$, and an income effect for taxpayers with income above z^*.

- *Mechanical effect net of welfare loss.*

As shown in Figure 3, every taxpayer with income z above z^* pays $d\tau dz^*$ additional taxes which are valued $(1 - g(z))d\tau dz^*$ by the government therefore the overall mechanical

17. Revesz (1989) has also attempted to express the optimal non-linear tax formula of Mirrlees in terms of elasticities. His derivation is similar in spirit to the one presented in the Appendix.

effect M net of welfare loss is equal to[18]

$$M = d\tau dz^* \int_{z^*}^{\infty} (1 - g(z))h(z)dz.$$

- *Elasticity effect.*

The increase $d\tau$ for a taxpayer with income z between z^* and $z^* + dz^*$ has an elasticity effect which produces a small change in income (denoted by dz). This change is the consequence of two effects. First, there is a direct compensated effect due to the exogenous increase $d\tau$. The compensated elasticity is the relevant one here because the change $d\tau$ takes place at level z^* just below z. Second, there is an indirect effect due to the shift of the taxpayer on the tax schedule by dz which induces an endogenous additional change in marginal rates equal to $dT' = T''dz$. Therefore, the behavioural equation can be written as follows

$$dz = -\zeta^c z^* \frac{d\tau + dT'}{1 - T'},$$

which implies

$$dz = -\zeta^c z^* \frac{d\tau}{1 - T' + \zeta^c z^* T''}.$$

It is easy to see that $1 - T' + \zeta^c z^* T'' > 0$ if and only if the curvature of the indifference curve at the individual optimum bundle is larger than the curvature of the schedule $z - T(z)$, or equivalently, if and only if, the individual second-order condition is strictly satisfied. Mirrlees (1971) showed that bunching of types occurs when this condition fails. I assume here that $1 - T' + \zeta^c z^* T'' > 0$. Note that this condition is always satisfied at points where $T''(z^*) \geq 0$.

Introducing the virtual density $h^*(z^*)$ and using equation (13), the overall effect on tax receipts (denoted by E) can be simply written as

$$E = -\zeta^c_{(z^*)} z^* \frac{T'}{1 - T'} h^*(z^*) d\tau dz^*,$$

where $\zeta^c_{(z^*)}$ is the compensated elasticity at income level z^*. The use of the virtual density h^* is useful because it allows to get rid of the complication due to the endogenous change in marginal rate $dT' = T''dz$. In other words, one can derive the above expression for E without taking into account the endogenous change in marginal rates by just replacing h by h^*.

- *Income effect.*

A taxpayer with income z above z^* pays $-dR = d\tau dz^*$ additional taxes. So, taxpayers above the small band $[z^*, z^* + dz^*]$ are induced to work more through income effects which reinforce the mechanical effect. The income response dz is again due to two effects. First, there is the direct income effect (equal to $\eta dR/(1 - T')$). Second, there is an indirect elastic effect due to the change in marginal rates $dT' = T''dz$ induced by the shift dz along the tax schedule. Therefore

$$dz = -\zeta^c z \frac{T''dz}{1 - T'} - \eta \frac{d\tau dz^*}{1 - T'},$$

---

[18]. The tax reform has also an effect on $h(z)$ but this is a second order effect in the computation of M.

which implies

$$dz = -\eta \frac{d\tau dz^*}{1 - T' + z\zeta^c T''}. \tag{18}$$

Introducing again the virtual density $h^*(z)$ to get rid of the endogenous rate change component and summing (18) over all taxpayers with income larger than z^*, I obtain the total tax revenue effect due to income effects responses

$$I = d\tau dz^* \int_{z^*}^{\infty} -\eta_{(z)} \frac{T'}{1-T'} h^*(z) dz.$$

As in Section 3, in deriving E and I, I have implicitly assumed that the set of taxpayers who might jump discontinuously because of the small tax reform is negligible. This amounts to assuming that only *local* incentive constraints bind at the optimum. Mirrlees (1971) proved that, assuming the single-crossing property holds, this is always the case except at bunching points.

Any small tax reform around the optimum schedule has no first-order effect on welfare. Thus the sum of the three effects M, E and I must be zero which implies

$$\frac{T'}{1-T'} = \frac{1}{\zeta^c} \left(\frac{1-H(z^*)}{z^* h^*(z^*)} \right)$$

$$\times \left[\int_{z^*}^{\infty} (1-g(z)) \frac{h(z)}{1-H(z^*)} dz + \int_{z^*}^{\infty} -\eta \frac{T'}{1-T'} \frac{h^*(z)}{1-H(z^*)} dz \right]. \tag{19}$$

Equation (19) can be considered as a first-order linear differential equation and can be integrated (see Appendix) using the standard method to obtain equation (14) of the proposition. Changing variables from z^* to n, and using the fact that, by Lemma 1, $z^* h^*(z^*)(1 + \zeta^u) = nf(n)$, it is straightforward to obtain equation (15) of Proposition 1. When changing variables from z^* to n, an additional term $1 + \zeta^u$ appears on the right-hand side to form the term $A(n)$ of equation (15). This counterintuitive term (higher uncompensated elasticity should not lead to higher marginal rates) should be incorporated into the skill distribution ratio $(1 - F)/(nf)$ to lead to the income distribution ratio $(1 - H)/(z^* h^*)$. Expressing optimal tax formulas in terms of the skill distribution instead of the income distribution can thus be misleading. ‖

4.2.2. *Interpretation and implications.*

• *Interpretation of Proposition 1.*

In the light of this direct proof, let us analyse the decomposition of optimal tax rates presented in Proposition 1. Analysing equation (14), it appears that three elements determine optimal income tax rates: the shape of the income (or skill) distribution, elasticity (and income) effects, and social marginal weights.

• *Shape of income distribution.*

The shape of the income distribution affects the optimal rate at level z^* mainly through the term $(1 - H(z^*))/(z^* h(z^*))$. The elastic distortion at z^* induced by a marginal rate increase at that level is proportional to income at that level times number of people at that income level ($z^* h(z^*)$) while the gain in tax receipts is proportional to the number of people above z^* (i.e. $1 - H(z^*)$). Therefore, the government should apply high marginal rates at levels where the density of taxpayers is low compared to the number of taxpayers with higher income. This is obviously the case at the bottom of the income distribution because $z^*h(z^*)$ is close to zero while $1 - H(z^*)$ is close to one. At the top, for a Pareto distribution with parameter a, the ratio $(1 - H)/(z^*h)$ is constant and equal to $1/a$. From the evidence displayed in Section 3, we expect the ratio to converge to a constant close to 0·5 (remember that a is around 2) for large z^*. Figure 4 presents the graphs of the ratio $(1 - H(z))/(zh(z))$ for years 1992 and 1993 as a function of z. These graphs are based on the same data and samples as the graphs of Figure 2. The ratios are U-shaped. The hazard ratio is very high for low incomes, it decreases until income level $80,000 and then increases until $200,000. Above $200,000, the ratio is indeed approximately constant, around 0·5, showing that the Pareto approximation is adequate. The fact that the ratio increases from $80,000 to $200,000 suggests that, with constant elasticities, optimal rates should be increasing in that range.

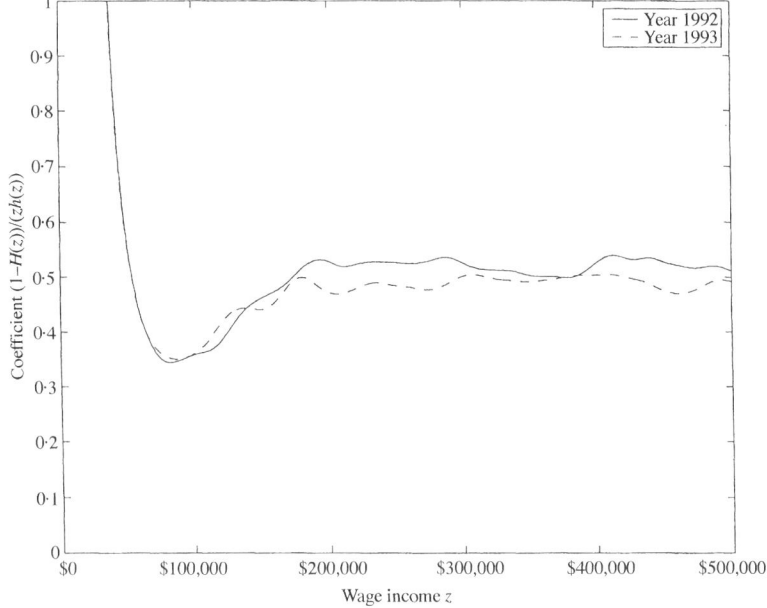

FIGURE 4
Hazard ratio $(1 - H(z))/(zh(z))$, years 1992 and 1993

Of course, the ratio $(1 - H)/(z^*h)$ is endogenous (because of behavioural responses, changing the tax schedule may change the income distribution). Nevertheless, directly using the income distribution allows a better understanding of the optimal tax rate formula. In the numerical simulations presented in the following section, the endogeneity issue is solved by estimating an exogenous skill distribution based on the actual income distribution.

- *Substitution and income effects.*

Behavioural effects enter the formula for optimal rates in two ways. First, increasing marginal rates at level z^* induces a compensated response from taxpayers earning z^*. Therefore, $\zeta^c_{(z^*)}$ enters negatively the optimal tax rate at income level z^*. Second, this marginal rate change increases the tax burden of all taxpayers with income above z^*. This effect induces these taxpayers to work more through income effects which is good for tax receipts. Therefore, this income effect leads to higher marginal rates (everything else being equal) through the exponential term in (14) which is larger than one. Note that this term is identically equal to one when there are no income effects (this case was studied by Diamond (1998)).[19]

- *Social marginal welfare weights.*

The social marginal weights $g(z)$ enter the optimal tax formula through the term $(1-g(z))$ inside the integral. Social marginal weights represent the relative value for the government of an additional dollar of consumption at each income level. More precisely, the government is indifferent between giving $1/g(z_1)$ additional dollars to a taxpayer with income z_1 or giving $1/g(z_2)$ dollars to a taxpayer with income z_2. These weights summarize in a transparent way the distributive objectives of the government. If the government has redistributive tastes, then these weights are decreasing in income. In that case, expression $(1-g(z))$ in equation (14) is increasing in z. Therefore, taste for redistribution is unsurprisingly an element tending to make the tax schedule progressive. If the government had no redistributive goals, then it would choose the same marginal welfare weights for everybody and thus equation (14) can also be applied in the case with no redistributive concerns. The shape of the income distribution and the size of both substitution and income effects would still matter for the optimal income tax.

The original Mirrlees (1971) derivation relies heavily on the fact that there is a uni-dimensional skill parameter which characterizes each taxpayer. Mirrlees (1986) tried to extend the model to heterogeneous populations where individuals are characterized by a multidimensional parameter instead of a single dimensional skill parameter. He adopted the same approach as he used in his original 1971 study and derived first-order conditions for the optimal tax schedule. However, these conditions were even more complicated than in the unidimensional case and thus it proved impossible to obtain results or interpret the first-order conditions in that general case. The direct proof using elasticities shows that it is not necessary to introduce a unidimensional exogenous skill distribution to obtain formula (14). Therefore, formula (14) might, in principle, be valid for any heterogeneous population as long as $\zeta^u_{(z)}$ and $\zeta^c_{(z)}$ are considered as average elasticities at income level z.[20] It is, in fact, possible to recover formula (14) using the first-order conditions of the general multi-dimensional case derived in Mirrlees (1986). Therefore, the elasticity method could be a useful step to take to extend in a fruitful way the Mirrlees (1971) model to heterogeneous populations. One important caveat should be mentioned: formula (14) is valid only at points where the first-order condition characterizes the optimal schedule. The small literature on multi-dimensional screening models has shown that assessing whether first-order conditions characterize the optimum schedule is much more complicated in the multi-dimensional case because non-local incentive constraints are likely to bind in these problems (see the analysis of Rochet and Choné (1998)). Therefore, in the multi-dimensional case, without additional restrictive conditions, formula (14) might not be valid. The difficult analysis of the singularities in the multi-dimensional case is beyond the scope of the present paper.

---

19. The heuristic proof shows clearly why negative tax rates are never optimal. If the tax rate were negative in some range then increasing it a little bit in that range would decrease earnings of taxpayers in that range (because of the substitution effect) but this behavioural response would increase tax receipts because the tax rate is *negative* in that range. Therefore, this small tax reform would unambiguously increase welfare.

20. Equation (13) linking the virtual density h^* to the actual density h can be generalized to the case of heterogeneous populations.

In any case, Proposition 1 suggests that the unidimensional skill distribution in the Mirrlees model should not be considered as a real economic element (which could be measured empirically) but rather as a simplification device to perform computations and numerical simulations. The skill distribution should simply be chosen so that the resulting income distribution is close to the empirical income distribution. This route is followed in Section 5.

Formula (14) could also be used to pursue a *positive* analysis of actual tax schedules. Considering the actual tax schedule $T(\cdot)$ and the actual income distribution $H(\cdot)$, and making assumptions about the patterns of elasticities $\zeta^u_{(z)}$ and $\zeta^c_{(z)}$, it is also possible to use equation (14) to infer the marginal social weights $g(z)$. Even if the government does not explicitly maximize welfare, it may be interesting to know what are the implicit weights that the government is using. For example, if some of the weights appear to be negative then the tax schedule is not second-best Pareto efficient.[21]

- *Links with previous studies.*

As discussed in Section 2, Roberts (2000) has obtained a formula equivalent to (19) using also a perturbation approach. His perturbation induces all taxpayers in a small band of income to bunch at the upper end of the band. His derivation is perhaps less transparent than the present one because it is obtained using Taylor expansions and does not decompose the tax revenue changes into income and substitution effects. Moreover, his approach relies on the assumption that there is only one type of individual at each income level as in the Mirrlees (1971) model.

The derivation presented here is also close to the demand profile approach used in the literature on optimal nonlinear pricing for a regulated monopoly (see Wilson (1993)). The nonlinear price problem is formally equivalent to the optimal income tax problem with constant welfare weights $g(z)$. Moreover, the non-linear pricing literature generally assumes away income effects. In that particular case, the non-linear pricing literature has been able to derive optimal pricing formulas directly in terms of demand profiles and express optimal pricing formulas as a simple inverse elasticity rule that is formally equivalent to formula (14) with no income effects and constant weights $g(z)$. In the income tax case, the demand profile elasticity becomes the elasticity of the number of taxpayers above a given income level z (*i.e.* $1 - H(z)$) with respect to (one minus) the marginal rate at z (*i.e.* $1 - T'(z)$).[22] In the case of the income tax problem, it is more convenient to express optimal tax formulas in terms of standard labour supply elasticities rather than the "demand profile" elasticity. Nonetheless, it is perhaps surprising that the optimal income tax literature before Diamond (1998) did not consider more seriously the case with no income effect which is standard in the nonlinear pricing literature because it is very convenient to solve and analyse.

- *Optimal asymptotic rates.*

It is possible to recover the high income optimal tax formula (9) from Section 3 using equation (14) for large z^*.[23] With large z, $g(z)$ tends to $\bar{g}$, and the ratio $(1 - H)/(z^* h^*)$ tends to $1/a$ when the tail is Paretian. Assuming that elasticities converge, the exponential term in (14) is approximately equal to $(z/z^*)^{1-\bar{\zeta}^u/\bar{\zeta}^c}$ and thus the fact that $h(z)$ is Paretian implies that the integral term in (14) tends to $(1-\bar{g})a/[a-(1-\bar{\zeta}^u/\bar{\zeta}^c)]$. Putting together these results, one can obtain (9).

---

21. This analysis has been used frequently in the commodity taxation literature where it is known as the inverse optimum problem (see *e.g.* Ahmed and Stern (1984)).
22. See Saez (1999*b*) for more details.
23. Saez (1999*a*) discusses this point in detail.

Diamond (1998) obtained this formula in the case with no income effects but expressed the formula in terms of the Pareto parameter of the *skill* distribution instead of the income distribution.[24] Using Lemma 1, it can be shown that the Pareto parameter of the income distribution is equal to the Pareto parameter of the skill distribution divided by $1+\zeta^u$. This shows that, as discussed in Section 3, the Pareto parameter a is independent of the limiting tax rate in the Mirrlees model. Roberts (2000) also obtained an asymptotic formula that is close to equation (9). However, the basic methodology of Section 3 is a much easier way to obtain the same optimal tax rate result for high incomes than going through the asymptotics of the general formula.

5. NUMERICAL SIMULATIONS

5.1. *Methodology*

As we saw in the previous section, there are three key elements that determine optimal tax rates: elasticities, the shape of the income distribution, and the redistributive tastes of the government. In the simulations, careful attention is paid to the calibration of each of these parameters.

Simulations are presented using utility functions with constant compensated elasticity ζ^c. This provides a useful benchmark because the compensated elasticity is the key parameter in empirical studies. Even though there is empirical evidence showing that elasticities may be higher at the low end and the high end of the income distribution (see *e.g.* Blundell (1992) and Gruber and Saez (2000)), it is useful to start with the case of constant elasticities in order to see how optimal tax rates should be set in that benchmark case. It is fairly simple to adapt the simulation methodology to the case of varying elasticities.[25]

As we saw, for a given compensated elasticity, varying income effects affects optimal rates. As most, though not all, empirical studies find small income effects relative to substitution effects (see *e.g.* Blundell and MaCurdy (1999)), it is useful to consider the case with no income effects. Therefore, in the simulations, I use two types of utility functions with constant elasticities. With utility functions of Type I

$$u = \log\left(c - \frac{l^{1+k}}{1+k}\right), \qquad (20)$$

there are no income effects. The elasticity (uncompensated and compensated) is equal to $1/k$. This case was examined theoretically by Atkinson (1990) and Diamond (1998).

Type II utility functions are such that

$$u = \log(c) - \log\left(1 + \frac{l^{1+k}}{1+k}\right). \qquad (21)$$

The compensated elasticity is equal to $1/k$ but there are income effects. The uncompensated elasticity ζ^u can be shown to tend to zero when n tends to infinity. Comparing the results of Type I and Type II utility functions will allow us to assess the impact of income effects on optimal schedules keeping constant substitution effects. It is important to keep in mind that the utility functions should be chosen so as to replicate the empirical elasticities and that l does not necessarily represent hours of work. As a result, Type I utility

---

24. That is why his table of high income optimal tax rates is not directly comparable to the results presented in Table 1. He also confused a and $1+a$ when selecting examples.

25. This is attempted by Gruber and Saez (2000) in a simpler four-bracket optimal income tax setting.

function, where l tends to infinity for large n, is clearly not realistic when l represents hours of work but is nevertheless appropriate if, as evidenced empirically, income effects are much smaller than substitution effects. As discussed in Section 3, there is controversy in the empirical literature about the size of substitution effects. I choose two values for the compensated elasticity parameters $\zeta^c = 0.25$ and $\zeta^c = 0.5$. These values fall within the middle range of empirical estimates.

I use the earnings distribution of year 1992 from tax return data to perform numerical simulations. Formula (14) cannot be directly applied using the empirical income distribution because the income distribution is affected by taxation. Therefore, it is useful to come back to the Mirrlees formulation and use an exogenous skill distribution to perform numerical simulations. The main innovation is that the skill distribution is calibrated such that, given the utility function chosen and the *actual* tax schedule, the resulting income distribution replicates the *empirical* earnings distribution. Previous simulations almost always used log-normal skill distributions which match globally unimodal empirical distributions but approximate very poorly empirical distributions at the tails (both top and bottom tails). Moreover, changing the elasticity parameter without changing the skill distribution, as usually done in numerical simulations, might be misleading because changing the elasticities modifies the resulting income distribution and thus might affect optimal rates also through this indirect effect.

Optimal rates simulations are performed using two different social welfare criteria, Utilitarian and Rawlsian. Because for both types of utility functions, $u_c \to 0$ as $n \to \infty$, $\bar{g}$ is always equal to zero and thus the asymptotic rates are the same with both welfare criteria. In the case of the Utilitarian criterion, social marginal weights $g(z)$ are proportional to u_c which is approximately decreasing at the rate $1/c$. Optimal rates are computed such that the ratio of government spending E to aggregate production is equal to 0.25. The original Mirrlees (1971) method of computation is used and the details are presented in the Appendix.

5.2. Results

Optimal marginal rates are plotted on Figure 5 for yearly wage incomes between $0 and $300,000. The curves represent the optimal non-linear marginal rates and the dashed horizontal lines represent the optimal linear rates (see below). As expected, the level of the optimal rates depends on the level of elasticities and on the type of the utility function. In all four cases, however, the optimal rates are clearly U-shaped.[26] Optimal rates are decreasing from $0 to $75,000 and then increase until income level $200,000. Above $200,000, the optimal rates are close to their asymptotic level. This U-shape pattern is strikingly close to many actual tax schedules. The high rates at the bottom obtained in the simulations correspond to the phasing-out of the guaranteed income level. As in actual systems, the simulations suggest that the government should apply high rates at the bottom in order to target welfare only to low incomes. In most countries, rates drop significantly once welfare programmes are phased-out and tax rates are in general increasing at high income levels because most income tax systems are progressive. In the simulations presented, tax rates increase at high income levels because of the shape of the income distribution (as discussed above) and because of the redistributive tastes of the government. Note that the increasing pattern of tax rates due to the U-shape pattern of the ratio

---

26. The rate at the bottom is not zero because labour supply tends to zero as the skill n tends to zero, violating one of the assumptions of Seade (1977).

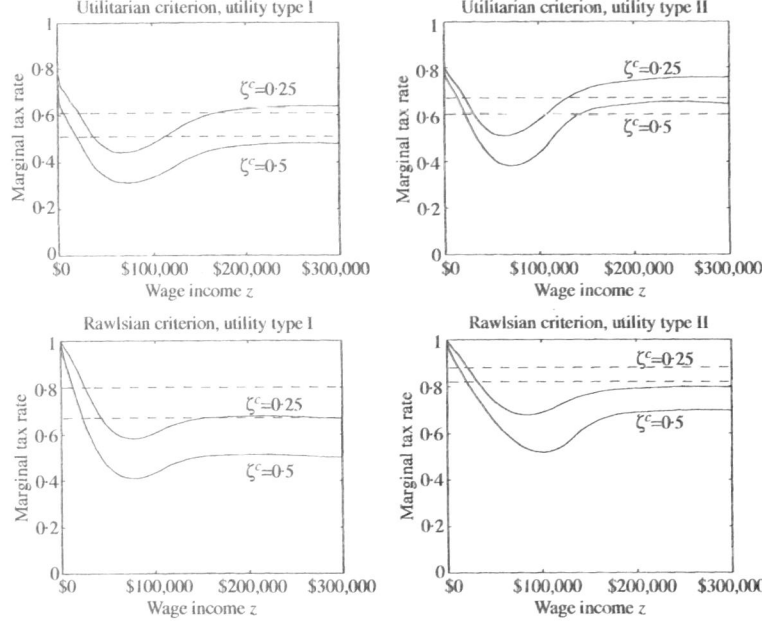

FIGURE 5
Optimal tax simulations

$(1-H)/(zh)$ cannot be obtained with a log-normal skill distribution because in that case, the ratio $(1-H)/(zh)$ is always decreasing. The increasing pattern of marginal rates at the high end depends of course on the assumption of constant elasticities and might be reversed if elasticities are increasing with income (Gruber and Saez (2000)).

As expected, the Rawlsian criterion leads to higher marginal rates. The difference in rates between the two welfare criteria is larger at low incomes and decreases smoothly toward 0 (the asymptotic rates are the same).

I have also reported in dashed lines on Figure 5, the optimal *linear* rates computed for the same utility functions, welfare criteria and skill distribution (the upper one corresponding to $\zeta^c = 0.25$ and the lower one to $\zeta^c = 0.5$). The optimal linear rates are also computed so that government spending over total earnings be equal to 0·25. Table 2 reports the optimal average marginal rates weighted by income in the non-linear case along with the optimal linear rate.[27] The guaranteed consumption levels of people with skill zero (who supply zero labour and thus earn zero income) in terms of average income are also reported. As average incomes differ in the linear and non-linear cases, I also report (in parentheses) the ratio of the guaranteed income for the linear case to the guaranteed income for the non-linear case: this ratio allows a simple comparison between the absolute levels of consumption of the poorest individuals in the linear and non-linear case.

The average marginal rates are substantially lower in the non-linear cases than in the linear cases. The guaranteed levels of consumption are slightly higher in relative terms in the linear cases (than in the non-linear cases) but as average earnings are lower in the linear cases, the absolute levels are similar. Therefore, non-linear taxation is significantly

27. The asymptotic rate in the non-linear case is reported in parentheses.

TABLE 2

Numerical simulations of optimal taxes

	Utilitarian criterion				Rawlsian criterion			
	Compensated elasticity				Compensated elasticity			
	0.25		0.5		0.25		0.5	
	Non-linear	Linear	Non-linear	Linear	Non-linear	Linear	Non-linear	Linear
	(1)	(2)	(3)	(4)	(5)	(6)	(7)	(8)
Panel A: Utility Type I (no income effects)								
Optimal Average Rate (Asymptotic Rate)	0·51 (0·68)	0·61	0·38 (0·51)	0·51	0·68 (0·68)	0·80	0·52 (0·51)	0·67
Guaranteed Income Level (linear over non-linear level)	0·33	0·36 (1·03)	0·21	0·26 (1·09)	0·55	0·55 (0·92)	0·42	0·42 (0·87)
Panel B: Utility Type II (income effects)								
Optimal Average Rate (Asymptotic Rate)	0·59 (0·81)	0·67	0·48 (0·69)	0·60	0·77 (0·81)	0·88	0·65 (0·69)	0·82
Guaranteed Income Level (linear over non-linear level)	0·40	0·42 (1·00)	0·31	0·35 (1·01)	0·60	0·63 (0·92)	0·50	0·57 (0·92)

In the non-linear case, optimal rates are averaged with income weights; asymptotic rates are reported in parentheses below average rates. The guaranteed income level is expressed in percentage of average income. The ratio of the absolute guaranteed level in the linear case over the absolute guaranteed level in the non-linear case is reported in parentheses.

more efficient than linear taxation to redistribute income. In particular, it is better from an efficiency point of view to have high marginal rates at the bottom (which corresponds to the phasing out of the guaranteed income level).

Mirrlees (1971) found much smaller optimal marginal rates in the simulations he presented. Rates were slightly decreasing along the income distribution and the levels around 20% to 30%. The smaller rates he found were the consequence of two effects. First, the utility function he chose ($u = \log(c) + \log(1-l)$) implies high elasticities. Income effects are constant with $\eta = -0.5$ and compensated elasticities are large with ζ^c decreasing from around 1 (at the bottom decile) to 0.5 (at the top decile). These high elasticities lead to low optimal tax rates. Second, the log-normal distribution for skills implies that the hazard ratio $(1 - H(z))/(zh(z))$ is decreasing over the income distribution and tends to zero as income tends to infinity. This implied a decreasing pattern of optimal rates.

Subsequently, Tuomala (1990) presented simulations of optimal rates using utility functions with smaller elasticities. As in Stern (1976) for the linear tax case, Tuomala (1990) used the concept of elasticity of substitution between consumption and leisure to calibrate utility functions. This concept does not map in any simple way into the concepts of income effects and elasticities used in the present paper. Tuomala's utility function implies that the compensated elasticity is around 0.5 but income effects are unrealistically large ($\eta \simeq -1$) implying a negative uncompensated elasticity. Unsurprisingly, he found higher tax rates but the pattern of optimal rates was still regressive, from around 60% at the bottom to around 25% at 99-th percentile because of the shape of the skill distribution. Kanbur and Tuomala (1994) noticed that it is important to calibrate the log-normal skill distribution indirectly so that the income distribution inferred from the skill distribution matches the actual distribution. They obtained optimal tax rates substantially higher than previous simulations and closer to those presented here.

6. CONCLUSION

Using elasticities to derive optimal income tax rates is a fruitful method for a number of reasons. First, it is straightforward to obtain an optimal tax formula for high incomes.

The literature following Mirrlees (1971) on optimal income taxation had not been able to obtain this simple formula. Using elasticity estimates from the empirical literature, the formula for asymptotic top rates suggests that marginal rates for labour income should not be lower than 50% and may be as high as 80%. Second, the elasticity method has the advantage of showing precisely how the different economic effects come into play and which are the relevant parameters for optimal taxation. The original maximization method of Mirrlees (1971) did not allow such a simple economic interpretation. Third, because optimal tax formulas are expressed in terms of parameters that can be observed or estimated, numerical simulations can be performed and calibrated using the empirical income distribution.

The analysis can be extended in several ways. First, the ratios $z_m/\bar{z}$ and $(1-H(z))/(zh)$ introduced in Sections 3 and 4 are closely linked to optimal pattern of marginal rates and can be fruitfully examined using empirical income distributions. It would be interesting to compute these ratios for other years and countries to see whether the U-shape pattern is universal of specific to the U.S. Second, the general framework under which the approach used here to derive optimal tax rates is valid, needs still to be worked out precisely. Last, it might be fruitful to apply the same methodology to other tax and redistribution problems. In particular, the issue of optimal tax rates at the bottom of income distribution deserves more attention in order to cast light on the important problem of designing income maintenance programmes.

APPENDIX

Deriving the Mirrlees optimal tax formula

Each individual chooses l to maximize $u(nl - T(nl), l)$, which implies, $n(1 - T'(z_n))u_c + u_l = 0$. Differentiating u_n with respect to n, we have $du/dn = -lu_l/n$. Following Mirrlees (1971), in the maximization programme of the government, u_n is regarded as the state variable, l_n as the control variable while c_n is determined implicitly as a function of u_n and l_n from the equation $u_n = u(c_n, l_n)$. The government maximizes equation (10) by choosing l_n and u_n subject to equation (11) and $du/dn = -lu_l/n$. Denoting by p and $\phi(n)$ the corresponding multipliers, we obtain (see Mirrlees (1971), equation (33))

$$\left(n + \frac{u_l^{(n)}}{u_c^{(n)}}\right) f(n) = \frac{\psi_l^{(n)}}{n} \int_n^\infty \left(\frac{1}{u_c^{(m)}} - \frac{G'(u_m)}{p}\right) T_{nm} f(m) dm, \qquad (22)$$

where $T_{nm} = \exp[-\int_n^m (l_s u_{cl}(c_s, l_s))/(s u_c(c_s, l_s)) ds]$. ψ is defined such that $\psi(u, l) = -l u_l(c, l)$ where c is a function of (u, l) such that $u = u(c, l)$. A superscript (n) means that the corresponding function is estimated at (c_n, l_n, u_n).

Proof of Lemma 1.

$\dot{z}_n/z_n = (l_n + n\dot{l}_n)/(n l_n)$ and $l_n = l(w_n, R_n)$ where $w_n = n(1 - T')$ is the net-of-tax wage rate and $R_n = n l_n - T(n l_n) - n l_n(1 - T')$ is the virtual income of an individual with skill n. I note $l(w, R)$ the uncompensated labour supply function. Therefore

$$\dot{l}_n = \frac{\partial l}{\partial w}[1 - T' - n(n\dot{l}_n + l_n)T''] + \frac{\partial l}{\partial R}(n\dot{l}_n + l_n)(n l_n T''),$$

and rearranging

$$\dot{l}_n = \frac{w_n}{l} \frac{\partial l}{\partial w} \frac{l}{n} + \left[w_n \frac{\partial l}{\partial R} - \frac{w_n}{l} \frac{\partial l}{\partial w}\right] \frac{n l_n T''}{n(1 - T')} [l_n + n\dot{l}_n].$$

Using the definitions (1) and (2) along with the Slutsky equation (4)

$$\dot{l}_n = \zeta^u \frac{l_n}{n} - \dot{z}_n \frac{l_n T''}{1 - T'} \zeta^c,$$

and therefore

$$\frac{\dot{z}_n}{z_n} = \frac{n\dot{l}_n + l_n}{nl_n} = \frac{1+\zeta^u}{n} - \dot{z}_n \frac{T''}{1-T'}\zeta^c$$

which is exactly (12). The second-order condition for individual maximization is $\dot{z}_n \geq 0$. Therefore, if (12) leads to $\dot{z}_n < 0$, this means that T' decreases too fast producing a discontinuity in the income distribution. ||

Proof of Proposition 1

In order to rewrite equation (2) in terms of elasticities, I first derive formulas for ζ^u, ζ^c and η as a function of the utility function u and its derivatives. The uncompensated labour supply $l(w, R)$ is obtained implicitly from the first-order condition of the individual maximization programme, $wu_c + u_l = 0$. Differentiating this condition with respect to l, w and R leads to

$$[u_{cc}w^2 + 2u_{cl}w + u_{ll}]dl + [u_c + u_{cc}wl + u_{cl}l]dw + [u_{cc}w + u_{lc}]dR = 0.$$

Replacing w by $-u_l/u_c$, the following formulas for ζ^u and η are obtained

$$\zeta^u = \frac{u_l/l - (u_l/u_c)^2 u_{cc} + (u_l/u_c)u_{cl}}{u_{ll} + (u_l/u_c)^2 u_{cc} - 2(u_l/u_c)u_{cl}}, \quad (23)$$

$$\eta = \frac{-(u_l/u_c)^2 u_{cc} + (u_l/u_c)u_{cl}}{u_{ll} + (u_l/u_c)^2 u_{cc} - 2(u_l/u_c)u_{cl}},$$

and using the Slutsky equation (4)

$$\zeta^c = \frac{u_l/l}{u_{ll} + (u_l/u_c)^2 u_{cc} - 2(u_l/u_c)u_{cl}}. \quad (24)$$

The first-order condition of the individual $n(1 - T')u_c + u_l = 0$ implies $n + u_l/u_c = nT' = -(u_l/u_c)T'/(1 - T')$. Therefore (22) can first be rewritten as follows

$$\frac{T'}{1-T'} = -\frac{\psi_l}{u_l}\left(\frac{1-F(n)}{nf(n)}\right)\int_n^\infty \left[1 - \frac{G'(u_m)u_c^{(m)}}{p}\right]\frac{u_c^{(n)}}{u_c^{(m)}}T_{nm}\left(\frac{f(m)}{1-F(n)}\right)dm. \quad (25)$$

The first part of (25) is equal to $A(n)$ iff $-\psi_l/u_l = (1 + \zeta^u)/\zeta^c$. ψ is defined such that $\psi(u, l) = -lu_l(c, l)$ where c is a function of (u, l) such that $u = u(c, l)$. Therefore, using (23) and (24), simple algebra shows that $-\psi_l/u_l = (1 + \zeta^u)/\zeta^c$.

The integral term of (25) is equal to $B(n)$ if it is shown that

$$T_{nm}\frac{u_c^{(n)}}{u_c^{(m)}} = \exp\left[\int_n^m \left(1 - \frac{\zeta_{(s)}^u}{\zeta_{(s)}^c}\right)\frac{\dot{z}_s}{z_s}ds\right].$$

By definition of T_{nm} and expressing $u_c^{(n)}/u_c^{(m)}$ as an integral

$$T_{nm}u_c^{(n)}/u_c^{(m)} = \exp\left[\int_n^m \left(-\frac{d\log(u_c^{(s)})}{ds} - \frac{l_s u_{cl}^{(s)}}{su_c^{(s)}}\right)ds\right]. \quad (26)$$

I note $J(s) = -(du_c^{(s)}/ds + l_s u_{cl}^{(s)}/s)/u_c^{(s)}$ the expression in (26) inside the integral. Now, $u_c^{(s)} = u_c(c_s, l_s)$, therefore $du_c^{(s)}/ds = u_{cc}^{(s)}\dot{c}_s + u_{cl}^{(s)}\dot{l}_s$. From $du/dn = -lu_l/n$, I obtain $u_c^{(s)}\dot{c}_s + u_l^{(s)}\dot{l}_s = \dot{u}_s = -l_s u_l^{(s)}/s$. Substituting $\dot{c}_s$ from the latter into the former, I obtain $du_c^{(s)}/ds = -[s\dot{l}_s + l_s]u_l u_{cc}/(su_c) + u_{cl}\dot{l}_s$. Substituting this expression for $du_c^{(s)}/ds$ in $J(s)$ and using again the expressions (23) and (24), we have finally

$$J(s) = [lu_l u_{cc}/u_c^2 - lu_{cl}/u_c]\left(\frac{l_s + s\dot{l}_s}{sl_s}\right) = \left(\frac{\zeta_s^c - \zeta^u}{\zeta^c}\right)\frac{\dot{z}_s}{z_s},$$

which finishes the proof. Note that on bunching intervals included in (n, m), $\dot{z}_s = \dot{c}_s = 0$, $J(s) = 0$, and all the preceding equations remain true, and thus the proof goes through. ||

Derivation of the formula for optimal rates (14) *from formula* (19)

I note

$$K(z) = \int_z^\infty -\eta\frac{T'}{1-T'}h^*(z')dz'.$$

Equation (19) can be considered as a first-order differential equation in $K(z)$, $K'(z^*) = D(z^*)[C(z^*) + K(z^*)]$, where $C(z^*) = \int_{z^*}^{\infty} [1 - g(z)]h(z)dz$ and $D(z^*) = \eta/(z^*\zeta^c)$. Routine integration using the method of the variation of the constant and taking into account that $K(\infty) = 0$, leads to

$$K(z^*) = -\int_{z^*}^{\infty} D(z)C(z) \exp\left[-\int_{z^*}^{z} D(z')dz'\right] dz.$$

Integration by parts leads to

$$K(z^*) = -\int_{z^*}^{\infty} C'(z) \exp\left[-\int_{z^*}^{z} D(z')dz'\right] dz - C(z^*). \tag{27}$$

Differentiation of (27) leads directly to (14). ||

Numerical simulations

Separability of the utility function in labour and consumption simplifies the computations. Therefore, for Type I utility, I use $u = c - l^{k+1}/(k+1)$, and $G(u) = \log(u)$ (in the utilitarian case). For Type II utilities, $u = \log(c) - \log[1 + l^{k+1}/(k+1)]$ and $G(u) = u$ (in the utilitarian case). For both types of utility functions, optimal rates are computed by solving a system of two differential equations in $u(n)$ and $\rho(n) = (n + u_l/u_c)/\psi_l$. The system of differential equations can be written as follows

$$\frac{d\rho}{dn} = -\frac{\rho}{n}\left(1 + \frac{nf'}{f}\right) - \frac{1}{nu_c} + \frac{G'(u)}{pn},$$

and $du/dn = -lu_l/n$.

The system of differential equations used to solve optimal rates depends on $f(n)$ through the expression $nf'(n)/f(n)$. $f(n)$ is derived from the empirical distribution of wage income in such a way that the distribution of income $z(n) = nl(n)$ inferred from $f(n)$ with flat taxes (reproducing approximately the real tax schedule) matches the empirical distribution. I check that the optimal solutions lead to increasing earnings z_n which is a necessary and sufficient condition for individual second-order conditions (Mirrlees (1971)).

Acknowledgements. This paper is based on Chapter 1 of my Ph.D. thesis at MIT. I thank Mark Armstrong, Peter Diamond, Esther Duflo, Roger Guesnerie, Michael Kremer, James Mirrlees, Thomas Piketty, James Poterba, Kevin Roberts, David Spector, two anonymous referees, the RES 1999 Tour participants and numerous seminar participants for very helpful comments and discussions. Financial support from the Alfred P. Sloan Foundation is thankfully acknowledged.

REFERENCES

AHMAD, E. and STERN, N. H. (1984), "The Theory of Reform and Indian Indirect Taxes", *Journal of Public Economics*, 25, 259–298.
ATKINSON, A. B. (1990), "Public Economics and the Economic Public", *European Economic Review*, 34, 225–248.
BALLARD, C. L. and FULLERTON, D. (1992), "Distortionary Taxes and the Provision of Public Goods", *Journal of Economic Perspectives*, 6, 117–131.
BLUNDELL, R. (1992), "Labour Supply and Taxation: A Survey", *Fiscal Studies*, 13, 15–40.
BLUNDELL, R. and MaCURDY, T. (1999), "Labour Supply: A Review and Alternative Approaches", in Ashenfelter, O. and Card, D. (eds.), *Handbook of Labor Economics* (Amsterdam: North-Holland).
DALHBY, B. (1998), "Progressive Taxation and the Social Marginal Cost of Public Funds", *Journal of Public Economics*, 67, 105–122.
DIAMOND, P. (1998), "Optimal Income Taxation: An Example with a U-Shaped Pattern of Optimal Marginal Tax Rates", *American Economic Review*, 88, 83–95.
DIXIT, A. K. and SANDMO, A. (1977), "Some Simplified Formulae for Optimal Income Taxation", *Scandinavian Journal of Economics*, 79, 417–423.
GRUBER, J. and SAEZ, E. (2000), "The Elasticity of Taxable Income: Evidence and Implications" (NBER Working Paper No. 7512).
KANBUR, R. and TUOMALA, M. (1994), "Inherent Inequality and the Optimal Graduation of Marginal Tax Rates", *Scandinavian Journal of Economics*, 96, 275–282.
MIRRLEES, J. A. (1971), "An Exploration in the Theory of Optimal Income Taxation", *Review of Economic Studies*, 38, 175–208.
MIRRLEES, J. A. (1986), "The Theory of Optimal Taxation", in Arrow, K. J. and Intrilligator, M. D. (eds.), *Handbook of Mathematical Economics* (Amsterdam: North-Holland).

PARETO, V. (1965) *Ecrits sur la Courbe de la Répartition de la Richesse* (Genève: Librairie Droz).
PIKETTY, T. (1997), "La Redistribution Fiscale face au Chômage", *Revue Française d'Economie*, **12**, 157–201.
REVESZ, J. T. (1989), "The Optimal Taxation of Labour Income", *Public Finance*, **44**, 453–475.
ROBERTS, K. (2000), "A Reconsideration of the Optimal Income Tax" in Hammond, P. J. and Myles, G. D. (eds.), *Incentives and Organization: Papers in Honour of Sir James Mirrlees* (Oxford: Oxford University Press).
ROCHET, J.-C. and CHONÉ, P. (1998), "Ironing, Sweeping, and Multi-dimensional Screening", *Econometrica*, **66**, 783–826.
SADKA, E. (1976), "On Income Distribution, Incentive Effects and Optimal Income Taxation", *Review of Economic Studies*, **42**, 261–268.
SAEZ, E. (1999a), "Using Elasticities to Derive Optimal Income Tax Rates" (Chapter 1, MIT Ph.D. Thesis).
SAEZ, E. (1999b), "A Characterization of the Income Tax Schedule Minimizing Deadweight Burden" (Chapter 2, MIT Ph.D. Thesis).
SEADE, J. K. (1977), "On the Shape of Optimal Tax Schedules", *Journal of Public Economics*, **7**, 203–236.
SEADE, J. K. (1982), "On the Sign of the Optimum Marginal Income Tax", *Review of Economic Studies*, **49**, 637–643.
SLEMROD, J. (2000) *Does Atlas Shrug? The Economic Consequences of Taxing the Rich* (Cambridge University Press).
STERN, N. H. (1976), "On the Specification of Models of Optimal Taxation", *Journal of Public Economics*, **6**, 123–162.
TUOMALA, M. (1990) *Optimal Income Tax and Redistribution* (Oxford: Clarendon Press).
WILSON, R. B. (1993) *Nonlinear Pricing* (Oxford: Oxford University Press).

Optimal Taxation and Optimal Tax Systems

Joel Slemrod

"Optimal tax formulas are either guides to action or nothing at all."

Frank Hahn (1973)

Should additional revenue be raised by introducing a value-added tax, increasing income tax rates, or by enforcing the existing income tax more effectively? Should the attempt to tax income progressively be abandoned? Should the income tax be scrapped entirely, and replaced with a consumption tax? A normative theory of taxation, as a guide to action, should illuminate these and other fundamental questions of current and future tax policy.

The theory of optimal taxation has, for the past two decades, been the reigning normative approach to taxation. During its reign it has generated several useful insights about the relationships between assumptions about the set of tax instruments available to the government, the structure of the economy, and the objectives of tax policy. However, I will argue in this paper that in its current state optimal tax theory is incomplete as a guide to action concerning the questions that began this paper and for other critical issues in tax policy. It is incomplete because it has not yet come to terms with taxation as a system of coercively collecting revenues from individuals who will tend to resist. The coercive nature of collecting taxes implies that the resource cost of implementing a tax system is large. Furthermore, alternative tax systems differ greatly in the resource cost of operation. Differences in the ease of administering various taxes have been and will continue to be a critical determinant of appropriate tax policy.

■ *Joel Slemrod is Professor of Economics, Professor of Business Economics and Public Policy, and Director of the Office of Tax Policy Research at The University of Michigan, Ann Arbor, Michigan.*

As a prelude to my argument, I will first walk the reader through three of the principal propositions of optimal tax theory, pointing out along the way the key assumptions of the restricted problem under consideration.[1] Next, I comment on the influence of the theory on recent tax policy developments. I conclude by sketching an alternative to optimal taxation, which I call the theory of optimal tax systems. This theory embraces the insights of optimal taxation but also takes seriously the technology of raising taxes and the constraints placed upon tax policy by that technology. A theory of optimal tax systems has the promise of addressing some of the fundamental issues of tax policy in a more satisfactory way than the theory of optimal taxation.

Three Cornerstones of the Theory of Optimal Taxation

Common Structure

A typical exercise in optimal taxation has three key aspects. First, there is an explicit representation of individuals' preferences, technology (usually constant returns to scale), and market structure (usually perfect competition). Second, the government must raise a fixed amount of revenue with a limited set of tax instruments which can be administered costlessly. Lump-sum taxes, for which the tax liability is unrelated to any economic decision, are often ruled out. Given the assumptions about the economy, any choice of tax instruments is associated with a consumption bundle for each individual. Finally, there is a criterion function which ranks outcomes and chooses the best ("optimal") tax system among the limited set available. In models with one representative individual, this criterion is simply his or her level of utility. In models with heterogeneous individuals, a utilitarian social welfare function is used to aggregate the individuals' levels of utility into a measure of social welfare.[2]

The spirit of the optimal tax literature is that the efficiency costs of taxation are potentially large, and therefore it is worthwhile to focus attention on how to minimize these costs. In the simplest of the models, minimizing efficiency costs is the only objective. In more sophisticated models, tax systems are also evaluated by how they affect the distribution of welfare, and the efficiency costs must be balanced against the distributional implications.

Optimal Commodity Taxation

In the basic problem of optimal commodity taxation, the government must raise a fixed amount of real resources and can levy only commodity taxes. All taxpayers are identical (in tastes and endowment), so the government need not be concerned with

---

[1] For more thorough surveys of the theory of optimal taxation, see Auerbach (1985), Stern (1987), and Stiglitz (1988).

[2] The theory of optimal taxation does not consider the political process that generates tax policy and does not deal with the possibility that policymakers' objectives may not be maximizing social welfare. It also attaches no weight to the pre-tax distribution of income. The desirability of any tax policy is judged solely by its consequences for individuals and is not judged independently on how closely it meets abstract principles such as fairness and efficiency. A concern for fairness may, though, be imbedded in the concavity of the social welfare function, and the desire for efficiency will be reflected in the decrease in individual welfare levels caused by inefficiency.

questions of vertical equity (how the tax burden varies across taxpayers of different means) or horizontal equity (how the tax burden varies across taxpayers of identical means). Any pattern of taxes can be raised without administrative or compliance cost.

What set of commodity taxes will raise the required revenue and leave the taxpayer as well off as possible? Or to put it another way, what set of taxes minimizes the efficiency cost of the tax burden? Frank Ramsey solved this problem more than 60 years ago, though its solution may still come as a surprise to those readers whose first instinct is to assume that the lowest efficiency cost will be achieved with the fewest distortions in relative prices. Ramsey (1927) showed that a uniform commodity tax system, which alters none of the relative prices of goods, is in general not optimal. Instead, efficiency cost minimizing commodity taxes will in general differ by commodity, such that more inelastically demanded goods tend to attract higher tax rates. In fact, with certain strong simplifying assumptions, an "inverse elasticity rule" applies exactly; the tax rate is inversely proportional to a good's own compensated elasticity of demand.

Why the apparently benign rule of uniform taxation is generally not optimal should become clear once the second-best nature of the problem is understood. The first-best solution is to impose a lump-sum tax on the representative taxpayer. In that way the required revenue can be achieved with no efficiency cost at all. Because lump-sum taxes are ruled out by assumption, any tax system will inevitably cause some distortions as individuals substitute away from relatively highly taxed goods to relatively lightly taxed goods. A uniform tax on all commodities (other than leisure) reduces the relative price of leisure with respect to each commodity, causing an inefficiently large consumption of leisure. The optimal tax pattern should take advantage of commodities' relative substitutability or complementarity with leisure. A complement to leisure, such as skis, should be taxed relatively heavily and a substitute for leisure (complement to labor), such as work uniforms, should be taxed relatively lightly. The extent to which this relative substitutability should be exploited is limited by the fact that non-uniform taxes do cause inefficiency in the consumption pattern of non-leisure goods. Uniform commodity taxation is optimal under very restrictive conditions.[3]

Can these prescriptions for optimal commodity taxation be made operational? Deaton (1987), for one, has expressed considerable skepticism. He first points out that common restrictions on preferences that are made to facilitate estimation presuppose the optimal tax solution. For example, given a linear expenditure system, uniform taxation is optimal regardless of the system's parameters. Thus, estimation done within that framework is pointless. With the right kind of data, preferences can be represented by a flexible enough functional form so that measurements are not merely assumptions in disguise. However, note that calculating the optimal commodity tax rates may require knowing price and income responses at points quite different from

---

[3] Uniformity is optimal only if there is implicit (also known as quasi) separability between leisure and goods; that is, when all goods complement leisure equally. Formally, two goods are quasi-separable from leisure if the expenditure function can be written $e(w, f, (q, U), U)$, where w is the wage rate, q is a vector of goods prices, and U is utility (Atkinson and Stiglitz, 1980, p. 379).

the current position or anything else previously observed. Deaton concludes that such global knowledge of preferences is probably unobtainable. Stern (1987) is less pessimistic. While he acknowledges the difficulties involved in estimation, he claims (p. 86) that we do know a lot about the relevant relationships [elasticities] and will therefore be "negligent... if we suppressed or ignored this information." Because predicting the effects of small changes from a given tax system requires only knowledge of the current position and derivatives of demand functions, some have suggested that the main use of optimal tax theory is for tax reform, and that policy should focus on tax reform.

If taxpayers have different endowments, then the optimal commodity tax structure must consider not only its efficiency cost, but also its effect on the distribution of consumer welfare. Not surprisingly, in this case the optimal tax on luxury goods is higher than otherwise and the optimal tax on necessary goods is lower than otherwise. Of course, when one can also choose an income tax at the same time as commodity taxes, then the income tax can accomplish much of the redistributional task. The presence of this additional instrument critically changes the nature of the optimal commodity tax structure. Atkinson and Stiglitz (1976) have shown that, when a general income tax structure is available, commodity taxes will not be part of the optimum tax structure whenever the utility function is weakly separable between labor and all goods together.[4]

In the past decade, Feldstein and others have argued that the quantitatively significant distortions caused by the tax system are intertemporal rather than intratemporal, and have focused attention on the taxation of capital income and away from the taxation of commodities at a point in time. By distinguishing goods according to date of consumption, the insights of optimal commodity taxation have been usefully applied to the question of whether capital income ought to be taxed. To see this, consider a two-period model with three goods: first-period consumption, first-period leisure, and second-period consumption. It is assumed that the individual chooses how much to work in the first period, but does not work in the second period. The government must raise a fixed amount of revenue in present value, and can levy commodity taxes on consumption in either period.

In this model the tax treatment of capital income is implicit in the relative tax impact on consumption in the two periods. Imposing equal tax rates on consumption in each period is equivalent to a wage tax or consumption tax. Similarly, when the tax rate on second-period consumption exceeds (is less than) the tax on first-period consumption, capital income is subject to a positive (negative) tax.[5]

---

[4]A utility function is weakly separable when the marginal rate of substitution between any two goods is not affected by the quantity of leisure consumed. Note that this condition is quite different than the quasi-separability required for optimal uniform commodity taxes (equivalent to a tax only on earnings) in a one-person world with no lump-sum taxes available.

[5]The lifetime budget constraint of a representative individual can be written as

(A-1) $$C_1(1 + t_1) + \frac{C_2}{1 + r}(1 + t_2) + wL = w,$$

The theory of optimal commodity taxation tells us that the efficient pattern of taxation depends on the relative substitutability of consumption in each time period for leisure. If first-period consumption is relatively more substitutable for first-period leisure, then it should be taxed relatively lightly, implying a positive tax on capital income. If, on the other hand, second-period consumption is relatively more substitutable, then a subsidy to capital income is called for. In the event they are equally substitutable, a zero tax on capital income (that is, a consumption or wage tax) is optimal, so that the tax rate on first-period and second-period consumption should be equal.

Feldstein (1978) argued that reasonable values for the wage elasticity of labor supply and the interest elasticity of savings imply that capital income was taxed too highly at that time. He estimated that eliminating capital income taxation and replacing the lost revenue with higher taxes on labor would reduce the efficiency cost of taxation by 18 percent of tax revenue. King (1980), though, points out that these reasonable parameter values used by Feldstein happen to imply the optimality of consumption taxation. In any event, Deaton's pessimism over the ability of econometricians to provide the parameters of optimal tax formulae applies even more strongly to the structure of intertemporal preferences than it does to preferences at a point in time. I am very doubtful that we'll ever know much about the relative substitutability of leisure with consumption of different periods. In fact, many attempts to estimate intertemporal preferences empirically begin with functional form restrictions that practically guarantee the dominance of consumption taxation over income taxation.

In a model of overlapping generations without bequests, the effect of taxation on the capital-labor ratio becomes an additional issue. When, in the absence of taxation, the steady-state capital-labor ratio would be below the level that maximizes utility, an

---

where C_1 and C_2 are first and second-period consumption, respectively, t_1 and t_2 are the two consumption tax rates, w is the wage rate, r is the rate of interest, and L is leisure (out of a unit time endowment). When t_1 equals $t_2 (= t)$, the budget constraint can be recast as either

(A-2) $$C_1 + \frac{C_2}{1+r} = w(1-L)\left(1 - \frac{t}{1+t}\right),$$

which shows the equivalence of uniform commodity taxes to a wage tax at rate $t/(1+t)$, or

(A-3) $$\left(C_1 + \frac{C_2}{1+r}\right)(1+t) = w(1-L),$$

which shows the equivalence to a general consumption tax. Rewriting (A-1) as

(A-4) $$C_2 = \left[w(1-L)\left(1 - \frac{t_1}{1+t_1}\right) - C_1\right]\left[(1+r)\left(1 - \frac{t_2 - t_1}{1 - t_2}\right)\right]$$

makes clear that when t_2 exceeds t_1, capital income is subject to a positive tax, and when t_1 is less than t_2, capital income is subsidized.

optimal tax policy must not only consider the distortion in the lifetime consumption pattern but also whether it moves the capital-labor ratio closer to or farther from its optimum level and how it affects the intergenerational distribution of welfare. Summers (1981) has suggested that the intertemporal elasticity of substitution may be so high that these other issues dominate the life cycle distortion issue. This occurs because tax-induced changes in the initial after-tax interest rate cause so much response in saving and, eventually, the capital-labor ratio that the new equilibrium after-tax interest is not much changed, so that life-cycle consumption decisions are not much affected. Then the critical question becomes what tax structure is most effective in raising the capital-labor ratio. This may depend critically on the timing of the tax liability and on the government's ability to use debt policy to affect saving.

Production Efficiency

Now suppose that, in addition to commodity taxes, the government can also raise revenue by levying various kinds of production taxes on firms and on suppliers of inputs. To what extent should these taxes be used to supplement (or replace) commodity taxes?

The short answer to this crucial problem, provided by Diamond and Mirrlees (1971), is that as long as commodity taxes can be set without constraints (and therefore optimally) and if there are no privately received economic profits (either because there are constant returns to scale or because of 100 percent profits taxation), then taxes should be set to achieve production efficiency. In other words, all firms (both private and government enterprises) should face the same vector of prices.

The intuition behind this result is straightforward. With no constraint on commodity taxes, any set of after-tax prices, including the optimal one, can be achieved with commodity taxes alone.[6] Any other taxes may increase the efficiency cost and cannot improve on the minimal efficiency cost achieved in their absence.

This result is potentially important because achieving production efficiency rules out a long list of taxes. On the proscribed list are corporation income taxes, origin-based commodity or capital income taxes, tariffs, sector-specific investment or employment incentives, taxes on intermediate goods, and the tax exemption of non-market labor supply.

However, the conditions necessary to seek production efficiency, and to therefore rule out such taxes, are not realistic. Production efficiency is in general not desirable when there are constraints on how commodities and profits can be taxed. For example, if a commodity tax cannot be imposed on some good, a tax on factor income earned in that sector may serve as a partial substitute. If certain commodities must be taxed at identical rates, then differential taxation on factors in those industries is generally desirable. Furthermore, if 100 percent taxation of profits cannot be achieved, differential taxation of factors can serve as a substitute for the profits tax; the greater the share of profits in an industry, the larger should the differential factor tax be. In

---

[6] The assumptions of the model imply that the welfare of any consumer depends only on his endowment and the vector of prices he faces.

the absence of 100 percent taxation of profits, the structure of optimal commodity taxes as well as the optimal structure of factor taxes is changed.

Administrative problems are often at the heart of why optimal commodity and profits taxation are not implemented, thus opening the way for taxes which interfere with production efficiency.[7] It is difficult to tax the rental value of owner-occupied housing and other consumer durables, consumption of family-provided domestic services, and consumption of nonmarketed agricultural produce. It is difficult to tax labor used in household production. The cost of administering any tax system increases with the number of different tax rates that are imposed, so that only a small number of tax rates may be desirable. It is difficult to distinguish between capital and wage income in unincorporated enterprises; therefore it is difficult to maintain different rates of tax. Because of the difficulty of separately measuring pure profits and capital income, 100 percent taxation of profits is problematic at best.

Thus, problems that arise in administering real tax systems may often make some forms of production tax appropriate, even if such a tax works against production efficiency. The importance of feasibility constraints in defining and collecting taxes will be a recurring theme of this paper.

Optimal Tax Progressivity

Many analyses of taxation address the problem of taxing a single representative consumer, but this convenient assumption sidesteps the thorny issues of interpersonal comparisons of welfare. When the assumption of a representative consumer is abandoned to face the reality of heterogeneous individuals, optimal tax solutions get more complicated. As mentioned earlier, the optimal commodity tax solution must be modified to account for the income elasticity of commodities and the social weight put on redistributing welfare through the fiscal systems. Production efficiency is no longer necessarily desirable (Dasgupta and Stiglitz, 1972).

Restricting attention to commodity taxes at various rates is surely inappropriate once redistributional issues are admitted. On the other hand, commodity taxes which vary with the circumstances of the buyer are conceivable but usually impractical. Personal income taxes, though, are flexible enough that the average tax rate may vary by individual (although not without cost), thus allowing the pursuit of redistributional goals.

Mirrlees (1971) initiated the modern debate on how progressive the income tax should be. In his formulation, the government seeks to maximize a utilitarian social welfare function, and must choose an income tax schedule subject to raising some given amount of total revenue.[8] A progressive tax on ability, which would cause no efficiency cost, is ruled out on the grounds that ability is impossible for the government to observe. Mirrlees first investigated what characterizes the optimal income tax for any set of assumptions about the social welfare function, the distribution of

---

[7] A formal model of the impact of costly administration on the desirability of production efficiency is presented in Heller and Shell (1974).
[8] Because a tax schedule may feature rebates rather than taxes at some levels of income, it is really the optimal tax-and-transfer system that is at issue.

endowments, and the behavioral response (utility) functions. He concluded that only very weak conditions characterize the optimal tax structure in the general case: that the marginal tax rate at all levels of income lies between zero and 100 percent, and that in most of the interesting cases some of the population will choose not to work at all. Clearly these requirements offer us little concrete guidance in the construction of a tax schedule.

But one result of this general literature is surprising—that the marginal tax rate at the highest level of income should be precisely zero.[9] This is true as long as there is a known upper bound to the income distribution and regardless of the form of the social welfare function, provided that the welfare of the most well off individual carries some positive weight.[10] To see the intuition behind this result, first consider an income tax schedule in which the marginal rate applicable to the highest observed income is positive. Now consider a second tax schedule which is identical to the first except that it allows the highest-earning household to pay no taxes on any excess of income over what it would have earned under the first tax schedule. When faced with the second tax schedule this household is certainly better off, works more hours, and pays no less tax than under the first schedule. All other households are at least as well off (and may be strictly better off if the top marginal tax rate is set to be slightly positive and the increased revenue from the highest-earning household allows a reduction in average tax rates in the lower brackets). In other words, raising the marginal tax at the top above zero distorts the labor supply decision of the highest earner but raises no revenue.

This result calls to mind Edgeworth's (undated, p. 9) comment about Marshall's discovery of the Giffen good: "Only a very clever man would discover that exceptional case; only a very foolish man would take it as the basis of a rule for general practice." The result does not imply that marginal taxes should be zero or very low near the top, only precisely at the top. In fact, numerical calculations by Mirrlees (1976, p. 340) suggest that zero "is a bad approximation to the [optimal] marginal tax rate even within most of the top... percentiles."

Although I feel that this result should not be taken seriously as a practical guide to tax policy, it does provide some insight into the question of optimal tax progressivity. It highlights the possibility that a utilitarian social objective function, even one that places a large weight on the welfare of the poor, is not necessarily maximized through high marginal tax rates on the rich. In fact, the poor can only be made less well off by a non-zero marginal tax rate at the very top. The numerical examples I discuss below indicate that, more generally, the poor may be best served by tax systems which are less leveling than intuition might suggest.

---

[9] Even more surprising is the result that, when there exist two types of labor (skilled and unskilled), the marginal tax on the most able individual should be negative. This causes a second-order efficiency loss, but redistributes welfare to less able individuals because it increases the relative wage of unskilled labor.

[10] Note that this result, when combined with Mirrlees' finding that the marginal tax rate must be nonnegative at all income levels, implies that the optimal income tax system cannot have continuously increasing marginal tax rates. It does not, though, say anything about what the average tax rate at the top should be.

The literature offers no other completely general results. In their absence, the approach has been to make specific assumptions about the elements of the model and in some cases to limit the class of income tax system under study (usually to linear or flat-rate schedules), and then to calculate the parameters of the optimal income tax system. This approach is meant to suggest the characteristics of the optimal income tax under reasonable assumptions and to investigate how these characteristics depend on the elements of the model.

Mirrlees pioneered this approach in his 1971 article. Assuming a simple utilitarian social welfare function, a lognormal distribution of ability, and an identical Cobb-Douglas utility function of goods and leisure for each individual, he calculated that the optimal tax structure is approximately linear (that is, it has a constant marginal tax rate and an exemption level below which tax liability is negative) and has marginal tax rates which were quite low by then current standards, usually between 20 and 30 percent and almost always less than 40 percent.[11]

Subsequent work investigated the sensitivity of the optimal income tax to the parametric assumptions. Mirrlees showed that widening the distribution of skills increased the optimal marginal tax rates, though he considered the dispersion of skills necessary to imply much higher rates to be unrealistic. Atkinson (1973) explored the effect of increasing the egalitarianism of the social welfare function. Even in the extreme case of the Rawlsian maximin social welfare function, where social welfare is judged solely on the basis of how well off the worst-off person is, the model generated optimal tax rates not much higher than 50 percent. Finally, Stern (1976) suggested that the degree of labor supply responsiveness implied by the Cobb-Douglas utility function is excessive and thus overstates the costs of increasing tax progressivity. He claimed that when a more reasonable estimate of labor supply responsiveness is used (with an elasticity of substitution of 0.4 rather than the unitary elasticity of the Cobb-Douglas formulation) the value of the optimal tax rate is substantially higher than otherwise, 54 percent in his central case compared to 20 or 30 percent in the Cobb-Douglas case.[12]

In sum, simple models of optimal income taxation do not generally point to sharply progressive tax structures, even if the objective function puts relatively large weight on the welfare of less well-off individuals. This conclusion does, though, depend on the wage elasticity of labor supply. Low elasticities, which imply a low marginal cost of redistributing income through the tax system, can imply highly progressive tax structures, so that lack of consensus about elasticities precludes consensus about optimal progressivity. Furthermore, the models that have been applied to this question have been very stylized, for the most part ignoring such issues as uncertainty, dynamic factors such as bequests and inheritance, tax evasion, and tax arbitrage.[13] For

---

[11] Note that, although the marginal tax rate is approximately constant, the average tax rate (tax liability divided by income) increases with income due to the presence of the positive exemption level.

[12] The revenue requirement in this example was about 20 percent of net output.

[13] Stiglitz (1988) has also criticized the literature's reliance on a utilitarian social welfare function which embodies value judgments about interpersonal welfare comparisons. He has advocated disentangling the latter from efficiency considerations, and concentrating on the characteristics of Pareto-efficiency tax structures.

example, considering only linear tax schedules (with one marginal tax rate and a demogrant) undoubtedly sacrifices some flexibility in redistribution. However, eliminating the graduated rate structure promises substantial simplification in the tax system by minimizing the incentive to arrange transactions to move income from high tax rate to low tax rate individuals. The tradeoff between the distributional flexibility of graduated income tax systems and the benefits of a flat rate is ignored in the standard models which either assume a flat rate or do not consider tax arbitrage.

The Guiding Principles of Recent U.S. Tax Reform

Recent changes in the statutory progressivity of the individual income tax are an apparent testimony to Keynes' statement about the policy influence of academic scribblers. When the optimal progressivity literature first surfaced in the early 1970s, the top marginal tax rate in the U.S. stood at 70 percent. (It had been 91 percent as recently as 1963.) As of January 1, 1988, the marginal tax rate on the highest income has fallen to 28 percent, a remarkably steep drop. In fact, the top marginal income tax rate has fallen in nearly every OECD country, in many cases quite substantially. The most recent drop in the top U.S. marginal rate was accompanied by broadening the tax base, in particular by subjecting realized nominal capital gains to full taxation, when only 40 percent of long-term gains had been taxable previously. The optimal progressivity literature does not directly address the appropriateness of lowered marginal tax rates when achieved by eliminating aspects of preferential tax treatment. Nevertheless, a key message of the optimal progressivity literature, that high marginal rates may not be appropriate even for egalitarian social welfare functions, has apparently won the day.

Judging by the recent debate over tax reform, the lessons of the optimal commodity tax literature have not had much of an impact on tax policy. The U.S. Department of the Treasury's initial proposal in 1984 favored a comprehensive income tax and defended it on, among other things, efficiency grounds (p. 25): "A comprehensive tax base is...necessary for economic neutrality, since...discrimination between various ways of earning and spending income distort economic decisions." This statement is incorrect if one interprets "economic neutrality" to mean causing no distortions, as that can be achieved only with a lump-sum tax. The theory of optimal commodity taxation suggests that minimal (as opposed to zero) distortion is achieved with a comprehensive income tax base only if utility functions satisfy fairly strong conditions which certainly have not been decisively established by econometric investigation. Yet the tax reform movement championed minimal tax differentiation of sources and uses of income. Interestingly, the Tax Reform Act of 1986 did not substantially change the average rate of tax on saving and investment, rejecting the intertemporal version of uniform taxation of goods which would exempt capital income from taxation in favor of a consumption base.

The desirability of production efficiency, usually referred to as a "level playing field," was a consistent theme of many tax reform proposals, including the Treasury's initial proposal and the Tax Reform Act of 1986. These proposals sought to reduce the apparently widespread disparities in effective capital income tax rates across industries and types of capital investments. Production efficiency precludes the differential taxation of the inputs to firms, whether the tax is differentiated by section of use or by type of input, since either would distort production decisions.

The apparent triumph of production efficiency as a goal is somewhat surprising in view of the strong assumptions needed to demonstrate its desirability. The wide acceptance of this goal led Feldstein (1985) to point out that as long as the income from some capital goods would be untaxed (as would characterize the return to owner-occupied housing in all the major proposals), it is not in general optimal to tax uniformly the income from those forms of capital which are taxable. Summers (1987) further argued that the potential efficiency gain from eliminating differential taxation of different types of capital income is small, and that attention paid to this problem diverts attention from the overall level of taxation of capital income, which in his view is far more important in determining the efficient operation of the economy.

Clearly the *spirit* of optimal taxation theory, that tax-induced inefficiencies are potentially large and must be considered in the design of policy, has infused the recent tax reform movement.[14] However, policymakers have been selective in adopting the lessons of the theory. Marginal tax rates have come down significantly, and a partial move toward undifferentiated capital income taxes has been accomplished. However, little attention has been paid to differential commodity taxes or to changing the effective rate of tax on saving and investment. I suspect that the ascendancy of uniform taxation, at least in its intratemporal version, is due to the lack of strong evidence pointing to a clear alternative and the sense that a uniform tax system is less susceptible to political pressures favoring tax changes that serve special interests and are unrelated to optimal tax considerations.[15]

What strikes me most about the tax policy debates of recent years is that many of the critical issues lie outside the usual domain of optimal taxation theory. Simplification, tax shelters, and inflation-induced problems were of major concern during the debate leading up to the Tax Reform Act of 1986. Since 1986 debate has focused on the appropriate level of enforcement of existing tax laws, the taxation of capital gains, and whether a value-added tax should be added to the federal arsenal of tax instruments. Although optimal taxation theory is useful for analyzing some aspects of some of these issues, in many cases it cannot address the principal questions.

One reason that the theory of optimal taxation is incomplete as a guide to action is that its models, like all models, are imbedded in stylized versions of the environment and tax systems. The usual stylizations exclude such potentially important features of the world such as imperfect competition, increasing returns to scale, and unemploy-

---

[14]See McLure (1984) for an interesting perspective on the effect of academic thinking on the tax reform movement. The policy influence of the high distortionary cost of taxation is somewhat ironic because the profession has since moved away from its belief in high behavioral elasticities. In particular, the median professional estimate of the intertemporal elasticity of substitution is undoubtedly much lower now than in the early 1980s. For example, compare Hall (1988) and Summers (1982).

[15]See Hulten and Klayman (1988) for a statement of this view.

ment. I believe that its critical problem is the failure to consider the technology of collecting taxes. In the next section I argue it is this omission which severely limits applicability of optimal taxation theory to many current policy problems.

Optimal Tax Systems and the Technology of Tax Collection

The leap from the blackboard to the real world is a large one when it comes to taxation. In the United States, operating the tax system requires the participation of over 100 million taxpayers, hundreds of thousands of tax professionals, and a multi-billion dollar budget for the Internal Revenue Service and its state counterparts. The resource cost of operating the income tax system alone, including the administrative cost borne by the government and the compliance cost borne by the taxpayers, has been estimated to be as high as $35 billion annually, or about 7 percent of revenue (Slemrod and Sorum, 1984). This cost is large both in absolute terms and relative to the distortionary costs of taxation. For example, it is more than twice as high as recent estimates of the efficiency cost of the nonuniform taxation of assets used within the corporate sector (Summers, 1987).

More important than the magnitude of the costs, though, the ease of administering various taxes has critical implications for the optimal structure of tax systems. As discussed earlier, tax codes which are based on unobservable and practically unmeasurable quantities (such as an ability tax) often look desirable on paper. The choice among real tax systems must confront the fact that some taxes can be administered more easily than others. If optimal tax theory is to be a reliable guide to action, it must consider the issues that arise in operating the tax system.

Integrating the issue of administrative ease into optimal tax theory will require a shift of emphasis away from the structure of preferences, which has been the principal focus of optimal tax theory, toward the technology of tax collection. In what follows, I will use the term optimal tax systems to refer to the normative theory of taxation that considers not only the structure of preferences but also takes seriously the technology of collecting taxes.

The Choice of Tax Instruments

With some exceptions, optimal tax theory has dealt with the issue of administering a tax by making extreme assumptions about what kinds of taxes are available to the policymaker. Each of the three cornerstones of optimal tax theory depends on implicit assumptions about which taxes can be administered and which cannot. The problem of optimal commodity taxation is interesting only because the possibility of lump-sum taxation is ruled out, presumably because it is infeasible. Production efficiency is desirable only if all commodities can be taxed and 100 percent taxation of profits is feasible (or if no profits exist). When consumers are not identical, an ability tax dominates an income tax because it causes no distortion in behavior. The study of optimal income taxation is appropriate when ability taxes are ruled out, usually by appealing to the difficulties of measuring ability.

Extreme assumptions about the feasibility of tax instruments are analytically convenient but incorrect. Ability can be measured, although with some expense and error. On the other hand, income cannot be measured perfectly, and the degree of accuracy in income measurement depends on the resources expended toward this goal.

Extreme assumptions about the feasibility of tax instruments may also preclude consideration of fundamental changes in policy.[16] For example, a common assumption made in optimal taxation models of developing countries is that income and consumption arising in the agricultural sector are not taxable, although marketable surplus is taxable. Much interesting analysis proceeds from this assumption, but none asks at what point it makes sense for a country to attempt to tax agricultural income, even assuming that it will have only limited success in doing so. There is strong evidence (Riezman and Slemrod, 1987) that countries with low literacy rates tend to rely on highly distorting but (relatively) easily collectable import and export taxes, and shy away from efficient but administratively difficult land taxes. Under what conditions should an imperfect land tax be tried? The answers to these questions depend on the resource cost of administering the new tax instrument relative to its effectiveness, or degree of success. This latter notion has several dimensions, including the true revenue yield and the extent and nature of the mistakes that are made in administration.

Some initial progress has been made in analyzing the optimal choice of tax instruments. Stern (1982) models the choice between two distinct tax systems: an optimal nonlinear income tax, where income is costlessly observable, and a system of differential lump-sum taxes based on characteristics of taxpayers which can be ascertained with some error. The lump-sum tax system is superior if there are no errors in classifying individuals but, when enough mistakes are made, income taxation may be the preferred system.

Stern's analysis recognizes that the two tax systems each have their own information requirements (the lump-sum system requires classifying individuals, the income tax system requires observing incomes). The two systems will also likely have different administrative costs as well, although Stern assumes these costs are identical for the sake of simplicity. Greater accuracy in the classification of individuals could be achieved with higher cost, as could more accurate measurement of income.

Yitzhaki (1979) investigates the optimal commodity tax base when there is a resource cost to adding goods to the tax base. If, as he assumes, preferences over all goods are Cobb-Douglas, then uniformity of rate for all taxed goods is optimal. Expanding the tax base to cover more goods will reduce the excess burden of taxation, but increase the administrative cost. The optimal tax system equates the marginal

---

[16] The desirability of making the choice between tax instruments an endogenous variable has been noted by, among others, Hahn (1973) and Atkinson and Stiglitz (1980, p. 363), who state that "for a complete theory of the choice of tax base, a fully articulated model is necessary of the information available to the government and cost of observing the different characteristics." Diamond (1987, p. 640) agrees that this would be ideal, but adds that the standard simplifications "may do little damage to the policy conclusions if the set of feasible policies is well chosen, although the problem of choosing well is a difficult one."

excess burden of the taxes to the marginal administrative cost, and thus minimizes the total resource cost of raising revenue.

The fact that changes in administrative costs are likely to be discontinuous with respect to changes in tax policy is troubling in more general treatments of the optimal set of tax instruments. The theory of optimal taxation tells us that, in general, all goods should be taxed at different rates. But administrative cost is likely to be lower whenever the rate on substitutable goods is uniform. It may be that the cost depends on the number of different tax rates, rather than the number of commodities taxed, as Yitzhaki assumed.

The cost of administering a commodity tax system undoubtedly depends not only on the number of commodities covered, but also on the number of different rates imposed. This is not an issue when a demand structure that implies uniform optimal taxes is assumed (that is, Cobb-Douglas), but is very important under a more general demand structure.

Many of these concerns are relevant to the debate in the U.S. over introducing a value-added tax to raise additional revenue. The cost of the new administrative machinery would not be trivial. The Treasury Department (1984) estimated it would cost about $700 million per year, and require about 20,000 additional employees. The British experience with the VAT (see Sandford, et al. 1981) suggests that the cost borne by taxpayers is probably five times higher, bringing the total collection cost to nearly 3 percent of the revenue raised from a 7 percent VAT.[17] Obviously these costs could be avoided if additional revenue came from existing taxes rather than introducing a new tax.

One argument for the value-added tax is that it can be self-enforcing. Under the invoice method of value-added taxation, each firm pays tax on its sales and receives a credit for taxes invoiced by its suppliers. Thus evasion by suppliers through understating tax collected is counteracted by purchasers' interest in ensuring that all tax paid is recorded. Similarly, evasion by purchasers in overstating tax paid runs counter to the interest of suppliers. Of course, this self-enforcement aspect of value-added taxes can be eroded by, for example, counterfeiting of invoices. Moreover, this tendency to self-enforcement is not effective at the retail level, which can comprise as much as half of the tax base. Although the European experience suggests that this advantage is not fully realized in practice, the revenue loss from evasion (estimated in the United Kingdom to be 1.5 percent of potential revenue (Hemming and Kay, 1981), is probably very low compared to the revenue loss from income tax evasion.[18]

---

[17]According to the U.S. Treasury Department (1984), the base of a value-added tax that excluded the rental value of housing, medical care, food, and certain other items would be $2.06 billion. Thus a 7 percent value-added would raise $144.2 billion, compared to an estimated collection cost of $4.2 billion. There is a large element of fixed cost, so that the collection cost per dollar raised falls as tax rates increase.

[18]Such high rates of compliance apparently do not apply to all countries. Evasion of the value-added tax in Italy, for example, has been estimated to reduce collections by as much as 40 percent (Pedone, 1981). Income tax evasion is notoriously high in Italy as well.

The European experience with the value-added tax also suggests that the potential simplicity of the value-added tax is seriously eroded when differentiated rates and exemptions (usually designed to lessen regressivity) are introduced, as they have been in all European countries and would likely be in the United States (Aaron, 1981). Thus, any desire to discriminate among commodities on optimal tax grounds must be balanced against the additional cost of administering such a system.

Although the apparent discontinuity of administrative cost functions poses analytical difficulties, a more profound problem is that the quality of tax administration is variable. Until now, in treating the question of whether to have or not have a particular tax, I've assumed that a tax is perfectly enforced after it is enacted. In fact, for any given tax structure more resources expended in enforcement can reduce the extent of tax evasion and therefore produce more revenue, reduce distortions, and improve horizontal equity.

Tax Evasion

The Internal Revenue Service (1988) has estimated that in 1987 noncompliance with the individual and corporation income tax cost the Treasury $84.9 billion, comprising over 20 percent of tax liability. Since 1973 the lost revenue had been rising faster than nominal income for each year until 1986. Although comparable studies for other countries do not exist, anecdotal evidence suggests that the extent of tax noncompliance is even larger in other countries.

Tax evasion is widespread, and its presence has serious implications for the equity, efficiency, and collection cost of alternative tax systems. Skinner and Slemrod (1985) discuss some of these implications. Yet its existence has not penetrated the standard (positive or normative) models of taxation, in which the effect of a tax levy is treated identically to an upward shift in the supply curve generated by, say, increased input prices. There is, though, a fundamental difference between the two cases. In the latter case the purchaser presumably must pay the higher price to continue to receive the good from the supplier. The higher equilibrium price is self-enforcing. When a tax is levied, though, neither party to the transaction has a direct incentive to collect the tax. In the absence of enforcement, only particularly dutiful individuals would forward the taxes to the government. Since no quid pro quo is attached to the payment of taxes, all parties would attempt to be free riders.

More generally, all taxpayers have the incentive to misrepresent their activities which have tax implications to reduce or eliminate their tax liability. For this reason no tax structure can stand alone without an enforcement mechanism supporting it. A theory of optimal tax systems must encompass not only the choice of tax rules but also how they are enforced.

Allingham and Sandmo (1972) were the first to analyze an individual's decision about whether and how much to comply with the tax law as a choice under uncertainty. An individual, by understating taxable income, receives the reward of a lower tax liability if the evasion is undetected, and pays a penalty if the evasion is detected. The decision will depend on the terms of the gamble (the chances of being caught, the penalty if detected) and on the individual's attitude toward risk. Subsequent work has modeled the labor supply decision and tax evasion decision jointly and introduced more general penalty and tax functions than considered by Allingham and Sandmo.

Sandmo (1981) built on this model of the taxpayer decision to evade to consider the simultaneous choice of the parameters of a linear income system tax and its enforcement structure. His model contains two types of people—nonevaders who work only in the regular economy, and evaders who divide their time among leisure, taxed work in the regular market and untaxed work in the underground economy. In this model, the presence of the underground economy will lower the optimal marginal tax rate if it implies that regular income is a less reliable indicator of economic welfare, because in this case a more progressive tax system accomplishes less redistribution from the truly well off to those truly not. It also lowers optimal progressivity if it increases the compensated wage elasticity of regular labor supply. The tendency for a higher marginal tax rate to increase the supply of labor to the underground economy is not, however, an argument for a lower marginal tax rate. If anything, the reverse is true, because the increased supply of labor is a move in the direction of the undistorted level of labor supply to the underground economy.

Sandmo also derives the condition characterizing the optimal amount of resources to be devoted to the detection of evaders, which unsurprisingly reduces to equating the marginal resource cost of increasing the probability of detection to its marginal social benefit. The trick here is correctly interpreting the marginal social benefit of strengthening enforcement. As stressed by Slemrod and Yitzhaki (1987), it does not directly include the revenue gained via increased voluntary compliance; that represents a transfer from the private to the public sector. Thus, there are no normative implications of the claim of every IRS commissioner that each additional budget dollar allocated to the IRS will return on the order of ten dollars in increased revenues. The marginal social benefit does, though, include the value to risk-averse taxpayers of paying the required expected tax payment in a less risky manner, which occurs because the higher probability of detection deters tax evasion gambling. In a more general model, the marginal social benefit of increased enforcement would also include such factors as the efficiency gain from reducing the resources attracted to evasion-facilitating activities and the reduced horizontal inequity from favoring people with relatively less risk-averse preferences.

Mayshar (1986), adapting a model introduced by Usher (1986), places administration and sheltering costs within a formal model of optimal taxation. The standard result from the theory of optimal commodity taxation continues to hold: any tax instruments that are used ought to equalize at the margin the excess burden per dollar raised. The measure of excess burden, though, must be modified to include the cost of administration and the resource cost of sheltering income from the tax authorities, which includes the uncertainty of tax payment. The optimal level of enforcement of the tax laws, viewed as one of several tax instruments, is similarly characterized at the margin—the ratio of excess burden (broadly defined) to revenue raised should be the same as the ratio that applies to increasing tax rates of existing taxes.

Can Capital Income Tax Be Collected?

The collection of taxes is greatly facilitated when it is based on easily observable transactions. This has important implications for the implementation of an income tax, because some income flows are not reflected in any transaction. This problem applies often, but not exclusively, to capital income. The service flow from owner-occupied housing represents income to the owner, but is not accompanied by a market transaction. The same story applies to the change in the value of an asset. Sometimes there is an observable transaction, but at a price which misrepresents the flow of real income. I have in mind the payment of interest on nominal bonds, where the interest payment exceeds the real flow of income because it does not take account of the decline in the real value of the principal.

Tax policy reflects this problem. The imputed income from owner-occupied housing is untaxed in the United States, although a few other countries attempt to tax it, usually ineffectually. Capital gains in the United States are taxed not upon accrual but only upon realization of the gain through sale or transfer to another party. The measurement of capital income is exacerbated by the presence of inflation, because it is nominal rather than real gains that enter the tax base.

The attempt to use transaction-based measures to measure income flows causes its own difficult problems, about which optimal taxation theory is virtually silent. An intertemporal version of the theory can, for a given utility function, prescribe the optimal tax rate on present and future consumption, and thus the optimal tax rate on capital income. But a tax imposed on, for example, capital gain realizations is not a tax on second-period consumption, but rather on the activity of adjusting one's portfolio or one way of drawing down one's assets for consumption. The apparent high responsiveness of capital gains realizations to taxation reflects the availability of highly substitutable financial strategies, and is not related to any characteristic of utility functions such as the elasticity of intertemporal substitution.

The difficulty of measuring capital income flows leads inevitably to a situation in which the effective rate of tax on capital income varies widely depending on the form and intermediation process for holding wealth.[19] Unfortunately, economic distortions and unintended distributional consequences arise whenever a tax system differentiates both on the basis of the financial arrangements for holding wealth and on the recipient of the income flow from that wealth, as it does under a progressive tax system. What tends to occur is high tax rate individuals using lightly taxed financial arrangements for holding wealth and low tax rate individuals using highly taxed financial arrangements. In the extreme case, individuals simultaneously hold a long

---

[19] Measurement difficulties are not the only source of differential taxation of capital income. The government often intentionally subsidizes particular strategies for holding wealth, as in the case of the exemption from federal tax of the interest from state and local government securities.

position in a lightly-taxed asset and a short position in an identical (or similar) asset that is highly taxed. The net result of these phenomena, generally referred to as tax arbitrage, is that the government may collect little or no revenue from its attempt to tax capital income progressively, although in the process cause significant economic inefficiency. Steuerle (1985) and Gordon and Slemrod (1988) argue that this state of affairs in fact characterized the United States of the early 1980s. The Tax Reform Act of 1986, by flattening the schedule of marginal tax rates and reducing the differentials in taxation of capital income, undoubtedly has mitigated this problem somewhat.

Differential taxation of financial assets and wealthowners will generally result in not only production inefficiency, but also inefficient allocation of risk-bearing and capricious distributional consequences. Positive and normative modelling of this phenomenon is in its infancy. A difficult fundamental problem is how to characterize an equilibrium, in particular what limits individuals' profiting from tax arbitrage opportunities.

The problems that stem from the difficulty of measuring income have led some scholars (notably Bradford, 1980) to advocate the scrapping of income taxation in favor of a consumption-based tax. Of course, the change from an income tax to a consumption tax might also be supported on optimal taxation grounds, depending on the nature of utility functions. The problem of tax arbitrage suggests that the rate of tax on capital income is not as important as its uniformity with respect to the financial structure, intermediation process, and the identity of the wealth owner. A move toward either a truly comprehensive income tax, which taxes capital income uniformly at a positive rate, or a move toward a consumption tax, which taxes capital income uniformly at a zero rate, may be an improvement. Which is preferable depends on which system is more likely to be able to sustain uniformity. Bradford argues that, because consumption is easier to measure than income, a consumption tax is superior. Graetz (1979) and the American Bar Association (1985), though, conclude that a consumption tax would not be significantly less complex than a comprehensive income tax.

From this perspective the winner of the great debate over the relative merits of the consumption versus the income tax rests on an issue of measurability and thus is firmly in the realm of optimal tax systems rather than optimal taxation. Earlier we saw that the question of whether to sacrifice the redistributional flexibility of a graduated tax system in favor of a flat-rate tax also rests heavily on the administrative advantages of the latter. A comprehensive income tax with a flat rate would arguably offer nearly as much gain in simplicity as would a tax based on consumption rather than income.

A Look to the Future: Some Speculation and a Research Agenda

Changing Technology

I have argued in this paper that future research in the normative theory of taxation ought to shift its focus from the structure of consumer preferences to the technology of collecting taxes and those aspects of the economy which affect tax collection, and from optimal tax rate structure to optimal tax systems. This is an exciting and challenging change in perspective. It is exciting because preferences (economists are accustomed to assuming) are relatively stable over time, but technology is clearly not stable, whether one is discussing the technology of producing steel or of collecting taxes. Changing technology implies that what is an optimal tax system today for the United States is not likely to be optimal 20 years from now.

Compared to 20 years ago, the Internal Revenue Service of today has a tremendously improved capacity to match information reports of parties to transactions to information reported on tax returns. It also faces an immensely more sophisticated financial system in which the transaction costs of hiding income have shrunk. This technological change may, for example, greatly diminish the ability of governments to cheaply enforce a residence-based capital income tax. When funds can evade taxation by crossing borders, countries may be forced to rely on origin-based taxes such as the value-added tax. Some have argued (like Bird, 1988) that the attempt to measure the portion of the income of multinational firms that originates in any country may have to be abandoned in favor of a formula apportionment rule similar to that used in state corporation income tax systems.

I have shown earlier that increasing financial sophistication places great strains on tax systems which attempt to tax capital income in an incoherent fashion and on any system of graduated tax rates. There is a growing awareness that the kinds of behavioral responses to taxation that matter in the real world have little to do with the structure of utility functions, but with the availability of financial strategies that circumvent the intent of the tax laws.

Scholars of the historical evolution of tax structure, notably Hinrichs (1966) and Musgrave (1969), have stressed the importance of tax administration issues. Modern tax structure development has generally been characterized by a shift from excise, customs, and property taxes to corporate income and progressive individual income taxes.[20] This shift has been made possible by the expansion of the market sector and relative decline of the rural sector, the concentration of employment in larger establishments, and the growing literacy of the population. Further changes in the technology of tax administration may now be pushing us away from progressive income taxes toward tax systems that rely more on broad-based consumption taxes such as the value-added tax and much flatter rate structures for income taxation.[21]

A Research Agenda

The shift in focus to a theory of optimal tax systems is challenging as well as exciting because it requires a rethinking of both theoretical and empirical research.

---

[20]Although Hinrichs points out that tax structure development began with direct taxes rather than indirect taxes. See also Kau and Rubin (1981).

[21]The Danish tax reform passed in 1985 is a fascinating recent development. It creates a separate tax schedule for capital income (interest, dividends, taxable capital gains, rents, and profits from business enterprises) and personal income (predominantly labor income). Capital income is taxed at a flat 50 percent rate, and capital income losses are not deductible from personal income. One objective of this system is to reduce the revenue losses from the kind of tax arbitrage discussed in the text.

The normative theory must come to terms with such issues as the choice of tax instruments, the optimal design of enforcement policy, the tax treatment of financial strategies (as opposed to goods or income flows) and more generally, must develop a descriptive and normative framework in which to evaluate the issue of tax arbitrage. These are difficult issues, although progress is being made.

To make the theory of optimal tax systems operational, empirical work must proceed on the technology of collecting taxes. (This is the analogue to the critical role for optimal taxation theory of the empirical investigation of the structure of individuals' preferences.) This effort includes estimating the collection cost of alternative tax systems (for example, Sandford, 1987; Slemrod, 1989). It is important that the inputs to this process be related to a multidimensional measure of output. More resources devoted to tax collection may certainly increase revenue, and can also reduce the horizontal and vertical inequities that accompany tax evasion. The deterrent effect of enforcement is another critical topic for empirical research. Of course this does depend critically on one aspect of preferences: taxpayers' attitudes toward bearing risk. Although plagued by data inadequacies, some research has begun on this topic (Clotfelter, 1983; Dubin and Wilde, 1986).

During its reign as the predominant normative theory of taxation, optimal taxation has generated many valuable insights about the relationships between policy objectives, the structure of the economy, and the availability of tax instruments. In the more general framework of optimal tax systems, optimal taxation emerges as a special case in which the set of tax instruments is fixed and enforcement of any available instrument is costless. These assumptions preclude the study of a variety of important issues. To be a guide to current and future tax policy action, the more encompassing framework of optimal tax systems is essential.

■ *For helpful comments on an earlier draft I would like to thank Henry Aaron, Richard Bird, David Bradford, Leonard Burman, Don Fullerton, Harvey Galper, James Levinsohn, Joram Mayshar, Pradeep Mitra, Joseph Pechman, William Shobe, Jonathan Skinner, Eric Toder, Shlomo Yitzhaki, and the editors of this journal.*

References

Aaron, Henry, ed., *The Value-Added Tax: Lessons from Europe*. Washington, DC: The Brookings Institution, 1981.

Allingham, M. G., and Agnar Sandmo, "Income Tax Evasion: A Theoretical Analysis," *Journal of Public Economics*, November 1972, *1*, 323–38.

American Bar Association, Committee on Simplification of the Section on Taxation, "Complexity and the Personal Consumption Tax," *Tax Lawyer*, Winter 1985, *35*, 415–42.

Atkinson, Anthony B., "How Progressive Should Income Tax Be?" In Parkin, M., and A. R. Nobay, eds., *Essays in Modern Economics*. London: Longman, 1973, pp. 90–109.

Atkinson, Anthony B., and Joseph E. Stiglitz, "The Design of Tax Structure: Direct Versus

Indirect Taxation," *Journal of Public Economics*, July-August 1976, *6*, 55–75.

Atkinson, Anthony B., and Joseph E. Stiglitz, *Lectures on Public Economics*. New York: McGraw-Hill, 1980.

Auerbach, Alan, "The Theory of Excess Burden and Optimal Taxation." In Auerbach, Alan J., and Martin Feldstein, eds., *Handbook of Public Economics*, Vol. 1. Amsterdam: North-Holland, 1985, pp. 61–127.

Bird, Richard, "Shaping a New International Tax Order," *International Bureau of Fiscal Documentation Bulletin*, July 1988.

Bradford, David, "The Case for a Personal Consumption Tax." In Pechman, Joseph A., ed., *What Should Be Taxed: Income or Expenditure*. Washington, D.C.: Brookings Institution, 1980, pp. 75–113.

Clotfelter, Charles T., "Tax Evasion and Tax Rates: An Analysis of Individual Returns," *Review of Economics and Statistics*, August 1983, 303–23.

Dasgupta, Partha S., and Joseph E. Stiglitz, "On Optimal Taxation and Public Production," *Review of Economic Studies*, Feb. 1972, *39*, 87–103.

Deaton, Angus, "Econometric Issues for Tax Design in Developing Countries." In Newbery, David, and Nicholas H. Stern, eds., *The Theory of Taxation for Developing Countries*. New York: Oxford University Press, 1987, pp. 92–113.

Diamond, Peter, "Optimal Tax Theory and Development Policy: Directions for Future Research." In Newbery, David, and Nicholas H. Stern, eds., *The Theory of Taxation for Developing Countries*. New York: Oxford University Press, 1987, pp. 638–47.

Diamond, Peter A., and James A. Mirrlees, "Optimal Taxation and Public Production, Part I: Production Efficiency," and "Part II: Tax Rules," *American Economic Review*, March and June 1971, *61*, 8–27 and 261–78.

Dubin, Jeffrey A., and Louis L. Wilde, "An Empirical Analysis of Federal Income Tax Auditing and Compliance." Social Science Working Paper No. 615, California Institute of Technology, Pasadena, CA: October 1986.

Edgeworth, Francis Y., *On the Relations of Political Economy to War*. London: Oxford University Press, undated.

Feldstein, Martin, "The Welfare Cost of Capital Income Taxation," *Journal of Political Economy*, April 1978 (Part 2), *86*, S29–S51.

Feldstein, Martin, "The Second Best Theory of Capital Income Taxation," National Bureau of Economic Research Working Paper No. 1781. Cambridge, MA, December 1985.

Gordon, Roger, and Joel Slemrod, "Do We Collect Any Revenue from Taxing Capital Income?" In Summers, Lawrence, ed., *Tax Policy and the Economy*. Cambridge, MA: National Bureau of Economic Research, 1988, pp. 89–130.

Graetz, Michael, "Implementing a Progressive Consumption Tax," *Harvard Law Review*, 1979, *92*.

Hahn, Frank, "On Optimum Taxation," *Journal of Economic Theory*, 1973, *6*, 96–106.

Hall, Robert E., "Intertemporal Substitution in Consumption," *Journal of Political Economy*, 1988, *96*, 339–57.

Heller, Walter P., and Karl Shell, "On Optimal Taxation with Costly Administration," *American Economic Review*, May 1974, *64*, 338–45.

Hemming, Richard, and John A. Kay, "The United Kingdom," In Aaron, Henry, ed., *The Value-Added Tax: Lessons from Europe*. Washington, DC: The Brookings Institution, 1981, pp. 75–89.

Hinrichs, Harley H., *A General Theory of Tax Structure Change During Economic Development*. Cambridge, MA: The Law School of Harvard University, 1966.

Hulten, Charles R., and Robert A. Klayman, "Investment Incentives in Theory and Practice." In Aaron, Henry J., Harvey Galper, and Joseph A. Pechman, eds., *Uneasy Compromise: Problems of a Hybrid Income-Consumption Tax*. Washington, D.C.: The Brookings Institution, 1988.

Kau, James B., and Paul H. Rubin, "The Size of Government," *Public Choice*, 1981, *2*, 261–74.

King, Mervyn A., "Savings and Taxation." In Heal, Geoffrey M., and G. A. Hughes, eds., *Public Policy and the Tax System*. London: Allen and Unwin, 1980.

Mayshar, Joram, "Taxation with Costly Administration," Research Report No. 158. The Hebrew University of Jerusalem, Department of Economics, June 1986. Processed.

McLure, Charles, E., Jr., "The Evolution of Tax Advice and the Taxation of Capital Income in the USA," *Environment and Planning: Government and Policy*, 1984, *2*, 251–69.

Mirrlees, James A., "An Exploration in the Theory of Optimum Income Taxation," *Review of Economic Studies*, April 1971, *38*, 175–208.

Mirrlees, James A., Optimal Tax Theory: A Synthesis," *Journal of Public Economics*, 1976, *6*, 327–58.

Musgrave, Richard A., *Fiscal Systems*. New Haven and London: Yale University Press, 1969.

Pedone, Antonio, "Italy." In Aaron, Henry, ed., *The Value-Added Tax: Lessons from Europe*. Washington, DC: The Brookings Institution, 1981.

Radian, Alex, *Resource Mobilization in Poor Countries: Implementing Tax Policies*. New Brunswick, NJ: Transaction, 1980.

Ramsey, Frank P., "A Contribution to the Theory of Taxation," *Economic Journal*, March 1927, *37*, 47–61.

Riezman, Raymond, and Joel Slemrod, "Tariffs and Collection Costs," *Weltwirtschaftliches Archiv*, 1987, *123*, 545–9.

Sadka, Ephraim, "On Income Distribution, Incentive Effects, and Optimal Income Taxation," *Review of Economic Studies*, June 1976, *43*, 261–68.

Sandford, Cedric T., M. R. Godwin, P. J. W. Hardwick, and M. I. Butterworth, *Costs and Benefits of VAT.* London: Heinemann, 1981.

Sandford, Cedric, "The Costs of Paying Tax," *Accountancy*, June 1987, pp. 108–11.

Sandmo, Agnar, "Income Tax Evasion, Labor Supply and the Equity-Efficiency Tradeoff," *Journal of Public Economics*, December 1981, *16*, 265–88.

Skinner, Jonathan, and Joel Slemrod, "An Economic Perspective on Tax Evasion," *National Tax Journal*, September 1985, *38*, pp. 345–53.

Slemrod, Joel, "The Return to Tax Simplification: An Econometric Analysis," *Public Finance Quarterly*, January 1989, *17*, 3–27.

Slemrod, Joel, and Nikki Sorum, "The Compliance Cost of the U.S. Individual Income Tax System," *National Tax Journal*, December 1984, *37*, 461–74.

Slemrod, Joel, and Shlomo Yitzhaki, "The Optimal Size of a Tax Collection Agency," *Scandinavian Journal of Economics*, September 1987, *89*, pp. 183–92.

Stern, Nicholas H., "On the Specification of Models of Optimum Income Taxation," *Journal of Public Economics*, July-August 1976, *6*, 123–62.

Stern, Nicholas H., "Optimum Taxation with Errors in Administration," *Journal of Public Economics*, March 1982, *17*, 181–212.

Stern, Nicholas H., "The Theory of Optimal Commodity and Income Taxation," In Newbery, David, and Nicholas H. Stern, eds., *The Theory of Taxation for Developing Countries.* New York: Oxford University Press, 1987, pp. 22–59.

Steuerle, Eugene, *Taxes, Loans, and Inflation.* Washington, DC: The Brookings Institution, 1985.

Stiglitz, Joseph E., "Pareto Efficient and Optimal Taxation and the New New Welfare Economics." In Auerbach, Alan J., and Martin Feldstein, eds., *Handbook of Public Economics*, Vol II. Amsterdam: North-Holland, 1988.

Summers, Lawrence H., "Capital Taxation and Accumulation in a Life-Cycle Growth Model," *American Economic Review*, September 1981, *71*, 533–44.

Summers, Lawrence H., "Tax Policy, the Rate of Return, and Savings," National Bureau of Economic Research Working Paper No. 995, September 1982.

Summers, Lawrence H., "Should Tax Reform Level the Playing Field?" National Bureau of Economic Research Working Paper No. 2132. Cambridge, MA, January 1987.

Usher, Dan, "Tax Evasion and the Marginal Cost of Public Funds," *Economic Inquiry*, October 1986, *24*, 563–86.

U. S. Department of the Treasury, *Tax Reform for Fairness, Simplicity, and Economic Growth: Volumes 1 and 3.* Washington, D.C., November 1984.

U.S. Department of the Treasury, Internal Revenue Service, *Income Tax Compliance Research: Gross Tax Gap Estimates and Projections for 1973-1992,* Washington, D.C.: March 1988.

Yitzhaki, Shlomo, "A Note on Optimal Taxation and Administrative Costs," *American Economic Review*, June 1979, *69*, 475–80.

Part III
Tax Reform

ON THE THEORY OF TAX REFORM

Martin FELDSTEIN*

Harvard University, Cambridge, MA 02138, U.S.A.

Revised version received September 1975

This paper focuses on the difference between de novo tax design and the reform of existing tax laws. Issues of efficiency and equity in optimal tax reform are discussed. Principles for balancing horizontal equity and efficiency are discussed. The paper also examines critically the utilitarian criterion of social choice that has been the basis of recent theoretical studies of optimal tax design. The Haig–Simons standard, as a principle of either design or reform, is criticized as both inefficient and inequitable in the light of optimal tax theory and the theory of tax incidence.

> *We shall deal with our economic system as it is and as it may be modified, not as it might be if we had a clean sheet of paper to write upon; and step by step we shall make it what it should be.*
>
> Woodrow Wilson

1. Introduction

Although there have been substantial contributions to both the theory and the policy analysis of optimal taxation, all of these studies have dealt with tax *design* rather than tax *reform*. Discussions of optimal taxation implicitly assume that the tax laws are being written de novo on 'a clean sheet of paper.' Such tax *design* is a guide for tax policy in the Garden of Eden, in Rawls' (1971) 'original position,' in the social contracts of Locke, Hume and Rousseau. Optimal tax *reform* must take as its starting point the existing tax system and the fact that actual changes are slow and piecemeal. Everything we know about the theory of economic policy in other areas reminds us that optimal piecemeal policies cannot be made by haphazard steps in the direction of the global optimum, that a constrained second-best policy cannot be guided by the conclusions of an unconstrained optimization [Lipsey and Lancaster (1956–57), Little (1956), Tinbergen (1952)]. Moreover, considerations of distributional

---

*This paper was prepared for the International Seminar on Public Economics, meeting in Paris, January 1975. I am grateful to the National Science Foundation for financial support and to John Flemming for helpful discussions.

equity make it important to consider the position of each individual before as well as after any proposed change. The primary purpose of this paper is to contribute to a theory of tax reform and to consider the implications for tax policy of the distinction between design and reform.

There has been a wide gap between the recent contributions to the theory of optimal tax design and the policy analysis of current tax reformers. One group of theoretical studies, originated by Mirrlees (1971) and Fair (1971), focuses on selecting the best rate schedule for the income tax, balancing losses due to decreased efficiency against gains due to a more equal distribution of after-tax income.[1] The other studies of optimal taxation, which extend early work by Ramsey (1927) and Boiteux (1956), seek the optimal rates of commodity excise taxes in a framework that balances efficiency losses and equity gains.[2] In contrast, the tax policy studies have been concerned with defining the appropriate *base* for the income tax, i.e. the appropriate exclusions and deductions, and with estimating the revenue implication and distributional consequences of departures from this base.[3] I believe that the analysis of the appropriate income tax base could benefit from some of the insights of optimal tax theory and of the theory of tax incidence. A second purpose of this paper is to begin bridging the intellectual gap between the theoretical studies and the policy analyses.

The paper thus deals with both theoretical and practical problems of tax reform. As I prepared this paper, I quickly found the subject spreading from my original starting point to issues of law, political theory and moral philosophy. As a result, I have only begun to develop what I would regard as a satisfactory structure for considering the question of optimal tax reform. Yet I believe that in territory that is as unexplored by economists as this, even the reflections of a recent traveler may provide both valuable information and some inspiration for future research.

The next section of this paper examines the criterion of social choice that has been used in the recent theoretical studies of optimal tax design. Section 3 considers the Haig–Simons standard for tax design in the light of optimal tax theory and the theory of tax incidence. The fourth section begins the discussion of the difference between optimal tax design and optimal tax reform. Section 5 discusses the principles of reform when actual compensation is precluded, including the balance of efficiency and horizontal equity and the optimal speed of reform. There is a brief final section that reviews the major conclusions.

---

[1]See also the papers by Atkinson (1973a, 1973b), Feldstein (1973), Phelps (1974), Rosen (1975) and Sheshinski (1972).

[2]Among the recent studies of this problem are Baumol and Bradford (1970), Diamond and Mirrlees (1971), Dixit (1970), Feldstein (1972), Kolm (1969) and Stiglitz and Dasgupta (1971).

[3]These studies, which build on the early contributions of Haig (1921), Simons (1938) and Fisher (1927, 1937), include Pechman (1971), Pechman and Okner (1972), Musgrave (1968), Surrey (1973) and Andrews (1974). Bittker (1967, 1973) provides a fundamentally different view. I will return below to the substance of these studies.

2. The social choice criterion and optimal tax design

The recent contributions to the theory of optimal taxation have added significantly to our understanding of the principles of tax design. The early insights of Ramsey (1927), Boiteux (1956) and Green (1961) have been extended to show how distributional equity and allocative efficiency can be balanced in the design of optimal excise taxes. Similarly, the research on the optimal progressivity of the income tax has elucidated how the optimal tax schedule depends on the elasticities of labor supply, the distribution of skill levels and the concavity of the social welfare function.

It is easy therefore to overstate the significance and generality of these recent results in the theory of optimal taxation. The specific excise tax formulae and income tax schedules reflect a whole series of assumptions that have not yet been fully explored. For example, studies of optimal income taxation (1) assume that all income is from labor services, (2) ignore the distortions that occur when untaxed benefits are substituted for wages, and (3) assume either that individuals invest in education but then supply a fixed amount of effort or do not invest in education but change their effort in response to taxes. The existing literature provides a framework within which to relax these and other restrictions. Elsewhere I have examined the implication of extending this framework to include a general equilibrium response of wage rates to factor supplies [see Feldstein (1973)]. Here I wish to focus on the more fundamental issue of the criterion of social choice that has been used in optimal tax theory.

Although I shall emphasize the restrictiveness of the social choice criterion that has been used in all of the recent contributions to the theory of optimal taxation, I do not wish to deprecate the general value of this work. The purpose of all applied welfare economics is to draw out the implications of alternative economic assumptions. Each individual's preferences among policies must reflect both his descriptive judgements about the behavior of the economic system and his value judgements about the appropriate criterion of social choice. My remarks in this section are intended primarily to clarify the nature of the social choice criterion that has been used in the recent studies of tax design and that will be used again in later sections of this paper.

2.1. The utilitarian principle

A generalized utilitarian social welfare function has been the criterion of social choice in all of the recent studies of optimal taxation. Each individual's utility is measurable on a cardinal scale with a unique zero. Utility depends only on the individual's own consumption, including the consumption of leisure and of public goods. Utility functions are identical and utility is interpersonally comparable. The optimal tax maximizes a quasi-concave function of these individual utilities, subject to whatever constraints are imposed by individual behavior, technology, the required government revenue and the restrictions on the allowable taxes (e.g. a linear tax on income only or an excise tax that cannot be levied on leisure).

It is important to distinguish this generalized welfare function from the classical utilitarianism of Bentham. The classical utilitarian maximand is the sum of individual utilities ($W = \sum_i U_i$), while the generalized utilitarianism of optimal tax theory allows other quasi-concave functions of the individual utilities. Rawls (1971) has objected to the utilitarian principle of distributive justice on the ground that it looks at the average utility (or sum of utilities) without regard to the distribution of these utilities. Although this criticism is correct only for the classical utilitarian maximand,[4] it is not correct for the generalized social welfare functions. Atkinson (1973b) has noted that the classical utilitarian criterion and Rawls' maximin criterion (i.e. maximize the utility of the worst-off individual) can be expressed as special cases of the social welfare function:[5]

$$W = \frac{1}{\alpha} \sum_i U_i^\alpha, \quad \alpha < 1. \tag{1}$$

As α tends to minus infinity, maximizing W tends to the maximin criterion.[6] More generally, with $\alpha < 1$, the distribution of utilities as well as their sum affects social welfare.[7]

There is a fundamental but irrelevant ambiguity about the interpretation of α that has caused unnecessary confusion. Unless there is deemed to be some empirical basis for assessing the concavity of the individual utility function,[8]

---

[4]Some individuals will of course share Bentham's view that the *correct* criterion is the sum of utilities.

[5]Note that this is closely related to the generalized mean [Hardy et al. (1934)] $[\Sigma_i U_i^\alpha]^{1/\alpha}$ and yields equivalent decisions.

[6]Rawls' 'difference principle' states that the distribution of incomes should be equal unless departures from equality increase the well-being of the worst off. Note that strict application of this requires only ordinal information (who is worst off and whether a given change improves his condition) and provides no guidance for choosing between options that do not affect the worst-off individual. Atkinson's reformulation of Rawls therefore has a greater informational requirement and provides additional results in return.

[7]I do not find Rawls' arguments for the difference principle to be very persuasive. Why should the amoral and self-interested decisions of men in the 'original position' take on such moral force as a basis for distributional justice? And even if one grants that such an original contract is morally compelling, why assume that rational self-interest in the original position would lead to a conservative maximin rule rather than maximum expected utility and therefore the classical utilitarian criterion? If expected utility is rejected because the 'continuity axiom' of Savage (1954) is denied in this context, might not rational men maximize expected utility above some floor rather than sacrifice expected utility to raise the minimum utility by an arbitrarily small amount?

[8]Fisher (1927) and others have of course attempted to measure the elasticity of the marginal utility of income function.

the value of α can either be incorporated directly into the utility function or the utility function can be assumed to be homogeneous of degree 1 while the value of α is incorporated into the welfare function. For example, if utility depends only on the consumption of a single good (C_i), the social welfare function can be written as

$$W = \frac{1}{\gamma} \sum_i C_i^\gamma, \qquad (2)$$

where either (a) $U_i = (1/\gamma)C_i^\gamma$ and $\alpha = 1$, or (b) $U_i = C_i$ and $\gamma = \alpha$, or (c) $U_i = (1/\beta)C_i^\beta$ and $\gamma = \alpha\beta$.[9] More generally, when utility depends on the consumption of the good and of leisure (L_i), the specification $U_i = C_i^\beta L_i^{1-\beta}$ combined with the social welfare function of eq. (1) does not really impose any meaningful restriction that individual utility is homogeneous of degree 1.

Before considering alternatives to the pure utilitarian principle, I should note the significance of ignoring externalities in consumption. In particular, this precludes incorporating the effects of either altruism or envy. This exclusion may explain why all of the studies of the optimal progressivity of the income tax have implied surprisingly little redistribution through the tax-transfer process.[10] Altruism by the rich toward the poor would of course increase the optimal degree of progressivity, a point stressed in a somewhat different framework by Hochman and Rodgers (1969). Similarly, envy by the poor of the rich, i.e. a situation in which the consumption of the rich decreases the utility of the poor, will also increase the optimal progressivity of the tax structure.

But if the implications of envy are to be admitted as part of a utilitarian calculation, so also should any other negative interdependence. The utility of the rich may be increased by their *relatively* high position per se just as the utility of the poor is decreased by their *relatively* low position. Such negative interdependence may imply that greater inequality and less progressivity is optimal. Consider for example the problem of distributing the fixed sum of $1 between two individuals. Let X be the amount given to the first individual. With no interdependence, let $U_1(X) = X^{1/2}$ and $U_2(1-X) = (1-X)^{1/2}$. An additive welfare function is maximized at $X = \frac{1}{2}$, a completely equal distribution. Consider by contrast the case of negative interdependence in which each individual's utility depends on his consumption relative to that of the other individual. Thus, $U_1 = [X/(1-X)]^{1/2}$ and $U_2 = [(1-X)/X]^{1/2}$. The additive welfare function is maximized when there is complete inequality, i.e. $X = 1$ or

---

[9]The objection of Blum and Calven (1953) that tax progressivity rests on the assumed diminishing marginal utility of income is therefore false.

[10]This is true even if the tax is used solely to finance redistribution, i.e. if no government revenue is needed. An increase in the required government revenue reduces optimal redistribution even further. See, e.g., Mirrlees (1971) and Feldstein (1973, section 4).

$X = 0$. Incorporating such a relative income measure into the general optimal income tax problem would presumably strengthen this conclusion.

2.2. Taste differences and horizontal equity[11]

The utilitarian criterion of eq. (1) can be applied even if individual utility functions differ. For example, the optimal income tax problem could be extended by (1) allowing the relative taste for goods and leisure to vary among individuals and (2) specifying the bivariate distribution of the taste parameter and the skill level. The design of optimal excise taxes would be feasible if the taste distribution could be assumed to be the same at every income level.

But the diversity of tastes raises the more fundamental problem of horizontal equity, i.e. of the injunction to treat equals equally [Musgrave (1959)]. With the assumption that individuals all have the same utility function, the principle of horizontal equity requires nothing more than that individuals with the same consumption bundle (including leisure) should pay the same tax or, equivalently, that all individuals should face the same tax schedules. Since violation of this condition would reduce aggregate social welfare, the equal taxation of equals is implied directly by utilitarianism and does not require a separate principle of horizontal equity.

All of this changed if we recognize the existence of a diversity of tastes. For concreteness, consider again an economy in which utility depends only on the consumption of a single good and of leisure. Leisure is measured so that its maximum is 1, i.e. $0 < L_i < 1$. There are two types of individuals, Consumption-Lovers whose utility function is $U_1 = C_1^2 L_1$ and Leisure-Lovers with utility function $U_2 = C_2 L_2^2$. All individuals have equal earning ability and face a common wage rate of 1, i.e. the individual budget constraint in the absence of any tax is $C_i = 1 - L_i$. Note that in the absence of any tax the individuals consume different amounts of the good and of leisure but enjoy the same utility level, $U_1 = U_2 = \frac{4}{27}$.

Consider the implication of an income tax at rate t used to finance necessary government expenditure. With a budget constraint of $C_i = (1-t)(1-L_i)$, the Consumption-Lovers obtain utility $U_1' = (1-t)^2(1-L_1)^2 L_1$ while the Leisure-Lovers obtain utility $U_2' = (1-t)(1-L_2)L_2^2$. Since the utility maximizing values of L_1 and L_2 are obviously unchanged, the tax reduces the utility of the Consumption-Lovers by a factor of $(1-t)^2$ while the utility of the Leisure-Lovers is reduced by only a factor of $(1-t)$. The Consumption-Lovers also pay more tax than the Leisure-Lovers.

This example suggests a useful formulation of the principle of horizontal equity:

---

[11]The discussion in this section benefited from the opportunity to hear a preliminary version of Richard Musgrave's paper for the current conference.

If two individuals would be equally well off (have the same utility level) in the absence of taxation, they should also be equally well off if there is a tax.

More generally, the introduction of a tax should not alter the ordering of individuals by utility level. It is clear that the income tax violates the injunction that taxes should not alter the utility ordering of individuals. Moreover, the example indicates the ambiguity and inadequacy of the usual definition of horizontal equity as 'the equal tax treatment of equally situated individuals.'

It is clear also that the principle of horizontal equity will in general only be satisfied completely by a lump sum tax. The problem for tax design is therefore to balance the desire for horizontal equity against the utilitarian principle of welfare maximization. Balancing these two goals requires an explicit measure of the departure from horizontal equity. I can offer no obvious or compelling solution to this problem. The rank correlation of utilities before and after tax emphasizes the notion that taxes should not alter the utility ordering but it does not reflect the magnitude of the change, e.g. it would be completely uninformative about the effect of the income tax in the previous example. A measure of the after-tax variance of utilities for individuals with equal before-tax utilities[12] would reflect the magnitude of the departures and would be sensitive to unequal treatment of equals but would not reflect the utility reversals as such. A product moment correlation would avoid some of these problems but would be distorted by nonlinearities, e.g. even if the utility ranking was perfectly preserved, the product moment correlation would be less than one if the utilities were altered by a nonlinear function.

2.3. The egalitarian principle

With the utilitarian criterion, optimal taxes decrease the inequality of income as a byproduct of maximizing a function of individual utilities. In contrast, the egalitarian principle regards equality as desirable per se. The resulting social welfare tradition is no longer based only on individual preferences in the traditional Bergson–Samuelson manner. But social ethics need not be individualistic. The Pareto principle is appealing but not inviolable.

The egalitarian principle may be required as an extension of Rawls' criterion of distributional justice. Equality is clearly of great importance in Rawls' ethics. According to Rawls' 'difference principle,' equality is to be sacrificed only to the extent that doing so increased the utility of the worst-off individual (or group).

---

[12]More specifically, this would be the sum of such variances over all of the equal before-tax classes; in the above example

$$(N_1(U_1' - \bar{U}')^2 + N_2(U_2' - \bar{U}')^2)/(N_1 + N_2),$$

where

$$\bar{U}' = (N_1 U_1' + N_2 U_2')/(N_1 + N_2).$$

No increase in inequality, no matter how slight, is allowed in exchange for any increase, no matter how great, in the well-being of others. But if equality per se is so important, why are we enjoined to accept any increase in inequality, no matter how great, if it increases the utility of the worst off, no matter how little?

Consider a situation in which the welfare of the worst-off group has been maximized by policies that yield a relatively narrow distribution of income. A new opportunity arises to raise the welfare of the least advantaged by a slight amount, but almost everyone else must be made substantially worse off, except for a few individuals who would become extremely wealthy. Can we really believe that there is a compelling moral argument for such a change? The discontinuities of the difference principle lead to unacceptable conclusions.

Would it not be better to introduce an explicit trade-off between the utilitarian measure (a function of the individual utilities) and equality per se? If E is some measure of the degree of equality of the income or utility distribution, the egalitarian principle implies that the social welfare function should be written as

$$V = V(W_\alpha, E), \tag{3}$$

where W_α is the value of the social welfare function of eq. (1) with the parameter value equal to α.[13] If the V function is defined with the Rawlsian value of $\alpha = -\infty$, the optimal policy would produce even greater equality than Rawls' maximin criterion. In less extreme cases, a higher value of α would imply the desirability of accepting greater inequality in exchange for a higher utility level even above the minimum, while the explicit inclusion of E and the concavity of the W_α function would limit the extent of such trades. Even with such a value of $\alpha > -\infty$, the optimal tax may be more progressive than with the Rawlsian criterion.

Rawls would object to the criterion of eq. (3) as an example of 'intuitionist' ethics, i.e. an ambiguous ethical norm that requires each individual to use his moral intuition to balance E and W_α.[14] But discretion and balancing can only be avoided by imposing an extreme criterion with unacceptable implications. Even in the utilitarian framework, there is an arbitrary choice of the patameter α. Moreover, this cannot be avoided by using the simple Benthamite criterion because the concavity of the individual utility function cannot be established empirically.[15]

---

[13]More generally, and I believe more accurately, descriptive of an important segment of current political preferences, the V function could be defined with several different equality variables for different types of consumption. Recent discussion of the distribution of health care and education suggest the importance of such measures of 'categorical equity'; see Feldstein (1975, section 1).

[14]See Rawls (1971, section 1) for a discussion of Rawls' objection to a criterion based on E and W_1, i.e., an intuitionist balancing of an equality measure and the Benthamite sum of utilities.

[15]See above p. 81.

Let me emphasize that I am not advocating the egalitarian principle. I have discussed it because I believe that it is attractive as an alternative to Rawls' difference principle and because it indicates another sense in which a restricted social choice criterion has been used in the design of optimal taxes. Perhaps those who have expressed surprise and disappointment with the optimal degree of progressivity implied by even the maximin criterion are in effect indicating a preference for the egalitarian principle.[16]

2.4. The entitlement principle

Nozick (1974) has recently presented an extensive criticism of the use of utilitarian principles to justify the redistribution of income and wealth. Nozick's analysis is an extension of Kant's dictum that people are ends in themselves and must not be used as means, and of Locke's analysis of the justification of private property. From Kant's injunction against using individuals as means, it follows that it is inadmissible to treat individuals' ability endowments as a form of common property to be exploited for the collective good by a system of optimal taxes. From Locke's notions, Nozick develops rules for entitlement to property. He emphasizes that a just distribution of property is defined not by the pattern of holdings but by the process that generated the distribution of property. In Nozick's words, 'justice in holdings is historical' and 'time slice' principles of justice are invalid.

According to Nozick, the common analogy between the fair division of a cake and the just distribution of income is inappropriate. The question of how society should distribute income is irrelevant because society as such has no income to distribute. Optimal tax policy is thus concerned not with the distribution of income but with the *re*distribution of income. Redistribution is just only to rectify the improper holding of property, and thus never to redistribute labor income.[17]

The problem of optimal taxation is thus narrowly restricted by the entitlement principle. But even if taxes are not to be used to redistribute income, there is still the question of how taxes should be levied to finance such public services as defense and police. Although a pure voluntary exchange process might be feasible for small communities from which exclusion is possible, a system of compulsory taxes is required for a large nation. In this context, the principle of benefit taxation or of tax schedules that impose equal utility sacrifice[18] have an appeal that is clearly lacking in the utilitarian framework. The early writers who suggested these principles derived optimal tax schedules on the assumption that taxes do not affect labor supply. The recent research on optimal tax progressivity

---

[16] See the discussion on this issue in Atkinson (1973a).
[17] Individuals may of course agree unilaterally to redistribute income because of altruism, in the manner of Hochman and Rodgers (1969).
[18] For a summary of these theories, see Musgrave (1959, chapter 5).

suggests how these rules could be revised to take individual behavior into account.

Those who are fully persuaded by Nozick will thus completely redefine the problem of optimal taxation. Others will reject Nozick completely because they find nothing objectionable in the notion that all property and all individual abilities should be regarded as society's common resource. Many will be persuaded that the entitlement principle limits the desirable degree of redistribution. Once again, optimal tax design involves a balancing of conflicting criteria.

2.5. The limits of optimal tax design

The comments of this section have emphasized the limited criterion of social choice that has been used in all of the recent theoretical work on optimal tax design: a utilitarian welfare function without externalities (altruism or envy) and with no regard for the problem of horizontal equity implied by differences in tastes. Neither equality per se (the egalitarian principle) nor property rights (the entitlemenent principle) has been considered.

I feel free to make this criticism because I have been as guilty as anyone else. Let me therefore reiterate what I said at the beginning of this section. My purpose here is not to deprecate the value of optimal tax theory but to emphasize that only a limited criterion of choice has been examined. The results of optimal tax design, like my applied welfare economics, are only as compelling as the criterion of social choice from which they are derived.

3. The Haig–Simons standard for tax design

All of the recent economic studies of practical tax reform have taken the Haig–Simons standard of optimal taxation as their guide.[19] Before examining the specific problems of tax *reform* (i.e. *changes* in tax structure), it is useful to consider the appropriateness of the Haig–Simons principle as a standard for tax *design*.

The Haig–Simons standard is concerned with the tax base rather than with tax rates. According to the Haig–Simons principle, every individual should pay tax on his total income from whatever source. For this purpose, income is to be defined as the value of consumption plus the increase in wealth. All departures from this comprehensive tax base, i.e. all exclusions and deductions, are to be regarded as 'tax preferences,' 'tax expenditures,' or more generally, 'erosion of the appropriate tax base.'[20] By implication, since taxes are to be based on

---

[19]See the references in footnote 2.

[20]Individual authorities differ in the specific list of current U.S. tax law provisions that constitute erosion of the tax base. Some of the amgibuous items are small but others (e.g. income splitting of married couples) are quite large. In contrast to Simons, all recent writers would exempt the receipts of gifts and bequests.

comprehensive income regardless of source and regardless of use, there is no general role for excise taxes as a source of revenue.

The basic justification for the Haig–Simons standard is its appeal to our sense of fairness that individuals with equal incomes are taxed equally, regardless of the source of income or of its use. Why should an individual who receives interest on municipal bonds pay less tax than an individual with equal income who receives his interest on a bank deposit? Why should homeowners be allowed deductions for housing expenses when renters are denied those opportunities?

Although these examples are striking, I believe that the *general* case for the Haig–Simons principle as a standard of tax design is not persuasive. In this section I will discuss (1) the conflict between the Haig–Simons standard and horizontal equity and (2) the inefficiency of the comprehensive tax base. Let me stress that I am not denying the possible value of the Haig–Simons standard as a *starting point* for practical tax design. My purpose is to explore some of the ways in which it may be desirable to modify that standard in order to improve both the equity and the efficiency of the tax structure. The problems associated with *changes* in tax structure are postponed until later sections.

3.1. Horizontal equity and the comprehensive income tax

The principle of horizontal equity in tax design implies that individuals who would be equally well off in the absence of the tax should be equally well off with the tax. The tax system should preserve the utility order of individuals.[21] Conversely, individuals who are not equally well off should pay different taxes.

Section 2.2 showed that when tastes differ (i.e. when individuals have different utility functions) any income tax will violate the principle of horizontal equity. The argument that a Haig–Simons tax yields horizontal equity must implicitly assume that all tastes (utility functions) are the same. I will make that assumption for the remainder of this section.

Even with identical utility functions, the Haig–Simons tax will violate the principle of horizontal equity when individuals differ in ability *if there is more than one type of ability*. Consider an economy in which individuals are endowed with varying amounts of two abilities, 'wit' and 'strength.' In such an economy, two individuals with different endowments and the same tastes may earn equal money incomes but, because of differences in the work that they do have different utility levels. More formally, each individual's abilities may be measured by the earnings per unit of physical effort ('strength endowment') and earnings per unit of mental effort ('wit endowment'). Each individual's utility is then a function of his money income, his level of physical effort and his level of mental

---

[21]Note that this also implies the 'equal utility sacrifice' rules of taxation. If two individuals have the same before-tax utility and the same after-tax utility, they have made the same absolute and proportional utility sacrifices.

effort.[22] With different endowments of strength and wit, two individuals may select supplies of effort that yield the same income but different utility. Taxing them equally would thus violate horizontal equity.

The multiple ability model suggests another way in which a comprehensive income tax may not satisfy horizontal equity. Consider now an economy in which each individual has an endowment of only one of the two types of ability. Utility depends on income and the level of effort, with no distinction between physical and mental effort. The distributions of these abilities are such that, with the wages prevailing in the absence of taxation, the corresponding income distributions overlap. The introduction of an income tax will in general change the relative aggregate supplies of the two types of labor and therefore the relative wage rates.[23] Two individuals with equal income and utility in the absence of taxes,[24] would have different pre-tax income after the tax system was introduced, and would therefore pay different taxes. The general equilibrium response of factor prices thus introduces a further source of horizontal inequity.

The assumption that individual utility depends on income and labor supply is only appropriate if the individual lives for a single short period. A more realistic description must recognize that the individual's utility depends on his entire lifetime path of *consumption* and labor supply. If every individual's labor supply is fixed and equal and tastes are assumed to be identical, the present value of the individual's lifetime income is an appropriate tax base;[25] with identical tastes, all individuals with the same present value of income will enjoy the same consumption path and therefore have the same utility level.[26] A tax based on the annual flow of noncapital income (i.e. labor income plus gifts received) will be equivalent only if it is a strictly proportional tax; the present value of the annual tax payments will then equal the tax at that rate on the present value of income.[27] Since consumption and income have the same present value, a proportional tax on consumption would also be equivalent to a tax on the present value of income.

Thus, with a proportional annual tax, the principle of horizontal equity does

---

[22]This is exactly analogous to the conventional single ability model in which utility is a function of consumption and leisure where leisure is measured on an arbitrary scale as one minus the supply of effort. Note that with a single type of ability and identical tastes, all individuals with the same ability would supply the same effort so that the problem of horizontal equity does not arise.

[23]There are of course tax schedules and utility functions for which this would not be true, but these should be regarded as special cases. I have examined this type of general equilibrium response to a linear income tax in Feldstein (1973).

[24]Equal income does not imply equal utility but the combination is consistent if the individual with the less valuable type of ability has a greater endowment so that he earns the same income with the same level of effort.

[25]Income must be defined to include gifts and bequests received.

[26]Note that this is still true even if utility is deemed to depend on the ownership of wealth as well as consumption.

[27]Note that the proper tax base excludes interest income and does not allow a deduction for interest payments.

not favor either an income base or a consumption base even though utility is a function of consumption only. But with a progressive annual tax, only a consumption base will achieve horizontal equity; any two individuals who enjoy the same utility of lifetime consumption must have the same path of consumption (given identical tastes) and therefore pay the same taxes under any tax schedule.

If two individuals can have the same utility with different consumption paths, either because tastes differ or because there are different rates of interest for borrowing and lending, even a consumption tax will not achieve horizontal equity. If the utility function can be regarded as separable, i.e. if lifetime utility is the sum of annual utilities, the principle of horizontal equity might be redefined to apply one year at a time; in this case, a consumption tax base would achieve horizontal equity even if tastes differ or the borrowing interest rate does not equal the lending rate.[28] Again, a comprehensive Haig–Simons tax on annual income would be a source of horizontal inequity.

A further problem of horizontal inequity in the Haig–Simons approach has been emphasized by Bittker (1967, 1973) who argues that no truly comprehensive tax base can be unambiguously defined. He supports this argument with evidence that advocates of the comprehensive tax base differ in their definitions and that various complex and detailed problems require arbitrary choices. Bittker then reasons that if there is no compelling standard for a comprehensive tax base, any attempt to use this as a criterion of tax policy will require arbitrary distinctions which are the essence of horizontal inequity.

As noted at the beginning of this section, it is clear that some departures from the Haig–Simons comprehensive tax base are sources of horizontal inequity. I have tried to show that a comprehensive income tax would also be a source of horizontal inequities. The use of a consumption base would probably be an improvement,[29] but it must be recognized that no tax will achieve full horizontal equity. The process of tax design must therefore balance the achievement of horizontal equity against other desirable features of a tax structure.

3.2. Economic efficiency

Departures from the Haig–Simons principle of the comprehensive tax base are often criticized as sources of distorted incentives and economic inefficiency. The exclusion of the imputed income of homeowners increases housing con-

---

[28] This is a different type of argument for a consumption base than Kaldor's (1955) notion of 'taxing individuals in what they take out of the pot'. Since the analysis here shows the superiority of the consumption tax to a tax on *labor* income only, the current argument is also different from the conventional opposition to the 'double taxation' involved in taxing interest income.

[29] Fisher (1937) argued for a consumption base with the same fervor that Simons (1938) argued against it. Musgrave appears to favor the Simons view but notes that reasonable men may disagree (1968). Andrews (1974) has recently shown how a personal 'consumption-type income tax,' i.e. a tax based on consumption, could be easily implemented and would avoid many of the problems in the current tax law.

sumption [Laidler (1969)]. The lower tax rates on capital gains distort the pattern of investment and financing. The exclusion of unemployment insurance benefits induces additional unemployment [Feldstein (1974)]. The list could be extended to great length.

There is no doubt that particular departures from the comprehensive tax base are inefficient and reduce economic welfare. It could nevertheless be wrong to conclude that a Haig–Simons comprehensive income tax would be the most efficient source of revenue. Since all taxes other than lump sum taxes distort behavior, a comprehensive income tax is itself a distortionary tax and therefore an inefficient tax. The problem is to select the set of tax rates (or tax schedules) on different sources of income that minimizes inefficiency or maximizes welfare.

Consider an economy with two distinguishable types of individuals. If there is a difference in their labor supply elasticities, an efficient tax would impose a higher tax rate on the individuals with the lower supply elasticity.[30] The exact optimal tax rates could be derived by analogy with Ramsey's optimal excise taxes. The analysis could also be extended to use a utilitarian welfare function to balance efficiency and distributional equity (although obviously not horizontal equity). The basic point is that such optimal tax rates would not be equal for all types of individuals.

The same conclusion applies to different types of income earned by a single individual. Rent on unimproved land is the obvious and extreme type of income that, on grounds of efficiency, should be taxed most heavily. If tax rates could be varied by occupation, it is again clear that equal tax rates would be inappropriate. Finally, there is no reason to expect that the optimal tax rates on labor income and capital income would be the same.[31]

Finally, tax subsidies may be a useful instrument of public policy for achieving desired increases in the consumption of particular types of goods and services. In a number of important cases, such tax subsidies may be more efficient than direct government spending.[32]

4. Tax reform vs. tax design

Tax reform is a change from the existing tax structure. In practice, tax reform is piecemeal and dynamic in contrast to the once-and-for-always character of

---

[30]An example that comes to mind is the higher supply elasticities of women than of men. See Rosen (1975).

[31]Under ceratin conditions, an optimal tax on labor income implies that no tax should be levied on the interest income earned on savings. It has been shown in a static context, that, if the utility function is separable into leisure and all other goods, an optimal income tax implies that no excise taxes should be levied; see Atkinson (1974). Since taxes on interest income are are equivalent to excise taxes (i.e. they distort the relative prices of consumption goods at different times), a similar separability in the dynamic case would imply that no taxes on interest income should be levied. This is developed in Atkinson and Stiglitz (1976).

[32]See Feldstein (1975b, 1975c) for discussions of the optimal use of tax subsidies to encourage particular types of consumption and investment.

tax design. In this section I will discuss why optimal tax reform differs from optimal tax design. Although several specific issues will be examined, there is a common theme: the optimal tax reform depends on the starting situation. Equivalently, the optimal tax laws for next year are not the same as they would be if taxes were being introduced for the first time. Optimal taxation depends on the historical context.

The growing literature on optimal taxation and on tax reform does not fully recognize this distinction. Even those who focus on piecemeal change rather than complete design merely compare alternatives as if tax reform were equivalent to de novo design subject to constraints on the admissible taxes. Moreover, reform is treated as a one-time change with the new tax law etched immutably in stone rather than as a process of change.

I start with the generalized utilitarian principle and ask how, given that criterion, optimal reform should be different from optimal design. I then examine the implications of horizontal equity and of legitimate property rights. Both types of considerations generally imply that optimal tax changes produce smaller differences from the current tax structure than would result from optimal de novo design. The next section will discuss how postponement can often be used to achieve more desirable tax reforms.

4.1. Utilitarian principles and tax reform

Although I am primarily interested here in how optimal utilitarian tax design must be modified, I shall first consider the implications of the utilitarian criterion for tax reform based on the Haig–Simons principle. Even if the Haig–Simons principle were an acceptable basis for efficient tax design,[33] it cannot be used as a guide for efficient tax revision. Consider, for example, an economy in which all income comes from the supply of a single type of labor, and the current tax system consists of an income tax and an arbitrary set of excise taxes. Both the Haig–Simons principle and the utilitarian criterion might agree that the excise taxes should be eliminated and the income tax increased.[34] In this situation, the Haig–Simons principle leads to correct design. However, any more limited change in the direction of the Haig–Simons optimum might actually decrease welfare. By an obvious extension of the theory of the second best [Lipsey and Lancaster (1956)] the first-order conditions for the maximum of the generalized utilitarian welfare function are generally all changed when an additional constraint (such as an arbitrarily fixed tax rate) is imposed. For piecemeal reform, the Haig–Simons principle cannot be a substitute for explicit maximization.[35]

---

[33]I limit my comments here to efficiency. Questions of horizontal equity, perhaps the primary case for Haig–Simons, are discussed in section 4.2.

[34]This would be optimal if the utility function were separable in such a way that the marginal rate of substitution between each pair of goods is independent of the individual's leisure.

[35]Bruno (1972) has shown that a proportional reduction in all distortions leads to an unambiguous welfare increase. But even a proportional reduction in all excise taxes may not raise welfare when the distorting income tax is present.

I return now to the difference between tax reform and tax design within the utilitarian framework. The theory of optimal tax design implicitly assumes a steady state or, equivalently, that each individual lives for only one period. A more general model would not alter the fundamental properties of the optimal *design* of a tax on labor income. But the analysis of optimal tax *change* requires a model in which utility depends on the path of consumption as well as on its level. Gradual changes in expectations, tastes and habits may make the long-run elasticity of the marginal utility function substantially less than the short-run elasticity.

The theory of optimal tax design has ignored our uncertainty about the parameters of economic behavior. Explicit attention to uncertainty is likely to be more important for tax reform than tax design. Although maximizing *expected* social welfare may yield an optimal tax *design* that is different from the current procedure of maximizing social welfare using the expected values of the unknown parameters, this is not necessarily true. To be more explicit, if the welfare loss that is associated with any set of taxes can be approximated by a quadratic function of the tax rates, in the manner of Hotelling (1938) and Harberger (1964), the expected values of the compensated price elasticities are certainly equivalents, i.e. minimizing the expected welfare loss is equivalent to minimizing the nonstochastic loss function obtained by replacing the uncertain price elasticities by their expected values [see Theil (1964)]. This example of the irrelevance of uncertainty in tax design is limited to taxes that are small enough to permit the quadratic approximation. More generally, a higher-order expansion is required and its expected value cannot be written in terms of the expected values of the price elasticities.[36] Parameter uncertainty is more important in the theory of tax *reform* because the dynamic process permits opportunities for learning. The selection of particular tax rates not only affects current social welfare, but also changes the information that is available for later choices. Maintaining current tax rates produces no information (unless tax rates were different in the past) while large changes in tax rates produce more information than small changes. This implies both that (1) the optimal tax structure in any period depends on the past history of tax rates and (2) the optimal tax change may be larger than it would be if the value of information were ignored. It is clear that the theory of adaptive control [e.g. Aoki (1967)] has interesting and potentially important implications for the theory of optimal tax reform that cannot be pursued here.

Another way to see the importance of uncertain economic information is to consider the implication of uncertain incidence. When the government changes a tax rate, it imposes a gamble on everyone. For some, the expected value of the

---

[36]There is the further problem of defining the government budget constraint when uncertainty is recognized. Should the problem specify expected value balancing or constraining the probability of a deficit (or surplus)?

gamble is positive; for others, it is negative. A tax change that leaves all expected incomes unchanged is inferior to the status quo because it imposes a gamble that lowers everyone's expected utility. A tax change is desirable only if the expected gain through increased efficiency and improved distribution outweighs the utility loss imposed by a gamble. This again implies that the optimal tax structure after the change depends on the existing tax structure before the change but, in contrast to the value of information analysis of the previous paragraph, the imposed gamble argument implies that the optimal tax change is always smaller than it would be if the uncertainty of economic parameters were ignored.

Because the theory of optimal tax design assumes that the new tax rules are permanent and immutable, an important implication of the dynamic process of tax reform is ignored. Tax changes make individuals uncertain about the future reliability of the tax laws. Their anticipation of future possible changes induces inefficient precautionary behavior. For example, the frequent proposals over a long period to eliminate the oil depletion allowance have made investors wary of investment in oil and have therefore raised the cost of capital to the oil industry (i.e. the investors' rate of return on oil shares), lowered the rate of investment, and increased the price of oil. Note that these effects occur even though the government collects no revenue.[37] The proposed change in the tax treatment of the profits of foreign subsidiaries of U.S. companies will deter foreign investment even though the law has not changed. The cost of capital to state and local governments, i.e. the rate of interest on the tax-exempt bonds that they issue, is higher because of any fear by investors that the tax exemption may be ended even for existing bonds. This list could be extended to great length. In each case, the possibility of a future tax change distorts behavior in a way that is contrary to current government policy without, of course, yielding any direct tax revenue.[38]

The implication of this for current tax changes depends on how a current change affects individuals' subjective probabilities of other changes in the future. If a current change would raise the subjective probabilities of future changes the disadvantage of this must be taken into account in assessing the desirability of the change. It is not inconceivable that a relatively small current change would affect the probabilities of many other changes, making the indirect effects more important than the direct effect. Of course, if a current tax reform alters one provision of the tax law but leaves another related provision unchanged, this may reduce the subjective probability of a future change in the second provision. (The relative importance of these two countervailing tendencies is an

---

[37]Since the oil depletion allowance is itself a 'distortion' to 'overinvest' in oil, it might be argued that this precautionary behavior is economically desirable. However, as long as the depletion allowance remains the expressed preference of the government, the precautionary behavior must be regarded as contrary to the aims of government policy.

[38]When individual action does not involve any future commitment, the fear of future adverse taxation may induce acceleration of some activity with a possible increase in tax receipts.

empirical question that should be considered as part of evaluating proposed tax changes.) This general discussion suggests the desirability of reducing the uncertainty about future tax laws. Although uncertainty must remain if the tax laws are to be revised, the impact of this uncertainty on behavior can be drastically reduced by enacting delayed changes in order to reduce the present value of their effect. There may be substantial virtue in a legislative procedure that frequently reexamines all of the provisions of the tax law but that requires that no change can become effective without a delay of, say, ten years.[39]

4.2. Absolute horizontal equity

I argued above that the process of optimal design requires balancing traditional utilitarian implications against concepts of hoirzontal equity. This is even more important in the process of tax reform. Tax changes that improve efficiency and make the distribution of income more equal may drastically violate the principle of horizontal equity. I will examine a number of examples of this in the current section.

Sections 2 and 3 showed that no income tax is consistent with horizontal equity if individuals differ in tastes or specific abilities. The horizontal equity of an income tax requires that it is legitimate to treat all individuals as if they had identical tastes and as if they differed only in the quantity of a single homogeneous type of ability. I will accept these assumptions for this discussion of tax reform.

Recall the definition of horizontal equity in tax design: the tax system should preserve the utility order, implying that if two individuals would have the same utility level in the absence of taxation, they should also have the same utility level if there is a tax. With the assumption of equal tastes and a single source of income (i.e. type of ability), any permanent existing tax structure will not violate horizontal equity if individuals are free to choose their activities and expenditures. Thus, if employees enjoy tax advantages denied to the self-employed,[40] all workers would become employees unless self-employment had other intrinsic advantages, If both arrangements coexist and individuals are free to choose, the net after-tax reward must be the same in both. Although the two groups may pay unequal taxes, there is no horizontal inequity. Similarly, although homeowners pay no tax on the imputable income on their gross housing capital, there is no horizontal inequity if everyone has the choice between owning and renting. With

---

[39]Alternatively, tax changes may be restricted to future actions, e.g. the elimination of accelerated depreciation might apply only to future investments. Although Congress has often behaved this way, it has not always done so and has never restricted itself to do so in the future. The proposed 'limited accounting loss' and 'minimum taxable income' are examples of effectively retroactive changes in the tax treatment of previous investments.

[40]These include pension arrangements, other forms of deferred compensation, and the tax exclusion of employer payments for health insurance, etc.

identical tastes, everyone would become an owner unless the price of houses adjusted to capitalize the tax advantage.[41] If individuals choose to rent because the nature of their employment makes rental intrinsically more desirable,[42] their net-of-tax earnings would compensate them for being renters.

Similar arguments apply to other activities that receive favorable tax treatment: investment in oil, municipal bonds, common stock, rental real property, etc.; the choice of occupations that provide high psychic income, pleasant working conditions or untaxed fringe benefits; and consumption of the services of consumer durables, medical care, certain types of education, etc. If horizontal inequities occur, it is because individuals differ in tastes or in sources of income. The argument that certain tax advantages are only available to those with high incomes (e.g. the yield on tax free municipal bonds is too low to induce investment by middle-income taxpayers) is irrelevant. If the opportunity is open to everyone with the high income, it is in effect a reduction in rate progressivity but not a source of horizontal inequity. If wealth is required to take advantage of the tax opportunity, there is a possibility of horizontal inequity, i.e. of reversing a utility ordering if capital markets are imperfect. With perfect capital markets and identical tastes, individuals with the same utility level must have the same wealth and individuals with more wealth must have higher utility levels. If differences in tastes or types of abilities are acknowledged, all taxation entails horizontal inequities. Any tax reform must balance changes in horizontal inequity against the utilitarian gains. As I noted above, I will adopt the assumptions of common tastes and a single type of ability for this discussion of tax reform.

The principle of horizontal equity *in tax reform* can now be defined. With the assumptions of common tastes and a single type of ability, a pre-existing tax structure is not a source of horizontal inequity. All horizontal inequities arise from *changes* in tax laws.[43] The principle of horizontal equity in reform thus requires that *if two individuals would have the same utility level if the tax remained unchanged, they should also have the same utility level if the tax is changed.*[44]

In practice, tax changes are a source of horizontal inequity because individuals make commitments based on the existing tax law. Commitments involving human capital may be irreversible (e.g. education level) or reversible either very slowly or at a substantial loss (e.g. occupation or location). Commitments

---

[41]Even if tastes were not identical, capitalization would remove any advantage of home ownership if everyone paid the same *marginal* tax rate. With a graduated income tax, the price of any house reflects the marginal rates of all potential buyers. With homogeneous tastes, all potential buyers have the same income and therefore the same marginal rate. But if tastes differ, an individual who buys a more expensive house than is common for his income level will pay for the tax advantage that would accrue to individuals with a higher marginal rate. Since this source of horizontal inequity depends on the *variability* of marginal rates at a *given* level of house value, it is likely to be relatively small.

[42]E.g., because their location is temporary.

[43]Of course, inequities may exist now because of changes in the recent past. I ignore this and assume that the pre-existing tax structure has existed unchanged for a very long time.

[44]More generally, the tax change should preserve the previous utility order.

involving property may be easily reversed but the sale of assets will involve a capital loss. In both cases, individuals who were equally well off before the tax change are not equally well off after the change. Some specific examples will clarify the nature of the problem and the reason why horizontal equity must be balanced against utilitarian gains.

Consider first the suggestion of Henry George to tax away all of the rent on unimproved land and lower other income tax rates to keep revenue unchanged. Since a tax on the income of unimproved land involves no distortion, there is a clear efficiency gain from such a substitution. The substitution would also tend to increase the taxes paid by high-income individuals and lower the taxes paid by low-income individuals. The generalized utilitarian principle would therefore favor such a substitution. Why then has such an obvious tax change had so few supporters among economists? A 100 percent tax on such rental income would make the property rights to that income valueless. Those individuals who happened to own land would suffer a capital loss equal to the value of the unimproved land. Such losses would be completely haphazard and arbitrary. Of two otherwise identical individuals, the one who happened to invest in land would suffer the capital loss while the other would be unaffected.

The effect is similar for any change in the taxation of capital income. Taxing the imputed income or owner-occupied houses would eliminate the inducement to overinvestment in housing[45] and increase the overall progressivity of the tax. But current homeowners would suffer a capital loss in the value of their homes equal to the present value of the increased future taxes. In many cases, the loss would exceed the individual's equity in his home. In contrast, renters would suffer no capital loss. Other changes in the personal income tax and the corporate income tax would be reflected in share prices. Thus, elimination of the depletion allowance would reduce the value of shares in oil companies; the immediate taxation of the profits of foreign subsidiaries would reduce the value of shares of companies with relatively large foreign earnings; and the taxation of capital gains at the full-income tax rate or the constructive realization of capital gains at death would reduce all share prices. Individuals who owned these shares would suffer a capital loss while others with equal income and wealth who invested in other assets would be unaffected.

Two individuals with equal ability and taste may enter two occupations that provide different combinations of after-tax income and untaxed benefits, but the same level of utility.[46] Although identical individuals pay different taxes there is

---

[45]As usual, the facts are more complicated. Local property taxes induce underinvestment in housing while the special features of the mortgage market induce overinvestment. It is not clear whether the current law exacerbates a problem or offsets a distortion.

[46]Although it may at first seem that individuals with the same ability and taste would all choose the same occupation, this is false if the relative productivity of the marginal workers in the two occupations depend on the relative numbers of workers in them. All workers are indifferent between the two occupations but equilibrium requires that they be divided between the two.

no horizontal inequity. If the value of benefits were taxed, there would be a long-run tendency to raise the pre-tax value of compensation in the occupation with the higher ratio of benefits to income (as well as to substitute income for benefits in both occupations). When the new long-run equilibrium is reached, both occupations must again offer equal utility to individuals of identical ability and taste. But in the short-run, the ability to change occupations is limited and relative compensation adjusts only partially. The taxing of benefits therefore lowers utility more for the individual in the occupation with the higher ratio of benefits to income.[47]

The basic conclusion is thus the same for changes in the taxation of both capital and labor income. In a long-run steady state there are no horizontal inequities if all tastes are identical and there is a single type of ability. Apparent tax advantages are offset by differences in wage rates or asset values. But in the short-run, a change in tax rules will cause individuals who were equally well off to suffer different losses. Optimal tax reform requires balancing these horizontal inequities against the usual implications of the utilitarian principle.

4.3. Legitimate property rights

Until now, I have implicitly asserted that a tax change is desirable if it increases the value of the general utilitarian criterion function and does not violate horizontal equity. But how should we regard a one-time lump sum tax on high income individuals with the proceeds distributed equally to everyone? Since it is a one-time tax, there is no efficiency loss. If tastes are identical and there is a single type of ability, the social welfare indicator must rise. Since all individuals at each utility level have the same change in income, there is no horizontal inequity. Yet such a tax may be criticized as an unjust taking of private property, a violation of individuals' property rights.

A respect for individual property rights is one of the oldest ethical precepts. In the *Nicomachean Ethics*, Aristotle defined justice as refraining from pleonexia, that is, from taking what belongs to others or denying them what is rightly theirs. This view is repeatedly echoed in later writers. Even Rawls (1971, pp. 11, 311) appears to accept this view, although he argues that it is relevant only after the establishment of social institutions and particular property rights and therefore does not conflict with his own conclusions about the establishment of a basic structure in the 'original position.'

This view that property rights are fundamental must not be confused with the utilitarian view that property rights and the reliability of unchanging rules are necessary for the efficient functioning of a capitalist economy. Writers from

---

[47]The primary reason to tax benefits is to eliminate the inefficient substitution of benefits for cash payments. The only inequity in the current system arises from the failure of the labor market to offset the value of benefits by corresponding changes in cash income.

Hume and Bentham to Coase (1960) and Michaelman (1967) have stressed the value of protecting property rights without any notion of inherent individual rights to property: 'Security of expectations is cherished, not for its own sake, but only as a shield for morale.' [Michaelman (1967, p. 213)].

Nozick (1974) has argued that the right to property makes all taxation unjust.[48] Against this view it may be argued that an individual who chooses to live in a country agrees thereby to accept its rules of income taxation. Moreover, what we know as property is no more than 'the instutionally established understanding that current rules governing the relationships among men with respect to resources will continue in existence' [Michaelman (1967, p. 212)]. The inherent right to private property therefore does not preclude established rules of taxation but does protect the individual from the arbitrary and unanticipated taking of property.

To the extent that such protection of private property is considered part of our legal tradition, tax reforms that frustrate expectations and reduce wealth unexpectedly must be considered unjust. This too, along with the utilitarian gains and losses and the effect on horizontal equity, must be considered in evaluating proposed reforms.

This section has emphasized the difference between optimal tax design and optimal tax reform. The optimal design is not a goal to be achieved as quickly as possible. The need for gradual changes is stressed even by Rawls when he writes: 'Of course, the pace of change and the particular reforms called for at any given time depend upon current conditions' [Rawls (1971, p. 261)].

5. Optimal tax reforms

For many worth-while tax reforms, the objections that have just been raised could be eliminated by compensating those who would otherwise lose.[49] The utilitarian argument that reforms create uncertainty about future reforms and therefore induce inefficient behavior loses its force if investors know that they will be fully compensated for any losses that result from reform, they can ignore future possible reforms. There is no horizontal inequity and no arbitrary taking of property when all losers are compensated. Unfortunately, such compensation would not be technically feasible for many important tax reforms, and may always be politically impossible. How then should taxes be reformed when compensation is precluded?

5.1. Postponement vs. reduction

Postponing the effective date of a tax reform can substantially reduce the horizontal inequities associated with the change. More specifically, there are

---

[48]See section 2.3 on the implications of the entitlement principle for tax design.

[49]Feldstein (1976) presents a more detailed discussion of the use and limits of compensation in tax reform.

three ways in which *enacting a tax change with a delayed effective date* can reduce the arbitrary losses incurred by individuals who have acted in reliance upon the current laws.

First, for tax changes that affect labor income, sufficient postponement can eliminate all horizontal inequities. If the effective date is in the distant future but the change is correctly perceived, all new entrants to the labor market will make their decisions in terms of the correct rules (both current and future). By the time the law changes, the only affected individuals would be those who had known of the new rules since they entered the labor force.

Second, any postponement lowers the present value of the individuals' losses. This benefit affects the taxation of both capital income and labor income. For changes in the taxation of capital income, individuals suffer an immediate capital loss even with a delayed effective date, but the capital loss is reduced by the postponement.

Finally, the knowledge that the tax law will change causes a reduction in the flow of resources into the less favored activity which raises the compensation to the factors already there. Even if the delay is not sufficient for the level of compensation to offset the tax change, these general equilibrium price changes will tend to reduce horizontal inequity.

I have emphasized *current enactment with a future effective date, and not merely postponed enactment*. Although postponement per se lowers the present value of the loss, the first and third advantages depend on 'advance warning' that (1) allows individuals to reduce their commitments and to avoid making commitments based on misinformation, and (2) induced price changes that reduce horizontal inequity.

The decrease in arbitrary individual losses that is achieved through postponement can also be achieved by reducing the size of the tax change. Those who would be affected by an immediate change in the tax law are indifferent between some current partial change and a subsequent total change. It is clear that if these individuals are the only ones affected, society should also be indifferent between the reduction and postponement.[50] But postponement has the advantage of preventing new commitments based on misleading information, thus eliminating a source of horizontal inequity without any reduction in welfare gain. Although the choice between postponement of the change and its reduction should involve an examination of the welfare effects of general equilibrium price changes, the current analysis does suggest that postponement is preferable to partial reform.

5.2. Balancing efficiency and horizontal equity

Any postponement in the effective date of a tax reform entails a greater traditional welfare loss. The problem of selecting the optimal postponement or

---

[50]This implicitly assumes an additive social welfare function.

optimal extent of partial reform requires balancing the traditional welfare loss against the horizontal inequities of arbitrary individual losses. There is no clearly compelling procedure for such a balancing, nothing that follows naturally from traditional economic theory in the way that the generalized utilitarian criterion of section 2 does for balancing traditional efficiency and distributional concerns.[51] Nevertheless, the generalized utilitarian criterion does provide an approach to this problem that will be examined in the current section.

Although much of the popular discussion of tax reform confuses the elimination of tax distortions with increases in tax progressivity,[52] careful economic and legal analysts always separate the two issues. Surrey (1973) emphasizes that defining the tax base is logically prior to setting the tax schedule, and Pechman and Okner (1972) show a variety of different rate structures that could be used with an expanded tax base to yield the current tax revenue. This emphasis that tax structure can be defined without regard to the tax rates suggests an approach to balancing horizontal equity and traditional utilitarian gains. This separation of tax base decisions from tax rate decisions is equivalent to ignoring income distribution considerations in defining the tax base, i.e. equivalent to treating all individuals as if they have the same income. This procedure of ignoring income differences is of course common to most legislative and judicial procedures: neither the law nor the courts take income into account in establishing liability rules and awarding tort damages.[53] This notion of an impersonal justice that is identical for all can provide a basis for balancing horizontal equity and utilitarian gains.

If all individuals are *treated as if* they have the same income, or, more specifically, that they are at the same point on the utility–income function, the optimal tax reform can be obtained with the help of the traditional utilitarian calculus. Let me illustrate this by means of a simple example. Consider an economy with N individuals of whom n currently enjoy a tax advantage that increases their real income by x dollars per individual per year over what it would be with a uniform tax. Because eliminating the tax difference reduces an excess burden, the aggregate gain to the $N-n$ nonfavored individuals exceeds xn dollars. Let the gain per nonfavored individual be z dollars per year, $z(N-n) > xn$. The traditional efficiency criterion would clearly favor the tax change. Yet if n/N is small, the individual losses that result are large relative to the individual gains. The concavity of the utility functions together with the assumption that everyone should be treated as if they had the same utility function and the same initial

---

[51]Although the generalized utilitarian criterion does provide a theoretically comfortable way of combining notions of equity and efficiency, it is not the only way. The discussion of the egalitarian principle in section 2.3 indicates the limits of the generalized utilitarian criterion.

[52]See, e.g. Stern (1973).

[53]That is, the damages paid by a tort feaser are not related to his own income. The earnings of the plaintiff may be relevant in assessing his losses, but this is a completely different matter.

income imply that the optimal tax change may be smaller than if horizontal equity is ignored.

To consider this more explicitly, note that postponed elimination of the tax advantage reduces both the individual losses and individual gain proportionately.[54] Let λx be the loss associated with a particular postponement and λz the corresponding individual gain. If current utilities are all written $u(y)$, where y is the common initial level of income, the revised welfare gain associated with the λ postponement is

$$G = (N-n)[u(y+\lambda z) - u(y)] + n[u(y-\lambda x) - u(y)]. \qquad (4)$$

Using a second-order approximation of the utility function implies

$$G = (N-n)[\lambda zu' - \tfrac{1}{2}\lambda^2 z^2 u''] - n[\lambda xu' - \tfrac{1}{2}\lambda^2 x^2 u''], \qquad (5)$$

where the derivatives u' and u'' are evaluated at the common initial income y. As usual, it is convenient to represent the concavity of the utility function by the Arrow–Pratt measure of relative risk aversion, i.e. the elasticity of the marginal utility function: $R = -u''y/u'$. Rewriting (5) in terms of R, taking the derivative with respect to λ and rearranging terms yields the first-order condition for the optimal tax change:

$$\lambda^* = \frac{1}{R} \frac{z - [n/(N-n)]x}{[n/(N-n)]x(x/y) - z(z/y)}. \qquad (6)$$

Eq. (6) has some immediate implications about the balancing of horizontal equity and efficiency gains. It is clear that an increase in the gain (z) or a decrease in the loss (x) increases the optimal λ^*, i.e. reduces the optimal postponement. The greater the concavity of the utility function (i.e. the higher the value of R), the smaller the optimal λ^* and the longer the optimal postponement. For the same reason, an increase in y makes the gains and losses *relatively* smaller, decreases the importance of the concavity of the utility function (with *fixed* relative concavity) and thus decreases optimal postponement.

To conclude this discussion, consider a numerical example of the optimal λ^*. Let the average loss be $x = 1000$ and the average gain be $z = 10$, but with only 9 losers per 1000 gainers, i.e. $n/(N-n) = 0.009$. Eq. (6) then implies $\lambda^* = y/8900R$. If R is low and y is high, total immediate reform is optimal. But if substantial concavity is assumed, the postponement may be significant. For example, if $y = 10,000$ and $R = 2$ (i.e. a 1 percent increase in income reduces the marginal

---

[54]With an immediate *partial* elimination, the excess burdens vary nonlinearly with the degree of reduction while with postponed *complete* reduction this is not true.

utility by 2 percent), $\lambda^* = 0.56$. With a six percent discount rate, this is equivalent to a postponement of about 10 years.

More general problems of tax reform will require more sophisticated models to balance horizontal equity against traditional welfare gains. Moreover, the discussion of section 2 indicated the inherent limits of any criterion for optimal taxation. It is with these limits in mind that I suggest the current 'equal income assumption' as a basis for balancing horizontal equity against traditional welfare gains.

6. Conclusion

In section 2 of this paper I examined the limited concept of optimality that has been adopted in the recent contributions to the theory of optimal taxation. Section 3 then discussed the Haig–Simons approach to tax design and criticized its potential conflict with both economic efficiency and horizontal equity.

The remainder of the paper focused on the important difference between de novo design of a tax structure and subsequent tax revision. The key argument is that optimal tax reforms will generally lead to a different tax structure than optimal de novo design. Three types of reasons for this were discussed: efficiency, horizontal equity, and legitimate property rights. The final section examined the principles of optimal tax reform when compensation is precluded.

The attractiveness of the recent contributions to the theory of optimal taxation is due in large measure to the power of a relatively simple model to yield bold and apparently precise implications for optimal tax policy. But the useful insights that can be obtained from such formal analysis should not be confused with a full consideration of appropriate tax reform. Optimal tax policy requires a more general balancing of conflicting aims than has been recognized by either the recent theoretical contributions or the Haig–Simons tradition. I hope that the current paper will increase economists' awareness of these issues and will encourage further analysis of the specific problem of tax reform.

References

Andrews, W.D., 1974, A consumption-type or cash flow personal income tax, Harvard Law Review 87, 1113–1188.
Aoki, M., 1967, Optimization of stochastic systems, in: Mathematics in science and engineering, 32 (Academic Press, New York).
Atkinson, A.B., 1973a, How progressive should income tax be, in: M. Parkin, ed., Essays in modern economics (London) 90–109.
Atkinson, A.B., 1973b, Maxi-min and optimal income taxation, unpublished paper.
Atkinson, A.B., 1974, Housing allowances, income maintenance and income taxation, in: M. Feldstein and R. Inman, eds., IEA Conference volume of papers presented at Turin, Italy, April 1974 (forthcoming).
Atkinson, A.B. and J.E. Stiglitz, 1976, The design of tax structure: Direct versus indirect taxation, Journal of Public Economics 6, 55–75 (this issue).

Baumol, W.J. and D.F. Bradford, 1970, Optimal departures from marginal cost pricing, American Economic Review 60, 265–283.
Bittker, B.I., 1967, A 'comprehensive tax base' as a goal of income tax reform, Harvard Law Review 80, 925–985.
Bittker, B.I., 1973, Income tax 'loopholes' and political rhetoric, Michigan Law Review 71, 1099–1128.
Blum, W. and H. Calven, 1953, The uneasy case for progressive taxation (University of Chicago Press, Chicago).
Boiteux, M., 1956, Sur la gestion des monopoles publics asteints a l'equilibre budgetaire, Econometrica 24, 22–40.
Bruno, M., 1972, Market distortions and gradual reform, The Review of Economic Studies 39, 373–383.
Calabresi, G. and A.D. Melamed, 1972, Property rules, liability rules and inalienability: One view of the cathedral, Harvard Law Review 85, 1089–1128.
Coase, R.H., 1960, The problem of social cost, The Journal of Law and Economics 3, 1–44.
Diamond, P.A. and J.A. Mirrlees, 1971, Optimal taxation and public production, I, II, American Economic Review 61, 261–278.
Dixit, A.K., 1970, On the optimum structure of commodity taxes, American Economic Review 60, 295–301.
Fair, R.C., 1971, The optimal distribution of income, Quarterly Journal of Economics 85, 551–579.
Feldstein, M.S., 1972, Distributional equity and the optimal structure of public prices, American Economic Review 62, 32–36.
Feldstein, M.S., 1973, On the optimal progressivity of the income tax, Journal of Public Economics 2, 375–376.
Feldstein, M.S., 1974, Unemployed compensation: Adverse incentives and distributional anomalies, National Tax Journal 27, 231–244.
Feldstein, M.S., 1975a, Wealth neutrality and local choice in public education, American Economic Review 65, 75–89.
Feldstein, M.S., 1975b, The theory of tax expenditures, Harvard Institute of Economic Research Discussion Paper.
Feldstein, M.S., 1975c, The efficient taxation of portfolio income, Harvard Institute of Economic Research Discussion Paper.
Feldstein, M.S., 1976, Compensation in tax reform, National Tax Journal, June.
Fisher, I., 1927, A statistical method for measuring 'marginal utility' and testing the justice of a progressive income tax, in: J. Hollander, ed., Economic essays (Macmillan, New York).
Fisher, I., 1937, Income in theory and income taxation in practice, Econometrica 5, 1–55.
Green, H.A.J., 1961, The social optimum in the presence of monopoly and taxation, Review of Economic Studies 29, 66–78.
Haig, R.M., 1921, The federal income tax (Columbia University Press, New York).
Harberger, A., 1964, Taxation, resource allocation and welfare, in: The role of direct and indirect taxes in the federal revenue system (Princeton University Press, Princeton, NJ).
Harberger, A. and M.J. Bailey, eds., 1969, The taxation of income from capital (Brookings Institution, Washington).
Hardy, G.J., J.E. Littlewood, and G. Polya, 1934, Inequalities (Cambridge University Press, Cambridge).
Hochman, H. and J.D. Rodgers, 1969, Pareto optimal redistribution, American Economic Review 59, 542–557.
Hotelling, H., 1938, The general welfare in relation to problems of taxation and of railway and utility rates, Econometrica 6, 242–269.
Kaldor, N., 1955, An expenditure tax (George Allen and Unwin, London).
Kolm, S., 1969, L'etat et le systeme des prix (Dunod, Paris).
Laidler, D., 1969, Income tax incentives for owner-occupied housing, in: A. Harberger and M. Bailey, eds., The taxation of income from capital (Brookings Institution, Washington).
Lipsey, R.G. and K. Lancaster, 1956–57, The general theory of second best, Review of Economic Studies 24, 11–32.
Little, I.M.D., 1957, A critique of welfare economics, 2nd edition (Clarendon Press, London).

Michelman, F.I., 1967, Property, utility and fairness: Comments on the ethical foundations of 'just compensation' law, Harvard Law Review 80, 1165–1258.

Mirrlees, J., 1971, An exploration in the theory of optimal income taxation, Review of Economic Studies 38, 179–208.

Musgrave, R.A., 1968, in defense of an income concept, Harvard Law Review 81, 44–62.

Nozick, R., 1974, Anarchy, state and utopia (Basic Books, New York).

Pechman, J.A., 1971, Federal tax policy (W.W. Norton, New York).

Pechman, J.A. and B.A. Okner, 1972, Individual income tax erosion by income classes, in: The Economics of Federal Subsidy Programs, a compendium of papers submitted to the Joint Economic Committee, Part 1, General Study Papers, 92nd Congress, 2nd session (U.S. Government Printing Office, Washington) 13–40.

Phelps, E.S., 1973, Taxation of wage income for economic justice, Quarterly Journal of Economics 87, 331–354.

Ramsey, F.P., 1927, A contribution to the theory of taxation, Economic Journal 37, 47–61.

Rawls, J., 1971, A theory of justice (Harvard University Press, Cambridge, MA).

Rosen, H., 1975, A methodology for evaluating tax reform proposals, mimeo.

Savage, L.J., 1954, The foundations of statistics (John Wiley, New York).

Sheshinski, E., 1972, The optimal linear income tax, Review of Economic Studies 39, 297–302.

Simons, H.C., 1938, Personal income taxation (University of Chicago Press, Chicago).

Stern, P., 1973, The rape of the taxpayer (Random House, New York).

Stiglitz, J.E. and P. Dasgupta, 1971, Differential taxation, public goods and economic efficiency, The Review of Economic Studies 38, 151–174.

Surrey, S., 1974, Pathways to tax reform (Harvard University Press, Cambridge, MA).

Theil, H., 1964, Optimal decision rules for government and industry, in: H. Theil, ed., Studies in mathematical and managerial economics, 1 (North-Holland, Amsterdam).

Tinbergen, J., 1952, On the theory of economic policy (North-Holland, Amsterdam).

THE EFFICIENCY GAINS FROM DYNAMIC TAX REFORM*

By Alan J. Auerbach, Laurence J. Kotlikoff
and Jonathan Skinner

The efficiency gains from dynamic tax reform are the object of increasing interest among academic economists and economic policy makers. This paper presents a new simulation methodology for determining the pure efficiency gains from tax reform along the general equilibrium rational expectations growth path of life cycle economies. The simulation model measures the efficiency gains from changes in the degree of progressivity of tax structures as well as changes in the tax base. It also distinguishes pure pareto efficiency gains from the welfare changes arising from simple economic redistribution among generations.

The principal findings of this study concern the effects of switching from a proportional income tax with average rates similar to those in the U. S. to either a proportional tax on consumption or a proportional tax on labor income. Given our assumptions about production technology and individual preferences, a switch to consumption taxation generates an efficiency gain sufficient to improve the welfare of all future generations by almost 2 percent of lifetime resources. This result is not greatly influenced by reason' ble changes in parameters of the utility and production functions. In contrast, a transition from an income tax to a wage tax generates an efficiency loss greater than 2 percent of lifetime resources for the same set of parameter values; however, this number varies substantially for moderate changes in preference parameters.

For a constant level of revenues, the consumption tax combines a one-time, nondistortionary lump sum tax with a wage tax. Since a wage tax itself is distortionary, it is natural to expect the consumption tax to be more efficient. It is this element of lump-sum taxation, and not the exemption from taxation of capital income *per se* that is crucial to the achievement of efficient tax reform.[1]

A second general result is that even a mild degree of progressivity in the income tax system (as measured by the steepness of the marginal rate schedule) imposes a very large efficiency cost. For example, in comparison with an equal revenue proportional income tax, a progressive income tax with average tax rates varying over the life cycle between .23 and .32 and marginal rates ranging from .23 to .43 imposes an efficiency cost greater than 6 percent of full lifetime resources.

Section 1 of this paper reviews selections from the voluminous literature on optimal taxation that are most relevant to the present analysis. Section 2 describes the basic simulation model. The model, which incorporates variable labor supply and endogenous retirement behavior, is a more elaborate version of the

---

* Manuscript received April 16, 1982; revised August 20, 1982.
[1] Chamley [1981a, 1981b] and Black [1981] emphasize this point in discussing tax efficiency for infinite horizon economies.

Auerbach-Kotlikoff [1983] simulation model. Section 3 describes the method of welfare analysis that permits one to distinguish economic efficiency from redistribution. The model is then used to determine the efficiency gains from switching from a proportional income tax to proportional consumption and wage taxes. Section 4 examines the sensitivity of Section 3's results to changes in the static and intertemporal elasticities of substitution in consumption and leisure demand as well as the elasticity of substitution in production. A similar analysis of the progressive tax is conducted in Section 5; this section considers both changes in the degree of progressivity of the income tax as well as changes in the progressive tax base either to consumption or wages. The final section discusses some of the implications of this paper for current tax policy.

1. SELECTED LITERATURE REVIEW

Both the measurement of excess burden and the calculation of optimal tax schedules have been extended recently to the intertemporal issues surrounding the taxation of capital income. Feldstein [1978] presents efficiency calculations based on a two-period model in which an individual supplies labor in the first period and consumes in both periods. Feldstein concludes that a proportional tax on labor income is significantly more efficient than a proportional income tax. While instructive, Feldstein's analysis ignores general equilibrium changes in prices due to changes in factor supplies and uses Harberger's [1964] local approximation formula to measure the efficiency effects of large tax rate changes (Green and Sheshinski [1979]). The single period of labor supply also raises problems. Summers [1981] demonstrates that uncompensated labor supply elasticities with respect to the net return to capital are markedly different for multi-period models than for one period labor supply models. The same point pertains to those compensated labor supply elasticities relevant for excess burden calculations. A final issue is the sensitivity of Feldstein's conclusion to the particular choice of preference parameters (King [1980]).

In studying the taxation of savings, an alternative to the static, two-period model is the dynamic, two-period model introduced by Diamond [1965]. Papers by Auerbach [1979] and Atkinson and Sandmo [1980] characterize tax structures that maximize the utility of individuals in the steady state of such an economy. While derived from a general equilibrium model, these results are still based on the simple two-period model of individual behavior with a single labor supply decision. Moreover, for purposes of analytical tractability, these papers ignore the effect of the tax structure on the welfare of earlier generations alive during the economy's transition to its steady state. Determination of the tax schedule that maximizes steady state utility is a quite different exercise from the standard optimal tax problem of minimizing excess burden; it is possible to improve the utility of steady state generations by switching from one efficient tax system to another by imposing a greater fraction of the economy's long-run tax burden on earlier, pre-steady state generations.

With a numerical simulation model, like that developed by Miller and Upton [1974], Summers [1981] compares steady state utility for a model with fixed labor supply, but a more realistic, multi-period description of life-cycle consumption behavior; his study also attempts to measure the efficiency consequences of an explicit transition from one tax system to another. His analysis demonstrates that proportional wage and consumption taxes with equal annual revenue have markedly different long run impacts despite the fact that the structures of these two tax systems in the long run are identical in the sense that neither imposes a distortion on intertemporal choice. The common assumption of steady state models that the government's budget be balanced at each instant implies a quite different inter-cohort distribution of the tax burden of financing government expenditures under the wage tax versus the consumption tax. While long-run tax structures are identical under the two tax systems, the inter-cohort distribution of the economy's tax burden is not[2].

Summers' transition analysis, however, like that found in the earlier work of Miller and Upton, is based on the assumption of myopic rather than rational expectations; it also assumes completely inelastic supplies of labor. The exclusion of variable labor supply in an analysis that purports to compare the efficiency of capital income taxation with consumption or wage taxation is an obvious shortcoming; the assumption of myopic expectations is also undesirable. The transition paths of myopic life cycle economies are likely to differ significantly from perfect foresight rational expectations paths.

These advances in the measurement of dynamic tax efficiency would, of course, be inconsequential if economic theory alone could provide a clear guide to efficient, dynamic tax structures. Unfortunately, theory provides little guidance for the choice of tax base even in static settings. Even in the simple static case where the welfare of a single generation alive for two periods with no initial endowment is considered, a particular argument advanced by Feldstein [1978] and others in favor of a zero tax on capital income no longer applies if leisure is a choice variable in the second period. As shown by Sandmo [1974], if utility is separable into the untaxed numeraire good and a homogeneous function of all other commodities, uniform taxation of these commodities is optimal. If the untaxed good is labor, and the remaining commodities are first and second period consumption, then Sandmo's conditions are met. The optimal tax structure is a pure consumption tax or, equivalently, a labor income tax. However, if a fourth taxable commodity, second period labor, is added, separability of the utility function into goods and leisure and homogeneity with respect to consumption is no longer sufficient to ensure the optimality of the pure consumption tax.[3] In fact, in this case, a

---

[2] See Summers [1981] or Auerbach and Kotlikoff [1983] for further discussion.

[3] Letting l_1, l_2, c_1 and c_2 be leisure and consumption in the first and second periods, respectively, a utility function of the form $u(l_1, l_2, \phi(c_1, c_2))$, where ϕ is homogeneous, would normally call for a uniform tax on c_1 and c_2 *plus* a tax on second period labor supply, assuming first period labor to be untaxed. Even if utility was of the form $u(\psi(l_1, l_2), \phi(c_1, c_2))$ with both ψ and ϕ homogeneous, a pure consumption tax would not be called for; it is homogeneity in *labor* rather than leisure that would suffice for such a result.

proportional income tax may be less distortionary than a proportional consumption tax. Given the failure of economic theory to guide the choice of an efficient tax base, let alone the choice of efficient dynamic tax rates, the efficiency properties of alternative tax structures remain a suitable object for study through numerical simulation.

2. THE BASIC MODEL AND ITS SOLUTION

The basic model extends the Auerbach and Kotlikoff [1983] life cycle simulation model by incorporating endogenous labor supply and retirement and by permitting the production technology to differ from a simple Cobb-Douglas specification. The model describes the evolution over time of an economy consisting of government, household, and production sectors. The household sector comprises fifty-five overlapping generations of individuals. The fifty-five period life span is intended to correspond roughly to the life span of an adult, that is, the years between ages twenty and seventy-five. In each generation, there is a single, representative individual, and individuals in different generations differ only with respect to their opportunity sets.[4] The population as a whole grows at a fixed rate n (assumed to equal .01 throughout the paper). There is no uncertainty in the model, so rational expectations is equivalent to perfect foresight.

2.1. The Household Sector.
Each household is a self-contained unit, engaging in life-cycle consumption and labor supply behavior with no bequests.[5] The lifetime utility of each household takes the nested, constant elasticity form:[6]

(1) $$u(c, l) = \left(\frac{1}{1-1/\gamma}\right) \sum_{t=1}^{55} (1+\delta^{-(t-1)})[c_t^{(1-1/\rho)} + \alpha l_t^{(1-1/\rho)}]^{\left(\frac{1-1/\gamma}{1-1/\rho}\right)}$$

$$\alpha, \gamma, \delta > 0$$

---

[4] Auerbach and Kotlikoff [1983] examine issues arising from intragenerational differences in ability, and intergenerational differences due to technological change. As discussed below, both of these extensions would be difficult to maintain in the current model and are not directly relevant to the questions being addressed.

[5] Recent research (Kotlikoff and Summers [1981]) has suggested that a substantial portion of the economy's capital stock may be attributable to non-life cycle saving. What influences such saving is not well understood, but its existence may have important implications for evaluating taxes that impose intergenerational transfers. Under certain conditions, older generations will act to offset changes in the tax system of a purely distributional nature (Barro [1974]). Further research is required to determine how realistic bequest behavior would influence the results presented here.

[6] For $\gamma=1$, the use of l'Hôpital's Rule yields:

$$u(c, l) = \left(\frac{1}{1-1/\rho}\right) \sum_{t=1}^{55} (1+\delta)^{-(t-1)} \log\left[c_t^{(1-1/\rho)} + \alpha l_t^{(1-1/\rho)}\right]$$

For $\rho=1$,

$$u(c, l) = \left(\frac{1}{1-1/\gamma}\right) \sum_{t=1}^{55} (1+\delta)^{-(t-1)} \left[c_t^{1/(1+\alpha)} + l_t^{\alpha/(1+\alpha)}\right]^{1-1/\gamma}$$

where l_t and c_t are the household's leisure (out of a unit labor endowment) and consumption at the end of year t, and δ, α, and γ are taste parameters. A large value of δ, the household's pure rate of time preference, indicates that the individual will consume a greater fraction of lifetime resources in the early years of life. The term α is the intensity parameter of leisure. Given prices, a larger value of α would lead to a greater fraction of full resources being spent on leisure. The terms ρ and γ are the household's elasticities of substitution between consumption and leisure in a given period and between consumption (or leisure) in different periods, respectively. Though this is an extremely general utility function, it does impose certain constraints on preferences, such as equal intertemporal substitutability of consumption and leisure.

The individual maximizes lifetime utility (1) subject to a budget constraint, the exact specification of which depends on the particular tax system in force. For a progressive income tax, the lifetime budget constraint is:

$$(2) \quad \sum_{t=1}^{55} \{\prod_{t=2}^{s} [1+r_s(1-\bar{\tau}_{ys})]\}^{-1}(1-\bar{\tau}_{yt})w_t e_t(1-l_t) \geq \sum_{t=1}^{55} \{\prod_{s=2}^{t} [1+r_s(1-\bar{\tau}_{ys})]\}^{-1} c_t$$

where r_s is the gross interest rate in period s, w_t is the gross wage rate (in output units) in period t, and $\bar{\tau}_{yt}$ is the *average* tax rate on income faced by the household in year t. The e_t terms are included to reflect the accumulation of human capital; these terms describe how many units of "standard" labor the household supplies per unit of leisure foregone in any given year. Thus, $w_t e_t$ may be interpreted as the individual's gross wage rate. The human capital profile e (the shape of which is discussed below) is the same for all households, and labor supplied by different generations, after adjustment for efficiency, is homogeneous.

In addition to this overall budget constraint, we impose the requirement that labor supply can never be negative, i.e., if the notional demand for leisure, l, exceeds one, the individual must "retire" for that period, supplying zero labor. This is represented by the inequality constraints:

$$(3) \quad l_t \leq 1 \quad \text{for all} \quad t$$

Construction of a Lagrangian from expressions (1), (2), and (3), and differentiation with respect to c_t and l_t, produces the respective first-order conditions:[7]

$$(4a) \quad (1+\delta)^{-(t-1)}\Omega_t c_t^{-1/\rho} = \lambda\{\prod_{s=2}^{t}[1+r_s(1-\bar{\tau}_{ys})]\}^{-1}\theta_t$$

$$(4b) \quad (1+\delta)^{-(t-1)}\Omega_t \alpha l_t^{-1/\rho} = \lambda\{\prod_{s=2}^{t}[1+r_s(1-\bar{\tau}_{ys})]\}^{-1}w_t *\theta_t$$

where λ is the Lagrange multiplier of the lifetime budget constraint,

---

[7] The derivation of this and of further results in this section is provided in the appendix to Auerbach, et al. [1981].

(5) $$\Omega_t = [c_t^{(1-1/\rho)} + \alpha l_t^{(1-1/\rho)}]^{\left(\frac{1/\rho - 1/\gamma}{1-1/\rho}\right)}$$

(6) $$\theta_t = \prod_{s=t+1}^{55} \left\{ \frac{1+r_s(1-\tau_{ys})}{1+r_s(1-\bar{\tau}_{ys})} \right\}$$

(7) $$w_t^* = w_t e_t(1-\tau_{yt}) + \mu_t$$

τ_{yt} is the *marginal* income tax rate in the year t, and μ_t is the multiplier of the period t labor supply constraint.

With progressive taxes, θ_t is less than one, and represents a reduction in the implicit price of year t consumption or leisure. This additional term reflects the fact that an increase in current consumption or leisure will reduce savings and, hence, income from assets in all future years, thus reducing all future average tax rates. The "effective wage" w_t^* equals the net marginal wage per unit of leisure foregone when $\mu_t = 0$. When μ_t differs from zero, no labor is supplied and the individual is "retired." In this case, w_t^* is the "shadow" or "reservation" wage at which the household would freely choose to supply zero labor.

Combination of conditions (4a) and (4b) yields:

(8) $$l_t = \left(\frac{w_t^*}{\alpha}\right)^{-\rho} c_t$$

Substitution of (8) into (5) provides an expression for Ω_t in terms of c_t; given this formula, (4a) yields the "transition equation":

(9) $$c_t = \left(\frac{1+r_t(1-\tau_{yt})}{1+\delta}\right)^\gamma \left(\frac{v_t}{v_{t-1}}\right) c_{t-1}$$

where:

(10) $$v_t = [1 + \alpha \rho w_t^{*(1-\rho)}]^{\left(\frac{\rho-\gamma}{1-\rho}\right)}$$

The interpretation of (9) is complicated by the presence of the term v_t/v_{t-1} that involves the effective wages in the two periods. Since the derivative of v_t with respect to the effective wage w_t^* has the same sign as $(\rho - \gamma)$, the effect of the slope of the wage profile on the slope of the consumption profile depends on whether the elasticity of substitution between consumption and leisure in the same period is greater than or less than the intertemporal elasticity of substitution. For the special case where $\rho = \gamma$, $v_t/v_{t-1} \equiv 1$, and (9) reduces to a simpler, more familiar formula in which the growth rate of consumption depends positively on the net rate of return and negatively on the pure rate of time preference, with the intertemporal elasticity of substitution determining the sensitivity of the consumption profile to these other parameters.

The corresponding transition equation for leisure follows from (8) and (9):

(11) $$l_t = \left(\frac{1+r_t(1-\tau_{yt})}{1+\delta}\right)^\gamma \left(\frac{v_t}{v_{t-1}}\right)\left(\frac{w_t^*}{w_{t-1}^*}\right)^{-\rho} l_{t-1}$$

It is straightforward to show that l_t/l_{t-1} is negatively (positively) related to the net marginal wage in period t (period $t-1$), regardless of the values of ρ and γ.

It is important to remember that equations (9) and (11) determine the shape of the consumption and leisure profiles, not their absolute levels. In general, no analytic solution for the actual values of c and l is possible, and values for c and l must be determined numerically.[8]

Two other tax systems examined here are progressive annual consumption taxes and progressive annual labor income taxes. (The proportional versions are special cases.) For these two tax systems, suitable redefinitions of the budget constraint (2) yield conditions analogous to (8) and (9).[9] If we redefine the effective wage to be:

(7') $$w_t^* = (w_t e_t(1-\tau_{wt}) + \mu_t)/(1+\tau_{ct})$$

where τ_{wt} is the marginal labor income tax and τ_{ct} the marginal consumption tax, then condition (8) is a general expression for all tax systems, and condition (9) becomes:

(9') $$c_t = \left(\left(\frac{1+r_t}{1+\delta}\right)\left(\frac{1+\tau_{ct-1}}{1+\tau_{ct}}\right)\right)^{\gamma}\left(\frac{v_t}{v_{t-1}}\right)c_{t-1}$$

where v_t remains defined by (10). Again, while no analytical solution for c and l is normally possible, a number of interesting points concerning these two tax systems are readily apparent. First, the "equivalence" between wage and consumption taxes disappears when taxes are progressive or marginal tax rates change over time. In particular, a rising consumption profile normally leads to a rising marginal tax rate schedule under a progressive expenditure tax. As a comparison of (9) and (9') indicates, this is equivalent to taxing the rate of return to savings. In general, the degree of progressivity of any of three tax systems is just as important as the tax base in determining economic efficiency.

2.2. *The Production Sector.* The economy's single production sector is characterized by the CES production function:[10]

(12) $$Y_t = A[\varepsilon K_t^{(1-1/\sigma)} + (1-\varepsilon) L_t^{(1-1/\sigma)}]^{\left(\frac{1}{1-1/\sigma}\right)}$$

where Y_t, K_t and L_t are output, capital and labor at time t, A is a scaling constant,

---

[8] It is not possible to obtain an analytical solution for the absolute level of consumption and leisure for the following reason: successive application of (9) yields an expression for c_t in terms of c_1; from (8) and the budget constraint (2), c_1 can be solved in terms of net average and marginal factor returns and labor endowments; given c_1, (8) and (9), one can solve for all other values of c_t and l_t. However, this procedure would yield an analytical solution for the consumption and leisure profiles c and l only if net factor returns actually were exogenous. There are two reasons why this is not the case. First, under a progressive tax system, tax rates are function of the vectors c and l. Second, even with proportional taxes, the multipliers μ_t may depend on the labor supply decision. Thus, the procedure just outlined would amount to no more than a solution for c and l in terms of some complicated nonlinear functions of c and l.

[9] See the appendix to Auerbach, et al. [1981] for a demonstration.

[10] As is well-known, this specification reduces to Cobb-Douglas when $\sigma = 1$.

ε is the capital intensity parameter (assumed throughout the paper equal to 0.25) and σ is the elasticity of substitution between capital and labor. L_t is simply equal to the sum of effective units of labor supply of all households. K_t is generated by a recursive equation that dictates that the change in capital stock equals private plus public savings. Competitive behavior on the part of producers plus constant returns to scale in production ensure that the gross factor returns r_t and w_t are equated to the marginal products of capital and labor and that factor payments exhaust output. This is summarized by:

(13a) $$w_t/r_t = \left(\frac{1-\varepsilon}{\varepsilon}\right)(K_t/L_t)^{(1/\sigma)}$$

(13b) $$r_t K_t + w_t L_t = Y_t$$

This specification of production makes no allowance for technical change. While productivity growth was incorporated by Auerbach and Kotlikoff [1983] in an earlier version of the model with fixed labor supply, it is impossible, in general, to retain this element once labor supply is endogenous; the steady rise of wage rates over time is not compatible with a steady state unless $\rho = 1$, i.e., unless the utility function of contemporaneous consumption and leisure is Cobb-Douglas.[11] Such a restriction seems undesirable in the present context.

2.3. *The Government Sector.* In this model the government's sole concern is the financing of a stream of public expenditures, G_t, that grow at the same rate as population.[12] For simplicity, the impact of these expenditures on individual utility is ignored in the analysis. Aside from various taxes, the government can issue one-period debt to help finance current expenditures; such debt is a perfect substitute for capital in household portfolios. If D_t is defined as the value of government's debt (taking a negative value if there is a national surplus), government tax revenue at the end of period t is:

(14) $$R_t = \bar{\tau}_{yt}[w_t L_t + r_t(K_t + D_t)] + \bar{\tau}_{ct} C_t + \bar{\tau}_{wt} L_t$$

where $\bar{\tau}_{yt}$, $\bar{\tau}_{ct}$ and $\bar{\tau}_{wt}$ are aggregate average tax rates on income, consumption, and wages, respectively, calculated as weighted averages of individual average tax rates and C_t is aggregate consumption. Given the government's ability to issue and retire debt, its budget constraint relates the present value of its value of its expenditures plus the value of its initial debt to the present value of its tax receipts:

---

[11] In a steady state both l_t and c_t/w_t^* must be constant over successive generations for any age t. However, from (8),

$$l_t = \alpha^{-\rho}(w_t^*)^{1-\rho}\left(\frac{c_t}{w_t^*}\right)$$

so that these conditions cannot simultaneously be met, if there is general wage growth, unless $\rho = 1$.

[12] Note that G_t corresponds to a different concept from that reported in the National Income Account, which includes government purchases of capital goods.

EFFICIENCY GAINS FROM TAX REFORM

(15) $$\sum_{t=0}^{\infty} [\prod_{s=0}^{t} (1+r_s)]^{-1} R_t = \sum_{t=0}^{\infty} [\prod_{s=0}^{t} (1+r_s)]^{-1} G_t + D_0$$

2.4. *Solution of the Model.* Determination of the economy's dynamic equilibrium behavior begins with a characterization of the initial steady state. The next step is to solve for the economy's transition to the new steady state that results from the adoption of a new policy or sequence of policies. (It is important to remember that the transition described is the one the economy would actually take if all agents had perfect foresight.) The actual solution technique involves iterating until a fixed point is reached. For further details, see Auerbach, et al., [1981].

2.5. *Parameterization of the Model.* To solve the model, it is necessary to choose values for the preference parameters, δ, α, ρ and γ, the production elasticity σ, the production scaling constant, A, and the human capital vector, e.

The human capital vector determines relative wages by age. The profile used in this paper is calculated from a cross-section regression of weekly labor earnings of full-time workers on personal variables including experience and experience squared, reported by Welch [1979].[13] The resulting wage profile peaks at age 30, with wages at that age 45 percent higher than at age one. The age 55 wage is 22 percent smaller than the age one wage.

For our basic parameterization, we set $\sigma=1$, thereby assuming a Cobb-Douglas production function. There has been a considerable amount of research into the elasticity of substitution between capital and labor in U. S. manufacturing (see, for example, Nerlove [1967], Berndt and Christensen [1973]) with the general finding that $\sigma \leq 1$; however, only a few studies have been able to reject the hypothesis that $\sigma=1$.

The intertemporal elasticity of substitution between goods (or leisure) in different periods, γ, has also been the subject of a number of studies, most focusing on consumption. Weber [1970] estimated γ to lie between .13 and .41. In a later study (Weber [1975]), he found a range of γ from .56 to .75. More recently, Grossman and Shiller [1980] estimated γ to lie between .07 and .35, and Hall [1981] found values generally below .1. In a study of both leisure and consumption, Ghez and Becker [1975] estimated γ to be at most .28. Based on these studies, we choose a value of $\gamma=.25$ for our basic simulations.[14]

There is little direct empirical evidence on the value of ρ, except for the results of Ghez and Becker [1975], who find an aggregate value of $\rho=.83$. Much evidence is available on the labor supply elasticities of both men and women with respect to the contemporaneous wage, with "standard" values for the un-

---

[13] The equation used, based on one reported by Welch [1979] for the earnings of high school graduates, is $e_t = 4.47 + 0.033t - 0.00067t^2$, where t is the number of years of experience. We take t to equal the age of the individual, since, by our measure, adult life begins at $t=1$.

[14] For a detailed survey of the empirical evidence relevant for the choice of γ, as well as other preferences parameters, see Skinner [1981].

compensated elasticity equal to near zero for men and at least one for married women (see, for example, Heckman [1974], Rosen [1976], MaCurdy [1981] and Hausman [1981]). However, the translation of these elasticities into estimates of ρ depends on the degree to which the underlying wage changes are permanent or temporary, and whether they are anticipated or unanticipated. A detailed discussion of this issue is provided in the appendix to Auerbach et al. [1981]. While a range of values seems plausible for ρ, .8 seems to be a reasonable compromise. Moreover, this value of ρ provides realistic age-earnings and age-consumption profiles in our simulation of the initial steady state. For lower values of ρ, consumption growth is too high in later years and retirement does not occur. For higher values, consumption actually declines during retirement. These effects occur because leisure is relatively cheaper in later years (e declines); the greater the elasticity of substitution, ρ, the greater the shift from consumption into leisure (see (8)).

The leisure intensity parameter, α, and the scaling constant, A, really depend on the choice of labor and output units. For convenience, we always choose output units so that the wage in the initial steady state is unity for age one individuals. This determines A. Adopting the convention of a labor endowment equal to 5,000 hours per year, we choose α so that prime age labor supply is about 2,000 hours per year, or 40 hours per week. This suggests a value of $\alpha = 1.5$, which is used in all simulations. Finally, there is scant empirical evidence on the appropriate value of δ. Since an increase in δ would reduce the steepness of consumption and leisure profiles (see (9) and (11)), it would lead to less saving and hence a lower capital-output ratio as well as a smaller likelihood of retirement in later years. We find that setting $\delta = .015$ gives realistic values both for the capital-output ratio and the age of retirement. Lowering δ eliminates retirement, while raising it makes the capital-output ratio unreasonably low.

The exact values of the key substitution elasticities remain uncertain. Hence, we also present simulation results for different values of σ, γ and ρ. The aim of this paper is not, however, to calculate exact estimates of the efficiency gains or losses resulting from particular policies, but rather to reach certain qualitative conclusions about the differences among alternative policies.

2.6. *Basic Simulation Results.* The initial fiscal structure used as the starting point for most simulations is a proportional income tax of 30 percent, with no national debt. The parameterization outlined above generates an initial, long-run equilibrium with a capital-output ratio of 3.04 and a gross interest rate of 8.22 percent. Retirement occurs at age 53, with labor supply peaking at a value of 0.468 (2,340 hours per year) at age 9. The solid and dashed lines in Figure 1 depict, respectively, the age-consumption and age-earnings profiles in this initial steady state. The age-consumption profile rises slowly over time, nearly leveling off before retirement. Earnings rise until age 20 and then begin to fall off. This drop in earnings becomes more rapid after age 30 as a result of the combination of lower labor supply and a decline in wages. The sudden jump in consumption during retirement results as a spillover from the retirement constraint placed on the individual's purchase of leisure.

Starting from this long-run equilibrium, we calculate the path of the economy to a new long-run equilibrium after the immediate adoption of either a proportional consumption tax or a proportional wage tax, with annual budget balance imposed in each year. Figure 2 presents the effects on cohort welfare of these two potential changes in tax regime. The various cohorts alive during the economy's transition are identified on the vertical axis by their year of birth, taking zero to the year of the initiation of the tax change. Welfare gains and losses are measured on the vertical axis as the fraction of full lifetime labor endowment required under the original income tax regime to generate the same level of utility actually achieved with the change in tax regime. For example, a value

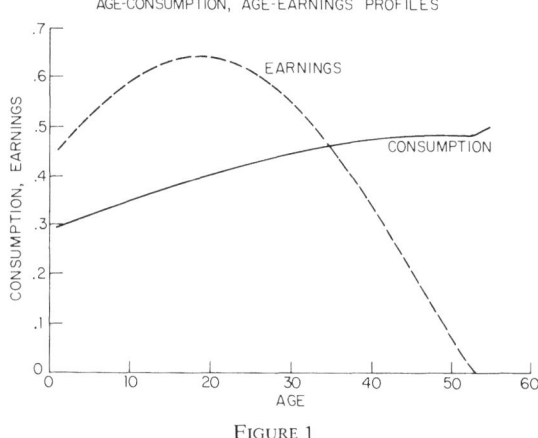

FIGURE 1

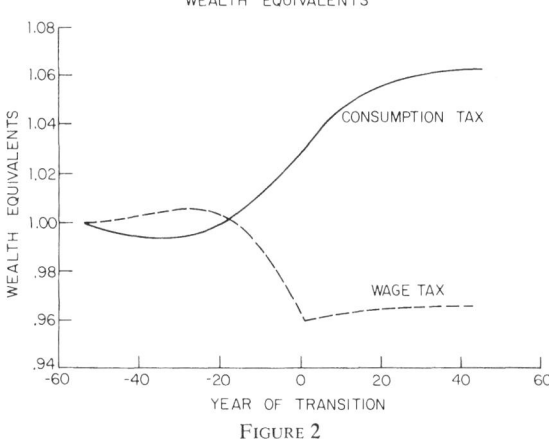

FIGURE 2

of 1.02 means that a cohort's utility is increased as a result of the tax change by the same amount as would have been induced by a 2 percent increase in human capital endowment under the income tax. We refer to these measures as "wealth equivalents." The two lines in Figure 2 represent the wealth equivalents under transitions to a consumption tax and to a wage tax.

As the diagram clearly demonstrates, the consequences for distribution of cohort welfare are markedly different under these two alternative "tax reforms." Along the consumption tax transition path, young and future cohorts achieve substantial utility gains, partly at the expense of older cohorts. The long-run steady state gain is over 6 percent under the consumption tax. Under the wage tax, older cohorts gain, while generations either young or unborn at the time of the policy switch are hurt. There is eventually a steady state welfare loss of almost 4 percent. Interestingly, the identity of gainers and losers under the two regimes is almost exactly opposite. Those above the age of about 18 at the time of the policy change gain from a wage tax and lose from a consumption tax, while all subsequent cohorts gain from a consumption tax and lose from a wage tax.

The shapes of these curves are readily understood. Under the consumption tax, elderly cohorts are faced with a much heavier tax burden than they would have experienced under the income tax. For these older cohorts, labor earnings are small, and consumption is financed by depleting accumulated savings. Thus, consumption far exceeds earnings, and the base of the consumption tax is far greater than that of the income tax. Young and future cohorts gain from a switch to a consumption tax because older cohorts have been forced to bear a larger portion of the present value of government expenditures.

The switch to a proportional wage tax raises the welfare of the elderly for much the same reason that a consumption tax lowers it. Here, taxes on capital income that would have been due under the income tax are eliminated. However, these gains must be supported by a greater tax collection from young and future generations.

Despite the very different effects these two tax regimes have on steady state welfare, both lead to a greater capital-output ratio by exempting capital income from taxation and hence encouraging savings. Under a consumption tax, which has a steady state value of 0.395, the capital output ratio rises so much, from 3.04 to 4.38, that the net-of-tax interest rate actually falls, from 5.75 percent (0.7×8.22) to 5.71 percent. Under a wage tax, which equals 0.411 in the new steady state, the capital-output ratio rises less, to 3.45. Because of this smaller rise in capital accumulation, the gross interest rate falls less, to a value of 7.25 percent.

These results beg the question of whether policies that increase capital accumulation also increase economic efficiency. Since some generations gain and some lose under each of the tax changes considered thus far, some method is necessary to isolate the substantial intergenerational transfers associated with "tax reforms" like these from any inherent gains in efficiency associated with these policies. One approach, explored by Auerbach and Kotlikoff [1981] is to seek combinations of wage and consumption taxes and deficit policy that raise the utility of all cohorts to at least the level enjoyed under the income tax. However, such "Pareto welfare paths" cannot offer an exact measure of the efficiency gain (or loss) resulting from a tax change. The next section presents a methodology for doing so.

3. DISTINGUISHING EFFICIENCY FROM REDISTRIBUTION: THE LUMP SUM REDISTRIBUTION AUTHORITY (LSRA)

The LSRA is a hypothetical construct used to measure the pure efficiency gains from tax reform. The LSRA is modeled as a separate, self-financing government agency that uses lump sum taxes and transfers to keep cohorts born before a specified date at their status quo level of utility, and to raise the utility of all cohorts born after this date by a uniform amount. Equalization of the utility of those born after a certain date, a policy analyzed in a two-period setting by Phelps and Riley [1978], seems to be a logical way of characterizing the infinite set of welfare paths the LSRA could generate.[15]

The simulation model was adapted to solve for the economy's general equilibrium transition path consistent with the behavior of the standard government fiscal authority as well as the lump sum tax-transfer activity of the LSRA. Thus, for example, household consumption decisions under a consumption tax transition take account of the LSRA lump-sum taxes and transfers. It is also important to note that the equilibrium path of consumption tax rates will differ from that generated in the absence of the LSRA, since changes in the behavior of households will necessitate modifications in the tax schedule imposed by the main government authority.

The LSRA faces a budget constraint requiring that its lump sum taxes and transfers sum to zero in present value. At any point in time, the LSRA holds net assets that may be positive or negative, but that equal the present value of its net future payments. These net assets are added to those held by the private sector to determine the economy's total stock of capital.

Lump sum taxes and transfers are collected and paid in year one (the first year of the transition) for all existing cohorts and in the first year of economic life for all subsequent cohorts. Equation (16) expresses the LSRA budget constraint, where v_i is the lump sum tax (negative, if a transfer) paid by members of generations born in year i, and n is the economy's population growth rate. The two pieces of the expression in (16) correspond, respectively, to the net taxes collected from existing and future cohorts.

---

[15] Because the LSRA is only a theoretical construct, there is still a potential problem, dating from the welfare analysis of Hicks [1940] and Kaldor [1939], in using it to make a comparison between tax systems. The "maximin" level of utility achieved by cohorts born after one date might be higher under tax regime A than tax regime B, while if a different date were chosen, all subsequent cohorts might do better under regime B. Unless one particular redistribution scheme is actually carried out, theoretical "as if" comparisons may yield ambiguous results.

$$\text{(16)} \quad \sum_{i=-53}^{0}(1+n)^i v_i + \sum_{i=1}^{\infty}(1+n)^i[\prod_{j=1}^{i}(1+r_j)^{-1}]v_i = 0$$

The method of simulation is essentially the same as that previously used. However, the budget constraints of existing and future cohorts now include the terms v_i, and updated guesses of these must be made in each iteration step along with those of factor prices, tax rates and shadow wages. In the first iteration of the simulation, all v_i's are given preliminary values of zero. In the course of each iteration, the model produces new estimates of the path of this vector v. A weighted average of the initial guess and this computed path generates a guess for the next iteration.

The calculation of v in each step is described in detail in the appendix of the working paper. It is important to remember that the vector v is included in the full general equilibrium solution of the model. Thus, policies leading to large transfers to older cohorts (as will be the case for a consumption tax) will lead to an accumulation of debt by the LSRA and hence crowd out some of the increase in capital that occurs in the basic simulation.

Starting in year one, the efficiency gains from switching to a proportional consumption tax are sufficient to raise the wealth of all future generations by 1.73 percent without harming the welfare of earlier generations. Delaying the gains until $i^*=20$ allows a per cohort gain of about 5 percent. While substantial, these gains are smaller than those achieved in the steady state without the LSRA, because the heavy tax burden levied on the elderly starting in year zero has been undone.

The LSRA transition to a wage tax involves a *loss* in efficiency. The sustainable level of utility for $i^*=1$ is 2.33 percent below what it would have been under the income tax. Delay of the loss until $i^*=20$ leads to a drop of almost 9 percent in full lifetime resources for all future generations.

This difference between the sustainable levels of utility at $i^*=1$ under the alternative tax regimes is remarkably large in light of the apparent similarity of the regimes themselves. Taking account of the fact that the present value of full lifetime resources is approximately four times as large as lifetime earnings for our simulations of the initial income tax, the 1.73 percent gain under the consumption tax and 2.33 percent loss under the wage tax represents a swing of about 16.25 percent of lifetime earnings. Except for the difference between the population growth rate and the individual rate of discount, this is also a measure of the annual loss as a fraction of total labor income. For the U. S. economy in 1980, total wage and salary compensation was 1,344 billion dollars,[16] 16.25 percent of which is 218 billion dollars, or about one-third the size of the federal government's budget.

The key to this difference lies in the pattern of tax burden each new system imposes on different generations. Aside from the differences in distributional

---

[16] *U. S. Economic Report of the President*, 1981; Table B–20.

EFFICIENCY GAINS FROM TAX REFORM

impact, which the LSRA neutralizes, the tax systems also differ in their excess burden because they tax different generations at different marginal rates. A consumption tax places high marginal tax rates on the elderly who, because they have few years over which to alter their consumption-leisure decisions, exhibit relatively inelastic behavior with respect to tax-induced changes in net prices. This allows a lower burden, and, consequently, lower distortionary marginal tax rates, to be placed on those with a more elastic response, the young. The wage tax does just the opposite, giving low marginal tax rates to the elderly, paid for through higher distortionary taxes on the young. It is thus crucial to the efficiency gain resulting from a consumption tax that the initial generations face high marginal tax rates.

4. SENSITIVITY ANALYSIS OF EFFICIENCY GAINS

As stressed in Section 2, the parameters chosen for the baseline simulations are subject to a great deal of uncertainty. It is important to examine the sensitivity of our results to changes in such parameters. Table 1 presents the sustainable

TABLE 1
SENSITIVITY ANALYSIS
Maximin Gain ($i^* = 1$)
Proportional Consumption Tax

	ρ		
	.3	.8	
γ = .1	1.81	2.06	1
.25	1.48	1.73	1
.25		1.18	.8

σ

Proportional Wage Tax

	ρ		
	.3	.8	
γ = .1	−1.17	−6.74	1
.25	0.03	−2.33	1
.25		−1.04	.8

σ

maximin wealth effects (for $i^*=1$) of movements from a proportional income tax to proportional consumption and wage taxes for alternative values of ρ, the intratemporal elasticity of substitution between goods and leisure, γ, the intertemporal elasticity of substitution, and σ, the elasticity of technical substitution between capital and labor.

For the wage tax, the results are quite sensitive to parameter changes, but in directions that intuition would dictate. Lowering γ, and, hence, the distortions associated with taxes on capital income, worsens the effects of going to a wage tax. Reducing γ from .25 to .1 increases the welfare loss from 2.33 percent to 6.74 percent at $\rho=.8$. Decreasing ρ, and, hence, the distortions associated with taxes on labor income, improves the outcome. With γ held at .25, a reduction of ρ to .3 is sufficient to neutralize the negative impact of the wage tax. Changing σ to .8 reduces the effect of the change in regime, since gross factor prices change more as a result of initial changes in factor supplies, thus making the general equilibrium changes in net prices, as well as associated behavioral responses, smaller.[17]

In contrast, the efficiency effects of moving to a consumption tax appear much less sensitive to the preference parameters ρ and γ, though the effect of a change in σ still appears important. To explain this result, it is helpful to recall why the consumption tax is more efficient than the wage tax in the first place. The consumption tax may be thought of as the combination of a wage tax plus a levy on the initial elderly population. Though these elderly individuals are relatively inelastic in their behavior, they can shift away from the consumption tax to a certain extent, by shifting resources to periods when the consumption tax may be lower (it is highest in the first year of the transition, and then declines steadily until the new steady state is reached). The extent to which they will do this depends on γ, the intertemporal elasticity of substitution. The higher is γ, the more they will shift and the less like a lump sum tax will be the initial levy on the elderly. Thus, the rise in γ makes the wage tax relatively more efficient, compared to the income tax, but it also reduces the efficiency advantage of the consumption tax over the wage tax.

5. THE PROGRESSIVE TAX: EFFICIENCY GAINS FROM SWITCHING TO ALTERNATIVE TAX STRUCTURES

Additional distortions are introduced with the progressivity of tax rates. It is important to see how the results of the previous section are influenced by allowing marginal and average tax rates to differ.

For each of the tax structures, marginal tax rates are determined by the following formula

(17) $$t = \Psi_0 + \Psi_1 B$$

---

[17] This sensitivity to σ has been examined carefully by Chamley [1981b].

where B is the tax base, either annual income, annual consumption or annual labor earnings. It follows that the average tax rates corresponding to (17) are

(18) $$\bar{t} = \Psi_0 + 1/2\Psi_1 B$$

As explained in Section 2, each cohort in each transition year faces a different path of marginal and average tax rates because of differences in behavior and differences in the tax schedule parameters Ψ_0 and Ψ_1. These rates are solved for in each iteration step along with factor prices and shadow wages.

To investigate reform of the progressive income tax, we specify an initial steady state with $\Psi_0=.22$ and $\Psi_1=.28$ for the income tax. This yields a profile of average tax rates that ranges from .282 at age 1 to .323 at age 26 to a minimum of .227 at age 55, and is concentrated around .30, the level of proportional income tax considered above. The marginal rates range from .234 to .426. The first experiment involves switching from this regime to a proportional income tax (roughly equal to .28 in the long run) to evaluate the excess burden due to the progressivity of the income tax. The sustainable welfare gain is larger than any of those reported in Table 1, equaling 6.15 percent of the lifetime resources. The size of this distortion may seem somewhat surprising, given the relatively small gap between marginal and average tax rates in the initial steady states. However, it must be remembered that, for any single tax, the magnitude of the distortion rises roughly in proportion to the *square* of the marginal tax rate. Moreover, a further efficiency loss is introduced here by the variation in marginal tax rates over time. Shifting to either a proportional consumption tax or a proportional wage tax also leads to a large welfare gain (7.08 percent and 4.24 percent, respectively) although, as before, the wage tax is inferior to the proportional income tax, while the consumption tax is superior; however, it may be more appropriate to compare the progressive income tax with alternative taxes possessing a similar degree of progressivity. To do this, we choose values of Ψ_1 for the alternative tax bases that give top marginal rates having roughly the same proportion to overall average rates as is the case for the income tax. For example, the progressive income tax resulting from $\Psi_0=.22$ and $\Psi_1=.28$ yields a top marginal rate of 0.43 compared to an overall average rate of about .3. In our previous simulations for proportional taxes, we had a consumption tax of .39 in the new steady state versus a wage tax of .41. Thus, we seek top marginal rates of about .55 and .58, respectively. These outcomes are roughly achieved by $\Psi_1=.6$ for the consumption tax and $\Psi_1=.4$ for the wage tax.[18] The values of Ψ_0 depend on the size of the annual tax bases; in the steady state, they equal .24 and .32, respectively.

Transition from a progressive income tax to a consumption tax with $\Psi_1=0.6$ still results in a substantial efficiency gain of 4.97 percent. However, the switch to a wage tax produces a loss of 3.14 percent; this loss is even larger than the loss

---

[18] The actual top marginal rates that occur in the final steady state are 0.572 at age 55 for the consumption tax and 0.553 at age 16 for the wage tax.

of 2.33 percent occurring with a switch under proportional taxation.

To summarize these results, a truly progressive income tax is substantially more distortionary than a proportional income tax. If progressive taxation must be used (for distributional objectives, presumably), the general efficiency results from the study of proportional taxation carry over. A transition to a consumption tax is considerably more efficient than a transition to a wage tax; the first generates a large efficiency gain while the second induces an equally large efficiency loss.

6. CONCLUSIONS

Because the model used in this paper does not incorporate a number of factors which might influence savings behavior (e.g., bequests, risk, etc.), the results must be regarded with some caution. However, there is much we have learned from them.

The simulations presented above suggest that a shift to a wage tax from an income tax can significantly reduce economic efficiency. While a consumption tax does offer efficiency gains, these arise chiefly from the placement (probably implausible, politically) of large marginal tax burdens on the relatively inelastic elderly when capital income taxes are reduced. Foregoing such taxes on the elderly effectively removes the distinction between a consumption tax and a wage tax. While wage taxation will also stimulate capital formation, it may reduce economic efficiency. Thus, it is important that policy makers not confuse programs that stimulate capital formation with those that increase welfare.

The paper also points out that the progressivity of a tax may be at least as important as the tax base itself in determining the efficiency of the tax system.

Harvard University and National
 Bureau of Economic Research
Yale University and National
 Bureau of Economic Research
University of Virginia

REFERENCES

ATKINSON, A. B. AND A. SANDMO, "Welfare Implications of the Taxation of Savings," *Economic Journal* 90 (September 1980), pp. 529–549.

AUERBACH, A. J., "The Optimal Taxation of Heterogeneous Capital," *Quarterly Journal of Economics* 93 (November 1979), pp. 589–612.

AUERBACH, A. J. AND L. J. KOTLIKOFF, "National Savings, Economic Welfare and Structure of Taxation," in M. Feldstein, ed., *Behavioral Simulation Methods in Tax Policy Analysis* (Chicago: University of Chicago Press, 1983), forthcoming.

AUERBACH, A. J., L. J. KOTLIKOFF AND J. SKINNER, "The Efficiency Gains from Dynamic Tax Reform," NBER Working Paper No. 819 (December 1981).

BARRO, R. J., "Are Government Bonds Net Wealth?" *Journal of Political Economy* 82 (November/December 1974), 1095–1117.

BERNDT, E. R. AND L. J. CHRISTENSEN, "The Translog Function and the Substitution of Equipment, Structures and Labor in U. S. Manufacturing, 1929–1968," *Journal of Econometrics* 1 (March 1973), 81–113.
BLACK, F., "When Is a Positive Income Tax Optimal?" NBER Working Paper No. 63, (February 1981).
CHAMLEY, C., "The Welfare Cost of Capital Income Taxation in a Growing Economy," *Journal of Political Economy* 89 (June 1981a), 468–496.
———, "Efficient Stationary Taxation and Intertemporal General Equilibrium," Cowles Foundation Discussion Paper No. 591 (May 1981b).
DIAMOND, P. A., "National Debt in a Neoclassical Growth Model," *American Economic Review* 55 (December 1965), 1126–1150.
FELDSTEIN, M. S., "The Welfare Cost of Capital Income Taxation," *Journal of Political Economy* 86 (April 1978), S29–S51.
GHEZ, G. AND G. S. BECKER, *The Allocation of Time and Goods over the Life Cycle* (New York: Columbia University Press, 1975).
GREEN, J. AND E. SHESHINSKI, "Approximating the Efficiency Gains from Tax Reforms," *Journal of Public Economics* 11 (April 1979), 179–195.
GROSSMAN, S. AND R. SHILLER, "Capital Asset Returns and Consumption," mimeo (December 1980).
HALL, R. E., "Intertemporal Substitution in Consumption," NBER Working Paper No. 720 (July 1980).
HARBERGER, A. C., "Taxation, Resource Allocation and Welfare," in *The Role of Direct and Indirect Taxes in the Federal System* (Princeton: Princeton University Press, 1964), reprinted A. C. Harberger, *Taxation and Welfare* (Boston: Little, Brown, 1974).
HAUSMAN, J., "Labor Supply," in H. Aaron and J. Pechman, eds., *How Taxes Affect Economic Behavior* (Washington: Brookings, 1981).
HECKMAN, J., "Shadow Prices, Market Wages and Labor Supply," *Econometrica* 42 (July 1974), 679–694.
HICKS, J. R., "The Valuation of Social Income," *Economica* N. S. 7 (May 1940), 105–124.
KALDOR, N., "Welfare Propositions in Economics," *Economic Journal* 49 (September 1939), 549–552.
KING, M., "Savings and Taxation," in G. A. Hughes and G. M. Heal, eds., *Pubulic Policy and the Tax System* (London: Allen and Unwin, 1980).
KOTLIKOFF, L. J., AND L. H. SUMMERS, "The Role of Intergenerational Transfers in Aggregate Capital Accumulation," *Journal of Political Economy* 89 (August 1981), 706–732.
MACURDY, T., "An Empirical Model of Labor Supply in a Life-Cycle Setting," *Journal of Political Economy* 89 (December 1981), 1059–1085.
MILLER, M. H. AND C. W. UPTON, *Macroeconomics: A Neoclassical Introduction* (Homewood, Ill.: R. D. Irwin, 1974).
NERLOVE, M., "Recent Studies of the CES and Related Production Functions," in M. Brown, ed., *The Theory and Empirical Analysis of Production* (New York: NBER, 1967).
PHELPS, E. S. AND J. G. RILEY, "Rawlsian Growth: Dynamic Programming of Capital and Wealth for Intergenerational 'Maximin' Justice," *Review of Economic Studies* 45 (February 1978), 103–120.
ROSEN, H., "Taxes in a Labor Supply Model with Joint Wage-Hours Determination," *Econometrica* 44 (May 1976), 485–580.
SANDMO, A., "A Note on the Structure of Optimal Taxation," *American Economic Review* 64 (September 1974), 701–706.
SKINNER, J., "Cost and Incidence of an Interest Income Tax," mimeo, (January 1981).
SUMMERS, L. H., "Capital Taxation and Accumulation in a Life Cycle Growth Model," *American Economic Review* 71 (September 1981), 533–544.
WEBER, W., "The Effect of Interest Rates on Aggregate Consumption," *American Economic*

Review 60 (September 1970), 591–600.

WEBER, W., "Interest Rates, Inflation and Consumer Expenditures," *American Economic Review* 65 (December 1975), 843–858.

WELCH, F., "Effects of Cohort Size on Earnings: The Baby Boom Babies' Financial Bust," *Journal of Political Economy* 87 (October 1979), S65–S97.

# [29]

Simulating Fundamental Tax Reform in the United States

By David Altig, Alan J. Auerbach, Laurence J. Kotlikoff,
Kent A. Smetters, and Jan Walliser*

This paper uses a new, large-scale, dynamic life-cycle simulation model to compare the welfare and macroeconomic effects of transitions to five fundamental alternatives to the U.S. federal income tax, including a proportional consumption tax and a flat tax. The model incorporates intragenerational heterogeneity and a detailed specification of alternative tax systems. Simulation results project significant long-run increases in output for some reforms. For other reforms, namely those that seek to insulate the poor and initial older generations from adverse welfare changes, long-run output gains are modest. (*JEL* H20, C68)

Fundamental tax reform has been a hot issue, and for good reason. The U.S. tax system—a hybrid of income- and consumption-tax provisions—is complex, distortionary, and replete with tax preferences. Recent "reforms" of the tax code, including the Taxpayer Relief Act of 1997, have made the system even more complex and buttressed the argument for fundamental reform.

"Fundamental tax reform" means different things to different people. The definition adopted below is the simplification and integration of the tax code by eliminating tax preferences and taxing all sources of capital income at the same rate. Several current tax proposals certainly deserve to be called "fundamental." They include Robert E. Hall and Alvin Rabushka's (1995) flat tax, the retail sales tax, and David Bradford's (1986) X tax. The flat tax and the retail sales tax are two alternative ways of taxing consumption. The X tax also taxes consumption, but places high-wage earners in higher tax brackets than low-wage earners. Another fundamental reform is to adopt a broad-based, low-rate income tax.

This paper uses a computable general-equilibrium simulation model to compare the welfare and macroeconomic effects of fundamental tax reform. The model is a substantially enhanced version of the Auerbach-Kotlikoff (1987) dynamic life-cycle simulation model.[1] The new model follows the significant lead of Don Fullerton and Diane Lim Rogers (1993) in incorporating intra- as well as intergenerational inequality. Specifically, it includes 12 different groups within each cohort, each with its own earnings ability (its own endowment of human capital).

Our new model approximates U.S. fiscal institutions much more closely than does its predecessor. It includes an array of tax preferences, a progressive Social Security system, and a Medicare system. Including tax preferences is not only crucial for studying fundament tax reform. It also permits our use of actual tax

---

* Altig: Federal Reserve Bank of Cleveland, Cleveland, OH 44101; Auerbach: Department of Economics, University of California, Berkeley, CA 94720; Kotlikoff: Department of Economics, Boston University, 270 Bay State Road, Boston, MA 02215; Smetters: The Wharton School, University of Pennsylvania, 3641 Locust Walk, Philadelphia, PA 19104; Walliser: International Monetary Fund, 700 19th St. NW, Washington, DC 20431. The views expressed here are those of the authors and do not necessarily reflect those of the Federal Reserve Bank of Cleveland, the IMF, or any other organization. We are grateful to Cristina DeNardi, Barbara Fried, Bill Gale, Jane Gravelle, participants in workshops at the University of Chicago, the NBER, the Federal Reserve Bank of Cleveland, Indiana University, the Federal Reserve System Committee on Macroeconomics, and two anonymous referees for comments on earlier drafts. Auerbach thanks the Burch Center for Tax Policy and Public Finance and Kotlikoff thanks the National Institute of Aging and the Smith Richardson Foundation for research support.

[1] A similar model, used to consider only steady states, is presented in Altig and Charles Carlstrom (1999).

schedules in calibrating the model.² Stated differently, omitting tax preferences would mean unrealistically low tax rates since the current federal income tax covers only 57 percent of national income.³ The improved modeling of Social Security and Medicare is also vital since both programs materially alter the intergenerational and intragenerational distributions of welfare and the initial set of fiscal distortions from which tax reform proceeds.

Like Auerbach and Kotlikoff (1987), we compute the economy's perfect-foresight transition path. Given the magnitude of factor-price and tax-rate changes along our simulated transition paths, permitting agents to think rationally about the future is of great importance. This and other advantages vis-à-vis the Fullerton-Rogers (1993) model, which assumes myopic expectations, must be set against some disadvantages. Our model has a simpler production and preference structure than does the Fullerton-Rogers model, which features multiple consumption and capital goods, intermediate inputs, and industry-specific capital-income taxation. As such, it cannot measure the efficiency gains from the removal of intersectoral and interasset distortions. Nor does it incorporate the externalities present in endogenous growth models, which might provide another source of efficiency gains from tax reform (e.g., Nancy L. Stokey and Sergio Rebelo, 1995).

Our model also omits the impact on labor supply of low-income programs such as the Earned Income Tax Credit, and several influences on saving, including earnings and lifespan uncertainty, transfer program asset tests, and liquidity constraints. The impact of these factors has been evaluated in simulation studies by R. Glenn Hubbard and Kenneth Judd (1987), Hubbard et al. (1995), and Eric M. Engen and William G. Gale (1996). The low intertemporal elasticity of substitution used in our simulations is, in part, a reflection of the fact that not all saving is driven by standard life-cycle concerns. However, the lack of a richer model should be borne in mind in assessing our findings.

We use our model to examine five fundamental tax reforms that span the major proposals currently under discussion. Each reform we consider replaces the federal personal and corporate income taxes in a revenue-neutral manner.⁴ The reforms are a proportional income tax, a proportional consumption tax, a flat tax, a flat tax with transition relief, and the X tax.

The proportional income tax applies a single tax rate to all labor and capital income, with no exemptions or deductions. The proportional consumption tax differs from the proportional income tax by permitting 100-percent expensing of new investment. One may think of it as being implemented via a wage tax at the household level plus a business cash-flow tax. The flat tax differs from the proportional consumption tax by including a standard deduction against wage income and by exempting implicit rental income accruing from the ownership of housing and consumer durables. The remaining two proposals modify the flat tax to address distributional concerns. The flat tax with transition relief aids existing asset holders by permitting continued depreciation of old capital (capital in existence at the commencement of the reform). The X tax aids lower-income taxpayers by substituting the flat tax's single-rate wage tax with a progressive wage tax. To recoup the lost revenue, its sets the business cash-flow tax rate equal to the highest tax rate applied to wage income. Alternatively, one can think of the X tax as a high-rate flat tax with a progressive subsidy to wages.

Each of the reforms broadens the tax base, permitting reductions in statutory marginal tax rates on labor supply and saving. And each reform imposes an implicit tax on existing wealth by introducing full expensing and, thus, shifting the tax structure toward consumption taxation. The expensing of new capital effectively eliminates the taxation of capital income at the margin. However, unlike the simple elimination of capital-income taxes, this tax reduction is available to new capital only, and, consequently, reduces the value of existing capital relative to that of new capital in a manner equivalent to that of a one-time tax on their

---

² The Fullerton-Rogers model, in contrast, assumes that all agents face the same marginal tax rate independent of income.

³ See Congressional Budget Office (CBO, 1997).

⁴ To be precise, in each tax reform simulation the levels of government purchases and outstanding debt are held constant through time when measured in effective units of labor.

wealth. As discussed in Auerbach and Kotlikoff (1987), this capital levy is crucial to both the efficiency and long-run welfare gains from switching to consumption taxation. It permits a permanent reduction in distortionary marginal tax rates and shifts the burden of paying for government spending from young and future generations to middle-age and older initial wealth owners.

As indicated, the five reforms differ in the treatment of marginal and inframarginal capital income, the extent of base broadening, and progressivity. These differences translate into different income and substitution effects on consumption and labor supply which, in turn, generate the different responses to the five policies. These responses depend on our choices of parameter values. In our base case results we find the following:

The proportional income tax raises the long-run level of output by almost 5 percent. It also generates sizable increases in the capital stock and the supply of labor. However, the reform hurts the poor, who face low effective rates of income taxation under the current federal income tax system due to its deductions and exemptions. The proportional consumption tax raises long-run output by over 9 percent. The implicit wealth tax generated by this reform reduces the welfare of the initial middle-aged and elderly. They respond to this and the increase in after-tax interest rates by consuming less and working more, which raises national saving and investment. The expanded capital stock and reduced fiscal burden make most of those alive in the long run significantly better off. However, eliminating tax progressivity lowers the welfare of the poorest members of society.

The flat tax's standard deduction alleviates some of the distributional concerns raised by the proportional income and proportional consumption taxes. But this deduction increases the tax rate needed to satisfy the government's intertemporal budget constraint. Consequently, long-run output rises by less than 5 percent. Although the flat tax's standard deduction insulates the poor from welfare losses, it hurts middle-income groups, especially in the short run but even in the long run. Its capital levy also hurts initial high-income elderly cohorts. Those welfare losses must be set against the welfare gains enjoyed by all groups in the long run.

Adding transition relief to the flat tax limits the welfare losses of initial capital owners. But this modification of the flat tax reduces aggregate income gains again, with long-run output now rising by less than 2 percent. Furthermore, because replacement tax rates must increase to compensate for the lost revenue associated with transition relief, all but the richest and poorest lifetime-income groups suffer welfare losses in the long run. The X tax, which raises long-term output by 6.4 percent, provides no transition relief. It also confronts the rich with higher effective tax rates on their labor supply. It is not surprising, then, that the X tax helps those who are poor in the long run by more than it helps those who are rich. Still, all long-run cohorts gain.

Thus, fundamental reform of the U.S. tax system offers significant long-run gains in output and general welfare, but these gains come at the expense of certain groups. Modifications that mitigate adverse transition and distributional effects also substantially reduce the long-run gains. In considering the plausibility of the results, one should bear in mind that these changes are generally much more radical than any U.S. fiscal policy change enacted in recent memory. Moreover, the structure of economic incentives and the distribution of resources are being altered in two ways—by the policies themselves and by their general equilibrium impacts on the time paths of factor prices. Hence, simple intuition about the expected magnitude of individual responses is difficult to apply to the reforms being considered.

I. The Model

A. *Demographic Structure*

The model's agents differ by their dates of birth and their lifetime labor-productivity endowments. Every cohort includes 12 lifetime-earnings groups, each with its own endowment of human capital and pattern of growth in this endowment over its lifetime. The lifetime-earnings groups also differ with respect to their bequest preferences. All agents live for 55 periods with certainty (corresponding to adult ages 21 through 75), and each j-type generation is $1 + n$ times larger than its predecessor. At age 21, each j-type cohort gives birth to a cohort of the same type. Population growth is exogenous, and each cohort is $(1 + n)^{20}$ larger than its parent cohort.

B. Preferences and Household Budget Constraints

Each j-type agent who begins her economic life at date t chooses perfect-foresight consumption paths (c), leisure paths (l), and intergenerational transfers (b) to maximize a time-separable utility function of the form

$$(1) \quad U_t^j = \frac{1}{1-\frac{1}{\gamma}} \left[\sum_{s=21}^{75} \beta^{s-21} \left(c_{s,t+s-21}^{j\,1-\frac{1}{\rho}} \right. \right.$$
$$\left. \left. + \alpha l_{s,t+s-21}^{j\,1-\frac{1}{\rho}} \right)^{\frac{1-\frac{1}{\gamma}}{1-\frac{1}{\rho}}} + \beta^{54} \mu^j b_{75,t+54}^{j\,1-\frac{1}{\gamma}} \right].$$

In (1), α is the utility weight on leisure, γ is the intertemporal elasticity of substitution in the leisure/consumption composite, and ρ is the intratemporal elasticity of substitution between consumption and leisure. The parameter μ^j is a j-type specific utility weight placed on bequests left to each child when the agent dies, representing a "joy of giving" bequest motive, a formulation of bequest preferences studied by Alan S. Blinder (1973) and others. The term $\beta = 1/(1 + \delta)$, where δ is the rate of time preference, is assumed to be the same for all agents.[5]

Letting $a_{s,t}^j$ be capital holdings for type j agents, of age s, at time t, maximization of (1) is subject to a lifetime budget constraint defined by the sequence:

$$(2) \quad a_{s+1,t+1}^j$$
$$= (1 + r_t)(a_{s,t}^j + g_{s,t}^j) + w_{s,t}^j(E_{s,t}^j - l_{s,t}^j)$$

$$- c_{s,t}^j - \sum_{k=1}^{K} T^k(B_{s,t}^{j,k}) - Nb_{s,t}^j,$$

$$l_{s,t}^j \leq E_{s,t}^j,$$

and

$$a_{75,t}^j \geq 0,$$

where r_t is the pretax return to savings, $g_{s,t}^j$ are inheritances received from parents, $E_{s,t}^j$ is the time endowment, $b_{s,t}^j$ are bequests made to each of the $N = (1 + n)^{20}$ children, and the functions $T^k(\cdot)$ (with tax bases $B_{s,t}^{j,k}$ as arguments) determine net tax payments from income sources $k = 1, \ldots, K$. All taxes are collected at the household level, and the tax system includes both a personal income tax and a business profits tax. There are no liquidity constraints, so the assets in (2) can be negative, although terminal wealth—the wealth left over after final period bequests are made—must be nonnegative.

An individual's earnings ability is an exogenous function of age, type, and the level of labor-augmenting technical progress, which grows at a constant rate λ. We summarize all skill differences by age and type via an efficiency parameter ε_s^j. Thus, the wage rate for an agent of type j and age s is $w_{s,t}^j = \varepsilon_s^j w_t$, where w_t is the real wage at time t. The term ε_s^j increases with age to reflect not only the accumulation of human capital, but also the technical progress that occurs over the course of each individual's life; i.e., the values of ε_s^j are set to establish a realistic longitudinal age-wage profile. To permit balanced growth without a further restriction of preferences (i.e., to keep the ratio of labor supply to labor endowment constant in the steady state), we model the growth in lifetime wages from one generation to the next as growth in time endowment rather than in the wage rate per unit of time; that is, we assume that technical progress causes the time endowment of each successive generation to grow at rate λ.[6] Thus, if $E_{s,t}^j$ is the endowment

---

[5] The relationship between γ, ρ, and the elasticity of labor supply with respect to the current wage is discussed in an unpublished Appendix, available upon request.

[6] Both of these adjustments, to the slope of the wage profile and to the time endowment, are needed to incorporate the impact of technical progress on wage growth, the

of type j at age s and time t, then $E_{s,t}^j = (1 + \lambda) E_{s,t-1}^j$, for all s, t, and j. Because E grows at rate λ from one cohort to the next, technical progress imparts no underlying trend to w_t.

Children receive transfers, with interest, at the beginning of the period after their parents make them. We restrict parental transfers to bequests, so that $b_{s,t}^j = 0$, for $s \neq 75$, and $g_{s,t}^j = 0$, for $s \neq 56$. In the steady state, therefore, $g^j = b^j$, for all j (with age subscripts dropped for convenience).

C. *The Government*

At each time t, the government collects tax revenues and issues debt (D_{t+1}) that it uses to finance government purchases of goods and services (G_t) and interest payments on the inherited stock of debt (D_t). Letting φ^j stand for the fraction of j-type agents in each generation, the government's official debt evolves according to:

$$(3) \quad D_{t+1} + (1+n)^t \sum_{j=1}^{12} \varphi^j$$

$$\times \sum_{s=21}^{75} (1+n)^{-(s-21)} \sum_{k=1}^{K} T^k(B_{s,t}^{j,k})$$

$$= G_t + (1 + r_t) D_t.$$

Government purchases are assumed to be either (a) unproductive and generate no utility to households, or (b) be fixed and enter household utility functions in a separable fashion. The values of G_t and D_t are held fixed per effective worker throughout the transition path. Any reduction in government outlays resulting from a change in the government's real interest payments is passed on to households in the form of a lower tax rate.

The model also has a Social Security system that incorporates Old-Age and Survivors Insurance (OASI), Disability Insurance (DI), and Medicare's Hospital Insurance (HI). Old-age benefits are calculated according to the progressive statutory bend-point formula. Disability and Medicare benefits are provided as lump-sum transfers. The OASI payroll tax is set at 9.9 percent and applied to wage income up to a limit of $62,700. HI and DI tax rates are set at 2.9 percent and 1.9 percent, respectively. Like the OASI tax, DI contributions apply only to wages below $62,700. The HI tax, by contrast, is not subject to an earnings ceiling.

Benefits are scaled to reflect spousal and survivor benefits using distributional information provided in the 1997 OASDI Trustees Report. We set the perceived marginal link between the OASI contributions and the OASI benefits at 25 percent. The perceived effective OASI tax rate is, thus, 7.4 percent—75 percent of 9.9 percent.[7] Lump-sum HI and DI benefits are provided on an equal basis to agents above and below age 65, respectively.

D. *Firms and Technology*

Aggregate capital (K) and labor (L) equal the respective sums of individual asset and labor supplies as indicated in equations (4) and (5).

$$(4) \quad K_t = (1+n)^t \sum_{j=1}^{12} \varphi^j$$

$$\times \sum_{s=21}^{75} (1+n)^{-(s-21)} a_{s,t}^j - D_t,$$

$$(5) \quad L_t = (1+n)^t \sum_{j=1}^{12} \varphi^j$$

$$\times \sum_{s=21}^{75} (1+n)^{-(s-21)} \varepsilon_s^j (E_{s,t}^j - l_{s,t}^j).$$

Output (net of depreciation) is produced by identical competitive firms using a neoclassical, constant-returns-to-scale production tech-

---

former because we assume that each cohort's time endowment is fixed at birth. See Auerbach et al. (1989) for a detailed discussion of this approach.

[7] See Chapter 10 of Auerbach and Kotlikoff (1987) for a more detailed discussion.

nology. In the base case, the aggregate production technology is the standard Cobb-Douglas form:

$$(6) \quad Y_t = AK_t^\theta L_t^{1-\theta},$$

where Y_t is aggregate output (national income) and θ is capital's share in production. However, in later simulations, we do consider the impact of a lower elasticity of substitution in production, σ, using a constant-elasticity-of-substitution (CES) function.

Another important aspect of the production technology is the assumption that it is costly to adjust the capital stock. Tax reforms, particularly those that eliminate the marginal tax on capital income, can induce large increases in demand for capital. The extent to which increased demand translates into more investment, rather than higher asset values, affects both the efficiency of the tax reform and its distributional consequences. We model adjustment costs as convex, indeed as a simple quadratic function of investment:

$$(7) \quad C(I_t) = [1 + 0.5\psi(I_t/K_t)]I_t$$

with the quadratic term ψ equal to 10, a value consistent with the recent results of Jason G. Cummins et al. (1994). With convex adjustment costs, investors will be induced to smooth out increases in investment, and the shadow price of new capital goods relative to their replacement cost—Tobin's q—will move in the same direction as investment.[8]

The competitive pretax, pre-expensing rate of return to capital at time t is given by the marginal product of capital (defined in terms of the capital-labor ratio, κ)

[8] The restriction of our model to a single composite capital good means that we are unable to study the differential revaluation of housing, equipment, plant, inventories, and other forms of capital arising from tax reforms. The fact that the market values of particular capital goods may change to a greater degree than those of others means that we may be under- or overstating saving and labor-supply responses to tax reforms, particularly if different capital goods are disproportionately held by particular age-groups and particular income classes within those age-groups.

$$(8) \quad R_t = \theta A \kappa_t^{\theta-1}.$$

In general, tax systems treat new and existing capital differently. Under the consumption tax, new capital is permitted immediate expensing, while existing capital receives no such deduction. Even under the existing income tax, the combined effect of accelerated depreciation and the lack of inflation indexing makes the depreciation allowances per unit of existing capital lower than those given new capital. We model provisions that treat new and existing capital differently using the mechanism of fractional expensing of new capital, at rate z. That is, we set z to account for the extent to which new capital faces a lower effective tax rate than does existing capital (with $z = 1$ under the consumption tax). If τ_t^K is the time-t marginal tax rate on net capital income (i.e., the tax rate applied to capital income net of expensing) then, given (7), arbitrage between new and existing capital implies that the latter has a unit value of

$$(9) \quad q_t = (1 - z_t \tau_t^K) + (1 - \tau_t^K)\psi(I_t/K_t),$$

assuming that adjustment costs are expensed. Equation (9) equals Tobin's q. Note that q depends not only on the strength of demand for new capital (via the second term), but also on the relative treatment of old and new capital. Tax reforms typically affect both of these terms.

The arbitrage condition arising from profit maximization implies that the posttax return is:

$$(10) \quad \tilde{r}_t = \frac{(R_t + 0.5\psi(I_t/K_t)^2)(1 - \tau_t^K) + q_{t+1} - q_t}{q_t}.$$

In (10), the total return to capital includes its after-tax marginal product[9] plus capital gains.

II. Calibration

Much of our model's parameterization is relatively standard. Exceptions include earnings-ability profiles and the fiscal structure. We

[9] This equals R_t, as defined in (8), plus the reduction in proportional adjustment costs due the increase in the capital stock. See Auerbach (1989) for a derivation of equations (9) and (10).

TABLE 1—BENCHMARK PARAMETER DEFINITIONS AND VALUES

Symbol	Definition	Value
	Preferences	
α	Utility weight on leisure	1.00
δ	Rate of time preference	0.004
γ	Intertemporal substitution elasticity	0.25
μ^j	Utility weight placed on bequests by income-class j[a]	
ρ	Intratemporal substitution elasticity	0.80
	Human Capital	
ε_s^j	Productivity of agent in income class j at age s.	
	Demographics	
n	Population growth rate	0.01
N	Number of children per adult, $(1 + n)^{20}$	1.22
φ^j	Fraction of agents of income class j[b]	
	Technology	
λ	Rate of technological change	0.01
ψ	Adjustment-cost parameter	0.10
θ	Net capital share	0.25
σ	Constant elasticity of substitution	1.00
	Values of Fiscal Variables in Initial Steady State	
—	Debt service as fraction of National Income	0.0310
—	Disability Insurance tax rate	0.0190
—	Medicare (HI) tax rate	0.0290
—	Social Security (OASI) tax rate	0.0990
—	Social Security replacement rate[c]	
—	Social Security marginal tax-benefit linkage	0.25
—	Payroll-tax ceiling	$62,700
τ^C	Proportional consumption tax	0.113
τ^K	Proportional capital-income tax	0.20
$\tau^W(\cdot)$	Progressive wage tax with deductions and exemptions[d]	
τ^Y	State proportional income tax less evasion adjustment	0.011
—	Reduction of wage base from itemized deductions[e]	0.0755
—	Reduction of wage base from fringe benefits[e]	0.1129
z	Expensing fraction[f]	0.20

[a] Calibrated in the initial state to match the level of bequests—as a fraction of mean national income—in Fullerton and Rogers (1993 Tables 3–8), in 1996 dollars.

[b] $\varphi^1 = 0.02$, $\varphi^2 = 0.08$, $\varphi^i = 0.10$ ($3 \leq i \leq 10$), $\varphi^{11} = 0.08$, $\varphi^{12} = 0.02$.

[c] The statutory progressive bendpoint formula for 1996, scaled up by a factor of 2 to account for the fact that other non-DI benefits (mainly spousal and survivors benefits) account for 50 percent of all benefits paid (see 1996 OASDI Trustees Report Table II.C7).

[d] The 1996 statutory tax function for a single individual with a deduction equal to $9,661 ($4,000 standard deduction, $2,550 personal exemption, and $2,550 · N exemption for dependents).

[e] Total proportional base reduction above the standard deduction therefore equals 0.18845.

[f] Deductions for new investment above economic depreciation and adjustment costs.

turn first to these elements and then discuss more familiar preference and technology parameters. Table 1 summarizes our selected parameters.

A. *Earnings-Ability Profiles*

The growth-adjusted earnings ability profiles in equation (5) are of the form:

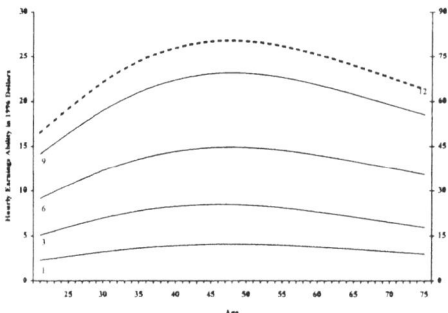

FIGURE 1. EARNINGS-ABILITY PROFILES

(11) $$\varepsilon_s^j = e^{\xi_0^j + (\lambda + \xi_1^j)s + \xi_2^j s^2 + \xi_3^j s^3}$$

where, as discussed above, λ is the constant rate of technical progress. Values of the ξ coefficients for j-type groups 1 through 12—in ascending order of lifetime income—are based on regressions fitted to the University of Michigan's Panel Study of Income Dynamics, using a strategy similar to that in Fullerton and Rogers (1993). The procedure involves (i) regressing the log of hourly wages on fixed-effect dummies, cubics in age, and interactions between age, age-squared, and a set of demographic variables; (ii) using the estimated coefficients from step (i) to generate predicted lifetime-wage profiles; (iii) sorting the data according to the present value of implied lifetime income, and dividing the sorted data into the 12 classes according to lifetime-wage income; and (iv) estimating the coefficients of (11) from the simulated data profiles of each of the 12 groups.

In sorting the data for steps (iii) and (iv), we divided the population into deciles. Groups 1 and 12 comprise the bottom and top 2 percent of lifetime-wage-income earners, and groups 2 and 11 the remaining 8 percent of the top and bottom deciles. Each other group constitutes 10 percent of the population. For example, group 3 is the second decile of lifetime-wage income, group 4 the third decile, and so on up to group 10.[10]

Figure 1 presents the estimated earnings-ability profiles (with group 12's profile scaled by the second vertical axis), adjusted to include the effects of technical progress. Given our benchmark parameterization, peak hourly wages valued in 1996 dollars are $4.00, $14.70, and $79.50 for individuals in classes 1, 6, and 12, respectively. More generally, steady-state annual labor incomes derived from the model's assumptions and from the endogenous labor-supply choices range from $9,000 to $130,000. As discussed below, these calculations include labor compensation in the form of fringe benefits.

B. *Fiscal Structure*

The model includes government purchases of goods and services, government debt, and distortionary taxes. The level of government purchases, G_t, was chosen so that the benchmark steady-state ratio of government purchases to national income equals 0.211. The level of government debt, D_t, was chosen such that the associated real interest payments equal about 3.1 percent of national income in the initial steady state. These values match the corresponding 1996 values for combined local, state, and federal government in the United States.

The benchmark tax system in our initial steady state is designed to approximate the salient aspects of the 1996 U.S. (federal, state, and local) tax and transfer system. It features a hybrid tax system (incorporating wage-income, capital-income, and consumption-tax elements) and payroll taxation for the Social Security and Medicare programs.[11] To adjust for tax evasion, we reduce income taxes by 2.6 percent. This adjustment is consistent with the degree of tax evasion reported in Joel Slemrod and Jon Bakija (1996). In the alternative tax-structure experiments we assume that evasion reduces the post-reform tax base (income net of deductions and exemptions) by the same percentage as before the reform. This is a simplifying assumption that merits exploration in future research.

We approximate the current U.S. tax system by specifying a progressive wage-income tax, a

---

[10] This procedure is described more fully in our unpublished Appendix.

[11] As the payroll tax in our model is used entirely to pay for current benefits, we set the rate slightly below its 15.3-percent statutory rate to account for the portion of payroll taxes devoted to trust-fund accumulation. See Table 2.

flat capital-income tax, a flat state income tax, and a flat consumption tax.

1. *Wage-Income Taxation.*—The wage-income tax structure has four elements: (1) a progressive marginal rate structure derived from a quadratic approximation to the 1996 federal statutory tax rates for individuals;[12] (2) a standard deduction of $4,000 and exemptions of $5,660 (which assumes 1.2 children per agent, consistent with the model's population growth assumption); (3) itemized deductions, applied only when they exceed the amount of the standard deduction, that are a positive linear function of income estimated from data reported in the *Statistics of Income* (Internal Revenue Service, 1996);[13] and (4) earnings-ability profiles that are scaled up to incorporate pension and fringe components of labor compensation.[14]

2. *Capital-Income Taxation.*—Since our model has a single capital good, we need to calibrate marginal and inframarginal capital-income tax rates based on the average values of these rates taken across different types of U.S. capital. Here, we follow closely the calculations in Auerbach (1996), who reports that income from residential capital and nonresidential capital is taxed at flat rates of 6 percent and 26 percent, respectively. Given that the U.S. capital stock is split evenly between these two forms of capital, the weighted average federal marginal tax rate on total capital income is about 16 percent. Because of the difference in treatment of new and existing capital, primarily in the nonresidential sector, U.S. capital faces a higher tax rate—roughly 20 percent for the capital stock as a whole, according to Auerbach's estimates. To incorporate these tax rates in our model, we assume that all capital income faces a 20-percent tax, but that 20 percent of new capital is expensed, thereby generating a 16-percent effective rate on new capital.[15] In addition to the federal taxation, both capital and wage income are subject to a proportional state income tax of 3.7 percent.

3. *Consumption Taxation.*—Consumption taxes in the initial steady state reflect two elements of the existing tax structure. First we impose an 8.8-percent tax on consumption expenditures, consistent with National Income and Product Account (NIPA) values for indirect business and excise revenues, a substantial component of which are state sales taxes. However, because contributions to both defined benefit and defined contribution pension plans receive consumption-tax treatment, we add an additional 2.5-percent tax on household-consumption expenditures to account for the indirect taxation of labor compensation in the form of pension benefits (Auerbach, 1996). This 2.5-percent tax replaces the wage tax that otherwise would apply if pension contributions were taxed as income.

C. *Preferences and Technology*

Our initial choices for the remaining technology, preference, and demographic parameters are summarized in Table 1. The value for δ, the pure rate of time preference—about which there is little evidence—is set equal to 0.004 to generate a realistic value for the capital-output ratio

---

[12] We use a quadratic approximation rather than the exact, discrete brackets to simplify the simulation problem. Using a differentiable tax function allows us to derive first-order conditions that do not involve kink points and shadow wages at these kink points. This simplification is particularly relevant because our household decision problem already has a kink point at the minimum taxable income level, and a potential corner solution at zero hours worked, both of which involve the calculation of shadow wage rates, as well as a nonconvexity at the point where the Social Security earnings ceiling is reached. These additional complications are discussed below in the section that discusses the solution of the model.

[13] The data used in this estimation were taken from all taxable returns in tax year 1993. The function was obtained by regressing deductions exclusive of mortgage interest expense on the midpoints of reported income ranges. (The deduction of interest expense on home mortgages was included in our calculation of the capital-income tax rate, as we will subsequently describe.) The regression yielded a coefficient of 0.0755 with an R^2 equal to 0.99.

[14] Benefits as a function of adjusted gross income (AGI) were kindly provided by Jane Gravelle of the Congressional Research Service and Judy Xanthopoulos of the Joint Committee on Taxation. Based on this information we regressed total benefits on AGI. The regression yielded a coefficient of 0.11295 with an R^2 equal to 0.99. In defining the wage-tax base, we therefore exempt roughly 11 percent of labor compensation from the base calculations.

[15] The absence in our model of heterogenous capital goods means that we not only fail to capture the differential revaluation of different capital goods, but we also fail to capture the additional efficiency gains that may arise from equalizing effective tax rates on different capital inputs, an issue studied by Fullerton and Rogers (1993) and others.

in the initial steady state. The values of γ, ρ, and n are those in Auerbach and Kotlikoff (1987). The intertemporal elasticity, γ, is set equal to 0.25, representing a relatively low degree of substitution between consumption at different dates. While some studies in the literature have found higher elasticities, most have not. One possible reason is the presence of liquidity constraints and other factors that may mitigate the responsiveness of saving to interest-rate changes. Our use of a low intertemporal elasticity of substitution serves as an imperfect proxy for such factors.

We choose α, the utility function's leisure intensity parameter, such that, on average, agents devote about 40 percent of their available time endowment (of 16 hours per day) to labor during their prime working years (roughly ages 21–55). As discussed in the unpublished Appendix, the combined values of γ, ρ (the intratemporal elasticity of substitution), and α generate labor-supply elasticities that are well within the range of empirical estimates. Still, as this range is fairly large, we also report results for values of γ and ρ that induce smaller behavioral responses. The bequest weights in the utility function, μ^j, are chosen to match bequests as a fraction of income in the initial steady state based on estimates by Paul L. Menchik and Martin David (1982) reported in Fullerton and Rogers (1993).

D. Solving the Model

Following Auerbach and Kotlikoff (1987), we solve the model with a Gauss-Seidel algorithm. The calculation starts with guesses for certain key variables and then iterates on those variables until a convergence criterion is met. The model's identifying restrictions are used to compute the remaining economic variables as well as the updates for the iterations. The solution involves several steps and inner loops that solve for household-level variables before moving to an outer loop that solves for the aggregate variables including the time paths of capital stock and aggregate labor supply.

The household optimization problem is subject to the constraint that leisure not exceed the endowment of time [equation (2)]. For those households who would violate the constraint, the model calculates shadow wage rates at which they exactly consume their full-time endowment. The household's budget constraint is kinked due to the tax deductions applied against wage income under the personal income tax. A household with wage income below the deduction level faces marginal and average tax rates equal to zero. A household with wage income above the deduction level faces positive marginal and average tax rates. Due to the discontinuity of the marginal tax rates, it may be optimal for some households to locate exactly at the kink. Our algorithm deals with this problem as follows. We identify a household that chooses to locate at the kink in particular periods by evaluating each period's leisure choice and corresponding wage income above and below the kink. We then calculate a set of period-specific shadow marginal tax rates from the period-specific first-order conditions that put such households exactly at kinks in each period in which being at a kink is optimal. This calculation of shadow tax rates for particular periods is simultaneous; i.e., a shadow tax rate in any particular period will influence labor-supply decisions in all other periods. The payroll-tax ceiling introduces additional complexity by creating a nonconvexity in the budget constraint. For those above the payroll-tax ceiling, the marginal payroll-tax rate on labor earnings is zero. For each period, we evaluate the utility on both sides of the nonconvex section and put households on the side that generates highest utility.

Aggregate variables of the model are solved with a forward-looking algorithm that iterates on the capital stock and labor supply over the entire transition path. Initial guesses are made for (a) the time path of aggregate demands for capital and labor, (b) each household's shadow wage and tax rates at each age, and (c) the endogenous tax rate (for which the program is solving), the payroll-tax rate, and Social Security and Medicare benefit levels. Given the initial guesses of the time paths of all these variables, the model calculates (a) the factor prices in each period that are consistent with the use by firms of the aggregate inputs assumed to be demanded, and (b) the remaining lifetime consumption and leisure choices for all income classes in each current and future cohort. Shadow wages and shadow taxes are calculated to ensure that the time endowment and the tax constraints discussed above are satisfied.

TABLE 2—KEY VARIABLES IN THE INITIAL STEADY STATE AND U.S. DATA

Model		Empirical estimate and calculation	
Concept	Value	Estimate	Calculation (using NIPA unless indicated)
Composition of National Income (fraction)			
Personal consumption	0.731	0.720	Personal consumption expenditures − housing services
Net saving rate	0.051	0.056	(National saving − capital consumption allowance)/NI
Government purchases	0.211	0.212	Consumption expenditures + gross investment for federal (defense and nondefense) and state and local − consumption of fixed capital
Tax Rates and Revenue			
Average marginal wage tax[a]	0.216	0.217	Auerbach (1996) based on the NBER TAXSIM model.
Government revenue	0.239	0.239	Total receipts − contributions for social insurance − property taxes (state and local)
OASDHI tax	0.146	0.147	1996 tax rate is 15.3 which includes trust-fund contributions equal to about 0.6.
The Capital-Output Ratio and the Pretax Rate of Return			
Capital-output ratio	2.562	2.660	(1993 current-cost net stock of fixed reproducible wealth − government-owned fixed capital)/1993 national income
Pretax rate of return[b]	0.083	0.093	The 1960–1994 average of the sum of interest, dividends, retained earnings and all corporate taxes divided by the replacement value of capital stock (Richard Rippe, 1995).

[a] Does not include the payroll tax.
[b] The social marginal rate of return (i.e., before corporate taxes).

Households' labor supply and assets are then aggregated across cohorts and, within cohort, across lifetime-income classes for each period. This aggregation generates a new guess for the time paths of the aggregate supplies of capital stock and labor supply.

In equilibrium, the factor-supply time paths for capital and labor must equal their corresponding factor-demand time paths. Hence, to form a new guess of the time paths of aggregate factor demands we form weighted averages of the initial guess and the supply time paths derived using the previous guess of the time path of factor demands. The time paths of the tax rate for which we are solving and the payroll-tax rate are also updated to meet the revenue-neutrality requirement and to preserve the pay-as-you-go financing of Social Security and Medicare benefits.[16] The algorithm then iterates in this manner until the capital-stock and labor-supply time paths converge; i.e., until the time paths of factors demanded are consistent with the time paths of factors supplied.

E. *The Benchmark Equilibrium*

Table 2 provides summary statistics for the initial steady state. Given our parameter choices, the model generates a pretax, pre-expensing interest rate of 8.3 percent,[17] a net national saving rate of 5.1 percent, and a capital/

[16] Note that the Social Security replacement rate and absolute level of Medicare benefits are exogenous.

[17] This number is somewhat lower than the estimated 1996 percent return to capital relative to replacement cost of 9.3 percent listed in Table 2. In our model with nonzero adjustment costs, the before-tax interest rate determined by expressions (9) and (10) differs from the return to capital, because market value differs slightly from replacement cost [see (9)] and because the total return to capital accounted for by the interest rate also includes the reduction in adjustment costs brought about by additions to capital [see the numerator in (10)]. Ignoring these two terms, the return to capital itself, equal to the term R in (8), is 9.7 percent.

national-income ratio of 2.6. Consumption accounts for 73.1 percent of national income, net investment for 5.1 percent, and government purchases of goods and services for 21.1 percent. These figures are close to their respective 1996 NIPA values.

The calibrated model's initial economywide average marginal tax rate on wage income is 21.6 percent, close to the figure obtained from the NBER's TAXSIM model reported in Auerbach (1996). The average wage-income tax rate equals 12.2 percent. For all individuals in the highest lifetime-income class (group 12), the average effective marginal tax rate on labor income is 29.2 percent. The highest realized effective marginal tax rate is 34.9 percent. For lifetime-income class 6—whose members have peak labor earnings of about $35,000—the average tax rate and average marginal tax rate are 10.7 and 20.0 percent, respectively. For the poorest class (group 1), the corresponding rates are zero and 11.1 percent.[18]

In this initial steady state, bequest wealth (the accumulated value of inheritances received summed over all households) depends on the age structure of bequest receipt. Our assumption that individuals receive bequests at age 56 is made primarily for simplicity.[19] With this assumption, and our calibration of bequests themselves to the data cited earlier, bequest wealth represents 30 percent of the capital stock. This percentage is smaller than that reported for 1974 for overall transfer wealth by Kotlikoff and Lawrence H. Summers (1981). The percentage would, presumably, be larger had we assumed an earlier age of bequest receipt, but still is in rough agreement with the Kotlikoff-Summers findings concerning the amount of wealth generated solely by bequests as opposed to *inter vivos* transfers, which we do not model explicitly. That said, the importance of bequests and *inter vivos* transfers for U.S. capital formation appears to have diminished through time because of the remarkable increase in recent decades in the degree of annuitization of the elderly (see Auerbach et al., 1995).

III. Initial Tax Reform Simulations

Table 3 summarizes the five tax reforms. Table 4 presents simulations for all five reforms for the base case assumptions. In each of these simulations, our initial steady state is the same, calibrated to the 1996 U.S. economy as described above. Table 4 also presents variables of interest for this initial steady state and for three transition years—1997, 2010, and 2145—meant to illustrate short-run, medium-run, and long-run effects. Subsequent tables, described in the next section, present the results of sensitivity analysis involving preference and technology parameters.

A. *A Proportional Income Tax*

Our first experiment replaces the progressive tax on wage income and the proportional tax on capital income with a proportional tax applied to all income. In addition, the proportional income tax eliminates the major preferences in the federal income tax, including the standard deduction, personal and dependent exemptions, itemized deductions, and the preferential tax treatment of fringe benefits. The last of these is implemented by decreasing the consumption tax rate by 0.025 and subjecting all compensation to the new proportional income tax. The investment expensing rate remains at its initial 20-percent level.

The first panel in Table 4 summarizes the aggregate results from this reform. The marginal tax rates required to satisfy the government's budget constraint stay close to 13 percent over the entire transition path. This value lies far below both the 21.6-percent average marginal rate applied to labor income and the 16-percent rate applied to capital income in the benchmark steady state. National income rises by 3.8 percent immediately and by 4.9 percent ultimately. In the early years of the transition, these output changes are dominated by increased work effort associated with the

---

[18] The average marginal rate for people with the lowest income exceeds zero due to positive shadow tax rates in peak earnings years.

[19] See Gale and Scholz (1994) for a discussion of the relative magnitudes of bequests and *inter vivos* transfers. While our choice of age 56 to receive inheritance seems reasonable, different ages could certainly be considered. However, each age of inheritance would alter the stock of inherited wealth and thus the economywide capital-output ratio. As this, in turn, would necessitate a recalibration of bequest preference parameters, the ultimate impact on our results would likely be small.

TABLE 3—KEY ELEMENTS OF TAX REFORM EXPERIMENTS

Experiment	Description

Proportional income tax	Eliminate all tax-base reductions
	  Eliminate the standard deduction, personal exemption, exemptions for dependents, itemized deductions, preferential tax treatment of all fringe benefits (the consumption-tax treatment of pension and the deductibility of nonpension benefits), and the deductibility of state income taxes at the federal level.[a]
	Flattening of tax rates
	  Replace progressive wage tax and proportional capital-income tax with a proportional equal tax rate on wage and capital income. Eliminate double taxation of capital income.

Proportional consumption tax	Eliminate all tax-base reductions Flattening of tax rates Full expensing Allow the deductibility of all new investment.

Standard flat tax	Eliminate all tax-base reductions
	Flattening of tax rates
	Full expensing
	Protection of housing wealth
	  Housing (including consumer durables) remain untaxed.[b]
	Standard deduction
	  Allow for a deduction for a single individual equal to $9,500.

Flat tax with transition relief	Eliminate all tax-base reductions Flattening of tax rates Full expensing Protection of housing wealth Standard deduction Transition relief All existing assets continue to receive depreciation allowances.[c]
X tax	Eliminate all tax-base reductions Preserve current-law progressive wage tax[d] Capital-income tax set at highest marginal wage-tax rate Full expensing Protection of housing wealth[e]

[a] Consumption tax treatment of pensions is eliminated by decreasing the consumption tax by 0.025 and subjecting all compensation to the new proportional income tax.

[b] About 50 percent of the capital stock is composed of housing and consumer durables whose imputed rent is not taxed. Hence, the proportional tax rate on capital income is set to half of the tax rate on wage income.

[c] As noted in Auerbach (1996 footnote 46), under current law and with current inflation, the present value of remaining depreciation allowances per dollar of net nonresidential capital is approximately half the value of the assets. Allowing for these depreciation allowances has the same impact as forgiving half of the cash-flow tax on existing assets. Hence, the cash-flow tax on capital income is set to one quarter of the replacement proportional wage-tax rate.

[d] General-equilibrium effects and the constant government revenue constraint requires proportional shifts in the wage-tax schedule (with an increase in the short run and a decrease in the long run). The average marginal tax rate is reported in Table 4.

[e] Since the highest marginal wage-tax rate in the final steady state equals about 0.30, the capital-income tax is set equal to 0.15.

lower marginal tax rates. In the long run, higher wealth levels mitigate some of the increase in labor supply. However, the accumulated effects on the stock of capital from the reform more than compensate for the reduced labor supply: in the long run the capital stock increases by 5.6 percent. The short-run decrease in the capital-labor ratio produces a short-run increase in the before-tax interest rate and a short-run decrease in before-tax wage rate. The long-run increase in the capital-labor ratio produces the opposite effects on factor prices. This reform's initial impact on the market value of our composite capital good (measured via Tobin's q) is posi-

TABLE 4—BASE CASE RESULTS, FIVE TAX REFORMS

	Year	National income[a]	Capital stock[a]	Labor supply[a]	Net saving rate	Before-tax wage[a]	Interest rate	Normalized Tobin's q	Tax rate[b]
	1996	1.000	1.000	1.000	0.051	1.000	0.083	1.000	0.216
Proportional income tax	1997	1.038	1.002	1.051	0.056	0.988	0.088	1.037	0.135
	2010	1.044	1.030	1.050	0.054	0.995	0.083	1.028	0.131
	2145	1.049	1.056	1.047	0.052	1.001	0.083	1.019	0.130
Proportional consumption tax	1997	1.044	1.010	1.063	0.073	0.987	0.079	0.960	0.142
	2010	1.063	1.108	1.054	0.067	1.013	0.076	0.934	0.138
	2145	1.094	1.254	1.046	0.059	1.046	0.073	0.906	0.127
Flat tax (standard)	1997	1.010	1.006	1.016	0.065	0.997	0.076	0.964	0.214
	2010	1.022	1.059	1.013	0.061	1.011	0.078	0.958	0.211
	2145	1.045	1.150	1.013	0.056	1.032	0.080	0.941	0.199
Flat tax (transition relief)	1997	0.995	1.003	0.994	0.059	1.002	0.081	1.001	0.241
	2010	1.005	1.031	0.998	0.057	1.008	0.080	0.994	0.234
	2145	1.019	1.083	0.998	0.055	1.021	0.078	0.983	0.226
X tax	1997	1.018	1.009	1.027	0.069	0.996	0.063	0.949	0.178
	2010	1.031	1.076	1.019	0.064	1.014	0.077	0.910	0.177
	2145	1.064	1.210	1.020	0.059	1.044	0.074	0.882	0.157

[a] Measured per effective labor unit and indexed with a value of 1.00 in 1996.
[b] Statutory federal rate; for 1996, this is the rate that applies to wage income.

tive, reflecting the increase in saving and demand for capital that results from two factors: the rise in short-run disposable income (due to higher labor supply) and, to a lesser extent (because it does not change much), the lower marginal tax rate on capital income. The second potential effect on q, associated with changes in the relative treatment of old and new capital, is small because the level of expensing has not changed and the effective tax rate on capital income has decreased only slightly (housing capital is no longer exempt).

Figure 2 shows the effects of the tax reform on remaining lifetime utility for different generations by lifetime-income group.[20] For ease of exposition, the figure reports the utility gains only for classes 1, 3, 6, 9, and 12. The horizontal axis of the figure lists the period the generation enters the model—reaches adulthood— relative to the period of the regime shift (period 0). For example, -1 refers to the generation that

[20] We focus on the welfare effects of tax reforms on members of different income groups and generations, rather than on the overall efficiency change that might be calculated by aggregating such individual welfare effects. As our model's disaggregation by income class is largely secondary in the context of an efficiency analysis, it seems unnecessary to repeat the extensive analysis of efficiency already provided in Auerbach (1996), based on the original AK model.

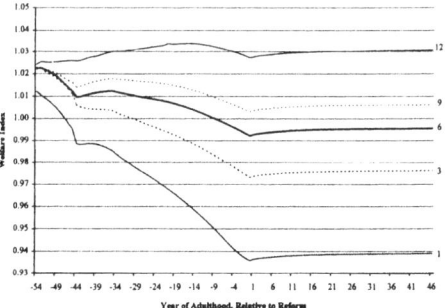

FIGURE 2. REMAINING LIFETIME UTILITY:
PROPORTIONAL INCOME TAX

reaches adulthood just prior to the regime shift, 0 to the generation that reaches adulthood in the period of the shift, 1 in the following period, and so on.[21] The change in remaining lifetime utility is measured as the equivalent variation of remaining *full* lifetime income. In interpreting these numbers, one should keep in mind that full lifetime income includes the value of leisure. In our model, full lifetime income is more

[21] For members of the 55 transition generations, an individual's age at the time of reform equals 21 minus the number on the horizontal axis.

than twice the size of remaining *actual* lifetime earnings. Hence, gains or losses will tend to be larger if measured relative to either realized earnings or consumption.

In the long run, only members of lifetime-income groups 8 through 12 experience increased utility from the proportional income-tax reform, the rise in aggregate output notwithstanding. The main reason is that average tax rates increase for income classes 1 through 7 due to the loss of deductions and exemptions. In the short run, however, the oldest agents at the time of the reform are slightly better off since the reform increases the after-tax return to capital.

B. *A Proportional Consumption Tax*

Our proportional consumption tax differs from the proportional income tax by including full expensing of investment expenditures. The government is now taxing income less domestic investment, which, in our closed economy, equals income less saving, i.e., consumption. Formally, we specify the consumption tax as a combination of a labor-income tax and a business cash-flow tax. The second panel of Table 4 summarizes aggregate effects. The first thing to note is the 4-percent drop in q—the value of the existing capital stock relative to new capital. This drop occurs even though the rate of investment surges, because the impact of investment demand on q is more than offset by the sharp increase in the tax advantage of new versus old capital. This second effect constitutes the one-time effective tax on existing capital assets mentioned above.

In the period just after the tax reform, labor supply increases by 6.3 percent, a higher effect than was observed under the proportional income tax. This is because there are now additional factors at work beyond the reduction in marginal labor-income tax rates. The rise in after-tax interest rates (because capital income is now essentially untaxed) produces substitution effects that encourage delays not only in consumption, but also in leisure, impacts reinforced by the negative wealth effect among those holding old capital.[22] These two factors

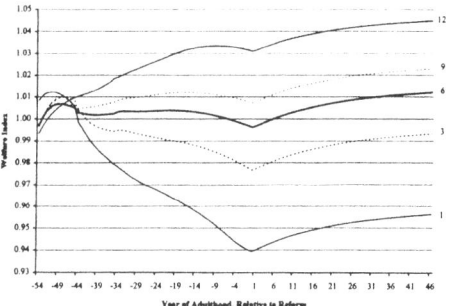

FIGURE 3. REMAINING LIFETIME UTILITY: PROPORTIONAL CONSUMPTION TAX

also generate a substantial short-run jump in the saving rate from 5.1 percent to 7.3 percent. However, as the initial negative wealth effects diminish over time and interest rates fall with the growth in capital, the saving rate eventually recedes to 5.9 percent. Fourteen years into the reform (in 2010), the capital stock (per effective unit of labor) is 10.8 percent larger than its initial steady-state value, and output is 6.3 percent larger. In the long run, the capital stock exceeds its initial value by 25.4 percent, and output exceeds its initial value by 9.4 percent, strong reactions that permit the consumption tax rate to fall over time, from 14.2 percent initially to a long-run 12.7 percent.

Figure 3 shows that, despite the large aggregate income gains, lower lifetime-income groups are hurt by the reform. Although these losses are not as large as those in the proportional income-tax case—indeed, several groups switch from being long-run utility losers to long-run utility winners—the regressive nature of the outcomes persists. The figure also reveals welfare losses for initial rich elderly, who own the lion's share of the existing capital stock.[23] In contrast, the initial poorest elderly gain from the tax reform. There are two reasons. First, this

---

[22] There is also an income effect associated with the rise in interest rates, equal to the reduction in the present value of future consumption less the present value of future labor

income. These income effects will generally be positive and discourage saving, though the effect will be much smaller than in the simple two-period life-cycle model with first-period labor supply, in which only the future-consumption term is present.

[23] Their welfare loss is less than the 4-percent capital loss they experience on their holdings of capital, because much of their welfare comes in the form of leisure.

group consumes almost entirely out of Social Security benefits, the real value of which are unaffected by the change in asset values. Second, this group also borrows against some of their Social Security benefits prior to retirement, and their slightly negative net worth in old age shrinks in magnitude due to the policy-induced fall in the value of existing capital.

C. *The Flat Tax*

Our flat-tax experiment modifies the proportional consumption tax by including a standard deduction of $9,500. In addition, it fully exempts housing wealth—about half of the capital stock—from taxation. Because policy makers are unlikely to extend the capital levy to housing, this exemption is an important step toward realism.[24]

As the third panel in Table 4 makes clear, the need to finance the standard deduction and tax exemption of existing housing increases the replacement tax rates well above those of the proportional consumption tax. As a result, the output effects under the flat tax are substantially reduced relative to its proportional counterpart. The long-run rise in the capital stock and level of output are, respectively, only 59 and 48 percent as large as those under the proportional consumption tax. The labor-supply response is lower as well, reflecting the higher short- and long-run levels of marginal tax rates. The revenue-neutral flat-tax rate equals 21.4 percent initially and reaches 19.9 percent in the long run. The short-run impact on Tobin's q is quite similar to that of the proportional consumption tax, but this masks two offsetting effects. Investment demand rises less under the flat tax, moderating the positive impact of this factor on q. On the other hand, as the flat tax exempts much of existing wealth from the implicit tax on old capital, it also moderates this factor's negative impact on q. In the longer run, as the first difference declines in importance (with net investment converging to zero in both instances), the second effect predominates, resulting in a higher value of q under the flat tax.

---

[24] To impose the capital levy on existing housing would require taxing current owners' imputed rent and eventual sale proceeds.

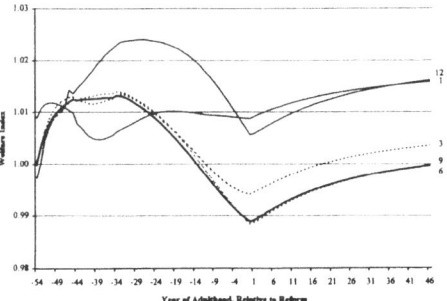

FIGURE 4. REMAINING LIFETIME UTILITY: FLAT TAX (STANDARD)

Figure 4 shows that the flat tax generates short-run utility effects that are similar to those of the consumption tax. The long-run utility changes are bunched much more closely than those of either of the proportional tax reforms. This reflects the flat tax's attention to preserving progressivity. Interestingly, the highest relative gains are for the richest and poorest lifetime-income groups, with the poorest gaining from the higher standard deduction and the richest from the flattened marginal-rate schedule.

The utility changes for the richest and poorest lifetime-income groups also differ from those of the middle groups throughout the entire transition path. Group 12 benefits the most from reduced marginal and average tax rates. Group 1, which pays very little taxes under either regime, benefits from the overall increase in wages. For those in income groups 3 through 9, the marginal and average tax rates initially change little or even rise. This stems from the revenue neutrality of the experiment, which requires a flat-tax marginal rate that initially exceeds the prereform tax rates for some agents in the middle-income classes in order to finance the lower tax rates at the top end. Those who belong to the lifetime-middle-income range and enter the workforce close to the time of reform suffer utility losses along the transition path. They face relatively high tax rates of 20 to 22 percent on labor income for 20 to 25 years of their working life before the growth of the capital stock becomes fully effective. Once the economy grows, though, tax rates fall and wages rise, which leaves group 3 better off and raises the lifetime utility levels of groups 6 through 9 to the point of indifference.

Neither the macroeconomic variables nor the welfare effects of the flat-tax experiment are substantially influenced by the existence of a bequest motive. We repeated the simulation by "turning off" bequests (setting the utility bequest weight $\mu^j = 0$ for all j), simultaneously reducing the rate of time preference slightly (from 0.004 to 0.002) to maintain the same initial steady-state capital-output ratio. The resulting transition path was nearly identical to that just discussed, with the long-run increases in national income, the capital stock, and labor supply equal to 4.6 (versus 4.5) percent, 15.3 (versus 15.0) percent, and 1.4 (versus 1.3) percent, respectively, and no significant differences in the remaining initial steady-state computations nor in the postreform changes in output or welfare.[25] While it might seem surprising that eliminating bequests has so little impact, it should be remembered that bequests are modeled here as basically another type of future consumption. Thus, the motivations for bequest saving and life-cycle saving are essentially the same.

D. *The Flat Tax with Transition Relief*

One important characteristic of consumption-tax reform is its treatment of existing assets and their owners. In contrast to the positive welfare gains they receive under the switch to proportional income taxation, older, higher-wealth asset holders lose with the adoption of the proportional consumption tax or the flat tax. Though these losses are moderated by the surge in asset demand that limits the decline in existing asset values, the presence of such losses may make transition relief for existing assets a political necessity. Our fourth experiment adds transition relief to the flat tax by extending prereform depreciation rules for capital in place at the time of the tax reform. Since the present value of depreciation allowances equals roughly 50 percent of the nonresidential capital stock, transition relief is

---

[25] Because of the extreme similarity to the simulation just presented, the results for this experiment are not shown separately in the table.

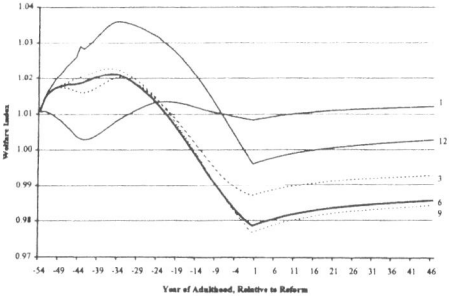

FIGURE 5. REMAINING LIFETIME UTILITY: FLAT TAX (TRANSITION RELIEF)

modeled by cutting the effective cash-flow tax rate in half.

As the fourth panel of Table 4 confirms, all of the salutary long-run aggregate effects of the standard flat tax are mitigated by the introduction of transition relief, which must be financed by permanently higher tax rates. The transition relief is, in some sense, excessive, in that the value of existing assets actually rises slightly in the short run. Still, the capital stock increases by over 8 percent in the long run, affording a 1.9-percent rise in the long-run level of output. Labor supply changes little following this tax reform, actually declining slightly below its initial steady-state level, reflecting both higher marginal tax rates (on average) and positive wealth effects.

Figure 5, which shows the welfare effects of the flat tax with transition relief, differs markedly from Figure 4, which shows the effects with no transition relief. Transition relief replaces the small short-run welfare losses of the wealthier initial elderly with sizable welfare gains, and raises the welfare gains of all income classes who are in their middle ages when the reform is begun. But these welfare gains come at the cost of smaller welfare gains for certain future generations and welfare losses for others. For example, with no transition relief, the long-run rich (members of groups 12 alive in the long run) experience more than a 1.6-percent gain in welfare. But with transition relief, these gains are cut nearly to zero. For middle-class households alive in the long run, the concession to initial wealth holders transforms the flat tax from having essentially no impact to a roughly

1.5-percent loser when measured in terms of its welfare impact. Indeed, with the exception of the very poorest and very richest members of society, transition relief transforms the flat tax into a bad deal for those alive in the medium and long runs. This is critically important to keep in mind in assessing calls for a flat tax. Many advocates of the flat tax favor transition relief, apparently without sufficient understanding that offsetting wealth effects are already present, and that short-run relief undermines the results they claim the flat tax will achieve in the long run.

E. *The X Tax*

The X tax, using the present-law standard deduction, maintains the progressivity of the present-law wage-tax schedule. It also sets the cash-flow tax rate equal to the highest marginal tax rate on labor income, in this case 30 percent.[26] An important reason for choosing equal rates of tax on labor and cash flow under the flat tax was that doing so eliminates the incentive for businesses to shift income. Under the X tax, the cash-flow tax rate cannot equal all marginal tax rates on labor income simultaneously, but setting it equal to the highest labor-income tax rate is nearly as effective, as most potential shifting would involve high-income executives and business owners in the top labor-income bracket. However, an interesting byproduct of this design feature is that it raises the levy on old capital above that imposed by the basic flat tax. This higher capital levy offsets the rise in marginal tax rates on labor income due to progressivity, for it reduces the present value of revenue that labor-income taxes must raise.

As shown in the bottom panel of Table 4, this reform produces large long-run output gains despite maintaining progressive wage taxation. Only the proportional consumption tax generates larger long-run output gains. The long-run welfare effects of the X tax are progressive. As shown in Figure 6, the long-run gains vary inversely with lifetime income. However, the percentage gains across groups are closer for

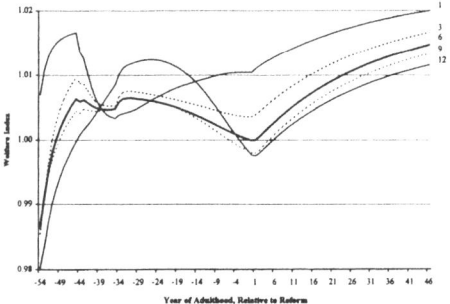

FIGURE 6. REMAINING LIFETIME UTILITY: X TAX

this proposal than for any other, suggesting that, in the long run, it is—as intended—the least disruptive in its distributional impact. All groups experience welfare gains of between 1 and 2 percent of full lifetime resources. In the short run, though, those in the highest income class who are old at the time of the reform suffer the largest welfare loss—reaching 2 percent of remaining lifetime resources—since they hold the largest share of physical assets. The poorest elderly, on the other hand, actually benefit from the capital levy since they live essentially on their Social Security benefits which are, in fact, a source of a slight amount of borrowing.

IV. Sensitivity Analysis

This section considers the impact of changes in assumptions regarding three key elasticity parameters for two of the tax reforms just considered, the standard flat tax and the flat tax with transition relief. In each instance, we make offsetting parameter adjustments to maintain the correspondence between our initial steady state and the benchmark economy. Table 5 presents the results of reductions in the production elasticity of substitution between labor and capital, σ, and the utility function's intratemporal elasticity, ρ, and intertemporal elasticity, γ.

The first panel of the table presents simulations for the CES production function,

(12) $Y_t = A[\theta K_t^{1-1/\sigma} + (1-\theta)L_t^{1-1/\sigma}]^{\frac{1}{1-1/\sigma}}$

in which the production elasticity of substitution, σ, is reduced from 1 (i.e., Cobb-Douglas)

---

[26] Recall that marginal wage-tax rates are a linear function of taxable labor income. The adjustments required to maintain budget balance are implemented by changing the intercept of this function, while holding the slope constant.

TABLE 5—SENSITIVITY ANALYSIS

	Year	National income[a]	Capital stock[a]	Labor supply[a]	Net saving rate	Before-tax wage[a]	Interest rate	Normalized Tobin's q	Tax rate[b]
$\sigma = 0.8$									
	1996	1.000	1.000	1.000	0.051	1.000	0.083	1.000	0.216
Flat tax (standard)	1997	1.009	1.006	1.014	0.064	0.994	0.077	0.967	0.215
	2010	1.022	1.055	1.013	0.060	1.010	0.078	0.952	0.210
	2145	1.043	1.136	1.015	0.056	1.032	0.078	0.936	0.198
Flat tax (transition relief)	1997	0.994	1.003	0.993	0.059	1.000	0.081	1.000	0.241
	2010	1.004	1.029	0.998	0.057	1.007	0.080	0.993	0.234
	2145	1.018	1.075	1.000	0.054	1.020	0.081	0.982	0.226
$\rho = 0.4$									
	1996	1.000	1.000	1.000	0.049	1.000	0.086	1.000	0.213
Flat tax (standard)	1997	1.008	1.006	1.013	0.063	0.998	0.081	0.971	0.213
	2010	1.016	1.057	1.005	0.059	1.013	0.081	0.953	0.211
	2145	1.028	1.136	0.996	0.055	1.033	0.078	0.935	0.203
Flat tax (transition relief)	1997	1.001	1.003	1.002	0.057	1.000	0.084	1.005	0.235
	2010	1.007	1.033	1.000	0.055	1.008	0.083	0.995	0.227
	2145	1.015	1.080	0.995	0.054	1.021	0.082	0.987	0.225
$\gamma = 0.1$									
	1996	1.000	1.000	1.000	0.051	1.000	0.083	1.000	0.216
Flat tax (standard)	1997	1.007	1.003	1.010	0.057	0.998	0.075	0.947	0.211
	2010	1.007	1.019	1.004	0.054	1.004	0.082	0.932	0.217
	2145	1.013	1.038	1.005	0.053	1.008	0.081	0.928	0.213
Flat tax (transition relief)	1997	0.990	1.000	0.986	0.050	1.003	0.077	0.974	0.239
	2010	0.985	0.985	0.984	0.047	1.000	0.083	0.965	0.244
	2145	0.969	0.920	0.983	0.049	0.983	0.088	0.975	0.256

[a] Measured per effective labor unit and indexed with a value of 1.00 in 1996.
[b] Statutory federal rate; for 1996, this is the rate that applies to wage income.

to 0.8, a reasonable alternative value to our base case assumption.[27] As one would expect, the lower elasticity of substitution means that the before-tax interest rate falls by more as capital accumulates, somewhat dampening the capital accumulation incentive. Thus, while the long-run interest rate is 8.0 percent in the base case for the standard flat tax displayed in Table 4, it is 7.8 percent in the corresponding run in Table 5 for $\sigma = 0.8$; the long-run gain in the capital stock is reduced from 15.0 percent to 13.6 percent. However, these differences, as well as those in other variables, are small. The same conclusion holds for the case of transition relief.

As discussed above, there is considerable uncertainty about the "correct" values of the parameters γ and ρ. It is therefore important to determine how sensitive the results presented thus far are to reasonable variations in these parameters. In each case, because we pose the question in terms of whether tax reform might *fail* to produce welfare and income gains, we consider *smaller* values of these elasticity parameters, which reduce the degree to which agents react to improved incentives. However, one can use these simulations to infer the effects of raising γ or ρ. The second panel of Table 5 presents results for each of the two flat-tax variants, with the value of the intratemporal elasticity of substitution, ρ, reduced from 0.8 to 0.4. The bottom panel covers the same two reforms, this time with the intertemporal elasticity of substitution, γ, reduced from 0.25 to 0.1.[28]

---

[27] As we reduce the production elasticity, we also change the capital intensity parameter, θ, from 0.25 to 0.312, and multiply the production efficiency parameter, A, by 0.962. It is a matter of simple algebra to show that these two changes ensure that the levels of capital and labor and the wage and interest rates in the initial steady state are the same as for the base case with Cobb-Douglas production.

[28] We adjust δ to -0.08 to preserve the initial capital-output ratio when changing γ. However, when changing ρ, we adjust the labor intensity parameter α to 0.2, in order also to maintain the appropriate share of labor supply in total labor endowment.

The experiment with a smaller intratemporal elasticity of substitution looks quite similar to the flat-tax case under our benchmark parameterization (in Table 4) in the early stages of the transition path. However, in the long run, the decreased willingness to substitute higher consumption for leisure results in a decline in aggregate labor supply relative to the higher elasticity case. The smaller increase in labor supply contributes to a smaller increase in the level of saving (even though the saving *rate* is similar) and capital accumulation. As a result, capital growth is smaller as well and, although real wage growth is similar to before, the slower growth in both labor and capital makes income growth smaller as well, only 2.8 percent in the long run, instead of 4.5 percent. The relative impact is similar when transition relief is added.

The effects of the smaller intertemporal elasticity of substitution are greater, because this change reduces the responsiveness not only of labor supply, but of consumption as well. Thus, in addition to the smaller labor-supply response just observed, we also see a smaller increase in the saving rate. As a result, short-run and long-run output gains are even smaller than in the second panel of the table. Under the pure flat tax, output rises by just 1.3 percent in the long run; with transition relief added, long-run output actually falls by 3.1 percent. Thus, there is no guarantee that a realistic consumption tax reform—the flat tax with transition relief—will raise output in the long run.

V. Summary and Conclusion

Proponents and opponents of fundamental tax reform wrestle with the same question: Are the gains to the winners worth the costs to the losers? The answer involves value judgments that go beyond economic science. But forming one's judgments requires knowing what fundamental tax reform will do to the economy and to its current and future participants. This paper tries to provide a better sense of those outcomes by simulating fundamental tax reform in a much-improved version of the Auerbach-Kotlikoff model—one that considers intra- as well as intergenerational equity and one that is closely calibrated to U.S. fiscal institutions and tax policy.

The model predicts significant long-run increases in output from replacing the current U.S. federal tax system with a proportional consumption tax. For our base case, output would rise eventually by more than 9 percent. For middle- and upper-income classes alive in the long run, this policy is a big winner. But older transition generations suffer from the imposition of an implicit capital levy, and low-income individuals, even in the long run, suffer a significant loss as growth fails to compensate for the decline in tax progressivity.

The flat tax, which modifies the basic consumption tax by exempting housing wealth from taxation and by providing a large wage-tax deduction, improves the welfare of lower-income individuals in the long run, but at a cost of more than halving the economy's long-run output rise, to 4.5 percent for the same economic assumptions. Even then, this reform leaves initial older generations worse off. Insulating them through transition relief, in the form of maintaining present-law depreciation allowances on existing capital, further reduces the long-run output increase—to just 1.9 percent.

Other reforms produce similar trade-offs. Switching to a proportional income tax hurts current and future low-lifetime earners but helps everyone else. The X tax, which combines consumption-tax and progressive wage-tax elements, makes everyone better off in the long run and raises output by even more than the flat tax. But this reform harms initial older generations who face an implicit tax on their wealth. Further, with smaller but still plausible labor supply and saving responses to tax changes, the potential gains and hence the scope for trading off efficiency for equity are reduced. Indeed, the last reform considered, a flat tax that offers transition relief, actually reduces output in the long run for a low intertemporal elasticity of substitution. Presumably, this is not what proponents of tax reform have in mind.

Thus, the view formed on the basis of our model is that fundamental reform of the current U.S. tax structure offers the possibility of significant macroeconomic expansion and welfare gains for many, but not without true sacrifice by certain groups. Adjustments that attempt to prevent adverse distributional effects yield much more modest aggregate effects. While we have not sought to identify more complicated policies that shield all losers from sacrifice, our findings do suggest that such policies, if they exist, are likely to yield much smaller output increases than those of policies that provide no such relief.

While we have adapted our model to accommodate many of the key issues that arise when considering tax reform, there are some that we have not addressed. In treating the economy as closed, we may have overstated the depressing impact of additional capital accumulation on the rate of return and, hence, understated the potential welfare and output gains from tax reform, a conclusion consistent with the open-economy simulations presented by Auerbach (1996).

Additional gains may also accrue under any of the tax reforms considered here as a result of the more uniform treatment of different types of capital and different sectors of production. There may also be welfare gains from tax simplification arising through reduced costs of compliance and enforcement. Gains from both of these sources, though, would depend on the reformed tax system maintaining not only its reduced rates and broader base, but also its lack of special-interest provisions that exist under the current tax system and could arise under at least some of the alternatives we have considered. Finally, as discussed recently by William M. Gentry and Hubbard (1997), the distributional and efficiency effects of tax reform might change somewhat in a richer economic model incorporating variation in risk and rates of return, for one would then need to consider the risk-sharing aspects of different tax systems and the extent to which the capital levy of the consumption tax hit not only the quasi-rents of existing capital, but also true economic rents. A challenging task for future research is to determine the relative importance of these factors.

REFERENCES

Altig, David and Carlstrom, Charles T. "Marginal Tax Rates and Income Inequality in a Life-Cycle Model." *American Economic Review*, December 1999, *89*(5), pp. 1197–215.

Auerbach, Alan J. "Tax Reform and Adjustment Costs: The Impact on Investment and Market Value." *International Economic Review*, November 1989, *30*(4), pp. 939–62.

_____. "Tax Reform, Capital Allocation, Efficiency, and Growth," in Henry J. Aaron and William G. Gale, eds., *Economic effects of fundamental tax reform*. Washington, DC: Brookings Institution Press, 1996, pp. 29–73.

Auerbach, Alan J.; Gokhale, Jagadeesh; Kotlikoff, Laurence J.; Sabelhaus, John and Weil, David N. "The Annuitization of Americans' Resources: A Cohort Analysis." National Bureau of Economic Research (Cambridge, MA) Working Paper No. 5089, April 1995.

Auerbach, Alan J. and Kotlikoff, Laurence J. *Dynamic fiscal policy*. Cambridge: Cambridge University Press, 1987.

Auerbach, Alan J.; Kotlikoff, Laurence J.; Hagemann, Robert P. and Nicoletti, Giuseppe. "The Economic Dynamics of Ageing Population: The Case of Four OECD Countries." *OECD Economic Studies*, Spring 1989, (12), pp. 97–130.

Blinder, Alan S. "A Model of Inherited Wealth." *Quarterly Journal of Economics*, November 1973, *87*(4), pp. 608–26.

Bradford, David. *Untangling the income tax*. Cambridge, MA: Harvard University Press, 1986.

Congressional Budget Office (CBO). "Comparing Income and Consumption Tax Bases." CBO paper, July 1997.

Cummins, Jason G.; Hassett, Kevin A. and Hubbard, R. Glenn. "A Reconsideration of Investment Behavior Using Tax Reforms as Natural Experiments." *Brookings Papers on Economic Activity*, 1994, (2), pp. 1–59.

Engen, Eric M. and Gale, William G. "The Effects of Fundamental Tax Reform on Saving," in Henry J. Aaron and William G. Gale, eds., *Economic effects of fundamental tax reform*. Washington, DC: Brookings Institution Press, 1996, pp. 83–112.

Fullerton, Don and Rogers, Diane Lim. *Who bears the lifetime tax burden*? Washington, DC: Brookings Institution Press, 1993.

Gale, William G. and Scholz, John Karl. "Intergenerational Transfers and the Accumulation of Wealth." *Journal of Economic Perspectives*, Fall 1994, *8*(4), pp. 145–60.

Gentry, William M. and Hubbard, R. Glenn. "Distributional Implications of Introducing a Broad-Based Consumption Tax," in James M. Poterba, ed., *Tax policy and the economy*, Vol. 11. Cambridge, MA: MIT Press, 1997, pp. 1–47.

Hall, Robert E. and Rabushka, Alvin. *The flat tax*,

2nd Ed. Stanford, CA: Hoover Institution Press, 1995.

Hubbard, R. Glenn and Judd, Kenneth. "Social Security and Individual Welfare: Precautionary Saving, Borrowing Constraints, and the Payroll Tax." *American Economic Review*, September 1987, *77*(4), pp. 630–46.

Hubbard, R. Glenn; Skinner, Jonathan and Zeldes, Stephen P. "Precautionary Saving and Social Insurance." *Journal of Political Economy*, April 1995, *103*(2), pp. 360–99.

Internal Revenue Service. *Statistics of income—1993: Individual income tax returns,* Washington, DC: U.S. Government Printing Office, 1996.

Kotlikoff, Laurence J. and Summers, Lawrence H. "The Role of Intergenerational Transfers in Aggregate Capital Accumulation." *Journal of Political Economy*, August 1981, *89*(4), pp. 706–32.

Menchik, Paul L. and David, Martin. "The Incidence of a Lifetime Consumption Tax." *National Tax Journal*, June 1982, *35*(2), pp. 189–203.

Old-Age and Survivors Disability Insurance Trustees Report (OASDI). 1996, 1997.

Rippe, Richard. "Further Gains in Corporate Profitability." *Economic Outlook Monthly,* Prudential Securities, August 1995.

Slemrod, Joel and Bakija, Jon. *Taxing ourselves: A citizen's guide to the great debate over tax reform.* Cambridge, MA: MIT Press, 1996.

Stokey, Nancy L. and Rebelo, Sergio. "Growth Effects of Flat-Rate Taxes." *Journal of Political Economy*, June 1995, *103*(3), pp. 519–50.